FORGING A UNITARY STATE

Russia's Management of the Eurasian Space, 1650–1850

Covering two centuries of Russian history, *Forging a Unitary State* provides a comprehensive account of the creation of what is commonly known as the "Russian Empire," stretching from Poland to Siberia. In this book, John P. LeDonne demonstrates that the so-called Empire was, for the most part, a unitary state, defined by an obsessive emphasis on centralization and uniformity. The standardization of local administration, the judicial system, the tax regime, and commercial policy was carried out slowly but systematically over eight generations, in the hope of integrating people on the periphery into the Russian political and social hierarchy. The ultimate goal of Russian policy was to create a "Fortress Empire" consisting of a huge Russian unitary state flanked by a few peripheral territories, such as Finland, Transcaucasia, and Central Asia. Additional peripheral states like Sweden, Turkey, and Persia would guarantee the security of this "Fortress Empire" and the management of Eurasian territory. LeDonne's provocative argument is supported by a careful comparative study of Russian expansion along Russia's western, southern, and eastern borders, drawing on vital but under-studied administrative evidence. *Forging a Unitary State* is an essential resource for those interested in the long history of Russian expansionism.

JOHN P. LEDONNE is a senior research associate at the Davis Center for Russian and Eurasian Studies, Harvard University.

JOHN P. LeDONNE

FORGING A UNITARY STATE

RUSSIA'S MANAGEMENT OF THE EURASIAN SPACE 1650–1850

UNIVERSITY OF TORONTO PRESS
Toronto Buffalo London

Toronto Buffalo London
utorontopress.com

ISBN 978-1-4875-0611-7 (cloth)
ISBN 978-1-4875-4211-5 (paper)
ISBN 978-1-4875-3332-8 (EPUB)
ISBN 978-1-4875-3331-1 (PDF)

Library and Archives Canada Cataloguing in Publication

Title: Forging a unitary state : Russia's management of the Eurasian space, 1650–1850 / John P. LeDonne.

Names: LeDonne, John P., 1935– author.

Description: Includes bibliographical references and index.

Identifiers: Canadiana (print) 20190222808 | Canadiana (ebook) 20190222875 | ISBN 9781487506117 (hardcover) | ISBN 9781487542115 (softcover) | ISBN 9781487533328 (EPUB) | ISBN 9781487533311 (PDF)

Subjects: LCSH: Russia – History – 1613-1917. | LCSH: Russia – Foreign relations – History – 18th century. | LCSH: Russia – Civilization – 18th century. | LCSH: Russia – Politics and government – 1689-1801. | LCSH: Imperialism.

Classification: LCC DK127.2 .L43 2020 | DDC 947/.06 – dc23

University of Toronto Press acknowledges the financial assistance to its publishing program of the Canada Council for the Arts and the Ontario Arts Council, an agency of the Government of Ontario.

Funded by the Government of Canada | Financé par le gouvernement du Canada | Canada

Vidia, chto nikto ne prinimaetsia, ia khotia ne svershu, odnako nachnu, chto drugim posle menia legche budet delat'

(an unknown eighteenth-century scholar cited in Lodyzhenskii, *Istoriia russkogo tamozhennogo tarifa*, x)

Contents

Part II. The Southern Theatre Reaches the Sea

Part III. The Eastern Theatre: The Advance toward the Mountains

Maps

Tables

Acknowledgments

There comes a time in the long life of a scholar when he can fully appreciate the profound influence some of his teachers had upon his future scholarly life. Two of them left a mark on me as early as high school. One taught me to structure my writing in order to shape a large amount of material into a convincing story; the other insisted that one could not study history without the help of geography. Later in life, there was Marc Raeff at Columbia, who guided my first steps in the study of Russian administrative history after I completed my dissertation on the formation of economic regions after the Revolution. Later still, Edward Keenan brought me to Harvard, and at numerous lunches challenged some of my conclusions with his usual inquisitive open-mindedness. These four scholars are no longer with us, but I owe them what I later became.

More recently, Serhii Plokhy supported a beginner's work in Ukrainian history and recommended the manuscript to University of Toronto Press. I also owe a great deal to Mikhail Dolbilov's profound knowledge of the Western Borderlands; to Erika Monahan, who taught me the difference between winter and spring wheat and many other things about Russian trade along the Irtysh River; and to Willard Sunderland, who introduced me to the vast grasslands of Siberia. My special thanks also go out to Paul Bushkovitch, who was the first to read the entire manuscript and gave it an early push; to Richard Wortman, with whom I have been exchanging books and ideas for some forty years; and to Donald Ostrowski for sharing many discussions in happier times.

I am most grateful for the publication grants and support I have received from both the Davis Center and the Ukrainian Institute and their directors, Rawi Abdelal and Serhii Plokhy, as well as from Executive Director Alexandra Vacroux and the ever busy but always hopeful Maria Altamore. At the Press, Richard Ratzlaff was the first to welcome the manuscript, and his successor Stephen Shapiro piloted it with ruthless determination across all the pitfalls of the acceptance process. I am also grateful to the Academic Committee who gave its final approval. Many thanks are also due to the redoubtable but generous copy editor Judith Williams and to Robin Studniberg, who gently but firmly kept reminding me that there were deadlines to meet. Since I am allergic to computers, I was fortunate to find two outstanding graduate students to digitize the manuscript. Michael Smeltzer digitized a first version, and the very professional Sara Powell digitized the last version and the maps.

There are also those who helped in a more personal way. I am deeply grateful to Lubomyr Hajda and Tamara Nary for their friendship and their help; to Mary Louise Corradino, who offered her time and generous support in times of great distress; to Yun Ji (Gigi), Sylvie Papazian, and Robin Yun for creating a cordial working environment, and last but not least, Penelope Skalnik, a genius with the computer and a wonderful friend.

I dedicate this work with love to Myroslava and our family, Zina, Tatiana, Randy, and Tad.

Note on the Text

A note on transliteration and geographic terminology: Since this is a historical study dating to the seventeenth century, attention has been paid to both historical precision (terminology most commonly used in original texts) and modern usage.

For non-Cyrillic languages, both in the text and bibliographies, the full spelling with diacritical marks is preserved for both personal names and for toponyms/hydronyms.

For Cyrillic languages in the text and notes, the simplified/modified Library of Congress Russian, Ukrainian, and Belarussian transliteration systems have been used for both personal names and toponyms/hydronyms. This system a) omits the (', ") primes used to transliterate the soft and hard signs (ь,ъ); b) masculine family name endings in ий (Russian/BR: ii, Ukrainian: yi) are contracted to "y" (thus Viazemsky, not Viazemskii, Khmelnytsky, not Khmel'nyts'kyi); and c) in initial positions, Ya, Yu, Ye, (for я, ю, є) are preferred to Ia, Iu, Ie (Yavorsky, Yakovlev, Yalta).

For Cyrillic languages in the bibliography and bibliographic citations, the full Library of Congress transliteration system is preserved (with the exception of the above noted initial "Y" in personal names and toponyms).

For toponyms and hydronyms on all territories under consideration, I have used current place and river names (followed, when first used, by the alternate historical form/s in parentheses), unless listing the historical term first made more sense. Hence, Lviv (Lwów, Lvov, Lemberg), Chernihiv (Chernigov), Hadiach (Gadiach), Myrhorod (Mirgorod), Vilnius (Vilna), but Elizavetograd (Kirovohrad, Kropyvnytsky), Ekaterinoslav (Dnipropetrovsk, Dnipro), Yurburg (Jubarkas). We have also retained a few more commonly used anglicized forms, such as Belorussia (Belarus), Kiev (Kyiv), Volhynia (Volyn), Podolia (Podilia), Polesia (Polissia), Dnieper (Dnipro), Dniester (Dnister), Odessa (Odesa).

For a work of this size, the density of biographical and topographical positions in the text would ideally require an appendix. We hope, therefore, that the readers will be satisfied with the author's choice of the key positions listed in the index.

FORGING A UNITARY STATE

Introduction

I offer this work as a sequel to my *Absolutism and Ruling Class*, published in 1990, where I discussed the public administration of what was still called "Russia" – the central provinces between the Urals and the western borderlands – from 1700 to 1825. It was my intention at the time to continue with another book to discuss the management of the borderlands, but the task proved harder than I expected. Ultimately, I decided to expand the time frame to include a longer period, from the mid-seventeenth to the mid-nineteenth centuries. One can certainly argue about when the construction of a Russian "Empire" began – during the reign of Ivan III (1462–1505), or that of Ivan IV the Terrible (1547–84) – but it was the reign of Alexei Mikhailovich (1645–76) that marks the beginning of sustained drive of territorial expansion that would continue with only some short interruptions until the First World War, if not even 1950.

The year 1650 is of course arbitrary, but also symbolic of a first period of Russian expansion until 1800. The year 1850 marks the zenith of a second period, that of the maximization of Russian power under Nicholas I (1825–55) and the completion of a structure of territorial administration began by Alexei Mikhailovich and his son Peter I (1689–1725), and the culmination of a unitary state. After the death of Nicholas I, a third period began, lasting until the First World War and characterized by the gradual loss of legitimacy by the Romanov house and the rise of nationalism among ethnic groups of what had by then become a Russian Empire. This work focuses on the first and second periods because they are the constructive ones, and also because the enormous volume of available materials makes it impossible for a single scholar to make a detailed analysis of the increasingly complex administration of such an enormous land mass.

I propose to discuss a number of topics largely ignored in most of our scholarship on the Russian Empire – focused as it is on ethnic identities, social tensions, and intellectual issues – and draw attention to what can be broadly called the history of its public administration. I mean here more specifically the policy of harmonization and integration, aimed at imposing a uniform system of local administration, judicial procedures, tax administration, and even social and religious integration. That policy, I argue, aimed at creating not an empire, but a unitary state across the vast expanse of Eurasia, of which Russia was the indisputable core. First of all, however, I need to definite the term "Eurasia."

"Eurasia" has become fashionable, but few scholars take the risk of defining its borders, especially in the West. It is sometimes misunderstood as a single continent combining Europe and Asia as if they belonged together. I do not hesitate to say that I remain a disciple of Sir Halford Mackinder, Geoffrey Parker, and Owen Lattimore. Eurasia is indeed a huge land mass, but one only partaking of both Europe and Asia. Its core consists of what is usually called "European Russia." Its western border follows the Scandinavian Alps separating Sweden from Norway; the Oder, the old boundary of the Holy Roman Empire and Hungary along the Morava, on the Dinaric Alps. The southern border follows the Taurus Mountains of Turkey and the Zagros of Persia; the eastern border is marked by the Hindu Kush, the Gobi Desert, and the costal ranges along the Sea of Okhotsk; the core is bounded in the west by Sweden and Poland, in the south by Turkey and Persia, in the east by Mongolia. Eurasia is thus nearly identical with Mackinder's Heartland.[1]

But these territories are of two kinds. Sweden, Poland, Turkey, and Persia I call core powers, and the lands between them and the Russian core I call frontiers. These frontiers, forming an "overlapping space" (*Überlappungsraum*), are shaped by four river basins draining into four seas – the Baltic, Black, Caspian, and Okhosk seas. Their geography makes them into zones of contention between opposing core powers that invited Russia's advance. These border regions I group into three theatres of Russian strategic activity: the western (the Baltic basin); the southern (the Black and Caspian basins); and the eastern (mainly Siberia and the basin of the Amur draining into the sea of Japan). I distinguish three states in the period under consideration: the creation of a unitary state in the Russian core; the integration of the frontiers into a single homogenous system; and the attempt to transform the outlying core powers into a glacis protecting the security of the imperial system, which I have called Fortress Russia, later a Fortress Empire. I discussed these stages in my *Russia and the World*. The expansion of the Russian core and the integration of the frontiers form the object of this work.

My definition of Eurasia raises the question of the extent to which Russia was, and is, part of Europe. Like a definition of Eurasia and of the location of its orders, the question is worth asking, especially after the fall of the Soviet Union. It is now taken for granted by most that Russia is indeed part of Europe, but it is my contention that it is not: it is the core of Eurasia. Carsten Goehrke, in his original and very valuable interpretation of Russian history, writes that Russia developed "the consciousness of an historical identity [*Besonderheit*] between East and West resting above all upon a European but also upon an Asiatic foundation."[2] Some of the fundamental features of its political culture have exercised, and will continue to exercise, a strong impact upon its relations with its immediate peripheries.

Byzantium, which did not emerge all naked from the sea like Botticelli's Venus, belonged to the Hellenistic tradition of the East, to Eastern Christendom; Europe to Latin Christendom, shaped by Roman and Germanic influences, as Nikolai Danilevsky contended in his famous book.[3] The division between Russia and Europe ran along the great and permanent fault line between the two branches of Christendom, in fact of the ancient world, between the Hellenistic and Roman worlds.[4] What Galina Yemelianova calls the grassroots of the Gingissid trend of Russian historical development deserves greater attention: the story of Muscovy and the Turkic peoples, its major interlocutors for 250 years in the immense space between the Carpathians and the Volga. Similarly, Istvan Vasary is convinced that the "Turco-Mongol overlords had fundamental influence on the nascence and fate of the Russian state."[5] The obsession with Byzantium has blotted out additional influences from Armenia and Georgia, as well as Persia.

But what does it mean in practical terms? Yemelianova, once again, writes that the Gengissid trend "was intertwined with the official byzantinization of the Russian state [and] that the interplay of these two cultural influences contributed to the sacerdotal make up of the tsar's authority, the fusion of the secular and religious domains, and the ruler's supremacy over the law."[6] The political geography of Eastern Orthodoxy shows that, in the Russian experience at least, the head of the Church nearly always resided in the political capital, and that, despite the proclaimed "symphony" between the two powers, the ecclesiastical power would inevitably fall under the control of the secular power – as happened in the seventeenth century. It means that the resulting sacralization raised the person of the monarch above all others on earth and made him unchallengeable on pain of losing all hope of salvation after death. It meant that, in sharp contrast with the Latin tradition in Europe, men could have no dual loyalty – to God and to Caesar – justifying challenge and rebellion. There could be no contest, no fruitful dialectic between Church and State, one of the defining markers of European civilization. No grand prince or tsar ever went to Canossa. Nor was he bound by his word, and here he was much like his Turkic interlocutors among the khans of the steppe, who looked upon treaties as personal arrangements without binding conditions.

It follows that there could be no contract between the ruler and his subjects, and this for another reason. Despite brave attempts by Soviet scholarship to claim it for three generations, Russia did not experience feudalism and subinfeudation. Feudalism rested on a contractual relationship defining both rights and obligations between higher and lower lords, between suzerain and subject.

The tsar-emperor (or his representative) did not take an oath before his subjects, as the Polish kings had done in the past. In 1654, when Vasilii Buturlin took the oath of allegiance from Hetman Bohdan Khmelnytsky, he refused to take a reciprocal oath on behalf of the tsar: representatives from the other side were not true sovereigns and, if they were at times of another faith, in effect they were aliens. Likewise, when the Duchy of Kurland was incorporated into the expanding Russian core nearly 150 years later (1795), its Protestant nobles submitted a list of charters and privileges granted by the Polish king, the feudal suzerain of Kurland, but did not ask for their confirmation: they merely placed themselves "at Her Majesty's mercy."[7]

Moreover, Muscovy's *Sonderweg* far from the open seas did not generate the gradual development of triangular structures between sovereign, town, and landed elites, the fertile ground for the creation of a public space and a socio-political dynamic conducive to the growth of democratic values. When, with the development of a money economy, serfdom was ebbing away in Europe, it spread from Poland on the edge of Eurasia into Russia to degrade even further the condition of the peasantry, deepening the chasm between Russia and Europe. Both continued to belong to two different civilizations, destined by an unchanging geopolitical situation to remain in a semi-permanent state of mutual hostility.

On the other hand, the issue of Russia's relations with Europe is linked with that of the country's role as a modernizing force. Those who insist on Russia being part of Europe cannot shy away from their assumption that it was an "inferior" part of Europe, in matters of government (autocracy), police administration (corruption), and economy (serfdom). European apologists see the incorporation of the borderlands, especially the western ones, as a step backwards in the course of their development until then shaped by Poland and Sweden, even Persia. But if Russia is seen not within Europe but as the core of Eurasia, it can also be characterized as a modernizing force. Indeed, anyone reading documents of the period soon becomes aware that some of the borderlands needed "modernization" not so much from Europe as from the expanding Russian core.

We discover, for example, that the Baltic provinces had no common system of weights and measures, that units varied not only from one district to another but even from one manor to another, a medieval situation that drove to distraction the officials of the Provision Chancery in Petersburg when it came to assessing the deliveries of grain to the capital and the army; that there existed seventeen separate taxes on trade in the small Sheki khanate of Transcaucasia alone, enough to paralyse commercial exchanges in the region; that the nomads, whose only source of wealth was in cattle, did not cultivate hay, which alone could save their animals against devastating frosts that killed most of them in winter; that the Cossacks in western Georgia had to teach the locals how to improve their diet (and their revenues) by fishing; and what are we to make of those "privileges" and local laws which so enthuse the supporters of the "differences," and which the Russian government supposedly encouraged? The Magdeburg Law in effect in the western provinces was adapted from the *Sachsenspiegel* of 1242; the third Lithuanian Statute of 1588, drawn up by and for the nobility, had largely become anachronistic by 1800, while the Russian *Ulozhenie* of 1649 (which the Statute influenced) had been amended by so much legislation as to become unrecognizable. Russian penal legislation was not much crueller than some borderland legislation,[8] and indeed the cruellest punishment in the Russian army – running the gauntlet – was a Swedish import. In a word, those famous "differences" were in fact remnants of a past designed to protect the status of Polish and German nobilities. That explains why the Russians met such resistance in trying to eradicate them in pursuit of "standardization." To champion a "Russian Empire of differences" contains the danger of supporting anachronistic backwardness.[9]

In the process of incorporating the peripheries, local laws and privileges were recognized only in so far as they did not deviate from the existing laws of the "empire," but the laws were made by the monarch independently of any constitutional restraints, and it was he who determined when the divergence was becoming unacceptable. That was the case in the Baltic provinces, but in Lithuania, on the other hand, they were not recognized, then were recognized, and finally abolished. In other words, all local privileges were seen as residual – whatever Moscow–St Petersburg chose not to take upon itself. That is why one cannot claim that the government ever violated its promises: they depended from the beginning on the supra-legal will of the ruler. Alexander II (1855–81) went even farther with his decisive "No one can take upon himself to petition me about the general welfare and needs of the state."[10]

There was in that statement the germ of the perception of a homogenous state. Jane Burbank may have been too forceful when she claimed there were no natural rights[11] – unless she meant in the Russian core alone, where the concept of natural law was always an oxymoron – but that perception also reflected an assertive policy towards the creation of unitary state. An interesting illustration is the treatment of the monarch's title. In 1785, for instance, the title included some thirty-seven possessions of Catherine II, including "All the Russias," and "others." There were sixteen "Russian" territories, four Tatar and Siberian, three Baltic and three Ukrainian, three Belorussian, and two Caucasian, all mixed together, not in accordance with their location or date of incorporation.[12] The 1817 title included Poland as a *tsarstvo* (tsardom, not kingdom) placed between Astrakhan and Sibir' (Siberian) among the five *tsarstva* (Kazan, Astrakhan, Poland, Siberian, and Tavrich). What can better explain this Russian perception of fluid homogeneity in a unitary state as a realm forming a whole (*tselost'*), as Richard Wortman calls it, "in which the boundaries between the metropolis and the peripheries tended to blur"?[13]

If the prevailing understanding of law assumed that differences were not accepted a priori but tolerated as a temporary aberration on the way to the creation of a unitary state, what then is a unitary state? It is one in which the government creates its territorial divisions, determines their number and boundaries, their authority and the scope of their operations; it also leaves them very little decision-making power. It seeks to minimize centrifugal forces, and downgrades the importance of the regional capitals, whose locations and historical importance may rival its own. Within those tightly circumscribed jurisdictions, a highly centralized government pursues a policy of harmonization and integration of the administration of justice, of tax collection, of economic management, and even, if possible, of religious unification.

During the period under study here, the Russian government pursued such a policy gradually but systematically, although hampered by enormous distances, low population density, and shortages of personnel in the counties and provinces.[14] From the days of Peter I, this policy of harmonization and integration intensified to reach the first peak during the reign of Catherine II (1762–96) and a second during that of Nicholas I (1825–55). It was immensely encouraged by the creation of ministries in 1802–11, which followed that of a hierarchical and integrated fiscal structure of tax collection by Catherine's great Procurator General Prince Alexander Viazemsky (1727–93) in the 1780s.[15] Ministries, being functional rather than territorial organizations, have a powerful interest in monopolizing the management of their specific functions and their related activities throughout the entire territory. Provincial agencies were subordinated to them alone, and ministries destroyed the regional and local bodies capable of challenging the uniform operation of their own agencies.[16] In the 1850s we witness the completion of the ministerial system and the apogee of the unitary state. A similar development had been taking place in France, with the pre-revolutionary intendants and the Napoleonic ministers and prefects also imbued with a military spirit and an obsession with uniformity.

In Russia, as in Napoleonic France, there existed a powerful incentive to create a unitary state. Maritime powers in search of luxury goods and raw materials built commodity chains resting on traditional trade networks going back to antiquity; they built decentralized empires consisting of production and trade hubs supported by naval stations. Russia, on the other hand, hemmed in by almost internal seas cut off by nature (harsh weather, narrow straits) or geopolitical factors from the same great oceans, as well as hampered by endemic shortages of capital and labour, needed to create a continental market, and a centralized management of scarce resources on a continental scale to guarantee the often insecure functioning of a military-industrial complex: it had to be capable of sustaining an expansive policy designed to unify Eurasia under Russian leadership. Hence the importance of finance and war ministries in the management of the space occupied by the expanding core. Russia already understood the importance of an alliance between geopolitics and economic power because it was so aware of the latter's weakness; to remedy it required a polity to enforce centralization and homogeneity in a unitary state.

A unitary state must not be confused with a nation state. A nation state is one in which political parties and interest groups converge to share in the political process and the elaboration of national policies. It is a state in which civil society has become strong enough to impose its views on the administrative state. The Russian unitary state could never make the transition to nation state because of the divisive influence of emerging ethnic centrifugal forces. What we call the formation of the Russian Empire was in fact a process of administrative, unitary state building from the Baltic to the Sea of Okhotsk, from the White to the Black seas. Beginning in the 1860s, however, the emerging liberal, conservative, and multi-ethnic movements acted together to undermine the administrative state, but could not create a nation state. The result was a political vacuum incapable of coping with the stresses of economic and social dislocation.

A unitary state must not be confused with an empire either. It is a world in itself, while an empire is a constellation of worlds revolving around that of the unitary state in the making. Was Russia then an empire or a unitary state? It was both, but at a different time. The Russian Empire was one in which the Russian core built a unitary state until it encountered unsurmountable resistance and went on constructing an empire. The incorporation of Finland, Poland, and Transcaucasia – and later Central Asia – was by necessity a type of imperial construction because these territories represented different worlds, a constellation of contiguous territories revolving around an expanding world reaching, at the beginning of the nineteenth century, the natural limits of its expansion. The expanding core sought to become largely Orthodox and Russian, a unitary confessional state and a unitary Russian society, despite the inevitable exceptions that only confirm the rule. Finland, Poland, and Transcaucasia could not possibly be integrated into the expanding core and unitary state, but the traditions of the unitary state remained so strong that the Russians persisted in seeking to integrate them while recognizing they could not (as in Poland). This dilemma would become the fundamental flaw of the Russian Empire during the last fifty years of its existence. In other words, I do not understand the words "Russian Empire" in the usual sense, but as a process begun with the systematic construction of a unitary state followed by that of an empire.

I also claim that the Russians were aware of the strategic limit of their expansion. I have discussed this in *The Russian Empire and the World* and *The Grand Strategy of the Russian Empire*. Russian policy exhibited a form of "aggressive defensiveness," perhaps unique in its kind. Spain, England, and France did not expand over long distances in order to protect the security of their homeland, but Russia did, and conceived the outer limits of its expansion to be those of Eurasia as I defined it here. As a result, we can postulate the existence of three consecutive zones of Russian activity in the three theatres: the core as a unitary state; the building of an empire in a first periphery; and an outer periphery encompassing Sweden, Poland, Prussia, Turkey, and Persia as satellites of the Russian empire. Thus did Russia manage the Eurasian space.

After defining Eurasia, examining the position of the ruler in the system, and claiming that Russia was building a unitary state until the beginning of the nineteenth century, there remains to examine yet another process, that of social integration and the governing of the unitary state.

I submit that the unitary state – the expanding core, as I call it throughout this work – was kept together not so much by a bureaucracy as by an interlocking mesh of patronage networks, combining to form a gigantic pyramid of which the tsar-emperor was the Grand Patron. Patronage networks are hierarchical rather than ideological formations, created for the purpose of sharing the spoils of office. An individual of some importance attracts a retinue of favour-seeking "creatures" who enhance his prestige. He, himself, seeks to integrate into a wider network, in which the original patron becomes the creature of a more powerful individual. And on to the top of the political hierarchy, where the last patron becomes the immediate client of the Grand Patron.[17]

In Russia's relations with its peripheries within the emerging unitary state, the existence of patronage networks implied the integration of local elites into the power structure of the Russian core. The process is usually called one of cooptation. I prefer to use "superstratification," a term coined by Sinologist Wolfram Eberhard in his studies of medieval China.[18] I believe it is more appropriate in a study of Russian expansion. Cooptation implies a certain equality between parties: it is mainly a process of horizontal integration. A Polish magnate of Right Bank Ukraine becomes Russia's foreign minister or curator of a university and director of an educational region. A Baltic aristocratic German enters the Russian army alongside Russians and becomes a general, a grade giving access, as I see it, to the ruling elite. But superstratification implies something else, and especially so in the eastern theatre. As Russia expanded, it incorporated nomads and hunters who were more often than not descendants of the Turkic interlocutors of Muscovite Russia, as in the former khanates of Kazan, Astrakhan, and Sibir', and others beyond the Yenisei river. These societies were undergoing a process of stratification in the seventeenth century, and a top stratum was crystallizing, claiming to become the unchallengeable ruling group of its people. Here Russians were intruders, armed with superior weapons, convinced of the superiority of the settler over the nomad, and determined to assert their authority over the native society. They became a new stratum superimposed over the leading stratum of local society.[19]

There would inevitably be conflicts between the Russians and the native "notables," even bloody ones, as in Bashkiria and Buriatia, but in the end, a compromise had to be negotiated between the Russians and the natives, because the Russians needed the native leaders to govern and the leaders needed the Russians to help them settle intertribal differences and put down resistance to their own abuses. But that was only half the process. Russian expansion must be placed in the much larger context of a massive rollback by the settler of the nomad, who had lorded over him for so long. The nomad now had to be integrated into a rigid structure of domination prevalent in the expanding core. Once the nomad had become a settler (hopefully), he could be be incorporated into a peasantry dominated by officials and landlords. Superstratification was thus not so much a process of horizontal cooptation as a form of vertical integration into a Russian-dominated social and administrative hierarchy. The native upper stratum was integrated into the lower ranks of the hierarchy, decorated with medals, and encouraged by tax exemptions to exploit their own people.

The research for this work was based largely on the *Collection of Laws of the Russian Empire* (*PSZ*), first series (1649–1832) and part of the second. The first series is not, as some claim, a collection of normative acts, but one of reports and even position papers, to which the ruler appended his or her signature. Therefore, many of these documents state a policy, and it is for the scholar to trace its continuity. My intention was to discover a certain strategic vision and the means to realize it among Russian policy makers seeking hegemony over the Eurasian land mass. Besides the *PSZ*, I have used the valuable *Review* of the Interior Ministry (*ZhMVD*), which contains many scholarly articles based on the ministry's archives. Many other published sources complement these basic collections.

Anyone embarking on the study of a large territory faces a dilemma – to follow a territorial or topical approach. I chose the former because it makes the work more manageable, and because Russian policy makers were clearly aware – and certainly continue to be – of the existence of these three theatres. Of course, there will be a repetition of certain topics in each theatre, but a topical approach would necessitate a repetition of each theatre when discussing too many topics. The territorial approach shows much more conclusively that a policy was adapted to different theatres but had the same purpose, and was therefore consistent.

I hope this work will stimulate a debate on the nature of the Russian administrative-military state. For example, it may help scholars abandon the old cliché that the Russians took part in the partitioning of "Poland" of 1772–95: they only incorporated the eastern marches of the Polish Empire (for the faint-hearted, the Polish-Lithuanian Commonwealth). We also need to reassess the reforms of Catherine II to understand her comprehensive, and perhaps unique, policy of decentralization. Much work has already been done by Nancy Kollmann on the judiciary, but I have in mind here the codification of local laws in the Baltic and western provinces. We need more work, modelled after Erika Monahan's, on the intracontinental trade within the Russian core and its impact on the economic integration of the peripheries. Last but not least, in a country where the army has been the structural shaper of the state, its territorialization would introduce us to Russian regionalism, one of the most challenging topics in the history of Russian public administration. This work can only be a beginning. But a beginning there has to be. May it encourage others to move one.

Map 1 The Southern and Western Theatres

PART I

The Western Theatre: The Struggle for Northwestern Eurasia

Map 2 The Western Theatre

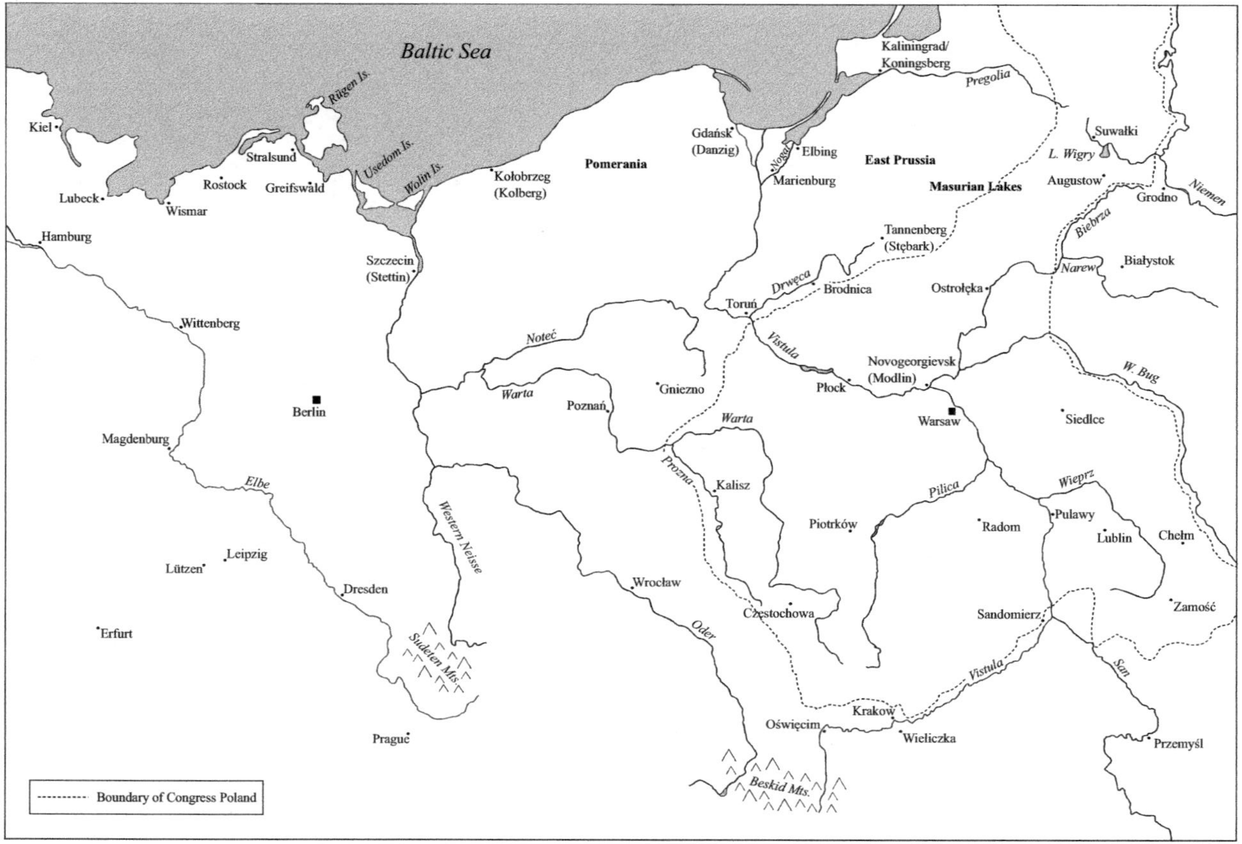
Baltic Sea
Rügen Is.
Usedom Is.
Wolin Is.
Kiel
Lubeck
Wismar
Rostock
Stralsund
Greifswald
Hamburg
Szczecin
(Stettin)
Kołobrzeg
(Kolberg)
Pomerania
Gdańsk
(Danzig)
Nogat
Elbing
Marienburg
Kaliningrad/
Koningsberg
Pregolia
East Prussia
Masurian Lakes
Suwałki
L. Wigry
Augustow
Grodno
Niemen
Biebrza
Tannenberg
(Stębark)
Drwęca
Brodnica
Toruń
Ostrołęka
Narew
Białystok
Wittenberg
Noteć
Vistula
Novogeorgievsk
(Modlin)
Płock
W. Bug
Berlin
Warta
Poznań
Gniezno
Warta
Warsaw
Siedlce
Magdenburg
Elbe
Prozna
Kalisz
Wieprz
Pilica
Western Neisse
Piotrków
Radom
Pulawy
Lublin
Chełm
Lützen
Leipzig
Dresden
Wrocław
Częstochowa
Sandomierz
Zamość
Erfurt
Sudeten Mts.
Oder
Vistula
San
Krakow
Oświęcim
Wieliczka
Przemyśl
Prague
Beskid Mts.
Boundary of Congress Poland

Map 3 Poland

Chapter One

Laying the Foundations, 1650–1775

The Geopolitical Setting

Geographical Environment

The western theatre was the smallest of the three, but also the most complex. More densely settled, it formed the transition from the endless and inhospitable continental land mass to the more compact and more varied landscapes of Europe, with their indented coasts bathed in the warm waters of the Atlantic Ocean. Transitional zones partake of the two core territories and civilizations which nature has imposed upon them to join. If the western theatre can and must be seen as the northwestern end of Eurasia, it was also the northeastern end of the Atlantic basin and Latin Christian civilization. As such it was also a geopolitical frontier, where Europe and Eurasia, Latin and Orthodox Christianity, fought for hegemony for centuries. To place Sweden and Poland in Eurasia, albeit as peripheral cores, may raise eyebrows, but it is an incontrovertible fact that while both belong to Europe culturally (as members of Latin Christian civilization), they constituted the western periphery of the Eurasian land mass geologically and geopolitically.

The western theatre was an oval-shaped territory centred on the Baltic Sea and the Gulf of Bothnia. Its western boundary was the crestline of the Scandinavian Alps separating Sweden from Norway. It crossed the Baltic to reach the Oder and followed the river to its source on the watershed separating the basin of the Baltic from that of the Danube, where Austria claimed to have an exclusive jurisdiction. It followed the Beskids past the headwaters of the San, reached the Western Bug, then followed the Pripiat, which formed the boundary with the southern theatre. It then ran along the Sozh to its headwaters near Smolensk, the strategic location controlling the watershed between the Dnieper and the Western Dvina. From there, it reached the Valdai Hills and Lake Onega, then followed the Karelian upland to Lapland on the foothills of the Scandinavian Alps. Of the three theatres, it was the only one fully situated in the forest zone: it had no steppe land and no Cossacks. It was about three thousand kilometres long and over one thousand across between Smolensk and Stettin, a theatre of transition between the great Eurasian land mass and maritime Europe, partaking of both Eurasia and Europe, a theatre of confrontation with the eastern marches of Europe and the western marches of Eurasia.

An observer situated in Moscow on the upper reaches of the Volga-Caspian basin who looked west would see the ground rise toward the Valdai Hills containing – so it was believed until the nineteenth century – the highest point on the Russian plain to the Urals, as well as the watershed between the sources of the Volga, the Dnieper, and the Western Dvina. The northern extension of the Valdai Hills, Lake Onega, and the ridges of southern Finland and Karelia enclosed the basin of Lake Ladoga, the largest lake between the Atlantic and the Urals, with a basin more than twice the size of England and more than half the size of France. A lake of rough waters with a circular current driving ice floes toward the southern coast and its exit via the Neva into the Gulf of Finland, it was rich in clusters of islands in its northern section, including one on which was built, perhaps as early as the tenth century, the Valaam Transfiguration Monastery, to stand guard for Orthodoxy against the ambitions of Scandinavians and Catholics.

The lake was for centuries the hub of the international trade linking the Baltic with the Black Sea and with the Caspian via the Volga. In the Middle Ages, traders brought goods from Constantinople up the Dnieper past Kiev to the Dvina. From there, they sailed down the river to Riga or down the Lovat to Lake Ilmen, where Novgorod the Great built a commercial empire based on the fur trade. From Novgorod they descended the Volkhov to Lake Ladoga – the so-called Novgorod route – and followed its southern coast to the Gulf of Finland. From the Dvina they could also go east to reach the Volga on the way to the great emporium in Kazan, the hub for the Caspian and Central Asian trade. Goods like wax, honey, and furs went the other way, to Constantinople and the Mediterranean.

The creation of Arkhangelsk in 1584 and the opening up of the Russian far north lessened the importance of Lake Ladoga, but the emergence of Sweden restored its importance. The Swedes saw the incorporation of the lake and its basin as a means to control the interior, deep into the Russian land.

The lake also received Lake Onega, eighteen times the size of Lake Geneva, via the Svir. With its two outstretched fingers pointing north, Lake Onega showed the way to the White Sea, as a king of Sweden would later discover and which the Soviet government would seek to develop – with disastrous results. But its importance lay in the connection it established via the Vytegra and the Kovzha with the White Lake (Belo-ozero), and south of it, via the Sheksna, with the Volga at Rybinsk. This was the route followed by caravans from Central Asia and the Caspian on their way to Novgorod. Those lakes and rivers, connected by portages[1] before the age of canals in the eighteenth and nineteenth centuries, were not easily navigable because of many obstacles: strong northern winds causing shipwrecks; low and swampy shores; rapids caused by glacial moraines; shallow beds with an imperceptible gradient, which froze for several months and had too little water in the summer. Nevertheless, the river beds and lake shores remained preferable to the unreliable trails across a forested land.

A second waterway linked the Volga with the Baltic, also starting at Rybinsk. Here, grain, salt, and iron came from the Urals, the mid- and lower Volga region, on their way to Petersburg. It followed the Mologa, then the Charodoshcha, a few smaller rivers, and then the Tikhvinka and the Sias, which drained into Lake Ladoga, a short distance east of the Volkhov estuary. These two routes became known in the nineteenth century as the Mariinskii and Tikhvinskii waterways respectively. The age of canals may be said to have begun with Peter I, who built a third route, shorter, more dangerous, and eventually less profitable. The Tvertsa drained into the Volga at Tver. It began in a swampy depression filled by Lake Mstimo, out of which flowed the Msta, which after a long detour, made dangerous by the twenty-six Borovichi rapids, drained into Lake Ilmen, and linked up with the Novgorod route on the Volkhov. It was built by hard labourers, including fifteen thousand Little Russian Cossacks, and many more sacrificed their lives to assert Russia's claim to hegemony in the eastern Baltic.

All these waterways, linked by portages, formed a continuous system stretching from the Caspian to the Baltic. The westernmost end of the system was also the westernmost rim of the Eurasian land mass centred on the Caspian basin. Petersburg may have been a European city, its glare fixed on Europe, but its survival depended on a constant supply of all its basic necessities from the interior of Eurasia: a European city, but the capital, not of European Russia, but of a Eurasian empire.

This Eurasian corridor continued westwards into Finland. Beyond Lake Ladoga the ground rose toward Lake Saimaa, draining into Lake Ladoga via the Vuoksi, a lazy river looking more like a succession of pools in an indifferent and sparsely populated landscape. The lake is at about eighty metres of elevation above sea level and is itself the drainage basin of other elongated and deeply incised lakes, stretching along the Karelian border to the east and beyond Kuopio in the north. West of this enormous waterway lay Lake Paijanne with its 640 sister lakes forming the watershed between Lake Ladoga and the Gulf of Bothnia. It drains into the Gulf of Finland via the Kiumenne (Kymi) at Lovitsa and Kotka. Further west lay Lake Nasi (Näsijärvi), draining into the Gulf of Bothnia at Björneborg (Pori).

Finland has been called the land of the one thousand lakes; in fact, there may be more than fifty-five thousand, most of them closely packed in the central Lake Region. Its appearance suggests "a level shore, recently forsaken by the tide,"[2] a striking similarity with the coast of the southern Ukraine (New Russia, Novorossiya), where inland shells remind the visitor that it once was under the waters of the Black Sea.

To the south of the Lake Region, an amphitheatre of three parallel ridges of glacial mud and gravel, called the Saupasselka, separates it from the coastal strip of the Gulf of Finland. Together with the southeastern coast of the Gulf of Bothnia, facing Sweden below Björneborg, the strip was the most populated part of Finland, where Swedes predominated. Only 8 per cent of Finland is arable and grassland, 46 per cent consists of forest and lakes, and the rest is largely swamp. The country's interior, the Lake Region, is unfit for agriculture. North of it, the ground continues to rise all the way to the headwaters of the Torneo and Muonio near the Swedish and Norwegian border.

But the whole of Finland beyond the basin of Lake Ladoga descends gently toward the Gulf of Bothnia, a large trough separating Finland from Sweden; at the Kvarken, it is only seventy kilometres wide and only twenty if one begins at the islands. Sweden is the land of another fifty-five thousand lakes, but many are mountain lakes.The Swedish coast rises rapidly toward the Scandinavian Alps.[3] They are difficult to cross, and several heights exceed 1,800 metres. The Crestline forms the boundary of western Eurasia, and beyond it lies the vast expanse of the Atlantic Ocean.

If we look back upon the topography of this northern sector of the western theatre, we find an almost completely self-enclosed world of Sweden and Finland bowing to each other across the Gulf of Bothnia, but on the whole forming a huge extension of the basin of Lake Ladoga. Its orientation was not western, was barely southern toward Baltic shores, but definitely eastern toward the Eurasian land mass, of which it constituted the westernmost end.

A short distance from the Pola descending toward Lake Ilmen and the Volga beginning its long voyage to the Caspian, the 920-kilometre-long Western Dvina turned southwest toward Beshenkovichi, from which a portage linked the river with the Dnieper. It then swerved abruptly westward toward Dünaburg (Dvinsk, Daugavpils) and then northwards toward Riga, the greatest port in the eastern Baltic from medieval days to the eighteenth century. Immense timber rafts steered by Russian Gypsies carried the products of Russian and Polish forests, and the hemp and flax so highly prized in Europe. It was a dangerous river to navigate because of its rapids, especially those between Kokenhusen (Koknese) and Jacobstadt (Ekabpils), which ranked in importance after those of the Msta and the Dnieper (Dnipro). But it had once been part of the waterway from the Black to the Baltic Seas, and Tsar Ivan IV could still say in the sixteenth century that its banks were made of silver and its bottom was made of gold.[4]

The Dvina was the first of a number of rivers draining toward the semicircular coast of the southeastern Baltic, each with a major port at its mouth. Beshenkovichi was near the confluence of the Ulla and the Dvina. The Ulla linked it via a portage, later a canal, with the Berezina, known in history as the river which Charles XII crossed on his way to Poltava and Napoleon crossed on his way back to France. The Berezina led to the heights of Minsk, where the Niemen began its nine-hundred-kilometre course across Lithuania to the swampy coast of the Kurisches Haff. Boats entered it to dock at Memel (Klaiped) in Prussia. Like almost all the rivers of this region, and like almost all the rivers of the Eurasian land mass, navigation on it was obstructed by rapids, low gradient, occasional boulders, dead trees, and sandbars, but the river was also the only means of communication after the thaw set in and the country became an impassable swamp. The Niemen also carried mostly timber and timber materials, typical products of Eurasia, for which there always was a great demand in the German lands.

The Niemen was easily connected with the Vistula. A string of lakes forming the Augustow canal led to the Bebrza (Bobr), which flowed into the Narew, the latter into the Western Bug descending from the Volhynian upland and draining into the Vistula downstream from Warsaw. The Narew could also be reached via the Zelvianka, a tributary of the Niemen, past the famous Belovezh Pushcha, an enormous hunting preserve known for the variety and abundance of its game, including the almost extinct bison. All these rivers were insignificant. Indeed, their importance was greater in olden days, when boats were smaller and loads lighter, than in the nineteenth century, and they flowed across a desolate swampland. The triangle formed by the Narew and the Bebzha formed the Byalystok region; Prussia, which acquired it in 1795, was only too happy to turn it over to Russia in 1807.

The Vistula (Wisla) was the longest (about one thousand kilometres) of all the rivers draining into the Baltic. The size of its basin, about two hundred thousand square kilometres, was almost as large as Great Britain and Northern Ireland. The Vistula gathered into itself all the rivers of Poland, if we also include the Warta descending from the Czestochowa-Kraków plateau at 535 metres of elevation.

The Warta once flowed into a swampy depression filled by Lake Goplo, now much smaller, which linked it with the Vistula. Some scholars still consider it reasonable to include the Warta among the tributaries of the Vistula, draining the western part of Poland to Silesia, the valley of the Oder.[5] But while the Vistula was the symbol of Poland, it was not very useful as a transportation medium. It took its source in the Beskids, a northern spur of the Carpathians on the Slovak border, flowed northeastward until it received the San, which divided Galicia into two halves, the Polish and the Ukrainian. It was navigable over a very short distance and prone to devastating floods. The Przemysl Gate separated it from the headwaters of the Dniester.

The river then turned north, picked up the Wieprz, where it became navigable for more than flat-bottom boats, and entered near Warsaw a low-lying corridor, which led to the sea. Before reaching the sea, it divided into two branches, the Vistula proper and the Nogat. The latter flowed into the Frisches Haff (Zalew Wislany) past Elblag (Elbing) and entered the Baltic west of Königsberg (Kaliningrad). The Vistula proper divided again into two branches, one called the Elbing Vistula, also draining into the Frisches Haff, the other, called the Danzig Vistula, named after the port of Danzig (Gdansk). With Riga, it was the most important port of the eastern Baltic and the outlet for Polish exports of grain and timber from all the way in Volhynia sent down the Western Bug.

West of the Vistula there remained only the Oder (Odra), about nine hundred kilometres long. It took its source a short distance west of the Vistula on the Czech border. It flowed northwest across Silesia, then turned sharply west and then north, to drain into the Stettin Haff, named after the port of Stettin (Szczecin), almost blocked from the sea by three large islands. A notable feature was that it received no affluents from the west: the Neisse, the present-day border between Germany and Poland, comes from the south and forms a kind of forward defence line protecting the Oder. The Oder "was a strong barrier protecting Poland against its western neighbors" (1942); it protected "Poland in the west, like a solid wall, against the Germans and other Slavs" (1803); the Holy Roman Emperor Frederick I Barbarossa (1135–90) regarded it as "the rampart of Poland."[6] Like the Scandinavian Alps in the north, it was the perfect boundary of western Eurasia in the south. From there, or at least from the Vistula, began the land of the forest – 70 per cent of Poland consisted of coniferous forests. "The prison of those Polish pines / How it shuts off from all things dear" (in Europe), bemoaned a German officer in 1915.[7] These coniferous forests continued without interruption across the whole of Eurasia all the way to the Pacific.

Each of the three theatres had its own sea, but if they eventually led to the great oceans, their shores were not hospitable to traders and the development of a flourishing maritime civilization. The Baltic Sea offered more favourable conditions than the Sea of Okhotsk or the Black Sea, but its major ports owed their development more to their being outlets for the raw materials of western Eurasia than to the economic growth of their local base, except for Petersburg. Shorn of its imperial attributes, however, the capital was no more than a great commercial city for the transit trade between Europe and Eurasia.

The Baltic Sea was once part of the Ancylus Sea, a marshy plain extending from the Atlantic to the Urals, until the ocean drowned the western part to form the North Sea, which merges with the Atlantic Ocean.[8] The remainder became the Baltic Sea, and Finland still continues to rise above its level at the rate of about ninety centimetres a century. The sea exits into the North Sea through three channels, the Sound between Sweden and Denmark, and the

Great and Little Belts of Denmark. The Sound is the major one because it is unencumbered by islands and sharp turns. Its depth does not exceed seven metres: it was used by sailing ships but can no longer be navigated by large modern ships. Baltic waters are almost entirely fresh; very little water enters from the North Sea, unlike the Black Sea where a strong Mediterranean current runs under the layer of lighter fresh water from the Dnieper and other rivers. Therefore, "the Baltic basin constitutes the selfcontained basin of a typical continental sea, almost completely cut off from other oceanic influences."[9] At least three consequences follow. Tidal movement is almost completely absent; ports freeze up for at least part of the long winters; marine life is poor: the celebrated Baltic herring of medieval days is in fact no bigger than a sardine and the cod only about one-fifth of the weight of those found on the Norway coast.

The sea is 1,700 kilometres long from Kiel to Haparanda at the far end of the Gulf of Bothnia. Its largest island is Gotland, its largest archipelago, that of the Åland Islands at the entrance of the Gulf. Its greatest depth reaches 300 metres off Gotland, but most of the sea is between 25 and 100 metres deep. At about the latitude of Stockholm, it branches out into the Gulf of Bothnia, 670 kilometres long, whose northern part is under ice for from six to seven months. It separates Sweden from Finland, and the latter's isolation did much to cultivate separatist sentiments among even the Swedes of Finland.

The other branch is the Gulf of Finland, about 430 kilometres long, under ice for from five to six months, at the tip of which the Swedes built a profitable commercial outlet in the seventeenth century and the Russians a capital in the eighteenth. The northern coast is sharply indented, the southern coast is smooth The existence of a rotating current, encouraged by westerly winds, emphasizes the nearly self-enclosed nature of the sea, and explains the creation of lagoons (each called a Haff), nearly blocked by great sandspits capped by dunes, with a narrow opening through which the rivers finally reach the sea. All in all the Baltic Sea was not an open sea in the traditional sense, but a large pool draining in circular fashion all the important rivers of western Eurasia. Only beyond its western exits did Europe's maritime civilization begin.

Geopolitics

The early political history of western Eurasia was marked in the thirteenth century by a concerted assault from Europe and Latin Christianity upon the Russian and Orthodox lands, the so-called *Drang nach Osten*. It was led mostly by German knights. Later came Polish and Swedish expansion within western Eurasia, converging on the Dvina and the Gulf of Finland, followed by a destructive war between Poland and Sweden, which opened the way for Russia's *Drang nach Westen* beginning in the seventeenth century.

There were six crusades between 1095 and 1229, inspired by a Latin Christian ideal to convert schismatics and infidels to the true faith, and give employment to idle knights, together with the chance of capturing booty and creating fiefs in lands that were much richer than those of Europe. The crusaders fanned out in two directions: toward the Holy Land, occupied by Muslims, and against Orthodox Christianity, whose capital, Constantinople, the most splendid medieval city, they sacked in 1204 at the end of the fourth crusade. This need not concern us here. In the north, the crusaders focused on the southern coast of the Baltic all the way to the Gulf of Finland, in order to convert native tribes in present-day northern Poland, Lithuania, Latvia, and Estonia, and to destroy the Orthodox stronghold in Novgorod, from where missionaries and traders were moving into the eastern Baltic and Finland.[10]

Germans had been coming from Westphalia (capital Münster) and Lübeck since the twelfth century via Visby on Gotland Island to trade and settle in Livonia (Livland), the land of the Latvians. The first bishop (1186–96) had his capital in Uxküll on the lower Dvina, but the third, Albrecht von Buxhoeveden (1199–1229), moved his see to Riga, which he founded in 1202.[11] His descendant would command Russian troops invading Finland six hundred years later. That same year, he founded the Order of the Sword Bearers headed by a master (*Meister*) with a mission to convert the pagans and fight Orthodoxy; he later became the pope's highest representative in the region with the rank of archbishop. Twelve years earlier, in 1190, the Teutonic Order was founded in Acre in the Holy Land to care for the German sick during the third crusade, but it later withdrew to Venice. It was headed by a grand master (*Hochmeister*), who governed with the help of commanders forming a council or chapter (*kapitul*).

Grand Master Hermann von Salza (1210–39) saw an opportunity in 1226, when Conrad of Mazovia, the Polish lord of the middle Vistula region, asked the Order to exterminate the Prussians, who blocked Poland's access to the Baltic. They did, settled down, founded Danzig in 1235 and Elbing in 1237, and established their capital at Marienburg (Malbork) on the Nogat. Also in 1237, they incorporated the Sword Bearers, who became the Livonian branch of the Teutonic Order, but the pope insisted that they must take the oath of fealty to the archbishop in Riga. The knights inaugurated a "continual crusade," "a permanent presence with a vested interest in growth,"[12] as the papacy's strike force against Novgorod and Orthodoxy), but they were decisively beaten in 1242 on Lake Peipus (Chud) by Alexander Nevsky. The lake and the Narova River would become and remain to this day the boundary between the Russian lands and the Baltic peoples south of the Gulf of Finland.

The Order, whose possessions extended from eastern Pomerania to the Gulf of Finland, formed a "state" (*Ordenstaat*), and imposed upon the native population an exceptionally brutal rule, especially in Livonia and Estonia (Estland), purchased from Denmark in 1347. But a triangle of rivalries soon developed between them and the Riga archbishop, from whom they sought their autonomy, and the merchants of Riga, who sought freedom from both Grand Master and bishop. As a result, a "state" did not truly develop in the Baltic provinces, but instead, a maze of conflicting jurisdictions which would mark the political life of those provinces until 1917.

But the Order's growth was constrained by the completion of the conversion drive, the resulting weakening of the Order's resolve, and the growth of Polish power. The Order attempted to convert Samogitia, "the heart of ethnic Lithuania ... and the last independent island separating German possessions in Prussia and in Lithuania," but could not keep it.[13] If the Order blocked Poland's access to the sea, Poland blocked the Order's inland expansion. Like the Little Russian Cossacks after 1775, the soldier-monks lost their raison d'être once their purpose had vanished. They began to marry – the celibacy rule had cultivated over the centuries a racism toward Slavs and others which never truly abated – had children and other heirs, and became landowners. In 1410, they were crushed by Poland at the famous battle of Tannenberg (Stetbark), and after a long war (1454–66) Poland gained West Prussia, Danzig, and Thorn (Torun). The Grand Master moved to Königsberg, but had to recognize himself a vassal of the Polish king. The territory would become known as Royal Prussia until 1772, and the remainder of the Order's possessions, as East Prussia.[14]

The sixteenth century was the great turning point. Martin Luther (1483–1546) posted his ninety-five theses on the door of the castle church in Wittenberg on the Elbe in 1517, and the Protestant Reformation began. Like the crusaders and colonists of past centuries, Luther's ideas quickly spread eastward and influenced Grand Master Albrecht von Hohenzollern (Brandenburg)-Ansbach (1511–68). In 1525, he transformed his lands into a secular state with himself as duke, while still recognizing the Polish king as his suzerain. He thereby seized the properties of the Catholic Church in his territory. Then Livonia fell prey to Russo-Swedish-Polish rivalries against which the Order was powerless. In 1561 the Livonian master, Gotthard Kettler, made himself Duke of Kurland, the southern rump of Livonia, and he too became a vassal of the Polish crown. The *Ordenstaat* had come to an end, but a new Prussia was being born, which one day would unite the lands of the German crusaders and destroy the Russian empire.

While the Germans were creating a "new Germania"[15] on the southern shores of the Baltic, a powerful state was emerging in Poland. The country managed to escape the German onslaught because its prince, Mieszko I (960–992), had converted to Latin Christianity in 966 and placed his lands under the protection of the Pope. Roman Catholicism had found a forward position against Russian Orthodoxy and a core area suitable for building an empire dedicated to the containment of an expanding Russian core. An archbishopric was created in Gniezno, with bishoprics in Poznan, Kraków, and Wroclaw (in Silesia) between

968 and 1000, two hundred years before the foundation of Riga. A Piast dynasty began with Mieszko's son Boleslaw I (992–1025), which would last until 1370. It united Little Poland (the valley of the upper Vistula with Kraków) in 1305 and Great Poland (the valley of the middle Oder and the Warta with Poznan) in 1314. Casimir the Great (1333–70) founded the University of Kraków in 1364, but left no son. Fourteen years later, the Poles accepted one of his nieces, Jadwiga, as their queen (1384–98), and arranged for her to marry Jagiello, the Grand Duke of Lithuania. They founded the Jagellonian dynasty (1386–1572). Jagiello ruled as King of Poland (1386–1434) and Grand Duke (1382–1401).[16]

The union of Poland and Lithuania was a momentous event. Among other things, it created a mortal threat to the Teutonic Order. The Grand Duchy of Lithuania had begun with Gedymin (1316–41), who resided in Vilnius. He united more closely the Lithuanian and Belorussian lands and forged a centralized military state which rapidly expanded eastward. It eventually reached the boundaries of the grand principalities of Moscow and Riazan and the republic of Novgorod.

Lithuania was an overextended territorial conglomerate which needed the superior resources of Poland. When Jagiello converted to Latin Christianity, the influence of Catholicism grew exponentially. The Grand Duchy drew Poland eastward, transformed it into a crusading state, much more capable of challenging Orthodoxy than the Teutonic Knights could ever do. The emerging conflict with Russia (and Sweden) helped define the western theatre within Eurasia. Poland acquired an eastern mission, which it would retain until it turned westward during the first decade of the twenty-first century.

The union of Krewo (Krevo) of 1386 was intended to be more than a personal and dynastic union; it was meant to be a complete incorporation of Lithuania into Poland, with Catholicism as the official religion and Lithuanian nobles enjoying the same privileges as the Polish ruling class (*szlachta*). But the Lithuanians had already developed a strong identity, and resentment brought about the election of Jagiello's cousin, Witold (Vitovt), as Grand Duke of Lithuania (1401–30). The Lithuanians had carried out attacks on Russian lands, including Moscow, in 1368 and 1370, and become involved in Muscovite politics. Witold seized Smolensk in 1395 and had designs on Novgorod, but he chose to focus on the Ukrainian provinces of Lithuania. He died in 1340 before he could succeed. By that time, it seemed that the policy of "gathering the Russian lands" would be carried out not by Moscow but by Lithuania: Witold's daughter married Vasilii I (1389–1425), who in his testament of 1423 left his wife and sons to the protection of the mighty Witold; soon afterwards, Tver and Riazan recognized Witold as their suzerain.[17]

But not for long. With the accession of Ivan III (1462–1505), Moscow assumed the leadership. It gathered Novgorod in 1478, Tver in 1485. Ivan's son Vasilii III (1505–33) annexed the frontier city of Smolensk in 1514 and Riazan in 1517. Meanwhile, Ivan III had married the only niece of the last Byzantine emperor (1449–53) and become the defender of Eastern Orthodoxy against Islam and Catholicism. Since Witold's death, the military efficiency of Lithuania had considerably declined and the natural attraction of Eastern Orthodoxy had much increased. A geopolitical rivalry between Russia and Poland over Lithuania was becoming a religious one as well. The Reformation found an echo in Lithuania, but the Catholic Church retaliated with the Counter-Reformation. It began with the creation of the Jesuit Order in 1540 and the summoning of the Council of Trent in 1545. The Jesuits, headed by a "general," became the soldier-crusaders of the papacy, worthy descendants of the Teutonic Knights, but without their brutality and racism. Instead, they relied on education in various "missions," schools and academies, which they opened in increasing numbers across Lithuania all the way to Polotsk on the Dvina facing Smolensk on the road to Moscow.

The turbulence created by the Reformation and Counter-Reformation in Lithuania and Livonia, and the resulting rapprochement between the two countries, worried Moscow. When Master Kettler and the Riga archbishop accepted the incorporation of Livonia into the Polish empire in 1561, Ivan IV (1533–84) in Moscow saw this as a *casus belli*, bringing about a twenty-year war between 1561 and 1582. The Polish empire during the reigns of Sigismund I (1506–48) and Sigismund II August (1548–72) marked the zenith of Polish political and cultural influence, the high-water mark of Polish Protestantism, but also the appearance of the Jesuits in 1565. The Union of Lublin (1569), when Sigismund II incorporated the Volhynian and Podolian provinces of Lithuania into the Polish core (*korona*), created an indivisible body politic between Poland and Lithuania.

It also shifted Poland's centre of gravity eastward and brought it into direct contact with the confessional frontier between Catholicism and Orthodoxy in Belorussia.[18] The stage was being set for the momentous conflict with Russia. Paradoxically, Sigismund's death brought about the end of the Jagellonian dynasty and introduced the period of the elective kings, beginning with the "Henrician Articles" of 1573, which transformed Poland into an elective monarchy ("republic"), fated to be torn apart by internal discord until it fell prey to the ambitions of Russia and Prussia (and Austria).

While these developments were taking place on the southern shores of the Baltic and the open plain between the Niemen, the Dvina, and the upper Dnieper, another conflict had been brewing for centuries between Scandinavians and Russians. Eric IX of Sweden (1150–60) launched a crusade against the pagan Finns in 1157, imposed Christianity in the Åbo region (Finnish Turku, meaning a trading place), and founded a colony. A century later, in 1240, the Swedes reached the mouth of the Neva, but were stopped by Alexander Nevsky (1220–63), prince of Novgorod. Novgorodians and Swedes became natural rivals in the basin of Lake Ladoga, where the fur trade had made the wealth of Novgorod. In 1249, the Swedes founded Tavastborg (Tavastehus) on the southern rim of the Lake Region and, in 1293, Vyborg on the Vuoksa, the centre of Finnish Karelia, where Orthodoxy had already made some inroads; they hoped to make it a springboard for the conquest of Lake Ladoga's basin. In 1300 they built Nienshants on a stream near where Peter I would lay the foundations of Petersburg four hundred years later, but it was destroyed by the Novgorodians in 1301. In 1310 they built Keksholm, a fort which gave them a foothold on Lake Saimaa and a backup position to defend Vyborg. The Novgorodians countered by building a fort at Orekhov (Noteborg), on an island formed by the two branches of the Neva exiting Lake Ladoga, but it was taken by the Swedes in 1328. An attempt was made to reach a *modus vivendi*. The Treaty of Noteborg in 1323, the year the fort was built, contained a vague attempt to establish a border running from the Narova River along the southern shore of the Gulf of Finland, across Kotlin Island to the Sestra stream, across the Lake Region to the end of the Gulf of Bothnia and to the Varanger fjord. Traders seem to have ignored it because the stakes were so high, but armed conflicts were avoided when both Sweden and Novgorod became torn by internal strife.[19]

The situation changed radically following the annexation of Novgorod by Ivan III. Muscovy inherited the city's claims in the Baltic sector, just as it would assume the inheritance of the Kipchak Khanate in the 1550s and that of Kievan Rus' in the 1650s. Muscovy was becoming a Eurasian power and would henceforth seek to assert its hegemony in western Eurasia. His grandson Ivan IV was drawn into the vacuum created by the secularization of the Teutonic Order and by Swedish and Polish rivalry. He invaded Livonia in 1558, but Estland placed itself under Swedish suzerainty, Livonia passed under Lithuania, Kurland became a fief of Poland, and Ösel Island went to Demark. Russia found itself at war with both Poland-Lithuania and Sweden.[20] In the meantime, a Swedish nobleman, Gustav Vasa, founded a new dynasty bearing his name (1523–1818). Sweden became Lutheran. The war, which had begun well for the Russians, turned against them, especially during the reign of Stefan Batory (1575–86), who inflicted disastrous defeats on them and even almost took Pskov. Moscow had to abandon all its acquisitions in Livonia in 1582, and give up the southern shore of the Gulf of Finland from Narva to Lake Ladoga to the Swedes in 1583. Muscovy had been cut off from the Baltic, but Arkhangelsk opened a new way to Europe.

The geopolitical situation became extremely confused between 1584 and 1612. Russian weakness, the end of Moscow's Riurikid dynasty – which went back to the Scandinavian chieftain Rurik, "invited" to rule over Novgorod in 862 – and the short and disastrous reign of Boris Godunov, followed by the so-called Time of Troubles (1605–12), invited Swedish and Polish intervention, but not always military. We encounter the first projects of union between the crowns of Poland, Sweden, and Russia, which came almost to fruition in 1809 and 1815, when the tsar-emperor became Grand Duke of Finland and King of Poland.

Finland was a duchy in an emerging Swedish empire, and Gustav Vasa's younger brother Johan became duke of that eastern land. He married Catherine, sister of Sigismund II August, and became King of Sweden as Johan III (1568–92). When Sigismund died without issue, and with him the Jagellonian dynasty in 1672, Johan inherited both crowns, creating, on paper, a formidable competitor for Russia, capable of uniting western Eurasia. The endemic rivalry with Denmark had already resulted in Sweden's acquiring Estland in 1572. When Johan died in 1592, his son became King of Poland and Sweden: he had already succeeded Batory in Poland in 1587. But the union would not last. Sigismund III (1587–1632) was narrow-minded, obstinate, and a staunch Catholic, who antagonized his Lutheran subjects. They deposed him in 1599, but he would remain King of Poland until 1632. He was succeeded in Sweden by his uncle Charles, who became king as Charles IX, not crowned until 1607, and who died in 1611. His son, Gustav II Adolf, would become Sweden's greatest king (1611–32).[21]

In 1586, Batory had sent a mission to Moscow offering a dynastic union: if he died before Fedor, Ivan IV's son (1584–98), the latter would become King of Poland and Grand Duke of Lithuania, while remaining tsar in Moscow. If Fedor died first, the reverse would apply. Nothing came of it: Batory died that same year and Moscow refused to consider the offer,[22] which was intended to harness Muscovy to fulfil one of Poland's greatest ambitions: to lead a crusade against the Ottoman Turks under the auspices of the Pope to create a Polish empire from sea (Baltic) to sea (Black). In 1600, Sapieha, a Lithuanian grandee, went even further: Muscovy would be included into the Polish empire like another Lithuania. This may have been directed against Poland's overbearing influence.

But by 1609, when Muscovy's disintegration was reaching its final stage, Sigismund III marched on Smolensk, where an agreement was reached in February 1610: his son Władysław would be crowned tsar in Moscow by the Orthodox patriarch, convert to Orthodoxy, and take an Orthodox bride. But Sigismund nullified it, when he announced that he himself wanted to be tsar. Muscovy would thus have a Catholic ruler, a non-negotiable position for the Russians. A foreign prince was acceptable, but not a schismatic one.[23] The Poles continued their advance and entered Moscow in August 1610, but were soon expelled by a violent reaction led by the Orthodox Church, and Michael I was elected the first tsar of the new Romanov dynasty in February 1613. The opportunity had passed to unite most of western Eurasia under Polish leadership; it would never return.

At first, the Russians were more successful against the Swedes. In 1590 they reoccupied the southern shore of the Gulf of Finland (Ingria), but could not take Narva. Charles IX too had vast ambitions: not only to keep Ingria but also to annex Novgorod and Pskov as well as Karelia and the Kola Peninsula on the White Sea. The Swedes then took both cities and entered Moscow in January 1610 – the decisive event which prompted the Poles to do the same. An agreement signed in July 1611 made Novgorod into a Swedish protectorate, and a Swedish prince would become tsar in Moscow. But Gustav Adolf, like Sigismund, overplayed his hand: he would not let his brother become tsar, but would seek the title himself. For the Novgorodians a schismatic prince from hated Latin Christendom was as unacceptable as it was for the Muscovites. He had to desist in the summer of 1612.[24]

And thus three centuries of rivalry, commercial, military, and diplomatic, had ended in a draw. But such a prolonged rivalry had shaped a strategic theatre in the northwestern end of Eurasia. Poles, Lithuanians, and Swedes had always moved east, Russians west, for the control of a common frontier including the basin of Lake Ladoga and the hydrographic infrastructure of Lithuania. A new phase in that never-ending rivalry was about to begin after 1613.

The Russian Advance

The new Russian dynamism manifested itself very quickly. By the end of 1614, there was already violent opposition to Swedish rule in Novgorod, and Gustav Adolf had to lift the siege of Pskov in the summer of 1615. In October, negotiations began at Stolbovo near Tikhvin, southeast of Lake Ladoga, but an agreement was not signed until February 1617. The Swedes abandoned Novgorod, but Russia had to cede Karelia, Ingria with the mouth of the Neva, and Kotlin Island. The country was once again cut off from the Gulf of Finland. The Swedes had created a strategic frontier running from Estland past the eastern shores of Lake Ladoga to the Karelian upland forming the watershed between the Lake Region of Finland and the basin of the White Sea. The agreement was not a disaster:[25] Russia's hold on the Neva had always been tenuous, and the circumstances in which Russia had regained it in 1590 had distinctly been unfavourable. On the other hand, Sweden was definitely on the defensive: it had not reached the White Sea and had lost Novgorod.

This appears clearly from two speeches delivered by the king before the Swedish parliament. In January 1617, he was confident that Lake Ladoga, the swamps of Ingria, and the "turbulent Narova" blocked Russia's access to the gulf, for war or trade purposes, "without our special permission." But in August, the emphasis had changed: he had become aware of the capabilities of "our enemy the Russian," his "appallingly large armies," and his ability to use the hydrographic network of western Eurasia to transport them "on the Caspian and up the Volga and down the Volkhov, and along the Dvina and the Niemen to

Livonia."[26] Was the king already aware that Russia was a Volga-Caspian-based power, capable of projecting great power across the whole of western Eurasia?

Poland too was on the defensive. Sigismund III did not recognize the election of Michael, but was willing to settle for Władysław. The Poles moved against Moscow once again, reached it in October 1618, but could not take it. An armistice was signed for fourteen years. Sigismund died in 1632 while preparing a religious crusade against Muscovy with the help of the Catholic and Uniate churches, but his son, now Władysław IV (1632–48), could only take Smolensk. Poland's ambitions no longer matched its capabilities. The "eternal peace" of June 1634 left Smolensk in Polish hands, but the king recognized Michael and gave up his claims to the Muscovite throne.[27] The threat now came from Ukraine, where turbulence among the Cossacks announced the great uprising of 1648, in which Russia would gradually become involved to begin the dismemberment of the Polish empire.

Swedish policy after Stolbovo focused on the old enemy, Denmark, and on northern Germany, where Gustav Adolf had fought to become the leader of the Protestant cause. It was there that he lost his life, at the battle of Lützen west of Leipzig in November 1632, seven months after Sigismund III. But his faithful chancellor, Axel Oxenstierna, shared the same ambitions in the Baltic. Sweden must become a great naval power capable of imposing its hegemony in what must become a Swedish lake.[28] But a naval policy is usually the handmaiden of a commercial policy. Sweden, with little good land and a small population, must gain control of all the estuaries of the rivers flowing into that sea and access to their hinterlands: Bremen on the Weser, Hamburg on the Elbe, Stettin on the Oder, Danzig on the Vistula, Königsberg and Memel (Klaipeda) on the Pregel and Niemen, Riga on the Dvina, and a still undeveloped location on the Neva. A Swedish merchant marine would drain the products of Muscovy and Ukraine, Lithuania, Poland, and Silesia. All trade routes would lead to Swedish-controlled ports. But such a policy contained the seeds of a permanent conflict with the Polish empire. The endemic conflict with Denmark was already consuming much of Sweden's energy and resources. In the end, the destruction of Poland would also eliminate one of Muscovy's major opponents and leave Sweden alone to face the rising Muscovite core, which would then destroy Sweden's hegemony.

Sweden was on the defensive during the long reign of Charles XI (1660–97). Its fifth war with Denmark was a disaster. The Danes took Wismar in 1675 and crushed the Swedish fleet off Oland Island in 1676. The Swedes lost control of the Baltic, of Wolin and Usedom, and Stettin capitulated in 1677. They lost Greifswald and Rügen Island. War on land and at sea exhausted the resources of the country, and the government had to raise the fiscal burden and, more importantly, turn against the nobility, both in Sweden and in Estland and Livland, who had encroached upon crown lands to enlarge their properties.

The so-called *Reduktion* antagonized the nobility as the ruling class of the provinces. The knights traced their origins to the Livonian and Teutonic Orders, and many were already anti-Swedish. By antagonizing the Baltic nobility, the Swedish government would encourage their switch of allegiance during the Northern War of 1700–21. Reducing the importance of the nobility in Sweden strengthened the monarchy; reducing it in Estland and Livland undermined the stability of the empire. Jan Sobiecki died in June 1696; Charles XI in April 1697; in May Peter I left Moscow for his grand tour of Europe. A new era was about to begin.

Peter I (1689–1725) was a strong and healthy youth, curious, enamoured of the sea and, unlike his predecessors, not distrustful of foreigners. Charles XII of Sweden (1697–1718) was a gifted and precocious youth of high morality, but obstinate to the point of obduracy; no one yet guessed that he possessed military talents of the highest order. As to August II (1697–1733), elected from among eighteen candidates partly as a result of Russian pressure, the most generous thing to be said about him was that he could bend a horseshoe in his bare hands and was "one of the most unscrupulous scoundrels ever to ascend the ill-fated throne of Poland."[29]

Sweden had been collecting significant revenue from its control of the Baltic ports and the channelling of the Russian trade toward Lake Ladoga and the Neva away from Arkhangelsk. There was a threat of Russia becoming economically dependent on Sweden. It had long been part of the "Great Eastern Program" of the Swedish monarchy to consolidate a Swedish takeover of the Russian trade in the region.[30] Commercial rivalry with Sweden created a natural alliance between Russia and Poland, but other ambitions created a potential conflict. Augustus wanted to regain Livonia with Riga; this would also put him on a collision course with Russia. Peter had visited Kurland on his way back and had become aware of its ports such as Libava (Liepaia) and Vindava (Ventspils), as well as of its rich oak forests, so suitable for shipbuilding. The reconquest of Livonia would strengthen the king's position in Lithuania, where the powerful Sapieha family refused to recognize him, but the Russians too had designs on Lithuania. Nevertheless, an alliance was forged in 1699 with Poland and Denmark: its major purpose was to expel the Swedes from their beachheads.

The high point of the Northern War of 1700–21 came in 1709. In the summer of 1707, Charles led "his magnificent army"[31] out of Saxony toward the east. The destination was Moscow. But the strategic picture had changed. The Russians had nibbled at the Swedish position. In 1703 they had taken the Neva and laid the foundation of a new capital at the site of Nien. They were once again on the Gulf of Finland. In 1704 they had retaken Narva, and they now threatened both the Baltic provinces and Finland. The king chose not to see. But the scorched-earth policy pursued by the Russians began to take its toll after the Swedes crossed the Dnieper in July 1708. Instead of moving north to find provisions and meet the Russians, who were now threatening his rear, the king turned south to winter in Little Russia with the support of Hetman Mazepa. The winter of 1708–9 was one of the coldest in living memory and inflicted more losses on the Swedes. The Russians checkmated them on the edge of the steppe. The result was the catastrophic battle of Poltava in June 1709.[32] The Swedish army was annihilated and the king forced to flee into Ottoman territory. Charles XII had lost the war.

The Russians then counterattacked in the north. Vyborg capitulated, then Keksholm, Reval, Riga, and Pernau, all in 1710. That same year, Peter married off his niece Anna to the Duke of Kurland and established a foothold in that Polish fief. The Danes joined the fray. The Russians built a fleet – the nightmare of Gustav Adolf – which defeated the Swedish fleet at the battle of Hangö in June 1714. The occupation of the Åland Islands brought the Russians within fifteen miles of Stockholm. Charles returned from captivity in November 1714, and turned on the Danes, who were threatening an invasion of Sweden, but he was killed, probably by one of his men, in December 1718. The Swedes still refused to surrender, despite the unravelling of their position and the loss of all their beachheads, until April 1721, when the Treaty of Nystadt gave Russia Ingria, Estonia, and Livonia, Ösel and Dagden (Khiruma) Islands, and the Vyborg district of Karelia. The Russians returned Finland, which they had occupied in 1714. Sweden would never recover from its defeat. Another war with Russia in 1742–3 resulted in another occupation of Finland, the stationing of Russian troops in Stockholm, and the annexation of another strip of Finnish territory by the Treaty of Åbo (Turku) of January 1743.

Hesitant Integration

Centre and Province

The annexation of Estland, Livland, and Vyborg provinces presented the Russian government with unprecedented problems. The Muscovite core had been steadily expanding across the forest zone and the steppe, incorporating territories which the ruling elite assumed would eventually become fully integrated. Those territories had been conquered by force of arms, like Kazan and Bashkiria, or brought in by treaties, like Little Russia, where religion and an emerging society of landowners facilitated a growing accommodation. The Baltic provinces had also been acquired by force, and had no right to claim more than what the conqueror was willing to concede. But their societies were more pluralistic, and their "rights and privileges" formed a dense web of relationships more capable of resisting outside pressures. Moreover, they were part of a wider world of the Swedish empire, of German cities on the Baltic, and of Protestant Germany in general.

Sweden had pursued throughout the seventeenth century a policy of administrative centralization, which had created much resentment among the elites. For the Russians to do the same carried the risk of incurring the same resentment on the shores of an immense continent, with dangerous implications. Likewise, a policy of full integration was certain to ring many alarm bells throughout the Germanic world, with which the Russians wished to remain on friendly terms, in their own endeavour to gain hegemony in the Baltic sector of their western theatre. Such concerns dictated caution, and a policy of full integration would have to be tempered by the need to keep recognizing a special status for the provinces within the expanding core, in order to conciliate the wider world of which these provinces remained a part. Such a policy would not come until the second half of the nineteenth century when, characteristically enough, the German danger raised its head.

It was in the field of territorial administration that integration became official policy from the beginning. Since the 1634 reform of the Swedish government, the Swedish kingdom, including Finland, had been divided into provinces (*län*). They included Estland, Livland, and Ösel Island; in Ingria, Noteborg, Kopore, Yamburg, and Narva; Karelia with Vyborg, and Kexholm, ceded by Russia in 1617, with a large Orthodox population soon forced to emigrate or convert to Lutheranism.[33] When the annexation took place in 1710, the territorial reform of the expanding core had already divided it into eight provinces (*gubernii*) in December 1708. Narva was incorporated into Petersburg province, as well as Ingria under a separate administration. Estland, Livland, and Vyborg were later merged with it. When the second territorial reform took place in August 1719, which divided the provinces into *provintsii*, an enormous Petersburg province was made to consist of eleven *provintsii*, including Ingria, Vyborg, and Narva, as well as Pskov and Novgorod and their environs, even Tver and Yaroslavl. Estland was recognized as a separate province with Ösel Island; so was Livland, which had already become a province in 1713. Smolensk was added to it as the capital of a *provintsiia*, even though the two were not even contiguous.[34]

There was something incongruous in the long term about such territorial division, but it found its justification in current strategic considerations and the need to channel the largest amount of available resources toward the new capital. Petersburg became the capital not only of an expanding Russia but also of an immense region in need of an administrative infrastructure to link the various parts of what was essentially the basin of Lake Ladoga. But distances and the difficulty of maintaining communications convinced Peter's successors of the need to concentrate agencies in smaller provinces. By 1727, Estland and Livland remained separate provinces, but the latter without Smolensk. A much smaller Petersburg province consisted only of Ingria, the Neva, and Karelia with Vyborg and Kexholm. The remainder, without Tver and Yaroslavl, became

Novgorod province, encompassing much of the old Novgorod territory reaching as far north as the White Sea.

The only other change until the annexation of Finland in 1809 was the incorporation of additional territory in 1743. The new Russo-Finnish boundary followed the Kiumenne River from its mouth near Kotka across the Saupasselke ridges, swerved east and then north to include most of Lake Saimaa, and rejoined the 1721 border at Nyslott (Savonlinna). It was a strategic border which incorporated into the expanding core the entire Swedish defence perimeter running from Fredrikshamn (Hamina) past Villmanstrand (Lappenranta) to Nyslott. The enlarged Vyborg *provintsia* was transformed into a separate province. The newly annexed territory became Kiumenegorsk *provintsiia* of Vyborg province, its capital in Kexholm.[35]

The Swedish monarchy had long pursued a policy of full incorporation into the kingdom and total assimilation of the non-Swedish peoples. Its agents in the provinces were the governor (*landshövding*) with a small chancery. Baltic Germans usually filled the higher posts; the languages were Swedish and German. The governor was responsible for civil and fiscal affairs, even though the latter were often the responsibility of a separate *Statthalter*. Military affairs depended on a governor general. Finland was for long a distant backwater, cut off from Sweden during the winter months. In 1581 it was made a grand principality, and a governor general was first appointed in 1623. He resided in Åbo. It was not a permanent post at first, but became increasingly so during the reign of Charles XI. There was another in Reval, a third in Riga, and a fourth in Narva, who was responsible for Kexholm as well.[36]

After the conquest and until Peter's death in January 1725, the administration of the new lands reflected the government's concern with the construction of Petersburg, to which many of the central agencies were transferred from Moscow in 1714 and reorganized on the Swedish model in 1717. The eastern Baltic remained a war theatre until the peace of Nystadt, and Peter was obsessed with the building of a navy to challenge Sweden's supremacy. Finland, occupied in 1714, was placed under General, later Field Marshal, Prince Mikhail Golitsyn (1714–20), who was then transferred to the southern theatre to become commander in chief of Russian troops facing the Tatar steppe. The top man in Vyborg was senior (*ober*)commandant Colonel, later Major General, Ivan Shuvalov (1714–32).

Petersburg was, from its foundation, under Peter's closest confidant, the capable and corrupt Alexander Menshikov, a field marshal since 1707, who remained in the post of governor general until 1728. He was also war minister from 1717 to 1724, and governor general of Livland (1710–13). He was followed in Riga by *stolnik* Prince Petr Golitsyn (1713–19), a cousin of Mikhail, as governor, and Prince Nikita Repnin as governor general (1719–26), who succeeded Menshikov as war minister (1724–6). Golitsyn then became governor general of Kiev (1719–22). Estland was combined with Livland under Menshikov until it became a regular province in 1719, then placed under Count Fedor Apraksin as governor general (1719–26). Apraksin was an admiral, who combined the post of governor general with that of navy minister (1717–28). He was placed above Major General Friedrich von Löwen, who had been vice-governor in Reval since 1711, when Estland was not yet a province, and who then succeeded Apraksin as a mere vice-governor, then as governor from 1730 to 1735, an unusually long tenure. Löwen, from an Estland family, had transferred from Swedish to Russian service in 1710. His brother Karl was Swedish navy minister in the 1730s.[37] The Russians thus incorporated the Swedish model of provincial administration by governor and governor general. A close association with the military and naval establishment – and with the Romanov house – reflected the strategic importance of Estland and Livland at the time, as a land bridge from which to launch offensive operations against Sweden and Poland.

After Peter's death, the importance of the post of governor and governor general was clearly downgraded. It was so partly because of the southern shift in Russian strategy, partly because the recognition of the privileges of the knights and burghers and the implicit rejection of the Swedish policy of integration and assimilation combined to leave Estland and Livland to their own devices, especially at a time when the importance of the "German lobby" was strong in Petersburg. On the other hand, the fact that the Vyborg area remained only a *provintsiia* until 1744 reflected the government's attitude that Vyborg's Karelia had once been a Russian land and that there were no "rights and privileges" to confirm. The Nystadt treaty confirmed only the tolerance of the Lutheran religion.[38]

There were few governors general; governors came and went. Of all those appointed between 1725 and 1762, six were governors and two vice-governors; their term of office was usually about three years; four had Russian names, three German and Swedish names. Gustav Douglas, of Scottish origin, had been taken prisoner at Poltava, entered Russian service in 1714, and had been governor general of occupied Finland in Åbo (1717–21). Only one governor was appointed in Vyborg, and he was a Russian, General Afanasii Isakov (1745–52, 1754–66). There were only three governors general. General, later Field Marshal Peter Lacy, an Irishman, had commanded the invasion of Poland in 1733, one army against the Turks in 1736, and the invasion of Finland in 1741. He was governor (1729–40) and governor general (1740–51) of Livland.[39] Little is known of Prince Vladimir Dolgorukov, governor general of Estland (1748–58) and Livland as well (1751–3). He was preceded and followed in Reval by Prince Peter von Holstein-Beck (1748–75), who had been governor of Estland (1743–53) under Dolgorukov. He was a relative of the future Peter III and married the daughter of Admiral Nikolai Golovin, the navy minister (1733–45).

But the real power holders in the Baltic provinces were the Germano-Swedish nobility. When Reval capitulated in September 1710, one of the requests was for a governor speaking German well, with a German-speaking chancery; other requests were that all directives be issued in German, and that only German be used in the chanceries and courts.[40] This was no more than maintaining the status quo, even though the use of Swedish had been rising. Higher posts, even in Finland, were often filled by Germans. The civilian governor general of occupied Finland in 1743 was Lt.-Gen. Johann von Campenhausen, from a Livland family, a former colonel in Swedish service who had joined the Russians in 1711.

The possessions of the Livonian Order had been divided into districts. In the middle of each stood a fort (*Burg*) on elevated ground. Each fort was run by a council (*konvent*) of twelve to twenty knights headed by a commander or *Vogt* (*fokht*). The council had jurisdiction over administrative, military, fiscal, and judicial affairs. Command in war was vested in the marshal, who resided in Wenden. The council of his district elected the *Meister*, who was then confirmed by the *Hochmeister*. The order was a feudal society of knights pledged to carry out military service. To discuss larger issues of domestic and foreign policy, an assembly (*Landtag*) met usually every three years, consisting of the Riga archbishop with the bishops of Ösel Island, Pernau, Reval, and Kurland, the *Meister* with his knights, and delegates from the entire nobility of Livonia and from towns. Following the secularization of the Order, the organization changed, but power remained concentrated in the knights to an even greater extent. The Catholic Church had disappeared and the towns went their own way. Livonia consisted of three separate territories: Estland, Livland, and Kurland. After the annexation, a *Landtag* continued to meet every three years in Reval and Riga. It elected a college of councillors (*Landrat Collegium*), twelve in Livland and four on Ösel Island, whose names were sent on to Petersburg for the tsar's confirmation.

In 1739 Ösel Island received its own executive agency in the form of a Land Captain (*Landhauptmann*). In Estland, twelve councillors formed a superior court (*Oberlandgericht*), which had the right to co-opt its own members without requiring the emperor's confirmation. When their decisions concerned only the internal affairs of the knights, they took effect immediately. If they had an impact on other issues, they were referred to the governor sitting in council with two provincial councillors (*Gubernamentsräte*) or were sent up to the emperor in Petersburg. There, two appellate instances existed, both staffed with Germans, who filtered matters coming up from the governor's offices before they reached the Senate. A separate College of Justice for Livland and Estland emerged in 1727, with jurisdiction over petitions and decisions coming from Vyborg added in 1735. In 1739 a separate board (*kontora*) for Livland and Estland fiscal affairs was merged with the college, and in 1744, after the creation of Vyborg province, the words "Finnish affairs" were added to the college's title. Like other colleges, this German institution was subordinated to the College.[41]

The Russians thus retained the institutional setup which had existed under Swedish rule – complete with the college of *Landräte* which Charles XI had abolished, a fact which the knights carefully concealed from the Russians. A thin stratum of Russian agents governed with the collaboration of the elite knights, who kept a tight grip on the population at large, and who were represented in the central government. From there they could influence the activities of the Russian agents, who were thus squeezed from below and from above. If an occupying power was ever checkmated in the territory it nominally controlled, the Baltic provinces provide a telling example. Nevertheless, the central government always retained the option and the capability to impose its will if it chose to – but was it in its interest to force the issue except in extraordinary circumstances?

The ability to maintain control depends, in the last analysis, on the ability to use force. To maintain its hegemony, Sweden had built an armed force consisting of over 60,000 regular troops, 24,000 mercenary troops, and some thirty capital ships. The mercenary troops were stationed mostly in fortresses and provincial garrisons. Some 23,000 regulars were stationed outside Sweden-Finland, but all of them were recruited on the basis of the so-called "allocation system" (*Indelningsverket*, from *indela*, meaning to assign). Nearly every province concluded a contract with the king to raise an infantry regiment of 1,200 foot. Crown farms, greatly increased in number by those recovered in the wake of the *Reduktion*, were grouped into pairs, and each pair had to deliver a recruit, between the ages of eighteen and forty, who was provided with food, clothing, quarters, and even an annual wage, in return for working on the farm of the pair. Those who could deliver a fully equipped horseman were exempted from this rule. Officers and non-commissioned officers were allotted their own land; the troopers and infantrymen were employed as farm labourers. When the soldier was at war, the farmer had to cultivate his land.

The Russian army relied on the conscription system, which the *ukase* of March 1712 extended to the entire expanding core.[42] It denied at the time the principle of territoriality, because it was a very mobile army operating anywhere between the Caspian and the Niemen, as Gustav Adolf had once feared. It was supported by the capitation, which, however, was not introduced in the Baltic provinces. Service was for life, and recruiting caused great distress in peasant communities, but it made serfs into free men and was a powerful tool of social integration, both vertical and horizontal. The Russians incorporated the allocation system of the Swedes into their military administration by levying troops in accordance with a variable ratio of one recruit per so many souls and requiring the delivery of grain to army stores in Reval and Riga. Troops stationed in the Baltic provinces would no longer be local troops, but a parasitic formation whose billeting caused a great deal of resentment.

But once the war with Sweden was over, Russian field troops were withdrawn in accordance with the strategic doctrine of the day, which required that the army be concentrated around Moscow; only garrisons remained. There were four garrison infantry regiments in Riga and another four in Reval (together nearly 11,000 men), another three in Vyborg, and a battalion in Kexholm (4,785 men). These troops were supplied from the capitation levied in Russian provinces of western and northern Russia.[43] The situation changed at the time of the Russo-Swedish War of 1741–3. The deployment of October 1743[44] listed three infantry regiments stationed in Fredrikshamn and Vyborg, including two moved forward from Tver and Vladimir; nine stationed in Stockholm to enforce the terms of the Treaty of Åbo, including six from Moscow province; five in Estland; and another five in Livland, including two infantry regiments transferred from Kaluga and Smolensk, a total of thirteen regiments in the Baltic provinces and nine in Sweden. These troops were later withdrawn, but it would seem that the Baltic provinces became gradually integrated into the territorial deployment of the army as a whole.

After the Seven Years' War (1756–63), the entire expanding core was divided into eight territorial "divisions," four of them in the Baltic sector. The Finland division consisted of six infantry and one cavalry regiments (in Kexholm); the Estland division, of five infantry and two cavalry regiments; and the Livland division, of eight infantry and five cavalry regiments. This meant a total of twenty-seven out of sixty regiments, equal in size to the Ukrainian division deployed against both Poland and the southern steppe.[45] The territorialization of the army had become official policy and, with it, came the increasing importance of the border territories: Petersburg (with its division of eleven regiments) and Kiev became the two strategic bases from which to launch offensive operations against Swedes, Poles, and Turks. From the administrative and military points of view, the Baltic provinces had been integrated into the structure of domination of the expanding core on the eve of Catherine II's reign, during which further integration in the social and fiscal domains would be pushed to the limit.

Superstratification

Perhaps nowhere else can one so accurately speak of "a gradation of authority"[46] than in the Baltic provinces, with a governor representing the centre of power, who himself often belonged to the upper tier of the provincial elite, who, in turn, represented the landowners exercising absolute jurisdiction over the peasant masses. Superstratification was a form of gradation of authority. In the eastern theatre it was mainly ethnic, binding the newly arrived Russian "elite" with the upper stratum of the non-Russian local society, a mostly nomadic society scattered over an enormous territory. In the southern theatre superstratification was above all social, because Orthodoxy transcended ethnic differences, already considerably muted by the fact that the intruder and the local population belonged to the same group of Eastern Slavs. In the Baltic provinces, it was both ethnic and social: Russian Slavs and Baltic Germans, ruling elite of service people bound together in their more densely settled society, descendants of knights proud of their membership in an exclusive corporation infused with a quasi-mystical veneration of their privileges. Paradoxically, however, it was in the Baltic provinces, where the clash was potentially more ominous, that the symbiosis was the most successful.

Before the Russian conquest, Sweden had an upper stratum of great families proud of their ancestry, with whom the kings had to struggle to establish and maintain their rule. There was also a noble plebe attached to the great lords, for whom making war was a profession and a business:[47] there was land and loot for the victors. That was especially true in Finland, where the poverty of the country did not attract the great lords, but where the petty nobility was given positions as officers in the territorial army and as landlords ready to answer the summons of the king, or who simply seized land in the basin of Lake Ladoga, where an ongoing struggle pitted them against the Orthodox Slavs. The Reformation gave the monarchy a considerable number of properties which it then could dispense among petty nobles to reward their allegiance. Gustav Adolf and his daughter Kristina also "packed" the aristocracy by bringing in distinguished foreigners, including Baltic Germans, whose allegiance would be to the king alone. Eventually, Charles XI would anchor his absolute rule on a service nobility sharing some features with the Russian.[48]

But this did not sit well with the nobility of the Baltic provinces. Swedish policy in Estland was more moderate because the land had not been conquered, unlike Livonia. Nevertheless, the Swedes were determined to integrate the Germano-Danish nobility into the Swedish and Finnish nobility – Finnish families were also being integrated into a common "Swedish" nobility – by giving them large tracts of land in Finland, with a view to creating a single integrated nobility bound to the king. In Livonia, the first act of Gustav Adolf was to seize one-third of the feudal properties of the Teutonic Knights and distribute them among Swedish families, including that of his own chancellor, Axel Oxenstierna, whose estates would eventually amount to about one-eighth of the whole area of the province.[49]

The first governor general of Livonia, Ingria, and Karelia, Johan Skytte, was not impressed by the privileges of the knights, calling them "the many legal wondrous conceits, of which this land is replete in every scattered corner."[50] He was an integrationist at heart, determined to create a single community under a single king and a single law. But under Polish rule, more tolerant of local particularisms, the knights – and the Swedish families which increasingly identified with them – won a charter from Sigismund August in 1561, which blindly confirmed all ancient privileges, known and unknown, assuming the existence of documents which may never have existed. After the return to Swedish rule, the knights continued to consider the document their great charter, even though the original had mysteriously disappeared.[51]

In the Baltic provinces, the beneficiaries from the confiscation of Catholic Church lands had been the knights, whose corporation became the largest landowner. Seizures of land, as well as land grants to Swedish and Polish families, eventually created a situation in which the Swedish treasury derived little income from a shrinking tax base. To carry out expansion in an age of fiscal austerity, the crown inaugurated a policy of "reversion" (*Reduktion*), the forceful reclamation of properties which it considered ought to be its lawful property, henceforth to remain inalienable. Its effect was devastating, and it may have reduced the noble share of cultivated land by half. It created unending challenges, left title insecure, and damaged the provincial economy, which had witnessed the creation of large and efficient farms. But the most important consequence was to build up an enormous reservoir of resentment against the Swedish determination to create a unitary state, which became even more obvious when an undeterred Charles XI abolished the post of *Landrat*, the *Landrat Collegium*, and the *Landtag* shortly before his death.[52]

After defeating the Swedes at Poltava in June 1709, Peter shifted his focus to the Baltic sector, and he announced that he would confirm the privileges, even those which had presumably existed before the reversion, in effect cancelling it. But much of the population remained loyal to Sweden, and Vyborg, Reval, and Riga provinces had to be conquered by force of arms. Peter, as ignorant as Sigismund August had been of the true content of the privileges, nevertheless agreed in September 1710 to confirm only those that were still compatible with current circumstances and the new form of government, that is, the Russian autocracy (*eliko onye k nyneshnemu Pravitelstvu i vremeni prilichaiutsia*).[53] The formula was highly equivocal. First, the privileges had to be set in writing and codified; then, it was necessary to determine which privileges had become archaic and which remained acceptable in the social conditions of the eighteenth century. A potentially explosive question was the compatibility of the privileges of a private corporation with an autocratic form of government which did not recognize the autonomous existence of such corporations. And finally, it was necessary to distinguish between the privileges of the descendants of the Teutonic Knights and those of other families that were not of Teutonic origin, but traced their ancestry to German, Swedish, and Polish families.

Such questions could not be settled in wartime, but Russian victories and the promise to abandon the integrationist policy of the Swedish monarchy induced well-positioned individuals to transfer their allegiance to the Russians and help shape a *modus vivendi* between them and the knights, who remained the core of the nobility of the Baltic provinces. One of these well-positioned individuals was Gerhard von Lowenwölde, from a German family which had settled in Livonia in the thirteenth century. A major in the Swedish garrison in Riga, he was a friend of Reinhold Patkul (who plotted for the secession of Livonia) and was sentenced to death with him, but escaped punishment. His family's properties were confiscated in the reversion, and he left Swedish service; in 1710 he was among the first to swear loyalty to Peter I and entered Russian service. He worked hard to help his fellow nobles regain their properties and to get the Russian government to recognize the privileges. It was he who, in 1710, summoned in Riga the first *Landtag* under Russian rule, as well as the next, in 1712. His zeal earned him the rank of secret councillor (the equivalent of a lieutenant general, the first rank in the ruling elite) and the position of grand master of the heir's court (1711–21). He married a von Löwen, relative of the Russian-appointed governor of Estland.[54]

In 1710, the Russians were about to deal with a caste such as they would not find anywhere else in the expanding Russian core. The Baltic German nobles have been harshly judged "as unpleasant a gang of robber barons as ever darkened the pages of European history."[55] They fought tooth and nail to retain their privileges, but they also knew they had to become parties in an unwritten contractual relationship with the Russians at two levels. The Swedes had tried to emancipate the peasantry – peasants were free in Sweden and Finland – but had desisted in the face of ferocious opposition. The Russians would have no objection to the landlords keeping jurisdiction over their serfs. The Swedes had tried to integrate the Baltic peasantry into a larger social world of free peasants. The Russians would integrate them into a wider world of an enserfed peasantry. The nobles would transfer their loyalty to the Romanov house, but in return they would want access to positions in the Russian military and nascent diplomatic service, where the Russians did not have enough qualified personnel. In return, the Russians would recognize their privileges and tone down their policy of building a unitary state. But they would also integrate the Baltic nobles into a wider world, that of Eurasia, to which they belonged by their location, and that of Europe, from which they originally came.

The agreements for the surrender of Riga in July 1710 and of Estland in September were negotiated between the Russian commanding general and the Swedish authorities, but they also took the form of a declaration by Peter answering requests presented by the *Ritterschaft* (*rytsarstvo*) and the *Landschaft* (*zemstvo*, the other nobility).[56] Between the two agreements the tsar issued a "universal," promising not only to keep the privileges inviolate (*sviato*) but also to increase them with "broader and more important ones."[57] The agreement of September promised to keep the privileges always "as understood orally and without any other interpretation" (*po slovesnomu razumeniiu, bez vsiakogo drugovo tolkovaniia*).[58] Since it was impossible to condense them in a single digest, the standard formula declared them to remain "as they existed from *Herrmeister* to *Herrmeister*, from archbishop to bishops, from king to king," including "all worthy customs [*dostoinye obyknoveniia*] and royal resolutions."[59] The declaration was a blanket endorsement of unknown privileges presumably given over time to the Teutonic Knights, the Church, and the towns. In a word, Peter gave the Baltic nobles what Charles XI had refused, and the annexation of Livonia was "welcomed by town and land as a happy event."[60]

The *Landräte*, individually and collectively in their collegium, regained their old power. Charles XI had been aware that they saw little difference between the management of a corporation and the public administration of a territory. With the restoration of the *Landtag*, the old system destroyed by Charles XI came back to life. But the *Landräte* also became an integral part of the new hierarchical structure of domination created by the Table of Ranks. The Russians, who realized their importance in the policy of stratification, gave them the rank of major general, a high rank at the time, and the Livland nobility asked that they be given not only a salary but also properties from which to derive an additional income. It was decided in 1713 that the collegium would meet twice a year, and the newly elected land marshal was given the rank of colonel.[61] The collegium also became closely associated with the post of governor. Governor von Löwen was an Estland *Landrat* from 1696 to 1721. One of his successors, General Gustav Douglas, the son of a Swedish colonel and full general in the Russian army, was also an Estland *Landrat* (1715–17). And Lt.-Gen. Johann von Campenhausen occupied the same post in Livland for a very long time (1721–47).[62]

The post-Petrine period running until the accession of Catherine II in 1762 witnessed not only the consolidation of the new system but also a sharpening of differences within the oligarchy. Catherine I, who was favourable to the Livland nobles, confirmed their privileges with the restrictive clause. The confirmation of 1728 also expressed dissatisfaction with the "ancient and obscure [*neiavstvennie*] rights" and called for their codification. The confirmation of 1742 did not include the restrictive clause, perhaps because of lingering German influence at the Court.[63]

It is difficult to say whether the conservative reaction of the 1730s was defensive or offensive: defensive in its attempt to create a caste within a caste, to stratify the nobility by upholding the existence of a core, access to which would be restricted to a specific number of families and excluding others, such as men of lowly origin who had moved up on the social ladder on account of their wartime achievements; offensive in its determination to create an upper stratum of aristocratic families in alliance with the Russians, especially the Saltykov patronage network, to support their foreign policy unconditionally in return for the maintenance of the status quo in Livonia. Whichever the reason, the conservative reaction fitted in very well with the Russian policy of stratification and anticipated by a century a similar policy by the Polish aristocracy in Right Bank Ukraine.

Until the 1730s the Baltic German nobility had not been a homogeneous body. There were native (*Eingeborene*, *Indigene*) nobles, largely descendants of the Teutonic Knights, with properties that were either divisible (*Erbgüter*) or indivisible fiefs (*Lehngüter*). There were Swedish and Polish families, some of which gradually entered the ranks of the "native" nobles. There were other "foreign families." There were also bourgeois families which had occasionally entered the elite. Last but not least, there were non-nobles who had risen through the ranks and claimed service, rather than landownership, to justify their desire to enter the nobility. By 1710, *Ritterschaft* and *Landschaft* had become two distinct categories, even though the distinction between them was not always clear. An attempt to "matriculate" the nobility had already begun in Sweden under Queen Kristina, but was never completed. Now left to themselves, the Baltic nobility was determined to create a *Matrikel*, a roster of families with exclusive access to elected positions, a ruling elite within a ruling class which would retain its dominion over the peasantry and, if possible, the towns as well.

The *Landtag* took up the issue in 1720 and again in 1727, with a view to retaining the Germanic and provincial foundation of the nobility. Approval came from Petersburg in 1728. In 1733, a commission was created, chaired by *Landrat* de la Barre (hardly a Germanic name!), to verify the claims submitted by noble families showing when the family first acquired landed property, and with a genealogical table. It took almost a decade to sift the evidence, and a first roster was published in 1742, a second in 1745 (which may have reflected Russian pressures for enlargement), with a supplement in 1747. The roster included 172 Livland families divided into four categories: 52 families from the Middle Ages to the sixteenth century; 16 from the days of Polish rule; 45 from the days of Swedish rule; and 59 from those families admitted between 1710 and 1747. It was found, meanwhile, that too many Swedish families had been included, and their number was reduced in the final version from 45 to 14(!).[64] All these families would have the right to be considered native nobles (*Indigenatsrecht*). In Estland, the *Matrikel* of 1756 included 120 families.[65] In Kurland, a similar *Matrikel* had existed since the beginning of the seventeenth century. From then on, only matriculated families would have the right to fill elective positions. They could not be only Germanic families, as was the original intention, but they certainly would form an exclusive caste.

The consequences of the *Matrikel* may have been unexpected. Once the matriculated nobility set itself apart from the rest of the nobility and gained a monopoly over the administration of Estland and Livland, a mutually "hostile attitude" (*feindliche Gegensatz*) developed between the "natives" and the "non-natives," which would poison the public life of the Baltic provinces for a century. The new men who had earned their officer patents in the service could no longer hope to be included. They became a service nobility without access to provincial service, and developed a "murderous hatred" toward the matriculated nobility. They were also denied the right to acquire local real property and the hope of becoming a "nobilis livonus," with the prestige attached to it.[66] There were precedents in Poland, Sweden, and the German states, with their closed noble corporations, to which state service did not give entry. The Baltic provinces were joining their ranks and diverging from the Russian pattern, but in so doing they exposed fissures in the nobility which the Russians would exploit during the reign of Catherine II. A chasm also opened between the matriculated nobility and the towns, where the burghers ceased feeling a duty toward the land, a common interest in its welfare, now a monopoly in the hands of the "natives."

Whatever internal differences may have developed, the Baltic elite played their role as men of the frontier to perfection. The policy of the expanding Russian core was to draw the elites of the borderlands into its power structure and give them positions befitting their status in their own societies. Baltic Germans – as well as Germans from outside the Baltic provinces, coming from German lands which had once launched the Teutonic Knights on their eastern march, like Burkhard von Münnich (1683–1767) and Heinrich Ostermann (1687–1743) – began to occupy leading positions in the colleges of war and foreign affairs, as well as in the College of Estland and Livland Affairs – with Karl Freiherr von Mengden (1706–61) – where they could defend the interests of their native provinces.

But it was also the core's policy to turn these men of the frontier outward by giving them appointments in which they could carry out their new masters' policies while remaining immersed in the outlook and traditions of their societies. Russian interests were made to coincide with their own. A vast field was opening in the Baltic region as well as in Poland. One thinks of Johann von Korff (1677–1766), Biron's agent in Kurland, President of the Academy of Sciences in Petersburg (1734–40), envoy to Denmark (1740–6 and 1748–66) and Sweden (1746–8). Another famous man of the frontier was Hermann von Keyserlingk (1696–1765), Vice-President of the College of Justice (1730–33), President of the Academy of Sciences in 1733, envoy to Warsaw (1733–44), where he succeeded Karl von Lowenwölde, Gerhard's son, envoy to Berlin (1747–8), Warsaw again (1749–52), Vienna (1752–61), and Warsaw once more (1762–5).[67] These men and their followers helped integrate an upper crust of Baltic Germans into the military and diplomatic establishment of the expanding core, together with the lesser men who filled the post of commandant in the numerous forts facing the steppe in Siberia.

Town and Country

Towns are communities which are not self-sufficient, particularly with regard to food; the density of their population is as a rule higher than that of the surrounding countryside. They may be staple cities in which trade is concentrated by government policy or which reach this status on account of special circumstances and facilities. They are usually found on the coast, and the sea links them with the great oceans. They specialize in imports or export or combine both. Others, "internal cities," are towns in name only and function as market towns, because their function is administrative or military, in areas where they could not generate enough economic activity as centres of trade and protection. Charles IX of Sweden (1604–11) added thirty-one towns to the thirty-three he found at his accession, populated by "townsmen by command,"[68] a policy which antedated Catherine II's of Russia by 170 years, in the wake of her reform of local government.

In Livonia, there were only two staple cities, Reval and Riga, with possibly Pernov and Narva. Pernov was founded in 1255 by the Ösel bishop and became the terminal point for the medieval trade route coming from Derpt, Pskov, and Novgorod – until Ivan IV destroyed it during the Livonian war. Narva, also in Estonia, was founded by the Danes in the 1220s, was burned by the Novgorodians in 1294, and was under Swedish rule from 1581 to 1704. It faced Ivangorod across the Narova River, the Russian fortress built in 1492. But Reval was much more important. Founded in 1219 by Waldemar II of Denmark on the site of an Estonian community overlooking the Gulf of Finland, it was settled by Germans from Lower Saxony and Westphalia, and became part of the Hanseatic League. Its importance grew after Ivan III destroyed the German entrepot in Novgorod in 1477. In 1561 it took the oath of allegiance to the King of Sweden, and surrendered to Russia in 1710.

The queen of the eastern Baltic trade was Riga, founded in 1201 by the third bishop of Livonia, on the Dvina, ten kilometres from the sea. It was the most important trading city of the eastern Baltic until the foundation of Petersburg in 1703, a member of the Hanseatic League since 1282, with its own troops and fleet. A fractious city, at constant loggerheads with the Teutonic Knights and the archbishop, it was, like Reval, a German city, an island of German civilization in a sea of Latvians, and the focus of Russian ambitions on the Baltic shore. Annexed to Russia in 1710, it was fated, again like Reval, to suffer from the rise of Petersburg. Toward the end of the eighteenth century, only five cities in the region had a population exceeding 50,000 inhabitants – Copenhagen, Stockholm (73,000), Königsberg, and Danzig – but the fifth, Petersburg, already had 191,000, even though this was far below the population of Paris (600,000) and London (959,000).[69] While it is true that the Baltic urban system was part of the European periphery with its large wastelands, low population density, very small secondary and tertiary economic sectors, and little growth potential,[70] it may just as well be said that it was also part of the Eurasian periphery with its diminishing wastelands, rising population densities, developing economic sectors, and promising growth potential.

The Baltic towns, implanted by German settlers on Estonian and Latvian soil, remained indifferent to the world about them. They modelled their institutions on the town or region of their origin. Livland towns followed the Riga model. Its municipal system went back to the thirteenth century, when the bishop gave the town privileges modelled after those of Visby on Gotland Island, later modified by the Hamburg municipal law, which gave Riga its entire system of municipal administration, its criminal and civil law, and its judicial procedure. Its municipal statute of 1673 codified much of this legislation, which also included Swedish ordinances. Reval followed Lübeck's municipal organization and became the model for the other Estland towns, including Hapsal in Livland, which abandoned the Riga for the Lübeck model. One cannot but notice the parallel with the Magdeburg Law in the Polish Empire. The Germans who settled in the Baltic towns came from northern Germany, the core of the Hanseatic League; those who settled in the Polish and Ukrainian towns came from Saxony. In both cases, their communities were islands of German merchants and artisans, ethnically different from the population around them. Town and country were not only economically and socially diverse, they were also ethnically alien and even hostile to each other.

To strengthen their identity against the surrounding natives, upon whom they depended for their food supply, the towns, despite their professed indifference, found it imperative to determine who had the right to reside in the towns and enjoy the status of townsman (*Bürgerrecht*) and who could take part in the management of the town. In effect, this meant the creation of a three-tier stratified society of Latvians and Estonians – the so-called non-Germans (*Undeutsche*) – German artisans, and German merchants.

There had long been a rule in medieval Europe, that "town air makes man free." Fugitive peasants, in Livonia as well, automatically became free if they could prove they had resided in the town for two years. This suited neither the landed nobility nor the German artisans who feared competition from outsiders. The Riga *magistrat* ruled in 1738 that all "non-Germans" had to dispose of their property in the city within one year, because the ownership of such property made it possible to claim the *Bürgerrecht* and the right to engage in trade. This stirred the opposition of the Latvian artisans, and the governor general vetoed the city's ordinance. But in 1752 Latvians were banned from acquiring the *Bürgerrecht*. On the other hand, foreigners, who had been forbidden to reside in the city, were finally allowed to do so in 1762, on condition they were not Jews.[71]

German merchants and artisans belonged to different guilds. In Reval, only the rich merchants could belong to the Great Guild; artisans joined the guilds of St Canute and St Olaf.[72] In Riga there was the Great Guild and the Small Guild, which coopted their members and controlled production, sale, and prices. Riga's population numbered about 10,000 in 1710 and grew to 27,800 by 1800. The growth was largely due to in-migration, and the share of the Latvians grew steadily, eventually reaching 31 per cent, and that of the Russians grew to 14 per cent, with the German share remaining under 50 per cent. Other Livland towns did not have much more than 2,000 inhabitants. Some seventy occupations were organized in forty-three guilds or brotherhoods; Latvians were admitted only to some, but were excluded from the Great Guild.[73] In Estland, Reval had a population of only 1,962 in 1710 – a consequence of the war and epidemics – but it rose phenomenally to 10,653 in 1782. The ratio of Germans to non-Germans was about the same as in Riga.[74]

Petersburg continued to uphold the "privileges," first in 1712 with the restrictive clause, later without it.[75] The social and municipal organization of the two provinces even became a model for the Russian government, beginning with the creation of a Central (*Glavnyi*) *Magistrat* in Petersburg in 1712. The result was a curious situation. Integration usually proceeds from the centre to the periphery. In the case of the Baltic provinces, it proceeded from the periphery: the Baltic system became a model for the unification of municipal administration across the entire core. This would become evident for all to see during Catherine II's reign.

All these German towns shared a similar administrative system. Germans who met the requirements of the *Bürgerrecht* – Russian citizenship (*poddanstvo*), the Christian faith, the condition of free men, lawful birth – but with the confirmation of the burgomasters, formed a community (*Bürgerschaft*), which assembled to elect the municipal government from its midst. The government of the town consisted of the *magistrat* of members of the Great Guild alone. In Riga there were four burgomasters, a council of twelve filled by cooptation, a chief secretary, and five ordinary secretaries. The Reval *magistrat* was similar, but had only three secretaries; Pernov and Narva had only two burgomasters and smaller councils. One of the burgomasters served as a burgrave (*Burggraf*), responsible for the administration of justice.[76] The *magistrat*'s jurisdiction was comprehensive: it managed the administration, the police and the judiciary, the economy and the finances of the town, even the affairs of the Lutheran Church. The Riga and Reval *magistraty* were also courts of appeal against the decisions of the *magistraty* of the smaller towns in their provinces. The members of the *magistraty* thus constituted the core of an urban oligarchy which controlled urban affairs as tightly as the matriculated nobility controlled rural affairs, two parallel administrative and social hierarchies, linked at the top by giving the members of the Riga *magistrat* the status of hereditary nobles. Ethnically, they sealed the Germans' dominion over the Estonian and Latvian population, and formed a powerful centre of resistance to attempts to create a unitary state in the expanding Russian core.

The overwhelming majority of the population of the Baltic provinces consisted of Estonians and Latvians (and Finns in the Vyborg area). It was estimated that in a total population of 525,100 in 1744, 318,500 were Estonians (including those in the northern districts of Livland province), or 60.6 per cent, and 167,900 Latvians (31.9 per cent). The German group was much smaller with 32,000 individuals of both sexes (6.1 per cent), and the Russian share (2,700) of 0.5 per cent was insignificant. Most of the other 3,800 (0.7 per cent) were Swedes, whose settlement on the Estonian shore and on the Dagö Island was encouraged by Gustav Adolf to establish a permanent Swedish presence on the southern shore of the Gulf of Finland, across from southern Finland.[77] The Swedes had been settling there since the thirteenth century – at the same time as the Germans were moving into Livonia – on the Åland Islands and in the Åbo and Helsingfors areas. Most of them were fishermen and free peasants, and formed islands of Swedish civilization in a sea of Finns, Estonians (both belonged to the same ethnic group), and Latvians – the so-called eastern Balts.

Serfdom and the manorial system were the characteristic features of European rural society from the eleventh to the fifteenth century. A lord held a manor populated by peasants who were bound to it and paid him fixed dues in kind, money, and services. The development of trade, the growth of towns, and the concentration of royal power in a ruling house helped transform the rural scene, undermined the self-sufficiency of the manorial economy, and weakened the power of the lords, while increasing that of the municipal authorities, the rising bourgeoisie, and the "third estate" spawned by the ancillary activities of urban life. By 1500, when the Renaissance reached its apogee in Italy, and the Reformation was about to engulf the city states and governments of Germany, the voyages of exploration were laying the foundation of an Atlantic economy. These developments brought about the demise of the manorial system, even if serfdom was not officially abolished until the end of the eighteenth century.

Livonia followed a very different course. The sixteenth century marked a turning point. The German knights and the Catholic Church had converted Estonians and Latvians by force and imposed an essentially military rule, but little is known about the type of rural economy which they built on their territory, although it was probably a variant of the manorial system. The natives were bound neither to the land nor to a master; servile status, where it was imposed, was not hereditary, and corvée labour did not appear until much later.[78] By 1500 again, however, an assumption had taken root that every peasant was a debtor and could not leave the manor without the consent of the lord. Serfdom began to crystallize. In the sixteenth century, while Europe looked increasingly westward across the great oceans, the rural economy of Eurasia's western periphery began to look increasingly eastward and to resemble that of the expanding Russian core.[79]

The gradual transformation of the *Ordenstaat* into a community of landowners, followed by the secularization of the Church's lands in the 1520s, the dissolution of the *Ordenstaat* in 1561, and the scorched-earth policy pursued by both sides in the Livonian war of 1561–82, pressured the fittest among the German families to survive. In the absence of royal power, they seized landed properties to create manors (*myzy, muizas*), populated by a ruined peasantry in desperate need of protection against the breakdown of order.[80] Serfdom had slowly crept over the land, with the first known example of the sale of a peasant without land going back to 1495.[81] Servile status became hereditary, and a trend became noticeable to bind the serf not only to the manor but also to a master, the last stage in the degradation of the peasantry, worsened by the racial haughtiness of a German caste toward the native peoples.

Paradoxically, the consolidation of serfdom went hand in hand with the consolidation of manors into larger units of production operating with forced labour to take advantage of the price revolution in Europe that followed an increase in population and the rising demand for goods and services. Livonia had much grain to export, and larger manors were more efficient. While economic growth was thus associated with the liberation of man in Europe, it was associated with his degradation in the western theatre (except Sweden). By 1600, serfdom had triumphed on the western periphery of Eurasia, at the very same time that it was officially established in Muscovy in the midst of the dreadful devastation caused by the civil war of 1605–13.

The seventeenth century was the time of Swedish rule. In Sweden itself, the manorial system had never taken root. The king's relationship with his peasants had always been a direct one, and peasants were legally free. Any attempt by the nobility to enserf the peasant would have met with the opposition of a peasantry supported by a strong royal power, which, by the seventeenth century, had become one of the strongest monarchies in the region. But the incorporation of Livonia into the Swedish empire by Gustav Adolf in 1621 raised problems with the German landowners. The manorial system kept expanding, and peasants ran away to Russia, Poland, and Sweden and revolted against rising obligations. The Livonian landlords lived up to their reputation as evil and cruel men, who called the natives dogs and tramps,[82] inflicted drastic punishments for small offences, and took over the monopoly of mills, distilleries, and breweries.[83] Trading in serfs became common, and the custom was officially recognized in Estonia in 1650, in Latvia in 1653.[84] The Security Regulation of 1671 gave official sanction to serfdom in Livonia by upholding the practice of binding the peasant to his place of birth.[85] The sharply deteriorating international economic situation, caused in part by the steep decline in the import of precious metals from the Americas and the Thirty Years' War of 1618–48, damaged the urban trade throughout the western theatre and resulted in a tightening of control over the towns by the landed nobility. The Baltic manors combined to form a separate state within the Swedish Empire, but a state founded on increasing exploitation and racism.

The Swedish monarchy had no choice but to resort to a policy of superstratification. Only the German landlords in their productive manors could maintain order, guarantee a regular supply of grain to feed Stockholm and other Swedish towns, and channel exports of timber and naval stores that were essential to sustain the emerging British navy – and a source of substantial revenue for the crown. Swedish aristocratic families were settled in Livonia in the hope that they could provide an alternative to the manorial economy run by the Germans. By 1680, they already owned over half of the land of Livonia. By and large, they only succumbed to the overarching influence of the German landowners and adopted the same methods.[86] But the Swedish government pursued both a policy of superstratification and one of assimilation, which eventually became contradictory. To gain and retain the loyalty of the German landlords, it had to, and did, sanction serfdom. To abolish it, if only on humanitarian grounds, and pursuant to a policy of assimilation which pervaded the whole of Sweden's imperial policy, ran the risk, in assimilating the Baltic with the Swedish peasant, of antagonizing the German landowners and forcing them to look eastward, toward Muscovy, which Gustaf Adolf had already recognized as Sweden's enemy.

Charles XI, both for fiscal reasons and to reassert the royal power against a nobility which had benefited from "donations" (of landed property) and the unlawful seizure of crown lands, carried out the "reversion" to bring back these lands into the reservoir of crown lands. He also proposed in 1681 to abolish serfdom in Livonia and introduce Swedish law. The nobles met this offer with "indignant incomprehension"[87] and threats to leave Livonia – one wonders where to. In Sweden itself, the policy of reversion brought about a drastic improvement in the lot of the peasant.[88] In the Baltic provinces, both the reversion and the threat to abolish serfdom only exacerbated tensions on the eve of the great war of 1700–21. Serfdom was not abolished, and the Russians would confirm the "privileges" of the Baltic nobility, including the retention of their lands and the enserfment of the peasant. In so doing, they reconciled the two policies and squared the circle: they won the loyalty of the German landowners and integrated the Baltic peasantry (except in Vyborg province) into the expanding world of Eurasian serfdom.

The eighteenth century marked the zenith of serfdom in the western as well as in the southern theatre. Figures for 1744 show that serfs made up 93.3 per cent of the population of Livland. The proportion of manors with a population exceeding eight hundred nearly doubled during the century from 29.8 to 50.1 per cent.[89] Moreover, the weakness of the money economy resulted in an increase in labour dues. In Estland and northern Livland, where serfdom was even harsher than in Livland proper, these dues reached 85 per cent of the peasants' obligations.[90] One consequence was the flight of peasants, despite the harsh punishments: after 1719 runaway peasants were punished with branding and cutting off an ear or the nose (in Kurland with the amputation of a foot). Another was the spread of a peasant movement influenced by the Moravian or Herrnhut Brethren, an evangelical communion which first appeared in Bohemia. They set up self-governing communities and opposed the Lutheran Church and the German landlords. The movement was banned in 1743, but remained underground. The flights and the Brethren did not deter *Landrat* Otto von Rosen from declaring in 1742 that the peasant was the lord's chattel and could not possess anything of his own.[91] Baltic serfdom was approaching slavery and had reached a dead end.

Trade, Religion, and Law

Trade

"The Baltic Sea was a kind of Mediterranean, without tides and without salt."[92] Salt determined the patterns of trade. A vital necessity, it had to be brought in to be exchanged for local goods. The forests of the vast Baltic hinterland yielded tar, potash, furs, honey, construction timber, and various wooden articles for domestic use. Livonia and Estonia produced grain, flax, and hemp. Amber was found along the coast of Kurland. The preservation of fish and meat required enormous amounts of salt, and Lübeck became the market for the salt of Lüneburg (now connected with Lübeck by a canal), and later for the so-called bay salt of France and Portugal. German traders in their fortified towns anchored on the Baltic coast became natural brokers in this maritime commerce linking Europe via the Volga basin with the trade of Central Asia and even India, at least until the opening of the sea routes in the sixteenth century. They traded local for European goods in the whole of northwestern Eurasia, all the way to Yaroslavl on the Volga.

The Dutch, who carried the goods, were the pioneers in this Baltic trade with Europe, followed by the English in the sixteenth century. Western Eurasia became a vast colony exporting raw materials and importing manufactured goods and colonial products. Conjuncture in the European economy determined the type and level of demand for various products – grain or timber – and imposed sometimes drastic changes in the economic standing of the landowners, not only in Livonia and Estonia but also in Poland and Lithuania, as well as in the prosperity of the towns. The rise of Sweden and Russia would alter the relationships.

The German traders would find themselves squeezed between the ambitions of both powers to control the Baltic trade, and the eastern Baltic zone would become a commercial frontier between Sweden and Russia. Its control would also give the stronger power the control of the sea – a Swedish or a Russian lake – much as the commercial rivalry between Russia and Turkey created a commercial frontier in the basin of the Black Sea, each power seeking to transform it into a closed sea.

The Swedes encouraged Russian trade. The Kardis Agreement of 1661 allowed[93] Swedish subjects to enter Russia to trade in Russian towns of the interior: Novgorod, Pskov, and Ladoga, Riga's natural hinterland; also Moscow, Yaroslavl, and Tikhvin, the last two towns on the periphery of Lake Ladoga, where it links up with the Volga-Caspian basin; even as far north as Kholmogory, a short distance from Arkhangelsk, linked with Yaroslavl via Vologda. The Russians, in turn, were allowed to trade in all the possessions of the Swedish Empire, in Riga, Reval, Vyborg, Finland, and Stockholm – a relaxation of the more exclusive policy of a generation earlier. The Treaty of Andrusovo of 1667 would allow trade relations between Riga and Smolensk, on the edge of the Belorussian and Ukrainian markets.[94] These two treaties deepened Riga's hinterland beyond the Dvina and the Dnieper, and went some way toward realizing Sweden's Great Eastern Program, aiming at the eventual integration of the entire western theatre into the Swedish Empire.

The Swedes also sought to create new ports to tap the hinterland of neglected rivers. The most dramatic example was the construction of Nien (Nienshants), later to become the Okhta suburb of Petersburg, near the Neva estuary. The river led to Lake Ladoga and the lake to Novgorod. The rivers descending into Lake Ilmen formed, with the Dvina and the Baltic coast, a huge circle encompassing the entire basin of Lake Peipus. This would deepen Riga's hinterland, which the Kardis agreement, thirty years after the founding of Nien in 1632, would deepen even further. It is easy to see in this commercial policy the realization of Gustav Adolf's commercial and strategic vision stated so eloquently in 1617. Nien became a phenomenal success, channelling the immense resources of the Russian interior toward the Gulf of Finland and – paradoxically – challenging the Russians to seize the new port and found on its site the capital of a new empire bent on destroying Sweden's hegemony.

By 1689, when Peter I seized power in Russia, Sweden's policy of deepening the Riga hinterland and stifling the competition of other ports (except Nien and Reval) had transformed the Russo-Swedish commercial frontier into a Swedish colonial market managed along mercantilist lines. Estonia had become an agrarian colony of the metropolis, and the mobilization of the Swedish army in 1700 would depend on supplies of Estonian rye. About 46 per cent of Sweden's state revenue came from the Baltic provinces.[95] The decline of the Arkhangelsk trade in the 1650s benefited Nien, to which much of it was diverted. A "self-sustaining boom" began, as demand rose in Europe for Baltic naval stores, and large forest areas of central Russia were turned over to tar and potash production.[96] A potential danger became palpable that Russia, "an underdeveloped country that was peripheral to the economies of Asia as it was to those of Europe,"[97] would also become a Swedish colony.

The Northern War (1700–21) was as much about controlling the thriving trade of northwestern Eurasia as about opening "a window on Europe" and gaining access to its technology, in order to build a war machine bent on destroying Sweden's hegemony and replacing it with Russia's own. It was the Russian merchants who benefited handsomely from the privileges given to them at Kardis and who opened Russia's Baltic window on Europe, and Peter's lasting achievement was to employ military means to keep it open.[98] But the devastation of the Baltic provinces and of much of Finland, poor as it was, accompanied by natural disasters, drastically reduced the region's trade, and one had to wait until the Nystadt Treaty and the Tariff of 1724 to see the emergence of a Russian policy in the region.

The accelerated development of Petersburg, to which government agencies were moved from Moscow in 1714, destroyed the Arkhangelsk trade, most of which was rerouted to the new capital. Between 1700 and 1718 the value of that trade shrank from 3 million to 300,000 roubles, while that of Petersburg rose from nothing to 4 million a year. The trend continued, and by the end of the eighteenth century, half of Russia's foreign trade passed through Petersburg and another quarter though Riga.[99] When they capitulated in 1710, Riga, Reval, and Pernov asked for the restoration of free trade in grain, interrupted by the war, and that they might remain staple cities, centres of small economic regions monopolizing trade with the outside world. Even though the English were displeased with the decline of the Arkhangelsk trade, to which they had become accustomed since the sixteenth century, they understood that Russia had now turned the tables on Sweden, and that the terms of trade in the commercial frontier would henceforth be set by the Russians.

The new geopolitical situation was clearly expressed in the Treaty of Nystadt. It proclaimed freedom of trade between the two former belligerents, subject to the payment of duties, and allowed the Swedish king to purchase duty-free every year in Riga, Reval, and Arensburg (on Ösel Island) fifty thousand roubles' worth of grain on condition that the grain was bought for the king or accredited persons. Russia, however, reserved the right to suspend the export of grain in years of poor harvests or for other important reasons justifying such a ban on exports to other nations as well. But by placing a value rather than a size on the shipments, Russia would export less if prices rose. This Article VI was followed by the ambiguous language of the next article, pledging Russia not to interfere in Swedish domestic affairs, but, at the same time, to do everything possible to block an attempt against the new constitution which downgraded the monarchy and upgraded the role of parliament. The grain purchase was a sword of Damocles suspended over the head of the Swedish monarch. Sweden would have to rely on regular grain purchases in its former granary until the middle of the nineteenth century.

The Tariff of January 1724[100] – like the Swedish Produktplakat of the same year – marked a turn to protectionism, and, in Russia at least, toward the creation of Fortress Russia.[101] Peter had visited France in 1717 and shown interest in its manufactures which produced goods for export in order to bring as much precious metal as possible into the country. However, after a trip across Russia in 1723, he became aware of Russia's industrial backwardness and of the impact made by imported manufactures on domestic production.[102] Peter had to confess, at least to himself, that Russia was still a colonial country, capable of exporting only agricultural products and raw materials. If Russia was to derive a profit from its foreign trade, it had to reduce imports of manufactured goods. His commercial policy would be an inverted form of mercantilism. Unfortunately, the lack of competition, while protecting domestic industries, would also stifle their development.

The tariff imposed very high duties of up to 75 per cent *ad valorem* on some articles which the government felt were produced in adequate quantities in Russia, such as some textiles and iron, and of 50 per cent on other textiles and silver. The duties were considered so high that the Prussian envoy to Petersburg declared the tariff to be "a knife to the throat of the entire trade."[103] Export duties were set at 3 per cent *ad valorem*. In Arkhangelsk, the duty was 25 per cent higher than in Petersburg. The tariff applied only to Petersburg, Arkhangelsk, and Kola, as well as to Vyborg and Narva, but was later extended to the trade across the Polish border.[104] The Baltic German staple cities, however, continued to form a separate customs zone, where the tariff remained more moderate. Foreign goods brought into these ports were taxed at a lower rate but could not be exported to Russia and across Russian territory to Little Russia. Goods brought from Russia into the customs zone were charged the regular export duty so that Reval, Riga, and Pernov would not enjoy a privileged position vis-à-vis the Russian ports. The domestic products of Estland and Livland entered Russian ports duty-free.[105]

Behind these complex tariff provisions, which scholars find it difficult at times to sort out, a clear policy was taking place. The entire trade of the basin of Lake Ladoga was integrated into that of the expanding Russian core, an integration all the more irresistible in that Petersburg was fated to become not only the largest city on the Baltic littoral but also a capital with a powerful impact on the whole of northwestern Eurasia. Petersburg replaced Stockholm, but Petersburg was also the capital of an expanding core with an enormous potential much greater than that of tiny Sweden. The maintenance of a customs zone, a kind of *porto franco*, for the three Baltic cities until 1782 merely reflected a desire not to offend a Baltic German identity, which believed that it formed a separate civilization – and Peter's desire to remain on good terms with that world for political reasons as with the Dutch and the English for commercial reasons. But the fact that Estonia and Livonia could export their products duty-free to Russia meant that the three cities had become isolated while their hinterland was being integrated.

The history of the tariff until the 1750s was marked by repeated requests by the Baltic landowners to develop grain exports against the resistance of the Provisioning Department in Petersburg to guarantee a regular supply for the army and the capital, expressed in periodic attempts to ban exports whenever there was a poor harvest. The "greed of some" ignored the prohibition, but one senses a permanent concern over the security of supply in the capital.[106] There were similar worries on the Finnish front. Good harvests and repopulation measures helped the Finns recover from the horrors of war, and sawmills using more advanced Dutch technology helped Vyborg overtake Narva as the principal export of sawn timber by 1740. But the danger of deforestation and a resulting shortage of construction timber and firewood in the capital caused the government to restrict the production of mills. By mid-century, Petersburg's population reached ninety thousand, and the city offered opportunities to Finns from the eastern districts, so much so that the Finnish community of 1,500 in the capital was larger than many Finnish towns themselves. While western Finland was still drawn to Stockholm, Swedish Karelia and even Savolaks were beginning to gravitate toward Petersburg.[107] Russian exports continued to grow, not only of timber, but also of iron, carried on river boats to Petersburg from the Urals, 2,600 kilometres away, which began even to compete with Swedish iron as early as the 1730s. The Swedes saw this expansion of Russian trade as an existential threat, and in July 1741, using as a pretext another prohibition of grain exports, declared war on Russia.

The same issues continued to confront policy makers and producers in the 1740s and 1750s, but a new one came to the fore in the 1750s. The government became concerned with the impact of internal duties on the flow of goods on roads, rivers, and bridges, and resolved to take the drastic step to abolish them all in 1753. To compensate for the loss of revenue, a single internal duty was introduced, no longer to be collected in the interior of the country, but at ports of entry and customs houses along the land border. Originally fixed at 13 per cent *ad valorem*, it was not uniformly applied in this amount, but within a range of from 6 to 16 per cent over and above the duties of the 1724 and 1731 tariffs. "There had never been before such a high tariff in Russia,"[108] and the incongruous position of the three Baltic *porto francos* became even more obvious. Only a continuous determination to maintain the "privileges" explains the retention of these exemptions from the new 1757 tariff. When the assault against the privileges finally began in the late 1770s, Reval, Riga, and Pernov were fully integrated into the tariff regime of the expanding Russian core.

A Confessional and Cultural Frontier

The expansion of the Russian core encountered confessional and cultural frontiers in all three theatres – with Islam in the east, with Catholicism in Right Bank Ukraine, and with Catholicism and Lutheranism in the west. Each frontier had its own distinct features, but the western frontier, where Russia also faced the Swedish and Germanic worlds, was the most peculiar of the three.

After Vladimir Sviatoslavich (St Vladimir), Grand Prince of Kiev (978–1015), converted to Byzantine Orthodoxy in 988, the new religion quickly spread north in the basin of the Dnieper and along the Varangian Route to Novgorod and the Baltic shores. Its progress was facilitated by the simplicity of the doctrine and of its practices and organization; by its ability to accommodate indigenous cultural traditions, certain ritual similarities such as the celebration of marriages and the mourning of death; and by the simplicity of its priests, who married and won acceptance among the native peoples.[109] The stronghold of Orthodox missionary work was the Valaam Transfiguration Monastery on a northern island of Lake Ladoga, from which Orthodoxy spread among the Estonians and the Karelians, while the Belorussians were drawn to the principalities of Polotsk on the Dvina, Pskov on Lake Peipus, and Novgorod on Lake Ilmen. The first experience of Christianity by the native population thus came from the Rus' principalities,[110] from their Orthodox priests and monks. By the time the new millennium began, it appeared that Byzantine Orthodoxy was in the process of winning over the basin of the Dnieper, the upper Volga, the Dvina, and Lake Ladoga, which led into Finland.

Latin Christianity was also expanding. The Catholic Church became established in Sweden in 1070, sixteen years after the Greek and Latin churches excommunicated each other. It converted not only the great families but also the general population, announcing the confessional homogeneity which would become a key feature of Swedish civilization.[111] Its archepiscopal see, founded in 1164, was in Uppsala, north of Stockholm. There was already an older one in Lund in Scania created in 1103, but then Scania was part of Denmark. In Rome, Pope Urban II (1088–99) called for the rollback of Islam in the Holy Land, and the First Crusade was crowned by the capture of Jerusalem. In the meantime, Pope Innocent III (1198–1216), the greatest and most ambitious medieval pope, who promoted the Fourth Crusade during which Constantinople was plundered by the crusaders (1204), bestowed crusading privileges on German knights who agreed to convert the pagans and roll back Greek Orthodoxy in the Baltic lands.[112] Bishop Albert founded Riga in 1202, and another bishop founded Dorpat. Catholic bishops were warrior-bishops, while Orthodox prelates never led troops in battle.[113] The Teutonic Order (Knights), founded in the Holy Land in 1191, moved to Europe and led a crusade against the Prussians, whom they exterminated in short order. The order then merged with Albert's Livonian Order to create a Baltic German crusading order, which crushed and converted Estonians and Latvians before it met its equal in Alexander Nevsky. He stopped their momentum on Lake Peipus in 1242, two years after blocking the Swedish advance on the Neva. The line had been drawn between Latin and Byzantine Christendom, and would remain largely unchanged until the present day. The expanding Russian and Orthodox core would never be able to breach it.

The Reformation gave the Order and the Swedish monarchy their chance. By breaking away from Rome and turning Protestant, they gained control of the assets of the Catholic Church, substantially enlarged their income, and incorporated the new Lutheran Church – which had become an Erastian church after Luther's excommunication in 1521 and his opposition to the Peasants' War of 1524–5 – into the civil administration of the Swedish monarchy and the collegial administration of Livonia. The latter *de facto* assumed the episcopal authority over the Lutheran congregations. By 1570 there was a Lutheran Church in Kurland headed by a thirteen-member General Consistory, presided over by a superintendent. There would also be one in Riga with six sub-consistories and about fifty parishes across Livonia.[114] In Finland, a second bishopric was created in Vyborg in 1554, not only to minister to the Lutheran population but also to convert the Orthodox in Karelia and Ingria and expel them if necessary, without arousing Russian opposition.[115]

In Sweden itself, Catholicism retained its hold – Queen Kristina would convert to Catholicism before she was forced to abdicate in 1654 – but it fought a rearguard action against a groundswell of support for Lutheranism. The break with Rome took place early, in 1527, and Gustav Vasa seized the assets of the Catholic Church. It was the first "reversion" carried out by the Crown, this time not against the landed nobility but against the Church. The vernacular was introduced in the service in 1537, and the Finnish branch of the Lutheran Church was placed under two bishops who had studied in Wittenberg and were wary of Russian Orthodox expansion.[116] A superintendent was appointed (but not a consistory), a post resembling that of minister of ecclesiastical affairs, and a state church was born. Its creation and integration into the machinery of government in a new monarchy ruled by a vigorous and ambitious king gave Swedish Lutheranism a "harsh, rigid, and combative character,"[117] and transformed the parish clergy into "propaganda agents" imbued with the spirit of the Old Testament and leading their congregations to sing "psalms of battle and psalms of hate."[118] Even if there was no General Consistory – which distinguished the German from the Swedish church – a small group consisting of the primate of Sweden (the Uppsala archbishop) and ten other bishops, all appointed by the king, upheld an uncompromising Lutheranism as a tool of unification in the emerging Swedish empire and as a military banner during Swedish expansion into northern Germany during the Thirty Years' War (1618–48).[119] Across the Russo-Swedish frontier, in Moscow, the Orthodox Church was also feeling the heavy hand of the state in the midst of the Livonian war, fought for the incorporation of the lands of the Teutonic Order into the expanding Russian core. Ivan IV ordered the assassination of Metropolitan Philip in 1569, who also believed in the subordination of the Church to the State – the Greco-Russian Church was always an Erastian church – but insisted that the Church should retain Philip's vast landed properties. Intolerance was helping to shape the contours of a confessional frontier.

It remained for Gustav Adolf and his successors to build on the solid foundations laid by the first Vasa king. The annexation of Estland and Livland brought about the Consistorial Regulation of 1634, which created in Livonia a General Consistory (*Ober-Konsistorium*) of two executive officers and six assessors. Its president, appointed by the king, accepted complaints, directed trials, and imposed sentences; a superintendent, later called General Superintendent, also appointed by the king, was in charge of ordinations and investitures, and directed visitations. The six assessors, three from the clergy, three from the lay community, were appointed by the governor general in Riga. The consistory met in Dorpat once a year for a month. It took on matters related to marriage and divorce, the sacraments, and church discipline. No appeals were accepted against its decisions. The king later ordered the creation of a second consistory in Riga.[120]

These agencies also pursued a policy of Swedification, seeking to integrate German into Swedish Lutheranism, which had become a symbol of Swedish nationality.[121] When Scania and its bishopric in Lund were annexed from Denmark in 1660, the Swedish church became an instrument to integrate the new land into the expanding Swedish realm. One cannot but be struck by certain similarities between Swedish Lutheranism and Russian Orthodoxy after the 1660s – both Erastian churches transformed into propaganda departments of expanding cores beginning to shape two rival identities in a common confessional frontier.

The Swedes were on the offensive in the seventeenth century. After 1617, their main effort was to extirpate Orthodoxy from Ingria and Karelia, where the population fled to Orthodox Russia in large numbers: of a total population of 160,000, only 21,000 remained.[122] In 1625, Gustav Adolf ordered that a Slavonic printing press be set up in Stockholm to help disseminate a translation of Luther's Catechism, and at the end of the century the Bishop of Vyborg demanded the total proscription of Orthodoxy, a step which the Swedish government was not yet willing to take.[123] Nevertheless, in their work of religious and political unification, the Swedes sought to break down the racial barrier created by the Teutonic Knights in Livonia. The Church Law of 1686, which made "the royal power into a theocracy,"[124] centralized the administration of the Lutheran Church by curtailing the autonomy of parishes and congregations, ordered the creation of a secondary school (gymnasium) in every diocese and rural elementary schools in the countryside, made the knowledge of Luther's Catechism a prerequisite for admission to communion and confirmation, and encouraged the training of Estonian and Latvian pastors and the translation of the Bible into the vernacular – into Latvian in 1638, into Estonian in 1643 (though this was not published until 1739).[125] Moreover, it strove to suspend labour services on the German manors so that the non-German peasants could attend church on Saturday afternoons and Sundays. Charles XI "was the first to take seriously the idea that Estonian and Letts were fellow Christians and entitled to be treated as such."[126]

Lutheranism's great contribution was in education, which it tightly controlled. By insisting that every member of a congregation must be able to read the Bible in the vernacular, it compelled the government and every congregation, at a time when education was not yet a fully public function, to hire private tutors to teach its children – a vicious circle, since tutors had first to be trained. Gymnasia were opened in Riga, Revel, Dorpat, and Åbo under Gustav Adolf. The teaching was in Latin, and religion permeated the entire system. Schools were in effect propaganda centres, where belief in Lutheranism was equated with loyalty to Sweden. But the major push toward the integration, unification, and Swedification of the empire had to come from the universities, which were also part of the religious establishment. The oldest university, that of Uppsala, dated from 1477, and had been a hotbed of Catholicism before becoming "a tragic victim of the Reformation."[127] It ceased to operate, but reappeared as a Lutheran hotbed in 1595. Most of its books came from Germany. Next was Greifswald University, founded in Pomerania in 1456, a popular centre for Swedish students on the northern periphery of the Germanic world. Åbo University was founded much later, in 1640, administered by the bishop of Finland. The third was Lund University, established in 1668 following the annexation of Scania. In the meantime, however, a fourth university had been created in Dorpat in 1632 to carry out the same work of integration and unification in the Baltic provinces.[128]

Dorpat was founded as the Academia-Gustaviana on the site of a gymnasium created two years earlier. It was granted the same rights and privileges as Uppsala University and had nineteen professors teaching in four departments. Its purpose was strictly utilitarian: to consolidate the hold of Lutheranism in Livonia and to train administrative cadres – pastors, officials, judges, teachers, and doctors. Unfortunately, the Russian invasion of 1656 forced it to close after graduating 1,061 students, an average of 40 a year. It reopened in 1690 as the Academia Gustaviana-Carolina with ten professors. It then became another tragic victim of unsettled times. At the beginning of the Northern War it moved to Pernau; when the Russians captured the city in 1710, professors and students left for Germany and Sweden, and the university would not reopen until 1802. It had graduated another 587 students in ten years.[129]

One must not exaggerate its importance. The Swedish Lutheran world remained a cultural dead end[130] on the far eastern periphery of Europe, and there seems not to have been much pressure to convince the Russians to reopen the Academia. The German nobility preferred to send their sons to European universities – Königsberg, founded in 1544, Rostock, founded in Pomerania in 1419, and as far as Leiden, created in 1575, a centre of science and Protestant theology – if only to express their opposition to the Swedification of Livonia. Nevertheless, Dorpat University during the thirty-four years of its existence laid the foundations of a cultural awakening in Estland and Livland[131] and consolidated the position of Lutheranism against which Russian Orthodoxy would remain helpless. A dead end on the cultural periphery of Europe was also a bright spot on the western periphery of Eurasia which would shed light on the bleak cultural landscape of the continent in the eighteenth century.

The Russians encountered a new situation in the Baltic provinces. In Karelia and Ingria, the Orthodox Church proceeded to reassert its influence, but there could be no question of persecuting the Lutherans (like the Muslims in the east), or incorporating them into the Orthodox Church (like the Uniates in Right Bank Ukraine). On the other hand, supporting Lutheranism meant supporting serfdom and the landlords, as well as consolidating Russian rule. Lutheranism, which demanded obedience and order, appeared as a parallel church serving the same purpose as Orthodoxy. A policy of social stratification found a natural companion in a policy of confessional superstratification in order to obtain the unconditional obedience of the peasants to their pastors and their lords. Having no university also served the same purpose. There would not be one in Russia until 1755, and Moscow University would be no great success until the nineteenth century.[132] Even as utilitarian institutions, universities could become centres where awkward questions were raised. Unlike the Swedish government which was readying drastic reforms to integrate the Baltic provinces ever more deeply, thereby antagonizing both clergy and landlords, the expanding Russian core abandoned the dream of integration in order to secure the maintenance of the status quo in what was essentially an alien society. That is why Moscow outlawed the Moravian Brethren, as soon as they aroused suspicions that their beliefs were likely to undermine the authority of the Lutheran clergy and the dominion of the landlords.

It was agreed that the consistorial form of church management would remain and would even expand, with four assessors in Riga and eight church and school inspectors (*prepozity*) in Riga, Pernau, Dorpat, and Wenden. The general superintendent was assisted by two superintendents in Riga and Arensburg.[133] The

Knights asked in 1725 that the college of *Landräte* be given episcopal authority because no bishop was appointed, but Petersburg demurred. It remained unclear who would appoint the members of the consistories.[134] Another question was what agency would replace the royal council in Stockholm with final authority. By the 1730s, a College of Justice for Estland and Livland Affairs (and Finnish Affairs after 1744) had emerged, subordinated to the Senate.[135] Thus, at the highest level, judicial and ecclesiastical affairs had become integrated into the structure of the imperial government, while local affairs remained in the hands of the *Landräte*. The creation of a separate and parallel line of authority for the administration of a territory resembled the system created for Little Russia (with this difference, that the college resided in Hlukhiv (Glukhov) and not in the capital) and may have served as a precedent for the administration of Muslim affairs in Orenburg and the Crimea later in the eighteenth century.

Toward the Integration of the Court System

The law is a set of norms created over time to maintain peace and order, a framework for a community to express its attitudes toward power relationships, economic competition, and social equality and inequality, and laws embody assumptions which have long been taken for granted.[136] Laws and religion define the civilization which created them. In Europe and Eurasia, there were four great systems of private law: the English (with the American); the continental with its two branches, the French and the Austro-German; the Islamic; and the Russian. For our purpose here, we need to consider the expansion of Swedish law, as a sub-system of Germanic law, in Finland and the Baltic provinces.

A characteristic feature of old Swedish law was that its custodian was not the priest, but anyone inclined to acquire a knowledge of it.[137] He would assume the role of leader in his community and help maintain its independence. Later, long after Sweden had become politically unified, the idea of the sovereign legislating at will, as in Roman law, was unacceptable.[138] It was the responsibility of the king to interpret the law, not to make a new one, for the basic law was God's will. Nevertheless, there could not be a politically unified Sweden without a single law, and local laws were gradually "melted together"[139] in the fourteenth century, even before the founding of the Vasa dynasty, into the "law of the land" (*landslag*), which remained in force until 1442. The man "who knew the law" (*lagman*) was at first elected, later appointed in each province, but he did not tell the law and impose sentence without the help of a "jury" (*nämnd*) of twelve persons, half elected by the *lagman*'s side, half by his opponent's. A majority of seven was required to render a verdict, but the judgment was the responsibility of the *lagman*. The jury decided questions of fact at first, but imperceptibly took up questions of law as well. Elected at first to sit on a particular case, it then became a permanent institution to assist the *lagman* in the county courts – a local reflection of the king telling the law with the assistance of his own lawmen.[140]

In the seventeenth century, a law school was created at Uppsala University (1620), and Sweden was the first in Scandinavia to develop a sizable legal profession in the wake of Gustav Adolf's reforms. A Supreme Court (*Svea Hovratt*) was created in 1614, consisting of a president and twelve professionally trained assessors, standing over a network of county courts, each headed by an appointed *lagman*. Courts of appeal (Swedish *Hofratter*, German *Hofgerichte*) were appointed in Stockholm and Jonköping, in Åbo, Riga, and Revel (where such a court was called *Ober-Landgericht*). A law professor at Uppsala who wrote a history of Swedish law in 1675,[141] during the reign of Charles XI, behaved in an "un-Swedish" manner by giving ample scope to the positive law, but also encouraged the codification of Swedish law, which contained many contradictions and needed adjustments to respond to changing social and economic conditions. The result was the Code of 1734, which would remain in force, with periodic amendments, for over a century.

The Code was not really a new law but the old *landslag* rewritten in strong modern vernacular Swedish, with only one foreign word in it (*testament*). Nevertheless, it was the outcome of serious and prolonged discussions which consulted canon and Roman law as well as German municipal law, but in the end, the old law prevailed, stripped of its medieval formalism. However, it followed German law in at least one feature of the civil law. Concerning the right of alienation, it distinguished between inherited and acquired land. The former could not be sold or given away by donation because the heir apparent possessed the *jus retractus* empowering him to step into the bargain and acquire the land.[142] A similar procedure was found in Russian law (*vykup*). Our scholarship would be immensely enriched with the publication of comparative studies of Germano-Swedish and Russian law, in order to bring out the similarities and differences as well as to illuminate the problems faced by the Russians in their attempts to create a unitary state. The Code also softened the harsh provisions of the old penal law. The dominant principle had been the *lex talionis* of the Mosaic law, the law of God, who must be appeased by the most severe penalties in order to frighten prospective criminals, a principle also found in Russian law (*v strakh drugim*). But the Code also retained the death penalty for sixty-eight offences,[143] ten years before its abolition in Russia.

Across the Gulf of Bothnia, the old *landslag* was translated into Finnish in the seventeenth century but was never published, perhaps because the judges were Swedes or knew Swedish. The Code of 1734 was translated in 1738, but was not published until 1759.[144] The Finnish judiciary, "which has been in existence in Sweden since ancient times," had two tiers. The lowest court, similar to the Russian county (*uezd*) court, was headed by a *haradshövding*, who had the rank of lieutenant, but whose position was considered highly respectable. He and his jury met twice a year in the fall and winter, in order not to disturb the peasants' field work. Appeals had to be filed within eight days to the *lagman*'s court, which tried cases with a jury. The *lagman*'s position was considered distinguished (*znatnyi*). He had the rank of lieutenant colonel and was appointed by the king. The court met once a year, and further appeals went to the Åbo *Hofgericht* if the value of the suit exceeded a certain amount. It was "a well organized judiciary."[145]

It was the opposite in the Baltic German provinces. Three basic kinds of law prevailed there. The first two were the canon law of the Church, and the German law, brought in by the Livonian Order and supplemented over time by the legislation of the German emperors, the Pope, and the Order itself. A major source of the German law was the Saxon Mirror (*Sachsenspiegel*), going back to the 1230s and regulating feudal relationships. A Livland Mirror partly brought it up to date in the fourteenth century. This Germanic law made up the "law of the land" (*Landrecht, zemskoe pravo*). In Estland, much of the law of the land was of Danish origin. After 1561, the canon law was superseded on the former properties of the Church, and the land law incorporated elements of Polish law during the so-called Polish period (1562–1625), when Livland was incorporated into the Polish Empire. With the incorporation of Estland and Livland into the Swedish Empire in 1561 and 1625 respectively, Swedish legislation penetrated the old land law, so that by the time of the Russian conquest of 1710, the Russians were faced with an impenetrable maze of "rights and privileges" of various ancestry.[146]

The third was municipal law. With the agreement of the Danish kings, Revel took as a model Lübeck's municipal law, and Revel in turn became the model for other Estland towns, although some chose the land law, like the Upper Town (Vyshgorod) overlooking the port of Revel. Eventually, the Estland land law would prevail under the impact of the jurisprudence developed in the *Ober-Landgericht*. Only the remainder of Revel would retain the old Lübeck law. In Livland, the towns took Riga for their model. There, Bishop Albrecht, the founder of the city, gave it rights and privileges borrowed from Visby, the entrepot on Gotland Island, but the town later adopted the Hamburg municipal law which gave Riga its entire civil and criminal legislation. Swedish ordinances made their contribution in addition to those of the city itself, and Riga received its municipal statute in 1675. It remained outside the jurisdiction of the *Hofgericht* sitting in the city itself.[147]

Sweden at the height of its power in the seventeenth century endeavoured to create a uniform legal system in its Baltic empire. This was especially the case during the long reign of Charles XI (1660–97), who looked on the positive law as a weapon of imperial administration to override regional "land laws" and create a single one that would be Swedish in spirit and content. Thus, the

Trusteeship Ordinance of 1669, the Promissory Notes Ordinance of 1671, the Church Ordinance and inheritance laws of 1686, and a number of procedural codes intended for the metropolis and Finland were also extended to the Baltic provinces.[148] The campaign reached its apogee with the imposition of Swedish law on Riga and the Livonian courts in 1690, and in Estonia in 1694. The change was for the better. For example, torture had never been legalized in Sweden, but it was in Livonia, in 1632. In 1686 Charles XI prohibited its use in all his domains.[149] At the same time, efforts were made on both sides to codify Baltic German law, not only to clarify it for the benefit of the Swedish administration but also to legitimize Baltic German resistance to increasing Swedification. Thus, Swedification created its own antithesis, a provincial backlash, which would facilitate the Baltic Germans' acceptance of Russian rule.

It required some time after the annexation of 1710, confirmed by the Treaty of Nystadt of 1721, for the Russian government to create a new judicial system. The confirmation of the "rights and privileges" meant the retention of the Livonian law of the land and whatever the Germanic establishment wanted to retain from Swedish legislation. It also meant the retention of the court system – that is, the *Hofgericht* in Riga and the *Ober-Landgericht* in Revel, and their subordinate county courts. In the wake of the 1717 reorganization of the central government (inspired by Swedish models), a College of Justice was created in Petersburg. It originally contained a desk to take up appeals from Riga and Revel. In 1727 a separate College of Livland and Estland Affairs was created, which later acted as the *Hofgericht* for the Vyborg territory, cut off from that in Åbo. In 1734, following a petition by a Lutheran who could not find a court to file suit for divorce in Petersburg, its jurisdiction was extended to include all religious disputes (including marriage and divorce) to which non-Orthodox subjects were a party anywhere in the empire, but representatives from the party's confession residing in the capital would have to attend the trial. Beginning in 1736, decisions of the college were appealed to the Senate.[150] In Estland, divorce cases went from the provincial consistory to a Superior Court of Appeal, and from it to the College of Justice.[151]

Despite this apparently simple solution, great confusion prevailed in the courts. There was at first only a judicial commissioner in Vyborg *provintsia*, who probably remained until the creation of Vyborg province (*gubernia*) in 1744, when the position of *lagman* was restored. His court received appeals only in civil cases; criminal sentences went directly from the five county courts (*haradshövding*, corrupted into Russian as *geratsgevding*) to the College of Justice. But three problems arose. Court proceedings were conducted in four languages: petitioners continued to write in German; the record (protocol) was also written in German; it was sometimes translated into Russian; extracts were written in Swedish; the jurors understood only Finnish or Karelian.[152]

Another problem arose after the annexation of additional territory in 1743, the corridor stretching from the Kiumenne River to beyond Neishlot. In the territory annexed in 1710, the old Swedish land law of 1442 and subsequent Swedish legislation applied, but the new territory had already received the Code of 1734 (also called in Russian sources the Frederician Code, after King Fredrik I of Sweden's Hesse dynasty). Much later, in 1787, the Vyborg procurator would praise it as shorter, clearer, and adequate, as well as imposing less harsh punishments, especially in family law cases.[153] Nothing was done, however, perhaps because the Russian government could not free itself at the time from its obsession with maintaining the territory's "rights and privileges," and its occasional "clarifications" only caused greater confusion and total chaos. Moreover, members of the ruling elite in Petersburg brought some of their serfs into the province, where the Karelian peasant was free. As a result, the peasant population found itself living under three legal systems.[154]

There was a third problem. Despite the existence of the "rights and privileges," the Russians assumed that the annexations of 1710 and 1743 were permanent, and that the new territories – often referred to in the 1740s as "the conquered territories" – had become part of an expanding Russian core, in which they would have to occupy a position commensurate with that of the other provinces. As early as 1718, Peter I decreed that in judicial cases the College of Justice would follow the *Ulozhenie* (the Russian Code of 1649) and the Swedish ordinances (*ustavy*), but in other matters concerning the political and administrative organization of the expanding Russian core (*gosudarstvennye poriadki*), the college and the Senate would have to match the ordinances against Russian practices (*obychai*) and determine what had to be changed. But the emperor was obviously pulled in different directions. He stated on the same day that there must be "only one *ustav* and one *ulozhenie*," which implied the creation of a single legal system for Russia and the Baltic provinces, in which Swedo-German legislation would be incorporated into the Russian *Ulozhenie*, perhaps in the form of amendments or additional articles. In the meantime, the immediate issue concerned translations. The Russians did not have translations of Swedish laws, and foreigners sitting in the College of Justice were not familiar with the Russian *Ulozhenie* and the Supplementary Articles of 1669–86. The *Ulozhenie* existed in Latin translation, but the Articles would have to be translated into German, and Swedish legislation into Russian. Once this was done, the judges in the college (and in the Senate) would have to work together to achieve "a rapid merger" (*skoroe soedinenie*) of both legal systems.[155]

Whether and when such translations were made is unclear. At any rate, the College of Justice found itself in the same situation in Vyborg in 1744: it was told to decide cases in the new territory in accordance with its "rights and privileges," but did not know what they were, nor did the Senate. The Vyborg governor was told to send certified copies for the college, which would forward them to the Senate.[156] We face here an ambiguous policy: there was a willingness to accept the "rights and privileges," without even knowing what they consisted of, if only to emphasize that the Russians would not follow in the footsteps of Sweden, which had also promised to recognize them, before shifting to a policy of Swedification that antagonized the regional elites and encouraged the Russian advance. On the other hand, the Russians also pursued a policy to create a unitary state, which manifested itself from time to time, and finally triumphed during the reign of Catherine II, before retreating again under her three successors, until the death of Nicholas I in 1855.

By the mid-eighteenth century we obtain a fairly clear picture of the court system. In Riga, the *Hofgericht* consisted of a president who was the governor general or, in his absence, the governor; a vice-president, twelve assessors, and a secretary. It received appeals from five county courts (*Landgerichte*) in Riga, Pernau, Dorpat, Wenden, and Arensburg, consisting of a judge and two assessors. In criminal cases, their decisions were automatically forwarded to the *Hofgericht*. In Revel, the *Ober-Landgericht* was also chaired by the governor general or the governor, but consisted of twelve *Landräte*, the executive agency of both the nobility and the province, and received appeals from three lower or "district" courts called *Manngerichte*, consisting of a judge and two assessors elected by the nobility, sitting in Revel, Leal, and Wesenburg. The provincial *magistraty* in Revel and Riga remained courts of appeal for burghers suing in the *magistraty* of their home towns. Thus the Swedish system had been retained, including the incorporation of the court system into the power structure of the province.[157] Administration and justice remained close relatives, especially in Estland.

Under Swedish rule, however, the members of the *Hofgericht* had served for life, and if they retired, they would retain their ranks: the vice-president that of colonel, the assessors that of major. The Russians introduced their own rule that the ranks attached to elective positions were valid for as long as their holders remained in office (*za uriad*). The *Hofgericht* won a concession from the Senate in 1726 that the Swedish practice would remain. The Estlanders were very keen on making sure that the *Ober-Landgericht* must remain under the control of the *Landräte*. In 1737, Petersburg decreed that when there was no governor, the provincial board would appoint a replacement, but the court obtained a ruling that the senior *Landrat* would stand in for the governor until a new one was appointed.[158]

Attempts continued to codify the law of the land. In 1728 the Livland nobility evoked the "inconveniences" of trying cases by relying on a confused jurisprudence resulting from an accumulation of local German and Swedish laws, not to mention the inevitable contradictions that crept in with changing social and economic circumstances. They asked for a commission to codify Baltic German law. This was granted in 1730, when Anna Ivanovna, favourably disposed toward the Baltic nobility, came to the throne. By 1740, much of the work on civil and criminal law and judicial procedure had been completed, but with Anna's death, the Senate asked for a new version, and the project was abandoned, even though it had already been approved by the *Landtag*. It was not even printed. Elizabeth was hostile to the Germanic world, but when a codification commission was created in Petersburg in 1755 to work on a new *Ulozhenie*, the project was taken up anew in a committee attached to the College of Livland and Estland Affairs. But nothing was accomplished, and despite continued efforts, a Code of Baltic Laws would not see the light of day until 1845 (the first two parts) and 1864 (the third and last part), by which time the separate status of the Baltic provinces would soon become anachronistic.[159]

As in Little Russia, the attempts to codify local laws foundered and for the same reasons. The Russians, who were also aware of the need to codify their own laws, could not afford to let peripheral elites get ahead of them and achieve what they still found too difficult to achieve for themselves – the first edition of the *Svod Zakonov* in fifteen volumes would not be published until 1832, nearly two hundred years after the *Ulozhenie*. There were other reasons. The Russian and local elites worked at cross-purposes. While it is true that both recognized the need to codify their laws to clear a path for judges through a growing maze, the local elites saw codification as a way to assert an identity against the brooding Russian presence, just as their grandparents had bridled against increasing Swedish pressures. Codification gave a feeling of confidence and pride in their past and the distinctive separateness of their civilization. But the Russians had to resist such a development for obvious reasons, all the more so in that it was easy to detect an unbending determination to eventually create a unitary state with a single legal system. Last but not least, there existed on both sides a shortage of expert opinion, of legal training for an immensely difficult task, exacerbated by endless arguments over the meaning of the "rights and privileges." Nevertheless, there is no doubt that during the first fifty years of Russian rule, the Baltic German nobility had every reason to be complacent about their position. The *Matrikel* had been a form of codification, and the "job market" for ambitious noblemen was expanding with the expansion of the Russian core.

Chapter Two

Full Integration, 1775–1815

Territorial and Administrative Integration

Belorussia

But clouds were rising over the horizon. Catherine II, a full-blooded German and a foreigner in her adopted country, came to the throne in June 1762, when the Seven Years' War was drawing to a close. Although the country's finances were in dire straits, Russia had scored impressive victories, had briefly occupied Berlin, and was contemplating the annexation of East Prussia, the land of the Teutonic Knights.[1] A new crop of ambitious and determined generals was filling the upper echelons of the civil and military establishment, with far-ranging visions of Russia's future strategic goals, especially in the southern theatre. The impending death of the King of Poland, Augustus III, acted as a catalyst. In October 1763, General Zakhar Chernyshev, the war minister, who had led the offensive on Berlin in 1760, submitted a memorandum to a conference held at the Russian Court.[2]

The further expansion of Russia would serve no purpose, claimed the general in a curious reasoning, because it would make it difficult to raise the population density of the core (*sredina*) and would compel the government to deploy troops on the periphery – as if the periphery could not be more densely settled and richer. Supporting such troops would place pressure on the government's budget, which should instead serve to increase the capability of the core and help develop its internal commerce. It was necessary to find "natural borders" (*natural'nye ukrepleniia i okruzheniia*), which must be rivers, because they are easier to defend with fewer troops. The revenues from such peripheries would improve the domestic budget, the size of the army could be reduced, and the budget would be better adapted to reflect the economic condition of the people. Therefore, the Russian core needed to expand (!) "in the direction of Europe" (*k storone Evropy*) to link the Dvina with the Dnieper and create a continuous waterway from Riga to Kiev. Russia would thus expand to include Polish Livonia, part of the Polotsk palatinate (*wojewodztwo*) situated on the the right bank of the Dvina, the Vitebsk palatinate, then follow a line from the confluence of the Ulla River to Orsha on the Dnieper and on to Rogachev, thus incorporating Vitebsk, Mogilev, and Mstislavl palatinates, and follow the Dnieper to the Little Russian border.

In order to carry this out, Russia would demand from Poland, after the death of August III (he died the same month), the election of the Russian candidate to succeed him, and would mount a converging attack from Livonia and Smolensk with backup troops from Petersburg and Moscow to compel acceptance of the Chernyshev proposal. It was not, however, a proposal to partition Poland but one to create a buffer state similar to the one in neighbouring Kurland, which had been a fief of the Polish king since 1561. The territory would retain its laws and its administrative system, and the nobility would be given the properties of the Polish king (*starostva*), which in different circumstances would become the property of the Russian empress. Troops would then be recalled, but garrisons would remain – all this on condition that the nobility agree to become vassals of the empress (*vasal'stvom obiazhutsia*).

Chernyshev's proposal was not carried out at the time, largely because of the political turbulence in Poland following the election of Stanisław Poniatowski in 1764, which embroiled Russia in a war with the Ottoman Empire in 1768. But the war was far from over when a secret convention with Prussia in January 1772 partitioned the Polish Empire.[3] The Russian share incorporated the territory included in Chernyshev's proposal, but it was a bit larger. The Dvina remained the border to a point between Beshenkovichi and Vitebsk, from which it ran to Tolochin, then followed the Drut flowing west of, and for the most part parallel to, the Dnieper to their confluence at Rogachev, and from there, along the Dnieper to Kiev. The new territory thus included Polish Livonia (ceded to Poland in 1660) with Dünaburg and Drissa on the Dvina, Rezhitsa and Liutsin in the central lake region, and the greater part of Polotsk palatinates, as well as Vitebsk, Mogilev, and Mstislavl palatinates.

Twenty years later, and after the conclusion of another Russo-Turkish war, in which Poland openly sided with the Turks, Russia and Prussia once again agreed to carry out a second partition in July 1793. While it had acquired 93,000 square kilometres and 1.3 million inhabitants in 1772 from the Grand Duchy of Lithuania, Russia now gained another 250,200 square kilometres and over 3 million inhabitants.[4] The partition line began at Druia on the Dvina, at the very eastern end of Kurland, reached and followed the Naroch to its confluence with the Vilia running into the Niemen, continued overland to Slobtsy near the headwaters of the Niemen, passed Nesvizh and Pinsk at the confluence of the Pina and the Pripiet, and finally crossed the swampy zone called Polesie to enter the lands of Right Bank Ukraine. The new territory thus incorporated

Minsk palatinate and the eastern half of the Novogrudok and Brest-Litovsk palatinates.[5] This was western Belorussia, while the lands acquired in 1772 constituted eastern Belorussia.

The focus in scholarly literature has been on the "partitions of Poland," but this neglects an important aspect. From a geographic and strategic point of view, the second partition completed the incorporation of the entire basin of the Dnieper into the expanding core. The Treaty of Andrusovo (1667) gave Russia the lands of Smolensk, Starodub, and Chernihiv (i.e., the basin of the Desna, the major left bank tributary of the Dnieper).[6] The Smolensk corridor gave entry to the middle Dnieper. In 1772, Russia reached the middle course of the river, and the Treaty of Kuchuk Kainardji (1774) incorporated the lower Dnieper. By 1793, the Dnieper and the Dvina had been brought into the expanding Russian core, and the Polish dream of an empire "from sea to sea" (i.e., from the Baltic to the Black Sea) had been realized for Russia's benefit.

The administrative-territorial integration of eastern Belorussia took place in two stages: from the annexation until the introduction of the local government reform in 1778; from then on until the death of Catherine II in 1796. The so-called Plakat of August 1772,[7] in which Chernyshev, appointed governor general of the territory, announced to the population the boundary of the Russian acquisition, promised religious toleration and the inviolability of property, and stated Catherine's determination to give her new subjects the same rights as her existing ones – effectively integrating them into the mass of the latter. It also divided eastern Belorussia into two provinces, Pskov and Mogilev. These provinces (*gubernii*) were in turn divided into *provintsii* as was the case elsewhere in the Russian core, and these into counties (*uezdy*). There could be no better manifestation of the impulse to integrate than the decision to incorporate the Polotsk palatinate into Pskov province, which was detached from the huge Novgorod province to form a separate (and a purely Russian) one. A Russian province now bordered on the Dvina, which had also become the boundary of the expanding core, an exceptional situation which could not last, because the internal, Russian, provinces required a peripheral buffer to protect them against outside contamination.

The local government reform took effect in the spring of 1778.[8] Polotsk province was divided into eleven, Mogilev province into twelve, counties. Before the annexation there had been only two *powiat* (county) centres (Vitebsk and Orsha); Polish Livonia, Polotsk, Mstislavl, and Mogilev palatinates had not been divided into counties. There were now twenty-three county centres, including some that were given the status of towns: they had been privately owned villages and *mestechki*. This represented a substantial implantation of state power, even though the elected land and county courts fell under the control of the Polish *szlachta* serving the interests of the great families of the Grand Duchy, such as the Sapiehas and Oginskis. Of the eleven county centres in Polotsk province, four were in the former Polotsk and another four in the former Vitebsk palatinate. The other three were in Polish Livonia, with Marienhausen renamed Liutsin and Dünaburg, Dvinsk. Of the twelve county centres of Mogilev province, three were in Vitebsk palatinate, six in the former Mstislavl palatinate, and three in the southeastern corner of Minsk palatinate.

The territorial reform was automatically extended to the territory occupied in 1793.[9] A Minsk province was created of thirteen counties – the palatinate had only three; it now contained five. The other eight consisted of lands acquired from Novogrudok (three), Brest-Litovsk (two), Vilno (two), and the remainder of Polotsk palatinate on the left bank of the Dvina (one). The new territorial division of Belorussia thus consisted of three provinces and thirty-six counties with a total population of 2.4 million thus distributed: Polotsk 725,725; Mogilev 811,770; and Minsk 882,848.[10]

The Plakat of August 1772 instructed Governor General Chernyshev, who also commanded the troops deployed in eastern Belorussia, to maintain order, conduct a census, and collect as much information as possible on the judicial and fiscal system, the sale of spirits (a major source of revenue), the distribution of salt (a vital necessity) among the population, and, last but not least, the location of the grain stores. The governor general was appointed for only two years, at the end of which the governors in Pskov (later Polotsk) and Mogilev would assume full responsibility for doing the same thing, each in his province. The appointment of a governor general over two provinces was a novelty. Until then, governors general, governors, and vice-governors had served in a single province, and their authority reflected the importance given by the government to the management of the province at a particular time. Moreover, the statute of April 1764 had given the governor full authority over his province. The two governors, both major generals, were placed under the jurisdiction (*v vedenie*) of General Chernyshev, but the meaning of the expression was not explicit. As long as the first two governors were officers in active service, they were in fact subordinated to Chernyshev as war minister, but when they were succeeded by civilians, these reported to the procurator general, who, during Catherine's reign, was a de facto prime minister. The true nature of the post of governor general would remain an object of contention for a very long time.[11] Some would even wear two hats and bear a dual responsibility, to the civilian authorities as well as to the war ministry. Of the eleven governors who served in eastern Belorussia between 1772 and 1796, seven were Russian, while the other four had family ties in the region.

In each *provintsia* capital – Polotsk, Vitebsk, and Dünaburg (Dvinsk); Mogilev, Orsha, Mstislavl, and Rogachev – a *voevoda* with his deputy, a procurator, and a secretary were appointed by the Senate as they were in Russia and with the same staff. *Voevodas* were usually in the rank of colonel or the civilian equivalent, and some came from the *szlachta*. The provincial administration was thus fully incorporated into that of the expanding core. The lowest territorial unit was the parish (*parafia*); it had lived an autonomous existence under the control of influential families.[12] In 1773 Chernyshev reported there were thirty-nine *parafias* in eastern Belorussia. They were combined into fourteen counties and placed under an appointed county commissioner (*komissar*) responsible for carrying out decisions – civil judgments and criminal sentences, the collection of taxes and arrears – made at the provincial level.[13] They probably were chosen from among the local *szlachta* but were removable at will. In Russian eyes, these reforms were intended to create a streamlined administration capable of ending "the anarchy of the Polish Republic." Order, declared the empress, was the soul of government (*dusha pravlenia*).[14]

The local government reform, with its multiplicity of agencies at the provincial level – the provincial board, the treasury chamber, the two judicial chambers with the intermediate courts – increased the Russian presence in Polotsk, Mogilev, and Minsk but also brought in a substantial number of Polish *szlachta*. They were indispensable to the relatively efficient functioning of a provincial administration in a territory where the official language had been Polish for centuries, much in the same way as German had been dominant in the Baltic provinces. This was even more the case at the county level, where the county court, the land court, and county treasurer had at least to understand Polish and even Belorussian.[15] The policy of superstratification would raise sensitive issues, because Russians and Poles were often allergic to one another, while police investigations, the adjudication of disputes, and the repression of crime depended on the two nationalities reaching an accommodation. At any rate, even if cooperation would soon be found wanting and the local personnel incompetent, the integration of the provincial administration resulted in a considerable increase in the presence of state power, especially in what had been a distant far eastern march of the Polish Empire. One is struck by the number of privately held towns and villages that needed to be bought by the Russian treasury to become county centres fit to administer a population which the statute of 1775 fixed at about 30,000 males in each county. While it was of course impossible to keep this norm everywhere, the reform succeeded: a population of 2.4 million in thirty-six counties meant an average of 66,700 males and females per county.

Much depended on the personality of the governor general. Chernyshev did not remain for two years but for ten. He descended from a Polish *szlachtich* who had transferred his allegiance to Muscovy in 1493. His father had been an adjutant of Peter I and his early career had been in the military and diplomatic service. He won fame in the Seven Years' War, at the end of which he was promoted to full general and became war minister in 1763, and in 1773 he earned the coveted rank of field marshal – the table of organization allowed for only three. Soon afterwards, however, the rise of Grigorii Potemkin forced him to retire in 1774. He was an honest and honourable man who cared for the good of the country, but his hot temper and arrogance caused Catherine to relieve him in 1782 and make him governor general of Moscow, where he died in 1784. He belonged to a proud and contemptuous elite, lived well, but treated his subordinates, even his governors, as if they were his orderlies. His contempt for subordinates – so characteristic of the age – resulted in the appointment of corrupt Russian officials brought in from the interior provinces, for whom corruption was not a crime but a way of life.[16]

His successor, Petr Passek, was of Czech origin: his ancestors had emigrated to Lithuania and the Hetmanate. His grandmother was Ukrainian; his father had been a judge in the Hetmanate's General Court and a Belgorod *voevoda*. He was a cousin of Chernyshev: both married Wedel ladies, but he was a Potemkin protégé. He was also a very ordinary man, who had joined the Orlov brothers (who helped put Catherine on the throne in 1762), had horse farms in Smolensk province and properties in Estland, and retired from Court service in 1766 at the rank of lieutenant general. In 1778, he became governor of Mogilev, where he remained until his appointment to replace Chernyshev in 1782. He too loved the good life, fawned on Potemkin and the procurator general, but, like Chernyshev and other grandees, he was "one of those highly placed people whose commands must be carried out as if they were of divine origin and who could in one instant destroy all the endeavours and accomplishments [of a man]."[17]

Passek's mediocrity and corruption mirrored the shift of Russian activities from eastern Belorussia to the territory acquired in the second partition. General Timofei Tutolmin was a very different man. He had served with distinction under Rumiantsev during the Turkish war of 1768–74, transferred to the civil administration, and was appointed governor in Tver and then Ekaterynoslav. There he had the misfortune of falling foul of Potemkin, who had him removed to serve as governor general of Olonets and Arkhangelsk in 1784. This semi-disgrace gave him at least a modicum of independence from the powerful favourite. After Potemkin's death in 1791, Tutolmin returned to favour, and the entire territory acquired in the second partition north and south of the Pripiet marshes was placed under his jurisdiction. The fact that he resided in Nesvizh may explain the fact that the command of troops in Right Bank Ukraine was given to someone else. He was an upright and dedicated member of the ruling elite. He remained in his post until Catherine's death, when he retired under a cloud (but demonstrated his innocence) and, like Chernyshev, ended his career as governor general of Moscow from 1806 until shortly before his death in 1809.[18]

A giant step had been taken by the end of Catherine's reign to integrate Belorussia into the expanding Russian core. As the Baltic provinces, Lithuania, Volhynia, and Podolia became an inner frontier of the core, Belorussia began to gravitate more and more eastwards. It began to be seen as another Smolensk province, still strongly Polonized but indubitably Russian. By the time the Polish rebellion of 1831 shook Russia's dominion in Lithuania, eastern Belorussia would be ready for full integration, as officially proclaimed in January of that year.

Table 2.1 Share of the three powers in the partition of Poland

	Area (km²)	Population (millions)
Prussia	141,400	2.6
Austria	128,900	4.2
Russia	463,200	5.4
Total	*733,500*	*12.2*

Sources: Martens, *Recueil*, 2:238–43; 6:175–81; Zhukovich, "Upravlenie i sud," 50–2; *Historical Atlas of Poland*, 28–9 (maps) and 18 (text); Magocsi, *Historical Atlas*, 58 and 70–1.

Lithuania

The Grodno agreement with Russia, by which a Diet specially convened for this purpose ratified the loss of Belorussia in September 1793, caused a backlash against the Russians in the eastern marches of the Polish Empire. An insurrection, triggered by an announcement by the Russians in Warsaw that the size of the crown forces (i.e., those of the Polish core and Right Bank Ukraine) would be cut by nearly two-thirds and those of Lithuania by half, broke out in March 1794 in Ostrołenka in eastern Poland. It quickly spread to Warsaw, where half of the Russian garrison was massacred, then into Lithuania and Volhynia. It was led by Tadeusz Kosciuszko, who won some early successes but was taken prisoner in October; Russian forces led by Alexander Suvorov occupied Warsaw in November. Prussia, Austria, and Russia then agreed to complete the dismemberment of the Polish Empire.[19]

By the Declaration of Petersburg of December 1794 (January 1795) and the Act of Demarcation of June (July) 1796, Russia claimed another 120,000 square kilometres with 1.2 million inhabitants. The new border (now with Prussia and Austria) ran from the 1793 Austrian border with Galicia on the Zbruch, continued northwestward past Beresteczko to the Western Bug below Sokal, and followed the river to the border of the Grand Duchy and then a straight line to Grodno on the Niemen. It then followed the river to the Prussian border with Samogitia and reached the Baltic coast near Polangen. Thus the new territory in Lithuania included most of the remainder of the Brest-Litovsk and Novogrudok palatinates, part of the Troki palatinate east of the Niemen, and Samogitia. It automatically also incorporated Kurland, the elongated frontier between Samogitia and Livonia. It is inexact to say that Russia took part in the partition of Poland: it incorporated almost entirely the northeastern marches of the Polish Empire in the Grand Duchy, while Poland, the Polish core, was partitioned by Prussia and Austria. The total share of the three powers can be found in table 2.1.

There never was any doubt about Russian intentions concerning the administration of the new territory. The manifesto of October 1794, when the insurrection was hardly over, divided it into three "parts," centred in Vilno, Kovno (or Kaidany), and Grodno. Prince Nikolai Repnin, governor general of Estland and Livland since 1792, was given jurisdiction over the three parts as well. However, it soon turned out that Lithuania was not quite populous enough to accommodate three "provinces," and Repnin was ordered in December 1795 to administer the oath to the population of two provinces, one centred in Vilno, the other in Slonim. There were no local rights and privileges, but the population was guaranteed the free religion "of its ancestors" and the use of their property.[20]

The original division into three parts was premature, but not unwise. Kovno on the Niemen had been a fortified stronghold of the Teutonic Knights from which to convert the Lithuanians of Samogitia – the Zhmud Principality – on the densely forested high ground overlooking the swampy (but fertile) valley of the Nieviazha River. The knights were not successful and stopped their incursions after 1410; nor were the grand dukes of Lithuania. Only the Jesuits would succeed in the sixteenth century. Kovno was also an important trade centre where traders from the Kurisches Haff unloaded their boats from larger vessels to smaller ones on their way to Vilno and Grodno.[21] North of Kovno, Kaidany on the Nievazha – forming the eastern boundary of Samogitia – was a major religious centre and the property of the Radziwill family. Eventually, Kovno would become a provincial capital, but not until 1842.

Troki, located on a picturesque lake slightly west of Vilno, was founded in 1321 by Grand Duke Gedimin, who lived there until he moved to Vilno shortly thereafter. Karaim Jews were strongly represented there, and Tatar prisoners of war were resettled in the area by Grand Duke Vitovt after his advance into the southern steppe in the 1390s. However, Vilno, better situated on the Viliia meandering its way toward Kovno where it drained into the Niemen, relegated Troki to the status of a market town gathered around a majestic Gothic castle reminiscent of a glorious past. It became the dominant cultural religious and cultural centre as well as the true capital of Lithuania. It was a natural choice for the capital of one of the two provinces, which incorporated most of the Vilno palatinate, the eastern part of the Troki palatinate, and Samogitia with its capital in Vorny (Varniai), south of Telshi.

Slonim province absorbed the southern part of the two palatinates and the remainder of the Novogrudok and Brest-Litovsk palatinates which had not been included into Minsk province. Grodno on the Niemen would have been a better choice, and did become a provincial capital in 1802. The city had long been the object of a bitter rivalry between the Teutonic Knights and the Grand Duchy, but Vitovt made it his second capital in 1398, and King Batory lived there for a while. One in three Diets of the Polish Empire met in the town after 1673.

But Slonim was chosen partly because it was better located at the centre of the province and was on the road from Minsk to Warsaw; while Grodno did not have enough buildings to house the new government agencies, Slonim had a palace of 116 rooms owned by the Oginski family and five stone-built Catholic monasteries.[22]

Finding seats for the eleven counties of Vilno province and for the eight of Slonim province presented Repnin with the usual problem found throughout the former Grand Duchy: there were too few towns worthy of the name, and too many of the large villages were privately held. The implantation of a new public power in a territory consisting chiefly of private properties and properties leased for life from the Polish monarchy – the so-called *starostinskie mestechki* – required the creation of artificial towns without adequate infrastructure. These *mestechki* were taken over by the Russian treasury and their owners compensated; so were other villages. Repnin did not quite succeed in mapping out counties with an average total population of 60,000: in Vilno province the average was 89,000 and in Slonim province it was 76,000. Population figures for 1795 give a Vilno province of 977,810 and a Slonim province of 608,102. Kabuzan estimated that the total population of Lithuania and Belorussia in 1795 was 5.2 million, of whom 3.2 million (61 per cent) consisted of Belorussians ("Ruthenians"), who made up 90 per cent of the population of Minsk and Mogilev provinces. Lithuanians were the second largest group of 624,000 (12 per cent). There were 493,000 Russians (9.5 per cent), chiefly Old Believers who were now brought back under the control of the official Orthodox Church. Poles made up a small minority of 280,000 (5.4 per cent). Ukrainians (224,000 or 4.3 per cent) were found mostly in the south along the Pripet marshes, but Jews (179,000 or 3.4 per cent) were more evenly distributed. Latvians (128,000 or 2.4 per cent) lived mostly in the old Polish Livonia.[23] We can thus distinguish a top stratum of Poles, a second of Lithuanians, and a great mass of Belorussians. It was with such a stratified society that the Russians would have to deal in their administration of the "lands returned from Poland."

The crushing of the 1794 insurrection in Lithuania placed the country under martial law, with Repnin in command of troops stationed in the Baltic provinces and Lithuania, two major generals as governors in Vilno and Slonim, brigade commanders in *powiaty*, and colonels and other field grade officers to administer the police in towns and rural communities until sheriffs could be appointed and land captains elected. The manifesto of October 1794 ordered the population to take the oath of loyalty to the Russian throne and show "passive" (*bezmolvnoe*) obedience to the new authorities. It also promised that the new subjects would retain the religious freedom which "all non-Orthodox tribes enjoy in the bosom of our capitals (*vse obitaiushchie v Derzhave Nashei inovernye Nam plemena v samikh nedrakh stolits Nashikh*), a curious expression to use for Catholic (and Calvinist) Lithuanians. It added that they would retain their property and the rights they had enjoyed in accordance with the laws of the Polish Republic. By 1795, however, they were told that they, like their brethren in Belorussia, would be incorporated into the great mass of "ancient Russian subjects."[24]

Moreover, the manifesto ordered the creation of a Supreme Lithuanian Government to sit in Grodno, Repnin's headquarters at the time, a pompous and meaningless title. As the executive authority of the territory, it would be no more than a truncated provincial government similar to the one introduced elsewhere by the local government reform of 1775, and it was considered temporary, until the two new provinces finally took shape.[25] And indeed, Repnin was ordered to introduce the full panoply of new agencies in the fall of 1796. The Vilno and Slonim agencies opened for business at the end of November, but Catherine had died on 6 November; Repnin had received the news on 11 November and was recalled to Petersburg two days later.[26] Russian policy had been, as elsewhere, a policy of full territorial and administrative integration, which reduced a proud and ancient Grand Duchy to the status of two provinces of an immense Eurasian empire to be managed, at least in theory, by the same uniform laws. The resulting resentment would cut deeply for a long time, and Lithuania, later called "the northwestern provinces," would remain a field of bitter rivalry between Russians, Lithuanians, and Poles.

If a concession was made to Lithuanian pride, it was the appointment of General Prince Nikolai Repnin as governor general. He belonged to one of the great families of the ruling elite, descending as he did from the princely house of Chernihiv in Kievan Rus', absorbed into the Grand Duchy in 1355, until it became part of the Little Russian Hetmanate in the seventeenth century. Repnin's grandfather had been governor general of Riga (1719–26), his father commanding general of the Artillery (1745–8). He had no sons, but one of his three daughters married a Prince Volkonsky, and the family became known as Repnin-Volkonsky. Their son, also Nikolai, would become governor general of Little Russia (1816–34) and marry the granddaughter of the last hetman, Kiril Razumovsky. Both were buried in Poltava province. Fine diplomat and forceful military commander (and freemason), Repnin was one of the great figures of the Catherinian age. Faithful to the spirit of his time, he was also a consistent believer in the full integration of the peripheral regions into the expanding Eurasian empire. What he would have done if his tenure had been longer – he had already abolished the Lithuanian Statute – we cannot tell. He remained commanding general of the troops deployed in Livland and Lithuania, but lived in Moscow, where he was promoted to field marshal and died of a stroke in May 1801. His wife had died and been buried in Vilno in 1798.[27]

The Russian position in Lithuania rested on a strong military presence. Since 1717, under pressure from foreign powers, the size of the "Lilliputian"[28] army had been set at 24,000 men – 16,000 for the *Korona*, 8,000 for Lithuania – but it never reached this figure. There had always been a strong distrust of a standing army as a potential tool of royal absolutism, even though, paradoxically, these troops became, in the hands of corrupt hetmans, "much more dangerous for the Poles than for the enemy."[29] In 1781, before the annexation of Lithuania, there had been a Belorussian Division commanded by Chernyshev, consisting of four regiments of infantry and three of cavalry: five of the seven were deployed in Belorussia, the other two in Pskov province. It was backed by the Smolensk Division, commanded by Repnin, who was at the time governor general of Smolensk: it consisted of three regiments of infantry and three of cavalry.[30] By the end of 1796, the Belorussian Division had ceased to exist, but the Smolensk Division remained, six infantry regiments, all deployed in Belorussia: one each in Polotsk, Mogilev, Vitebsk, and Rogachev, and two in Minsk. There was also a new Lithuanian Division of seven regiments of infantry, three of cavalry, and five battalions of chasseurs,[31] about 14,000 men, and these were battle-hardened troops. Lithuania had become the other periphery of the deployment of the Russian army, facing East Prussia in Königsberg and the Prussian share of the Polish core in Warsaw, and backed up by troops deployed in Smolensk and the Baltic provinces.

Ruling Class versus Ruling Class

Following the annexation of the Grand Duchy (and much of the Polish core twenty years later), the ruling elite of the expanding Russian core faced new and intractable problems, which would continue to torment it until the end of the imperial period. It has been said that "in Poland there was both a nation and a state, but the former, by its own free will, was an aristocracy of a handful of magnates and a few thousand squires, while the latter, though preserving the forms of constitutional monarchy, had lost its power to function."[32] In other words, there was a ruling class with a ruling elite at its core, but one undisciplined and turbulent. It was a ruling class with a strong sense of identity and superiority – as befitted that of a core area – over the "barbarians" of the Eurasian continent, of which it was nevertheless an intrinsic part. As a result, it would be highly reluctant to accept its demotion in the context of a policy of superstratification. Moreover, the Polish-Lithuanian ruling class was closely associated with Roman Catholicism, much as the Russian ruling class was identified with Eastern Orthodoxy, and the two confessions harboured an implacable hostility toward each other. This interpenetration of ethnic, cultural, and religious factors created a highly combustible mixture that would preclude the successful development of a policy of superstratification and result in the disastrous uprisings of 1831 and 1863, both followed by brutal Russian repression.

The Polish-Lithuanian ruling class (*szlachta*) owed its unchallenged and unchallengeable position to the absence of a civil society of burghers and an active peasantry. Rousseau may have exaggerated when the wrote that the Polish nation consisted of three estates – nobles who are everything, townsmen who are nothing, and peasants who are less than nothing – but he was not far off the mark. Between 1496 and 1543, when European discoveries of the world were bringing about an economic transformation that loosened the shackles tying the European peasant to the land, peasants in the Polish Empire were tied down to seignorial land, forbidden to appeal from seignorial courts, and required to perform a minimum amount of corvée labour every week,[33] all this at least half a century before the official introduction of serfdom in the Russian core. The worsening of economic conditions in the seventeenth century caused the peasant to sink into "the most abject kind of bondage," in which "the landowner was the lord of his [the peasant's] land his property, his life, and his conscience,"[34] and the situation became worse as one moved deeper into the Grand Duchy. Towns were hardly in better shape. The devastations caused by the wars with Sweden and Russia reduced their population and shattered their economies. A contemporary wrote in 1744 that "the ruin of the cities is so universal and so evident that with the single exception of Warsaw the first ones in the country can well be compared with caves of robbers," and a governmental commission noted in the 1760s that "every street is an open field, every square a desert."[35] The situation improved in the last quarter of the eighteenth century, but in the Polish Empire, "as scarcely anywhere east of the Elbe, was there a widely-flourishing urban sector."[36] Towns suffered not only from an unfavourable economic situation but also from oppression by the *szlachta*, on whose lands many "small towns" (*miasteczka*, Rus. *mestechki*) were located and transformed into villages in all but name.

The size of the *szlachta* vis-à-vis the rest of the population – about 8 per cent – placed it in a class apart (even though similar figures were found in Spain). By contrast, the percentage of nobles across Europe ranged from 0.3 to 1 per cent, and in the Russian core it reached 0.6 per cent. It was not until the end of the eighteenth century that fairly reliable figures became available, and they show 720,000 nobles in a population of 8.8 million people, or 8.2 per cent, but with great regional variations.[37] Since it is not always clear what "Poland" encompasses, we may use Kabuzan's figures of 1795 for the Grand Duchy. For the five new provinces he gives a total population – males multiplied by two – of 4 million, 89.4 per cent of whom were peasants, and 6 per cent of whom were classified as townsmen. The overwhelming majority (85.8 per cent) of the peasant population consisted of serfs, with another 12.7 per cent of "state peasants." The nobility numbered 244,184 persons; if added to the 4 million, their share of the total was 5.7 per cent, somewhat below the figure given for the Polish Empire as a whole. Within the Grand Duchy, variations were also substantial. Vilno province (including at the time the future Kovno province) had 56,445 nobles, while Grodno had only 11,538, Vitebsk 11,382, Mogilev 12,807, and

Minsk 23,470.[38] Thus, 23.1 per cent of the nobility was concentrated in Old Lithuania (especially in Samogitia), and only 9.9 per cent was found in eastern Belorussia. Being *szlachta* and Catholic was considered at the time to be Polish; as a result, the nobility is usually referred to as the Polish nobility.[39]

The *szlachta* was originally a military order, summoned by the king and the grand duke to fight their battles. That mission crystallized a strong sense of identity grounded in a belief that all its members were equal as well as distinct from the rest of the population. With the passing of time, and certainly after the monarchy became elective in 1573, equality became a myth. In Poland proper, more and more *szlachta*, like the Teutonic Knights in Livonia, concentrated on the management of their properties. Economic disparities created social ones, which only a stubborn belief in the myth could conceal from the *szlachta*, while they became obvious to everyone else. The increasing weakness of the royal power transformed the *szlachta* into a ruling class in the full sense of the term, but also added political dissensions to social and economic disparities. An even greater belief in the myth would help keep the ruling class from disintegration. Nevertheless, by the time of the Russian annexation, the *szlachta* had become a stratified ruling class exercising its dominion over a dependent population as well as over a weakened monarchy hobbled by tentacles spun by a ruling elite of magnates. Out of this highly unstable situation came "the insane maxim" that Poland subsisted through its anarchy and that its impotence was the best guarantee of its security.[40]

At the top stood some sixteen families, among whom the better known were the Czartoryskis from Volhynia, the Potockis from Podolia, and the Radziwills from Lithuania. Their properties were enormous, their wealth immense. They were called "kinglets" because they behaved like princes of the Holy Roman Empire, fought one another for power and plunder, and did not shirk from calling for help on neighbouring monarchs.[41] They cared so little for the fate of the Polish Empire, despite the fact that they controlled its government, that the Baltic German negotiator of the Grodno Treaty of 1793, Jakob Sievers, marvelled at the festivities they carried on in the town while their nominal country was being partitioned.[42] The fact that these magnates came for the most part from the eastern marches suggests that the political centre of gravity of the Polish Empire was not in the Polish core, but in the old Grand Duchy north and south of the Pripiet, as in the days of Grand Duke Jagiello, who pulled Poland eastward, deeper into the Eurasian continent.

The second stratum consisted of well-to-do landowners (*zamozna szlachta*), most of them living in western Poland, where magnates were few. They were also called the *folwarczna szlachta* because they owned a demesne (*folwark*, Ger. *Vorwerk*) worked by serfs. In the eighteenth century this medium gentry exhibited little independence, followed the leadership of the magnates in the Diet, and obtained in return a monopoly of lesser positions in the palatinates. As late as the second half of the century, "the style of their dress was distinctly Asiatic in appearance": they shaved their heads, leaving only a tuft on the crown. Lithuanian hetmans favoured the same style. This medium gentry was "boorish and provincial," and little interested in the outside world.[43]

Well over half of the *szlachta* consisted of poor nobles with little or no property. They were the *szlachta golota*, the "barefoot *szlachta*," found chiefly in the north, in Podliachia palatinate (capital Drohiczyn) and, across the border, in the Grand Duchy, especially in Samogitia. They consisted of a rural and an urban group. The rural group generally lived in villages consisting mostly of noble holdings. They were "almost indistinguishable from the peasants themselves except in their pretensions and their ability to read and write and in drunkenness."[44] In some areas, Polish was not their native speech, but they insisted on calling themselves Polish, a mark of superiority. They were, in other words, the "white trash" of the Polish Empire. They served in menial capacities at the courts of the magnates, who herded them to the dietines in order to vote on their lords' motions.

The other group lived in towns, or what passed for towns. They were reluctant to enter the Catholic Church because the parish clergy was recruited mainly from the peasantry, but there were few alternatives in an overwhelmingly agrarian society. Engaging in trade and industry was considered degrading. They could at least invoke the Lithuanian Statute, Section 3, Article 37, according to which a *szlachtich* was the equal of a grandee. They could also join the sons of the *folwarczna szlachta*, whose fathers could not afford to pay for their education, to form the rudiments of an urban proletariat and an urban intelligentsia. The "constitution" of 1775 finally allowed them to overcome their prejudices and engage in economic activities. They and other nobles could also band together to form the so-called *jurydyki*,[45] large enclaves within a town or in a suburb, which they then withdrew from municipal authority and made into a noble town within a town, enjoying the privileges of the nobility, especially in the manufacture of vodka and exemption from tolls, which eventually weakened if not destroyed the municipal economy.

The term "magnate," seldom used in documents and even in political writings, referred to a social and historical category, the elite of a certain period stretching over some eight generations, or about two centuries. The Union of Lublin (1569) took place during the so-called Price Revolution (1500–1620), when prices across Europe rose exponentially with the arrival of cargoes of gold and silver from the Americas, a steady increase of population, and rising demand for foodstuffs and services in a growing network of ports and inland cities.[46] The Union opened large swaths of land in the southern steppes to be colonized by ambitious lords, some of whom became magnates, and caused an influx of Ukrainians from Galicia. The process affected the Lithuanian lords as well, but the great families there owed, if not their entire wealth, at least their social standing, to their closeness to the house of Jagiello. The general economic improvement and social transformation was dealt a sharp blow by the Thirty Years' War in Europe (1618–48) and the wars between Poland, Sweden, and Russia in the middle of the century, which caused a recession and crippled the Polish economy. In the eighteenth century, the magnates, who had formed an ascending and relatively open class, in which 70 per cent of the magnates married outside the group in the seventeenth century, was becoming a caste in which only 18 per cent now brought in outsiders a century later.[47] Their growing conservatism helped bring down the Polish Empire which had been the source of their wealth.

The magnates and their courts were the power centres of the empire. Their wealth was staggering, and it was displayed wantonly. When a Czartoryski set out from his family residence in Pulawy on the Vistula for his Volhynian estates, he needed four hundred horses and fourteen camels in his train, and a hundred wagons as escort when he "went to the waters" in Bardejov,[48] in the Western Beskids, 300 kilometres to the south. Karol Radziwill's family estates covered 27,000 square kilometres, about the size of Belgium, with sixteen towns and 383 villages, and it was said that he could travel from Vilno to Kiev without ever having to step out of his properties – while six thousand nobles in Lithuania in the 1770s were too poor to own serfs.[49] Equality was indeed a myth. In 1748, the public revenue of the Polish Empire amounted to eight million *zlotys*, which exactly matched the combined income of Michael Radziwill (five million) and Felix Potocki (three million), and this did not include additional wealth from free labour services and dues in kind. But the vast country residences with their magnificent furniture and costly internal decorations (so out of place in the bleak landscape of western Eurasia), as well as the pleasures of the table, concealed a contempt for the public good, brutishness, and excessive indulgence in strong drink. Karol Radziwill showed his true colours when he entered Warsaw in 1764 seated in a chariot pulled by bears, the royal beast of the Eurasian forest.

The magnates of Lithuania, who seem to have been more politically motivated than their brethren in Right Bank Ukraine, had often exhibited a separatist streak. The Sapiehas, built up by King Jan Sobiecki (1674–96) as a counterweight to the once omnipotent Pac family, sought to transform the Grand Duchy into a private satrapy in such a way that "the naked brutality of their methods at the *sejmiki* and in the courts alarmed even their own clientele."[50] The opposition rallied behind the Oginski family and assassinated the clan's leaders, but the family remained strong. Charles XII used the opposition, which was anti-Russian, to foment civil war in Lithuania. The Radziwills sought Swedish support to set up their own principality under Swedish overlordship.[51] Such dissensions weakened the ruling elite within Lithuania and within the Polish Empire, and encouraged the Russian advance.

Relations between the magnates and the *szlachta* were a complex combination of dependence and resentment. After 1569, the Lithuanian *szlachta* was given the same rights as the Polish nobility; it never had to fight for them as the Polish *szlachta* had to during the reign of the Jagellons. The magnates imposed themselves on the *szlachta*, and built up their economic power, especially in Lithuania, where there was no steppe land to plough. They seized the land of the less fortunate *szlachta* and impoverished them, a process exacerbated by the devastations of war, to the point where "the great lords showed little compunction in overcoming labor shortages by forcing serf obligations onto the poorest of their younger brethren."[52] Nevertheless, magnates and *szlachta* were united in the defence of the "golden liberties" and in their opposition to a hereditary and "absolute" monarchy (*dominium absolutum*): the kings could not turn to the *szlachta* to break the stranglehold of the magnates and, in the absence of towns, were left isolated and powerless.[53]

The magnate's court was also a refuge and an opportunity. In a climate of growing insecurity, the magnate (who often kept his own troops) guaranteed the security of life and property. Sometimes he paid an annual pension in return for the poor *szlachtich*'s vote at the dietines. Large magnate properties needed the services of administrative personnel, copyists, accountants, lawyers, carriers, servants, clergy, and soldiers. Linking one's fate to a magnate house was an important decision.[54] It saved the capable *szlachta* from the final degradation of a serf tilling the land. The majority of magnates in the seventeenth century went through a process of "self-Polonization,"[55] of cultural Polonization which did not exclude separatism, while Jesuit schools taught the supposed perfection of the Polish system, with the cult of the equality of the members of the "*nation nobiliaire*" as the "keystone" of the empire's special and political thought.[56]

Despite the process of cultural homogenization, the Russians found a fractured elite and fractious ruling class, and a policy of superstratification was certain to face serious obstacles. The great families of the eastern marches had long felt the pull of the growing power of the expanding Russian core. Some remained anti-Russian, some were pro-Russian, especially in eastern Belorussia, where economic interests dictated cooperation. Families that refused to take the oath of allegiance to the empress saw their properties confiscated on Chernyshev's orders, but Catherine enticed young nobles by appointing them to serve in the governor general's suite, and children of fathers found reliable were given access to a military career and educated free of charge in Petersburg. Nobles who served in elective posts were given ranks which integrated them (while they were in office) into the administrative machinery of the expanding core. This was especially true of the provincial and county marshals who all wore Polish names. Catherine's chief secretary, Alexander Bezborodko, noted that "all their ambition is to receive Russian ranks and to register their children in the Guard"; in March 1776 Jozif Chodkiewicz thanked Catherine for giving his son the rank of ensign in the Guard, and added that "he will live and die for Your Majesty."[57] But the great families remained wary. They continued to intermarry and very few seem to have entered the ranks of the imperial ruling elite.

Nevertheless, the great families and the Russians had a common interest in their determination, not only to maintain serfdom, but also to purge the *szlachta* of its "barefoot" proletariat. The dietines were replaced by county and provincial assemblies meeting every three years to elect people to local offices. The territorial division cut across the magnates' properties, and "Russian" governors represented a strong government that was notoriously allergic to unruly public meetings. To continue to use that proletariat would be counterproductive and highly offensive to the Russian authorities; removing it from the *szlachta* rolls would legalize its transformation into a serf-like labour force on the magnates' properties. Moreover, the charter of the nobility (1785) was extended to the Grand Duchy, and elections were governed by the statute of December 1766, which banned landless nobles and those without rank from electing and being elected to local office; elections also required the confirmation of the governor general.

The question came up in eastern Belorussia in 1784 of the meaning of owning property, in view of the widespread practice in the Grand Duchy of leasing and mortgaging land. Could nobles leasing *starostva* for a given term or for life be considered as landowners at election time? The Senate resolved that lessees could take part and be elected, but that those holding mortgaged property and living outside the county or the province were barred from taking part. The decision of 1795 went further, and decreed that even those owning land "temporarily" had no right to take part in elections, unless the local noble society (*obshchestvo*) agreed to admit them into the county or provincial *szlachta*. It also encouraged nobles to enter the service, earn rank, and acquire property which would make them eligible, and it opened the door to those who had been given Polish ranks before the annexation.[58] The decision was a major one, because it raised the portentous question of showing proof of nobility in a land without the equivalent of the Baltic German *Matrikel*, a question that would plague the Russian government for half a century. In the meantime, it was clear by the end of Catherine's reign that the introduction of the local government reform of 1775 and the noble charter of 1785 showed the determination of the Russian elite to compel the *szlachta* to act in conformity with Russian usages as well as to integrate the administration and the ruling class of the Grand Duchy into the expanding core.

Religion and Economy

Catholicism and Orthodoxy

But there was more to the integration of the Grand Duchy than the creation of provinces and the "domestication" of its ruling class. The old Grand Duchy, before its amputation in 1569, had always been a confessional frontier between Roman Catholicism and Orthodoxy, between Rome and Moscow, and, like all frontiers, was fated to become a zone of contention between the two cores of political and religious power. The Reformation, which brought about a geopolitical revolution in the Baltic region, penetrated the Polish Empire as well, especially in its Calvinist form and in Lithuania, where Prince Nicholas Radziwill ("the Black," 1515–65) converted to it in 1553. A synod held in Vilno in 1557 brought into being the Calvinist Lithuanian Evangelical Reformed Church. Calvinism owed its greater appeal in the Polish Empire to the fact that, unlike Lutheranism – the Protestantism of the Germans and the Swedes – it did not invest the secular power with control over the church and protected the nobility against the increasing claims of kings and princes upon the loyalty of their subjects.[59]

The Reformation, we know, brought about a swift Counter-Reformation and the creation of the Jesuit Order in 1534 to be the vanguard of the papacy's determination to regain the lost ground and deepen the Church's implantation in the eastern marches of the Polish Empire. That was a time when Russian power was growing, with the emergence of a potential threat under Ivan III (1462–1505), who married Sophia Paleologue, the niece of the last Byzantine Orthodox emperor in Constantinople – where the ecumenical patriarch of the Greek Orthodox Church resided – and of a real threat under Ivan IV (1533–84), crowned the first tsar in 1547, whose mother was a Lithuanian princess. Three hundred years earlier, the papacy had encouraged and supported a crusade by French and English knights against the Muslims in the Holy Land and against Constantinople, and another by German knights against Orthodoxy in the basin of the eastern Baltic. In the sixteenth century, it used Spanish "knights" (the Jesuits were a military order founded by a Spaniard and headed by a general) to fight in the Grand Duchy a Russian Orthodoxy which had become an autocephalous church in 1448 and would have its own patriarch from 1589 on.[60]

The Order's administrative-territorial unit was the province: a Polish one was created in 1574, and a separate one for the Grand Duchy was carved out of it in 1606, with a sub-province for eastern Belorussia. The provincial head was not subordinated to any diocesan bishop or even to the archbishop in Vilno, who had jurisdiction over all the Catholic churches and monasteries, but reported directly to the general in Rome.[61] The Jesuits believed in the power of education, and they quickly built a network of colleges (secondary schools) all over the Grand Duchy: in Kovno, Grodno, and Novogrudok in Lithuania proper, and in Niesvizh, Minsk, Brest-Litovsk, Polotsk, Vitebsk, Pinsk, and Orsha in Belorussia; their numerous "missions" spread education farther afield.[62]

Their most durable legacy was the foundation of Vilno University. Created as a college in 1569, it was raised to university status as an "academy" by Stefan

Batory and Pope Gregory XIII in 1579, thirty-five years after the founding of Königsberg University (1544) and half a century before that of Dorpat University (1632). It joined the 144 colleges and universities of the Order in Europe and the Americas. By 1618, it had 1,210 students.[63] The other great success of the Order was the creation of the Uniate Church by the Union of Brest (1596). Its longstanding advocate had been Piotr Skarga (1536–1612), a Jesuit father and the first rector of the Vilno Academy, who believed that the Orthodox in the Grand Duchy ("the Greeks") should be allowed to keep their liturgy if only they recognized the authority of the pope. Skarga (and others) "undoubtedly saved Poland for the Vatican."[64]

Jesuit education had a political purpose: to complete the Christianization of the eastern marches, especially of Samogitia, which had resisted for so long all efforts to extirpate the paganism of its Lithuanian population. The integration of the marches into the Latin world would draw a line along the eastern border of the Polish Empire, "separating not only two states but two different types of civilization,"[65] Poland-Lithuania from the expanding Russian core, Latin from Eastern Christianity. Latin had to be the language of instruction. Polish was at first excluded, later included, and only the better colleges taught the sciences and humanities. Jesuit education, almost exclusively for the *szlachta*, inevitably became associated with the defence of Sarmatism, that diffuse ideology which idealized the Jagellonian state in the sixteenth century, called for expansion against Orthodox Muscovy and Muslim Turkey in the seventeenth, and, in the wake of the disasters of mid-seventeenth century, degenerated into xenophobia and conviction of the *szlachta*'s superior way of life.[66]

An eighteenth-century quip would later say that Prussia was not a state with an army, but an army which had found a state; in the century from 1550 to 1650 the Polish Empire was, likewise, not a state with a religion, but a religion which had found a state. It is no less true that the triumph of the Counter-Reformation "began to petrify Catholicism and the spirit of tolerance."[67] Nevertheless, Catholicism experienced a renewal in the second half of the eighteenth century, but it was a Piarist monk, Stanisław Konarski (1700–73), who made his order the leader in the field of education, when he founded in 1740 a Collegium Nobilium in Warsaw to teach sons of magnates to become the future leaders of a reformed Polish Empire – to teach the sons to reject the political traditions of their fathers. And it was the last king, Stanisław Poniatowski, who founded a Warsaw Cadet Corps in 1765 with an offshoot in Vilno, which would teach, sadly enough, an entire generation of patriots and military leaders, including Kosciuszko (who was born in Slonim),[68] to die on the battlefield against insuperable odds.

The first partition of 1772 marked the beginning of the rollback of Catholicism and Jesuit influence in the Grand Duchy and of an offensive against the Uniate Church, which would eventually result in its abolition, leaving Orthodoxy and Catholicism face to face. Russia did not have its knightly orders, but it had bishops, governors, and governors general backed by the full power of the Russian state. Indeed, the counteroffensive had begun with the Russo-Polish agreement of October 1686, which stated that the Orthodox religion would be freely practised in the king's domains, and that the Orthodox clergy would come to the Orthodox Metropolitan of Kiev and Galicia for "blessing and ordination" (*blagoslovenie i poviashchenie*).[69]

The ukaze of December 1772 distributed the newly acquired Orthodox population among two separate dioceses: that of Pskov, which included eastern Belorussia on the Dvina (with Polotsk, Vitebsk, and Dvinsk), and that of Mogilev, to include eastern Belorussia on the Dnieper (with Orsha, Mogilev, Mstislavl, and Rogachev). It had been until then the only Orthodox see in the Polish Empire. In Mogilev, the Russians retained Bishop Grigorii Konisskii (Konysky, 1717–95), a remarkable Ukrainian born in Nizhyn, who had studied in the Kiev Mohyla Academy and become a professor of liturgy and rector there.

Konisskii had been consecrated Belorussian bishop in 1755 and was elevated to archbishop in 1783. He had founded in 1757 a seminary in Mogilev with a printing press, which he used to vigorously oppose the Catholic and Uniate churches.[70] Both dioceses were placed under the direct authority of the Holy Synod in Petersburg – that is, they were fully integrated into the administrative hierarchy of the Russian Orthodox Church.

The first enemy was the Uniate Church. The partition brought some 1.4 million Uniates into the expanding core, leaving some 2.6 million in "Poland."[71] The Uniate Church also had its Metropolitan of Kiev, who was at the time Fylyp Volodkovych (1762–78), but the affairs of the church were in the hands of Lev Sheptytsky (Szeptycki, 1717–79), who succeeded to the post in 1778 and died the following year. Pressure was placed by the Russian government to return to the Orthodox Church the monasteries and churches which the Uniates had seized from it when Orthodoxy experienced a period of decline, and this pressure played a role in the dismissal of Iason Smogorzewski, the Uniate archbishop of Polotsk, the most important diocese, who was expelled in 1780.[72] Two consistories were created in Mogilev and Polotsk until a new archbishop could be appointed. The Russians took advantage of the vacancy to bring the Uniates back into the fold by imposing Orthodox priests on some eight hundred Catholic and Uniate parishes. Pope Paul VI protested, but Catherine was able to obtain his approval to elevate Herakly Lissowski to archbishop of Polotsk in 1785.[73] Sheptytsky retained jurisdiction over the Uniates of "Poland" and Galicia (annexed by Austria), and the pope elevated Smorgoszewski to Metropolitan (1780–99). The hierarchy remained Polish, but it was now cut off by imperial orders from contacts with outside hierarchies. As the Russian core kept expanding, it also became a confessional Fortress Russia, fenced off from the outside world by an iron curtain.[74]

The Russian government followed the same policy toward the second, but major, enemy, Catholicism and the Jesuits. Only 100,000 Roman Catholics were incorporated in 1772,[75] but eastern Belorussia would become the first battleground in the Russian-Orthodox offensive. The instruction to the two Belorussian governors ordered them in May to conduct a census of Jesuit monasteries and schools and warned them against the Order, "the most crafty of all the Latin orders, because in that order subordinates cannot undertake anything without the agreement of their superiors,"[76] an amazing statement from a government in which subordinates were often paralysed for fear of their superiors. But the Jesuits, true to form, immediately took the oath of allegiance in their magnificent Polotsk cathedral. Then the papacy played into Catherine's hands. For reasons of European politics, Pope Clement XIV ordered the dissolution of the Jesuit Order in July 1773. Catherine's own craftiness saw an opportunity to domesticate the Order. She refused to publish the papal bull in Belorussia, and had already decided in December 1772 that henceforth it would be subordinated to a Catholic bishop who would do her bidding. The Jesuits sent a delegation to Petersburg, where their craftiness earned them significant tax exemptions for their properties in January 1774.[77]

Catherine II not only turned the tables on the papacy but also pursued a very realistic school policy. The closing of the Order raised the acute question of what to do with the Jesuit school properties. Data for 1780 showed that they owned 11,700 serfs in eastern Belorussia, from whom, as well as from forests and mills, they derived a substantial revenue.[78] To close the schools would have been counterproductive, and the Russians did not have the means to replace them yet. In the remainder of the Polish Empire, the reaction was led by an Education Commission, created in Warsaw in October 1773, on which Lithuanians were strongly represented. The commission built on the work of Konarski and created a network of "main" and secondary schools, in which Jesuit properties were used an endowment (*fundush*). The Vilno Academy became a main school, whose rector was Martin Poczobut (1728–1810), a well-known astronomer and former Jesuit.[79] The reform of the Polish school system was closely followed in Petersburg, where a school reform based on similar principles was introduced in 1786 and extended to Belorussia in 1789.[80] It created main schools in Polotsk and Mogilev, and "small" schools in eight county seats. Jesuit schools were reorganized to follow the Russian organization and curriculum, and Jesuit properties also became their endowment. Instruction had to be in Russian. Thus the abolition of the Jesuit Order resulted in the integration of the eastern Belorussian school system into that of the expanding core. That was, indeed, "a major work of internal unification."[81]

There remained to elaborate a policy toward the Catholic Church as a whole. Before 1772, Catholics were found only in Petersburg and certain German colonies on the lower Volga. Appeals against local decisions went to the

College of Livland, Estland, and Finland Affairs, and the church in Petersburg was governed by the statute of February 1769.[82] Catholics in the Grand Duchy belonged to the Vilno diocese, but Polish Livonia had its own diocese, whose bishop resided in Kreslavka,[83] east of Dünaburg. The annexation thus gave the Russians the chance to build a new organization on virgin soil. The ukaze of December 1772 only stated that a bishop would be appointed with jurisdiction over all (including Jesuit) churches and monasteries in the empire, that he would invest fathers and parish priests and adjudicate disputes between church authorities and parishioners; appeals would go to the same college. A Catholic bishop was finally appointed in November 1773, to be called Belorussian bishop of Catholic churches. He would reside in Mogilev, perhaps because Catherine did not want the presence of a high Catholic prelate too near the Court. It is easy to see in the documents of the period a certain anxiety grounded in the fear of Catholic proselytism and superior influence. The appointment was made "at Our discretion" to assert Russian independence from the Vatican. The annexed provinces forming White Russia (*Belaia Rossiia*) would form a new Catholic diocese with its bishop Stanisław Sestrentsevich (Siestrzencewicz-Bohusz, 1731–1827), who was elevated to archbishop by the empress in January 1782 but was not confirmed by the Vatican until 1784. His consistory also became the final court of appeal, supplanting the college.[84]

Sestrentsevich reminds us in some ways of Feofan Prokopovych in the Orthodox Church, who also had a chequered career, and finally put his great talents at the service of the Russian autocracy. He was the son of a Lithuanian nobleman, attended Calvinist school, where he attracted attention, and was sent to France to prepare himself for a clerical career. He spent three years abroad (1748–51), then served in the Prussian army, and returned to Lithuania, where he served in the Radziwill household. He studied canon law, became a Catholic priest in 1763, and was given the temporary administration of the Vilno diocese in 1771. He was recommended to Catherine by Kaspar von Saldern, Russia's envoy to Warsaw (1771–2), who had his own views on the organization of the Catholic Church in Russia – which may not have endeared him to the Russian leadership. Sestrentsevich was a man of the Enlightenment, who hated the Jesuits for their "fanaticism," and who would do all he could to destroy the Uniate Church.[85] He would become a willing tool of a policy to create an independent Russian Catholic Church.

That policy had been stated in 1779, if not already in 1772, but it was more definitely expounded in the ukase of January 1782. The Mogilev archbishop would receive his orders only from the Senate and the empress, and no foreign clergy would be allowed into Russian territory; if any were found, they must be deported; all monastic orders were under his jurisdiction; no papal bull could be published in Belorussia, but would have to be sent by the governor general to the Senate to see if everything in it was in conformity with Russian "civil laws and the rights of the Autocratic power given to Us by God."[86] Catherine thus presented herself as God's representative on earth, on an equal footing with the pope, with full authority (except in matters of dogma) over a Russian-controlled Catholic Church without any ties with the wider Catholic world where a fundamental tenet was the "autocratic power" of the pope. In the age-old duel between the Vatican and Russia for hegemony, the Russians were turning the Vatican's policy against itself: the papal-Jesuit drive to bring Roman influence to the banks of the Dvina and the Dnieper had become a Russian policy of projecting Orthodox influence westward into the Grand Duchy. There could hardly be a better example of confessional integration.

Most interesting was the fact that the Polish government was thinking along similar lines. During the Four-Year Diet of 1788–92, which sought to channel a national resurgence into a program of radical reforms and produced the Constitution of 3 May 1791, an attempt was made to create an independent Polish Orthodox Church, to be governed by an archbishop-metropolitan and three diocesan bishops. It would be placed under the jurisdiction of the Patriarch of Constantinople, who gave his approval in 1790. But the proposal encountered the violent opposition of the Catholics and the Uniates, and came to naught.[87]

In September 1795, two new Catholic dioceses were created, one in Pinsk, the other in Polish Livonia, where the incumbent had fled to Warsaw. The Pinsk bishop would have jurisdiction over monasteries and churches in Minsk province and Volhynia, and was told to follow scrupulously the injunctions of the ukase of January 1782. The Vilno diocese, renamed the see of Polish Livonia (*Infliantskoe*), with jurisdiction over churches and monasteries in Lithuania, was entrusted to Jan Kossakowski (1755–1808), "who has shown his dedication to serve our purposes." He too was enjoined to follow the ukaze of 1782.[88] Thus the entire Catholic Church in the Grand Duchy was brought into a new Russian Catholic Church[89] and, although this was nowhere stated explicitly, under the overall authority of Sestrentsevich. Earlier in the year, the empress had told the Synod in Petersburg that she was "in a hurry" to restore the Orthodox Church wherever its parishes had been seized by the Uniates. The archbishop of Minsk was leading the offensive. That of Mogilev and Polotsk was told to follow his example. Viktor Sidorski, the "Minsk, Iziaslav, and Bratslav Orthodox archbishop, co-adjutor of the Kiev Metropolia, and archimandrite of the Slutsk monastery" in southern Belorussia, had sent a pastoral letter asking his flock to return to the true faith; Catherine added that resistance by Uniate and Catholic clergy as well as by landowners would be treated as a crime and punished by the sequester of their properties; she found this to be "the most convenient way to extirpate the Uniates."[90] The battle for the unification of the Orthodox world in the Grand Duchy and the domestication of the Catholic Church was about to begin in earnest.

Trade and Taxes

The trade of the Grand Duchy was poorly integrated with that of the Polish core because the hydrographic network hindered the creation of a homogenous commercial region. While the relief shaped latitudinal zones running from east to west, as western Eurasia slowly edged into Europe, rivers flowed northward across those zones, thereby negating the centripetal effects of the land surface. Thus the Polish core was the basin of the Vistula, Lithuania the basin of the Niemen, and Belorussia that of both the Dnieper pulling south and the Dvina pulling north. Overland routes connected them, but they were not practical, and trade followed the course of the great rivers, so much so that Russo-Polish trade was insignificant. When Russian traders were asked in 1773 whether they wanted to continue supporting a consul in Sklov on the Dnieper below Orsha, they answered in the negative; they did not even want one in Vilno, the trade was too small.[91] There were not even customs houses on the Russo-Belorussian border until 1730, when one was set up in Smolensk on the overland route from Orsha to Moscow, and another in Toropets on the route from Polotsk on the Dvina to Novgorod via the Lovat River, with three-week fairs in both places, in December and July respectively.[92]

Geography and history created a situation in which the trade of the Polish Empire fell hostage to the politics of other, and potentially hostile, powers. Danzig and Elbing controlled the delta of the Vistula, Poland's "economic jugular."[93] The Niemen flowed into the Kurisches Haff, whose exit ran past Memel and whence a short route led to Königsberg. The Dvina drained into the Baltic Sea at Riga. Both Danzig and Riga were proud German cities which set their own terms of trade, because the power that controls the estuary of a river controls the trade of its hinterland. Elbing, Königsberg, and Memel had once been possessions of the Teutonic Order and, by the eighteenth century, had become incorporated into the expanding Prussian core. Frederick II charged exorbitant duties on the Vistula trade, and after 1772, controlled it entirely, forcing a reorientation of Polish trade toward the Black Sea. Königsberg and Memel became prosperous from the duties they charged on the Lithuanian trade, and Riga, insulated in its own tariff zone, channelled that of northern Belorussia.

The region exported articles from the forest (masts, timber, wax, and potash, the so-called naval stores) as well as furs, grain, honey, flax, and hemp, in return for colonial goods, salt, and manufactured articles. But these exchanges were commerce, not trade: they did not benefit the local population. The Lithuanian peasant lived at the subsistence level, and had few needs beside the most elementary ones. Goods were produced by serf labour and exported by Germans and Jews, because the nobles considered engaging in trade a degrading occupation.[94] Poland and Lithuania were in fact peripheral colonial markets. Towns and countryside had been devastated during the Northern War of 1700–21, and the partial recovery that began in the 1730s, following the rise of prices in Europe, could not compensate for the losses: by the end of the eighteenth century, production remained inferior by one-third to the level of 1580(!),[95] and the situation in the Grand Duchy was even worse. A contemporary traveller wrote of "entirely neglected roads, little better than by-paths, winding through the thick forest without the least degree of artificial direction," and of "bridges so weakly constructed and so old that they seemed ready to crack."[96]

Chernyshev's memorandum of October 1763 took full advantage of the hydrographic network of eastern Belorussia. The annexation of the territory, which he came close to advocating, would incorporate the entire valley of the Dvina and of the upper Dnieper into a peripheral but internal market gravitating toward northern Russia and Left Bank Ukraine, and fully integrated into the expanding Russian one. After the annexation, the governor general proceeded to carry out his intentions with the full support of Petersburg. In January 1771, the import of Polish goods into Russia was forbidden, on the spurious ground that Russian territory needed to guard against the epidemic of plague.

The prohibition remained in effect after 1772. "Since the new border with the Polish Republic now follows largely navigable rivers and goods are sent not into the Russian interior but along the border to sea ports," Polish goods were allowed not into the Russian interior but to river landings, from which they would reach Riga by means of the Dvina through Russian-controlled territory. The Russian government declared unofficially that it intended to place the two new provinces on the same footing as other Russian provinces concerning the trade with Riga.[97] A prohibitive customs barrier had risen along the border between Russia and eastern Belorussia on the one hand and Poland and the Grand Duchy on the other.

The Senate edict of February 1773 confirmed the trend toward integration. Raw materials from Poland, Lithuania, and Belorussia shipped in transit would reach Riga duty-free. Belorussians would pay on the imports of foreign goods the full duty paid on imports in Petersburg. Russian manufactured goods sent to Little Russia would enter Belorussia duty-free, as if the two territories had become part of a single market. Although the Russo-Polish agreement of March 1775 declared the trade between the two powers to be free – while the Prusso-Polish treaty of the same date imposed an official, but in fact much higher, duty of 12 per cent *ad valorem* on Polish goods – it is obvious that it upheld the decisions of 1771, 1772, and 1773, with the longest article devoted to navigation on the Dvina. Finally, the introduction of the new Russian tariff of September 1782, which abolished the separate status of Riga and brought the trade of Estland and Livland under the provisions of the so-called European Tariff, completed the process of integration. The Baltic trade was merged with that of Belorussia and Little Russia, as well as with that of the provinces of Smolensk and Pskov (and that of other Russian provinces) to form a single "internal market."[98] The second and third partitions brought no change in policy. The customs houses set up in 1783 in Polotsk and Tolochin (on the Drut' River as one approaches Orsha from Minsk) were closed and replaced by seven new ones along the 674-kilometre-long new border with Austria's and Prussia's possessions in partitioned Poland; they included Grodno, Iurburg, and Polangen in Lithuania, with an additional two, Libava and Vindava, on the Baltic coast of Kurland annexed in 1795. The new territories became part of the internal market to which the provisions of highly restrictive tariffs of April 1793 and September 1796 applied in full.[99] The entire Grand Duchy, together with the three Baltic provinces, had become an integral part of the expanding core's single market west of the Urals.

With the policy to create an integrated market came the attempt to harmonize tax legislation. The total revenue of the Polish Empire in 1790, before the Four-Year Diet substantially raised taxes, amounted to 19.6 million *zlotys* (Polish florins), of which 5 million were collected in Lithuania.[100] The main tax was the general poll tax, payable by all males and females from the age of ten. It was paid by all, including the *szlachta*, but not the clergy, who contributed a "subsidy" (*subsidium charitavum*) fixed at the discretion of the Catholic Church hierarchy. The Jews were taxed separately. Nobles paid an annual average of two *zlotys*, peasants one *zloty*. Receipts were earmarked for the army, and the *szlachta* either passed on the tax to their peasants or ignored it altogether, especially in Lithuania. The tax was introduced in 1717 and was based on tables compiled in 1674 and 1676, which had become obsolete. In practice, fixed quotas were assigned to given areas.[101]

Other taxes included the *hiberna*, paid in the winter (hence its name) by the peasants of the Grand Duchy crown lands, and the *kwarta*, or one-fourth of the revenue collected from properties granted by the king to magnates or *szlachta* in lifelong tenure (*starostva*). These included one or more towns with some villages. Unfortunately, the tax was assessed again on obsolete valuations. Thus the annual *kwarta* quota for the Grand Duchy was 6,000 *zlotys*, but Hieronim Radziwill managed to squeeze ten times that amount from only one *starostvo*.[102] Both taxes went to support the army, small as it was, and in the Grand Duchy, the artillery. There was a hearth tax (*podymnaia*), also called the chimney tax, confined to Lithuania before the partition, but rendered general in 1775: it was a tax on houses in both towns and villages, from palace to peasant cottage, but a regressive tax whose burden fell much more heavily on the latter. Customs duties yielded a very modest revenue.[103] All these taxes were supplemented by others paid in kind, called *gvalty* (manuring fields, repairing roads), corvée labour on the lords' lands, and the quitrent paid in money called not *obrok* but *chinsh*. The tax burden was most oppressive in Lithuania, "the most unfortunate part of the empire [*Reich*]." The *szlachta*'s rule was harsh, and many villages were so poor that travellers "could not even find a piece of bread."[104]

Chernyshev made no secret of his determination to introduce the Russian fiscal system into eastern Belorussia. In his report of September 1772, he called for the extension of Russian weights and measures and of the currency, and the introduction of the capitation of seventy kopecks then in effect in Russia, to include a contribution of one *chetverik* (26.2 litres) of flour valued at fifteen kopecks. However, the capitation was assessed differently in Russia: only males from the day of their birth to the day of their death were taxable. The Russians decided to keep the Polish word for something now quite different, and, perhaps in deference to Catholic sensibilities, called the tax not a "soul tax" (*podushnaia*) but a head tax (*pogolovnaia*). No mention was made of the *obrok*.[105] Since the Russian capitation was intended to finance the needs of the army, the head tax combined the Polish tax, the *hiberna* and the *kwarta*, and may have been much heavier.

At any rate, Russian authorities quickly found out that the Belorussians could not pay. In December 1772, the rate was reduced by one-half, to thirty-five kopecks, or twenty kopecks in money and one *chetverik* of flour. This was confirmed in April 1773. In February 1774, the tax was abolished for six months, then for eight years, although deliveries of flour continued, with a *chetverik* now valued at thirty-five instead of fifteen kopecks. The conversion of the poll tax into a tax in kind pleased both nobles and peasants.[106] This seems to have remained the case until 1783, when it was estimated that agriculture had sufficiently recovered after a string of bad harvests – although agriculture was never profitable in eastern Belorussia.

In May of that year a major reform took place, similar to the one introduced in Little Russia at the very same time.[107] Its purpose was "to achieve uniformity with adjacent (Russian) provinces," that is, to integrate Belorussia fully into the Russian fiscal system. Peasants, both serfs and state (*kazennye*) peasants, would have to pay seventy kopecks per male a year, which would include a charge for the right to distil. The *obrok* payable by serfs was left to the discretion of their owners, but state peasants would pay one rouble a year, a much lower rate than that in effect in Russia (three roubles). Merchants (*kuptsy*) were charged 1 per cent on their declared capital, a tax introduced in Russia in March 1775; townsmen would pay the capitation of 1.20 roubles, as in Russia. The government recognized that, although the reform integrated eastern Belorussia into the fiscal system of the expanding Russian core, the rates would remain lower until the economic standing of the Belorussians approached that of the Russian peasant. In June 1794, the capitation was raised from seventy kopecks to one rouble. This applied to Polotsk and Minsk provinces as well, but in Mogilev, with less profitable agriculture and a better river network, the additional thirty kopecks would be charged in the form of fifteen kopecks in money plus one *chetverik* of rye and one or two *garnets* (one *garnets* equalled 3.3 litres) of groats from state peasants and serfs respectively. In December 1797, Lithuania was placed on the same footing as Minsk province. The fiscal integration of the Grand Duchy was complete.[108]

Steps were also taken to integrate the delivery of salt into the internal market of the expanding core. Polish rock salt from Wielicka (east of Kraków) served the needs of the Polish core, but was not suitable for export to the Grand Duchy for the same reason that hindered the commercial integration of the ducal market into the Polish core: rivers flowed northward, and overland transportation was too expensive. The salt of Staraia Russa, south of Lake Il'men, went to Novgorod, Pskov, and Petersburg. As a result, the Grand Duchy (as well as the Baltic provinces and Finland) received their salt from overseas. The prosperity of the Hanseatic League had rested to a great extent on the export of products from the western part of the Eurasian land mass, well irrigated by a river network facing Europe, and the importation of products of maritime Europe – cloth from Flanders and England, salt from the Atlantic coast of France, Spain, and Portugal. The salt brought to Memel and Riga was rafted upstream into Lithuania and Belorussia. It was sold on the free market by merchants in towns and itinerant peddlers in the countryside, together with needles, thread, and buttons. Indeed, salt was the only imported good with a mass market, because it was essential to human health; fresh water predominated in the entire region, and the low salinity of the Baltic Sea made the water unsuitable for salt boiling.[109]

Russia had experimented with the free sale of salt at the beginning of the eighteenth century, but production and sale became a state monopoly in 1731. Salt was sold from government stores at the fixed price of 50 kopecks a *pud* (16.38 kilograms) beginning in 1756.[110] Chernyshev recommended that the monopoly be introduced in eastern Belorussia, if only to bring down prices. Imported salt sold at the warehouse in Polotsk for 57 kopecks, but in the countryside prices reached 64 and 67 kopecks, and in some places around Vitebsk as much as 70 kopecks.[111] But the governor general encountered the opposition of the procurator general (who was also finance minister) and the Commerce Commission: they feared the monopoly would hurt the Riga trade. Catherine opted for a compromise: the sale of salt would remain free, but Russian stores would also be built in six places in Mogilev and four in Polotsk provinces to guard against shortages. It was decided in 1774 to bring Perm salt, produced from natural brines in the Urals, the favourite salt of Russian consumers. It soon turned out, however, that the operation was not profitable: the local population was not accustomed to the taste of Perm salt, and overland distances were enormous.[112]

This became more and more obvious with the passage of time, and by 1794 Governor General Passek asked the government to stop the sale of Russian salt. The delivery of 200,000 puds in Mogilev and 50,000 in Polotsk was causing excessive losses to the treasury: the salt was selling at the time for 45 kopecks a *pud*, but contractors were asking 70 kopecks alone to bring Crimean salt to Mogilev and 80 kopecks to bring it from Ekaterynoslav to Polotsk. Following the incorporation of Lithuania in 1795, shortages developed, and Catherine ordered the opening of a store in Pinsk on the Pripet capable of holding 600,000 *puds*, which had to come from the Crimea. The Salt Code of 1781 was introduced, and the salt would sell at 80 kopecks a *pud*, or twice the official price at the time. The purpose was "to replace foreign salt with our own."[113] Thus the policy of integration did not give up the original intention to fully integrate the sale of salt into the expanding Russian market.

There would be more opposition, but on different grounds, to the policy of integrating the production and sale of spirits into the Russian system. It would not have been the case if the system had not changed in the middle of the eighteenth century. Until then, nobles, merchants, and the government had the right to produce vodka (*vino*), but in 1754 the nobility gained a quasi-monopoly over production, and the sale was farmed out to merchants who pledged to pay the government a fixed amount for (usually) four years with the revenue they earned from the sale at a fixed price of three roubles a *vedro* (12.2 litres) by 1794.[114] In the Grand Duchy, nobles, townsmen, and Jews and royal domains produced and sold on the free market, but nobles possessed an additional right, the so-called *propinatsiia* (from the Latin *propinare*, to drink to someone's health). This referred to the exclusive right of a landowner to prohibit the production and sale of vodka to outsiders on his properties, giving him a monopoly not only on his lands but also in towns and *mestechki* he privately owned. Since the sale of vodka was the major source of cash in western and southern Eurasia, a landowner could derive a substantial revenue from his monopoly, so much so that estates came to be valued according to the size of the revenue earned from the sale of vodka. Moreover, the nobility was exempted in 1629 from the *czopowe*, an excise tax charged on the sale of vodka, beer, and mead, and collected by Crown officials.[115]

Chernyshev did not call for the introduction of the Russian system in eastern Belorussia but recommended a mixed system. He insisted that landowners must retain their right to distil and sell their vodka and beer and keep the taverns already existing on their properties. However, landowners would be charged, for the retention of this right, 50 kopecks per male peasant registered in his name by the current census. Sale prices would be set in December by the governor and representatives of the nobility. In the towns, burghers were no longer allowed to sell spirits on their own. The sale was vested in the town council (*magistrat*), which would farm out the sale by asking for bids, but on condition that the value of the farm be no less than 1.5 roubles – 75 kopecks in *mestechki* – multiplied by the number of "heads" registered in the census.[116] These rates, like those of the capitation, were soon found to be too high and were reduced in 1779: landlords would be charged only 20 kopecks; in towns the value of the farm must not be under one rouble, in *mestechki* 50 kopecks, multiplied by the number of heads. In government-owned villages, spirits were sold by village authorities and the funds deposited in the local treasury.[117] The reform of 1783 introduced no changes, but recognized the landlords' right of *propinatsiia*. The system in effect in eastern Belorussia was extended to Minsk province in 1795. In Lithuania proper, the Polish system remained in force;[118] it was too late in the reign of Catherine to expect changes which might upset landlords and townsmen.

An examination of provincial budgets suggests interesting conclusions. The revenue from eastern Belorussia in 1795 amounted to 894,321 roubles, of which 669,032 roubles (74.8 per cent) remained for local expenditures, mainly salaries and expenses connected with the shipment and storage of salt; only 50,000 roubles went to the Commissary, and 150,000 roubles to the Treasury in Petersburg and Moscow, while neighbouring Smolensk province, with a population of 451,626 males, smaller than the combined population of Polotsk and Mogilev provinces (640,567 males), contributed 830,000 roubles to both the Commissary and the Treasury. Some 10 per cent came from the renting of state properties (*obrochnye stat'i*), 12.6 per cent from the sale of salt, and almost nothing from the sale of spirits. That may be due to the fact that by the 1790s charges for the right to distil and sell were included into the capitation, since they amounted in fact to a tax on peasants and townsmen. Comparisons with Smolensk province are revealing. There, 44.8 per cent of the revenue came from the capitation (against 77.2 per cent in eastern Belorussia), but 31.6 per cent came from the sale of spirits and 17.4 per cent from the sale of salt. Figures for Minsk province and Lithuania were not included in the tables, but partial estimates for 1796 show a revenue of 596,953 roubles for Minsk and 859,468 roubles for Lithuania.[119]

The Jews

"In our route through Lithuania we were struck with the swarms of Jews, who, though very numerous in every other part of Poland, seem to have fixed their headquarters in this duchy. If you ask for an interpreter, they bring you a Jew; if you come to an inn, the landlord is a Jew; if you want post-horses, a Jew procures them, and a Jew drives them; if you wish to purchase, a Jew is your agent; this perhaps is the only country in Europe where Jews cultivate the ground; and we frequently saw them engaged in sowing, reaping, mowing, and other works of husbandry."[120]

Thus wrote a contemporary traveller in the 1770s on his way from Warsaw to Moscow. Nevertheless, the Jewish population of the Grand Duchy was not exceedingly large. Out of a population of about 2.5 million Jews in the world in 1800, it was estimated that about 800,000 lived in the "Polish Republic" in 1789,

200,000 in the Austrian share of the first partition, 15,000 in the Prussian share, and 40,000 in eastern Belorussia, or about one million in the former Polish Empire.[121] Similar figures (750,000 to 800,000 Jews) show that they made up 9 per cent of the total population of "Poland," of whom 15 per cent lived in Great Poland, 35 per cent in Little Poland, and 50 per cent in the eastern marches, where they constituted from 70 to 90 per cent of the urban population.[122] In eastern Belorussia, there may have been no more than 30,000 Jews in 1764, or perhaps 45,000,[123] but in 1793 and 1795 Russia annexed (in the Grand Duchy and Right Bank Ukraine) another 289,000 Jews,[124] making up a total of about 330,000 Jews under Russian suzerainty. If we follow Kabuzan's figures for the sake of consistency, there were 160,000 Jews in Lithuania and Belorussia in 1782, 179,000 in 1795 – figures not considered reliable – but it was estimated that they made up about 8 per cent of the population. By 1850, the Jewish population had grown to 509,000, still 8 per cent of the total population of Belorussia and Lithuania (6.1 million). Thus the Jewish population of the former Grand Duchy, which had been smaller than that of Right Bank Ukraine in 1795, had become slightly larger by 1850, when its 538,000 individuals made up 11 per cent of the Right Bank's total population.[125]

The high percentage of Jews among the urban population shows that indeed the urbanization of the "eastern territories" would not have been possible without their participation,[126] but the term "urbanization" must be qualified. The bulk of the Jews did not really live in or near towns at all, but on *szlachta* estates, and especially in the *mestechki*, so distinguishing a feature of the Grand Duchy's social landscape: "the diminutive Jewish towns often created especially for them by landowners, with close economic ties with the surrounding countryside."[127] They were also found, but in lesser numbers, in the towns belonging to the Catholic Church. These *mestechki* functioned as market towns which yielded substantial revenues to their owners, and there existed a symbiotic relationship between the ruling class, the Jews, and the peasants, which served the interests of all three constituent parts of the territory's society. Paradoxically and often tragically, however, the symbiosis also generated an envy and hatred stimulated by ethnic, economic, and religious animosities.

Polish law considered the Jews to form a people apart from the rest of society, one which could not be assimilated. It forbade them to own land, but the Lithuanian Statute did not.[128] That may be the reason why the Jews, who "lacked room"[129] not only in their *mestechki* but also in the larger towns where their competition was resented, moved to villages where they could engage in agriculture, to an extent large enough that their farming activities caught the attention of the passing traveller. But their major activity was that of middleman, and they played a major role as managers or lease-holders (*arendarz*, *arendatory*) on the properties of nobles who were often absentee landowners. The lease functioned as a farm which transformed the lease-holder into the manager of an estate. In return for giving the owner a certain sum for the lease, the lessee was left free to extort as much as he could from the property, which was not his own, and which he would eventually have to return to its owner. He also used serf labour, and the serfs were Christian Lithuanians and Belorussians, a situation that bred considerable resentment. The Jewish lease-holder brought in other Jews as sub-lessees, and a small Jewish community arose on the estate, an alien body in a sea of natives.[130] This contributed to the "geographic spread of ruralization" of the Jews – the counterpart of the "urbanization" of the Grand Duchy. The noble landowner, secure in the fixed income the lease gave him, could afford to neglect his property and care little for capital improvements; thus landowner and Jewish lessee collaborated in the destruction of the Grand Duchy's agriculture and the impoverishment of its population.

Jews were also active in the production and sale of spirits. Landlords farmed out both production and sale. The sale took place in "the ever-present tavern, mainstay of the village economy, meeting place and battleground of Jews and Poles … entrance to the cavernous world of demonic activity." By the mid-eighteenth century, 10 to 20 per cent of Polish Jews engaged in some aspect of alcohol production. Taverns were owned almost exclusively by Jews and represented the "intrusion of the 'other' into the countryside."[131] Here too, farming out the spirits trade had a deleterious effect on the well-being of the population, even if drinking was for many a form of entertainment. Landlord and Jew worked in tandem to maximize alcohol production. Whenever there happened to be a grain surplus, it was used in the production of vodka; the Jewish farmer (*otkupshchik*) paid the landlord a fixed sum and then tried to sell as much as he could. In towns, he competed with Christian burghers, for whom selling vodka was often the only possible source of revenue. The result drew the attention of the commission set up to prepare the fiscal reform of May 1783; the "limitless" sale of vodka caused a corrupting "drunkenness and idleness" and "extreme poverty [*nedostatok*] everywhere."[132]

Such was the situation facing the Russians in eastern Belorussia in 1772. They had had little contact with the Jews until then, and they would have to work out a new policy on a tabula rasa.[133] They would have to choose between a policy emphasizing the territory and one emphasizing the personality of the law, and would have to create an economic environment capable of sustaining a fiscal policy seeking to harmonize taxation in order to pave the way for the integration of the territory into the expanding Russian core. It would take a long time to find a solution, one which would never be satisfactory and which would, in the end, give birth to the "Jewish question" in the former Grand Duchy and the Ukrainian provinces of the old *Korona*.

Chernyshev was a man in a hurry, who was determined to integrate eastern Belorussia as rapidly as possible. His report of September 1772, which contained a comprehensive plan of reforms, imposed on the Jews a head tax of one rouble, against the 70 kopecks charged on peasants, who would also have to pay the quitrent, even if it was not mentioned in the text. Burghers were charged 1.20 roubles per head. The Jews were also told to register in Jewish governing bodies (*kahals*), and where these did not exist, to create some under the governor's direction. The *kahal* was at the time undermined by serious internal strains, both economic and religious, but by giving it support under the authority of the provincial governor, the government followed its traditional policy of superstratification, in which the position of the top stratum was strengthened against the rank and file, and order would be maintained – the major concern of the Russian authorities.[134] Nevertheless, the Russians would remain ambivalent about the value of the *kahal* until the 1840s, when it was finally abolished. This is evident from the report of Major General Mikhail Kakhovskii, the governor of Mogilev (1773–8), who suffered "a cultural shock" when he had to deal with it.[135]

Chernyshev instructed the two governors in 1773 to conduct a general census, including one of the Jews. Census takers would have to register Jews at their place of residence; those wishing to travel for business purposes (*dlia promyslov svoikh*) would receive their passport from the *kahal*, which would also collect the head tax and deposit it in the provincial treasury. Jews who converted to Christianity would be registered separately, would not be taxed as Jews, but would have to choose a social category (*rod zhizni*), and would be taxed as a member of it; they would be allowed to enter military and civil service. Such Jews were also a free people, and could not be enserfed (by being registered as the property of a landlord).[136] Such a policy thus distinguished between Jews who converted and those who did not. The former – bound to remain a small number – were removed from the jurisdiction of the *kahal*, entered a local society being restructured along Russian lines, and became integrated into the larger society of the expanding core. They became "Russians." The latter remained a category apart, as they were under Polish law, forming a social cluster resembling the millet in Ottoman lands, which would continue to generate a mixture of envy and contempt.

The Jews benefited from the reduction in tax rates which the Russians found themselves forced to concede following a string of bad harvests and their becoming aware of the extreme poverty of the territory.[137] But there were clouds on the horizon. The reform of 1783 gave to the *szlachta* a monopoly of the production of vodka and of its sale on its properties and a similar monopoly to the *magistrat* in non-privately owned towns. The measure may have been intended to eliminate the Jews from this profitable branch of the economy, but it did not make it illegal for landlords to keep leasing their right, as they had always done. However, the new governor general, Petr Passek, interpreted the law to mean that people without the right to distil and sell could not obtain it under a lease,[138] although one must wonder how realistic such an interpretation was, since the Jews owned most of the taverns. Moreover, Passek soon found himself on the defensive. A senatorial inspection conducted in 1785 heard many complaints from the Jewish communities. Jews received no satisfaction in the new courts created by the local government reform of 1775 but still staffed with Poles. *Magistraty* kept Jews from electing and being elected to fill municipal positions, despite the fact, as the senators noted, that in almost all towns the number of Jewish merchants and burghers exceeded the number of Christians.[139] The Jews referred to the reform of 1783, which stated that they must be taxed in accordance with the social category they had joined without distinction of ethnicity and religion (*zakon i narod*).

That reform, which took place in a decade of radical transformation of Russian local administration, embodied a major shift in policy toward the adoption of the territoriality of the law (i.e., that the law applied to all the inhabitants of a given territory) and the rejection of individual and group exemptions. But there was considerable resistance among the Christian population to the reform, partly because it rejected the traditional Polish policy of treating Jews as a separate group, partly because Christians did not want Jews to enjoy the same privileges as themselves. The issue became acute in 1786 in the wake of the introduction of the Municipal Statute of April 1785, which had a profound effect on the urban social landscape. It drew a sharp line of demarcation between the urban and the rural population by requiring those engaged in urban occupations to move to towns, whose number had by then been reduced to the number of county seats; the others became rural settlements. This meant that Jews living in the countryside had to relocate to the official towns. The resulting increase in the Jewish urban population, in towns where they already constituted a substantial percentage, threatened to give them control at election time of the councils (*dumy*), courts (*magistraty*), and mayor's (*golova*) offices. Passek was not sure that they could take part in elections but was told by the empress that they must, "with the agreement of the Christian community," a qualification which made the 1783 law inapplicable. It turned out that few Jews were elected; only one in Polotsk, none in Mogilev and Orsha, although more in the smaller towns. There was an especially bitter conflict in Vitebsk, where the Jewish population was 4.5 times more numerous than the Christian. The Jews were barred from electing to a number of positions in 1786, the *kahal* complained, and the provincial board (chaired by the governor) had to order the *magistrat* on four separate occasions to relent; so great was the "stubbornness of the Christians" that the governor had to file criminal charges against the *magistrat*.[140]

It was in that same year that the government finally took up the "Jewish question." The Jews had petitioned the empress to redress their grievances, and she had the report of the senatorial inspectors to corroborate their views. The Senate handed down its decision in May and took up four issues. Jews must be allowed to participate in elections to fill municipal positions on the same footing as Christians. They must enjoy the same privileges in bidding for contracts and in engaging in crafts and trades. As a result, they might not have separate courts, since they would have their representatives on the *magistrat*. Litigation involving rabbis, synagogues, and religious issues would be adjudicated in county and provincial *kahals*, forming a hierarchy parallel to that of the municipal and provincial *magistraty*. In matters of taxation, Jews would register as merchants (*kuptsy*) and burghers (*meshchane*) and pay the same taxes as other members of these groups. Jews were refused their request to register as "outside merchants" (*inogorodnye kuptsy*) in the Riga suburb (*Vorstadt*) because there existed no Russian law allowing the registration of Jewish burghers in towns outside Belorussia. Concerning the production of vodka, beer, and mead, the Senate upheld the reform of 1783 and the Liquor Code of 1781 requiring them to bid for farms (*otkupy*) on the same footing as Christians, and rejected Passek's interpretation: landlords must remain free to farm out stills and taverns to Jews on their properties if they so desired. The old right of *propinatsiia* remained in force.[141] Thus the decision of 1786 marked the triumph of the principle of the territoriality of the law and of a policy of dual integration: of the Jews into the new social structure of eastern Belorussia, and of the latter into that of the expanding core.

The policy of integration was still in force in 1790, when Passek was reminded that he had violated the edict of June 1789 by allowing the Mogilev *kahal* to import religious books from Poland. The edict did not permit the import of books, but in view of "the significant number of Jews" in Belorussia, it would be more appropriate "to set up a local printing press for the publication of such books."[142] One can detect here the same approach as that proclaimed by Petersburg toward the Catholic Church: there must be a "Russian Catholic Church," and there must be "Russian Jews" integrated into the expanding core, with as few links with the outside world as possible. Integration thus meant isolation behind a great wall, as Fortress Russia reached the final stage of its consolidation.

It has been alleged that Russian policy began to change in the 1790s.[143] The French Revolution came as a shock, and the proclamation of the Polish Constitution of May 1791 was seen as a Jacobin plot against the foundations of the Russian policy. The war of 1788–92 was expensive and severely strained the Russian budget. The partitions of 1793 and 1795 brought in a much larger Jewish population than the first one in 1772. As the core suddenly expanded to reach an unprecedented size, the diversity of the Grand Duchy's population raised the issue of its mobility within a much larger space. If there must be integration and isolation from the western fringe of western Eurasia, pressures would rise to let the population move eastward, deeper into the interior of the core. People must be allowed to travel and resettle into the interior, toward the two great capitals, Petersburg and Moscow, as well as Kiev and Kazan on the edge of the steppe, which still led to the great intercontinental trade routes. However, Petersburg was not ready to take that step when the Jews were concerned.

In June 1794, several edicts increased taxes on individuals and industry, including the capitation, but singled out the Jews, now considered full-fledged urban residents, by charging double the rate imposed on *meshchane* and *kuptsy*.[144] This was certainly a discriminatory decision, which brings to mind the double tax on Old Believers and also was a mild reassertion of the principle of the personality of the law. Another feature of the edict was the mention for the first time of the territory to which the Jews would be confined. It included eastern and western Belorussia (three provinces), Right Bank Ukraine, Little Russia, and New Russia with the Crimea. Payment of the double tax was required for joining the new social structure of the expanding core: it implied choosing integration; it was an admission fee for Jews wishing to enjoy the privileges associated with the status of urban resident. Those who did not wish to join would have to leave the country. Lithuania, not yet annexed, was of course not included.

It is an exaggeration to see in this edict a cornerstone of a policy to create what later came to be known as the Pale of Settlement.[145] It did not create a new policy, only confirmed an old one. The concept, the principle of a pale of settlement, was born in the edicts of December 1742 and January 1744,[146] expelling the Jews from Great Russia, Little Russia, and the "conquered" Baltic towns, unless they chose to convert to Russian Orthodoxy and thereby became "Russians." If the Jews could not live there, it follows that they must be confined to the Grand Duchy and Right Bank Ukraine, where they had lived for centuries. These territories were still beyond the boundary of the expanding core. Once they became incorporated into it, the policy need not change. The census ordered by Chernyshev in 1773 bound the Jews in eastern Belorussia to their place of residence and allowed them to move only on business trips with the appropriate passport. The Senate decision of May 1786 stated that Russian legislation did not allow Jews to register in towns outside Belorussia. This was repeated and confirmed by the empress in December 1791, following Jewish petitions to register among Smolensk and Moscow *kuptsy*.[147] The same edict, however, granted residence rights to Jews in Ekaterynoslav province and the Crimea, a mere extension to the right granted to Jews to settle in the much smaller province of New Russia in 1769, which was not quite yet a part of the expanding core.

The government was thus feeling its way, as two policies began to converge. One was a policy of integration into a new urban world created by the reforms and the reduction of the role of the *kahal* to the arbitration of purely religious disputes;[148] the other was a policy of territorial separation, which kept confining the Jews to a specific territory. But by maintaining their territorial concentration rather than allowing their dispersion in the larger space of the expanding core, it encouraged the festering of internal strains between Jews and Christians, which boded ill for the future, when the Grand Duchy became embroiled in bitter disputes between Russians and Poles.

The Baltic Provinces

Administrative Integration

While Governor General Chernyshev was carrying out the integration of eastern Belorussia, a comprehensive assault on the privileges of the Baltic German matriculated nobility was being prepared in Petersburg, with a much greater resonance throughout the western theatre. The reasons were both general and specific. Russian policy had been consistent since the middle of the seventeenth century in seeking to create a unitary state, in which the expanding core would whittle down differences and divergences in the newly annexed peripheries, after incorporating their elites into an ever-growing ruling class. It was a paradox (and a source of strength) that the increasing social diversification of the ruling elite paralleled increasing harmonization – or, as one would say in a later and infamous age, a *Gleichgestaltung* – of different administrative, judicial, and fiscal legislations. The policy of harmonization was immeasurably strengthened by the philosophy of the Enlightenment, which swept across Europe and wafted into western Eurasia from the 1750s until the French Revolution forty years later. It called for a structuring of government and society in the name of rational principles, and influenced the policy of cameralism, obsessed with the collection of data and the intensification of geographical knowledge. Cameralism would reorganize the economy in order to create conditions fostering the common good and would also call for fiscal reforms to simplify taxation and maximize revenue collection, not only to pay for the common good, but also to create resources for ever more expensive wars.[149]

There were also specific reasons. Serfdom was more oppressive in the Baltic provinces than anywhere else in the region. Catherine II was brought up on Enlightenment ideas during her years of solitude in her gloomy Petersburg chambers, and toyed with abolishing, or at least alleviating, serfdom in Russia, until she found herself facing political realities. But it might be less dangerous to address the emancipation of the serfs in the Baltic provinces. Perhaps she remembered the ambitions of Charles XI of Sweden, for whom the emancipation of the serfs was part of a program of systematic integration into the Swedish Empire. The policy had not been without dangers; the king's attacks on the privileges of the Baltic German caste had undermined their loyalty to Sweden and they had accepted Russian rule. The decision had been a vote against Sweden, not a vote for Russia.

Catherine II came to the throne at the end of a bloody and ruinous Seven Years' War, and relations with Prussia were not friendly. But Prussia was a rising core, Frederick II would be its greatest king, and the Hohenzollern house evinced ambitions to gather the German lands. Prussia was strongly influenced by the Enlightenment, and its influence was felt in Königsberg, with its university founded in 1544, where Immanuel Kant began to teach in 1755, the year when the expanding Russian core finally found enough confidence to create its first university in Moscow. The Pietism of Halle was spreading in the Baltic provinces, with its emphasis on self-development, on inculcating a sense of dignity and duty toward one's fellow men. The Baltic provinces were becoming a political and cultural frontier between Prussia and Russia, but the ruling class was German. There was a danger of the Swedish experience repeating itself there, and Russia had to get ahead of Prussia and integrate the provinces beyond a point of no return, where they would "stop looking like wolves to the woods."[150]

Provinces (*gubernii*) had existed since the 1710s; only their internal divisions needed to be adjusted to meet the standards set by the local government reform of November 1775. The reform was carried out in Estland and Livland in 1783. Counties (*Kreise*), named after their territory, were renamed after the county seat, and called *okrugs* or *uezds*, as in the Russian core. Revel province (Estland) would consist of five counties, including Baltic Port (Rogervik) cutting deep into the land. The many islands were incorporated into the neighbouring county, but Ösel Island (its seat in Arensburg) would constitute a separate county in Riga province (Livland). The decision taken in 1765 to include it into Estland was not retained, although Arensburg was more accessible from Revel than from Riga. Estland's five counties were divided into 46 parishes (*Kirchspiele*), the basic territorial, administrative, and ecclesiastical division. The same procedure was followed in Livland. Its nine *Kreise* became nine *okrugs*, divided into 119 parishes. Most of the county seats were former castles (*zamki*) built in the days of the Teutonic Order, including Wenden, the residence of the *Herrmeisters* for three hundred years. When Kurland was annexed and made into a third Baltic province in 1795, it was immediately divided into nine counties, from its narrow eastern end along the Belorussian border to Libava and Vindava, the two ports on the coast, and including Pilten (in Vindava county), the ancient residence of the Kurland bishops, by then an impoverished place buried in the sands.[151]

The three Baltic provinces occupied an area of 92,232 square kilometres, with a total population of 1.2 million in 1795. See table 2.2 for how this population is distributed. If we add Vyborg province, where the reform was carried out also in 1783 and the province was divided into six counties – including three in the territory annexed in 1743 – with an area of 31,404 square kilometres and a total population of 185,756, we see that the Baltic periphery of the expanding Russian core comprised 123,636 square kilometres with a population of 1.4 million, much smaller than those of the five provinces of the former Grand Duchy

Table 2.2 Distribution of population in the Baltic provinces, 1795

	Area (km²)	Population
Estland	19,694	212,942
Livland	45,514	569,166
Kurland	27,024	409,922
Total	*92,232*	*1,192,030*

Source: Kabuzan, *Narody Rossii v XVIII veke*, 174–5, 218, 228.

of Lithuania at the same time.[152] The population was homogeneous: Latvians made up 50 per cent and Estonians another 40 per cent, but Germans only 6.5 per cent, and Russians a bare 1 per cent.

Two governors were appointed in Estland and four in Livland between 1783 and 1796. All but one bore German names, so that the German elite, now integrated into an extensive hierarchy, retained influence, if not power, in the management of the provinces. But the dominant figure was General George Browne, Governor General of Livland (1762–75) and of Livland and Estland (1775–92). He was born in Ireland in 1698, on the eve of the Northern War, and died in 1792, on the eve of the second partition of the Polish Empire. He had entered Russian service in 1730. During the War of the Polish Succession (1733–4), he had served under General, later Field Marshal, Peter Lacy, another Irishman, Governor General of Livland (1740–51), then under Field Marshal Burkhard von Münnich in the Turkish War (1735–9). He had been taken prisoner and sold three times in Constantinople, managed to escape, and served in the Swedish War of 1741–3. By 1758, at the outset of the Seven Years' War, he had become a full general. At the end of the war, Peter III gave him a well-deserved rest by appointing him governor general in Riga. He owned huge properties in Livland. His first wife was Lacy's sister, but the second was a Baroness von Mengden, who gave him three children who married into the Baltic German aristocracy. The Browne family became "Germanized."[153]

That may be why Catherine did not fully trust him and occasionally rebuked him. Like other governors general with a long tenure, he developed affinities for the milieu in which he lived, and this did not sit well with the ruling elite in nearby Petersburg, always wary of centrifugal yearnings. The empress appointed a Russian to carry out the reform in Livland, Major General Alexander Bekleshov (1745–1808). He had risen under the protection of Alexei Orlov, with whom he served in the naval expedition against the Turks in 1771, and had been in the Finland Division since 1779. He would later serve as governor general of Little Russia and then of Right Bank Ukraine. He remained single, but his mother came from a family that would give birth to Field Marshal

Mikhail Kutuzov, the hero of the war of 1812. Faithful to the policy of territorial administration so characteristic of Catherine's reign, Bekleshov opposed the creation of the ministries in 1802, and was packed off to the Senate. It was said of him that he was "un vieux Russe, de formes brusques et grossières," who did not know French and hardly understood it, but who "sous une écorce très rude avait un coeur droit, ferme et compatissant aux peines d'autrui." Untouched by corruption, he came out "pur et intact."[154]

Kurland had its own governor, Major General Gustav von Lambsdorff, ancestor of the Russian foreign minister from 1900 to 1906, but also a governor general, Peter Freiherr von der Pahlen (1745–1826) from the Estland nobility, who had been instrumental in the annexation of Kurland. He possessed an "uncanny ability to get himself out of the greatest troubles and always managed to advance his interests," but that eventually doomed him. As military governor of Petersburg and commanding general of troops deployed in Finland, Petersburg, Livland, Lithuania, and Smolensk, he obtained extraordinary powers, but also led the conspiracy that resulted in Paul I's murder. For that he was banished to his properties until the end of his life.[155] Vyborg province had its own governor, but its proximity to Petersburg was such that the real power was the governor general of the capital. During the Swedish war of 1788–90, Lt.-Gen. Count Yakob Bruce (1729–91), the descendant of a Scot, was governor general of both provinces.[156]

An extensive development of troops underpinned the Russian presence throughout the region. In 1781, a Finland Division of five infantry regiments was stationed in Vyborg province. The Petersburg Division linked it with the Estland Division of four infantry regiments and two of cavalry, with headquarters in Revel, and the Livland Division. The latter was commanded by the governor general of Petersburg, and included four infantry regiments and three of cavalry deployed all over Livland.[157] These "divisions," with the Guard in the capital, formed a defence perimeter around the capital. Together with other troops in Belorussia and Lithuania, they were part of a strategic deployment guarding the coast from Finland to the Polish border against a potential Swedish aggression; they also served to remind the servile population that they must obey their masters.

The administrative reform was a relatively easy matter, but the test of a policy of integration would be the treatment of Baltic German law. There were also certain procedures which were now found to be at variance with the Statute of November 1775. It had long been customary to pay fees (*aktsidentsii*) to judges and clerks, a practice which encouraged corruption. Browne was told in 1784 that since judicial personnel now received a regular salary determined by the table of organization (*shtat*), the fees must be abolished. Appellate procedures must follow those given in the Statute and the old ones must be abandoned, because the Baltic provinces must be brought into a state of complete uniformity (*sovershennoe edinoobrazie*) with other provinces. The old courts had their own house lawyer (*fiskal*) who watched over the observance of the law but was subordinated to the president of the *Hofgericht*. He was replaced by a provincial procurator and a provincial hierarchy of *striapchie* appointed by the Senate – a key feature of the reform – and the procurator was the "eye" of the procurator general, who was responsible for the uniform interpretation of the law (*razumen odinakovo*) throughout the expending Russian core.[158]

But if the law had to be interpreted in a uniform fashion, local laws had to be bent in order to accommodate Russian law. The Russians had to be cautious when it came to striking down the former, because they were part of the "privileges" which Petersburg had pledged to observe since 1710. Nevertheless, even the Baltic nobility could accept the amendment of some privileges if it served their interests. One example will illustrate the nature of the issue. The Manifesto of May 1783 extended to both provinces the abolition decreed in March 1731 of the difference between properties held in return for service (*pomest'ia*) and ancestral properties (*votchiny*). The former were known in Estland and Livland as *Mannlehen*, transmissible only in the male line and with the ruler's approval. The manifesto gave their owners the freedom to bequeath, and otherwise dispose of, all their real properties as they wished. Thus a feature of Russian property law was introduced in the Baltic provinces, where there existed, as of 1777, 329 allodial estates and 139 *Mannlehen*.[159]

Russian authorities may have been active in the field of criminal law, where they sought to confirm local laws while mitigating the harshness of punishments. A case reached Browne from the Estland criminal chamber, which had sentenced to death by decapitation a young woman (*devka*) for murdering her child. Russian law had suspended the application of the death penalty in 1754 by insisting that governors could not carry out death sentences on their own authority, but must forward them to the Senate in Petersburg. This was construed as a violation of the "privileges," restricting the jurisdiction of the *Oberlandgericht*, but was nevertheless accepted later. Browne refused to confirm the sentence, and the chamber commuted it to twenty-five lashes of the *knut*. Browne then objected that the *knut* was unknown in the province, and asked if he could commute the sentence to whipping with birches (*rozgi*), as already practised in Livland. The Senate merely told him that capital sentences must be carried out in accordance with the local laws in effect in each province.[160] A short time before, Browne had told Petersburg that Estland local laws punished criminals for serious crimes committed for the first time with forty pairs of twigs (*prut'ia*) administered three times, or 120 lashes in a single day, followed by release or a time at hard labour. He found such punishments excessive and degrading (*obezuvechit chelovechestvo*), and asked that the punishment be staggered over three weeks. The Senate concurred, since Estland local laws did not specify whether the punishment must be administered on the the same day or over three weeks. Here the governor general clarified the "privilege" for the benefit of the defendant.[161]

We find the same issues in "Russian Finland" (Vyborg province), but they were more complicated owing to the existence of two penal systems in the two parts of the province, one annexed in 1721, the other in 1743. The Swedish Code of Punishments of 1653 imposed the death penalty for the theft of objects valued at less than the equivalent of twenty roubles, even for the first time, but the Frederician Code of 1734 greatly mitigated the punishment by imposing a fine equal to three times the value of the stolen object. Children who offended (*provinilis*) their parents were sentenced to death after 1653, to whipping with twigs after 1734. Which of the two laws, both part of the "privileges," should apply? In 1779, the Senate concurred with the opinion of the College of Justice that the Code of 1734 must be applied throughout Vyborg province because the population of both parts was of the same faith and customs. However, the Senate decision applied only to criminal cases, as it appeared from a discussion held in Vyborg by a joint session of the provincial board with the judicial chambers in the 1780s. They claimed that the decision to extend the penal law of 1734 to both parts, first in 1763 and again in 1779, did not say that it applied to civil litigation as well. The provincial procurator concluded that this should be the case, all the more so since the Frederician Code was also published in Finnish. What would happen if a peasant living on one side of the internal border between the two parts sued another on the other side? The Senate expressed its irritation: the population had not expressed any dissatisfaction with the situation and no litigation was involved. The Senate merely stated that the Frederician Code did not apply to civil litigation in the older part of the province. It may be that the senators suspected that the introduction of the later and more liberal Swedish civil legislation there would upset Russian landowners who had been bringing their serfs into it.[162]

The government also sought to mitigate the harshness of the Swedish penal law. A peasant boy was sentenced in Riga for committing sodomy to decapitation and the burning of his body. A higher court found that he was a minor, and commuted the sentence to whipping with ten pairs of twigs on three separate holidays, to be followed by one year of hard labour. It also placed him under church observation until he repented (*pokaianie*). The Senate concurred because he was ignorant of the "Christian law"; he should first be taught that law – he may have been a Latvian pagan boy – until he repented. The empress ordered him tried in the newly created court of equity (*sovestny sud*) for minors and the mentally retarded. Similar cases were treated in similar fashion. Sodomy was not as serious a crime as premeditated murder and crimes against public security; their authors must not have to suffer the harshness of Swedish laws inspired by the Mosaic law that imposed beheading with burning of the body, but they must be explained by the primitive way of life of the defendants (*nevezhestvo*). Historical experience, wrote the senators, showed that criminality increased with the harshness of punishments. Sodomy and incest, and other such crimes, must be tried before the courts of equity, which did not have to follow the letter of the law, but in which the judges followed their conscience. Of course, this conscience reflected the attitudes of their society, and some, like the chairman of the criminal chamber, a Baltic German (Ungern-Sternberg), objected that leniency would open the way to "unnatural vices."[163]

The local government reform of the Baltic provinces exposed the complexities inherent to a policy of integration. There was a determination to achieve a full institutional integration, but the individuals who would fill the new positions had grown up in the pre-reform world and remained attached to it. The reform of the law proved much more difficult to achieve, because law was the cement of social and economic relationships, and to upset these relationships would be counterproductive. On the other hand, a policy of integration assumed, in principle, that the maintenance of the older institutions was unacceptable if they were at variance with the new agencies. The *Landrat* College, the heart of the old power structure, was abolished. The policy clung to the clause, first introduced in the early confirmations of the privileges, that they must be in accord with the political organization and principles of the expanding Russian core. If they were not, but if it was not politically acceptable to abolish them, they would remain as a favour (*milost'*) granted by the monarch, who could also withdraw them if circumstances so required. In the meantime, the Russian government would clarify the privileges, smooth out contradictions when cases came up before the Senate, or modify them in order to infuse them with the spirit of the times – many years had passed since the medieval customs and the sixteenth-century legislation upon which these privileges rested. The policy of integration was only partially successful in the Baltic provinces, and its inevitable completion would have to wait for another day.

Resistance to Social Integration

The publication of a *Matrikel* for Livland in 1742, and for Estland in 1756, had in fact undermined the legitimacy of the German nobility in the Baltic provinces, at a time when the expanding Russian core was becoming steadily stronger and more self-conscious. The expression "the conquered provinces" and "the conquered towns" disappeared after the death of Elizabeth in 1761, but Catherine II, brought up a German, had to proclaim her Russian and Orthodox allegiance to strengthen her own legitimacy. There would hardly be any German names among the high officials of her reign, and Prussia was still seen as a Russian satellite, but a dangerous one, whose influence radiated all over the German *Kulturgemeinschaft* in the east, all the way to the Gulf of Finland.[164]

After 1747, the matriculated nobility became more and more selfish and set itself apart from the non-matriculated nobles, and even more from the rest of society; in so doing, it lost its awareness of, and responsibility for, the common good of the provinces.[165] *Landräte* became the representatives, less of the nobility as the ruling class of the provinces, than of the executive agents of a caste. There had always been two distinct groups – the *Ritterschaft* (the knights), registered on the *Matrikel*, and the *Landschaft* (*zemstvo*), the non-matriculated landowners. The *Ritterschaft* banded together in exclusive corporations (*Mitbruderschaften*), whose members claimed that they alone could be called noblemen.[166] This was resented by the *Landschaft*, consisting of *Landsassen*, poor noblemen living in isolation on their rural estates, conscious of their social degradation, not unlike the middle and lower *szlachta*. Catherine II was determined to reassure them, and announced in January 1763 that both *Ritterschaft* and *Landschaft* belonged to the noble estate (*blagorodstvo*).[167]

The striking difference between the two groups was vividly described by Alexander Igelstrom (from a Swedish family of West Gotland, ennobled by the king in 1645). Some of us, he wrote, lived a very frivolous and extravagant life, in close touch with the outside world (*Ausland*), especially France, and with few contacts with the "East." The greater part of their youth began its education at home with a learned teacher from one of the German lands, who taught philosophy and foreign languages, and completed it in a German university. They then went on to serve in the French army or navy, and France even kept for them a regiment of "royal Swedes." They returned as libertines or lyric poets and fought duels. They lived lavishly and wasted their fortunes. The *Landschaft* was in a different world. Their lives were frozen in the simplicity of their fathers' customs, their houses were furnished as they had been as far back as one could remember. They were no more educated than their fathers had been, and kept marrying in the same world. They cared nothing about the land and its institutions, and both groups cared only about themselves.[168]

This nobility was very small, as shown in table 2.3. In Estland and Livland, its percentage of the total population was minuscule, very similar to that prevailing in the Russian core in 1782 (0.6 per cent).[169] Only in Kurland was it much larger, but Kurland had long been under Polish suzerainty. It was also a land of Latvians ruled by Germans, but it resembled Belorussia more than its neighbour to the north. Grodno, with its large Belorussian population, reminds us of Belorussia as a whole, but in Lithuania, the percentage of nobles exceeded 10 per cent, one found nowhere else in the expanding Russian core at the time. It would be no coincidence that the uprising of 1831 would make its greatest impact there. Thus, before the annexation of Kurland in 1795, the Russian government had to deal with a very small ruling class of some 1860 men, even much less in fact, if we consider only the adults.

Table 2.3 Percentage of nobles in the Baltic, Belorussian, and Lithuanian provinces, 1795

	Nobles	Population	%
Estland	1,590	212,942	0.7
Livland	2,546	569,166	0.4
Kurland	8,592	409,922	2.1
Subtotal	*12,728*	*1,192,030*	*1.1*
Polotosk	22,764	725,725	3.1
Mogilev	25,614	811,770	3.1
Minsk	46,940	882,848	5.3
Subtotal	*95,318*	*2,420,343*	*3.9*
Vyborg	1,102	185,756	0.6
Vilno	49,778	977,809	11.5
Kovno	63,112	–	–
Grodno	23,076	608,182	3.8
Subtotal	*135,966*	*1,585,991*	*8.6*

Sources: Kabuzan, *Narody Rossii* (1990), 172–5; Kabuzan and Troitskii, *Izmeneniia*, 162–4.
Note: Figures for nobles are males multiplied by two.

The Baltic provinces sent their representatives to the Legislative Commission, which met in 1767, and their instructions tell us about their concerns at the time. The Livland *Landschaft* asked for an end to the constant disputes (*raspri*) with the knights and for the merger of the two groups into a single body – showing that Catherine's declaration of January 1753 had had little immediate effect against ingrained prejudices. Officers who had served or were serving in the Russian army should also be incorporated into the nobility, even if they had no land. Others called for a discussion of the recently translated code (*Ulozhenie*) of Baltic German privileges. The Vyborg nobility asked for similar things, the preparation of a separate *Matrikel*, and the codification of their privileges "to the extent that they are in accord with Her Majesty's autocratic rights."[170]

The administrative reform was carried out in 1783 with considerable, but passive, resistance. The knights sat on their hands. A worse shock came with the introduction of the Charter of the Nobility of April 1785. In 1782, Browne had asked the opinion of the nobility about the impending reform: he was met with a blunt refusal to accept it. Much of the opposition centred on the appointment of a procurator to replace the *fiskal*: the final interpretation of the law would depend on an official appointed by the central government.[171] The Manifesto of May 1783, giving the nobility the full ownership of every type of land in their possession, was seen as an olive branch. Some nobles indeed had no legal title to their land. They had acquired former properties of the Teutonic Order after its dissolution, but these were transmissible only to the fifth generation, after which they would become "state" properties – that is, properties of the Swedish and then the Russian government.[172] The nobles were also much concerned with the more liberal provisions of the Charter, which allowed a noble woman who married a non-noble to retain her personal rights to buy and sell real estate and peasants: this threatened the monopoly of the *Ritterschaft* and *Landschaft*, and the decision of 1787 only confirmed their fears.[173]

Moreover, the creation of provincial assemblies of the nobility elected on the basis of entirely new principles to replace the traditional *Landtag*, and their right to elect deputies (*deputaty*) to pass on the qualifications of aspiring nobles, subject to the confirmation of the Heraldry Office in Petersburg, were a flagrant attack on the concept of *Matrikel*. In October 1783, a Major Blumen, in the name of the Livland *Landschaft*, complained to the Senate that the knights were blocking the *Landsassen* from the assembly and neutralized their right, given to them by the Organic Statute of 1775, to elect their candidates to provincial and county positions. That same year, the Livland knights submitted a petition asking that the Protestant Church remain under the direction of a *Landrat*; that judicial procedure be conducted in German; that all officials must be recommended by the Collegium and elected for life (a turnover every three years would expose "a shortage of intelligent people"); that the *Landtag* must remain an assembly of knights; and that a *fiskal* must remain in every court, and an *ober-fiskal* in the *Hofgericht*.[174]

Catherine's answer came in August 1786, with the introduction of the Charter: the position of *Landrat* belonged to another age (the Swedes had already abolished it in 1694!). The protection of the privileges now depended on agencies "created by our autocratic power." The position was abolished, and the Collegium ceased to exist. *Landräte* were placed in class 4 of the Russian civil service (the equivalent of a major general, which was also the usual rank of a provincial governor), and would be appointed to other positions if they were found fit for them.[175] No wonder that the hurt pride of a powerful caste caused such a backlash that one of Paul I's first decisions was to cancel his mother's reforms and restore the old order (but the procurator and the provincial board remained!). In Kurland, the nobility did not have the time to resent the reforms. Their main concern was that Duke Peter, who had several daughters to endow, was preparing a latter-day "reduction" by a land survey, which would reveal that many private titles to land were fraudulent. They wanted to abolish the duchy and join Poland, and transform feudal properties into *starostva*, which the king would then lease to them. In 1795, they turned to Russia.[176]

The cities too felt the blow.[177] In fact there were only two, Revel and Riga, ruled by a burgher caste proud of its ancestry, and which had long fought to resist the encroachments of the *Hofgericht*. The reform removed from the *magistrat* most of its administrative and police duties, and its economic activities fell under the purview of the provincial treasury chamber. It changed the electoral rules to break the hold of a caste on those who could not gain admission into it, and left the *magistrat* as mainly a court subordinated to the civil and criminal chambers. In so doing, the reform "democratized" urban society – as it democratized the nobility – by bringing fresh blood into it. All this took place at a time when the new tariff of September 1782 abolished the customs zone that had isolated Riga from the market of the expanding core. As in Belorussia, the population of Riga and Revel became integrated into the new social structure being built in the core.

The Russians also had to deal with the "peasant question." Paradoxically, the Enlightenment coincided with the worst abuses of serfdom. The rising demand for grain in Europe and Petersburg caused a constant pressure to increase output while little progress was being made in agricultural technology still practising the slash-and-burn method. Rising production also resulted in the growth of alcohol production. In the absence of improved technology, the landlords enlarged their demesne by incorporating the individual strips of their peasants and intensifying corvée labour, threatening to transform the peasants into a landless proletariat. These developments went hand in hand with growing interference in the family life of the peasants, the widespread sale of individual peasants and the breakup of families, and the pervasiveness of the unrestricted resort to corporal punishment and imprisonment in the houses of correction. By the beginning of Catherine's reign, the Estonian and Latvian peasant was being degraded to the status of a slave.[178]

It was not until the 1780s that the censuses carried out in Russia since 1719 were extended to the Baltic provinces. The 1782 census showed that 77.9 per cent of the peasantry consisted of serfs; in Estland the percentage reached a staggering 93.2 per cent, while in Vyborg province it was only 25.6 per cent: these peasants must have been brought in by their Russian owners, since the peasantry had traditionally been free in Swedish Finland. By 1795, the situation had only got worse: 95.7 per cent of the Estland peasantry were serfs, 80.9 per cent in Livland, but only 56 per cent in Kurland. In Vyborg it had grown to 33.7 per cent. But these high percentages were of the same order as those in the former Grand Duchy: in 1795, 75.3 per cent of the Polotsk peasants, 86.4 per cent of the Mogilev peasants, 75.8 per cent in Minsk, 61 per cent in Vilno, and 85.5 per cent in Grodno provinces were serfs.[179] Thus in both territories the overwhelming majority of the peasantry (and the population) lived in a degraded condition, at the mercy of a very small ruling class which also happened to be, ethnically, sharply different from its subjects.

Much has been made of Catherine's visit to the Baltic provinces in 1764, her conversations with Pastor Johann Eisen (1717–79) and Karl Schoultz (1720–82), the owner of the Ascheraden estate (in southern Livland near the Dvina), to help launch a program to reform what the publicist August Schlözer (1735–1809) called the "barbarism of serfdom."[180] It is true that the empress thought that an improvement in the conditions of serfdom, if not its complete abolition, was possible in an age when Reason was expected to guide humanity toward a better future. But serfdom was not a theory but a practice, a deeply ingrained way of life, the support for an elite which had been deeply shaken by the policies of the Swedish kings in the seventeenth century aiming to abolish serfdom and "reduce" their landholdings. The development of serfdom had been a process, and its abolition could only be a reverse process, away from the 1739 declaration of Livland *Landrat* Otto Freiherr von Rosen (1693–1764) – who died, symbolically, the same year Catherine visited his homeland – that the peasant was no more than his lord's chattel. It is likely that her visit was directed against the *Ritterschaft*, the real power holders in the provinces. She sought to strike an alliance with progressive landowners, like Schoultz, and the Lutheran clergy, among whom there were some, like their colleagues in Sweden, who deeply cared about improving the lot of the peasant. After the Reformation, the pastors had begun to preach to their Estonian and Latvian flocks in their native tongues without changing the status quo. Now, they, with other publicists of the Enlightenment, demanded the abolition of serfdom – a radical restructuring of the status quo – as a prerequisite of the development of an enlightened personality.[181] The Moravian Brethren had already paved the way. And the younger publicists, like Garlieb Merkel (1769–1850), the contemporary of Johann Herder (1744–1803, who taught in Riga in the 1760s), no longer looked upon the Estonians and Latvians as *Undeutschen* but as two nations with a right to their separate development. Merkel's *Die Letten* appeared in Leipzig in 1797 and caused an international stir.[182]

But the *Ritterschaft* withstood the onslaught. Eisen and Schoultz were ridiculed and ostracized. Schoultz published a compendium of peasant law (*Bauernrecht*) for his serfs in 1764, in thirty articles. Among other things, it granted the peasant the ownership of his movable property, of which he could dispose at will, providing it remained within the estate. The land remained the property of the lord, but the peasant's allotment was transmissible to his heirs, also as long as they remained on the estate. He could not be sold by his master. His obligations would be set down in the so-called *Wackenbuch*; he gained the right to complain against his lord – but to whom if not the courts controlled by the knights? The peasant remained a serf but ceased to be a chattel.[183]

In January 1765, Browne summoned the Livland nobility to a *Landtag* and submitted a number of proposals which were incorporated into the "patent" of 12 April. They were largely borrowed from Schoultz's *Bauernrecht*, and took up the four major issues about which the debate on serfdom was bound to take place. The *Landtag* had little choice but to accept them, because the governor general had expressed Catherine's strong displeasure with the condition of the peasantry during her trip. Peasants gained the ownership of their movable property and could no longer be sold; corporal punishment was limited to whipping with ten pairs of twigs (without specifying how many times); the amount of corvée labour and the rate of other duties were fixed; and peasants were given the right to complain against their lords for abusing their power. But who would guarantee that these modest changes would be carried out?[184]

Next to nothing was done until after Catherine's reign. After 1765 came the Legislative Commission, which resolved nothing; then the war with the Ottomans and a higher burden of taxation; then the introduction of the Organic Statute and the Charter of the nobility, which restructured government and nobility: those were no times to debate the rights and wrongs of serfdom. But in 1792, Friedrich von Sievers (1748–1823), from a family which gained prominence owing to Russian patronage, was elected Livland provincial marshal (1792–7). He and his friends, notably the Wenden county marshal Carl von Transehe-Roseneck, who had been in America, "the utopia of the eighteenth century," and had met Washington and Hamilton, decided to face down a still very strong reactionary party.[185] However, that was also the time when the Polish Constitution of May 1791 and the increasing violence of the French Revolution were raising fears of Jacobin subversion. Finally, Catherine passed away in November 1796, but the die had been cast: the publicists had done their work. When Alexander I (1801–25) acceded to the throne in 1801, his "liberal" views gave the final push that paved the way for the reforms of 1804–19.

There was also another reason for the lack of progress. Catherine's government did little to improve the fate of the serfs (and state peasants) in Russia proper, so why should it endeavour to improve the lot of the Baltic peasantry? To do so would undermine the hold of the *Ritterschaft* in the political life of the provinces by encouraging an alliance between the *Literatenstand* of publicists and pastors, who so deeply felt that the enserfment of the overwhelming majority of the population was an affront to enlightened public opinion. But courting them and the progressive landowners threatened the foundations of a policy of superstratification. This policy rested on the premise that a community of interests was possible between the intruder (the Russians) and the top stratum of local society to strengthen the status quo and facilitate Russian rule. To undermine the *Ritterschaft*, a caste of power holders, by "democratizing" both nobility and society was a dangerous policy: it would not integrate, but create an emancipated social structure, very different from that of the expanding core, eventually fated to turn against that of the core, where ruling elite and ruling class still believed, and would continue to believe for the next three generations, that serfdom was the foundation of the social order. A Russian policy to support the emancipation of the Baltic serfs would destroy the policy of superstratification, especially if it was supported by a belief that Russians and natives had a common interest against the German ruling class. Only if the *Ritterschaft* became convinced, as it eventually would be, that emancipation was in its economic interest and would guarantee its continued control in alliance with the Russians could progress be made. Then a compromise would be possible between superstratification and "modernization."

Trade and Taxes

Commercial integration encountered much less resistance, largely because economic imperatives demanded a unification of tariff rates throughout the region. The rapid growth of Petersburg revolutionized the situation by creating a huge customs zone in the eastern Baltic, in which geography and politics combined to transform the northern capital into the staple city, leaving far behind Revel, Narva, Riga, and Vyborg and, increasingly, even Danzig. Out of necessity, the Russians pursued a staple policy serving the so-called passive trade; traders allowed the merchants of other countries to bring and take out goods instead of themselves carrying the goods to foreign places and bringing others back.[186] Russia never developed a merchant marine worthy of the name. By the end of the 1770s, it had only a dozen large vessels, mostly captained by foreigners, while Åbo alone, facing Stockholm across the Bothnian Gulf, had at least another dozen of long-range merchantmen to supplement the coastal trade (*kabotazh*) with other Finnish towns. And in 1792, 756 British ships, mostly in ballast because local demand was so low, visited Memel to load up with balks and beams from the forests of the Lithuanian interior.[187]

There was hardly any domestic trade, both a cause and a consequence of the insignificance of the inland towns. Until General Browne issued his patent in 1765, peasants did not even own their surplus production. Even after the trade became free, we learn of the conditions in which it was conducted from the Police Regulations of May 1766. Artisans and other townsmen must give the peasant a good price, must not make him drunk but trade with him only when he was sober, and must not beat him if he refused an offer in favour of another.[188] Small towns remained impervious to Physiocratic ideas. Trade was thus mainly commerce, as it was in the Grand Duchy. Goods crossed the land on their way to the ports, but such commerce depended on the level of external demand and the policies of the core area governments. Much progress had been made during the reign of Elizabeth with the abolition of internal customs houses, but a good deal of harm had also been done by the activities of private trading companies and monopolies, some run by members of the elite. Catherine, a free trader, encouraged grain exports, and, to the extent that this was possible, the export of Russian manufactures as well. And indeed, Russia's trade greatly increased. In 1762, exports had reached 12.7 million roubles; in 1792 they reached 40.7 million, with a permanently positive balance throughout the reign.[189]

The expansion of trade also raised the question of removing exemptions from the general tariff, the so-called European Tariff. Petersburg had been given privileges by Peter I to help divert the trade from Arkhangelsk to his "new Paradise." They were removed in 1762, and the government discussed the possibility of abolishing the special position of Riga as well. The encouragement of grain exports suffered a setback whenever a bad harvest raised the price of grain and threatened shortages. This happened in July 1762, soon after the beginning of Catherine's reign, when grain exports from all Russian ports were prohibited, although Polish grain transiting to Riga was not affected. But this greatly affected the income of the knights and merchants, who protested and claimed that if an adequate amount were stored in the good years, there would no longer be any shortages, The clergy noted that there was no trade in Estland except in grain for export and that "countless amounts" of Polish grain and more grain from neighbouring Russian provinces would meet any shortages. The prohibition was lifted in April 1763, but would be reinstated from time to time in later years. These periodic shortages encouraged those who felt that a unified grain market was becoming a necessity and that the special position of Riga had become obsolete.[190]

The export of timber was also encouraged. Browne reported in 1764 that it had been forbidden on and off as far back as 1721 out of fear that the deforestation would deprive the Navy of the precious "naval stores" and Petersburg of firewood. Baltic forests were endangered not only by exports but also by the primitive technology of agriculture. Rather than resorting to the three-field division of the allotments, peasants followed the slash-and-burn method, clearing forests to enlarge the arable area. Browne and the Commerce Commission asked for a uniform duty in Arkhangelsk, Narva, and Pernov, which had once greatly profited from the timber trade under Swedish rule. A count conducted in 1754 had revealed that there were enough trees in the environs of Pernov for ninety-seven years. He also called for the creation of a water link between Pernov, Derpt, and Lake Peipus,[191] using the tributaries of the Pernov and Embach Rivers, which would facilitate the otherwise difficult overland transportation of goods from the Gulf of Riga to the Russian hinterland – another way of saying that the Estonian counties of northern Livland should be gradually integrated into the market of Pskov, Novgorod, and Petersburg.

The new tariff of September 1766[192] retained the separate status of the Baltic ports. It sought to reduce, if not eliminate, the contraband trade (*vorovskii torg*) between those ports and Russia by taxing imports *ad valorem* instead of according to size and weight, and separated raw materials from manufactured goods in order to encourage the export of the latter while hindering the import of the former, which Russia possessed in abundance. The tariff followed by less than a year the Tariff Regulations (*Ustav*) of December 1765 for the Riga trade,[193] which may have influenced similar policies in the other Baltic ports.

They allowed Poles, Kurlanders, and Lithuanians to bring their goods to Riga overland or on the Dvina duty-free, and gave them equal rights with the Riga merchants in the export of their goods. Thus they created a nearly single market for the commerce of the Grand Duchy and the Baltic provinces, but still moderately protected it against the Russian market by imposing a 2 per cent duty on Russian goods entering the Baltic ports from the hinterland.

Economic conditions had changed by the late 1770s, and access to the Black Sea, gained in 1775, promised rich dividends. The government embarked on a policy of across-the-board integration across the entire expanding core. Domestic production had much increased, and Russia was eager to develop its exports not only of manufactured goods but also of raw materials, competing with Sweden on the international market for iron and copper, while seeking to reduce its imports of luxury and colonial goods. The new Tariff of September 1782 was a relatively liberal one,[194] reflecting growing Russian self-confidence. It reduced duties to an average of 10 per cent *ad valorem*, while the average rate in Riga was still 12 per cent. In other words, commercial developments and governmental policy had been converging, and a separate tariff for the Baltic ports was no longer justified. In one respect, however, the Riga rates remained separate: duties and port charges would still have to be paid in silver talers (*efimki*), because the Russian currency still did not circulate in Riga. An annex to the 1782 tariff governed the export through Riga of Polish and Lithuanian goods.[195] The reaction was mixed: some feared that the price of certain imported goods would rise, while others calculated that the very small export duty would stimulate the production of grain on their estates.[196] At any rate, both policies – commercial and administrative unification – must be seen as part of a general assault on the Baltic privileges with the goal of seeking the full integration of the Baltic provinces into the expanding Russian core.

The fiscal system was extremely complex, but this complexity merely reflected the extreme fragmentation of the Baltic provinces' social and economic life. The matriculated nobility descended in large part from the Teutonic Knights, conquerors who had settled on the land and built castles around which they created estates, which then became their own, following the secularization of the Order in the sixteenth century. Each estate followed its own way under the benevolent monopoly of *Landräte* and their Collegium. Weights and measures varied from one province to another, from one district, even one estate, to another. So did the rates of corvée labour and other in-kind taxes. Estland and Livland peasants did not pay head taxes and were not drafted into the Russian army when periodic levies were announced in Russia. But there was a land tax, its rate about the same as that of the head tax in the Russian provinces. The lord's demesne was exempted, and the full burden fell on the peasantry. The land was valued according to censuses conducted by the Swedes under Charles

XI; obligations were fixed in *Wackenbücher*, which had not kept up with the times since the Swedish period and were largely ignored.

The Baltic provinces were not paying their share. From the larger province of Livland, the Russian treasury collected 130,000 talers in the 1740s, but only 117,000 in 1782. The reason was simple. The lords kept enlarging their demesne by annexing peasant land, and that land ceased to be taxable. A new valuation became imperative, but it met with the fierce opposition of the landlords because it would demarcate more clearly peasant land from the demesne and turn the expansion of the latter into an unlawful enterprise, raising the spectre of another "revision." Government-owned properties were given away to favoured members of the elite and turned into private properties, which then underwent the same process of change. The extension of the demesne was accompanied by the intensification of corvée labour, since the dominant philosophy of the day, until the 1770s at least, taught that the use of free labour was much less profitable (by half) than corvée labour. The sad consequence was that the Baltic nobility "felt like the owners of sugar plantations in the American colonies."[197] It was not unusual that a peasant had to work six days a week in the demesne: in Estland the basic unit of taxation was the *Haaken* (*gak*), equal to the work of one household for six days, and this with a horse. Other in-kind taxes belonged to a medieval economy. The peasant had to sell his grain for salt, metal, and tobacco belonging to the lord, or spend it in a tavern run by the same landlord, who brewed and sold beer and spirits as well as ran the mills.[198]

The most important tax payable to the government was the delivery of grain, called *Zollkorn* in Estland, *Station* in Livland. The landlord paid it, then collected from the peasant households an amount greater than that he had paid to the government. The grain was delivered into the account of the Provision Chancery in Petersburg, responsible for the provisioning of the army, but the valuation of the grain (rye or barley) caused endless disputes and the delivery painful logistical problems. The harvest was uncertain and it was impossible to determine grain prices ahead of time. Payments were made on delivery, sometimes after long delays, in copper instead of in silver as contracted for. While suppliers waited for their receipts, they incurred expenses in town and "vexations" on the part of military personnel. The creation of a systematic network of military stores in April 1766 sought to facilitate the deliveries of grain. Until then, the grain had been collected in county seats and transported at the supplier's cost to Revel, Riga, and Arensburg (from points on Ösel Island). Then it was delivered on regimental carts to the headquarters of regiments and companies. But the distances were so great that the horses could not cope with the long trip. Following the decision in 1763 to assign permanent quarters to the military units, which would no longer be kept secret but were made public by the governor general, the grain would be shipped directly from the estates to the headquarters, based in individual contracts between the estates and the units, and would be delivered at prices set by the government, as had been the case under Swedish rule. In Vyborg province, where the harvest was generally poor, grain was replaced by hay and was delivered at ten kopecks a *pud*.[199]

The scope of the policy of fiscal integration becomes quite clear when we realize that the same edict of May 1783, which we encountered in Little Russia and eastern Belorussia, also took effect in the Baltic provinces. There, it replaced the land tax based on the size of allotments with a head tax of 70 kopecks per male peasant and a 1.20-rouble tax per townsman (*meshchanin*). Merchants (*kuptsy*), who were exempted from the capitation, were charged 1 per cent on their declared capital. The reform also spelled out that the yield of the new tax must not exceed that of the old land tax and must include the grain deliveries. Thus the key question was to assign a given value to those deliveries, as was done in Belorussia, but there the government set the price; in the Baltic provinces it preferred to wait. Nevertheless, the intent of the reform was not in doubt: to create a single fiscal system for the Baltic provinces so that "they may be integrated as fully as possible into the fiscal system of the empire" (*chrez to koliko vozmozhno k edinoobraziiu s glavnym korpusom imperii priblizheny byli*).[200]

The reform of 1783 changed the fiscal system fundamentally.[201] It contributed to the monetization of the economy by replacing a land tax with a head tax assessed according to the number of males registered in regular censuses, instead of according to the size of land allotments. It may have encouraged the lords to keep enlarging their demesnes by incorporating peasant land. It was hard on the towns, already in a sorry state. Before the reform, townsmen had had to pay only a small excise tax for the right to sell spirits; now they had to pay, in addition, a high personal tax, and the merchant, a tax on his capital. It was hard on a peasant with four sons and little or no land. Landlords did not like the head tax, because they had to pay the full amount assessed against their peasants as a whole, and if the peasants could not pay it, the landlords would have to pay the balance out of their own pockets. Nevertheless, the reform had a modernizing effect, even if it did not encourage urban development. It accelerated the transformation of agriculture and the proletarianization of the peasantry. In so doing, it also made the reform acceptable to the ruling class and paved the way for the acceptance of landless emancipation thirty years later.[202]

A glance at the provincial budgets[203] reveals the dominant position of Livland among the Baltic provinces and the overwhelming supremacy of Petersburg in the eastern Baltic. The share of the capitation (28.7 per cent) was lower than in Belorussia because of the importance of the customs revenue (1.1 out of 1.3 million roubles or 61 per cent) in Estland and Livland. Estimated revenue from Kurland in 1796 added another 263,585 roubles from the capitation and 480,814 roubles from other sources, a total of 724,399 roubles. Added to the 1,825,702 roubles from the other three Baltic provinces, we have a total revenue of 2.5 million roubles for the region, or about 3.8 per cent of the 66 million for the entire expanding Russian core. The central government received practically no revenue from the sale of spirits and salt because both products were sold on the free market – as in Belorussia, the salt came from France and Portugal. But the contribution of the Baltic provinces to the central treasury was substantial: 858,612 roubles or 47 per cent remained in the provinces to pay for the salaries of both elected and appointed personnel. This represented a new and important infusion of capital in the local economies, and contemporaries were quite aware of it. This no doubt may have convinced at least part of the nobility that the reform had something in it for them. But the central treasury also derived a great profit from the reform, much greater, relatively speaking, than in Belorussia: 210,000 roubles went to the Commissary and the Navy and 757,089 roubles (41 per cent) to the Treasury in Petersburg.

The hegemonic position of the northern capital was obvious. While the three Baltic provinces yielded a revenue of 1.8 million roubles, Petersburg collected 7.5 million. Its position was due to two factors: 3.4 million came from the sale of spirits by the government and 3 million (out of 3.6 million) from the customs revenue. The customs revenue from Riga was only 838,522 roubles, from Revel 242,883 roubles. Even if we add the estimated total revenue from Kurland of 724,399 roubles, the total for the four provinces pales against the 7.5 million collected in Petersburg. By 1795, the commerce of the region was revolving around the northern capital as the staple city of the eastern Baltic, and a separate fiscal regime would have been an anachronism. Only the salt trade and the lucrative trade in spirits retained, as in the western theatre as a whole, their traditional peculiarities, the product of a certain commercial environment and of the economic privileges of the nobility which it would still have been counterproductive to abolish.

Chapter Three

Unitary State or Empire? 1815–1855

Civil Administration and the Army

Finland

If the establishment of a Russian presence in eastern Georgia in 1801 (or even in 1783) marked the first stage in the creation of a Russian Empire, the annexation of Finland in 1808 was the second. Petersburg recognized from the beginning that Finland was a different world which could not be integrated into the expanding Russian core, but must continue to be governed by its own institutions and its own laws. It would be linked with the emperor not via the ministerial hierarchy but via a separate line of authority. However, this was easier said than done. The Russian elite's proclivity to shy away from clear and binding agreements and procedures would mean, in fact, that a natural and age-long impulse to create a unitary state would struggle with the recognition that it was not possible for a long time to come. Nevertheless, the steadfastness of the Finnish people and its Swedish elite, ethnically and culturally so different from their Eastern Slav neighbour, would guarantee that Finland would remain a major constituent element in the emerging empire, one that may not have been, in the western theatre at least, a mere "great robbery."

The invasion of Finland in February 1808 was a result of the Tilsit agreement of July 1807 between Alexander I and Napoleon, according to which the French and Danes would invade Sweden from the south and the Russians from the east, a repeat of their invasions of 1714 and 1742. By the Treaty of Fredrikshamn of September 1809, Sweden ceded to Russia the whole of Finland to the Torneo River, including the Åland Islands. The Russians acquired another 300,466 square kilometres (331,870 with Vyborg province added to "Swedish Finland" in 1811). Alexander I declared Finland annexed forever, and boasted that he had defeated his country's "geographic enemy": geography had dictated the invasion of Finland to ensure Russia's hegemony in the eastern Baltic, "the basin of St. Petersburg."[1] The population was solidly Finnish. A Swedish census of 1806 gave a population of 909,025; that of 1850 (including Vyborg province) gave 1,637,000 inhabitants, of whom Finns made up 1,387,000 or 84.7 per cent. Swedes accounted for 214,000 or 13 per cent, and Russians (mostly in Vyborg province) a mere 34,000 or 2 per cent. Swedes were found mostly on the southern coast between the Vyborg border and Åbo (45 per cent) and in the Vasa region of Ostrobothnia, where their share did not exceed 30 per cent. They predominated on the Åland Islands and, across the Gulf of Finland, on Mohn Island facing Estland.[2] The Russian government retained the Swedish division into *län*, but by 1831 the term had been replaced by *gubernia*, of which there were eight: Niuland, including Helsingfors, Finland's "main city"; Åbo-Björneborg and Vasa as well as Vyborg provinces formed a coastal semi-circle along the Gulf of Bothnia and the Gulf of Finland. Tavastehus, Sankt Michel, and Kuopio provinces occupied the lake region in the interior; and Uleaborg (with Lapland) included the northern half of the country to the Swedish and Norwegian borders. Each province was administered by a governor (*landshövdingar, Landsgevding*) appointed by the emperor.[3]

One of the major problems after 1808 was to create institutions to administer the new territory. In June 1808, deputies were summoned to give their opinion on the needs of the country, and a *Landtag* met in Borgå in February 1809. It would not meet again until 1867, and Finland would not have a legislature until after the reign of Nicholas I. It would merely have an administrative body called a Governing Council (*Conseil de régence*), then Senate, beginning in 1816. Created in 1809, it consisted of two sections, justice and political economy, with fourteen Finnish members, half coming from the nobility, half from the other three estates, the clergy, the burghers, and the peasants. They were chosen and appointed by the emperor and served for three years. The Council's powers were residual: it could do only what the emperor chose not to do. It could not impose new taxes or defray expenditures above those authorized in the approved annual budget. It could not make new laws, annul old ones, or even interpret them, but had the right to recommend amendments to the emperor, the only source of law. The judicial section was Finland's new high court, with the former jurisdiction of the Swedish High Court in Stockholm, and received appeals from three *Hofgerichts* in Åbo, Vasa, and Vyborg. The political economy section managed the police, finances, military, and ecclesiastical affairs, in the tradition of the eighteenth-century *Polizeistaat*.[4]

The Council grew in importance with the passage of time, and by 1814 it had become "a fully equipped central administration"[5] for Finland with a population which, in 1850, was about the same as that of the three Baltic provinces. The Council was chaired by the governor general, who merely presided over the deliberations, took no part in the "substance" of civil and ecclesiastical affairs, and, with the procurator subordinated to him, made sure that procedures – the old Swedish ones of before 1808, including the *Landsgevding* Instruction of November 1734 – were fully observed. Decisions were made by majority vote, but if he disagreed with any of them, he had no right to suspend its execution; he could only send his comments to the emperor. In certain cases, such as personnel matters and imperial orders affecting Finland, he summoned a joint meeting of both sections to hear their comments. All this seems to show that Finland had indeed been given its own administration, separate from that of the other provinces of the expanding core. But anyone familiar with the history of Russian administration will immediately recognize a disturbing similarity between the sections, the joint meeting, and the role of the governor general on the one hand, and the administration of the internal Russian provinces, with their provincial boards, three chambers, and joint sessions and procedures, on the other. This similarity offers convincing evidence that some in the Russian government were already thinking about the eventual administrative integration of Finland into the expanding core.

But other factors pointed to a determination to maintain a separate status for the territory. The first governor general, Georg Sprengtporten (1808–9), a Finn already sixty-seven years old, was a controversial figure. He had long been known, together with other Swedish and Finnish officers, for separatist tendencies, and had ambitious plans for an independent Finland under Russian protection, ambitions that did not square with the more modest, and more realistic, plans of other Finnish leaders, notably Carl Mannerheim, who feared that the general hoped to create a "pashalik" for himself. Sprengtporten was removed in 1809 after a series of sharp disagreements with General Gotthard von Knorring, the commanding general of Russian troops in Finland.[6] He was succeeded by General Michael Barclay de Tolly (of future 1812 fame) for merely a year, who was then recalled to prepare for the imminent Napoleonic invasion of Russia. But then a happy choice was that of Lt.-Gen. Fabian von Steinheil (1810–23) from the Estland nobility, whose background was in staff and cartographic work, and who had commanded Russian troops on the Åland Islands in 1809, a Finlandophile who spoke fluent Swedish, but not a strong personality. He was particularly successful in convincing some one hundred Swedish officers to enter the Russian military.[7]

The status of the governor general began to change with the appointment of Lt.-Gen. Arsenii Zakrevsky in 1823, an ambitious and younger man (born in 1786), who inaugurated a harder line toward Finnish autonomy. He had been for eight years director of the Personnel Department of the Main Staff (the top military agency), and was a great friend of Alexei Ermolov, the governor general of the Caucasus (1816–27). His reputation for firmness resulted in his appointment as minister of the interior (1828–31), one of the most sensitive positions in the civilian administration. He resided in Petersburg most of the time, so that the position of governor general became subordinated in his person to that of interior minister, following a similar trend in other regions placed under the authority of a governor general. Zakrevsky's tenure embodied a trend in Russian attitudes very much in evidence everywhere during Nicholas I's reign.[8]

The status of his successor was even more exceptional. Alexander Menshikov was the great-grandson of another Alexander, Peter the Great's favourite. Appointed chief of staff of the Navy in 1828, he would remain in this post until the end of the reign. He succeeded Zakrevsky in 1831 and was governor general for twenty-four years (1831–55). However, his many other duties forced him to delegate most of his functions, if not his powers, to Lt.-Gens. Alexander Thesleff (1833–47) and Platon Rokasovskii (1848–54), who later himself became governor general (1861–6).[9] The incorporation of the governor generalship into the naval ministerial establishment – away from the interior ministry – illustrated the true nature of Russia's interest in Finland: a Russian presence on the northern shore of the Gulf of Finland and the eastern shore of the Gulf of Bothnia, together with the annexation of the coast of Estland, sealed the entrance into the Gulf of Finland and protected Petersburg. It also gave Russia an offensive posture against Sweden – the Åland Islands were within thirty kilometres of Stockholm.

Such a perception may explain why a relatively large number of troops was stationed in the territory. The *indelningsverk* system was abolished after 1810, to be replaced by a small force of volunteers numbering from 1,600 to 4,500 men. But the Russian presence rested on the Baltic fleet, responsible to Menshikov, and garrisons, reorganized in 1835 into nine line battalions of 920 privates each. Two battalions were headquartered in Vyborg, one in Helsingfors, two in Sveaborg (guarding the entrance to Helsingfors), one each in Hango, Åbo, and Vasa, and only one in the interior, in Tavastehus.[10] Menshikov was a supporter of Finnish autonomy – as a bailiwick of the Navy – but the interior ministry did not forget that it once had had jurisdiction over Finland and had taken a harder line. When Lev Perovsky was interior minister (1841–52), he fought in the State Council in 1846 for the introduction of Russian laws, institutions, and language in the borderlands, including Finland. However, the influence of Menshikov and the Swedo-Finns in Petersburg convinced Nicholas that the time had not yet come to alter Finland's status.[11]

What gave Finland its special position as a major building block in the emerging empire was not so much the existence of a governor general and a Finnish Senate, as the presence in Petersburg of influential members of the Finland ruling elite. A commission set up in 1765 to survey Vyborg province and fix the amount of *obrok* to be paid by the peasants merely collected statistics and recommended no substantial changes; "the province remained as poor as it had been in 1710." This commission was closed in May 1802 and replaced by a Special Commission, later renamed Committee, for Finnish Affairs, reorganized in October 1811 to consist of Finnish officials. It was closed in April 1826 and downgraded into a state secretariat, which would remain in existence until 1918. It was headed by Robert Rehbinder (1811–41), followed by Alexander Armfelt, for thirty-five years (1841–76). The reorganization of 1826 – pushed by Zakrevsky – was welcomed in some quarters. Senator Pavel Divov wrote in his diary that "it seems to herald the fusion or full union of the duchy with the empire." In December 1834, the state secretary was renamed minister state secretary,[12] but the change only reflected the emperor's esteem for Rehbinder rather than an administrative upgrade.

Three men stand out among many other Finns and Swedes who had properties in Finland and identified with the country, and who created a kind of feudal fraternity of officers and officials who transferred their allegiance not so much to Russia as to its emperor. Gustav Armfelt himself once said that "he had nothing in common with Russia and that his [personal] relations were with Alexander I, the benefactor of my Fatherland."[13] He was born in 1757 near Åbo, the son of a Swedish general. He was a companion of Gustav III and saved his life twice during the Russo-Swedish war of 1788–90, but he also felt uneasy about the king's dictatorial tendencies. Like many other men of the frontier, above all those living in an aristocratic age that knew no national boundaries but only the exuberance of a cosmopolitan universe, he began to toy with the eventuality of another Finland, independent but allied with Russia, in which the tax burden would be low and conscription no longer necessary. At the end of 1788 he made overtures to Catherine II, but without success. He continued to serve Sweden, and in 1806–7 commanded Swedish troops in Pomerania and Norway. But personal rivalries at court and the Russian occupation of Finland in 1808 finally convinced him to pledge allegiance to Alexander I in 1811, and within a year he was a full general in the Russian army and chairman of the Committee for Finnish Affairs. He died suddenly in 1814, and a Russian warship took his body back to Åbo, facing a Sweden which now considered him a traitor.

Alexander I greatly trusted him, and he was in turn trusted by those in the Swedo-Finnish elite who were determined to achieve a modus vivendi with the expanding Russian core and to protect Finnish autonomy – no longer independence – against the persistent intrusions of the new Russian ministries (reorganized in 1811), all great believers in the superiority of the unitary state. Armfelt had a decisive influence in the decision to merge Vyborg province with the main body of Finland – a major concession by the Russians which created enemies for him in the capital – in the formation of the Finnish government, and in transforming the Committee for Finnish Affairs into an advisory body operating in the capital, close to the Court and the emperor. A rivalry inevitably developed between the Committee and the governor general. Steinheil expressed his frustration when he felt bypassed in matters belonging to his jurisdiction, and Zakrevsky would later claim that the Committee's influence had gone far beyond Alexander's intentions in 1812. Only Armfelt's early death prevented an inborn rivalry from developing into an open conflict.[14]

Armfelt's son Alexander (1794–1875) followed in his father's footsteps as a defender of Finnish interests in Petersburg, and his friendship with Menshikov made for smooth cooperation. He was born in Riga, attended Uppsala and Edinburgh universities, graduated with a law degree from Alexander University in Åbo, and became director of the Bank of Finland in 1831. But he served in very different circumstances. He was merely a personal secretary (*stats-sekretar'*) of the emperor with a special responsibility for Finnish affairs, but had no authority to pass on proposals submitted for the emperor's approval. Nevertheless, he remained a trusted helping hand as his long tenure so clearly attests; influence can be exercised in many subtle ways.[15]

Robert Rehbinder (1777–1841) was the second most important public figure after Gustav Armfelt. His family was a branch of the von Rehbinders from Estland, whose members served in both Sweden and Russia. He was born in Åbo, the heart of Swedish Finland, spent four years at Åbo University (the precursor of Alexander University in Helsingfors), served in the Åbo *Hofgericht*, and became known at Borgå for his knowledge of Swedish laws. In 1811 he was attached to Gustav Armfelt with the title of *stats-sekretar'*, and after a short interval succeeded him as chairman of the Committee for Finnish Affairs until 1826. He remained as *stats-sekretar'* until his death. Rehbinder was a lawyer and a man of the world rather than a politician like Gustav Armfelt, and this made him perfectly suited to occupy his post for so long. He too exercised influence on Menshikov to convince him that it was in Russia's interest to maintain Finland's status in the emerging empire.[16]

But what exactly was this status? It remained unclear, if only because the Russians themselves did not know. Contradictions abound. One often encounters in official texts the expression "Finland and the empire,"[17] as if they were different entities, but, if that was the case, how could Finland be considered a part of the empire? When a debate began in the 1830s to answer that question, the Finns argued that the Borgå assembly met before the conclusion of peace with Sweden and that, as a result, Finland had become a state, and that its representatives had negotiated a settlement on equal terms with the Russians. This was a legal argument, but the Russians did not think in legal terms. Alexander I wrote to Gustav IV while the *Landtag* was in session that "Finland is incorporated into Russia by right of conquest and victory on the battlefield" (*po prave zavoevaniia i po zherebiu bitvy*). The title of the emperor relegated Finland to a secondary position after the *tsarstva*, and proclaimed the emperor to be "Grand Duke of Smolensk, Lithuania, Volhynia, Podolia, and Finland."[18]

There were claims that Alexander I (and Nicholas I after him) had confirmed the "basic" (*osnovnye, korennye*) laws of the Grand Duchy, but what were they? For the Finns, they were the Swedish Constitution of 1772 and the Act of Union and Security of 1789, which gave the king extensive powers, including the exclusive right to initiate legislation, but denied him the crucial power to tax. To call upon the Russian emperor to confirm constitutional documents recognizing the existence of a permanent parliament (*Riksdag*) representing the four estates of the Grand Duchy and restricting the "absolute" powers of the ruler was to demand the impossible. The emperor, Eurasian ruler that he was, could not accept any restriction on his "autocratic and unlimited power" – unless it was self-imposed. The Borgå assembly was not an embryonic parliament, but a meeting of notables (*Landtag*) called upon to bring their needs to the ruler's attention.[19]

All power in the Grand Duchy would reside in the emperor, and whatever authority remained in the provincial agencies was residual. What the Russians considered as basic laws referred to the Naval Regulations of 1667, the Church regulations of 1686, the *Ulozhenie* of 1734, the Land Survey rules of 1775, and the Act of 1789 as far as it gave greater rights to the peasantry.[20] Their observance by Russia would depend on the emperor's good will – or that of the key members of the ruling elite who concealed their motives behind the will of their autocratic master. No parliament was created after the Borgå assembly disbanded. As a result, there existed no legislative authority in the Grand Duchy, only the Senate's administrative acts, which the emperor could suspend or annul, if he chose to consider them in violation of the laws and institutions of the empire. That had been the purpose of the restrictive clause imposed on the Baltic nobility in 1710. No wonder that the Finns felt uneasy, with a sword of Damocles constantly suspended over their heads.[21]

Poland

Five years after the occupation of Finland, in January 1813, Russian troops marched into the Polish core in pursuit of Napoleon, and Alexander I declared his determination to incorporate into his domain the Duchy of Warsaw, created by Napoleon in July 1807 out of the Prussian and Austrian shares. Back in 1808, after Prussia's defeat by Napoleon, the expanding Russian core had annexed the Bialystock territory, which was not strictly Polish land: populated by Lithuanians, it had been the western, trans-Niemen part of the Troki palatinate in the old Grand Duchy, and its acquisition merely rounded out the lands annexed in 1793 and 1795. The partition of Poland at the Congress of Vienna (1814–15) marked the first time that Russia took part in the dismemberment of the Polish core, which must always be distinguished from its eastern marches in the Grand Duchy and Right Bank Ukraine.[22] The annexation of the entire Duchy of Warsaw was not acceptable to Russia's allies, Prussia and Austria, and a compromise was reached in 1815 giving Russia so-called Congress Poland. It consisted of part of the Austrian and Prussian shares, and was bound by a line running from the lower San to the Western Bug south of Zamość; to the west the boundary ran from Oswieczyn (Auschwitz) to the Prosna River and to its confluence with the Warta. The northern boundary went from that point across the Vistula upstream from Torun, followed the Drweca River, and then linked up with and followed the southern border of East Prussia to the Niemen, Lithuania's border.

The territory of Congress Poland greatly suffered during the Napoleonic invasion of Russia: its population of 3.3 million in 1811 had been reduced to 2.6 million in 1815, a loss of nearly 8 per cent.[23] By 1850, however, in part because of a substantial immigration of colonists mostly from the German lands, it had risen to 4.8 million, of whom 3.4 million (71 per cent) were Poles. The second largest group was Jews, with 564,000 inhabitants (11.7 per cent) followed by Germans, Lithuanians, and Ukrainians, slightly over 5 per cent each.[24] The Lithuanians were found mostly in the northeast, which merged imperceptibly with Old Lithuania; the Ukrainians were concentrated in so-called Chervonnaia Rus between the Wieprzh and the Western Bug. The eastern border of Congress Poland, running along the Niemen, the Bobrza, the Narew, and the Bug, was thus not quite an ethnic boundary, but incorporated a substantial number of people who had belonged to the Grand Duchy. The western boundary, on the other hand, cut right through the heart of Poland.

In Congress Poland the Russians acquired another 126,948 square kilometres, a territory much smaller but more compact than Finland, with a much larger and less homogenous population. It was divided in 1815 into eight provinces (*wojewodstwa*), the latter into thirty-nine districts (*obwódy*) and seventy-seven counties (*powiaty*). The Russians felt the impulse to create a unified territorial grid to support the creation of a unitary state more in Poland than in Finland. In May 1837, the *wojewodstwa* were renamed *gubernii*, and the *obwódy* were abolished in September 1842: the Polish territorial division became identical with that of Russia. Presidents of provincial commissions became civil governors, and their commissions provincial boards. Finally, in August 1844, the eight provinces were consolidated into five by merging three with their neighbours. There remained Warsaw – the capital had then a population of 139,600 – Plotsk and Suwalki (the capital of Avgustov province), Radom, and Lublin.[25]

As in Finland, a major preoccupation was to give Poland a type of government which would preserve its identity, keeping in mind that its status as an "inseparable part of Russia" had been negotiated at Vienna between the Russians, Prussians, and Austrians. At the time, there was still no intention to integrate Poland into the expanding Russian core, as was being increasingly done in neighbouring Lithuania and Belorussia. The expanding core was in the process of becoming an empire. A Constitutional Charter was granted by Alexander I in November 1815, as unrealistic as it was liberal.[26] The kingdom had a bicameral Diet: a Senate consisted of princes of the blood, bishops, and castellans, nominated for life by the emperor as King of Poland; a chamber of delegates consisting of 77 "envoys" chosen by the county assemblies and 51 deputies from the communes (*gminy*), a total of 128. Membership in the Senate could not exceed half the total number of deputies, or 64, elected for six years. The Diet would meet every year for sixty days, summoned and prorogued by the emperor. There was also a State Council consisting of an Administrative Council and its general assembly; it included the five ministers and persons chosen by the emperor and would discuss projects of laws to be submitted to the Diet and try officials for abuses of power.

The day-to-day administration of the kingdom was vested in five ministers heading governmental commissions: interior and police; finance; justice; religion and education; and military. The ministers were all Poles; the language of administration was Polish. There was also, as in Finland, a *stats-sekretar'*, renamed in 1820 minister state secretary, who resided in Petersburg.[27] In his absence, the emperor was represented by a viceroy (*namestnik*), who exercised his powers and reported to him through the secretary. The constitution was considered liberal, not only because it provided for a parliament, but also for its generous (for the time) protection of civil liberties and an independent judiciary. Incongruously enough, the Russians hoped it would unite Poles "forever with a magnanimous people in brotherly relations on account of their ancient kinship in the glorious and common appellation of a Slavic [*Slavianskii*] people."[28]

But a constitution granted by a Russian monarch can be amended or even withdrawn at will, and no time was lost in so doing. What should Poland's place be in the tsar-emperor's title? Poland was not called a kingdom (*korolevstvo*, which struck a dissonant chord in a Russian ear) but a *tsarstvo*, and Alexander became "tsar of Kazan, Astrakhan, Poland, Siberia, and Crimea." Poland's place may seem odd, but did not the title express a conviction that Russia had finally vanquished its traditional enemies in Catholicism and Islam and united the former domain of the Golden Horde and (most) of the Polish empire under its hegemonic leadership?[29]

The Diet would not meet every year but only in 1818, 1820, 1825, and, for the last time, in 1830. As in Finland, the country lost its legislature, and legislation became indistinguishable from the decrees of the Administrative Council. The Charter did provide for a commander in chief of the Polish army in the emperor's absence, but much depended on the personality of the appointee. Alexander I made the fatal error of appointing his brother Constantine – a tragic figure, unbalanced, and incapable of controlling his arbitrary behaviour. He did not want the appointment, disliked Poles but, eventually, came to like them – when it was too late. But his rank, as brother of the tsar, made him the first personality in the *tsarstvo* and the real viceroy.[30] The appointment of the nominal one was a farce: he was a "creature" of Constantine. General Józef Zajączek was already sixty-three in 1815. He was born in Right Bank Ukraine, served in the troops of the Targowica Confederation, then in the French army, commanded a division in the Napoleonic invasion, then won the trust of Constantine for his submission and servility toward the Russians. He disliked the Charter, calling it a "code d'anarchie."[31]

When he died in 1826, he had no successor until 1832, when a very different viceroy would impose a dictatorial regime on Poland for nearly twenty-five years. A sinister figure accompanied Constantine, with the title of imperial commissioner, unknown in the charter. Nikolai Novosiltsev (1761–1836) also disliked Poles and had opposed the creation of the *tsarstvo*. He had been a friend of Adam Czartoryski, who expected to become viceroy, but whose strong personality was incompatible with Russian expectations of obedience. Novosiltsev became the grand inquisitor of Congress Poland until 1831. The charter did not need more enemies to become as early as 1816 "une pénible et inutile comédie."[32]

Discontent with Russian misrule and the humiliation of a proud people caused the Poles, mostly the *szlachta*, to rise up against the Russians. The uprising of November 1830 in Warsaw nearly cost Constantine his life – he died of the cholera shortly afterwards – and Novosiltsev managed to disappear. A massive invasion of the *tsarstvo* began in 1831, Polish resistance was crushed, and the Russians were back in Warsaw by September. A very different order was about to begin.[33]

The Charter of 1815 was replaced by the Organic Statute of February 1832,[34] intended to create between Poles and Russians (*Rossiane*) "the harmonious brotherhood of a single people" (*edinyi narod soglasnykh bratii*). It retained the Administrative Council, chaired by the viceroy, but now consisting of only three ministers (interior, with religious and cultural affairs; finance; and justice), the comptroller general and other members appointed by the emperor at discretion. It was the executive branch of the new Poland; it selected candidates for the posts of bishop and high state officials to be submitted to the emperor, drew up projects of new laws, and took up administrative matters in general. Decisions were made by majority vote, but if the viceroy disagreed, he stopped further proceedings and reported the matter to the emperor. A semblance of legislature was also retained, called a State Council, which was, in fact, no more than an enlarged Administrative Council. It was a copy of the State Council in Petersburg. It examined projects of new laws and the estimates of the Polish budget drawn up in the Administrative Council, and tried officials for abuses of power. A separate Department for Polish Affairs was created in the Imperial State Council, chaired by the viceroy when he visited Petersburg, and consisting of seven persons, including Novosiltsev, Minister State Secretary Stefan Grabowski, the chief of gendarmes in Poland, and Prince Francisek Drucki-Lubecki, who had been finance minister in Warsaw (1821–30), whom Nicholas I greatly trusted.[35]

The elimination of every form of election in the organization of the new government, the creation of an administrative structure resembling the imperial one, the key position of the viceroy, who had the controlling say in every operation of government, pointed to a double trend. Power was being concentrated in Warsaw, and the governing of Poland was becoming increasingly integrated into the all-imperial machinery of government. This became obvious when it was stated in April 1842 that the purpose of the Polish Department was to examine projects of legislation for their "compatibility" (*soobrazhenie*) with similar legislation in force in other parts of the empire and with its general interests (*polzy*).[36] The next stage in the administrative integration of Poland was the creation of two departments of the Senate in September 1841.[37] The Ninth would take up civil litigation, the Tenth, criminal cases. The Polish State Council was closed, and its jurisdiction was taken over by the general assembly of the two departments, chaired by the viceroy, except for the examination of the estimates, which went to the Polish Department in Petersburg. Thus the examination of the entire gamut of Polish laws and regulations became integrated into the machinery of the imperial government.

At the same time, Poland retained its separate status, which makes it possible to claim that it was not becoming just another region of the expanding core. The term viceroy (*namestnik*) had had several meanings in Russian administrative history, but it acquired a distinctive one during the reign of Nicholas I. There were only two such viceroys in the nineteenth century – in Poland and in the Caucasus – and one toward the end of the dynasty, in the Far East, in 1903. Elsewhere, a governor general had jurisdiction over a region and usually had no military command. He was an organ of territorial administration, but was gradually transformed into the regional agent of the interior ministry. Ministries were agents of functional administration, to a large extent incompatible with territorial administration. Ministries kept chipping away at the jurisdiction of the territorial agent, and provincial and regional administration began to resemble central administration – a collection of functional agents without a strong coordinating agent. As a result, the governor general eventually retained only a political responsibility (to the emperor) for peace and security in a given frontier territory.[38] On the other hand, a viceroy was an agent of pure territorial administration. Ministers could not bypass him, but had to send their directives to him to be forwarded to their local agents, and these had to send their reports to the viceroy to be sent on to the respective minister. The battle between the proponents of territorial administration and those of functional administration continued throughout the nineteenth century and was a major feature in the policy to create a unitary state.

The new viceroy was Field Marshal Ivan Paskevich, who was given the title of Prince of Warsaw for crushing the Polish uprising. He was born in Poltava in 1782, possibly of Polish descent. His grandfather was a Cossack officer; his father served in the new judiciary in Ekaterynoslav and Voznessensk in the 1790s, but, like many others of his generation, understood that the future of ambitious families lay in entering the Russian elite. Ivan was admitted to the Corps of Pages in 1793, was already a major general in 1810, and commanded a Guard division and later the Caucasus Separate Corps from 1827 to 1832. He died in Warsaw in 1856.[39] He managed to forge an unusually close relationship with Nicholas I, fourteen years his junior, who had served under him when he was still a grand duke, and who always called him his "father-commander."

Paskevich was a great believer in the creation of a unitary state, despite the fact that his own position denied the possibility. When he was in the Caucasus, he had called for the full integration of eastern Georgia into the expanding Russian core. When he arrived in Warsaw, he was eager to introduce the Russian administrative system. "Unfortunately," he was told to proceed by the Organic Statute of 1832, which restricted his full freedom of action. But he knew that Poland needed to be ruled with exceptional powers (*iz'iatiia iz zakona i otstupleniia ot form*) established by the laws – a concise description of the essence of the rivalry between territorial and functional administration: a power above the law versus the ministerial defenders of legality. Such a power was necessary because the land between the Oder and the Niemen was "the nest of all disturbances for Russia" and "the ulcer" (*iazva*) of the empire. Ministers were too far away to administer efficiently the distant borderlands like Finland, the Caucasus, Siberia (and Poland).[40] Thus the creation of an extra-legal regional jurisdiction was deemed better able to bring about the full integration than the delegates of distant, functional, law-bound ministries with which it was incompatible.

Paskevich did not entirely get his way, but Nicholas I gave him virtually dictatorial powers. A major reorganization of the army took place in the 1830s. Two field armies had been created with the return of Russian troops from Europe in 1814–15, the First and Second, headquartered in Mogilev in Belorussia and Tulchin in Podolia. The Second Army was abolished in July 1830, the First in July 1835, and both were replaced by an Active Army. This active (and overstretched) army consisted of six infantry corps. The I guarded the entire Baltic coast from Petersburg to Vilno; the II and III garrisoned Poland and the neighbouring provinces of Grodno and Volhynia. The IV was deployed in the Russian interior, and the V in Kiev, Podolia, and Poltava. Finally, the VI watched the Turkish border in Bessarabia and Kherson province,[41] under the overall command of the war minister. The first four were subordinated to the viceroy, who was thus the commander in chief of the Russian army in the entire western theatre except Finland. He possessed extraordinary jurisdiction for a regional authority (one is reminded of Potemkin under Catherine II) and, in addition, he often ruled by martial law: it was imposed in 1831 and lifted later, but unofficially, it was reintroduced in 1846 and would remain in effect until

1856. There were also four battalions of garrisoned troops in Warsaw, Novogeorgievsk, and Zamość (and Brest-Litovsk). They formed the Tenth Region of the Corps of Internal Troops, but were subordinated to the viceroy.[42] The separate corps of gendarmes, created in 1827, was also divided into regions, of which Poland formed the Third beginning in 1832. It was given its own statute in July 1844. The gendarmes too were subordinated to the viceroy, but their commanding general (and head of the infamous Third Section) had a say in personnel matters.[43]

The existence of these two military regions represented an intrusion of functional military administration into the territorial jurisdiction of the viceroy. There was more to come. In November 1839, Polish schools and institutions of higher learning had been combined to form a Warsaw region of the Ministry of Education under its own regional agent.[44] In December 1846, the Administration of Roads and Waterways created a new, Thirteenth, Region for Poland, "fully dependent" on the viceroy, with centres in Avgustov, Warsaw, and Radom.[45] In January 1848, Russians weights and measures were introduced "in view of the increasing trade and industrial relations" between "the empire and the *tsarstvo*."[46] In January 1851, the Polish postal administration was subordinated to the director of the Imperial Postal Department.[47] In 1850, the customs barrier between the two was abolished,[48] and Poland became integrated into the larger market of the expanding Russian core.

This gradual penetration of the institutions of the core into Poland was not necessarily imposed against the viceroy's will because they contributed to the integration of the territory, but he could not but be aware that the arrival of regional directors of various ministries was undermining his authority. He complained in 1847 that education, finance, the judiciary, the political police, and all the important matters were being integrated into the imperial administration and that his full authority was constricted as a result. Finland, he wrote, was less dependent on the ministries than Poland.[49]

A paradox indeed, but one inherent to Paskevich's own position: he could not strive to integrate Poland and retain his undiluted authority. In a very subtle way, the viceroy was slowly becoming, like his colleague Vorontsov in the Caucasus, the regional agent of the war ministry, much as the governor general in Finland had already become the regional agent of the navy ministry. Functional administration, the bearer of the unitary state idea, was slowly gaining the upper hand, and would triumph in the 1860s and 1870s.

The Western Provinces

Russia's orientation toward the German states, anchored in a close alliance with Prussia, together with the annexation of Congress Poland and the transformation of Sweden into a Russian satellite until the 1840s, had the effect of making Lithuania, Belorussia, and the Baltic provinces into internal frontiers of the nascent Russian empire. Despite the efforts of Paul I to restore the "privileges," the old impulse to create a unitary state reasserted itself right after his death, and a bundle of complex and at times contradictory policies endeavoured to complete the full integration of those provinces, begun by Catherine II, but suspended by her son. It is customary to distinguish the "northwestern" provinces – a term that came into being in the 1840s – from the provinces of the "Eastern Sea" (*Ostzeiskie*) – a German word for the Baltic – but in this short survey it will be more appropriate to combine them into a single region of "western provinces" along the inner periphery of western Eurasia, facing west indeed, but increasingly drawn eastward under the impact of Russian rule.

In December 1796, Paul I ordered the merger of Vilno and Slonim provinces to form a single "Lithuanian" province, capital Vilno, and that of Polotsk and Mogilev to form a "Belorussian" province, capital Vitebsk, considered more "convenient." Minsk province remained separate.[50] By 1802, however, there were five provinces once again, with Vilno, Grodno (replacing Slonim), Vitebsk, Mogilev, and Minsk as provincial capitals. Nevertheless, Vitebsk province continued to be called "Belorussian" until 1840. The annexation of the Bialystock territory in July 1808 added a sixth, but one called *oblast* because of its small size.[51] There were no further significant changes until December 1842, when the *oblast* was abolished and incorporated into Grodno province. At the same time, six northern counties of Vilno province and part of a seventh were separated to form a new Kovno province, including Samogitia between the Niemen and the Vindava Rivers, together with the triangular land between the Sventa and Viliia Rivers.[52] In December 1819, the port of Polangen had been transferred from Lithuania to Kurland province.[53] Situated two kilometres from the Prussian border, the port had a Lithuanian population, and had historically been part of Lithuania. It also had given Samogitia an outlet to the sea. The transfer made Kurland contiguous with East Prussia and blocked Lithuania's direct access to the outside world.

The western provinces numbered nine, including the three Baltic German ones. They covered an area of 401,745 square kilometres, or about three-fourths of France. The administration of their heterogeneous population would cause the Russians much trouble, and the emergence of a national consciousness among the various groups would wreck all hopes of creating stable societies within a unitary state. Table 3.1 shows the size and share of the various nationalities (in thousands) in 1850.[54] These nearly eight million people represented only 11.4 per cent of the total population of the Russian "empire" (69,731,800), but their importance was far out of proportion to their small share because of their strategic location, different faiths, political clout, and an existential struggle between Poland's Catholic and Russia's Eurasian civilizations.

Table 3.1 Sizes and shares of nationalities in the western provinces, 1850

	Population size (thousands)	%
Poles	369.4	4.6
Germans	131.3	1.6
Russians	690.8	8.7
Estonians	673.1	8.4
Latvians	931.4	11.7
Lithuanians	884.6	11.1
Belorussians	3,462.1	43.4
Jews	531.4	6.7
Others	296.4	3.7
Total	*7,970.5*	*100.0*

Source: Kabuzan, *Narody Rossii v pervoi polovine XIX v.*, 122–3, 125.

Paul I disliked the institution of governor general because it constituted an intermediate level between himself and the provincial governors, the equivalent of his divisional commanders in the army. However, he created the position of military governor, which would become the core of the new governor generalships during the reigns of his two sons. The distinguishing responsibility of a military governor was the command of the garrison, which placed a military force at his disposal in the event of popular disorders in the provincial capital or in the surrounding countryside. He resided in the provincial capital together with a civilian governor but, at times, also combined both military and civilian jurisdiction without the assistance of a civilian governor. There was a military governor in Riga, assisted by a "civilian commander in chief" for Livland and Estland (who never went to Riga), and military governors in Vyborg, Vitebsk, and Vilno. Minsk was combined with Kiev under a military governor residing in Kiev.[55] Their tenure was for the most part very short.

Paul's reign would not be worth mentioning in this matter, were it not for the fact that the emperor was determined to undo the work of his mother, not only for personal reasons, but also for reasons of policy. His orientation was pro-German and pro-Polish, and this required a new attitude toward the western provinces. He restored their privileges, and Alexander Gradovskii, in a typically Russian misunderstanding of European history, would write that the Baltic provinces fell prey once again to the knights and burghers, "the two plagues of feudal Europe."[56] Paul also closed the agencies created by Catherine II's reforms, and this, at first glance, seemed to mean a departure from a policy of integration. There was a significant reservation, however. The provincial board and the treasury chamber would remain and continue to operate in accordance with "general state legislation" (*ustanovleniia*).[57] Thus there would be two parallel systems: the most important (general administration, police, and finance) would follow Russian laws, while the judiciary and the government of the estates – the *Landräte* and their Collegium were restored – would operate in accordance with their privileges.

With the accession of Alexander I in March 1801, a difficult period began, dominated by the conflict with Napoleon. The creation of the Duchy of Warsaw raised hopes in Lithuania of an eventual recovery of the borders of 1772, and the threat of a French invasion raised insecurity in the Baltic provinces. After Napoleon's army was rolled back into Poland, the German nobility gained considerable influence in the military establishment; many scores had to be settled in Lithuania, which was subjected to a regime of arbitrary police power, denunciations, and confiscations,[58] while Poles, Lithuanians, and Russians sought to create a new equilibrium that would finally bring peace to the territory.

In the Baltic provinces, there was at first a governor general – the title reappeared – for Livland, Estland, and Kurland from 1801 to 1808, then a separate governor general for Estland alone and another for Livland and Kurland until 1819, when the three provinces were again combined under a single governor general residing in Riga, who was given additional jurisdiction over Pskov province from 1823 to 1829. He was General Filippo Paulucci (1779–1849), the former commander in chief in the Caucasus, who had been military governor of Riga and governor general of Livland in Kurland from 1812 to 1819.[59]

In Belorussia, Vitebsk and Mogilev provinces remained combined under a military governor in Vitebsk until 1822, save for a short interval between 1807 and 1811, when each province had its own civil governor. Minsk remained joined to Kiev until 1816, when a civil governor took over in Minsk. Beginning in 1823, Vitebsk and Mogilev were combined with Smolensk and Kaluga under a governor general, Lt.-Gen. Prince Nikolai Khovansky. Minsk was added later. Further west, in Lithuania, the Russians pursued a different policy. Belorussia was a land to be fully integrated as soon as possible, but they recognized the continued administrative gravitation of Lithuania toward Poland. The two provinces had each a civil governor subordinated to a military governor in Vilno continuously from 1801 to 1831. The leading figure was General Alexander Rimsky-Korsakov (1753–1840).[60] In June 1822, in the wake of concerns over the growth of a revolutionary movement, Grand Duke Constantine in Warsaw was given the powers of a commander in chief in wartime, in accordance with the statute of January 1812, over Vilno, Grodno, and Minsk provinces. The decision had the effect of placing the provinces under martial law; they remained in that state until the outbreak of the Polish uprising in December 1830.[61]

Alexander's reign witnessed a revival of the old assumptions in certain parts of the ruling elite about their privileges as well as of an unconcealed resentment against "the Germans." The most articulate spokesman of the critics was Dmytro Troshchynsky, the justice minister from 1814 to 1817. He went back to the "capitulations" of 1710 and emphasized the importance of the restrictive clause in the relationship between the privileges and the legislation of the expanding core. "No matter how you look at them," he wrote, "privileges are nothing but exemptions from the general laws, and they are justified [*spravedlivye*] only so long as the advantages resulting from them exceed the disadvantages from the non-execution of the general laws."[62] While his criticism was directed against the Baltic Germans, it applied just as well to the Poles in the Grand Duchy. Privileges were essentially static, while "imperial" legislation was dynamic, because it was engaged in a process of constant adjustment to changing circumstances. The rights of local bodies and estates to regulate their affairs were residual rights, valid only so long as the ruling elite so decided. The highly tense international situation during Alexander's reign dictated caution in any systematic attack on the privileges, but it would come with full fury during the reign of his brother, Nicholas I.

That reign began with the Decembrist uprising and the discovery of Polish underground societies opposed to Russian rule. The Warsaw uprising came five years later. The antagonism of the Poles, contrasted with the loyalty of the Baltic Germans, and the death of Constantine, helped an incipient Russian policy to finally crystallize. Lt.-Gen. Karl Freiherr von der Pahlen, nephew of the first governor general of Kurland in 1795, was appointed to succeed Paulucci in 1830, four years after the selection of Alexander von Benckendorff to head the Third Section and the Corps of Gendarmes. The alliance of the two men, the nucleus of a Baltic German network – described sarcastically by Iurii Samarin, an official of the interior ministry, as the "ministry of Baltic Affairs in the capital" – guaranteed that the privileges would not suffer irreparable harm. Benckendorff's death in 1844 and Pahlen's recall in 1845 were followed by the appointment of Lt.-Gen. Evgenii Golovin (1845–8), who supported a more active policy, but his short tenure showed the continuing strength of the German lobby and its support by the emperor, who once remarked that the Baltic German families had contributed 150 generals to the Russian army. His successor, Lt.-Gen Count Alexander Suvorov-Rimniksky – grandson of the famous field marshal – would remain for thirteen years (1848–61). He was a Germanophile who sympathized with the privileges and accepted the view that their retention was more advantageous than their removal, in order to create a unitary state.[63]

In Belorussia and Lithuania, however, Nicholas I pursued a very harsh policy. In January 1831, when the Russian counteroffensive began, Kaluga was removed from under Khovansky's jurisdiction, leaving only the three Belorussian and Smolensk provinces (still very Polonized) in the governor generalship.[64] At the same time, but in eastern Belorussia alone, Russian administrative and judicial agencies were introduced; procedures would have to follow those introduced in the expanding core in 1775, and the operation of the Lithuanian Statute was terminated. This was extended in October to Vilno, Grodno, and

Minsk provinces, but the Lithuanian Statute remained in effect there until June 1840. That year, the emperor decreed that the terms “Belorussia” and “Lithuania” must no longer be used in official correspondence.[65] In September 1831, a Committee for the affairs of the western provinces had been created in Petersburg to examine the privileges and prepare the full integration into the expanding core. It was closed in 1848, when the northwestern provinces were finally integrated into the unitary state (*obshchii poriadok*), and provincial agencies would have to deal with the relevant ministries in the capital.[66]

The emperor's visceral hatred of the Poles was no secret. One of his most faithful disciples was Mikhail Muravev (1796–1866), the governor of Mogilev from 1828 to 1831 and thirty years later governor general of the northwestern provinces and commanding general of the Vilno Military Region (1863–5), who earned then the infamous title of “the Vilno Hangman” for his brutal repression of another Polish uprising in Lithuania. He advocated the appointment of a viceroy in Lithuania, anticipating the appointment of Paskevich in Warsaw, free from ministerial interference, in order to impose a “solid and uniform foundation” (*prochnoe i edinoobraznoe osnovanie*) grounded in the Statute of 1775, as had already been done in financial administration everywhere. All governors and provincial officials must be replaced by native (*korennye*) Russians depending on the viceroy, and none must be appointed without his approval. Polish place names must be replaced by Russian ones. The Lithuanian Statute must be abolished in order to achieve a “moral rapprochement” (*sblizhenie*) with the expanding Russian core.[67]

No viceroy was appointed, but Muravev's recommendations in this and other matters became official policy. The Lithuanian provinces were placed under hard-line governors general: Lt.-Gens. Prince Nikolai Dolgorukov (1831–40), Fedor Mirkovich (1840–50), and Ilia Bibikov (1850–5), brother of Dmitrii, the hard-line governor general of the Southwest (1837–52).[68] These governors general could not but feel the influence and pressures emanating from Warsaw, where Paskevich outranked them and commanded the troops stationed in their provinces. They also carried out the directives of their administrative superior, the interior minister, especially Lev Perovsky (1841–52), a strong believer in administrative integration, who was succeeded by Dmitrii Bibikov (1852–5) and by Muravev as both minister of crown properties (*udely*) and state domains (1856–62). These men formed a team under the emperor, dedicated to the eradication of the privileges, the extirpation of Poland's political, religious, and cultural influence, and the full integration of Lithuania, following that of Belorussia in the 1830s.

The military integration of the northwestern provinces had already taken place with the creation of the First Army in October 1814. The headquarters of its I Corps was in Mitava (Kurland), with four divisions in Kurland (two), Riga, and Vitebsk, and two divisions of the Lithuanian Corps, the latter under the command of Constantine in Warsaw, deployed in Lithuania and based in Bialystock. After the creation of the Active Army in 1832, troops in the former Grand Duchy belonged to the III Corps. The recruiting system had been introduced everywhere during and after the reign of Paul I, but the Regulation of June 1831 retained some exceptions for the Baltic provinces "so long as they are not at variance with these provisions."[69] Garrisons were combined to form regions, as elsewhere in Russia proper. Estland, Livland, and Kurland (with Petersburg and Pskov) were in the First Region, Vitebsk and Mogilev (with Smolensk, Kaluga, Moscow, and Orel) were part of the Sixth; Vilno, Grodno, and Minsk of the Eighth. The Tenth included the Polish *tsarstvo*. This region was reorganized in November 1833, but, unlike the others, it was under the command of the viceroy, despite the fact that it was part of the Separate Corps of Internal Troops. Also as everywhere else, the Corps of Gendarmes had its own regions: the three Baltic provinces belonged to the First Region, and the five provinces of the former Grand Duchy to the Fourth, with detachments in Dünaburg and Bobruisk.[70]

In civilian administration, Dorpat and Vilno universities became centres of regions of the education ministry in 1803. The Vilno region was much larger and included the northwestern and southwestern provinces under Czartoryski (1803–23), who was often absent and abandoned his duties to Tadeusz Czacki, who did not quite grasp that the provinces had been annexed to Russia. After a short interval, Czartoryski was succeeded by his nemesis, the notorious Novosiltsev (1824–32). In the wake of the uprising, Vilno University was closed in May 1832 (it would not reopen until 1918), and Dorpat became the only university in the entire western theatre. The region was broken up, with Minsk annexed in January 1831 to a new Belorussian region created in 1829 with Vitebsk and Mogilev provinces detached from the Petersburg region; Vilno and Grodno provinces were added to it in 1832. In 1850, however, the Vilno region was recreated, Vitebsk and Minsk were returned to the Petersburg region, and the Belorussian region was abolished. The new Vilno region was placed under the authority of Governor General Bibikov (1850–6).[71] The northwest provinces had thus been fully integrated into the regional network of the education ministry.

Ten regions of the Administration of Roads and Waterways had been created in November 1809, centred on river basins which cut across provincial boundaries. A part of Mogilev province was in the Fifth region, the other in the Seventh with the Baltic provinces, Vitebsk province, and part of Vilno province; the remainder was in the Sixth Region with Grodno and Minsk. The reorganization of November 1843 retained only two regional headquarters, one in Riga, the other in Mogilev. The reform of the postal administration of 1830 placed the three Baltic provinces in the First Region, Vilno, Grodno, and Minsk in the Fifth, and Vitebsk and Mogilev in the Sixth. The regional division was abolished in 1853, and all the provinces of the western theatre, except Poland, were henceforth administered directly from Petersburg, together with the Russian provinces of the interior.[72] We can see in this string of reforms throughout the reign of Nicholas I the operation of a systematic policy of integration – muted in the Baltic provinces – in the pursuit of the eventual creation of a unitary state.

Society, Law, and Trade

The Failure of Superstratification

Russian policy toward the ruling class of the various provinces of the western theatre was very complex, because there were significant structural differences both between the provinces and within them. It was not so much that Russian policy was contradictory, reflecting as it did the views of various groupings within the ruling elite, as that the situation on the ground often required different responses, creating an impression of internal contradictions. Moreover, as integration proceeded apace, policies in the frontier followed similar developments within the core. Briefly stated, beginning with the reign of Paul I, certainly after 1815, and above all during the reign of Nicholas I, we witness the emergence of a military state, in which the monarchy drew its legitimacy from the support of an enormous military establishment and a stratum of large aristocratic landowners, but ignored the lower strata of the ruling class, now considered irrelevant to its good fortunes. Ruling elite and ruling class became estranged, and the monarchy developed into an exclusive military and administrative state. The result would be to destabilize the system, beginning in the late 1860s, when the lower strata began joining up with the emerging intelligentsia to monopolize politics and challenge the supremacy of the administrative state, eventually rendering the monarchy totally irrelevant.

The general purpose of the Charter of the nobility granted in April 1785 had been to create corporations of nobles in the new provinces to take up the tasks of local government for their own benefit. It was granted in the context of a general backlash against the growth of the administrative state after Peter's reign. The Statute of December 1831 regulated the provincial elections by the nobility but was inspired by different motives. The basic assumption was that the nobility was indeed a ruling class – as long as it was properly purged – comprising those who had served in the army and the upper ranks of the administration. Both Paul I and Nicholas I stated at various times that the landlords were their police agents in the countryside. The government had extended the Charter to all the provinces of the expanding core; the Statute applied everywhere save in the Baltic provinces, where the *Landtags*, which gradually assimilated the

Russian practice of meeting every three years, continued to elect to positions found nowhere else.[73]

The Statute increased the number of elective positions, but also gave civil service status to those elected. It raised property qualifications, and restricted the right to elect and be elected to those with at least one hundred serfs or 3,000 *desiatin* (3,300 hectares or 8,100 acres), a very large area indeed. The supplementary legislation of 1836 gave an extraordinary advantage to those who had achieved high rank in the service but had little property: those who reached grade 5 (state councillor or former "brigadier," between a colonel and a major general – the rank no longer existed) needed to have only five serfs or 100 *desiatins* of land. All other nobles, including hereditary ones, who did not meet these qualifications were disfranchised.[74] Finally, the Manifesto of June 1845 sharply restricted access to the status of hereditary noble: while the 1831 Statute had retained the old provisions of the Table of Ranks of January 1722, which gave hereditary status to all officers and to civilians who reached grade 8 (college assessor or army major), the manifesto gave that status only to officers who reached grade 8 and civilians who reached grade 5 (instead of 8).[75] In those three documents, the ruling elite carried out a political purge by coopting the upper stratum of the ruling class and disfranchising the rest.

A peculiar feature of the ruling class of the western provinces was that it was already an alien intruder before the arrival of the Russians: the Swedes in Finland, the Germans in the Baltic provinces, the Poles in the Grand Duchy. As elsewhere, the Russians needed to consolidate the position of those elites over the native peoples, Finns, Estonians and Latvians, Belorussians and Lithuanians, thereby reaching an accommodation in which loyalty to the expanding core was traded for the retention of local domination. But, as nowhere else, if that original and alien stratum refused such an accommodation – and even if it did not – the temptation could become irresistible to use the dependent native population against their masters, especially where old historical ties and the Orthodox confession created affinities between the new intruder and the native peoples. If the Russians chose that course, however, they were certain to antagonize the very top stratum upon which they depended to administer territories where the Russian population was insignificant. No policy of superstratification would be possible, and destructive tensions were certain to follow. Such a situation explains the hesitations of Russian policy against a clear determination to carry out the full integration of the western provinces.[76]

Tensions were least in evidence in Finland. Swedish settlements – some going as far back as the thirteenth century – were concentrated in the coastal strip east and west of Helsingfors, the skerries off Åbo, and on the Åland Islands. Their society was highly stratified, the Swedes higher up on the socio-economic scale regarding with "vast disdain" the fishing and farming population.[77] Nevertheless, it was a pluralistic society which had never known serfdom and the brutalization of relationships it always entails. Since early times, there had been a class of independent peasantry which, under Swedish rule, had been represented in the *Riksdag*. The ownership of land was not a noble monopoly, clergy and burghers (also represented in the Swedish Parliament) had been allowed to own noble land since 1723, and peasants, more recently, since 1789. "Many parsonages and peasant estates were comparable to noble ones in wealth and stateliness."[78]

Beginning in the seventeenth century, the nobility had chosen the army as a career to fight in the Swedish army building a Baltic empire, but they retained an independent streak: there always had been a separatist sentiment in the Grand Duchy, nurtured during the long winter months, when Finland was completely cut off from Sweden. Nevertheless, the Swedish ruling class, including Swedified Finns, was also known for its exploitation of the Finnish people, so much so that General Barclay de Tolly, the "Russian" commander in chief and governor general of Finland (1809–10), himself a "German" from Livland (but of Scottish origin), wrote in 1809 that he opposed the creation of the governing council as "the pernicious project of the first class of inhabitants with the malicious design to later seize the reins of government in order to oppress and suck [the blood of] the inferior class."[79]

The nobility underwent a crisis in 1809, when Alexander I disbanded the Finnish troops who had served in the Swedish army, and left some fifteen thousand officers and non-commissioned officers without a living. However, he granted them generous pensions the following year, thus ensuring their loyalty, and even encouraging them to serve in the Russian army, and many did. Other nobles made a career in the new agencies created by the Russian government, and by the 1820s about half of the higher officials were nobles.[80] When the Table of Ranks was introduced in Finland in January 1842,[81] these Swedo-Finnish officials were incorporated into the ruling class of the expanding core. They formed a small coterie of men – fewer than two thousand in number – who administered the land and dispensed justice, honest, deeply conservative, and loyal, consisting of interconnected families resembling "the branches of family trees, interwoven through the trellis-work of the rank system."[82] The paradox was striking: a natural internal evolution in a land which retained so many of its laws and customs brought about the very same result which the legislation of the expanding core was seeking to achieve everywhere else.

In the Baltic provinces, old tensions remained. The nobility was described by a German traveller in 1841 as consisting of many "independent kings" but organized in corporations represented in the *Landtags*. These still elected for life an executive committee called the *Landtagskollegium* in Estland and Livland, the *Ritterschaftskomite* in Kurland, which appointed nobles to enforce law and order, dispense justice, run the affairs of the Lutheran Church, and take up any matter which they found needed their attention. The triennual *Landtags* were chaired by the *Landmarschall* in Livland and the *Ritterschaftshauptmann* in Estland, and the corporation kept a "resident *Landrat*" in Riga. The corporation on Ösel Island was modelled after that of Livland.[83] These men were staunchly loyal to the Romanov house, but their loyalty was of a feudal kind – understandable among families most of which descended from the Livonian Knights – not to Russia as such. They also expected loyalty to work from the top down, taking for granted that the monarchy would respect their privileges.

But the nobility, taken as a whole, was not a homogeneous body, and suffered from internal strains. There was the matriculated nobility, previously described, the core of the estate, possessing large tracts of land cultivated by Estonian and Latvian serfs. These nobles were the equivalent of the upper stratum which Russia was seeking to create, who combined wealth and power, and would be the natural ally of the Russian ruling elite. Here, as in Finland, a process of social integration had been taking place, and it would accelerate with the military integration of so many of its members into the Russian army. There were also nobles who resented being kept out of the *Matrikel*. They too were landowners and sat in the *Landtag*, but were "kept strictly on the margins," allowed to vote on matters of taxation – this only in Livland – but given little else to say or do.[84] A third group consisted of landowners who were not noble, but they would be in Russia, where the nobility enjoyed a monopoly of serf ownership. These people were inclined to seek Russian support to bring about a closer integration of Russian and Baltic social legislation. A fourth group included nobles who acquired their status in the service by promotion in accordance with the Table of Ranks, but had neither land nor serfs. There had been some accommodation, however: in 1774, the Livland *Landtag* authorized non-noble landowners to acquire noble land unless it was redeemed by other nobles within a certain time. All these people challenged the legality of the *Matrikel* and formed a latent opposition to the hegemony of the matriculated nobility.

A fifth group consisted of certain Russian aristocratic families which were barred from acquiring estates in the Baltic provinces, did not understand the caste-like mentality of the matriculated nobility, and felt that since Germans had the same rights as Russians to acquire estates in Russia, they too should have the same rights in the Baltic provinces – another factor encouraging social integration. And finally, there were Russian officials in nearby Petersburg who also felt socially excluded. The exclusive privilege of the matriculated nobility was gradually whittled down during the first half of the nineteenth century, and all social groups eventually gained the right to acquire land, with Estland, the most conservative of the three provinces – which kept insisting that the matriculated nobility alone had this right – finally giving in during the reign of Alexander II.[85] All these groups had an interest in seeking closer integration with Russia in order to break up the hegemony of the matriculated nobility. The ruling elite of Catherine II's Russia had understood this simple fact, and

Table 3.2 Population of nobility in the Grand Duchy of Lithuania, 1834

	Population		Population		Population
Vitebsk	16,004	Vilno	24,887	Estland	1,193
Mogilev	16,794	Kovno	37,722	Livland	6,033
Minsk	35,110	Grodno	23,255	Kurland	979
Subtotals	*67,908*		*85,864*		*8,205*

Source: Kabuzan and Troitskii, "Izmeneniia," 163–4.
Note: The nobility in Vitebsk, Mogilev, Minsk, Vilno, Kovno, and Grodno made up 5.5 per cent of the total population of those provinces; in the Baltic provinces of Estland, Livland, and Kurland, the nobility made up 1 per cent of the total population.

had ordered the elimination of the *Landrat* system. Neither Alexander I nor Nicholas I was willing to go that far; if they broke up the hold of the caste of *Landräte*, who would govern the Baltic provinces? Even the most important social development of the period – the emancipation of the Estland, Livland, and Kurland peasantry between 1816 and 1819[86] – created misgivings, and the Russian government left the drafting of the statutes to the matriculated nobility, which used the opportunity to reinforce its police and judicial power over a now largely landless rural proletariat, causing rising peasant unrest in the 1840s. There was no need for Petersburg to purge the ruling class of the three provinces: the matriculated nobility had been doing it for a long time.

Tensions were much greater in the former Grand Duchy of Lithuania, and became highly destructive. The nobility (*szlachta*) was much more numerous than in the Baltic provinces and its percentage of the total population much higher, as shown in table 3.2 for 1834.[87]

As we already know, the *szlachta* was a highly heterogeneous body despite its insistence that all its members were equal. There were the magnates, who owned enormous properties, like the Radziwills, the Oginskis, and the Sapiehas, "independent kings" like the Baltic German aristocrats, a middle group of landowners, and a large noble proletariat, who paid rent on the land of other lords, served in a magnate household, or were no more than vagrants. The noble proletariat were a coarse lot, uneducated and stubborn, and prone to rebel against established authority. But they had voted in the old provincial assemblies, bribed by the more powerful lords. Catherine II chose to ignore the differences and recognized them all as nobles with the same rights as the Russian nobility, but doubts were soon raised about the validity of their titles, when new assemblies were required to draw up rolls of nobles in their provinces. The Russians did not like the practice of electing officials for life, the noisy demonstrations as in the old days of the Polish Empire, and the universal franchise enjoyed by the *szlachta*. There also existed a deep-seated (and reciprocal) antagonism and resentment between Poles and Russians, and the behaviour of the Polish army in 1812, including the sack of Smolensk and Moscow by Polish units in Napoleon's army, "reawakened ancient hatreds."[88]

In 1802, the new assemblies were required to follow the Statute of 1775 and elect their judges and marshals for three years, with the confirmation of the governor; in 1804, participation was restricted to landowners whose annual revenue was at least 150 roubles or who had held positions in the civil or military service. In 1809, nobles found responsible for causing disorder when assemblies were in session were ordered disfranchised. Some officials began to think of turning to the native population. A memorandum of possibly 1810, found in the war ministry, expressed hope that the Belorussians would eventually become completely Russified: "the hatred of Russia, found in all of Poland, comes not from the native population; the source is in the Polish families, the irreconcilable enemies of Russia, the descendants of the old conquerors of Rus'."[89]

The offensive against the *szlachta* took the form of a requirement, stated and restated again and again at least until the 1840s, that all members of the *szlachta* must give evidence of their status, not an easy task in any case following the scattering of the archives in the territory of three powers and the destruction of property during the first decade of Alexander I's reign. The final confirmation of the evidence was vested in the Heraldry, a department of the Senate in Petersburg. The process could take a long time. Then came the uprising of 1831, which found active support among the petty *szlachta* in the "turbulent frontier" between the Polish and the German worlds north of the Vistula and in the large Vilno province, including Samogitia. Support for the rebellion brought about the completion of the purge of the *szlachta* that had been going on for a generation. The Statute of October 1831 degraded nobles who could not prove their status to the condition of townsman (*grazhdanin*) if they lived in towns, or of *odnodvorets* if they lived in the countryside, a category of state peasant in Russia. They were deported en masse to the southern theatre to the Caucasus or to Siberia, and were declared liable to military service in a proportion four times, later reduced to twice, as high as for other classes.[90] What impact all this had on the size of the *szlachta* is difficult to say.[91] The decree of October 1835 was directed against the *szlachta* who refused to serve in the civil or military service: if they did not serve ten years in it, they would be disfranchised, and the interior ministry would fill vacancies with appointed officials.[92]

But all this did not break the hold of the Polish *szlachta* on the political, social, and economic life of the Grand Duchy, above all in Lithuania. There was no question of emancipation, and serfdom of the worst kind remained, as the Decembrist Andrei Rosen wrote in his memoirs in the 1830s: landlords treated the dependent population with "insolent haughtiness" (*derzkoe vysokomerie*) and the peasants as slaves.[93] It could still be said in 1858 that 95 per cent of the landowners in Vilno province, 94 per cent in Minsk province, and 82 per cent in Kiev province were Poles. "Twenty years of anti-*szlachta* policy in the western provinces obviously had not broken the back of Polish social and economic power."[94] In Lithuania, where the Russian population was not much higher than in the Baltic provinces, there was no alternative to relying on the Polish *szlachta*, but these people belonged to a Polish civilization which was that of a core fighting for its survival. The Poles were indeed the irreconcilable enemies of Russia, and compromise was possible only in individual cases. The policy of stratification was bound to fail, and its failure would bring much suffering to both Poles and Lithuanians.

The Russo-Polish antagonism was strongest in the *tsarstvo*, where the Russians discovered in 1813 that they were not welcome, while they had been well received by the Swedish ruling class in Finland. There was "tedium and coldness everywhere," wrote one of their commanders.[95] The antagonism flared up in 1831, when the Russians felt betrayed, prompting Nicholas I to vent his visceral hatred of Poles and tell them in Warsaw that, at the slightest disturbance (*émeute*), "I will destroy [the city] and I will not be the one to rebuild it," a statement strikingly reminiscent of Repnin's warning in 1766.[96] Neither one could anticipate that not the Russians but the Germans would commit the dastardly act a century later. The Poles responded by giving themselves over to "a messianic creed,"[97] which only deepened a now unbridgeable divide. Confiscations and deportations did the rest. Yet, it was impossible to govern the *tsarstvo* without Poles. There were enough members of the aristocracy willing to work with the Russians, while the middle *szlachta* and the professionals could not accept the permanent loss of the "borders of 1772." About five-sixths of the *szlachta* belonged to a depressed class dependent on employers. They were the carriers of Polish hatred of Russia. Those who chose to work with the new government after 1832 had to fight against the "sullen non-cooperation" of other Poles, and earned "great unpopularity for their submissiveness to the viceroy." Nevertheless, they performed a great service to Poland, whose economy benefited from its proximity to, even integration into, the huge market of the expanding core. Superstratification could work only with a common interest in crushing peasant unrest, but the "deep fissure"[98] within the *szlachta*, together with an ethnic and religious antagonism between the two core civilizations, meant it never really had a chance to work.[99]

Codification

The failure of a policy of superstratification in Poland and the former Grand Duchy of Lithuania did not dampen the determination of the Russian government to harmonize the laws and institutions of the borderlands with those of the expanding core. Minister of the Interior Lev Perovsky, in his passionate call in December 1846 for the integration of their legal systems into a single "Ulozhenie of Nicholas I" – the *Ulozhenie* of 1649 was usually referred to as the Ulozhenie of Alexei Mikhailovich – rejected the concept of separate law codes for the borderlands: legal materials drawn from old charters and judicial precedents might be retained only as footnotes in a single Digest (*Svod Zakonov*), and this work must be done, not by a German or a Pole, as was being done, but by a Russian. However, Perovsky weakened his own case by ignoring the existence of separate nationalities with separate identities (*otdel'naia samobytnost naroda*) and calling for their integration into a single Slavic (*Slavianskii*) *narod* "stretching from the Baltic to the Adriatic Sea, from the Oder to Kamchatka, and from the cliffs of Finland to the approaches of the Balkans," merged to form "a single awesome power" (*odno tseloe groznoe mogushchestvo*).[100]

Institutional integration had long been in progress. The Russian Senate was the highest court of the expanding core. It had been divided into departments since 1763; by 1832, there were eight – four in Petersburg and three in Moscow.[101] The Third Department in Petersburg was the court of civil appeals from the three Baltic, three Belorussian, two Lithuanian (three after 1842), three Right Bank Ukraine, and two Little Russian provinces, and the Fifth Department, also in Petersburg, was the court of criminal review for the same thirteen provinces. Finland remained outside the system. Petitions for review against decisions of the Finnish Senate went to the minister state secretary. Poland had a High Court of Appeals in Warsaw, and petitions in cassation also went to the Polish minister state secretary in Petersburg. However, two additional Senate Departments were created in Warsaw in September 1841, the Ninth and Tenth for civil and criminal affairs respectively, and the Court of Appeal was abolished. The viceroy chaired the general assembly of both departments, to which belonged ex officio the members of the Administrative Council and the Warsaw military governor. Overall jurisdiction over this new Polish Senate was vested in the Polish "minister of justice," Ksawery Kossecki (1832–43) succeeded by Onufry Wyczechowski (1844–54).[102]

The task of codifying Russian law had a long history,[103] but it was becoming increasingly urgent by the end of Alexander I's reign, following the creation of the ministries and the growing scope of legislation – the first series alone of the *Complete Collection of Laws of the Russian Empire* (1649–1825) (which was almost complete) contains 30,600 documents, and there would be another 29,042 for the reign of Nicholas I alone. The laws had to be accessible to the ever greater number of officials and also to interested members of society, who all needed an authoritative version of what was still in force and what had been discarded with the passage of time: most of the 1649 *Ulozhenie* was no longer in force. To that effect, Nicholas I decided to concentrate the work of codification in a Second Section of his personal chancery in January 1826, immediately after his accession. Its director, Mikhail Speransky (1826–39), guided the work of publishing the first Digest in 1832. He was followed by Dmitrii Bludov (1839–61), who also chaired the Department of Laws of the State Council (1840–61).[104] The Second Section was given the task of also codifying the laws of the western and southern borderlands, but the task varied in each. Thus it is important to note that the codification of the borderlands' laws was part of an ambitious and comprehensive attempt to collect and systematize the legislation of the entire expanding core, including Russia.

The task was relatively easier in Finland, yet it failed. The Second Section decided that an eventual Finnish Code would have to follow the organization of the Digest, so that jurists would benefit from a concordance between both. A Finnish Codification Commission chaired by Carl Walleen proceeded to follow the instructions from the capital, but in so doing included a section on "basic laws" (*osnovnye zakony*) intended as an equivalent of the basic laws of the Digest. They were the Form of Government of 1772 and the Union and Security Act of 1789, which the Russians had never accepted because their principles were anathema to the government of an autocratic tsar-emperor. Bludov rejected the section in 1842. Moreover, there was opposition in the Finnish Senate and in Alexander University in Helsingfors to the way the Swedish Code of 1734 had been reworked and amended, if only to avoid citations which the Russians would feel were not "in accord" with Russian legislation.

This Code of 1734 consisted of nine parts dealing with marriage and inheritance law, land tenure, buildings, commerce, and market towns, crimes and punishments, and court procedure, but it omitted many provisions important in social and political life.[105] Filling those would have to be the work of subsequent legislation. Nevertheless, the Finns considered the Code to be "the irrevocable safeguard of their civil rights."[106] Menshikov, the governor general, was responsive to the rising opposition; as Chief of Staff of the Navy he wanted no trouble in a society of loyal and conservative Swedes and Finns who, unlike the Poles, never revolted and guaranteed the security of the northern shore of the Gulf of Finland. Nicholas agreed, and the commission was told to work only on an equivalent of the Complete Collection of the Laws of the Russian Empire, beginning with the Code of 1734 and containing subsequent amendments by the Swedish *Riksdag* and, after 1816, the Finnish Senate. But even this work was never completed: the Code of 1734 remained in force until the twentieth century, although a criminal code was published in 1899.[107] The status quo benefited both sides.

The task was much harder in the Baltic provinces, but it was there, and only there, that the drafting of a code of local laws was finally published. It had long been a work in progress. There had been a plan at the end of the sixteenth century, when Livland was part of the Polish Empire (1561–1621), to combine Polish-Lithuanian law with the old *Ritterschaft* law, but it never succeeded. When Sweden incorporated Estland into its empire (1561–1710), as well as Livland (1629–1710), it proposed to remove Polish laws which violated the privileges, but then proceeded to introduce Swedish law systematically until united opposition forced it to desist; Swedish law became only auxiliary law to fill the gaps which local law had ignored. The Swedish approach anticipated the Russian by more than a century: local law had to be identified and published, then had to be harmonized with Swedish legislation. In other words, local law was residual: it retained its value only so long as Swedish law did not supersede it. Some progress was made in Kurland, where the old Germanic Teutonic law continued to prevail and eventually produced a code of civil and criminal procedure in 1718.

During the Russian period, after 1710 in Estland and Livland, more attempts to codify Baltic German law led nowhere. There were two problems. The task was monumental. By the time the drafting of a code began in earnest in the 1830s, there were already twenty-three volumes of privileges written in Latin, German, and Swedish.[108] They were based on medieval papal bulls, statutes of the Holy Roman Empire of the sixteenth century, decisions of the empire's High Court (*Kammergericht*), medieval Saxon law, Swedish statutes, and also laws addressed to specific places or even individuals, such as the Pilten statute, the law of the Danish king Waldemar-Eric, the Lübeck law, the charters of Archbishop Silvester and of Bishop von Hellinghausen.[109] This immense body of laws and charters had first to be published in an easily available form, then systematized to follow the organization of the Digest. The other problem which impeded the production of a code for so long was that the confusion served the interests of parties ready to invoke more privileges, unknown to others, and whose original had supposedly disappeared. Without access to a systematized code, there was no way to challenge their claims. But there was also a danger. When all the privileges had presumably been published and systematized, there followed two consequences: parties to a suit could no longer invoke other privileges and the Russian Senate would be in a position to refer to the concordance between the local code and the Digest to challenge the validity of its provisions by claiming that the Russian "imperial" law had superseded the privileges and revoked their residual status.

Speransky hesitated between two methods: either drawing up a full code, even one modelled after the Digest, or adding footnotes (as would later be done for the Lithuanian Statute in Little Russia) to relevant articles indicating the existence of separate provisions for the Baltic provinces based on the privileges. Choosing the latter solution would de-emphasize the autonomous status of the region and reduce it to that of provinces of the Russian interior, to which a temporary exemption from the general law had been granted. The emperor, as a token of loyalty to his loyal *Ritterschaft*, eventually ordered the Second Section to prepare a full code. The work was entrusted in 1829 to *Landrat* Reinhold Samson von Himmelstiern (1778–1858), who had studied law in Leipzig (1796–8), had served in the chancery of the *Landratskollegium*, and was at the time vice-president of the Livland *Hofgericht* (1824–34, later president, 1851–6) and a member of the Livland legislative commission (1824–9). He was thus an authoritative figure, a member of the Livland ruling elite. There seem to have been some heated debates in the Second Section between Germans and Russians, and it was even claimed that the "capitulations" (*akkordnye punkty*) of 1710 had never been ratified by the emperor, that the originals could not be found, and that copies could well have altered the original text.[110]

Nevertheless, the edict of July 1845 announced the publication of a partial code in two parts, one dealing with local institutions, the other with social classes (*sosloviia*). It explained that what had been done in Little Russia in 1842 could not be repeated in the Baltic provinces because of the "complexity and diversity" (*mnogoslozhnost' i raznoobraznost'*) of the privileges. The project had been drawn up in the Second Section and examined in provincial committees and in a general commission of delegates in the capital, and finally in a general assembly of senators and members of the State Council. The decree announced the preparation of another three parts, for the civil law, and for civil and criminal procedures. The first was not published for another twenty years, in 1864, when a major reorganization of the Russian judiciary took place in Russia. The other two never were. The reform was extended to the Baltic provinces in 1889 and rendered much of the 1845 Code obsolete. In the end, it was the second method that prevailed: separate provisions for the provinces were appended as footnotes to the relevant articles of the Digest.[111] What struck some observers of the Code of 1845 was that it was no code at all, but a systematization of the privileges granted to "the most brilliant baronial properties": rights granted to one family were extended to the fortified manor (*zamok*), and stopped at the border of the neighbouring property. The Code was indeed a victory for the *Ritterschaft*'s particularism within a small German Fatherland that was no part of the expanding core.[112] The integrating impulse had stopped at the border of Estland, Livland, and Kurland.

A half-hearted effort was made in the former Grand Duchy of Lithuania. The Lithuanian Statute remained in force after Catherine II's death. There had been in pre-partition times a High (*Glavnyi*) Lithuanian Tribunal which met semi-annually alternately in Vilno and Grodno. Abolished in 1795, it was restored in 1797, but only as a provincial court for the single province of Lithuania. Vitebsk and Mogilev provinces formed a single Belorussian province which had its "main court." After 1802, when the two provinces were broken into two each (Vilno, Grodno, Vitebsk, and Mogilev), the main court in each continued to apply the Lithuanian Statute in their decisions. The edition of 1588 had been translated from "Ruthenian" into Polish in 1786, but the translation was considered very corrupt. Nevertheless, it was translated from Polish into Russian in 1811. The Committee of Ministers considered it unsatisfactory, and ordered the Ministry of Education to prepare a translation of the Polish edition of 1616 This was not done until 1834, too late to be of any use after the Polish rebellion of 1831. In the meantime, the decree of January 1831 had ordered that in criminal and administrative cases the courts could cite (*vmeshivat'*) "Polish laws," that is, "constitutions" passed by the Sejms to occasionally amend the Lithuanian Statute, only when Russian laws were found to be "deficient" (*nedostatochnye*).[113]

The rebellion was still in its early stage when the decree of January 1831 announced that in view of "the true needs of and the present situation in" the region, eastern Belorussia must be governed in the same way as the internal provinces of the expanding core, and the Lithuanian Statute was abolished.[114] The text of the decree contained verbatim some of the recommendations of Mikhail Muravev, the governor of Mogilev, who left his post that same month. The equalization of political rights, he wrote, must serve as the foundation for the merger (*slitie*) of Belorussia with Russia; "why should Belorussia be an exception to the rule that the entire state must be administered by Russian laws?" The decrees of October 1831 and January 1832 imposed Russian names on local agencies and courts, and those which had no equivalent in Russia were closed.[115]

So much for eastern Belorussia. An effort was made, however, to codify the laws of the "northwestern provinces" Vilno, Grodno, and Minsk, as well as those of the "southwestern provinces" Kiev, Volhynia, and Podolia.[116] The work of codification was vested in the Second Section, even before the outbreak of the rebellion. A specialist was brought in, as was done for the codification of Baltic German laws. He was Ignacy Danilowicz (1787–1843), jurist and historian, who graduated from the Bielostock gymnasium in 1807 (then under Prussian rule), then joined the Vilno law faculty.[117] He made his specialty the study of Polish and Lithuanian law, and began to work on their codification. He ran afoul of the Russian authorities for political activities, and was "banished" to a professorship in Kharkiv University in 1824. Six years later he was called to Petersburg to join the Second Section. He submitted a voluminous code of Lithuanian laws in 1835, 298 pages long and containing 2,070 articles.[118] By then, however, the tide had turned in Petersburg. Danielowicz was "banished" again that same year to teach in Kiev University, where he remained until 1839. The project remained in limbo, faced with the violent opposition of Dmitrii Bibikov, who became governor general of Right Bank Ukraine in 1837, and of the same Muravev; Perovsky's views must have already been known. Last but not least, Nicholas did not feel the need to conciliate either Poles or Polonized Lithuanians. In June 1840, the Lithuanian Statute was abolished in the six provinces north and south of the Pripet marshes. The legal integration of the former Grand Duchy was complete.[119]

There remained Poland. In their shares of the Polish core after the partitions, the Prussians and Austrians had introduced their civil and criminal laws. Russia – it bears repeating – did not take part in the partitions of the Polish core until the Congress of Vienna. By then, Polish courts had to deal with four systems of law: Polish, Prussian, Austrian, and French. After the creation of the Duchy of Warsaw, Napoleon had introduced his Code Civil in May 1808. It was considered at the time to be alien to local traditions, if only because it abolished serfdom and introduced important changes in marriage and property law. Nevertheless, Napoleon's civil system would remain in force until the twentieth century. The French also introduced their commercial code of 1809, their judicial organization and procedure.[120] One can easily see that the three powers, Prussia, Austria, and France, like Sweden in an earlier day in the Baltic provinces, were much more determined than the Russians would ever be until much later in the century to override native Polish law in favour of their own legislation.

In the new Polish *tsarstvo*, a "civil committee" was created in 1814 and told to draft a new civil code, but it accomplished little, save for submitting a law on mortgages, which was passed by the Sejm in 1817. Some Poles even wondered about what law was best for Poland. Tomasz Wawrzecki, who had served with Czartosyski, Novosiltsev, and Drucki-Lubecki on a Temporary Council set up in March 1813 to prepare for the creation of a new government in liberated Poland, and briefly served as minister of justice in the new government (1815–16), was convinced that the Lithuanian Statute was better than the Code Civil and should be the law of the new Poland![121] A legislative commission was created in 1820 to draft a new code, but the Code Civil had by then been accepted by public opinion: it was, after all, much more liberal – as the child of the French Revolution carried all over Europe by Napoleon's armies – than the legislation of conservative Prussia and Austria. The Sejm approved a penal code in 1818 and a civil code in 1825, which merely amended the Code Civil by restoring the sanctity of marriage and replacing the common property clause between spouses with one restoring the individual property of the wife in the form of a dowry. The French Code of military justice was translated in 1824 to guide Polish courts martial.[122]

The Sejm of 1830 heard strong criticism of the judiciary and especially of administrative interference in the operations of the courts, of violations of the rights of property, of long detentions in prisons and the use of torture.[123] In 1833, after the arrival of Paskevich, a Codification Commission for Poland was created in the Second Section, which, as for the Baltic provinces, drew on the assistance of native jurists, such as Ignacy Turkull (d. 1856), the future minister state secretary (1839–56), and Romuald Hube, who would later serve as Polish minister of Church affairs and education (1861–2). The Commission collected a substantial amount of material, but the work received no official sanction, although some of it, a new penal code, essentially no more than a literal translation of the Russian penal code of 1845, replaced that of 1818 and took effect in Poland in 1848. In the meantime, Paskevich had submitted his recommendations for the creation of the two Senate departments in Warsaw in September 1841; their operations were governed by the statute of March 1842.[124]

Little was in fact accomplished. Poland's civil law had been borrowed from the Code Civil, its penal law from Russian legislation. Its high court was integrated into the high tribunal of the expanding core. But Polish would remain its official language until 1872; the senators were Polish; and how much the courts made of this mishmash of Polish, French, Prussian, Austrian, and Russian legislation must await the completion of scholarly studies of the interpretations handed down in the Petersburg Senate and State Council. But Polish law would never be codified under Russian rule.[125]

Trade versus Integration

Trade binds but also divides. It binds when the economies of a core and its periphery are complementary; it creates tensions and divides when a new core emerges in the periphery and begins to rival the economy of the old core on which it was originally dependent[126] – as in Poland. Trade also contributes to increasing resistance to integration when a recently annexed periphery retains strong ties with a core now excluded from an economic system exercising a strong centripetal pull on that periphery – as in Finland. The Tariff Act of September 1782 had created a single export-import market incorporating the Baltic provinces and eastern Belorussia. The partitions of 1793 and 1795 further extended it to include western Belorussia and Lithuania (i.e., the entire former Grand Duchy of Lithuania), which had traditionally gravitated not so much toward the Polish core as toward Memel and Riga. The wars with France, the Tilsit encounter, and the nefarious inclusion of Russia into the Napoleonic Continental System, followed by the catastrophe of 1812, were disastrous for Russia's foreign trade, and it was not until the Congress of Vienna and the incorporation of Finland and much of the Polish core that Petersburg could afford to frame a coherent trade policy.

During the remainder of Alexander I's reign and throughout that of Nicholas I, there were no appreciable changes in the volume, composition, and direction of Russia's foreign trade, which would remain a small share of the international volume of trade – about 3.5 per cent.[127] Russia's merchant marine remained practically non-existent, especially if one excludes Finnish ships engaged in coastal trade. The bulk of trade continued to flow through the Baltic ports – about 80 per cent – staple cities where foreigners brought in and took out goods without the involvement of domestic commercial houses. The bulk of Russian exports consisted of raw materials, the bulk of imports of manufactured and colonial goods. Fifty-seven per cent of the exports consisted of grains, animal fats, flax, and hemp, and over 55 per cent of the imports, of cotton, woollens, dyes, colonial goods, and tea. In a word, the western theatre remained a fringe of Eurasia, poorly integrated in a world economic system being inexorably shaped by British manufactures. It was the western fringe of a semi-closed world increasingly dominated by Moscow's textiles and manufactures, supplying non-competitive articles to a population still steeped in an overwhelmingly agricultural market.

The Tariff Act of December 1810 was already protectionist and that of March 1816[128] even more so: it even included prohibitive duties. The aim of a protectionist policy, at a time when the Industrial Revolution was about to transform the world economy, was to protect nascent domestic industries against the competition of more advanced economies. Russian policy was defensive, seeking to transform the western periphery of Eurasia into the periphery of its own economic system, to build a Fortress Empire in which its industry and manufactures would occupy a hegemonic position. Here was one of the roots of the conflict that would pit Russia against Britain for a century of cold war. The period from 1810 and 1819 was dominated by Interior Minister Osip Kozodavlev, who vigorously pursued a policy of factory building, which eventually failed because of inadequate demand in Russian towns and villages.

Protectionism created its own backlash, which exposed the fragility of Russian industries. The Tariff Act of November 1819[129] retained a fairly high level of protective duties and removed all prohibitions on imports: Kozodavlev's factories collapsed while landed proprietors lamented the loss of foreign markets. Free trade was exposed for what it was, "the hypocrisy of the export interest,"[130] as John Stuart Mill would put it, and yet another tariff act, that of March 1822,[131] restored high protective rates and the prohibitions of 1816. Leadership passed to the finance ministry, where a department of foreign trade had been created in 1811 and a department of manufactures opened in 1819. Finance Minister Georg von Cancrin would become the architect of a steadily protective policy until his death in 1844. The excesses of Cancrin's policies kept on the black list iron, pig iron, metal articles, sugar, and cotton and woollen articles – which had made up over a third of Russian imports at the beginning of the century. They raised much opposition, and the Tariff Act of October 1850,[132] which would remain in effect until 1865, granted some remedies. It is in the context of these policies that trade relations with Poland and Finland must be examined.

The extensive border with Poland perplexed the Russian government for a long time. The finance ministry administered the collection of customs duties in coastal and inland districts organized around a major customs house. There were two such districts in the northwestern provinces with headquarters in Yurburg and Brest-Litovsk. The statute of January 1811[133] created a customs police (*strazha*) to patrol the border between customs houses and checkpoints (*zastavy*). The border ran over 150 kilometres from Polangen to Yurburg at the confluence of the Niemen with the Yura River, from which goods were shipped to and from the former princely residence of the Radziwills in Keidany, a major trading centre for Samogitia. From Yurburg, boats sailed on the Niemen over 142 kilometres to Vershtany in Vilno province and another 162 kilometres to the confluence of the Niemen with the Losona, on the major road linking Vilno with Warsaw. The border followed the Losona to the Bobr River and the latter to its confluence with the Narev, and up the latter to Khoroshche, another 165 kilometres, encompassing the Bialystok *oblast*. From there it ran along the Narev to Nemirov on the Western Bug on the Polish border, west of Brest-Litovsk. This 780-kilometre-long border was patrolled by only five regiments of Cossacks.

The Continental System, which Russia was forced to join after the Tilsit interview of 1807, was a disaster for the region. Large shipments of grain, seeds, flax, wool, timber, and "naval stores" had been sold to British merchants in Königsberg, Memel, and Riga, who brought into the region, integrated into the expanding Russian core since 1795, colonial goods, spirits, and cloth, essentially luxury goods. The region had no industry, and customs duties were almost the only source of revenue and the only underpinning of the *szlachta*'s way of life.[134] The Continental System destroyed the economy of Belorussia and Lithuania, and the 1810s not only became the golden age of smuggling but also paved the way for a deeper integration of the former Grand Duchy into the expanding Russian core.

The three partitioning powers, Russia, Prussia, and Austria, agreed at Vienna in 1815 that they would seek to retain the integrity of the Polish core's economy, ensconced in the basin of the Vistula, into which we may also include that of the Warta and its tributary, the Prosna, which had once flowed into the Vistula before turning west to join the Oder. The Polish economy had been in dire straits in the eighteenth century, but had experienced a sharp recovery after Catherine II's death, and outlived the catastrophe of 1812. But the three powers were eager to integrate their share of Polish territory or destroy what they could not integrate. Partitioned Poland had become completely cut off from the sea, and Prussia, for example, was determined to downgrade Danzig, the commercial jewel of old Poland even if it was a German city, to a city of shipyards and civil servants, and divert its trade to Stettin on the Oder's estuary. Prussia also controlled Königsberg on the Pregel and Memel on the exit from the Curonian gulf (Kurisches Haff), into which the Niemen brought timber and other raw products of the forest and the land from the Lithuanian interior, as far back as the Minsk upland. Prussia was also determined to protect against competition the powerful Junkers of Brandenburg and East Prussia, the backbone of its officer corps, thereby diverting Polish grain to Odessa on the Black Sea, a policy it had pursued since the 1760s.[135] Poland's southern trade, across Galicia, on its way to Budapest on the Danube and to Odessa via the San River, through Lvov, and via the Dniester, was at the mercy of Austria's own protectionist policies and Austro-Russian cooperation. Such constraints imposed by the Germanic powers made the development of the Polish economy and foreign trade dependent on Russia's goodwill. The situation was well understood by the architect of Poland's industrial renewal after 1815, Prince Ksawery Drucki-Lubecki (1778–1846). Educated in the First Cadet Corps in Petersburg, he had served in a Russian infantry regiment in 1799, was Grodno provincial marshal (1813–15), Grodno civil governor in 1816, then Vilno governor from 1816 to 1823 (but never assumed office). In 1821, he became the *tsarstvo*'s finance "minister," and remained in that post until 1830. He later became a member of the Imperial State Council. He won the trust of both Alexander I and Nicholas I, and might have become imperial finance minister, had he not been both a Catholic and a Pole.[136]

There was progress in agriculture when corvée labour began to be replaced by money rents, and sheep breeding diversified a sector traditionally specialized in the production of grain for export. The introduction of the potato not only improved the peasantry's diet, but also created a new industry, the production of vodka based on the new tuber, and a major source of income for the producers. The sugar beet industry reduced the need for imports of colonial sugar. A Land Credit Society was created in 1825. But the core of the reforms was the development of the textile industry, and a gradual transition from charcoal to hard coal and from water energy to steam power in the metal industries. In 1829, the ninety-eight-kilometre-long Avgustov canal was completed, linking the Vistula with the Niemen; it brought much good to the region by facilitating the marketing of Polish products in southern Lithuania. The so-called Old Polish Basin was becoming the heart of the new Polish economy. Located between the Pilica and the upper Vistula, it contained coal and iron within short distances, and a little further north, Lódź was emerging as the centre of the textile industry producing cloth for the Polish and Russian army.[137] An integrated Polish economy was emerging, based on a strong agricultural and industrial sector, capable of creating a core economy in what seemed to have been a mere periphery of the expanding Russian core. Therefore, the inevitable competition with the Russian textile industry based in Moscow, Vladimir, and Kaluga was bound to place the Russian government in a quandary.

The Supplementary Act of August 1818[138] still sought to retain the economic integrity of old Poland by reiterating that navigation on all rivers and canals within the borders of 1772 would be free. But such a convention ran counter to the fact that the former Grand Duchy of Lithuania had already been integrated into the market of the expanding Russian core, which extended to the Niemen and the Western Bug. The Russians could not have their cake and eat it too. As a result, a customs cordon (*cherta*), created between the *tsarstvo* and the expanding core, essentially abrogated the promise of 1818. But the Tariff Act of 1819, which embraced free trade, abolished the cordon and opened the Russian market to the competition of Polish textiles. These soon became a major threat to the textile manufacturers of Russia's so-called Central Industrial Region around Moscow.

The backlash took the form of the protectionist and even prohibitive tariff of 1822, which restored the cordon and abolished the administration of customs houses in Warsaw, which had managed the entry points along the outer periphery of the expanding core. In other words, the tariff of 1819 had sought to create an integrated common market between the *tsarstvo* and Russia, while that of 1822 backed away from that intention and created two entities, the "*tsarstvo* and the empire," as the finance ministry's documents of the time put it. There would be two tariff barriers: an external barrier with Prussia and Austria and an internal cordon between Russia and the *tsarstvo*. Customs houses and checkpoints were built facing East Prussia and the Duchy of Posen (Poznań), now part of Prussia, and along Galicia facing Right Bank Ukraine. The cordon ran from Grodno to Ustilug (Ustyluh) on the Western Bug via Brest-Litovsk, and would separate "the two states." The decree of August 1822 retained free trade in natural products (*syrye proizvedeniia*), if they were intended for internal consumption; articles manufactured from local raw materials would be charged a 1 per cent duty *ad valorem* when they crossed the internal cordon, a 3 per cent duty if the raw materials were of foreign origin.[139] Special arrangements had already been made for the transit of Polish and Prussian cloth to China and of Polish grain and other goods from Brody-Radzivilov on the Austrian border to Odessa.

The uprising of 1831 upset an arrangement which clearly favoured Polish interests. The Tariff Acts of November 1831 and November 1834[140] raised the tariff and restored a number of Polish goods, mainly textiles, which could again be imported into Russia, while also favouring Russian manufactures. They also precipitated a slump in the Polish economy, aggravating a worsening situation at a time when the Drucki-Lubecki program of over-investment in the textile industry made Polish industry more dependent on the Russian market. There no longer was a Polish army, and the Russian army would depend on its own supplies of cloth.

The creation of the Bank of Poland in 1828 made matters worse by facilitating credit to encourage a production that could no longer find domestic outlets: Poland remained an overwhelmingly agricultural country where more than half of the peasant population still did corvée labour or had no land. Urbanization had barely begun. In 1830, of the 453 places classified as towns, 242 were owned privately and 211 by the government:[141] they were no more than large and small villages. Tariff policy began to change after Cancrin's death in 1844, with the abandonment of prohibitive duties and the lowering of duties in general. The Tariff Act of October 1850 did not fundamentally change the system, but it abolished the internal cordon and enlarged the network of customs houses and checkpoints along the outer boundary of the *tsarstvo*. Thus, it finally created a single common market between the *tsarstvo* and the expanding Russian core. The Polish economy and its credit infrastructure remained more advanced than the Russian, but the latter's size and growing strength enabled it to incorporate its rival. The *tsarstvo* had again become a periphery ready for integration into the enormous market of western Eurasia.

The Baltic provinces, integrated into that market since 1782, experienced the same fluctuations from a tariff policy made in Petersburg. A protectionist tariff, let alone a prohibitive one, only encouraged smuggling, and Riga suffered from the competition of Prussian Memel, which sought to divert the exports of Livonia and Lithuania by imposing much lower duties. The Revel customs district included customs houses in Revel and Hapsal and two checkpoints on the Gulf of Finland; the Riga district, three customs houses in Riga, Pernau, and Arensburg with a checkpoint in Mitava for goods shipped inland on the Aa from Riga; and a Libava district had only two, Libava and Vindava. Grain, flax oil, bristles, and feathers as well as timber came from Kurland and Lithuania, and imports included salt, herring, spirits, and colonial goods.[142] The trade of the three provinces was not so much with the Russian interior as with Europe, as in the days of the Hanseatic League, but it had been incorporated into the trade balance of the expanding Russian core. Moreover, it was more commerce than trade: it yielded little benefit to the towns of the interior, whose conditions remained dismal during the first half of the nineteenth century, as Governor General von der Pahlen reported in 1830 when discussing the sale of spirits.[143]

Finland was a different case. The Treaty of Fredrikshamn (1809) recognized that Finland had long been integrated into the Swedish market, and allowed the importation of minerals, construction stones, and pig iron from Sweden in exchange for cattle, fish, beams, wooden utensils, and timber from Finland. Exchanges were duty-free because the imported and exported goods were complementary. An important sector was the coastal trade (*kabotazh*) linking Finnish coastal towns among themselves (to avoid the difficult inland travel) as well as with Sweden. But this situation slowly began to change. The Supplementary Act of August 1817[144] cancelled the right of the Finns to export agricultural products to Sweden duty-free, and they would have to pay the duty charged on other powers. But there was an even more important reason for this change. The emergence of Petersburg as the heart of an industrial region was diverting Finnish trade eastwards, along the Gulf of Finland and across Lake Ladoga. By 1820, Petersburg had a population of about 400,000, while that of Stockholm in 1810 was only 65,500, and the largest Finnish town, Åbo, had a mere 10,225 inhabitants.[145] All Finnish exports were in demand in the capital and were becoming less so in Sweden, which was reaching agricultural self-sufficiency and was practising a protectionist policy of its own.

The Act of June 1835[146] was a step toward greater integration. Finnish goods imported directly from Finland on Finnish ships or sent via Lake Ladoga were imported duty-free, but foreign goods imported into Finland and re-exported to Russia would have to pay duties in accordance with the Tariff Act of 1822.

By contrast, Russian goods exported to Finland entered the country duty-free, as if they had been shipped from another port of the expanding Russian core. Russo-Finnish exchanges continued to grow, and by 1840, 40 per cent of Finland's foreign trade was with Russia. That same year, Swedish currency was withdrawn from circulation, and the rouble became the only medium of exchange.[147] The Act of June 1850[148] accepted the importation via Lake Ladoga only of a fixed quantity of copper and an unlimited amount of tin, if these metals had been smelted in Finland. But despite those concessions Finland would remain a separate tariff zone. Being a small and poor country, it needed to import raw materials, but its manufactured articles faced a customs barrier along the Russian border, while Russian manufactures were free to enter the Finnish market. The asymmetry between the trade of the two countries, and the necessity to maintain the peace in Finland, made full integration possible.

On the Road to Disintegration

Education versus Integration

While the western theatre was the closest to the northern capital and thus the most exposed to the centripetal forces pulling it away from its anchors in Åbo, Riga, Vilno, and Warsaw, its resistance to integration into the expanding Russian core was all the greater, even turning into open violence, and generated a growing self-consciousness which would collide with a similar development in Petersburg and Moscow. The victory over Napoleon, the projection of Russian power into Europe, and the completion of Russia's rise to occupy a hegemonic position in the whole of Eurasia released a tremendous energy among the ruling elite and its ruling class. It found its expression in the "slogan of Nicholas I's reign," Orthodoxy, Autocracy, and Nationality, first formulated officially in 1832 by Minister of Education Count Sergei Uvarov (1833–49).[149] The glorification of Orthodoxy not only served to emphasize for all to see the subordination of the Church to the autocratic rule of the emperor, but also to identify Russia with Orthodoxy, and the Russian core with the autocracy of the Romanov dynasty. Such association had to be taught in schools and universities to strengthen the identity of the younger generations; it also ended up by creating a Hegelian antithesis of sprouting local and regional identities all across the western theatre, and eventually a synthesis, which would cause the expanding Russian core to implode.

The creation of a Ministry of Education in Petersburg in September 1802 was followed by the school reform of January 1803, which built upon the work of the Main Commission of Schools appointed in September 1782. Two universities were opened in the western theatre, one in Vilno, the other in Derpt.[150] The Vilno Jesuit Academy, reorganized into the Main School of the Grand

Duchy of Lithuania in 1780, became Vilno University in 1803. The creation of educational regions, each under a curator residing in Petersburg, made Vilno the regional educational centre for all the "former Polish provinces," two in Lithuania, three in Belorussia, and three in Right Bank Ukraine. Like other universities, it was managed by a rector, assisted by a council of senior professors who elected him. As the centre of an administrative region, it managed the Polish secondary school system, and also functioned as a normal school preparing teachers whom it then appointed to serve in the region. Elementary schools remained under the responsibility of the Church (Catholic and Uniate). Vilno University was thus designed to become the educational and cultural centre of a vast territory, where the Russian presence was still minimal. Unfortunately, it would also become a hotbed of Polish nationalism, which subverted many youths among the *szlachta* and became one of the causes of the rebellion of 1830–1.

The Act of Incorporation of April 1803[151] described Vilno University as a "temple of the sciences" (*khram nauk*) and expressed the hope that it would exercise "a useful influence on the national enlightenment [*narodnoe prosveshchenie*] and the good of the empire." It was given considerable autonomy, even in judicial and economic matters, but its professors were integrated into the civil service of the expanding core: they were given grade 7, the equivalent of a lieutenant colonel in the army. They were coopted by majority vote, but their election required the confirmation of the curator and the minister of education. The university's golden age was between 1815 and 1830. It was able to attract distinguished professors from abroad, and local faculty included Joachim Lelewel (1786–1861), who taught history, and Ignacy Danilowicz, who taught local law and, as we saw, took an active part in the work of codification. Its mathematics, medical, and theological departments became well known beyond the borders of the former Grand Duchy.[152]

The region's secondary schools had some 20,000 students in 1815, more than in all the other five regions, but they were growing up in a Polish world, and all was not well. Governor General Prince Nikolai Khovansky (1823–36) complained that Russian was poorly taught in eastern Belorussia and that an anti-Russian spirit prevailed in the Polish schools there. As a result, Vitebsk and Mogilev provinces were transferred in 1824 to the Petersburg educational region, where curator Dmitrii Runich (1821–6), a conservative Russifier, nearly destroyed all vestiges of university autonomy and academic freedom. In fact, things were going from bad to worse in the region. Its first curator, Adam Czartoryski, was much too busy on the international scene and seldom visited Vilno. He was a controversial figure among the Russians, who looked upon him as a Polish nationalist dreaming of restoring the Polish Empire to its 1772 borders on the Dvina and the Dnieper.[153] In his absence, the true curator was Tadeusz Czacki (1765–1813), a highly educated firebrand who looked upon the school system as an instrument of Polonization. Russian General Staff officers detailed to Vilno complained that the Lithuanian Corps had become a purely Polish outfit and of meeting the "hostility and crudity" of the Polish landowners.[154] The intellectual effervescence throughout the former Grand Duchy resulted from the exhilaration which agitated the Polish world after 1815, when the creation of Congress Poland and Alexander I's vague hint that he might contemplate the reunion of Lithuania with Poland released powerful energies. It also was a time when student associations in the German and Italian states revelled in liberal ideas of German and Italian unification.

A conservative reaction was not long in coming. In October 1817, the ministry of education assumed responsibility for ecclesiastical affairs under Prince Alexander Golitsyn (1816–24), mystic and freemason, who started a crusade against liberal and "ungodly" ideas and preferred Latin to the natural and political sciences. A campaign began against the cosmopolitan Czartoryski, who was forced to resign in 1823 and was followed by Novosiltsev (1824–32), the grey eminence of Grand Duke Constantine. Golitsyn's successor was Admiral Alexander Shishkov (1824–8), a reactionary if there ever was one.[155] The scene was set for a dramatic confrontation between Russian and Polish school policies. Education in the *tsarstvo* was in the hands of a Commission (ministry) of Religious and Educational Affairs chaired by Count Stanisław Kostka Potocki (1815–20), whose relative was curator of the Kharkiv region from 1803 to 1817, and Count Stanisław Grabowski (1820–30), a relative of the minister state secretary. The Sejm that met in 1830 found that education was in excellent condition, but the elementary schools were falling apart despite their increasing number. A military school for the training of officers for the Polish army was opened in Kalisz for two hundred students.[156]

The rebellion marked a dramatic turning point. Nicholas I was determined to destroy every institution of higher learning in the former Polish provinces. Warsaw University (together with the Kalisz military school) was closed in 1832, and it would not reopen until 1869 in very different conditions. To compensate for the loss, a network of middle schools was created in every major town with an eight-year curriculum, the last two years devoted either to training for the civil service and preparing to enter Russian universities, or to military training for officers to serve in the Russian army or follow careers in industry and mining. In 1840, law classes were added in the gymnasia to train lower-ranking judicial officials, and two Polish chairs were opened in Petersburg and Moscow with a broader curriculum. They were closed in 1846, and Polish students increasingly went to the two Russian capitals. In November 1839, schools in the *tsarstvo* were integrated into a new Warsaw Educational Region, whose curators, Nikolai Okunev (1839–50) and Pavel Muchanov (1851–61), both Russian, were responsible to both Paskevich and the minister of education. Beginning in 1835, curators were required to reside in the capital of their region. Russian and Polish educational systems had been placed on "a uniform and solid foundation" (*edinoobraznye i tverdye nachala*). In April 1850, the Warsaw Censorship Committee was subordinated to the Main Censorship Administration in the Ministry of Education in order to create uniformity (*edinoobrazie*) in their procedures.[157]

In the former Grand Duchy, Vilno University was closed in May 1832; its medical department was reorganized into a Medical-Surgical Academy under the jurisdiction of the interior ministry in Petersburg, and its theological department became an Ecclesiastical School. The schools of the region were incorporated into the Belorussian Educational Region created in January 1829, with Vitebsk and Mogilev separated again from the Petersburg region, and Minsk was added to it in January 1831. Only Vilno and Grodno remained, but the Vilno region was abolished in May 1832 and the provinces were added to the Belorussian region, under Curator Grigorii Kartashevsky (1829–35), a Russified Ukrainian of Polish descent from Poltava, who won the praises of Governor Muravev, followed by Evarist Gruber (1835–50). However, the Vilno region reappeared in May 1850 with Vilno, Grodno, Kovno, and Minsk provinces and was placed directly under Governor General Ilia Bibikov (1850–6), and the Belorussian region was abolished. Vitebsk and Mogilev provinces returned to the Petersburg region.[158] These shifts reflected a desire to punish Vilno for its role in the rebellion and to concentrate the execution of educational policy in eastern Belorussia, closer to the Russian core, but in the end, Vilno won again.

In November 1833, Uvarov won the Committee of Ministers' approval of a policy that would make sure that "the youth of the Western provinces must be educated totally in the Russian spirit, and that the Russian language must be taught in the lower schools in order to be used in everyday conversation [*narodnyi*]"; Muravev had claimed that it was already the case in Mogilev province. In July 1834, the Russian school statute of December 1828 was introduced in Vilno, Grodno, and Minsk provinces; it had already taken effect in eastern Belorussia. In January, the middle schools had been reorganized from Catholic into Russian state schools to be supported by revenues collected from the properties of Roman Catholic monasteries closed in 1832.[159] But these forceful measures of integration ran against a powerful countercurrent which they would be helpless to overcome in the end. Education and Polish Romanticism would combine to generate a virulent nationalism capable of resisting a no less virulent Russian nationalism, and the yearning for national emancipation inspired by the teachings of Herder would counter the brutal policies of educational integration. Administrative integration was possible, but Polish nobles and the emerging Lithuanian and Belorussian intelligentsia could not be made into Russians in an age of nascent nationalism. A policy of educational integration contained the seeds of its own destruction.

The situation was much less tense in the Baltic provinces, but the resistance to integration was no less strong. Dorpat University, created by Gustav Adolf in 1632, was closed in the wake of the Russian annexation of the provinces in 1710, and never reopened in the eighteenth century; nobles in search of a higher education had to attend German universities. When Paul expressed his concern over the "pernicious [*zlovrednye*] ideas firing up immature minds"[160] abroad under the influence of the French Revolution, and forbade the German youth to leave the country, a substitute had to be found: the emperor instructed the nobility of the three provinces to discuss the creation of a new university. Dorpat must have been in dire straits by then, because Mitava was first chosen as the proper site, but Alexander I chose Dorpat on account of its central location and lower cost of living.[161]

The university opened in December 1802. Its Act of Incorporation[162] created four departments: theology, philosophy, medicine, and law. It was amended in June 1820[163] to tighten discipline over an unruly student body influenced by student corporations in the Germanies agitating for the unification of Germany. In Dorpat, they formed corporations calling themselves "Livonia" and "Estonia," evidence of a rising historical and national consciousness. This second statute would remain in force until 1865. As in Vilno, the university enjoyed full judicial and economic autonomy under the overall jurisdiction of the Ministry of Education. Dorpat became the centre of an educational region including the three Baltic provinces and Vyborg province ("Finland"),[164] but, with the incorporation of Vyborg into Finland in 1811, the latter was kept out of the regional system. The act of incorporation called the university a "sanctuary [*sviatilishche*] of the sciences," but gave it a somewhat narrower mission, in accord with the original intention of the Swedish king, not only to disseminate knowledge but also "to train youth to serve the Fatherland" – an implicit claim that in educational matters, the Baltic provinces were part of the expanding Russian core. Under its first two curators, Major General Friedrich von Klinger, a distinguished poet (1803–17), and Karl von Lieven (1817–28), later minister of education (1828–33), the university, which opened with a mere nineteen students, became a first-class institution. It also trained professors for positions in Russian universities, in Petersburg, Moscow, Kazan, and Kharkiv.[165]

The fundamental difference between the situation in Lithuania-Belorussia and the Baltic provinces was that Dorpat University did not become a hotbed of anti-Russian feeling preaching rebellion. The German ruling elite and ruling class, because they did not feel, like the Polish *szlachta*, the radical influences radiating from a geopolitical core, remained loyal, and the *Ritterschaft* kept a tight control over the student body. The Russian university statute of July 1835 strengthened the powers of the curator over his region. It was extended to the Baltic provinces in January 1837 and raised the authority of Curator Gustav

Craffstrom (1835–54), who succeeded Karl Freiherr von der Pahlen (1828–35); the latter briefly combined the post with that of governor general (1830–45). The Ministry of Education gained the right to appoint professors, and the election of the rector was abolished in March 1850.[166] The teaching of Russian was encouraged: the circular of January 1837 required all county schools to teach Russian and Russian history four and two hours a week respectively; by the mid-1840s, all students matriculating in Dorpat University were required to pass a rigorous examination in Russian.[167] The German ruling elite accepted the increasing integration of Dorpat University into the Russian educational system because it served its own interests as well as it did those of the Russian ruling elite – there was no open, active, opposition. However, it strongly resisted Russian penetration of the middle and lower elementary schools. Such a penetration ran contrary to the policy of superstratification: if Latvian and Estonian children became bilingual and even trilingual, the Russians might use them later to challenge the political authority of the German landowners and the religious authority of the Lutheran Church. Moreover, they might even use the printed word to develop a national consciousness that would turn, not only against the Germans, but against the Russians as well. It may not yet have become clear that such a policy of Russifying the lower strata contained the seeds of destruction of both the superstratification, on which the entire system rested, and of Russian rule itself.

The dilemma – and the danger – for the Russians was epitomized by Adolf Arwidsson, the most prominent representative of the so-called "Åbo Romantics," who said: "Swedes we are not, Russians we do not wish to become, therefore let us be Finns."[168] Finland was a poor and small country, where only 15 per cent of the population spoke Swedish, but the Swedes, who dominated the cultural scene, had on the whole accepted Russian rule in 1809. Queen Cristina had founded a Royal Academy in Åbo in 1640, but it made little progress, overshadowed as it was by the Swedish universities in Lund and Uppsala, once the coronation place of the Swedish kings. Following the great fire of 1827, the university was moved to Helsinki (Helsingfors) and renamed the Imperial Alexander University, funded in part by Lutheran pastorates and a share of the customs revenue from the export of timber.[169] The university remained closely associated with the Lutheran Church, which, like Orthodoxy, preached obedience to the secular and political elite. Instead of a council, as in other universities, it had a consistory of twelve professors who elected the rector. The statute of 1828, which replaced that of 1655, gave it an extraordinary privilege. The university was not integrated into the regional organization of the Ministry of Education, but was headed by a chancellor, who was none other than Nicholas I himself, represented by a pro-chancellor. From 1803 to 1817 he was Jacob Tengstrom (1755–1832), a many-sided man, who had switched allegiance in 1809, and gave up his post in 1817 to become the first archbishop of Finland.[170]

The university served purely utilitarian ends. Noble officers had rejected a university education for over a century and a half, and only two professions dominated the "third estate," the clergy and the lawyer-official. After 1809, one notices the development of, on the one hand, a closer relationship between the nobility, the clergy, and the burghers, who would be entitled to a university education and to graduate officials for the new Finnish government created under Russian auspices, and, on the other, an increasing distance separating them from the peasantry – a conservative development found all over the western theatre (and in Right Bank Ukraine) as well as in the Russian core itself during the reign of Nicholas I. The development also brought about an increasing alienation between the Swedish-speaking upper classes and the Finnish-speaking peasantry. The paradox, however, was that it was the Swedish-speaking intellectuals who would shape a Finnish national consciousness until the 1850s, when Swedicized Finns would finally rediscover their roots. It was not until 1858 that the first Finnish-language high school leading to the university was opened.[171]

But the growing alienation of Finns from Sweden did not favour the Russians, who feared that rising Finnish consciousness would lead to separatism. Despite the introduction in the 1840s of a uniform secondary school system, in which Swedish was the language of instruction, there was a recognition that the Russian language was becoming a prerequisite for university graduates wishing to enter state service: the edict of August 1834 gave those graduates the same rights as those of other Russian universities to enter the service and be promoted in it.[172] Nevertheless, Russian made little progress, and repression did not help: the Finnish Language Act of 1850 banned Finnish publications except those "aiming at religious edification or economic application." It has been said that the Act aimed more at social than political control.[173] The Russians appeared to be upholding their policy of superstratification at the risk of alienating the Finns. That would indeed be the case later in the century.

An Existential Struggle

In the final analysis, a policy of full integration was bound to founder on the rocks of confessional conflict between Orthodoxy and Catholicism in Lithuania, and between Orthodoxy and Protestantism in the Baltic provinces and Finland. Every country, and perhaps every institution, remains faithful to the principles and goals that justified its creation and would preside over its development. It bears repeating that the Christianization of the Russo-Polish and Russo-Swedish frontier was a work of conquest directed by Latin Christendom against a Byzantine and increasingly Russian Orthodoxy spreading its wings over the vast river network of western Eurasia. The superior power of Latin Christendom eventually crumbled before Russia's rising might in the seventeenth century, but the confessional rivalry remained and would turn into a deep hatred of a Russian core inexorably expanding into the frontier. Russia became the standard bearer of a Russian way of life (*narodnost'*) and of Eastern Orthodoxy, Poland the standard bearer of Polonism and Catholicism. In both Poland and Russia, it became difficult to distinguish between religious and national objectives. The Uniate Church in between was seen by Poles as a projection of Polish Catholicism into Russian Orthodox territory and by the Russians as a barrier to Russian expansion and an obstacle to Orthodox integrity. For both powers the rivalry became an existential struggle, and Polono-Catholic resistance would create insuperable barriers to the progress of administrative integration.

The central administration of non-Orthodox (*inovertsy*) confessions – mostly the Protestants of the Baltic provinces and the Uniates – had been vested since February 1734 in the College of Justice, later in a separate College for Livland and Estland Affairs. After the annexation of eastern Belorussia in 1772, appeals from the territory also went to this college; so did those from western Belorussia and Lithuania, acquired in 1793 and 1795.[174] In February 1797, a separate Department for Roman Catholic Affairs was created alongside the College of Justice. In November 1801, the department was reorganized into a Main Ecclesiastical College, chaired by the Mogilev archbishop. In July 1810, in the wake of the reorganization of the central government along ministerial lines, a Main Administration for the Affairs of Foreign Confessions was created, incorporating both the College for Livland and Estland Affairs and the department, under the appellate jurisdiction of the Senate.[175] In October 1817, educational and ecclesiastical matters were combined under Prince Alexander Golitsyn (1773–1844), and the Main Administration became one of its departments until 1824, when they were separated once again. The Main Administration remained autonomous until February 1832, when it became a department of the Interior Ministry.[176] The ministry was seeking to create a parallel ecclesiastical hierarchy for non-Orthodox confessions, while the senior procurator of the Holy Synod became the "minister for the affairs of the Orthodox Church." Golitsyn became director of the Postal Department (1819–42), another section of the interior ministry. The administration of the Catholic and Uniate churches in the western provinces had become integrated into the ministerial system of the expanding Russian core.

Roman Catholicism was the religion of the overwhelming majority of Poles in the *tsarstvo*. It was estimated in 1840 that out of a total population of 4.5 million, 3.6 million were Roman Catholics, almost all of them Poles, and only 1,874 (!) Orthodox, while 235,966 were Uniates, most of them Ukrainians. On the other hand, 474,598 were registered as Jews, with 234,642 Protestants, and some 6,235 "others."[177] The Catholic population was distributed among seven dioceses. In 1815, some older ones passed under Russian jurisdiction: Chełm

(Kholm) along the Volhynian border; Kujawa along the Prussian border; Plock facing the Grand Duchy of Posen (Poznan) in Prussian-occupied Poland; and Warsaw, created in 1698. There were also more recent ones founded in 1805: Lublin in southeastern Poland, like Chełm, with a Ukrainian Uniate population; Wigry along the Lithuanian border; and Kielce-Sandomir. In March 1817, the Warsaw diocese was raised to the status of an archbishopric, the Chełm diocese was abolished, the Kujawa and Wigry dioceses were renamed Kalisz and Augustów (Sejny) respectively, and a new one was named after Janow near the Austrian-Galician border.[178] The archbishop, bishops, and other high prelates in this "Polish Catholic Church" were appointed by the emperor, but the nature of their relations with the Vatican remained undefined. The Russian government under Alexander I remained friendly to the Polish church for at least two reasons: the high church belonged to the aristocracy whom the emperor sought to win over to Russian policies; and they were in turn expected to uphold the conservative order against revolutionary ideas from abroad and against resistance in Poland itself, especially in the monasteries, where religious orders were often at odds with the high church, and which "had always been hotbeds of sedition."[179]

In the former Grand Duchy of Lithuania, the edict of April 1798 organized the "Catholic Church in Russia" in six dioceses, four of them in Lithuania and Belorussia: Mogilev, Minsk, Vilno, and Samogitia (the other two were in Volhynia and Podolia, in Lutsk and Kamenets). The Minsk and Mogilev dioceses had not existed in Polish days, and the Vilno diocese had been abolished. There had been only one diocese, in Samogitia, for its solidly Catholic population. In Vilno, Minsk, and Mogilev, the Catholic population was a minority: the Uniate population predominated. Sestrentsevych, the Mogilev archbishop, was raised to metropolitan of the Catholic Church in Russia, a position he would retain until 1826, shortly before his death. He also chaired the Department of Roman Catholic Affairs and became so powerful that it was said that "those who complained or appealed from one instance to another found him everywhere."[180] Leaders of monastic orders were forbidden to have relations with the Vatican and other powers outside Russia. The post of metropolitan had been unknown in the Polish Catholic hierarchy, and the Vilno and Samogitian dioceses had been subordinated, not to the archbishop and primate of Poland in Gniezno (now in Prussian Poland), but to the pope through the papal nuncio in Warsaw.[181] The edict thus consolidated the Catholic Church in the former Grand Duchy under the leadership of a metropolitan fully integrated into the central apparatus of the Russian government. It was one more step toward the creation of a "Russian Catholic Church."

The Orthodox Church was less well represented. There were only two dioceses in 1801. One was the Belorussian diocese for eastern Belorussia, its bishop in Mogilev, later called the Vitebsk and Mogilev archbishop. The other was the

Minsk diocese, its bishop called the Minsk and Lithuanian bishop because his jurisdiction included Vilno and Grodno provinces. It was not until 1833, after the crushing of the rebellion, that a third diocese was created, called the diocese of Polotsk and Vilno; Grodno province remained associated with Minsk.[182] These dioceses were, of course, fully integrated into the diocesan organization of the Orthodox Church headed by the senior procurator and the Holy Synod, the ecclesiastical equivalent of the Senate. The monastic clergy, however, was more deeply implanted in the territory. The interior ministry claimed in the 1830s that, while there was one monastery for 100,000 faithful in the Russian core, the ratio in the western provinces was one to 8,567. The "exorbitant" number of Roman Catholic monasteries, with their monastic orders "alienated from everything Russian,"[183] which controlled secondary and elementary education, became an obsession with the Russian authorities waiting for an opportunity to unleash a violent reaction.

The crushing of the rebellion of 1830–1, followed by the deportation of many members of the *szlachta*, the confiscation of their properties, and the mass degradation of many more to the status of burghers and peasants, resulted in two mutually reinforcing reactions. There developed among the *szlachta* – without which a policy of superstratification could not succeed – a form of messianism. It represented Poland "as the Christ of nations, who redeemed through her national Golgotha not only herself but all mankind," the innocent victim of "Asiatic" Russia, but also contrasted her with a Europe "contaminated by the diabolical forces of money."[184] This messianism, which merged Polonism with Polish Catholicism, found its bard in Adam Mickiewicz (1798–1855), Poland's greatest poet but born in Lithuania. It found its counterpart in a similar Russian messianism combining Russian identity (*narodnost'*) with the Orthodox Church, which found its bard in Alexander Pushkin (1799–1837), Russia's greatest poet. He warned "the "slanderers of Russia" to stay out of the Russo-Polish struggle to be fought and settled in western Eurasia by Russia's superior strength. Since both camps associated identity with religion, each treated the other as a confession of schismatics and infidels – as it had been the case since 1054! – and the Russo-Polish struggle turned into a vicious encounter between the Orthodox and the Catholic churches.[185]

Catholic monasteries were closed and later turned over to Orthodox communities. By 1842, 200 of the 291 religious houses in the former Grand Duchy had been taken over. The property of the church was seized by the new Ministry of State Domains (created in December 1837), but more often than not it was sold to Russian officials and dignitaries, who were expected to bring in Russian peasants. The edict of December 1841[186] dealt the church a devastating blow. It invoked Russian precedents of 1721 and 1764, when the properties of the Orthodox Church were secularized on the ground that the management of landed properties was detrimental to the performance of religious duties.

This redistribution of power over economic resources hit the high church especially hard – another blow to the policy of superstratification. From an economic point of view, the Catholic Church was downgraded to the level of the Orthodox Church and integrated into the Russian ecclesiastical system. Its clergy became dependent on a salary paid from the coffers of the ruling elite of the expanding Russian core, and "the religious life of the Catholic community was reduced to vegetation." The attack on the church was also directed against Polonism and created "a calamity for the general culture and civilization of the eastern marches, from which they never recovered."[187] The Orthodox Church had little to offer; its priests were openly despised by the *szlachta*. The Concordant signed in Rome in August 1847[188] seemed to soften Russian official policy. It confirmed the existence of the archibishopric of Mogilev, which included Finland and the dioceses of Vilno (Vilno and Grodno provinces), Samogitia (or Telshi created in October 1840) for Kovno and Kurland provinces, Minsk, Zhytomyr (Kiev and Volhynia), and Kamenets (Podolia), and the creation of a new one, the seventh, in Kherson, later moved to Tiraspol in Bessarabia. The nomination of bishops required the preliminary approval of the Vatican and Petersburg, but the appointment of parish priests by the bishops required the approval of the Russian government.

If the Catholic Church greatly suffered from the Russian counteroffensive for hegemony in the Russo-Polish confessional frontier, the Uniate Church was the major loser. Russia had refused to sanction the election of a successor to Smogorzewski as metropolitan of Kiev with jurisdiction over the church in the former Grand Duchy, and the Uniates had to wait until 1806, when Herakly Lissowski, archbishop of Polotsk (1806–9), was confirmed as "Metropolitan of the Greco-Uniate Church in Russia" (without reference to Kiev), a position he would retain only for a short time, until his death in 1809. The last metropolitan was Jozafat Bulhak (1758–1838), bishop of Brest-Litovsk (1798–1818) and Kiev (1818–38), who had been dismissed by Catherine II as bishop of Pinsk (1790–5). In April 1798, the government confirmed the existence of three Uniate dioceses: Polotsk for eastern Belorussia; Brest-Litovsk for western Belorussia and Lithuania; and Lutsk for the Uniates of Right Bank Ukraine. In February 1809, at Lissowski's urging, a Lithuanian metropolitan diocese was created in Vilno, to be administered by a suffragan bishop. Four years earlier, in 1805, a Greco-Uniate Department had been carved out of the Roman Catholic College in Petersburg.[189]

But this emancipation of the church was misleading. As early as 1798, Anastasii Bratanovskii, the Orthodox bishop of Polotsk, was already planning for the complete reunion of the two churches. In 1828, the Brest-Litovsk and Lutsk dioceses were closed, and in 1829, Iosif Semashko (Siemaszko, 1798–1869), the son of a Ukrainian village Uniate priest, educated at Vilno University, joined the department and became Uniate bishop of Lithuania. But he betrayed his church and wrote proposals to carry out the reunion. He then convened a church assembly in Polotsk in March 1839 to proclaim the dissolution of the Union of Brest (1595), which had created the church. The decision caused a painful split. Of the 2,000 priests and 342 monks forming the Uniate clergy, 1,305 signed the petition. Over a hundred of the others were deported to Siberia, and more were interned in Orthodox monasteries. Resistance among the population of 2 million Uniates was brutally put down.[190] Uniates remained only in the diocese of Chelm in the *tsarstvo*, which had been under the jurisdiction of the metropolitan of Halych in Galicia and later passed under the protection of the Vatican. They would be closely watched by the Orthodox bishop of Volhynia across the border and the vicariat of Warsaw, created in April 1834 and raised to a separate Orthodox diocese in October 1840.[191] The Uniate Church, called by Muravev the antechamber (*predverie*) to Catholicism, had not been integrated – it had been erased from the confessional map of the former Grand Duchy of Lithuania.

In the Baltic provinces, Lutheranism, like the Orthodox Church, had imposed on its parishioners a stultifying formalism.[192] The Lutheran pastor in his parish, like the German lord on his demesne, had a common interest in maintaining social control, and was the natural ally of the Russian authorities. The result was a deep chasm between ruling class and peasant, ethnic, religious, and cultural. Alexander Igelstrom from Estland, originally from Sweden, caught the mood very well. Pastors had been teaching morals rather than religion, and morals were inseparable from the maintenance of the status quo. Only the Moravian Brethren managed to attract the peasant and "caught in their nests the souls abandoned by their pastors."[193] Their membership more than doubled, from 31,554 in 1818 to 66,330 in 1839.[194]

The organization of the Lutheran Church centred on the consistory, mainly a judicial body, dealing with matters of faith and morals and, above all, marriages and divorces. The consistory was invariably chaired by a *Landrat*. The Lutheran Church was an appendage of the civil government and helped the College of *Landräte* administer the country. There were provincial consistories in Estland and Livland (called there the Superior Consistory – *Ober-Consistorium*), and in Kurland, as well as in Derpt and Pernau, on Ösel Island, and in the Pilten district of Kurland. Members were elected, some by the nobility, others by the clergy. There were also two municipal consistories, in Revel and in Riga. While a *Landrat* chaired the sessions, the administration of the church was in the hands of a superintendent, called general superintendent in Livland.[195] The Lutherans in the capital were placed in January 1803 under a new general superintendent.[196] These church officials were integrated into a new hierarchy headed by the Main Administration for Foreign Confessions in July 1810. Thus, the Lutheran, Catholic, and Uniate churches were incorporated into the ecclesiastical organization and ministerial system of the expanding Russian core, together with the Orthodox Church under its senior procurator.

But there were powerful forces within the Lutheran Church and the German ruling elite insisting on retaining a certain autonomy. After the failure to set up an episcopal system, as in Finland with its three bishops in Åbo, Borgå, and Vyborg, a committee was appointed in Petersburg to draw up a major reorganization of the Lutheran Church. The result of its work was the statute of December 1832.[197] A General Consistory was created for the entire church in Russia, with new consistories in Petersburg and Moscow. Local consistories remained in Estland, Livland, and Kurland, Riga and Revel, and on Ösel Island. The consistories were grouped into five regions (*okruga*), divided into districts (*probstva*) consisting of a number of parishes. The Consistory was headed by a lay president (Georg Freiherr von Meyendorff, 1845–79), so that the *Ritterschaft* remained in command. But the church was subordinated to the emperor, "the highest guardian [*bliustitel*] over order and discipline," who confirmed or rejected the decisions of Lutheran synods, the unfrocking of pastors, and deviations from church teachings "at his discretion."[198] The church thus regained a measure of administrative autonomy, only to fall directly under the emperor's supervision. The "feudal" nature of the relationship between the Romanov dynasty and the *Ritterschaft* was clearly in evidence here as well.

The alienation of the Lutheran Church from the peasantry explains at least in part the decision of a large number of Estonian and Latvian peasants to convert to Orthodoxy in the 1840s, encouraged by the new governor general, Lt.-Gen. Evgenii Golovin (1782–1858), who succeeded Pahlen in 1845. The movement fed on deep grievances of the peasantry against the terms of their emancipation in the 1810s and their treatment by the Lutheran lords and pastors. But the conversion made no significant headway, and Golovin was replaced after only three years in office.[199] A forceful movement to convert the peasants would have struck a blow to the policy of superstratification. The boundary between Orthodoxy and Lutheranism remained insuperable, and lords and pastors remained, at least for the time being, in full control of their dependent population. Garlieb Merkel, who had worked for the emancipation of the Latvian peasantry, had written at the end of the eighteenth century that "there is no Protestant country giving such example of arrogance of the clerical class [*soslovie*] as Livland," and in a veiled reference to the conquest of the country by the Livonian knights, "this can happen only in a country where the nobility owes its existence to the clergy."[200] That was still true at the end of the reign of Nicholas I.

Conclusion to Part I: The Western Theatre

The western theatre was a self-enclosed space bounded by the Scandinavian Alps, the Oder, the Sudeten Mountains, and the Vistula facing down the Baltic Sea, a fresh-water lake rather than a sea. The "lake" stretched from the Sound to the Åland Islands and branched off into the Gulf of Bothnia and the Gulf of Finland. It received little water from the North Sea, but was fed by the small rivers of Sweden, by Lake Ladoga and its satellites, and by the rivers of Lithuania and Poland. Geographically, the region was in certain ways the northeastern periphery of Europe, but it was much more the northwestern periphery of the Eurasian land mass, bound with it by latitudinal vegetation zones, by the great pine forests stretching from Poland to eastern Siberia, and by brutal continental winters. The western theatre was a corridor linking the dense land mass with the indented coasts of Europe looking outwards toward the Atlantic Ocean, while Poland and Sweden looked east to realize their destinies.

Largely because it was a self-contained world, dominated by the two cores of Sweden and Poland, it was a zone of perpetual conflict for hegemony between them, and also between the cores outside the territory, first between Catholic Europe and Orthodox Russia, much later between a rising Prussia and a rising Russia. It has been said that "Poland's geopolitical position [was] at the juncture between East and West, where two supranational communities overlapped." Poland was long regarded "by the Latin West as a somewhat primitive outpost of civilization, useful at one time for repelling Tatar and Turkish invasions and later for providing an obstacle to Russian territorial ambitions. The Slavic East viewed Poland – in language Slavic but in religion Roman Catholic – as a traitor to the Slavic nation and the Orthodox church."[1] It was the Latin West, with its power centre in Rome, which took umbrage at the progress of Greek Orthodoxy along the water route linking Constantinople with the Gulf of Finland and launched the northern crusades, led mostly by Germans, that planted the Vatican's flag on Baltic shores. It was the Catholic Counter-Reformation, led again from Rome, which launched another crusade three hundred years later under the leadership of another crusading order, the Jesuits, to check the progress of Protestantism, which had wrecked the unity of Latin Christendom. They Christianized Samogitia at last, but the schism could not be healed, any more than that of 1054 between the Latin West and the Greek East could have been healed. Religion became associated with national identity – Catholicism in Poland, Lutheranism in Sweden – and the two estranged sisters fought for hegemony in the Baltic basin, only to end up weakening each other. Paradoxically, it was also then that projects were floated to unite both with their other sister in the east, but to no effect.

By the seventeenth century, Russian Orthodoxy, which had settled its own schism by losing its independence and becoming identified with the rising Russian core and its ruling political elite, was also giving additional strength to that core. It was Russia which now fought both Sweden and Poland, and it was Russia, in alliance with Poland, which launched the so-called Northern War which destroyed Swedish hegemony and launched Poland on its path to self-destruction. Later in the eighteenth century, it incorporated the entire Russo-Polish frontier and was poised to annex Finland as well. How would it manage these new territories?

The Russian core, as it expanded to unify the basin of the Volga, had become a unitary state governed by an autocrat, for whom all power flowed from his person, and who, for fiscal and military reasons if for no other, had sought to harmonize administrative, military, fiscal, and judicial policies and convert his subjects to the Orthodox faith – to the extent that this was possible at a time of difficult communications and limited personnel. The Code of 1649 applied in all Russian territories, and their ruling class was submerged into a supra-provincial elite tightly controlled by the dynasty and capable of carrying out its policies on an all-Russian scale. The Swedish kings had been integrationists at heart; so were the Polish kings in Right Bank Ukraine after incorporating the territory into the *Korona*. Polonization was not always the organic process it has been made out to be. Russian rulers would follow the same path.

In the Baltic provinces, to which the expanding core remained limited until the last quarter of the eighteenth century, it was stated from the beginning of the annexation that the "privileges" were a residual juridical category and would be retained for as long as they were not inconsistent with an evolving Russian legislation – that is, for as long as the autocrat, as a true Eurasian ruler, found it fit to retain them. The plenitude of the legislative, administrative, and judicial power remained vested in the tsar-emperor, who could tolerate no deviation unless he had chosen to do so. The concept of residual local privilege versus the plenitude of central monarchical power would remain part of the political discourse throughout the eighteenth century; it was reasserted with new force at the beginning of the nineteenth in Troshchynsky's memorandum. Indeed, Catherine II, more than any other Romanov ruler, insisted without the least ambiguity that a policy of full integration served the interests of the expanding core, and that privileges, at least those found inconsistent with stated government policy, must make way before the supremacy of those interests. But policies, even clear ones, are not free from occasional contradictions. The German *Ritterschaft* was bound to the Romanov house by ties of loyalty, the loyalty of a warrior class to its commander in chief. The German nobility and clergy had created a Little Germania in an environment of natives with whom they had little in common and whom they had enserfed. Loyalty to the ruling house was essential to their survival. But they were also a conquered people, conquered by a people they had come to conquer, as an assertive Empress Elizabeth and her government reminded them on occasion. The government had to tread carefully, for loyalty worked not only from the bottom up, but also from the top down. To declare the privileges to be inconsistent with government policy was tantamount to declaring that the loyalty of the German ruling class had become irrelevant. That could open a Pandora's box of unforeseeable consequences. To preserve the status quo as long as possible was preferable, as the government of Paul I, Alexander I, and Nicholas I found out.

In eastern Finland, it was not necessary to mention privileges. The territory was considered an old Russian one, and Russian lands did not have privileges. The recovery of the Grand Duchy of Lithuania, whose people consisted of "ancient Russian subjects" and which had presumably been "taken away" from the Russian patrimony, did not require the recognition of privileges; the territory was immediately incorporated into the Russian administrative system.

A policy of integration must be accompanied by a policy of superstratification. Every "intruding" ethnic group faces the same problem, but success depends on circumstances which are peculiar to each territory. In the western theatre, these circumstances were varied and complex. In the Baltic provinces, society was already stratified by the time of their annexation. There were descendants of the Livonian and Teutonic Knights, who had become landowners when the Order converted to Protestantism; there were other Germans, some also landowners, some not; there was a native population of Estonians and Latvians. The Germans formed a separate *Kulturgemeinschaft* on the western fringe of Eurasia, looking outward to the North German world, but highly vulnerable to pressures from the east, conscious of their class differences and of their racial superiority over the native population.

A policy of superstratification presupposes the existence of a stratified society over which the Russian intruder will impose his rule and behaviour, but the intruder will also seek a *modus vivendi* with the top stratum of that society. The Swedes had neglected this crucial factor. By striking at the wealth of the top stratum in the "reversion" and even raising the possibility of abolishing serfdom – the foundation of the social order – they antagonized the German and Germano-Swedish ruling class and encouraged it to accept the Russians, who promised to confirm the privileges. In so doing, the Russians had to desist from pursuing a policy of integration, even though the existence of serfdom on both sides of the territorial divide already created a strong social bond. But the Germans themselves had been intruders, had conquered the indigenous population. The Russian intruders thus imposed their rule on other foreign intruders, creating a strong temptation, in times of differences between Russians and Germans, to turn the native population against the Germans – a temptation the Russians resisted until after the middle of the nineteenth century, because it was too dangerous to break a relationship based on loyalty. Catherine II's policy went some way toward upsetting the relationship. Her reforms "democratized" German society by diluting the power monopoly of the *Ritterschaft* and empowering other Germans who had been kept out of the structure of domination. Integration and superstratification were becoming contradictory policies, and her successors withdrew to a policy of superstratification in which the Russian elite and the *Ritterschaft* recognized their mutual interest in maintaining German social control.

In the Grand Duchy of Lithuania, where the population was overwhelmingly Belorussian, there were not two but three intruders. Lithuanians had built an overextended political conglomerate of Belorussians north of the Pripet marshes and Ukrainians south of them. The union with Poland of 1386, confirmed in 1569, brought Poles into the territory, who imposed their superior civilization and their Roman Catholicism. And then came the Russians, who sought to impose their way of life and Eastern Orthodoxy on both, in the name of a historical legacy which went back to Kievan Rus' and to which the Russians claimed they were entitled because it had been taken away from them, also in the name of a peculiar Orthodox pretension which bound religion with a dominant ethnicity: Belorussians and Lithuanians were Russian and should be converted to Orthodoxy or vice versa, as circumstances demanded.

This tortuous circular logic had to be grounded on the use of force. Unlike the situation in the Baltic provinces and Finland, where the German and Swedish nobility accepted Russian rule and cooperated with it because it was in their interest, the Polish *szlachta*, if not the Lithuanian one, was hostile to Russia. It saw its role as that of a *Kulturträger*, the carrier of a superior civilization, that of a core which for centuries had radiated a beneficent influence on a vast territory in the Russo-Polish frontier against Russia's "eastern barbarism," that soothing slogan of the Germans as well.

The *szlachta*'s opposition was not only cultural but also political. They strove to recover the "borders of 1772," a feat which could be achieved only on the battlefield, a hopeless pursuit. Hence the sombre hostility of the two peoples. The *szlachta* could not be expected to be loyal, and both policies of superstratification and integration were bound to fail. Or were they? In the face of systematic *szlachta* hostility, the Russians chose a policy of full integration in the former

Grand Duchy, playing upon the hostility between the Belorussians and the two intruders, Poles and Lithuanians, in the cultural and religious spheres. But that raised other problems.[2]

The western theatre had been a confessional frontier since the Middle Ages. For Roman Catholicism, the religion of Europe, it was the land of missionary activity, where monastic orders brought a message of love and brotherhood while slaughtering or converting the natives. The task, originally a German one, became a Swedish and a Polish one after the Reformation. Swedish Lutheranism was no less militant than Polish Counter-Reformation Catholicism. Both branches of Latin Christianity became associated with a civilizational core, Polish and Swedish. But Swedish Lutheranism preached obedience and subservience to the secular power, while Polish Catholicism remained part of a larger supranational church preaching the creed and European civilization to natives the world over. As to Russian Orthodoxy, it had long since become a xenophobic agent of the secular power, and the schism of 1666, the reforms of Peter I, and the secularization of 1764 only deepened its association with and subservience to that power. Its mission was to convert the natives of the Eurasian land mass, from the Baltic Sea to the Pacific Ocean. But it was bound to encounter, no longer Islam, but, on the western fringes of Eurasia, the determined opposition of Swedish Lutheranism and Polish Catholicism. A compromise was possible with the former, but Catholicism did not owe its allegiance to an ethnic ruling class. It drew its strength from an external power, no less determined and no less intolerant than Russia's political Orthodoxy. Here there could be no compromise. Both sides would continue to claim hegemony, and both would render impossible any policy of stratification and of integration.

If the confessional hostility was certain to block any durable compromise and prevent integration (a union of churches), a policy of educational integration contained the seeds of its own destruction. Such a policy would have to be directed to instil the "Russian spirit" in the Belorussian and even Lithuanian youth – Polish students in the same school might end up "Polonizing" their friends. Even if it emphasized the teaching of Russian and the natural sciences (instead of the humanities), it was certain to instil in the native youth a consciousness of their historical heritage, their literature and folklore, which had been smothered by their Swedish, German, and Polish teachers. But such a consciousness, grafted upon a resentment of Russian methods and intolerance, was certain to generate a mood of opposition to Russian rule and even a yearning for separatism. Education is everywhere potentially subversive. There was a danger that to educate the native population by creating a school network integrated into that of the expanding Russian core would only create an agent of disintegration. Catherine II, who did much for Russian education, had such a premonition when she wrote to Governor General Alexander Prozorovskii in Moscow (1790–5): "My dear Prince, do not bemoan the fact that our Russians have no desire to learn. The policy to create schools in my empire is not for us, but for Europe, in order to uphold among foreigners the good opinion they have of us. As soon as the Russian people truly become educated, I will no longer remain empress or you governor."[3] The effect was certain to be even more devastating in the western theatre.

But were Russian rulers truly creating an empire on the western fringe of the Eurasian land mass? The concept of empire rests on the acceptance of administrative diversity, the recognition of separate local institutions, separate legislation in the field of law and taxation, separate procedures, even separate religions. It is a combination of all these differences which distinguishes an empire from a unitary state, where the overriding concern, even obsession, of the central leadership is to erase differences and create a single state organism ruled by the same laws from one end to the other of a usually considerable territorial space. It is quite clear that the expanding Russian core was determined to incorporate and destroy that combination of differences in the former Grand Duchy of Lithuania. Catherine II's government pursued that policy in a paradoxical way. It closed most central agencies in a massive decentralization drive resulting in a well-concentrated central and local government, which, at first glance, should have upheld local peculiarities. But at the same time, it also insisted on extending Russian laws and procedures to the new territories acquired during the powerful expansionist urge so characteristic of the eighteenth century. Even the Baltic provinces felt the devastating blow.

Catherine's two grandsons were strong believers in the unitary state; the creation and development of powerful ministries were the best proof. Ministries are specialized institutions with their own specialized agencies, distrustful of local variations in laws and procedures. They are by definition the creators of the unitary state. Both the Grand Duchy and the Baltic provinces were integrated into the regional networks created by each ministry, but the Baltic provinces remained a case apart. Their privileges were defended by a caste of warriors well connected with the centres of power; the warriors swore a personal oath of loyalty to the Romanov ruler, and welcomed their integration into the military establishment of the expanding core. There, integration, superstratification, and the protection of privileges combined to create an exceptional case in the history of Russian public administration.

But the expanding core stumbled at the beginning of the nineteenth century against an obstacle it could not afford to overcome, and the unitary state had to concede the necessity of creating an empire. Finland, sturdy and loyal, suffered little interference, created its own elite, and kept its own laws. Poland, much larger, less stable, and fundamentally disloyal because of its past, was also given a separate administration, not seen anywhere else other than in the Caucasus, from which ministries were largely excluded because the regional institution of viceroyalty was fundamentally antithetical to the functional hierarchies of ministries. It also kept its own laws even if they were largely based on the Code Napoleon. Only in the case of both Finland and Poland, despite their differences – the essence of diversity – can we speak, not of a unitary state, but of an empire, yet one unstable at best. The urge to integrate was so old and so powerful that ministries kept chipping away at the fringes of imperial administration, and a generation after the death of Nicholas I, the empire was on the verge of becoming a unitary state, until it was realized that the power of resistance was too strong. But by 1850, the expansion of the unitary state had stopped at the boundaries of Poland and Finland, and an empire had been born in the western theatre.

There, as in the southern theatre, we observe the unfolding of the same policy. The expanding Russian core created an imperial cushion, both for self-protection and as a base from which to project power further afield. Poland and Finland served that purpose. Beyond that zone lay Sweden and Prussia. Sweden, domesticated after 1815 by the Russian embrace, was turned outward toward Norway to forget the days of its past grandeur, when it was a threat to Russia. But Prussia, although tied to Russia by close dynastic unions, remained a recalcitrant client fated to increasingly reject Russian tutelage; it was also turned westward to unite the German lands. There, Russian policy would fail; its management of the western fringe of Eurasia would disintegrate, and a renewed German *Drang nach Osten* would destroy the Russian drive to unify and integrate the Eurasian land mass into a single territorial and political conglomerate capable of rivalling the rising United States in the Northern Hemisphere, as Alexis de Tocqueville so dramatically prophesied in the 1830s.[4]

PART II

The Southern Theatre Reaches the Sea

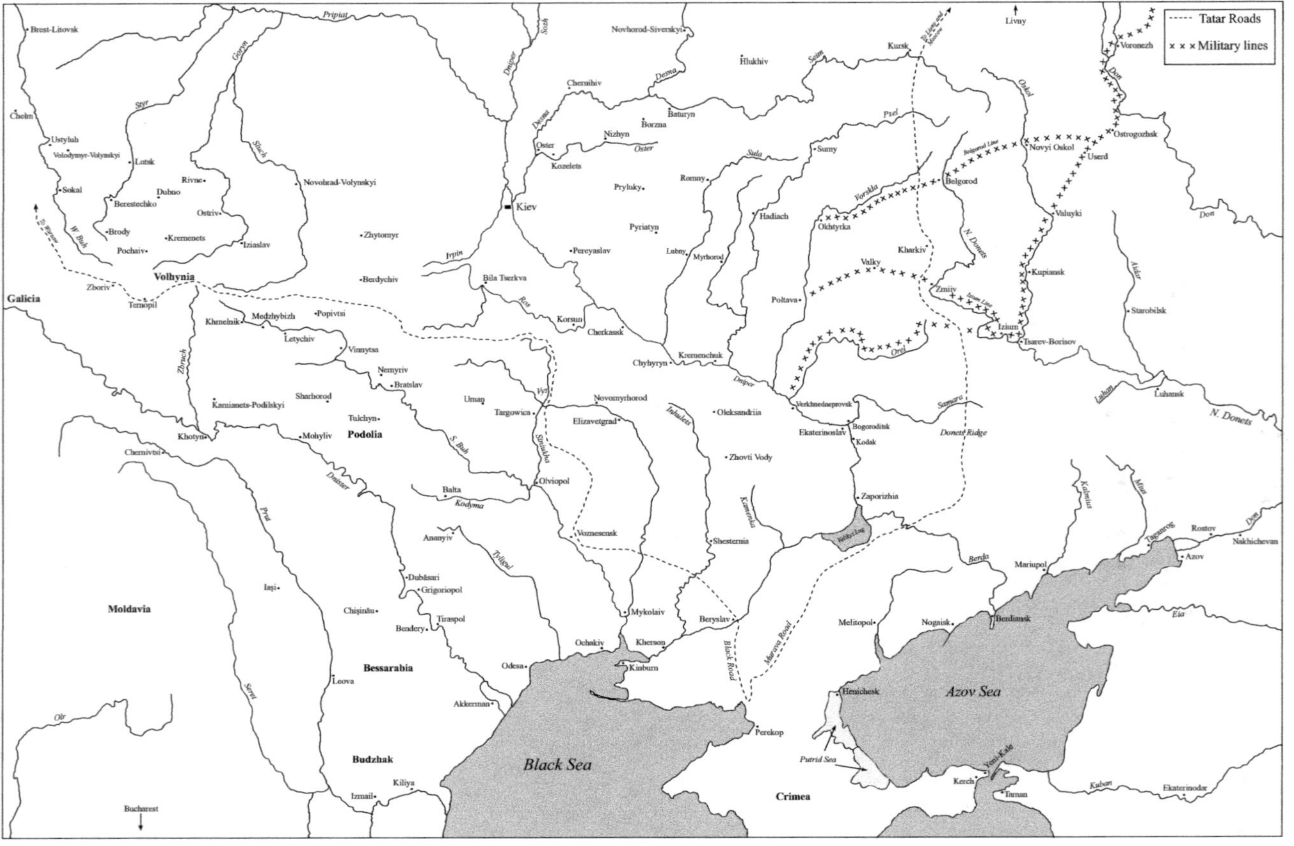

Map 4 The Southern Theatre

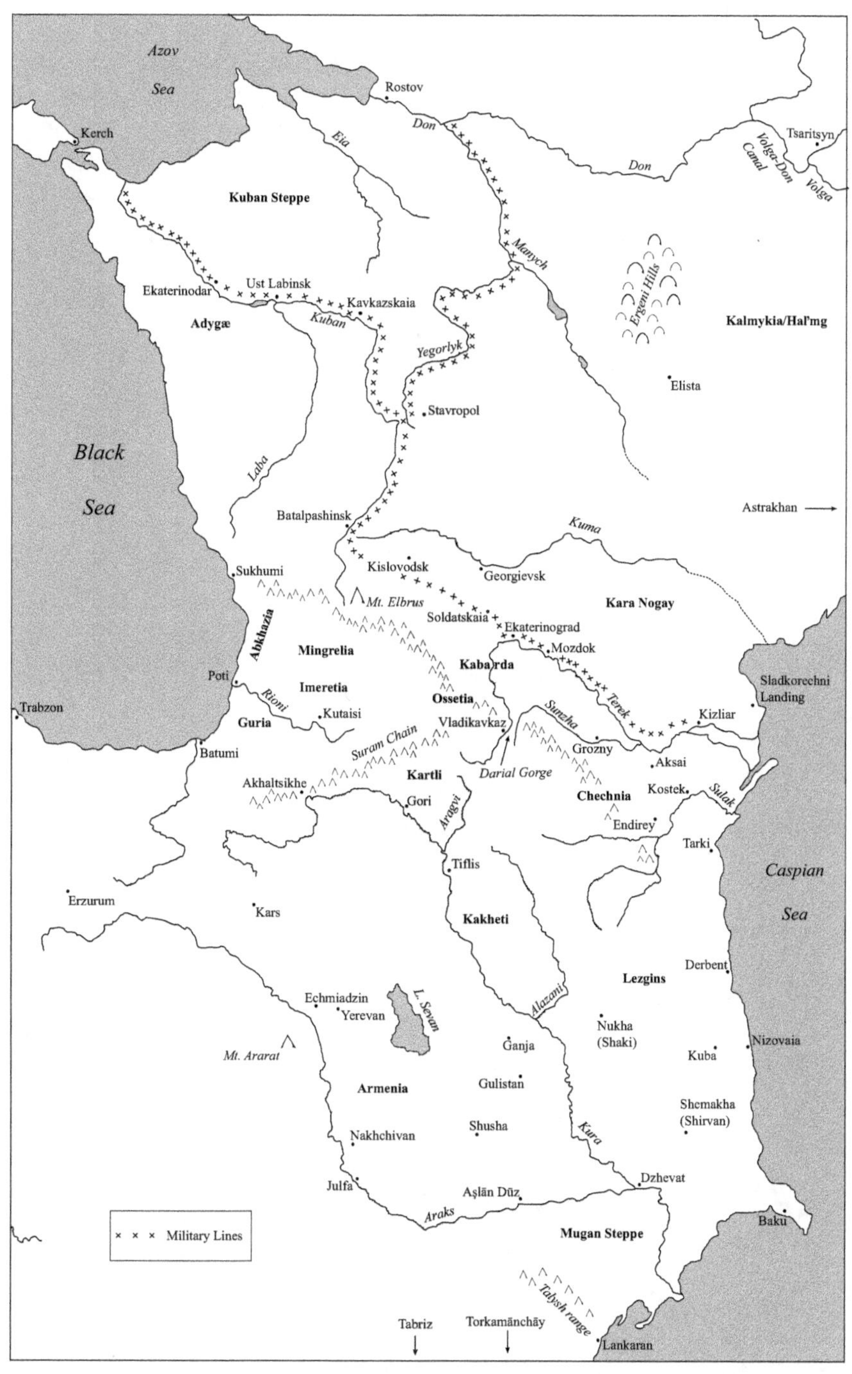

Map 5 The Caucasus

Chapter Four

Laying the Foundations, 1650–1725

The Geopolitical Setting

Geography and Geopolitics

The southern theatre resembled a crescent with points in Bessarabia and western Transcaucasia, connected by an outer semicircle running north of Lviv (Lwów, Lvov), Kiev (Kyiv), and Chernihiv (Chernigov), east past Kursk and Voronezh, south past Kalachna on the Don (where the river flows closest to the Volga), along the watershed between the Black Sea and Caspian basins, and across the Caucasus to Batum; its inner semicircle followed the northern Black Sea coast with a detour to include the Crimean peninsula. The crescent was about 1,200 kilometres long as the crow flies and 800 kilometres across. Most of it was steppe land, for long the unchallengeable domain of the nomad as far north as the Oka River, the northern boundary of the wooded steppe zone. The southern boundary of that zone ran from the northern corner of Bessarabia to Ananev (Ananyiv) on the Tiligul (Tylihul) along the Kodyma and Tashlyk Rivers past Elizavetgrad (Kirovohrad, Kropyvnytsky) to Kremenchuk on the Dnieper, crossed the river to Poltava, continued south of Kharkiv (Kharkov) to Valuiki on the Oskol and Borisoglebsk on the Vorona, reached the Volga north of Saratov, and followed the river to the confluence of the Samara, where the Orenburg Territory began. South of the wooded steppe zone, characterized by fertile soils and forests of birches and oaks (until the advancing settlers cut them down), began the treeless steppe, covered with luxurious vegetation of tall feather grass growing on black earth of varying humus content, but everywhere the best soil for the cultivation of cereals, at least where the climate permitted. The steppe extended as far south as the piedmont of the Great Caucasus and to the watershed with the semidesert of the Caspian basin.[1]

The southern theatre can conveniently be divided into five natural and historical regions superimposed upon the latitudinal zones of wooded steppe and pure steppe. The first was the territory north of the Dnieper, between the Pripiat marshes of Belorussia (Belarus) in the western theatre and the Orel River flowing into the Dnieper, downriver from Kremenchuk. Its northern boundary was the watershed between the basin of the Volga and that of the Dnieper, between that of the Caspian and that of the Black Sea. It ran from Briansk deep in the forests of the Desna valley past the headwaters of the Oka to the Don valley north of Voronezh. The transit zone between the higher ground of Tula and Kaluga provinces and the Dnieper depression stretched latitudinally between the Desna and the Don, as if to protect the Muscovite centre against threats from the south. Indeed, it warded off the cold northeasterlies known as *sukhovei* or, with a touch of humour, the Muscovites (*moskovskie*), which dried up the top layer of moisture, causing repeated droughts and poor harvests.

Beyond the transition zone was Kursk province with its southern town of Belgorod on the very fringe of the Dnieper depression. To the west flowed the Desna through forests of oaks and pines, but navigable only for flat-bottom boats carrying timber and iron goods from Smolensk province to Kiev, connecting the manufacturing region of central Russia with the agricultural provinces of the south. The river was of potential strategic importance as an invasion route for a river flotilla descending the Dnieper to attack Turkish possessions in the river's estuary, notably Ochakov. Unfortunately, the rapids on the Dnieper presented a nearly insurmountable obstacle to free access to the Black Sea, as Peter I found out when he planned his war against the Turks in 1711. The other left-bank tributaries of the Dnieper (the Sula, the Psël, and the Vorskla) were less obstructed by countless water mills that helped irrigate the "kingdom of orchards" that began as far north as Kursk, famous for their apples and pears, then cherries and plums.

These two lands of Chernihiv and Poltava were known as Little Russia[2] or the Hetmanate, because they were administered by a hetman after the uprising that resulted in their annexation to Great Russia, or the Muscovite centre. Both fronted the Dnieper, which, between Kiev and Ekaterynoslav (Dnipropetrovsk, Dnipro), became a lazy river forming a multitude of parallel channels. They greatly reduced the volume of water in the main channel, and created some three hundred large and small islands, with additional sand bars obstructing navigation. East of Poltava, the Ukrainian lands also included the Kharkiv corridor. It did not quite belong to the valley of the Dnieper save for the headwaters of the Psël and Vorskla. Its axis was the Northern Donets, a tributary of the Don. The corridor contained the Murava trail used by the Tatars on their way to Moscow. The route began on the Perekop Isthmus separating the Crimean Peninsula from the mainland, followed the great bend of the Dnieper, then the Northern Donets past Belgorod, on to Livny, from which the trail led straight to Tula and on to Serpukhov on the Oka. The soil consisted almost entirely of black earth, but the climate was drier and colder than in Poltava.

Across the Dnieper was the second region known as Right Bank Ukraine, rising from the flood plain of the Dnieper toward the Podolia Plateau, dissected by countless streams descending into the Dniester, beyond which the valley of the Prut announced the Carpathian Mountains. Right Bank Ukraine was not only a historical creation, it was also shaped by nature. It bordered on the southeast, along the Kodyma, the Syniukha, and the Vys, on the so-called "Khan's Ukraine," the domain of the Crimean Khan, a pure steppe watered by the lower course of the Southern Buh (Bug), the Inhul (Ingul), the Inhulets, and other steppe streams. The northern part was a flat and swampy land crossed by rivers, notably the Styr and the Horyn (Goryn) with its tributary, the Sluch, feeding the Pripiat marshes, the so-called Polesie (Polissia), drained by the Pripiat of Belorussia flowing into the Dnieper some ninety kilometres north of Kiev.[3] From this poorly drained and heavily forested region the ground rose rapidly southwards on the Volhynia upland, whose black earth appeared along the upland's perimeter from Volodymyr-Volynsky (Vladimir-Volynsk) to Novohrad-Volynsky via Rivne, and the Podolian Plateau overlooking the Dniester's valley with its gardens and vineyards. This rich Right Bank Ukraine was ideally suited to become both a granary and a zone of transit trade. Its grain was exported northeastwards to the Western Bug, forming Poland's natural eastern border, and on to the Vistula to Danzig on the Baltic coast, from which it went to the European markets. The grain also travelled along the Southern Buh to the Black Sea and on to Transcaucasia and the Turkish Straits, from which it reached the Mediterranean. Moreover, the timber of the region's northern part was floated down the Pripiat to the Dnieper to meet the demand of the steppe region for boat- and house-building, even for firewood. As far back as antiquity, the Greeks had a colony at Akkerman (Bilhorod-Dnistrovskyi) on the estuary of the Dniester, where the export trade of the entire region was concentrated.

One hesitates to place that part of Moldavia located between the Dniester and the Prut, known as Bessarabia. From its high point near Khotyn in the narrow passage between the two rivers, the ground descended toward the steppe. The soil and vegetation of the northern part continued those of Right Bank Ukraine; the southern part, known as Budzhak, belonged to the feather grass steppe of New Russia. The boundary followed approximately the so-called Upper Trajan Wall, built by the Roman emperor (98–117), between Leova on the Prut and the confluence of the Botnia with the Dniester near Bendery.

The third region was New Russia (Novorossiya), now better known as southern Ukraine. It was an immense steppe stretching from the Dniester to, and including, the Donets Ridge overlooking the lower Don valley and the Gulf of Taganrog to the north of Berdiansk, and from the Orel River to the southern perimeter of the Kharkiv corridor.[4] It consisted of two latitudinal zones, one of feather grass steppe on black earth, the other, with the Crimean peninsula, of feather grass dry steppe on southern black earth (with a lower humus content) and brown chestnut soils, descending to the Black Sea coast. It was divided longitudinally into two unequal parts by the lower Dnieper ending in a long lagoon (liman) shared with the Southern Buh leading through a narrow channel into the Black Sea. It was a flat sedimentary plain where the rivers had cut through to the basement rock to produce a series of rapids: they were found across the Dniester near Yampol, at Voznesensk on the Southern Buh, at Shesternia on the Inhulets, and above all across the Dnieper, near present-day Zaporizhia ("beyond the rapids"), where the ten-kilometre-long Khortytsia Island became the headquarters of the Zaporozhian Cossacks. The rapids were so many markers forming the base of two triangles, the northern one on higher ground more attractive to settlement, the southern slowly merging with the sea along a desolate shore studded with seashells and patches of salt, as if the sea had only recently receded from the land. The desolation reminded some observers of the approaches to the Caspian Sea on the north Caucasian steppe.

If southern Ukraine had excellent soils, it suffered from a dreadful climate which repelled peasant settlers for a long time. The "Khan's Ukraine," which became Kherson province, was exposed to dry winds in the summer and to the northeasterlies in the spring and fall, which brought stifling heat and extreme cold, with hardly any snow cover to renew the moisture but just enough to turn it into the same destructive icy crust. The eastern part, which became Ekaterynoslav province, suffered from heavy rains in April and May, which often decided the fate of the harvest. At other times, a drought ruined the settlers' hopes, and to make matters worse, clouds of locusts could ruin a good harvest in a matter of hours.

The Dnieper was the heart of southern Ukraine, but it was an anemic one. The rapids occupied a ninety-six-kilometre-long section at the very beginning of the region. There were nine of them, leaving a narrow passage just deep enough for flat-bottom boats, but underwater boulders were a constant danger everywhere. Boats had to be unloaded and carried overland past the rapids.[5] Then came a huge, low, swampy island (*plavnia*) called Velykyi Luh, which drew water from the main channel and reduced the water's velocity, already slowed by the flatness of the land. Below Kherson, the Dnieper did not end in a broad estuary one would expect from such a majestic river, but divided into branches (*girly*), and the depth of the main channel did not exceed 2.7 metres, barely enough for boats engaged in coastal trade. The river then had to flow through a fifty-six-kilometre-long lagoon, which was not deep enough for large ships, including the warships which the Russians built for their Black Sea fleet, and which had to be anchored at Sevastopol. The Dnieper could not realize its potential until the Soviet period, when dams raised the water level above the rapids.

East of southern Ukraine and the Kharkiv corridor began a fourth region consisting of the broad basin of the Don. It was bounded in the south by the valley of the Kuban, descending from the western section of the Great Caucasus. The Don's major and only right-bank tributary was the Northern Donets, the axis of the Kharkiv corridor, whose eastern districts merged imperceptibly with the black earth steppe of the lower Don valley. The Northern Donets used to be navigable from Izium well into the eighteenth century for large barges, which, in the event of war, conveyed supplies to the army attacking the Crimea from the east, but the growing number of water mills subsequently obstructed navigation over most of its course, reducing the Don's potential as a shipping route.

The Don picked up several left-bank tributaries, notably the Khoper and the Medveditsa, both taking their source in the Penza upland, where the eastern theatre began. Both flowed across dense oak forests, which did not become steppe until the trees had been systematically cut down for shipbuilding. Their soil was rich black earth, ideal for the production of grain and the raising of cattle. The river took its source near Tula and flowed past Voronezh, located on one of its affluents. Peter I made the town a shipyard for the building of a Don flotilla to operate against the Turks in the Azov Sea. Its delta was a malaria-infested area of black earth, where the Turks built a fortress at Azov (known to the Greeks as Tana), near which Rostov was built in the eighteenth century.

The Don was also a boundary beyond which began a steppe of salt marsh that already belonged to the Caspian depression. Jan Potocki, travelling in the early 1800s, thought that even the Khoper separated Russia from "a scene of extreme desolation,"[6] where the Nogais roamed, who would later make way for the Kalmyks. But the Trans-Don (Zadonsk) steppe between the Manych and the Kuban had a redeeming feature in a fertile zone, excellent for the cultivation of wheat, whose only "inhabitants" until the end of the eighteenth century were the Tatar hordes roaming the entire region from the Budzhak to the Kuban. But the climate was unhealthy and became more so as one approached the swampy Azov coast and the Taman peninsula, a large waterlogged "plavnia" overgrown with reeds and surrounded by a cluster of deep bays, which the Russians long thought formed an island. Malaria and "fevers" killed off entire settlements along the Kuban and in the deep and humid valleys across the river.

But then the ground rose toward the western Caucasus, the fifth region, which began at Anapa and stretched southeastwards in three parallel ranges until it rose abruptly toward Mount Elbrus, where the Kuban took its source, at an elevation of 5,635 metres, the highest point in the Caucasus, overlooking the watershed between the southern and eastern theatres. South of the mountains, crossed via the Mamison Pass at 2,900 metres, began the fifth and last region of the southern theatre, western Georgia. It was a highly fragmented land from Abkhazia to Adzharia, facing chains running northwards from the Taurus Mountains of Turkish Anatolia. It was bounded in the east by the Suram range connecting the Greater with the Little Caucasus, leaving only a narrow corridor linking the Black Sea with the Caspian via Tiflis (Tblisi). Most of the relief consisted of heavily forested spurs, inaccessible in many places, and descending abruptly either to the sea or to the plain below. This plain was known as the Colchian Lowland, watered by the lower Rion River. It stretched from the Kodori River to Kobuleti north of Batum. Its soil was not suitable for agriculture, but the tropical climate favoured the cultivation of tea, tangerines, and bamboo.[7] Much of the coastal region, however, was another swampy and spongy land which caused the fevers so deleterious to human life in much of the land south of the lower Don.

Mongols and Crimean Tatars

The Mongol invasion was the greatest geopolitical event of the thirteenth century in the southern theatre. The defeat of 1223 on the Kalka (Kalmius) River was a portent of things to come, as the east-west alignment of the steppe kept driving the Mongols onwards. They destroyed Kiev (already much weakened by internecine struggles among the princes) in 1240, and crossed the Carpathians into the Hungarian steppe, which would also protect their right flank should they decide to move into Europe, as the Huns had done some eight hundred years earlier. The offensive never took place, but the Kipchak Khanate, with its capital in Sarai built in 1242, remained in control of the northern basin of the Black Sea to the Prut, the lower Danube, and Bulgaria, and to the watershed between the Black and Baltic basins.

But the khanate's hold on the western peripheries remained fragile. It was challenged, though not always openly, by the princes of Galicia and those of Chernihiv, and further north by the rise of Lithuania deep in the forest zone. The geography of the Mongol empire was that of the steppe and semi-desert, with few inroads into the forest zone, alien to the horseman and hostile to pastoralism. The rise of Lithuania was not a threat in itself, because friendly relations would open up an alternative route to the Novgorod connection with the Baltic coast, and the Muslim merchants who managed the trade of central and southern Eurasia had a strong interest in developing an international market between the Baltic, Black, and Caspian Seas linked with that of distant China and India, an inter-oceanic global economy linking the European with the Asian coastland.

But the Grand Duchy of Lithuania, founded in about 1235 around Novogrudok and Volkovysk in so-called Black Russia, quickly developed an interest in Galicia and Volhynia, and dynastic marriages promised to create a lasting alliance and a larger state between the Baltic and Black Seas. The Mongols retaliated by conducting devastating raids in 1285–6 to reassert their hegemony in the Black Sea basin, where the Crimean ports, especially Soldaia (Sudak), largely in the hands of Venetian and Genoese merchants, promoted trade not only in the Black Sea but also in the eastern Mediterranean and with Egypt. In 1271, Nogai, a chieftain given responsibility by Sarai for Black Sea affairs, launched a campaign against Constantinople, the Byzantine capital, where he married an illegitimate daughter of the emperor in 1273, after gaining the right to let the Mongols use the Straits to send diplomatic missions to Egypt. Nogai's bailiwick was the steppe between the lower Dnieper and the Danube – the future Kherson province and Bessarabia – and he sought in vain to annex Sandomerz and Kraków in Poland, but went on to occupy Serbia, as if to repeat the campaign of 1241. However, he ran afoul of the Kipchak khan, who defeated and killed him in battle near Kremenchuk in 1300. The disappearance of this powerful chieftain left a political vacuum which would invite the Lithuanian advance toward the Black Sea.

The fourteenth century, during which the khanate reached its apogee before entering a long period of decline beginning in the 1360s, witnessed a radical redistribution of space in western Eurasia. It was under Grand Duke Gedimin (1316–41) that Lithuania became a great power, and his grandson Vitovt (1392–1430) concentrated his efforts on reaching the Black Sea and incorporating into a Greater Lithuania what had been Nogai's domain a century earlier. Volhynia and Kiev were annexed, and Vitovt built forts along the lower Dnieper to carve out a realm that would roll back Mongol power beyond the river. By the end of the century, Lithuania had become a huge territorial entity reaching down to the Dniester and along the river to the Black Sea, up the Dnieper to and along the Vorskla, from which the border ran east of Briansk and Kursk to the Oka near Kaluga.

Other momentous events were reshaping the map of western Eurasia. Casimir the Great of Poland (1333–70) incorporated Galicia into the "Crown of the Kingdom of Poland" (*korona*), and advanced into Podolia, bordering on Moldavia, which, via the Seret and the Prut, led to the lower Danube and the Black Sea. But the Piast dynasty became extinct in the male line in 1382, and the young Queen Jadwiga married Jagiello, Vitovt's first cousin, the Grand Duke of Lithuania, in 1386, creating the Jagellonian dynasty, which would last until 1572. The union was a fateful event because it drew Poland deeper into western Eurasia and set the stage for the long conflict with Muscovy. Vitovt already thought of a possible alliance with the Kipchak khanate in what could have become a triangular struggle for hegemony in western Eurasia. But it was too late: after Tamerlane's destruction of Sarai in 1395, the khanate could not be a strong and reliable ally – in fact it could never have been reliable, what with the nomad's reluctance to form commitments that would go beyond raiding and plundering.

Yet another development was about to reshape the geopolitics of the southern theatre. In 1355, a small detachment of Ottoman Turks crossed the Dardanelles and established themselves in Gallipoli, a base from which to start the conquest of the Balkan peninsula. As the Turks followed the alignment of rivers and mountain chains to move from east to northwest, the Poles and Lithuanians followed the river valleys to expand southeastwards, until they and the Turks would inevitably meet. The Turks outflanked Constantinople by taking Adrianople (Edirne) in 1361, defeated the Serbs at Kosovo in 1389, and annexed Bulgaria in 1393, but were defeated by Tamerlane at Ankara in 1402, where the sultan was taken prisoner.[8] Nevertheless, the great expansion of the Ottoman empire was yet to come.

In the north, the Grand Princes of Moscow, notably Ivan I (1325–41) and Dmitri (1359–89), were fashioning another warrior state. Contained by Lithuania in the west and by Mongol power in the steppe, Moscow had been expanding northwards toward the Onega and Northern Dvina Rivers in the direction of the White Sea in search of furs and other products of the forest zone. Ivan I ingratiated himself with Sarai in order to build a power base in the Volga-Oka mesopotamia, which provided access to the interior lines of western Eurasia. In more favourable circumstances, they would make it possible to strike in three directions, against Lithuania, toward the Black Sea, and toward Kazan and beyond. Khan Mamai reached an agreement with Jagiello in 1380 to crush Moscow and divide its lands, and concentrated troops near Kolomna, where the Moskva flows into the Oka. But Dmitri went on the offensive and defeated the Mongols, even though they too had firearms, at the battle of Kulikovo. The victory was merely of great symbolic value because the Muscovites suffered heavy losses, but it earned Dmitri the name of Donskoi after the battlefield near the Don, southeast of Tula. The Lithuanians had come too late to make a difference, and Moscow had shown its mettle.

Moscow's locational advantage became clear in the fifteenth century, when the grand principality was blessed with a succession of three forceful leaders, whose reigns spanned over thirty years each: Vasilii I (1389–1425), married to Vitovt's daughter, Vasilii II (1425–62), and especially Ivan III "the Great" (1462–1505), the gatherer of the Russian land. The marital alliance with Lithuania served only to justify Moscow's subsequent claims to the northern and central lands which had once been part of Kievan Rus' and had been incorporated into an expanding Lithuania. The existence of three rivals in the southern theatre – Muscovites, Lithuanians, and Tatars (as the Mongols and Turco-Mongols were now known) – placed Muscovy in a position to play one off against the other, as Lithuania had tried to do under Vitovt, but Moscow's location now gave it a decisive advantage.

The world of the steppe nomad was slowly disintegrating. Endless struggles for the succession in Sarai strengthened centrifugal forces; individual chieftains began to offer their services to Lithuania or Moscow, which offered both rewards and security, and some even founded a small principality south of Kursk in 1438. The following year, the khan occupied the town of Belev on the upper

Oka, which at the time belonged to Lithuania but stood on the very border with Muscovy. From there, the khan appeared before Moscow, but a ten-day siege failed, he had to withdraw, and he lost face. Tatar strength was clearly ebbing. Other drives against Moscow failed in 1451 and 1472, eight years before the famous encounter on the Ugra River, which flows into the Oka a short distance upriver from Kaluga. Like Tula, it stood on the very fringe of the forest zone.[9] Like the battle of Kulikovo, the encounter on the Ugra was largely symbolic, but by then there no longer was any doubt that the Kipchak khanate had become but a mere ghost of its powerful ancestor. Plundering the "upper towns" (in the Oka basin) served only to sweeten the bitterness of defeat.

But the nomad had not yet made his last stand. About 1430, several Tatar bands roaming in the southern theatre broke away from Sarai and organized a separate horde in the Crimea under Haci-Giray, who became the first Crimean khan (1449–66). His son, Mengli-Giray (1478–1514), left a legacy as the most forceful of the khans and a deep imprint in the history of the Ukrainian steppe. The Crimean Tatars lived off plundering and the proceeds of the slave trade in the Black Sea; their expeditions would terrorize the inhabitants of the fringe of settlement until 1769, and Mengli's attack on Kiev as part of his war on Lithuania in 1482, as well as other raids in Podolia and Volhynia, created "a devastation worse than that of Batu," from which Right Bank and southern Ukraine would not recover for generations.[10]

The Crimean Tatars became the greatest offensive power in the entire southern theatre after being forced to recognize the sultan's suzerainty in 1478. The Turks had finally captured Constantinople in 1453, transforming the Black Sea into a closed sea, and they destroyed the Italian colonies which had controlled the Crimean trade for so long. In 1484, the Turks seized Kilia on the Danube delta and the gate to Moldavia and Hungary, and Akkerman on the estuary of the Dniester, the gate to Poland. This damaged the commerce of Lwów (Lviv), Kraków, and even Lublin, and neutralized Poland's position in Moldavia, which the Turks would transform into their own protectorate in 1513. Lithuania likewise lost its access to the Black Sea coast. In 1471, the Turks had seized the Genoese entrepot on the delta of the Don and renamed it Azov. But it was Mengli, who was not always a reliable vassal, who built Ochakov on the Dnieper-Buh lagoon in 1492; it later became a major Turkish fortress.[11] By the end of the century the Turks and Crimean Tatars controlled the exits of all the major rivers flowing into the Black Sea, the Danube and the Dniester, the Dnieper and the Don. They barred the way not only to the Poles and Lithuanians, their closest neighbours, but to the Russians as well. The transformation of the Black Sea into a Turkish *mare nostrum* dealt a sharp blow to the intercontinental trade route running from east to west, at the very time when the exploration of the world across the oceans was about to begin. The expanding Muscovite core would inherit a continental economy that had nearly closed its doors to the expanding maritime economy.

During much of the fifteenth century, the major thrust of Polish foreign policy was directed against Hungary and the Germanic possessions on the Baltic littoral, although King Władysław III (1434–44) had the grandiose dream of leading a crusade to expel the Turks from the Balkans and reconciling Catholicism with Orthodoxy, to be followed, no doubt, by the establishment of a protectorate over Muscovy which would give Poland hegemony in western Eurasia. He was killed fighting the Turks at Varna on the Black Sea coast of Bulgaria.[12] Moscow was completing the gathering of the Russian lands with the annexation of Novgorod in 1478 and Tver in 1485. But Ivan III also made an alliance with Mengli the cornerstone of his West Eurasian policy.[13] He encouraged the Crimean Tatars to weaken the Lithuanian state by repeated attacks which yielded countless slaves, to be sold in Kaffa (Feodosiia), then shipped to Turkey, Egypt, and Italy, while the Turks got their supply of slaves from western Georgia. There, they built a powerful fortress at Akhaltstikhe, their forward position ahead of the great Anatolian trunk road from Ankara to Erzurum via Sivas, and the gate to Transcaucasia.[14]

In 1505, the year of Ivan III's death, Mengli destroyed what was left of the Kipchak khanate, and the Crimea became the most powerful Tatar state all the way to Kazan. The khan no longer felt he had to accommodate Moscow, which he began to fear, as the gathering of the Russian land threatened to turn into the gathering of the legacy of the Mongol empire. In 1512 he allied with Lithuania, and his son reached the outskirts of Moscow in 1521. It was then that he may have extorted a promise that Moscow would pay him an annual tribute, which, in the traditions of the steppe, would make Muscovy a vassal state of the Crimean khanate. Poland was already paying an annual contribution,[15] and the khan could claim that, nominally at least, he had become the master of western Eurasia. At the same time, the Turks kept expanding westwards, inflicted a crushing defeat on the Hungarians at Mohacs in 1526, and reached the gates of Vienna in 1529. King Sigismund I of Poland and grand duke of Lithuania (1506–48) signed a treaty of friendship with the sultan in 1533. The first half of the sixteenth century thus marked the apogee of Turco-Tatar power.

But Moscow was now determined to assert its power in the Central Upland between the Desna and the Don. The policy was a defensive one – to protect Moscow against raids – but with a strong offensive component aimed at projecting Muscovite power into the "Wild Fields" (*Dikoe Pole*), which had been the nomad's realm for so long. When Ivan III died, the southern border of Muscovy was still only the periphery of the forest zone. Moscow built a fortified line – the prototype of many subsequent similar lines – from the forests and swamps of Briansk on the Oka near Riazan via Belev, along the Upa River, and on to Venev and Riazan. The line mapped out a zone contained within the great bend of the Oka between the confluence of the Ugra and Riazan, which guarded the approaches to Serpukhov, where the Tatars usually crossed the Oka a short distance away from Moscow. As a rule, a line sought to follow the course of a river or even a stream. It consisted of a series of abatis (*zaseki*), obstacles of tree trunks with sharpened branches directed against the enemy. In open spaces, earthen ramparts connected forested areas. The line was designed to check the rapid advance of the Tatar cavalry and give enough time to the main forces in the rear to advance and meet the Tatars on the line.

The Crimean khanate came under threat not only from the north but from the west, and even from within itself as well. The sixteenth century was a time of expansion for the Polish economy, whose cereal production, shipped down the Vistula and exported through Danzig, found eager buyers on the European markets, where prices quintupled in the course of the century. However, increased demand resulted, not in the commercialization of agriculture, but in the spread of a servile economy. By 1550, corvée labour on *szlachta* properties already exceeded three days a week. Moreover, pressures to increase production favoured the development of large properties (latifundia), not by mid-level noblemen, but by a rising class of magnates who increasingly dominated Polish politics, especially after the monarchy became elective in 1572. The magnates of Little (southern) Poland began to build latifundia in Podolia and Volhynia and to encourage the migration of peasants, who, like their brethren in Muscovy, would become increasingly bound to the land, in order to guarantee both a reliable source of labour and the regular payment of taxes. The trend culminated in the Union of Lublin of 1569, when Poland stripped Lithuania of much of its population and territory by annexing Volhynia and Kiev province, as well as Left Bank Ukraine to the Murava route and the Northern Donets. The poor *szlachta* who followed the magnates became their power base, and magnates would play a crucial role in the geopolitics of the region.[16]

But the new development had unexpected consequences. Peasants who moved into the Wild Fields got a taste of free life in river valleys where they could hunt and fish to their hearts' content. They ran away as other peasants did from Muscovy and for the same reasons. They became Cossacks, from a word known even before the Mongol invasions to denote one who lived on booty. They formed communities in the basin of the middle Dnieper, which the Polish government sought to transform into irregular troops deployed in territorial regiments. It also sought to restrict their number and made those who were not on the "register" (*reestr*) into peasants. King Stefan Batory (1576–86) was the first to pursue such a policy, which was continued by his successors until the 1640s.

Other Cossacks moved "beyond the rapids" of the Dnieper, where a petty Ukrainian prince built a fortified camp (*sich*) on Khortytsia Island; it became headquarters of the so-called Zaporozhian Cossacks. Some had families, but many did not marry and lived on booty, which they used to decorate their Orthodox churches. As early as 1560, the sultan and the khan were already complaining about their incursions. Tatars joined their host (*voisko*), and as the two societies intermingled, their rivalries over the share of the booty and the lucrative slave trade had the effect of destabilizing the Turco-Tatar presence on the mainland.[17]

Finally, a third group of Cossacks found refuge in the basin of the Don, notably along the Khoper and Medveditsa Rivers. Their first headquarters was at the confluence of the Northern Donets and the Don. They were mostly of Russian, rather than Ukrainian, origin and came first from the Riazan principality after its annexation by Moscow in 1529. They too did not marry at first, and their communities kept replenishing themselves with more runaways from the heavy fiscal burden of an expanding Muscovy. They lived on hunting and fishing – the lower Don and the Azov Sea were rich in fish – neglected agriculture, but raised horses and cattle. They, perhaps even more than the Zaporozhians, developed a strong *esprit de corps* which made them into "knights" (*bohatyri*) in the eyes of the peasantry and defenders of the faith against the infidel Muslims. The sultan aroused the Nogais against them, and the "Dontsy"'s hatred of the nomad became proverbial.[18] The Turco-Tatars had blocked the exits from the main rivers, but it was there that the Cossacks would challenge their hold, despite Moscow's reluctance to let them push their luck too far.

Russian Expansion

While the expansion of the Muscovite core into central Eurasia was the defining event of Ivan IV's foreign policy, Muscovy remained under severe constraints in western Eurasia as a whole and in the southern theatre in particular. Polish, Crimean (and Swedish) power combined to split the expansionist impulse in three directions, towards the Baltic, toward Smolensk and the Polish core, and toward the Black Sea.

The Turks and Tatars did not recognize the Russian annexation of the Astrakhan khanate in 1556, because the city was a strategic place of the first order for the Turks and a strategic threat to the Tatars: it brought Russian influence into the northern Caucasus and the lower Don valley, which led to the Azov Sea and the Crimea. For the Turks, still focused on the east-west alignment of their empire, the lower Don led to the lower Volga and Astrakhan, and Astrakhan to the northern provinces of Persia, from which they might restore a link with their brethren in Central Asia and surround Persia, their permanent enemy. But the expedition of 1569 failed because the crucial link in the chain, the portage between the Don and the Volga near present-day Volgograd, could not be turned into a canal. Turkish ambitions (like so many Russian ones) fell victim to logistics and unrealistic hopes.

As if to compensate for the failure before Astrakhan, the Crimean khan launched devastating raids almost every year between 1569 and 1591, but all failed to take Moscow, including that of 1571, when the Tatars burned the outskirts of the city and retreated with over a hundred thousand captives. The Tula Line did not fulfil its purpose, but Moscow emerged the stronger power nevertheless. Ivan IV (1533–84) not only brought Kazan, Astrakhan, and western Siberia into the expanding Muscovite core; he also aspired to bring Russian power to the shores of the Baltic Sea in the wake of the disintegration of the Livonian Order, as the Reformation moved deeper into the western theatre. In this he failed, but the so-called Livonian War (1558–82) raised for the first time the issue of priorities: whether Moscow should concentrate its forces for an attack on the Crimea or counter Polish and Swedish ambitions in the Baltic – or even do both at the same time. Ivan IV chose to do both and overestimated Moscow's capabilities, but the tsar hoped, not without some justification, that military pressure should be just strong enough to cause or exacerbate dissensions among the Crimean leadership and bring out supporters of a pro-Moscow orientation. This had always been a well-tested method of interfering in steppe politics. Not only was the Tula Line declared obsolete, but a new perimeter was built in a bold move into the steppe with Belgorod on the Donets and Valuiki on the Oskol, both built in 1598 (after Ivan's death), and, in an even bolder move, with Tsarev Borisov (Tsar Boris Fort), built in 1600 at the confluence of the Oskol and the Donets, later replaced by Izium. These forward positions did not yet form a new line, but they were a threat to the Tatar routes and, conversely, bases for future attacks on the Crimea along these same routes.

Ivan IV was succeeded by Fedor (1584–98), a feeble-minded and sickly child, with whom the Moscow branch of the Riurik dynasty came to an end. Fedor's successor, Boris Godunov (1598–1605), did not succeed in founding a new dynasty, and Moscow descended into chaos after his death, until the Romanov dynasty came to power in 1613 with Tsar Mikhail Fedorovich (1613–45), followed by his son Alexei Mikhailovich (1645–76), Peter the Great's father. While Muscovy's power was weakening, a dynastic union placed Poland, Lithuania, and Sweden under the same crown, that of Sigismund III, King of Poland (1587–l632) and King of Sweden (1592–9). His reign witnessed the apogee of Polish power in western Eurasia: the king supported pretenders to the Russian throne, and Polish troops reached Moscow in 1610, when his son Władysław IV (1632–48) was elected tsar of Muscovy. There was more to Polish policy than placing a Vasa prince on the Moscow throne. Poland pursued a dual objective: to convert the heretic Muscovites and launch a campaign against Turkey and the Crimea, which, if successful, would establish Polish hegemony in most of western Eurasia.[19] But a strong Russian reaction against the Poles, fuelled by the exhortations of an Orthodox patriarch, expelled them from the capital in 1612. From that time on, the Romanovs would steadily engineer Russia's ascent to hegemonic status in the whole of western Eurasia by destroying both Polish and Swedish power.

The establishment of a new dynasty in Moscow did not bring peace to the southern theatre, if only because Polish power declined precipitously in the seventeenth century. A growing power vacuum released social hatreds and caused a political upheaval, which radically altered the geopolitical situation and brought about the incorporation of Left Bank Ukraine into the expanding Muscovite core. While Muscovy and Poland were fighting over Smolensk and preeminence in Lithuania in 1632–4 and again in 1654–67, the Don Cossacks, who had been an important factor in the expulsion of the Poles and the victory of the Romanovs, were leading an offensive against the Crimean Tatars, who supported the Poles. The Don Cossacks quickly assumed a privileged position – Russians who fled to the Don were not considered fugitives subject to repatriation, and regulars were even sent to bolster their host when circumstances required. In 1623 they were placed under the Board of Foreign Affairs, a first step toward their official integration into the body of irregular troops, which Moscow increasingly looked upon as the pathfinders of Russian expansion into the steppe and standard bearers of Orthodoxy among alien peoples. They received a salary, but it was plundering – they became the mirror image of their enemies, the steppe nomads. In 1637 they seized Azov and offered it to the tsar, but Muscovy feared a war with the Turks, which it could not afford. They withdrew in 1642 and were then besieged by a coalition of Crimean Tatars and Nogais. They moved their capital to Cherkassk in 1645.[20]

The Dnieper Cossacks had a different history. The "registered" Cossacks were subjects of the Polish government, or perhaps more accurately, of the magnates in Right Bank Ukraine as well as across the Dnieper, where the Vyshnevetsky (Wiśniowiecki) family owned enormous properties in the Poltava region on the border with Muscovy. They were irregular troops for the maintenance of the peace and the protection of the population against Tatar raids, while the enserfment of the peasantry proceeded apace. These Cossacks supported the Polish intervention during the Time of Trouble, but social tensions with their Polish overlords grew rapidly, beginning in the 1620s.[21] The Zaporozhians kept going their own way as a quasi-independent force, to the point that the Poles built a fortress in 1635 at Kodak, where the Dnieper rapids began, upriver from Khortytsia Island. Its purpose was to separate the Ukrainian peasants from the Zaporozhian Cossacks, whose camp (*sich*) kept moving downriver to the maze of streams (*plavnia*) on the right bank of the river between the Buzuluk and Tomilovka Rivers, west of the Velykyi Luh. The Zaporozhians were in some ways similar to the Dontsy – they were the mirror image of the Tatars, whom they hated and with whom they intermingled at the same time. They were even better placed to raid Crimean and Tatar towns, without having to fear Moscow's reprobation. In 1605 they took Varna on the Bulgarian coast and captured Turkish galleys; in 1607 they plundered Ochakov and Perekop; in 1612 they took Kaffa and devastated the entire Crimean coast; in 1613 and 1616 they even crossed the Black Sea to burn Sinop and Trebizond on the Anatolian coast, a daring challenge to Turkish power.[22]

But the most dramatic events were about to take place in Little Russia and Right Bank Ukraine, where the Polish presence was more oppressive and where discontent had been seething since the crushing of the Nalyvaiko uprising against the Poles of 1595–6. The uprising, short-lived but encompassing a huge territory, took place while the Orthodox Church, the church of the Ukrainian people and the Cossacks, was dealt a major blow by the creation, largely at the instigation of the Poles, of the Uniate Church, which retained the Slavonic ritual but recognized the supremacy of the pope.[23] The Council of Brest of 1596 created what amounted to a religious frontier between the Roman Church in Warsaw and the Orthodox Church in Moscow, which would be fought over bitterly until 1839. The tensions it generated added to the social enmities between Poles and Ukrainians to form a highly combustible mix, which a mere spark could ignite into a major conflagration.

The entrance of Bohdan Khmelnytsky (1595–1657) on the historical stage was "almost accidental." By 1645 he had settled on a small estate given to him by a Polish magnate and become a captain in the Chyhyryn (Chigirin) regiment of registered Cossacks. In 1646, local magnates raided his property, killed his youngest son, and abducted his bride. The event transformed him into a "raging rebel."[24] He rallied Cossacks and peasants, and even allied with the Crimean Tatars, always ready to go on a plundering expedition, who contributed their cavalry. The Zaporozhians joined the fray as well. The rebels aimed straight for the Polish capital. From the Zaporozhian encampment on the Dnieper they moved rapidly westwards, crushed a Polish advance guard at Zhovti Vody in April 1648, and annihilated an entire Polish army near Korsun in May. The advance was accompanied by widespread massacres during the summer. In September, a new Polish army was decimated at Pyliavtsi in Podolia. In October, the rebels reached Lviv, and in November, Zamość, in Poland proper. But Khmelnytsky, for reasons that remain unclear, accepted an armistice from the new Polish king, Jan Casimir (1648–68), and returned to Kiev.

Then the Poles went on the offensive, but to no avail. Their entire army of over a hundred thousand men would have been crushed at siege of Zbarazh and the battle of Zboriv near Ternopil in the spring of 1649 if the Crimean khan had not betrayed the Ukrainians, partly for a bribe, but also because it was not in his interest to assist the creation of a Cossack state on the very border of the Crimean steppe. The Treaty of Zboriv (Zborov) concluded in August enlarged the register from eight thousand to forty thousand Cossacks, and banned Polish nobles and Jews from the provinces of Kiev, Bratslav, and Chernihiv, where only Cossack *starshyna* (*starshina*) and Orthodox noblemen were allowed to hold office. The peasants were sent back to servitude. The treaty thus represented a compromise between the new Cossack elite and the Polish magnates.

But the war was not yet over. Jan Casimir was determined to crush the uprising and did so at the battle of Berestechko in Volhynia, in June 1651. It was followed by the Bila Tserkva (Belaia tserkov) agreement of September, which reduced the Cossack register to twenty thousand and forbade the hetman to keep foreign contacts. The Cossacks took their revenge at Batih on the Southern Buh downriver from Bratslav in June 1652, but the victory had no immediate consequences. Both sides were exhausted, and Poland was about to become embroiled in the catastrophic Thirteen Year War (1654–67) with Russia and Sweden, which finally destroyed Polish power in western Eurasia.[25]

The uprising had created a perfect frontier situation, in which the lands controlled by the Cossacks *de facto* (until a final settlement with Poland could be reached) were caught between core powers, namely Muscovy, Turkey, and Poland. The distinguishing feature of a frontier is that it becomes an area of contention until one of the core powers finally prevails, or two agree to partition it. Anticipating Poland's future policy, Khmelnytsky had to turn to Turkey and Russia. The religious issue had played a major role in the uprising, and the creation of the Uniate Church had made it even more complex. The Turks were Muslims and so were the Tatars, who, in addition, were not willing to share with the Cossacks the dominion of the steppe. Khmelnytsky, in the political world of the time, remained a rebel against his Catholic king. To gain legitimacy, he needed a new overlord.

There remained Muscovy. In January 1654, it was agreed that the Orthodox tsar would be the most suitable overlord, and a meeting took place at Pereiaslav, sixty kilometres southeast of Kiev, between the Cossack elite and the tsar's representative, Vasilii Buturlin. The agreement later became controversial but it need not be, although it was based on a misunderstanding. The Cossacks wanted the tsar to accept the existence of the new Cossack state which they had created in their own interest, and to confirm the "rights and privileges" which the Polish kings had granted to the registered Cossacks since the 1560s. In return the Cossacks would swear the oath of loyalty (*virnist'/vernost'*) to the tsar and his descendants, which clearly implied that they were his subjects, required to obey his orders. But Buturlin refused to take a similar oath, on the ground that the Great Sovereign recognized no equals, that there were no contractual relationships between ruler and subject, and that the subjects possessed only the rights which he had consented to give them. The Cossacks thus took the oath unilaterally and sealed their fate. If the tsar chose of his own free will to alter the details or the fundamentals of the Cossack state and society, which he had only promised to keep at the time but had not sworn to respect in the future, the Cossack elite had no right to disobey, because they had taken the oath to accept the tsar's will unconditionally. If they did disobey, they would commit a mortal sin (because the oath was a religious pledge made before a common Orthodox God) and would be traitors before the Great Sovereign on earth and God in heaven. Thus each side entered into the Pereiaslav agreement with different assumptions, but the Cossacks took the unilateral oath because they had no choice, and in so doing they dug for themselves a trap from which there was no escape.[26]

Khmelnytsky's successors did not understand this simple truth, and kept behaving like steppe nomads who formed alliances for the needs of the moment and discarded them when circumstances changed, or like men of the frontier who thought that their only chance to maintain some independence lay in playing off one core power against another. Hetman Ivan Vyhovsky (1657–9) was an educated Orthodox nobleman who had joined the Cossacks, but who also favoured the rising *starshyna* against the rank-and-file Cossacks, and was drawn to Poland. He deluded himself in thinking that the nobiliar government of the Polish empire would favour a similar type of government in an autonomous Ukraine. In negotiating the Treaty of Hadiach (Gadiach) in September 1658, which would have created a Ukrainian principality as an equal partner of Poland and Lithuania, Vyhovsky not only violated the oath of 1654 but gave Moscow a justification for stirring up the anti-Polish population against him. Muscovite troops marched into the Left Bank but had barely crossed the border when they suffered a major defeat near Konotop in July 1659. Paradoxically, the Cossack victory created a backlash against the hetman, led by pro-Moscow colonels who accused him of selling out to the Poles, and he fled to Poland in October.[27]

The *starshyna* then elected Khmelnytsky's son Yurii (1659–62). On the one hand, he pledged loyalty to the tsar, agreeing to the stationing of Russian garrisons in all major towns and to the election of the regimental colonels with Moscow's approval; he also agreed to refrain from conducting foreign relations. On the other, he recognized the continuing pull of Poland and decided to return the Ukrainian lands to the Polish fold in 1660, even though there remained a separate hetman on the Left Bank. The decision confirmed the growing split between the Polish and the Russian spheres of influence in the Ukrainian frontier, and the emergence of three Ukraines: one on the left bank, one on the right bank, and the Zaporozhian lands trying to maintain a balance between Poland and Muscovy. Each bank elected its own hetman. On the left bank it was Ivan Briukhovetsky (1663–8), the first hetman to journey to Moscow, where he was made a boyar and given for wife a princess Daria Dolgorukova – whose brother would become the grandfather of Vasilii Dolgorukov, the conqueror of the Crimea in 1771 – but where he also had to sign new "articles" in December 1665. They reduced the "rights and privileges" recognized in 1654 and added new provisions, such as allowing tsarist officials to collect taxes and letting Moscow appoint the head of the Ukrainian Orthodox Church. Henceforth, hetmans would have to be elected in the presence of representatives from Moscow and would have to journey to the capital to obtain confirmation in office.[28]

Briukhovetsky unknowingly wrote the script for the Polish and Russian delegates who met at Andrusovo near Smolensk to negotiate an armistice that brought the Thirteen Year War to an end. In January 1667, the two core powers split the frontier among themselves: the Poles gave the Russians a free hand on the left bank, while the Russians gave a free hand to the Poles on the right bank. Kiev, overlooking the right bank of the Dnieper, was ceded to Russia for two years, but never reverted to the Poles. The Zaporozhian lands were placed under the joint overlordship of Poland and Muscovy to serve as a buffer against the Crimean Tatars.[29] Thus, just over one hundred years after the annexation of Kazan and Astrakhan inaugurated the expansion of the Muscovite core into the non-Russian lands of the former Mongol empire, the annexation of Left Bank Ukraine inaugurated the expansion of the Muscovite core into the lands of the last successor khanate of the Mongol empire and into those of the Polish-Lithuanian Commonwealth which had once belonged to Kievan Rus'.

This struggle over the Ukrainian lands took place within the Polish empire. But other decisive developments were taking place in the Russo-Crimean frontier. In 1635, the Russians built a fort at Kozlov (Michurinsk) on the Voronezh River at the same latitude as Orel, on the Nogai route. For the next eighteen years they built twenty-five towns and some two hundred forts along the river, the Don, across the steppe to Belgorod, and on to Okhtyrka (Akhtyrka) on the Vorskla near what was still the Polish border. This Belgorod Line was eight hundred kilometres long and was commanded by the Belgorod *voevoda*, who became a kind of regional military commander for the defence of the Russian south. The line was well ahead of the towns which had borne the brunt of the Tatar raids, and followed roughly the southern perimeter of the Central Upland, beyond which the Dnieper depression began. Its completion in 1653 preceded by only one year the acceptance by Moscow of Khmelnytsky's offer to place the Cossacks under the Great Sovereign's "high hand." The two events were more than a coincidence. The establishment of a Russian presence in Left Bank Ukraine and the promise of Cossack help had the effect of extending the Belgorod Line along the Vorskla to the Dnieper.[30]

At about the same time, the civil war in Ukraine created an exodus of peasants and Cossacks across the Dnieper into the left bank, where they settled along the Vorskla and into the nearly empty steppe to the east along the Donets and Oskol in the Kharkiv corridor. These migrants were organized into Cossack communities called *slobody*. The corridor was still a dangerous place, and to protect the new settlements a so-called Izium Line, 350 kilometres long, was built in the 1670s from the Vorskla south of Okhtyrka through Valki to Zmiev on the Donets, on to Izium and upriver along the Oskol to Userd, where it linked up with the Belgorod Line.[31] A fourth Ukraine was coming into being, called the Ukraine of Settlements (Slobodska Ukraina).

The Cossacks

The Hetmanate

The management of Left Bank Ukraine – the Hetmanate and the Kharkiv corridor, over which Moscow acquired an exclusive dominion in 1667 – presented the Russians with a new set of problems. They were reluctant to proceed to a full integration of the territory into the expanding Muscovite core, and experimented with various administrative models, which preserved the goal of full integration while retaining existing structures. The striking fact, which must have given Moscow pause, was the very size of the new acquisition. According to later figures from the first census, the population of the compact Left Bank territory reached 1.8 million people or 11.6 per cent of the approximately 15.7 million for the entire expanding core – about the same population as that of the distended former khanates of Kazan and Astrakhan.[32] Moreover, the Russian population made up an infinitesimal 2.1 per cent of the Left Bank population, a situation radically different from that prevailing in the eastern theatre, where the Russians were on their way to constitute a majority. Such a situation required a cautious approach, all the more so since the internal politics of the Hetmanate remained in a state of turmoil.

The Hetmanate, also called the Cossack state,[33] not because the population consisted of Cossacks but because it was ruled by Cossacks, was divided into ten territorial regiments. Four were in Chernihiv country – Kiev, Chernihiv, Starodub, and Nizhyn (Nezhin) – and the other six in Poltava country – Poltava, Pereiaslav, Pryluky, Lubny, Myrhorod, and Hadiach. Each regiment was commanded by a colonel who resided in the town in all but three cases: the Kiev regimental headquarters was in Kozelets on the Oster, on the road from Chernihiv to Kiev; the Lubny colonel resided in Romny, higher up on the Sula, and the Myrhorod colonel in nearby Sorochyntsi.[34] He was elected by the Cossack assembly (*rada*) for an indefinite time, but he increasingly became an appointee of the hetman. The quartermaster (*obozny*), who commanded the artillery, ranked after the colonel and replaced him in his absence. The regimental judge tried cases which were then referred to the colonel for further disposition; the adjutant (*esaul*) carried out the colonel's orders, and the *khorunzhii* kept the regimental standards. A clerk (*pysar*) functioned as the regimental secretary. These six men constituted the so-called regimental *starshyna*, whose role would be crucial in the evolution of the Cossack state. Each regiment was usually divided into companies of unequal size called *sotni*, commanded by a *sotnik* with his adjutant, standard bearer, and clerk.[35] The number of companies varied from one regiment to another, as shown in table 4.1 with the number of households (*dvory*) in each regiment. The table shows two unequal clusters of regimental territories. The Chernihiv group, in the forest zone, contained the

Table 4.1 Numbers of Cossack companies and households per regiment

	Companies	Households		Companies	Households		Companies	Households
Kiev	7	12,229	Poltava	16	18,529	Lubny	11	28,760
Chernihiv	16	22,297	Pereiaslav	16	17,929	Myrhorod	15	15,823
Starodub	9	29,571	Pryluky	8	26,051	Hadiach	10	16,448
Nizhyn	20	32,178						
Subtotals	*52*	*96,275*		*40*	*62,509*		*36*	*61,031*

Source: Kirilov, *Tsvetushchee sostoianie*, 170.
Note: Grand total = 128 companies, 219,815 households comprising about 68,415 Cossacks

larger units, including the largest, based in Nizhyn, a commercial town linked to the great markets of central Europe, the coastal towns on the Black Sea, and the larger Turkish market. But nearly 60 per cent of the companies and 56 per cent of the households were in Poltava country, in the woodland zone, which was thus the true centre of gravity of the Hetmanate.

The hetman resided in the capital, originally Chyhyryn (Chigirin) (1648–63), then Hadiach (Gadiach) for a short time (1663–8), and finally Baturyn (1669–1708). He was elected in theory by the entire *rada*, but in fact by the *starshyna* that surrounded him, consisting of the same officials as those at the regimental level. But the tsar was beginning to play an increasingly crucial role in the election, because it had to be confirmed when the hetman travelled to Moscow "to gaze upon the shining eyes of the monarch."[36]

The hetman's powers were never set in any constitutional document, but he commanded the Cossack army or host (*voisko*), granted estates as a reward for service, appointed *sotniki* and colonels, was the supreme judge with powers of life and death over rank-and-file Cossacks, and conducted foreign relations. He ruled without limit of tenure, which in practice meant until he died or was removed by force.[37] Moreover, his effective powers were severely circumscribed by the *starshyna* whom he had created and who eventually created him, and by the imperatives of the Muscovite government and its agents in the field. In Moscow, there was a Little Russian Chancery (*prikaz*), first mentioned in 1649, with an undefined but overall jurisdiction over the region's affairs, and which corresponded with the hetman in foreign policy matters. Toward the end of the seventeenth century it was incorporated into the Chancery of Foreign Affairs, of which it became an internal subdivision. It remained in existence until 1717 and had about twenty clerks.

The *starshyna* (and their families and clients) controlled the three agencies responsible for the management of the Hetmanate. A civil chancery consisted of the quartermaster general, the secretary, a treasurer, two judges, two adjutants, and two standard bearers. With the addition of three regimental colonels and their staffs, it became the "Council of Officers" (*starshynska rada*). And a military chancery consisted of a treasury, a court, and an accounting office. After 1669, in the wake of anti-Russian uprisings, the *starshyna* gained the right to maintain one of its members in Moscow as a permanent representative, for the stated purpose of transmitting to the tsar complaints about the behaviour of Russian troops, always a sore point in relations between the Russians, the Cossacks, and the urban population.[38]

In the Kharkiv corridor, the population which had emigrated from the Right Bank to escape the horrors of the civil war was gradually organized into similar territorial regiments. By the 1670s, there were five such regiments, headquartered in Sumy on the Psël, Okhtyrka on the Vorskla, both along the Hetmanate's border, and in Kharkiv, Izium, and Ostrohozhsk, near or on the Izium Line, across the entire space between the Vorskla and the Don, the first line of defence against Tatar raids ahead of the Belgorod Line. These regiments followed the pattern of the Hetmanate's regiments, but the colonel was elected for life, and he too, like the *sotniks*, had his own *starshyna*. The colonel also combined civil and military responsibilities, and was subordinated to the Belgorod *voevoda*, who commanded the Belgorod *razriad* or military region, under the overall jurisdiction of the Military Chancery (*Razriad*) in Moscow. Beginning in 1688, border relations with the Crimean Tatars and other steppe nomads were placed under the Great Russian Chancery (*Velikorossiiskii Prikaz*), another subdivision of the Chancery of Foreign Affairs.[39] These Sloboda Cossacks – their number was fixed at 3,500 in 1700 – did not have a hetman, if only because the proximity of the Belgorod *voevoda* made one unnecessary, and Moscow most likely did not want one: it always resisted the hetmans' attempts to extend their jurisdiction over the Cossacks. As a result, they were integrated from the very beginning into the military infrastructure of the southern theatre and constituted an intermediate group between the Don Cossacks to the east and their cousins in the Hetmanate.

The Zaporozhian Cossacks, who came under the undivided sovereignty of Moscow in 1686, ceased to play the central role which had been theirs since 1648. They truly became relegated to "beyond the rapids" and began to concentrate on their own affairs, while watching with increasing concern the consolidation of Cossack society in the Hetmanate and the Ukraine of Settlements as well as the destruction of the Cossack organization on the Right Bank under Polish rule. They could raise up to thirty thousand men, but seldom had more than ten thousand available for service. But they liked to think that their dominion extended from the Syniukha to the Azov Sea on the confines of the Don Cossack lands, even if that territory was largely uninhabited until the 1750s, a claim which Moscow found congenial: if the Zaporozhians should ever become integrated into the military infrastructure of the southern theatre, Moscow would "inherit" their land, and the expanding Muscovite core would approach the Black Sea coast.

The host retained its distinctive social organization, democratic for some, anarchic for others. The basic unit was the *kuren*, of which there were thirty-eight spread along the right bank of the Dnieper from Perevolochna at the confluence of the Vorskla and the Dnieper to Kizil-Kermen (Berislav) near where the estuary of the river began. The Cossacks met in a "circle" (*kolo*, *krug*) to deal with the business at hand. In the "camp" they elected a *koshevyi otaman* (*koshevoi ataman*), a chief executive officer for one year, who operated with a small staff. But the host still looked askance at agricultural pursuits, and Cossacks continued to live on hunting, fishing, beekeeping, and the booty from raids on Ottoman and Tatar possessions.[40] The *otaman* was a powerful individual with nearly dictatorial powers, but only for a short term of office. He resisted attempts by the hetman in Baturyn to maintain the unity of the "Zaporozhian Host." He recognized only the tsar as his ruler, but his personal fealty was highly vulnerable to pressures created by changing political circumstances, and a false step could threaten the existence of the host as Russian power grew, as we shall see presently.

The disastrous tenure of Hetman Briukhovetsky created both mutual recriminations and a hardening of Moscow's position. The three hetmans who served between 1669 and the even greater disaster of 1708 had to deal not only with a more assertive Moscow but also with a deepening fissure between the hetman and the *starshyna* at all three levels. Demian Mnohohrishny (Mnogogreshny) (1669–72) had been the acting (*nakaznyi*) *otaman* for the Left Bank of Petro Doroshenko, who began his career as hetman on the Right Bank, but then turned against Poland and then toward the Turks and Tatars. The Turks and Tatars, however, turned against him instead, and in 1672 incorporated the Right Bank east of a line running from the Kievan border to Khotyn overlooking the Dniester, where they would stay until 1699.

This alone made Moscow suspicious when Mnohohrishny sent his envoys to Moscow to pledge his loyalty, but he was nevertheless recognized hetman. In accordance with an agreement signed in Hlukhiv, Moscow would station garrisons not only in Kiev but also in four other towns (Chernihiv, Oster, Nizhyn, and Pereiaslav). Their *voevody* would try complaints against abuses committed by Russian troops; the number of registered Cossacks was reduced from sixty thousand to thirty thousand, but they would continue to receive a salary. On the other hand, Russian troops would be billeted only in the houses of burghers and peasants, not in those of Cossacks; Moscow would no longer send tax collectors to conduct a census; Russians would stop calling Ukrainians "traitors." Last but not least, the Great Sovereign would consider petitions submitted by the hetman and the *starshyna* to grant patents of nobility, most likely to themselves and their clients: such a privilege had already been granted to Briukhovetsky. Moscow was taking steps to speed up the integration of the Hetmanate into the expanding core.

Yet, the hetman managed to antagonize all his major supporters. His insistence that the Hetmanate was not a conquered province but had submitted voluntarily to Moscow in 1654 did not sit well with the Russians. The sharp reduction in the number of registered Cossacks antagonized the Cossack masses, for whom the hetman was "a peasant's son." The fact that he was indeed "a simple and unlettered man" did not enhance his standing among the *starshyna*, who saw themselves as a political and social elite, still inspired by the Polish culture which so deeply marked the intellectual life of the entire region. His use of special Cossack troops, paid by and subordinated to the hetman alone – the so-called *kompaneiski* or *okhochekomonni* regiments, of which there were five with a total of about 2,500 men – raised the spectre of a praetorian guard to help the hetman develop an independent power base. The *starshyna* quickly turned against him, and accused him in Moscow of seeking Ottoman overlordship, an accusation which in 1672 was tantamount to a charge of high treason. They petitioned for his execution, thereby putting their interests well ahead of those of the Hetmanate, but Moscow banished him to Selenginsk, where he was still alive in 1692, engaged in negotiations with the Manchus.

The case of his successor, Ivan Samoilovych (1672–87), provides a vivid illustration of the failure to reunite a frontier which has already been partitioned by core area powers. In order to achieve that hopeless goal, the leader must be willing to betray his friends, join his enemies, and betray them to return to his friends. The twists and turns of the hetman's career are too involved to be told here, but an outline will suffice. Samoilovych was the son of a priest, a man without a stable position in the elite. He had supported Briukhovetsky when the latter turned against Moscow, then rallied to Mnohohrishny, and took the loyalty oath to the Great Sovereign. Then he took part in the hetman's overthrow and was rewarded with the office in 1672. He then moved against Doroshenko in an attempt to reunite both banks of the Dnieper, but stood by the fallen hetman when he took refuge in the Hetmanate in 1676. He encouraged the emigration of families from the Right Bank, even though many would settle in the Kharkiv corridor, which began to attract even migrants from the Hetmanate. He vainly sought from Moscow jurisdiction over the Ukraine of Settlements, but Moscow was determined to keep it subordinated to the Belgorod *voevoda*. He reluctantly joined Vasilii Golitsyn with fifty thousand Cossacks in a huge campaign against the Crimea, when Moscow, after making peace with Poland in 1686, moved the following year against the Tatars and failed. Moscow remained too far from the Black Sea coast, even on the Belgorod Line, to send a hundred thousand men across the empty steppe, which the Tatars only had to set afire to paralyse the advance of men and wagons. Golitsyn found a scapegoat in the hetman, who was dismissed on Moscow's orders and banished to Tobolsk, where he died in 1690. One of his sons, accused of making derogatory statements against the tsar, had already been executed in 1687.

But there was more to Samoilovych's fall than the cowardice of Golitsyn and the enmity of Moscow. The *starshyna* had already become afraid of powerful hetmans. The Hlukhiv agreement was confirmed in 1672, but with an addendum that the hetman could not execute or remove from office anyone without a trial by the host's court. The *kompaneiski* regiments were disbanded, and the hetman was forbidden to engage in diplomatic correspondence and carry out military operations without the *starshyna*'s approval. The *starshyna* won from him generous grants of land and enlarged its membership by creating the new posts of "companions/fellows of the standard" (*bunchukovi tovaryshi*), who were supposedly being trained to assume responsible positions in the Cossack state. Thus, we find in the Hetmanate a socio-political evolution similar to that taking place in Poland and Lithuania – the rise of a nobiliar republic distrustful of the king/hetman and determined to rule the country without the restraints of monarchical power. Samoilovych did not help his cause by his haughty behaviour toward the *starshyna*, all the more galling because it came from a *popovych-hetman* (son of a priest) and because of his cupidity, which corrupted the administration of justice.[41] The fissure between the ambitions of the hetman and the interests of the *starshyna* was becoming a chasm, and it was a denunciation by the *starshyna* that Samoilovych aimed at transforming the Hetmanate into a separate realm which precipitated Moscow's action. Both Mnohohrishny and Samoilovych had resisted a powerful social current capable of sweeping away any ambitious hetman, and Moscow could only rejoice at the determination of the *starshyna* to dig the grave of even an autonomous Hetmanate.

The third hetman, Ivan Mazepa (1687–1708), has become a legend, reviled by some, revered by others. Yet his career as hetman had much in common with that of his two predecessors, despite very different origins. Born in an old noble family in Bila Tserkva, he received a solid education in the Mohyla Collegium in Kiev, then in the Jesuit College in Warsaw, where the king later sent him on a grand tour of Holland, Germany, Italy, and France. In 1669 he entered the service of Doroshenko, whose adjutant he quickly became. Sent to the Crimea in 1674, he was seized on the way by the Zaporozhian Cossacks, who delivered him to Moscow. There he betrayed Doroshenko by revealing the latter's pro-Ottoman and pro-Crimean sympathies. Moscow sent him to Samoilovych, whom he betrayed after becoming his adjutant, by intriguing with Golitsyn. His extraordinary abilities as a political intriguer served him well with the young Peter, about thirty years his junior, who seized power in 1689. But then Mazepa got caught in the maelstrom of the Northern War with Sweden (1700–21). Forced to choose in 1708 between Peter and Charles XII of Sweden, who had established his headquarters near Novhorod-Siverskyi in Chernihiv country, he betrayed Peter in October 1708, but the Russian victory at Poltava in June 1709 sealed his fate, and he had to flee with the king into Ottoman territory, where he died in Bendery in August. Baturyn, his capital, was burned to the ground, and the Zaporozhian Cossacks, whose *otaman* had sided with Mazepa, were wiped out or expelled; they founded a new "camp" at Oleshky (Aleshki) on the lower Dnieper.

Mazepa's plans for the future of the Ukrainian lands remain uncertain. He may have wanted to secure Charles XII's support and a guarantee for an independent hetmanate on both sides of the Dnieper, but he was also willing to surrender part of the Left Bank to the Polish king to secure his own skin. Such poker playing for high stakes in an emergency situation in an already partitioned frontier was extremely dangerous and could not possibly succeed, even if the Swedish king had won the battle of Poltava. Other considerations doomed Mazepa's ambitions from the start. The *starshyna* never accepted him, despite his attempts to win them over with extensive land grants, and few followed him in his flight. Among those who fled, some soon returned to seek Peter's pardon, including a future hetman, Danylo Apostol. To the *starshyna* he was a Pole and an outsider, and he never succeeded in building a power base. His attempts to win the support of the *starshyna* served these officers well: it would have to be bought by land grants and other concessions to help create the nobiliar republic they wanted. Among these concessions was greater control by landowners over their manorial peasants, a trend pointing toward the introduction of serfdom. The bargain between Mazepa and the *starshyna* was a fool's bargain, and at the decisive moment, when they had got from him all they could expect, they deserted him.[42] We thus find here the same sets of problems which had dogged Mazepa's two predecessors: the hopeless attempt to reunite a frontier already partitioned by two core powers, and the irreconcilable antagonism between a hetman whose activities were a source of discord and upheaval and a *starshyna* who craved security in their possessions. By 1709 it was becoming obvious that the *starshyna* and Moscow had converging interests.

The Petrine Reforms

Two months after Mazepa's flight, in preparation for the great battle which was certain to settle the fate of the two protagonists, Peter I and Charles XII, Moscow divided its territory into eight large provinces, each headed by a governor with undefined powers, but with the major responsibility for levying recruits and collecting taxes. Most of these provinces were in fact military regions, and their borders were drawn up in accordance with their distances from the regional capital. The Hetmanate was unceremoniously incorporated into Kiev province with Prince Dmitri Golitsyn as its governor. The province consisted of fifty-six "towns," chiefly forts in the wooded steppe, reaching as far north as Belev on the old Tula Line, and including towns gravitating toward Orel and Kursk. The eastern part of the Kharkiv corridor (along the Oskol River) was included into neighbouring Voronezh province, to which it geographically belonged, the western part into Kiev province.[43] The population of the province was almost equally divided between that of the Hetmanate (1.4 million males) and that of Orel and Kursk provinces in their nineteenth-century borders (1.3 million males), in other words between Ukrainians and Russians. The Kharkiv corridor was much smaller, with a population of 424,426 males.[44] The Hetmanate was thus integrated into the administrative-territorial structure of the Muscovite core.

These military regions were found to be too large for the purpose of day-to-day administration after the Swedish danger had passed and negotiations had begun to bring an end to the Northern War. But the war effort had been costly to the Hetmanate, as it had been to the Muscovite core as a whole: problems were the stationing of troops – some ten regiments of dragoons or about ten thousand men in the Hetmanate – who behaved without much restraint on the part of their commanders; the requisition of horses and carts that were never returned to their owners and of provisions without compensation; the deportation of peasants to build Petersburg and the Ladoga canal; and the drafting of Cossacks into the body of regular forces. These forces represented a significant extension of the strategic force subjected to exhausting deployments from one end of the core to another. Some relief had to be granted and some moderation imposed on the excesses of military rule. The reform of May 1719 brought the provincial authorities closer to the population and sought to make them more responsive. Kiev province was divided into four *provintsii*, Kiev, Belgorod, Sevsk, and Orel, each administered by a *voevoda*. Dmitri Golitsyn was replaced by his cousin Petr Golitsyn (1719–22), then by Prince Ivan Trubetskoy (1722–7), both with the title of governor general. The Kharkiv corridor became an autonomous territory, not dependent on any provincial authority, but subordinated to the commanding general of troops in the region, known as the Ukrainian Corps.[45]

The territorial reform helps us place the political reform of the Hetmanate in a broader perspective: the downgrading of the post of hetman accompanied by partial integration into the administrative infrastructure of the expanding core. In November 1708, under strong Russian pressure, the *starshyna* elected Ivan Skoropadsky as the new hetman. He was already sixty-two years old, but he had a beautiful and younger wife, of whom it was said that she carried the mace (the hetman's symbol of office) while he wore the ceremonial clothing.[46] The couple surrounded themselves with relatives, including their son-in-law, who became the chief judge and was corrupt beyond measure. The hetman may have been the largest landowner in the territory with 19,882 properties; even Mazepa could boast of no more than 19,654.[47] He was only too willing to do the tsar's work, even though he had no choice. After his election the tsar appointed a "resident minister" with two Russian regiments; he had orders to arrest the hetman on any suspicion of disloyalty. Thus, by the time the battle of Poltava took place, the hetman had been neutralized; his capital was moved from Baturyn to Hlukhiv, closer to the Russian border.

Skoropadsky continued the old policy of making land grants not only to old members of the *starshyna* but also to new ones, especially among regimental colonels like Serbs, who had emigrated to the territory after the disastrous campaign on the Prut (1711). The tsar made more grants to his officers, including German ones, but also to Russians like Alexander Menshikov and Count Petr Tolstoi, who became colonel of the Starodub regiment after marrying Skoropadsky's daughter.[48] The hetman's place in the hierarchy remained unclear: while he was subordinated to the tsar directly through the minister resident, he may also have been accountable to the governor in Kiev, who was responsible for the security of the territory as a whole.

Complaints against a system mired in corruption with unclear lines of authority convinced Peter, not to replace Skoropadsky with a forceful hetman, but to bypass him altogether by introducing a military administration staffed with Russian officers. The imperial order of April 1722 told the hetman that many complaints had been received from the "*starshyna* and the colonels," and that injustices were committed in the courts, where parties competed to pay large bribes to the judges to sway the decisions in their favour, but it also blamed the *starshyna* for widespread abuses. The colonels ruined the Cossacks and peasants by taking away their land, forests, and mills, and by confiscating their provisions, which they then sold for a profit. They compelled the Cossacks to build their houses, farm buildings, ponds, and dams for their mills, and gradually turned them into "subjects" (*poddannye*). Another reproach tells us how fast the *starshyna* had taken over the governance of the Hetmanate: many universals (hetman's decrees) issued in the hetman's name had in fact been signed by clerks, who could not have done so without the *starshyna*'s approval. Peter invoked the Khmelnytsky Articles to subordinate the administration of justice to the *voevody* of the five towns, who would function as courts of appeal against the decisions of the local courts. A new Little Russian College – a local territorial version of the colleges created in 1719 in the centre, each responsible for a separate sector of administration – was created in Hlukhiv. It consisted of one officer in the rank of major and up from each of the five garrison towns, with a procurator (to watch over the proper interpretation of the law and most likely to encourage the introduction of Russian law), and a president, Brigadier (General) Stepan Veliaminov. The college, like other colleges in Moscow, was subordinated to the Senate, the highest administrative body in the Petrine state.[49]

The college had to examine complaints against the *starshyna* ("chanceries") at all levels including the extortion of grain and money, and to make sure that the hetman would sign in person the decrees sent in his name. It developed into a high court of appeal for the entire Hetmanate as well as a parallel government and a rival to the *starshyna* hierarchy. It was called upon to take to heart the interests of the "Little Russian people" (*narod*), an ambiguous but not unusual policy in Russia's administration of its internal frontiers. On the one hand, order had to be imposed on the *starshyna* for its own benefit at a time of rapid social transformation. On the other, the interests of the *narod* had to be defended in order to keep the *starshyna* in line by undermining its power base and blocking the development of mass movements, like those which took place in the Don region and the Lower Volga. Such a policy was contradictory and could only be a temporary expedient, inspired as it was by Peter's resentment of the hetman and the *starshyna* since 1709. The socio-economic development of the Hetmanate was beginning to resemble that of the Russian lands – the spread of serfdom and the transformation of the service class into a landed nobility. Moscow could not appeal to the support of the *narod* against the emerging ruling class without defeating its own purpose to create a unitary state.

The reform also downgraded the status of the governor general of Kiev by creating a province within a province, both equally subordinated to the Senate. The governor assumed responsibility for border affairs, diplomatic correspondence, and intelligence gathering in the steppe, while the college concentrated on the administration of the Hetmanate. Essentially it made the post of hetman superfluous. Skoropadsky understood the implications of the reform, and travelled to Petersburg to complain to the tsar, but to no avail. He could only return to Hlukhiv to die later that year (1722). And indeed, he had no immediate successor. The tsar refused to confirm the election of Pavlo Polubotok, the colonel of the Chernihiv regiment, who fought corruption in the courts and asserted his autonomy against the encroachments of the college, but Veliaminov found enough *starshyna* to petition the tsar against the putative hetman, who was arrested and died in a Petersburg prison in 1724.[50] The college now had a free hand in the administration of the former Hetmanate.

The administrative-territorial reform, with its attendant consequences for the fate of the Hetmanate, cannot be separated from the reorganization of the Russian army and its deployment in the expanding core. The strategic force engaged against the Swedes was constantly on the move between 1703 and 1721 in the Petersburg-Copenhagen-Poltava triangle. Some of it was also engaged against the Turks beyond the Dniester in 1711. The Northern War was barely over when troops were sent on an expedition along the Caspian shores, which was directed as much against Turkey as it was against Persia.[51] By 1723, when it was over, a so-called Southern Corps remained in the eastern theatre between Astrakhan and Resht, and a Ukrainian Corps was stationed between the Dnieper and the Volga in the southern theatre. Both corps were deployed to form a huge crescent directed against the Crimean Tatars and the Turkish position on the Azov Sea.

In the meantime, a so-called land militia had been created in 1713 for defence against the Crimean Tatars. It consisted of five regiments drawn from peasants settled along the Belgorod Line. In 1722, *odnodvortsy* were drafted into it, and the militia was transformed into a cavalry unit of six regiments of 1,500 men each, each commanded by a colonel. The reform was explained by concern over the possibility of a Crimean Tatar attack expressed by the new Russian resident in Constantinople, Ivan Nepliuev (the future governor of Orenburg), in connection with the Russian invasion of Persia, which also threatened to affect the Crimean khan's position in the northern Caucasus. The militia was placed under the Kiev governor general, save the units stationed in neighbouring Azov province, which depended on the provincial governor.[52] Two years earlier, in 1720, after the division of Kiev province into *provintsii*, the *sloboda* regiments of the Kharkiv corridor, which had been commanded by the Kiev and Azov governors, were placed again under the authority of the Belgorod *voevoda*.[53]

The militia and the regiments had complementary missions: the regiments set up patrols and warned of Tatar raids, the militia formed a second line of defence for the same purpose. The *voevoda* ruled by martial law and was responsible, like the Kiev governor general, for the collection of intelligence on Turkish and Crimean activities (as well as on those of the Zaporozhian Cossacks), which he forwarded to the Senate and the College of Foreign Affairs, and in purely military matters, to the College of War. Whenever he sent troops into the steppe, he had to inform immediately the Kiev governor general and the hetman – proof that the Little Russian College engaged only in the domestic affairs of the Hetmanate. Peter also counted on 60,000 registered Little Russian Cossacks, as had been agreed with Khmelnytsky in 1654, not all of whom, of course – perhaps only half – served at any one time. He also contemplated the creation of mercenary troops (*serdiuki*) numbering 15,000 men.[54] The Cossacks depended on the hetman, but by then their operational assignment depended on the emperor alone. The command hierarchy of the mercenaries was unclear, but as troops consisting chiefly of immigrants from central Europe and the Balkans, they must have been looked upon as a type of regular troops, except that they were drawn from a distinct category of the population. In fact, they may have never been created. There were also about 3,500 Sloboda Cossacks. Finally, there were in Kiev province six regiments of "garrison dragoons" numbering about 6,000 men and seven of garrison infantry with about 9,300 men.[55]

This hodgepodge of military units of various origins and composition required a unified command if it was to be effective. In April 1723, General Prince Mikhail Golitsyn (Dmitri's brother, who would later combine the post with that of president of the College of War) was appointed commander in chief of all regular and irregular troops in Little Russia and the Kharkiv corridor, as well as over the Don Cossacks and the small "regiment" of Chuhuiv Cossacks (214 men), who were chiefly converted Kalmyks commanded by a *murza*.[56] Golitsyn was authorized to deploy troops at his discretion in the event of a Tatar raid. The Little Russian College, the Voronezh governor, and the Belgorod and Sevsk *voevodas* were subordinated to him in military matters.[57] This immense territory, incorporating the entire wooded steppe of the southern theatre, was that of the Ukrainian Corps (also called Division).

Peter's reform of the Little Russian and Kharkiv Cossacks must be seen in the context of the evolution of Russian strategy in the southern theatre. After 1686, the only enemies in that region were the Crimean khanate and the Ottoman Empire, against which Russia, Austria, and Poland were mounting a counteroffensive. The Muscovite advance had proceeded apace since the creation of the Belgorod and Izium lines, and the Cossack lands were increasingly becoming an inner frontier of the expanding Muscovite core, a zone of assimilation like all frontiers, in as much as the internal evolution of Cossack society was creating a stratified society seeking to resemble the Polish one at first, but one becoming increasingly closer to the Russian. If there had not been a Russo-Swedish war, which stretched the resources of the Muscovite core to the limit, the reform might not have gone so far and so fast. But the intensity of the struggle created a unified playing field for the Petrine government, which rejected local claims to separate status, and Mazepa's betrayal was the decisive event which broke whatever restraint Peter may have felt and unleashed his fury. If the great battle of the war had not been fought in the Hetmanate, where Swedish and Russian ambitions fought for hegemony in western Eurasia, the reforms might not have been so brutal. But the Hetmanate was transformed by war into a small but crucial sector in Russia's theatre strategy, where military rule prevailed and local elites had to bend or be crushed. When the danger had passed, and the khanate and the Ottoman Empire once again became the major enemy, a partial return to the old order would not be able to change the fact that Left Bank Ukraine was being integrated by forces beyond anyone's control into a Muscovite core steadily expanding toward the Black Sea.

The Don Cossacks

In the basin of the Don, whose left-bank tributaries watered the Riazan-Kalachna[58] corridor descending toward the Azov Sea, of which it formed the natural hinterland, the Don Cossacks were emerging as the most powerful irregular force in the southern theatre. By the mid-seventeenth century the Dontsy lived in families clustered in some 125 towns, villages (*stanitsy*), and forts (*gorodki*) strung along the Khoper, the Medveditsa, and the Northern Donets at the entrance of the Kharkiv corridor, as well as on the Don itself. They still formed a highly democratic society. In towns and villages, the Cossacks formed a circle (*krug*), named after the practice of meeting on horseback in a circle in the field to discuss the final dispositions before giving battle. The circle elected an *otaman*, an *esaul* (deputy), and a clerk for one year and re-elected them at discretion. The host likewise elected a *voiskovyi otaman*, deputies, and a clerk. One *otaman*, Frol Minaev (1682–1700), was re-elected twenty times. In wartime, the host elected a campaign (*pokhidnyi*) *otaman* and sometimes a *nakaznyi otaman* as well, who remained in Cherkassk in charge of the host's civil administration.

The host *otaman* was the executive agent of the circle, and as a result received unlimited powers – subject, of course, to review by the assembly at the end of the one-year term. In wartime he had powers of life and death over his men, but, in peacetime as well, those who opposed his decisions ran the risk of being sewn into a bag and thrown into the river or hung upside down on a tree. The circle had all the virtues and defects of a large popular assembly which took its role seriously: democratic inclusiveness and intolerance of opposition. Its "sentences" (*prigovory*) were announced as those of the entire Great Don Host (*Velikoe Voisko Donskoe*).

The origins of the Don Cossacks explained the distinctive role they played in the history of the Cossacks of the southern theatre. The Ukrainian Cossacks of the Hetmanate and Zaporizhia, despite their mixed origin and their Orthodox religion, had grown as part of the Polish empire in the wooded steppe, and had been structured to serve its security needs. Even the Sloboda Cossacks, shaped by the expanding Muscovite core, came largely from beyond the Dnieper. But the Don Cossacks had come from the north, and vagrants kept escaping from the core, including Old Believers after the Church Council of 1666–7. They kept looking for a secure haven in the still densely wooded basin of the Don, where Moscow, until 1695, chose not to pursue them. Thus the Don Cossacks were not so many ethnically different communities encountered in the process of expansion, but extensions of the core itself, with which they remained inextricably linked.

Close ties were facilitated by the Cossacks' dependence on Moscow for deliveries of grain, which they did not want to cultivate, in exchange for fish and Turkish and Tatar goods. They sent to Moscow parties of Cossacks (*zimovye stanitsy*) to bring intelligence on the steppe nomads' intentions, and their *otamans* were received in great honour by the tsars. Unlike the Ukrainian hetmans, the Don *otamans* were trusted, even though some were more trusted than others, like Kornelii Yakovlev, who helped put down the Razin rebellion in 1671, Frol Mineev, and Rodion Kaluzhin: these last two were even invited to attend the military councils seeking to shape Russia's policies in the region. Conversely, *otamans*, rough frontier types, came under the spell of "white-stone Moscow" with its elaborate court and dazzling entertainments. There, they got used to comfort and luxury, and took precious cloth and furs back with them to Cherkassk. But the Cossacks also had to entertain the envoys Moscow occasionally sent to Constantinople via Cherkassk, Azov, and Kerch, as well as the troops stationed from time to time in the vicinity. All this cost money and contributed to a growing social differentiation between the emerging *starshyna* and the rank-and-file Cossacks. There was still much booty to be shared when the host sent small and large detachments, the latter divided into regiments, *sotni*, and half-*sotni*, to attack Crimean towns at night on swift boats (*chaiki*) that gave them the advantage of surprise. If the raids did not suit Moscow's purpose, they could always be disavowed. If they did, they served to test Muslim defences on the Black Sea coast and contributed a wealth of experience for the future in managing coastal operations.

The emergence of a community of interests between the *starshyna* and the Muscovite government was visible in other ways. The Razin rebellion, short and brutal, which shook Muscovite power in the mid-Volga region in 1670–1, threatened to spill into the Don lands, from which Razin originated and to which he sought to return, only to be seized by Otaman Yakovlev and delivered to the Muscovite authorities. The *starshyna* would not tolerate a rebellion by its "rabble." Yakovlev's action symbolized the transformation of the Don Cossack leadership from descendants of vagrants and runaways fleeing the advance of serfdom and the rise of the fiscal burden in the Muscovite core into a social group cooperating with Muscovite troops to extend the range of serfdom, although not in the Don lands. To consecrate the new alliance between the Don *starshyna* and the Muscovite *voevody*, the tsar sent two high-ranking members of the ruling elite (*stolniki*) to administer the oath of allegiance to the host and to initiate a policy by which the *starshyna* and the host would renew their oath at the accession of every new tsar. Then, during the reign of Fedor Alexeevich (1676–82), the Dontsy began to receive a permanent salary, but only for 3,250 men, chiefly for the main force around Cherkassk, because the Dontsy could already put 10,000 horsemen and infantry in the field by the time Peter came to the throne in 1689. A major step had been taken toward the integration of the Don Cossacks into the irregular forces of the Russian army.[59]

Peter's wars accelerated their transformation into an elite formation among the Cossack forces, while destroying the independence that they had cherished for a century. Peter's wars did not begin with the attack on the Swedish possession at Narva in 1700, but with the expedition of 1695 against Azov, captured the following year. It required the creation of a Don flotilla built at the new shipyards of Voronezh and sent down the Don with troops, equipment, and provisions, to compel the Turks to surrender the fortress and establish a Russian presence in the Azov Sea. The Don River became the axis of a war zone, and the Don Cossack settlements in the river's basin were required to man a communication infrastructure linking the units in the field with Voronezh. The burden was heavy, because the region remained sparsely populated and the

Don was not always a reliable shipping route because of sandbars, at Boguchar, for example, which obstructed the progress of "caravans" bringing grain and timber to Azov and later to Taganrog. So many Cossacks were drafted to carry messages in addition to the 7,000 taken into the army for the siege of Azov that few remained to cope with Tatar threats from beyond the Don.[60]

Moreover, the turbulence already created by Peter's violent temper and ruthless determination to carry out a program of reform in the face of any opposition was beginning to be felt among the Don Cossacks. Flights of serfs increased toward the border regions, while the need for more troops increased by the day, even before the war with Sweden had begun. In 1695, the tsar demanded that fugitives would henceforth have to be returned, a threat to the well-being of the Don *starshyna* for whom the fugitives were a source of cheap labour. Peter took away the Bakhmut saltworks from the Don Cossacks and gave them to the Izium Cossacks, who were in greater need of them, and demanded that the Don Cossacks carry salt from beyond the river to Azov. The peace treaty with the Ottomans of June 1700 gave Azov and Taganrog to the Russians, but also forbade further Cossack expeditions against the Crimea's coastal cities, the old source of booty. Peter did not like the headstrong spirit and chaotic politics of the Don Cossacks, and he even forbade them to navigate the Azov Sea and fish in it – and fishing had been a major source of their income. Yet, the Cossacks remained faithful, and ten thousand even joined Russian troops to put down the Astrakhan rebellion in 1705, while others served in the Swedish war at a great distance of their homeland.[61]

But compulsion steadily applied against the interests of a social group inevitably generates a backlash. When the *starshyna* refused to surrender the fugitives, the tsar sent Colonel Yurii Dolgorukov to carry out the order. The decision was the precipitant of the Bulavin rebellion. Kondrat Bulavin was a campaign *otaman* who patrolled the border on the Donets Ridge at the end of the Kharkiv corridor. He was also receptive to Mazepa's ambitions to draw the Dontsy into the alliance with Sweden and Poland against Muscovy. Dolgorukov facilitated his task by resorting to brutal methods to send back some three thousand runaways. But in the winter of 1707 Bulavin moved up the Khoper to Uriupinsk, where he massacred a thousand Russian troops including Dolgorukov, then moved to Bakhmut to seal his alliance with Mazepa, less than a year before the Ukrainian hetman made his fateful move.

Peter took forceful measures to put down the rebellion, and sent twenty thousand regulars from Tula under Dmitri Golitsyn, who was about to become governor general of Kiev. He was soon replaced by Vasilii Dolgorukov, Yurii's brother, who also took command of the Dontsy who had refused to join the rebels. *Otaman* Lukian Maksimov (1700–8), a weak leader, suffered a severe defeat on the Kalmius River, the western "boundary" of the Don Cossacks, and had to surrender Cherkassk, where he was beheaded. Bulavin was proclaimed *otaman* of the host. But Dolgorukov crushed the revolt in April 1708, and Bulavin committed suicide in Cherkassk in July,[62] leaving the Don land utterly devastated, three months before Mazepa moved to the Swedish camp and caused a similar devastation to be visited on the Hetmanate. The two events cannot be separated, and both inaugurated a new period in the history of the Cossacks of the Don and the Hetmanate.

From that time on the election of the *otaman* would require the tsar's approval, if he did not choose the *otaman* himself. When Peter came to Cherkassk after the crushing of the revolt, he chose Petr Ramazanov as "temporary *otaman*" (*vpred do ukaza*). Ramazanov died in 1715, and was followed by Maksym Kushmatsky (1715–16), with whom Moscow did not interfere. In 1716, the circle elected Vasilii Frolov (a son of Frol Minaev), whom Peter proclaimed permanent *otaman* in 1718 because he had shown his mettle in fighting the Tatars; he died in 1723. Peter then imposed Andrei Lopatin, who remained in office until 1735. That same year, in 1723, the host, which had been under the jurisdiction of the "ministry" of foreign affairs for a century (since 1623), was subordinated to the College of War – it became one more formation in the growing military establishment, and one that was promised a great future.[63]

The crushing of the Bulavin rebellion coincided with the introduction of the administrative-territorial reform in the basin of the Don. Azov province was given a governor who resided at first in the old Ottoman fortress, but who moved to Voronezh after the disastrous campaign on the Prut in 1711 and the return of Azov to the Ottomans. The first governor was Fedor Apraksin (1700–6), who was also in charge of the nascent Russian navy and was the tsar's brother-in-law. He was followed by Ivan Tolstoi and Petr Izmailov. The province contained fifty-two "towns" and an additional twenty-five "attached" to the Voronezh shipyards. It absorbed the entire basin of the Don including the Ukraine of Settlements in the basin of the Donets. It stretched as far north as the Oka and as far east as the Medveditsa Rivers, leaving the Volga corridor with Saratov in Kazan (later Astrakhan) province in the eastern theatre.[64] One result, as in the Hetmanate, was to incorporate the land of the Don Cossacks into the territorial grid of the expanding Muscovite core and to subordinate de facto the *otaman* to the Russian governor in Azov/Voronezh.

But not for long. In 1719, Voronezh province was divided into five *provintsii*: Voronezh, Tambov, Shatsk, Elets, and Bakhmut, the latter an elongated and shapeless promontory that kept the saltworks outside the jurisdiction of the Don Cossacks. The land of the Don Cossacks, which now regained its territorial autonomy, was huge – larger than the Hetmanate. It bordered in the east on the Ergeni Hills overlooking the Caspian depression, and in the south on the Manych River and salt lakes, beyond which began the Kuban and North Caucasian steppe. It was still very sparsely populated. The 1719 census, most likely unreliable here because it did not include the vagrants and Old Believers, gave a population of 58,000. Tambov *provintsiia* – which became Tambov province much later – together with Voronezh province, had a population of only 680,422 within their nineteenth-century borders, about half the size of the population of Orel and Kursk provinces bordering on the Hetmanate.[65]

But like the Hetmanate and the Ukraine of Settlements, this second sector remained highly vulnerable to Tatar raids from the Crimea and the Kuban. They followed the left bank of the Don and kept devastating the valleys of the Medveditsa and the Khoper, which led to the Penza Upland and the eastern section of the Belgorod Line. To block such raids, the government began in 1717 the construction of the so-called Tsaritsyn Line running from Kalachna on the Don to Fort Mechetny, twelve kilometres from Tsaritsyn on the Volga. Regular troops were stationed there, and five hundred Dontsy were sent each year to patrol the line. But this projection of a permanent military presence to the portage between the Don and the Volga, together with the subordination of the Don *otaman* to the College of War (and to General Golitsyn), had the effect of transforming the land of the Don Cossacks into an internal frontier of the expanding core, which now bordered on the Crimean khanate between the middle Dnieper and the lower Don. Even after the return of Azov to the Ottomans, Peter was preparing for Russia's reemergence. Azov had been a suitable site for the Turks coming from the sea, but its soil was swampy and its climate deleterious. Two kilometres below Cherkassk and sixty from the sea, Peter set up a fort called Tranzhament and stationed a large garrison in it. Its commandant was instructed to watch over the Cossacks and the Turks and to decide disputes between them and with the Kalmyks and Tatars. A new Cossack regiment, later called Azovskii, was added to the garrison,[66] and the fort displaced the Cossack capital in strategic importance to become the local headquarters of the Russian military. The choice of the site was successful. The fort was later called St Anna, then St Dmitri, and finally Rostov-on-Don, which would become one of the most important cities and communication hubs of the late Russian empire.

The Petrine policy of destroying the independence of the Cossack formations in the Hetmanate and the Don basin was largely motivated by the equivocal role they played in the larger conflict between Russia and Sweden, and between Russia, the Crimean Tatars, and the Turks, for hegemony in western Eurasia. Their subsequent fate would be different, however. The Cossacks of the Hetmanate were already part of a more densely settled and agricultural society undergoing a transformation marked by the rise of a landowning class and the spread of serfdom, a social revolution that shaped Ukrainian society throughout the eighteenth century. With the growth of Russian power against Poland, Turkey, and the Crimea and the growing importance of the infantry in determining the outcome of battles, the Ukrainian Cossacks became relegated to the condition of auxiliary formations for reconnaissance and foraging operations, which only earned them a poor reputation, or they were simply incorporated into new regiments of regular cavalry.

By contrast, the importance of the Don Cossacks grew as their settlements became the mother house of other Cossack formations in the eastern theatre. They served in the Persian war of 1722–3 (and suffered heavy losses), yet in 1723, 1,000 families were sent to reinforce the Greben and Astrakhan Cossacks in the delta of the Terek and in the valley of the Sulak.[67] Later, they would serve in large numbers on the Caucasian Line. Don Cossacks also established relations with their brethren on the Ural River. It was as if they were destined to migrate southeastward as the advance formation of the Muscovite core relentlessly expanding in the direction of the Caucasus. It was indeed their natural destiny, because their settlements in the basin of the Medveditsa and the Khoper stood about halfway in the great corridor of Russian expansion from Riazan via Tambov and Tsaritsyn to the foothills of the Caucasus, between the Black Sea and the Caspian depressions. At the end of Peter's reign, the Ukrainian Cossacks still constituted the larger group, with perhaps 60,000 in the Hetmanate and 3,500 in the Ukraine of Settlements. The Don Cossacks numbered 14,266, and there were another 244 in the "Vasiliev regiment" (Azovskii) in Tranzhament. The Cossacks were backed by six regiments of regular dragoons (about 6,800 men) in Tambov and Shatsk *provintsii*, forming the southern perimeter of the army's deployment in Voronezh province. In addition, three regiments of garrison infantry (about 3,800 men) were stationed in Voronezh and Elets *provintsii*.[68] The Don Cossacks thus played a major role in guarding alone the entrance to the Riazan-Tambov corridor, which led straight to Moscow.

Society, Religion, and Trade

Stratification

The process by which the intruder group established its dominion over an already stratified society – creating a community of interests with the dominant stratum of the native society – was at work in the southern theatre. In the Hetmanate and the Kharkiv corridor a new society was taking shape and creating its own upper stratum while becoming increasingly stratified. Before we turn to an examination of that process, let us briefly consider the origin of the new society.

The sixteenth century was very favourable to the Polish economy. There was a great demand for wheat and cattle in Europe. Wheat was shipped down the Vistula to Danzig and large herds of oxen were driven to Silesia on their way to the great fair in Leipzig. But the growth of the Polish economy was not accompanied by the commercialization of its agriculture. On the contrary, economic expansion was followed by social regression with the intensification of serfdom beyond the Polish core. The magnates built large latifundiae in Right Bank Ukraine, incorporated into the Polish core in 1569, but Ukrainian peasants resented the increase in the tax burden (in the form of corvée labour) on those properties, and began to migrate eastward toward the Dnieper and then beyond the river, where the census of 1552 found a still largely uninhabited country. Peasants sought freedom in the open country, but with freedom came danger from the Tatars in search of booty. The Tatar danger explained the rise of the Cossack free-booter, the mirror image of the nomad, and the only one capable of standing up to him. That early frontier society consisted of two still largely undistinguishable elements, the Cossacks who fought and the peasant who worked the land, but who was also likely to join the Cossacks when his distress became unbearable.

The migration of Cossacks and peasants across the Dnieper in search of freedom attracted Polish noblemen in search of new land. They came largely from Volhynia, with its outlet on the Western Bug, which led to the Vistula, even though the Left Bank was far away. The most prominent of these families was the Vyshnevetskys (Wiśniowieckis), Orthodox Ukrainians who had converted to Catholicism. The Polish king gave them title to an enormous "wilderness" containing the region of the Udai, Sula, and Solonytsia Rivers, between the Dnieper and the still undefined possessions of Muscovy.[69] Other Ukrainian families and Polish *szlachta* joined them from the Right Bank. Poltava on the Vorskla to the east was already an isolated Cossack regimental capital in 1514, and became the centre of the Vyshnevetsky private empire, which resembled in some ways that of the Russian Stroganovs in the eastern theatre. The northern part of what would become the Hetmanate, north of the Oster River, with Chernihiv its major city, had belonged to Moscow since 1503, and its soil and dense forests were not attractive to settlers from the south in search of good land or to the Tatars, whose trails ran much farther to the east. As a result, a third element emerged in the Poltava region, the heart of the future Hetmanate – a stratum of large and small landowners, Polish and Ukrainian, Catholic and Orthodox, but all bent on extracting resources from the peasantry, whom they viewed as their future serfs. They were also determined to control the Cossacks, who, if they served a useful military purpose, were also developing as a dangerous fringe of doubtful loyalty and becoming a magnet for the resentful peasants who eagerly joined them.

The Khmelnytsky uprising and the subsequent civil war destroyed the landowning stratum and left two groups face to face – the Cossacks and the peasantry (*pospolstvo*) – but they were no longer equal. The Cossacks had borne the brunt of the fighting and had developed into a warrior class with its hierarchy of officers at the hetman, regimental, and *sotnia* levels, the so-called *starshyna*. Khmelnytsky destroyed the large landed properties where the peasants had performed corvée labour, but these private properties became the collective property of the host (*svobodnaia voiskovaia zemlia*). The *starshyna* stepped effortlessly into the shoes of the former landlords and began to detach parcels from the common land or seize still unoccupied land, and transformed these lands into private properties.[70] The Cossacks thus built the rudiment of a stratified society, Cossack ruling over peasant (the despised *muzhik*), *starshyna* ruling over the rank-and-file Cossack. The more fortunate peasant managed to retain the ownership of the land he had tilled on the magnate properties, but Cossacks, *starshyna*, and peasant were now in a state of incipient war for the control of the land. Recent arrivals from the Right Bank became only tenants on Cossack and peasant land, adding another stratum in the Left Bank society.

To this social distinction created by war and revolution was added an economic transformation in which the *starshyna* began to accumulate wealth while the rank-and-file Cossack had to be content with common property or whatever he was able to acquire, like the *starshyna*, by hook or by crook. The peasant found himself again at the bottom of the social hierarchy, paying taxes and dues and performing corvée labour, from which the Cossack was exempt. The peasant began to find his freedom of movement limited by his *starshyna* overlord with his monopoly of force, while the Cossack still retained his full freedom. Khmelnytsky and his successors carved estates from the common land and attached them to certain offices in the Cossack administration (the so-called *rangovye imenia*),[71] and granted others to faithful followers for services rendered to the host. Peasants on the attached properties paid one-tenth of the harvest to the host's treasury and worked on them two days a week.

The process of stratification affected the Cossacks as well as the larger society. The *starshyna* as a whole, combining Cossack officialdom and the increasing number of favourites gathered around the hetmans and the regimental colonels, began to imagine themselves as a privileged class scattered across the entire country and living off the back of the peasants.[72] As is often the case in such situations, the Cossack rebels endeavoured to create a new society modelled after that of their former masters, the Polish *szlachta*. Polish influence remained strong, and some hetmans came to be associated by the Orthodox Cossacks and peasants with the Catholic Poles, thus widening the gulf with the mass of the population. This undermined the legitimacy of the hetmans and facilitated a rapprochement between the Ukrainian peasantry and the Muscovites with whom they shared a common Orthodox religion.

The hetmans' legitimacy was threatened in another way. As long as Polish influence remained strong, the *starshyna* modelled itself after the Polish *szlachta* and, if possible, even after the magnates. Indeed, the *starshyna* began to call itself *shliakhetstvo*, a transliteration of *szlachta*, which later, with the waning of Polish influence later in the eighteenth century, became *dvorianstvo*, as in the Russian core. A corollary of this early infatuation with Polish ways was a reluctance to accept a strong hetman, much in the same way as the magnates and their nobiliar republic with its *pacta conventa* distrusted a strong king.[73] Paradoxically, Polish influence was paving the way for an accommodation with Moscow, which remained suspicious of the hetmans' Polish proclivities.

Among the Don Cossacks, a stratified society was already very much in evidence by the end of the seventeenth century. The officers who joined the *starshyna* by virtue of their office kept the title after their term expired and constituted a privileged group. The rank-and-file Cossacks were divided into two groups, the well-established (*domovitye*), who had come to the Don much earlier, and the recent immigrants (*golitvennye* or *golit'ba*), who formed the raiding parties that plundered merchant caravans on the Volga and held a grudge against Moscow. It was the *domovitye* who turned against Razin and delivered him to the Russians. And there were the runaway peasants who did not join the Cossacks but worked the land for the benefit of the *starshyna* and the *domovitye*, who exploited them with the threat of a return to the *voevody* on the Belgorod Line. The *starshyna* and the *domovitye* were referred to as the "downriver" (*nizovye*) Cossacks, because they were concentrated in Cherkassk, Razdory, and other strategic points; they had already reached an accommodation with Moscow and persecuted the Old Believers, who made up most of the *golit'ba* and were called the "upriver" (*verkhovye*) Cossacks, chiefly Old Believers in the wooded areas.[74] Cossack society on the Don was already more stratified than that of the Hetmanate, and therefore more receptive to the process of superstratification.

Cossack service was onerous, what with the great distances in open country and patrol duty during the summer months. The Cossack often had no time to earn a living from his land, and the occasional salary was not enough. The Polish authorities had already distinguished between the "registered" Cossacks and the others, who received no salary at all. Gradually, a distinction emerged in the Hetmanate between the Cossack who served and the Cossack who did not, who became a "helper" (*podpomoshchnik*), responsible with his community in the *stanitsa* and the regiment for supplying the Cossack in active service with his clothing, his provisions, and his equipment.[75] The struggle for the land, combined with the burden of Cossack service, forced Cossacks who were landowners to sell their land and join the category of privately owned peasants (*vladelcheskie pospolitye*) on the land of a Cossack official or that of the private landowners, who resurfaced in the Left Bank. These peasants were not serfs, even though the *starshyna* already assumed they were, if only because they retained their freedom to move. When they sold their land and moved to someone else's property, including that of monasteries, they became *podsusedki* and paid a share of the harvest to their new lord. Thus Cossack society became stratified within a society undergoing a process of stratification, from hetman to *starshyna*, to Cossack on active service, Cossack helper, and *podsusedok*, barely above the peasant stratum. The *starshyna* kept replenishing itself by natural growth, but also kept increasing as enterprising Cossacks managed to acquire land, while others, not so fortunate, lost theirs. Less than a generation after Khmelnytsky's death, Left Bank society was in the throes of a momentous transformation.

It was estimated that at the beginning of the eighteenth century the *starshyna* consisted of about one thousand families in a population of 1.1 million.[76] If we assume that a three-generation family included about ten people, the *starshyna* made up at least 1 per cent of the population. By then, it included all those who had been given properties by the hetmans or the tsars. In addition, some of these families combined landownership with a monopoly of certain offices, which passed from one generation to the next. For example, one *sotnia* in the Nizhyn regiment would remain in the hands of the same family for one hundred years, while another was "owned" by a different family for ninety years.[77] Thus the *starshyna* was emerging by the time of Peter's reign as a managerial class of landowners in control of the administration and the courts of the Hetmanate. It was at this point that the process of superstratification began.

There was hardly any Russian peasantry in the Hetmanate, and the Russian presence was found in a few garrison towns and among the *voevody* and their staffs. For Russian rule to be effective, without resorting to violent means which can only be temporary and become counterproductive in the long run, the Russian authorities needed the support of the *starshyna*, and the *starshyna* needed the support of the Russians to legitimize its newly acquired social status and ownership of land. Properties had been granted by the hetmans *do laski*, for as long as the holder retained the hetman's favour. Such lands remained under the threat of confiscation. It was therefore necessary to obtain Moscow's confirmation of the title to landed properties in the College of Landed Affairs (*Votchinnaia Kollegiia*), which grew out of the College of Justice to become a separate agency in 1722.

Of course, such properties might also be confiscated by the Russians for political disloyalty or for being on the wrong side of Muscovite politics, but this only added more urgency to the need for cooperation between the ruling class of the Hetmanate and that of the Muscovite core. Moreover, members of the Russian elite, like Alexander Menshikov, Boris Sheremetev, Gavril Golovkin, Petr Tolstoi, and Petr Shafirov, were granted large properties by the tsar and became de facto members of the *starshyna*, creating a form of superstratification within the elite. Land titles in the Hetmanate were often undocumented, either because the original documents had been lost or destroyed or because there had been no documents at all.[78] This explains the already common complaints about endless litigation over the ownership of real estate, but those who had registered their titles in Moscow had an advantage; so did those who managed to enter the patronage networks of high Russian officials. The College of Landed Affairs would soon emerge as the final arbiter of land disputes, bypassing the hetman.

All this served to downgrade his importance and created an unwritten understanding by the *starshyna* and the Russian elite that they had some common interests. Serfdom was already a fact in the Muscovite core. It formed the social foundation of the ruling class's power. It was also a fact in the Polish core, including Right Bank Ukraine. It would inevitably spread to the Hetmanate as well. At early as the time of Samoilovych (1672–87), the Cossack officers already spoke about the servile duties of the peasants. The heavier charges imposed on the landless new settlers from the Right Bank were gradually extended to the early settlers who had their own land. If they refused to accept the new and heavier charges, they were deprived of their land. A 1701 universal of Mazepa referred to corvée labour as being legal in the Hetmanate, fixed at two days a week.[79]

The enserfment of the peasantry had been steadily taking place since the second half of the seventeenth century. When a peasant moved, he did not lose the ownership of his land, but if he decided to sell it to someone outside his lord's domain, the new owner (who may or may not have been a peasant) did not assume the charges which his predecessor had to pay, and the land ceased to be within the lord's jurisdiction. To prevent such losses, the owners began to demand that the peasants who wished to leave could not sell their land without their approval, and they gained the support of Mazepa, even though this violated the established customs of the country. Then in 1723, the host's government (chancery) decreed that the lord's approval was mandatory in accordance with Chapter 29, article 27 of the Lithuanian Statute, which forbade the sale of anything without the *pan*'s approval. The order amounted not only to a restriction of the peasants' property rights, but also to a limitation of his right to move: a peasant who could not sell his land would not be able to obtain the capital he needed to finance his move and purchase new land elsewhere. It also facilitated the acquisition of peasant land by the *starshyna*.

Attempts were made to prevent the peasants from joining the Cossacks, as the Poles had done before 1648. The policy began toward the end of the seventeenth century and was sanctioned by the ukaze of April 1723.[80] Peasants were forbidden to register as Cossacks unless they could prove that their fathers and grandfathers had been in Cossack service or had been forced (*po nevole*) by the *starshyna* officers to become their "subjects," a clear hint that the degradation of the Cossacks to the status of privately held peasant was already taking place. Nothing was said about prohibiting the Cossacks from joining the peasantry without being compelled to do so. Lower-ranking Cossack officers, who could not hope to get land grants from the hetman or the tsar for "services," took advantage of the poverty of the Cossack rank-and-file and peasants to buy their land for a song – as they did in Bashkiria from the natives – or simply seized it by violent means, although it remains unclear whether Cossacks could sell their land if it remained part of the common land.

Thus, social stratification in the Hetmanate was beginning to resemble that of the Polish and Muscovite core, in the sense that a rising class of landowners was transforming the free Cossack and the free peasant into "subjects," until the abolition of their right to move would convert them fully into serfs. To legitimize the process, the *starshyna* needed the concurrence of the Russian authorities. Both had a mutual interest in the enserfment of the peasantry, but the process was bound to generate widespread opposition, as it did in the Muscovite core, where peasants were running away toward the peripheries, as well as in the Hetmanate, where free men would soon begin to run away to the Don *stanitsy*, where Cossacks and peasants remained free men.

But this social development, which left a profound imprint in the frontier along the fringe of Russian settlement from the Baltic to Bashkiria, had important consequences for the future of the *starshyna*. Edward Thaden claims that the Russians pursued different policies in the Baltic provinces and in the Hetmanate.[81] But this is to misread the issue. In the Baltic provinces, a caste of intruding German knights Christianized and enserfed the natives and remained an alien body in native society, conscious of its "privileges," even though it did not always know what they were. The consciousness of their privileges gave the knights a strong sense of separateness and identity. In the Hetmanate, however, a class of Cossack officers arose out of its own free people, and then gradually enserfed the peasantry and downgraded the status of its own warriors to near servile status. In both regions, the Germanic ruling class and the *starshyna* sought an accommodation with the Russians to maintain their hold over their population. But the former could always uphold its identity by returning to the historical origins of its power – the crushing of a native society. The *starshyna* could not invoke privileges because they had been those of a free people which it betrayed in alliance with Muscovy, and it had no legitimate ground on which to stand to represent its own people. The *starshyna* began among a free people, but it transformed it into a dependent population, very much as the Russian nobility had been doing with the peasantry since the reign of Ivan IV. In the Hetmanate, superstratification ended up by identifying the *starshyna*, not with a past when its people had been free, but with an evolving present, in which it lost its identity to become an integral part of an imperial ruling class dominated by Russians.[82]

Orthodoxy

The Orthodox religion, common to both Russians and Ukrainians, was a powerful agent fostering the integration of the Left Bank into the expanding Muscovite core. While religion can be a source of endless discord, belonging to the same religion, especially one surrounded by a hostile Roman Catholicism and a hostile Islam and closely associated with the secular power in Moscow, hostile to both Poland-Lithuania and the Crimean khanate, created a siege mentality, which encouraged rapprochement and, eventually, a fusion for a common cause. It also fostered the development of an ideology transcending socio-ethnic differences and creating uniform standards of behaviour vis-à-vis one's fellow men and the secular power. Orthodoxy also fostered the development of an ecclesiastical superstratification, when Russian and Ukrainian clerics discovered they had some common interests.

The Ukrainian lands between the San and the Dnieper belonged to the metropolitanate of Kiev, created at the end of the tenth century under the jurisdiction of the ecumenical patriarch in Constantinople. After the destruction of the city by the Mongols, the metropolitan moved north and settled first in Vladimir in 1299, then in Moscow in 1328. The common residence of the head of the church and the grand prince recreated the Byzantine pattern of church-state relations, in which the church was a state within the state (and not outside it) and remained vulnerable to arbitrary interference by the emperor. It also helped to identify the fate of the church with that of the grand prince, and turned the territory into a holy land. The expanding Muscovite core would be sanctified by being also a metropolitan see, and the church would have to destroy any deviations obstructing the development of a unitary ecclesiastical state.

Poland-Lithuania attempted to convince the ecumenical patriarch to recreate a separate metropolitanate for its Ukrainian and Belorussian lands, to create an Orthodox Church within the Polish empire, but this did not take place until 1458, when an Orthodox metropolitan was appointed in Lithuanian Novogrudok; he later moved to Kiev. Ten years earlier, in 1448, Moscow, angry at the decision of its metropolitan Isidor to accept the union of the Latin and Greek churches, had a synod of bishops elect its own metropolitanate of Kiev (but residing in Moscow) without the approval of the patriarch. This was a major step toward the creation of an autocephalous Orthodox Russian Church, and another synod would elect a Russian patriarch in 1589, this time with the approval of the ecumenical patriarch, who was visiting Moscow at the time. In 1453, Constantinople had fallen to the Turks, and the patriarch would henceforth be under the jurisdiction of an infidel sultan.[83] This momentous event and the growing independence of the Russian church split Orthodoxy in two, one part dominated by Greek, the other by Russian clerics, and eventually by Russian and Ukrainian clerics. Moreover, the Russian Church, unsullied by its incorporation into an infidel empire, naturally expected, together with the tsar, to become the protector of the Orthodox faith in the lands of the Polish and Ottoman empires, a claim with serious implications for the international relations of western Eurasia.

The Union of Brest (1595), which created the Uniate Church in the Polish-controlled metropolitanate, outlawed Orthodoxy, but the king legalized it again in 1632, when anxiety spread in Poland lest the Orthodox clergy turn to

Moscow for support during the imminent Russo-Polish war (1632–4). This was also the time when large numbers of Orthodox Ukrainians began their migration across the Dnieper into Little Russia and the Kharkiv corridor to escape both the extension of serfdom and religious persecution on the Right Bank. The Khmelnytsky uprising was not only a social upheaval but also a religious revolt by Cossacks and peasants against Catholicism. The Pereiaslav agreement of 1654 (whose ideological foundation was the Orthodox discourse)[84] pledged that the metropolitan and clergy in the Polish empire could "come under the blessing" of the Moscow patriarch, who promised not to interfere in ecclesiastical matters.[85] But the Kiev metropolitan, Sylvester Kosiv (Kosov), a man of Polish and Latin culture, remained close to Poland. Kosiv and his episcopate resisted the idea of joining with Moscow, and he refused to swear allegiance to the tsar. He insisted that the clergy had not asked for "protection," and that any association with Moscow must recognize the privileges of the largely Ukrainian Church; that it must remain under the jurisdiction of the ecumenical patriarch in Constantinople; that the high clergy must keep their posts; and that all disputes in Little Russia must be tried in local ecclesiastical courts and appealed to the metropolitan, who would have the final say, without the possibility of an additional appeal to Moscow.[86]

But Moscow's gravitational pull was becoming stronger. The metropolitanate had become an ecclesiastical frontier between Moscow on the one hand, Warsaw and Constantinople on the other, but frontiers are vulnerable to pressures exercised by the cores that surround them. The ecclesiastical frontier on the Right Bank was dominated by Warsaw. The frontier on the Left Bank was torn between Moscow and Constantinople, but the latter's influence was waning, while Moscow's was growing. Kosov died in 1657. His successor, Dionsii Balaban (1657–63), a candidate of Hetman Vyhovsky, suffered from his association with the fallen leader. Hetman Iurii Khmelnytsky (1659–63), a son of the first hetman, was already willing to accept the submission of the metropolitanate to the Moscow patriarch. Balaban's successor, Lazar Baranovych (1593–1694), the archbishop of Chernihiv, was installed by Prince Alexei Trubetskoy, the commanding general of Russian troops on the Left Bank, not as metropolitan, but as "administrator," and was consecrated by Moscow in 1661. Then Moscow instructed Hetman Samoilovych in 1675 to summon a synod of bishops to elect a metropolitan who would recognize the Moscow patriarch as his superior. In the meantime, the Russo-Polish treaty of Andrusovo of 1667 (confirmed in 1686) had recognized Moscow's suzerainty over the Left Bank and over Kiev on the Right Bank. The metropolitan's residence had been included into the expanding Muscovite core, and the Kievan monks were already the strongest supporters of the Muscovite tsar.[87]

In 1685, the Bishop of Lutsk in Volhynia, Gideon Sviatopolk-Chetvertynsky, was elected metropolitan of Kiev with the support of Hetman Samoilovych.

He had told the tsar the previous year that "he had experienced much evil in the lands of the Polish king and could take it no longer";[88] he was ready to ask the tsar for his protection and patronage. He then travelled to Moscow to be consecrated by the patriarch. Not only did the ecumenical patriarch not oppose the decision, but he also abdicated his rights to the Kievan metropolitanate, and the formal annexation to the Moscow patriarchate took place in June 1686. After that date, the ecclesiastical frontier with Constantinople ceased to exist. The metropolitanate became a constituent part of the autocephalous Moscow patriarchate. This suited the patriarch and the tsar, both anxious to "reunite" the Orthodox world of the Eastern Slavs. The move also gave Moscow a powerful weapon with which to interfere in the religious affairs of the Polish empire. Forty years earlier, Bohdan Khmelnytsky had already invoked "the mirage of a vast Orthodox empire,"[89] including even the Balkans and Greece, to be under the rule of the Muscovite tsar. A common Orthodoxy was creating a community of interests between the core area government and the Cossack frontier against Poland and Turkey.

In the meantime, a schism had been taking place in Moscow. Nikon's election to the patriarchate in 1652 and the assumption by tsar and patriarch of the title "of all the Great and Little Russia" created uncertainty. On the one hand, it was clearly Moscow's intention that Russia and Little Russia be part of a single expanding Muscovite core and a single Orthodox Slavic patriarchate. On the other, Nikon wanted Moscow to become the leader of the Orthodox world in its entirety. There were bound to be tensions between the narrower view of the political establishment and the "ecumenical" ambitions of the patriarch, who wanted to raise the educational level of the Moscow clerics by Hellenizing the Russian Church. Revising the ritual and correcting the Church books were intended to serve a higher goal, to raise the prestige of the Russian Church in the Orthodox world.

When Kosiv died in 1657, the tsar and the boyars wanted a metropolitan they could accept, but Nikon refused on canonical grounds, claiming that the election of a metropolitan still required the approval of Constantinople. But Nikon's reign was short. The ruling elite imposed its will on the Church, and Nikon's position had already been much weakened by 1660, six years before his banishment to Beloozero.[90] There were three consequences. Old Believers split from the official Church and fled into the forests of the Chernihiv region and to the Don, where they actively opposed Moscow's policies. Another was the strengthening within the Russian official Church of the association between religion and Russian identity, so that the Orthodox faithful became Russian ipso facto. A paradoxical result of this nativist backlash was to encourage the migration of better-educated Ukrainian clerics to Moscow to improve the Church's management. Thus, the integration of Little Russia into the patriarchate inaugurated a process of superstratification, in which Muscovite and Ukrainian clerics found they had a common interest in strengthening the authority of the Church within the limits set by the ruling elite.

Chetvertynsky died in 1690 and was succeeded by Varlaam Yasynsky (1690–1707). His reign coincided with Mazepa's hetmanship (1687–1708). The hetman gained his support by building monasteries and richly decorated churches to promote religious and educational work. He encouraged the hierarch to maintain his autonomy vis-à-vis the patriarch – all this to build a power base and counter rumours that Mazepa was a Catholic and a Pole. Indeed, Mazepa had close ties to the Catholic Church: his mother was an abbess and his sister a nun. Yasynsky had opposed submission to Moscow in 1685, yet it was during his rule that a sharp reorientation of Ukrainian culture toward Moscow took place.[91] The Muscovite elite gathering around the young Peter, who came to the throne in 1689, was imbued with the spirit of reform, including that of the Church, associated with Russia's backwardness. The Kievan theological "Collegium" (later Academy), founded in 1632 by Metropolitan Petro Mohyla (1632–47) from Moldova (who had been consecrated in Lviv), had trained a new generation of clerics who went to Europe to taste the forbidden fruit of Catholicism, and even converted to it, before returning to the Orthodox fold.[92]

Thus Stephen Yavorsky (1658–1722), who came from a Galician family, travelled after his graduation from the Academy to Lviv and Poznan, and attended the Vilnius Academy in Lithuania. He was a man of Polish, Latin, and Catholic culture, yet Peter appointed him "keeper and administrator" of the patriarchal see when he chose not to accept a successor to Adrian, the last patriarch, who died in 1700. That a former pupil of the Jesuits could hope to become patriarch of the Russian Church showed how radically the religious and intellectual climate had changed, and how attractive career prospects had become for ambitious and capable Ukrainian clerics.[93]

Yavorsky remained in this post of *locum tenens* of the Church until 1721, and had to accept, with the creation of the Senate in 1711, that the consecration of bishops would require the approval of the new institution, which assumed jurisdiction over the domestic affairs of Muscovy. The reform of 1721 abolished the patriarchate and created instead a Holy Synod of bishops to manage the affairs of the Church. The Synod was supervised by a chief procurator, who was appointed by the tsar from among army officers, an unheard-of humiliation for the Church. The Kiev metropolitanate, over seven hundred years old, was downgraded to the status of a diocese headed by a bishop.[94] Among the Don Cossacks, priests had come from Russia in the seventeenth century, and with them, fugitive monks and teachers of the Old Belief. The "church" had depended on the Moscow patriarch. After the reform, the Don Territory was incorporated into the diocese of Voronezh.[95]

The president of the new Synod was none other than Yavorsky. Its two vice-presidents were Teodosii Yanovsky and Feofan (Teofan) Prokopovych

(1681–1736). Prokopovych was a graduate of the Mohyla Academy, who then went to Poland, where he converted to the Uniate Church. He spent three years in Rome, returned to Kiev in 1702, and repudiated his conversion. He was ambitious and ruthless, like a typical man of the frontier, always highly receptive to changes in the political climate of the neighbouring core. Only the new Russia offered career opportunities to satisfy his intellectual talent. He was a great orator: the eloquent sermon which he delivered before Peter in 1709 to celebrate the Poltava victory attracted the tsar's attention, and his career was made. It was he who drafted the Church statute of 1721, which "reads in part rather like a political satire than the constitutional charter of a Christian Church."[96] In 1724 he was made archbishop of Novgorod, the highest post under the Synod. In return he would become one of the fiercest defenders of autocratic rule. Thus the hierarchs of the Ukrainian Church, like the *starshyna*, had accepted the process of superstratification, by which they gained a strict control of their church in exchange for accepting the supremacy of the ruling elite in the expanding Muscovite core.

Trade

Trade between economic regions binds but separates as well. It becomes a factor of integration, not only when geography creates natural zones of exchange, but also when the core power, the larger region, imposes its will on the frontier and fashions economic patterns in both core and frontier to form a single economic universe. While a common Orthodoxy and converging social developments were building a community of interests between the Muscovite core and the Left Bank, it required the forceful interference of Moscow to reorient the frontier's trade patters toward the Russian capital.

And yet, the economy of the two regions was complementary. Moscow in the forest zone was becoming an industrial centre producing manufactured goods for sale within the core and even for export. The Left Bank on the edge of the steppe was a chiefly agricultural region cultivating wheat, raising cattle, and marketing agricultural products largely for export to and across Poland, all the way to Europe. But geography had not created a favourable river network. The basin of the Black Sea channelled goods westward and southward, that of the Volga channelled them eastward. The only link between the two was the road from Moscow to Kiev via Tula, Orel, Baturyn, and Nizhyn, and the Desna River from Briansk to Kiev, which encouraged Russian merchants from the core to penetrate the frontier rather than Ukrainian merchants to go north. The reason was that the trade routes in the southern theatre, like those of the eastern theatre, had long followed a latitudinal direction. Kiev and the Left Bank formed the distant hinterland of the Polish empire, and trade routes ran from Kiev to Lutsk in Volhynia, to Lublin across the Western Bug, to Kraków on the upper

Vistula, to Breslau on the Oder, on the periphery of Europe, and on to Leipzig and Frankfurt/Main in the European coastland.[97] If a trade route went south it was that of the Dnieper, which linked Kiev with the Black Sea rather than with the Muscovite core, although the Dnieper route also led northward to Orsha and across the Dnieper-Dvina corridor to Beshenkovichi on the Dvina and to Riga. The economy and trade of the Ukrainian frontier thus depended on the evolving relationships between the three cores, Moscow, Warsaw, and Istanbul.

The expansion of large-scale Polish landholding on both sides of the Dnieper, the development of agriculture accompanied by the introduction of a "new serfdom" in the late sixteenth and early seventeenth centuries,[98] channelled the Ukrainian wheat trade toward the Western Bug and the Vistula, which carried enormous amounts of grain to Danzig (Gdansk) for transshipment, together with timber, to Europe via the Baltic to meet a growing demand for foodstuffs and building materials. This trade route was a north-south one and a latter-day version of the old Varangian route between the Baltic and the Black Seas, destroyed by the Mongol invasion. Ukrainian wheat and cattle, chiefly oxen, which also crossed Poland westward, contributed a major share to the wealth of the empire, but the trade benefited chiefly the magnates and some rich merchants. Like the China trade in the eastern theatre, it was commerce rather than trade, carried on between the source and the terminal hub, and of little impact on the market towns in between, where local fairs were the main place of exchange. Polish wealth and Polish power created strong centrifugal forces encouraging Polonization and even the creation of a religious frontier – the Uniate Church – between Orthodoxy and Catholicism. Moscow was traumatized by the Time of Trouble and, engaged in a constant struggle with the Crimean Tatars, had little to offer.

The Khmelnytsky rebellion and the subsequent period of "Ruin" (1657–86) had the same effect as the "Deluge" (1655–86) in Poland – they destroyed a flourishing but superficial economy and intensified the decline of the towns, which had always occupied a secondary role in the socio-economic order, below the magnates and the *szlachta*, the ruling class of the Polish empire. A measure of the catastrophic decline in Polish (and Ukrainian) trade was the size of Polish exports through Danzig: 1.5 million metric tons in 1645, 45,500 tons in 1715,[99] by which time the Polish economy was suffering another devastating blow in the form of the Northern War and a new Swedish occupation. The decline of the Ukrainian economy was compensated in part by an increase of trade with Moscow after 1654 and especially with Turkey and the Crimea. The Left Bank sent Istanbul meat, furs, and grain, and imported luxury textiles and carpets, cotton materials, and dried fruits; with the Tatars it exchanged grain for horses, cattle, and sheep, but the intermediaries were not Ukrainian merchants but Armenian, Greek, and Jewish traders based on the Crimean coast. The Left Bank thus restored a tentative connection with the east-west transcontinental route which still linked China and Central Asia with the Black Sea and the Mediterranean.

Peter's policies, so deeply marked by the war with Sweden (1700–21), sought to achieve a dual purpose. They sought to deprive Sweden (and Poland, allied with Sweden between 1704 and 1709) of basic supplies like hemp, necessary for its war effort, and create a new economic space conterminous with the expanding Muscovite core that would constitute the foundation of a Fortress Russia,[100] with its strategic force supported by the local population among which it was deployed, and ready to strike in any direction whenever the ruling elite chose to move against Sweden, Poland, and Turkey. Petrine policies toward the Left Bank cannot be understood without placing them in this larger context. The forced economic integration of the Hetmanate into the expanding core was designed to compensate it for the loss of markets in Poland and beyond and to broaden the core's economic base as the foundation of Russia's military power.

We need to distinguish three periods. One extends to 1710 when Riga, the major supply base of the Swedish army, was occupied by the Russians, while the eastern end of the Gulf of Finland had already been incorporated in 1703, when Petersburg was founded at the site of a very profitable Swedish customs house. Much trade was still conducted with Poland: it was estimated that in 1710 more than one million roubles' worth of goods entered Poland, but it is impossible to determine how much of this total came from the Left Bank. The enormity of this sum becomes obvious when we consider that the revenue of the Muscovite state was 3.4 million roubles in 1708.[101] Yet political consideration always trumped economic realities in Russian strategic thinking, and the economy of the Left Bank had to be redirected toward the centre.

Much has been made of the ukaze of January 1701[102] ordering Istanbul Greeks and Little Russian merchants who were about to leave for Moscow to go to Azov instead and sell their goods at the newly created fair. They were forbidden to trade with Russians in Kursk and other places. This was not an "absurd" decision,[103] but it was certainly an arbitrary one. Peter had high hopes for Azov, and it would become a provincial capital in 1708. Its hinterland included the land of the Don Cossacks and the Kharkiv corridor. The Hetmanate would only pursue the same economic policy as it had in the 1680s, and Greek merchants, well placed in Istanbul and Nizhyn, in the heart of the Hetmanate, would be the chief beneficiaries. No doubt they would spread the good news among their co-religionists in Greece and the Balkans, in which Peter had developed a strong interest. The focus on Azov – the type of "staple city" dear to the mercantilists, who strove to channel trade through a small number of towns, chiefly on the coast[104] – bypassed the Crimea and looked to the creation of an economic region including the Hetmanate and the valley of the Northern Donets and the Don, the outer periphery of the expanding core. The policy failed because Peter's war with the Turks was a disaster, and Azov was surrendered in 1711.

No less controversial was the ukase of August 1701[105] instructing traders in Little Russian towns (and that meant not so much Ukrainians as Greeks and Armenians, who had long been active in the trade across Poland with Breslau and Leipzig), who took hemp for sale in Polish towns and in Riga, to desist from exporting carded hemp (*chistaia pen'ka*) but ship it instead to Arkhangelsk via Yaroslavl and Vologda, presumably overland through Moscow. Protests in the Hetmanate, including some by Mazepa himself, did not convince the tsar to rescind the order until 1711 – after the annexation of Riga.[106] The choice of Arkhangelsk was certainly detrimental to the Left Bank economy, but the city was, until well after the founding of Petersburg, the only staple city for Russia's trade with Europe. Peter aimed at making the Muscovite core a transit zone for commerce between the south and the north, very much as he also wanted to redirect the Armenian silk trade from the Caspian-Mediterranean route to a north-south route following the Volga from Astrakhan via Kazan to Yaroslavl and on to Vologda and Arkhangelsk. Once again, the tsar's Hetmanate policy must be placed in a larger context – to deprive the Swedes of a vital necessity and to give the core an infrastructure of routes linking north and south beyond the grasp of Poland and Sweden. In that vision Arkhangelsk and Azov were the two poles of an integrated commercial space, in which the Left Bank, far from being a "colony," could play a major role, much as both sides of the Dnieper had once been a major source of wealth for the Polish empire.

The second period ran from 1711 to 1714, when the Swedish king returned from his "house arrest" in Bendery to Stralsund, intent on prosecuting the seemingly endless war with Russia. The ukaze of August 1713[107] encouraged the Hetmanate to increase its production of saltpetre (used in making gunpowder) and sell it at the market price to local traders, who would bring it to Moscow and nowhere else, let alone export it. While this measure was directed against Sweden, it also opened up a large market in Russia, where the army was growing rapidly in the frantic search for a decisive superiority over Sweden. That same year it was also discovered that foreigners working for Sweden had been sending agents to the Hetmanate (*Cherkasskie goroda*) to obtain hemp, *iuft* (soft leather), and lard (*salo*) on the free market. The ukaze of January 1714 reiterated that such goods must be taken to Riga and other suitable Russian ports on the Baltic coast, because Russia was determined to develop its trade in the region. In April the list was extended to include potash, pitch and tar, bristles, and other goods.[108] The ukaze did not say what route the goods would have to follow but insisted that they must be shipped only via Russian landings (*pristani*). In that case, the Dnieper-Dvina route would have to be abandoned in favour of the Desna via Briansk, then overland to Smolensk and the Kasplia, which flows into the Dvina at Vitebsk. But goods would still have to be carried across Polish-held territory in Belorussia. Such vague wording did not endear the new policies to the traders, and the decision to hold the hetman responsible for their behaviour did not help either.[109] One thing was clear, however: the determination to reorient the trade routes within the expanding core in the name of higher political and strategic requirements, even in disregard of geographic constraints and economic realities. The two ukazes dealt a severe blow to the Hetmanate's economy.

The third period, from 1715 to 1725, witnessed no changes in policy. In April 1719 the sale and export of all kinds of foreign brocades was allowed in Riga and Livland, but their importation into Russia and Little Russia was forbidden.[110] The measure was designed to encourage the development of the native textile industry in the core, especially in Moscow. In June 1724, the government announced that the recently created cloth factories (for the production of chiefly army uniforms) needed a large supply of sheep's wool. Since the Hetmanate was blessed with favourable conditions, it should focus on raising sheep. Not only saltpetre but also wool would be assured of an expanding market. But the local wool was found to be of poor quality and was sold for a song. Peter had told Skoropadsky shortly before his death in 1722 of the need to import Silesian (Breslau) methods for woolmaking, but nothing had been done. Meanwhile, Russian landowners and the Ukrainian regiments in the Kharkiv corridor were making a large profit from using these methods, and the market price of their wool had doubled from a miserable 1.10 to 2.20 roubles a *pud* (36 kilograms); there was no reason why the Hetmanate could not do the same. The order was repeated in November 1727,[111] but seems to have encountered resistance. At any rate, the Kharkiv-Voronezh region would later become a major centre of production of raw wool for the army and other needs.

Three years earlier the government had apportioned the Baltic export trade among three ports, Riga, Narva, and Petersburg, the new capital, which had by then replaced Arkhangelsk as the great staple city of Russian trade, and gave each a hinterland from which goods had to be shipped to the coastal hub. Goods from the Pskov region would go to Narva. The entire basin of the Volkhov River and Lake Ilmen, and the upper Volga, constituted the southern part of the Petersburg hinterland. An important landing on the Gzhat marked the beginning of navigation to Tver and then to Novgorod and Petersburg via the Vyshnii Volochek canal, built between 1719 and 1723. As to Riga, it would remain the hub for goods "which have always been taken there," including those coming from the Hetmanate.[112] If the Dnieper to Orsha remained off limits, there is indeed some justification for claiming that this represented a "radical altering of trade routes" which did "incalculable damage" to Ukrainian trade. But one must also consider that if "Ukraine now [1725] is but a shadow of what it once was,"[113] this was more the result of the terrible devastation caused by troops criss-crossing the country, seizing carts, horses, and provisions, and draining the money supply from towns and villages than from an alteration of Ukrainian trade patterns.

The impact of Petrine legislation on the Left Bank economy and trade remains controversial. What is not is that it was inspired by political considerations which served strategic purposes. The Hetmanate had to be integrated into a single economic space, even if barriers would remain until 1755 in the form of a tariff within the expanding core, which favoured Russians coming from Moscow and Tula to sell their manufactured goods. The redirection of trade routes between the Hetmanate and Riga did indeed create difficulties for Ukrainian export, but it served a strategic and mercantilist policy of concentrating production and circulation within a single economic space tightly controlled by the central government. Briansk and Smolensk were not *terra incognita*, and the Desna could easily accommodate two-way traffic. But it is quite possible that economic realities reasserted themselves in the end, and that the Dnieper-Dvina route became the preferred route once again after Peter's death. The Orsha-Beshenkovichi segment was commercially and strategically so important that it would figure in a plan to annex eastern Belorussia less than forty years later along a line following the Ulla and Drut' Rivers.

There is some validity in claiming that Petrine policies played a major role in extending the Russian social and economic system into the Hetmanate, but one does not see how they ought to have promoted the creation of manufactures in an overwhelmingly agricultural country while their creation was being promoted in the forest zone between Petersburg and the Urals. Indeed, Petrine policies took advantage of the natural division between the forest and the woodland zones. Ukrainian exports before Peter had consisted chiefly of agricultural products, not manufactures. The decline of the towns in the Hetmanate, as well as in the larger Polish empire – the result of the Deluge and the Ruin – certainly did not encourage the creation of industrial centres. The Hetmanate did not need Petrine policies to fall victim to "peasantization"[114] – the *starshyna* that had been introducing serfdom on the Left Bank in alliance with Russian landlords was doing its utmost to create an agrarian order in the entire region between Tula and the Dnieper. If the Hetmanate became a "colony," so did the Orel and Kursk upland. It was serfdom which became the most effective agent of integrating a social order common to the entire woodland area, whether Russian or Ukrainian.

Economic interdependence encouraged integration, and Petrine policies, brutal as they were in their attempts to transform a society in the midst of a war that lasted nearly a generation, redirected the economy of the Hetmanate inward into the expanding core, where it became an economic region, matching the Moscow-Vladimir, Petersburg, and Ural industrial regions. There was a looming danger, however. Russia's industrial development in general was geared not so much to the development of the country's productive forces, to create more wealth, and to urbanize the country, as to support the war effort and the military establishment. For the ruling elite, as for mercantilists in general, the economy was a zero-sum game, in which to favour one sector required the neglect of others. Russian industrialization, remarkable in itself, showed little interest in producing quality consumer goods that could possibly rival those of Europe, which had once come into the country when Kiev was trading with Kraków, Breslau, and Leipzig. Integration here meant relative impoverishment, because the Russian market could not compensate for that of Europe, and only the *starshyna* could still hope to obtain on occasion the luxury goods to which their ancestors had become accustomed. The economic integration of the Hetmanate meant its subordination to the imperatives of the war machine of a warrior state, now based not only in Moscow but also in Petersburg, its window on Europe.

It was there, and no longer in the Hetmanate, that contact with a higher civilization would develop, reducing the Hetmanate to the economic backwater it would remain until the last quarter of the nineteenth century.

Chapter Five

Toward Full Integration, 1725–1796

Civil and Military Administration

1725–1762

The decade following Peter's death witnessed a conservative backlash against his impulsive reforms, and the uncertain state of domestic politics in Moscow and Petersburg favoured a relaxation of the tensions that had marked the great emperor's reign. There was at first no change in the territorial division of the southern theatre, but the government decided to restore the Hetmanate in 1727, and its choice for hetman fell on Danylo Apostol (1654–1734), who had been close to Mazepa, had fled with him, but had then returned to Little Russia with the promise of a pardon. In fact, the decision may have originated with Menshikov, the destroyer of Baturyn, and one of Little Russia's richest landlords, who had expected to become hetman himself.[1] His banishment in 1727 did not change what must have already become a consensus among the ruling elite. Trubetskoy, the governor general of Kiev, was recalled, and the Little Russian college was closed. But Senator Fedor Naumov was sent to Hlukhiv to watch over Apostol's election and behaviour; he remained until 1728 as the imperial representative attached to the hetman. He then went on to Bashkiria to supervise the construction of the Trans-Kama Line. He was followed by Semën Shakhovskoy (1728–30) and Semën Naryshkin (1732–4), who remained until the hetman's death. They headed the so-called Ministerial Chancery.[2] Ukrainian affairs were transferred back to the College of Foreign Affairs, giving the hetman a status similar to that of a Kalmyk or Kazakh khan. Apostol was already an old man and became a faithful servant of the empire – his son was kept hostage in Petersburg – who enriched his relatives, persecuted his opponents, and slowly sank into decrepitude, which is why the imperial government expressed its satisfaction with his rule and disappointment at the time of his death.[3]

The Articles of August 1728[4] placed more restrictions on the hetman's authority. He could no longer appoint colonels and new members of the *starshyna* without the agreement of the existing *starshyna*, who had to submit candidates for the ruler's approval. And the hetman could not remove them from office. He was of course forbidden to correspond with foreign rulers and had to report to the College of Foreign Affairs whenever couriers arrived from Poland or the Crimea. At the end of Apostol's reign, the Russians purged the *starshyna* by reducing their number and demanding that those who had not taken the oath of fidelity to the empress be dismissed.[5]

However, the restoration of the Hetmanate inevitably resulted in a reorganization of the Left Bank administration. A Belgorod province was created in 1727 consisting of three *provintsii* of the old Kiev province which had not been part of the Hetmanate (Belgorod, Sevsk, and Orel), but Voronezh province remained divided into the same five *provintsii*.[6] Without the Hetmanate, Kiev province became a mere rump, the city and its environs on the right bank of the Dnieper. The Hetmanate was divided into twelve territorial regiments, including one for Kiev. It seems that not even a governor was appointed after Trubetskoy's recall. The four territorial regiments of the Kharkiv corridor – Okhtyrka, Kharkiv, Sumy, and Izium – were subordinated to the Belgorod governor,[7] as they had been to the Belgorod *voevoda* until 1708 and to the Kiev governor thereafter. In the Don Territory, where *Otaman* Andrei Lopatin was still in office, the government's policy was to increase the number of Cossacks by encouraging, as in 1731, the settlement of outside families in its eastern part as far as the Volga, which was still largely empty.[8] They would have to register as Cossacks, both in order to increase the number of men available for service and to facilitate the patrolling of the Tsaritsyn Line and the detachment of Cossack parties to the northern Caucasus.

But the most important authority in the southern theatre was the commanding general of the Ukrainian Corps. General Golitsyn became president of the College of War with a promotion to field marshal in 1728, but retained his regional command until 1731. He was followed by General Johann von Weissbach (who came from Bohemia and had entered Russian service in 1707). He had previously commanded troops in the region between 1711 and 1723. He was also appointed governor general of Kiev in 1731. He died in 1735 on his way to the Crimean front.[9] Weissbach's jurisdiction extended to all regular and irregular troops in the southern theatre. The lines of authority were never clearly spelled out, but governor, hetman, and *otaman* were ultimately subordinated to him in matters of military deployment and security.

Three important events took place during Weissbach's tenure. At the time of the Polish succession crisis of 1733, Russian troops were sent into Poland to support the Russian candidate, August III, against the French candidate to the Polish throne, Stanisław Leszczyński, who had once been installed as King of

Poland by Charles XII in 1704 and had corresponded with Mazepa. They were joined by Cossacks as auxiliary troops, who also helped the Polish landowners put down the so-called *haidamak* uprising in Right Bank Ukraine.[10] The intervention in Poland and the support given to Leszczyński by the Crimean khan created an urgent need for more irregular troops to fight both Polish irregulars and Crimean Tatars. Weissbach's solution was to recommend the reintegration of the Zaporozhian Cossacks.

They had not been well treated by the khan since their arrival at Oleshky in 1709, and their deep attachment to Orthodoxy caused them to resent their subordination to a Muslim ruler and long for a return to their old territory. Weissbach obtained the empress's approval, and when the khan ordered them into Poland, they moved instead up the Dnieper into Russian-controlled territory, and set up a new camp on the Podpolnaia River, a small right-bank tributary of the Dnieper, a short distance downriver from the Velykyi Luh.[11] In 1735, their land was divided into five districts (*palanki*). It bordered on the Ottoman empire and the Crimean khanate on both banks of the Dnieper, to the east along the Konka River (Konskie Vody) to near the estuary of the Mius, and across the Dnieper from the Kamenka River (another small tributary of the Dnieper) to the Southern Buh.

However, the return of the Zaporozhians – who numbered hardly more than seven thousand men at the time[12] – did not stabilize the frontier situation. Conflicts with the Tatars became endemic, and there were endless land disputes and bloody fights with Little Russians and Poles who had settled on lands the Zaporozhians had abandoned in 1709. Moreover, the long history of Muscovy's relations with the Zaporozhians had left a legacy of mutual distrust, and Weissbach's successors, Generals Ivan Leontev (1738–41) and Mikhail Leontev (1741–52),[13] must have rued having to deal with an insoluble problem in an already all too turbulent frontier. In 1735, the Russians built a fort in the camp (Nova Sich/Novaia Sich) with a commandant subordinated to the governor general, and restored the old fort of Novo-Bogoroditsk, built by Vasilii Golitsyn in 1688 at the confluence of the Samara and the Dnieper but later abandoned, now called Ust-Samarsk. They also built a succession of redoubts along the Dnieper, effectively splitting Zaporozhia into two parts, east and west of the river.[14]

The third event was the construction of the so-called Ukrainian Line. It began at the confluence of the Orel and the Dnieper, followed the Orel to the confluence of the Berestova, then crossed over to the Bereka, a right-bank tributary of the Donets, which led to the Don.[15] It had been a century-old ambition to link the Dnieper with the Don, but the alignment of the Dnieper had made it impossible to reach the river except via the Vorskla. The Ukrainian Line represented a projection of Russian power an additional 150 kilometres to the south, to where the Dnieper and the Don flowed closest to each other. It finally closed the trails used by the Tatars on their way to Little Russia and the Central Upland. A result was a rapid increase in the population of the Sloboda Ukraine with the resettlement of *odnodvortsy* from the Belgorod region. By 1740 the line consisted of 18 forts linked by 140 redoubts, and the 1744 census registered a population of nearly twenty-five thousand men and women.[16]

The construction of the line also brought about the closer integration of the entire Left Bank Ukraine into the expanding Muscovite core. After Apostol's death in 1734, the Hetmanate was abolished, and Little Russia was placed under a board answerable to a Little Russian chancery in the Imperial Senate – a return to the 1722 situation. The board consisted of two Russian officers and three Ukrainian members chosen by the *starshyna*, under the authority of Lt.-Gen. Alexei Shakhovskoy (1734–6), who had six successors until 1745, including Lt.-Gen. Alexander Rumiantsev, father of the future governor general. To emphasize their equality, the Russian and Ukrainian members sat opposite each other across the same table. The territory would continue to be ruled in accordance with its customs and the Articles of Bohdan Khmelnytsky and Apostol. It is unclear whether a resident minister continued to be appointed in Hlukhiv.[17] Also in 1734, the administration of Sloboda Ukraine was removed from the jurisdiction of the Belgorod governor and placed under Shakhovskoy,[18] who thus gained what no hetman had ever been able to obtain from Moscow – the unification of Little Russia and the Kharkiv corridor. A commission consisting of two Russian officers was put in charge of judicial and military matters, the former to be appealed to the Senate, the latter to the College of War, to which the regiments had been subordinated since 1726.

To provide a military force in a theatre of low-intensity threats, when the Russian army was still deployed in the central provinces or engaged in large-scale operations in Poland, Sweden, or against Turkey (as in the Russo-Turkish war of 1735–9), the land militia was considerably expanded. In 1729, the existing six regiments grew to ten, and in 1731 to twenty including sixteen of cavalry. The militia was called "Ukrainian" to distinguish it from the similar force being built beyond the Kama River in the eastern theatre. In 1736 all twenty regiments became mounted, and the force was called the Ukrainian Landmilitia Corps, under the command of Lt.-Gen. Prince Vasilii Urusov, stationed in Kiev, who received his orders from Shakhovskoy and to whom the entire land militia was subordinated, all the way to Bashkiria. Each regiment had a strength of 910, including 880 privates. When combined with the Russian garrisons and the Cossacks, these irregulars – not a very impressive force despite the numbers – were deployed in the following manner. The militia was distributed among the forts of the Ukrainian Line. From its western end in Little Russia there were six regiments of garrisoned troops, from its eastern end between Voronezh and Fort St Anna on the lower Don, another six; and the Don, Sloboda, and Little Russian Cossacks were distributed in their respective territories.[19]

The Empress Elizabeth (1741–61), the grand patron of the Naryshkin-Trubetskoy network which now had a long history of involvement in the affairs of the southern theatre – the two Leontevs, for example, belonged to it – was more sympathetic to Ukrainian "autonomy" than the Saltykov network and its German allies, who had been so prominent during Anna Ivanovna's reign. However, she was in no hurry to restore the Hetmanate, partly because she knew that the expansion of the Muscovite core was inimical to the retention of local "rights and privileges," partly because her candidate for the post of hetman was still very young and not eager to leave the splendours of Petersburg for the rural comforts of Hlukhiv. He was Kiril Razumovsky (Kyrylo Rozumovsky), born in 1728, brother of the empress's morganatic husband Alexei, of the most obscure Ukrainian origin. It was not until 1750 that Razumovsky was finally appointed hetman of Little Russian Cossacks both sides of the Dnieper. In October, the Zaporozhian Sich (Sech) and its *koshevyi* (supreme commander) were subordinated to him, as had been the case since 1708, but his relations with the Kiev governor general remained undefined once again. The latter was relegated to the rank of "acting governor general," and the regional command was handed over to a separate general, while Razumovsky was promoted to field marshal, the highest post in the military establishment. He in turn was subordinated to the College of Foreign Affairs, but his poor personal relationship with Chancellor (Foreign Minister) Alexei Bestuzhev-Riumin convinced him to ask in 1756 to be placed under the Senate instead.[20]

Razumovsky openly interfered in the affairs of the Sich, and sent Little Russian Cossacks into its territory, where they did not always behave well, as the antagonism between the Little Russian and Zaporozhian Cossacks grew with the passage of time. He confirmed the election of the *koshevyi*, but was not empowered to replace him without Petersburg's approval. He greatly resented having to deal with a lower-ranking governor general in Kiev, who also wanted to have his say in Zaporozhian affairs, handled relations with Poland and the Crimea, kept collecting valuable intelligence from secret informants at the Nikitin crossing in the middle of the Sich, where merchants congregated to exchange goods, and set up "border commissions" with Poles and Tatars to settle land disputes and conflicts over salt lakes in the estuary of the Dnieper, which the Zaporozhians considered their own. Razumovsky behaved like other grandees of his day, held court in Hlukhiv, which he endeavoured to model after the imperial court, and gave away land and estates, as other hetmans had done before him – until Petersburg grew annoyed in 1754 and stripped him in March of his authority to promote to colonel and grant villages in hereditary tenure without the empress's approval. To add insult to injury, a resident minister was sent once again, and Lt.-Gen. Ivan Glebov was appointed in 1760 with the full title of governor general.[21] Sloboda Ukraine had been returned in 1743 to the jurisdiction of the Belgorod governor.[22]

It is evident that the imperial government did not wish to create a unified command over the Left Bank in the person of the hetman, and that the government gradually cut him down to size. When Elizabeth died in 1761, his days were numbered. His role must remain controversial. As a member of the ruling elite, he could not but be a proponent of further integration into the expanding core. But he also had a genuine feeling for his homeland and encouraged the development of Ukrainian values and culture. On the other hand, as an ex officio member of the *starshyna* he was caught in the inexorable consolidation of the upper stratum of landowners seeking to strengthen the status quo by binding the rank-and-file Cossacks and peasants to the land.[23]

The building of fortified lines and, to some extent, the annexation of the Hetmanate had been part of a defensive policy against Tatar raids, which did so much damage over the centuries by their endemic threat to human settlement. But a defensive policy may also have an offensive intent: to create a logistical infrastructure to sustain the steady advance into frontier territory. Peter's forward policy was premature. Making war on the opposite Turkish core by a flanking attack – first against Azov, later on the Prut – overestimated Russia's capabilities and underestimated the strength of the Turks' own defensive policy along a perimeter running from Khotyn to Azov via Bendery, Ochakov, and the Crimean khanate. By the 1730s, however, it was felt that the expanding Muscovite core had built a sufficient logistical infrastructure between the Belgorod and Ukrainian Lines and could afford to engage, no longer in a flanking, but in a frontal attack on the Crimean khanate. The war was a tactical success in that the Russians occupied the Crimea, but a strategic disaster because they suffered enormous casualties, caused largely by the same logistical problems in a waterless steppe between the Ukrainian Line and the peninsula. The only gain was the agreement to raze Azov, whose district became a treeless, snake-infested wasteland devastated by malaria and other "fevers."[24] From then on, Russian strategic thinking would return to the Petrine policy of a flanking advance via the Azov Sea in the east and the Ottoman principalities of Moldavia and Wallachia in the west.

In the Don Territory, the government kept pursuing a systematic policy of integrating the Cossacks into the infrastructure of the expanding core. Beginning in 1738, when Danilo Efremov (1738–53) was appointed by the College of War, all *otamans* were given the title of "acting *otaman*" (*nakaznyi otaman*) to emphasize that their tenure depended on retaining the government's favour. At the same time, the importance of the *starshyna* kept growing, and that of the circle (*kolo*, *krug*) gradually disappeared. Danilo's tenure ended with his promotion to major general (grade 4) and, later, to privy councillor (grade 3 in the Table of Ranks). His son Stepan succeeded him for nearly twenty years (1753–72), and it was during his tenure, in 1754, that the government assumed the exclusive right to appoint members of the *starshyna*.[25] This complete integration of the Cossack elite into the officer corps of the irregular troops was accompanied by the progress of serfdom, when that same elite transformed itself into an upper stratum of landowners in no way different from their brethren in the core.

In the western wing of the southern theatre, the advance into the Russo-Turkish frontier entered a new phase. Toward the end of 1749, the Russian ambassador to Vienna was told to express Petersburg's concern over the forced conversion of Serbs to Catholicism. They were invited to emigrate to Russia. Serbs and Hungarians, as well as Bulgarians and Wallachians (Rumanians), first arrived in 1752, and were settled along the Russo-Turkish border, which followed the Syniukha and Vys Rivers. They formed a military settlement called New Serbia, its capital in a new town called Novomyrhorod. In 1753, another party of Serbs was settled along the Donets in a new settlement called Slaviano-Serbia, a prolongation of Sloboda Ukraine to the Luhanchyk River, between the Donets River and the Don Territory. Both settlements were divided into territorial regiments, named after the colour of their uniforms. In 1754, Fort St Elizabeth (Elizavetgrad) was created on the headwaters of the Inhul River, a tributary of the Southern Buh, and became the headquarters of the new so-called Slobodskii territorial regiment, formed three years later.[26] Anxiety in Constantinople delayed the development of the fort on the eve of the Seven Years' War with Prussia (1756–63), but the government had taken a decisive step in the settlement of the steppe south of the Turko-Polish border and the Ukrainian Line. The expanding core was staking a claim to the steppe all the way to the Black Sea, a claim fulfilled twenty years later at the conclusion of the Russo-Turkish war of 1768–74.

1763–1782

The reign of Catherine II (1762–96) brought about a massive transformation of the geopolitical situation in the southern theatre. It began with another succession crisis in Warsaw and the intervention of Russian troops to bring about the election of Stanisław Poniatowski in 1764. The pursuit of "confederates," who opposed the election, resulted in a party of Cossacks crossing the border at Balta and provoking the Turks to declare war on Russia in October 1768.[27] But, independently of the events in Poland, the expansion of the Muscovite core, blocked in the western theatre by the intervention of Peter III, Catherine's husband, in 1762, was recovering the momentum it had gained in the first half of the century. Nothing was more indicative of the intentions of the ruling elite than the 1763 deployment of the Russian army at the end of the Seven Years' War.

Troops deployed on the Left Bank belonged to the so-called Ukrainian Division under General Petr Rumiantsev. Of its twenty-one regiments, six were stationed in the Chernihiv region, nine in the Poltava territory, and another six in the Kharkiv corridor, all facing the Dnieper between the Belorussian border and the Northern Donets. These troops had a dual mission. Those stationed in Chernihiv were on, or had easy access to, the road leading to Kiev and, beyond Kiev, into the Right Bank to the Western Bug and southern Poland. Those in Poltava and the Kharkiv corridor faced the Dnieper between the Sula and the Vorskla and, across the Dnieper, Elizavetgrad and the headwaters of the Syniukha-Southern Buh and the Inhul Rivers, which led to the Black Sea. Both deployments could easily be combined for operations either in the Right Bank or into the steppe toward the Crimea. Never before had so many regular troops been stationed on the Left Bank in peacetime. Russian strategic thinking was shifting toward the creation of operational theatres, of which the Black Sea basin would remain the most important for the duration of Catherine's reign. The arrival of troops was not entirely unwelcome, as long as they were billeted in towns, where they would stimulate the marketing of grain, spirits, and textiles, but there was concern over their being stationed in villages, where they would only abuse the villagers and bring disease.[28]

The deployment also brought about the elimination of the land militia, which had become obsolete. Peter III had already abolished the term, and the force was simply called the Ukrainian Corps. In June 1764 it was reduced by half, reorganized into an infantry force of ten regiments (with one regiment of cavalry), and gathered into the towns. They were sent to the front during the Turkish war, where they performed well, and, on Rumiantsev's recommendation, the entire force was merged into the regular army in 1770.[29] The land militia had ceased to exist. The same fate befell the Cossacks of the Kharkiv corridor. The deployment of a substantial number of regular troops cancelled the threat from Tatar raids, already blocked by the construction of the lines and the creation of Slavic settlements, and transformed the corridor into an internal frontier of the expanding core, which now needed to be fully integrated.

In the spring of 1765 the government decided to transform the territory of the Sloboda regiments into a new province called Sloboda Ukraine, divided into four *provintsii* and headed by an acting governor, Guard Major Evdokim Shcherbinin. He was instructed to follow the recently promulgated instruction of April 1764 for the guidance of all other governors in the core. The territory would be governed in accordance with the general laws of the country, unless they violated some remaining privileges. The *voevody* and the procurator would be Russian officials.[30] The Cossack regiments were reorganized into four hussar regiments incorporated into the twenty-one regiments of the Ukrainian Division. Cossack helpers who had not been part of the select (*vybornye*) Cossacks were downgraded to the status of state peasants (*voiskovye kazennye obyvateli*) or serfs (*vladelcheskie poddannye*). This amounted to the nearly complete integration of the corridor into the expanding core.

A complex restructuring of the Slavic military settlements had been taking place at the same time. In the spring of 1764, New Serbia (or the "New Serbian Corps"), consisting of the Black and Yellow hussar regiments, and the territory of the Slobodskyi regiment (renamed and enlarged in 1769 to become the Moldavian hussar regiment) were combined to form a province of New Russia, its capital in Kremenchuk. The following year, Slavianoserbia was added to it, together with the land on both sides of the Ukrainian Line, which was abandoned. The province was divided into two *provintsii*, Elizavetgrad, centred in the fort after which it was named, and Ekaterininsk, east of the Dnieper, centred in Fort Belev (Konstantinograd). The entire province from the Syniukha to the Luhanchyk and Donets was placed under the command of Lt.-Gen. Alexei Melgunov, followed by Lt.-Gen. Yakov von Brant (1766–7), and finally, during the Turkish war, by General Fedor Voeikov, the governor general of Kiev (1767–75), all three with the title of commanding general (*glavnyi komandir*). The *provintsii* were administered by colonels. The commanding generals came from the headquarters staff of the Ukrainian Division.[31]

There had been dissatisfaction with the Ukrainian Line. It was considered too long (385 kilometres), across a steppe landscape, too open and flat to support fortified outposts, short of water and timber; it was becoming obsolete "as our borders expand with political circumstances."[32] It was proposed to build yet another line from the confluence of the Samara and the Dnieper to the Luhanchyk – about 45 kilometres southward – incorporating two Zaporozhian *palanki* and creating considerable annoyance among the Zaporozian Cossacks, whose *otaman*, Petro Kalnyshevsky (1765–75), was incautious enough to state in 1766 on a visit to Petersburg that the situation had become hopeless and that the time might have come to seek Turkish overlordship.[33]

To fill the void created by the abandonment of the Ukrainian Line, *pikineer* (lancer) regiments were created of 3,000 horsemen or 1,000 footsoldiers in twenty companies of military settlers, each given thirty *desiatins* of land. Three such regiments were settled between the Dnieper and the Donets (Dniprovskyi, Luhanskyi, and Donetskyi), with two regiments of settled hussars of 2,208 men each (Samarskyi and Bakhmutskyi). West of the Dnieper, in Elizavetgrad *provintsiia*, there were three regiments of hussars and one of *pikineers* (also called *uhlans*).[34] New Russia remained a huge military settlement facing the open steppe, extending across the Zaporozhian lands all the way to the Crimea, and backed by the full force of the Ukrainian Division. It represented a fringe of settlement in the southern theatre, unstable like all such fringes, with its own expansive dynamism, and a challenge to the Tatars and the Turks behind them. The stage was set for a conflict of major proportions.

The Zaporozhians were caught in the middle. No one knew their exact number on the eve of the war. The *voisko* had changed a great deal since its early days when it was a community of single warriors who did not till the land, but only hunted and fished. Most now lived in villages with peasants on land that was the common property of the *voisko*. It was estimated that the total population reached 59,637 in thirty-eight *kureni*, including peasants, but that only 12,247 were active warriors. They were probably even less, while the total population may have reached 100,000, because the Sich had always been a refuge for runaways of all kinds. The Zaporozhians were not above supporting insurgencies in Right Bank Ukraine and forming ephemeral alliances with the Crimean khan. Like the Tatars, they were a source of constant instability. During the Russo-Turkish war of 1735–9, General Christoph von Manstein had called them a "republic of thieves and vagabonds," and William Coxe wrote fifty years later that they had been "barbarous and unruly banditti," whose continued presence had been a source of "perpetual depredations" for the trade of the region.[35] The creation of the fringe of military settlement was a mortal threat to them, and when rumours reached Petersburg that they had been in touch with the Tatars and had refused to help the Elizavetgrad garrison when the Tatars launched their last destructive attack in 1769, their fate was sealed.

The creation of the province of New Russia and the integration of the Kharkiv corridor were part of a theatre strategy in which there no longer was any room for a Hetmanate and its Little Russian Cossacks. The Hetmanate and the Zaporozhian lands had once constituted a frontier between the expanding core and the Crimean khanate, and all were part of an even larger Russo-Turkish frontier. The raison d'être of the Cossacks had been to protect the Polish and Russian cores against Tatar raids, but this role was now performed by the military settlements and the Ukrainian Division. Moreover, Cossack society in the Hetmanate and Zaporizhia had developed along different lines. The Hetmanate had become an agricultural land of *starshyna*/landowners and Cossacks/peasants sharply differentiated by their access to land. Serfdom in all but name had made considerable progress, and the social structure of the Hetmanate was increasingly resembling that of the Russian agricultural provinces.

The "strongly worded petition" of a council consisting of *starshyna* and Razumovsky held in Hlukhiv in September 1763 to set up a parliament of nobles modelled after the Polish Sejm – which by then had become a symbol of anarchy – not to mention a proposal to make the hetmanate hereditary in Razumovsky's family,[36] was inopportune at best and a challenge to the theatre strategy the Russians were embarking upon at the time. Razumovsky was forced to resign in November 1764, and Rumiantsev was immediately appointed governor general of Little Russia in Hlukhiv, where he would remain until 1775, when he moved to Kiev and the post of Kiev governor general was abolished. Rumiantsev presided over a new Little Russian College consisting in the 1760s of seven members, including three other Russians and four Ukrainians, who no longer sat facing each other but in order of seniority, as if to demonstrate that the Ukrainian members had been integrated into a provincial administration subordinated to the theatre commander. The merger of civil and military responsibilities in the hands of a full general (who would soon become a field marshal) clearly illustrated the process of superstratification at work in Hetmanate society. But the creation of the college was only a temporary development to ease the transition to the full administrative integration which would take place in the 1780s.

The war of 1768–74 was the decisive event in the history of the southern theatre. Rumiantsev assumed the command of the army advancing across Moldavia and Wallachia toward the Danube and destroyed Ottoman hegemony in the Black Sea, after imposing a puppet khan in the Crimea in September 1771. The Treaty of Kuchuk Kainardji of July 1774 gave the Russians a triangle of land between the lower Southern Buh and the lower Dnieper, a tenuous access to the Black Sea, beyond the Zaporozhian lands. The Zaporozhian Cossacks were the first victims of Russian victories. They were scattered in the summer of 1775 (after some were used to fill two *pikineer* regiments), the *starshyna*, considered unreliable, was banished to various monasteries in the interior, and Koshevyi Petro Kalnyshevsky would spend over twenty-five years in the Solovetskii monastery in the far north until his death in 1803 at the age of 112.[37]

The offensive went on against the Crimea and other Tatars under the leadership of Catherine II's favourite, Grigorii Potemkin, appointed in January 1776 governor general of the New Russian province, the former lands of the Zaporozhian Cossacks, and the land of the Don Cossacks, as well as of Astrakhan province, thus linking the western with the eastern theatres across the Don-Volga watershed. The following year he was given the command of all the irregular troops in the country, including the Cossacks, and became the rival of Rumiantsev, relegated to the rear, behind Potemkin's forward position which formed the arc of a circle facing the Crimea.

Potemkin carried out a radical reorganization of the post-war territory. New Russia province was confined to the area west of the Dnieper, between the river and the Southern Buh, its capital still in Kremenchuk, together with the *sotni* of the Little Russian regiments of Poltava and Myrhorod on the Left Bank, which had been part of the old province of New Russia. Kremenchuk on the Dnieper was an important crossing from the valley of the Psël and Vorskla to the steppe on the river's right bank. The capital was moved to the new town of Ekaterynoslav in 1778. East of the Dnieper, Slavianoserbia and the entire territory between the Dnieper and the Donets, including the old Zaporozhian lands to their border along the Konka and Berda Rivers, together with the Don Territory, were combined to form a new Azov province, extending as far south as the Eia River flowing into the Azov Sea. A governor was appointed in Azov, Major General Vasilii Chertkov, who, together with his colleague in Kremenchuk, Major General Matvei Muromtsev, was subordinated to Potemkin.[38]

The new arrangement was awkward. Azov was too far away from the Dnieper, and the Don Cossacks had developed such a separate identity that they could not be combined with the Slavic settlements into a single administrative unit. Cherkassk, the capital of the Don Cossacks, was only a short trip upriver. Yet there was a reason for the creation of Azov as a provincial capital: it was meant to be the administrative headquarters for the coastal towns, poorly integrated with their hinterland, which had been captured from the Turks: Kerch and Enikale, which controlled the exit from the Azov into the Black Sea, as well as Taganrog, the forts on the Dnieper Line along the Konka and the Berda built in 1770,[39] and, most curious of all, Fort Kinburn, on the promontory enclosing the estuary of the Dnieper. The new arrangement had a clear purpose: it was to integrate the new lands, including the Don Territory, "in such a way that by the application of the same laws, they may henceforth constitute one state body [*gosudarstvennyi korpus*]."[40] There could be no clearer statement that the expansion of the Muscovite core aimed at creating a unitary state all the way to the Black Sea.

The new province was also intended to become the crucial link in the extension of the eastern wing of the Russian offensive against the Crimea. The wing would now extend to the Caucasus and, across the mountains, to western Transcaucasia, the Ottoman foothold in the region. In 1769 the Russians, in accordance with their usual strategy of flanking movements converging toward the heart of the enemy's country, had sent an expedition across the mountains to Tiflis, from which the troops advanced on Poti only to fail, not unlike Peter I in Persia in 1722–3, because of the deleterious climate and the "fevers."[41] The tip of this eastern wing would also meet the tip of the western wing of the similar flanking movement in the Caspian basin directed against Persia and the Kazakh steppe. Thus the Russian advance during Catherine's reign was directed not only against the Crimea, but also against all the Ottoman possessions in the Black Sea basin. The extension or the western wing would take place later in the reign.

The first step was the reorganization of the Don Cossack administration. Potemkin dismissed *nakaznyi otaman* Stepan Efremov, "who was not trusted by the *starshyna*," and replaced him with Alexei Ilovaisky, who had served in the Turkish war and had commanded Don and Iaik Cossacks pursuing Pugachev. He would serve for twenty-two years (1775–96) and would be the first Don Cossack leader to be promoted (in 1796) to full general. To raise his prestige, Potemkin, who was empowered to appoint him, nevertheless asked for the empress's formal approval, and a *sotnia* of Don Cossacks was sent to join the Imperial Guard.[42] But in a perverse way, the reorganization also reduced the *otaman*'s powers. Potemkin noted that the *otaman* enjoyed "unlimited power" in both civil and military affairs. He separated the two jurisdictions and created a civil chancery for administrative, judicial, and fiscal affairs, chaired by the *otaman*, but consisting of two permanent members from the *starshyna* appointed by the governor general, and another four elected for one-year terms. It would administer in accordance with the laws and regulations of the realm and "local privileges." The new *nakaznyiotaman* was given the rank of major general – the usual rank of a provincial governor – and Catherine later promoted him to lieutenant general. In military affairs the *otaman* would also be subordinated directly to the governor general, with a small "field [*pokhodnaia*] chancery" consisting of only one clerk. Cossack officers who commanded smaller Don regiments (usually five hundred men) were given higher ranks (from major to colonel) to end their humiliating subordination to army officers, but Potemkin was not yet ready to propose a table of equivalent ranks between army and Cossack officers. This would not happen for another generation.

The second step was the creation of another fortified line linking the Don with the Terek, the western with the eastern theatre. In April 1777, Potemkin submitted a proposal to connect Azov with Mozdok. There had been great turbulence in the region in the 1770s, caused by the Kuban Tatars resisting Cossack inroads and incited by the Crimean Tatars. Together with Azov province the line would cut overland communications between the Crimea and the Kuban and facilitate Russian penetration of the Caucasus in order to find and exploit "the ores and metals of Ossetia."[43] The line would run northwards from Mozdok to the headwaters of the Egorlyk (near modern Stavropol), follow it to its confluence with the Manych, and follow the latter to its own confluence with the Don near Cherkassk. Potemkin estimated that the line would reduce the distance between Moscow and Mozdok by 500 kilometres to 1,400. Cossack settlements would also interdict access to the salt lakes of the Manych valley to the highlanders, who had no salt in the mountains.

The deployment of 1781[44] showed a vast increase in the size of the regular army and the military settlements. Rumiantsev in Kiev still commanded the Tenth (Ukrainian) Division of nineteen regiments (twelve of infantry and seven of cavalry, including six of hussars now incorporated into the regular army). There were also two regiments of Little Russian Cossacks and a larger Chuhuiv (Chuguev) Cossack regiment of 1,341 men, including 1,200 privates. The Eleventh Division, commanded by Potemkin, was deployed in New Russia, Azov, and Astrakhan provinces. In New Russia there were eight regiments of infantry (with two *Jäger* battalions), two of dragoons, six of hussars, and three of *pikineers* in their settlements; in Azov province, three regiments of infantry, one of dragoons, three of hussars, and three of *pikineers* in their settlements. Don Cossack regiments were incorporated into the division and stationed in both provinces. Thus in the southern theatre there were now deployed twenty-three regiments of infantry and twenty-five of cavalry (not counting the Cossacks but including fifteen regiments of military settlers of 10,404 men, who were required to serve for fifteen years). In addition, Don Cossack regiments were building the Mozdok-Cherkassk Line, but the resettlement of hundreds of families caused great distress and even open revolt.[45] Unlike the situation in the early 1760s, the military settlers were no longer an advance formation ahead of the army's deployment: they were combined with it and strengthened each other, the army guaranteeing the security of the settlements, the settlers giving the army staying power in a territory that remained largely uninhabited.

1783–1796

The restoration of peace in 1774 cleared the way for the great administrative-territorial reform of the entire expanding Russian core, which began in the interior provinces and then spread to the outlying regions. It took effect in Orel province in January 1779, in Kursk and Voronezh, as well as in the Sloboda Ukraine, in December 1780.[46] Little Russia was divided into three provinces, Novhorod-Siverskyi, Chernihiv, and Kiev, where the new agencies opened for business between January and April 1782.[47] There were now in Left Bank Ukraine four provinces divided into forty-eight *uezds*. The new territorial division cut across the old regimental boundaries, but followed the natural declivity of the land, sloping down in a succession of terraces toward the Dnieper. To the south, New Russia province became Ekaterynoslav province in March 1783, but Azov province was abolished, and the Don Territory regained its autonomy once again. Taganrog, Azov, and Rostov, however, although separated from the province, were placed under the jurisdiction of the Ekaterynoslav governor.[48] Ekaterynoslav province was divided into fifteen *uezds*, but the Don Territory retained its traditional divisions until 1802.

In the meantime, the expansion of the Russian core had retained its momentum. The Treaty of Kuchuk Kainardji had left the Crimean question unsettled, even though it had always been the crucial factor in Russo-Turkish relations. The establishment of a protectorate over the khanate – which consisted of both the peninsula and the mainland from the Dnieper to the Kuban around the Azov Sea – could only postpone the inevitable. Only its full incorporation could give the core an extensive coastline on the Black Sea and naval bases for what had been until then a largely landlocked southern theatre. This incorporation took place in April 1783, and the khanate became the Crimean *oblast*, because its insufficient population did not justify giving it the status of a province, even though a governor was appointed as in any other province.[49] The mainland part was now confined to the land between the Dnieper and the Konka-Berda Rivers, along which the Dnieper Line, now obsolete, had been built in 1770. The *oblast* was divided into seven *uezds*, including one for the Taman peninsula ("island"). Its incorporation was followed by a bloody – although unintended – encounter between the Russian authorities and the Nogais nomadizing in the Kuban steppe between the Eia and Kuban Rivers, following which the nomads deserted the land, which would remain unsettled until the arrival of the Cossacks in 1794.[50]

As a result, the old southern theatre was divided into six provinces and seventy *uezds*, with the Don Territory and the Kuban steppe standing apart. The four governors in Kiev, Novhorod-Siverskyi, Chernihiv, and Kharkiv were subordinated to Marshal Rumiantsev, as governor general of Little Russia and commanding general of the Ukrainian Division. The Little Russian College was abolished. The other two governors, in Ekaterynoslav and Simferopol, and the *otaman* of the Don Cossacks were subordinated to Marshal Grigorii Potemkin as governor general in Ekaterynoslav and commanding general of the New Russian Division. He combined these two posts with that of president of the College of War, an unprecedented and never to be repeated concentration of power in a single regional authority. He was also grand admiral of the new Black Sea fleet, which won such brilliant victories during the Russo-Turkish war of 1787–92. Rumiantsev died shortly after the empress, in December 1796; Potemkin preceded him in October 1791.

The annexation of the Crimea destroyed Ottoman hegemony in the Black Sea basin, and could only cause rancour in Constantinople, exacerbated by the flaunting of Russia's power and Catherine II's visit to the Crimea, including the new naval base at Sevastopol, in 1787. The Turks still retained Ochakov, a huge fortress blocking the exit from the estuary of the Dnieper and the Buh, which became the focus of the Russo-Turkish antagonism. A determination to regain the lost territory resulted in a Turkish declaration of war in August 1787, and this second Russo-Turkish war of Catherine's reign would last until the Treaty of Jassy, signed in January 1792.[51] The Russian core expanded further west to absorb the so-called Ochakov steppe (the "Khan's Ukraine") between the Buh and the Dniester, bounded in the north by Right Bank Ukraine along the Kodyma River. The new territory was added to Ekaterynoslav province, still joined with the Crimea, but under a new governor general, Platon Zubov, the empress's last favourite, appointed in July 1793. Less than two years later, Zubov reported that Ekaterynoslav province had become too large for a single governor to administer, and a second province was officially opened in May 1795.[52] Its capital was Voznesensk on the Southern Buh, from which much was expected. The province included the three western *uezds* of Ekaterynoslav province, and stretched as far east as the Buzuluk River, the headquarters of the old Zaporozhian Camp.[53] It was divided into twelve *uezds*, and included Kherson on the Dnieper, where the Russians planned to build shipyards for the Black Sea fleet, and Odessa, then a modest Turkish fishing port but destined to become Russia's greatest commercial port on the Black Sea coast.

The population of the southern theatre had grown enormously during Catherine's reign, as shown in table 5.1 (in thousands of people). In 1762, it numbered 2.6 million people; by 1795, it had nearly doubled to reach 5 million.

Table 5.1 Population (in thousands) of the southern theatre, 1762 and 1795

	1762	1795
Orel-Kursk-Voronezh	1,069	1,542
Chernihiv-Poltava-Kharkiv	1,342	1,697
Right Bank	23*	1,738
New Russia	105	520
Don Territory	71	164†
Total	*2,610*	*5,661*

Source: Kabuzan, *Izmeneniia*, 87–94, 107–18.
* Kiev *uezd*
† and Black Sea Host (14,726 people)

In 1762, 2.4 of the 2.6 million were in the three Russian provinces and Left Bank Ukraine. By 1795, the Right Bank alone accounted for 34.3 per cent of the total, and the Ukrainian provinces on both sides of the Dnieper for 56 per cent, not including New Russia (Ekaterynoslav and the Crimea), and the three Russian provinces for another 30.4 per cent. In Left Bank Ukraine the population was overwhelmingly Ukrainian (93 per cent), and more Ukrainians lived in the three Russian provinces, except Orel. The Russian share was 5.2 per cent, that of Jews less than 1 per cent. In Right Bank Ukraine the population was also overwhelmingly Ukrainian (87.8 per cent), with Poles (7.7 per cent) and Jews (3.6 per cent), adding up to 99.1 per cent of the total. There were hardly any Russians (0.1 per cent). The picture was different in New Russia, where the population was much more varied. The region grew in part by absorbing an outflow from the Left Bank. Yet, the Ukrainians made up only 52.4 per cent of the total, followed by Russians (19 per cent), Tatars and Kalmyks (11.1 per cent), and Jews (1.5 per cent). Moldavians escaping the yoke of the Phanariot Greeks made up another 11.7 per cent. There was a mass reverse emigration of Tatars after the annexation of the Crimea, but it later stopped, and Tatars made up 86 per cent of the population in some *uezds* of the peninsula, 96 per cent in others. The share of Armenians, Greeks, and Germans was insignificant.[54]

The administrative integration of the new provinces modelled after those of the core, and the proclamation that they would be governed in accordance with the same laws, created the uniform civilian infrastructure needed to support a new deployment of the army in the southern theatre. The hussar and lancer regiments, which had been settled for nearly half a century between the Syniukha and the Donets, no longer served their original purpose and were abolished in June 1783, when Potemkin carried out a major reorganization of the cavalry.[55] The regiments of military settlers, created to hold territory and consisting largely of heavy cavalry, were transformed into regiments of light cavalry (*legko-konnye*) of 930 officers and men in six squadrons each (ten Ekaterynoslav regiments and six from the Sloboda Ukraine), and the Little Russian Cossacks, who also no longer served their original purpose, were transformed into eight regiments of carbineers and ten of dragoons. The military settlers became a mobile force fully integrated into the Russian army, which had now reached the periphery of the expanding core. Its mission was no longer defensive (against the Tatars), but offensive (against the Turks). With the disappearance of the frontier in southern Ukraine, the old lines were abolished; the forts, notably St Elizabeth (Elizavetgrad), became "internal towns." The perimeter of the core merged with the coastline and the remainder of the Ottoman and Polish boundary in the west. New coastal forts were built at Olviopol, where the Kodyma and the Syniukha drained into the Southern Buh, at Kinburn, Kherson, the mouth of the Inhul (the future Mykolaiv/Nikolaev) facing Ochakov, at Evpatoria, Sebastopol, Balaklava, Feodosiia, and Perekop in the Crimea, and at the mouth of the Eia on the edge of the Kuban steppe.[56] The military perimeter enclosed the new provinces of the expanding core, where the work of integration would proceed at an accelerating pace. In the Kuban region, the eastern wing of the southern theatre, the Don-Mozdok Line was placed in 1784 under the command of the new governor general of the provinces of Caucasus and Astrakhan, Lt.-Gen. Pavel Potemkin, Grigorii's cousin. The line thus demarcated the boundary between the southern and eastern theatres, leaving the Kuban steppe under the jurisdiction of the governor general in Ekaterynoslav.

The Turkish war of 1787–92 exposed the limits of Russian capabilities in the southern theatre, aggravated by the rivalry between Potemkin and Rumiantsev, and by Potemkin's own shortcomings as a military commander. Nevertheless, the incorporation of the Ochakov steppe and the partitions of the Polish empire created another radically new situation, not unlike that following the annexation of the Crimea. Polish troops who surrendered to the Russians in 1793 joined the Russian army. Greeks and Albanians, who had served in the Russian navy in the Aegean Sea, about 350 men, were settled in the environs of Odessa in April 1795 to form another squadron (*divizion*). A "corps" of Little Russian Cossacks numbering 5,600 men was created in April 1794 to be trained as sharpshooters (*Jägers*) while serving as "irregular" infantry.[57] But it was in the Kuban steppe that colonization accelerated after Potemkin's death.

The Mozdok-Azov Line created a triangular frontier with the Kuban River and the Azov coast. Of its three sides only the Kuban remained unfortified, but it had to be, if the Kuban steppe was to become safe for settlers against the raids of "trans-Kuban" natives (Zakubantsy), inhabiting the foreland sloping upward to the Main Caucasus and watered by countless mountain streams running through impassable forests. During the Turkish war, General Ivan Gudovich, who took Anapa in 1791 and would soon become governor general of the Caucasus, proposed building forts along the river before inviting Cossack settlement. In 1792 he was allowed to do so from Konstantinograd (near Georgievsk) to the confluence of the Laba with the Kuban. Six regiments of Don Cossacks were ordered to the new Kuban Line, but they mutinied when they discovered that no accommodation had been built for their families (as they had been promised it would be), and three returned home. Military force had to be used, and only one thousand families eventually settled there. Their task was to form cadres for additional military settlements along the line.[58]

That same year, in 1792, the Black Sea Host and part of the Ekaterynoslav Cossacks were combined and transferred to the Kuban steppe. These Cossacks resembled the old Zaporozhians. They were no longer raiders in the steppe, but had settled down and tilled the land; they were also becoming a haven for runaway serfs. The authorities, faced with the conflict between encouraging settlement and creating a threat to the social order based on serfdom, opted, now that Potemkin was no longer on the scene, for the removal of the Cossacks to the Kuban steppe, which remained uninhabited. Their "*koshevyi*, *starshyna*, and host" in forty *kureni* were given a charter in February granting them the "island of Fanagoria" (the Taman peninsula), which was part of the Crimean *oblast*, with the entire steppe between the Kuban and the Eia River (the Don border), and all the way to the confluence of the Laba with the Kuban. Their civil administration would follow that of the internal provinces, but they would remain under the overall jurisdiction of the governor of the Crimea in Simferopol.[59] With the remainder of the Ekaterynoslav host, Zubov planned to create a Voznesensk host, but nothing came of it because Catherine II died five months later.

Immediately after her death, Paul I announced a new deployment of the army in the southern theatre, which did away with Potemkin's reforms and returned to the more traditional division of the army into infantry and cavalry units. It reflected the situation in the field following the third partition of the Polish Empire, but also pointed to the emergence of new priorities, as the expansion of revolutionary France increasingly threatened the Germanic powers and Russia itself.[60] The Ukrainian Division of sixteen regiments was largely concentrated in Volhynia and Podolia, with only five regiments stationed in Orel, Kursk, and Kiev. The Ekaterynoslav Division of fifteen regiments was concentrated in the Ochakov steppe, along the Dniester, and all the way to Novo-Myrhorod and Elizavetgrad. There was also a small Crimean Division of five regiments stationed along the Crimean coast, with one regiment in Karasubazar on the postal road from Sevastopol to Kerch via Simferopol. The deployment meshed with the new infrastructure of provincial and *uezd* agencies to consolidate the hold of the expanding Russian core on its outlying peripheries and their integration into a single unitary state. Such at least was still the program of the ruling elite at the end of Catherine's reign.

Ecclesiastical and Legal Integration

The Church

The ransacking of the Mohyla Academy, the abolition of the office of Kiev metropolitan, and the ukaze of 1720 forbidding Ukrainian publications, except religious books (which had to follow Russian editions), were not only acts of revenge for Mazepa's betrayal of the trust Peter had placed in him. They were also symptoms of a policy of unification of the Russian and Ukrainian churches, separated, not by matters of dogma, but merely by institutional rivalry. The increasing influence of the Russian language, which reflected the rising power of the Russian core after Poltava, while that of Poland was steadily decreasing on the Left Bank, merged with the growing willingness of most of the hierarchs to join their Russian colleagues and of the *starshyna* to discover a common interest with the Russian nobility. Both sides implicitly agreed on restructuring the Orthodox Church and Cossack society in order to facilitate the integration of the Russian periphery into the larger, but, paradoxically, more confined and xenophobic, Russian core. Fifty years later, in 1769, in the reign of an enlightened empress, a Kiev monastery petitioned the Holy Synod for permission to publish a Ukrainian grammar. The Synod refused, adding that even the old Ukrainian church books had to be removed from circulation and Russian books substituted.[61]

Integration was rapidly progressing in Sloboda Ukraine. Its Cossacks had long been subordinated to the Belgorod *voevoda*; its hierarchy belonged to the diocese of Belgorod (*eparkhiia*), but the Ostrohozhsk regiment to that of Voronezh. Even though the bishops were usually graduates of the Mohyla Academy and Chernihiv College and kept alive a Ukrainian atmosphere, the province's church had been integrated into the "All-Russian" church. The creation of a Kharkiv College by Bishop Yepyfanii Tykhorsky of Belgorod in 1722 could not neutralize the gravitational pull of Belgorod and Voronezh. Kharkiv College was modelled after the Mohyla Academy, and its professors were graduates from it and from the Chernihiv and Pereiaslav colleges, but its curriculum was mostly theological and its purpose was to train priests for parishes in the southern theatre. The Latin-Slavic school created in Ostrohozhsk in 1733 was a smaller version of its Kharkiv sister. In the faraway Don Territory, the appointment of priests and deacons depended on the Moscow patriarch, and beginning in 1720, the territory was incorporated into the diocese of Voronezh, where a seminary trained future priests, largely because the *otamans* could not find the will to create one in Cherkassk or enough students willing and able to attend it.[62]

The situation was more complex in Little Russia, with its three dioceses of Chernihiv, Kiev, and Pereiaslav. All three depended on the archbishop in Kiev.

In 1733, the Pereiaslav see was subordinated directly to the Holy Synod, but in 1743 the office of Kiev metropolitan was restored owing to the benevolence of a deeply religious empress and the efforts of Archbishop Rafail Zaborovsky (1731–47), born in Galicia, trained in the Mohyla Academy, but also at the Moscow Theological Academy, a former chaplain in the Russian navy, and bishop of Pskov. He became the first metropolitan "of Kiev, Galich, and Little Russia." His successor, Tymofii Shcherbatsky (1748–57), had been archimandrite of the Cave Monastery, and became embroiled in a running dispute over the appointment of professors and the establishment of a printing press. He ended his career as metropolitan of Moscow (1757–67), and a member of the Holy Synod. It was under his successor, Arsenii Mohyliansky (1757–70), former archimandrite of the Trinity monastery north of Moscow, member of the Holy Synod, and official court preacher, that "Little Russia" was removed from the title, as if to confirm that, after the resignation of Razumovsky and the abolition of the Hetmanate, the territory had become integrated into the ecclesiastical unitary state, with Galich remaining in Polish hands. Another metropolitan worthy of mention was Havryil (Gavril) Kremianetsky (1715–1783), who served in high church positions in Petersburg and Moscow before becoming metropolitan (1770–83). All four were Ukrainians and graduates of the Mohyla Academy, but became "socialized" into the All-Russian church to the point where they no longer saw any distinction between the sees of Pskov and Pereiaslav.[63]

But at the same time, by what might be called a complementary process, the Ukrainian church continued to suffer from its close association with the *starshyna*, whose power was growing, and from the gradual enserfment of the peasantry. In 1734, the three bishops were forbidden to consecrate priests and deacons who came from *starshyna* families, without the permission of the chancery, and Shakhovskoy was ordered to confiscate the property of those who entered the priesthood without it. The Cossack influx into the clerical estate ran counter to the Russian policy of creating a closed estate, in which sons succeeded their fathers and daughters married into other priestly families.[64] The clerics so chosen often did not have any vocation and only corrupted the priesthood. They also became monks and abbots (called archimandrites in the larger monasteries), and the monks gained an unsavoury reputation for their greed in seizing peasant and Cossack land, woods, and fishponds. Bishops were not above excommunicating their rivals when cases came to court.[65] The extension of *starshyna* power into the clergy called for a Reformation that could not take place in Orthodoxy, although the brotherhoods in Right Bank Ukraine had done remarkable work raising educational standards and challenging church corruption. Under Russian rule, they would have been considered subversive, but the church would pay a heavy price in the 1780s for stifling dissent.

There was a crying need for educational opportunities. The Mohyla Academy, the jewel of Ukrainian education in the latter half of the seventeenth century, spawned similar institutions, such as the Chernihiv College in 1700, the Kharkiv College in 1722, and a third one in Pereiaslav opened in 1738. But all four, despite the addition of courses in more modern and useful subjects, could not escape their basic religious orientation, and, as such, were drawn into the centripetal pull of Moscow and Petersburg, with the hierarchs becoming the willing agents of a policy of integration. Grigorii Vinsky, who studied at the Mohyla Academy in the mid-1760s, was not impressed by what he was taught. Arithmetic he learned from a local artillerist, French in a private school in Starodub, but he remembered having learned Polish and Latin well,[66] hardly useful subjects to help him make his way in the world of the expanding core, where the emphasis was on preparing for a military career.

The instructions of the Little Russian nobles sent to the Legislative Commission in 1767 all have one thing in common. Education is needed to fight Old Belief, superstition, and ignorance, but there are no schools. Families of means send their children to Moscow and Petersburg (where they learn the majesty of Russian power and the need for unity as the foundation of strength), or even abroad, and often become impoverished as a result. Those without means have no opportunities, and there is no mention of the colleges. They all ask for the creation of schools for the nobility (*dvorianskie korpusa*), like those in Moscow and Petersburg to help young men become military commanders, civil servants, and "useful citizens." They also want schools for girls, whose education was completely neglected.[67] The instructions show that the nobles were aware of Catherine's plans to reform Russian education and wanted similar reforms in Little Russia. They also show that for the nobility the religious colleges had become irrelevant, except for the training of priests.

It may not have been a coincidence that the reform of Russian education and the final integration of the Orthodox Church in Little Russia were announced the same year, in 1786. Of course, the latter was also the natural corollary of the administrative integration carried out in 1782 with the introduction of the Organic Statute of 1775 and the division of Little Russia into three provinces. The School Statute of August 1786 called for the opening of schools in each provincial and *uezd* capital of the Russian core, with a curriculum that included the teaching of Russian grammar and history, even though it would take a long time to reach such an ambitious objective.[68]

The ukaze of April frankly stated that, following the creation of the new provinces, "We wish to introduce uniformity in the maintenance of the episcopal sees and monasteries" and free the hierarchs from taking part in litigation "inappropriate" for their rank.[69] The church was stripped of most of its real properties, which amounted to the extension to Little Russia of the legislation of February 1764 for the Russian core. The Pereyaslav diocese was already part of it. The hierarchs and monasteries were given an establishment and a salary. The Kiev Cave Monastery was placed on the same level as the Trinity

Monastery north of Moscow, and the metropolitan was its ex officio archimandrite. A monastery attached to the St Sophia Cathedral was transformed into a provincial school, and the cathedral was equated in the establishment with the Arkhangelsk Cathedral in the Kremlin. Monasteries and convents not retained in the establishment were closed or became *uezd* schools, hospitals, and houses for the poor, placed under the jurisdiction of a new board of public welfare, as in the rest of the Russian core. A university was planned for Chernihiv, close to the Russian border, but it was never created. The only university in the core, that of Moscow, created in 1755, was not yet ready for competition, let alone from a university in the periphery with a strong ethnic identity. There would now be three dioceses, Kiev, Chernihiv (where the cathedral was equated with St Sophia in Novgorod), and Novhorod-Siverskyi, but there would be no bishop in Kiev: the metropolitan was given the same salary as the bishop of Moscow.

The annexation of the Crimea and the Ochakov steppe, together with the creation of three provinces of Ekaterynoslav, Voznesensk, and Crimea (*oblast*) brought about the same systematic integration into a single unitary church. New Serbia had been subordinated to the Pereiaslav bishop, and Slavianoserbia to that of Belgorod. The Ekaterynoslav diocese was created in 1784 with an associate (*vikarnaia*) diocese in Feodosiia beginning in 1787, to which the Black Sea Cossacks were subordinated in 1794. It was abolished in 1799. The bishop of "New Russia and the Dnieper" resided in Novomyrhorod with jurisdiction over the entire region.[70]

The Crimea, especially its southern part, where the Muslim Tatar population was concentrated, resisted full integration. The *mufti*, as chief Islamic cleric, had full authority over all religious affairs, including the management of the vast *vakif* lands that belonged to various mosques and religious foundations – they comprised nearly a third of all the lands of the peninsula. The *kadiasker* was a Muslim official appointed, not by the clergy, but by the sultan, to oversee the judiciary, and the *kadis* (judges) were subordinated to him. Catherine promised religious freedom, and gained the strong support of the upper ranks of the "clergy." Here too, superstratification was favouring the progress of integration. When the *mufti* died in 1791, the Russian authorities obtained the selection of the *kadiasker* as the new *mufti*, and an "ecclesiastical assembly" was created in 1794 to consist of six clerics, with the *mufti* as chairman, similar to the agency created in Orenburg in 1788. It retained jurisdiction over the *vakif* lands, a potential source of great tension with the new Russian landowners and settlers.[71]

But it was in Right Bank Ukraine that the great battles would have to be fought. The Ukrainian lands had always been a religious frontier between Orthodoxy and Roman Catholicism, two religions associated with two powerful cores vying for supremacy in western Eurasia. The Treaty of Andrusovo and the Eternal Peace of 1686 delivered Kiev and Little Russia to the former, the

Right Bank to the latter. While Moscow then set about Russifying the hierarchy of the Left Bank church, the Poles were even more forcefully Polonizing and Latinizing the remaining Cossack leaders and gentry of the Right Bank. Polish Catholicism, reinvigorated by the Counter-Reformation, understood that education must play a decisive role. The Uniate Church, an orthodox church but one recognizing the pope as spiritual leader, was an instrument of Polish rule to draw the upper strata of the Orthodox Ukrainian population into the fold of the Polish empire, and the Poles were so successful that by the end of the seventeenth century they had destroyed the infrastructure of the Orthodox church. The Uniate church had triumphed, with its own metropolitan (who did not always reside in the same place) and diocesan sees in Lutsk (Volhynia), Lviv, and Peremyshl in Galicia.

A century earlier, in 1596, the Sejm had already decided that all official documents must be written in Polish. Polonization often preceded joining the Uniate church. For the Ukrainian Orthodox nobility, abandoned to its fate by the partition of 1686, learning Polish opened the door to participation in the activities of the government in Warsaw and even promised entry into the magnate world.[72] Like all men of the frontier, they gravitated toward the core that exercised the greater pull. After the final partition at the end of the eighteenth century, Russian influence would supplant that of Poland, but many Ukrainians would remain torn between the two for a long time. Joining the Uniate church, which retained the Eastern rite, was easier than to convert to Catholicism, but the Polish government never recognized that church as the equal of their own Catholic church, and Uniate metropolitans had to resist Polish efforts to convert the Ukrainians. In so doing it undermined its policy of creating a single state (*korona*) including both Right Bank Ukraine and the Polish core.

The progress of Polonization and Latinization depended not only on compulsion but on education as well. The Uniates, influenced by the Jesuit example, set up an extensive network of schools run by the Basilian order. After the Union of Brest (1596), the Uniate metropolitan, Yosyf Rutsky, combined the monasteries that had accepted the Union into one congregation of the Holy Trinity (also called the Lithuanian Congregation), independent of the bishops, and subordinated to a protoarchimandrite. In 1739, a congregation of the Protection of the Mother of God (the Ruthenian Congregation) was created in Lviv. Both were merged to form a Basilian Order; its first general assembly was held in Dubno in 1743. A major role was placed by the Uniate metropolitan, Atanasii Sheptytsky (1686–1746), the bishop of Lviv, which after 1686 emerged in Galicia as the Uniate counterpart of Kiev, the guardian of Orthodoxy. In 1790, a general assembly held in Tarakaniv (Volhynia) divided the order into four provinces (Lithuanian, Belorussian, "Crown," or Right Bank Ukraine, and Galician). By then, the order had 1,235 monks in 155 monasteries. The Basilians ran colleges for young men – the most famous one was in Volodymyr-Volynsky, west of

Lutsk – and schools for the sons of impoverished nobles. They also took over the Jesuit schools, including their main one in Ostroh, east of Lutsk; and their main publishing centre was in Pochaev, south of Lutsk, whose diocese thus became the educational headquarters of Right Bank Ukraine.[73] But the Uniate church had an Achilles heel. Its creation had been divisive, because the peasants remained deeply attached to Orthodoxy. A religious schism was grafted onto a social one, and religious intolerance fuelled social antagonisms. They erupted during the *haidamak* uprising in the 1730s and 1760s, when Orthodox and Uniates fought cruel and obscene battles in the name of the Prince of Peace.[74] The Uniate church was becoming a church without a people, the Orthodox a people without a church.

The partitions of the Polish Empire closed the Russo-Polish religious frontier and transformed the Uniate church into a minority church within the larger unitary Orthodox universe. The Russian church would eventually destroy it (1839). Catherine II may have been ambivalent about the course to follow, but so much resentment had built up during the seventeenth and eighteenth centuries that events forced her hand. Twenty years earlier, in 1773, she had proclaimed the tolerance of other religions, and had inaugurated a policy of accommodation toward Islam, if only to better integrate it by a process of ecclesiastical superstratification. In Right Bank Ukraine, the Polish magnates had been favourable to the partitions, which put an end to the unnatural union between the Polish core and the Right Bank frontier and opened up great commercial opportunities in the Black Sea basin. The Russian authorities would need the magnates and the *szlachta* to administer the country. The Uniate church had become the church of an inner frontier. A cautious approach was needed.

By the spring of 1794, however, one year after the second partition, the empress was receiving reports that the Ukrainian peasants "who are in the Union with the Roman church" and had been converted by force were returning to Orthodoxy. She ordered Governor General Tutolmin to announce everywhere through the rural police that attempts by landowners and Uniate clergy to hold them back and use violence against them would be treated as crimes against the official church and "Our will," punishable by the sequester of their properties. The Uniate metropolitan, Feodosii Rostotsky (1788–1805), the first Uniate hierarch to sit in the Polish Senate (and who would eventually be deported to Petersburg in 1796), was enjoined to desist from placing obstacles to the sinking of his ship. The return of the peasants, added Catherine, would facilitate the "uprooting" (*udobnoe iskorenie*) of the Uniate church.[75] In the absence of an Orthodox infrastructure, it was still enough to let the Ukrainian masses express their religious preferences and elect their own priests. But the reestablishment of the Orthodox church and difficult relations with the Polish *szlachta*, which did not welcome its integration into a superstratified society – because it belonged to a core, and core elites could not be successfully integrated into the expanding Russian core – would soon convince the Russian government that Roman Catholicism was a more dangerous enemy than Islam, and that a policy of open repression was in order.

In the fall of 1795, with Russian troops in occupation of most of Right Bank Ukraine, a new Orthodox diocese was created for the three provinces of Bratslav, Volhynia, and Podolia, as well as for Minsk province in Belorussia, annexed in 1793. It would be under an archbishop, who was also the ex officio archimandrite of a monastery in Slutsk, south of Minsk. The Kiev diocese, now enlarged with parishes from the Right Bank and still ruled by the metropolitan, was given an associate bishop, to be called bishop of Pereiaslav and Boryspil (east of Kiev), who remained subordinated to the metropolitan.[76] After the third partition, when "one million Russian people" (*Rossiiskii narod*), who had been "corrupted from the true path by Polish blandishments and violence," voluntarily returned to their "true Mother, the Orthodox Eastern Greco-Russian Church," and would no doubt inspire their compatriots (*edinoplemennye*) – in Galicia? – to follow their "path to salvation" (*spasitel'nyi primer*), a new organization took place. Bratslav and Podolsk provinces were combined to form one diocese with a bishop in Sharhorod, later transferred to Kamianets-Podilskyi, and an associate bishop for Volhynia was appointed in Zhytomyr, subordinated to the Archbishop of Minsk and Volhynia. In 1799, he gained his independence from Minsk, and a Bishop of "Volhynia and Zhytomyr" was appointed in Ostroh (Ostrog). Another diocese was created in Chyhyryn on the Right Bank, whose bishop resided in the Golden Domes Monastery in Kiev. The metropolitan retained the title of "Kiev and Galicia," but Yerotius Malytsky (1796–9) was the last Ukrainian to occupy the office.[77] Sloboda Ukraine became a separate diocese with a bishop in Kharkiv. The Don Territory remained associated with Voronezh, whose bishop wore the title of Bishop of Voronezh and Cherkassk. The Ukrainian Orthodox church had been fully integrated into the Orthodox church of the expanding Russian core to form, with it, a single unitary ecclesiastical state.

The Courts

The courts also fell victim to the process of both integration and superstratification, one similar, as in the case of the church, to developments in the Ukrainian lands that became part of the expanding Polish core (*korona*). On the eve of the Khmelnytsky uprising (1648), the Polish judiciary on both sides of the Dnieper consisted of civil courts (*sądy ziemskie*), which tried cases in each district (*powiat, povet*), criminal courts (*sądy gorodskie*), and land courts (*sądy podkomorskie*), which settled boundary disputes. The civil courts had a judge, an associate judge (*podsudek*), and a clerk chosen by the king from among twelve candidates submitted by each district. They met three times a year. In the criminal courts three judges and a clerk sat under the chairmanship of the *starosta*, who administered the district. They met during the winter for a few weeks, and their decisions were referred to a court consisting of the associate *voevoda* and three judges sitting in each palatinate, of which there were five in Ukraine (Volhynia, Podolia, Bratslav, Kiev – on both sides of the Dnieper – and Chernihiv). The land court was at first an arbitration court, before it became a section of the civil court: its judge (*podkomorzy*) was appointed by the king. The highest appellate court was the so-called Crown Tribunal, created in 1578. Its twenty-seven judges were elected by the *szlachta* in the palatinate assemblies; it was chaired by a marshal (*marszalek*).[78] The Tribunal met twice a year, once in Piotrków for cases originating in Great (northern) Poland, the second time in Lublin for those coming from Little (southern) Poland and the Ukrainian lands. Decisions were reached by majority vote.

Some towns were governed by the Magdeburg Law, brought into Poland by German colonists beginning in the thirteenth century. It was mainly a charter of urban self-government and provided for an elected council (*magistrat*), headed by a mayor (*wojt*), usually appointed by the king. The council combined administrative, judicial, and financial responsibilities, owned properties, and kept a budget. Its jurisdiction was restricted to the town's burghers (*mieszczanie*), and its judicial decisions were appealed to the Crown Tribunal. Those of the Lwów (Lviv) council seem to have created precedents for the other councils to follow. The official language was Polish, sometimes Latin, and procedure was oral. The motivation behind granting such charters was to encourage the immigration of artisans in order to develop a degree of urban life in an otherwise depressing agrarian landscape. The policy, however, was to make the burghers into a separate and closed group in accordance with the Polish socio-political system (here strikingly similar to the Russian in many ways), which recognized the necessity to break down society into autonomous categories defined by their occupations: the *szlachta* fought and owned serfs, the clergy prayed, the burghers engaged in trade and crafts, the peasants tilled the land. But in a society increasingly dominated by the magnates and the *szlachta* in the sixteenth century, the effect of such a policy was to place the burghers at the mercy of the landlords.[79] That was certainly the case in the other towns without Magdeburg Law charters: there, a smaller council called *ratusha* managed the towns, many of which became the private property of the landlords in the seventeenth century.

Seven towns were given a charter in Right Bank Ukraine – Volodymyr-Volynsky near the Western Bug, the major trade artery for Volhynia and Podolia to the Vistula and Danzig on the Baltic coast; Lutsk and Dubno, also in agriculturally rich Volhynia, forming the hinterland of the Bug; and Zhytomyr, the the capital of the Kiev palatinate after Poland lost Little Russia in 1686. The other three were in Podolia – Kamianets-Podilskyi with its huge fort facing the Turkish Khotyn across the Dniester; and Letychiv and Khmelnyk on the Southern Buh, both fortified towns and trade centres. But there were twelve such towns in Little Russia, ten of them in the forest zone, north of a line running from Kiev to Karachev via Baturyn – Oster, Kozelets, and Nizhyn, all three on the Oster River, trade centres forming the hinterland of Kiev; Chernihiv and (possibly) Novhorod-Siverskyi (Novgorod-Seversk);[80] Pochep and Pogar on the Desna and its tributary the Sudost, the waterway linking Kiev with the basin of the Oka; Starodub and Mglin, linking Little Russia with Belorussia; and of course, Kiev. Only two were in the woodland zone – Pereiaslav and Poltava on the edge of the steppe. Thus, the urban councils (acting as courts) were found overwhelmingly in the forest zone, where large landed properties were the exception, and where urban activities were connected with river traffic and the manufacture of forest products such as tar and potash, as well as the cultivation of hemp.

Following the Khmelnytsky rebellion, the Treaty of Andrusovo, and the creation of a Cossack state superimposed upon a population of peasants and burghers, a new judicial hierarchy gradually came into being. At first, the Polish system was retained, and appeals were now taken to the hetman, but in towns where Russian *voevodas* were appointed, appeals were taken to them, with the possibility of a further appeal to Moscow, especially in criminal and politically sensitive cases.[81] In Sloboda Ukraine, *sotniki* and colonels continued to function in their judicial capacity, and appeals were taken to the Belgorod *voevoda*. In Little Russia, Cossack agencies soon replaced the Polish courts, and the ten regimental colonels – four in the forest zone (Nizhyn, Starodub, Chernihiv, and Kiev on the border), six in the woodland zone (Pereiaslav, Myrhorod, Lubny, Hadiach, and Pryluky, with Poltava on the boundary) – became the most important judicial authorities, whose decisions were appealed to the hetman. A "general court" was created in Hlukhiv in 1654, which was then subordinated to the chancery of the host, creating, with the hetman, a three-tiered appellate system.[82] It caused endless delays, but also gave the *starshyna* a chance to fight their battles over the acquisition and disposal of landed properties, the major source of civil litigation. These courts handled both civil and criminal cases, but the land courts disappeared, to the great satisfaction of the *starshyna*, who preferred to leave the boundaries of their properties uncertain as long as it suited their purpose. The municipal councils remained in existence. Thus the judicial system of Little Russia consisted of a network of twenty-two basic courts, subordinated to the general court and ultimately to the hetman.

After Skoropadsky's death in 1722, the Little Russian College (and its successors) became the highest court of appeal, replacing the hetman, and a final appeal was allowed to the Senate directly or through the College of Foreign Affairs, depending on the times. This meant that the highest judge in Little Russia became a Russian (Brigadier General Veliaminov, Lt.-Gen. Shakhovskoy), whose major task was to begin the integration of the appellate system into the Russian one. The Apostol Articles of 1728 called the empress "the chief judge of the All-Russian Empire, who wishes to administer justice [*pravosudie*] everywhere,"[83] a clear hint that the central government was guided by the ideal of a unitary state. Even Sloboda Ukraine was placed under Shakhovskoy, but this was revoked in 1743,[84] only to reaffirm the integration of its judiciary by proclaiming that litigants dissatisfied with the decisions of the Belgorod *voevoda* were free to appeal to the College of Justice and against it to the Senate, "in accordance with the provisions of the gubernatorial instruction of 1728" in effect in the internal provinces of the Russian core.

As had already happened in the Polish core, a struggle developed between the urban councils and the authorities of a basically agrarian state. The Cossack state was a warrior state, and although Cossacks, burghers, and peasants had been united in the struggle against the Polish magnates and *szlachta*, it was in the nature of things that the Cossack authorities representing agrarian interests should try to assert their control over the towns and neutralize the self-government granted by the Magdeburg Law. When Elizabeth came to the throne in 1741, she announced a return to the policies of her father, Peter I, including the restoration of a Central Council (*Glavnyi Magistrat*) with an exclusive jurisdiction over the urban councils everywhere, which were thus removed from the jurisdiction of the governors and *voevodas*.[85] This made a conflict with the Cossack authorities inevitable. It was behind much of the rivalry between Hetman Razumovsky and the governor general of Kiev. The hetman eventually emerged as the victor, when the Kiev council was subordinated to him in May 1762, "like the councils of other Little Russian towns."[86]

In 1763–4, as if again in imitation of the Polish model, Little Russia was divided into twenty districts (*povity/povety*), the civil and land courts were restored, and the regimental courts were transformed into new criminal courts. These courts were elected by the *starshyna* – and became excellent sources of patronage – except for the criminal courts, where the colonels remained the chair and appointed two or three judges from among the *starshyna*. Very few judges seem to have been re-elected, and the tendency was to make these courts hereditary plums for well-placed members of the *starshyna*. In November 1760, the general court was made to consist of two judges and ten "deputies" elected for one year, but Rumiantsev, dissatisfied with the neglect of their duties, replaced them in 1767 with permanent members.[87] The court was kept separate from the new Little Russian College but remained subordinated to Rumiantsev as the chief judge of Little Russia. The reform remained in force for twenty years, until the 1780s, when the judiciary, like the church, became finally integrated into that of the expanding core.

In each of the four provinces of the Left Bank (Novhorod-Siverskyi, Chernihiv, Kiev, and Kharkiv for Sloboda Ukraine), civil and criminal chambers were created as courts of appeal from the new district (*uezd*) courts, which combined the jurisdiction of the Polish-style civil and criminal courts. The *uezd* became the equivalent of the *poviet*. An additional level of appellate courts was added between the chambers and the district courts, a cumbersome and totally unnecessary intermediate level, but an important source of patronage. The reform amounted to a large-scale redistribution of the spoils among the *starshyna*, with colonels and *sotniki* finding a cozy place in the new hierarchy of courts, all elected, in part by the nobility, in part by the better-off burghers. The chambers, however, were appointed by the government, though almost all their chairmen, at least at first, were Ukrainians. A hierarchy of land surveyors (*zemlemery*) was created to replace the old land courts.

Municipal councils were established in an increasing number of towns raised to the status of district capitals, but they lost their administrative jurisdiction, as well as their properties, to become merely urban courts of law, still called *magistraty*. Appeals went to an intermediate council, also elected by the burghers, and on to either the civil or the criminal chamber, where the burghers were not represented. Appeals from the chambers went to the Senate. The reform thus recognized the validity of the status quo, in which the *starshyna*, as the ruling class of Little Russia, managed to integrate urban life into its power structure, very much as it already had integrated the rank-and-file Cossacks and peasantry into its manorial economy dominated by serfdom.

The reform also created peasant courts (*raspravy*) at the district and intermediate levels to try cases to which state peasants were a party, but they did not exist in every district, only in those where there was a sufficient number of such peasants. These courts were thus given jurisdiction in a number of cases over more than one district, even though in the four provinces state (and former church) peasants made up, in 1795, 52.7 per cent of the peasant population (and the urban population a mere 2 per cent of the total population).[88] In summary, the reform of the Left Bank judiciary, which created forty-eight counties, replaced ten regimental courts with forty-eight county courts, the twelve municipal councils with forty-eight new urban courts, but created only twenty-six peasant courts. It also replaced the appellate hierarchy centred in the general court with twelve intermediate courts and eight chambers.[89] It was a remarkable achievement, which made the courts much more accessible to the general population, but also strengthened the *starshyna*'s hold over the dependent population.

The court hierarchy could not be separated from the new administrative structure, into which it was deeply embedded. Governors reviewed the sentences of the criminal chambers and forwarded the case to the Senate, if they disagreed with the decision. Most were Russians, with the notable exception of Lt.-Gen. Andrei Miloradovich in Chernihiv – a descendant of Serbs from Slavianoserbia – who had an exceptionally long tenure from 1782 through 1796.

The governor general had the overall responsibility to make "justice" prevail. Procurators at the provincial and intermediate levels were expected to reconcile Russian and Ukrainian law, and make Russian law prevail in the event of conflicts. Rumiantsev, the governors, and the procurators in the four provinces, together with their staffs, formed the upper stratum of an administrative hierarchy engaged in a process of superstratification, in which the *starshyna* would continue to share the spoils of judicial office in return for accepting its integration into the power structure of the expanding core's ruling class and its multiethnic, but largely Russian, ruling elite.

Elsewhere in the region, the same process was at work. In the pre-reform New Russia province, the commanding general was the equivalent of a governor, and he applied law from the beginning. The Bakhmut urban council, which had been dependent on the Voronezh council, was subordinated to him in 1772, as an exception to the general rule that urban councils were subordinated to the Central Council in Petersburg.[90] Among the Zaporozhian Cossacks, the *koshevyi* retained his traditional authority as the judge of last resort, but the Kiev governor general stripped him of his power to impose and carry out death sentences, which had been "suspended" in the core since 1754.[91] A similar restriction applied in the Don Territory as well, but both the *koshevyi* and the *otaman* fought to circumvent that restriction.

The enormous expansion of the core in 1774 and 1792 and the administrative integration that followed also resulted in the creation of new courts identical with those already in operation in the Russian core. Ukrainians and Russians moving into the territory to join the remaining Crimean Tatars were placed under the same courts, where the written procedure followed Russian law and appeals moved along the same channels. The territory was divided into three provinces (Ekaterynoslav, Kherson, and the Crimean *oblast*) and thirty-one districts with thirty-one county courts, nine intermediate courts, and six chambers. There were also thirty-four urban courts: in the Crimea, where towns had a long history along the southern coast, an additional three were planned for Vospor, Sevastopol, and Feodosiia. There were also only twenty-seven peasant courts: in the Crimea again, they were established in only three district capitals, although 63.1 per cent of the peasant population consisted of state and church peasants (and 8.8 per cent of the total population were burghers, an unusually high percentage, and the highest in the entire southern theatre).

The integration of the mainland part of New Russia was a simple matter: the territory was a *tabula rasa*, upon which the expanding core rolled and absorbed without encountering physical or human obstacles. The Crimean Peninsula was another matter. The khanate had a long history and a strong sense of identity, based on the fact that, after Kazan and Astrakhan, annexed by Russia two centuries earlier, it was the last remaining khanate to have broken off from the old Mongol empire in western and central Eurasia. It was a Muslim state governed by Muslim law, fundamentally different from the Ukrainian and Polish political and social world. Nevertheless, there were some interesting similarities. The *kadi-asker* (who was appointed by the sultan) gave patents of office to forty-eight *kadis*, who administered justice, each in his own *kadilik*. The *kadis* of Kaffa (Feodosiia), Sudak, Mangup, and Enikale were appointed by the sultan. The nobility had their own courts, whose decisions were confirmed by the *kadi-asker*, with the *mufti*'s advice. There were also separate courts for the Muslim clergy, for Christians, and for Jews, as well as urban courts for burghers. Cases which for some reason did not come under the jurisdiction of these courts were decided in the state council (divan), consisting of the *kalgan* (the khan's heir apparent), the *mufti*, the heads of the five clans, and representatives of each branch of these clans. Procedure was oral.[92] The Russian reforms also retained the ecclesiastical courts (consistories) and courts for the nobility and the burghers, and, as we shall see, would also recognize the existence of separate courts for ethnic and religious minorities.

In Right Bank Ukraine, the court system of the expanding core was introduced with some hesitation at first, then with ruthless determination. At the time of the annexation of 1793, the Polish civil and criminal courts had been replaced by the so-called confederate courts (*marshalkovskie sudy*), created by the Constitution of 3 May 1791; they were immediately closed. The civil and criminal courts were then restored in order to win over the magnates, against whom the Constitution had been directed, but were soon closed again, and replaced by the Russian system of courts already in force in Little and New Russia. By 1796, in the three provinces of Bratslav, Podolia, and Volhynia, divided into thirty-eight counties, there were six chambers, nine intermediate courts, thirty-eight county courts, and thirty-eight urban courts, but only nine peasant courts. The peasantry consisted overwhelmingly of privately held serfs – state and church peasants made up only 14.8 per cent of the peasant population, a figure that set the Right Bank apart from the rest of the region. The share of the urban population was 5.9 per cent, placing the Right Bank between Little and New Russia, which stood out for the much higher percentage of townsmen.

The entire judiciary after the reform remained staffed with Polish *szlachta*, who often did not know any Russian, but would have to cooperate in a process of reluctant superstratification. It was assumed that oral procedure would be replaced by the written form in usage in the Russian courts, but this was easier said than done. The Russian authorities would for a long time have to rely on interpreters and translators. The courts would receive their instructions in Russian, and decisions written in Polish would be sent with translations to the higher courts and the governors. Documents would show the Russian double eagle, the death penalty was abolished, the gallows, which had been a feature of the urban landscape, were taken down, and the swords were removed from the walls of the county courts.[93] But in both Left and Right Bank Ukraine, which had been so profoundly marked by Polish influence, a major question facing the Russian authorities was: what kind of law would this uniform court system apply in reaching decisions?

Legal Systems

Two legal systems existed side by side in the Ukrainian lands at the time of the Khmelnytsky uprising. West of the Dnieper, most of the territory bounded by the river, the Western Bug, and the middle Dniester had belonged to the Grand Duchy of Lithuania until the Union of Lublin (1569); so had the Left Bank between the Desna, the Donets, and the Tatar borders. The grand dukes had promulgated a large body of legislation which, by the early sixteenth century, was greatly in need of codification for at least two reasons: to eliminate the inevitable contradictions, and to bring the law to reflect the consolidation of a social situation in which the nobility had been usurping more and more princely power in order to establish a republic of nobles, both magnates and rank-and-file *szlachta*.

A First Lithuanian Statute (*Litovskii Statut* or simply *Statut*) was promulgated in 1529.[94] It contained many archaic provisions and harsh penalties for violations of the public order, and was not yet particularly favourable to *szlachta* interests. A Second Statute, chiefly for Volhynia, received the approval of Sigismund-August, King of Poland and Grand Duke of Lithuania, in 1566, on the eve of the Union, which required the publication of a Third (and last) Statute in 1588.[95] By then, the Ukrainian lands which had been part of the Grand Duchy had been incorporated into the Polish core, but the Statutes were recognized by Warsaw as the corporate law of the Polish nobility on both banks of the Dnieper, subject to amendments by the Polish parliament in the form of "constitutions." After the incorporation of the Hetmanate into the expanding Russian core, the Russians recognized the legal validity of the Third Statute, but it also became subject to interpretation by Muscovite and later imperial authorities. Both the Poles and the Russians looked upon the Statute as an intrinsic part of their jurisprudence, but one expected to satisfy the interests of the ruling class of a specific region, with its own social relationships and economic landscape. The Statute thus represented a jurisprudential frontier between the legal philosophies of the Polish and Russian cores, exposed to pressures from Warsaw and Moscow-Petersburg, both seeking to create within their territorial jurisdiction a unitary science of law. Nevertheless, the Statute became the basic law (*korennyi zakon*) on both banks of the Dnieper, and was still recognized as such, at least in the former Hetmanate, as late as 1842.[96] It was originally written in the contemporary Ruthenian chancery language, which was a mixture of Church

Slavonic, Ukrainian, and Belorussian. A first Polish translation appeared in 1616, but a partial Russian translation was not printed until 1811 for the use of senators in Moscow and Petersburg.

By the eighteenth century, however, there already was a growing feeling in the Hetmanate that the Statute no longer embodied the aspirations and practices of a new age. There was no republic of nobles in Left Bank Ukraine, even if the *starshyna* would have liked to create one, but the region was being integrated into an expanding unitary state ruled by an autocratic emperor, whose prerogatives were immensely greater than those of the Polish king. If "man lives his laws before he frames them,"[97] the situation had been reversed; the Statute had framed laws by which men lived less and less. A different social situation had developed (without magnates for example), prices imposed on the compensations for injuries were obsolete, borrowings from the legislation of "other Christian lands" that had been incorporated into the Statute were irrelevant to Ukrainian life in the Left Bank, and imperial orders emanating from Petersburg were not coordinated with the provisions of the Statute, without expressly annulling them. Last but not least, the original language of the Statute had become incomprehensible, and even Polish translations presented problems because, "with the passage of time, the study of Polish had become neglected."[98] In 1767, the Chernihiv nobles instructed their representative to the Legislative Commission, which was expected to draw up a new code of laws for the expanding Russian core, to state that Little Russians, "as the most important constitutent member of the Russian people [*Rossiiskii narod*]," wished to become incorporated into it under the authority of a single law" (*prisovokupleny telu k pervomu ego v soobshchestvo edinogo zakona*), while keeping the rights and privileges which had been recognized by Russian authorities since 1654, "in order to strengthen the mutual friendship and accord [*edinodushie*] between us and the Russian people."[99] This came very close to saying that the Statute had become obsolete, although it is worth noticing that the wish came from the northern half of the Hetmanate, where Polish and Lithuanian influence had never been strong.

Forty years earlier, in 1728, the Apostol Articles had called for a review of the civil and criminal legislation guiding the courts of the Hetmanate, and a committee was created consisting of eight members of the *starshyna*, three clerics, and two urban leaders, to whom a Russian was added in 1735. The committee, which does not seem to have begun to meet until 1734, would labour for a decade to produce a code of Hetmanate law under the name of "Laws by which the Little Russian people are tried" (*Prava, po kotorym suditsia malorossiiskii narod*).[100] It was a serious effort by competent people to achieve a synthesis between the Lithuanian Statute, the Magdeburg Law, and Ukrainian customary law, suggesting that such customary law had been used for the guidance of at least the lower (regimental) courts alongside the Statute, to which the higher courts probably resorted in order to maintain a certain uniformity in the settlement of similar categories of cases.

The proposed code, consisting of 531 articles (the Statute had 488) was sent to the Russian Senate in 1744, but was never confirmed, even though the Hetmanate was about to be restored. A new effort was made in 1761, when a Russian commission, created in 1754 to draw up a new code of laws, observed that the Statute was not carved in stone, and clearly stated that if it lacked provisions for the settlement of a given case, it was permissible to borrow from other "Christian" legislation – which in this context could only be Russian.The hetman was instructed to appoint a new committee with the task of purging the Statute of its inconsistencies and redundancies and sending the Senate a new version.[101] But nothing seems to have been done – Elizabeth died at the end of 1761, and the 1767 Commission made little progress in the work of codification.

There was a variety of reasons for the failure to codify Ukrainian law. The Russians had long been trying to bring some order in the increasing chaos of their own legislation, but to no avail, and the first Digest (*Svod Zakonov*) would not see the light of day until 1832. It was they who took the initiative in urging the authorities in the Hetmanate to bring up to date a basic law which was already over six generations old, and which had not successfully integrated into the Statute the "articles" granted to every new hetman as well as imperial legislation, of which it was not always clear what parts applied to Little Russia and what parts did not. In other words, the codification of Ukrainian law, to be politically acceptable, could not be divorced from that of Russian law, and since the latter made so little progress, the former could not be expected to reach completion. There was resistance on both sides as well. The very idea of codifying regional law, of particularizing the legal system of a given territory, was anathema to those who believed that the expanding core must remain a unitary state. The period between 1725 and 1762 may have been an exception in its acceptance of some diversity, but with the reign of Catherine II the pressure toward the restoration of unity became stronger than ever. There was also resistance on the part of the more conservative members of the *starshyna*, who feared that the changes would not be in their interest by depriving them of some of the privileges they derived from the Statute, which had been the expression of a social order dominated by magnates. Central and local politics combined to keep on hold the codification of both Russian and Ukrainian law.

The other legal system existing side by side with the Statute, and which complemented it as well, was the so-called Magdeburg Law. The charters that granted it to various towns did not spell out its contents, which had to be found in various handbooks, of which the most authoritative were those of Bartosz Groicki (*Porządek sądow*, 1566) and Pawel Szczerbic (*Speculum Saxonum*, 1581). These early handbooks were based on the Saxon Mirror (*Sachsenspiegel*), the most influential legal code of the German Middle Ages, which also influenced the law of the Livonian Knights. By the middle of the eighteenth century, when the knowledge of Polish was ebbing away in the Hetmanate, judges, lawyers, and agencies were drawing up their own handbooks in Ukrainian, and they probably added their own interpretations, which resulted in the creation of a composite Magdeburg Law that accommodated the customary law of the major towns, a process resembling that taking place with the Statute. A hodgepodge of legal norms must have given everyone what he wanted to find. The litigious spirit often ascribed to the Little Russians may not so much have been a national trait as the product of a chaotic condition in the substantive and procedural law.[102]

The Magdeburg Law was originally the law of the German settlers who were encouraged to immigrate into Polish-held territory and who sought a guarantee that they would be tried by their own laws and their own officers. Its jurisdiction was gradually extended to include the entire population of the town, even to outside traders and artisans who happened to reside in it at a given time. But Cossacks resented being tried by urban courts, because the ruling class of the territory could not agree to accept decisions made by its social inferiors, and the *starshyna* made it a point to interfere in urban affairs. Regimental courts assumed jurisdiction over townsmen, invoking both the Statute and the Magdeburg Law. A similar phenomenon was taking place in the Right Bank, where the creeping agrarianization of the region transformed towns into the private holdings of individual lords and stifled urban life. The continued existence of the Magdeburg Law was contingent upon the existence of a social order, but that social order was radically transformed by the local government reform and the municipal charter of 1785. The Law seems to have died a natural death. It was not formally abolished at the time, but when Emperor Paul restored the old institutions in December 1796, he made no mention of it. When a case dealing with a commercial dispute reached the Senate in 1824, the high court sent it back to the Poltava general court on the ground that the latter court had decided it in accordance with the Statute instead of the Magdeburg Law. But it was then discovered that no handbook had been available to guide the court's decision. Petersburg concluded that the law was no longer in use. Mikhail Speransky, who was in charge of the codification that resulted in the publication of the *Svod Zakonov*, agreed that the Magdeburg Law had been replaced in part by the Statute, in part by Russian legislation. The Madgeburg Law was formally abolished in 1831 and, in Kiev, in 1834.[103]

East of Little Russia, in the Kharkiv corridor, which had always been under the jurisdiction, not of the hetman, but of the Belgorod *voevoda*, the law of the Russian core prevailed, i.e, the Code (*Ulozhenie*) of 1649, amended and supplemented by an extensive body of legislation. The Code (in 967 articles) was drafted in the summer and fall of 1648, and printed in the spring of 1649. Such speed explains why it was not the product of extensive deliberation, but the product of a less than consistent combination of sources, such as the decisions of the individual *prikazy* (ministries), each for its own jurisdiction, the Duma, and the tsar himself. It left important gaps concerning the organization of the Muscovite core's government, its civil law was focused on landed property law for the benefit of the emerging ruling class, and it gave preeminence to criminal legislation.[104] This was understandable, since the five members of the commission had grown up during the Time of Trouble and were living through the uprising of 1648, which raised the threat of another civil war.

More important for our purpose was the importance of the Lithuanian Statute as a source of the *Ulozhenie*. It may well have been the single most important source. Some of its articles were reworked to take certain specific Russian considerations into account; others were taken over wholesale.[105] Such was the influence of the jurisprudence of the eastern marches of the Polish core over that of the Russian core expanding westward toward those same marches, at a time when the Polish Empire had reached the zenith of its power. One of the major features of the Statute had been the juridical recognition of serfdom as the foundation of the social order in the magnate-ruled Ukrainian lands. The *Ulozhenie*, which followed the Statute by sixty years, also recognized serfdom as the social foundation of the new Russia which had emerged from the crucible of the Time of Trouble. Serfdom was thus the poisoned gift of the Polish core to the Ukrainian lands, and the Russian law of May 1783, which some once considered as having introduced serfdom in the Left Bank, was in fact only the law by which men had lived or had aspired to live for a long time.

In this jumble of laws, gravitating around the Statute and the *Ulozhenie*, judges and administrative authorities, who often used the law for political purposes, had a choice when required to settle civil litigation or pronounce criminal sentences. One example will suffice. A case reached the desk of Governor General Rumiantsev concerning the punishment of an official in the Kiev administration. Rumiantsev found he had a choice between an article of the Statute, a Russian ukaze, and an ordinance of the city of Kiev, perhaps based on the Magdeburg Law, if not on customary law. He chose the latter because it called for a less severe punishment.[106] The Senate for its part did not always choose a law; it also created new law by interpreting existing law, although this usually required the ruler's approval.

In 1759, for example, the Senate took up a case brought by the widow of Brigadier General Vasilii Kapnist concerning the division of his property among his sons. Kapnist (who was killed in Prussia two years earlier) was a Greek who had entered Russian service in 1711, and later become a *sotnik* in the Izium regiment, a colonel of the Myrhorod regiment, and a brigadier general in the Sloboda regiments. He had been granted three villages in three different *sotni*, but his widow claimed that, although his properties were in Little Russia, they should not be divided in accordance with the Statute but with Russian law, because he was not a native of Little Russia.[107] The Senate agreed that since the Greek Kapnist had taken the oath of fidelity (*vechnoe poddanstvo*) to the Russian ruler, he and his heirs must be considered Great Russians, even if their properties were in Little Russia. The Senate thus asserted the preeminence of the personality over the territoriality of the law, and, in the event of a conflict, of the ethnic origin and service record of an individual over the territory where he had permanently resided. The law of the expanding core prevailed over that of the native inhabitants of a given territory.

Little Russia had been a relatively small territory, where Russian and Statute law, Magdeburg and customary law, coexisted in uneasy partnership, while Russian influence kept growing until the end of the eighteenth century, when the creation of a uniform court system tilted the balance in Russia's favour. The second and third partitions of 1793 and 1795 brought into the expanding core a Right Bank Ukraine, whose evolution had been profoundly shaped by the Polish core for two centuries. The creation of a uniform system of courts – even if the names were different – staffed with Polish noblemen (because so few Russians would ever move there) already evoked the possibility of an internal jurisprudential frontier with strong powers of resistance against the momentum of the expanding core bent on creating a one and indivisible Russia. Moreover, it turned out that the experience gained in Little Russia would be of little use. In western Podolia, approximately between the Zbruch and the Southern Buh west of Vynnytsia, and between the watershed of the upper Zbruch and the Dniester, annexed by Poland from Lithuania in 1454, Polish law was the prevailing law. In most of Volhynia, incorporated into the Polish core in 1569, the basic law was the Second Lithuanian Statute of 1566, also called the Volhynian Statute because the Volhynian nobility had exercised a dominant influence over its preparation, and the Statute had been amended and supplemented by subsequent Polish "constitutions."[108] If we overlook the Magdeburg Law and customary law, the Russians were faced with three major legal systems – two Lithuanian Statutes and Polish law – administered by a uniform system of courts.

Not only was such a situation confusing to the Senate's appellate departments, which had to reconcile the local laws and also the local with Russian law, but it also ran counter to the strong impulse toward administrative centralization during Alexander's reign, with the creation of the ministries and their regional authorities. Centralization and increasing militarization called for greater uniformity. There was more. Once it had been incorporated into the expanding Russian core, the Right Bank, as an age-long frontier between Poland and Russia, remained a subject of contention between the Polish core, which could not accept its loss, and the Russian core, which looked upon the resulting tensions as an existential threat to its unity and the law as the vehicle of litigious dissent. The Polish uprising of 1831 under Nicholas I, who showed little empathy for regional autonomy, resulted in the complete integration of the court system and the abolition of the "Lithuanian Statute" in 1840.[109] Not only the courts but also the law had become fully integrated into the expanding Russian core.

The Ethnographic Map

The Poles

Poles had been in the region since the days of Kievan Rus' and were found along its western boundaries – in Galicia, Volhynia, the Kholm region, and Podliashe. Later, during the reign of Casimir III "the Great"(1333–70), the Polish core embarked upon a systematic expansion to confiscate the estates of the Ukrainian nobility and grant them to Polish noblemen. New villages were built with relocated Ukrainian and Polish peasants, and towns were created by enticing German, Polish, and Armenian craftsmen with the privileges of the Magdeburg Law. The Polish eastward advance was followed, as befitted the policy of a core, with the Polonization of the Ukrainian local elites. A Roman Catholic archdiocese was created in Lviv in 1412, with diocesan sees in Volhynia and as far as Kiev. But the Polish advance stopped at the borders of Podolia, which was more exposed to Tatar raids. Poles and Russians alike were influenced by the same *Drang nach Süden*, a response to the challenge of the steppe nomad based on the Black Sea coast.

The growth of Polish influence accelerated after the Union of Lublin (1569), when Right and Left Bank Ukraine (less the Kharkiv corridor) – extending all the way to the Murava Trail which the Crimeans followed on their way to Belgorod, Orel, Tula, and the Oka – were incorporated into the expanding Polish core. The territory was divided into five provinces patterned after those of Poland, and large tracts of land were granted to Polish nobles, who built estates (latifundia, *folvarki*) to produce great quantities of grain for the booming European trade. There was much land but a sparse population: in 1572, the density of central Poland stood at 16 persons per square kilometre, that of Volhynia and Podolia at 6.4 persons, and the Kiev region had less than half this amount. The expansion into Left Bank Ukraine did not begin until about this time.

The *Drang nach Süden* received a new impetus during the reign of King Stefan Batory (1575–86), who decreed that the "wastelands" of Volhynia, Bratslav, and Podolia provinces be distributed in perpetuity to Polish magnates and nobles, and an additional impetus under Sigismund III Vasa (1587–1632), who raised the Polish Empire to the zenith of its power. The magnates settled their estates with serfs, used petty gentry and Jews as estate managers, and rented out taverns to the Jews who had followed them. In 1619, the Chernihiv region, occupied by the Poles in 1618, was parcelled out in reward for military service largely to settlers from central Poland, and in the 1630s, Lithuanian officers received holdings in the Novhorod-Siverskyi region further north. The magnates became the ruling elite of Ukraine – it was no coincidence that they were often called "kinglets." Largely independent of the royal power in Warsaw, yet playing an increasing role in the politics of the core, they consolidated their properties in ever larger latifundia, and induced peasants with promises they did not keep, such as twenty- to thirty-year exemptions from serfdom. Two magnates even became Polish kings – Michael Wiśnowiecki (1666–73) and Jan III Sobieski (1674–96). One of the largest landowners was Jeremiah Wiśnowiecki, who ruled over 38,000 households and 230,000 subjects. The petty nobility, despite its poverty and the downgrading of many of its members to the position of lackeys in the magnates' households, claimed equality with the magnates in accordance with an ideology which bound the entire *szlachta* together into one social corporation. They constituted the ruling class of Ukraine, which antagonized the Orthodox peasantry and Cossacks, and built up the resentment that exploded with the Khmelnytsky uprising of 1648.

The uprising was a disaster for Polish rule. The massacres of the Poles rivalled those of the Jews. Those who escaped were forced to flee the country, unless they managed to convince the Cossacks of their newly discovered support of their cause, and became integrated into the emerging Cossack elite. Following the truce of Andrusovo (1667) and the Eternal Peace of 1686, the Polish presence on the Left Bank was obliterated. But by the 1710s the Poles had regained full control of the Right Bank, which Ottoman and Cossack forces had thoroughly devastated. The magnates, pressed for cash, increased the corvée obligations of their serfs, who had been emancipated in the uprising but now fell again into servitude. The result was a series of *haidamak* uprisings directed against the new Polish rule in the 1730s, which culminated in the Koliivshchina rebellion of 1768. It caused the death of many Polish landlords. On the other hand, the fragility of Polish rule and the general insecurity brought about the creation of an extensive administrative system and private armies, which together built a political infrastructure with which the Polish ruling class exercised a tight control of the Ukrainian population.

But the Poles also built a lasting cultural universe which left a strong imprint in the region. It would successfully rival that of its eternal rival in the expanding Russian core. Polish life and culture were inseparable from Roman Catholicism with its advance formation, the Jesuit Order. The Order emphasized the education of the elites in order to bring about, if not conversion, at least Polonization. Some of the major Polish seventeenth-century writers lived in Ukraine, and the magnates built in the midst of the steppe fortified castles with large art collections, libraries, and archives. It has even been claimed that the Polish centres in Ukraine rivalled, and in some cases, even surpassed, their counterparts in central Poland.[110] Jesuit schools and Basilian colleges trained Poles and Ukrainians of noble birth; Piarist schools paid greater attention to the petty nobility. Basilian printing houses in Pochaev, and Dominican and Carmelite ones in Lutsk and Berdichev respectively, with their substantial libraries, transformed the estates of the magnates into political centres of domination and cultural centres of Polonization.

The partition of the Polish Empire, in which the expanding Russian core acquired the eastern marches of the retreating Polish core, created an entirely new situation. The separatist tendencies among the magnates facilitated, even encouraged, the Russian advance. Already during the Turkish wars of 1768–74 and 1786–92 the Russian army had been dependent on Polish grain from Right Bank Ukraine, which formed the natural hinterland of the battlefield along the lower Danube.[111] Prussian ambitions in northern Poland, seeking to cut off Poland from the Baltic coast and connect with East Prussia – this was achieved by the first partition of 1772 – interfered with Polish exports down the Vistula to Danzig, and Polish magnates in Right Bank Ukraine found a ready market in the Russian army operating west of the Dnieper. They also looked forward to the opening of Black Sea ports to ship grain across the sea to the western Caucasus and through the Straits to the Mediterranean. It was therefore no coincidence that the leaders of the pro-Russian policy of reorienting Polish trade toward the Black Sea, like Felix Potocki, Ksawery Branicki, and Seweryn Rzewuski, came from among the magnates. They and the Russians found a common interest, and the partitions gave them a place in the aristocratic elite of the expanding Russian core.

The Poles remained heavily concentrated in Right Bank Ukraine. It was estimated that in 1782 they numbered 243,300 there, with only 200 in Left Bank Ukraine, and 1,800 in New Russia. In 1833, 264,000 were found in the Right Bank, 2,000 in the Left Bank, and 9,600 in New Russia; in 1856, 297,100, 3,300, and 16,600 in the three regions respectively. This amounted to a small minority of 9.1 per cent of the 2.7 million Ukrainians in the Right Bank in 1782, and 7.2 per cent of the 4.1 million in 1856. By their very presence in the Right Bank, their long history as the ruling class of the territory, and the near-absence of Russians as late as 1850 (16,900), they controlled the police and the courts.[112] At the beginning of the nineteenth century, their control of the rural police gave them a stranglehold on communications between Russian military units in the area.[113] Serfdom became more oppressive for the greater benefit of the estate owners shipping their wheat to Odessa. Polish culture remained dominant, with Polish as the official language of education, the administration, and the courts. Right Bank Ukraine became the most industrially developed region of Ukraine until the mid-nineteenth century.

It seemed, at first glance, that the post-partition situation was perfectly adapted to the pursuit of a policy of superstratification. The Russians belonged to the higher military and administrative (and ecclesiastical) stratum of the ruling class. They intruded upon a highly structured society with its own network of new agencies introduced by the Russians themselves, but which the Poles controlled, and of old fortified castles and estates which guaranteed their domination of the dependent Ukrainian population. In order to maintain this rule and crush opposition to it, they needed Russian support, and the Russians needed them to consolidate their rule in the territory. The ruling elite, which had so shamelessly betrayed its own country, was easily integrated into the elite of the expanding core, and received positions at court, in the administration, and in the military. The economic interests of important landowners matched the strategic ambitions of the Russian elite.

But superstratification did not work in Right Bank Ukraine. Alone in what was becoming the Russian empire, and no longer merely the expanding Russian core, the local elites, even if their properties and churches were in the Russo-Polish frontier, were not men of the frontier but of a core. A core is distinguished from a frontier by its ability to radiate influence beyond its borders, to set up distinctive and durable institutions which can enforce their own laws without the interference of outsiders. It is capable of conquering, dominating, and transforming as well as leaving its imprint on other peoples. The people of a core can always return to their fundamental values in times of stress and find succour in their reassertion. Only one core was ever incorporated into the Russian core and empire – Poland. Polish civilization had been Russia's rival for dominance in western Eurasia, anchored as it was in the basin of the Dnieper and the Black Sea, while Russia's was anchored in the basin of the Volga and the Caspian Sea. The incorporation (in 1815–22) of much of the Polish empire (with the exception of the territories annexed by Prussia and Austria) into the Russian empire[114] was intended to reconcile the two peoples, but it only made matters worse by forcing a showdown that eventually would destroy Polish influence.

There was Catholicism embodying the beliefs and aspirations of the Polish people, much as Orthodoxy embodied those of the Russian people. Both were core religions and had excommunicated each other in 1054, creating a Manichean world in which, until the secularization of values in the modern age, one must not compromise with, but must prevail upon, the other. There was the old strategic competition for hegemony in western Eurasia, in which Poland must plant its flag on the Kremlin, as it did in 1610, or Russia plant its own on Warsaw's Belvedere, as it did in 1814. There was a sense of superiority over the other on both sides, and of foreboding as well, at the thought that Poland was a conduit for European influences that threatened the integrity of Russian values, and that Russia was the westernmost outpost of Oriental barbarism. And there was the split among the Polish *szlachta*. Most of the magnates were loyal to the Russian elite, but they had pursued a policy of social stratification which destroyed the old solidarity between them and the petty nobility. Many of the latter had been downgraded to the status of peasants, and compensated for their social abasement by becoming fervid supporters of an acute form of Polish nationalism. The ethnic factor, which had been muted under the rule of the magnates before the arrival of Romanticism, asserted itself against the transnational elite solidarity of the eighteenth century. A similar phenomenon was taking place in the Russian core, and ethnic antagonism raised its ugly head in the frontier, destroying all hopes of successful superstratification.

The situation was already serious before the Napoleonic invasion, when the creation of the Grand Duchy of Warsaw raised Polish hopes of reestablishing the Polish empire in its borders of 1772 – an act of war against the Russian core. Poles from the Grand Duchy were fomenting resistance to Russian rule, and the situation had become so serious by 1809 that the government drafted Poles detained at the border into the Siberian line battalions and confiscated their property. Two years later, General Petr Bagration (a Georgian!), the commander in chief of the army on the Danube, reported that the "leading people" in Volhynia and Podolia were not devoted to Russian interests, and that they were influential in Warsaw as well; he recommended that they be deported into the Russian interior before their influence could spread any further. The creation of the Polish Kingdom (*tsarstvo*) in 1815 – which joined the *tsarstva* of Kazan, Astrakhan, and Sibir in the nomenclature of the Russian emperor's titles – broke down the artificial walls created by the partitions between the Polish core and its Ukrainian marches. The activities of educators like Tadeusz Czacki were so openly anti-Russian[115] that one can only marvel at the suicidal proclivities of the middle and lower *szlachta*. By creating the Kremianets Lyceum in 1805, which became the leading centre of Polish education and culture, and linking Right Bank Ukraine with Lithuania in the Vilno educational region, the Russian government had shown forbearance on the assumption that a policy of superstratification could succeed, but in fact, it had been playing with fire.

The fire broke out in Warsaw in November 1830, following a rumour that Nicholas I was planning to despatch Polish troops to crush the July Revolution in France. The revolt escalated into an effort to restore a Polish state within the pre-partition borders, which pitted Poles not only against the Russians, but against the Prussians and the Austrians as well. It reached Right Bank Ukraine in the spring of 1831, when some Polish gentry formed armed detachments, which had no chance against Russian regulars. The Orthodox clergy and the Ukrainian peasantry were indifferent or hostile to the insurrection, and it was quickly put down. It was worse than a revolt of peasants. A political system resting on the enserfment of the population – 1.4 of the 1.8 million male peasants of the Right Bank in 1833, or 78 per cent, were privately held serfs, while many of the 383,000 state peasants had been the property of monasteries[116] – had to accept recurrent outbreaks of peasant discontent, and also took it for granted that they had to be mercilessly crushed. But the Polish uprising was a revolt within the ruling class of the territory and, by extension, a revolt within the imperial ruling class: it was high treason threatening to destabilize Russian rule in the region and confirmed the failure of the policy of superstratification.

The government of Nicholas I, who, unlike his predecessor and brother, Alexander I, had no sympathy for the Poles, inaugurated a policy of de-Polonization directed against the middle and lower gentry. The owners of the larger estates had understood that it was not in their interest to rock the boat at a time of economic prosperity; they escaped, on the whole, the wrath of the government. But thousands of participants were exiled to the Kuban and Siberia, and their properties were confiscated. Their serfs became state peasants, soon to become the wards of a new Ministry of State Domains created in 1837. The Kremianets Lyceum was closed, and its library was transferred to the newly created Kiev University, whose major purpose was the de-Polonization and the Russification of Right Bank Ukraine.

The Poles responded by forming conspiratorial societies to prepare for a new insurrection, which would break out in 1863. But the interests of the magnates continued to match those of the Russians, and not only in economic affairs. Both had an interest in purging the ranks of the *szlachta* by expelling those who had no land or peasants, and who could only justify their holding a patent of nobility by referring to old documents which were now considered irrelevant or fraudulent. The *szlachta* had always been larger than the Russian nobility. The purge, the product of an alliance between Russian and Polish conservatives, reduced the share of the nobility in Right Bank Ukraine from 7.8 to 3 per cent between 1795 and 1858, while on the Left Bank it remained steady at 1.2 per cent between those two dates.[117] It created a new and more homogenous social corporation with which a policy of superstratification could perhaps work, and without which the Russians would have been forced to rule by martial law. But the conflict between the intransigence and the pride of two core nobilities and the need to accept the inevitable would continue to maintain an unstable situation serving the interest of neither side.

The Jews

We find in the southern theatre, as we do everywhere else, the coexistence of two principles: that of the territoriality and that of the personality of the law. The former incorporated the latter in order to create a harmonious system that mitigated conflict and reconciled differences. Such coexistence also existed in the southern theatre. The expanding Russian core, forming a community of believers, in which the acceptance of Orthodoxy created supra-ethnic "Russians," had to cope with religious communities which would never convert to the core religion, and with other communities which, even if they were

Christian and Orthodox, could never be integrated into the Russian social order and would remain fundamentally alien. The acceptance of the principle of the personality of the law did not imply the abandonment of the supremacy of the territorial law of the expanding core; it only created exceptions which confirmed the rule, and which were expected (vainly as it would turn out) to disappear in the distant future. Among these communities in the southern theatre, the Jews were the most important.

They had long been found on the northern coast of the Black Sea, from which they moved inland even before Right Bank Ukraine was incorporated into the Grand Duchy of Lithuania in the fourteenth century, but the great migration came later. While the Polish magnates and *szlachta* followed the Ukrainian peasantry who were seeking to escape the progress of serfdom and fleeing eastward toward and beyond the Dnieper, the Jews followed the magnates as stewards on the estates sprouting in the steppe, as tax farmers who collected tolls, managed water mills and taverns, and, in general, became the intermediaries between the landlords and the peasantry. Tax farming was the bane of the entire system: while it guaranteed the lords a steady revenue from profitable sources, it also gave the tax farmer a licence to maximize his profit by collecting more than was economically and even morally acceptable. The lords also leased some properties, and as a result, the Jews acquired administrative and judicial authority over the peasantry, and over the artisans in the small towns and in the villages, where most of them lived. However, they remained outside those communities and did not pay the communal taxes or perform the communal services required of these communities. The solidarity of the Jews in trade gave them a strong competitive advantage at the local fairs and the small-town markets, even though many Jews remained desperately poor. Added to the religious antagonism between Judaism and Orthodoxy, this situation created intense resentment, which turned the Jews into scapegoats at times of social unrest.[118]

Such was the case at the time of the Khmelnytsky uprising, when Poles, Catholics, and Jews became the enemy to be destroyed at any cost. The warrior state that emerged in the Hetmanate long retained a memory of the passions that had done so much harm during the uprising, even if it would remain ambivalent about the Jews, as it recognized their important contribution to the economic life of the territory.[119] In the expanding core, however, there was no such ambivalence. Religious intolerance, on the rise since the reign of Ivan IV, continued unabated throughout much of the seventeenth century, even though it was not always specifically directed against the Jews but against all the non-Orthodox, including Muslims. It abated somewhat under Peter because the acceptance of foreigners became acceptable and the Church was harshly treated, but it returned after the tsar's death. In April 1727, perhaps at the suggestion of Feofan Prokopovych,[120] the Ukrainian cleric who had done so well in the hierarchy of the core's Orthodox Church, the Jews living in the Hetmanate and "other Russian towns" were ordered expelled and forbidden to take out their gold ducats and silver coins, which had to be exchanged for Russian copper coins.[121] But in August 1734, Jewish traders were allowed to come to the Ukrainian fairs to engage in retail trade.[122] During the Russo-Turkish war of 1735–9, the ambivalence of the Hetmanate authorities became very noticeable. It turned out that Jews had remained in the territory, and that Cossacks had even hired Jews to run taverns and had leased other property to them. To expel them in wartime ran the risk of the Jews taking out sensitive information to the Tatars and Turks. Nevertheless, Petersburg insisted in July 1740 that they must be expelled.[123] Elizabeth too, who, like Anna Ivanovna, pursued a strongly anti-Islamic policy in the eastern theatre, gave her orders a religious colouration. In December 1742, she upheld her mother's order of April 1727 and called the Jews "the haters of Christ the Saviour." In December 1743, she rejected the request of the Cossack chancery to let the Jews at least come to trade, if not to live, with the famous statement that from the enemies of Christ she did not intend to make a profit.[124] Catherine II's more tolerant policy allowed the Jews to reside in the three new provinces of Kiev, Chernihiv, and Novhorod-Siverskyi in 1794,[125] but they remained excluded from the Kharkiv corridor, which had never been part of the Hetmanate, and the exclusion policy remained in force in Russia proper. The partitions of Poland brought large numbers of Jews into the expanding core and required the elaboration of a uniform policy for the Jews in general.

They were unequally distributed. In Left Bank Ukraine there were none in 1762, only 35 in 1782, but 10,500 in 1795, although none in Kharkiv province. They made up 0.3 per cent of the total population. By 1833, they numbered 37,500 and in 1856, 63,000 or 1.3 per cent of the total population. The bulk of the Jewish population was concentrated in Right Bank Ukraine. In 1782 they numbered approximately 164,500, but 123,500 (3.4 per cent) in 1795 – the difference probably due to concealment from the census takers and migration to New Russia. Even if the statistics raise questions about their accuracy, the Jewish population had more than doubled to 489,700 (8.5 per cent of the population) in 1833, including the Jews of Bessarabia, annexed in 1812. By 1856, there were more than half a million Jews in the region (601,500) out of a population of 2,039,400 Jews in "Russia," against 576,200 in 1795. In New Russia, in which the Jews were allowed to settle in 1785, there were already 12,200 in 1782, 24,300 in 1795 (1.5 per cent of the population), 106,300 in 1833, and 194,700 in 1856. They had already been allowed to settle in the old New Russian province in 1769, and Jews already lived in the Crimea. Most settled in Kherson county, which included the new town of Odessa, where the grain trade attracted large numbers of merchants, and they did not begin to move into Ekaterynoslav province until 1841.[126]

The territorial distribution of the Jews helps us place the so-called Pale of Settlement into some perspective.[127] The Russian authorities, accustomed for centuries to dealing with people of the steppe, had long sought to bind them to a definite territory, in very much the same way as it was the essence of serfdom to bind the peasantry to a definite location and the townsmen to a definite town, save for the merchants registered in the guilds, who were not required to pay the capitation and the quitrent, though even they had to obtain passports to travel on business. The assimilationist policy of the Catherinian government sought to incorporate the Jews into the general categories of merchants (*kuptsy*) and townsmen (*meshchane*), and it followed that the Jews who registered into these categories would be subjected to the same restrictions. The government would often resort to brutal measures of coercion to remove them from the countryside, where many of them had settled. It simply confined the Jews to the territory which they already occupied; from the administrative point of view, such a policy was not fundamentally different from that pursued toward the Bashkirs, Kalmyks, and Kazakhs. It is not far-fetched to see Russia's creation of the Pale as part of a general policy pursued by the expanding core toward its subjects in the steppe. Eventually, the Pale would include fifteen provinces, of which nine were in the southern theatre (with three in Belorussia and three in Lithuania).[128] Within that well-defined territory, the law of the expanding core, which would subsequently be uniformly applied, would have to accept the personality of the law as an exception enforced by the harsh reality that the bulk of the Jewish population could neither be converted nor assimilated.

The Jews were organized into communities which elected governing bodies called *kahals*. They were first created in the Polish Empire as local government organs in 1495 with jurisdiction over religious affairs, the settlement of disputes, the creation of schools, and the support of the poor and the old, but their primary justification was to assume collective responsibility for the payment of taxes on behalf of each community. The *kahals* had a central agency called the Council of the Four Lands (Great and Little Poland, Galicia, and Volhynia), which met alternately in Jarosław and Lublin to apportion the responsibility for taxes and to decide matters of concern to the Jewish community.[129] It was abolished in 1764. Each *kahal* had from eight to thirty-five members depending on the size of the community, and from three to five "honorary members," including the rabbi, who served as judges and treasurers and carried out various other functions.

The *kahal* system had functioned well until the disasters of the mid-seventeenth century followed by the *haidamak* revolts of the eighteenth century, which culminated in the Uman catastrophe of 1768, when Jews and others were massacred in large numbers. The impoverishment of the Jewish communities placed severe strains on the *kahals*' ability to pay taxes to the landlords and the government for which they were collectively responsible. It created dissensions between the Jews living in the towns and those living in the countryside, upon whom the *kahals* sought to transfer most of the tax burden, as well as between the Jewish masses and the *kahal* leaders, who gradually became an oligarchy more concerned with keeping good relations with the government than with caring for the needs of the masses. When Right Bank Ukraine was incorporated into the expanding core, the *kahals* became unpopular, and pressure was mounting to abolish them.[130]

For the Russian government, it was tempting to follow the wishes of the masses and to proceed to the Jews' immediate integration into the social structure of the expanding core. On the recommendation of Governor General Tutolmin, the Jews were allowed to register in the category of merchants or townsmen, or had to leave the country. Those who remained, however, would have to pay twice the amount charged to their peers – a "penalty" not unlike that visited upon the Old Believers – and it remained in force until 1807. The *kahal* was not abolished, but its jurisdiction was restricted to religious affairs, a policy similar to that followed toward the Muslims in the eastern theatre. And Jews were allowed to elect and be elected to positions in the management of the towns.[131]

In different circumstances, the *kahal* would have found its place in the policy of superstratification which we have encountered elsewhere, including the Hetmanate, and which the Russians sought to replicate in the Right Bank as well. There, however, the Polish nobility and the Jewish leaders were unwilling to play the game, because it was not in their interest. Fostering integration into the expanding core would displace each group's position as the ruling stratum in its territory, not strengthen it. The government was left with a policy which neither displaced the leading group nor integrated it. Perhaps that is what Ivan Aksakov, sent by the interior ministry to investigate conditions in the southern theatre in the 1840s, meant when he wrote that Russia's policy toward the Jews was in total chaos.[132]

The statute of December 1804[133] was the first to address the "Jewish question" as a whole, and it emphasized integration. Jews were to register into one of the four social categories, merchants, townsmen, "manufacturers" (*fabrikanty*) and artisans, and free peasants, but could leave one to enter another. Landlords could not enserf Jews settled on their land and had no judicial authority over them. Jews were tried in the ordinary courts in civil and criminal cases, but no mention was made of violations of Jewish law, which it must be assumed remained under the jurisdiction of the rabbi. The *kahal* remained responsible for the collection of state taxes without arrears; it was elected for three years with the confirmation of the provincial board chaired by the governor. All Jewish children had to be taught in Russian schools (unless their parents were willing to pay a tax to support their own schools) and must learn Russian, Polish, or German: all public documents had to be written in one of these three languages. Jews, as free settlers, were allowed to buy, sell, and mortgage lands in the three provinces of the Right Bank and the three of New Russia, but not in the former Hetmanate (Chernihiv and Poltava provinces), or in Astrakhan and the northern Caucasus, where they were now allowed to settle (until the permission was rescinded in 1835). They were forbidden to sell spirits except in provincial capitals and county seats, and to keep taverns and lease property from landlords.

Despite the bare reference to the *kahal* as a tax-collecting agency, the government continued to rely on it to keep an internal census of the Jewish population, to bind the poor Jews to communities so that they would not become vagrants – always an object of concern to the Russian authorities – and even to select recruits for military service, to which the Jews became subjected beginning in 1827. But the old conflict between the oligarchy that ran the *kahals* and the old and destitute Jews, who had no labour to contribute to the community, became acute in the wake of the Napoleonic wars and the troop movements in Right Bank Ukraine. In Podolia the issue came to a head when the *kahal* refused to accept them, register them as its own, and pay their taxes. The provincial *kahal* was forced to reach a compromise with the Treasury Chamber and agree to take in the poor and the old who had relatives in the community, while the others would be distributed among the other communities in accordance with their size. The enforced registration of all the Jews in the communities, with their collective responsibility to pay the taxes of those who could not pay, was extended to the entire Pale in February 1819.[134] But the problem persisted in view of the continued resistance of the *kahals* to accept newcomers. As a sop to them, the government decided in July 1824 that those Jews who found no community to accept them would be turned into workers (*rabochie liudi*) in the county seats, there to be taxed like ordinary townsmen.[135]

The government of Alexander I was relatively favourable to the Jews, and much of the reign's legislation often originated in local politics, in which religious tensions between the Jews, the Catholics, and the Orthodox combined to poison the atmosphere. To this was added the issue of the sale of spirits, which, in an agrarian economy, was often the major, if not the only, source of cash, and that of the contraband trade along the Polish and Austrian border. Aksakov painted a vivid picture of the beneficial influence of the Jews at the Ukrainian fairs, but also noted that the Jewish traders sold below cost and put the local traders out of business, even though, to his satisfaction, they were also the major buyers of Russian manufactured goods.[136] But the reign of Nicholas I resembled that of Elizabeth in its virulent anti-Semitism. The emperor was also determined to integrate the Jews into the social fabric of the core, especially after the Polish rebellion of 1831, which aroused Russian nationalism and lumped Jews, Poles, and Uniates into the common pool of enemies of the policy of centralization aiming to create a one and indivisible Russia.[137]

The incarnation of the Nicholaevan policy was the statute of April 1835,[138] which further restricted the movement of the Jews and shrank the Pale of Settlement, but retained the *kahal* organization as it existed at the end of Alexander I's reign: a tax-collecting, welfare, and recruiting agency. It devoted much greater attention than the 1804 Statute to the role of the rabbi and the application of Jewish law. But the days of the *kahal* were numbered. It was finally abolished in April 1844, five years after the closing of the Uniate Church and four years after the abolition of the Lithuanian Statute. Jewish affairs were placed under the jurisdiction of the municipal authorities accountable to the Interior Ministry. The policy of integration had reached its logical conclusion.[139]

The Jews of the Crimea, called Karaites, deserve special mention. Their origin was obscure, and as late as the 1840s, the Interior Ministry still distinguished the Jews of the southern theatre by religion and ethnic origin. The Karaites, unlike the Rabbinites (or Talmudists), were not of Semitic but of Turkish stock, descendants of the Khazars, who had once set up a khanate in the region encompassing much of southern Ukraine, the Don Territory, and the northern Caucasus to the Caspian Sea. Judaism became its state religion at the beginning of the ninth century. Aksakov noted that many of their customs were not Jewish: their women lived in seclusion, their clothing was fully oriental, they spoke a Turkic language.[140] Their numbers were small: perhaps five thousand in "Russia" (there was another community in Lithuania) in the 1870s, with another one thousand in Galicia, Constantinople, and Egypt. They were, on the whole, well-off traders.[141]

The Russians had distinguished them from the Rabbinites as far back as 1795, when Governor General Zubov won from the government an exemption from the double tax imposed on the other Jews. They were placed in the same fiscal category as merchants and townsmen, allowed to dispose of their real property in accordance with Jewish law, but in other civil and in criminal matters they were tried in accordance with the general laws of the Russian core.[142] In 1843 and again in 1850, foreign Karaites were told to follow the same rules as other foreigners if they wished to become Russian subjects, and in 1863, they were officially recognized as a distinct religious group and exempted from the laws that applied to Jews.[143]

In fact, the statute of March 1837 had already recognized them as a separate religious group, after the Karaites themselves petitioned the government to give them some of the same rights enjoyed by the Muslim community.[144] The Karaites of the Crimea and Odessa were placed under a *gakham* living in Evpatoria and elected by the various communities. The results of the election were sent to the governor, who submitted two candidates to the interior ministry through the office of the governor general of New Russia. He was confirmed in office by the Senate. Each synagogue had two *gazzans*; those living in the Evpatoria synagogue formed, with the *gakham*, a Karaite Ecclesiastical Board. They took the oath of office in Russian, with a translation in Hebrew and Tatar, and had to be judged politically reliable. The board's jurisdiction was strictly religious, but petitioners were allowed to appeal its decisions to the governor general and the interior minister. The similarities with the Muslim boards in Orenburg and the Crimea are obvious. In all three cases, Muslims and Karaites were being integrated in civil litigation and criminal affairs with the other subjects of the expanding core, under the overall supervision, as was the case with the Russian population, of the interior ministry.

The Tatars

The Tatars represented the third of the ethnic minorities which played a major role in the history of the southern theatre. The Poles had been the ruling class of Right Bank Ukraine since the sixteenth century, and remained in that position after the annexation of the territory. The Jews had always been among the major actors in its economic life. The Tatars, who had struck terror in the entire region for nearly three centuries, became, after the incorporation of the peninsula in 1783, largely confined to its southern part, or fled into the Ottoman Empire to escape retribution. Of all the nationalities that were being absorbed into the expanding Russian core, none aroused more hatred, not so much on the part of the government as among the Slavic settlers, nobles and peasants alike, whose ancestors had suffered from plundering Tatar raids. These raids, in search of human booty, had systematically burned villages, towns, and churches and blocked the progress of settlement in the steppe.

It is true that the economy of the Crimean khanate was not sufficient to provide enough resources for a people which occupied a special place among the other vassals of the sultan by the fact that its dynasty was Gingissid and that booty was needed.[145] Slaves were sold on the Kefe market and sent on to fill the harems, to serve as janissaries, and to become civil officials. Slaves did not come from Ukraine and southern Russia alone, but also from western Georgia, which had to pay a tribute in human beings until the end of the eighteenth century. They were the major staple of the Black Sea trade, and the khanate derived a substantial share of its revenue from their sale. Each raid yielded anywhere from ten thousand to sixty thousand captives,[146] and much else besides; the booty was distributed among the raiders, and the khan took his share. The legacy of this hatred must be kept in mind when deploring the burning of Bakhchysaray in 1736, the systematic destruction of Muslim architecture on the orders of Governor Vasilii Kakhovsky (of Polish ancestry, 1797–1801) and Governor Alexander Kaznacheev (1829–37). Elena Druzhinina had a point when she wrote that Kakhovsky was no better than his Mongol and Tatar predecessors,[147] but it can also be said that the Crimean Tatars were being paid in the same coin.

Large-scale emigration, some of it encouraged by the Russians, had a deleterious effect on the size of the Tatar population. The fact that it began in the early 1760s adds some justification to the contention that Russian foreign policy was already shifting from a focus on the western theatre to one on the Black Sea basin.[148] In 1762, there were about 275,000 Tatars (both sexes) in New Russia, but only 125,000 in 1782 on the eve of the annexation. The emigration may have been caused by a fear of Russian invasion as well as by the migration of the Nogai Tatars to the lower Don and Kuban region. Despite another wave of emigration after 1783, they still numbered 166,000 in 1795 and 283,000 in 1833, 320,000 in 1849, but 296,000 in 1856, right after the Crimean War of 1854–6 and before the mass emigration of 1860–2. By 1862, there were fewer Tatars than in 1783 – maybe as few as 85,000. Nevertheless, they remained highly concentrated in the peninsula, where Slavic immigration may have encountered an ethnic wall blocking interpenetration between Slavs and Tatars for some two generations. In 1783 the Tatar share of the population was 83 per cent, but it had dropped to 54 per cent by 1833. From then on, the Russian and Ukrainian population would quickly become a majority, and by 1897 the Tatar share was down to 15 per cent.[149] This proud – and destructive – people, the last remnant of the Kipchak khanate, had been swamped into Slavic settlements, much as other peoples in the eastern theatre were being integrated into the expanding Russian core.

The Crimean Tatars were a mixed lot, and the Russians distinguished between those of the interior (*stepnye*) and those living on the coast (*pribrezhnye*), a conglomerate of Kipchaks, Khazars, and Seldjuks who had intermarried over the centuries with Greeks, Armenians, and Genoese, not to mention the slaves they had acquired. Those of the interior were ethnically more homogenous, known for their self-esteem, their honesty and cleanliness, and their hard-working habits. They lived in houses, cultivated grain, and raised cattle. They even paid taxes to the khan's government, which earned them the contempt of the Nogais, who were pure nomads, a contempt reciprocated by the more civilized Crimeans.[150]

The khans were Gingissids from among the Girei family, but, like that of the steppe nomads in general, their government was not autocratic. They were elected by the clan leaders called beys, who participated in a government which operated by consensus. The backbone of the clans' organization consisted of *murzy* (nobles), who were of two types: the descendants of the old conquerors of the Crimea, and those who had been raised to that status when their ancestors reached high positions. Each clan had a territorial base. The Sirin (Shirin) clan, the largest, lived between Karasubazar and Kerch; the Batins in Karasubazar (they would later leave the country); and the Argin clan, the second largest, between Karasubazar and Akmecet (Simferopol). These three clans constituted the aristocratic core of the Crimean nobility, and their beys were called the Karaci beys, whose collective power was greater than that of the khan.[151] Two other clans were based near Bakhchysaray, the khan's capital, and in the basin of the Salgir River, known for its orchards, north of Karasubazar. Their base was thus in the elevated woodland zone of the peninsula, and in the winter and spring, they sent their herds down into the grassy steppe north of the Salgir River in the western part of the peninsula. More clans, but of lesser importance, were scattered between Karasubazar and the river.

In theory, the *murzy* held their lands as grants from the beys – they were a kind of service nobility. In fact, with the passage of time, these grants had become hereditary possessions. Some even held properties as fiefs from the sultan, who sought to transform the *murzy* into the social base of Ottoman power on the peninsula. Such a policy would undermine the power of the clan leaders, who wanted to retain their control of the politics of the peninsula and did not shrink from interfering in the politics of Constantinople itself.[152] The *murzy*'s natural allies were the clerical establishment of mullas, headed by the *mufti*, elected by the clergy, but accountable to the khan and eventually to the sultan, as the caliph of Sunni Islam. Paradoxically, and not unlike the Jewish *kahal*, the *mufti*'s office was neither judicial nor theological, but financial. It controlled the *vakif* lands (owned by religious institutions), which made up almost 30 per cent of the peninsula's productive land.[153] The *murzy* and clergy combined were the largest group of landowners. Among them was also another influential group, that of the *chelebi*, the descendants of *muftis* and important clerical leaders. Such was the society with which the Russians would have to deal.

The khan was replaced by the governor general of New Russia, who resided in Kherson, with his deputy, the governor of "Tavrida" in Simferopol. Prominent members of the elite, which now included Ukrainians, were given extensive properties in the most attractive parts of the peninsula, which happened to be where the great clans resided, although the lands came mostly from the properties of the Girei house. The old animosities remained close to the surface, especially after the marshal of the provincial nobility, who was invariably a Russian, became, in accordance with the Charter of 1785, its highest representative. The clan leaders were left with the choice of emigrating to Turkey, accepting their shrunken role under Russian rule, or entering the officer corps with the possibility of joining the imperial elite. Even before the annexation, Potemkin had secured the approval of the empress to appoint the khan captain of the Preobrazhensky regiment of the Guard, of which the ruler was the colonel.[154] The most successful career was that of Lt.-Gen. Alexander Rudzevich, the son of a former Tatar official (Iakup Aga), who had joined the civil administration of the Crimea in the 1780s: he became chief of staff of the Second Army (1815–19) stationed in Podolia facing the Ottoman Empire on the Danube.[155] The general was an exception, however; the days when Turco-Mongol princes had entered the Russian elite and were given high positions had long been over. The centre of gravity of the expanding Russian core had been shifting westwards, and as the core became an empire of largely Christian peoples in the nineteenth century, they had more than enough candidates than did the "backward" Muslim peoples, which remained associated in the Russian mind with devastating raids and plunder.

However, Russian policy was at first conciliatory. Catherine's commanding officer in the Crimea, General Igelstrom, a Baltic German who would later pursue a similar policy in the Orenburg Territory, believed that Russian rule would not succeed until it managed to gain the allegiance of the Tatar elite. While the military authorities must remain Russian, the civil administration would be staffed with Tatars, and the *murzy* would become the new nobility of the peninsula and elect and be elected to local posts under the overall authority of the civil governor. Local agencies would register the *murzy* who met the criteria established by the Charter of 1785. They would become integrated into the nobility of the expanding core.[156] How successful the policy was is hard to say. In 1782, when there were hardly any Russians in the peninsula, the noble population was estimated at 952 males. By 1795, it had reached 1,857 males, most of whom were still Tatars. By 1834, it had reached 3,458 males, and then became stable: they numbered 3,491 in 1850.[157]

The reasoning behind Russian policy was made clear in the ukaze of November 1794. It stated that the Crimea had become upon its annexation a province like any other in the expanding core, but that those who owned real property would retain their right to it, even if they were not allowed to do so by the general laws of the core, such as clergy, merchants, and simple Tatars. It was hoped, however, that such properties would gradually pass into the hands of those who had earned noble status in the service, and would then be governed by the general laws. There could be no clearer statement of a unitary policy: Tatars, and especially *murzy*, were invited to become integrated into the society of the expanding core if they wanted to retain their property.[158] It was among the clergy that the Russians found their greatest support – as they had in Orthodox Ukraine. The situation was rather paradoxical in view of the age-long antagonism between Orthodoxy and Islam, but the clergy found its interest in supporting Russian rule. The *mufti* remained the general manager of the *vakif* lands and was given a salary of two thousand roubles. The lower clergy was also put on the government's payroll. In return, they were expected to win over the common people to accept the rule of the infidel.

Serfdom was expressly forbidden in the Crimea, as any attempt to introduce it among a people used to free movement across the steppes would have created an explosive situation. The statute of September 1827[159] made this clear. Tatars were a free people who contracted out their labour on privately held lands and retained their freedom to move from one landowner to another. Landowners had no judicial authority over their Tatar workers. However, Tatars constituted a separate category of state peasants, and their freedom to sell their real property was restricted if the local financial authority and the finance ministry had doubts about the legality of their claims; but they were free to dispose of property acquired separately after the ukaze of November 1794.

The statute of 1827 was followed by that of December 1831,[160] which reorganized the Muslim Ecclesiastical Board created in 1794, but which does not seem to have been very active. Its jurisdiction was extended to include the western provinces, especially Lithuania, where a Muslim population had lived since the fourteenth century. It was subordinated to the governor of the Crimea, and complaints against its decisions were sent through his office to the Main Administration of Foreign Faiths of the interior ministry, from which substantial issues were referred to the Senate and the emperor himself. It consisted of the *mufti*, the *kadi-asker*, and the *kadis* of Simferopol, Feodosiia, Evpatoria, Perekop, and Nogaisk counties. These five *kadis* tried cases in accordance with Muslim religious law. The *mufti* was elected by an assembly consisting of the higher Muslim clergy of the Crimea and the senior members of the parish clergy; the provincial marshal of the nobility; the *murzy* of the entire province; and the heads of each Muslim canton (*volost*). From the list of those who received the largest number of votes, the governor selected three candidates, and the emperor appointed the *mufti* and the *kadi-asker* from among them. The county *kadis* were elected in similar fashion and were appointed by the Senate. Removal from office took place, as a rule, with the approval of the appointing authority. In the Crimea and the western provinces, the Board had jurisdiction over the mosques and their schools, the *vakif* lands, litigation over private property arising from the interpretation of wills, and the division of property among heirs in accordance with Muslim law. It also had jurisdiction over family law, including marriage and divorce, and parent-child relationships, although this was not specifically stated. All other matters, civil and criminal, came under the jurisdiction of the ordinary courts.

A policy of integration, coupled with one of superstratification, did not and could not succeed in the Crimea. Despite the existence of powerful clans, Crimean society – a community of warriors and pirates of the steppe – was not truly stratified. The beys forming the elite of that society could not find a common interest with the new Russian super-stratum – they lost much of their power and could not compensate for their loss by gaining greater authority over their own people incorporated into the great mass of state peasants, upon whom the Russians exercised direct rule. The annexation of the Crimea destroyed these Tatars' way of life, and to create a new one within the alien society of the Russian intruder was more than could be expected of them. And the Russians did not really want them to stay. Elsewhere, and certainly in the eastern theatre, they lived among the natives and reached an accommodation based on a policy of superstratification. In the Crimea, the Tatars ended up by living among the Russians and Ukrainians, and were made to feel like aliens in their own land, always a potential fifth column for the hated Turks. The natural consequence was emigration, a return to the land of the Turks, with whom, once upon a time, they had shared a common homeland in the Eurasian steppe. The orchards and vineyards and spectacular scenery of the peninsula became the land of villas and palaces reserved for the elite, including the governor general and the emperor himself.

There remains to briefly discuss the Nogai Tatars, who roamed on the mainland between the Danube and the Kalmius, the western boundary of the Don Territory. They were named after a prominent military leader of the Kipchak khanate who had died in 1300. They were first found in the northern part of the Kazakh steppe, but in the sixteenth century, they split into two hordes, the Great Horde, which settled in the lower Volga region, and the Small Horde, which migrated into the mainland steppe of the Crimean khanate, where they became nominal vassals of the khan and the sultan. The Great Horde was expelled by the Kalmyks in the 1630s and reunited with the Small Horde. Then they divided into four smaller hordes, each headed by a khan. They made up about 40 per cent of the khanate's population.[161]

The Budzhak (Belgorod) Horde settled in the lowland of Bessarabia (Budzhak) between the Dniester and the lower Danube. They lived in large settlements, and their way of life resembled that of the Crimean Tatars. The Yedisan Horde, the largest, roamed between the Dniester and the Dnieper, on both sides of the Southern Buh. They raised cattle and engaged in plunder. Across the Dnieper was the Yedickul Horde, which also combined a pastoral economy with plunder, and was constantly at odds with the Zaporozhian Cossacks over fishing grounds and the share of booty. The Jamboyluk Horde, the smallest, roamed close to the coast from the estuary of the Dnieper to the Berda River. All four hordes occupied a zone in the Russo-Turkish frontier, in which the peninsula constituted a second frontier, the Zaporozhian and Little Russian Cossacks and third and a fourth between the Russian core and Anatolia.

The Porte entrusted the government of the hordes to the Crimean khan, who appointed representatives called *seraskers*, who were, however, unsuccessful in gaining the allegiance of the nomads. They took part in the politics of the Girei family, even supporting the election of a khan opposed by the Porte. They were not a particularly warlike people, but they were major participants in the raids into Ukraine and the Russian core, while at the same time being receptive to Russian offers to change their allegiance.[162] Figures for the sizes of the hordes are not reliable. It was estimated that, at the beginning of the eighteenth century, the Yedisan Horde consisted of 4,655 males, the Jamboyluk Horde of 1,922 males (which would make it the second largest), and the Yedickul of 1,188 males. The Budzhak Horde was still in Ottoman-held territory. It crossed the

Dniester to the Russian side in 1807, with a population of 6,404 (both sexes). Nevertheless, these figures give an approximate idea of their respective size.[163]

The Treaty of Kuchuk Kainardji of July 1774 created a radically new situation. In 1770, the Yedisan Horde had already signed a treaty of friendship with the Russians, but it did not help them. The Nogais, as a people, were deported to the Kuban steppe between the Don and Kuban Rivers. Before the annexation of the Crimea in 1783, in anticipation of disturbances following the abolition of the khanate, Potemkin decided to deport the hordes farther east, between the Ural and Volga Rivers, where they had once roamed before they migrated into the Crimean steppe. The operation was entrusted to Alexander Suvorov, the commander of the Caucasian Line, and Alexei Ilovaisky, the *otaman* of the Don Cossacks, who had always hated the Nogais. The encounter of June 1783 on the Eia River proved deadly, and many Nogais perished.[164]

Those who survived were allowed to settle in the Kuban valley. Of the others who had managed to remain in the steppe or returned to the Kuban, some 9,422 males were given 50,000 desiatins (1.3 million acres) of land between the Molochnye Vody and Berda Rivers (most of it soon grabbed by the Don Cossacks and the Mennonite colonists) and became known as the Melitopol Nogais.[165] Those who remained in the northern Caucasus were distributed among reservations (*pristavstva*) stretching from the Kuban to the Caspian coast, where they numbered 64,232 of both sexes in 1838. Those who roamed between the Terek and the Kuma Rivers were called the Black (Kara) Nogais, described by John Baddeley in 1908 as "strictly religious [Sunnis], hospitable, thievish, dirty, not over brave, and miserably poor."[166] They had been relegated to the outer fringes of the civilized world.

Chapter Six

Unitary State or Empire? 1796–1855

Regional Integration

Governors General and Ministerial Regions

The local government reforms of the 1780s, which established a uniform provincial administration across the entire expanding core, might also have laid the foundation of a federal system, if circumstances had been more propitious. The institution of governor general, even if it never was properly worked out, had the potential of becoming the major structural element of a regional administration – meaning supra-provincial administration – between the centre and the provincial capitals. This was especially true in the core's outlying territories, where regions easily meshed with the existing "countries" (as they were called from time to time), or ethnic communities occupying relatively well-defined areas. One can certainly claim that Rumiantsev and the two Potemkins (Grigorii and his cousin Pavel) saw themselves, not only as members of the high command of the army, but also as representatives of their territory in Little Russia, New Russia, and the Caucasus respectively, not to mention Chicherin in Siberia, among others. That such a state of affairs, allowed to develop, was perceived as a danger to the stability of the unitary state easily explains Paul I's aversion toward the post of governor general, which he abolished immediately after ascending the throne.

But Petersburg still had to deal with the intractable fact that the expansion of the core kept bringing into it people who were not Russian – even if conversion to Orthodoxy created the fiction that converts were supra-ethnic Russians – and could not erase the fact that some people were nomads, and thus had a different type of economy and different customs that translated into different legal systems. These could not be abolished outright without striking at the heart of an ethnic identity and creating major problems of internal security. As we saw, the territoriality of the law of an expanding core seeking to remain a unitary state had to accept the parallel existence of the personality of the law, as least as a temporary expedient. The very fact that these countries and territories bordered on hostile empires raised diplomatic and military issues which had no counterpart in the internal provinces, and required the appointment of regional authorities with a specific set of powers, together with the overall responsibility for an ongoing evaluation of the political situation, and with direct access to the emperor.

The solution was found from the very beginning of Alexander I's reign in the restoration of the post of governor general. The usual formula was that a general was appointed military governor of the province where he resided and governor general of usually two other provinces. In his province, he commanded the garrisons and irregular troops, and, in some cases, was also given the responsibilities of a civil governor. Otherwise, a separate civil governor was appointed in his province. A controversy soon developed, however, over his responsibilities as governor general. The appointment of governors general in the 1780s had been followed by the closing of the central agencies of government responsible for functional administration (finance, customs, education), so that the governor general was eventually bound to become a true territorial manager for the second time in modern Russian history – the first time had been between 1708 and 1717. Territorial administration prevailed over functional administration.[1] This is why Catherine's reforms had the potential of creating a true system of regional administration, which, if grafted upon ethnic territories, could have evolved into a federal system.

But the restoration of the post of the governor was accompanied by that of its nemesis in the form of ministries, which became much more powerful than the old colleges had ever been. Territorial administration was incompatible with functional administration, and ministers quickly proceeded to curtail the managerial responsibilities of the governors general by establishing direct links with their local agencies – the finance ministry with the provincial treasury chambers, for example – bypassing the governor general's office. As functional administration began to prevail decisively, the post of governor general became integrated into the ministerial hierarchy: he gradually became the regional representative of the interior ministry, while retaining access to the emperor in political matters which transcended the responsibilities of individual ministers.[2] If a governor general was given the command of a separate corps, he also became the regional delegate of the war minister. The exception was the post of viceroy (*namestnik*), of which there would be only two: in the Caucasus and in Poland. A viceroy was a truly territorial administrator: all directives from the centre had to reach provincial authorities through his office, and their reports also required his preliminary approval.

The Russians did not recognize a single Ukraine, even after the third partition of the Polish Empire, but three historical ones, and each received a governor general: one in Poltava for Left Bank Ukraine (Chernihiv and Poltava or the old Hetmanate, and, at first, without Kharkiv); another in Kiev for Right Bank Ukraine; a third for southern Ukraine (New Russia) in Kherson. The Don and Kuban Cossack territories were autonomous, even though the latter remained under the jurisdiction of the New Russian governor general until 1819, and western Georgia, despite its natural orientation toward the Black Sea, was placed from the beginning under the authority of the governor general of the Caucasus in Tiflis. Yet, within the three governor generalships, the three historical Ukraines would gradually develop an all-Ukrainian identity beginning in the middle of the nineteenth century, and they emerged at the end of the imperial period with a new identity – the old one had been lost following the "Ruin" of the post-Khmelnytsky uprising in the seventeenth century. Moreover, historical Ukraine had never included the Black Sea coast and the Crimean peninsula. What is striking among the governors general of the three Ukraines is their high rank and distinction as members of the ruling elite, proof enough that the basin of the Dnieper was seen as one of the most important constituent parts of the expanding Russian core, which finally reached the limits of its expansion during the reign of Nicholas I.

Eight governors general of Little Russia were appointed between 1801 and 1856, when the post was abolished. Their tenure ranged from one to nine years, with the exception of Nikolai Repnin-Volkonsky, who remained eighteen years (1816–34) as military governor of Poltava and governor general of Chernihiv, to which Kharkiv province was added in 1835. Kharkiv became his residence in 1837.[3] He was the grandson of Marshal Nikolai Repnin, who had made his mark as ambassador to Warsaw (1764–9) and as a leading military commander in the Turkish wars of 1768–74 and 1787–92. The marshal's wife was the granddaughter of Boris Kurakin, Peter I's brother-in-law, and aunt of Alexei Kurakin, who had preceded Repnin-Volkonsky in Little Russia (1801–7). The Repnin family had always been small, and the marshal had only one daughter, whom he married off to Grigorii Volkonsky; the two names became hyphenated. He also arranged the marriage of his grandson to Varvara Razumovskaia, the granddaughter of Kiril Razumovsky, the last hetman. Repnin-Volkonsky's uncle was Ivan Gudovich, another Ukrainian, who had been military governor of Kiev and commanding general in the Caucasus, as well as governor general of Moscow.[4]

Across the Dnieper, civil governors were appointed in Kiev, Podolia, and Volhynia, but there was also a military governor in Kiev and another in Kamianets-Podilsky, who functioned as a de facto governor general of Podolia and Volhynia. Three were appointed in Kiev between 1803 and 1818, when the post became vacant until 1827, and two more were appointed between 1827 and 1832. Bessarabia, annexed in 1812, had its own viceroy, but the title was held by the military governor of Kamianets-Podilsky between 1816 and 1820, and later, from 1823 on, by the governor general of New Russia. The three provinces of Right Bank Ukraine were then combined under the authority of the military governor of Kiev, who was also governor general of Podolia and Volhynia. Another three were appointed between 1832 and 1852, among whom one stood out with the longest tenure, Dmitrii Bibikov (1837–52), the nephew of Marshal Mikhail Kutuzov of 1812–13 fame.[5]

Bibikov left a reputation as a hard-liner, but he was also the faithful executor of a government policy to complete the integration of the Right Bank into the Russian core. In 1840, the emperor thanked him for the assistance he had given to the execution of a policy "seeking to merge [*sliiat'*] the western Russian region with the ancient fatherland of its native inhabitants" – an expression which sounds ironic to modern ears, since the native inhabitants were not Russian but Ukrainian; of course, in the terminology of the day, Ukrainians, as Orthodox Eastern Slavs, were assumed to be Russians. He dismissed Polish officials whom he did not consider loyal enough to Russia, and proposed to give state lands to new Russian officials with the provision that such lands might not be divided, sold, mortgaged, or leased to Polish *szlachta* for sixty years. He also sought to improve the lot of the Ukrainian peasantry by introducing the so-called inventories (*inventary*), which regulated the amount of corvée labour they had to give to their landlords.[6] And it was during his tenure that the Lithuanian Statute and the Jewish *kahals* were abolished, and the Uniate Church was forced to close its doors.

The third Ukraine, New Russia, was divided in 1802 into the three provinces of Ekaterynoslav, Crimea (Tavrida), and Mykolaiv, but the latter was renamed Kherson province the following year. Mykolaiv (with its shipyards) was placed under a military governor, who was also the admiral commanding the Black Sea fleet. A military governor of Kherson and Crimea was followed in 1805 by one for the three provinces, who was a de facto governor general; then, beginning in 1814, by a military governor of Kherson, a governor general of New Russia and, after 1828, a governor general of New Russia and Bessarabia. Six "governors general" were appointed between 1801 and 1854, three of them for relatively long periods, who made their mark on the administration of the region.[7]

The decision to appoint Armand Emmanuel, Duc de Richelieu, governor general in 1805 was a lucky one. The settlement of the region was so new and the population so varied, with Russians, Poles, Jews, and Tatars, as well as Greeks, Armenians, Italians, Frenchmen, and others, that a foreigner was better placed to make peace among them and harness their energies for the common cause of developing both settlement and trade. The duke had emigrated to Russia after the outbreak of the French Revolution, and had been town governor (*gradonachalnik*) of Odessa since 1803, a new post in Russian administration, which showed the importance the government attached to the growth of coastal towns in the region.

It was he who transformed an insignificant Turkish fishing village into a city, which in time would become the third largest port after Petersburg and Riga. He created a commercial court to settle differences among traders unfamiliar with Russian laws, and wanted to integrate Odessa into the network of free economic zones (*porto franco*) including Marseilles, Genoa, Livorno, Trieste, and others. He opened a lycée for the children of traders and an institute for the sons and daughters of the nobility; the two were combined in 1817 to become the Richelieu lycée. He encouraged sheep-raising and salt production, and was fortunate to escape falling victim to the plague of 1813, which killed 2,660 of the 36,000 inhabitants of Odessa – so great had been the growth of the city since its founding in 1794. He returned to France in September 1814.[8] His successor, Louis Alexandre, comte de Langeron, another French émigré, continued his work. In 1815 he was appointed military governor of Kherson, town governor of Odessa, and governor general of the three provinces, as well as commander of the Buh and Black Sea Cossacks. But his temperament often placed him at odds with other Russian commanders and with the emperor himself, and he resigned from the army at the end of the Turkish war of 1828–9. He died of cholera in Petersburg in 1831, and was buried in Odessa.[9]

In May 1823, he had already been replaced by the "star" of the southern theatre governors general, Mikhail Vorontsov. He had served in Georgia under the legendary Tsitsianov, had entered Paris with Langeron in 1814, and had commanded a corps of Russian troops left in France from 1815 to 1818. He was the nephew of Alexander, former "minister of commerce" (1773–93) and of foreign affairs (1802–5), and the son of Semën, envoy to Great Britain (1784–1800). Semën was married to a cousin of Admiral Dmitrii Seniavin, who advocated a strong Russian naval province in the eastern Mediterranean. Vorontsov was married to Elizabeth Branicka, the daughter of Ksaweri, the Polish magnate who had been one of the first to join the Targowica confederation of 1791, which paved the way for the annexation of Right Bank Ukraine in 1793–5.

Vorontsov was governor general of New Russia and viceroy of Bessarabia in the rank of full general (from March 1825), and in December 1844 he was appointed commanding general of the Caucasian corps and viceroy of the Caucasus, where he would remain until October 1854. Two years later, he was promoted to field marshal, shortly before his death.[10] During his absence from New Russia, the acting governor general was Lt.-Gen. Pavel Fedorov, an invalid who had been seriously wounded during the 1813 campaign. After serving as chief of police in Mykolaiv and working in the Black Sea naval department, he had been Mykolaiv and Sevastopol military governor, Bessarabia civil and then military governor, and Izmail town governor.[11] He also retired in 1854, and a new governor general was appointed to succeed Vorontsov. Bessarabia became an ordinary Russian province.

While the governor general increasingly became the regional delegate of the interior ministry, other ministries created their own regional authorities, responsible, not to the governor general, but to their minister in the capital. Such regions were not conterminous with the governor generalships, and the southern theatre was divided into overlapping administrative regions, which denied the existence of "countries" while the governor generalships sought to maintain the acceptance of such countries, with their specific political and security problems. The result was confusion, but one that barely concealed the fundamental principle that the expanding core was a unitary state managed by central ministries, for which centralization and uniformity were objects to be pursued systematically.

When four universities were opened in 1802–4 on the periphery of the Russian core, to add to the single university created in Moscow in 1755 and the Academy of Sciences in Petersburg, each university was given a region (*okrug*) with jurisdiction over the secondary and primary schools on its territory. Of the six universities and region, one was in Kharkiv; its region included the three Ukrainian provinces on the Left Bank, the three New Russian provinces, the territory of the Don and Black Sea Cossacks, and the three Russian provinces of Kursk, Orel, and Voronezh. The three provinces on the Right Bank were included into the Vilno region. The curator of each university, in Kharkiv and Vilno, was the regional delegate of the education ministry. In December 1830, an Odessa region was created for the Odessa and Bessarabian schools (with the Richelieu lycée being given the status of a university), to which Kherson and Crimean provinces were added in December 1832, At the same time, a university was finally created in Kiev, called the University of St Vladimir, for Right Bank Ukraine. Between 1848 and 1856, the governor general in Kiev was also the curator, one of the rare instances in which a governor general was given jurisdiction over the regional delegate of another ministry, and one justified by the tense political situation in the region.[12]

In 1809, the Main Administration of Roads and Waterways created its own regional administration, but one that did not follow provincial boundaries; instead, it incorporated river systems. Of the ten regions, two included Ukrainian territory.[13] The Postal Department had followed suit in October 1830 with the creation of thirteen postal regions, each under a postal inspector. Kharkiv province was included into the Voronezh region; Volhynia and Podolia into the Vilno region; Kiev, Chernihiv, and Poltava into the Chernihiv region; and the three New Russian provinces with Bessarabia into the Odessa region.[14]

These ministerial regions gave little consideration to the "countries" of the periphery as such. Boundaries were drawn in accordance with administrative convenience, and regional delegates were given the same authority everywhere, while governors general perpetuated the legal fiction that the border regions of the expanding core were separate entities. The inclusion of Russian and non-Russian provinces into the same ministerial region showed that the ministries made no distinction between them. Their view was that of a unitary state. If governors general became the regional delegates of the interior ministry – and Bibikov became interior minister after leaving Kiev – it was also largely for reasons of administrative necessity: local tensions required a regional approach to problems of internal security. Nevertheless, governors general slowly became irrelevant: the Little Russian and the New Russian governor generalships were abolished in 1856 and 1874 respectively, completing the process of full administrative integration. If that of the Right Bank remained in existence until 1914, it was largely because of the existence of Kiev, which ranked with Moscow and Petersburg as one of the three "political" capitals of the Russian core.

Military Deployment

At the close of the Napoleonic wars, when the troops returned to their homeland, they were distributed in 1814 among two armies and four "separate corps." Each army was commanded by a full general and divided into a number of territorial corps, each under a lieutenant general, whose rank corresponded to that of a governor general, and each corps consisted of a number of divisions, each commanded by a major general, equal in rank to a provincial governor. Separate corps (in Finland, the Caucasus, Orenburg, and Siberia) were outside the army hierarchy, and were directly subordinated to the chief of staff and the emperor, like the two commanders in chief.[15]

The location and composition of the two armies showed the full extent of Ukraine's integration into the territorial infrastructure of the Russian army, and how regional administration was more conducive to greater uniformity than to the recognition of diversity in the peripheral regions of the expanding Russian core. The First Army, with headquarters in Mogilev on the Dnieper in Belorussia, was commanded between 1818 and its dissolution in 1835 by General Fabian von der Osten-Sacken and his chief of staff, Hans von Diebitsch (1815–23), who then became the army's chief of staff. It consisted of five army corps, one corps of grenadiers, and four of reserve cavalry.[16] Of the five army corps, one was headquartered in Moscow, another in Vladimir, and a third in Mitava (Kurland); the grenadiers were posted in Moscow, Smolensk, and Kaluga provinces, with their headquarters in Kaluga. The reserve cavalry was concentrated in Orel, Kursk, and Voronezh provinces, along the northern edge of Little Russia, with a *uhlan* division of four regiments in the Kharkiv corridor. As a rule, a cavalry division consisted of four regiments; an infantry division, of four regiments of musketeers and two of sharpshooters (*Jägers*).

Of the two other corps, the Third was commanded by General Mikhail Gorchakov in Kremenchuk, and consisted of a hussar division of four regiments stationed in Ekaterynoslav province, two infantry divisions with headquarters in Romny and Poltava, and a third infantry division in the vicinity of Elizavetgrad in Kherson province. The headquarters of the Fourth Corps was in Kiev under General Nikolai Raevskii. Like the others, this corps consisted of one division of cavalry (dragoons) stationed in Poltava province (Pryluky and Piriatin) and Chernihiv province (Borzna and Nizhyn). One infantry division was in Kiev and its province, the other in the northern part of Chernihiv province in the vicinity of Starodub. The third infantry division was in Mogilev (Belorussia) across the border with Chernihiv. The deployment of the First Army, which encompassed the whole of central Russia from Riazan and Tambov to the Belorussian border, and from it to the Polish border, thus incorporated Little Russia and the old zone of Serbian settlements between the Dnieper and the Syniukha. The remainder of Right Bank Ukraine and Bessarabia, annexed in 1812, were incorporated into the area of deployment of the Second Army.

This was a much smaller army, commanded from Tulchin, a former estate of the Potocki family in Podolia, by General Peter von Sayn-Wittgenstein (1818–28) and his chief of staff, Major General Pavel Kiselev, between 1818 and 1829; it was dissolved a year later, after the conclusion of the Russo-Turkish war. While the First Army's mission, with its vast hinterland in the Russian core, was to make a show of force in central Europe and even project Russian power to the Rhine in the event of French revanchism, that of the Second Army was to launch an invasion of Moldavia and Wallachia, cross the Danube, and move on to Constantinople (with the help of additional forces from the interior). It consisted of two army corps and one of reserve cavalry settled in Voronezh province under the command of Lt.-Gen. Ivan de Witt. The headquarters of the Sixth Corps was in Tiraspol on the Dniester, across the river from Bendery, which had been, with Khotyn and Ochakov, one of the three major Ottoman fortresses barring access to the Black Sea between the Prut and the Southern Buh. The six regiments of infantry were all stationed in Kherson province, including Kherson and Odessa, and the other six of its second infantry division were all in Bessarabia, including two on the delta of the Danube.

The Second Army corps in Kamianets-Podilsky under Lt.-Gen. Alexander Rudzevich, who had preceded Kiselev as chief of staff, consisted of a division of dragoons in Medzhibozhe in Volhynia, and the eighteen regiments of its three infantry divisions were concentrated in Podolia facing the Dniester. There was also a so-called Lithuanian Separate corps, detached from the Polish Army, with headquarters in Bielostock, and consisting of two infantry divisions, one in Volhynia (in the vicinity of Dubno), the other in Bielostock itself, in the northern corner of the Polish core, annexed in 1807. This corps did not face the Turkish front, but was intended to serve as a reserve formation capable of converging on Warsaw in support of Grand Duke Constantine in an emergency.

We can thus see that much of the Ukrainian lands had been fully integrated into the territorial military administration of the expanding Russian core. Four army corps headquarters (Kiev, Kremenchuk, Tiraspol, and Kamianets-Podilsky) assumed jurisdiction over Left Bank and much of Right Bank Ukraine, leaving only southern Ukraine (New Russia) denuded of troops. The army as a whole was a multi-ethnic organization dominated by Russians, in which non-Russian ethnic groups, notably Germans and Georgians, were well represented in the command posts. The army contributed to the integration of native groups into a supra-ethnic organization, and its territorial distribution contributed further to the integration of historical territories into the expanding core.

The reign of Nicholas I witnessed some important changes. The Russo-Turkish war of 1828–9, in which the Second Army was fully engaged, ended with the Treaty of Adrianople, which established a Russian protectorate over Moldavia and Wallachia, and fulfilled Russian ambitions in the region for the foreseeable future. Its mission accomplished, the Second Army was abolished, and its units were distributed among other army corps.[17] In November 1830, an uprising broke out in Warsaw against the Russians, in which units of the Polish Army took part. The uprising was crushed in the summer of 1831, after Grand Duke Constantine died of cholera. It also claimed the life of Diebitsch, who had led Russian troops against Warsaw.[18] Both the Lithuanian Corps and the Polish Army were disbanded, and a major reorganization of the infantry and cavalry took place soon afterwards. By 1835, it was decided to abolish the First Army as well, and to keep only a single Operational (*Deistvuiushchaia*) Army with reserve infantry divisions.[19]

The Operational Army was placed under the command of Marshal Ivan Paskevich, the new viceroy of the Polish Kingdom (1831–56), and his chief of staff, General Mikhail Gorchakov (1832–54), who then succeeded him between 1856 and 1861. It consisted of five infantry corps (I–IV and VI) and infantry reserve divisions attached to the infantry corps. Other troops were subordinated to the war minister, including the V infantry corps and cavalry units settled in the Ukrainian and New Russian military colonies. The VI Corps, although part of the Operational Army, was also subordinated to the war minister. The commanders of these two corps (V and VI) were given the authority of a separate corps commander. As a result, the old First and Second Armies were first combined and then split into two "armies," one commanded from Warsaw, the other from Petersburg, the latter consisting of units stationed in central Russia and Little Russia with military colonies beyond the Dnieper.[20]

The reform was not as innovative as it appeared at first glance. It built upon an earlier state of affairs. In June 1822, Grand Duke Constantine, commander in chief of the Polish Army and commander of the Lithuanian Separate Corps, who resided in Warsaw, had been given the powers of a commander in chief in wartime, in accordance with the statute of January 1812, over troops stationed in Lithuania and Minsk province, as well as in Podolia and Volhynia.[21] The decision amounted to the creation of two armies in Russia proper and in

Poland and its former borderlands, except Polotsk, Mogilev, and Kiev provinces, in addition to the Second Army in the south. It meant the recreation, but in a roundabout way, of the old Polish Empire within the Russian Empire.[22] Paskevich was given an even broader jurisdiction, since his army included troops stationed in the Baltic provinces as well. The Operational Army, to be true to its name, had to have a dual mission. It was the "army of the West," and its deployment recognized the importance of the Polish core and the extent of its influence in its former empire. It was intended to crush more Polish and Polish-inspired rebellions, and keep watch on the Baltic shores and the Danube, while the troops placed under the war minister formed an "army of the centre" to maintain order and manage the military colonies. The Ukrainian lands were thus split between two armies and duly integrated into both. The Operational Army also had an offensive mission: to operate in Prussia and the Austrian Empire (as it did in 1849) to quell rebellions and keep both monarchies within the Russian fold.

The Crimea and the northern coast of the Black Sea had once been a major strategic sector, when the strongest power in the region was the Crimean khanate supported by the Ottomans. With the annexation of the peninsula in 1783, a territory which had once been the northernmost stronghold of Ottoman power became the southernmost projection of the expanding Russian core against Turkey. A decision was soon taken to build a Black Sea fleet that would be the counterpart of the Baltic fleet. And indeed, that fleet did play a brilliant role during the Russo-Turkish war of 1787–92. A Naval Department (Admiralty) modelled after that built in Petersburg became autonomous under Potemkin, was downgraded under Paul, but was restored in 1808. The statute of December 1831 created a Main Administration of Black Sea Fleet and Ports under a commanding admiral (*glavnyi komandir*), who was also the military governor of Mykolaiv and Sevastopol with the powers of a separate corps commander.[23] He was responsible to the chief of staff of the Navy, Admiral Alexander Menshikov (1828–55), who also happened to be the governor general of Finland.

The fleet consisted of between fifteen and eighteen ships of the line with a number of supporting frigates; its ports were Kilia and Izmail on the northern branch of the Danube delta; Akkerman on the Dniester liman; Kherson, Mykolaiv, and Sevastopol; Taganrog and Rostov. The shipyards were in Mykolaiv, and Sevastopol was the fleet's anchorage. Although it was considered one of the most beautiful and secure naval ports in the world, its waters, infected with worms, were dangerous to wooden ships if their hulls were not protected by copper plates.[24] Despite all the hopes placed on them, the fleet and the ports contributed nothing to the region's economy. The timber came from Belorussia and was rafted down the Dnieper past Kiev and Ekaterynoslav and down the Dniester past Odessa a short distance away; the iron and copper came from the Urals down the Volga and the Don. The ports and shipyards constituted an economic region, but one drawing its sustenance from distant sources of production.

They were an artificial creation for another reason. A navy and merchant marine are the two sides of the same coin in a state's maritime policy. They support and reinforce each other in the projection of naval and commercial influence. But the Russians, who remained the people of an essentially fluvial civilization, never built a merchant marine in the Black Sea. Merchantmen had flown the flag of other powers since antiquity: Greek and Italian city states, France, Britain. In peacetime, the fleet's mission was only to show the flag to the Ottomans in an essentially closed sea (unlike the Baltic), since the treaties forbade Russian warships to cross the Straits into the Mediterranean. Contemporaries noted the depressing contrast between the rich and populous Sevastopol, with its fifteen thousand naval personnel and closed to merchantmen, and the neighbouring town of Balaklava, its great bay without a single well-built merchantman, peopled by Greeks who fished and sailed as if they were living on the banks of a pond or lake in the Russian interior. The few Russian merchantmen, built of vulnerable pinewood, sailed without map or compass and were thrown by contrary winds and currents on the desolate coast of Abkhazia, where they lost their way.[25]

A study of regionalization as a tool of integration of the core's periphery cannot overlook two other military networks, which supplemented the territorial distribution of the army into army corps. When the garrisons and other semi-military units consisting of old soldiers no longer fit for active duty were combined to form battalions of a corps of Internal Defence in April 1811, the troops were distributed among eight regions, each under a regional commander (*okruzhnoi general*) in the rank of major general and with the powers of a divisional commander. The corps commander was later given the authority of a separate corps commander. He was responsible to the war minister. The main responsibility of the regional commander was to supply provincial governors with troops to put down peasant revolts, convoy prisoners sent into exile, and transport funds to Moscow.[26]

By 1818, there were already twelve regions, three of them including the Ukrainian provinces. The Third Region in Kiev consisted of Kiev, Chernihiv, Poltava, and Kharkiv provinces, but also Kursk; the Fourth in Kherson, of New Russia and Bessarabia. The Twelfth in Vilno combined Volhynia and Podolia with Lithuania across the Pripiat marshes. The new distribution of September 1829 reduced the number of regions to nine.[27] The Seventh Region in Kiev included the same provinces but with the addition of Volhynia, and the Eighth was the old Fourth with the inclusion of Podolia. The link between Right Bank Ukraine and Lithuania had been severed. These regions were much closer to the governor generalships in Kiev, Poltava, and Kherson, a fact easily explained by the close relationship between the Internal Defence battalions and the provincial administration. These troops were a militarized police force at the disposal of governors and governors general, and facilitated the execution of operations which the civil administration, in the absence of its own civilian police force, would otherwise have been unable to carry out.

There was another police force, but one of a very different kind. The gendarmes were a military police created in June 1815 and operated within the army. Gendarme squads were attached to divisional and corps headquarters, and remained a military police organization throughout the reign of Nicholas I. But their jurisdiction was vastly expanded to cover the investigation of every form of dissent among the population and the collection of information not only on actions deemed subversive by the local gendarmes but also on the mood of the population in general. Gendarmes were also attached to the staff of provincial battalions of the corps in Internal Defence. After Nicholas' accession in the wake of the Decembrist uprising, a Third Section ("of His Majesty's Personal Chancery") was created, and gendarme units (*komandy*) were combined to form a separate corps, headed by the chief of the Third Section, General Alexander von Benckendorff (1826–44), followed by General Alexei Orlov (1844–56).[28]

In April 1827, gendarme units were distributed among five regions (the term *okrug* was the usual term for these "ministerial" regions), raised to seven in July 1836.[29] The Fourth in Vilno combined Lithuania and Belorussia with Right Bank Ukraine (Kiev, Podolia, and Volhynia); the Fifth in Poltava included Little Russia and New Russia, but Kharkiv province was in the Sixth Region in Kazan. In each province the gendarmes were commanded by a colonel responsible to the regional commander, usually in the rank of major general, with the rights of an army divisional commander. There were separate gendarme units in Sevastopol, Mykolaiv, Odessa, Kerch, and Taganrog. These regions, more than any other, recognized the existence of historical territories, with Right Bank Ukraine in one region and the remainder of the Ukrainian lands in another. The Kharkiv corridor, as usual, was incorporated into a predominantly Russian region. Gendarme regions, like governor generalships, were essentially political constructs, which identified peripheral territories with special political problems. As a result, they were more likely to coincide with those territories than any other type of region.

Military Colonies and Cossacks

Even a short survey of the military deployment in the southern theatre cannot overlook the peculiar institution of the military colonies or "military settlement," according to which a substantial part of the Russian army was eventually settled in villages among a population of state peasants, whose primary responsibility became to provide recruits and provisions to support the soldiers stationed in their midst. In fact, the policy had a long history, but the experiment had taken various forms from one generation to another, from Peter's decision to settle the entire army following the introduction of the capitation to the settlement of Serbs, Hungarians, and Moldavians on the edge of the steppe from the Syniukha to the Donets under Elizabeth. And indeed, the Cossacks were no more than other colonies settled along the Dnieper and in the Kharkiv corridor.

The basic concept behind the military settlement was to create, at a minimal cost to the government, an armed force consisting of those on "active" duty, either along the border or campaigning with the regular army, and those who remained "settled" at home but provided the clothing, the provisions, the equipment, and even the horses. Such colonies were thus self-financing with the proceeds from in-kind taxes, and saved the government considerable amounts of money. The other side of the coin was that such troops, while excellent at foraging and partisan warfare, were not disciplined enough to fight a well-trained enemy on the open field.

The nineteenth-century version of military settlement began in July 1810, when Alexander I visited the estate of his alter ego, General Alexei Arakcheev, and was impressed by the order prevailing in a battalion stationed on it. He thought it could provide a social model for the improvement of the peasants' lot. A first experiment was made in the Belorussian province of Mogilev with a regiment of infantry. Each soldier of a designated battalion was given ten *desiatiny* (twenty-seven acres) of land, as well as cattle and tools, and was made responsible for supporting two "active" soldiers of the other two battalions, who in turn would help with the farming when they were not campaigning. The state peasants, who had occupied the area where the regiment was stationed, were forcibly relocated. The Napoleonic invasion interrupted the reform, which was resumed in 1816, but only three regiments had been settled by the end of the year. Beginning in 1817, the pace of reform accelerated, and by 1825, the colonies included some 265,000 soldiers, or about a third of the army, and some 375,000 peasants assigned to them.[30] The deportation of state peasants had been stopped: they were needed as a source of recruits and to develop agriculture. Some ninety infantry battalions were settled in Novgorod province, twelve in Mogilev province, and thirty-six in the southern theatre, while 240 squadrons of cavalry were settled north of Kherson and east of Kharkiv. A separate corps of military colonies was created in 1821, commanded by Arakcheev until 1826, then by General Peter Kleinmichel (1826–42) and General Nikolai von Korff (1842–52). In June 1835, the central administration of the military colonies was integrated into a department of the war ministry.

In Left Bank Ukraine, ten villages of state peasants in Zmiev and Volchansk counties (Kharkiv province) were selected in April 1817 for the settlement of the Third Uhlan Division. That same year, the Chuhuiv Cossacks (numbering

7,646 men in 1803), who had become a regular *uhlan* regiment, were added to the settlement.[31] In March 1824, more villages were placed under military administration for the settlement of the Second Cuirassier Division in Izium, Kupiansk, and Starobelsk counties. In each regiment, six squadrons remained "active" and three became "settled."[32] Policing and the collection of taxes were removed from the civilian administration, and commissions were appointed consisting of surveyors, one officer, and one representative of the county nobility, to survey the land adjacent to the military settlement. These counties filled the space between the Donets and the Aidar rivers, steppe country with its usual bleak uniformity and excellent soil, but suffering from repeated droughts and producing unreliable harvests. No wonder the *uhlans* revolted as early as June 1819, but the revolt was put down with the usual brutality by the commander of the Second Uhlan Division, Lt.-Gen. Grigorii Lisanevich.[33]

In New Russia, the area of military settlement was found chiefly in Alexandriia, Olviopol, and Elizavetgrad counties (Kherson province), and Verkhne-Dnieperovsk in neighbouring Ekaterynoslav province. These counties happened to have been the territory allocated to the Serbo-Hungarian hussar regiments in the 1760s; these regiments had been settled troops, but before they became incorporated into the regular army. No doubt, memories remained of what had once been a close relationship between active troops and peasants, even though the new relationship would assume a different nature in a military settlement integrated into a tightly hierarchical structure based on the unconditional obedience of lower-ranking commanders to their superiors. In 1817, the Ukrainian Uhlan Division, created in October 1816, was broken up to form two divisions, the smaller one combined with the Buh Cossack Host to form a Buh Division, each of its three regiments consisting of six active, three settled, and three reserve squadrons.[34] The settled troops of both divisions were assigned fifteen (later forty-two) state-owned villages in Olviopol and Elizavetgrad counties with the former town of Novomyrhorod and Arkhangelsk *posad*, which used to be along the boundary of the hussar regiments with Right Bank Ukraine. In 1821, the four regiments of the Third Cuirassier Division were settled in forty-five villages in Alexandriia, Elizavetgrad, and Verkhne Dnieperovsk counties, and a separate command was created for the military settlement in the four counties of the two provinces under Lt.-Gen. Ivan deWitt, who also commanded the Buh Uhlan Division.[35] In November 1826, he was given the authority of a separate corps commander.[36]

But all was not well in the military settlements, and the brutality with which the reform was carried out was the major cause of the rebellion that broke out in 1832 in the Novgorod settlement. Once it had been repressed, an attempt was made to alleviate the lot of the peasants and the settled troops, who were now called "farming soldiers" (*pakhatnye soldaty*), a term which had long been in use in other parts of the country – like Nizhnii Novgorod and Kazan provinces – for soldiers who had become unfit for active military service, and were given a plot of land to make a living for the rest of their lives. By 1838, there were also military settlements in Kiev province and Podolia, with a population of 76,777 males in five districts (*okrugi*) containing 250 villages. In New Russia, the number of districts had risen to twelve. Despite some opposition, Nicholas I was determined to retain the policy of military settlement, and it was not until the early years of Alexander II's reign that the colonies were abolished and the "active" forces incorporated into regular military units, the farming soldiers joining the state peasantry under the jurisdiction of the Ministry of State Domains.

What of the Cossacks? The annexation of the Black Sea littoral from the delta of the Danube to the estuary of the Rion between 1783 and 1829 radically transformed the geopolitical situation in the southern theatre and substantially affected the position of the irregular forces in the territory. The Little Russian Cossacks, deeply rooted in the soil of the former Hetmanate, had been relegated to the status of state peasants by the reform of May 1783, but remained a separate group within that peasantry with their rights to own land and dispose of it. During the war of 1812, they filled some fifteen new Cossack regiments, which fought with regular units, but these regiments were disbanded after the war. During the Polish rebellion of 1830–1, they mustered eight regiments, but this number was reduced to two, which were later transferred to the Caucasus. In 1832, an annual draft of five men out of every thousand was instituted in the two provinces of Chernihiv and Poltava, exclusively for the purpose of staffing cavalry regiments in the army, and no longer infantry regiments as well.[37] It was a compromise which continued to recognize the Little Russian Cossacks as a special group (and their skills as horsemen), while refusing to create more Cossack regiments. These Cossacks were fully integrated into the regular army. To continue to recognize the Little Russian Cossacks as a territorially based social group required finding a new mission for them along the internal frontier of the expanding core: that is why large numbers of them were moved to the northern Caucasus, along the boundary of highland country beyond the Kuban River, as we shall see presently.

In Right Bank Ukraine, the old Cossack organization had long been gone, but memories remained. The government invoked them in 1812, when a Cossack host of four regiments was created with Ukrainian serfs on the estates of Polish nobles living in Kiev province and four eastern counties of Podolia. Each regiment consisted of eight squadrons, each squadron of 150 men.[38] The men were promised that they would be sent home when the emergency was over, but they would always have to remain in a state of readiness to reconstitute the host at the next emergency. In fact, this "Ukrainian Host" became the Ukrainian Cossack Division, reorganized into the Ukrainian Uhlan Division in October 1816, consisting of three regiments: they were incorporated into the Kherson military settlement.

There was greater variety in New Russia. At its western end, some of the Zaporozhians, who had fled their old settlement on the Dnieper in 1775, had settled in Moldavia, but with the progress of the Russian advance toward the Danube, culminating in the annexation of Bessarabia in 1812 and the establishment of a protectorate over the remainder of Moldavia in 1829, they expressed a wish to return to South Ukraine, perhaps for sentimental reasons, or, more likely, because they feared to be considered vagrants or even deserters. In February 1807, at the outset of the Russo-Turkish war, the commander in chief of the army on the Danube had created a "Danube-delta Host" (*Ust-Dunaiskoe voisko*), which remained in the delta.[39] But in 1828, when these Zaporozhians and others beyond the river faced the possibility of having to fight in the Ottoman army against their co-religionists (and frightened by the rumour that the sultan might deport them to Egypt), their *otaman* took them back into Russian-held territory. After the war, they were reorganized, first into a Danubian Cossack regiment, then into an Azov host settled on the Azov coast, in a picturesque region between Berdiansk and Mariupol, east of the Mennonite colony in Melitopol on the Molochnye Vody River and of the Nogais settled between that river and the Berda.[40] Their colony reflected a policy of implanting settlers along the Azov coast between the Putrid Sea of the Crimea and the Kalmius River, where the Land of the Don Cossacks began. The soil was black earth, and the sea was rich in fish. Two Nogai Cossack regiments had been created in 1801 of five hundred men each in each *sotnia*, modelled after the Don Cossack regiment.[41] They would create a prosperous community in Nogaisk, a town on the Azov coast, about thirty kilometres west of Berdiansk.

In the interior of New Russia, the Buh Cossack Host created by Potemkin was disbanded by Paul I, and its men became state peasants: they numbered 6,383 males in 1803, settled in Olviopol, Elizavetgrad, and Kherson counties. Their petition to restore the host was granted in May 1803, with the addition of 300 Bulgarians, to consist of three regiments of five *sotni*, each under an elected *otaman*. It was hinted that they might be given additional land between the Southern Buh and the Inhul Rivers, the old triangle of land acquired from the Turks in 1774, which was still largely empty.[42] The host functioned as an active military organization under the authority of the commander of the Crimean "military region," and its duty was to patrol the border along the Dniester. In 1817, it was merged with part of the Ukrainian Uhlan Division to form a Buh Division, and its territory was incorporated into the Kherson military settlement.

The world of the Ukrainian Cossack had practically disappeared, the victim of the elimination of the Crimean khanate and the end of steppe warfare. Any future war in the region would involve Ottoman forces and require the use of regular infantry and cavalry, with Cossack units integrated into the army's structure and playing only an auxiliary role. Cossack units fighting independently would henceforth have to confront an enemy, no longer in the steppe, but in the river valleys and the high ridges of the Caucasus.

It was paradoxical that such a changing geopolitical situation worked to the advantage of the Don Cossacks, who had long been closely integrated into the regular army's infrastructure. They managed to carve out a distinctive role for themselves as brave (and destructive) fighters in wartime, as a police force operating outside its territory in peace time to put down peasant revolts, and as a nursery of other Cossack settlements to which they supplied cadres and a basic settlement.[43]

In January 1801, Paul I ordered the full mobilization of their forty-one regiments for an invasion of India, an expedition which might very well have destroyed the host had it not been for the emperor's death two months later. In 1805, their *otaman*, Lt.-Gen. Matvei Platov (1801–18), moved their headquarters from its unhealthy location in Cherkassk to Novocherkassk on a higher site, forty-five kilometres from Rostov. During the Napoleonic wars they mustered sixty thousand men between the ages of fifteen and sixty, of whom fifteen thousand fell in battle. The war, their success in harassing the retreating enemy and preventing him from foraging, and their victorious march across Europe all the way to Paris strengthened their esprit de corps and their commitment to elite military duty. In 1798, their ranks had been equated with those of army officers, the *starshiny* given the rank of major and their *sotnia* commanders that of lieutenant.[44] Not only were they integrated into the army, they also joined the ranks of the nobility, the core's multi-ethnic ruling class.

Potemkin had broken up the administration of the host into two agencies, one headed by the *otaman* as military commander with great powers, the other consisting of permanent and elected members with collegial decision-making powers which restricted the *otaman*'s powers in civil matters (like grants of land, for example). Paul restored the single chancery and increased the powers of the *otaman*, but a procurator was appointed in 1802 to make sure that the chancery's decisions would conform to the general laws of the expanding core. The reform of July 1802[45] also retained the single chancery, now doubly subordinated to the College of War in military matters (including the confirmation of court martial sentences), and to the Senate in civil matters. It consisted of two permanent members and assessors elected for three years, and did away with Paul's decision to appoint a general from outside the host to command it, thus relegating the *otaman* to the position of second in command.

But the Don Cossacks were not only a military formation. Like the Little Russian Cossacks in the eighteenth century, they also ruled a territory. They owned land, and they needed peasants to farm it. Peasants kept flocking to the Don to escape the fiscal and other constraints in the interior provinces. Social differentiation gradually emerged, similar to that which had plagued the life of the Hetmanate. By 1811, there were some seventy-seven thousand serfs on the properties of Don landowners, who also belonged to the *starshyna*. A struggle emerged between the simple Cossack and the *starshyna*, between the peasant and the noble. In October 1818, the new *otaman*, Adrian Denisov (1818–21), asked Alexander I to set up a special commission of four members to meet in Novocherkassk to examine a more equal and rational distribution of the land, and put some order in the host's finances. The emperor agreed, but added Lt.-Gen. Alexander Chernyshev (the future war minister from 1827 to 1852) and an official from the Justice Ministry. Denisov supported the rank-and-file Cossack, Chernyshev the landowners. Denisov was forced to retire, Chernyshev became chair, and the commission moved to Petersburg.[46] The result of its labour was the monster statute of May 1835.[47] It again divided the chancery into two offices and fixed the term for field service at twenty-five years, with an additional five for internal duty. Cossack villages were given thirty *desiatiny* (seventy-one acres) of land per male and officials fifteen *desiatiny* for each male peasant they owned. The statute also forbade the Cossacks to keep their beards and trade in vodka and grain, a decision which had a deleterious effect on the Don trade and favoured the landowners. Two years earlier, in June 1835, the Don and other Cossack hosts were subordinated to the Department of Military Settlements.[48] A policy of superstratification was at work here again, by which the Russian government catered to the needs of the upper stratum in return for the consolidation of its socio-economic interests and the abandonment of its dream of autonomy within a unitary state.

The only Cossack settlement which still preserved Cossack traditions was the Kuban (Black Sea) host, and it was no coincidence that its members were descendants of the Zaporozhians who had not fled to Turkey and Little Russian Cossacks. Its early years, after 1792, had been years of deprivation, illnesses resulting from an inhospitable climate, and heavy military duties between the land of the Don Cossacks and the highlanders beyond the Kuban, who descended into the plain and challenged the Cossacks' claims to the land. In 1808, five hundred former Zaporozhians had been sent there from the Budzhak, but that could not be enough. That same year, the host had no more than twenty thousand men and ten thousand women – figures significant enough to show there must have been much wife hunting across the Kuban and that the Cossacks were being "nativized," a phenomenon found in the internal frontier all the way to the Altai. That year, another twenty-five thousand Little Russian Cossacks were deported to the Kuban, but the relocation was brutally done at the cost of considerable suffering. They were settled in five *stanitsy* along the Kuban, upriver from the confluence of the Laba.[49]

Some contemporaries were impressed with the results – the Cossacks did not engage in agriculture (and imported their grain from peasant settlements further east), but had large herds, plenty of timber, and excellent fishing grounds. They struck terror in the heart of the highlanders, but adopted their clothing, weapons, and customs. The government, however, forbade them to cross the river, out of fear they might bring in the plague. Others were less impressed, and saw poverty all around.[50] The establishment of 1808 called for a host of ten mounted and ten regiments of foot, each consisting of five *sotni*. In 1820, Lt.-Gen. Pavel Kiselev, the chief of staff of the Second Army, was sent to inspect the host, and recommended the resettlement of yet another 25,000 Little Russian Cossacks. At the time, the host had 37,050 males plus officers. The administration was chaotic, largely because the residence of the governor general of New Russia was too far west in Kherson, and the host was placed under the command of Lt.-Gen. Ermolov in Tiflis in December 1819.[51] The statute of July 1842[52] required them to muster twelve regiments of cavalry and nine battalions of infantry. The host had a brilliant future: in 1860 its population reached about 200,000. Its settlement was part of the eastward migration of the Ukrainian peasant, who would eventually colonize much of the northern Caucasus and the northern part of the Kazakh steppe, the internal frontier of the eastern theatre.[53]

Fiscal and Commercial Integration

Direct Taxation

Taxation was a powerful tool of integration. On both banks of the Dnieper, before their incorporation into the expanding core, taxation had served the needs of essentially private authorities, like the magnates and other estate owners on the Right Bank, the hetmans and colonels on the Left Bank. West of the Dnieper, there was hardly any public economy and public activities – witness the difficulties the Russians encountered during the implementation of the territorial reform in finding suitable locations and buildings for the new governmental agencies. East of the Dnieper, the administrative infrastructure was better developed because the headquarters of the territorial regiments and *sotni* had required the building of facilities to house the administration and the courts. But it was symptomatic of the semi-official nature of these military headquarters that landed properties, the so-called *rangovye imenia* attached to the office of hetman, colonel, and *sotnik*, often turned into their own private property after they left office. The revenues collected from these properties, in an overwhelmingly agrarian economy, were essentially delivered in kind or in the form of services (building houses, carting goods, maintaining bridges and ferries) which resembled those of an earlier, medieval, economy, when the public power was non-existent, and the execution of public duties was vested in individuals acting primarily in a private capacity.

In Little Russia, where Moscow had never since 1654 been able to determine how much revenue was being collected annually, the first attempt to introduce the core's system of direct taxation must be traced to 1765, when Governor General Rumiantsev imposed a tax of one rouble per household (*khata*), usually assumed to consist of three census-registered males. At that time, the capitation collected in the core amounted to 70 kopecks and the quitrent to 40 kopecks, a total of 1.10 roubles. Townsmen paid 1.20 roubles. But in 1679, before Peter's reforms, the unit of taxation had been the household (*dvor*) and the rate 1.30 roubles. Rumiantsev's tax was thus very similar to that of 1679, but the rate was much lower by perhaps a third than the rates introduced by the reform of 1722–4. The direct tax was collected from state peasants – on privately held land the rate of the quitrent depended on the landlord, but that of the capitation was the same – and from townsmen, but not from Cossacks, who performed military service and were fed and equipped by their communities, a form of collective tax. The same applied in the Kharkiv corridor, where Cossacks, state peasants, serfs, and townsmen constituted the four major categories of taxpayers.

A decisive step was taken in May 1783,[54] when the one-rouble tax was abolished and replaced by the capitation and quitrent in force in the core provinces: the capitation of 70 kopecks, the quitrent of 3 roubles (raised to this also in May 1783); the capitation of 1.20 roubles on townsmen (*meshchane*); and the 1 per cent tax on assets declared annually by merchants (*kuptsy*). The Cossacks, with the exception of those who had been drafted into the eight regiments of regular cavalry, were downgraded into the general category of state peasants, even though they remained a separate group and remained liable to perform Cossack service whenever called upon to do so by the Russian government. However, the legislation of May 1783 taxed them at a lower rate, equal to that of townsmen (1.20 roubles), and looked upon the reform as imposing a more just and equal burden than had previously been the case, when the rate of the tax depended on the whim of their colonels. This harmonization of the tax burden within the expanding core would "eventually lead to a complete uniformity which is useful to the empire."[55] The inevitable consequence was the cancellation of the right to move (unless authorized by the landlords and the authorities) and the final consolidation of serfdom in Left Bank Ukraine and the Kharkiv corridor.

The equivocal position of the Cossacks continued to preoccupy the government. In 1812, Governor General Yakov Lobanov-Rostovskỳ was ordered to recreate a Cossack host (*voisko*) to join the struggle against Napoleon; eighteen thousand men were eventually drafted. What is curious is that the governor general promised to exempt them from the payment of all taxes, except the "household tax" (*podymnyi sbor*) of one rouble paid by each household (*dym*, *izba*, *khata*). This suggests either that the old tax had not been abolished in practice, or that the new one was still collected from each household as a taxable unit, but assessed according to the number of males in each. At any rate, the governor general's action provoked a strong reaction in the Committee of Ministers, where the finance minister, Dmitrii Gurev, attacked him for deviating from state policy, which was that "our government had always [*izstari*], and especially during Catherine II's reign, sought to unite as much as possible all the provinces annexed to Russia into one administrative body, including Little Russia, which is why the Cossack regiments had been abolished, as an irrelevant [*nesposobnoe*] body of troops."[56]

But the issue remained latent. In 1831, during the Polish rebellion, the government called on another governor general, Nikolai Repnin-Volkonsky, to create eight regiments of Little Russian Cossacks to join the reserve cavalry, each consisting of 576 Cossack rank and file, to be fed and equipped in traditional fashion (i.e., by their communities).[57] This in-kind support was considered part of the quitrent. As a result, the Cossacks, except those drafted into the new regiments, remained liable for the capitation, which by then amounted to three roubles, and to a quitrent of four roubles, or half the rate paid by state peasants in Poltava and Chernihiv provinces. In Kharkiv, the rate was ten roubles, as in the adjacent Russian provinces. As a result, it may be said that the legislation of May 1783 inaugurated a process of fiscal integration of Left Bank Ukraine into the fiscal system of the expanding core, with the Cossacks remaining a special case as a source of manpower for several regiments of irregular troops. This gave them a privileged position, as other peasants who paid higher rates were in reality subject to the levies of soldiers for the regular army.

In Right Bank Ukraine, which had been administratively part of the Polish core, and where, by 1830, 1.4 of the 1.8 million peasants were serfs, the Russian government assumed at first the collection of the revenue that had been delivered to the Polish treasury. By 1795, however, it had already been decided to introduce the capitation and the quitrent as of 1 January 1797.[58] It was a major step toward the full integration of the region into the Russian core's fiscal system. Jews who effectively became peasants and lived in their own villages were taxed like other free people, such as the peasants emancipated under the provisions of the law of February 1803. Jews thus continued to be considered a free people. Those who remained townsmen were taxed like other townsmen.[59]

Separate provisions were made for former Polish *szlachta* who had been downgraded to the status of *odnodvortsy* similar to those who, on the northern fringe of Little Russia, especially in Voronezh province, had been settled by Moscow to man the defence line against the Crimean Tatars. They had not been able to convince the government that they should be included into the nobility in the 1760s and had been lumped together into the general category of state peasants. The Polish rebellion of 1830–1 forced the government's hand, and a "purge" of the *szlachta* was announced in October 1831.[60] These *odnodvortsy* were of two kinds: the settled and the migrant (*neosedlye*). The former lived on their own land or paid a quitrent (*chinsh*) on state or privately held land. They paid a household tax (*podymnaia podat'*), and were registered in each *uezd* on lists submitted to the treasury chamber, regardless of whether the household consisted of more or less than three males. This new tax took effect on 1 January 1833. Its purpose was to contribute to the maintenance of troops stationed in Kiev, Podolia, and Volhynia provinces. *Odnodvortsy* who lived on their own land paid three silver roubles per household; those who lived on other land or became townsmen paid two silver roubles, but did not pay the quitrent. The migrant *szlachta* who hired themselves out for domestic work paid paid a single rouble each. With the exception of this small category of former *szlachta* turned into state peasants (not unlike the Little Russian Cossacks), Right Bank Ukraine had also been integrated into the direct taxation system of the expanding core.

The situation was more complicated in New Russia, because the territory was largely empty at the time of its annexation, but would gradually include non-Russian and non-Ukrainian settlers who were attracted by privileges and exemptions, such as Greeks and Armenians, as well as settlers from Moldavia and Wallachia, Bulgaria, and the German states. The Tatar population of the Crimea already constituted a very distinctive group. The statute of February 1820 recognized that New Russia was in an entirely different situation from that of the interior provinces, where the land had already been surveyed and owners had received the confirmation of their holdings and where stock raising was little developed. It was found that the simplest way to attract settlers had been, since the creation of New Russian province in 1764, to grant tax exemptions for a number of years and to tax the settlers' land rather than their persons. In Ekaterynoslav and Kherson provinces, except the territory between the Buh and the Dniester (Podolia) and the mainland districts of the province of Crimea, the treasury charged an annual 2.5-kopeck tax per *desiatina* (2.7 acres), based on a grant of 15 *desiatiny* per male as long as the land remained unsettled. Once it was settled by Russians transferred from the interior provinces, the land tax was replaced by the capitation and the quitrent. The owner who had been given such state land had ten years to settle it. Officers of territorial regiments which had been stationed there (the hussar regiments, for example) were given a lifetime tax exemption, but their widows and children one for ten years only, unless they sold their land to a non-military person, who would have to pay the land tax upon taking possession of the land.[61]

In the country between the Buh and the Dniester, grants of land followed the norm of thirty *desiatiny* per male, and the owners and their peasants were encouraged to raise cattle and sheep, for which they were granted two *desiatiny* per head of cattle and one *desiatina* per head of sheep. Once the land had been settled, the peasantry would be taxed with the capitation and the quitrent. Once stock raising had become established – no deadline was set – the land would be taxed 2.5 kopecks per *desiatina*. If the owner did not settle his land or develop stock raising, the tax would rise to 10 kopecks per *desiatina*.[62] German colonists who immigrated to New Russia, especially the Mennonites in the Mariupol district, paid a tax of 3 roubles and a quitrent of 9 roubles.

In the Crimea, a special committee appointed to study the situation recognized the natural distinction between steppe land in the northern part of the peninsula and mountain land in the southern districts of Simferopol and Feodosia. Mountain land, which contained rich pastures and timber for construction and heating, would be taxed, in accordance with the legislation of January 1824, at 5 kopecks per *desiatina* a year; cultivated land and hayfields at 2.5 kopecks; Orchards at 2 kopecks; vineyards at 2.5 roubles a *desiatina*. These taxes would be assessed by the nobility of the districts to make sure that its interests would be well protected.[63] Eight years later, in January 1832, the government doubled the tax burden of the Tatars living in villages, the capitation from 1.5 to 3 roubles; those living in towns as *meshchane* saw their tax rate raised by a lesser amount, from 3.8 to 5 roubles, and they were also given the right to engage in retail trade. They and other Tatars within and outside the Crimea were de facto incorporated into the general body of tradesmen by being required to obtain the same certificates (*svidetelstva*) as other merchants and peasants in the core.[64] Tatars would still pay less than state peasants in general, but the legislation made clear that the raise of the tax rate was but a step toward the harmonization of rates across the entire expanding core. Only special circumstances, such as the existence of orchards and vineyards not found in the colder and forested centre and north, required the retention of taxes not applicable elsewhere.

The recognition of the necessity to personalize the law was even more in evidence in the fiscal treatment of the ethnic minorities. The Greeks who settled in Kerch and Enikale on the strait linking the Azov and Black Seas after the Russo-Turkish war were given a charter in March 1775 exempting them from the payment of taxes for thirty years; they were later promised another exemption, but after Catherine II's death, they were forced by the fiscal authorities in the Crimea to join the general body of townsmen and state peasants This was rescinded in 1812, but in 1829, they claimed that the exemption applied also to the charges they would have to pay, not as Greeks, but as members of one of the three merchant guilds if they wished to engage in trade. The governor general of New Russia convinced the government in February 1830 to opt for a compromise. Greeks who had settled in Kerch and Enikale for over thirty years (or in Taganrog, Feodosia, and Odessa for over twenty-five years) would have to pay taxes because their exemption had expired, but those who had settled in the other three cities after 1805 would retain their exemption. They would then join the general category of taxpayers.[65] The Armenian community in Nakhichevan (on the Don) was given a similar tax exemption. Armenian townsmen in Grigoriopol on the Dniester paid only two roubles per household (*dvor*).[66] The Mariupol Greeks paid on their land ten kopeck per *desiatina* a year, the Nakhichevan and Grigoriopol Armenians five kopecks.

The government used tax policy not only to attract settlers, whether from Little Russia or the provinces of the interior, and to retain members of ethnic communities who had long resided in the territory; it also encouraged their compatriots to immigrate. Tax was personalized not only to give them favourable treatment, but also to facilitate the development of towns on the coast or along rivers with some economic potential. But the personalization of fiscal legislation must not blind us to the uniformity of the territorial law, to the fact that its ultimate goal was the harmonization of the fiscal rates across the entire territory of the expanding core. Finance ministers were always great centralizers and unifiers, and Gurev and Cancrin were certainly no exceptions – the more unified the tax rates, the easier it was to keep the accounts, and the more revenue was siphoned off from the provinces to fill the central treasury. In an expanding core, where agriculture was the main source of wealth, where the industrial base remained so narrow, where the level of urbanization created few incentives to the development of domestic trade and the treasury was always short of funds, a policy of centralization and uniformity was the only one capable of sustaining the expanding core's great power ambitions.

Even in the distant western Caucasus, the committee of ministers did not see "any necessity to deviate from the general rule" according to which every source of state revenue must belong to the central treasury. In February 1823, it decreed that all the revenue of Imeretia, a recently acquired territory of the emerging empire beyond the expanding core, whether already known or which might become known in the future, must be incorporated into the total mass of state revenue and included into the annual estimate.[67] In December, it accepted Ermolov's recommendation that the time had come to bring the territory's fiscal system closer to that of the core. Since its annexation in 1810, Imeretia had been paying the same taxes as under its previous kings (tsars). They were collected in money, grain, and cattle, but many inhabitants had been granted charters (*tarkhanstva*) of tax exemption (which had already been abolished in eastern Georgia since 1807). These charters had been rewards for support in the slippery world of mountain politics or simply for prayers for the souls of departed members of the royal family. Ermolov had already experimented with a partial reform in 1822 on the estates of noblemen who had been denounced as traitors to the imperial cause. Their peasants were incorporated into the category of state peasants, and were taxed one silver rouble per capita, but a distinction was made between peasants who had not been the noblemen's personal property and those who had. The latter were taxed only fifty kopecks, perhaps in order to encourage them to denounce their masters. The committee approved the cancellation of the charters and the abolition of a great variety of taxes which yielded little revenue in favour of the new capitation, and extended Ermolov's reform to all other peasants, who were now declared state peasants, except those belonging to nobles considered loyal to the imperial government.[68]

It was only at the western end of the southern theatre that the government trod cautiously in the matter of tax reform. In September 1815, three years after the annexation, it was announced that until the administration of Bessarabia was placed on a permanent footing, the population would continue to pay the same taxes as it had under Turkish rule.[69] Bessarabia had been part of Moldova, and continued to gravitate more toward the latter than toward neighbouring Podolia and Kherson provinces. Caution dictated that Bessarabian and Moldovian sensitivities be catered to. But Bessarabia quickly became, as the southeastermost corner of the empire, a refuge for vagrants and deserters from Right Bank Ukraine and for Old Believers as well. The government set about creating a Russian presence by transferring large numbers of state peasants from the interior. As early as 1824, the governor general insisted that taxes must be paid no longer in Turkish but in Russian currency. All Bessarabians, except nobles and clergy, were taxed 10 roubles per family; those settled on state land had to pay an *obrok* of 23.5 roubles per family. Moldavian law, which did not tax single men, was superseded in January 1829, and they were taxed like other family members.[70] Gypsies were taxed 10 roubles per head (*po golovshchine*), and Bessarabian Jews who converted to Christianity were given a three-year exemption, at the expiration of which they would be taxed like other Bessarabians.[71] But Bessarabia was only the exception from the general rule that the government had engaged throughout the southern theatre in a policy of tax harmonization which placed the local population on the same basis as that of the interior provinces.

Consumption Taxes and Budgets

As elsewhere in the emerging empire, the salt trade was of crucial importance, if only because salt was an item of vital necessity for human beings. It was especially important in the southern theatre because of the abundance of salt lakes along the Black Sea coast and in the lagoons, which formed one of the most distinctive features of the landscape. The Crimean khans had owned a monopoly of salt production, and the sale of salt had provided one of the major items in the khanate's budget. After the annexation of the Crimea, a mixed system was introduced. Russian and Ukrainian landowners who received large grants of land gained the right to own the salt lakes and marshes (*solonchaki*) on their properties and the privilege of selling salt as they wished, while the transportation and sale of the salt from the other lakes to Right Bank Ukraine and Belorussia was farmed out. In September 1802, the farming-out system was abandoned, and the government took over the operation.[72] The statute of August 1818 retained the existing system, but imposed an excise (*aktsiz*) on the private producers of salt. At the same time, a salt board (*pravlenie*) was created in Perekop for the production and sale of state-owned salt, and a second one for

Bessarabian salt in May 1830. Both were subordinated to the Mining and Salt Department of the Finance Ministry.[73]

State-owned lakes in the Crimea were of two kinds. "Internal lakes," within the peninsula, were in the environs of Evpatoria, Feodosia, and Kerch. Some of the "external lakes" were near the Perekop Gates, on the narrow isthmus connecting the peninsula with the mainland; others, near Genichesk, on the strait separating the mainland from the spit called the Arabat Needle (*strelka*) extending over one hundred kilometres to the eastern neck of the peninsula and containing the so-called Putrid Sea (*Gniloe More* or *Sivash*). The third group was truly outside the peninsula, on the Kinburn spit: the so-called sulphate (*progoinye*) lakes, which had once been the site of the oldest Cossack settlements in the region, and a battlefield between the Zaporozhians and the Tatars. The government kept large stores for the wholesale market in Kerch, Feodosia, Genichesk, and Perekop, as well as in Berislav, where transports crossed the Dnieper on their way to Right Bank Ukraine and Belorussia, and in Odessa. Stores were built at Kriukov on the Dnieper facing Kremenchuk for shipments into Little Russia, and at Rostov to provision the Don Territory. Salt was also exported to the highlanders on the eastern shores of the Black Sea, including those living in Abkhazia.[74]

The Statute of August 1818 made it clear that its provisions applied to the entire country, but also had to recognize that sources of salt were not found everywhere. Most of them were in the southern periphery, from the Black Sea coast to the Altai Mountains, in what had been a huge sea in geological times. It had dried up and left a multitude of salt lakes scattered over the land. The Caucasus Mountains, the interior of the core, and much of the western theatre did not have their own sources of salt. Nature had thus created two complementary markets, one for the production, the other for the consumption, of salt. The trade was nevertheless hampered by high transportation costs between the two, which sharply reduced profits. The government's role was not only to make a profit, but mostly to guarantee that salt would be available everywhere because shortages were deleterious to human health and were likely to cause social unrest.

The government fixed the sale price of salt everywhere in the country once a year. The price was considered modest so that private producers could not raise prices much higher to increase their profits or compensate for losses. The price was intended to cover the production and administrative costs, and a surcharge of 10 kopecks per *pud* (16.4 kilograms) was added to maintain bridges and ferries at Berislav and Nikopol higher up on the Dnieper, and the wells in the steppe between Perekop and the Dnieper. Salt was exported from the Crimea either overland into the provinces of the interior or by sea to other Black Sea ports or even to Turkish Anatolia. Overland carriers were charged an excise of 80 kopecks per *pud* at the Perekop Gates and at Genichesk, and the salt was then sold in provinces of the southern and western theatre at a price fixed by the government for each town. In 1821, for example, customers had to pay 1.80 roubles a *pud* in Kursk, 1.90 in Orel, and 1.50 in Voronezh. No price was set for the Little Russian provinces because salt was sold on the free market. If the salt was exported by sea, the carrier paid a customs duty of 75 kopecks added to the price paid in the Crimea, which in 1821 ranged from 73 to 80 kopecks a *pud*.[75] The government thus sought to make a profit by taxing the transportation of salt and fixing the sale price in the provincial capitals and county seats.

While the government's revenue from the sale of salt had nevertheless been declining and made up only 6.4 per cent of the total revenue in 1825, the vodka trade was much more profitable: in 1825, its share had risen to 32.7 per cent of the total. It had been an established principle since 1754 that the distilling of vodka was a monopoly of the nobility, and that the sale was farmed out to merchants who had to pay the government the amount fixed in the contract. They had to sell the vodka at a price set by the government, but they also could sell as much as they could once they had fulfilled their contractual obligations. But in Little Russia, Cossacks also had the right to sell vodka, and this was one of their most treasured privileges: the sale of vodka was the major source of cash. Restrictions were imposed beginning with Peter's reign. In 1721, the colonels and *starshyna* were allowed to produce and sell only on their properties and Cossacks only in their houses. They were forbidden to sell in towns. In May 1783, distilleries were banned from towns, and a strict demarcation was introduced between town and countryside: vodka was produced in the countryside and sold in towns (as well as in villages of state peasants).[76] It was easier said than done, and nobles continued to distil in towns on the ground that the loss of this right would infringe on the full enjoyment of their real estate in those same towns. The situation was similar in New Russia, but in Right Bank Ukraine, where the Cossacks had nearly disappeared, the landed *szlachta* and magnates distilled on their estates, and merchants, for the most part Jewish, took out farms to sell vodka in the numerous taverns found in every town and village.

In April 1817, the farming out of the sale of vodka was abolished, but it was restored in October 1826 for Right Bank Ukraine and introduced in the military colonies.[77] Farms were for the usual term of four years. Elsewhere, the government set up an elaborate network of authorities to take over the sale. Seven years before this new statute, which would remain in force until 1860, the government had complained that it had been collecting no revenue from the provinces annexed as a result of the partitions of Poland, where the vodka trade had been a purely private undertaking in which the government took no part. As a result, a sales tax (*poshlina*) of 60 kopecks per *vedro* (12.3 litres) was introduced in September 1810 in Right Bank Ukraine,[78] in Little Russia, in the five counties of Voronezh province, and in the villages of Kursk provinces, where the sale of vodka had also been free. This was cancelled in October 1826, when the sale of vodka in Right Bank Ukraine became free once again. By the 1830s, when the production and sale of spirits was finally codified, in Little Russia and the Kharkiv corridor as well as in Kiev province – leaving out Podolia and Volhynia in the Right Bank – only landowners were allowed to distil, and this on their properties alone. The same applied in New Russia and Bessarabia. In the colonies of foreign settlers, the right was given to their inhabitants by their original charters. Among the Don Cossacks, the population had the right to distil, but the sale was farmed out. Elsewhere, the local authorities appointed by the Finance Ministry took over the sale. Little Russian Cossacks and the former Cossacks of Kharkiv province, who had become state peasants for fiscal purposes, paid a capitation of two roubles in addition to the regular capitation of three roubles for the right to continue to distil in their homes. In the same three provinces and in Right Bank Ukraine as well as in the Don Territory, landlords paid a capitation of two roubles for each male serf, also for the right of their serfs to distil.

The legislation on the sale of spirits in the southern theatre was bewilderingly complex. Vodka, made from grain, was the most important staple of the trade. But there were also grape wine and various kinds of liqueurs produced in the orchards and vineyards of Little Russia and the Crimea. The legislation regulated their production, storage, and sale, both in large amounts and by the cup (*charochnaia*) in the taverns, and determined who was entitled to produce and sell them. The essential point, however, was that the government looked at the production and distribution of spirits (and salt) as forming a single market regulated by a single statute. Of course, the statutes contained exceptions for certain territories – it obviously made no sense to regulate the production of salt where there were no sources of salt or the production and sale of wine where there were no vineyards. But this personalization of the law did not in any way deviate from the general principle that both statutes on the salt and alcohol trade applied to the entire expanding core and contributed their share to the building of a unitary state. The expanding core was viewed as a single market of complementary parts in the case of salt and a much better-integrated one in the case of spirits, because vodka could be produced everywhere and wines and liqueurs were easily transported from one region to another. As in other areas of legislative activity, the central government continued to view the expanding core as a unitary state where local exceptions only confirmed the rule.

Turning now to the revenue collected in the southern theatre in 1795 (see tables 6.1 and 6.2), we can assess its relative importance in the expanding core's fiscal position and its contribution to the creation of a central budget from which funds were allocated for the army and navy and, increasingly, for the civilian administration as well. It will be useful to include the three Russian provinces of Orel, Kursk, and Voronezh, which formed the northern periphery of the

Table 6.1 Provincial revenues in the southern theatre, 1795

	Head taxes		Vodka		Salt		Other		
	Roubles	%	Roubles	%	Roubles	%	Roubles	%	Total (roubles)
Orel*	925,544	40.1	1,046,564	45.5	240,000	10.4	92,492	4.0	2,304,600
Kursk*	1,170,506	55.3	649,769	30.6	206,959	9.7	95,328	4.5	2,122,562
Voronezh*	867,566	55.6	482,409	30.9	126,000	8.1	84,388	5.4	1,560,363
Subtotal	*2,963,616*		*2,178,742*		*572,959*		*272,208*		*5,987,525*
Kharkiv†	472,560	66.1	63,892	9.0	119,796	16.8	58,192	8.1	714,341
Chernihiv†	374,964	89.3	7,039	1.7	–	–	37,926	9.0	419,930
N.-Seversk†	326,122	88.8	6,112	1.7	–	–	34,889	9.5	367,122
Kiev†	437,835	80.2	4,316	0.8	–	–	103,660	19.0	545,810
Subtotal	*1,611,481*		*81,359*		*119,796*		*234,667*		*2,047,203*
Ekaterynoslav‡	166,720	14.1	656,000	54.9	–	–	364,355	31.0	1,177,075
Tavrich‡	27,490	5.9	186,000	39.7	172,901	37.0	81,332	17.4	467,723
Subtotal	*194,210*		*832,000*		*172,901*		*445,687*		*1,644,798*
Total	4,769,307		3,092,101		865,656		952,562		9,679,526
Grand total for all three theatres	25,657,426		24,123,576		5,535,755		10,773,289		65,990,047
% from southern theatre	18.5		12.8		15.6		8.84		14.6

Source: *SIRIO*, 1871, 6: 284–92.

Note: Total population (males) in the southern theatre = 3,759,106. The grand total population (males) for all three theatres = 18,168,574. The southern theatre forms 20.7 per cent of total male population.

* Population (male) for Orel, Kursk, and Voronezh = 1,542,332

† Population (male) for Kharkiv, Chernihiv, N.-Seversk, and Kiev = 1,696,824

‡ Population (male) for Ekaterynoslav and Tavrich = 519,950

Table 6.2 Disposition of provincial revenues in the southern theatre

	Retained for provincial expenses (roubles)	Sent to Commissary (roubles)	Sent to Admiralty (roubles)	Sent to Treasury in Moscow and Petersburg (roubles)	Other (roubles)	Total (roubles)
Orel	616,942	250,000	400,000	800,000	237,658	2,304,600
Kursk	594,895	350,000	500,000	520,000	157,667	2,122,562
Voronezh	379,454	400,000	300,000	380,000	100,909	1,560,363
Subtotal	*1,591,291*	*1,000,000*	*1,200,000*	*1,700,000*	*496,234*	*5,987,525*
Kharkiv	306,996	100,000	100,000	150,000	57,435	714,341
Chernihiv	152,035	250,000	–	–	17,895	419,930
N.-Seversk	199,001	150,000	–	–	18,121	367,122
Kiev	221,123	300,000	–	–	24,687	545,810
Subtotal	*879,155*	*800,000*	*100,000*	*150,000*	*118,048*	*2,047,203*
Ekaterynoslav	544,713	120,000	100,000	–	412,356	1,177,075
Tavrich	232,269	50,000	90,000	–	95,460	467,723
Subtotal	*776,982*	*170,000*	*190,000*	–	*507,816*	*1,644,798*
Total	3,247,428	1,970,000	1,490,000	1,850,000	1,122,098	9,679,526
Grand total for all three theatres	22,966,837	13,780,855	5,349,617	14,762,737	9,129,997	65,990,047
% from southern theatre	14.1	14.3	27.8	12.5	12.2	14.6

Source: *SIRIO*, 1871, 6: 284–92.

southern theatre. The inclusion of adjacent Russian provinces exposes the contrast between these provinces and the non-Russian (or less Russian) provinces.[79]

The total population of the southern theatre, including the three Russian provinces, had reached 3.7 million males by the time of the census of 1795, 1.5 million of them in the three provinces, 1.7 million in Left Bank Ukraine (including the Kharkiv corridor), but only 519,950 in New Russia. The share of the theatre's population was thus 20.7 per cent of the 18.1 million males in the expanding core, but the revenue collected in the theatre of 9.6 million roubles amounted to only 14.6 per cent of the total (66 million roubles).

The capitation and the quitrent yielded the largest revenue: 49.5 per cent of the total collected in the three Russian provinces; the revenue from the sale of vodka yielded another 36.3 per cent, and that from the sale of salt 9.5 per cent. The remainder came from miscellaneous taxes and rents, including rents from forests, mills, fisheries, etc., leased by the government, the so-called *obrochnye stat'i.* The situation was sharply different in Left Bank Ukraine, where the tax burden was lighter than in the Russian provinces. In Chernihiv province, for example, where the population was smaller than in Kursk province, the capitation and the quitrent yielded 374,964 roubles, but they yielded 1,170,506 roubles in Kursk province. Only in Kharkiv province (183,688 roubles) was revenue collected in any amount from the sale of salt and vodka, and it amounted to only 21.4 per cent of the same revenue collected in neighbouring Kursk province (856,728 roubles). Kiev province was in the same situation as the other Ukrainian provinces on the Left Bank; it was part of it until 1797. The share of the capitation and the quitrent remained higher in the three provinces of the former Hetmanate than in Kharkiv and the three Russian provinces – close to 90 per cent in Chernihiv province. New Russia was a case apart. From a population of 520,000 males the government extracted 1.6 million roubles, but only 194,210 roubles (11.8 per cent) came from head taxes and 832,000 (50.5 per cent) from the sale of vodka. The sale of salt was free and contributed nothing to the Treasury, except in the Crimea. In Ekaterynoslav province the large item of 364,355 roubles consisted of 117,075 roubles of customs duties and 242,780 roubles from other sources, including rents from state-owned properties. There were no data for the recently acquired Right Bank Ukraine.

The disposition of these revenues tells us about the contribution of the southern theatre to the national budget. These funds were divided into four categories, of which those retained for local expenditures (mainly for the operation of the vodka and salt monopolies) usually, but not always, made up the largest share. If we take the region as a whole, 33.5 per cent (3.2 million roubles) of the total revenue of 9.6 million remained in the province of origin, 20.3 per cent went to the Commissary and the Navy for the salary and provisioning of troops and sailors, and another 19.1 per cent was transferred to the National Treasury for other expenditures. Thus the provinces retained more for their internal administration and sent less to Moscow and Petersburg for the needs of the expanding core as a whole. Within the region, however, there were noticeable differences. The three Russian provinces kept 1.6 million roubles (26.5 per cent of their receipts) and sent 28.8 per cent (1.7 million roubles) to the central treasuries; the Ukrainian provinces kept 43.3 per cent (1.6 million roubles), and only Kharkiv sent anything to the Treasury (150,000 roubles). If we add to these contributions the transfers to the Commissary and the Navy, the three Russian provinces sent 65.1 per cent of their receipts (3.9 million) to Moscow and Petersburg, the Ukrainian provinces only 38.1 per cent (1.4 million).

These figures show that the southern provinces still paid much less to the Imperial Treasury than the Russian provinces. The difference was due in part to the fact that, on the one hand, the revenue from the sale of vodka and salt was insignificant and even non-existent in some provinces, and, on the other, the contribution of the southern provinces to the Commissary and the transfers to the Treasury were lower. While the fiscal system was uniform in both the Russian and Ukrainian provinces and had become integrated, its operation still resulted in major differences, largely because the emerging ruling class of the Ukrainian provinces retained significant privileges of a private nature that still set them apart from the original Russian core.

Commercial Integration

The economic and commercial situation in the southern theatre was calling for a drastic solution by the beginning of Catherine II's reign in 1762. The tariff of December 1755 had closed the customs houses on the Hetmanate's border with Russia to complete the commercial integration of the territory into the expanding core. But the attempt to reorient the domestic trade of the Left Bank toward the internal provinces, and its foreign trade toward the Baltic, continued to run against geographical obstacles: The Black Sea and Baltic basins were not connected by rivers deep enough to carry a substantial flow of goods, raising costs and reducing competitiveness with similar products like hemp, flax, and grain, which Riga and Petersburg could obtain more easily and more cheaply from Livonia.[80] While Moscow's iron and textile industry and Left Bank agriculture remained complementary, the gap between them was growing wider: Russian industry, fuelled by the resources of the Urals and fed by the grain from the mid-Volga provinces, easily transported by means of the Volga, was becoming ever more powerful, while Left Bank agriculture, unable to dispose of its surpluses, was being contained against the great bend of the Dnieper between the Belorussian forests and the open steppe of the Zaporozhian Cossacks, with the prospect of becoming a backwater.

The situation was not better in Right Bank Ukraine. Its agriculture was also turning into a closed economy, likewise unable to market its surpluses. A French diplomat observed in 1771 that there were piles of wheat, large enough to feed the whole of Europe, but rotting in the fields of Volhynia and Podolia because the grain could not be sold.[81] Transporting grain westward to the basin of the Vistula had always been a problem: the Southern Buh, despite its seven hundred kilometres, was not navigable within the Polish-held Right Bank Ukraine. And the Prussian king was placing obstacles to the shipment of Polish grain down the Vistula to Danzig. The canal begun in 1770 at the order of Prince Michal Oginski of Lithuania to connect the Niemen and the Dnieper (and completed in 1784) was not capacious enough to provide another suitable export route for the products of Right Bank agriculture.[82] As a result, much of the grain surplus was used to produce vodka, which only worsened the condition of the peasantry while enriching their lords.

The Ukrainian economy, on both sides of the Dnieper, thus remained hostage to a geopolitical situation in which the Ottoman Turks and the Crimean Tatars hampered its further development by blocking access to the Black Sea, into which all the main rivers drained and which alone could create a wider market for the manufactured goods of the expanding core. On the eastern shore of the sea was Poti, where Georgian merchants came to market their goods (as well as slaves); then Trebizond and Sinop, coastal towns like Tokat, where the caravans from Persia assembled and separated before proceeding by different roads to Constantinople and Smyrna, past Angora (Ankara), the only place known at the time for "camel's hair" (in fact, fine goat hair), from which the best camlets were manufactured. The trade was in the hands of Greek and Armenian merchants, who exchanged Russian and European products for honey, wax, animal skins, raw and manufactured Persian and Turkish silks, cotton goods, rice, saffron, dried fruit, salt, and salt fish. On Tinos Island, the Turks kept a dock for the repair of their ships, thus creating a demand for cordage, anchors, and other naval stores. On the western shore was Varna, which supplied Adrianople, the sultan's summer capital, deep inland. Further north, there was Kilia on the northern branch of the Danube's delta, Akkerman (Bilhorod-Dnistrovsky) on the Dniester's estuary, downriver from the massive Turkish fortress of Bendery, and Ochakov, which controlled the Dnieper estuary. The same products were traded, with the addition of Hungarian, Moldavian, and Greek wines, rich Turkish carpets, fresh fruit, and spices.[83]

As a result, there emerged a common understanding between the Right Bank magnates, the Cossack *starshyna* on the Left Bank, and the Russian army and political establishment, that the future lay in the destruction of Ottoman hegemony in the Black Sea.[84] The Russo-Turkish war of 1768–74 deployed a Russian army of some one hundred thousand men in Moldavia and Wallachia, who could not be supplied from Little Russia by ox-driven wagons, because it was too far. But the *chumaki* (ox-drivers), who for generations had carried whatever grain was exported to the Western Bug, were now requisitioned to carry Right Bank grain to the front. The same thing happened during the war of 1787–92, by which time the Ottoman hegemony had largely been destroyed. Then the partitions of 1793 and 1795 incorporated Right Bank Ukraine into the expanding core. The Crimea and the Kuban valley had been annexed a decade earlier. The entire northern shore of the Black Sea was now in Russian hands.

We can thus understand the tremendous importance of the Treaty of Kuchuk Kainardji (July 1774), even though it gave Russia only a small triangle of land between the lower Dnieper and the Inhul and Southern Buh Rivers. It was followed by the Tariff of August 1775,[85] specifically crafted to favour Turkish imports of gold and silver brocades from Constantinople and Chios. The duty on such imports was set at three-fourths that of the 1766 tariff on similar imports in Petersburg. However, European goods imported via Constantinople would be charged the same duty. The Polish magnates well understood the implications of Russia's gaining access to the Black Sea. It was largely for them that the Russians built in 1778 a port at Kherson on the left bank of the

Dnieper, seemingly well situated near a stone quarry and the terminal point for shipments of timber from Belorussia. It was made a free port (*porto franco*) in December 1784.[86] But the Russians would soon discover that the northern coast of the Black Sea was inhospitable territory. The air of Kherson was unhealthy, and the Dnieper was navigable for only seven months and too shallow: sea-going ships drawing more than 1.8 metres could not reach the town.[87]

Four years later, the general Tariff of September 1782[88] incorporated the southern ports and inland points of entry into a single customs zone, and sharpened the distinction between the "European" and "Asiatic" tariffs. However, it retained the provision of the 1775 Tariff reducing by one-fourth the duty on imported goods "in favour of our subjects." In 1783, the annexation of the Crimea transformed its inhabitants into "our subjects," and that of Right Bank Ukraine in 1793–5 added its Poles, Ukrainians, and Jews to the list. The entire southern theatre was thus included into an expanding "European" tariff zone. Ten years earlier, in November 1784,[89] Polish magnates, not yet Russian subjects, were allowed to export their grain across Russian territory by paying three-fourths of the duty, but on condition that their trade take place in Kherson, which the Russians still considered their "staple city" in the region. However, the founding of Odessa in 1794 at the site of a Turkish fishing village, already known for its roadstead, revolutionized the foreign trade of the northern Black Sea coast. Situated at a convenient distance from the estuaries of the Dniester and Southern Buh, Odessa's location was ideal for exports from the Podolian upland and as the terminal of a transit route from Poland, Austria, and Hungary. The destruction of the Polish Empire had restored the natural gravitation of Left and Right Bank Ukraine toward the Black Sea. But the protective tariff of April 1793 and prohibitive measures taken between then and 1796 did not bode well for the development of the Black Sea trade, which still made up at the end of the eighteenth century only about 5 per cent of the total Russian foreign trade.[90] Protectionism was not only a response to the changing international situation in the wake of the French Revolution; it was also a disturbing marker in the emerging transformation of Fortress Russia into Fortress Empire.[91]

The reign of Alexander I (1801–25) witnessed many changes in the infrastructure of Russian ports in the southern theatre, notably the accelerated development of Odessa under the direction of Richelieu (the Kherson military governor), the appointment of separate governors (*gradonachalniki*) in some of the more important ports (Odessa, Taganrog, and Kerch), and the build-up of Sevastopol as the headquarters of the Black Sea fleet, with its shipyards in Mykolaiv on the Southern Buh, a better location than Kherson. The legislation of November 1804 and August 1818 regulated the transit trade across Right Bank Ukraine with customs houses in Dubossary and Mogilev on the Dniester for wagons proceeding into Moldavia and Wallachia; in Radzivilov for those entering Austria at Brody on the Austrian side; and in Ustilug in Volhynia on the Western Bug for those going into Lithuania and Prussia via Brest-Litovsk. That of 1818 imposed a transit duty of thirty silver kopecks per *pud* on a long list of goods.[92]

Hopes ran high for the growth of grain exports not only through the Turkish Straits (as in antiquity, when Greek colonies sent their grain to Attica and the Morea) but also to the western Caucasus, where another transit route began toward Tiflis and Persia, and even Central Asia. And since latitudinal trade routes in the southern theatre had always been complemented by longitudinal ones, there were hopes that not only would the Dnieper, now flowing across the expanding core in its entirety, facilitate the transportation of Russian manufactured goods to the ports, but also that the Volga would bring iron and iron articles from the Urals to Tsaritsyn, from which they would be portaged to the Don and the Azov Sea. In other words, the Black Sea would become the great integrating agent, drawing out its hinterland in both the Russian and Anatolian core to create a vast commercial zone. Some contemporaries waxed enthusiastic about the prospect. One anonymous observer wrote in the *Asiatic Journal* of 1824 that "the south of Russia will, at no distant period, form one of the most powerful empires in the world … under a government distinct from that which may then rule at St. Petersburg or Moscow … as powerful as the United States."[93] Odessa would dominate the western Black Sea trade, Taganrog would draw the iron from the Urals, and Kerch would incorporate the western Caucasus into the eastern Black Sea market.

Such exaggerated hopes had been encouraged by the creation in 1818 of a free port in Odessa, which opened in August 1819. A ditch (*cherta*), twenty-two kilometres in circumference, was dug around the city, with only two checkpoints to inspect transports crossing into New Russia. All goods, except vodka, were allowed into the port duty-free, but had to pay the duty in accordance with the Tariff of November 1819 (replaced by that of March 1822) if they were exported to Russia.[94] The immediate results were very encouraging, as the prospects of trading in duty-free goods were stimulating. But there was opposition in the Finance Ministry, upset at the loss of revenue, while traders abused the privilege and engaged in widespread smuggling. In June 1822, the area of the port was reduced to encompass that of the town alone, and a duty equal to one-fifth of the tariff was collected on all goods entering the port. Exporters of the same goods would have to pay the remaining four-fifths if they took the goods into Russia. This decision, based on fiscal considerations alone – which often ran counter to those of Russia's foreign trade – "broke the momentum"[95] created by the opening of the port, inspired distrust abroad, and slowed down emigration from the interior provinces into New Russia of an active and industrious population. Nevertheless, the free port, largely reduced to an entrepot, would remain in existence until 1859.

Other developments contributed to dashing some of the most exuberant hopes. Trade requires a peaceful international setting, but Russia and Turkey remained hostile. They were even at war between 1806 and 1812 and again in 1828 and 1829. In the meantime, the Greek uprising, which began in 1821 and did not end until the proclamation of Greek independence in 1832, damaged trade relations, since much of the shipping was in Greek hands, and even brought it to a halt when the Turks closed the Straits to merchantmen. The plague, endemic in Turkey, struck several times, despite strict quarantine controls. The slave trade had been banned. Russian and Ukrainian traders showed little enterprising spirit and no interest in the carrying trade from port to port.[96] Foreign traders quickly discovered that the Black Sea hinterland was not populated or economically developed enough to constitute a substantial market capable of absorbing potential imports. Trade in the entire Ukraine was still conducted in market towns and at regular fairs, chiefly for the satisfaction of local needs, and most of the peasantry had no surplus cash.[97] Foreign trade did not expand and diversify enough to include more than agricultural products, especially grain. Commerce, like that of the eastern theatre, was the transit trade, here of Right Bank Ukraine, carrying Prussian, Polish, and Austrian manufactures, textiles above all, and did not affect the economy of the region they traversed.

Russia's tariff policy remained what it had been in the eighteenth century, largely protectionist and at times even prohibitive, as if consciously designed to restrict the development of international trade. It was matched by a similar policy among the Ottomans. The Tariff of 1819,[98] which removed all prohibitions on imports, caused such distress among core merchants, who could not withstand the competition of essentially British goods, that the Tariff of 1822[99] restored high protective rates and the prohibitions of the Tariff of March 1816.[100] No major changes took place during the reign of Nicholas I (1825–55), despite a steady rise of Russian foreign trade beginning in 1836, following the cancellation of a number of prohibitions in the 1822 tariff in 1836 and 1838, and a revision of the tariff in November 1841,[101] which abandoned a prohibitive for a merely protectionist tariff. Grain exports, which made up most of the exports of the southern theatre, depended on the Ukrainian harvests and the fluctuation of demand in western Europe. As a result, it remained vulnerable to changes over which the authorities and the traders had no control.

By the end of Alexander's reign, the situation had become catastrophic. A French consul who sailed in the Black Sea after 1819 saw no trace of navigation and was struck by "the silence of death" hovering over the ports.[102] The governor general reported in 1825 that the region's merchants deserved the government's "full compassion" (i.e., tax exemptions): the harvest had been poor and demand had collapsed; the men had lost their capital in the Ottoman Empire, their social degradation was extreme, they fled abroad to escape their creditors, and their destitution was "hardly credible."[103] That same year, the former interior minister, Viktor Kochubei, wrote to Speransky in Petersburg that no trade was to be seen even in the provinces of the interior, that Russian industry was stagnant, that locusts had destroyed the harvest, and that poverty was "extraordinary." A "deep gloom" had descended on Odessa, where the trading houses were closing and the foreign merchants were leaving.[104]

Another observer pointed to another cause of the decline of the Black Sea trade as early as 1822, only three years after the opening of the free port which had generated such enthusiasm. There had once been Genoese and Venetian colonies on the Crimean and Azov coasts. They had been the terminal cities of the intercontinental route to and from India and China. Now, it was all "ruins and emptiness," because the overland commerce had been destroyed by the sea route around the Cape of Good Hope.[105] And indeed, the Russian and Black Sea trade had fallen victim to the fundamental shift of the trade routes following the great voyages of discovery of the sixteenth and seventeenth centuries. The ensuing rivalry between continental and maritime economies was relegating the emerging Russian Empire to the position of a backwater in the world economy, and Russian tariff policy helped transform the expanding Russian core – which by then had ceased to expand in the southern theatre – into a Fortress Empire. There had been no change by 1832, when another observer visited Odessa and was appalled by what he saw: a "somber, wild and melancholy place," in "wretched condition," with filthy peasants and stupid- looking soldiers, this in a town of 41,552 people, including 33,646 Christians and 7,906 Jews. No bustle or activity was to be seen, and he hastened "to quit this melancholy abode for the smiling shores of the Bosphorus, where Turkish despotism has not, at least, degraded the human species to the condition of the brute."[106]

Yet, the region's potential was enormous, and the exploitation of the coal mines of the Donbas and the iron ore of Kryvyi Rih (Krivoi Rog) would revolutionize the Ukrainian economy. Paradoxically, this transformation and the resulting revolution in foreign trade, not unlike that of the 1770s, would require a deeper integration into the core by means of railroads.[107] Except for the iron transported from the Urals in barges down the Volga and the Don to Taganrog, most of the grain and other agricultural products were transported across the steppe in ox-driven wagons, which exercised a quasi-monopoly of the Ukrainian overland transport.[108] Ukrainian rivers, including the Don, were not suitable for reliable transport because of their low gradient, shallowness, and ice in wintertime.[109] But costs and the volume of exchanges had so risen by the end of Nicholas I's reign – what with the growth of population and industry after the slump of the 1820s, and the gradual transformation of fairs into permanent towns – that this type of transportation, which had always been the least efficient, was becoming obsolete.[110] Railroads would transform Kiev, Ekaterynoslav, and Rostov into major transportation hubs. The Black Sea economy of the future would not be one in which the Ukrainian provinces would be drawn out into a single market with the Anatolian towns, but one more deeply integrated into the economy of the expanding Russian core.

The First Cracks

Schools and Universities

Ever since the establishment of a protectorate over Left Bank Ukraine in 1654, which committed the expanding core to advance into the Ukrainian lands and face the Polish core already settled in them, it had been the Russian government's policy to steadily dismantle local institutions in order to eventually create a unitary state. The implementation of that policy accelerated during the reign of Catherine II, and reached its completion during that of Nicholas I. But, in truly Hegelian fashion, the victory of the unitary state, which the creation of universities was expected to crown, coincided with the first challenges from below. They constituted a regional backlash against the uniformity imposed from Moscow and Petersburg, and would themselves create another backlash in the form of repressive policies, thus compounding the problem.

There was a great yearning for a higher education in Left Bank Ukraine during the reign of Catherine II, as we can easily see from the instructions given by the local nobility to their delegates to the Legislative Commission.[111] This was to be expected from a rising class of landowners consolidating its power over the peasantry and eager to join the multi-ethnic ruling class of the expanding core. They complained that universities were far away; some managed to send their children to Moscow and Petersburg (which did not have a university) and even abroad, but at a ruinous cost. One detects a very utilitarian approach to education: they sought an education, not so much in order to ask great questions and to participate in the debate generated by the Enlightenment, as to join the ranks of military commanders, civil officials and judges, and "useful citizens." They were also for the education of a select group of women. They bemoaned the fact that Catherine was laying the foundation of an extensive network of schools and that the former Hetmanate was not included in it: they were thus calling for the integration of a new Ukrainian school system into that of the expanding core.[112] The brilliant careers of Alexander Bezborodko and Petro Zavadovsky, both patronized by Governor General Rumiantsev in the 1760s, invited others to seek entry into the civil and military hierarchy. There had been a time when the Ukrainian Church had given the Russian Church a large number of capable bishops who had graduated from the Mohyla Academy; the demand was now for young Ukrainians educated in the sciences.

As a result, the nobles called for the creation of a university in the region. Hetman Razumovsky had proposed one in Baturyn, his headquarters. The nobles called for one in Chernihiv or Pereiaslav, "which had been the capital of a principality and the place where Bohdan Khmelnytsky had placed Little Russia under Russian suzerainty [*poddanstvo*]."[113] In 1786, Catherine did agree to build one in Chernihiv, but her intention was never realized.[114] There could also be one in Kiev, and Potemkin wanted one in Ekaterynoslav, but it was the Austrian emperor, Joseph II, who built the first university on Ukrainian soil, in Lviv in 1784. The most likely reason for the reluctance may have been that the creation of a university required the existence of a network of elementary and secondary schools to train students for a higher education, and these did not exist until the end of the eighteenth century. Vinsky tells us how haphazard his education had been: in the local parish school, where thrashing the boys seems to have been the major activity, then learning Latin from a Polish landowner, going to Polish school in Chernihiv to age fifteen, then to the Mohyla Academy for a year to learn more Polish and Latin in preparation for a clerical career which he did not want. His parents chose to send him to the Guard instead, where he began a new life in Petersburg.[115]

There were only a few intermediate schools. There was, of course, the venerable Mohyla Academy in Kiev, founded in 1632 as an institution of higher learning modelled after the Jesuit schools, but it saw itself as the defender of the Orthodox Church, not as an institution of secular learning. It stressed the humanities, but without the contributions of the Renaissance and the Reformation, and neglected the sciences. It was, at first, called only a college of secondary education and not an academy until 1701, because only an academy could teach philosophy and theology, and the Polish king did not want to create a rival of the Jesuit-run Polish academies. In the second half of the eighteenth century, courses in mathematics, medicine, geography, and history were added to the curriculum, but the abolition of the Hetmanate and the secularization of the Left Bank monasteries in 1786 deprived the academy of its chief sources of financial support. By the end of the century, it had been relegated to the rank of a diocesan seminary. In 1811, 1,069 of its 1,198 students were candidates for the priesthood; it was closed in 1817, but reopened two years later as a theological seminary. The Academy had neglected secular culture and even the Ukrainian vernacular – the courses were taught in Latin – and had become irrelevant outside the church hierarchy.[116]

There was the Kharkiv College (Collegium), founded in 1722 as a diocesan seminary in Belgorod, transferred to Kharkiv in 1726. Modelled after the Mohyla Academy, it trained candidates for the priesthood, and was called a college in 1734. Among contemporaries, its prestige was second only to that of the Mohyla Academy. In 1737, French and German were added to the curriculum; mathematics, drafting, artillery, and land surveying in 1765, physics and natural history in 1795. However, its role in secular education declined after the founding of Kharkiv University in 1805, and it became simply a theological seminary in 1817. There was another college in Pereiaslav founded in 1738, also to train Orthodox clergy. Its six-year program followed that of the Mohyla Academy; it taught Polish and Latin, rhetoric, music, and mathematics. In 1785, a branch of it was transferred to Novhorod-Siversky and reorganized into a seminary, and the college itself eventually became another theological seminary. Thus, the three major schools in Left Bank Ukraine did not outgrow their religious mission. The secular trend in education passed them by and required the creation of a new set of institutions. As Catherine's school reform took hold in the Left Bank, the new secular schools, Russian- and no longer Polish-oriented, dominated the field of education. The old religious schools became more tightly integrated into the hierarchy of the Orthodox Church, and the new schools became the local agencies of a new education ministry in Petersburg.

But the creation of a central agency did not preclude the foundation of new separate institutions. In 1817, a Richelieu lycée – named after the former governor general – was founded in Odessa, which drew children primarily from aristocratic and wealthy merchant families. French was the only language of instruction until 1820, when some classes began to be taught in Russian. Its eight-year program emphasized philosophy and juridical-political studies and ignored technical or professional specialization. But in the late 1820s, the curriculum was broadened to include mathematics, physics, chemistry, biology, and geography, and a pedagogical institute was also created to train teachers for county and commercial courts. It remained a secondary level school (gymnasium) until 1837, when it became an institution of higher learning, with an Eastern-language institute for the training of interpreters for the army, and in the 1840s its mandate became the training of government officials. It was the precursor of Odessa University, created in 1865.

In Nizhyn, once the great commercial hub of the Hetmanate, another lycée was founded in July 1805 (but did not begin to function until 1820), named after Ilia Bezborodko (brother of Catherine II's former secretary), who contributed 210,000 roubles to its endowment. It was originally a gymnasium for sons of the nobility, with a nine-year program offering a classical education in ancient and modern languages, geography, history, mathematics, physics, and military science. Its most famous graduate would be Nikolai Gogol. But in 1832, the gymnasium was transformed into a technical lycée for the training of military officers, and in 1840, it became a law school for the training of officials in the Justice Ministry; a veterinary school was added in 1839. The school was well supplied with a surgical laboratory, mineral collections, and a botanical garden. Like the Richelieu lycée, it became a specialized school on the margin of the regular school hierarchy of gymnasia in the provincial capitals and county schools, but also one with a mandate not limited to the the education of Ukrainians but of others as well, who would serve in the administrative apparatus of the expanding core. They were integrated into a hierarchy which did not recognize ethnic boundaries within the unitary state.

The crowning event was the creation of Kharkiv University in 1805. It was significant that it should have been founded in the corridor which had never been part of the Hetmanate but had depended on Belgorod, as if to emphasize that its own work of regional integration in the Left Bank and New Russian provinces (but not the Right Bank) would take place within the larger policy of integration carried out by the core's central agencies. The university was founded on the initiative of Vasilii Karazin, born near Bohodukhiv (between Okhtyrka and Kharkiv) in 1773, who had studied mining and metallurgy in Petersburg, and had been director of schools in the Ministry of Education from 1801 to 1804. He convinced the nobility and merchants of the province to contribute funds for its upkeep; forty years earlier, their parents had already been eager to pool their resources to support a university. The instruction was in Russian, and the professors were foreigners for the most part. It consisted of four faculties (mathematics and physics; history and philology; law; and medicine), to which a veterinary school was added in 1839. In the 1830s, the university lost its jurisdiction over the New Russian schools, which passed under the supervision of the Odessa educational region, and was given a new charter (1835), which increased the powers of the Education Ministry. Like other Ukrainian institutions, Kharkiv University felt the repercussions from the Polish uprising. Censorship grew worse, and the scholars' freedom to travel was curtailed. But the university had already played a major role, not only as an institution of learning but also as a cultural centre for a Ukrainian public increasingly conscious of its separate identity.

In Right Bank Ukraine, a major reform of the school system had taken place after the suppression of the Jesuit Order in 1773. Its properties were entrusted to an Education Commission, which assumed jurisdiction over the entire educational establishment and classified schools as academies ("main schools"), district (*okruzhni*), local (*pidokruzhni*), and parish (*parafialni*) schools. It divided the Polish Empire into nine regions (*okrugi*), five of them in the kingdom (*Korona*), including a Volhynian (capital Kremenets) and a Ukrainian (capital Vinnytsia). Each region had one district and two or more local schools, supported by funds from the former Jesuit schools (the so-called *fundusz* properties). The new school system was given a statute in 1783, three years before a similar reform was introduced in the Russian core. The academies were university-level institutions, while the district schools taught the humanities and sciences, agriculture and gardening, arts and crafts.[117] Parish school education, however, was neglected, for lack of both funds and teachers, and because the "people," consisting largely of serfs, continued to live in a parallel universe, sunk in ignorance and superstition.

The annexation of the Right Bank was viewed favourably even by some among the Polish clergy, as when a Polish priest wrote that "Russian domination [*vladychestvo*] opens to us the most favourable perspectives."[118] It was impossible, and would have been counterproductive, to introduce the Russian school system into the territory. In the parish schools, the teaching monks, mostly Basilians and Piarists, were placed under the authority of the bishops, and a statute was promulgated for the Roman Catholic churches and monasteries. The other schools were subordinated to the governor and the board of public welfare (one in each province), which financed the schools elsewhere in the Russian core. Teaching was addressed chiefly to the sons of Polish nobles, but Orthodox sons of clergy and burghers preferred the Russian gymnasium in Kiev. The three schools in Kremenets, Vinnytsia, and Nemirov had 806 students in 1801; 613 were nobles, and 112 were sons of clergy, both groups making up 90 per cent of the total enrollment; 66 were sons of burghers, and 15 were of diverse origin. All subjects were taught in Polish; Russian, like French and German, was considered an elective, and was even taught in Polish! Yet, despite the strong noble character of the Polish schools, about 20 per cent of the student body was Orthodox and Uniate.[119]

The creation of a Ministry of Education in 1802 tightened the school hierarchy in the expanding core, and made it possible to engage in a policy of integration while recognizing the need to retain a certain diversity created by historical circumstances. It is worth noting that the first minister was Petro Zavadovsky (1802–10), who had been one of Catherine's secretaries and chairman of the School Commission (1782–99) that drafted the school reform of 1786: he was thus the main figure in the formulation of an educational policy for eighteen years. He was the descendant of an old Polish family, whose members had become Russian subjects at the beginning of the seventeenth century. His father was a poor landowner from Starodub county, who sent his son to study in a Jesuit school in Orsha (Belorussia), then to the Mohyla Academy. Petro then served in the Little Russian College and in Rumiantsev's chancery, and the governor general introduced him to Catherine in 1775. He was thus by nature and by training well disposed to the maintenance of Polish influence in the Right Bank. Karazin, we saw, was the director of schools in the ministry from 1801 to 1804. Zavadovsky's successor was Alexei Razumovsky (1810–16), the son of the last hetman and former curator of the Moscow educational region. And we cannot overlook the fact that Adam Czartoryski, whose family came from Volhynia and who played such an important role in Russia's relations with Poland during the first quarter of the nineteenth century, was curator of the Vilnius educational region (which included the Right Bank) for twenty years (1803–23), even though he was often away on other official business. Seweryn Potocki was his counterpart in Kharkiv from 1803 to 1817.

Such a favourable environment played a part in the creation of the Kremenets (Krzemieniec) Lyceum in October 1805, when Czartoryski was also foreign minister (1802–6). The town was one of the oldest in the Ukrainian lands – Greek and Roman coins were found there. It had been one of the strongholds of the principality of Galicia-Volhynia and had withstood sieges by Hungarians, Poles, and Mongols before being destroyed in 1261. But it recovered and flourished in the fifteenth and sixteenth centuries as a county seat of the Volhynia *voevoda*, and fought Tatars and Turks. In the seventeenth century, it had a monastery, a brotherhood school, and a printing press. Between 1725 and 1839, the Uniate monastery was run by the Basilian Order. It fell victim to the Cossack wars of the mid-seventeenth century and never recovered its former greatness, but its history and location on a ridge forming the watershed between the basins of the Dnieper, Dniester, and Vistula made it a natural bastion of Polish influence in the region.

The lyceum was the brainchild of Tadeusz Czaski, Czartoryski's deputy and the de facto curator. It was soon called "the colony of Vilnius University" and the "Volhynian Athens."[120] The school was housed in the monastery, and Czaski bought for it the library of the last Polish king. He intended the lyceum to serve as a university for the young nobles of the entire Right Bank. Polish was the language of instruction in the humanities and sciences, as well as in Latin, German, and Russian. It also had several science collections. Most of its six hundred students in 1821 were Poles: only thirty-four were Ukrainians, but they became intoxicated with the Polish indoctrination they had received and joined the 1830 uprising. As a result, the school was closed, and its library was transferred to Kiev, where St Vladimir University was founded in 1834 (at present Taras Shevchenko National University).

Until the outbreak of the rebellion, the Russian government had accepted the dominance of Polish culture in the Right Bank, which it had combined with Lithuania to form a single educational region. That policy ran hand in hand with the policy of superstratification, which relied on the cooperation of the magnates with the Russians. But the rebellion convinced the new emperor, Nicholas I, that both policies had failed and that the Right Bank had to be Russified. The territory was separated from Lithuania to form a separate region under the supervision of the new university in Kiev. The university's beginnings were modest. It had only one faculty, divided into two departments: history and philology; physics and mathematics. A law faculty was opened in 1835 and a medical faculty in 1841. The university's four-year program was designed to give a general, not a specialized, education. Its autonomy was restricted: the elected professors and deans had to be approved by the minister of education (Sergei Uvarov from 1833 to 1849), and the rector by the emperor, who also appointed the curator. Of its original sixty-two students, thirty-four were Catholic and mostly Poles, with some Uniates.[121] It was symptomatic of the cultural importance of the Polish (and Polonized) upper stratum that a university created to counter Polish influence would have a majority of Polish students until the 1860s. Most of the others were Ukrainians from the Left Bank.

Paradoxically, and for reasons to be examined presently, an instrument of Russification became instead a centre of revolutionary activity and national awakening. In 1838, a clandestine student society was discovered, and in 1845, Nikolai Kostomarov founded the Cyril and Methodius Brotherhood. Then came the revolution of 1848, which shook most of central Europe and brought about a Russian military invasion of Hungary. Kiev University was caught in the storm. The philosophy faculty was closed, the rector and deans would have to be appointed by the emperor, foreign scholars were denied teaching positions, and the enrolment of self-supporting students was limited to three hundred. Darkness fell upon Fortress Empire, and when it cleared during the following reign, the legitimacy of the core area government had been shattered beyond repair.

The Challenge to Integration

This network of schools and universities was fated to exercise the most destabilizing influence in the Ukrainian lands, because it created a political infrastructure for the crystallization of yearnings, ambitions, and resentments directed against that policy of integration, with its accompanying emphasis on uniformity and the promotion of intolerance. By the 1840s, that policy had run its full course, but only to discover that it faced an existential threat in the form of Polish nationalism and Ukrainian self-consciousness.

The Ukrainian lands were a religious frontier between Polish Catholicism and Russian Orthodoxy until the destruction of the Uniate Church. They remained a political and religious frontier between the Polish and Russian cores. They had once been an internal frontier of the expanding Polish core before they were split along the Dnieper to become a similar frontier between the expanding Russian core to the east and a receding Polish core to the west. After 1795, they were an internal frontier of the expanding Russian core. Twenty years later, when most of the Polish core was incorporated into the Russian Empire, both core and frontier became part of the Russian Empire. The Polish core continued to exert a powerful influence, as befits a core area, over territories located far beyond its natural borders, capable of blocking the progress of Russian influence. Ukrainian self-consciousness grew under the wings of Russian autocracy. It was a home-grown phenomenon, but one no less subversive of the ideals of uniformity and integration which had sustained the expansion of the original Russian core for nearly two hundred years.

The policy of integration had rested on the assumption that a mutual interest existed between the Russian ruling elite and ruling class on the one hand, and the existing (or aspiring) ruling class, on the other, in the various territories incorporated over the years into the expanding Russian core. The policy recognized the existence, but denied the importance, of ethnic differences, accepted the leading members of the upper strata of those territories into the core area government, and gave them opportunities to realize their ambitions while they consolidated their position in the home territories. The dominant feature of the social and economic history of the large frontier belt running from the Baltic to the Caspian from the 1650s to the end of the eighteenth century was the development and triumph of serfdom. The transformation of these upper strata into a single core area ruling elite was accomplished on the back of a peasantry downgraded to the lowest level of their society. Therefore, the policy of integration rested on a class foundation. Russian and non-Russian elites were bound together into a single patronage network and a single multi-ethnic ruling elite and ruling class by their exploitation of the "people" – that is, the peasantry, which made up some 90 per cent of the population, and the burghers in towns, which often were barely visible spots in a uniform agrarian landscape.

But in the 1770s Johann von Herder (1744–1803) began to preach in the German lands a new gospel rejecting the principal tenet of classicism – the equality (in the elites) and rationality of all men in a cosmopolitan universe – in favour of the glorification of the same "people" who lived in oppression, as the carriers of a "spirit" peculiar to each.[122] The people was no longer understood in a class, but in a territorial, sense. A belief in the people (*Volk*) as the carrier of its own individual spirit (*Volksgeist*) was a belief in diversity instead of uniformity, in liberation instead of integration, in equality rather than stratification. Herder and the Grimm brothers collected folksongs, which harked back to a distant past, and the distant past evoked an idealized state of nature, which had been whittled down by the intervention of the core powers and their policy of integration in the name of their own "spirit." This reaction took the form of nationalism, that destructive force which shattered the cosmopolitanism of the eighteenth century and challenged head-on the policy of integration, to create a world of warring nation states which would eventually commit collective suicide in the horrors of the twentieth century.

The new gospel was given the name of Romanticism, which carried in Poland and Ukraine a heavier and more emotional historical baggage than perhaps anywhere else. The Poles hardly needed it, it is true, because a core area is an indestructible cultural epicentre which never ceases to project influence far and wide. But the partitions caused greater pain because they sought to destroy an age-long mission to Polonize subject peoples in Ukraine, Lithuania, and Belorussia, and subjected the core to Russian cultural hegemony, with its apparatus of compulsion in all areas of public and even private life. The Poles forgot that they had been conquered, and proceeded to assert their cultural mission through the school system created by the Russians. They sought to use

Russian or Russian-approved institutions to destroy the hegemony of the Russian core, only to create a disaster for themselves and, unfortunately, for many others as well.

The leader of the Polish offensive was the same Tadeusz Czacki, born in 1765 in Volodymyr country of Volhynia, a short distance from the Western Bug. By his Jesuit teacher he was taught to love Polish history and ethnography, and he could not remain indifferent to the political death of Poland. He was one of the major authors of the Constitution of 3 May 1791, which sought to modernize the Polish political system by giving greater rights to the "people." He became embroiled in the 1793 uprising in Kraków, and his properties were confiscated by the Russians, but were later returned. He made a name for himself by publishing two works on Polish and Lithuanian law, and in 1803 Czartoryski chose him as his deputy in the Vilnius educational region. His inspection tour of the region disclosed dilapidated buildings and poorly respected teachers, and he learned that Russian history was taught, but not Polish. His reaction was to deepen the Polonization of the region and induce even Russian officials to speak and write Polish with the assistance of the (redoubtable) Polish ladies. Polish became fashionable even among the Orthodox clergy. He insisted that those who did not want to speak Polish must speak French, and never Russian. The Kremianets Lyceum was created to radiate Polish influence and extinguish the Russian presence. Every Polish landlord was encouraged to build a school on his property to teach Polish history to the children of his Ukrainian serfs and to convert them to Catholicism.[123]

The Russian authorities were aware that a *Kulturkampf* had been launched against them. The minister of the interior, Alexei Kurakin, stated in 1809 that, unlike the peasant in Krylov's fable, Zavadovsky did not realize how many snakes he was bringing into the western territories, and that Czaski was working for no less than the restoration of Poland. With all public education in the hands of the Poles, he was creating enemies of Russia every day.[124] Czaski died after a nervous breakdown in Dubno in 1813, but not without leaving a legacy of anti-Russian hatred among Polish youth. They would reject the very principle of integration into the Russian core, not in the name of a new Ukrainian national consciousness, but in the name of a Polish policy of restoring the *Korona*, which had always pursued its own policy of integration and Polonization.

The policy of integration was challenged by the Ukrainians as well. In the 1760s, Rumiantsev expressed his surprise that the upper stratum of Cossack society remained devoted to their own separate nationality, "even if they had acquired a higher education abroad."[125] For the governor general, yearnings for autonomy smacked of republican subversion, as in Semen Divovych's *Conversation of Great Russia with Little Russia* (1762), which pitted one against the other and called for a separate status for the latter. Rumiantsev's reaction was typical of the age of classicism, which proclaimed that the triumph of reason over obscurantism was inseparable from the spread of cosmopolitanism and the creation of a supra-national elite, which kept the people and the vernacular in the lower ranges of human consciousness. In the second half of the eighteenth century, the higher stratum of Left Bank society became Russified and, by extension, "internationalized," while the townsmen, common people, and village clergy "remained as silent as death" – as was the case elsewhere in the expanding core.[126]

But Divovych was pointing the way to the future. A generation later, Herder's influence was being felt across the Dnieper. In Novhorod-Siversky, a "patriotic circle" of Left Bank autonomists was discussing the revival of a state and the rebirth of a Ukrainian culture wallowing in "a sea of Russianism."[127] Its members were graduates of the Mohyla Academy but also of foreign universities. They called for the creation of a university in their home town and of a Ukrainian academy of sciences. They collected materials on Ukrainian history and language, and championed the rights of a separate nobility and of the much downgraded Cossacks. They went farther by calling for a new independent Ukraine which would unite both banks of the Dnieper as well as New Russia, where the Ukrainians formed an overwhelming majority. They distributed propaganda among the carbineer regiments, which had been Cossack regiments until 1783, and may even have sent Vasyl Kapnist to Berlin in 1791, at at time of acute tension between Russia and Prussia, to raise the possibility of a Prussian-Ukrainian alliance – a dangerous move harking back to Mazepa's suicidal move in 1709. That such a new Ukraine would acquire a "Polish question," with potential disastrous consequences, must have remained moot.

The same region – in the very margin of the Russian, Lithuanian, and Polish worlds – may have been the home of the anonymous author of the *History of the Rus'*, written possibly at the end of the eighteenth century. The work circulated in manuscript form, was first mentioned in 1825, and was published in 1846. It depicted the development of Ukrainian history until 1769, but was not intended to be an objective history. Written in the Russian language of the day with a strong admixture of Ukrainian words, its underlying idea was that each nation, defined as the bearer of its own spirit found in folksongs and historical ballads, had a right to an independent political existence.[128] By implication, the creation of a Ukrainian nation required the rejection of the policy of integration and uniformity, whether Polish or Russian, and, in the geopolitical circumstances of the time, would inevitably bring about a civil war with the Polish magnates and the Russian army. But those were still the heydays of illusions, when the implications of one's words were ignored or brushed away. Only when ideas create and animate an organizational construct are intellectuals faced with the implications of their follies.

The awakening of a Ukrainian self-awareness and patriotism, which would eventually turn into a nationalism marking the transformation of an ethnic community into a politically conscious nation, incompatible with the maintenance of a unitary state, already began to create a split among the Ukrainian nobility and intelligentsia slowly emerging out of the lower strata of the Cossack world. Among other beneficiaries of the policy of integration was Dmytro Troshchynsky (1754–1829), one of Catherine's secretaries – who followed Zavadovsky and served with Bezborodko and the Tatar poet from Kazan, Gavril Derzhavin – and minister of justice (1814–17), who asked Alexander I to abolish the Lithuanian Statute twenty-five years before it was formally superseded by Russian law.[129] There was also Viktor Kochubei (1768–1834), a descendant of Vasyl Kochubei (executed on Peter I's order to settle a sordid quarrel with Mazepa), envoy to Constantinople (1793–8), minister of the interior (1802–7, 1819–23), chairman of the State Council and Committee of Ministers (1827–34) – in effect, the most powerful member of the civil government in Petersburg, who was made a count in 1799 and a prince in 1831. He once told the Ukrainophile Nikolai Repnin-Volkonsky, the governor general of Little Russia (1816–34), that "although I was born a *khokhol*, I am more Russian than anybody else … I look at the affairs of your province from the point of view of the common interests of our country. Microscopic views are not for me."[130] And there was Nikolai Gogol of a later generation (1809–52), who was deeply influenced by Troshchynsky: he yearned for fame but also knew he could find it only in Petersburg.[131] For all these men, a deep attachment to their native land was not incompatible with loyal service in the imperial government and identification with its multi-ethnic ruling elite. They easily wore two identities, and it may very well have been that, for some, one strengthened the other.

But the Romantic movement was pulling others in the opposite direction. It spread from Europe to Poland and Russia at the beginning of the nineteenth century. The first manifestation of its influence was the publication (in Petersburg) of Oleksii Pavlovsky's *Grammar of the Little Russian Dialect* in 1818 and of Nikolai Tsertelev's *Attempt at Collecting Little Russian Songs* in 1819. A major event was the publication (in Moscow) of Mykhailo Maksymovych's *Little Russian Songs* in 1827. There also appeared "Ukrainian schools" in Russian and Polish literature. In Russian literature the leading members of the Ukrainian school were not only Russians like Konrad Ryleev, hanged in 1826 for his participation in the Decembrist uprising, but also Ukrainians writing in Russian, especially Gogol. The Russians were enthralled by the exotic nature of things Ukrainian, like nature, history, folklore, or mores.[132] The Romantic movement competed with the neoclassicism influencing architecture and the arts in Russia, the legacy of the Napoleonic empire. The divide between the two mirrored the divide between the Ukrainians who joined the ruling elite or identified with it and those who believed in a separate way for Ukraine, almost entirely unified at last, but under Russian auspices.

Particularly influential was the so-called Kharkiv Romantic School, referring to a group of young poets and professors gathered at Kharkiv University in the 1830s and 1840s by Izmail Sreznevsky (1812–80), a Ukrainophile Russian scholar and ethnographer. Imbued with an incipient national consciousness, they studied Ukrainian ethnography, collected and published folk songs and legends, and developed their own historical themes. While their predecessors had not yet sloughed off their supercilious attitude toward the "people," they looked upon the peasant and the lowly Cossack, now downgraded to the level of state peasants, as a source of spiritual renewal and poetic inspiration. They in turn were the precursors of what would be called a Ukrainian messianism.[133]

The Kharkiv Romantic School remained politically innocent, but it sprouted Nikolai Kostomarov (1817–85), born in Voronezh province in an old Russian noble family. His father had been receptive to the ideas of the French Revolution, and the son was strongly influenced by Herder's philosophy. In Kharkiv University he became an ardent student of history. He later moved to Kiev, where he became a teacher and met Pantaleimon Kulish, born near Novgorod-Seversk in 1819, who wrote the *Black Council*, a historical chronicle of the events of 1663 (when Briukhovetsky was elected hetman), of which excerpts were published in Moscow in 1845–6. It was at the very same time that Kostomarov crossed the Rubicon, when he founded, with others, the Cyril and Methodius Brotherhood. The secret society lasted barely a year, and may have had some one hundred members, but it never reached the organizational stage. Denounced by one of its members, it was closed in March 1847 – an event which may have convinced the government to appoint Governor General Bibikov curator of Kiev University the following year.[134]

The society's program was formulated in the Books of the Genesis of the Ukrainian People, influenced by the *History of the Rus'* and *The Books of the Polish Nation and of the Polish Pilgrims* by the Polish-Lithuanian poet Adam Mickiewicz (1798–1855).[135] It aimed at transforming the social order in accordance with Christian principles of justice, freedom, equality, and brotherhood – the great slogans of the French Revolution – and the unification of the Slavic peoples in a federation, of which Kiev would be the capital and the seat of an all-Slavic parliament. But behind this cloud of dreams there was a hard core of political ideas which struck at the foundation of the Russian policy of integration. The emperor was a despot who ruled over three Slavic peoples – Russian, Ukrainian, and Belorussian – with the help of "Germans," the standard bugbear of the Slavophiles, a notion which evoked Slavic memories back to the days when the Scandinavians had come to rule over Rus'. Ukraine will rise from the grave, and so will the Slavic world (*Slavianshchyna*). Ukraine and each Slavic people will form a republic (*Rechpospolita*) with its own administration, not merged with another (*ne slito s drugimi*). It is curious that Kostomarov used the term by which the Poles called their empire, which had become synonymous with anarchy and the despotism of the *szlachta*, especially in the Ukrainian lands. Perhaps Kostomarov followed Mickiewicz too closely and overlooked the implications of his choice of words. The program also called for the abolition of serfdom, the education of the broad masses, and the development of the national language and culture of each Slavic land.[136] Indeed, the abolition of serfdom fifteen years later would destabilize and delegitimize the entire system and give free rein to the forces of nationalism, which would eventually destroy both core and empire. The program was thus a revolutionary document, and the alarm it caused in the government was justified, but that government, basking in the triumph of its policy of integration, was already on the defensive. The 1840s did mark a turning point.

One of the brotherhood's possible members was Taras Shevchenko (1814–61), born a serf in Kiev province, one of the few leaders of the Ukrainian revival to be born in the Right Bank. The "bard of Ukraine" showed an early talent for drawing and painting, and was apprenticed in Petersburg by his master, who agreed to emancipate him. He returned to Ukraine in the early 1840s, befriended the wife of Repnin-Volkonsky,[137] but was dismayed by the impact of Russian rule on the region. He wrote satirical poems, including one directed against Nicholas I, and, as a result, was given in 1847 a harsher sentence than the other members: detention in Orsk on the Ural River and, later, in a desolate outpost on the Caspian coast. In an act of vindictiveness he was forbidden to write and even to sketch. He returned in 1857, but was not allowed to visit his homeland: he died in Petersburg.[138]

Shevchenko made a clean break with the Romantic yearnings of his contemporaries. Although his first collection of poems, published under the title of *Kobzar* (The Minstrel) in 1841, still dealt with Romantic themes, the epic poem *Haidamaky* (1841) invoked the Cossacks' struggle against the Poles in the 1760s. The poet began to see himself as the spokesman for the Ukrainian nation, and could not forgive Khmelnytsky for the agreement of 1654, although he praised Doroshenko and Mazepa, overlooking the disastrous consequences of their rule.[139] *The Dream*, written in 1844, was "one of the most violent and effective attacks on [Russian] tyranny"; it exposed the burden of the Russian yoke, its harshness and corruption; even if it was not openly stated, Shevchenko was calling for the independence of Ukraine. After his death, which coincided with the abolition of serfdom, the Ukrainians embarked on a dangerous struggle with the Russian overlord, based on a recognition of a separate identity for the basin of the Dnieper, where "Orchards bow down, richly laden, / Poplars, standing straight / Like sentinels in the open land / Are speaking with the plain."[140]

Conclusion to Part II: The Southern Theatre

While the eastern theatre consisted mostly of the basin of the Caspian Sea, the southern theatre was definitely that of the Black Sea. Drained by the Dniester, the Southern Buh, the Dnieper, and the Don, it extended southwards to include the valley of the Rion across the Caucasus, as well as the lower Danube, which led, along the border of modern Rumania and Bulgaria, to the river's Iron Gates and Serbia in the land of the Southern Slavs. All these rivers flowed into the Black Sea, the little mediterranean connected with the great one by the Turkish Straits, closed by the Ottomans to the ships of other nations and, after 1774, open to their own warships alone. The southern theatre was the hinterland of the Ottoman Empire north of the Black Sea and the hunting grounds of the Crimean Tatars. They raided for human booty as far west as Kremienets, as far north as the approaches to Moscow, and as far east as the northern fringes of the Caucasus in the valley of the Terek.

This fan-like hinterland was the scene of permanent conflict with Poland-Lithuania in the west and the expanding Muscovite core in the north, all the way to the approaches to the eastern theatre, where other Turkic peoples raided Russian settlements in a similar fan-like strategic space stretching from the Volga to the Altai Mountains. The expansion of the Russian core took place against Poland-Lithuania and the Crimean khanate, and eventually against the Turkish core as well, in an enveloping movement shaped by the contours of the Black Sea, one prong directed against Adrianople and Constantinople, the other against Erzerum and Anatolia. By the early 1850s, when our story ends, Russia had become the hegemonic power in the southern theatre as well, and its policy had been one of harmonization and integration aiming at the eventual creation of a unitary state in an expanding Russian core.

"Integration" is a term likely to be misunderstood. In the southern theatre it did not mean that the Russians introduced a replica of their administrative, social, and legal system immediately upon the incorporation of a new territory into the expanding core. Such a policy would have been impossible to carry out, if only because they often knew little about the new lands and did not have enough personnel. On the other hand, if it had been possible to carry it out, the policy would have been counterproductive because of the resentment of the local population at the sudden imposition of a new way of life. The harmonization of institutions and procedures and social organization was gradual, but the Russians expected it to result in such integration in the future, the speed of the process depending upon the situation in each territory.

Moreover, integration was not only a horizontal process; it was also a vertical one. The depth of its penetration depended on the ability to restructure the lower levels of society. The introduction of Russian administrative agencies (courts, fiscal agencies) in a newly incorporated territory was a form of integration, but at a superficial level. The adoption of Russian law, taxation, and education, which affected social relations at the deeper levels, was another form of, or, better, a more advanced stage in the process of, integration. But no matter how fast the policy developed, the ruling elite in the capital, despite the fact that it was a multi-ethnic one, had no doubt that the expansion of the Russian core would create in the end a single, uniform, and integrated community governed by the same rules.

One may argue over the relative importance of commercial incentives and geopolitical imperatives in Russia's expansion toward the Black Sea, but, on closer analysis, the southern advance of the Russian core must be placed in the larger context of the broad offensive against the largely nomadic Turkic world which had "begun" in spectacular fashion with the conquests of Ivan IV. The Crimean khanate was the last remnant of the Kipchak khanate, and its annexation in 1783 marked the conclusion of that offensive. But it also resulted in a declaration of permanent war with the Ottoman Empire, with which the expanding Russian core fought more wars than with any other power. Ottoman territories from the Balkans to the Transcaucasian border with Persia became a "domain of war," a Dar-el-Islam in reverse, where the expanding core would some day transform Anatolia into a Russian protectorate.[1]

The military establishment, closely embedded in the ruling elite, determined the pace of Russian expansion and cleared the field on which to build the foundations of a unitary state. The construction of the Belgorod Line across the Central Upland brought about the incorporation of the Kharkiv corridor and its Cossacks into the military infrastructure overlooking the Left Bank of the Dnieper, and the protectorate imposed in 1654 marked the completion of the line to the Dnieper and closed the gap between the river and the Don. The annexation of the Crimea for military and naval reasons, followed twelve years later by that of Right Bank Ukraine, revolutionized the geopolitical situation in the southern theatre: the closing of the outer frontier entailed the elimination of the Little Russian and Zaporozhian Cossacks. Only the Don Cossacks survived, but as a separate arm of the Russian army and the nursery of other

Cossack formations in the Caucasian frontier. Once this was accomplished, it was left to the ruling elite to proceed to the next stage in the formation of a unitary state.

Next to the army – a unitary "state" within the expanding Russian core – which ended up creating, with a blissful disregard of the historical foundations of the newly acquired territories, a uniform network of military regions integrating the southern theatre into an expanding military infrastructure of empire, the Orthodox Church was another major agent of integration. Its metropolitan had once moved from Kiev to Moscow, from where the Church radiated influence over all other Orthodox believers, especially after the creation of the patriarchate in 1589, a generation or so after the conquests of Ivan IV. It was in the nature of things that the Church would want to return to its place of origin when it ceased to be a frontier church to become the ecclesiastical underpinning of an expanding Muscovite core. Here was a situation unique to the southern theatre: the population of the Ukrainian periphery did not have to be converted, like the Bashkirs, Kalmyks, Buriats, and Yakuts in the eastern theatre. It already belonged to the true Orthodox Church, which claimed to be the only one to have maintained its purity after the Turkish conquest of Constantinople in 1453. It alone could create a community of believers capable of accepting a uniform organization in parishes and dioceses under a single head.

As early as 1654, it was agreed that the Kiev metropolitan would come under the "blessing" of the Moscow patriarchate, and in 1685 the metropolitan travelled to Moscow to be "consecrated" by the patriarch. The Ukrainian hierarchy quickly understood that recognizing Moscow's leadership gave them opportunities to participate in Peter's reforms of the church and to obtain posts in the eastern theatre as well, where their intolerance, honed in the Kiev Monastery of the Caves which stood guard against the Crimean Tatars, could be used against the Tatars of Kazan, Bashkiria, and Western Siberia. The hierarchs (and the monks) became the strongest supporters of integration, and their work was crowned by the reform of 1686, which created a single and integrated organization for the church of the expanding core. There remained one enemy against whom Orthodoxy had always pitted its small-mindedness and rejection of the modern world: Polish Catholicism and its advance formation, the Uniate Church. The latter was abolished in 1839, but the struggle against Polish Catholicism would never be satisfactorily settled. The Polish enemy would remain the scarecrow warning Orthodoxy to cultivate its intolerance and deepen its integration among clergy and parishioners alike.

Changes in Ukrainian society were also working toward integration and uniformity. Cossack society, triumphant during the Khmelnytsky uprising, quickly became stratified and went on the defensive. After 1667, the Cossacks nearly disappeared from the Right Bank, and the Zaporozhian and Little Russian Cossacks became alienated from each other. In both the Right and Left

Banks, serfdom proceeded apace and, with it, the struggle for landed properties which gave status to the emerging class of landowners. In the Left Bank, the Cossack *starshyna* turned into landowners eager to obtain title to the land they had acquired by hook and by crook or seized from the Cossacks and the peasants. The struggle created a triangular relationship between landowners, hetman, and tsar, in which Moscow emerged as the arbiter of disputes and guarantor of titles. The loser was the hetman, who became irrelevant and was bypassed in contentious cases. The progress of serfdom encouraged the process of superstratification, in which the Russian intruder group came to depend on the landowning stratum to administer the territory in return for accepting the enserfment of the peasantry. Self-interest and the development of patronage networks encouraged the landowners to join the wider world of the expanding core and to trade their "microscopic" views for the macroscopic perspectives of a continental civilization.

This was not the case in Right Bank Ukraine, however. There, a critical mass of the magnates accepted the principle of superstratification because it served their material interests, namely gaining Russian support to open an export market in the Black Sea as well as the possibility of entering the highest levels of the Russian government. But the position of the magnates as the top stratum of a stratified society was undermined by the antagonism of the middle and lower *szlachta*, who, despite the assumption that all Polish nobles were equal, were in fact downgraded to the level of peasants and servants in major magnate households. This middle and lower level could not accept a process that did not serve their interests, and rejected the principle of superstratification on which the policy of integration depended. They were crushed in the revolt of 1830–1 (and again in 1863), but the policy had been irremediably damaged. The cultural and religious antagonism between the Russian and the Polish cores did the rest.

The administrative integration of the Ukrainian lands accelerated with the passage of time. By the end of the seventeenth century, the Kharkiv corridor had already become an extension of the Belgorod military region, even if a governor was not appointed until 1765. The Hetmanate was incorporated into Kiev province in 1708, although the decision was later rescinded, until a governor general replaced the last hetman in 1764. The geopolitical revolution of 1783 resulted in the wholesale extension of the provincial reform of 1775 to the entire Left Bank – an integration which was not only horizontal but also vertical, because it reached as far down as the county level and was further deepened by increasing the number of counties as well. The administrative reform was also a social reform. The personnel of the new agencies was almost wholly Ukrainian, and Ukrainian landowners became ipso facto members of the multi-ethnic ruling class which managed the expanding core. People like Zavadovsky, Troshchynsky, and Ivan Gudovich, among many others, were the best examples. The reform also rested on a new territorial division into provinces and counties, which recognized no distinction between the Left Bank and the rest of the expanding core. The creation of ministerial regions in the first decade of the nineteenth century marked the completion of the administrative-territorial reform and the final integration of the Left Bank. The same must be said about New Russia, and, above all, of Right Bank Ukraine. The government stated right after the "return" of the Right Bank territories that they would become an organic part of a single political body, that is, the expanding unitary state.

The harmonization of the law raised difficult issues. If people truly live by the laws before they are drawn up and promulgated, it can just as well be said that for the intruder group to change the law implied that the local population must change its way of life. Marriage and relations between parents and children, property and inheritance law, form a tissue of private assumptions and relationships binding families and communities together. These change very slowly and, sometimes, not at all. To force changes is to strike at customs and destroy social bonds which keep the peace and confer legitimacy. For these reasons alone, the Russians could not afford to impose the norms of Russian law at the early stages of integration. Only the criminal and penal law was quickly extended, because crimes were violations of the social peace and often acquired a political colouration to which the Russians could not remain indifferent.

The Lithuanian Statute was the law of the eastern marches of the Polish Empire. The third version (1588) had been the work of the *szlachta* and embodied its interests, the law by which it lived. The same was true of the Magdeburg Law, which was largely town law. The peasantry lived by its own laws, but enserfed peasants lived outside the social order and, from the standpoint of the ruling class, were legal outlaws. But the Magdeburg Law was a medieval relic, which had become increasingly redundant as towns became the private property of landowners. The charter of 1785, which extended the municipal reform to the entire core, dealt it the final blow. The Lithuanian Statute was also the archaic product of an age of nobiliar freedom in a republican empire. Russian law, gradually modernized by an endless stream of ukazes (despite the confusion this created), invaded the jurisdiction of the Statute, which was abolished in 1840. The decision reflected the social integration of the Ukrainian landed ruling class into that of the expanding core. But the Statute and Russian law still contained many lacunae, and one reason for the creation of the State Council in 1810 had been to close them, clarify, improve, and harmonize the laws to form a single one. Social and administrative integration was creating new expectations which became embedded in an evolving law valid for the entire core.

The introduction of the core's fiscal system also marked the logical conclusion of a long social transformation. Left Bank society, born out of a conservative war against Polish overlordship, gradually but inexorably joined its two neighbours, Muscovy and the Right Bank, among the serf-owning territories. In the

Right Bank, where the public power was nearly non-existent, the peasantry had been transformed into a dense social mass of privately held serfs. In southern Muscovy, the peasantry was divided between privately held serfs and those held in trust for the ruling class, until they were finally transformed by the passion for uniformity of the fiscal authorities into state peasants or, more accurately, in accordance with the terminology of the time, peasants of the Treasury. The progressive enserfment of the peasantry began right after Khmelnytsky's triumph and was nearly complete by the 1760s. Binding the peasant to the land and to his master and the introduction of the core's fiscal system in 1783 merely recognized the state of affairs the peasant had been living in for some time. Social, administrative, and fiscal integration went together hand in hand.

Trade did not play a major role in integration because of the location of the Ukrainian lands. The economy of the steppe and that of the forest zone were complementary, but poor communications (until the construction of railroads) limited exchanges between the Muscovite core and the valley of the Dnieper. The Left Bank agrarian economy became an extension of that of the "central agricultural region" and did indeed become integrated into the core. But the Right Bank's orientation faced the Black Sea, the Caucasus, and the Turkish Straits, and, beyond them, the Mediterranean. Odessa played a major role in siphoning off the trade toward Europe's maritime economy, rather than inward, toward Moscow. The poor condition of the Black Sea ports, the inhospitable hinterland of the northern shores of the sea, and the shallow waters of the Azov Sea did not encourage the development of a vibrant maritime economy, a transition zone for the flow of goods into the core and the outflow toward the sea capable of creating a single well-integrated economy, both within the Ukrainian lands and between those lands and the core. The fairs remained the major centres of trade and did not create a truly urban economy.

The incorporation of the Ukrainian lands did not belong to the stage of Russian empire building but only illustrated the progress of the Russian core's expansion. One cannot but be impressed by the systematic way in which Muscovy gradually incorporated nearly all sectors of human activity into a single unitary state. A unitary state is not a nation state. A nation state is a construct requiring the awakening of a popular consciousness intent on creating a polity defined in national terms. In a multi-ethnic unitary state, the emergence of such a political awareness is a prescription for disaster, because it denies the very foundations of the unitary state. Unitary state and nation state can merge if administrative integration (understood in the broadest sense) can coexist with the development of a consciousness transcending territorial and class particularisms, and develop an allegiance to the "people" and some abstraction like the "republic" or "democracy." Without such a transformation, the development of political consciousness is the bitter enemy of integration. In the Ukrainian lands, the 1840s witnessed the development of such an ethnocultural nationalism, against both the Poles and especially the Russians, since they formed the intruder group which had guaranteed the continued existence of a superstratification and denied the legitimacy of such a classless construct as the "people." In the Ukrainian lands, the Russian presence was very small and, in the Right Bank, infinitesimal. One may claim that the incorporation of these lands belonged to the imperial phase. But systematic administrative integration and social transformation into a serf-owning world, with only slight differences from the condition of the core, mean that we are dealing with a unitary state. The question must also be asked whether one can accept as an empire a territory peopled by the same ethnic stock (Eastern Slavs) and inspired by the same Orthodox religion as that of the expanding core.

PART III

The Eastern Theatre: The Advance toward the Mountains

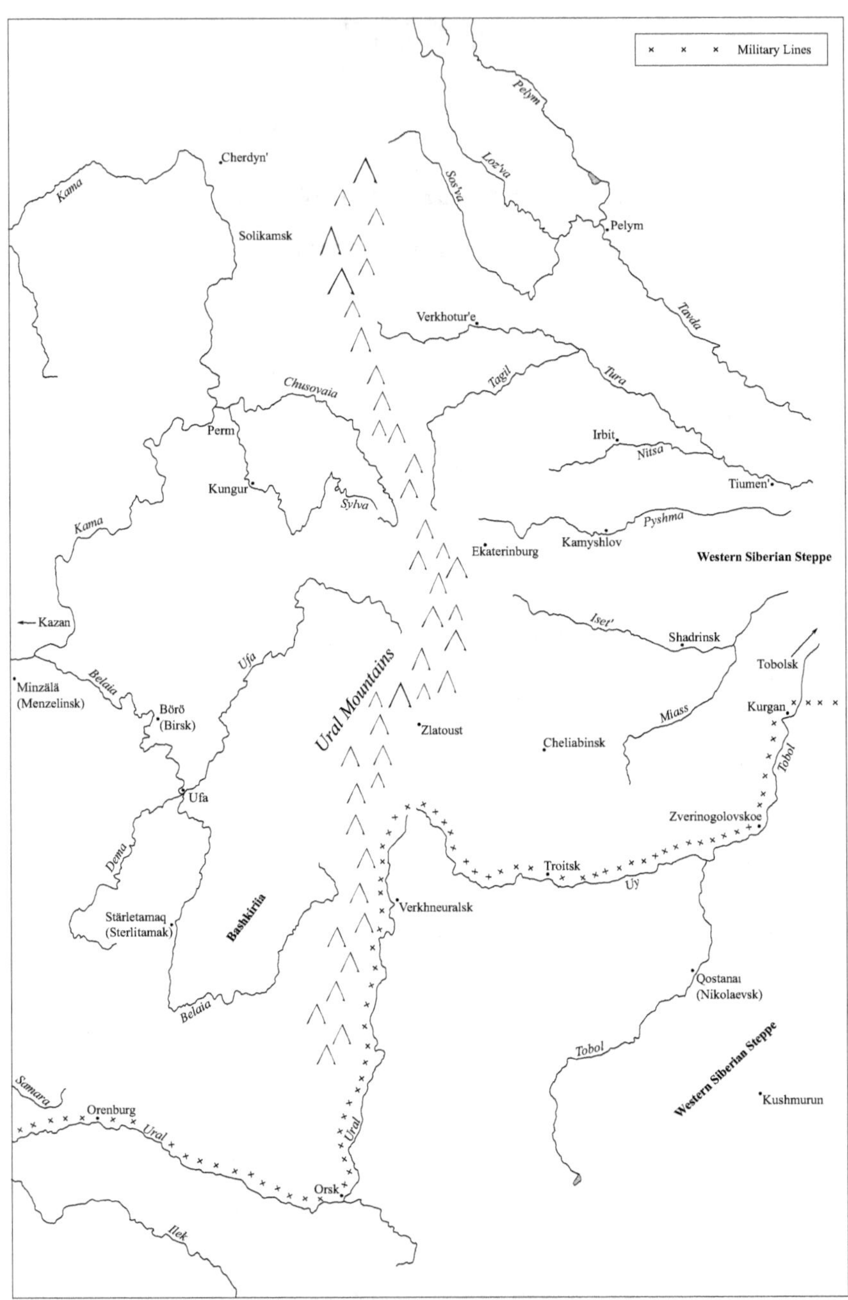

Map 6 The Urals and Bashkiria

Map 7 The Kazakh Steppe

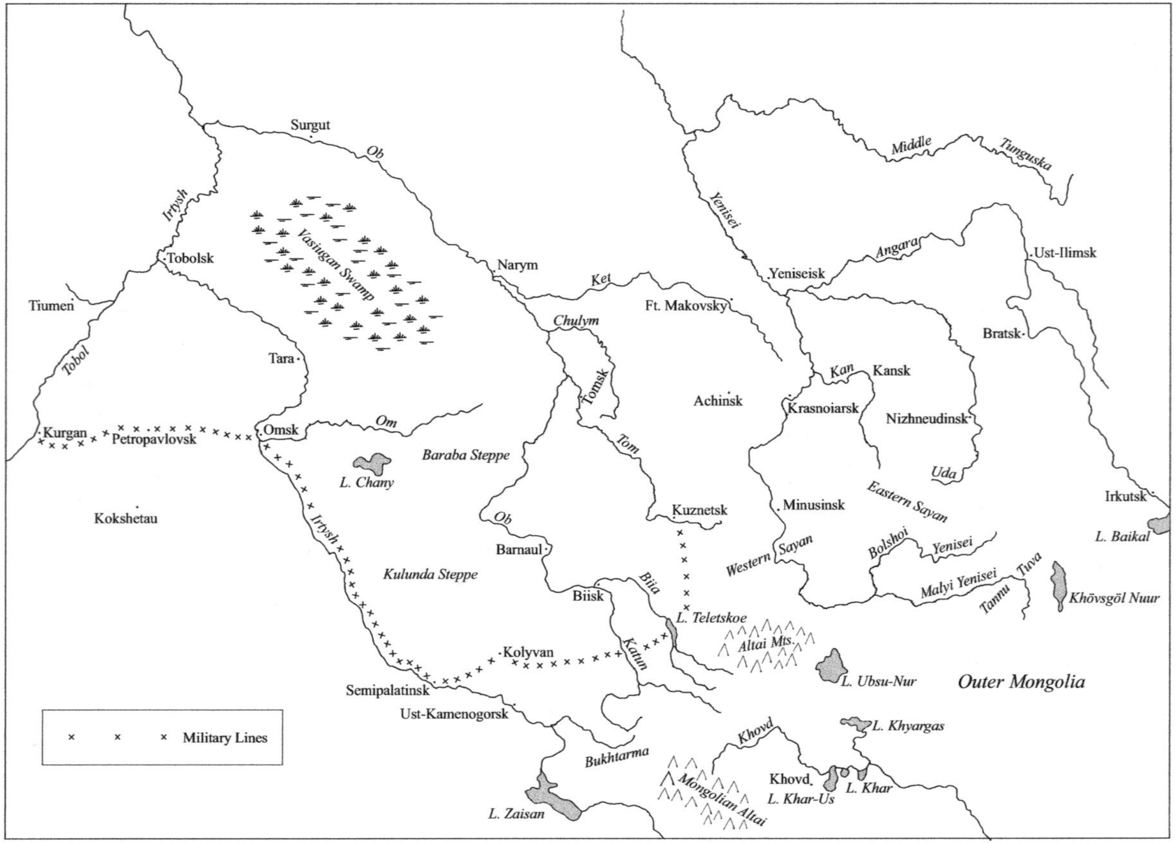

Map 8 Western Siberia

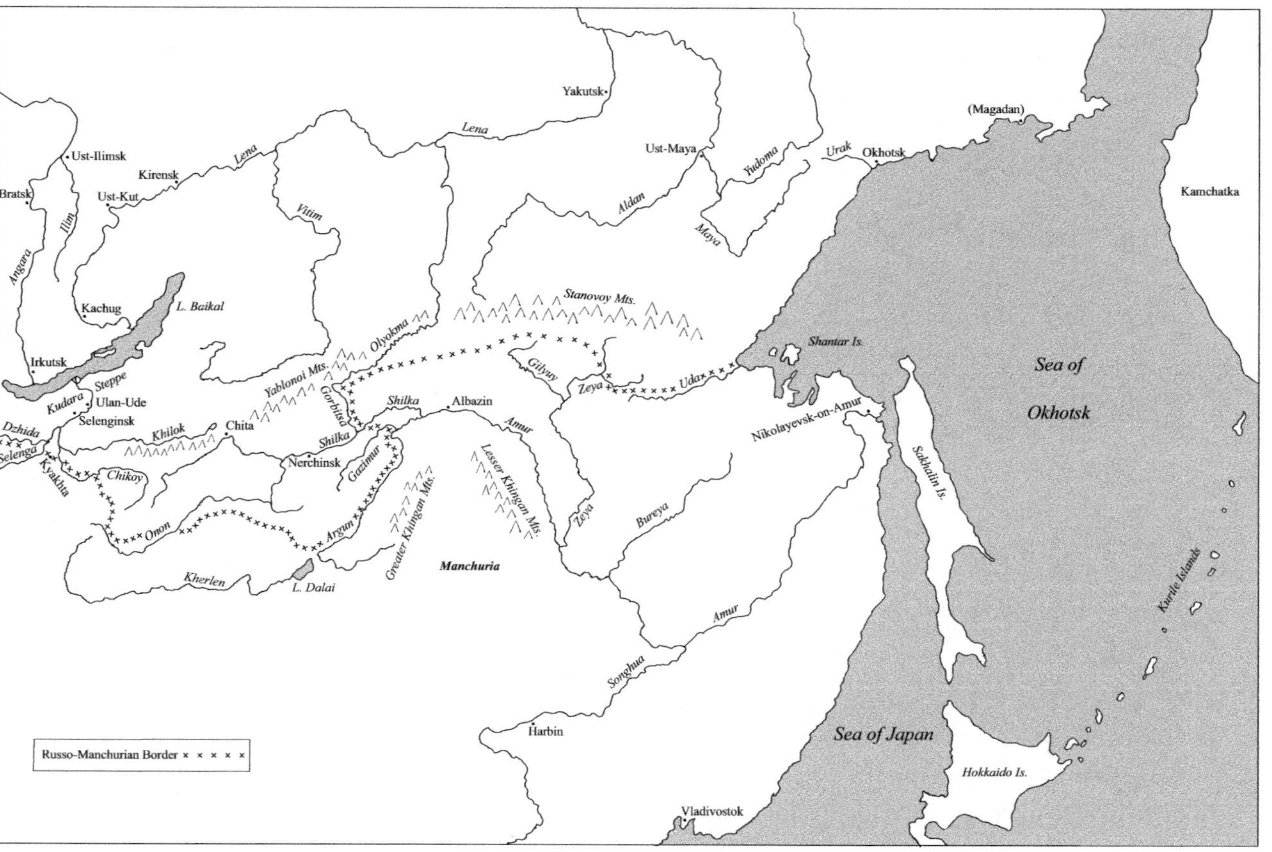

Map 9 Eastern Siberia

Introduction to Part III: The Eastern Theatre

The greater part of Eurasia made up the eastern theatre, distinguished from what I called the southern theatre, centred on the Black Sea, and the western theatre, held together by the Baltic Sea. However, its immense territory – the continental United States would easily fit into it – was landlocked, as its own peripheral sea, the Sea of Okhotsk, was of very difficult internal access. It was the land of nomads who roamed all over its southern steppe lands and of hunters who survived in the harsh environment of the taiga. Because it was a self-contained world which had once dominated the emergent Muscovite core and subsequently was overwhelmed by the settler on the march, it provides fertile ground for an examination of Russian policies of spatial domination and their retroactive application to the other two theatres.

Was Russia an imperialistic power, and must its imperialism be understood as a variant of the same developments which propelled certain European powers across the seas beginning in the sixteenth century? If the answer is positive, it must nevertheless be accepted with substantial reservations. European expansion, whatever its motives, whether political ambition, curiosity, or the search for economic profits, was a process of naked aggression. The Aztec of Mexico and the Inca of Peru no more threatened Spain than did the Mughals of India threaten England. But the Muscovite core had once been invaded by Turco-Mongol nomads, who dominated it for 250 years. When that world collapsed in the late fifteenth century, the Muscovite core found itself facing the hostility of three successor khanates in the Crimea, Astrakhan, and Kazan. Therefore, Russian expansion must be seen as a "response to the stimulus of pressures"[1] in the everlasting ebb and flow of the geopolitics of the Eurasian land mass. In its "struggle for the inheritance of the Golden Horde,"[2] Russia set off a process of identity formation leading eventually to the creation of a unitary state. Western imperialism did not result in the transformation of an expanding core into a state encompassing core and peripheries, and to equate Russian expansion with it is a form of deceptive reasoning reflecting a fashionable application of

Eurocentric concepts of historical development elsewhere in the name of world history.[3] We may apply the same reasoning to China's relations with Mongolia and Xinjiang, from which nomadic invasions so often threatened the country, including invasions of the same Mongols who imposed their rule upon Russia, also in the thirteenth century.

Do we not witness here developments similar to those we witnessed in the southern theatre, where the Crimean Tatars were still capable of burning Moscow in 1521 and kept raiding the southern steppes until the middle of the eighteenth century? Do we not also recognize that same ebb and flow as in the western theatre, where the Teutonic Knights launched a crusade against the Orthodox Novgorodians in the 1240s, the Jesuits fought the Orthodox in the sixteenth century, the Swedes cut off Russia's access to the Baltic Sea, and the Poles burned Moscow in 1610? The student of Russian expansion across the centuries finds the same defensive aggressiveness, the same response to the stimulus of pressures.

It has been said that "Tatars and Mongols have always stopped where the grass ended,"[4] and there was no more obvious confirmation of that statement than the declaration of the chief of the Western Mongols in 1714 that the boundary of their pastures ran along the Om River, beyond which the steppe gave way to the Vasiugan Swamp of Western Siberia.[5] This ecological boundary was also that of Russian expansion in Western and Central Siberia. It was within that territory, and not in the taiga zone where so few sedentary people can survive, that Russian expansion, and not Russian imperialism, implanted colonists and Russian rule. The grasslands were the battleground for both the sedentary agriculturalist and the nomad, where the nomad first won, but later became integrated into the world of the sedentary peasant, as was clearly the case in the Ukrainian steppe and Western Siberia. Even beyond the grassland proper, in eastern Eurasia, the Russians found patches of black earth in the Minusinsk steppe and the valley of the Lena, where gardens and orchards still grace the landscape.

But if we cannot speak of the Russian advance into the grasslands, favourable to both nomad and peasant, as a traditional form of imperialism, we must admit its existence where the Russians fell victim to "the curse of a distant horizon,"[6] in the frontier zones separating Russia from the peripheral core areas, here Persia and China, even if the latter was not part of Eurasia.

Russian expansion stopped for a long time along a line stretching across the steppe from the eastern foothills of the Urals to Omsk on the Irtysh, but then advanced toward the upper Ishim, where the ground begins to rise and tillable land gives way to grazing land inimical to agriculture. The Kazakh steppe ended along a string of deserts stretching from the Caspian to Lake Balkhash, beyond which began the oasis civilization of Central Asia. When the Russians kept advancing toward the Syr and Amu Daria and reached Bukhara, the cultural centre of the Russo-Persian frontier, and then debated whether to make the Persian core into a satellite (protectorate) at the beginning of the twentieth century, they engaged in blatant imperialism. Likewise, when they crossed the Eurasian boundary, joined the European powers in the partition of China, and laid claim to northern Manchuria, they followed in the footsteps of those powers, but they suffered a major defeat by the Japanese in 1905. Thus, by Russia's management of the Eurasian space in all three theatres, I mean the creation of a unitary state in the steppe and woodlands of that enormous land mass, and in the forested zone of the western theatre giving access to the Baltic Sea. That unitary state was turned during the reign of Nicholas I into a Fortress Empire from which the Russians created an imperial glacis of neutral states along the Eurasian periphery, beyond which, however, they would never be able to establish a permanent presence. If there ever was a Russian empire, it was one of short duration – like the Swedish Empire – quickly built and quickly destroyed.

The unitary state's ideology was Orthodoxy. The great empires professed a religion with a universal mission, Christianity, whether Catholic or Protestant, and Islam. Orthodoxy remained shackled to the Russian state and became identified with it. Outside of Eurasia, its faithful were found only among the diaspora of the Eastern Slavs. It never could make headway against Catholics and Muslims by its own superior strength, but only when it invoked the support of the secular power. Only in the eastern theatre was it partly successful against the animist peoples of steppe and taiga, and even there, Buddhism offered serious resistance. Orthodoxy was not an "imperial" religion fit for an empire, but as an instrument of state policy it helped strengthen the foundation and the constitution of the unitary state. Its internal mission hardened the cohesion of the unitary state and neutralized centrifugal forces which might otherwise have loosened the organic unity of centre and periphery. Imperialism may have contributed to the process of globalization elsewhere, but Russian expansion and Orthodox proselytism only resulted in the creation of a Russian world isolated from the rest of the "greater world" and frowning on the dangerous diversity of the latter's maritime economy.

If one cannot truly speak of Russian imperialism in the traditional sense during the period covered in this work, can one affirm that Russia was a colonial power during the same period? Colonialism is usually associated with imperialism, but Jürgen Osterhammel is convinced that there can be imperialism without a major colonial empire, and cites Russia as an example.[7] He also feels that colonization (colonialism) is anyway a phenomenon of "colossal vagueness."[8] There is no obvious answer to that question, but one thing is clear. The native peoples of Siberia at the time of the Russian intrusion, when much of the territory was a *terra nullius* for the future Russian agriculturalist, had been swamped by 1850 by Russian and other Slav settlers. The census of that year estimated that the Russian population of Siberia had reached 2 million out of

2.7 million people of both sexes. Can we speak of a colonial situation, characterized by the domination of a majority of natives by a minority of intruders (outsiders), when the natives have been overwhelmed by the intruders? While French Algeria certainly could be called a colonial state, can the same be said about the United States and Russia?[9]

In order to conform to fashionable and ephemeral theories, however, attempts have been made to insert the history of some borderlands into a post-colonial context. Yarolav Hrytsak has denied that this applied to contemporary Ukraine, for example. "One has to be rather cautious when applying the term colony to the Ukrainian territories under the Russian empire," he writes, because "Kyiv and central Ukraine were seen as the core of Russian lands and the Russian government" saw Ukraine as belonging to the imperial core.[10] He thus tacitly accepts the proposition central to this work, that the expanding Russian core was a unitary state.

It has been claimed that the colonial state brought about "the universal acceptance of the territorial principle."[11] In the eastern theatre, such a claim can only mean that the movement of nomads was restricted to specific areas (reservations?) to facilitate their sedentarization and their transformation into agriculturalists modelled after the settler from the core power. But such acceptance resulted in fact in the creation of administrative territories resembling those of the "colonial power" and facilitated the creation of a unitary state, as we shall see presently. A unitary state cannot admit the existence of a distinct system of administration in its peripheral areas, unless specific problems created by their location, or domestic and external threats, require exceptions from the general norms of territorial administration, and these exceptions can only be temporary. In the final analysis, how could one speak of two systems of law in a territory where the Russians made up such a high share of the population? Only if we include the "colonies" in eastern Transcaucasia, much of the Kazakh steppe, and Central Asia conquered after 1850 can we speak of multiple legal systems.

While the dissemination of the core's public and private law may not have been the primary goal of the expanding core, the spread of Orthodox Christianity certainly was, and the mother country and the colony did not remain "two separate entities."[12] As a rule, the Russians introduced their criminal law from the beginning, and gradually sought to force their civil law into the interstices of Muslim and Mongol law. It is only with serious reservations that one can speak of two legal systems. It is easy to see a determination to introduce uniform norms from the beginning of the conquest, one based on the assumption that "laws and privileges" as they existed in the Baltic, Lithuanian, and eastern borderlands would become residual constructs tolerated by the tsar-emperor only so long as he found them expedient and consistent with the maintenance of domestic peace. Conversion played a contradictory role. It made natives into Russians, as Speransky famously claimed in 1822, and thus subject to the "laws of the land," but religion also helped maintain a separate identity which resisted assimilation (i.e., the acceptance of the laws of the conqueror).

A colonial regime implied the existence of a certain type of economy based on forced labour – the native Inca in the mines of Spanish Peru, imported Black labour on the sugar plantations of the Antilles. The labour we find in the copper mines of the Altai Mountains and the silver mines of Nerchinsk did not consist of natives but of Russians (and others), including convicts deported from the Russian core to Central or Eastern Siberia to serve terms of penal servitude. In no way can this type of economy be described as colonial. On the other hand, the extraction of copper in Eastern Georgia in the 1830s and the forced cultivation of cotton in Central Asia by a small minority of Russians for the exclusive benefit of the empire were a form of colonial exploitation beyond the boundaries of the unitary state in the forest, woodland, and steppe.

Did the population of the eastern theatre form a colonial society? To answer that question, we must continue to distinguish between the territory constituting the unitary state and what I call the imperial peripheries. At least one thing is certain. The Russians did not proceed against the natives as the Spaniards and the English did in their colonies. The former "destroyed nine-tenths of the Indian population and enslaved the survivors, and the latter steadily drove the Indians off their lands until, after the conquest of New France, they were at last able to embark on a policy of genocide with impunity."[13] The Russians viewed the natives as taxpayers and as military auxiliaries in the intertribal conflicts that often disturbed the peace of the steppe – Bakshirs, Kalmyks, and Kazakhs engaged in bloody conflicts over pastures. We cannot apply to the eastern theatre the harsh words of the French-Antillean revolutionary during the Algerian war, Frantz Fanon, that *the* defining feature of colonial situations is the total, unbridgeable chasm between two cultures.[14] We are closer to the truth when we follow Owen Lattimore, who wrote convincingly about the changing attitudes of the Russian crossing Siberia on his way to China. The European, he writes, who boarded ship in Southampton or Amsterdam remained immersed during his entire trip (which could take months before the opening of the Suez Canal) in European customs, sounds, and smells. When he reached the first Chinese port, he suffered a culture shock which was likely to set off a hostile reaction. But the Russian leaving Moscow soon met Tatars in Kazan, Bashkirs in Ufa, Kazakhs in Orenburg, Bukharans in the steppe, Buriats before and beyond Lake Baikal, and finally Mongols. By the time he reached Beijing, he had grown accustomed to the sights, sounds, and smells of the East, and took them for granted. The Orient had lost much of its mystery and its potential hostility.[15] Even if they hated each other, Kazakhs married Kalmyk women and sold their children to Russians in times of need. In the most distant parts, as in Yakutia, the Russians became integrated into the native society. Even if conflicts existed, it is difficult to speak of a colonial society in the unitary state of the East.

This is not to say that there were no sources of conflicts. They were especially acute in Bashkiria, largely because of conflicts over land between the Russians and the native Bashkirs, who were, in part, also landowners. Nomads did not transform the land in order to exploit it. Their cattle consumed the grass as it grew, then moved on to new pastures according to the seasons. The allocation of pastures was therefore a weapon of crucial importance in the hands of clan leaders – and the Russian authorities. The Russians' goal was eventually to settle the nomad and transform him into a land tiller, like the Russian peasant who had immigrated from the core of the unitary state. If colonialism is a relationship "in which an entire society is robbed of its entire line of development, externally manipulated and transformed according to the needs and interests of the colonial rulers,"[16] we have here a form of colonialism. This view must be balanced against the realization that an area in which the population consists overwhelmingly of immigrants who swamped the native population can hardly be called a colonial territory. In the Bashkir lands, the natives were antagonized by the activities of the Russian industrialists eager to develop the mining industry of the southern Urals, which required the purchase (a euphemism for seizure) not only of Bashkir lands but also of forests as a source of fuel; their quick destruction and the resulting elimination of Bashkir apiculture (a major part of the Bashkir economy) caused armed rebellions which were cruelly put down. Nevertheless, the inexorable advance of Russian colonization threatened by the end of the eighteenth century to downgrade the Bashkirs to the level of state peasants; their reaction was to form Cossack-like units to guard the border against Kalmyk and Kazakh incursions and retain their dignity in a world of despised dependent peasants. Even in distant Buriatia, where the Russian imprint was much lighter, joining the ranks of the irregular forces was a way to preserve the nomad's dignity and even become integrated into the sociopolitical structure of the unitary state.

The topic of "collaboration" (an unfortunate word) is an important one in the study of colonialism. If we accept the proposition that there existed no fundamental opposition between the intruder and the native, cooperation was the only alternative. Cooperation will be passive if it does not alter anything in the relation, providing both parties have similar intentions.[17] I have used in this work the term "superstratification," which I find more relevant, because it characterizes a more dynamic process of the joint operation of similar intentions. Without recognition of a common interest, Russian rule would never have become established in any of the three theatres. The Russians did possess overwhelming power, whether in the form of firearms over the less effective weapons of the East or of modern armies in the south and west, but they would not have been able to rule without the cooperation of Swedish and Polish elites in the West or tribal chiefs in the East. The Russians had something to offer in return: the elite's participation in the process of social stratification taking place all over Eurasia from the seventeenth to the first decade of the nineteenth century. We encounter everywhere the rise of an upper stratum against the power of the dominant clan. Russian opposition to the institution of khan in the steppe, of hetman in Left Bank Ukraine, and of duke in Kurland matched the yearnings of a rising subordinate group for full power, and the emergence of a new ruling class in the peripheries matched similar developments in the core society. Moreover, while the intensification of serfdom was a characteristic feature of the new emerging social order from the Baltic provinces to the northern Caucasus, the social downgrading of the simpler tribesman in the nomadic societies of the East brought nomadic societies, even if they were still resistant to sedentarization, closer to the core society. It substituted a *modus vivendi* for a state of mutual hostility among a critical mass of those new societies. Only the dreadful impact of nationalism on social and tribal consciousness would later destroy the development of a potentially stabilizing convergence and fail to bring about the transformation of a unitary state into a nation state.

Among fine contemporary authors writing about the history and administration of Siberia, two deserve mention in the anglophone world (I do not include here the late outstanding Anatolii Remnev, who wrote mostly about the late imperial period): Erika Monahan on the Siberian merchants and Christoph Witzenrath on the Siberian Cossacks, both confining their work to the seventeenth century and the reign of Peter I. They discuss different subjects, but also one in common: the existence of corruption, widespread not only in Siberia but also in the entire Russian-dominated world. Both agree that it was ingrained in Muscovite culture, but we also know that it was found in late imperial, Soviet, and post-Soviet culture. But why? An explanation remains elusive.

I think there is a simple answer if one looks at the nature of Russian politics. We all agree that there existed a Russian ruling elite in the capital surrounding the tsar-emperor, but also partaking in his autocratic power. Indeed, that was the secret of Russian autocracy: members of the elite supported and encouraged the ruler's autocratic power because it strengthened their own. We are less willing to accept the existence of a ruling class because of the persistence of certain ideological prejudices, even though there cannot be a ruling elite without a ruling class. It was assumed in that Eurasian state, and especially in its eastern theatre, where there had never been any form of feudalism, that the wealth of the land belonged to the ruler (was his *otchina*) and, by extension, to the ruling class spreading its tentacles all over the land, bound to the ruling elite by vast networks of patronage, as Witzenrath concludes. In this case, helping oneself to the wealth of the country was taken for granted, and so was sharing the booty with others. What was not acceptable was exceeding certain limits, sometimes defined in the law, depending on the status of the taker. Russian politics was a vast mafia operation, in which corruption was taken for granted, and therefore was not a crime but a way of life. It was a family affair, as Montesquieu so delicately put it. It was only in the eyes of the beholder. That is an issue which both authors should have explored in greater detail if they had been willing to face the obvious.[18]

I still need to answer the question posed in the title of this work: were the Russians building a unitary state or an empire in the eastern theatre between 1650 and 1850? Those who claim that it was an empire agree with Karl Werner that "a kingdom is a country, an empire is a world"; that it consists of a metropole and subordinate peripheries; that the creation of an empire marks the completion of a process called imperialism; that an empire is a large conglomerate in which one people imposes its dominion over other peoples; that the "concept of empire presumes that different peoples within the polity will be governed differently"[19] (is that to say that France and the United Kingdom were empires at one time? A plausible claim). There may be many other attempts at defining what cannot truly be defined, because, as Osterhammel posited about colonialism, the term "empire" is a term of colossal vagueness, in which scholars compare not only apples and oranges but also bananas and plums. If the Russian Empire consisted of 180 nationalities (another specious argument, because I see nothing comparable between Samoyeds and Ukrainians), what can it have in common with the post-1871 German Empire, solidly German, with only a small Danish minority in the north and a larger Polish minority in the east? Rather than attempting to force a uniform typology into the Procrustean bed of world history concepts borrowed from Eurocentric history, it may be more profitable to turn to administrative history to find out what the Russians actually did rather than to what Western scholars, guided by ever-changing imagined concepts, think they saw.

It can be argued, for example, that certain borderlands (Siberia, the mid-Volga region) were administered by separate agencies headquartered in Moscow, but that argument does not stand close examination. Even before the creation of the provinces (*gubernii*) all across the Muscovite territory, there had existed a substantial number of territorial jurisdictions, even if the agency chief, unlike the future governor, resided, not in the regional capital, but in Moscow. Although the *prikaz* organization was very complex, largely because these agencies were often created ad hoc and closed when the circumstances that necessitated their creation had ceased to exist, one can distinguish two major principles underlying their creation. Some were functional agencies, whether they were given a single or several functions – the administration of justice, the collection of taxes, or even responsibilities for certain classes of people – while others had a territorial jurisdiction and were named after a certain city or territory. The former were the ancestors of the eighteenth-century colleges and the ministries of the nineteenth, the latter those of the provinces. Some others were even of both types. They were the successors of the *chetverti* (*cheti*) created in the latter half of the sixteenth century to administer the lands under the jurisdiction of the grand princely houses and integrate them into the growing Muscovite administration.

As this Muscovite inner core began to expand, *prikazy* emerged to assume the greater responsibilities of the Muscovite government. They were agents of administrative integration, first of the Russian lands, later of the peripheries. There was a *Pomestnyi Prikaz*, responsible for granting land to the servitors of the Muscovite state; there were a *Razriad* and territorial *razriady*, responsible for the military administration of certain peripheral territories. *Prikazy* were created to administer the affairs of the Smolensk Principality, for Little Russia (Left Bank Ukraine), for Lithuania, for Kazan, and for Siberia. The *prikaz* organization, despite its confusion, clearly shows that the Muscovite authorities made no distinction *in principle* between the administration of the core and that of the peripheries.[20]

That became even more obvious after 1708 when the provincial grid was imposed not only on the Muscovite core but also on the Baltic territories, Left Bank Ukraine, the mid-Volga region, and Siberia, and, later in the century, in every single territory acquired in the wake of the partitions of the Polish Empire. But the governor, as the head of a province, was required to reside in the provincial capital, even in distant Tobolsk. Colleges were created in Petersburg and Moscow to take over the various functions of government from the former *prikazy* and exercise them all over the country, subject to the self-imposed restrictions concerning the expediency of their immediate execution. The White Tsar, like the old khan, possessed the unlimited power to fashion his domain at his pleasure, and simplicity and uniformity were more appealing to him than the confused jurisdictional jumble of old.

Paradoxically, however, the passion for uniformity stood in constant opposition to the tsar-emperor's obsession with the retention of his arbitrary power. The result, in Richard Wortman's memorable phrase, was that "the permanent law in Russia was one of impermanence."[21] Privileges were never guaranteed, and institutions had no constitutional foundations, since the emperor was above the law: he made it, abrogated it, and adjudicated conflicts. But the influence of Enlightenment ideas and military thinking, which preached the necessity and the value of uniformity, strengthened the determination to create a unitary state in a political and administrative environment that was becoming increasingly complex.

The task became even more pressing in the nineteenth century with the creation of powerful ministries with large staffs, especially the Finance Ministry, determined to project their influence to the far ends of the unitary state. It was also at that time that the traditional rivalry between functional and territorial administration reached its peak before it eventually declined with the former's victory, as when the authority of governors general was systematically undermined by the Interior and Finance Ministries, among others. The old struggle had begun in the seventeenth century over the creation of a unitary state, when the *voevoda* sent to govern Russian cities as well as towns and forts in the distant peripheries had brought with his clerks and his soldiers the *Ulozhenie* of 1649 to administer his territory, dispense justice, collect taxes, and build a military infrastructure to initiate the process of integration. A Kazakh scholar who has written extensively on Russian policy toward the Kazakh steppe has summed up quite accurately the general principles governing Russian administrative policy toward the peripheries of the expanding core: "Russian authorities gave priority in the construction of the empire [*sic*] to the creation of new administrative territories by means of incorporating the traditional administrative agencies into a single political system." Despite the differences between the regions of the interior and peripheral ones like the mid-Volga region and the Caucasus, we can see that "the government used similar administrative structures [everywhere] ... These were part of a process of gradual integration of the peoples of these territories into a single [*edinaia*] system of state administration."[22] If that was truly the case, as I believe it was, then the Russians were not building an empire but a unitary state.

There must be individuals to articulate such policies and to carry them out, and to imprint upon their successors the need to continue them. Scholarship has neglected a potentially crucial topic. It was said of the Romans that it was an ancestral custom among them for the commander who had defeated an enemy in the peripheral regions of the Roman core to become his patron, and that this patronage was hereditary.[23] This assertion brings up two issues. Anyone perusing the list of *voevodas* sent to Siberia in the seventeenth century will recognize families that would give leading figures in the elite a century later. To take one example: the Gagarin family gave the first governor of Tobolsk, who was executed on Peter I's order in 1721 for defrauding the Treasury. But ten Gagarins had been *voevodas* in Siberia in the seventeenth century. Gagarin later married into the ruling house.[24] Prosopography may well reveal networks of Russian families in the administration of Siberia. In addition, archival research might disclose the existence of patronage networks between those families and tribal chieftains among the Kalmyks (who were well represented at the Petersburg Court), the Bashkirs, the Yakuts, and even the Mongols, like a Prince Gantimur, who abandoned the Manchus and went over to the Russians in 1666, and one of whose descendants reached the rank of colonel in the Russian army. Since the Russians used Tatars, whom they trusted and respected, to bring into nomadic territory the laws and procedures of their administration, they must certainly have used such networks to teach the nomads the vision of a unitary state bringing peace in the turbulent periphery, as well as rewards for those willing to play the game.

The expanding Russian core, as I have chosen to call the emerging unitary state, was indeed a pyramid of patronage networks stretching from the Baltic to the Pacific under the leadership of a Grand Patron in Petersburg, ruling by manipulating networks in a state of constant rivalry. Anyone familiar with "autocratic politics" cannot but be struck by its slippery and dangerous nature, as when an all-powerful Alexander Menshikov became a non-person in a matter of days and was sent to die in the snows of distant Berezov, or when an Artemii Volynsky, related to the last khan of Sibir', was executed to make way for his enemies. But the great secret of autocratic politics and the great strength of the Russian system – unlike that of the Polish Empire in the eighteenth century, for example – was the existence of a tacit understanding that the maintenance of the autocracy was fundamental: it secured the interest of the ruling elite as a whole and guarded against the nefarious disintegration that plagued the nomadic confederations. Alexander I's finance minister, Dmitrii Gur'ev, put it almost seditiously when he stated that the ruler was indeed an all-powerful inspector, but that it was not he, but the ministers, who managed the unitary state.[25] Such a system had an uncanny ability to maintain the status quo and resist rapid change, but also to be reborn as a phoenix, as in 1613, 1921, and 2014.

Because it was fearful of change, the expanding core was wary of coming too close to the sea. This is paradoxical. The entire course of Russian foreign policy from 1650 appears to be an uninterrupted "urge to the sea,"[26] a propulsion that began as a response to the stimulus of pressures. But as Russia prepared in 1850, when this work ends, to launch its last push toward the Pacific with the appointment in 1847 of General Nikolai Muravev as governor general of Eastern Siberia, there were voices, like those of Karl Nesselrode, the foreign minister, and Petr Gorchakov, the governor general of Western Siberia, who feared the influx of republican ideas from America moving up the Amur River to subvert Russian rule in the East.[27] In the western theatre, the government needed Finland and the Baltic provinces to keep Russians away from the winds and smells of the Baltic, beckoning away from Eurasia toward Europe and its own republican ideas. I have referred to the expanding core as "Fortress Russia" and to its empire (after the incorporation of Finland and Poland) as "Fortress Empire,"[28] because Russia did not expand in order to open up to the world across the Eurasian periphery, but to drop a curtain sharply demarcating its possessions from the rest of the world. Maurice Duverger referred to the Roman Empire as an "archaic variety of isolationism."[29] The same applied to the Russia of 1850, on the eve of its increased exposure to European ideas for technical and economic reasons, which upset its internal political equilibrium and destroyed the system two generations later.

The unitary state kept its internal cohesion not only because its ruling elite was able to transform Russia into the hegemonic power in the eastern theatre, creating a state of hegemonic stability. It also succeeded because its peripheries were trapped. Buriats might resent Russian rule and flee to China, but the Chinese were worse taskmasters than the Russians, and it was Manchu-Chinese, not Russian, troops, who massacred one million Western Mongols in 1757. Kazakhs had no place to escape except into deserts and oasis societies to which they did not belong. In Transcaucasia, the alternative to Russian rule was Turkish and Iranian brutality. Moreover, despite the lack of alternatives, the Russians were favoured by the full decline of the peripheral cores throughout the nineteenth century, and the orography of Anatolia and Persia blocked access to the sea from the interior. The expanding Russian core, the peripheral cores, and the frontiers were caught in a geopolitical nightmare. Russia's Eurasian policy sought to create a fortress within a fortress to secure its rule. Only when it violated the cardinal rule that it must not seek to expand beyond the outer periphery of the Eurasian land mass did it encounter the backlash of the maritime powers, which destabilized the entire system on which its security depended.[30]

I now turn to the creation of the unitary state in the eastern theatre, and will follow the same outline as I did in the previous volume for the southern theatre in the Black Sea basin and the western theatre in that of the Baltic Sea.

Chapter Seven

Laying the Foundations, 1650–1730

The Geopolitical Setting

Geography

The eastern theatre was by far the largest of the three. It stretched from Kazan to the Sea of Okhotsk across the whole of Siberia; from Kazan to the Araks River, beyond which the Taurus of Anatolia merged with the Zagros Mountains of Iran; from Kazan across the Aralo-Caspian depression to the Pamirs, the Roof of the World, overlooking the Hindu Kush and the Tien Shan Mountains, which formed, with the Taurus and the Zagros, Eurasia's southern periphery. The Altai, Saian, Iablonoi, and Stanovoi chains were its eastern periphery to the Sea of Okhotsk. From Kazan to Krasnoiarsk on the Yenisei River via Cheliabinsk, Omsk, and Novosibirsk, the distance is 3,270 kilometres; from Krasnoiarsk to Irkutsk, 1,064 kilometres; from Irkutsk to Yakutsk, another 2,653 kilometres, with still another 1,000 to the Sea of Okhotsk across desolate wastes, a total of nearly 8,000 kilometres. Kazan was also the starting point for projections of Russian power into Central Asia: Tashkent is 2,803 kilometres away via Orenburg, and there are another 679 to the Afghan border. Kazan led to the Caucasus along the Volga to Astrakhan, 1,480 kilometres away. From Astrakhan on the Caspian, a coastal road led to Baku, and from there to Tiflis and Erevan near the Araks, a total of 1,700 kilometres from Kazan. A shorter but more difficult road led along the Terek and across the mountains via Vladikavkaz to Tiflis, 2,430 kilometres from Kazan.

The geography of the eastern theatre was that of a plain, barely interrupted by the central and southern Urals, sloping into the Aralo-Caspian depression below sea level, then rising toward Eurasia's periphery. Further east, it inclined in the opposite direction to merge into the Great Lowland of Western Siberia to the coast of the Kara Sea. That plain ended along the Yenisei River, beyond which the ground rose to an elevation of over 2,500 metres in the Iablonoi-Stanovoi upland, south of which stretched the basin of the Amur River in the Asian coastland. The eastern theatre was thus well defined, a self-contained world in which the Russians would advance across the plain toward a periphery of nearly impassable mountains, displace the nomad, and interact with Iran and China.

This enormous area can best be represented as a triptych, the Ural range forming one of its hinges, the Yenisei valley the other. Its western panel was the basin of the Caspian drained by the Volga, the Kura (with its tributary, the Araks), and the Ural Rivers. The Volga flowed through the forest zone as if in a trough, picking up the Kama and its tributaries descending from the western slopes of the Urals, the Sura and the Sviiaga in the hinterland of the Volga Hills running parallel to the river, and further downstream, the Samara flowing along the boundary of the wooded steppe. East of the Volga, ensconced between the Belaia and the Samara, was a deeply dissected eroded upland known as the Obshchii Syrt, forming the watershed between the basin of the Volga and that of the Ural River, the northernmost end of what had once been the Caspian's bed.[1]

South of a line running from the Volga below Saratov to the Ural River began the semi-desert, bordered in the west by the escarpment of the Ergeni Hills and in the east by the Mugodzhary Hills, the southernmost extension of the Urals. Trees disappeared, saltmarshes became the dominant feature of the landscape, agriculture became increasingly difficult despite the presence of chestnut brown chernozem, until the land became a complete desert on both sides of the Volga. But the desert came to life where water was available, in the valley of the Ural River and the Volga below Tsaritsyn, where the Akhtuba, which flows parallel to the river over five hundred kilometres, formed a rich tissue of meadows and fish ponds attractive to nomads and their enormous herds, with salt available aplenty.

Nevertheless, the intersection of a north-south axis (the Volga) with latitudinal vegetation and soil zones gave this region a crucial strategic and commercial importance. Turco-Mongol nomads moving westward across the steppe zone found the lower course of the Ural and Volga a natural stopover on their way to the Ukrainian steppes or along the Volga to the periphery of the forest zone inhospitable to the horse-riding nomads and their herds. The confluence of the Volga and the Kama as well as the Volga delta attracted traders from east, west, and south along the transcontinental transit route connecting the trade of northern India and western China with the Baltic and Mediterranean since the days of the Bulgars in Kazan and the Khazars in Itil (Astrakhan). But the emergence of Moscow in the twelfth century created a built-in antagonism between that city and the two commercial and political centres downriver, as Moscow sought to become the core city of the forest zone, facing south and east rather than west, and to remove rivals that obstructed its advance into the steppe. The

Mongol invasion would counter Moscow's ambitions: it was the last thrust to assert the primacy of the nomad in Eurasia, before the world of the settler moving down the Volga toward the Kama and Astrakhan would wrest supremacy from the nomad in the latitudinal zones and shape a strategic theatre for a Russian core in full expansion.

The desert zone around the northern shore of the Caspian ended along the Terek River. From there, the ground rose rapidly toward the Main Caucasus, over 110 kilometres wide where the Georgian Military Highway now crosses it into the synclinal valley between the Great and Little Caucasus and the Armenian Plateau overlooking the Araks River. The valley, through which flows the Kura, was bounded in the west by the Suram range linking the two chains and forming an ecological watershed between western and eastern Georgia, one gravitating toward the Black Sea, the other toward the Caspian, one overwhelmed by heavy rains and luxuriant forests, the other struggling against drought which made the cultivation of crops impossible without irrigation. The Great Caucasus, which extends unbroken over 800 kilometres from the Black Sea to the Apsheron Peninsula on the Caspian, formed a nearly complete barrier to exchanges between north and south, but it did not isolate Transcaucasia from channels of trade and political rivalries. The Suram range could easily be crossed at 923 metres, and the Kura and the Rion formed an almost continuous (although not very serviceable) water route between the Caspian and the Black Sea.

Transcaucasia's east-west alignment made it a natural corridor of expansion for nomads from the east, including the Mongols, and a theatre of choice for the Turco-Persian rivalry, with devastating consequences for the welfare of the region. But the eastern end of Transcaucasia was also at the intersection of a north-south route between the Caspian desert and northern Persia, and Derbent on the Caspian earned its name (the "Gate of Gates") from its location, where the road narrows down to a ten-kilometre-wide passage between the coast and the mountains.[2] That road would never bring Russians into Transcaucasia in large numbers, but it would eventually link the Georgians and Armenians stranded among the Sunni and Shi'ite Muslims with the rising Christian power in the forest zone, and complete the logistical line running from Kazan to Astrakhan: that line would support Russian operations against both Turks and Persians and contribute to the establishment of Russia's supremacy in the entire western panel.

The triptych's central panel, the drainage basin of the Kara Sea, which merged with the Arctic Ocean, faced north. It filled the great depression between the Urals and the Yenisei River, known to Mackinder as the Great Lowland, and its four major arteries were the Tobol, the Irtysh, the Ishim, and the Ob Rivers. The Tobol, 1,575 kilometres long, received several rivers descending from the eastern slopes of the Urals before flowing into the Irtysh at Tobolsk. To the east, the Ishim, 2,200 kilometres long, which took its source in the Kazakh Upland, flowed parallel to the Tobol during much of its course before merging with the Irtysh. The 4,260-kilometre-long Irtysh rose in the Mongolian Altai, felt its way through Lake Zaisan and along the foothills of the Great Altai, then became a lazy steppe river that skirted in a huge bend the immense Vasiugan'e swamp, and flowed into the Ob, about 450 kilometres downriver from Tobolsk. Finally, the Ob, the fourth largest Siberian river (after the Lena, the Yenisei, and the Irtysh), began at the confluence of the Biia and Katun, both descending from the Great Altai. After forming a long detour around an upland dominated by the Selair range, it entered the Great Lowland, and after a sharp turn, where it received the Irtysh, flowed on to lose itself into the Kara Sea, 3,700 kilometres from its source.

At first glance, it seemed that the northward flow of the main rivers would be a major obstacle to the Russians' advance into and across Siberia. In fact, it facilitated it, because the latitudinal tributaries combined to create a nearly perfect hydrographic network in the entire panel. Armed men and traders sailed down the Tura, the Tobol, and the Irtysh, then up the Ob to the confluence of the Ket, a nine-hundred-kilometre-long river linked with the Yenisei by a ninety-kilometre-wide portage. Moreover, if these four Siberian rivers led into the Great Lowland and the useless Kara Sea, they also led out of the forest zone into the rich steppe to the south. The zone of dense conifer forest ended along a line running approximately from Cheliabinsk on the Miass (a tributary of the Tobol), past Omsk and Novosibirsk to Krasnoiarsk on the Yenisei. South of it was a broad band of wooded steppe with black and chestnut-brown soils, followed by the open steppe, the easternmost extension of the Ukrainian and North Caucasian steppe, also blessed with good soil and watered by the Tobol, the Ishim, and the Irtysh. As in the western panel, the north-south axis of the main rivers combined with latitudinal vegetation zones to create a communication grid encouraging the eastward expansion of the Russians and the westward migration of the nomads, but also the southward advance of the Russian settler out of the inhospitable forest into the enticing steppe. It also set the stage for an enduring conflict between settler and nomad. The sparsely populated forest zone was the home of Voguls, Ostiaks, and Samoeds, whose resistance to Russian inroads could only be sporadic and ineffectual, but the steppe supported the Kazakhs, the largest nomadic people in the entire eastern theatre, and the Kalmyks, their bitter rivals. Geography dictated that the Irtysh valley, cutting across the entire steppe, would become Russia's invasion route toward Altai and Mongolia.

The Kazakh Upland ended along a string of deserts consisting of the Ust Yurt Plateau, the Hunger Steppe (also Bet-Pak-Dala, the Cruel Steppe), the Lake Balkhash depression to the Zungharian Gate, the "Gate of Nations," between the Zunghar Alatau and the Tarbagatai range: Huns and Mongols crossed it at the outset of their long journey across the Ukrainian steppe to the Danube. Beyond these deserts were more deserts: the Kyzyl-Kum (Red Sand Desert), which occupied much of the area lying between the Amu Daria and the Syr Daria, very dry and little utilized except along the margins; and the Kara-Kum (Black Sand Desert), the most extensive sand desert in Central Asia, with shifting dunes of loose sand and totally unfit for agriculture. Beyond the great deserts that inclined northward into the Turanian Lowland, matching on a lower scale the Great Lowland across the Kazakh Upland and the Turgai tableland, was the Kopet Dag, marking the northern periphery of the Persian core bound further south by the parallel chains of the Zagros Mountains. But the land also rose again toward the TienShan Mountains and its several spurs, including one encompassing the Ferghana valley, where the Naryn and the Kara-Daria merge to form the 2,220-kilometre-long Syr Daria, flowing along the fringe of the Kyzyl Kum to end in the Aral Sea. The other great river of Central Asia, the Amu Daria (known in antiquity as the Oxus), rose in the Pamirs and flowed along the foothills of the Hindu Kush, before turning northwestward to end, like the Syr Daria, in the Aral Sea, 2,580 kilometres from its source.

The elevated ground between the two great rivers, often called Transoxiana, was a land of nucleated and mostly settled urban population and irrigation farmers. It was the land of Samarkand, Bukhara, and, in the large alluvian fan of the Amu Darya's delta, Khiva (Urgench). The west-east alignment of the mountains and the uniform pattern of latitudinal valleys bordered by mountains and deserts encouraged the migration of people and the caravan trade linking Persian with Indian and Chinese civilizations.[3] But here, as elsewhere in the central panel once again, rivers also created a longitudinal orientation. Bukhara was the hub toward which converged caravans from the western end of the Great Wall of China via Kabul in the south, Kashgar and Yarkend in the centre, and Kulja on the Ili River in the north. But Bukhara was also the starting point for one caravan route to Tobolsk and another to Kazan, while others further west along the Syr Daria led to Astrakhan, either across the Caspian or around its northern end. As a result, the Kazan-Astrakhan corridor, which led to Tiflis and northern Persia, also found another natural extension via the Amu Daria to Bukhara, from which yet another route via Aksu reached the upper Irtysh on its way to Tobolsk.[4]

The triptych's eastern panel was a different world. East of the Yenisei River, the ground rose to the Central Siberian Upland, a roughly dissected territory with canyon-like valleys, but never higher than 1,000 metres above sea level. The natural environment was so harsh that no extensive settlement has been possible to the present day. Fully contained in the permafrost zone showing the lowest recorded temperatures on earth, it was also a land of clear winters and little snowfall (unlike western Siberia), with a thick cover of conifers, chiefly larch, which were alone capable of finding sustenance in the thin layer of topsoil that thawed during the summer. But, as the ground rose toward the Saian Mountains to the south, patches of steppe and even black earth appeared in river valleys, where Buriats kept their herds and Turkic groups engaged in agriculture and the working of metals from local ore. The Upland abutted against Lake Baikal to the southeast and dropped toward the Lena valley farther east, beyond which a series of ranges rose to over 3,000 metres, separated by the valleys of rivers flowing northward into the Arctic Ocean, with the Kamchatka chain jutting out into the Pacific. East of Lake Baikal and south of the Lena, the ground kept rising to between 2,500 and 3,000 metres to form a broad upland dominated by the Iablonoi range, a desert of deep and swampy canyons, followed by the Stanovoi range, a succession of bare pyramidal heights (called *goltsy*) separated by deep narrow gorges. The Stanovoi continued northeastward along the coast of the Sea of Okhotsk to form a nearly impassable barrier between the interior and the sea. Such was Eurasia's eastern periphery.

But this inhospitable land, closed to the warm winds of the Pacific, contained an invaluable resource, more so than western Siberia in the central panel – fur-bearing animals, especially sables and foxes – and the fur trade became the stimulant to Russian expansion across Siberia. Moreover, the river network facilitated passage from the Yenisei to the Sea of Okhotsk. The portage between the Ket and the Yenisei took soldiers and traders to the confluence of the Angara, the Angara took them to the Ilim, and a short portage led to the Kuta, which flowed into the Lena. That queen of the Siberian rivers, 4,300 kilometres long (against the Yenisei's 4,020 kilometres), began on a ridge adjoining Lake Baikal and drained the central part of the panel before flowing into the Laptev Sea, which, like the Kara Sea, merged into the Arctic Ocean. It also flowed across a broad valley, the largest agricultural settlement in Eastern Siberia, created by the Yakuts, a Turkic people that migrated from the foothills of the Saian with their tools and horses. At the confluence of the Aldan began a difficult water and overland route to the Sea of Okhotsk, one of the most difficult passages on earth. The Aldan led to the Maia, the Maia to the Yudoma winding its way across an uninhabited upland covered with deep snows, and a portage led to the Urak that flowed into the sea.

The river network also led southward. Past the confluence of the Ilim, the Angara led to Lake Baikal (from which it issues), and across the lake, to the Selenga, which rose in the Khangai ridge on the edge of the Gobi Desert and flowed across the well-irrigated plain of central Mongolia. One of the Selenga's tributaries, the Khilok, descended from the Iablonoi, and a short portage connected its source with the Ingoda beyond the chain, which flowed into the Shilka, which merged with the Argun to form the Amur. This river flowed eastward toward the Tatar Strait into the Sea of Japan. The Amur could also be reached from the middle course of the Lena: one of its tributaries, the Olekma, descended from the watershed between the Iablonoi and the river's valley. The

Amur and its tributaries, notably the Sungari, which watered the Manchurian plain, belonged to the basin of the Pacific and formed a fourth panel, but it will figure little in our story and can be overlooked. Not until the Russians acquired the left bank of the Amur and the right bank of the Ussuri in 1858–60 did this region truly become an intrinsic part of the eastern theatre.

Geography dictated the pattern of trade routes between east and west. Caravans followed the Ob, the Ket, and the Angara, negotiated a difficult passage around the western end of Lake Baikal, followed the Khilok and the Ingoda, skirted the eastern end of the Gobi Desert and reached the Great Wall of China at Kalgan before moving on to Beijing. Lake Baikal could also be reached from Lake Yamyshev on the upper Irtysh by following the valley of the upper Yenisei. A third route took caravans from Lake Yamyshev past Lake Zaisan across northern Mongolia to the valley of the Tola on the southern edge of the steppe, and from there crossed the Gobi Desert to the Great Wall west of Kalgan. While the latitudinal alignment of mountain chains created natural channels of trade and corridors of expansion across Central Asia from Transcaucasia to Afghanistan, the same alignment of the tributaries of the major Siberian rivers drove the Russians across Siberia from the Urals to Lake Baikal, from which a sharp longitudinal detour took them across the desert to the periphery of the Chinese core.

The eastern theatre of effective Russian operations can thus be represented not only as a triptych but also as an amphitheatre sloping upward from the Russian plain in the vicinity of Kazan toward the Caucasus and Zagros complex, the Tien Shan, and the Altai-Saian complex extending eastward to form the Iablonoi and Stanovoi ranges. It was to a large extent a self-contained theatre with no access to the great oceans, a continental world protected against the influence and the countervailing power of the maritime empires, a world in which the Russians would build their own empire and develop a Eurasian identity.

Geopolitics

Two great developments marked the history of the eastern theatre. One was its rapid unification by the Mongol invasions of the thirteenth century. The Mongols were a people of the steppe who descended from the Eurasian periphery into the plain and imposed their rule all the way to the Hungarian depression, which formed the westernmost extension of the Eurasian steppe. The other was its gradual reunification, following the disintegration of Mongol power, by the Russians, a people of the plain moving toward the mountainous periphery and the elevated steppes of Mongolia.

In 1206, a general assembly (*kurultai*) of Mongol clans met near the sources of the Onon River and elected one of their leaders "supreme emperor" (Chingis

Khan). Five years later, he launched a first wave of invasions into northern China, gaining a logistical base and a staff of military engineers to give his nomads the necessary skills to conduct siege warfare. In 1219, he led his armies across the Gate of Nations into Central Asia to destroy the Khorezm empire dominated by Urgench (Khiva), then conquered Samarkand and Bukhara, but did not venture farther west. Instead, he sent two of his generals to reconnoitre the western lands: they entered the Transcaucasian corridor, crushed in 1221 the Georgian empire, which had stretched under Queen Tamar (1184–1212) from the Black Sea to the Caspian, and went as far as the Crimea, but were recalled following his death in 1227.[5]

Before his death, Chingis Khan had assigned to each of his four sons by his first wife a portion of the nascent empire as his respective appanage or *ulus*, thereby creating four dynastic branches and a source of potential conflicts. He selected his third son, Ugedei, as his successor, and gave him Zungharia, including the valley of the upper Irtysh. Tului, his youngest son, received the central and western part of Mongolia; his second son, Jagatai, the basin of Lake Balkhash; and Juchi, his eldest son, the newly conquered regions north of the Aral Sea. But he died before his father, and his *ulus* passed to his second son, Batu. The second wave of invasion began in 1237, when Batu, with a force of fifty thousand Mongols and seventy thousand Turkic auxiliaries, destroyed the capital of the Volga Bulgars, burned Moscow, and took Vladimir by storm in 1238. The invasion stopped one hundred kilometres from Novgorod at the approach of the spring thaw, but the Mongols ravaged central Russia before taking a rest in 1239. The following year, they took Kiev, looted Hungary, and reached Croatia in 1241. But the death of the Great Khan, Ugedei, forced Batu to call off preparations for an offensive into western Europe.[6]

The Mongols gradually discovered the value of regional administration, and found it expedient to give one of the princes the title of grand prince with responsibility for the collection of taxes and for the administration of other principalities on behalf of the khan in Sarai, whose own suzerain was the Great Khan of China and Mongolia in Beijing. The khan gave the charter to the prince he found the most accommodating and effective at a given time. He soon found, however, that his choice was largely limited to the princes of Tver and Vladimir-Moscow. Later, in the first half of the fourteenth century, wary of the rise of Moscow, he sanctioned the division of the Russian land into four grand principalities, Tver, Vladimir (Moscow), Nizhnii Novgorod, and Riazan. Tver dominated the approaches to Novgorod and the upper Dnieper; Moscow, the Volga-Oka mesopotamia; Nizhnii Novgorod, the confluence of the two rivers; and Riazan, the Don-Volga corridor, which led from Moscow to Sarai. The grand princes had become so many Russian khans in the Mongol world order, but the Moscow "khan" was by far the most important. His principality was the largest, with fifteen *t'my*, a *t'ma* consisting of 200,000 people, well ahead of Tver and Nizhnii Novgorod with five each, and Riazan with two, giving a total of 5.6 million people.[7]

Despite its power, which impressed contemporaries, the Mongol empire, and the Kipchak khanate in particular, was fragmented along potentially destructive fault lines. The cleavage between nomad overlord and settled population was one of them. Ethnically, the Mongols were a minority in the midst of a population that was largely Turkic (Tatar) and were gradually Turkicized and, in China, Sinicized. They might have become Russified as well, had not religious exclusiveness prevented it. The Mongols were tolerant of other religions. Batu had been a sky-worshipper, his son embraced Christianity, and Batu's brother, the third khan in the house of Juichi, converted to Islam, but his successors returned to sky-worship. The reign of Khan Uzbeg (1313–41) is considered to have been the heyday of the Kipchak khanate, but it was he who took the fateful step of making Islam the official religion.[8] As a result, Muscovy acquired a Muslim overlord and became part of an increasingly Tatar-Muslim empire, for which the Orthodox Church, exclusive and xenophobic, with its metropolitan in Vladimir, nevertheless had to pray, at least so long as the eastern Russian princes could not shake off their allegiance to the khan in Sarai. The emerging religious antagonism strengthened an underlying antagonism between Russians and Tatars as Moscow's power grew and the Muslim empire began to weaken in the fourteenth century.

The disintegration of the Kipchak khanate accelerated in the fifteenth century. Tokhtamysh, a chieftain of the house of Jagatai proclaimed himself khan of Kazan in 1445 and one of his cousins khan of the Crimea in 1446, who became a vassal of the Ottoman sultan in 1475. In alliance with Moscow, Tokhtamysh destroyed what was left of the Kipchak khanate in 1502, leaving behind a small khanate of Astrakhan. In the meantime, a fourth khanate had emerged in Siberia toward the end of the fifteenth century, headed by a member of the house of Tului. Its capital was at the confluence of the Tobol and the Irtysh. All these khans were no longer Mongol, but Turco-Mongol or simply Tatar, the name given to the Turkic peoples in the eastern theatre who had been overrun by the Mongols two centuries earlier.[9]

While Tokhtamysh was undermining the Kipchak khanate in an attempt to restore its past glory, the grand principality of Moscow was ruled by Vasilii I (1329–1425), the son of Dmitri Donskoi, the hero of the Kulikovo battle, which had been the first open and successful challenge to Mongol rule. Despite the victory, the grand principality remained open to Tatar raids for another century, but the grand prince derived strength from the endemic threat. Political strength offered opportunities, and Tatar princes and high officials, accompanied by armed retinues, began to offer their services to the grand prince, converted to Orthodoxy, were rewarded with positions at court, married into elite families, and brought Tatar influence to bear on Moscow's domestic politics and relations with the steppe.[10] The Orthodox Church, which had greatly benefited from the tolerant policy of the Mongols, supported the growth of grand princely power. The metropolitan, who had moved from Kiev to Vladimir in 1300, transferred to Moscow after 1325, and the Church became autocephalous in 1448, when it elected a metropolitan in defiance of the patriarch in Constantinople. Its emphasis on external observance and blind obedience, its rejection of rational discourse in the discussion of sacred matters, and its insistence that the power of the ruler was similar to God's gave a religious underpinning to the grand prince's bid for greater power.[11]

It was under Ivan III (1462–1505) that the consolidation of the grand princely power reached a decisive stage with the creation of a service class possessing landed property, whose allegiance was to the ruler alone.[12] This crucial development gave him a power base that enabled him to face down opponents in his own house and in other princely families. The service class also became the core of a military force, chiefly cavalry, required to assemble whenever the grand prince chose to summon them. His appointments gave him a foothold beyond the lands held by his house, to a point where he could justifiably call himself the grand prince of "all Russia."[13] Such a claim was the ultimate challenge to the authority of the Kipchak khan, who burned Russian cities in 1472 and sent an embassy to Moscow in 1476 demanding that the grand prince appear in Sarai, but he refused. Gone were the days when Ivan I (1325–41) had journeyed nine times to Sarai during his reign.[14] The khan, bent on restoring his suzerainty and reimposing the annual tribute, which Moscow had stopped paying in 1452, led an army against Moscow; the two armies met on the Ugra River (a tributary of the Oka) in 1480, but the Tatars met strong resistance from the Russians, who were equipped with firearms. The khan did not force the issue and retreated to Sarai, thereby forsaking forever his claim to Moscow's vassalage.[15]

This prestige victory must be placed in the context of Ivan's dynamic "foreign" policy on two fronts. He pursued the "gathering of the Russian land" with the annexation, in the west, of Novgorod in 1478 and Tver in 1485, and in the east, of the land of Perm in 1472 and the Viatka republic in 1489. Riazan, however, would not be incorporated into Moscow's domain until 1517. But Ivan was also on the offensive against the Tatar lands. His father, Vasilii II (1425–62), had created a puppet khanate on the Oka between Riazan and Nizhnii Novgorod under Kasim (who gave his name to the town of Kasimov), a son of the Kazan khan and a Jagatai, who collected the *iasak* (fur tax) from his Mordvinian and Meshcherian subjects. It was Ivan's intent to use Kasim to manipulate Kazan politics, where the khan's power was limited by the heads of aristocratic Tatar clans, in order to eventually bring the Kazan khanate into Moscow's orbit. In 1487, he took the city and deported the khan to Vologda, yet failed to keep his prey.[16] But these moves also brought Moscow into the orbit of Chingissid politics. The Moscow "khan," the former subject of the Kipchak khan and subvassal of the Great Khan in China, had become the suzerain of a Chingissid khan and sought to extend his suzerainty over another Chingissid in Kazan. In so doing, Ivan became the founder of a policy of gathering the lands of the Mongol empire which eventually resulted in the reunification of the Kipchak khanate; his successors as late as the eighteenth century would be known at the Chinese court as the White (Western) Khans, the successors of the khans of Juchi's *ulus*.

In Chingis Khan's grandson Hulagu's and his son Jagatai's portions of the Chingissid inheritance, Mongol rule gave way to new constellations of power. An uprising in Transoxiana brought to power Timur (Tamerlane), a Turk from the family of a vizier in Jagatai service. He established his capital in Samarkand, restored Hulagu's empire, to which he added part of the Jagatai *ulus* to the borders of Kashgaria, and even crossed the Hindu Kush to loot Delhi in northern India. He died in 1405, while preparing an invasion of China. The Timurid empire barely outlived its founder. A long time of trouble in the fifteenth century came to an end with the establishment of the Shabanid Uzbek dynasty, whose founding khans belonged to the house of Tului. They placed their relatives in Bukhara, Khiva, and Tashkent. But the major event was the founding of the Safavid dynasty in Persia by Ismail I (1502–24), who restored the centrality of the Persian core over the peripheral regions in Transcaucasia, Central Asia, and the mountain cities of the Hindu Kush.[17]

Thus by the 1530s, when Ivan IV, Ivan III's grandson, came to power, Moscow had created a powerful core ready to stake a claim to the Chingissid legacy east of Nizhnii Novgorod. The Safavid dynasty (1502–1736) and the Ming dynasty (1368–1644) reinvigorated the Persian and Chinese cores. Unlike the "universal," tolerant, and inclusive Mongol empire, the three cores did not have universalist ideologies, but were all xenophobic and prisoners of a religious-cultural exceptionalism: Russia with Orthodoxy, Persia with Shi'ism, China with Confucianism. Their rise created a frontier over which they would struggle until at least the eighteenth century. That frontier was the eastern theatre of the expanding Russian core.

The Russian Advance

Ivan IV came to the throne in 1533 at the age of three and was not crowned until 1547. That same year, Moscow launched the first of four campaigns against Kazan, which ended in 1552 with a successful siege. There were two major reasons for this determination to take that city. It blocked Muscovy's advance down the Volga, which drained Moscow and its dependencies irresistibly eastward. The growing grand principality could not stop at the confluence of the Volga and the Oka; it needed to incorporate the confluence of the Volga and the Kama as well, another pivotal point from which it could develop its full potential in the Caspian basin. The second reason was local dissension in the khanate, which Moscow kept taking advantage of and even inciting, between the khans and the clan leaders and among the clans themselves, as well as the activities of the Crimean khan, who saw himself as a worthy successor of the former Kipchak khan in Sarai. After the conquest, the khan in Kazan converted to Orthodoxy and, in accordance with the norms of the day, was expected to bring his subjects into the Christian fold. The issue was not pressed at the time, but it remained in the background: the religion of the prince was also that of his subjects.[18]

The annexation of Kazan was followed by that of Astrakhan in 1556, and outposts were built along the Volga between the two cities: Saratov and Tsaritsyn in the late 1580s, Simbirsk in 1648. Astrakhan led to the Caucasus. A fort (Terskii gorodok) was built on one of the branches of the Terek's delta before 1586, and detachments of Russian troops appeared in the mountains, in Kabarda, where the princes pledged allegiance in 1557. A Kabardian princess became Ivan's second wife in 1561, and her family, the Cherkasskys, became one of the most prominent members of Muscovy's ruling elite. But the appearance of Russian troops set the stage for a prolonged conflict with the Crimean khan and his suzerain, the Ottoman sultan, who launched a campaign against Astrakhan in 1569, hoping to make it into an operational base against the hated Shi'ites and a link between the Ottoman empire and the Central Asian khanates, as well as an obstacle to Russia's advance toward the Caucasus.[19] The campaign failed, and it was the Russians who would transform Astrakhan into an assembly point for operations in eastern Transcaucasia and on the Persian shores.

But this remarkable projection of power nearly two thousand kilometres from Kazan to the Terek paled in comparison with the conquest of Siberia. Kazan led not only downriver to Astrakhan, the Caspian, and the Caucasus; it also led along the Kama to the western slopes of the Ural Mountains. In 1558, the Stroganov family of salt merchants was given a charter to colonize and administer unoccupied land between the Kama and the Chusovaia, which flows across the middle Urals. The Stroganovs were also allowed to have a private army, with which they sought to establish control over the Voguls (Mansi) and the Ostiaks (Khanty), nomads of the forest, who had been paying tribute to the Siberian khanate. Sable pelts were a source of both great profit and bitter rivalry among contenders for the allegiance of the peoples of the forest, whose only activity was hunting. Kuchum, the Siberian khan, who disposed of his rivals by 1571 and was a Muslim and a Chingissid, challenged the Stroganovs' inroads across the Urals by sending scouting expeditions into the Kama valley. By the late 1570s, the Stroganovs had engaged a force of Cossack freebooters who had been looting merchant caravans on the Volga. Led by their *ataman* Ermak, some five hundred men, armed with firearms, went up the Chusovaia, crossed over to the Tura and the Tobol Rivers, and seized Kuchum's capital at the confluence of the Irtysh and the Ob in 1582. Ermak then sent a delegation to Moscow asking Ivan to take possession of the new lands, but the Cossacks were then defeated, and Ermak was killed in 1585, one year after Ivan's death.

What had been until then a private undertaking now became a government enterprise. Reinforcements of infantry (*streltsy*) were sent every year as soon as the weather permitted, and Kuchum was eventually killed near present-day Novosibirsk on the Ob in 1598.[20] The establishment of an administrative-military infrastructure proceeded at a rapid pace. Tobolsk was founded in 1587 on the site of Kuchum's capital and gradually became the capital of Russian Siberia; Tara was founded on the Irtysh in 1594 against Kuchum's last desperate raids; Narym, at the confluence of the Ket and the Ob in 1596; Fort Makhovsky, on the portage between the Ket and the Yenisei in 1618; Tomsk and Kuznetsk, in 1604 and 1618. The time of trouble in the Russian core, which shook the foundations of Muscovy, did not stay the Russian advance, and the accession of the Romanov dynasty in 1613 could only encourage it. Yeniseisk was founded in 1618 and Krasnoiarsk in 1628; Ilimsk on the portage between the Angara and the Lena in 1630 and Ust-Kut the following year. The Russians reached Lake Baikal in 1631, built a fort that became Yakutsk in 1632, sailed up the Aldan and managed to reached the Okhotsk coast. In 1644–5, they sailed down the Amur River and northward along the coast to build a small outpost at Okhotsk; in 1652, they founded Irkutsk, destined to become the second capital of Siberia.[21]

In the sixty-five years between 1582 and 1647, the Russians travelled eight thousand kilometres of difficult country to reach the first of the three seas forming a transition zone to the great oceans.[22] But in fact they had laid claim to what was essentially an immense extension of the core. It has been said that in crossing Siberia the Russian is not making for new land at all. "He is shifting from one environment to a very similar one, and he may walk if he so pleases from Petrograd to Eastern Siberia without setting foot outside of Russia or of Russian climatic conditions."[23] Kazan also led across the Kama into Bashkir country, where the Russians built in 1574 a fort (Ufa) at the confluence of the Ufa and Dema Rivers with the Belaia, on the very edge of the forest zone. They had rapidly built an empire of the forest (with a projection into the steppe of the lower Volga and the northern Caucasus), but was it truly an empire or an extension of the core? The question needs to be asked, because it will become central to an understanding of Russian imperial policy. The Russians themselves would hesitate between building an empire consisting of core and peripheries or rounding out a unitary state, obliterating the differences between them.

When Ivan was crowned tsar in 1547, he abandoned the title of grand prince for that of tsar. In the past, the title had been given to the khan in Sarai. There are references as early as the thirteenth century to the "Tatar tsar," and it was said that Ivan III showed "no fear of the tsar" before the showdown of 1480.[24] By 1547, the Kipchak khanate was no more, and the title was vacant. Ivan IV assumed the succession, and by the time of his death had indeed reunified the khanate under Moscow's leadership, save for the Kazakh steppe now occupied by the Kazakh dynasty descending from a cousin of Akhmed, the last khan of the house of Juchi. While the title of the Moscow tsars (and later Russian emperors) never included a reference to the Kipchak khanate, it clearly stated that the tsar (emperor) was also "Tsar of Kazan, Tsar of Astrakhan, and Tsar of Siberia," the three major component parts of the old Kipchak khanate outside of the Russian lands.[25]

The administration of this enormous territory was vested in 1599 in the Kazan Chancery (*Prikaz Kazanskogo Dvortsa*), which did not reside in Kazan but in Moscow, a central office with a territorial rather than a functional jurisdiction. In 1637, a Siberian Chancery (*Sibirskii Prikaz*) was carved out with responsibility for Siberia, and the Kazan Chancery continued to manage the lands of the former Kazan and Astrakhan khanates. The Siberian Chancery included a separate department for sorting out pelts sent from Siberia, with a staff of appraisers who kept the best for the ruling house and placed the others on the domestic and export markets. In the towns, which were often not much more than a fort and a small number of houses, there were *voevody*, two in the larger settlements, one in the others, who represented the tsar and combined civil and military powers. Their major task was to consolidate Russian influence over the native population and secure a regular collection of the tribute in pelts. They usually served for two years, and were expected to fend for themselves ("feed themselves") from the limited resources of the forest zone.[26] This assumption created a major contradiction between their duty to win the allegiance of the natives and their unrestrained greed. The consequences included rebellions, which were put down with unnecessary cruelty. To carry out their duties, the *voevody* relied on servicemen consisting of tax collectors, *streltsy*, and gunners, who gave the Russians overwhelming superiority over natives armed with bows and arrows. They numbered about five thousand in 1635. Another four thousand native auxiliaries and Cossacks gave the Russians additional mobility, and provided a link with the natives often scattered over enormous distances.[27] If such a small force gave the Russians superiority over the natives in any local encounter, its success would ultimately depend on the inability of the natives to form an organized opposition in such a sparsely settled territory. The task of the central government was to settle the land with Russians and encourage the formation of a melting pot, in much the same way as expansion into the lands of Ugro-Finnish settlement had already created a hardy race in the Russian north. This would not be achieved until the nineteenth century.

In the middle of the seventeenth century, the ethnographic composition of the eastern theatre was already very diverse. The Russian population did not exceed forty thousand and consisted of peasants resettled more or less forcibly from the forest zone of European Russia, convicts banished to Siberia, either to settle in forts of rural communities or to do hard labour, and prisoners captured in Russia's wars with the Livonian Knights and the Poles. Many were men, and the conversion of native women served to provide brides and encourage settlement.[28]

To these Russians must be added (because they were Orthodox) Cossacks of various denominations, consisting of fugitive peasants, Old Believers, former rebels, and all types of criminals, who found a refuge in Muscovy's wooded periphery and sought to preserve their independence from the *voevody*, while often serving Moscow's interests by acting as pathfinders of Russian expansion. Along the Terek were the so-called Greben Cossacks, who also included immigrants from the valley of the Don, the mother house of many Cossack settlements. They are first mentioned in 1569. To the east were the Ural Cossacks along the lower course of the river, a den of thieves like the those of the Don, already in existence in 1580. They were a mixed lot, consisting not only of Russian fugitives but also of Tatars, Bashkirs, and Kalmyks. Fiercely independent, perhaps more than any other Cossack community, they also sent detachments to serve in the Russian army fighting the Crimean Tatars in 1629 and the Poles in 1634. The Siberian Cossacks were of a different kind. They were mostly an artificial creation of the government and never developed a tradition of freedom from central authorities. Their main source of recruitment was the "wanderers" (*guliashchie liudi*), who were pressed into Cossack service and did mostly garrison duty.[29]

While the Cossacks, despite their differences, represented a definite social category found along the periphery of the eastern theatre, native groups occupied definite locations in each of the triptych's panels, but many were hunters and fishermen scattered in the heavily forested far north, whose societies never developed close contact with the Russians.[30] We shall limit ourselves to the more important peoples. In the western panel, the Caspian basin, we find the Kazan Tatars, whose origin is controversial, but they were a Turkic people who came into their own with the creation of the Kazan khanate in 1445. The khanate occupied the entire valley of the Volga from the confluence of the Vetluga to the portage between the Don and the Volga, from the Moksha in the west to the upper course of the Ufa and the Belaia in the east. These Tatars were Muslim, agriculturalists and traders who controlled the entire trade of the region, a society dominated by powerful clans. They also lorded it over the Mordva and the Chuvash on the right bank of the Volga, and the Cheremis (Mari) and Votiaks (Udmurts) on the left bank in the forest zone to the Cheptsa River, idol worshippers for the most part, and at various times over the Bashkirs as well. Memories of their distant ancestry, of the fact their khans had been Chingissids and Sunni Muslims, would play a powerful role in the development of an identity separate from that of the Russians, but also willing to accommodate the policies of the White Khan in Moscow.[31]

Further down the Volga were the Astrakhan Tatars of the former khanate, many of whom offered their services to the government as guides, interpreters, and auxiliaries, and who assisted the *streltsy* and Cossacks. These Tatar auxiliaries were called *sluzhilye iurtovye* because they had become servicemen and lived in settlements called *iurty*. They were not nomads. One must also include here the Large Nogai Horde, which had once been powerful east of the Volga, but pledged allegiance to Ivan IV and was later contained between the Volga and the Ural Rivers.[32] In the Caucasus were the Kabardians, a Circassian people, who straddled the middle course of the Terek, and sought a protector in Moscow against their enemies in the mountains. In Transcaucasia were the Georgians and Armenians, both Christian peoples, who saw in the rising Orthodox power in the north a possible counterweight to the Ottomans and Persians, who ravaged their country in pursuit of hegemony in the old dependency of Hulagu's empire.[33] The rich rolling hills of Bashkiria had long attracted the envy of other peoples, and the Bashkirs found themselves under the rule of the Kazan Tatars or the Nogais. They were a Turkic people, Muslim, who had migrated from Siberia to settle between the Volga and the Urals on the upland that had once overlooked the bed of the Caspian Sea. Some had remained on the Siberian side of the Urals. There were steppe Bashkirs, who carried Mongol blood, and forest Bashkirs, who retained their Turkic appearance, more proud and more daring, who lived in the southern Urals. They were neither full settlers nor full pastoralists, but engaged in both agriculture and stock raising; they were also hunters, and apiculture was a substantial source of revenue.[34]

In the central panel between the Urals and the Yenisei there were more Tatars, in the Baraba steppe, in the Altai massif, and in the valley of the Chulym between the Tom and the Yenisei. But they formed small, scattered, and isolated communities, which would easily become integrated into the settler population. The ethnographic history of western Siberia would be dominated for two hundred years (until 1771) by the great rivalry between the Kazakhs and the Western Mongols. The Kazakhs, called Kirgiz in Russian sources, were a mixed but predominantly Turkic people, whose khans belonged to the house of Juichi. They branched off in the fifteenth century from a disintegrating Uzbek khanate; some remained in the basin of Lake Balkhash, others crossed the steppe to the Ural River. Late in the sixteenth century they agreed on a common khan, who sent an envoy to Moscow in 1594, offering to become subjects of the White Khan, but nothing came of it: long distances and intermittent contacts could only render such relationships meaningless.[35] But the offer was of great symbolic significance: that a Chingissid roaming the steppe so far away from Moscow could offer to become a subject testified to the vitality of a perception widely held in the steppe that the Russian tsar had become the successor of the Kipchak khanate, of which the Kazakh steppe had been such an important part.

The Western Mongols (Zunghars) were not Chingissids, and their ruler was therefore illegitimate. In the sixteenth century they formed a confederacy of four major tribes centred in the Kobdo depression between the Mongolian and Main Altai. They later spread out to become the leading nomadic power between the Altai, the Tien Shan, and the Gobi Desert as far as Lake Kokonor. But one of the four went west and appeared in 1606 before Tara on the Irtysh; they were allowed to pasture their herds in return for agreeing to become Moscow's subjects. Their envoys were given an audience in 1608, and they became known as Kalmyks. They were fierce warriors, although they were Buddhist of the Tibetan persuasion, and became the most destabilizing element in the politics of the steppe. They kept moving west, reached the Volga in 1620, crossed the river below Tsaritsyn, made it to the Terek, but were crushed in 1644 by the Kabardians, against whom they would nurture a long-lasting enmity. They found themselves at war with the Kazakhs and the Bashkirs, chiefly over the occupation of pastures, and there was still little Moscow could do, beside trying to enlist them as auxiliaries and promising them the tsar's "gracious favor."[36]

In the eastern panel of Eastern Siberia, the largest ethnic group was the Tungus, true nomads of the forest, who were hunters; they roamed across the immense area between the Yenisei and the Stanovoi. They were related to the Manchus, who were soon to play a decisive role in blocking the Russian advance toward the Pacific. But the Tungus, like other peoples of the Siberian far north, played no role in the formation of the Russian empire except as tribute payers. We must therefore leave them behind to turn to the Buriats, a subdivision of the Eastern Mongols, whose land was the basin of the upper Selenga. They were found west of Lake Baikal, in the land between the eastern Saian and the upper Lena, well drained by rivers with valleys rich in meadows and even patches of black earth; and also east of the lake, in the valley of the lower Selenga, the so-called Kudara steppe. The Russians encountered them first in 1612 and again in 1628 on the Angara, where they built Fort Bratsk in 1631. The forceful collection of the tribute did not sit well with the Buriat leaders, who already collected it from their Tungus subjects, and early relations were marred by violence in the 1640s.[37]

Below the confluence of the Olekma, the Lena enters a broad valley of larch forests with clearings of meadowland, where spring cereals and even watermelon flourish. That was the land of the Yakuts, a Turkic people who moved, not west like so many of their brethren, but north with their horses and cattle, "to become the only stock-breeding people of the Siberian north."[38] An energetic people, they kept expanding in all directions early in the seventeenth century and assimilated many Tungus and others, and would eventually assimilate the few Russians who chose to settle in such an otherwise inhospitable environment. The Russians founded Yakutsk in 1632, and the fort became the starting point for expeditions seeking a passage to the Sea of Okhotsk. Early relations were not friendly either, and the Yakuts revolted in 1642 against an order to conduct a census of their cattle.[39] They stood no chance against Russian firearms.

The Expanding Russian Core

Siberia

We may properly trace the renewal of an expansionist urge – which would continue unabated for three hundred years until the Korean War of 1950–3 – to the reign of Alexei Mikhailovich (1645–76), when the Romanov dynasty finally overcame the domestic crisis brought about by the interregnum of 1598–1613, and, in Siberia in particular, to the founding of Irkutsk and Nerchinsk in 1652 and 1653 and Albazin and Selenginsk in 1665 and 1667. Across the whole of Siberia the Russians were steadily pushing out of the taiga into the grassy steppe with chernozem and chestnut soils adaptable to agriculture – a land that had supported nomadic civilization for centuries but now beckoned to the advancing settler. The expansion of the core was about to assume geopolitical implications as the Russians found themselves facing a resurgent China, after the Manchus overthrew the Ming dynasty in 1644 and set up their own, which would last until 1911, six years before the collapse of the Romanov dynasty. Russian activities in Siberia could no longer remain the responsibility of individual *voevody* reporting separately to a chancery in Moscow, but required coordination at the regional level, as the politics of the steppe ceased to be the result of an encounter between Moscow and the nomad and became part of a relationship between a Russian and a Chinese empire advancing toward each other across a now common frontier.

In 1708, Moscow and its holdings from the Polish-Lithuanian border to Eastern Siberia were divided into eight provinces (*gubernii*), with Siberia forming one of them, but a Siberia which retained memories of its conquest: the province included land west of the Urals, the old properties of the Stroganovs on the upper Kama with Solikamsk and Cherdyn, and stretched as far as Viatka. In 1719, it was recognized that some of the provinces were too large, and they were divided into *provintsii*, of which there were five in Siberia: Viatka and Solikamsk west of the Urals, and Tobolsk, Yeniseisk, and Irkutsk in Siberia proper. The old division into districts (*uezds*) was retained. The entire province was divided into twenty-five *uezds*, of which six were in Viatka and Solikamsk *provintsii*, ten in Tobolsk, five in Yeniseisk, and four in Irkutsk *provintsii*.[40]

Siberia, like other provinces, was headed by a governor. The first to hold that post was Matvei Gagarin, from an old princely Russian family that had given ten Siberian *voevody* in the seventeenth century. Gagarin had been the last chief of the Siberian chancery, which was abolished when he moved to Tobolsk in

1711. He was recalled in 1719 and hanged in 1721 for defrauding the Treasury. His successor, Alexander Cherkassky, from the princely Kabardian family that had given Ivan IV his second wife, remained until 1724; he was also the brother of the last Tobolsk *voevoda*. The third, Mikhail Dolgorukov, from another old Russian princely family, was sent to Tobolsk as a form of punishment, a fairly common practice among members of the ruling elite who fell out of favour in the politics of the Court. Like Cherkassky, he remained only three years, too short a time to accomplish anything constructive. These first three governors were all closely related to the Romanov house by ties of marriage, a status which gave them great authority but not necessarily great power.[41]

After 1727, governors no longer came from the great families. Following Peter's death, some of the old principles of Muscovite administration reasserted themselves. The subordination of the *provintsia voevoda* to the governor caused unacceptable delays, as when the Solikamsk *voevoda* reported to Tobolsk and the governor then reported to Moscow via Solikamsk! In 1727, Viatka and Solikamsk *provintsii* were removed from the jurisdiction of Tobolsk, and in 1730 the Siberian Chancery was restored but subordinated to the Senate, implying a drastic reduction of the governor's status. Nevertheless, he remained the coordinating authority for most governmental activities in Siberia and Petersburg's representative in relations with China. By then, Siberia consisted of a single province, divided into three *provintsii* and twenty-three districts.[42]

Ambitious governors who had the ear of the ruler could easily become proconsuls with a vision of empire born of long experience with Muscovy's peripheries. Such was the case with Gagarin. Soon after his arrival, he heard that gold dust could be obtained at Yarkend on the Silk Road in Kashgaria. He sent an agent into Zunghar country, who travelled as far as Lake Kokonor and brought back confirmation of the rumours. At a time when Russia lacked its own sources of precious metals and faced enormous expenditures during the war with Sweden, the prospect of laying a hand on a source of gold was exhilarating. Gagarin convinced Peter I to send an expedition to Yarkend. He was certain it could reach the city within three months. The Russians would build forts along the Irtysh, manned by garrisons of Tatars commanded by Russian officers. However, he underestimated the dangers of challenging the Zunghars, who were then engaged in a bitter struggle with the Manchus over the control of the Kobdo depression east of the Mongolian Altai.

The tsar appointed Lt.-Col. Ivan Buchholz in 1714 to command an expeditionary force of 3,000 men with 1,500 horses and 70 guns. Its mission was to build a fort overlooking the Yamyshev salt lakes near the Irtysh, a major meeting point between Russians and nomads, to move on to Yarkend (whose location was unclear), take the town, and build a fort. The enterprise had a commercial purpose: to lay claim by force of arms to a city known for its wealth and establish a commanding position on one of the major trade routes with China and India. But the expedition did not go well because its planners neglected the logistical difficulties inherent in crossing unknown territory, most of it sheer desert. Buchholz left Tobolsk in July 1715, built a fort at the Yamyshev lakes in October, but soon found himself surrounded by Zunghars. A caravan bringing provisions and funds was seized by the Kalmyks and its men taken into captivity. By the spring of 1716, Buchholz's force had been reduced to 700 men. The Zunghars allowed them to retreat to the Om River, which the nomads considered to be the natural boundary of the Russian world.[43]

The expedition's failure was nevertheless rich in lessons for the historian. One was that the nomads, especially the Mongols (Zunghars and Kalmyks), still looked upon the Russians as a people of the forest and upon themselves as the lords of the steppe. Another was that the Russians were beginning to claim a decisive voice in the politics of the steppe. In February 1716, before the news of the disaster could reach him, Peter sent an envoy to the *kontaisha* (the Zunghar leader) to tell him that he had nothing to fear from Gagarin's mission to build "towns" on the Irtysh, and that he could turn to the governor for assistance should he feel threatened by his neighbours. This was a highly ambiguous offer. The Zunghars' neighbours were the Kazakhs, and relations between the two peoples were always tense. But the offer may have been intended to counter the offer by a Chinese embassy to the Kalmyks seeking an alliance against the Zunghars. It had reached the Kalmyk camp in June 1714. Most striking of all was an offer to the *kontaisha* to recognize the tsar as his sovereign, who would send him five thousand trained horsemen for his defence. The offer was so unrealistic in the circumstances that it only angered the *kontaisha*, who kept the envoys for several years in his camp.[44]

Buchholz's expedition also revealed a certain spatial vision of eastern Eurasia. In December 1716, Peter reinterpreted the goal of the expedition for the *kontaisha*'s benefit in a charter (*gramota*), which the Zunghar ruler did not receive until March 1718. It contained no mention of Yarkend, but referred to the gold, silver, and copper ore found along the Irtysh and the Lake Zaisan area – which obviously meant the Altai – lands which belonged to "our Siberian kingdom [*tsarstvo*]" where the Zunghars were merely tolerated as long as they lived peacefully.[45] Peter overlooked the military lesson of the encounter – that Russia could not defeat the Zunghars in battle – and resorted to the legal argument that the upper Irtysh had been part of the Kipchak khanate, which the Russians had inherited when Ivan IV assumed the title of tsar, and that the Zunghars (who were not even Chingissids) were essentially foreigners on Russian land.

That vision had been refined earlier, in February 1715, when Gagarin answered the *kontaisha*'s objections to the activities of the Tara *voevoda* who collected the *iasak* from the Baraba Tatars, south of the Om River, whom the Zunghars claimed as their subjects. Gagarin invoked both geography and history. The great rivers like the Ob (of which the Irtysh was a tributary), the Yenisei, and the Lena defined Siberia, which had belonged to Russia since time immemorial (*iskoni*). The Russian realm included their entire basin, from their mouth on the "Northern Sea" to the mountaintops where they took their source – "and the *kontaisha* knows this."[46] In other words, Gagarin was claiming that the Russians were indeed a people of the forest and the plain advancing on rising ground in an immense amphitheatre bound by the Altai, the Saian, the Iablonoi, and the Stanovoi – Eurasia's inner periphery – where the great rivers took their source, and from where Turkic and Mongol nomads had once descended into the steppe to build an empire which the Russians were now claiming as their own.

That such a vision of Russia's spatial claims was widespread in the Russian capital, to the point that one may say it imbued government policy, can be seen from the history of Russo-Chinese relations in Eastern Siberia. Russia's advance to the Amur River triggered a Manchu-Chinese reaction. The Amur provided easier access to the great oceans than the impossible overland route from Yakutsk to Okhotsk, but its occupation would threaten the homeland of the Manchus across the river. Likewise, the advance along the Selenga represented a threat to the Manchus' hold on the Eastern Mongols, whose land was the river's well-drained basin, which formed the southern extension of the steppe to the Hangai Upland and the Tola River, beyond which the Gobi and other deserts stretched to the Great Wall of China. As a result, Russia's penetration into the steppe, which almost brought about an armed conflict with the Zunghars, also aroused the anxiety of the Eastern Mongols, and called for the intervention of the Chinese core, now led by an ambitious dynasty and one of its two greatest emperors. Beside these larger issues of geopolitical importance, there were other, smaller, but more urgent ones. The Cossacks began to collect the *iasak* south of the Stanovoi, in areas where the finest sables and black foxes were found, from Tungus hunters whom the Manchus assumed were their subjects. Turbulence in the frontier caused temporary migrations of Buriats and Mongols from the Russian to the Manchu-Chinese side and vice versa, usually the result of oppression by local officials, but in the absence of a linear boundary it was impossible to determine at what point a migration became a cross-border flight. The most famous of these flights was that of a Tungus prince, Gantimur, with his family and people in 1666; they were given asylum in Nerchinsk, and the Russians refused to surrender them after they converted to Orthodoxy. The issue would poison Russo-Chinese relations for twenty years.[47]

By 1680, the Russians had built a number of settlements south of the Stanovoi, the most important of which was Albazin, a short distance from the confluence of the Shilka and the Argun, where the Amur began. It was then that the Manchus, who had been busy consolidating their rule in China, turned north to face the Russians. In 1683, the settlements were destroyed, and Albazin was razed in 1686. The Manchus then claimed that the Sino-Russian border must run along Lake Baikal and the Lena all the way to Yakutsk, thereby bringing into the empire most of the land of the Tungus, to whom the Manchus were related. Moscow had already decided to negotiate a settlement. It was enshrined in the famous Treaty of Nerchinsk of August 1689.[48]

The Russians showed great skill in the negotiations, considering that their embassy was at the mercy of the Manchus, who, however, were concerned lest the Russians form an alliance with the Zunghars against them. The Russian scaled back their claims, but insisted that the Outer Khingan – essentially the watershed between the Arctic and Pacific Oceans – should form the boundary. In the end, however, they had to concede that the boundary must run far to the west, along the Argun, but then skirt its confluence with the Shilka by following the lower Gazimur River to the Little Gorbitsa and to the valley of the Uda. The Russians had indeed been kept out of the Amur valley, but gained the valleys of the Argun and Shilka. No wonder the treaty was celebrated as a victory in Moscow. It gave them a foothold in the Pacific basin and, given the right circumstances, an opportunity to regain access to the great river at a later date.[49]

There remained to delineate the Russo-Mongol border. This was not done until 1728 with the signature of the Treaty of Kiakhta. The Russians were aware that the Manchus wanted to renegotiate the Treaty of Nerchinsk by claiming once again that Lake Baikal must be the boundary between the two empires, bringing the territory between the lake and the Argun into the Manchu empire. They also intended to build a fort on the upper Irtysh to gain a foothold in Zunghar country. But the Russians countered such claims, arguing, like Gagarin, that Russia's claims extended to the headwaters of the Siberian rivers. The lake had been a Russian possession since time immemorial (*izstari*), and all the rivers flowing into it belonged to Russia's domain.[50] The Russian Senate possessed the same spatial vision as Gagarin. The Selenga was the only significant river flowing into Lake Baikal. Its basin was the land of the Eastern Mongols. Therefore, Russia must claim suzerainty over them, in the same way as Peter had claimed jurisdiction over the basin of the Irtysh, where the Western Mongols were only tolerated. Consequently, the imperial government was not only claiming to have reunited the Kipchak khanate in the eastern theatre but was also staking a claim to the Mongol homeland from which the great invasions had come.

However, the Russians could not compel the Manchus to accept such claims. The new Russo-Mongol border was made to run from the upper Argun (where the 1689 border began) across the Onon valley and south of the Chikoi and Dzhida Rivers, leaving the Eastern Mongols under Manchu rule, and no Chinese fort was built on the Irtysh. But the Russians kept a long-term perspective: following the collapse of the Manchu dynasty in 1911, their interests in

Mongolia grew exponentially, and the country later became a Soviet satellite. And in 1944, the Soviet Union annexed the Tannu Tuva territory, which was no more than the headwaters of the Yenisei. It was only then that Gagarin's vision was fully realized: all the great rivers of Siberia, from their mouths to their headwaters in the mountains, had become Russia's possessions.

A major consequence of the border settlements of 1689 and 1728 – the former remained unchanged until 1858, when the Russians finally acquired the left bank of the Amur – was to eliminate the possibility of an armed conflict between the two empires. Their relations would henceforth be dominated by disputes over cross-border flights and trade, which never threatened to escalate to a dangerous level. The Russians could then concentrate on the internal policing of Siberia and the establishment of satisfactory relations with the Zunghars and Kazakhs. They had at their disposal garrisons, Cossacks, and auxiliary formations from the native population. No combat troops were stationed in Siberia at the time.

In Eastern Siberia, there were three areas of concern. One was the corridor formed by the Yenisei River across the Kobal and Minusinsk steppes, rich agricultural country bounded by the Kuznetsk Alatau and the Eastern Saians, where Russian settlers were entering Tatar country. East of Lake Baikal, several forts faced the Russo-Mongol border, including Selenginsk and Nerchinsk. The third area was the northeast, where a serious effort was made beginning in 1731 to develop a port from which to supply Kamchatka, of difficult overland access. In those forts and *uezd* centres, there were Cossack units of various sizes, from twenty to several hundreds, for a total of forty-five hundred. There were two regiments of garrison infantry in the Selenga and Yenisei valleys, and three regiments of Buriats and Tungus created after 1728 to patrol the Russo-Mongol border, about five thousand horsemen.[51]

In Western Siberia, the Russians faced the problem of creating a largely artificial boundary with the Kazakh world. They pursued a policy that both created a defensive perimeter against nomadic raids into already settled areas and staked out new territory for future settlement. Buchholz's expedition had not been totally in vain. On his way back, he built Fort Omsk at the confluence of the Om and the Irtysh, destined to become Russia's military headquarters facing the Kazakh steppe. Additional forts were subsequently built at Zhelezensk, Semipalatinsk, and Ust-Kamenogorsk on the Irtysh, the building blocks of what would soon be called the Irtysh Line. All these forts were manned by Cossacks, of whom there were 4,980 in the 1720s, including 1,000 each in Tobolsk and Tomsk. They sought to separate the Kazakhs from the Zunghars, who roamed beyond the Irtysh and staked a claim to the approaches to the Altai. To block access to Russian settlements emerging out of the forest zone into the Ishim steppe, the Russians built a line of forts stretching from the Irtysh below Omsk to the Tobol. It crossed the Ishim at Korkin (later called Ishim) and followed the upper course of the Vagai River and the middle course of the Tobol to end south of Tsarev Gorodishche (Kurgan). These forts created the Ishim Line.

In addition to the Cossacks there were in Western Siberia two regiments of garrison infantry and one of garrison dragoons stationed in separate companies in Kungur, Ekaterinburg, Omsk, Yamyshev, Semipalatinsk, Tomsk, and Kuznetsk. The dragoons, who operated as both infantry and mounted troops, were used to patrol the line between the forts, a task they shared with the Cossacks. In towns of the Siberian interior, Cossack detachments served as a police force. Four regiments of field infantry were stationed in Viatka and Solikamsk *provintsii*, but these were separated from Siberia in 1727. Altogether there were in Siberia in the late 1720s 5,000 garrison troops, nearly 9,500 Cossacks, and a few thousand native auxiliaries, a very light presence indeed in such an immense territory, but one shielded from great power conflicts.

The Caspian Basin

The Irtysh, Ishim, and Ui Lines represented the westernmost extension of a military perimeter designed to mark out a Russo-Chinese frontier: the history of the Kazakhs from the 1650s to the 1750s would be largely determined by the course of the great conflict between the Manchu dynasty and the Western Mongols, which played into the hands of the Russians. West of the Ural River, a different world began, unstable and extremely complex, which became part of an emerging Russo-Persian frontier. The Russians moving into Bashkiria and down the Volga were leaving the forest zone behind to enter the open steppe and approach the deserts and the mountains, beyond which lay Transcaucasia, the Persian core, and the nucleated societies of Transoxiana. It was a land of settled Bashkirs, nomadic Kalmyks and Nogais, Caucasian highlanders, but also of Russian Old Believers, runaways from the core, unruly Cossacks and bandits who raided merchant ships on the Volga – where the level of violence rose with the attempt by the Muscovite government to extend the reach of its activities in a slowly expanding Russian core.

A succession of uprisings exposed the underlying tensions. There were three rebellions in Bashkiria between 1662 and 1711. The first (1662–5) took place on the territory's northern fringes between the Kama and the Iset Rivers. It was a response to encroachments by Russian landlords, the forceful methods used in the collection of the *iasak*, and the building of the Transkama Line, which blocked Bashkir raids across the river. The rebels also sought to enlist the support of a great-grandson of Kuchum, the last khan of Siberia, as if remembering that Bashkiria had once been part of a much larger community. The rebellion was put down by the Russians operating from Kazan. A second one (1682–4) took place in the heart of Bashkiria as a backlash against a policy of forced conversion of the natives by clergy sent by the Kazan archbishop. It was crushed on the Ufa River. The third (1704–11) was longer and more serious: fiscal, land, and religious issues were joined. There was mass resistance to the fiscal policies of the Moscow government, always short of funds, especially in wartime, which imposed an indiscriminate number of new taxes, including one on black eyes; and there was opposition to continued land encroachments and the use of forests to fuel the new Ural industry. More ominous was the emergence of a religious leader in southern Bashkiria, who called for the restoration of a Muslim state as in the days of the Kazan khanate. He even got in touch with the Crimean khan and the Ottoman sultan. The rebellion encompassed the whole of Bashkiria and was crushed with the help of the Kalmyks; it left the territory a waste land.[52]

These rebellions were an echo of similar extensive disorders west of the Volga. In 1670, Stenka Razin, a Don Cossack who had made a reputation as a pirate on the Caspian shores, channelled widespread opposition to landowners and corrupt officials in the old Kazan khanate. The nomads joined the fray, but the rebellion was defeated by combat troops in 1671 and turned over by some of the Cossack leaders to the Russians.[53] The Razin and Bashkir rebellions had one common feature: they were largely violent, anarchic outbursts which exposed the cleavage between the masses and an emerging upper layer of leaders, who had an interest in collaborating with the authorities in the name of peace and order and whom the Russians favoured, because supporting their social conservatism helped the Russians consolidate their own political power in the region. In 1705–6, Astrakhan was in full revolt against fiscal oppression and abuses committed by garrison officers, and yet another rebellion in 1707 threatened to merge with the so-called Bulavin rebellion among the Don Cossacks (1707–9). Clearly something had to be done to implant an administrative infrastructure in the Caspian basin that would obviate the necessity of sending combat troops to put down domestic uprisings and would open up channels of communication between the authorities and disaffected Russians and nomads.

An answer was found in the reform of 1708–19, which not only created a provincial administration closer to the population than the Kazan Chancery in Moscow could have ever been, but also established a territorial base for the concentration of combat troops to be used against Persia and Central Asia in a bid to establish Russian hegemony in the entire Russo-Persian frontier. A governor was appointed in Kazan with jurisdiction over what was in effect the old Kazan khanate, and the Kazan Chancery was closed. In 1717, a separate province of Astrakhan was carved out, including the steppe on both sides of the lower Volga and the river's valley all the way to Saratov. In 1719, Kazan province was divided into four *provintsii*: Kazan with the valley of the Viatka; Sviiazhsk, straddling the Volga to the border of Nizhnii Novgorod province; Penza, with the basin of the Sura; and Ufa (Bashkiria) with the basin of the Belaia. In 1727, Viatka and Solikamsk *provintsii* were added. These six *provintsii* were divided into twenty-one *uezds*. Astrakhan province was not divided into *provintsii*, but it contained thirteen *uezds*, from Saratov in the north to Kizliar on the Terek. The Caspian basin was thus divided into two provinces and thirty-four *uezds* or, to put it differently, the khans of Kazan and Astrakhan had been replaced by two Russian governors.[54]

As in Siberia, these early governors were members of the ruling elite and were closely related to the Romanov house by ties of marriage, but an additional characteristic needs to be mentioned. Of the four governors who served in both cities, one was an Apraksin, from a family that originated in the so-called Great Horde – what remained of the Kipchak khanate after the secession of Kazan and the Crimea; two were Saltykovs from a family of Turkic origin, possibly Kazakh. Artemii Volynsky was a Russian, but he married a Naryshkina, a first cousin of Peter I, from a family of Crimean origin. Their ancestors had transferred their allegiance to Moscow and entered the orbit of the Court. Through his wife, Volynsky was related to the Princes Sibirskiis, descendants of Kuchum.[55] Moreover, two of these three families had given *voevody* who had served in the eastern theatre in the seventeenth century: thirteen Volynskys and four Saltykovs. After Peter's death, Volynsky moved to Kazan and was replaced, somewhat incongruously, in Astrakhan by Ivan von Mengden, a Baltic German from Livland, whose ancestor had been taken prisoner by the troops of Ivan IV and converted to Orthodoxy against his will.

Buchholz's expedition was only one prong of an enveloping movement directed against Central Asia and the transcontinental trade routes linking India and China with the Mediterranean. News arrived in Astrakhan in 1713 that gold dust was panned in the waters of the Amu Daria, which, it was claimed, used to flow into the Caspian Sea;[56] that it was feasible to build a fort where the river's mouth used to be, and to convince the Khiva khan to tear down the dam which had once diverted the river's course toward the Aral Sea. In May 1714, two days before Buchholz's appointment, Peter selected Prince Alexander Cherkassky – who had grown up in the house of Prince Boris Golitsyn, the last chief of the Kazan Chancery – to head an expedition to Khiva and Bukhara with a mission stated in one of the most succint of Peter's succint orders: to find the location of Yarkend; how far it was from the Caspian; and whether a river route connected it with that sea.

It was left to the Kazan governor, Petr Saltykov, to provide the wherewithal for the expedition – boats, provisions, and Cossacks – and Cherkassky did not leave Astrakhan until April 1715. How difficult it would be to carry out such a mission soon became obvious, largely because the original mission was broken into two, both of which eventually failed. Cherkassky was subsequently ordered to build forts on the Caspian's eastern coast before moving against Khiva. In 1715, he built one on the Mangyshlak peninsula and sailed on to the old mouth of the Amu Daria, where he built Krasnovodsk, and sent a detachment to explore the river's old bed. He did not move against Khiva until June 1717, too late in the season, with only 3,500 men, including 1,900 Cossacks. From Gurev, at the mouth of the Ural River, the expedition marched to the Emba River, where it found the caravan route to Khiva, covering 1,350 kilometres in sixty-five days across a grassless and waterless steppe at the hottest time of the year. The Kalmyks, who had not forgotten that the Kabardians had once decimated their forces in the northern Caucasus, had already warned the khan that Cherkassky's intentions were hostile. Unable to defeat the Russians in the field, the khan resorted to a ruse, and Cherkassky allowed himself to be deceived into splitting his force. Nearly all his men were then massacred in August; he himself perished with them. His head was stuffed and sent to the khan in Bukhara. In the meantime, the garrisons on the Caspian coast could not cope with the insalubrious climate and had to be withdrawn. The expedition had been an unmitigated disaster.

But it needs to be placed in a larger context. Cherkassky received an instruction in February 1714, spelling out the true scope of his mission, but also showing how unrealistic were the tsar's expectations. The Russians simply underestimated logistical difficulties and allocated inadequate resources to the realization of what was a truly grandiose vision of empire. In Khiva, Cherkassky would be Peter's ambassador (*posol*), but one who would obviously manage the khanate: if possible, he would restore the old course of the Amu Daria and close all the channels leading into the Aral Sea, and he would build a fort and a town. He would induce the khan to become a subject of the empire by promising that Russia would support his hereditary rights to the throne. If he agreed, the khan would be given a guard of perhaps five hundred men or more to protect him against his own people. Cherkassky would try to do the same in Bukhara because Peter knew that in both khanates the khans "live in fear" (*bedstvuiut*) of their subjects. Moreover, Russia's establishment in Transoxiana would also mark the beginning of a commercial thrust toward India. Cherkassky would have to send merchants along the Amu Daria "as far as one can go" and then overland to northern India, and he was given a charter for the Great Mughal in Delhi, who was a descendant of Tamerlane.[57]

This obsession with reaching India, whose wealth would soon become a source of rivalry between Britain and France, coupled with a geopolitical vision that would bring Russian influence to bear on Eurasia's periphery, also explained Russia's war with Persia in 1722–3. It was the third prong in Russia's advance into what had been Hulagu's and Tamerlane's empires. In 1715, when the tsar had already ordered Buchholz and Cherkassky to converge on Yarkend from the Irtysh in the east and Astrakhan in the west, he sent Volynsky on a mission to Persia. Its ostensible purpose was commercial: to negotiate a trade agreement and obtain compensation for the disaster of 1712, when Caucasian highlanders had sacked Shemakha in Persian Transcaucasia, causing enormous losses to Russian merchants. In fact, it was an intelligence mission to assess the military capabilities of the Safavid dynasty; to discover the country's waterways (was there a route from the Caspian to India?); to establish links with the Armenians and other Christian peoples; and to evaluate the state of Turco-Persian relations. That Volynsky was to find out how to reach Gilian province – where the best Persian silk was produced – gave a hint of Peter's intentions.[58]

Peter's interest in the Armenians was commercial and fiscal. They had been favoured at the Persian court by Shah Abbas I (1587–1629) but had fallen out of favour by the 1660s and were in need of a new protector. They shipped their silk via Aleppo to the Mediterranean, but some were receptive to the tsar's ambition to redirect the trade across Russia from Astrakhan via Moscow to Petersburg, from which the silk would be shipped to western Europe.[59] Russia would benefit by collecting customs duties and acquiring foreign exchange. Volynsky was in Isfahan, the shah's capital, from March to September 1717 – when Cherkassky was about to move on Khiva – and signed a trade agreement in July. But he brought back unfavourable impressions of the dynasty, sensing, rightly so, that it was on its deathbed. He concluded that, although Russia was still at war with Sweden, a small force would be enough to conquer for Russia the three provinces fronting the southern coast of the Caspian, Gilian, Mazanderan, and Astarabad, where not only silk was produced but also excellent cotton, the basic raw material for Russia's textile industry. Astarabad also led to Bukhara and via Balkh to Delhi. The tsar was not yet ready to move, and appointed Volynsky the first governor of Astrakhan.[60]

The Safavids' weakness also shook the dynasty's hold over eastern Georgia, where Tsar Wakhtang VI was ready to side with the Russians in order to gain independence for his country and political support against his fractious nobility. Volynsky was ordered to seek the support of the Tarku *shamkhal* (ruler), whose possessions controlled the coastal defile between Kizliar and Resht – Gilian's capital – via Derbent and Baku. Events then moved very quickly. Soon after the conclusion of the war with Sweden in August 1721, Peter ordered combat troops to assemble in the mid-Volga valley for the winter. In July 1722, he led an army of one hundred thousand men (including thirty thousand Tatars and twenty thousand Kalmyks) out of Astrakhan and took Derbent in August, but disaster struck: the flour for the troops got wet, and the advance stopped. It was renewed in 1723, and concluded with the capture of Baku in July. In the meantime, the Afghans had invaded Persia from the east in 1722 and deposed the shah in October. But Peter signed a treaty with the shah's young son Tahmasp, giving Russia the three provinces, although only Gilian was actually occupied. The Russians failed to link up with the Georgians, who suffered reprisals, and Wakhtang VI emigrated to Russia with his court in 1725.[61]

But the Russian success was of short duration. Tahmasp, who was hardly more than a Russian puppet, had to accept the growing role of one of his commanders determined to overthrow Afghan rule, who eventually made himself shah under the name of Nadir Shah and overthrew the Safavid dynasty in 1736. He was also intent on restoring Persian hegemony in eastern Transcaucasia and Transoxiana, and the Russians wisely cut their losses: they abandoned Gilian in 1732, Derbent and Baku in 1735, and the Terek became the unofficial boundary between the Russian and Persian empires.[62] But the war, coming after the Buchholz and Cherkassky expeditions, with which it was so closely connected, clearly revealed Russia's imperial vision in the Caspian basin: the incorporation of a Russo-Persian frontier in Transcaucasia and Transoxiana by bringing their peoples into the expanding category of imperial subjects, and the transformation of the Persian core into a satellite of the empire. Such a vision would continue to inform Russian policy until the end of the imperial period.

If the creation of a secure boundary with even a powerful and expansionist China and the low-intensity threat along the Kazakh and Zunghar "border" made it possible to withdraw combat troops from Siberia, the war with Persia and the country's instability, coupled with endemic turbulence in Bashkiria and the Caucasus, required a substantial military presence along the eastern edge of the Russian core, where the army was deployed when peace returned in 1724. Such a deployment enabled part of the army to live off the Persian provinces on the one hand and the more settled Russian provinces west of the Volga and north of the Kama on the other, and kept troops out of Bashkiria, where they were likely to cause trouble among the natives, who already had enough grievances against the extortions committed by *voevody* and other local officials.

As a result, combat troops were concentrated in two areas. One was the western *provintsii* of Kazan province. There were two infantry regiments in Viatka and Solikamsk, and seven dragoon regiments in Kazan, Sviiazhsk, and Penza *provintsii* – where the Razin rebellion had been the most violent. This meant a total of 13,800 men. At the other end of the Caspian basin, there was the Southern Corps (*Nizovy Korpus*), commanded in the later 1720s by General Vasilii Dolgorukov. Its headquarters was at Nizovaia Landing between Derbent and Baku, the only suitable place on that desolate coast. The corps consisted of ten infantry regiments or 14,320 men stationed along the corridor between the mountains and the sea and in Gilian province. The commanding general was the most important figure in the region: the Kazan and Astrakhan governors were subordinated to him, so that the entire valley of the middle and lower Volga formed another corridor for the logistical support of the troops: boats came from Kazan in the forest zone, weapons and ammunition from the Urals, and provisions from the market towns in the basin of the Sura. When the Russians withdrew behind the Terek in 1735, the corps was disbanded and its regiments reassigned elsewhere.

The two major cities, Kazan and Astrakhan, had substantial garrisons: 5,140 men in Kazan (three regiments of infantry and one of dragoons) and 6,318 in

Astrakhan (four of infantry and one of dragoons), but these garrisons were broken up into companies stationed in the Volga towns like Tsaritsyn, Kamyshin, and Saratov, and in Kizliar. There were about 12,500 Cossacks as well. The largest single group was the Ural (Iaik) Cossacks (3,195 men), stationed along the lower course of the Ural River to the sea, where they made a living from fishing, sending fish and caviar as far away as Petersburg or trading it for grain in the Volga towns. There were also 500 Cossacks on the Terek and about 1,000 Volga Cossacks settled between the elbow of the Don and that of the Volga, along the Tsaritsyn Line begun in 1717 and completed in 1732. In addition, there were 3,615 "soldiers and children," whom Kirilov included among the irregular troops, on the old Transkama Line built along the ethnic boundary between the Kazan Tatars and the Bashkirs, and another 4,165 in four "land militia regiments" stationed on the new Transkama Line linking the Samara with the Ik River, the western boundary of Bashkiria. Finally, the Russians counted on some 30,000 Kalmyk auxiliaries to separate and hold in check Bashkirs and Kazakhs and serve in their wars, not only in the eastern theatre but elsewhere as well. Thus, in the late 1720s there were in the Caspian basin 28,000 combat troops, 11,600 garrison troops, and 12,500 Cossacks, a total of 52,000 men, not counting the auxiliaries.

If we combine Siberia and the Caspian basin, we obtain for the eastern theatre a total of 28,000 combat troops, 16,600 garrison troops, and 22,000 Cossacks. Since the army in all three theatres consisted of 109,450 regulars, 68,450 garrison troops, and 69,000 Cossacks, we may conclude that the eastern theatre absorbed 25.6 per cent of the regulars, 24.3 per cent of the garrisons, and 31.8 per cent of the Cossacks.[63]

Russians and Natives

Three governors in Astrakhan, Kazan, and Tobolsk and thirty-four *uezd voevody* with a minuscule civilian staff relying on the assistance of twenty thousand garrison troops and another twenty thousand Cossacks spread across the immense territory of the eastern theatre were hardly enough to consolidate Russian rule and integrate both Siberia and the Caspian basin into what was assumed from the beginning would be a unitary state. It had been shaped by the iron will of the grand princes and tsars in Moscow and was transformed from Petersburg by Peter I's determination and brutal policies into a hegemonic power in eastern Eurasia. The advance of the Russians, a partly elemental phenomenon, but also one largely encouraged and controlled by the authorities themselves, resulted in the creation of a social system marked by ethnic superstratification, in which the conquerors added an ethnic and dominant layer to already stratified societies.[64] The early encounter was often violent because the top layer of those societies resented the loss of its privileges and the resulting political and social degradation. But continuing resistance was hopeless, what with the Russians' superiority in firearms, and the prolonged use of force was certain to be counterproductive, for the fundamental reason that the Russians looked upon the natives, not as alien societies to be eradicated, but as tribute-paying communities. The collection of the *iasak* would inevitably require the consent and cooperation of those who hunted the animals and brought the pelts to collection centres.

Moreover, Russian society itself was becoming highly stratified between a ruling elite in the capitals, a ruling class of civil and military managers in the provincial and *uezd* centres, and a dependent population of townsmen and peasants, whose existence was justified by the need for taxes and services to meet the growing needs of the expanding core. It was a society based on status distinctions, which became superimposed upon native societies based on similar distinctions. The recognition by both sides of that elementary truth facilitated an accommodation based on a common interest, in which native leaders obtained the confirmation and strengthening of their leadership positions in return for a willingness to become agents of imperial consolidation in their territories. The census of 1719–24, which introduced the poll tax and the quitrent (*obrok*), the foundations of the new fiscal system, sought to classify the entire dependent population in a few social categories – townsmen, Court peasants, privately held serfs, and state ("Treasury") peasants. Subsequent censuses would pursue such a policy relentlessly, to a point where the natives became identified, wherever possible, as state peasants as well, while the tribute became another form of quitrent similar to that paid by those peasants. Consequently, superstratification resulted eventually in the integration of the native leaders who were willing to cooperate into the power structure of the ruling class and the degradation of their peoples into the broad mass of the dependent population, creating a more or less uniform social structure in a multi-ethnic but unitary state. One thinks of Prince Gantimur, who brought his *ulus* of Tungus into Russian territory in 1666, whose princely title was confirmed by Moscow, and whose descendants would rule their people well into the nineteenth century and pay the *iasak* on their behalf.

Before we turn to these stratified societies, it will be useful to examine the results of the 1719–24 census. No matter how incomplete they may have been, they give an approximate picture of the place occupied by the Russians and the natives in the eastern theatre. It was estimated that the population of Siberia had reached 482,000 people, among whom the Russians numbered 323,000 or 67 per cent, the "Tatars" 27,800. Who the other 132,000 were is unclear, but they included about 35,000 Buriats and 32,000 Yakuts. The largest other group was the Tungus, the nomadic hunters of the taiga. In the Caspian basin one needs to distinguish between Kazan and Astrakhan provinces. Settlement in the former was already extensive, with 1.6 million Russians in a total population of 2.2 million or 71 per cent. The 216,000 Tatars were not even a majority of the native population, but a close second behind the 218,000 Chuvash. Other groups were much smaller: 77,000 Mordva, 62,000 Mari, 48,000 Udmurts, followed by a miscellanous group of 24,500. Across the Volga and the Kama, in the Orenburg territory, which at the time consisted mostly of Bashkiria, the Russian population of 36,500 was a poor second behind 172,000 Bashkirs with 23,000 "others." In Astrakhan province there were only 33,000 Russians among 114,000 Tatars and 200,000 Kalmyks. Thus the population of the eastern theatre was still overwhelmingly concentrated west of the Volga and north of the Kama. With 3.2 million people, it made up 21 per cent of the 15.6 million inhabitants of the empire. It formed a core group in Kazan province with two wings, one in Astrakhan and the northern Caucasus, the other in Siberia.[65]

The Kazan khanate had been a multi-ethnic society but one dominated by a Tatar minority. These Tatars were led by aristocratic families and their princes, who had circumscribed the authority of the khans. Their power rested on the support of landowners called *murzy* and their Tatar subjects. This Tatar ruling ethnos was Muslim and deeply so, since Kazan had been until the Russian conquest a major centre of Islamic learning. It pursued a dual policy: a social policy designed to extract resources from the non-Tatar majority transformed into a dependent population; and a religious policy to convert a majority of animists and idol-worshippers to Islam. A policy of "Tatarization" had long been in effect before Russification began to replace it.[66] The arrival of the Russians and their steady increase to a point where they practically swamped the native population by the 1720s was a perfect example of ethnic superstratification, but one bound to create tensions, because Russians and Tatars were rivals in the pursuit of similar aims.

The Code of 1649 sought to keep Russian and Tatar landholdings separate, but it was difficult to do so in practice. Conversion gave access to the new top layer superimposed upon the Tatar ruling group, since anyone who converted became a Russian, a member of the new power structure with the same obligations to serve the ruling elite of the empire and the same privileges over the dependent population. In 1713–19 *murzy* and other landlords who converted were allowed to own Russian peasants, while the natives who had not paid the *iasak* were required to pay the poll tax and the quitrent as well as to deliver recruits whenever a new levy was announced. But downgrading the Tatar ruling group following the creation of an administrative infrastructure dominated by Russians reinforced the importance of religion as the test of a Tatar identity and would continue to create frictions between the Russians and the Kazan Tatars, which would reach a boiling point in the 1750s. Elsewhere, in Astrakhan and Siberia, the coexistence of the Russian settler and the Tatar nomad postponed the latter's integration into the ruling class of the expanding core, but the

Russians were already allowed to buy Tatar men to become servants and peasants to work their fields and Tatar women as wives and servants.[67]

The unhappy history of the Bashkirs tells a somewhat different but similar story. Bashkir society was multi-ethnic, with Chuvash and Cheremis who had migrated from the Kazan khanate, as well as Meshcheriaks (Mishar), who were Tatars from the Meshcheria along the lower Oka, and Teptiars, who were Tatarized Volga Finns and Chuvash. Tradition had divided their lands into four *dorogi* subdivided into *volosts* corresponding to various clans. The Bashkirs did not constitute a super-ethnos in their land, however, but were themselves the dependents of others. After the breakup of the Kipchak khanate, Bashkiria was split between the Kazan khanate, the Siberian khanate, and the Nogai Horde (based on the lower course of the Ural River), a powerful confederation of Turkic peoples, which was eventually destroyed by the Kalmyks in the seventeenth century. The three khans inherited the ownership rights to the entire land which had once been the prerogative of the Kipchak khan, and which the White Khan in Moscow inherited after the conquest of the three khanates. The Bashkirs paid the *iasak* to all three, according to which *doroga* they were in, but the right to collect it was given to Tatar *murzy*, who were given land, which they rented out to Bashkirs and immigrants from across the Kama and the Volga.[68]

Here then was a certain similarity with the situation in the Kazan khanate, where Tatars had once dominated, but with this difference: the Bashkirs constituted a much larger and more compact ethnic group, whom the Tatars could hope to rule only from afar. There was another difference. The major economic activity of the Bashkirs was stock raising, but they also owned land and forests, with all the resulting gradations of wealth and influence. The khans had favoured "better people," among whom emerged a landholding nobility of representatives of clan or tribal leading families. They were called *tarkhany*, and the khans had given them charters (*iarlyki*) conferring ownership rights. The Russians inherited this right to create a class of native landowners and were generous with it: it was estimated that there were about 130 *tarkhany* in 1646 and 773 in 1735.[69] The Russians also sought to draw this privileged class into military service, which was a source of pride, because the semi-nomad Bashkir with his bow and arrows was also a born horseman and a born horseman was a trained warrior. It was in Bashkiria perhaps more than anywhere else in the frontier that the Russians sought to replicate the social order that was crystallizing in the core, with Bashkir and Russian landowner integrated into the power structure of the expanding core and a Bashkir population gradually transformed into their serfs or into state peasants, like their Russian brethren. It was a policy designed to create a unitary state rather than an empire, and explains why there would be six rebellions in Bashkiria between 1662 and 1773: the territory was part of a frontier of freemen who rebelled for a century against the relentless advance of a core area social order based on serfdom.

The Kalmyks were a separate case because they were still beyond the jurisdiction of the Russian authorities. They were a very fragmented people of clans, all resistant to the establishment of a central authority. They lived in *kibitki*, several *kibitki* formed an *aimak*, and a group of *aimaks* formed an *ulus* (*khoshun*), the basic political unit, whose leaders, called *taishi*, behaved in autocratic fashion toward the rank and file. It was not until the 1690s that one of them, Aiuka, who had been able to overcome such fragmentation for a while, obtained the title of khan from the Dalai Lama – the Kalmyks were lamaist Buddhists – which Peter recognized in 1707. Aiuka had consolidated his authority in 1672 and governed with an advisory body called the *Zargo*, which functioned as a highest court and consisted of eight members representing chiefly Aiuka's clan.[70] But Aiuka had to govern by compromise and was often unable to control his *taishi*, who went their own way in the perpetual pursuit of booty in human beings and cattle that characterized nomadic society in the great arc of steppe and semi-desert stretching from the Terek to the Irtysh Rivers.

And yet, Russian policy was friendly toward the Kalmyks despite the depredations which they committed west of the Volga as far as Tambov and Riazan, capturing thousands of Russians whom they later sold on the slave markets of Central Asia. The Kalmyks represented a redoubtable military force, which the Russians sought to enlist into an army of auxiliaries to hold the Bashkirs and Kazakhs in check and help them crush the Bashkir rebellions. Despite several attempts to induce them to become subjects of the empire, the nomads refused to accept the consequences of a binding oath, but the agreement of 1708 between the Kazan governor and Aiuka stated that Russians and Kalmyks now had a common sovereign, and that the Kalmyks would keep no contact with the Turks, Crimeans, and Persians. In 1713, Aiuka accepted a Russian representative at his headquarters with a detachment of six hundred men. In 1722, at the ripe age of eighty he travelled to Saratov to meet Peter on his way to the Persian campaign and sought the tsar's support for his eldest son in the impending succession. But the Russians now had the upper hand. Anticipating the destructive consequences of Aiuka's death (he died in 1724), they sided instead with a weaker man.[71]

In Eastern Siberia, the Russians came into contact with already well structured societies. Among the Buriats, a clan was a group of *ulusy* and was headed by a *shulenga*, and several clans were headed by a *taisha*, sometimes also known as khan, while the backbone of the social order consisted of rich herd-owners called *noyons*. West of Lake Baikal, leaders were referred as chiefs (*kniaztsy*). On the other hand, the Buriats were not united under a single political authority, but remained nomadic communities scattered over enormous distances, each grounded in a particular river valley, like the Selenga, the Uda, and the Aga. Nevertheless, *taishi* ruled a multi-ethnic society in which the Buriats imposed their rule on smaller ethnic groups like the Samoeds, Kets, and Tungus. The bond that tied ruling group with dependent population was called *kyshtymstvo*, from the word *kyshtym* meaning, significantly, to oppress. It meant the dependent population had to pay the *iasak* in sables, beavers, and squirrels, which the Buriats then bartered for cloth, ornaments, and utensils with Central Asian, Mongol, and Chinese merchants; it also meant they had to supply auxiliaries when the Buriat clan went to war. The Buriats also kept slaves, who were prisoners of war or wanderers caught in the steppe.[72]

The encounter with the Russians west of Lake Baikal was a violent one because the Russians claimed a monopoly over the collection of the *iasak* and sought to convert the Buriats by force. The result was a migration of Buriats back to Transbaikalia, from which they originally came, which alarmed the *voevody* who were losing *iasak* payers. East of the lake, the encounter was more peaceful, partly because the Russians had learned a lesson, partly because the Buriats there were themselves *iasak* payers to the khans of eastern Mongolia. The question became one of choosing between two overlords, and the Russians were often the winners because Mongol rule was even harsher. A gradual accommodation was reached in three ways: by farming out the collection of the *iasak* to Buriat leaders and exempting them from paying it; by granting them land allotments that resembled the *pomesties* of the Russian core; and by creating units of Buriat horsemen to patrol the new border with Mongolia after 1727.[73] The more pliant members of the Buriat aristocracy and their "subjects" became associated with the power structure of imperial rule.

In faraway Yakutia, the Yakuts had expanded on both sides of the Lena River to establish their dominion over Tungus, Samoeds, and Yukagirs, whom they assimilated rather than dominated, as was the case with the Buriats, and in the process created a multi-ethnic society of Yakut language and culture. Yet, they too had not reached by the time of the Russian conquest the stage of political union with a centrally based leadership. Yakut society remained fragmented among clans led by *toyons*, who were social as well as military leaders. Clans combined to form *volosts* (*naslegi*), of which there were about thirty-five in the seventeenth century, of very different sizes, ranging from less than a hundred to five thousand persons, and several *volosts* formed an *ulus*. Some *toyons* were obviously more powerful than others. Their power over their clansmen was very great and tended to become hereditary in a family, and it rested on their wealth as owners of herds of cattle.[74]

As everywhere else, the arrival of the Russians and the collection of the *iasak* had the effect of hardening social relationships between the native elite and its people. The *toyons* resented the imposition of the *iasak*, which they had not paid before because of the isolation of Yakutia, and at first led resistance to Russian rule. But their history taught them that the Russians, who were few and all men, could be assimilated – and indeed, a process of "Yakutization" began, which reached its completion in the middle of the nineteenth century. It was facilitated by the easy acceptance of Orthodoxy, which made Yakuts into "Russians." The Russians in turn pursued the same policy as in Buriatia: they farmed out the collection and delivery of the pelts to the *toyons*, who, as is usually the case in all such operations, managed to keep some of the pelts for themselves, and sold them to an emerging class of Yakut traders who would play a major role in east Siberian commerce. Some *toyons* were even integrated into, not simply associated with, the power structure of the expanding core, when they were granted the rank of "boyars' son" (*deti boiarskie*), given to the leading members of the Siberian administrative staff. In so doing, the Russians elevated the *toyons* to the status of a hereditary aristocracy, a policy which resulted in the corresponding abasement of the ordinary members of the clan to the status of serfs.[75]

By the late 1720s, the outlines of Russia's policy toward the native peoples were clearly visible. There could be no question of exterminating them because the Russians themselves were a melting pot and, most important, because the natives were viewed as *iasak* payers. The extension of Russian rule across the entire eastern theatre marked a return to a situation that had once prevailed centuries earlier, when the Mongols had superimposed a thin layer of Mongol power holders over native peoples and reached a mutually acceptable accommodation with the native elites. But, of course, there were significant differences. The Russians were settlers, who came to stay and till the land and multiply, and eventually overcome the natives by their sheer numbers. They brought with them the social order of the core, without the enserfment of the population, Russian or native, to individual members of the ruling class, but with a collective subjection to the ruling class as a whole, which managed Siberia as the tsar's private domain (*gosudareva votchina*), but in fact for their own benefit. This was also true in the southern part in the Caspian basin, while serfdom took hold in the former Kazan khanate. The powerlessness of the native, without political organization, without firearms, and without a compact economic base, facilitated both the acceptance of the new superstratification by their elites and the integration of the elites and the common people into the social and political order of the expanding core. Barriers would remain to full integration: religious ones with Islam and Buddhism, and in the way of life, with pastoralism. But even so, there was no doubt that the Russians were building in the eastern theatre not an empire but an extension of the core, a multi-ethnic unitary state.

Agents of Integration

Religion

While religious strife can tear apart human communities, religious belief can create a powerful incentive to integrate smaller ethnic groups into a larger community, especially if that community offers attractive rewards in the form of social acceptance, political advancement, tax exemptions, and land grants. As the strength of the Kipchak khanate began to ebb in the fourteenth century, Tatar and Mongol chieftains took their *ulusy* with them into the Russian core, converted to Orthodoxy, and received positions at court in the multi-ethnic elite gathering around the grand princes and tsars. Tsar Boris Godunov (1598–1605) was a descendant of such a chieftain, and it was estimated a century later that 25 per cent of the ruling elite consisted of such Tatar and Mongol families.[76] By converting, they became "Russian," a term that gave a super-ethnic identity to an elite consisting of an increasing number of ethnic backgrounds. Conversion and integration had been articles of faith when the Muscovite core expanded northward toward the White Sea, absorbing the Ugro-Finnish tribes into a great mass of peasants belonging, some to the monasteries, others to landowners, the government, or the Court. Conversion entailed integration into the social hierarchy of Muscovite Russia, the chieftains and their retinue into the upper layer of the managerial class, the other natives into the peasantry of an agrarian military and administrative state, a transition that also entailed social degradation.

It was assumed, as it also was in faraway western Europe after the declaration of Augsburg of 1555 – eight years after Ivan IV's accession – that the religion of a prince must be that of his people. The shah of Persia assumed that the religion of his subjects must be the Shi'ite branch of Islam. And when Khan Uzbek of the Kipchak khanate converted to Islam in the 1330s, he imposed Sunni Islam in the khanate and in Transoxiana as well. In 1383, Stefan, a monk from Ustiug, applied his "frenzied zeal" to convert the Zyrians (Komi) in the basin of the Kama, destroyed their idols and profaned their shrines in the name of Christianity's injunction to love thy neighbour as thyself, but also learned their language, created an alphabet for them, and eventually became known as St Stefan of Perm.[77] The policy of conversion, often but not always by force, of the Voguls, Ostiaks, and Yakuts, who all lived in the forest zone, was but a natural continuation of St Stefan's missionary zeal. The brutality with which some of the conversions took place reflected not only the ascetic intolerance of the monk, but also the determination of the Muscovite government to make Orthodoxy the agent of integration for ethnic groups being brought into the core and the test of a subject's loyalty to the crown.

And yet, it may very well be that a compromise solution gradually took shape, perhaps because there was no other choice. In the forest zone, where all the natives were at the mercy of their environment, it was natural for them to venerate the sky, the sun, the rivers, and the lakes; to see in animals like the goose, the swan, and the eagle the incarnation of spirits that must be propitiated with the help of shamans, who played the role of intermediaries in asking for the recovery of the sick, the healing of cattle and horses, and success in wars.[78] Russian Orthodoxy would of course reject such "unclean" beliefs, but it had little else to offer. It emphasized ritual over belief and merely asked the parishioners to come regularly to church, go to confession, and take communion at least once a year. Many of the natives (and Russians as well) found no incompatibility between the observance of Orthodox ritual and belief in spirits and the power of the shaman, in a world where the priests were few and distances great. Among the natives in already structured societies, Orthodoxy appealed because it taught unconditional obedience, and clan leaders could only welcome a religion that strengthened their authority and promised the backing of the secular state against revolts from below.

To carry out this policy of conversion and integration, the Orthodox Church began to build an administrative infrastructure immediately after the conquest of Kazan. A Kazan diocese was inaugurated in 1555, not only to serve the needs of the military and civilian establishment, but also to launch a missionary movement to convert both Tatars and non-Tatars. Its head had the title of archbishop of Kazan and Sviiazhsk, and his jurisdiction included the three old khanates of Kazan, Astrakhan, and Siberia. An "Astrakhan and Terek" diocese was first created in 1602 and administered by an archbishop until 1659 and a metropolitan thereafter until 1715. It was then renamed "Astrakhan and Stavropol" diocese under a simple bishop. The list of archbishops included Makari (1627–37), who was accused of trying to separate Astrakhan from Moscow in order to become the patriarch of a new Astrakhan kingdom (*tsarstvo*).[79]

A Siberian diocese was opened in 1620 under an archbishop, who became a metropolitan in 1664. The first archbishop found his flock in a deplorable moral condition and was shocked by the shortage of priests and monks. Building churches and monasteries became an urgent necessity for all his successors, as Orthodoxy and the "Russian spirit" (*Russkii dukh*) spread eastward all the way to Kamchatka, which they first reached in 1705. Most of the prelates remained but a few years, hardly enough to inspect their diocese, and some saw as a form of punishment their appointment to a cold and inhospitable continent that offered few rewards and little peace of mind. The early archbishops came from Russia, but Metropolitan Filofei (Leszczyński), a protégé of Peter I, was the first of several Ukrainian prelates who would dominate the Siberian church until the reign of Catherine II.[80] They were all well educated, but also possessed the "frenzied zeal" to do the work of both church and state, perhaps because their origin in the Russo-Ottoman frontier had instilled in them a clear perception of the strength of Islam.

But the Church, which triumphed with the election of its first patriarch in 1589 and rallied the tsardom against the Poles in 1611, suffered a major defeat in the 1660s, with two important consequences: it became an object of bitter dissension among the Orthodox, and lost a crucial opportunity to reinvigorate itself at a time when it was coming into increasing contact with the pagans,

Muslims, and Buddhists, whom it was its mission to integrate into a "Russian" community of believers. The election of Nikon, from a family of Mordvan converts, to the patriarchal see in 1652 marked a turning point. The Russian Church, while Orthodox and convinced of its superiority after the conquest of Constantinople by the infidel Turks in 1453, had developed practices and produced religious texts which were at variance with those of other Greek churches. The controversy involved not questions of dogma but the phrasing of certain texts and minor points of ritual, like the use of three fingers instead of two in making the sign of the cross, and the direction to be followed by religious processions (according to the movement of the sun or against it), concerns which would have been of great interest to any shaman. Nikon imposed his reforms with a brutality and intolerance which eventually led to his dismissal by a church council in 1666, but they had already caused a schism within the Church. Nikon's opponents became known as the Old Believers, who were declared heretics worthy of death by fire, and their leader, the archpriest Avvakum would indeed be burned at the stake in 1681.[81]

As a result, thousands fled deeper into the forests in the basin of the White Sea, to and beyond the Urals into Siberia, and down the Volga toward the Don and the northern Caucasus, where they made converts among the Cossacks, vagrants, and natives, whom they joined during the Razin rebellion and the Bashkir revolts. Gradually, Old Belief became as much a religious as a political issue, and the victory of the Romanov house and the ruling elite over an overly ambitious prelate served notice that the church existed to carry out state policy. Peter's abolition of the patriarchate and its replacement by a committee of bishops called the Holy Synod in 1721 only confirmed that assumption.[82] Old Believers were not only religious schismatics, they were also political heretics who must be converted or destroyed. The ukaze of 1684, following the participation of the Old Believers in the *streltsy* revolt of 1682, was a broad and vicious attack upon them, but persecution only resulted in mass suicides by burning to avoid being caught by punitive expeditions.[83] Since Old Believers were found for the most part in the same forested areas as the natives, their reconversion became enmeshed with the conversion of the pagans: this confusion may explain why the government's policy of friendship toward the natives whom it hoped to convert was carried out brutally at times by local priests and monks, who ignored the difference between natives, who had to be induced to join the community of believers, and heretics and traitors, who had left it.

A church weakened by internal dissensions, but so politicized that the conversion of native elites gave access to various rungs of the ruling class, remained a powerful agent of integration. However, it was at a disadvantage in its search for acceptance and legitimacy among the non-Orthodox population at large. The government's perception of its domain as a constantly expanding core with a social order based on serfdom, into which new ethnic groups must be made to fit, was challenged by the Church's inability to make a substantial contribution to a dual policy of Christianization and enserfment. The reasons were complex, but may be subsumed under two headings.

From a geopolitical point of view, the eastern theatre was an immense frontier between the Muscovite, Persian, and Chinese cores, in which Russia, whose ascending curve began with Ivan IV and continued steadily after 1650, eventually reached hegemony. It is also possible to speak of a confessional frontier, more diffuse but no less real. Orthodoxy dominated the Muscovite core. Sunni Islam dominated the Kazan core until its conquest in 1552. Thereafter, Muslim scholars fled to Dagestan, the Crimea, and even Constantinople/Istanbul, where the Ottoman sultan stood as the defender of the faith. Shi'ia Islam remained largely confined to Persia, where it became the state religion under Shah Ismail I (1502–24). The conquest of Kazan destroyed a Tatar urban civilization in the mid-Volga region as well as the perception of a common book culture among the Muslims of the eastern theatre. A renaissance came from Dagestan, where the absence of state control encouraged the study of law, rhetoric, literature, and Arabic. From Dagestan, scholars returned to Kazan with manuscripts and a new confidence in their ability to shape an Islamic view on basic questions of life and death, love and sorrow. Via Dagestan and Kazan, the Tatars "reentered the cultural and geographic orbit of Islam" toward the end of the seventeenth century.[84] This was a time when the Orthodox Church, weakened by the schism, retreated into a conservative refusal to engage the world save as the repressive arm of a government, which had long been suspicious of a potentially dangerous link, not only between Kazan and the Crimea, but also with the Ottoman empire, Russia's most formidable rival in the southern theatre.

The second reason derived from the first. The Russian priest was imposed upon his parish by the bishop. He was often totally uneducated, and his own ignorance made him suspicious of any innovation and distrustful of strangers. He enjoyed little respect, if only because he had to till his own plot and his usually large family was at the economic mercy of his parishioners. The landowners openly despised him.[85] Peter's government made great efforts to raise the educational level of the priesthood by creating theological academies, including one in Kazan, but education never enjoyed a high priority in an agrarian military state that had never been exposed to, or generated its own, religious and cultural disputes over the great questions of church-state relations, man's place in society and the political community. The parish priest at the bottom of the ecclesiastical hierarchy and the monk who came from a distant monastery in the core were not well prepared to win the acceptance of the non-Orthodox whom they had to convince of the superior values of the Orthodox religion.

By contrast, Islam among the Tatar community was a congregational religion which placed great emphasis on learning, and selected as imams (mullas) men who had earned the respect of their communities. These men did not constitute a clergy as in the older Christian churches, and there was no hierarchy. They formed instead a horizontal confraternity of scholars who had studied the Koran. They often held different views that were propitious to an exchange capable of enriching the theological content of Islam, and instilled in the parishioners and the children who studied in their religious schools a respect for learning.[86] In such conditions, it is not surprising that priests and monks were often on the defensive in spite of the Church's offensive in the religious frontier between the Muscovite core of Greek Orthodoxy and the great centres of Muslim learning beyond Moscow's reach.

Contemporary texts tell us of the allure (*soblazn'*) of Islam among the pagans, testifying to the fact that the Orthodox Church's determination to convert the Muslims was blunted by its need to compete with Islam for the allegiance of the pagans, like the Mordvins among others. They also tell us that in Tobolsk itself, the capital of Siberia, with its imposing St Sophia cathedral, Tatars mocked the Orthodox going to church, drowned out their singing during the liturgy, and did not take off their hats when a procession passed through their part of the city.[87] They were told to show respect to the holy icons, but the local *Ostiak* must have wondered why he was ordered to revere an old man painted on a piece of wood while the Church destroyed his idols representing a goose or a swan. Where the Church was more likely to be successful was in the more distant and isolated communities in the Altai and Saian mountains: the Chulym Tatars, for example, eventually converted, because their exposure to Islam had been less intense and the demographic pressure of the Russians much greater.

Elsewhere, it was the propertied families that were more likely to embrace Christianity, because they had little choice. In 1713, they were given six months to do so or lose their holdings. They were not allowed to keep as their personal property their own people who had converted. Ordinary Tatar converts were given tax exemptions and were spared the obligation to supply recruits for the army. Muslims who had Russian peasants on their estates could retain them only if they abandoned Islam. If they refused, their estates were confiscated and given away to Russians and new converts or became state property. The laws of succession were amended so that property might pass into the line of new converts.[88] This concerted attack on property rights threatened to destabilize families as well as the social order: it was counterproductive because the Russians could not govern without the support of the notables. On the other hand, conversion and the offer to enter the service (i.e., the managerial class of an expanding core where they already were men of influence) offered attractive opportunities. The combined effect of Russian policies (which were not always consistent) was to encourage the integration of the Tatar elite into a social order in which serfdom was progressing rapidly, and widen the gap between the landed elite and a population of merchants and peasants which resisted

Christianization. A paradoxical situation ensued, as Russian pressures brought about the integration of an entire non-Orthodox social structure into the social order of the core, while creating a religious chasm between the religion of the ruling class and that of its dependent population.

There existed a second religious frontier, but one that did not begin to develop until Peter's reign. A branch of Buddhism known as the Yellow Hat Sect had established itself in Tibet, a syncretic religion which absorbed many shamanistic practices. Its core tenet was a belief in the reincarnation of its leader, the Dalai Lama; its priests were called lamas, hence the name of Lamaist Buddhism by which it is also known. The institution of the Dalai Lama was of recent origin. It went back to 1578 – on the eve of the Russian conquest of Siberia – when the line of "Living Buddhas" began, which has continued to the present day. The Dalai Lama resided in Lhasa, and Lamaist Buddhism became the religion of both the Eastern and Western Mongols. The Eastern Mongols set up their own Living Buddha in Urga (Ulan Bator), a lineal descendant of Chingis Khan, who became the most influential figure in both the secular and ecclesiastical affairs of these Mongols.[89]

From eastern Mongolia, Lamaist Buddhism entered Buriat country east of Lake Baikal, where the first monastery-temple (*datsan*) was founded in 1710, followed by the arrival of 150 lamas two years later. Lamaist monasteries were usually built in commercial centres and became wealthy enterprises. But progress was slow, partly because the Buriats were not eager to encourage a growing Mongol influence among them, partly because shamanism and Lamaist Buddhism were not incompatible, and the Buriats saw no reason to abandon their ancient practices. Nevertheless, there were already eleven *datsans* by 1740. No progress was yet made west of the lake. From western Mongolia, Buddhism spread to the basin of the upper Irtysh, where a monastery was built near Ust-Kamenogorsk, and there were Buddhist chapels on the Bukhtarma.[90] It was customary for a new new Zunghar ruler to travel to Lhasa to obtain his investiture from the Dalai Lama. The Kalmyks, who migrated to the basin of the lower Volga, were also Buddhists.

As a result, a religious frontier between Russian Orthodoxy and Tibetan (and Mongolian) Buddhism was superimposed upon the geopolitical frontier between the Russian and Chinese cores. The Orthodox offensive against Buddhism would take the form of an attempt to convert the Kalmyks – the power base of Orthodoxy in Eastern Siberia was still too weak, and preserving the peace with China was an imperative of Russian policy – but it had no more success than the policy of converting the Muslims. In both cases, the strength of Islam and Buddhism resided in the fact that they emphasized learning among their religious leaders and combined in relatively compact ethnic communities a powerful sense of identity with a sense of belonging to a wider world, which assigned to them a place in a religious universe, where they could share their hopes and fears with a wider community of believers. The attempt of Russian Orthodoxy – self- contained within a Russian-dominated core, and intolerant of contacts with the outside world – to integrate both religions into a vibrant and rejuvenated Orthodox community of believers was bound to fail.[91]

Taxation

The government was much more successful in using taxation as an agent of integration. The Russian economy was largely agrarian and nearly closed. In the eastern theatre, it consisted in fact of two still largely separate economies, that of the Russian settlers, and that of the natives, who were either partly settled and partly nomadic, or nomadic altogether. As peasants migrated toward the Volga and the Urals, and beyond the mountains, into Siberia, they brought with them their familiar crops, their tools and implements, and their methods of cultivation. The result was to integrate the region into a single agricultural core, where rye became king. The fisc followed the settler, and taxation bound together what nature and human effort had steadily created.

In Muscovite Russia, taxes were apportioned according to the number of *sokhas*, a territorial unit comprising either a specific area of land or a definite number of households (*pososhnaia podat'*). The rate of the tax varied greatly depending on the productivity of the land and the taxpaying capacity of the population, and rural communities were held collectively responsible for the fulfilment of their quotas. Beginning in 1680, the household (*dvor*) became the basic fiscal unit: it was easier to identify and more uniform than the *sokha*. Periodic censuses fixed the number of households in each district (*uezd*), which received its own quota. But taxpayers responded by combining to form larger households, resulting in a curtailment of the tax base.[92] The government continued to search for a nuclear fiscal unit that could not be manipulated, and settled in 1718 on the individual male ("soul"). A new census conducted in 1719–24 yielded a total of 5,570,000 souls, who were required to pay a capitation (*podushnaia podat'*) of 74 kopecks (reduced to 70 kopecks in 1725), and a quitrent (*obrok*) of 40 kopecks, a total of 1.10 roubles. Townsmen were charged 1.20 roubles per soul. The two taxes would remain the backbone of the Russian fiscal system well into the nineteenth century.[93]

Their origins differed, however. The capitation was intended to defray military expenditures, and its proceeds went directly into the coffers of the army (and navy) establishment. The *obrok* was a form of tribute, paid for the use of the land whose only legitimate owner was the ruler, as it had been in Mongol times. By the 1720s, ownership was becoming divided between the ruling house and the ruling class as a whole, and a trend developed, giving its members the right to own such land with the peasants on it, who became the subjects of the landowner and the sub-subjects of the ruling dynasty. Peasants on estates belonging to members of this ruling and managerial class would accordingly pay the capitation to the military and the *obrok* to their masters. A second consequence was the accelerated consolidation of the dependent population into two categories, peasants held by individual members of the ruling class, and peasants held by the ruling class as a collective entity ("state peasants," with a smaller group owned by the Court and the Church), and the abolition of the category of slaves (*kholopy*).

A third consequence was to increase the stratification of Russian society. The assessment method did not change. The census assigned so many souls to each district, and the *voevoda* was expected to collect an amount equivalent to the number of souls multiplied by the rate of the tax. It was left to the community to apportion the individual contributions. The *voevoda* and the officers became fiscal agents collecting funds which paid their salaries and supported their activities, with all the abuses resulting from such a combination of functions. Moreover, the capitation was imposed on all males, including babies and old men, who obviously could not pay. The principle of collective responsibility meant that the other males would pay more, and that some within the community would have to pay for several others, who became their debtors. Not only did the capitation and the *obrok* help serfdom crystallize as the foundation of the social order; they also encouraged the further development of an authoritarian society, in which the wealthy and powerful members of the dependent population found a common interest with the lower rungs of the managerial class in the fiscal exploitation of the peasantry and the urban citizenry.

Such a fiscal system expanded with the core to the Volga and the Urals, but the very size of Siberia and its climate required some amendments. The *posochnaia podat'* was introduced there probably in the 1620s,[94] but the *obrok* took different forms. The ruling house had claimed the ownership of the land after Kuchum's defeat, but Moscow's sway did not extend far beyond the forest zone, where agriculture was possible only in well-defined and isolated areas. The southern boundary of Russian settlement still followed a line running along the Miass and Iset Rivers, crossed the Tobol to the headwaters of the Vagai River and reached the Irtysh near Tara, skirted the Vasiugane swamp to the Tom River and ran on to Krasnoiarsk. From there it followed the foothills of the Saian Mountains to Lake Baikal and beyond the lake to the Uda River. The rich steppes to the south were not reached until the late 1720s. As a result, there were only three widely separated agricultural regions, where the fisc could follow the progress of settlement: one around Tiumen and Tobolsk, a second around Tomsk, a third around Krasnoiarsk, with patches of tilled land along the upper Lena and Yenisei rivers and around Nerchinsk.[95]

The census registered a total taxable population of 119,895 males, 14.8 per cent of whom were considered urban population. Among the peasantry, 88.3 per cent belonged to the category of state peasants, and the Church ranked

Table 7.1 Taxable souls in 1719 (males)

	Tobolsk	Tomsk	Irkutsk	Total
Serfs	1,375	875	1,847	4,097
State peasants	62,348	15,214	12,736	90,298
Church peasants	5,890	424	1,461	7,775
Urban	6,308	5,764	5,653	17,725
Total	*75,921*	*22,277*	*21,697*	*119,895*

Source: Kabuzan, *Izmeneniia*, 64–6.

well below the "state" as an owner of human beings. The peasantry in Siberia thus constituted the collective property of the managerial class of *voevody*, civil officials and military officers, and private ownership was almost non-existent. At the time, few landowners had ventured across the Volga and the Urals: land was still aplenty in Simbirsk and Penza *provintsii* and needed to be settled first. Siberia was unknown country and too far away. But the fact that private land ownership would never substantially develop in Siberia reflected suspicions among the ruling elite that it might eventually encourage centrifugal tendencies and the development of a Siberian "regionalism" that would threaten the quasi-military discipline of the ruling class. The relative share of various categories of taxable souls in the provinces within their nineteenth-century borders appears in table 7.1.

The major problem facing the Siberian authorities after the conquest was to make the continent self-sufficient in grain production. At first, grain was shipped from the northern towns of the core across the Urals and transported by military units, merchants, and settlers, but chiefly for their own needs, and the government had to contract out grain deliveries at high prices. Grain took five years to travel from Velikii Ustiug, the great commercial city on the Northern Dvina, to the Pacific, and by then, it had spoiled.[96] Shortages were common and hunger was not unknown. The government had no choice but to compel the resettlement of free peasants from the north, who were incorporated by the census into the dependent population. For taxable purposes, this peasant population was required to pay the *posochnaia podat'*, like their brethren in the core from their own allotment (*sobinnaia pashnia*). In addition, the government gave them a separate allotment called the *gosudareva desiatina* (one *desiatina* equals 1.1 hectare or 2.7 acres) or *desiatinnaia pashnia* equal to one-fourth of their own allotment. The authorities supplied seed grain, supervised the sowing, harvesting, and threshing, and took the entire product. In addition, the peasants were required to pay an *obrok* in grain (*obrochny khleb*) equal to three *puds* (one *pud* equals 16.4 kilograms or 36.1 pounds) per *desiatina* from their own allotment. The pressure was so great to extract a maximum of resources from the peasantry that the authorities would sometimes requisition the entire surplus (*vydelnoi khleb*).[97] This type of economy was very close to a hard labour economy, but it was considered necessary in the emergency conditions of early settlement.

With the passage of time, more and more land was brought under cultivation, and the rudiments of a market economy developed with a growing surplus and the emergence of market towns which were also administrative and military centres. As a result, compulsory contributions were gradually replaced by fixed money payments. The introduction of the capitation and the *obrok* merely adjusted the fiscal system to changing conditions, although Siberia was so vast and conditions were so diverse that compulsory in-kind deliveries remained in various places, especially beyond the Yenisei River.[98] Nevertheless, the uniform application of the fiscal reform integrated the peasantry, not only in Siberia but in the entire eastern theatre, into the fiscal administration of the core, which now grew to include all the territories settled by Russians.

The second economy of the forest zone contained a major resource, the valuable fur-bearing animals that retreated deeper into the forest before the noise, the smoke, and the raising of crops in the settlers' clearings.[99] To tax that resource, the Muscovite government collected the *iasak* from the native population, but the operation was so complex and so much depended on ethnic diversity, natural environment, and way of life that we must restrict ourselves here to an examination of the *iasak*'s place in Moscow's policy of fiscal integration into a unified core.

The government did not possess a monopoly over the fur trade in Siberia. The continent's early settlement originated in two relatively independent flows of people, one of peasants heading southeast toward the open steppe (with no valuable animals), the other of trappers (*promyshlenniki*), officials, and Cossacks heading east via the Ket and the Kuta toward the Angara and the Lena into Yakut country and Transbaikalia. These lands quickly became known for the high quality of the sable pelts, which became the standard unit against which to assess the value of other pelts. It was the trappers' greed that hunted the animals to near-extinction and developed a fur trade within Siberia, and with Moscow and China at both ends, that rivalled and damaged the government-sponsored trade. It was estimated that, in the first half of the seventeenth century, three-fourths of the fur trade was in private hands, on which the government imposed a 10 per cent tax (*desiatinaia pushnina*) until the 1670s, when the destruction reached such a point that the private trade ceased to be profitable for the Russian trappers. In 1684, the government forbade them to hunt sables beyond the Yenisei River, and from that time on, the government's share of the trade became paramount.[100]

The Russians had long known the *iasak*, a Turkic term for tribute (*dan'* in Russian, *alban* among the Mongols), because they had once paid it to the khan in Sarai and were still paying it to the Crimean khan in the seventeenth century.

After the collapse of Mongol rule, the khans of Kazan, Astrakhan, and Siberia had collected it from their subjects, and the Buriats from their *kyshtymtsy*. The Bashkirs paid it to one of the three khans depending on their location, and the *iasak* they paid to the Siberian khan was particularly heavy. The Eastern Mongols collected it from the southern Buriats, the Western Mongols from the Baraba and Kulunda Tatars, and the Manchus from the Tungus beyond the Amur. Some were unfortunate enough to pay it to both sides (in the Altai, for example) and were called *dvoedantsy* (those who paid double tribute).[101] The *iasak* was so common in the eastern theatre that we need to inquire what it meant for the Russians.

The *iasak* consisted of typical products of the payers' land, as was also the case among the nomads and others who populated the peripheries of the Chinese core and paid it to the Manchu dynasty.[102] In Siberia, it consisted of pelts – sables, brown, black, and polar foxes, squirrels, and rabbits – but, if no fur-bearing animals were available, horses and cattle, reindeer skin, or finely chiselled arrowheads were acceptable. In Bashkiria, where apiculture was developed, honey was another substitute.[103] The natives exchanged gifts (*pominki*) with the tsar, *voevody*, their retinue and secretaries – pelts (*pominochnaia pushnina*) for trinkets, beads, and inexpensive jewellery, but also grain, knives, axeheads, copper kettles, and cloth.[104] The exchange embodied the recognition of a relationship which the native may have considered an equal one, but which the Russians viewed as the acceptance of their superior status, as when the *voevoda* received the natives in his parade uniform.[105] The decision to bring gifts was for the native a free choice at the early stages of his encounter with the Russians.

The *iasak* was a required contribution for permission to use the land, rivers, and forests, which had become the property of the Muscovite ruler as the successor of the Mongol khan and of the latter's own successors, who had collected it from their own subjects, and who were now relegated to form the second tier of a superstratified society in which the Russians had become the new rulers. There was a definite implication of inferiority attached to paying it, so much so that the Buriat *zaisang*, for example, who now had to collect the *iasak* on behalf of the Russians, preferred to call it *pominki*, thereby keeping to the fiction that it represented a free choice.[106] One cannot but see here a similarity with the *obrok*. The settler paid it in grain, the native in pelts or some equivalent. Both settler and native became subjects of the Muscovite ruler by assuming tributary obligations (*pod-dan-stvo*), and in the eyes of Moscow became inherently separate but equal in the structured society of an expanding core. The *obrok* and the *iasak* had the same juridical foundation, a payment of tribute for the right to till the land, to hunt, and to fish. They became a powerful agent of fiscal integration in the eastern theatre. The obstacle, especially in the deeper recesses of the taiga, was the chasm between the way of life of the settler and that of the hunter and nomad. But it was Russian policy to restrict the nomad's freedom of movement, to tie him to the land, to tighten the control exercised over him by his own leaders, thereby creating a social order that would approximate that of the original core. A policy of fiscal integration must be placed in the context of a broader policy of social and religious integration bent on creating not an empire but a unitary state.

It took a long time to establish a more or less consistent set of rates for the collection of the *iasak*. In the early years, the *voevody* were told to collect it on an annual basis according to the ability of the natives to pay. *Pominki* were also unregulated. Money was rare, and most of the natives had no concept of it as a medium of exchange. They would laugh at the naivete of the Russians, who were delighted to receive for a cooking kettle as many sable pelts as could be stuffed into it or barter an iron axehead for eighteen pelts.[107] However, the Russians set out to systematize the collection of pelts by introducing *iasak* books, which they intended to serve not only as payment records but also as census rolls for the taxable native population, defined as males between the ages of eighteen and fifty – when they were considered able-bodied enough to hunt in the forest during the long winter months when the fur was richest. *Pominki* became mandatory, and in the end indistinguishable from the *iasak*.[108] The *iasak* became a heavier burden, because a tax that is collected regularly is resented as a greater imposition than one collected haphazardly, as it had often been before the Russians' arrival. *Iasak* books also recorded arrears which tended to accumulate with the vagaries of the hunting season, causing greater resentment.

But it remained impossible to establish uniform rates because conditions were so different from one region to another. At the beginning of the seventeenth century, the *iasak* amounted, in general, to ten to twelve sables per man, but it could reach twenty-two and was often from five to seven sables. By the middle of the century, it had dropped to three sables in Western Siberia. A possible alternative was to place a money value on the pelts and set the *iasak* at between two and four rubles, but the *voevody* tended to undervalue them. The natives protested and the attempt was abandoned. In the southern fringes of Siberia, where a money economy already existed, what with the proximity of the Mongolian and Chinese markets, the natives delivered the cheaper pelts (valued at between thirteen and fifty kopecks) as *iasak*, but sold the more valuable ones for seven or eight roubles, if not more.[109] If the sable, rather than the kopeck or the rouble, was the standard unit of valuation, it was necessary to establish a relationship between the sable and other animals: in Yakutia for example, a wolf or ten squirrels equalled one sable, a black fox or a beaver two sables. Elsewhere, different rates applied.[110]

The collection of the *iasak* required the creation of an administrative infrastructure. The authorities divided the territory occupied by a native people into *volosts* – there were thirty-four in Yakutia, for example. The *volosts* were divided into *iurts* and were themselves integrated into the standard administrative division of the core, the *uezd*, administered by a *voevoda*, who kept the *iasak* books. Nomadic people could not so easily be integrated, because they tended to disappear at collection time. Among them, the *ulus* served as the equivalent of the *volost*, but it remained a social rather than a territorial unit.[111] The *iasak* books fixed the number of *iasak* payers at a given time. Each *volost* was assigned its share, and it was for the clan leaders to apportion the tax among their people, who were collectively responsible for the delivery of the pelts. As among the Russians, such a system guaranteed that some would have to pay more than others, and strengthened the authority of the clan leaders, who were also likely to be the richest members of the community. The collection of the *iasak* thus contributed to the creation of a common interest between them and the Russian authorities. If they did not collect the *iasak* themselves, and the natives were required to bring it to the collecting points, it was the *toyons*, *zaisangs*, and *taishi* who were the most likely to do so, and in the process they formed relations with the Russians. And if the authorities decided to collect the pelts themselves, their agents were, in Western Siberia certainly, former *murzy* of Kuchum's khanate who had entered Russian service and became known as "service Tatars" (*sluzhilye iurtovye Tatary*).[112] With the near-extinction of the animals in some areas and the growth of a money economy during Peter's reign, the *iasak* began to be converted into a money payment, as in Bashkiria, where a fox was valued at seventy-five kopecks, a beaver at one and a half roubles, and eight *puds* of honey at one rouble.[113] The *iasak* was fully becoming an *obrok* by another name, completing the integration of the native into the fiscal system of the expanding core.

Trade

The exchange of goods was a powerful incentive to foster closer relationships, and unequal exchanges between a core area partner and a multiplicity of peripheral communities created centripetal currents pushing toward integration into a larger and expanding economic zone. Market towns, with a territorial or areal orientation, served the needs of the subsistence economy of an agrarian administrative and military state and its ruling class. These towns were implanted into the countryside to create points of encounter between the rural population in need of basic tools and articles of clothing and a community of craftsmen in need of food beyond the yield of their "urban" plots. They were also collecting points to siphon off the surplus production of the rural population to satisfy the needs of garrisons and civil personnel.

In the Caspian basin, there had long been local markets in Terki and Tarku for weapons, precious stones, copper objects, especially kettles from Dagestan, carpets from Chechnia and Dagestan, and horses from Kabarda. The Russians supplied needles, knives, buttons, and mirrors, but above all, they controlled the sources of salt, on which the highlanders were totally dependent because none was available in the mountains. And they needed horses, both for domestic and service use, that were also shipped into the interior of the country.[114] But it was the slave trade that sealed the relationship between Russian and native. The sale of human beings had a long history in the Caucasus, where Tarku and Enderi were the chief markets for slaves from Georgia, Chechnia, and Ingushetia, who were sent either to the Crimea or eastward to Khiva and Bukhara, the great slave markets of Central Asia. The instruction of 1697 told the Terek *voevoda* that men, women, children, and horses captured in armed struggles with nomads were to be sold in the Terek bazaar, and the instruction of 1720 allowed the Astrakhan governor to buy adults and children offered for sale by their own people.[115] The fact that both instructions forbade the forceful seizure of the wives and children of Kalmyk and Tatar subjects and other friendly (*neprotivnye*) peoples clearly showed that such practices were common. The slave trade helped Russian officers and soldiers and even settlers, who were often unmarried runaways, to put down roots and form military settlements projecting Russian power in the region, which in turn pursued religious and fiscal policies encouraging integration.

Further north, in the Kama basin, the building of forts, the stationing of garrisons, and, above all, the development of the Urals industry created a regional cluster of market towns where troops, workers, and craftsmen found a meeting ground with Bashkirs, notwithstanding the hostility toward the implantation of Russian settlements in a pastoral or semi-pastoral economy. These developments both encouraged the settlement of Russians in the future Viatka and Perm provinces and exerted a gravitational pull on the Bashkirs of the Belaia valley, who shipped their grain to the Kama and then upriver as far north as Solikamsk and the Chusovaia, the industrial artery of the Urals. The Volga, below the confluence of the Kama, exercised a similar pull on the economy of the Ural Cossacks. These Cossacks did not engage in agriculture but derived all their resources from fishing. To supplement their fish diet, they travelled in armed detachments to Samara and Syzran on the Volga, the two grain markets for the garrisons of the Transkama Line. There, they bartered their frozen and salted fish, caviar, and fish glue for grain, which they took back to their settlements twice a year. But the trip was a dangerous one. In 1725, for example, 30 Cossacks returning from Samara were attacked by 150 Kazakhs and Karakalpaks, who killed some of them and took the others prisoner for seven years.[116] The hostility between Cossack and nomad on the most sensitive edge of the encounter between nomad and settler would delay for a long time the integration of the nomad into the settler's economy, but the trend was already irreversible by the 1720s and would quickly accelerate during the following decades.

Distant Siberia to the Yenisei River was in fact imperceptibly linked with the Urals – the headwaters of the Chusovaia are only thirty kilometres from

Ekaterinburg on the Iset, founded in 1721, the administrative capital of the Ural and Siberian industry, and the Ui Line was about to integrate the Trans-ural Bashkirs into the fortified perimeter of the Siberian Lines. Russian settlements became a magnet for traders from Central Asia, known collectively as Bukharans, although many did not come from that city.[117] Kazan and Bukhara had long been connected by trade routes, either down the Volga to Astrakhan and across the Caspian and via Khiva, or across the steppe via Ufa. Bukhara also led directly to Tobolsk across the steppe and along the valley of the Ishim or indirectly via the Yamyshev salt lakes on the Irtysh. Another route branched off the Silk Road at Yarkend and led to the Irtysh past Lakes Issyk Kul and Balkhash. Bukharan caravans monopolized the Zungharian trade with Siberia and took to Russian settlers cotton fabrics of various makes, colours, and patterns, tobacco, and rhubarb.

Cattle were an important article of trade. The nomad had more horses and cattle than he needed, and the Russian settlers and military needed draft animals, mounts, and meat to supplement their grain diet. Salt and slaves created, as in the Caucasus, a common bond between nomad and settler, mediated here by the Bukharans. The Yamyshev lakes drew Russians from Tobolsk and Zunghars from the Altai, as well as Bukharan caravans with textiles and sheepskin coats. The military and civil officials in the Irtysh forts were eager to get slaves, and had them baptized – it was state policy that prisoners and runaways who converted could not be returned – married them, or incorporated them into their households. Mongol (Zunghar and Kalmyk) women and girls were especially in demand.[118] Miscegenation encouraged the Russians to create similar military settlements and paved the way for the integration of some nomads into the world of the settler and for the creation of a Siberian ethnicity with its own specific characteristics.

All that trade focused on immediate sale and consumption in market towns emerging along the perimeter of Russian agricultural settlements or inland towns in the Urals. Bukharan trade created a grid of routes crisscrossing the Kazakh steppe, and laid the foundation of a regional economy gravitating northward, toward the manufacturing industry of the Urals. One can thus understand the true purpose of the Buchholz and Cherkassky expeditions: to transform much of the eastern theatre (to the Yenisei River) into a vast commercial region supplementing that of the original Muscovite core and integrated into an expanding core. But there was also the transcontinental commerce of cities on an east-west path, from northern India to the Mediterranean. It was dominated by Indian, Persian, and Armenian merchants. From Lahore and Multan, commercial routes crossed the Hindu Kush via the Khyber and Bolan Passes to Qandahar and ran on to Herat, Mashad, and Nishapur. From there, one route led to Shiraz and the Persian Gulf, another to Isfahan (the Safavid capital), Ardabil, and Tabriz, to Shemakha in Azerbaijan, the richest province of Persia. Shemakha was the entrepot of the entire trade in raw silk produced in Gilian province. From Shemakha, this continental overland route led to Tiflis and Gori, two flourishing Armenian colonies, and to Erzerum, and ended in Aleppo (Halab) and Smyrna (Izmir), where the Armenians exchanged without intermediaries their Asian goods for European ones, which they took back into Inner Asia.[119]

These routes formed a single corridor, a linear constellation of interconnected centres,[120] engaged not so much in local trade as in transcontinental commerce, independent of the galaxy of market towns along the way. The chief staple of that trade in the Persian sector was raw silk. But it also included silk and cotton fabrics, rice, dried fruits, Indian spices, carpets, luxury articles like precious stones, pearls from the Gulf, china from Persia and the Far East, weapons, and gold and silver objects. The merchants who controlled that commerce were organized in companies, the best known of which was that of the Julfa Armenians. There were Armenian, Persian, and Indian colonies in Astrakhan, the gateway to the Russian market. They formed a multi-ethnic community following its own rules and competing on its own terms.[121] There had been little trade between Russia and Persia so long as the Kazan and Astrakhan khanates barred the way, and Russian merchants were in no hurry to flock to Persian cities after the conquest.[122] For Persia, Muscovy was a distant and backward land, but one of potential interest: that may explain why Shah Abbas I was said to have loaned seven thousand roubles to Mikhail, the first Romanov tsar, who found his treasury empty in 1613.[123]

But the situation changed very rapidly during the second half of the seventeenth century. The first merchants had come to Astrakhan in the 1610s, settled down, and married local women. Later, they took their goods up along the Volga to the Makarev fair near Nizhnii Novgorod, and went on to Yaroslavl and Moscow, even as far as Tver.[124] In so doing they created a commercial route linking Moscow with the Caspian, which branched off from the transcontinental route between India and the Mediterranean, in much the same way as Central Asian traders created a similar diversion between Bukhara and Tobolsk. The Indian merchants' exploration of a transit route that might eventually lead, beyond the attractive market of the Muscovite capital, to northern Europe matched a Russian interest in redirecting at least part of the transcontinental commerce across Russia in order to create a similar route between east and west, an alternative corridor that promised to yield substantial revenue in transit fees to the Treasury, always at a loss to find additional income and without any domestic sources of gold and silver. This convergence of interests resulted in the elaboration of plans at the end of the seventeenth century to make Astrakhan a vast mart, the hub of Oriental merchandise on its way to Europe,[125] and to create not so much an overland route as a water route taking advantage of a network of rivers and canals.

Such an ambitious transformation of trade patterns required a drastic improvement in Russia's geopolitical situation, including gaining access to the Baltic Sea. Russia's early victories in the war with Sweden and the foundation of Petersburg in 1703 created an outlet for exchanges between the Russian economy and those of Britain and Holland. A canal cut above Tver linking the Tvertsa with the Msta, completed in 1709, inaugurated a continuous water route between the Baltic and the Caspian. Peter was obsessed with the silk trade, because raw silk not only was in high demand in Europe but also promised to be the most profitable staple in Russia's commerce with Persia. He wooed the Armenian merchants who controlled the trade, offering them privileges to send their silk to Moscow instead of Aleppo or Smyrna. Gilian silk and Mazanderan cotton, as well as saffron and madder (used in making dyes), were also needed to help Moscow develop a major textile industry capable, like the Ural iron and copper industry, of producing the manufactured goods which alone could integrate the peripheral economies into the expanding core. But the Armenians were Persian subjects, and those from Julfa were not eager to abandon a well-tested route for an unknown experiment, which they (rightly) suspected might not be in their interest.[126] The commercial treaty of 1717[127] did not grant the Russians that major concession, and the war of 1722–3 was basically a commercial war to gain it by other means. It gave them Gilian, if not quite Mazanderan and Astarabad, province, and did bring about a redirection of the silk trade across Russia. However, this attempt to integrate the western and southern littoral of the Caspian into the economy of the core came to an end when Russia returned the provinces in 1732.

Relations with China after the Treaty of Nerchinsk (1689) had the potential of creating a second corridor of commercial cities across Siberia. The treaty itself had little to say beyond the opening of free trade across the new boundary, but it gave a tremendous boost to the fur trade beyond the Yenisei River, and furs became the major staple in the China trade, accelerating the destruction of the animals in the region.[128] Beginning in 1693, the Russians were allowed to come to Beijing in caravans not exceeding two hundred merchants, who would be fed and housed by the Chinese, but could not stay beyond eighty days. However, the trade quickly degenerated into a free-for-all, when state-sponsored caravans had to compete with private traders, including *voevodas* trading in a private capacity, who undermined the trade of their own government.[129] Caravans and traders left Nerchinsk for the Amur, which they crossed to follow the Nonni River, and continued across southern Manchuria to reach Beijing via Kalgan on the Great Wall, the point of entry into the Chinese core. It was a long trip of 150 days, but the Chinese allowed the caravans to proceed from Selenginsk and Urga across the Gobi Desert to Kalgan beginning in 1704, a trip of only 70 days.[130] From Selenginsk, the corridor ran to Irkutsk, Yeniseisk, and Tobolsk, before reaching Verkhoture on a tributary of the Tobol, the only officially recognized point of entry between Russia proper and Siberia. There was another route from Tobolsk along the Irtysh to Lake Zaisan past the Yamyshev lakes, which crossed the entire length of Mongolia to Urga, but Kazakh raids and warfare between the Manchus and the Zunghars kept it unsafe.

The Russians had little else to sell beyond pelts, yet the caravans made substantial profits. They brought back brick tea, which became their favourite beverage, as well as precious silks. They were also on the offensive, even though many of the traders were Bukharans, whose commercial ambitions, like those of the Indians and Armenians, were continental in scope. In 1719, Petersburg proposed to the Chinese to allow Russian traders to enter freely all river and coastal ports, to trade wholesale and retail not only with Chinese but with others as well – a concession which they refused to make to non-Russians in Russia. The Chinese countered that they did not understand the meaning of free trade, and that there were already too many Russians in China.[131] But this Russian commerce, relying on the export of a single commodity and the import of very few, was in fact a fiscal operation in search of gold and silver, even though the discovery of silver ore in Nerchinsk in 1704 slightly improved the situation of a state completely devoid of precious metals. Traders were told to sell their pelts for gold and silver, and gold brought back by private traders had to be turned over to the government, either by purchase or in the form of customs duties. As early as 1692, the Russians had proposed to the Chinese to bring one thousand *puds* (16.38 tons) of silver to Moscow in order to exchange it for Russian and "German" goods, but the Chinese showed no interest.[132] Curiously enough, they behaved much like the Russians in the Caspian trade, who waited for the Indians and Armenians, while they themselves waited for the Russians.

In fact, both sides had an interest in keeping a high degree of control over their commerce – the Russians, because they wanted to maximize their government's profit by monopolizing the trade in precious metals, the Chinese, because they looked upon trade as a political weapon. Difficult negotiations over the delineation of a Russo-Mongolian boundary resulted in the interruption of commerce in 1722. The Treaty of Kiakhta (1728) upheld the Russians' right to send a state-sponsored caravan to Beijing every three years, but also closed off both China and Mongolia to Russian private trade. Just as Western traders were confined to Canton, the Russians became restricted to Kiakhta on the new border. Thereafter they lost interest in the caravan trade, which the Chinese did all they could to hinder anyway. A miserable border outpost, rather than the magnificent capital of the Manchu empire dominating the Asian coastland, became the terminal of the Petersburg-Moscow-Irkutsk-China corridor.

It was already apparent by the late 1720s that these corridors of transcontinental commerce would benefit the Russian economy but would never rival the oceanic commerce that was bringing such great wealth to northern Europe, as Peter himself had witnessed during his tour of 1697. If trade relies on land transport restricted to radii of exchange on relatively short distances, commerce relies on water transport, at sea best of all, or on navigable rivers supplemented by canals.[133] At first glance, the expanding Russian core within the confines of Eurasia possessed a splendid hydrographic network, which inspired Peter's vision of two commercial corridors across the entire eastern theatre. But the splendid network was only a mirage: rivers often froze for two-thirds of the year, were too shallow in the summer and obstructed by sand bars and fallen trees, portages were necessary to connect the major rivers, the canal was largely a bottleneck, and the Caspian was a dangerous sea. These corridors could not compete with the sea routes across the Atlantic, around the Cape of Good Hope and the Strait of Magellan, continuous, unobstructed, and relatively safe. Larger and larger ships were carrying cargoes to and from coastal cities and plantations whose commerce knew no bounds. These developments downgraded the importance of the transcontinental routes, and the victory of the sea over land doomed the economy of the eastern theatre to become a backwater within the growing world economy. The Russians could not subdue geography, which worked against them in this case.

Other developments ruined the potential of both corridors. Commercial cities were usually found on maritime littorals or in regions that might be best called frontiers between core powers, against which the cities always sought to maintain their independence, because their social structure, way of life, and perceptions of their own interests were radically different from those of the agrarian military and administrative state that constantly sought to encroach upon their freedoms. The east-west corridor from India to the Mediterranean ran along the periphery of the Persian and Turkish cores, and a history of relative independence allowed them to develop an urban society sharply different from that of the nomad.

But cities were also very vulnerable, and the disorders that marked the last fifty years of the Safavid dynasty damaged the trade substantially. Rerouting the corridor across Russia and building a new one across Siberia only compounded the problem: seeking to develop commercial societies in a political environment that had always been hostile to the independence of cities and the culture of negotiation, compromise, and trust that encourages the development of commerce and the buildup of safe surplus capital was tantamount to trying to square the circle. Moreover, neither the Indian nor the Chinese market was receptive to Russian penetration – one can only buy so many furs. While the market towns from the Terek across Bashkiria to the Irtysh were promoting integration between the settler's subsistence economy and that of the nomad, the commercial cities could not hope to develop their potential to integrate the economy of the eastern theatre into the larger economy of the expanding core.

Chapter Eight

The Progress of Integration, 1731–1782

The Military Structure

1731–1744

The next fifty years from about 1730, when Russia began to recover from the shocks administered by Peter's rule, to the early 1780s, when a comprehensive administrative-territorial reform took place across the entire Russian realm, were a period of consolidation, deepening integration of the expanding core, and preparation for future expansion in the eastern theatre. Anna Ivanovna's reign (1730–40) marked a partial return to pre-Petrine administrative organization and hierarchy, but the reform of 1708–19, which had been a major step toward the integration of the core, remained fundamental, and the governors continued to be the central government's regional delegates until the 1780s, when regional military commanders began to assume a dominant role. These regional delegates were not so much delegates of the central government as a whole as of the War Ministry (called in the eighteenth century the College of War), and their assumption of a leading role not only gave added impetus to the drive toward integration and uniformity, but also did much to militarize the management of the borderlands.

However, the governors' status suffered considerably from the creation in 1719 of the colleges, to which they became subordinated instead of to the Senate as a body, and from the decision of 1730 to allow provincial *voevody* located closer to Moscow (and Petersburg) than their governor to correspond directly with the colleges.[1] This was the reason for removing Solikamsk and Cherdyn *provintsii* from the jurisdiction of the Tobolsk governor and subordinating them to the Kazan governor. The creation of the colleges fragmented the governor's jurisdiction, which had been universal in 1708, and left him in the role of a regional coordinator of the colleges' activities in his province and commander of the garrisons, Cossack units, and, in some cases, combat troops as well. As a result, we find among the governors only a very few members of the ruling families, who preferred to stay in the capitals, close to the power centres. In Astrakhan, governors followed one another in quick succession, and one has to wait until the 1740s to find governors who stayed at least four years.[2] In Kazan, they remained much longer, perhaps because the religious conflict between Orthodoxy and Islam required some continuity of tenure. In both places, they remained subordinated to the commanding general of the Southern Corps until 1732, if not 1735.

The southward migration of the Russian peasant beyond the Sura and over the watershed between the basin of the middle Volga and that of the Don continued. While the census of 1719 had registered 1,195 male serfs and 489 male state peasants in the future Saratov province, that of 1744 registered 59,897 and 26,276 respectively.[3] Vasilii Tatishchev, the Astrakhan governor (1741–5), recommended the creation of new *uezd* centres along the Volga between Saratov and Tsaritsyn to form the administrative infrastructure necessary to integrate those peasants and their owners into the expanding core by means of police supervision, judicial unification, and the collection of the capitation and the *obrok*. He also called for the colonization of the trans-Volga steppe – the future Samara province – the Kalmyk steppe between the Volga, the Samara, and the Ural, where the black earth zone of the Ukraine and the Don continued to the valley of the middle Ural and even beyond it, to the Ilek River.[4] Tatishchev, who had been Petersburg's delegate in Bashkiria a few years earlier, envisioned a systematic assault on the domain of the nomad, as the Russians kept advancing out of the forest to which they had been confined until Peter's reign. The advance brought serfdom with it, the social foundation of the core, and aimed at either displacing the nomad or integrating him into that social order by compelling him to settle or enter the ranks of the irregular forces.

South of Tsaritsyn, where chestnut soils alternated with *solonchaks* unsuitable for agriculture, the Russian presence was still insignificant: the 1744 census listed only forty-eight male state peasants in the future Astrakhan province. But beyond this North Caucasian steppe, a multi-ethnic society was taking shape along the Terek, beyond which a black earth zone stretched almost to the Caspian coast. The steppe remained the domain of the nomad, but he had to be contained to stem raids against the new settlements on the right bank of the Volga. Indeed, dealing with the Kalmyks, highlanders, and Nogais was among the major responsibilities of the Astrakhan governor. To contain the nomad, a sixty-kilometre-long Tsaritsyn Line connecting the elbow of the Don with that of the Volga was begun in 1717 and completed in 1732 with the creation of a Volga Cossack Host made up of Cossacks transferred from the Don and Little Russia.[5] Across the steppe, the Greben Cossacks were joined after 1735 by the Terek Cossacks withdrawn from the Agrakhan peninsula and the estuary of the Sulak after the treaty with Persia and settled on the Terek's delta, where

Kizliar began to develop as a major administrative, military, and trade centre. It had a commandant subordinated to the senior commandant in Astrakhan, who reported to the governor. Kizliar had a mixed population of Armenians, Georgians, and Persians, as well as Tatars and highlanders who came to trade.[6] There were also Astrakhan Cossacks consisting of converted Kalmyks and all the riffraff the authorities could press into the service, from which the Kalmyks regularly ran away, and who seemed to have existed largely on paper.[7] These forces, together with the garrisons, were subordinated to the governor, but the three regiments of infantry (one in Astrakhan and two in Tsaritsyn) were part of the field army.

The offensive against the nomad had begun earlier in Bashkiria, with its dense chernozem between the Volga and the Belaia, although the Bashkirs were semi-nomads: some were sedentary stock raisers and owned land, and many lived in the forest zone. The crucial event was the decision by the khan of the Western Kazakh Horde to pledge allegiance to the Russian empress in 1730 and to make those Kazakhs "external subjects," who were not required to pay the tribute. The khan had asked in return for a Russian pledge to build a fort at the confluence of the Or and Ural Rivers, where he could find asylum in the event of his overthrow. The government sent the Senate's secretary, Ivan Kirillov, who arrived in Ufa in the fall of 1734 with two regiments of combat troops and some irregulars with an instruction to induce Bashkirs to join them in building the fort, which was completed in 1736. Kirillov's organization was called the Orenburg Expedition, renamed Commission in 1739.[8]

Ivan Kirillov (1691 or 1695–1737) was a child of the Petrine era. He had done work in Russian geography, had drawn up a map of Siberia based on older Russian and Chinese maps in 1724, had taken part in the compilation of the first general atlas of Russia in 1734, and had been senior secretary of the Senate since 1727, when he completed his immensely useful *Flourishing Conditions of the All-Russian State* (which was not published until 1831). Before his departure for the steppe, he completed a series of proposals ("projects") exhibiting a remarkable vision of Russian ambitions, concrete but premature, in the entire eastern theatre. These ambitions rested on a fundamental premise: the government must begin by building strategic cores (*opornye punkty*) along the periphery of the expanding Russian core. Originally forts with a substantial garrison, they would be given tax exemptions to attract settlers, and must have access to the most important trade routes. They would then become regional economic centres capable of supporting expansion further afield and the eventual annexation of outlying territories.

The Okhotsk project envisaged the building of Okhotsk, just west of Magadan, built three hundred years later as the capital of the GULAG empire in the Far East. The original settlers would be "service peoples" stationed in Yakustsk and convicts from Russia's internal provinces. The port would thus be built with forced labour, like Magadan. It would have shipyards to build boats with a view to engaging in commerce with Kamchatka and Japan and, around the peninsula, with America. Kirillov played an important role in the preparation of the Second Kamchatka Expedition commanded by Danish Captain Vitus Bering (1681–1741), charged with reconnoitring the so-called Northern Route from Arkhangelsk to the Anadyr River and the coast of America.

There was also a Central Asian project purporting to follow the realization of the Orenburg project. Once the Russians had created an equilibrium (*balans*) in alliance with China to maintain peace among the quarrelling Bashkirs, Kazakhs, and Kalmyks, they would seek to build another strategic core on the Syr Daria flowing into the Aral Sea. The Karakalpaks living in the estuary of the river would have to be annexed, and secondary forts would be built along the river to form so many strategic bases from which to control the Central Asian trade centred on Bukhara in the west and gold-rich Badakshan (Pamirs) in the east. Here Kirillov was living in a dreamworld, but a century and a half later would not the Russians be installed in Central Asia and in Vladivostok, the "Ruler of the East"? All these projects were inspired by a global vision of systematic expansion, in common with the Saltykov project of 1712, the expeditions of Buchholz and Berkovich-Cherkassky in 1715, and, much later, in the 1790s, General Yakobi's similar pincer movement directed against Persia in the west and Mongolia and Korea in the east, but they were doomed to fail. Siberia could not yet create an industrial base to produce competitively manufactured goods for the Chinese and Japanese markets, and the nomads were not numerous enough to create a substantial one. Furs were the major article of export, and they were useless in "India" and most of China. There was no labour to produce goods in the first place: convict labour was hardly enough, and large-scale immigration was not yet possible. But while these projects show the Russians' remarkable spatial vision, they were no more utopian than those of some Europeans who dreamt in the 1920s of irrigating the Sahara and transforming Africa into an American Far West, where certain Europeans would one day "live in world cities on the shores of the Congo River."[9]

The Orenburg project is of course central to our story. Kirillov planned the creation of a similar strategic core on the Ural River (Iaik), in the corridor controlling the movements of nomads from the Kazakh upland into the trans-Volga steppe. The city would be given trade privileges and tax exemptions to attract nomads and merchants from east and west. Settlers would come from the Russian interior, willingly or not. But as they moved deeper into Bashkiria they would also provoke ethnic conflicts as they squatted on Bashkir lands and became involved in the tripartite conflicts between Bashkirs, Kazakhs, and Kalmyks. The Bashkir rebellion of 1735–41 was the result, as we shall see presently.[10]

The founding of Orenburg brought about an administrative-territorial reorganization of Bashkiria. Ufa *provintsiia* had been removed from the jurisdiction of the Kazan governor in 1728 and its *voevoda* placed directly under the Senate, following complaints by the Bashkirs that they did not receive fair treatment from Kazan. The governor won it back in 1733, but it passed under the jurisdiction of the Orenburg Expedition in 1737, the year of Kirillov's death. That same year, a new Iset *provintsiia* was created, its capital in Cheliabinsk, to include the valley of the Iset and the Miass and the lake country to the Ui River, blessed with chernozem inviting Russian immigrants. Although the *provintsiia* belonged to the basin of the Tobol and the governor of Siberia coveted it, it was included into the Orenburg territory to become its major source of grain.[11] It was natural to expect that the territory would become yet another province, and it did in 1744, when Bashkiria was finally separated from Kazan province. Both the Ufa and Cheliabinsk *voevody* were subordinated to a governor, Privy Councillor (grade 3, the equivalent of a lieutenant general) Ivan Nepliuev, who had been a resident minister in Constantinople (1721–35) and was a full-fledged member of the ruling elite. He was given the command of all garrisons, Cossack units, and even combat troops in the province, and full powers over relations with the Bashkirs and Kazakhs.[12] The reform created a unified civil and military command, and Nepliuev outranked every other regional delegate in the eastern theatre. In the meantime, the original site of Orenburg had been found unsuitable – it was in the middle of nowhere, and there was no construction timber nearby. The fort was moved downriver in 1739 and to its present site near the confluence of the Sakmara and the Ural in 1743.[13]

The projection of Russian power across 600 kilometres of Bashkir territory to the mid-Ural River was accompanied by the building of fortified lines, which represented a declaration of war on the nomad well beyond the edge of the forest zone. By the mid-1740s, nine forts and eighteen outposts (*forposty*) had been built along the lower course of the Ural to its mouth, where Fort Gurev was removed from the jurisdiction of the Astrakhan governor and placed under the Orenburg governor. One of the forts, near the Inderskie hills, was built at the suggestion of the Kalmyk interim khan (*namestnik*) for protection against the Kazakhs, who forded the river at that point to attack their pastures. There and at the early site of Orenburg (now called Orsk) the advance of the Russian military perimeter was inextricably connected with tribal politics in the steppe. West of Orenburg, nine forts and three redoubts along the Samara River linked the new headquarters with the Volga at Samara. East of it, ten forts and sixteen redoubts on the Ural River linked it with the watershed between the basin of the Caspian and that of the Kara Sea in the triptych's central panel, where the Ui River took its source. Along this river, 770 kilometres long, more forts were built to Zverinogolovsk near the confluence of the Tobol, a small fort which also passed under the jurisdiction of the Orenburg governor.[14] From

Gurev to Zverinogolovsk, what became known as the Orenburg Line stretched along river banks over 1,600 kilometres of sparsely populated territory, from which the Kazakhs were expelled, and within which the Bashkirs were contained. Another 620 kilometres of fortified outposts along the Samara River separated Kalmyks from Bashkirs and pushed the former deeper into the semi-desert zone. To man these forts and outposts, Nepliuev consolidated Cossack units in the province which resembled the detachments of "town Cossacks" in Siberia to form an Orenburg Cossack Host, whose size was fixed at 4,882 men in 1755.[15] One-fourth consisted of converted Kalmyks, Bashkirs, and Meshcheriaks. Together with the Ural Cossacks these units formed the nucleus of a future Orenburg Corps, into which the garrisons were incorporated. Orenburg, located on the very perimeter of the expanding core, unlike every other provincial capital, was destined from that time on to become the assembly point for a general offensive against the nomad on the way to Central Asia.

The importance given to the integration of Bashkiria brought about the downgrading of Siberia until the mid-1740s. The Siberian Chancery was restored in December 1730, a move clearly designed to provide a sinecure for some members of the ruling elite who shunned appointments to distant Tobolsk, let alone Irkutsk.[16] But, in the battle over turf between proponents of functional and those of territorial administration, the Chancery lost out to the former, when it was subordinated not only to the Senate but also to the colleges of revenue and audit in 1734.[17] In-fighting at the centre and the incompetence of the governors in Tobolsk gave a free hand to local officials, whose abuses finally led the Senate to draw up a new instruction for the Siberian governor. However, the instruction, which the Senate approved in 1741, was only a throwback to that of 1697 for the Tobolsk *voevoda*, and does not seem to have been carried out.[18] Major General Ivan Shipov, chosen to be the new governor, wanted to be subordinated to the Senate directly and no longer to the Siberian Chancery, which he felt was unable to act on its own authority, but was rebuffed, and had to accept his immediate subordination to each college separately. He never really served in Tobolsk, however, and in 1742 the government appointed Brigadier Alexei Sukharev, promoted on the occasion to major general, who had been senior commandant in Tobolsk, to whom all commandants in Siberia were subordinated. He would remain until 1752, despite the Senate's request in 1744 that he be replaced on grounds of incompetence.

In Eastern Siberia, the government raised the status of Irkutsk *provintsiia* by appointing in 1731 State Councillor (grade 5, the equivalent of a brigadier) Alexei Zholobov as vice-governor, a title which in the parlance of the day meant a second-class governor, but outranking a *provintsiia voevoda*. The appointment was a form of banishment from the Court, where Zholobov had sided with the supporters of the future Empress Elizabeth against those of Anna Ivanovna the preceding year.[19] He was subordinated to the Siberian Chancery and the College of Foreign Affairs and given responsibility for relations with China, although the treaty of 1728 provided that these relations must be conducted between the Russian Senate and the Manchu "Tribunal" via the Tobolsk governor.[20] His key subordinate was the same Colonel Buchholz who had led the expedition of 1716 against the Zunghars, and who was now commandant in Selenginsk, where he would retire in 1740 in the rank of brigadier. Zholobov became one of the most corrupt members of the ruling class ever to disgrace the administration of Siberia, and he was beheaded in 1736 following an investigation conducted by Volynskii, the former governor of Astrakhan (who himself would be executed in 1740). But the government persisted in appointing a vice-governor in Irkutsk directly subordinated to the Siberian Chancery,[21] a decision which in effect considerably reduced the jurisdiction of the governor in Tobolsk by dividing Siberia into provinces, although the governor would always outrank the vice-governor in Irkutsk and retain overall responsibility for the entire continent.

The governor also commanded the garrisons and Cossack units manning the forts along the Irtysh and the Ob, although a separate officer had jurisdiction over the line. He was a mere colonel, however, and was subordinated to the governor. The population of Western Siberia was rising, encouraging migration beyond the Ishim Line, which by the 1730s already consisted of sixty settlements between Kurgan on the Tobol and Omsk on the Irtysh, and ran along the very edge of the forest zone.[22] The Baraba steppe beckoned beyond the Irtysh, but the area was still claimed by the Zunghars and was insecure. The peasant population of Western Siberia numbered 86,126 males in 1719 but 125,467 in 1744 (of whom 77,562 and 115,281 respectively were state peasants), most of them in the future Tobolsk province (69,613 and 92,408 males respectively).[23] Since most of the province north of the capital was inhospitable to Russian settlement, most of the population was concentrated between the Irtysh and the Tura in the north and the Ui River in the south, and the purpose of the Ishim and Ui Lines was to protect the settlers against raids by Kazakhs, who had always considered those lands to be theirs.

By the early 1740s, there were three clusters of garrisons: a Tobolsk cluster of thirty-one outposts with 3,410 men including a new dragoon regiment created in 1736; an Altai cluster of ten outposts with 1,242 men, stationed chiefly in the Kuznetsk area to guard against Zunghar raids; and between the two, the Irtysh corridor with five forts and seven outposts with 1,356 men, a total of 6,008 garrison troops.[24] With the growth of outposts on the lines came a gradual distinction between the "town Cossacks" who remained in the interior, in towns like Tiumen, Tara, and Surgut for example, and the "line Cossacks" serving on the Irtysh and Ishim Lines. A third category appeared in the form of "imported" (*vypisnye*) Cossacks, who were simply peasants (or natives) drafted into Cossack units: they numbered 7,700 in 1751.[25] They were supernumeraries who assisted the line Cossacks. Even though they were mounted irregulars, these Cossacks could not cope with the patrolling of such an endless perimeter: the Ishim Line from Zverinogolovsk to Omsk was 580 kilometres long, the Irtysh Line from Omsk to Ust-Kamenogorsk another 1,036, a total of 1,618 kilometres, along which it was simply impossible to interdict all Kazakh and Zunghar raids. The forts and outposts served mainly as a means of deterrence, because the nomads, once they had crossed the line, might find their retreat cut off and lose their booty.

The situation became alarming in the 1730s when the Russo-Persian and Russo-Chinese frontier became more turbulent than ever. After signing a peace treaty with Russia in 1735, Nadir Shah set about recreating Tamerlane's empire: he invaded Afghanistan in 1738 and northern India in 1739, and imposed his rule over Bukhara and Khiva in 1740. Central Asia was the area where Zunghar, Kazakh, and Persian interests overlapped. The Zunghars, now at peace with the Manchus, were determined to assert their rule over the entire Kazakh steppe: their success would restore a link with their Kalmyk brethren and create a Western Mongol empire stretching to the Volga, a prospect no less terrifying to the Russians than their ambition to reunite Mongolia was to the Manchus. The Eastern Kazakh Horde in the basin of Lake Balkhash already paid tribute to the Zunghar ruler. Zunghar raids into the pastures of the Central Horde in the 1720s explain why its khan and that of the Western Horde sought Russian support and pledged allegiance to the empress in 1730 and 1731. The unrest in the steppe was aggravated by Kazakh raids into Bashkir pastures. In addition, Abulkhair, the khan of the Western Horde and the last great Kazakh khan, sought to reunite the three hordes under his leadership, a prospect attractive neither to the Russians nor to the Zunghars. The Russians themselves in the person of Kirillov had worked out a vast program of expansion – which merely systematized Peter I's ambitions – to assert Russian rule in Central Asia;[26] it presupposed the integration of the Kazakhs into the Russian realm. The Russians knew the khans were weak and that they must be further weakened to facilitate their own penetration of Kazakh politics.

In this welter of conflicting ambitions, the Zunghar raids of 1741–2 across the steppe as far as the Tobol and the Or Rivers became the catalyst that prompted the Russian government to act. A joint session of the Senate and College of Foreign Affairs discussed reports sent by Nepliuev and Sukharev in 1743 and resolved to send a "corps" of 10,000 combat troops to Siberia. Only five regiments (about 5,820 men) were actually sent and arrived in 1745, commanded by Major General Christian Kindermann: two of infantry were stationed in Tobolsk, three of dragoons in the Altai between Semipalatinsk and Kuznetsk. Local commanders were told that there would henceforth be two generals in Siberia: one residing ("stationary," *nedvizhimyi*) in Tobolsk, the other on the line. Both were of equal rank and corresponded by memoranda (used between agencies of equal status).[27] This decision marked the emancipation of the military from the civilian authorities in Siberia and the emergence of Omsk as the second military headquarters (after Orenburg) facing the Kazakh steppe.

1744–1780

There were few changes in the administrative-territorial division of Siberia between the mid-1740s and the great reforms of the 1780s. In 1764, the government finally decided to raise Irkutsk to the status of a full provincial capital,[28] and the vice-governor, Major General Wulf von Frauendorff, appointed in 1753, became its first governor, and would remain in Irkutsk until his death in 1767. Also in 1764, the governors were given a new instruction,[29] which did not quite supersede that of 1728, but gave them greater authority over the provincial agencies of the colleges and chanceries in Moscow and Petersburg, a step away from functional toward territorial administration, which would become the defining feature of Catherine II's reforms. Irkutsk province was divided into two *provintsii*, one in Nizhneudinsk west of Lake Baikal, the other in Iakutsk east of it, each with its own *voevoda*.

In the meantime, the "governor of Siberia in Tobolsk" had risen in rank, beginning with the appointment of Lt.-Gen. Vasilii Miatlev (1753–7), who had been quartermaster (intendant) of the Baltic fleet and had retired in 1743 at the conclusion of the war with Sweden, but would return to the fleet at the outset of the Seven Years' War in 1757. There may have been a reason for sending a navy man to Tobolsk: the Russians were seeking ways to explore the Amur River and establish a water route to the Sea of Okhotsk and the Pacific, and the vast hydrographic network of Siberia required the attention of a trained eye to overcome the limitations imposed by the Treaty of Nerchinsk.[30] He was followed by Privy Councillor Fedor Soimonov (1757–63), who had grievously suffered at the end of Anna Ivanovna's reign and been deported to Okhotsk, whence he was brought back to serve under Miatlev before succeeding him. The third governor, and the one with the longest tenure in Siberia, was Lt.-Gen. Denis Chicherin (1763–80), a brother of the chief of police in Petersburg, who, like Soimonov, left a legacy of forceful administration keen on expanding Russian settlement, but, unlike Soimonov, behaved like a great lord who lived in style and did much to raise the cultural level of Tobolsk, if not of Siberia as a whole.[31] Raising the rank of the governor went hand in hand with the promotion of the corps commander to the rank of lieutenant general, as tensions rose in the Russo-Chinese frontier as well as in Russo-Chinese relations. These commanders, also with long tenures, were Johann von Springer (1762–71), Johann Clapier de Colongue (1771–7), and Nikolai Ogarev (1779–89).

The same joint session of the Senate and College of Foreign Affairs which had met in 1744 coupled the sending of additional forces with another declaration of war on the nomad east of the Ural River. Sukharev proposed to shorten the Ishim Line by drawing a straight path from Chernolutsk to Zverinogolovsk, bringing into the expanding core the so-called Kamyshlov lake district with its good land suitable for agriculture, and cutting across a zone of salt lakes, despite objections that the settlers might suffer a shortage of fresh water. The Senate did not give its final approval until 1752, but local authorities had already made the necessary preparations. Petropavlovsk on the Ishim was founded that year, a strong fort with a custom house destined to become the terminal on the line for the caravans from Tashkent, Bukhara, and as far away as Kuldja and Chuguchak in Zunghar country. The New Ishim Line – also called Bitter (*Gorkaia*) because of the salt lakes – advanced the periphery of the Russian core between fifty and two hundred kilometres into the Kazakh steppe.

The joint session also discussed even more ambitious proposals concerning the upper Irtysh and the Altai. A new 450-kilometre-long line would run from Semipalatinsk to Lake Teletskoe along the Abakan chain dividing the basin of the Ob from that of the Yenisei, and cut off the Zunghars from their Tatar subjects who paid them the *iasak* in the Baraba and Kulunda steppes. In conjunction with the Irtysh Line, it would also keep the Kazakhs from those same steppes, into which they were attracted by their rich pastures, despite the hostility of the Zunghars. The construction of such a line would indeed be tantamount to a declaration of war on both Kazakhs and especially Zunghars, who had told Gagarin forty years earlier that their claims extended as far north as the Om River. The decision to send additional troops was designed as a precautionary measure against a possible Zunghar counteroffensive. Sukharev, supported by Nepliuev, went even farther and recommended abandoning Ust-Kamenogorsk and moving the periphery upriver to the confluence of the Bukhtarma, on the edge of the Lake Zaisan depression forming a transition zone from the steppe to the semi-desert of the eastern Kazakh steppe. No decision was made at the time and the Russians were soon overtaken by events.

Galdan Tsering, the last great Zunghar ruler, died in 1745, leaving a thirteen-year-old son who was unfit to rule. Weakness at the top always sounded the death knell of nomadic confederacies, and the Zunghars never recovered. In 1753, Dawachi, the son of a cousin of Galdan, was chosen to rule but was challenged by a rival, Amursane, who defected to the Manchus. They had long waited for an opportunity to destroy the confederacy. Their troops captured Dawachi in 1754, but Amursane then tried to restore Zunghar unity and betrayed the Manchus, who forced him to flee to the Russians; he died of smallpox in Tobolsk in 1757. Tensions rose along the border as the Russians refused to surrender his remains. By 1759, the Manchus had finally destroyed the confederacy, and their patrols were found within seventy kilometres of Ust-Kamenogorsk and Semipalatinsk. The destruction of the Zunghars was only the most momentous event reshaping the geopolitics of the Russo-Chinese frontier. In 1748, Abulkhair, the khan of the Western Horde, was murdered by another clan leader who resented the khan's efforts to consolidate his power and reunite the Kazakhs. He left six sons, a prescription for disaster, and one of them, Nur Ali (1749–86), was chosen khan with the backing of Nepliuev, from whom he received his investiture in Orenburg. The entire power position of the nomad between the Ural and the Ob Rivers had collapsed, and the advance of the settler was becoming irresistible.

While Zunghar power was disintegrating, the Russians went on the offensive. In 1747, the gold and silver mines of the Demidov family in the Altai were taken over by the Cabinet, the economic management office of the Romanov house, and their security became a high priority for the central government. By the end of the 1750s, a new eight-hundred-kilometre-long Kolyvan-Kuznetsk Line spanned the entire space between the Irtysh and the Ob Rivers from the confluence of the Shulba to the Biia, and continued to Kuznetsk along the Kondoma to its confluence with the Tom River, creating a new "international" boundary with the Manchu empire.[32] The core had expanded another one thousand kilometres from the Om to the Shulba below Semipalatinsk; the Chinese and the Russians had partitioned the Zunghar territory among themselves. Now the Russians faced a Manchu empire at the height of its power, and the creation of a new geopolitical isobar[33] between them generated a certain turbulence, a sort of cold war, as is usually the case when such realignments take place. The last Russian trade caravan reached Beijing in 1757, and the Russo-Chinese trade was interrupted during much of Catherine II's reign, a clear sign of Chinese displeasure.

The Russians were uncertain of Chinese intentions, and the deployment of 1763 showed a regiment of infantry in Ust-Kamenogorsk and another in Selenginsk, seven regiments of dragoons on the Ishim and Irtysh and Kolyvan Lines, and another two in Irkutsk and Selenginsk. Never before had so many combat troops been stationed in Siberia, and although they were few compared with those available to the Manchu commanders, they were intended to act as a deterrent. The Russians were also pushing their luck. General Springer, the new commander on the Siberian Line, was given an instruction in 1763[34] which showed Russian concerns over the possibility that Chinese forces might sail down the Irtysh and claim the legacy of the Zunghars between the river and the Ob, provoking an open clash. But parties he sent across Lake Zaisan into the Black Irtysh reported that the river and the banks of the lake were so overgrown with reeds that the Chinese could not possibly mount a naval expedition from there. He was also instructed to build a fort at the confluence of the Bukhtarma to guard the approaches to Ust-Kamenogorsk and serve as a trading station to develop exchanges with Chinese merchants in western Mongolia. The fort was built, but trade never developed, and plans to build a line from it to Lake Teletskoe were finally abandoned on account of the unforgiving terrain in the

Altai. The Russo-Chinese border in this region would remain undemarcated until 1864.

The Russians quickly understood that the Manchus had no ambitions beyond Lake Zaisan, and combat troops were later withdrawn. By 1781, there remained a Siberian Corps, but it consisted only of so-called infantry battalions, created following the disbandment of the "light field units" created in 1771, whose dragoons were combined to form a single regiment.[35] There were also seven garrison battalions and Cossack units in Western and Eastern Siberia. The territory had become a zone of low-intensity threats, ready for full integration into the expanding core.

A similar situation was developing in the Caspian basin. At the very same time that the Manchus were launching their first offensive against the Zunghars, Nepliuev was facing the last Bashkir rebellion in 1755.[36] The census of 1744 had revealed that there were already more Russians than Bashkirs in the territory, and conflicts over land had become acute. Moreover, the rebellion acquired a distinctly religious tone when its leader railed against the Russian "onslaught" (*nashestvie*) on the Muslim communities and called upon the world of Islam to rise up in defence of the faith. The Chinese faced the same type of resistance in Kashgaria, which they put down in 1760; the Zunghars were Buddhist and had gone their own way. Some fifty thousand Bashkirs, or half their number, fled into the Kazakh steppe. Those who were not massacred would eventually return when the government granted them a general pardon. The rebellion lasted but one year, but it was the Bashkirs' last gasp before the invincible advance of Russian settlements and military colonies within the expanding core.

The Kalmyks, those fierce warriors of the steppe, made their last stand fifteen years later. They had been of great help to the Russian government in contributing manpower during its wars in the southern and even western theatres, but they were also the sworn enemies of the Bashkirs and Kazakhs and a major cause of instability in the valley of the lower Volga below Tsaritsyn. Even though there were so few Russians in the area – less than 50,000 against 200,000 Kalmyks – the nomads, accustomed to roam over great distances across nearly empty spaces, felt increasingly hemmed in by the building of fortified lines, resented the interference of the Russian authorities in their fractious politics, disliked having to pay for salt if only because they had so little money, and feared Christianization and even enserfment following the appearance of Russian (and German) settlements along the Volga. And there was nostalgia for the alpine pastures of the Altai and a willingness to listen to the siren song of the Tibetan lamas. In January 1771, some 150,000 Kalmyks set out to return to their ancestral land in now-deserted Zungharia. Most were massacred on the way by the Kazakhs, and the Manchus settled the survivors in the Ili valley.[37] The Western Mongols as a power factor in the Russo-Chinese frontier were no more.

Turbulence in the Caspian basin sharpened long-lasting dissensions within the Ural Cossacks, who, unlike the Orenburg Cossacks, had not been created by administrative order but had a long tradition of independence from the central government. With the passage of time, two parties had developed among them. One upper stratum saw its interest in integration into the advancing power structure of governors and *voevody*, because they hoped to gain the government's support in their determination to acquire land (and peasants) and fisheries, thereby joining the ruling class of landowners; the larger group of rank-and-file Cossacks remained faithful to their traditional independence (or anarchy) and resented the partiality of their superiors in selecting men for service on the line. The Cossacks' lack of zeal in stopping and pursuing the Kalmyks who crossed the Ural River under their noses was interpreted as a neglect of their duty. Their refusal to obey an *ataman* imposed by the Russian authorities in Orenburg and to send men to Kizliar brought about an open rebellion, in which the *ataman* and a major general sent from Orenburg were murdered. The rebellion was put down in 1772 and was followed by a ferocious repression. Cossack administration was abolished and a commandant was appointed in Uralsk, the host's headquarters.[38]

This sorry tale of savage massacres found its culmination in the Pugachev rebellion of 1773–4. Led by a Don Cossack, it brought together in an unholy alliance Cossacks, Bashkirs, Kazakhs, Old Believers, Polish Catholic confederates banished by the hundreds in the 1760s, peasants, and "wanderers" against the growing hold of the core area government that brought with it taxes and serfdom but paradoxically was unable to offer an alternative, since Pugachev claimed to be Peter III, who had been murdered in 1762. The map of the rebellion bears an uncanny resemblance to that of the Kazan khanate and that of the Razin rebellion. Despite its scope, brutality, and the anxiety it caused in Moscow, the rebellion was a last-ditch and hopeless attempt to reverse the course toward the greater integration of the expanding core. From the Volga to Lake Baikal and the Altai, the Russians would henceforth encounter only local disturbances calling for mere police operations. The eastern theatre was now ready for a comprehensive territorial and administrative reform abolishing the distinction between core and periphery.

However, troubling developments were emerging in the northern Caucasus. A fort called Mozdok was built on the middle Terek in 1763, in response to a plea by a Kabardian prince who had fallen victim to interclan politics in the mountains and had come down into the plain to find Russian support. The resemblance to the founding of Orenburg/Orsk and the fort on the Ural cannot be overlooked. Local leaders, for reasons of personal or more general security, sought to pin down a Russian presence at specific points where they could count on Russian support in emergencies. Mozdok became the terminal of a Terek Line which the Russians had been building since 1736 from Sladkorechie on the Caspian coast, but its garrison would come from Kizliar until 1770 when it got its own: that was the time when the Russians were sending an expedition across the mountains into Georgia to engage the Turks at Poti on the Black Sea coast during the Russo-Turkish war of 1768–74. In 1765, the Kizliar commandant, Major General Nikolai Potapov, had won the government's agreement to set up in Mozdok a unit of 214 converted highlanders (*gorskaia komanda*) under the prince's command. They would be given land and encouraged to settle down.[39]

The Terek was over three hundred kilometres to the south of Astrakhan, and terrain and climate did not facilitate communications. As a result, it was decided in 1763 to set up a separate command on the line under Major General Johann von Medem (1763–71), whose relationship with the Astrakhan governor, Nikita Beketov, remains unclear. Beketov was a lieutenant general, and Medem and Potapov were either subordinated to him or, most likely, independent in the chain of command. Both solutions had been tested in Siberia and Orenburg. There, Governor Dmitrii Volkov, also appointed in 1763, was only at the rank of a real state councillor (the equivalent of a major general), but a lieutenant general commanded the Orenburg Corps. Volkov protested his appointment (which had been a form of banishment), saying that Orenburg needed a general of imposing appearance to take charge of both civil and military affairs, because the population consisted of Russian military personnel and Kazakhs, who would respect only a general but despise a civilian.[40] His two successors were lieutenant generals who also commanded the Orenburg Corps.

In the northern Caucasus, the rising threat from the mountains enhanced the importance of military commanders, especially after Grigorii Potemkin was appointed de facto war minister in 1774 and governor general of New Russia and Astrakhan in 1776, a joint appointment which resulted in the temporary integration of the northern Caucasus into the southern theatre and gave the military establishment a decisive voice in shaping Russian policy in the region. Despite its importance and the size of its garrison (two battalions or 1,500 men) Kizliar was attacked by highlanders in 1770, 1773, and 1777. The Terek Line blocked access to the salt lakes in the steppe and caused great resentment in the mountains. Even if Cossacks and highlanders intermarried and lived a way of life with some common features, they lived in different worlds, and religion was not the least cause of discord and enmity. The occupation of the Black Sea littoral sent Tatar hordes that had been roaming the steppe between the Danube and the Don into the north Caucasian steppe, and the rising enmity between Russians and Turks reverberated in the mountain valleys and incited the highlanders to rise up against the Russians.

Such was the background of the decision to build a line from Mozdok northwestward to Azov on the Don. The Volga Cossacks were transferred in 1777 to the line, joined by converted Kalmyks, who, however, continued to live their own independent life. The Cossacks were settled across the watershed between the Terek and the Kuban. The line was built under the leadership of Alexander Suvorov, the commander of what now became the seven-hundred-kilometre-long Caucasian Line from Kizliar to Azov, completed in 1782.[41] It was a vast undertaking, which delineated a new space in the north Caucasian steppe along an arc of circle with a radius of some five hundred kilometres from Astrakhan, protected against raids from the mountains and ready for peasant settlement. The expanding core nearly reached the boundary of agricultural land. But unlike the relative peace that had descended in Siberia, in Bashkiria, and on the lower Volga, the establishment of a military presence (without combat troops yet) along a mountainous periphery signalled the future expansion of the Russian realm beyond the natural limits of the expanding core and the creation of an empire.

The Administrative-Territorial Reform

The great reform of the late 1770s and early 1780s brought about the most comprehensive and most systematic transformation of the structure of Russian government in the eighteenth century. Inspired by Enlightenment ideas that emphasized the importance of reason, system, and coherence in human affairs, it also seemed to reflect a perception in Petersburg that the expanding core was indeed about to reach its natural limits and needed to be fully integrated into a single and uniform whole, guided by identical structures and procedures within more or less identical territorial units – unlike the provinces created in 1708, which were of such different sizes that they had little in common.

The statute of November 1775 announced the division of the realm into provinces (*gubernii*) including between 300,000 and 400,000 males registered on the census and the division of these provinces into *uezds* containing between 20,000 and 30,000 males. The boundaries of each territory had to be drawn in such a way that its capital would occupy a central location equally accessible to the entire population, such as between 100 and 120 kilometres in each province. As a result, the larger provinces were broken up into smaller ones, the *provintsii* were abolished, and some of their capitals were raised to the status of provincial capitals. The number of governors increased accordingly. The reform originally planned to have a governor general in each province, but it had been decided by 1781 to appoint a governor general over two or more provinces, a compromise with the old order, in which the old governor became the governor general and the *provintsiia voevoda* the new governor. The ranks of these delegates of the ruling elite were also higher. Governors general were either lieutenant generals or full generals, the governor was a major general, although the post was a civilian one, and governors also had the equivalent civil rank.

The reform totally transformed local administration. In place of the governor or *voevoda* with a small chancery, it created a Provincial Board, a Treasury Chamber, and a civil and a criminal court. The personnel of the first two consisted of appointed officials and a staff of clerks; the courts were elected by the local nobility with an appointed procurator. The reform decentralized and deconcentrated the central government, where the colleges were gradually closed, and where the procurator general, the de facto president of the Senate, became the highest civilian official, whose power was balanced by that of the war minister (president of the College of War). Governors general were the regional delegates of both. At the *uezd* level, the simple *voevoda* was not replaced by a single official but by a land court of three officials (including a land captain in charge of the police), a *uezd* court elected by the nobility, a *magistrat* elected by the merchants, and a *rasprava* chosen by state peasants, from which appeals were taken to the upper courts in the provincial capital before the final decision was made in the provincial board or the civil and criminal court. There was also a government-appointed *uezd* treasury. This multiplicity of posts, the perfect spoils of office, reflected the main purpose of the reform: to decongest the two capitals (Moscow and Petersburg) and speed up the redress of the local population's grievances; to facilitate the exercise of power by the ruling class over the dependent population; and to improve the collection of taxes. The reform was intended to take effect uniformly across the entire realm, from the Polish border to the Sea of Okhotsk.[42]

In the eastern theatre, it began with the breakup of Kazan province in 1780–1 into five provinces: four new ones, Perm and Viatka in the north and Simbirsk and Penza in the south, with the new Kazan province constituting the remainder. Perm Province straddled the Ural chain – that is, the watershed between the basin of the Volga and that of the Tobol, between the larger Caspian basin and that of the Kara Sea. Perm was a new town, founded near a copper plant that had once belonged to the Stroganovs. Another four new *uezd* centres were created, former forts which had served as observation points against the Bashkirs on the Kama and the headwaters of the Ufa River, but one was the site of a monastery and was chosen to provide an administrative centre in Komi country west of the Kama. The location of Perm province on both sides of the Urals required the creation of Ekaterinburg *oblast*, a new subdivision that resembled the old *provintsiia*. Ekaterinburg was founded in 1721, both as a fort against the Bashkirs and as a centre of the mining industry. Since 1763 it was, like Kungur, on the new southern route leading into Western Siberia. It was too important to be a *uezd* capital, but the civil administration of the *oblast* was subordinated to the Perm governor. Only one of its *uezd* centres was old: Verkhoture, 404 kilometres east of Perm, had been in the seventeenth century the only official point of entry from Russia into Siberia and back, with a customs house and a fort, but it was eclipsed by Ekaterinburg. The others were either metallurgical plants or agricultural settlements that had developed around monasteries; Irbit was the site of a famous fair, usually abandoned for ten months of the year. Viatka province was more compact. Seven of its thirteen *uezds* were old ones; four of the other six were on the lower Kama in Udmurt country, and one (Glazov), 210 kilometres from Viatka, was an Old Believer stronghold.

The norms of the 1775 statute had been set much too low. Viatka province had a population of 414,620 males and Perm province one of 393,820 males in accordance with the 1782 census, and all their *uezds* had a population approaching the maximum of 40,000 males or even exceeding it.[43] However, this peasantry was of different composition. In Viatka province, 89.2 per cent were state peasants but in Perm only 66.2 per cent, still a substantial majority. If we consider the entire population, male and female, and non-peasant groups, we obtain 857,305 people in Viatka province and 813,751 in Perm province, a total of 1,671,056 people, among whom the Russian share already reached 84.5 per cent.

A second group consisted of the three provinces of Kazan, Simbirsk, and Penza. All three were in the wooded steppe, with a deep black earth cover to its periphery running slightly north of Saratov. The territory had been a battlefield between nomads launching raids from the south and southeast until the Tsaritsyn Line barred the way, and the settlers coming from the original core and the Voronezh region. It was also a multi-ethnic land where most of the *uezd* centres had been forts set up among native groups of Mari, Chuvash, and Mordvins, which then became administrative centres, *iasak* collection points, and small trading towns. The influx of Russians gradually transformed the territory into an extension of the core in which the natives, who had once been dominated by the Kazan Tatars and partly tatarized, were being integrated and partly Russified. Once a frontier long exposed to external dangers from the steppe, it had become by the middle of the eighteenth century a land of internal tensions resulting from the social and political superstratification imposed by the Russian presence.

Nineteen new *uezd* centres were created in the territory, most of them former villages and small trading towns that would never grow in that overwhelmingly agrarian universe. Kazan stood apart with its history as the capital of a khanate, then a province; an archbishopric see; a large garrison, with some industry revolving around the shipyards building boats for the Caspian flotilla, and a junction where the road from Moscow branched north toward Siberia and southeast toward Ufa and Orenburg. In 1782, Kazan province had a total population of 775,156, Simbirsk province 764,278, and Penza province 655,446, a total of 2,194,880 people. Among the peasantry, 51.7 per cent consisted of state peasants, but they were more heavily represented in Kazan province (77.6 per cent) and least in Penza province (33.8 per cent). The ethnic composition was very mixed, but the Russians were already the largest group by far with 1.4

million or 65.3 per cent. The 277,600 Chuvash came next, then the Tatars with 262,000, and the Mordvins with 143,000. Among the others the Mari were the largest group. The numerical superiority of the Russians over the Tatars, who used to be the masters of the land, is especially significant and vividly illustrated the process of superstratification.

Orenburg was a case apart. Its capital was moved inland to centrally located Ufa, and Orenburg became the capital of an *oblast* within the province, reflecting the continuing duality between the centre of Bashkiria and the military headquarters on the periphery. Only three of its thirteen *uezds* were old ones. The others were forts or villages selected more for their location than for their importance. Its total population of 560,088 was the smallest in the group of provinces which had once been part of Kazan province, and most of its peasant population (74.3 per cent) consisted of state peasants, showing the continued resistance of landowners to resettle their serfs in a territory which had experienced so much violence in the preceding fifty years. Ufa/Orenburg province was the only one where the Russians were a minority (37.2 per cent or 219,000), followed by the Bashkirs (138,900 or 23.6 per cent), the Tatars (82,700), the Chuvash (44,100), the Mordvins (19,100), and 84,200 "others," but even there the Russian share still exceeded that of the former dominant group.

One can think not only of Kazan as the key city in the western panel of the triptych but also of its pre-reform province as a large building with two unequal wings, one stretching southwards along the Volga toward the Terek River, the other, much longer, from the Urals to the Yenisei River, with Eastern Siberia forming a yet indeterminate extension. The southern wing was the former Astrakhan khanate and province, which the reform broke up into two provinces, Saratov and Caucasian (Astrakhan). The elongated form of Saratov province makes it hard to place. The province is usually combined with Astrakhan to form the lower Volga region with the northern Caucasus because of the southern orientation of Astrakhan, but the bulk of its population was in the black earth zone between the upper Khoper and the Volga: this places it in the same group as Penza and Simbirsk. Five of its seven new *uezds* were in the north, former forts on the Belgorod Line that had once stalled raids by Kuban Tatars and Kalmyks. The capital of the new Caucasian province was Ekaterinograd, a recently built fort on the Caucasian Line, and Astrakhan became the capital of an *oblast* within the province, but it would become a provincial capital again in 1790. The total population of the "lower Volga region" was 725,341 in 1782, 567,815 of whom in Saratov province, where only 36.8 per cent of the peasant population were state peasants. In Astrakhan province there were only 6,434 peasants. In both Saratov and Astrakhan provinces, the Russians were also a majority of 65.1 per cent (447,000), followed by Mordvins and Tatars (86,800), German colonists (28,204) and, in the steppe south of the Volga, 74,300 Kalmyks. Only in the northern Caucasus were the Russians still a minority of 16,500 against 115,500 "Tatars" and 6,800 others.[44] There, the periphery of the expanding core, patrolled by Cossacks on the Caucasian Line, was still waiting for its contingent of settlers to take the nomads' place.

In Siberia, Tobolsk province contained the entire western part, as had been the case since the creation of Irkutsk province in 1764, but the Tomsk region formed an *oblast* within it. Nine new *uezd* centres were created, and their location clearly showed the consolidation of Russian settlement along the Old Ishim Line and the advance into the steppe. Yalutorovsk was the largest of the new *uezds*, its centre near the confluence of the Iset and the Tobol, 340 kilometres south of Tobolsk; Ishim, at the same distance from the provincial capital, was on the river of that name and could be called the capital of the Ishim steppe; Omsk on the Irtysh was emerging as Tobolsk's rival and a major military headquarters. All three were on the Siberian trail that began in Moscow and ended in Irkutsk. Kurgan, where navigation began on the Tobol, was another agricultural settlement given the status of a town, but one destined to grow into a major trading centre, unlike many other *uezd* centres. But the largest *uezd* was that of Berezov, 1,015 kilometres north of Tobolsk in desolate Ostiak country, an old *iasak* collection point and trading town, from which the Russians had overwhelmed the natives; it had also been a place of exile for members of the elite in the 1730s, like Alexander Menshikov (who died there) and Alexei Dolgorukov. Surgut on the Ob was a way station on the Ob and a fort from which the Russians had penetrated into Ostiak country.

The fate of Tomsk region was curious, but was determined by strategic considerations. The town was the natural capital of the Altai, but the emergence of a separate industrial area in the mountains between the upper Irtysh and the Katun created a strategic sector along the border with Mongolia, which remained undemarcated. As a result, the Altai, under the name of Kolyvan province, was linked with Irkutsk under a separate governor general in Irkutsk, who acquired jurisdiction over the entire Russo-Mongol and Russo-Manchu border, at a time when relations with China remained tense. The decision also embodied a new latitudinal perception of the periphery of the realm connected with the rise of Potemkin as head of the military establishment and governor general of the territories acquired from the Ottomans in the southern theatre. Instead of envisioning the periphery as so many sections forming the ends of separate corridors of expansion, the frontier was now seen as a continuous territory running from west to east, along the natural limits of the expanding core. The remainder of the Tomsk region between the Ob and the Yenisei formed Tomsk *oblast*, extending as far north as Narym near the confluence of the Ket and the Ob, and other new centres in Kainsk and Achinsk were old forts, both on the Siberian trail.

Eastern Siberia was so huge that Irkutsk province had to be divided into its four natural regions, each forming an *oblast*. The region around Irkutsk included the western end of Lake Baikal with the Kudara steppe of the Transbaikal Buriats and Selenginsk, whose commandant was the key figure in the region after the governor. But it also extended as far north as Kirensk on the Lena, 1,030 kilometres from Irkutsk. In Siberia, distances had nothing in common with those encountered in the old Muscovite core, and the population was much sparser. The size of the *uezd* population was often close to the minimum and sometimes even below it, while Irkutsk *uezd* had over one hundred thousand people. The second *oblast* was that of Nerchinsk, the centre of silver mining and the main place of exile for hard-labour convicts. Joining Irkutsk and Kolyvan provinces under a governor general also had the effect of placing the entire industry of Siberia (metal working was also found among the Buriats) under a single authority. Two new *uezd* centres were Cossack settlements. The third was Yakutsk *oblast* or the land of the Yakuts, with additional *uezd* centres along the lower Lena in the midst of a desolate landscape supporting Yakuts, Tungus, and their reindeer. Half of the population of ninety-eight thousand lived in Yakutsk *uezd*. The fourth was Okhotsk *oblast* or the Siberian northeast with Kamchatka, where the Russians had fought a long conflict with the Koriaks, the Chukchis, and the Kamchadals from forts which now became *uezd* centres.

The 1782 census gave for the whole of Siberia a total population of one million, among whom the Russians numbered 693,500 or 67.6 per cent.[45] Tobolsk and Tomsk provinces (in their nineteenth-century borders) had a combined total population of 573,095 and Irkutsk one of 452,319. The most striking feature of the peasant population was that it consisted almost entirely of state peasants: 99.1 per cent of the peasantry in Western Siberia, 99.8 per cent in Eastern Siberia. Settlement had taken place either at the initiative or with the support of the government. Such an overwhelming presence of state peasants raises the question whether the expansion of the core truly resulted from a flow of settlers leaving the forest zone to find better conditions in the steppe, who then had to be protected against nomadic raids by building fortified lines. The central government and the ruling elite may well have long understood that their mission was the reconstruction of the Kipchak khanate and then encouraged or forced the resettlement of peasants in the steppe to create the social infrastructure of a Russian core expanding toward its natural limits along the mountainous periphery enclosing the great plains. Gagarin in 1715, the Senate in 1725, and the College of Foreign Affairs in 1763 certainly had such a vision: it only needed settlers to be carried out. In all likelihood, the expansion of the core resulted from a combination of that vision with the elemental migration of the Russian peasantry. A second striking feature was the small size of the native population. In the whole of Western Siberia there were only about 35,862 Tatars and 27,502 Ostiaks (Khanty); in Eastern Siberia about 98,478 Buriats, 86,606 Yakuts, and 29,518 Tungus, with eleven other small peoples numbering

22,868 people of both sexes. Everywhere, the Russian nationality had prevailed; in so doing, it paved the way for the introduction of a reform which, despite the inevitable adjustments due to local conditions, remained applicable to the entire realm. Distance and population size could not so easily be matched as in the original core, and in Astrakhan and Siberia, the absence of a landed nobility meant that the courts could not be elected but had to be filled by appointing members of the ruling class in the service, a multi-ethnic ruling class, itself the result of a long process of integration.

To cap the administrative-territorial reform, the provinces were combined under six governors general: Kazan was linked with Viatka; Perm with Tobolsk; Simbirsk with Ufa; Penza with Nizhnii Novgorod. Astrakhan and the northern Caucasus were linked with Saratov for a while, but then formed a single province under its own governor general; Kolyvan was linked with Irkutsk. Governors general were lieutenant generals everywhere except in Tobolsk (a major general), as if to emphasize the decline of that city in the administrative hierarchy, what with the shifting of the military and commercial centre of gravity toward Omsk. These high-ranking officers, members of the ruling elite, were responsible to the empress and the procurator general in civil affairs, and to the war minister in military affairs, but their primary responsibility was to the latter, both because their careers depended on him and because the management of the frontier with its foreign policy implications was becoming a responsibility of the military establishment, as Russia was about to embark on a course of empire building. Volynsky, Gagarin, Tatishchev, and Nepliuev had all been civilians; Otto von Igelstrom, Pavel Potemkin, and Ivan Jacobi were all general officers.

Land, Peoples, Religions

Bashkirs

While the core kept expanding and administrative integration proceeded apace, the government and its local agents were determined to complete the process of superstratification and bring about the social integration of the native population into the Russian-dominated social order. This could not be done, however, without severe convulsions, which caused great damage to the social fabric and created tensions that exposed the limits of the possible in Russia's policy of religious integration. The first catastrophe was the Bashkir rebellion of 1735–41.[46] To build Orsk/Orenburg, Bashkirs were impressed into labour gangs and turned hostile. The building of more forts along the Ural and Samara Rivers established an "international" boundary, which brought Bashkirs into the expanding Russian core with all the fiscal and social implications, of which the Bashkirs quickly became aware. Another, older, cause of Bashkir hostility was the advance of the settler toward the Kama River and into the basin of the Ufa River, into lands which the Bashkirs had long roamed in search of booty. The settlements included the metallurgical plants of the middle Urals, first built during Peter's reign; they required substantial amounts of fuel in the form of charcoal, and large areas of forests were declared off limits (*zapovednye*), thereby damaging Bashkir apiculture.[47]

Among the leaders of the rebellion were *abyzy*, "those who knew the Koran by heart," although the term was applied in the eighteenth century to all the mullas and people who could read and write and had deep roots among the Muslim Bashkirs.[48] They were best placed to channel their discontent by associating Russian behaviour with an attack on Islam and a traditional way of life, especially among the mountain and Transural Bashkirs. The rebellion lasted six years and had to be put down by regular troops commanded by the governor of Kazan in person, father of the future marshal Petr Rumiantsev, who would break Ottoman hegemony in the Black Sea forty years later. It resulted in the destruction of hundreds of villages and tens of thousands of Bashkirs killed or banished into the interior of the core, their wives and children distributed as so much booty among officers and men, baptized, and integrated into the emerging frontier society of the expanding core.[49]

The rebellion cannot be looked upon merely as a bloody encounter between Russians and Bashkirs. The rebellion and the ferocity with which it was put down may not have been unavoidable. Nikolai Petrukhintsev has offered a serious explanation. He points to the isolation of Bashkiria, its self-contained ethnic and religious population on the boundary separating the steppe from the woodland, the call of the good land of the steppe. The encounter between Russians and Bashkirs was a "clash of civilizations," pregnant with bitterness and resentment. Petrukhintsev blames the Bashkirs for initiating the rebellion, but also points out that the cruelty of the repression was part and parcel of Kirillov's Orenburg project. The nomad had to be removed by force to make way for Russian military men to build the strategic core and for Russian settlers from the interior to create the economic foundation of a springboard into and beyond the Kazakh steppe, to the Aral Sea. The bitterness was aggravated by serious ethnic, social, and economic conflicts.[50] Bashkiria's population was deeply fragmented among Bashkirs, Tatar Meshcheriaks, Tatarized Teptiars, animist Chuvash, and Mordvins (if not already converted to Islam or Orthodoxy). Bashkir landowners had been the territory's ruling class. Other natives rented (*kotormili*) land from them in return for the payment of an *obrok* and the delivery of services, and had the same reason to resent the Bashkir landowners as the Russian peasant had to resent the oppression of his lord (and run away to Bashkiria). Upon this stratified society the Russians imposed a new ruling class of landowners, officers, and government officials, a process of superstratification, which could only incur Bashkir hostility. The reversal in the position of the two peoples was striking. The census of 1719 gave 36,500 Russians and 113,500 Bashkirs, that of 1744, soon after the rebellion, 172,000 Russians and only 106,200 Bashkirs, the only case in the eastern theatre where the native population declined, showing the devastating demographic impact of the repression.

The ukaze of February 1736[51] struck at the foundations of the Bashkir socio-economic position. Meshcheriak tenants (who on the whole had supported the Russians) on the land of rebellious Bashkirs were declared owners of the land and the *obrok* was cancelled. *Teptiars* and *bobyli*, whose status was close to that of serfs, were emancipated (*otreshit' ot poslushaniia*), but would have to pay the *iasak* to the treasury. Bashkir villages were forbidden to keep blacksmiths, who could reside only in towns. Bashkirs, whether nomads or land tillers, who recently converted were offered a place in Cossack service and won an exemption from the *iasak*. But the deadliest provision of the ukaze was to annul an earlier law prohibiting the purchase of Bashkir lands by Russians (a prohibition that had made Russian settlements merely squatters on Bashkir land) and to register deeds, providing that the new owners did not keep *iasak*-paying natives or "free Russians." The result was an increase of the Russian population to 219,000 by 1782 and the purchase of thousands of acres for a song – the Bashkirs had no concept of a quantified area, the land was not surveyed, and boundaries were set in accordance with a few physical features (*urochishcha*) like a wood, stream, or gully, so that the Bashkirs never knew at the time of purchase how much they had sold for trinkets or a supply of vodka. However, the Russians seem to have recoiled from the implications of destroying the economic position of even the rebellious Bashkirs, and it seems that the law was not fully carried out by local authorities who were better able to assess its potential damage.

But the government also appealed to the loyalty of those who had realized that the rebellion had been doomed from the beginning, or who had switched sides at the right moment. By the time the rebellion was over, each of the one hundred *volosts* was administered by a *starshina* appointed by the *uezd voevoda* from a list of elected candidates, and the authorities ceased to grant *tarkhan* charters. Moreover, the number of *akhuns*, members of the higher clergy who administered the Muslim law and to whom the imams and the mosques were subordinated, was fixed at four, and they were required to accept a new role by becoming the political agents of the new ruling class and reporting the suspicious behaviour of their Muslim brethren.[52] These two decisions were of great importance. One was a form of socio-political engineering seeking to create and integrate a new breed of notables into the hierarchy of the core area government. The other initiated an evolution of official policy toward Islam in Bashkiria, from a situation in which Islam had received no official status to one influenced by the Bukharan model, in which the Muslim "clergy" were recognized an an intrinsic part of the political hierarchy and were domesticated to become loyal agents of the government in maintaining the peace. Such a new policy amounted to a recognition of the singularity of Islam and implicitly admitted the impossibility of converting but a small number of Muslims. Orthodoxy and Islam had checkmated each other in Bashkiria, but the result was the integration of both into the hierarchical structure of the ruling class.

In Kazan province (less Bashkiria), the hostility of the Orthodox Church was much more pronounced; so was its determination to convert the natives, thereby completing the process of making them into "Russians." However, much seems to have depended on the energy of the metropolitans of Kazan (1589–1731, 1762–82) or its bishops and archbishops (1732–62). After an initial spurt of missionary activity, the Church had relaxed its vigilance, and Metropolitan Germogen had discovered in 1593 that Russians and Tatars lived together in the same villages, intermarried, and even drank together[53] – the ultimate proof of integration into the Russian world short of conversion. Renewed activity had taken place under Peter, closely connected with the persecution of Old Belief. In 1731, a commission was set up in Sviiazhsk to launch missionary work in Kazan and Nizhnii Novgorod provinces, but its work was so sloppy that its claims to have converted 27,362 natives in two years were not credible. It offered emancipation from bondage to native landowners who refused to convert, a three-year tax exemption and a similar one from the draft, the cancellation of tax arrears, and a money payment of one and a half roubles for an adult who converted and fifty kopecks for a child. But a radical change – and the second catastrophe – began with the arrival of Bishop Luka (Konashevich) in 1738. He may have been the first Ukrainian to occupy the post, and had received an excellent education in the Kiev Ecclesiastical Academy, but he may also have learned there a hatred of Islam nurtured by the activities of the Crimean Tatars supported by the sultan in Constantinople, who was also the caliph of Sunni Islam. He launched a systematic onslaught on the Muslims of Kazan, Nizhnii Novgorod, and Voronezh provinces, which provoked such discontent that he had to be recalled in 1755 to avoid an open rebellion on the eve of the Seven Years' War. There were also concerns that the continued persecution of the Tatars might have repercussions in Muslim lands with large Christian populations. The bishop's tool was the Board of New Converts, which replaced the commission in 1740.[54]

One may speculate about other reasons for such an aggressive policy. Much of Luka's work of converting the natives by force, including the razing of 418 of the 536 mosques in Kazan and its *uezd* alone,[55] took place during the reign of the Empress Elizabeth, who was a devout supporter of the Church. In the provinces east of Moscow to the Volga River, there remained a substantial minority of non-Russians, and Kazan was still a powerful religious core from which Islamic influences radiated and rivalled Orthodoxy in the conversion of non-Tatars. We know for example that in Sviiazhsk *uezd* itself the Tatars were converting Chuvash, including the women they married, and raising their children in the Muslim faith. The Board ordered the execution of the Tatars (but they were pardoned) and the separation of the children from their mothers unless they converted to Orthodoxy.[56] Such activities were unacceptable because they threatened the very process of superstratification. There was also fear and a feeling of inferiority at the thought that the uneducated Orthodox priest, imposed on his parish from the outside by the bishop, was at a disadvantage before the mulla, the guardian of the values and traditions of a Muslim community, who knew The Book better than the priest. This certainly explains why the documents of the period repeatedly mention the "temptations" (*soblazn'*) of Islam and the need to isolate the new converts in separate villages or resettle them in Russian villages, away from the temptations of their former co-religionists – instead of looking at them as the new carriers of a vibrant faith in hostile territory.[57]

The emancipation of new converts from their Muslim landowners was intended not only to provide an incentive to convert but also to strike a blow at the dominant social and political position of the Tatars. Some must have felt that a pro forma conversion was the better compromise to save their holdings and gain an opportunity to join the new Russian-dominated ruling class, which offered rewards in the management of the realm, its primary function and defining feature. Those who resisted ran the risk of social degradation. Such a policy, therefore, was not so much a religious one as the mark of a political determination to break the hold of an established and autonomous ruling class over a dependent native population by integrating it into the ruling class of the realm and completing the process of superstratification. But if conversion offered rewards, it also entailed a loss of identity, and required the development of a new one. It was understandable that nothing should be said about the fate of the new converts. Once converted and emancipated from the Muslim landowner – and if he did convert, his serfs remained in bondage (*kholopstvo i krestianstvo*)[58] – the native had almost no choice but to join the state peasantry or become the serf of a Christian landowner. Conversion meant for him continued serfdom, but also integration into the social order of the expanding core.

How successful the Kazan authorities were in implanting Orthodoxy among the native population is extremely difficult to determine, if only because the emphasis was placed throughout the eighteenth century on registering as many new converts as possible, while neglecting the depth of their commitment, so that the converts were often likely to return to their old faith whenever they were given a chance. Until the Orthodox priest became better educated, he could not serve as an example. Bogoslovskii claims that, in Kazan and Simbirsk provinces, 575,104 natives had been converted by the beginning of the nineteenth century, but his table is extremely revealing: it includes 350,818 Chuvash, 118,958 Mordvins, and 66,650 Cheremis – 93.3 per cent of the total – and only

33,812 Tatars.[59] The campaign had been successful in this Orthodox-Islamic frontier in converting and integrating the great mass of the non-Tatar and non-Muslim population, but had made little headway against the adherents of the other core area religion. Its goal to serve as a factor of integration of the old dominant native group had largely failed.

That the official attitude toward the Tatars was governed not so much by religious incompatibility as by political considerations appeared clearly from what was happening in Bashkiria after the rebellion, while Bishop Luka was persecuting Islam in neighbouring Kazan province. One of the major problems faced by Governor Nepliuev was to find settlers to populate the valley of the Ural River and traders to initiate from Orenburg trade relations with the Kazakhs and the Central Asian oases. The Russians showed little interest at first. The governor won the government's permission to resettle two hundred families of Kazan Tatars eighteen kilometres from Orenburg, on a stream called Qarghali, which gave its name to the new settlement, also called Seitovskii *posad* after one of its founders. The Tatars were given land and the right to build mosques and schools – an exceptional concession – on condition that no Russians would live among them, as if the Russians might be tempted to abandon Orthodoxy. They built water mills, cultivated cotton for the first time in the region, and sowed grain. The Tatars also became Russia's diplomatic agents, traders, and interpreters in the steppe.[60] Despite the strong criticism later levelled against Nepliuev (and Governor General Igelstrom, his successor in the 1780s) for allowing the Tatars to become religious propagandists as well,[61] Nepliuev inaugurated a new policy toward Islam, which announced Catherine II's. The emergence of Orenburg and of Seitovskii *posad* – which would become the major centre of Muslim learning in the region by the end of thee eighteenth century – created a counterpart to Bukhara, with which the Russians were seeking to develop relations, if only because the city was the hub of the Central Asian trade. It was natural that the influence of Bukhara would grow, especially after the crushing of yet another, but this time, short-lived, Bashkir rebellion in 1754–6, led, interestingly enough, by an *akhun* inspired by the Dagestan model of autonomous Muslim communities suffused by an almost millenarian *Weltanschauung*.[62] The rebellion, like all rebellions, threatened the position of those who benefited from the status quo and had no interest in contributing to the destruction of Russian rule, and created a backlash that favoured the rise of Bukharan influence. Nepliuev was the founder of a policy of "statification" (*ogosudarstvennanie*)[63] of Islam. His religious policy was made easier to carry out by the fact that in Bashkiria and the steppe he did not have to break the hold of a Tatar ruling class and the Bashkir notables had been humbled in the 1730s.

The early years of Catherine's reign saw no major changes of policy save for the closing of the Board of New Converts and the abandonment of compulsion in bringing the natives into the Orthodox fold. A child of the Enlightenment, she was also more inclined to believe in the importance of education and less willing to accept the guiding light of "superstitions" in human affairs. Significantly, she was the first ruler since Ivan IV to visit Kazan (in 1767), and it was she who would eventually abandon the practice of appointing Ukrainian prelates to Kazan and Tobolsk, whose intolerance had become counterproductive. The conquest of the Crimea in 1771 and the attempt to create an "independent Tatar nation" that would include the former khanate and the mainland to the Kuban required the adoption of a policy friendly not only to Islam but also to the Tatars, a dual policy once again, with a religious and a political component. When the question was raised by a number of bishops that mosques were being built near Orthodox churches and that new converts still lived with their former co-religionists – in a word, that Islam was on the offensive, as it also was in Tobolsk, where the Tatars openly ridiculed the Orthodox – the empress declared in June 1773 that since God tolerated a multiplicity of faiths, languages, and beliefs on earth, she wished to do the same in her realm. Moreover, she told bishops that matters concerning other faiths, including the building of prayer houses, were none of their business, because she wanted to see "love, peace, and harmony" prevail among her subjects. This "toleration edict"[64] announced a new attitude toward the "Muslim Question" in general. The Orthodox world would remain closely integrated under the leadership of its bishops and the Holy Synod, itself tightly controlled by a lay procurator and a member of the political elite. In the eastern theatre, policy toward Islam and the Tatars and Bashkirs would no longer be in the jurisdiction of the Synod but of the governors responsible to the procurator general, and in the nineteenth century, the minister of internal affairs. The bishop of Tobolsk was given a sharp reminder in 1775 that "the governor alone was accountable to Her Majesty" in such matters.[65]

While the new attitude implied that the government understood the futility of converting Muslim Tatars by missionary work, it did not affect the policy of integrating the natives into the social order of the expanding core. The administrative-territorial reform imposed a uniform grid across the entire eastern theatre and made no provisions for separate territories to recognize the separate status of individual "nationalities." It assumed the full integration of all subjects into the various social categories of the core: nobles, townsmen, peasants, and their subdivisions. For the great mass of Tatars, Bashkirs, and others, who for the most part were not nomads, it meant integration into the peasantry. This appears quite clearly from the decision to introduce the reform in Orenburg province in 1782. The governor general was instructed to set up lower *raspravy* in native areas, to be named, not according to the nationality of their members, but after the location of the court, thus obliterating the difference between Russian and native.[66] Cases would move up a single hierarchy to end in the same provincial board or judicial chamber subject to the review or interference of the governor or governor general, who then could raise confessional issues with the procurator general and the empress.

There remained to work out a jurisprudence for the handling of cases subject to Muslim law, because it was impossible at this early stage either to supersede Muslim law (and achieve full legal integration) or seek compromises between Russian and Muslim substantive law. Legal issues were delicate matters, because they deeply affected the relationships of individuals with their communities and their conception of justice. Mishandling them was likely to cause an unwelcome backlash, as the activities of the Orthodox church had already shown. But the administrative and social integration carried out by the reform created the prerequisites for negotiating a mutually satisfactory encounter not only between the three religions of the eastern theatre, but also between its three legal systems, the Russian, the Muslim, and the Mongol.

Kalmyks and Kazakhs

Beyond the Bashkir Upland into the depression that had once formed the northern end of the Caspian Sea and beyond the Ural River toward the Kazakh Upland, the Syr Daria, and Lake Balkhash, Russian authorities in Orenburg and Omsk held only a tenuous and precarious hold over the native peoples. However, the half-century that followed Peter I's death witnessed the slow disintegration of the powerful Kalmyk and Kazakh confederacies that had reached the height of their power under Khans Aiuka (1690–1724) and Tauke (1680–1718). That disintegration, caused largely by succession crises and endemic rivalries between powerful clans, invited Russian interference. The growth of Russian military power was unevenly matched by the increasing political weakness of the nomad and his inability to resist the advance of the settler. The result was the political inclusion of the Kalmyks into the Russian core expanding toward its natural border along the Terek and the Sunzha, and the end of Kazakh resistance to a subsequent Russian expansion toward the natural perimeter of the agricultural zone in the Kazakh steppe.

On the face of it, the successions in the Kalmyk khanate were relatively smooth. Aiuka was succeeded by one of his sons, Cheren Donduk (1724–35), then by the latter's son, Donduk Ombo (1735–41), who then was followed by his second cousin Donduk Dashi (1741–61) and the latter's son Ubashi (1761–71).[67] The location of Kalmyk pastures meant that the Kalmyks' main interlocutor was the Astrakhan governor, who reported to the College of Foreign Affairs. The Kalmyks were thus still "external subjects" not yet quite penned in between the lower Volga below Tsaritsyn and the Ural River. They could still pretend to be the allies of Russia; they had contributed troops to serve in the Russian army in the Swedish War (1700–21) and the Persian War (1722–3), when they had suffered heavy losses; and they would contribute troops again during the Turkish wars (1735–9, 1768–74). But Aiuka's succession did not in fact go very well. There had been five candidates for the succession, including Aiuka's wife Darman Bala, who favoured her grandson Donduk Ombo. But Governor Volynsky imposed her son Cheren Donduk, a weaker man, when faced with the possibility of a bloodbath between the supporters of the other four male pretenders.

The decision caused a split between father and son, and Donduk Ombo took his clansmen and supporters to the Kuban, where he married a second wife, the Kabardian princess Dzhan. He had threatened to move to the Crimea and become an Ottoman subject, a disturbing possibility for the Russians, who always sought to keep the eastern and southern theatres separate, while the Ottomans always wanted to establish communications between them, but never could. However, Donduk could not find adequate pastures for his twenty-eight thousand *kibitki*, and asked permission to return in 1734. The request suited the Russians well on the eve of their war with the Turks. They knew that Cheren was incompetent and enjoyed little authority, and had recognized him only as "interim khan" (*namestnik khanstva*), but then gave him the full title when they learned that a Chinese embassy was on its way to do the same.[68] The Kalmyks were at the time the perfect example of a frontier people caught between three core areas, the Russian, the Persian, and the Chinese, but the Russian core was already the stronger. That Cheren had opened negotiations with Nadir Shah did not help his cause. In 1735, he was summoned to Petersburg, and the Russians made Donduk Ombo the interim khan.

Donduk Ombo was both intelligent and ruthless, not above killing members of his own family if he feared their rivalry. But he too had to receive the regalia of his office from the Astrakhan governor, a sword, a coat of mail, a sable coat, and a fox hat,[69] although he chose to keep his distance from the Russians. Perhaps in order to find supporters against his rivals among his own people, he brought in six thousand Turkmen families from the Mangyshlak Peninsula across the Caspian from Astrakhan and another eight thousand families of Nogais from the North Caucasian steppe, creating one last steppe empire between the Don, the Terek, and the Ural Rivers.[70] But his death in 1741 unleashed new disorders. He had chosen his ten-year-old son by Dzhan to be his successor, and had sent an embassy to the Dalai Lama in Lhasa to obtain his confirmation. However, both actions encountered strong opposition from the supporters of the first wife, and Dzhan fled back to Kabarda, where she appealed to Nadir Shah for help. She received none, and later went over to the Russians and converted. As Princess Vera Dondukova, she became the founder of a new lineage in the Russian elite, and her three sons became Russian army officers. Meanwhile, Tatishchev, appointed Astrakhan governor in 1741, gave the investiture to Donduk Dashi, who would not become khan until 1757.

After Donduk Dashi's death in 1761, the Russians modified the composition of the *zargo*, the Kalmyk governing body which functioned chiefly as a court. They chose to believe that the khan was a major part of the problem of Kalmyk internal insecurity and decided to "democratize" it. The *zargo* would no longer consist of members of the khan's family alone but would become a popular (*narodnoe*) body consisting of members elected by each *ulus* who would then be confirmed by the governor. Decisions would be made by majority vote, and if the khan disagreed, he had to refer the controversy to the governor.[71] In view of the constant squabbles between clans and the refusal to accept a strong khan of Aiuka's lineage, the reform was intended to facilitate the growth of Russian influence throughout Kalmyk society. It naturally annoyed Ubashi, who responded to his people's hopes and frustrations: hope for a return to the ancestral lands in the Altai Mountains and the Ili valley, encouraged by the Buddhist lamas; fear of the settlers, including the German colonists in Sarepta, near Tsaritsyn; anguish at increasingly feeling trapped between the Don and the Ural Cossacks. In January 1771, most of Ubashi's people decided to leave, but few made it to the Ili valley, where the Manchus resettled them on former Zunghar land: the others were massacred by the Kazakhs on the way.[72] In the 1740s, the Kalmyk population had numbered about two hundred thousand individuals of both sexes; in 1782, it was down to seventy-five thousand.[73] The khanate was abolished, and most of the remaining Kalmyks were later transferred to the right bank of the lower Volga, in what came increasingly to resemble a Native American-style reservation. Such was the end of a proud people who, 150 years earlier, had led the last migration from "Asia" into the southern steppe, and whose women contributed so much to the creation of a distinctive Slavic Siberian and Turkic Kazakh ethnic type.

While the Russians were gradually bringing the great mass of the Kalmyks into the expanding core and assigning them places within it to which settlers would not go, they were also experimenting with an attempt to convert and settle some of them. As early as 1725, after Aiuka's death, a number of Kalmyks petitioned the government to be allowed to join the Ural Cossacks, but were told they first had to convert to Orthodoxy.[74] In 1727, a *taishi*, suitably renamed Petr Taishin, asked to be given land for himself and his forty *kibitki* (176 males and females). He offered to enter the service in order to escape persecution (*obidy*) by other Kalmyks, a clear reference to the disorders that accompanied Aiuka's succession. His widow, Anna Taishina, was made a princess in 1737 and was granted land between the Sok and Cheremshan Rivers, where Fort Stavropol was built in 1738. The Kalmyks who had joined her would form the Stavropol host (*voisko*), patterned after other irregular Cossack formations, under the jurisdiction of the fort commandant, Colonel Andrei Zmeev.[75]

When the question arose of what to do with the peasants already living on that land (who turned out to be mostly runaways from across the Volga), the colonel recommended that they not be removed, because the Kalmyks would learn from them how to build houses, till the land, and grow hay. Moreover, the experiment would encourage intermarriage and integrate the Kalmyks into the "Russian nation" (*meshat' ikh s Rossiiskoi natsiei*). The college of foreign affairs demurred at the thought that Princess Taishina and her *zaisangs*, who, after all, remained nomads, would not know how to manage peasant settlers, but the Senate supported the colonel.[76] Thus, conversion – all Kalmyks in the settlement would have to convert – erased ethnic differences and created a Russian nation defined not by its ethnicity but by its religion. The colonel's approach was quite traditional.

Nepliuev followed the same reasoning and went further in 1745. The host was divided into eight companies, and a Kalmyk court was created, chaired by the commandant and consisting of the host's colonel (Nikita Taishin), a judge, a clerk, three *zaisangs* elected annually, and an interpreter. It would try cases between Kalmyks and Russian claims against Kalmyks – leaving unclear how Kalmyk claims against Russians would be handled. It would follow Kalmyk custom, except in cases of highway robbery and murder, where Russian law would apply. But the commandant was also enjoined to introduce "from time to time" Russian law and procedures, "so that the court's decisions do not violate them" – in other words, the court would endeavour to bring about the full legal integration of the Kalmyks into the Russian legal system.[77]

The experiment was largely a failure; it affected only a small number of Kalmyks. One reason was the poor location of the settlement. The Astrakhan governor, Nikita Beketov, himself the son of a Kabardian notable and a Swedish mother, reported in 1764 that one thousand families of converted Kalmyks had gone back to their *ulusy* because they could not cope with the climate of Stavropol (which was in the wooded steppe zone) and wanted to resettle between Tsaritsyn and Astrakhan, in the Akhtuba valley, a water labyrinth with a rich vegetation which had always acted as a magnet on the Kalmyks.[78] But in a larger sense, it failed because Orthodoxy could not hope to make inroads into the core religions of Islam and Buddhism – only in the religious frontier of idol worship and even shamanism did it have a chance to succeed. The Kalmyks could not be made into "Russians."

Russia's relations with the Kazakhs were tense throughout this period. Even the number of their *kibitki* was unknown, but the first census of 1834 would estimate their total population to be about 1.4 million.[79] They were thus the largest ethnic group in the eastern theatre. They were also Chingissids of Turkic stock, and Khan Tauke was the direct descendant of Ezhen, the khan of the White Horde and Juchi's son, who had received his *ulus* in the Kazakh steppe before his brother Batu went on to conquer the Russian lands and western Eurasia. The Kazakhs were surrounded by the Zunghars in the east, the Kalmyks in the west, the Bashkirs in the north, from whom they seized pastures, and the Russians, whose settlements and fortified lines were advancing into Kazakh pastures between the Ural and the Irtysh Rivers, and the Central Asian khanates of Khiva and Bukhara in the south, with which they often fought after they were forced out of Tashkent in 1723. The Kazakh lands were a typical frontier within a larger frontier – the Russo-Chinese and to a lesser extent the Russo-Persian, especially during the reign of Nadir Shah.

The immensity of the Kazakh steppe – two thousand kilometres across between the Ural River and Semipalatinsk on the Irtysh – had encouraged the dislocation of the Kazakhs and the emergence of three hordes that remained nominally under a single khan. After Tauke's death, however, each horde proclaimed its own khan, while the Central Horde kept claiming precedence in the Chingissid line. Tauke was followed by his son Sameke (1718–39), the latter's son Abulmamhet (1739–71), and Abulmamhet's cousin Ablai (1771–81). They ruled over a horde consisting of four major clans, of which the Naiman was the most poweful. In wintertime, those Kazakhs took their herds into the lowland between the Turgai tableland and the estuary of the Syr Daria. In summer, they moved to the headwaters of the Tobol, the Ishim, and the Irtysh between Semipalatinsk and Omsk. The Eastern Horde roamed between the middle course of the Syr Daria and the Chirchik (on which Tashkent is located), Lake Balkhash, and the Zungar Alatau, a land of semi-desert drained by the Chu and the Ili Rivers. Its very location made it a dependency of the Zunghar ruler, to whom they paid tribute. The khan presided over three major clans and belonged to another Chingissid branch. The Western Horde roamed between the Ural, Emba, and Turgai Rivers, and consisted of three major clans. Its first khan was Abulkhair (1748), whose father was a distant cousin of Tauke; he was followed by his son, Nur Ali (1749–81).[80]

All three khans were elected by assemblies of notables representing the clans, but none was secure if he upset the consensus upon which his election had depended. His ability to control the clans was limited: they rode away beyond the khan's reach if they chose no longer to support him. This was the major source of instability which prevented the creation of a political organization transcending both clan and regional differences. A second source of instability was the absence of linear boundaries between the pastures of the hordes or even of clans, between the pastures of the nomads as a whole and Cossack settlements, and between the Cossacks and the Zunghars. Patterns of transhumance very much depended on climatic conditions. A drought or the feared winter frosts that turned the topsoil into an icy crust and buried the grass could decimate a herd and force clans to find pastures elsewhere. Instability and economic insecurity fostered hatreds between Kazakhs and Kalmyks, Kazakhs and Bashkirs. Kazakhs raided Cossack settlements, rustled horses, and took prisoners, whom they kept in slavery or sold to the oasis cities of Central Asia in need of unfree labour to man their irrigation works. Cossacks sent parties into the steppe, burned the grass, raided graves in search of buried treasures, and took their own prisoners.[81]

The personal and political weakness of Sameke and Abulmamhet of the Central Horde enabled Abulkhair of the Western Horde to give full play to his ambition to reunite the three hordes under the authority of a single khan. One of the two great Kazakh leaders of the period, he knew that he would need the help of the Russians against his enemies within Kazakh society and against the Zunghars, who, increasingly checkmated in Mongolia, dreamed of creating a steppe empire that would include the three hordes – and they had already subjugated the Eastern Horde and taken Tashkent. To guard against his internal enemies, he asked the Russians to build a fort at the confluence of the Or and Ural Rivers (Orenburg) and to accept his people as subjects of the empress. There was much opposition to the khan's policy, especially in the matter of sending hostages to Orenburg. The Russians were willing to recognize Abulkhair as the "main khan," but that was not included into the charter of February 1731, in which the Western Horde pledged to serve the Russian government, pay the *iasak* "as the Bashkirs do," and no longer attack caravans in the steppe. The Russians pledged not to conduct punitive raids into the Kazakh pastures and to defend the horde in case of attack, presumably by the Zunghars.[82]

The khan's position was ambivalent. While he needed the Russians, he also knew that they were dangerous rivals, what with the arrival of Kirillov, Tatishchev, and Nepliuev in Orenburg, all hard liners determined to expand the range of the core into the steppe. While the Russians were grateful in 1734 for his efforts to convince the Middle and Eastern Hordes to join his Kazakhs and become Russian subjects,[83] the Russians had no interest in recreating the unity of the Kazakhs under a single khan. They saw the Kazakh clan leaders (*starshina*) as so many clients helping to strengthen Russian influence in the hordes, but without an intermediary in the person of a "regional khan," who could bestow favours on his own. Nepliuev found an ally in Barak, the chief of the Naiman clan with its forty thousand *kibitki*, who opposed both the khan's ambition to strengthen his position vis-à-vis his rivals and his plan to place his son Nur Ali on the Khivan throne, left vacant by the execution of the khan by Nadir Shah in 1740, thereby consolidating his influence around the Aral Sea, where Barak wished to rule alone. The khan fell victim to the rising triangular antagonism between himself, Nepliuev, and Barak: he was murdered on Barak's orders in 1748.[84]

The murder of a Chingissid created shock even in Orenburg, and may have explained the smooth transition. Nur Ali succeeded his father, but also became the first khan to receive his investiture from Orenburg. The khanship was retained, but on Russian sufferance. His reign began shortly before the final Manchu onslaught against the Zunghars. Their victory cast a shadow over the steppe, and Nur Ali established relations with the Manchu court in 1762 – men of power in the frontier must hedge their bets. He gave asylum to the Bashkirs in 1754–5, and some of his Kazakhs joined the Pugachev rebellion. He was removed from office by Catherine II in 1786 for his inability to put down an anti-Russian uprising. By then, whatever remained of the Western Horde's independence had become a fiction, and the horde was ready to share the fate of its bitter rivals, the Kalmyks.[85]

The death of Abulkhair gave Ablai of the Middle Horde a chance to claim the leadership of the Kazakhs. He had long been the most influential notable in the horde under the weak rule of his cousin Abulmamhet, and his leadership qualities made him the second great Kazakh leader of the period.[86] He took the oath of allegiance to Catherine in 1762, but was already a Manchu subject. The Manchu emperor had declared in 1757 that the Kazakh pastures would not become part of the territory to be administered by Manchu officials after the crushing of the Zunghars, but that they would be tributary states like Annam and Siam – their leaders brought tribute and received their investiture from Beijing.[87] The Russians so distrusted Ablai that they refused to give him the title of khan until 1771. When he died ten years later, the Central Horde was neither fish nor fowl: some of its notables opted for a Chinese protectorate, but the supporters of Vali, Ablai's son, began to look upon the Russians as their protectors.[88] The Russo-Chinese frontier had slowly been breaking up and was about to disappear in the Kazakh steppe, but, as the Manchu empire began to decline after 1796, the Central and Eastern Hordes were doomed to fall into Russia's orbit. The former was integrated into the newly created Semipalatinsk *oblast* in May 1854, the latter in the Semirech'e *oblast* in July 1867.

Buriats and Yakuts

In distant Buriat country beyond Lake Baikal, to the border with Mongolia and Manchuria negotiated in 1728, similar processes were at work. Irkutsk on the Angara had been the power centre of the expanding core beyond the Yenisei River, and Nerchinsk was the most important point in Transbaikalia. The importance of Irkutsk grew throughout the eighteenth century: the city became the capital of a province in 1764, and a governor general was appointed there in 1783.

The extension of the local government reform of 1775 to the whole of Siberia resulted, as everywhere else, in increasing the number of local officials, including Buriat chieftains who became integrated into the command structure of the expanding core, with police and fiscal powers supported by the higher authority of the Russian intruder. Great distances and a sparse population of nomads constantly on the move made the Russians dependent on the cooperation of appointed and elected Buriat officials, the *taishi* and *noyons*. Ignorance of the exact number of nomads made the Russians dependent on farming out the collection of the *iasak*, a destructive system in which Buriat officials were required to deliver a reliable number of pelts in return for being allowed to collect as many more as they wanted. Here was an example of the "concession economy" at work, in which the resources of the territory were assumed to belong to the Great Sovereign, who generously allowed his faithful and obedient subjects – as long as they remained obedient – to partake of the wealth in return for the confirmation of their privileged position. Likewise, the distribution of pastures was done, not in accordance with the number of nomads, but according to the size of the herds,[89] so that the upper stratum, endowed with administrative, fiscal, and judicial powers, kept getting richer while the dependent population became poorer – a phenomenon characteristic of the whole of Eurasia in the eighteenth century. The policy of superstratification as a form of integration was supplemented with extensive co-habitation between the Russians, mostly men, and native women.[90]

Military integration played a crucial role in cementing the compact between the Russian intruder and the upper stratum of Buriat society. The establishment of a Russo-Mongolian border necessitated the construction of outposts and the creation of border troops to patrol the great distance between the Argun and the Irkut Rivers via Kiakhta, where Russians and Chinese traded pelts for tea and textiles. The Russian presence was still too weak to supply enough troops. In the 1730s, there were already – supposedly – five thousand mounted Buriats patrolling the border, but they must have been inferior troops because they were reorganized into four Buriat Cossack regiments in 1764 (of usually five hundred men each) who served on a permanent basis, and were exempted from paying the *iasak*. There was also a Tungus regiment, also of five hundred men, commanded by Prince Gantimur, a descendant of that Tungus prince who had so disturbed Russo-Chinese relations in the 1680s. The regiments were commanded by *noyons*, who gradually began to look on their command as a hereditary charge. The regiments were incorporated into the Transbaikal Cossack Host in March 1851.[91] While the Russo-Mongol border was not one of high-intensity threat, the reliance of the Russians on native troops to patrol the border reflected their trust in the compact with the Buriat leadership, which was now given an additional tool to maintain its dominion over the native population.

Other factors also encouraged integration. Russian authorities facing the nomadic world visualized a universe in which the nomad would settle down to till the land, side by side with the Russian peasant. There was always something disturbing for a person born and raised in the plain, and bound by a collective responsibility to pay taxes in accordance with registers assigning to each a fixed place of residence, to live with nomads who did not have any. To compel the nomad to settle on the land was the settler's civilizing mission, his revenge against the nomad who had oppressed and threatened him for three hundred years. Agriculture developed on patches of better land, especially in the Kudara steppe along the lower Selenga River, and around Irkutsk on the other side of the lake, not only among Russian settlers, "vagrants" (*guliashchie liudi*) who had crossed the whole of Siberia in search of a better life away from the Muscovite *voevody*, but also among the Buriats.[92] These Buriats gained from the proximity of the Russians: they learned to keep hayfields and build stores against the ravages caused by bad weather and the Siberian plague, which destroyed entire herds, the nomad's only source of subsistence. Agriculture began to bind Buriats to fixed places of settlement, and reduced migrations. Those who gathered around monasteries received seed grain and implements to raise grain for a guaranteed market, and if they chose to convert, they became "Russians" and were given exemptions from paying the *iasak*. They also entered the slippery road to serfdom: even if state peasants were not serfs, they became attached to a fixed abode and equated with Russian settlers, made into a dependent population at the mercy of an institutionalized ruling class of officials, Russian and Buriat alike, who oppressed them as they were oppressed everywhere else in the expanding Russian core. In the eighteenth century, the spirit of serfdom shaped attitudes toward both peasant and nomad.

Relatively few Buriats chose to change their way of life – perhaps not more than 15 per cent – on account of the rising demand for food products on the part of the Russians manning the forts scattered across the land. Nevertheless, the Buriats had to respond to changing circumstances, especially along the Irkutsk-Kiakhta corridor. The growing trade with China, in caravans or by individual traders, required guides, drivers, carts, axles, road maintenance, and the servicing of boats crossing the lake to avoid the long detour around its western tip. These activities transformed some of the nomads' pastoral economy into a money economy, and a government report of 1792 stated that the Buriats now preferred to pay the *iasak* in money, thus transforming the *iasak* into a form of quitrent similar to the one paid by the Russian peasant.[93] Thus, the Buriats most exposed to Russian activities – military, commercial, and mining (in Nerchinsk) – began to be drawn into the economy of the expanding core, where money rather than barter was making significant inroads beginning in the 1750s.

The slow political, social, military, and economic penetration of Buriat country in the eighteenth century reflected a utopian vision of transforming nomadic societies into one of settlers and its full integration into the expanding core. The same vision inspired Governor General Ivan Jakobi in the 1790s to imagine Eastern Siberia becoming the economic centre of eastern Eurasia and projecting power over Mongolia, northern China, and Korea – an unrealistic one, then and now.[94] Even if the Russian population increased to the point where it would absorb the Buriats, full integration would encounter an insuperable obstacle. The creation of a "Russian" society in the region would require, as elsewhere, the conversion of the native population to Russian Orthodoxy in order to create a unitary state. But Orthodoxy was certain to collide with the countervailing force of Tibetan Buddhism, well established in neighbouring Mongolia.

Tibetan Buddhism radiated a powerful influence all the way to Lake Baikal and was even carried by the Kalmyks to the Volga and even beyond Astrakhan. Its lamas formed a numerous class – they comprised as much as 15 per cent of the population – settled in the many monasteries built in every suitable place. They were not highly educated, and were even "grossly ignorant of the tenets of their own superstition,"[95] as a European smugly put it, but were close to their own people. They incarnated its collective identity in the great world of Tibetan Buddhism, with its local leader in neighbouring eastern Mongolia and its god, the Dalai Lama, in distant Lhassa. The books and images came from China, whose dynasty originated in Manchuria. The Russians treated the Buriats with contempt "because they were not Christians,"[96] and a good many Buriats converted, wore crosses around their necks, and learned to despise their unbaptized brethren. Here was an excellent example of superstratification at work, in which native leaders converted to the religion of the intruder to gain access to its ruling class and enhance their status vis-à-vis the dependent population. But behind this misleading façade of superstratification and integration, Mongol itinerant teachers visited villages and taught reading and writing, strengthening the gravitational pull of Mongolia,[97] then a dependency of China. Thus did Mongolia and Transbaikalia form a confessional frontier between Russia and China. The fact that Buriats and Mongols were ethnically much closer to the Chinese than to the Russians gave China a considerable advantage. Being a core religion, Buddhism could never be subjugated to Orthodoxy, and would constitute, like Latin Christianity in the western theatre and Islam in the mid- and lower Volga region and the Caucasus, a formidable barrier to the full integration of the Buriats. Superstratification and religious integration were mutually incompatible.

By contrast, Yakutia, even farther away, became one of the most interesting laboratories for a policy of superstratification. The journey from Moscow to Yakutsk took more than a year, and the round trip required from three to four years. Yakutsk, on the northernmost periphery of the Eurasian land mass, was four thousand kilometres from Kiakhta, six thousand from Tiumen at the entrance of Siberia, and eight thousand from Nizhnii Novgorod. No wonder that it was "one of the most lawless of all the Siberian provinces,"[98] where the Russian intruder fought the Yakut to establish his dominion, and the Yakut fought other native peoples to assert his own. Despite its abominable climate – the coldest in the world outside Antarctica – Yakutia was an attractive country in the basin of the Lena, rich in fish, with broad meadows and patches of fertile soil. Spring wheat, rye, and barley grew there, as did watermelons, and the taiga abounded in sables. Its Turkic population raised reindeer and horses rather than the horned cattle of the Buriats. The Russian-Yakut encounter had unexpected results.

The Russians did not bring slavery into Yakutia; it was already there when they arrived. *Toyons* had enslaved some of their own people, and other slaves came from tribes defeated in war. The Russians tried to abolish it in May 1733, but the practice continued, if only because slavery and enserfment were not always easy to distinguish. A local edict had to remind the *toyons* in 1750 that slavery was unacceptable. At the same time, the Russians were increasingly forced to rely on the Yakuts to administer the territory. In the 1750s the *toyons*' right to adjudicate small disputes and inflict corporal punishment was confirmed. They were in effect given police duties which integrated them into the command structure of Russian administration. They gained almost absolute power over the tribesmen, who were specifically deprived of the right to complain to the Russian authorities against unfair treatment by their own leaders.[99] Even if it was not recognized officially, a form of serfdom came to prevail in Yakutia.

It was also in 1733 that collective responsibility was introduced for the payment of the *iasak*, as it was in the Russian core for the capitation and the quitrent. The payment of the *iasak* was made mandatory for every male aged eighteen and over. This equation of the *iasak* with the main direct taxes paid by Russians had the same effect. It reinforced the *toyon*'s position as the representative of the Russian ruling class. It was he who became responsible for the collection of the tax and who had to pay for those who could not pay.[100] In so doing he created with the dependent population ties akin to serfdom. When the Yakuts were forbidden to travel beyond their districts without a permit delivered by a *toyon* or a Russian official, the structure of Yakut society came to resemble the Russian in more ways than one. In such conditions, the infrastructural reform of the 1780s integrated the Russian land captain and the *toyon* into a single stratum of administrative managers with extensive powers over the social and economic life of the Yakuts, undisturbed as they were by faraway Irkutsk. That the *toyons* also managed to acquire the best meadows and became the richest men in the territory was so obvious that it hardly needs to be mentioned.

Yakutia's location was not favourable in some respects. The valley of the Selenga connected a great lake with a major trading outpost on the margin of the large Chinese market. But deep snows and mountains difficult to negotiate separated Yakutsk from the bleak coast of the Sea of Okhotsk with its eponymous port, the home base of the "Pacific" navy until it was closed in December 1849 and replaced by Petropavlovsk on the eastern shore of the Kamchatka peninsula. Travellers had to sail down the Lena to its confluence with the Aldan, sail up this river and into the Maia and the Yudoma, and cross the mountains to reach the Urok draining into the sea. Goods and equipment were carried on pack horses, which often died on the way. The portage was one of the most difficult on earth. Yakut guides and porters (and Russians too) had to bear the burden. These demands only strengthened the apparatus of coercion, and may have contributed to the establishment of slavery and the existence of a state of semi-serfdom.

These demands were especially great during the so-called Kamchatka Expeditions.[101] Both the First (1725–30) and the Second (1733–43) were voyages of exploration – to study the physical geography of the land between Lake Baikal and Okhotsk, to determine whether Siberia and Alaska were connected or separated by a strait, and to charter the waters between Petropavlovsk and Alaska. Shipbuilding in Okhotsk required transporting food and heavy equipment like anchors, carts, and boats. It may not have been a coincidence that one of the headquarters of the Gulag would be built at Magadan, to the east of Okhotsk, but better situated for the time.

In such a context, it may seem surprising that *toyons* should petition Catherine II in 1789 to be given the status and rights of Russian noblemen, "a case almost unique in Siberia."[102] In fact it was not surprising, because Yakut society had become quite similar to that of its masters, and it was there that the fusion between Russian and native became close. The Yakuts asked for the right to elect their own representative – a marshal of Yakut *toyons* now transformed into noblemen. The petition must be understood in two complementary ways. If the *toyons* were recognized as nobles, they would gain the right, not only to protect themselves against the exactions of the Russians, but at the same time to treat their tribesmen the same way Russian landlords were treating their serfs. They asked to annul the practice of land redistribution (*peredel*), which meant in effect asking that their holdings become their private property. Even though the empress was favourable, the petition was not granted. It was too much to expect from a ruling class of settlers to accept as equals even the elders of a nomadic society. The nomad had once despised the settler; the reverse had now become the norm. Such a recognition was acceptable in individual cases, but it could not be a matter of policy: superstratification required that the upper stratum of the local society remain subordinated to the intruder's representatives.

But while elsewhere in the expanding core religious differences generated powerful resistance to integration, religion in Yakutia helped foster a process of integration. Yakutia was included into the new Irkutsk diocese in 1731, and the Orthodox Church sent out missions into the territory. Converted Yakuts were given a five-year exemption from paying the *iasak* and making contributions to the in-kind services (road repairs, supplying carts, etc) which weighed so heavily on the population. The missionaries were a hardy and intelligent lot, who earned the praises of posterity for their interest in Yakut culture – they were the first Russians to study the native language. Orthodox churches began to dot the landscape of the Lena valley, and by the end of the eighteenth century the bishop of "Irkutsk and Nerchinsk" could boast that the entire native population had been converted to the true faith.[103] Triumphant Church statistics may not have been truly reliable, but there were obvious similarities to the situation in the Kazan diocese, where the entire non-Muslim native population had become Christianized and "Russian." At the same time, the tax exemptions were cancelled, not only because of the success of the missionaries, but also because of the decreasing revenue from the *iasak* and the growing shortage of free carts. The success seems to have been long lasting if only because of the remarkable qualities of the bishops sent to Irkutsk. Veniamin (Bagrianskii) was a highly educated man of integrity, although short-tempered. He had visited Europe and preached before Catherine II. He was sent to Irkutsk in 1790 and died there in 1814. His successor, Mikhail (Bardukov), was a Siberian, born in Tobolsk, dedicated and modest, a great believer in education who had a hard time convincing his flock of the value of educating their children. He was raised to archbishop in 1826.[104]

There were several reasons for the success of Orthodoxy in Yakutia. The greater concentration of the population, a social order less nomadic than that of the Buriats, and the existence of a state of semi-serfdom made the Yakuts more receptive to the message of Orthodoxy. The Church was not on the defensive as it was when it faced Buddhism, Islam, and Catholicism, but was convinced of its superiority. There was no confessional frontier, but a territory ready to accept the message of a transcendental faith which promised integration into the wider world of the Orthodox Russian core. While it always felt insecure when it faced the other three core religions of Eurasia (leaving Protestantism aside), the Church was determined in Yakutia, with the help of the secular power from which it was indistinguishable, to conquer the world of the shamans. Shamanism was an animist cult of spirits and demons created by the native and surrounding him in his daily life. It was found all over Siberia, even west of the Urals, where the Orthodox Church managed to create in its work of conversion a synthesis between its own beliefs and those of the pagan world. Shamans were mostly men, but women were also found among them. In their behaviour, shamans resembled witches, and worked as intercessors between the native and the mysterious and immense universe in which he had found his way of life.[105] Shamanism was vulnerable to the efforts of a religion preaching to liberate the native from his fears and offering the promise of a better world. Nowhere else in the Eurasian land mass was Orthodoxy so successful as in Yakutia and the mid-Volga region in implanting its authority and, with it, that of the expanding Russian core.

Fiscal and Commercial Integration

Direct Taxation

Taxation remained during this second period the most effective agent of integration in the eastern theatre. The advance of the Russian settler deeper into the steppe and his overwhelming share of the total population west of the Volga and in the grasslands of Western Siberia brought about a natural extension of the fiscal system prevailing in the original core to its expanding peripheries in the agricultural zone. The rate of the capitation remained 70 kopecks until 1794, when it was raised to one rouble, but that of the *obrok* charged to state peasants rose significantly from 40 kopecks to 1 rouble in 1760, 2 roubles in 1768, and 3 roubles in 1783, raising by then the personal tax to 3.7 roubles per male of any age registered on the census.[106] The increase was officially justified by claiming that the landowning members of the ruling class had benefited from the improvement of the economic situation since the beginning of the 1750s, and had been charging similar rates from their serfs. It was felt that state peasants, as the collective property of the ruling class, must make a similar contribution to the treasury of the ruling elite which financed its army, its navy, and its officials in the capitals and the provinces. Registered townsmen continued to pay 1.2 roubles until 1794, when the rate was raised to 2 roubles. These rates applied to all Russian peasants and townsmen in the expanding core, but it had always been government policy to extend them to the native populations, in order not only to create a single fiscal system but also to integrate them into the broad mass of the state peasantry and create a uniform social structure throughout the expanding core. The original decree of 1724 applied the capitation and the *obrok* to all state peasants and Tatars, except those Astrakhan and Ufa.[107]

In the old Astrakhan khanate and the North Caucasian steppe, where peasant settlers were still so few and the Kalmyks roamed freely, it was premature to even think of extending the fiscal system to the periphery. Yet, the Kazan Tatars residing in the city paid a personal tax of 1.1 roubles, raised to 1.7 roubles in 1761, perhaps because their deliveries of horses for the dragoons and the train had become converted into a money payment. Since Astrakhan was a commercial city with a population of Tatars, Armenians, Georgians, and Indians, in addition to Russian merchants, the policy was to exempt them from the capitation until they chose to become "permanent residents" (*vechno poddannye*) – when they would be taxed like other Russian merchants – but to require them to pay an annual lump sum to "help" the Russian merchants, who had to pay the capitation until 1775 (when they won a permanent exemption) and contribute to a municipal fund for the housing of local troops and other needs.[108]

In the Orenburg Territory, which included Bashkiria, whose population, Russian and non-Russian, was largely engaged in agriculture, there was greater pressure to unify the fiscal system, and Tatars, Chuvash, Mordvins, Udmurts, and other natives who had not converted already paid both the capitation and the *obrok*. To extend the personal taxes to Teptiars and Meshcheriaks and Bashkirs generated considerable resistance precisely because fiscal integration was perceived as a device to achieve social integration into the core's social order defined by serfdom. Kirillov wanted a rapid integration of the Bashkirs by introducing the capitation, but such an intention became a factor in the outbreak of the terrible rebellion of 1735–41 and had to be abandoned, in as much as the Bashkirs had been told in 1728 that they would not be charged any taxes beside the *iasak* of 25 kopecks.[109] But there were other ethnic groups in Bashkiria which might offer less resistance. In 1747, the government accepted Nepliuev's recommendation to impose a poll tax of 80 kopecks on Muslim Teptiars and *bobyli* who had settled on Bashkir lands and had paid an *obrok* to their Bashkir landowners and, in addition, to continue drafting seven hundred men every summer for construction work in Orenburg and other forts on the line. The government also decided to place the Meshcheriaks in the same category as the Bashkirs, but these "Ufa Tatars" claimed that they had never paid such a tax before before, and refused to pay it.[110] Kazan Tatars, who had been invited to settle outside Orenburg, when there were still no Russian merchants, were charged 1.80 roubles, but also had to carry out certain services like carrying the mail. In 1766, the procurator general recommended they be placed in the same category as state peasants, but the Senate left their status unchanged, so that they actually paid more than Russian merchants. This inequality was justified by the fact that they were not subject to the draft.[111]

In Western Siberia, there was a definite trend to abandon forced grain deliveries in favour of a money payment. Governor Soimonov did not believe in the agricultural potential of Siberia and insisted on retaining the old system in effect since the conquest, consisting of tilling a separate acreage for official needs or forcing the peasants to deliver their production on their own carts to the forts on the line, at considerable distances from their fields. The governor refused to believe that this form of compulsory labour, and not the peasants' "laziness," explained why the peasants abandoned their fields and ran away or sought employment in the towns. He was fighting a rearguard action, however.[112] By the 1760s, no more than 10 per cent of the peasants worked on the *desiatinaia pashnia*, which was replaced first by a grain *obrok*, then one payable in cash. Only in Eastern Siberia, where there was so little agricultural land, was the *desiatinaia pashnia* retained, to guarantee a grain supply for the workers, many of them hard labour convicts, in the Nerchinsk silver mining district, and for the Cossacks and Buriat military units along the Mongolian border. The Senate rejected Soimonov's arguments for Western Siberia in 1762 and extended the *obrok* of one rouble per male to all state peasants – that is, nearly the entire peasant population of the territory. It argued that if the peasant could keep all his production, he should be encouraged to produce more in order to sell more in the market towns and raise his income, and the more he did, the lighter his tax burden would become.[113] The decision completed the integration of the West Siberian peasants into the fiscal system of the core: they had had to pay the capitation everywhere since 1724; they would now also have to pay the *obrok* in cash everywhere, except in Eastern Siberia. Only the Bashkirs and the native peoples of Siberia still paid the *iasak*.

But the *iasak* was increasingly equated with the *obrok*. A decision of 1731 concerning peasants of the Trinity Monastery north of Moscow, who had run away and settled in a *iasak*-paying village in Penza *uezd*, stated that the natives were paying a *iasak* of 40 kopecks, which happened to be the amount of the *obrok*.[114] Obviously, the *iasak* was already collected in money west of the Volga, but it was kept in a separate account (*iasachnyi oklad*), which preserved the fiction that Mordvins, Chuvash, and others remained a separate category of taxpayers, while in fact they had already been integrated into the fiscal system and the social order of the expanding core.

The Bashkirs remained attached to the *iasak* because it seemed to guarantee their status as a separate people with a right to own, lease, and sell land that distinguished them from the Russian peasantry. This became very clear when Nepliuev and the government decided to change their approach to fiscal integration. In 1754, on the eve of another Bashkir rebellion which was in part a consequence of that decision, Bashkirs and Meshcheriaks were given a permanent exemption from the *iasak*, but were not required to pay the capitation and the *obrok*. Instead, they were told to buy salt from the government monopoly at the official price of 35 kopecks a *pud* (16.4 kilograms or 36 pounds), in effect everywhere else in the region.[115] The reaction was fourfold. The Bashkirs claimed that salt lakes had been no one's property until then, and they had always obtained salt free of charge; that the government's taking over the lakes and the establishment of a monopoly on the sale of salt were therefore attacks on tradition and unjustified. They also claimed that the purchase of salt would cost them six times more than the *iasak*, and that the abolition of the *iasak* implied the abolition of their property rights (*votchinnoe pravo*). Some were convinced that the new policy was a back-door approach to the transformation of the Bashkirs into state peasants, which would them make them subject to the capitation, the *obrok*, and the draft. At best, it would transform the Bashkir communities into so many Cossack settlements, exposed to the arbitrary power of the governor and the fort commandants. The Senate, however, refused to change course, but took note of the Bashkirs' fears, and promised that their property rights would not be infringed.

In Siberia, especially in Eastern Siberia, the collection of the *iasak* continued to be a major source of abuses which poisoned relations between the Russians and the natives, but also strengthened the bond between the Russians and the clan leaders. Until the 1760s the collection was largely unregulated and left to the whims of the local authorities. Hostages were kept in forts to guarantee a steady supply of pelts, and the male population between the ages of eighteen and fifty remained responsible for bringing the pelts to the collection points or delivering them to the Russian and Cossack collectors who visited the camps and settlements. It was usually forbidden to accept the *iasak* in the form of a cash payment, and natives who did not engage in hunting had to buy furs at market prices and deliver them as their *iasak* contribution. A sore point was the method of collection. Russian officials and merchants as well as service Tatars who visited the camps committed abuses and violence, seized more pelts than they had been instructed to collect, and sold the difference on the free market. In 1740, they were prohibited from visiting the villages and *ulusy* unless the natives refused to deliver the pelts themselves. Clan leaders and notables were encouraged to bring the better-quality pelts with a promise of ranks in the service.[116] And natives were reminded that they could sell on the free market the additional pelts on condition of paying the 10 per cent tax on the sale.

By the 1750s, reports on the long history of abuses had reached the higher echelons of the government, and Catherine II appointed a commission in 1763 chaired by Guard Major (the equivalent of an army colonel) Alexei Shcherbachev to investigate the plunder of Buriats, Tungus, and Yakuts, and recommend measures to improve the collection of the *iasak*.[117] The result was a significant improvement, albeit a temporary one, as the old abuses reasserted themselves. The hostage system was cancelled, if only because it did not work, as clan leaders abandoned their relatives to their fate. The government conceded that the *iasak* could be paid in cash, and its yield was fixed at 122,075 roubles, raised to 156,590 roubles in 1769. Shcherbachev conducted a census of the natives of Siberia and found 90,520 males,[118] so that the contribution of each male amounted to about 1.75 roubles, almost identical with the poll tax–*obrok* combination of 1.70 roubles until 1768, but less than that of 2.70 roubles afterwards. The admission that the *iasak* was payable in cash or its equivalent in furs (in Buriatia it was also paid in *kitaika*, a blue or black cotton cloth imported from China) marked a recognition, not so much that the supply of animals was dwindling (it was), as that some of the natives were settling down and turning to agriculture on pockets of good land and to the cultivation of hay for the herds, an innovation that reflected in part the growth of Russian influence. The fur trade remained active, and the delivery of pelts as *iasak* contributions represented only half of it: in the seven years between 1775 and 1782 Siberia exported to China furs valued at 1,176,000 roubles, an average of 168,000 roubles a year.[119] The natives were obviously becoming integrated into the fiscal regime of the core, despite the fact that Eastern Siberia was a distant periphery, where soil and climate attracted but few Russian settlers beyond the Irkutsk area.

The reform of the *iasak* also affected the structure of native society, especially among the Buriats and the Yakuts. The collection of the pelts was finally vested formally in the clan leaders and notables, who were allowed to keep 2 per cent of the amount collected, whether in pelts or money. If the market price was low, they would pressure their clansmen to deliver more pelts; it it was high, it was preferable to demand a payment in cash.[120] Either way, the clan leaders could now develop a closer relationship with the Russian authorities, while keeping a free hand in the non-*iasak*-driven fur trade, from which they derived substantial wealth. The development of a money economy stimulated the growth of animal husbandry, an activity that favoured the constitution of large herds and the creation of wealthy and powerful owners. The native leaders used their power to control the allocation of hayfields, which were divided into five categories in the 1770s, the share of each clansman to depend on his ability to deliver a quota of sables and foxes.[121] This caused a trickling-down effect that increased inequality in native societies, but also facilitated the integration of the *toyons* and *noions* into the social hierarchy of the core, when temporary ranks (*za uriad*) were given to them in return for a cooperation in which both sides had a common interest.

The integration of the native into the fiscal and social system of the expanding core may be examined from another standpoint. A social system based on the ownership of half of the population by a small group forming the essential element of the ruling class, and the tight control exercised over the other half by the ruling class as a whole, showed little respect for human dignity, strivings for social autonomy, and the "general good," but sought instead to maximize the extraction of resources from the dependent population. The poll tax, *obrok*, and *iasak*, together with taxes on the consumption of basic necessities like salt and vodka (!), combined to form the lion's share of tax revenues.[122] An agrarian society with a weakly developed urban sector did not generate the substantial exchanges between town and countryside needed to create an elastic tax base capable of yielding steadily increasing revenue. As a result, the ruling class of the expanding core resorted to compulsion to carry out some essential services, compulsion that applied equally to Russians and non-Russians, assuming in the process that they were all *pod-dan-nye* required to pay tribute to a leadership that viewed governing as indistinguishable from conquest.[123]

A shortage of inns and the near-absence of barracks required that officers and officials, whether travelling on business or stationed in the towns, be given quarters in private homes and that soldiers be distributed among the villages. This was the norm everywhere, and one equally resented. Exemptions were considered a great favour.[124] Tatars, Bashkirs, Mordvins, and other nationalities of the mid-Volga region were not exempted. Tatar homes were known for their cleanliness, but Cheremis homes were shunned. The best merchant houses, "with a stone foundation," as the saying went, were reserved for the *voevoda* and his family. In Siberia, there were many complaints against officers, officials, and couriers travelling to and from the Chinese border who literally requisitioned merchant houses and forced the owners to find a refuge elsewhere. If they were allowed to stay, living conditions could become unbearable if there were women at home, and when visitors consumed expensive firewood and candles without regard to cost.

The postal service was also resented. In parts of Siberia, peasants and natives were simply drafted to become carriers (*iamshchiki*) and lived in separate settlements. The postal service was closely connected with other services that required long absences from home and the use of their own carts and horses by peasants and townsmen. The Kazan Tatars living in Astrakhan complained of their being sent as interpreters to Persia and Central Asia and as couriers to Moscow and Petersburg. Some Astrakhan Tatars carried the mail and bulky loads (*tiazhesti*) to Kizliar, 500 kilometres away.[125] Bashkirs had to transport construction materials from the mountains to the forts on the Orenburg Line. After the uprising of 1754–6, they won an exemption from this back-breaking occupation, and postal stations in sparsely populated places were closed. The Tobolsk and Tara townsmen complained that they had to work the entire summer on the boats transporting provisions for the troops on the Irtysh Line, and also had to carry the mail – a stupendous obligation when we realize that Semipalatinsk was 1,400 kilometres away from Tobolsk. Those of Krasnoiarsk complained that transporting the mail required them to leave their families and businesses behind for a long time and their fields unattended. The postal service also included supplying horses and carts for travelling officials.[126] The worst sufferers were the Yakuts, who had to contribute about fifteen hundred men every year and between six thousand and ten thousand horses to transport supplies from Yakutsk to Okhotsk across nearly impassable mountains.[127]

Resorting to compulsion to obtain unpaid-for services from Russians and non-Russians raises important questions about the nature of Russian rule. These services were a form of corvée labour in an economy which remained a natural one throughout the expanding core. Complaints often refer to the excessive amount of time devoted to the delivery of those services, so that too little time was left to earn money to pay for the personal taxes. Such a subsistence economy remained throughout the eighteenth century a largely hard-labour economy that integrated the entire population into a world marked by a common servitude. This was particularly true in the eastern theatre, where the population was sparse, distances often unimaginable, and climatic conditions unfavourable, and where the proximity of nomads ignorant of money did nothing to stimulate the growth of the money supply. On the other hand, this type of in-kind taxation provides a strong argument against the claim that Russian rule was another form of colonial despotism. While the fur trade might be used as an argument in its favour, the resort to compulsion to obtain services from

Russians and non-Russians alike certainly disproves it. If colonial rule had a distinguishing feature, it was that a ruling class of outsiders separated its own people from the natives, who were considered of inferior status. It did not mistrust its own people or use them to work in the mines, as the Russian authorities did in the mines of the Altai – one more reason to demonstrate that the Russians were not yet building an empire, but were merely seeking to preserve the internal integrity of an expanding core.

Consumption Taxes and Budgets

There were few other sources of revenue, but among them profits from the sale of salt and vodka were the most important. In 1724, both contributed 20 per cent of the revenue budget against 54 per cent from the poll tax and the *obrok*; in 1769, 29.8 per cent against 42.7 per cent; and in 1781, 41.2 per cent against 33.8 per cent respectively. Profits from the sale of vodka made up 31.6 per cent of the total in 1781. While the production, transportation, and sale of salt combined to constitute an economic and fiscal operation designed to improve the general welfare, the sale of vodka encouraged depravity among Russians and non-Russians and siphoned off funds which might be better used in productive investments. Both, however, also operated as powerful agents of integration within the expanding core.[128]

The entire core formed a large market for the sale of salt. Human beings and cattle needed salt in order to survive; salt was a basic preservative in curing meat and fish, and the frequent and long Orthodox holy days raised the demand for salted fish. Salt was also used in industry, in tanning for example. But salt was not found everywhere. There was boiled salt in Perm province (Solikamsk), produced by serf labour on the properties of the Stroganov family since the sixteenth century by boiling brines. There was rock salt, mined chiefly by hard-labour convicts near the Iletsk River in the steppe facing Orenburg; and there was lake salt, extracted by Kalmyks from Lake Elton in the Astrakhan steppe, and from the many salt lakes which had once been part of the enormous sea including the Aral, Caspian, and Black Seas. The lakes attracted nomads and their herds as well as Russians. Hence the importance of the Yamyshev lakes near the Irtysh, which formed a kind of oasis drawing Russians, Zunghars, and Kazakhs, and forced them to reach an accommodation of sorts, until the Manchus destroyed the Zunghars and the Russians built lines to keep the Kazakhs out. In the northern Caucasus, the steppe lakes of the Manysh depression drew the highlanders into the plain because there was no salt in the mountains, until the Russians built other lines to bar the way if the highlanders refused to find their place in the social order of the expanding core.

The three major sources of salt in the eastern theatre – indeed in the entire core – were Perm province (4.3 million *puds* in 1788), Lake Elton and other

Astrakhan lakes (5.3 million), and the Iletsk salt dome (700,000), giving a total of 10.3 million *puds* out of a grand total of 12.9 million. Siberia, chiefly Tobolsk province, yielded another 600,000 *puds* and was largely self-sufficient. The Yamyshev and other salt lakes in the vicinity supplied the whole of western Siberia, and the Irtysh between Tobolsk and Semipalatinsk had long been the major artery of the salt trade. But Perm province faced west, and its salt that was not marketed among the factories and mines of the Urals was shipped, like its metal production, via the Kama and the Volga to the northern provinces as far as Smolensk and Pskov, while the Elton and other Astrakhan salt was transported overland to the southern provinces, even though there was no clearly defined boundary between the two markets. Iletsk salt provisioned chiefly Nizhnii Novgorod and Ufa provinces, while Kazan got most of its salt from Lake Elton.

The government hesitated between two methods of provisioning the expanding core. One was to create a monopoly, assume the transportation charges (which could be quite high), and sell the salt in government-owned stores, from which traders hawked the salt to the villages and market towns. The other was to leave the trade free and charge a tax on the sale. But the market was so large and the sources of salt so far away that the free market could not be the preferred method, as the Physiocrats would find out in the grain trade of France: in a subsistence economy exchanges remained limited for the most part to connections between landed estates and villages with market towns nearby.

The sale of salt was declared a monopoly in 1705, and the sale price was pegged to twice the cost of the salt to the government upon delivery, but the operation proved too costly, and free trade was restored in 1728. The rising cost of military expenditures during and after the Turkish and Swedish wars induced Petr Shuvalov, the chief of the artillery, to call for the restoration of the monopoly with a uniform sale price of 35 kopecks a *pud* in 1750, raised to 50 kopecks in 1756 at the outset of the Seven Years' War, while calling for increased production by harnessing the resources of Lake Elton. This contradictory policy had the effect of reducing consumption and increasing smuggling. The price was reduced to 40 kopecks in 1762, and in 1781, following the administrative-territorial reform, the treasury chamber in each province assumed responsibility for the operation of the monopoly. The system remained in effect until 1817. Its consequence was to integrate the production of the peripheries into a market that included almost the entire expanding core, except perhaps Siberia, where distances from the centre created a regional market, but where salt was nevertheless sold at the same price.

The vodka monopoly had the same effect, but in different ways. Vodka was produced from rye, and rye was the staple crop everywhere from Pskov to Nerchinsk. The Russian settler brought the seeds with him to the clearings and patches of good earth that had never known the plough and in so doing carried out the agricultural unification of western and eastern Eurasia. Vodka did not need to be transported over long distances, unless it was produced commercially on large estates for the needs of Moscow, Petersburg, the army and navy, and a multitude of small regional markets, where production was inadequate. On the face of it, vodka was not a vital necessity, although it kept the body warm in cold weather, but its consumption could be raised by opening an ever-increasing number of taverns. Unlike the consumption of salt, which remains relatively constant, the consumption of vodka can be stimulated, even at the cost of damaging health and encouraging profligacy and debauchery. The government and the Church were often at loggerheads on this issue, one eager to find a tax with an increasing yield, the other more concerned with its impact on the parishioners' behaviour.

The government faced difficult problems in trying to extract the maximum yield from the sale of vodka. Since the proceeds represented a major source of cash in an economy always short of it, the nobility, as a ruling class engaged in the costly process of "Westernization," was given a monopoly over production, but it could not keep up with the demand, let alone an artificially stimulated one. As a result, merchants and townsmen were allowed to produce for the market in 1728. By 1753, nobles produced 1.7 million *vedra* on their estates (one *vedro* equalled 12.3 litres or 3.25 gallons), townsmen another 1.7 million, and government-owned distilleries 500,000 *vedra*, a total of 3.9 million *vedra*, but the share of the nobility had been declining. As a measure of self-defence, the government restored the nobility's monopoly in 1754, but townsmen were still allowed to keep producing only so long as the nobles could not meet the entire demand. The improvement of the economic situation beginning in the 1750s justified the government's expectations. In Siberia, where there were no noble estates, the government remained the exclusive producer of vodka, and had to be concerned over balancing the interest of the monopoly with that of provisioning the population, especially the troops, when the harvest was poor.

The sale of vodka presented different problems. The merchants sold vodka on behalf of the government, an additional type of in-kind taxation which they resented because they were charged with shortfalls; it was also sold directly in taverns "on trust" (*na vere*), or by agencies of municipal government (*magistraty*). The sale price was not uniform until 1750, when the price of a *vedro* was fixed at 1.88 roubles, raised to 2.54 in 1763, and 3 roubles in 1769. The statute of 1781 created a mixed system. It vested the operation of the vodka monopoly in the Treasury Chambers, which negotiated usually four-year contracts with the nobles for a mutually acceptable price at which to buy their production. The chamber then asked for bids by tax farmers to sell so many *vedra* at the official price. In order to guarantee the merchants a profit, they were allowed to keep the proceeds from additional sales, a decision that encouraged them to open as many taverns as they could.

The introduction of a single sale price throughout the expanding core played the same major role as the uniform price of salt as a factor of fiscal integration. No one will deny the deleterious influence of strong spirits, not only on Russians, who had grown used to consuming them, but also on the natives, who had not. Vodka helped the settler defraud the Bashkir of his land, the Buriat and the Yakut of his pelts. It debilitated human beings, although it does not seem to have affected the birth rate, as the size of the native population kept growing steadily. But moral considerations apart, the unifying influence of vodka was there for all to see. From the end of the sixteenth century, when the Kazan metropolitan complained that Tatars and Russians were already drinking together, to the end of the eighteenth century if not later, vodka brought Russians and non-Russians into a single community that cut across ethnic boundaries. Salt and vodka, even more than the capitation and the *obrok-iasak*, played a major role in the fiscal integration of the expanding core.

When we turn to the structure of the revenues collected in the ten provinces of the eastern theatre, two striking facts are immediately apparent. Direct taxes yielded almost half of the total, except in Astrakhan and Irkutsk, where the large nomadic population was tax exempt. It is unclear whether the revenue included the *iasak* collected in Siberia. It was included in the 1780s but was no longer shown on the tables for the 1790s. The other striking fact is the high percentage of the revenue from the sale of vodka, which reached almost half the total amount, especially in Siberia and the old Astrakhan khanate. Other large sources of revenue, but found only in individual provinces, included the revenue from the Urals industry in Perm province – especially from the minting of copper coins in Ekaterinburg – and the revenue from the China trade in Irkutsk. The salt monopoly yielded high returns in Astrakhan province for obvious reasons: salt was available in large amounts from local salt lakes and was sold to the local fishing industry. But on the whole, these two sources of revenue – from the head taxes and from the sale of vodka – made up some 80 per cent of the provincial revenue almost everywhere.

If we compare the relative share of the revenue with that of the population, it appears that the eastern theatre contributed more than was warranted by its share of the population. The population made up 17.7 per cent of the total for the "empire" but contributed 26.3 per cent of its total revenue. Half of that population (1.7 million) lived within the approximate borders of the old Kazan khanate, where the Russians had already settled in considerable numbers, but only less than 600,000 taxable males were found in enormous Siberia. Most depressing was the fact that the highest share of the revenue from the sale of vodka was also found there.

Among expenditures, the overwhelming share went to pay salaries in the provinces and the operating expenses of the salt and vodka monopolies (not shown on the tables). It had been assumed from the days of Peter I that the revenue from the head taxes would pay for the army, and it still did in the eastern theatre: 3.1 against 4.8 million roubles. Outlays for salaries, operating expenses, and the army alone added up to 12.8 million against a revenue from the head taxes of 7.3 million. In the southeast and Siberia, 2.3 million went for military expenses. The remainder of the revenue that was not assigned to the Commissary and the Navy was transported to the civilian Treasury in Moscow and Petersburg to defray administrative expenses. The six northern provinces contributed 1.5 million, the old Astrakhan khanate only half a million, and Siberia nothing. A separate account was kept in both treasuries for part of the revenue from the sale of vodka earmarked to pay the foreign debt. Tables 8.1 and 8.2 show the revenue from various sources and the expenses for various services in the eastern theatre at the end of Catherine II's reign.

The Persian, Orenburg, and China Trade

While the integration of the expanding core was proceeding apace, the prospects of using trade to integrate the core's outer peripheries, which had appeared so promising during Peter's reign, were growing dimmer with the passage of time. Relations with eastern Georgia made little progress, despite the large emigration of Georgians with Tsar Wakhtang in 1725 and the creation of a Georgian colony in Kizliar, which seemed to augur well for the establishment of sustained relationships. But Georgia's economy was largely a natural one operating on barter, and the country kept gravitating toward the Caspian and Persia. Trade was in the hands of Armenians, who peddled their wares in the mountains, in the market towns of Dagestan (such as Enderi, Aksai, and Kostek), and the major article of trade remained slaves, who were transported to the Crimea. However, a turning point was the opening of a custom house in Mozdok in 1764, followed by the Totleben expedition across the Darial Gorge into eastern Georgia in 1769–71. The expedition exposed the Georgian economy's backwardness, but also stimulated the local agriculture to supply provisions and forage for the troops.[129] It announced not so much the integration of the territory into that of the core as the development of a local economy geared to supplying the necessities of a modern army, an "ambulant city," dependent for its subsistence on local deliveries – in a word, the integration of the Georgian economy into the expanding market of the Russian army. It also contributed to the growth of Kizliar as the future major transit point between Astrakhan and Tiflis.

Trading with Persia, i.e, the attempt to tap into the transcontinental trade between the Caspian and northern (Mughal) India, offered at first bright prospects to realize Peter's ambitions, and the treaty of 1732, by which Russia renounced the provinces won (largely on paper) in 1723, gave Russian traders considerable privileges: it allowed them to travel freely in all the territories that

Table 8.1 Provincial revenues in the eastern theatre, 1795

	Head taxes		Vodka		Salt		Other		Total
	Roubles	%	Roubles	%	Roubles	%	Roubles	%	(roubles)
Viatka†	1,594,086	63.2	636,255	24.2	211,400	8.5	78,346	3.1	2,520,087*
Perm†	1,188,512	36.3	852,946	26.0	191,640	5.9	1,039,776	31.8	3,272,874
Kazan†	1,216,728	55.0	683,981	31.0	180,604	8.2	129,127	5.8	2,210,440
Simbirsk†	809,295	52.9	483,472	31.6	181,815	11.9	55,989	3.6	1,530,571
Subtotal	4,808,621		2,656,654		765,459		1,303,238		9,533,972
Astrakhan‡	156,187	14.0	608,593	54.7	235,703	21.3	111,479	10.0	1,111,962
Saratov‡	654,959	43.3	651,462	43.1	119,773	8.0	85,029	5.6	1,511,223
Orenburg‡	477,962	37.7	489,008	38.5	141,832	11.2	159,518	12.6	1,268,320
Subtotal	1,289,108		1,749,063		497,308		356,026		3,891,505
Tobolsk§	727,767	48.6	637,924	42.5	92,753	6.2	40,159	2.7	1,498,603
Kolyvan§	266,356	43.2	297,987	48.4	32,252	5.2	19,310	3.2	615,905
Irkutsk§	276,076	14.8	758,126	40.6	49,147	2.6	781,668	42.2	1,865,017
Subtotal	1,270,199		1,694,037		174,152		841,137		3,979,525
Total	7,367,928		6,099,754		1,436,919		2,500,401		17,405,002
Grand total for all three theatres	25,657,426		24,123,576		5,535,755		10,773,289		65,990,047
% from eastern theatre		28.7		25.3		26.0		23.2	26.3

Source: *SIRIO*, 1871, 6: 284–92.

Note: Total population (males) in the eastern theatre = 3,222,240. The grand total population (males) for all three theatres = 18,168,574. The eastern theatre forms 17.7 per cent of total male population.

* There is an error of 606 roubles between revenue and expenditures in Viatka province due to a typographical error in the table which I have been unable to identify.

† Population (males) of Viatka, Perm, Kazan, and Simbirks = 1,751,422

‡ Population (males) for Astrakhan, Saratov, and Orenburg = 876,200

§ Population for Tobolsk, Kolyvan, and Irkutsk = 594,618

Table 8.2 Disposition of provincial revenues in the eastern theatre

	Retained for provincial expenses (roubles)	Sent to Commissary (roubles)	Sent to Admiralty (roubles)	Sent to Treasury in Moscow and Petersburg (roubles)	Other (roubles)	Total (roubles)
Viatka	487,491	890,000	–	1,000,000	141,990	2,519,481*
Perm	1,996,924	270,000	–	–	1,005,950	3,272,874
Kazan	482,479	500,000	800,000	300,000	127,961	2,210,440
Simbirsk	503,820	620,000	80,000	200,000	126,751	1,530,571
Subtotal	*3,470,714*	*2,280,000*	*880,000*	*1,500,000*	*1,402,652*	*9,533,366*
Astrakhan	427,315	500,000	–	–	184,647	1,111,962
Saratov	869,314	250,000	–	260,000	131,909	1,511,223
Orenburg	526,451	300,000	–	300,000	141,869	1,268,320
Subtotal	*1,823,080*	*1,050,000*	–	*560,000*	*458,425*	*3,891,505*
Tobolsk	463,499	870,000	–	–	165,104	1,498,603
Kolyvan	277,090	250,000	–	–	88,815	615,905
Irkutsk	749,547	200,000	–	–	915,470	1,865,017
Subtotal	*1,490,136*	*1,320,000*	–	–	*1,169,389*	*3,979,525*
Total	6,783,930	4,650,000	880,000	2,060,000	3,030,466	17,404,396
Grand total for all three theatres	22,966,837	13,780,855	5,349,617	14,762,737	9,129,997	65,990,047
% from eastern theatre	29.5	33.7	16.4	13.9	33.2	26.3

Source: *SIRIO*, 5: 284–92.

* There is an error of 606 roubles between revenue and expenditures in Viatka province due to a typographical error in the table which I have been unable to identify.

were part of the shah's dominion without paying any duty on goods brought in from Russia for sale or barter, and if they wished to go to India either by land across Persia, or by sea, they would pay no duty on this transit trade. It is unclear whether many Moscow merchants took advantage of these privileges, but Armenians, Georgians, and Indians certainly did by claiming to be Russian merchants, an abuse which aroused the strong opposition of the Persian trading community.[130] Yet, those were challenging if difficult times, what with the rise of Nadir Shah and his ambition to recreate a Persian empire stretching from the Suram range to the Hindu Kush, which would bring back security to the transcontinental route. The value of Russo-Persian exports, stimulated by the logistics of Persian military operations, averaged 450,000 roubles a year between 1737 and 1745, and that of imports 300,000 roubles, the commercial balance in Russia's favour providing a handsome source of gold and silver. The "Russians," it was said, "had no competitors."[131]

But the death of Nadir Shah in 1747 was followed by forty years of internal disorders, of which trade was the major victim. The richer Armenians left for Turkey and India and even Holland, and took their capital with them. The Russian traders who ventured into Persia were robbed of their goods, and ceased to go to Enzelinsk on the Caspian coast, the port of entry into Persia for the sea route from Astrakhan. Persian traders who went to Astrakhan encountered the traditional Russian prohibition against foreign traders entering Russia – they were confined to the border cities of Astrakhan, Arkhangelsk, and Petersburg. They could hire Armenian and Russian agents, but these were poor substitutes for employing their own skills in Saratov, Kazan, and Moscow.[132] The abolition of internal customs duties in 1754 contributed greatly to the unification of the expanding core, although the costs of inland transportation remained a major obstacle to the creation of a single, fully integrated, market. Until 1750, the Astrakhan trade remained unregulated. That year, the 1731 tariff in effect in western Eurasia was extended to cover Russian exports to Persia and "other Asiatic places," and Russian imports were taxed at 5 per cent *ad valorem*. The custom regulations of 1755 imposed a duty of 13 per cent on the transit trade to Persia and on Persian imports into Russia, a high duty which, combined with restrictions on foreigners entering Russia, was hardly calculated to develop exchanges with "Asia."[133]

To make things worse, ominous developments were taking place on the Indian subcontinent. The Seven Years' War (1756–63), which the Russians fought against Prussia, was part of a world-wide conflict between Britain and France in North America and India, where the East India Company emerged without competitors. The accompanying disturbances induced Indian traders to seek to revitalize the transcontinental route. Catherine II, who came to the throne in 1762, saw an opportunity "to return to Peter's idea of extending our borders to Persia's detriment";[134] one only had to find a reliable location for an emporium, from which to direct the Indian trade along the internal waterways to Petersburg. Such an ambitious program was so unrealistic that it was quickly abandoned, although the attempt made in 1781 to establish a naval and commercial base at Astarabad, as well as the Georgievsk treaty of 1783 with eastern Georgia, showed that it remained part of Russia's global vision in the eastern theatre. But a radical redirection of the trade routes had already taken place. It had become cheaper to ship textiles from Bengal to Petersburg than to send them overland via Astrakhan. The cost advantage of sea transportation threatened to create a centrifugal reorientation of the Persian and "Asiatic" trade away from the Russian-dominated continental market toward a British-dominated transoceanic market.[135] Paradoxically, however, the resulting destruction of the Central Asian transit trade and economic stagnation of the Central Asian economy were bound to reorient the economy of the oasis cities toward the Russian market and raise the possibility of an eventual integration into the economy of the expanding core.

By 1767, the "once flourishing" city of Astrakhan was reported to be in a state of "astonishing decay," and the Astrakhan governor reported in 1771 that the trade was in full decline, with ships lying idle in the harbour, and that both Russian and Persian traders – the latter now used to getting long-term credit from the East India Company – were showing no interest in the trade.[136] Yet the trade did not die. The average value of Russian exports during the four years between 1777 and 1781 amounted to 338,927 roubles, in which the lion's share belonged to two articles: foreign cloth (40 per cent) and dyes (30.5 per cent), mostly madder grown in the Caucasian highlands, followed far behind by metal and woollen goods, sugar, and "spicy roots" (about 5.2 per cent each). The import trade was even more lopsided. Silk and silk articles occupied 67.3 per cent of the annual average of 315,100 roubles, followed by cotton and cotton goods (13.9 per cent), and furs (7.5 per cent).[137] These figures point to two characteristic features of the trade: the overhelming importance of foreign cloth – with no mention of Russian-manufactured cloth – in what was essentially a transit trade, and the crucial role of silk imports. Russia imported one basic commodity and exported another, but one produced by foreigners rather than in its own factories. The Astrakhan custom revenue for 1783 was a paltry 410,000 roubles, against 183,000 roubles in Arkhangelsk, and 974,682 roubles in Riga.[138]

The fiscal and economic integration of the old Kazan khanate – what with the "rising tide" of Russian settlers, the centripetal flow of salt and iron up the Volga from Lake Elton and down the Kama from Perm and Solikamsk, and the transformation of Kazan into a hub for the supply agencies of the army in the region and as far south as the Caucasus – created centrifugal forces toward and beyond the periphery of the expanding core, whose limits were still cautiously being mapped out. The existence of the frontier exposed the interdependence of the economy of the settler and that of the nomad – the settler needed cattle and horses, the nomad needed grain and metal goods, among which cauldrons and knives occupied pride of place. The Russians, who disliked uncontrolled activities, channelled the trade with the Kazakhs through Orenburg on the Ural River and Troitsk on the Ui River, which became "staple cities," in order to maximize its benefits among the population of the forts along the Orenburg and Ui lines. The growing importance of Orenburg acted as a magnet for the Ural Cossacks, who, like the nomads they resembled in so many ways, brought wild boars, the hides and horns of steppe antelopes (a supposed aphrodisiac), wolf and fox pelts, and live hawks and eagles to hunt more wolves and foxes. Since money was unknown in the region, they bartered their goods for honey and cattle with the Bashkirs and Kazakhs.[139]

But all was not well with the Orenburg trade. Nepliuev reported in 1749 that it had not reached the expected levels, even though it was very profitable for Russian merchants, who brought to the town goods valued at nearly 140,000 roubles a year. Yet few Russians were coming, and the trade was largely in the hands of the Tatars whom the governor had invited from Kazan, who also took Russian goods into the steppe. The trade attracted Khivan and Bukharan merchants, who also bartered their goods. If gold and silver were nearly unknown in their monetary form, they were sold as commodities in the form of bars or bags of gold dust. The rate of exchange varied. In 1763 one *zolotnik* (4.26 grams or 0.15 ounce) of gold sold for 2.75 roubles, one of silver for 19.5 kopecks. To the Russians, the great value of the Orenburg trade was in the opportunity to barter their own goods for pure gold and silver at a time when the Cabinet had just acquired the gold mines of the Altai, the only source so far of native gold.[140]

The great obstacle to the integration of the edge of the nomadic frontier was the refusal to lift the old restrictions on the acceptance of non-Russian traders into the core and on Russian merchants selling their goods retail in the towns they visited: they were required to sell them wholesale to local merchants (*grazhdane*), who would then resell them retail in their own stores. This assumed the existence of well-to-do merchants with enough capital to participate in wholesale trade, but there were no such people in Orenburg, let alone Troitsk, and Russian merchants coming from the interior faced the prospect of bankruptcy – perhaps the major reason they were not coming. In 1752, the government opted for a compromise, and applied to the Orenburg trade the rules in effect at fairs (which were temporary towns) until Orenburg had enough well-off merchants. It invited European, Bukharan, Khivan, and Kashgarian merchants and all the steppe nomads to engage in wholesale and retail trade, although Europeans coming from the ports and border towns would have to pay the 10 per cent transit tax.[141] The custom regulations of 1755 required "Asiatic" merchants who brought goods from Asiatic places to pay only a 5 per cent duty; Russian merchants who brought goods from abroad had to pay an 18 per cent duty. The regulations retained the prohibition that Asiatic merchants might not bring foreign goods to Kazan and other Russian towns unless they were willing to pay a 28 per cent duty (including the 10 per cent transit duty). Asiatic traders who took Russian goods abroad were charged the 5 per cent duty, but the Russians 13 per cent.[142]

Orenburg faced south, toward the Aral Sea and, via the Amu Daria, toward Khiva and Bukhara, but trade routes were insecure because caravans had to cross Kazakh territory, and the nomads had always looked upon them as an object of plunder. For that matter, Cossacks were not above doing the same thing, if they could get away with it. The route was also difficult because no firewood and sometimes no water were found in the steppe. Nevertheless, the trade grew because it met the needs of all parties, the Russians, the Central Asian traders, and the nomads themselves. The same situation prevailed in Western Siberia, bound with the Orenburg Territory by the same line of forts facing the Kazakh steppe. There, one needs to distinguish between the 1730s and 1740s, on the one hand, and the period following the destruction of the Zunghars, on the other.

Caravans from Central Asia reached the Irtysh in the fall, and followed the river on the way to the Irbit fair held in January and February, from which the goods went on across the Urals to Kazan and Moscow. The overland commerce was supplemented by the trade of the market towns which grew with the number of forts and the increasing population of Russian settlers. This local trade contributed to the integration of the edge of the frontier between settler and nomad, separated only by the artificial boundary of the line of forts. Kazakhs came to the line to barter horses and cattle, including oxen, for grain and flour, ribbons, yarn, and needles. Horses were in great demand because of recurrent epidemics of Siberian anthrax, and dragoon horses often had to be replaced every year. Slaves were also sold. A seven-year-old Kalmyk boy was bartered for goods valued at 15 roubles, a twelve-year-old Kalmyk girl for 20 roubles; a dragoon horse cost the equivalent of 18 roubles, a gelding was bartered for five *arshin* (140 inches, 355 centimetres) of "Silesian" cloth valued at 4.57 roubles.[143] The eastern Kazakhs roaming close to the Irtysh traded with the Zunghars, exchanging fox pelts for grain. The Zunghars were also the intermediaries between the Russians, the Kazakhs, and the Chinese traders in Mongolia. To draw the Kazakhs closer to the Irtysh forts, General Kinderman established marts in Semipalatinsk and Yamyshev in 1745, but the trade grew very slowly.[144]

The disturbances accompanying the disintegration of the Zunghar khanate caused the Russian authorities that same year to forbid their merchants to trade in the Kazakh *ulusy* and with the Zunghars. By 1760, Zungharia had been laid waste and was eliminated as a trading partner. But Petropavlovsk on the Ishim, founded in 1752, was opened for trade in 1759. It grew steadily and would eventually become the major trading centre for the Russians and the Central

Horde, although it would always lag behind Orenburg with its well-known "exchange market" and the presence of a high-ranking personage representing the central government. Petersburg thought the Russians could replace the Zunghars as the trading partners of the Chinese, and toyed with the idea of creating a trading outpost at the confluence of the Irtysh and the Bukhtarma, but it would never grow, largely because the Manchus refused to accept the opening of a second staple city (beside Kiakhta) for the Russo-Chinese trade.[145] The consequence of the Zunghars' elimination was to leave the Kazakhs hemmed in commercially between the Russians and the Central Asian oasis cities, the latter being increasingly drawn into the orbit of the expanding core, while Persia was being pulled into the commercial orbit of British India.

The volume of the Central Asian trade (from Orenburg and the Siberian lines) remained inferior to the Russian trade with Persia (and Asiatic Turkey). During the four years between 1768 and 1772, exports averaged 212,712 roubles a year. As in the trade with Persia, the main article was foreign cloth (57 per cent) with only a very small share of Russian cloth. It was followed by dyes (12.4 per cent) and soft leather (*iuft*, a Russian specialty, 9.4 per cent), and some metal goods. Imports for the years 1777–81 averaged 227,944 roubles a year, with the lion's share belonging to cattle and horses (63.9 per cent), followed by cotton goods (26.1 per cent). The Orenburg custom revenue in 1783 reached 60,957 roubles, that of Tobolsk (for the trade on the line) a mere 1,440 roubles.[146]

The Russo-Chinese trade remained the best example of international commerce in the eastern theatre which failed to develop its potential. There were at least four reasons: the inability of the Siberian waterways to offer a commercially profitable trade route; the Chinese insistence on conducting trade at Kiakhta alone – Tsurukhaitui withered away – and their view of trade as a weapon to gain concessions from the Russians in border disputes; the rampant corruption in the Siberian administration; and the costs of overland transportation, which gave an edge to the sea traders in the northern Pacific.

The Manchus closed the trade in 1737 and 1738 and for fifteen of the forty-seven years between 1744 and 1791, sometimes for a few weeks or months at a time, once for five years in a row (1768–73). The government-run caravan trade came to an end in 1757 and free trade was proclaimed in 1762, with some negative consequences, such as the lifting of restrictions on the export of certain valuable furs.[147] The volume of trade varied considerably from one year to the next, but its composition remained remarkably constant. It was even more lopsided than the Russo-Persian and Russo-Central Asian trade. The annual average of Russian exports for 1777–81 was 1,518,209 roubles, of which furs made up 77.4 per cent, followed (again) by foreign cloth (13.8 per cent) and soft leather (5.8 per cent). Annual imports of 1,594,097 roubles were dominated by cotton goods (66.8 per cent), followed far behind by tea, usually associated with

Table 8.3 Russia's trade in the eastern theatre, 1777–81*

	Persian trade†		Asian trade‡		China trade	
	Exports	Imports	Exports	Imports	Exports	Imports
Foreign cloth	125,323	–	121,390	–	210,134	–
Russian cloth	–	–	8,500	–	4,239	–
Cotton	2,275	43,763	5,998	63,037	481	1,065,077
Wool	17,414	796	–	2,375	1,461	–
Silk	11,704	218,973	9,276	488	708	211,174
Dyes	103,509	13,306	26,433	–	–	359
Cattle and horses	209	680	34	145,613	12,545	–
Furs	2,164	23,727	2,778	16,431	1,175,364	–
Metal goods	20,137	–	5,307	–	1,800	–
luft	3,297	–	20,105	–	97,899	–
Sugar	17,665	–	1,920	–	–	8,913
Tea	–	–	–	–	–	266,735
Other	35,230§	13,855**	10,971††	–	13,488‡‡	41,839§§
Total	*338,927*	*315,100*	*212,712*	*227,944*	*1,518,119*	*1,594,097*

Source: Semenov, ch. 3, 450–71.
* annual averages, in silver roubles
† and with Asiatic Turkey
‡ annual averages for 1768–72
§ including "spicy roots" (17,870), linen (12,775), grain (3,138), and paper (1,447)
** including dried fruit (9,461), grain (4,102), "beverages" (184), tobacco (108)
†† including grain (9,433), mirrors (750), wax (389), paper (234), spices (125), and tobacco (40)
‡‡ including antlers (rogi, 7,810), mirrors (4,235), linen (1443)
§§ including precious stones and pearls (32,223), tobacco (6,182), and dishes (3,434)

the China trade (16.7 per cent), and silk articles (13.2 per cent). The customs revenue was 522,987 roubles in 1783, still far less than that of Riga.[148]

Nevertheless, the China trade made a powerful impact on the life of the Siberian settlers. Despite the transportation difficulties, it was still easier to travel in Siberia, where the nomads posed no threat, and where land and water transportation combined to give an advantage to free travel across the sandy wastes separating the Central Asian oases from the Kazakh steppe. A type of Chinese cotton good, the *kitaika*, was sold everywhere in the market towns and even served as a medium of exchange. Siberian women learned to appreciate Chinese silk scarves and ribbons, and the official chanceries wrote their reports with Chinese ink. Almost the whole of Siberia dressed up in Chinese (and Bukharan) cloth, and Chinese green tea (which the Russians did not like) was resold to the Kazakhs, who preferred it to black tea.[149] Thus the overland commerce of Siberia had the effect of integrating eastern Eurasia into

Table 8.4 Summary of eastern theatre trade, 1778–80 (annual averages)

Total "Asiatic" trade (roubles)	
Exports	2,069,748
Imports	2,137,141
Total	*4,206,889*
Total European trade (roubles)	
Exports	16,494,106
Imports	11,695,103
Total	*28,189,209*
% from eastern theatre (Asiatic trade)	
Exports	12.5
Imports	18.3
Total	*15.0*

Source: Author's personal computations.

the Chinese rather than the Russian commercial orbit. Moreover, the Russians faced another threat similar to the one they faced in Persia. British whalers in the northern Pacific began to bring furs to Canton, the other staple city where the Chinese traded with foreigners. The pelts which the Russians brought back from the Aleutian Islands to Okhotsk had to be transported over the hellish route from that port to Yakutsk, shipped up the Lena to Irkutsk and then up the Selenga to Kiakhta. During that time, British traders could make several trips between Northwest Canada and Canton at lower cost.[150] While Chinese merchants were slowly integrating Siberia into the commercial orbit of the Asian coastland, maritime commerce threatened to accelerate the process by destroying the major prop of the Russian export trade.

Chapter Nine

Unitary State or Empire? 1782–1830

The Administrative Infrastructure

Regional Integration

The 1780s marked a decisive turning point in the history of the eastern theatre. The Georgievsk Treaty of 1783, which established a protectorate over eastern Georgia, heralded a return to Peter I's forward policy in the Caucasus, and the short occupation of Tiflis (Tbilisi) by Aga Mohamad Khan, the founder of the Qajar dynasty (1796–1925), in 1795 threw down the gauntlet to Russia in what had been Persia's advanced position in Transcaucasia against the Ottoman empire beyond the Suram range. The disintegration of the Georgian dynasty, however, resulted in the annexation of eastern Georgia in 1801 and the creation three years later of a new military headquarters in Tiflis facing Persia in the east and the Turks in the west. Such a dramatic change in the geopolitics of the Caucasus was associated, in addition, with the arrival in 1804 of a new proconsul, Pavel Tsitsianov, related to the Bagratid royal house of Georgia, who stated that it was his ambition to recreate the Greater Georgia of Queen Tamar (+1213?), whose realm had once linked the Black Sea with the Caspian.[1] War with the shah, whose capital had moved from Shiraz to Tehran in 1789, was inevitable.

The first war of 1804–13 ended with the Treaty of Gulistan, which conceded to Russia all the Muslim khanates between eastern Georgia and the Caspian coast, together with those of Kuba and Derbent and the whole of Dagestan between the crests of the Great Caucasus and the sea, drained as if in a great fan by the four rivers which converged to form the Sulak. In effect, the treaty expelled the Persians from Caucasian Azerbaidjan, separated from Persian Azerbaidjan by the Araks River and the Talysh range, the northernmost extension of the Elburz Mountains embracing the southern coast of the Caspian to the mountain periphery of Khorasan and the Kopet Dag, beyond which Central Asia began. The second war of 1826–8 ended with the Treaty of Turkmanchai, which gave Russia the two Armenian khanates of Yerevan and Nakhichevan, and established the Russo-Persian border along the Araks to the fording place Gdibuluk, then followed the Talysh range to the Astara River. From that time on, Persia gradually fell into being a semi-protectorate of Russia, which gained the right to approve the selection of the shah's heir, who, as custom dictated, had to reside in Tabriz, a mere 125 kilometres from Djulfa on the Araks.[2] But the annexation of eastern Transcaucasia, completed in 1828, exposed the Russians to the same raids which had devastated eastern Georgia for generations, incited by Turks and Persians alike, who had an interest in destabilizing a country with a warlike tradition, and much effort and considerable resources would be wasted in subduing the highlanders.

At any rate, one thing was certain. Russian settlers would not move in any significant numbers beyond the valley of the Terek into the mountains and across the mountains into the desolate basin of the Kura between the river and the Alazani, or into the Mugan steppe, which bloomed in wintertime and attracted large numbers of nomads, but became in the summer a waterless, treeless, and saline snake-infested steppe. Nor would they want to move into the Armenian highlands of narrow valleys and upland basins severed from one another by difficult mountain barriers without any sizeable area of arable land.[3] Transcaucasia, save for a few blessed places, was a land of fevers, caused for the most part by sharp temperature changes within a single day.[4] The Russians, as men of the plain, were allergic to the entire physical environment of the Caucasus, even if it stimulated the literary creativity of a Pushkin, a Lermontov, or a Bestuzhev-Marlinskii. The core could not expand here; integration would be counterproductive. The expanded core was becoming an empire, but it would take time to recognize the obvious.

The Emperor Paul I (1796–1801) did not like regional authorities who interfered with direct links between the central agencies – which he restored and which would become ministries in 1802 – and the provincial governors. As a result, governors general were abolished, yet it was already understood that provinces bordering on the open steppe or the Russo-Persian or Russo-Chinese frontier faced intrinsic problems unknown to those situated in the interior of the core; above all, military problems with a bearing on the strategic posture of the central government. Paul appointed instead military governors in Astrakhan, Orenburg, and Irkutsk, to command both regular and irregular troops in their provinces, while the Siberian Corps commander functioned as a de facto military governor in the southern part of Tobolsk province. The post was unknown in the Russian provinces, except in those of the two capitals.

In the Caspian sector, eastern Georgia was transformed into an ordinary province immediately after its annexation in September 1801. It was divided into five *uezds*, and the khanate of Ganzha, renamed Elizavetpol, became a sixth *uezd* in 1813. In 1802, two separate provinces were created north of the

Caucasian Line, Astrakhan and Caucasian. The latter's capital in Georgievsk was moved to Stavropol in 1824. The nine *uezds* in both provinces were reduced to eight in 1822. Each province had a civil governor (called *pravitel'* in Georgia until 1811), subordinated to the military governor, who operated in accordance with the Statute of November 1775 with the help of the same provincial agencies as elsewhere in the core, but somewhat simplified in view of the still limited volume of business. In Tiflis, there was a Supreme Georgian Government, an extravagant title for a provincial agency that resembled a general assembly of the Provincial Board, the Treasury Chamber, and the civil and criminal courts, with some Georgian princes and nobles among their members. In Georgievsk, there was a "provincial government" largely identical with its equivalent across the mountains.[5]

The Muslim khanates annexed in 1813 were not integrated into the provincial system. Sheki (Nukha), Karabag (Shusha), and Shirvan (Shemakha) retained their khans as long as the title remained in the family in power at the time of the annexation or as long as they were not found guilty of "treasonable" activities. The khans continued to consider themselves clients of the Persian shah, and when they got into trouble with the Russians, they were likely to cross the Araks. Yet, the Russians, busy consolidating their rule in eastern and western Georgia, remained at first very tolerant. The khans lost their power to impose the death penalty, which had been abolished in Russia in 1753, but continued to govern their Azeri Turkic subjects as they pleased.[6] In 1824, however, the three khanates were renamed *provintsii* (harking back to the old eighteenth-century Russian term for the subdivision of a province), each under a commandant, with a translator of "Tatar" and Armenian, a policemaster, a court, and a treasury. All three were combined under a district military officer (*voennyi okruzhnoi nachalnik*). A second district incorporated the Baku, Kuba, and Derbent khanates. Thus, the Muslim provinces, stripped of their khans, were placed under military administration. Dagestan, still unpacified, was essentially a war zone. The Yerevan and Nakhichevan khanates were combined in 1828 to form an Armenian *oblast*, and the Talysh khanate remained a separate entity. Both were placed under the authority of majors general but retained considerable internal autonomy.[7]

To cap this "provincial" administration, the government was forced to resort to a regional authority similar to that which had been abandoned in 1796. Lt.-Gen. Karl von Knorring, the military governor of Astrakhan, was appointed military governor of Georgia in 1801, but the title was not retained. Tsitsianov, his successor, a full general and the first such high-ranking officer to become a regional delegate of the central government in the eastern theatre, was appointed chief administrator (*Glavnoupravliaushchii*) and commanding general of all troops in the Caucasus. He resided in Tiflis, where he was the de facto military governor. This remained the situation until 1844, when a viceroy (*namestnik*) was appointed. The leading figures among these proconsuls, beside Tsitsianov, were also full generals: Alexei Ermolov (1816–27) and Ivan Paskevich (1827–31), who left to become viceroy of Congress Poland for twenty-five years (1831–56).[8]

Paskevich is known, among other things, for perhaps the first attempt to face the issue of territorial administration beyond the expanded core, as well as his failure to realize that an empire was in the making. Unlike Ermolov, a charismatic figure for his troops, who left a controversial legacy because of his ruthless determination to crush the resistance of the highlanders, Paskevich believed that the flagrant disorders he had noticed could be remedied by introducing the agencies and personnel of the core provinces and discontinuing military rule, including the trial of criminal and even civil cases by court martial. He claimed that military rule only delayed the process of enlightenment. Administrative, fiscal, and legal unification (by superseding local laws and customs) would serve an educational purpose, reduce the local peoples' feeling of alienation among themselves and toward the Russians, and instil the "Russian spirit" among them (*priblizit' narod k obshchemu dukhu Rossiian*).[9] Such a prescription flew in the face of reality both in the mountains and in Transcaucasia, but it heralded what would become the myth of a "one and indivisible Russia," the failure to accept the fundamental distinction between a core, which was reaching its natural limits, and other lands beyond it, which constituted the new Russian empire in the eastern theatre.

Elsewhere in the Caspian basin, administrative, fiscal, and legal unification had already taken place in the provinces that had once been part of the Kazan khanate, and the Orenburg Territory remained Ufa province with a civil governor. The retention of a military governor in Orenburg, who also commanded the regular and irregular troops in the province, was justified, not so much by the multi-ethnic composition of the population, as by the unsettled conditions in the Kazakh steppe beyond the Ural River and Russian ambitions in Central Asia. These were imperial ambitions, unrelated to the internal situation in the province.

Further east, in Siberia, the government also faced the consequences of the abolition of the post of governor general. Kolyvan province was merged with Tobolsk, now disassociated from Perm. Tobolsk province encompassed the whole of Western Siberia, Irkutsk province the whole of Eastern Siberia. But the Altai was so clearly a separate territory that a new Tomsk province was detached from Tobolsk in 1803.[10] Nevertheless, the enormous size of Siberia – in which the continental United States can easily fit – raised problems common to the whole of eastern Eurasia, such as the sensitive issue of keeping the troops provisioned, the maintenance of communications, and in general, the coordination of responsibilities from one territory to another. In 1803, the government created the new post of governor general of Siberia, and its first incumbent,

Lt.-Gen. Ivan Selifontov, was instructed to administer Siberia in accordance with the statute of 1775 – clear indication that Petersburg looked upon Siberia as a part of the expanding core.[11] He was given some additional (but very vague) powers which dealt chiefly with the administration of the Nerchinsk territory (the Amur question and relations with China), Yakutia (Russia's presence in the Sea of Okhotsk), and Kamchatka (relations with Alaska and Russia's presence in the northern Pacific). Here too, these responsibilities were essentially imperial in nature, with hardly any connection with the internal administration of the three Siberian provinces. Selifontov's successor, Ivan Pestel, was a civilian – he had been director of the Moscow Post Office. After visiting Irkutsk in 1809, he returned to Petersburg, where he would remain until his dismissal in 1819, leaving the de facto administration of Siberia in the hands of the three governors.[12] Endemic corruption, arbitrary power in isolated communities, and the autonomy of governors (especially in Irkutsk), unchecked by a governor general residing in a distant capital, compelled the government to appoint Mikhail Speransky, with a mission to draw up statutes for a drastic overhaul of the entire Siberian administration.[13]

The product of Speransky's efforts was twelve statutes,[14] of which the first is of particular interest here. It divided eastern Eurasia into two governor generalships, Western Siberia with its capital in Tobolsk, Eastern Siberia centred in Irkutsk. The governor general of Western Siberia was also the commanding general of the Siberian Corps, thereby ending the division of responsibilities between a civilian and a military official which had been in effect since 1745. However, the post of commanding general was so much more important that the governor general moved his residence to Omsk in 1838.[15] Thus, a governor general was considered necessary to deal from Omsk with Russia's ambitions in the Kazakh steppe and Central Asia, very much in the same way as a military governor was needed in Orenburg. However, both governors general were lieutenant generals, while the Orenburg military governor was, as a rule, a full general, showing that Orenburg outranked Omsk in the formation of imperial policy in the region.

To help the governors general cope with their responsibilities – and to check the arbitrary use of their power – the statute created two Main Administrations consisting of the governor general and a council (*sovet*) of six members, all appointed by the emperor, three on the governor general's recommendation, the other three representing the Ministries of Interior, Finance, and Justice. Other officials were invited when matters came up in which they had a particular expertise. Each council had a chancery of twenty-six clerks, including two translators of "Tatar" in the west, one of Manchu and one of Mongol in Irkutsk. Since the governor general was the regional delegate of the War Ministry, the council functioned as a kind of regional assembly of ministerial delegates, in which that of the War Ministry and his three candidates had the dominant voice – showing once again that the new regional authorities were designed to serve the needs of an expanded core turning into an empire – as it would indeed later become with the conquest of Central Asia, and the annexation of the Amur valley with the Maritime Province. The council had no funds and no executive power. It deliberated without the governor general, who was empowered to reject even a unanimous recommendation. However, other regional delegates could appeal the decision to their respective minister.

To the Western Siberian Main Administration were subordinated the civil governors of Tobolsk and Tomsk, and a major general in charge of a new Omsk *oblast*, who functioned as a military governor. In Eastern Siberia, the civil governors of Yeniseisk (a new province), Irkutsk, and Yakutsk *oblast* reported to the Main Administration in Irkutsk; so did the Border Administration at Troiskosavsk near Kiakhta, the Okhotsk Coastal Administration under a naval officer, and the Kamchatka Coastal Administration based in Petropavlovsk. The provincial administration followed the model in effect in the core of Western Eurasia, but there were also provincial councils, which, however, were no more than permanent general assemblies of the three main provincial agencies.[16]

The Siberian statutes were intended not so much to supersede the Statute of 1775 as to create agencies and procedures designed to take into consideration the special conditions of Siberia. These included the native peoples scattered across enormous distances, the Kazakhs of the Central Horde, the "town Cossacks," the exile system, transportation and in-kind services, and grain stores. Are we then justified in claiming that Siberia was no longer considered part of the core? It seems that the question was often on the mind of Siberian administrators, as we learn from a decision of 1831, when the Siberian Committee ruled that, unless a general ordinance (*postanovlenie*) specifically annulled provisions of the Siberian statutes, these must continue to prevail. Regional law seemed to prevail over imperial law.[17] However, the statutes essentially created procedures to govern the operations of agencies for which there was no need elsewhere in the core, and did not create a body of substantive Siberian law, nor was one needed in a region where the Russians formed an overwhelming majority by the 1830s. Fiscal legislation, the civil and criminal law, as well as the penal law, remained in force across the entire core. Siberia never had its own budget, unlike Transcaucasia and even Turkestan later in the century. There was no contradiction between the existence of an integrated core and the creation of agencies and procedures to deal with specific problems of a regional nature. The Siberian Committee itself, created in 1822 to examine Speransky's proposals – a restricted committee of ministers for Siberian affairs – was closed in 1838, as if to signify that Siberia no longer needed a defender for a non-existent special status.

The enactment of the first Siberian statute created a momentum for an attempted administrative unification of the entire eastern theatre save for the

Orenburg Territory. The statute was introduced with some modifications in the northern Caucasus in 1827, with a Caucasian *oblast* subordinated to a Main Administration in Tiflis, but the statute left its composition and powers undefined, because it would have to wait until the reorganization of the Transcaucasian administration itself.[18] This took place with the statute of 1840, which extended the 1822 statute to that territory as well. The chief administrator was assisted by a military governor in Tiflis, who was the chairman of a council of five members appointed by the emperor, with other members invited when needed.[19] A Caucasian Committee was created in 1842, which would remain in existence until 1882. But the resemblance to Siberia went no further. Fiscal and judicial legislation did not extend to Transcaucasia, where the Russian settler population was non-existent. The chief administrator commanded a substantial number of regular troops, and stood outside the council, which itself was outside the ministerial hierarchy. Transcaucasia remained a war zone, beyond the core, in the new empire.

By the 1840s, however, deeper administrative integration was taking place. The statute of April 1840 on the administration of Transcaucasia introduced the territorial division of the core into the region, which was divided into two provinces (*gubernii*), one uniting the Georgian lands ("Gruzin-Imeretinskaia"), the other called an *oblast* ("Caspian") for the Muslim territories. With the arrival of a viceroy, General Prince Mikhail Vorontsov (1844–54), a further division took place in December 1846. Eastern Georgia became Tiflis province, and the Caspian *oblast* was divided into two provinces, Derbent and Shemakha. In January 1849, the Armenian *oblast* became Yerevan province. In the meantime, the "Caucasian *oblast*" north of the mountains had become Stavropol province in May 1847. By 1850, the Caucasian territory that was part of the eastern theatre had been divided into six provinces and a number of smaller units under the viceroy residing in Tiflis.[20]

The territorial reform affected Siberia as well. It was a prerequisite to the introduction of an administrative infrastructure paving the way for further integration during the tenure of the governor general of East Siberia, Nikolai Muravev (1847–61). In January 1851, the Kamchatka peninsula with a long stretch of the Okhotsk coastline was made into an *oblast* under a military governor. In July, the counties (*uezds*) of Irkutsk province beyond Lake Baikal were combined to form a Transbaikal *oblast* administered by a military governor in Chita. Yakutia remained an *oblast*, and Irkutsk province became a much smaller one; both were placed under a civil governor. East Siberia had now been divided into two provinces (with Yeniseisk) and three *oblasts*. West Siberia still consisted of Tobolsk and Tomsk provinces under a governor general residing, no longer in Tobolsk, but since 1839 in Omsk on the edge of the Kazakh steppe. There, a Semipalatinsk *oblast* was created in May 1854, extending Russia's presence beyond Lake Balkhash to the approaches of Central Asia. On the western edge of the steppe, a Samara province was created in November 1850, incorporating the land between the Volga and the Ural Rivers.[21] The military governor in Orenburg now became governor general of Orenburg and Samara. Not only was the territorial reform laying the foundations for a deeper Russian integration in the region; it was also setting the stage for the assault on Central Asia about to take place in the 1860s.

Army and Cossacks

These administrative reforms and the changing perceptions they represented on the management of the core and the imperial periphery required adjustments in the deployment of the troops. After the first Turkish war of 1768–74, the peacetime army had been deployed in territorial "divisions," of which there were twelve in the 1780s. During the second Turkish war and the partitions of Poland of 1793–5, the territorial system was abandoned in western Eurasia, and the army was deployed in operational sectors, whether in the Danubian Principalities or in eastern Poland.[22] With the return of peace and the accession of Paul, the army was again divided into territorial formations called "inspections." Three of the twelve were in the eastern theatre: the Caucasian and Orenburg Inspections under their respective military governors, and the Siberian under its separate commander. The inspections of western Eurasia were abolished in 1806 and became operational divisions, combined into corps, created in 1810. The Caucasian Inspection became a division in 1807, the other two in 1808. As the war with Napoleon became imminent, the corps were in turn combined to form armies. When it was over, in 1814, two armies were deployed in western Eurasia, each consisting of army corps. Each army was under a commander in chief, one residing in Mogilev in Belarus, the other in Tulchin in Podolia. They reported to the emperor and the chief of staff. In addition, "separate corps" (*otdelnye korpusa*) were deployed in the imperial peripheries. Three of them were in eastern Eurasia: the Caucasian, originally called Georgian until 1820, the Orenburg, and the Siberian. Separate corps commanders had no commander in chief and reported directly to the emperor and the chief of staff. They were given a set of powers slightly inferior to those of a commander in chief.[23] In Tiflis and Orenburg, the corps commander was also the chief administrator and the military governor respectively; in Omsk, he was also the governor general of Western Siberia beginning in 1822.

As the new Russian empire grew to unprecedented size in western Eurasia, the disparities between its two theatres and the third in eastern Eurasia became more pronounced, and showed quite conclusively that, except in the Caucasian sector, a Russian military presence was primarily designed to defend the edge of the expanding core, which in the Kazakh steppe was about to reach its natural limits, against nomadic raids by the Kazakhs. These raids were already losing their intensity, and frontier defence was becoming hardly more than a form of police control.

There were still regular troops in Siberia in the 1780s – one regiment of infantry, two of dragoons, two battalions of *Jägers*, and six field battalions, no doubt intended to show a token presence facing a China which remained, if not hostile, at least haughty and strong in former Zungharia. Chinese influence was so pervasive in the Kazakh steppe, especially in the Central and Eastern Hordes, that Catherine II justified the appointment of a senior commandant as far west as Troitsk in 1783 by the need "to handle border affairs with the Chinese state,"[24] at a time when Tobolsk had ceased to be a border province and was becoming an "internal" one – fully integrated into the core. The deployment of 1801 showed three regiments of infantry, two of them stationed along the Irtysh and on the Kolyvan Line; two of dragoons on the Ishim Line and interspersed with the infantry on the Irtysh Line; and two of *Jägers* along both lines. There were also eight battalions of garrison infantry between Petropavlovsk and Biisk. A third regiment of *Jägers* was created in 1805.[25]

This deployment would not last. In 1808, when the Siberian Inspection was renamed the Twenty-Fourth Division, it was ordered to withdraw all regular troops from Siberia and to create a ten-regiment Siberian Line Cossack Host of 5,950 officers and men.[26] By the late 1780s, the line Cossacks – distinguished from the town Cossacks – numbered about 2,000 men, but it was a poorly integrated force without its own commander, patrolling the lines between beacons (*maiaki*) at random and keeping communications open. Two thousand soldiers' children (*soldatskie maloletki*) who remained in Siberia after the departure of the troops were incorporated into the new host and were joined by various other people without a definite place in society. The host was given an artillery complement (twenty-four guns) and an *ataman* subordinated to the commander of the Siberian lines, who could then assign Cossacks to serve anywhere along a 2,400-kilometre-long line as circumstances required. These Cossacks, who had been until then without a sense of mission, began to develop an *esprit de corps* and a comprehensive vision of Western Siberia and the steppe, when they were sent to convoy caravans to Turkestan, Tashkent, Kokand, and Kashmir and do topographical work in the steppe. By 1838, the Siberian Separate Corps (by then the Twenty-Third Infantry Division) consisted of fifteen line battalions in four brigades. To three of the battalions were attached a number of *uezd* invalid units and convoying troops (*etapnye komandy*) to handle the despatch of exiles. The fourth brigade consisting of four battalions was in Eastern Siberia, under the jurisdiction of its governor general. In March 1851, border troops in East Siberia were consolidated to form a Transbaikal Cossack Host of four Russian and two Buriat mounted regiments of 750 Cossacks each, under an *ataman* subordinated to the governor general.[27]

In the Orenburg Territory, whose periphery merged imperceptibly with that of Western Siberia – to the point that Governor General Igelstrom recommended in 1788 that the Orenburg and Siberian Corps be merged to constitute a single formation facing the Kazakh steppe – there were still in 1801 three regiments of infantry stationed in Kazan, Ekaterinburg, and Orenburg, one of dragoons in settlements which had once been forts on the Transkama Line, two battalions of garrisoned troops in Kazan and another two in Orenburg, and six battalions along the line beginning at Simbirsk. Three years later they were reduced to four and renamed settled line battalions. These battalions served as military colonies, very much like the old land militia. They consisted of descendants of "ploughing soldiers" (*pakhatnye soldaty*) no longer fit for active service, who had been settled in the Kazan region and the Orenburg Territory since the middle of the eighteenth century. These troops were expected to build houses, raise families with Russian, Kalmyk, or Kazakh women, engage in agriculture and animal husbandry, and do basic training three or four weeks a year "so that they do not lose the military habit."[28] Regular troops seem to have been withdrawn from the territory as well, because the deployment of 1819 mentions only line battalions, whose number had reached twelve by then.

Cossacks had always played an important role in the history of the Orenburg Territory and the valley of the Ural River. While a distinction had emerged in Siberia between the town and the line Cossacks, some Cossack regiments in the Orenburg Territory were incorporated into the regular army, while others remained "irregular," settled, Cossacks. Thus by 1787, the Orenburg Cossacks already supplied two regiments to the regular cavalry. The Orenburg Host of irregular cavalry numbered at the time 5,156 officers and men, the smaller Ural Host, 4,027.[29] In 1798, the Orenburg Host was divided into five "cantons" to make it easier for the Cossacks to serve closer to their homes.[30] In 1807, a separate Cossack regiment of 1,000 men was created outside the canton system, called originally the *ataman*'s regiment (*Atamanskii*); it was renamed "permanent" (*nepremenny*) in 1821. Stationed in the environs of Orenburg, it had to be ready to leave on short notice for the front – it made it to Paris in 1814. By then, there were four such regiments, but three were disbanded after the war. In 1835, a "First Orenburg Cossack Regiment" was formed with disbanded regiments of native troops. The Host was given a new statute in 1840.[31] Its duties increased with the construction of the Ilek Line beginning in 1810 to convoy salt shipments from the local salt mines to the Volga. The Cossacks were strongly opposed to moving, and it would take more than ten years to compel them to resettle. A second "New Line" was built in the mid-1830s between Orsk and Troitsk, while the Cossacks kept advancing into the agricultural land of the western Kazakh steppe.[32] As to the Ural Host, it was reorganized to form ten regiments in 1803 from a total population of 14,618 males, but these regiments never seem to have joined the regular cavalry. They were used instead to patrol the lower course of the Ural River, where tensions were growing between the Western Kazakhs and the Kalmyks.[33]

By 1838, the Orenburg Separate Corps (called the Twenty-Second Infantry Division) consisted of ten Orenburg line battalions in two brigades, with thirteen *uezd* invalid units and two *etapnye komandy*. The Cossacks consisted of the Orenburg Host (the First and Permanent Regiments), a Cossack brigade of mounted artillery; the Ural Host; and two hosts of native troops, the Kalmyk and the Meshcheriak.[34]

While the centre of gravity of Russian military activity in the eastern theatre had been the Orenburg Territory in the eighteenth century – what with the Bashkir rebellions, the Pugachev rebellion, and Kazakh pressures in the wake of the Manchu conflict with the Zunghars – it decisively shifted to the Caucasus in the nineteenth century, when the Russians began to build an empire beyond the core's natural limits. Two battalions of infantry were sent beyond the Caucasus in 1784, when Vladikavkaz was built on the Terek, marking the entrance to the road linking the headwaters of the Terek with those of the Aragvi flowing into the Kura near Tiflis. They were withdrawn at the beginning of the war with Turkey of 1787–92, but the annexation of eastern Georgia in 1801 was accompanied by the deployment of five regiments of infantry, four of dragoons, and two of *Jägers*.[35] They were stationed on both sides of the mountains, not only to establish a military presence in Transcaucasia but also to face the highlanders from north and south, in anticipation of what would become the longest military conflict Russia would ever face – a guerrilla war in the mountains that lasted nearly eighty years, from Sheikh Mansur's revolt of 1785 to the surrender of Shamil in 1859. A Georgian Corps was created in 1811, combining the Nineteenth Division deployed on the Caucasian Line and the Twentieth in Transcaucasia. When Ermolov arrived in Tiflis in the fall of 1816, the Georgian Corps consisted of three regiments of infantry (about 6,500 men) and three of *Jägers* on the line (about 2,170 men), five of infantry and one of *Jägers* in Georgia with a regiment of dragoons in seven squadrons (1,260 men), and fifteen regiments of Don Cossacks (about 8,300 men). The corps had an artillery park of 132 guns. If we add two battalions of garrisoned troops in Astrakhan, three in Vladikavkaz, and two in Kizliar, reserve troops, and the local Cossacks, the corps numbered up to 45,000 men.[36] Nowhere in eastern Eurasia had such a Russian force ever been deployed, even if the high mortality rate among the troops considerably reduced its effective strength. Eventually, the corps would be given the status of an army with a strength of about 100,000 men. In 1834, the line battalions were reorganized into Georgian, Caucasian, and Black Sea battalions, the last formation stationed in western Georgia.[37] The fifteen Georgian battalions were stationed in Transcaucasia, from Akhaltsykh on the Suram range to the Caspian coast; the eleven Caucasian battalions, on the Caucasian Line and in the mountains, with one stationed in Astrakhan and commanded by the military governor.

As to the Cossacks, they numbered 5,828 men in 1812, divided into settled and line Cossacks. The settled Cossacks went back to the sixteenth century and consisted of the Grebentsy (684 men), the Terek-semeinye (432 men), and the Terek-Kizliar (143 men), forming three hosts on the Terek River. The line Cossacks were organized in regiments (sometimes also called hosts): the Mozdoksky (1,286 men) facing Little Kabarda and part of Chechnia; Volzhskii (781), moved from the Tsaritsyn Line in 1777, facing Great Kabarda between Georgievsk and Mozdok; Khoperskii (867 men) in Stavropol, but moved to the Kuban and the Kuma in 1826; Kubanskii (765); and Kavkazskii (813 men). The Mozdok unit of highlanders (*gorskaia komanda*) still existed, but consisted of only 57 men, and faced the rest of Chechnia. In addition, there were three regiments of Astrakhan Cossacks, combined to form a host in 1817 and consisting of about 1,600 men, a grand total of 7,400 Cossacks.[38]

By 1838, the Caucasian Separate Corps consisted of the Nineteenth Infantry Division in the northern Caucasus and the Twentieth in Transcaucasia, each consisting of two regiments of infantry and two of *Jägers*. There were in addition two regiments of cavalry and one of grenadiers forming a reserve and two artillery brigades. The sixteen Georgian line battalions were apportioned among the general officers, who also administered the several Muslim provinces and the Armenian *oblast* (but not eastern Georgia), with two attached to the reserve. The eleven Caucasian line battalions were commanded by the commandants of Piatigorsk, Vladikavkaz, and Kizliar, and the Astrakhan military governor.[39]

Unlike the situation in the Orenburg Territory and Siberia, the mission of these troops was not to police borders and keep the peace in provinces ending along the edge of settlement. In the northern Caucasus, their major duty was to cope with the resistance of the highlanders to accepting the incorporation of the plain below into the expanding core. Relations grew worse after Ermolov's decision to move the line from the Terek to the Sunzha, which was a more suitable periphery of the agricultural zone, because the land between the two rivers was fertile black earth. It had already been settled by the so-called "peaceful" Chechens.[40] The war in Chechnia – the "Caucasian" War was chiefly a war to conquer the mountain fortress of Dagestan – was fated to be a desperate one, because neither side could win a decisive battle, at least until 1859. The Russians could not commit large forces in the mountains – the terrain and dense forests precluded the use of cavalry and restricted the scope of the search-and-destroy operations to battalion- or regiment-size units, which struck quickly and withdrew as soon as their work was done. The mission of those troops was to achieve the impossible – to integrate into the agricultural zone a mountain massif with an irreducible population that could never become integrated politically, socially, religiously, or economically. Beyond the Terek and the Sunzha, a one and indivisible Russia came to an end and an empire began.

In Transcaucasia, Russia was likewise building an empire by simply annexing part of another empire. The Treaty of Georgievsk brought about the sack of Tiflis twelve years later. The creation of a regional military headquarters in the city in 1802 led to war with Persia two years later. The first war of 1804–13 began as a fight over the control of the Armenian church. The Persians had 20,000 men, the Russians not more than 10,000, but they relied on a Georgian militia and their superior artillery. They also suffered from a lack of provisions in a region where a money economy was almost unknown. The Muslim khanates fell into Russian hands one after the other, but the Russians failed to take Baku and Resht with their flotilla based in Astrakhan. In 1806, Tsitsianov was treacherously assassinated by the khan of Baku, who had offered to surrender, and was replaced by Ivan Gudovich, who had served in the northern Caucasus in the 1790s. He now had 12,000 men and forty-eight guns against much larger Persian forces commanded by Abbas Mirza, the heir to the Persian throne. Hostilities were nearly suspended between 1807 and 1811, when Russo-Persian relations became intertwined with Russia's relations with France and Britain, but they resumed in 1812, when Abbas Mirza sought to reoccupy the Muslim khanates. He was decisively defeated at Aslanduz on the Araks in October. The Russians then occupied Baku and Lenkoran, and negotiated the peace of Gulistan a year later.[41]

However, Russian successes still amounted to no more than a tactical victory, because the Persians retained possession of the khanates of Yerevan and Nakhichevan, from which they could make a rapid advance up the valley of the Akstafa and Borchala Rivers against Tiflis.[42] Abbas Mirza struck in 1826, taking Ermolov by surprise, although it was well known in Tiflis that Persia would seek to recover its hegemony in eastern Transcaucasia. He and his allies had about 100,000 men, but it was an undisciplined force, no match even for a Caucasian Separate Corps of nominally 45,000 men, which was 12,000 men under strength, and could not put more than 15,000 men in the field, the others doing garrison duty all over the Caucasus. By September, Paskevich, who had replaced Ermolov as corps commander, crushed the Persians before Elizavetpol. In 1827, the Russians, now numbering 24,000 men, took Yerevan and moved on toward Tabriz, Abbas Mirza's residence.[43] The Treaty of Turkmanchai of February 1828 destroyed Persia's hegemony in eastern Transcaucasia once and for all, and established Russia's own. None of the conquered territories could ever be truly integrated into the expanding core. They were imperial possessions beyond a one and indivisible Russia, despite a persistent assumption, born of a long history, that they eventually could.

The creation of separate corps, whose commanders were directly responsible to the chief of staff of the army (after 1832, the war minister), amounted to the development of regional agencies for a central ministry. It is possible, indeed quite likely, that this phenomenon served as a model for the creation of similar regional authorities by other ministries, even though some of these authorities actually antedated the creation of separate corps as territorial institutions. After the creation of the Ministry of Education in September 1802, its operations were made to rest on a network of five universities as regional centres for a number of provincial educational networks. Education in the eastern theatre was still so undeveloped that there was no separate region for the Caucasus and Siberia. Education was left to the discretion of governors and governors general. The Caucasus did not form a separate region until December 1848, the Orenburg Territory until May 1874, and Western Siberia until March 1885, seven years after the foundation of a new university in Tomsk. The integration of the eastern theatre was depressingly slow, but only because economic and social conditions remained so primitive.[44]

The administration of roads and waterways was divided into ten regions in 1809, reduced to five in 1836. Viatka and Perm provinces were in the Second Region with headquarters in Vytegra; Kazan, Simbirsk, and Astrakhan in the Third Region (Moscow), but Siberia remained the responsibility of provincial governments. The postal administration was reorganized into thirteen regions in 1830: Kazan and Simbirsk provinces were in the Third (Nizhnii Novgorod), Astrakhan and the Caucasus in the Sixth (Odessa), Viatka, Perm, and Ufa provinces in the Tenth (Perm), and Siberia in the Eleventh (Tobolsk). The military and political police (gendarmes) also had their own regions, eight in 1838: the Caucasus in the Sixth Region (Tiflis), the mid-Volga provinces in the Seventh (Nizhnii Novgorod), Siberia in the Eighth (Tobolsk, later Omsk).[45] These regional authorities, responsible to their respective headquarters in the capital, cut across historical boundaries and served as an excellent example of administrative integration of the expanding core into a unitary state, even though the attempted integration of Transcaucasia, as an imperial territory, was bound to remain a pious wish.

Peoples

Progress continued to be made toward the creation of a "one and indivisible Russia," but the emphasis was now placed on military and judicial integration, a natural consequence of the administrative integration of the 1780s. It seemed that the goal of social integration was being reached, with non-Russians drawn, at least formally, into the great mass of the peasantry, while the more tolerant religious policy, if it recognized that the conversion of the adherents of the other two core religions was only a distant possibility, nevertheless created an administrative organization with a definite place in the political infrastructure of the emerging empire.

In Transcaucasia, where the prospects of integration were the bleakest because the land was inhospitable to the Russian settler, and which was therefore an imperial territory beyond the expanded core, eastern Georgia was the exception. The Georgians were Orthodox, and the church was quickly integrated into the hierarchy of the Orthodox Church, not without some opposition rooted in the vested interest of the bishops, traditionally close relatives of the Bagratid house and powerful landowners. There was also opposition to the policy of reshaping the Georgian nobility after the Russian model, doing away with the excessive number of princes (*tavadi*) and nobles (*aznaury*), who could submit no evidence of their social status.[46] But once the dynasty had been removed by the Russians, it was relatively easy to appeal to the national pride and martial spirit of the Georgians, and induce them to serve in the civil and military administration in order to recreate a Greater Georgia under Russian auspices. Indeed, it had been claimed that "Russia assured the physical survival of Georgia": Georgia (eastern and western) had a population of 413,929 in 1800, but it had been a million on the eve of the Mongol invasion. By the 1830s it had risen to 750,000.[47] A similar policy was pursued toward the Armenians, who were also Christians, but whose church was monophysitic (recognizing only one nature in Christ); its separate status was recognized in 1836, not only for religious but also political reasons: to help the imperial government project Russian influence among the Armenian communities in the Ottoman empire. The Armenians were a mercantile people – Tiflis was largely an Armenian city – but the Orbelianis became major figures in the imperial administration of Transcaucasia, and Lt.-Gen. Raton (Valerian) Madatov (1782–1829) from Karabakh was one of the most fiery commanders of the Russian cavalry. Among both peoples, the church became a tool of integration. The Georgian Church was one of the oldest denominations of the Eastern Church, and its bishops were consecrated in Constantinople. It was in fact an autocephalous church. Its head was the "Catholicos of Mtskheta and Iberia" residing in Mtskheta, Georgia's religious capital in 1811; he was the son of Tsar Erekle (Heraclius). The existence of an independent Orthodox church within a unitary Russian church was unacceptable to the Russian authorities in Tbilisi. The autocephaly was revoked in 1811, and an exarch was appointed, who, beginning in 1817, would invariably be a Russian bishop, member of the Holy Synod in Petersburg managed by its senior procurator, the de facto "minister of the Orthodox Church." It would then be easy to strip the Georgian church of its properties and make it an instrument of Russian policy to weaken or silence opposition to the government.[48]

Domesticating the Armenian Church was more difficult, because the church was an international one: the Armenians were scattered throughout a vast territory extending well beyond the area incorporated by the Russians in 1828. The Armenians were the first to recognize Christianity as a national religion in the third century, closely followed by the Georgians. The church later fell victim to the Turco-Persian struggle over the Armenian lands. After 1453, there was a patriarch in Constantinople closely controlled by the Ottoman government and a Catholicos in Echmiadzin near Erevan, under Persian overlordship, so that the church was not only the church of a people but territorially also a transnational church. After 1828, Echmiadzin passed from Persian to Russian control, and eight years later, the Russian government published a statute on the administration of the Armenian church in Russia.

It amounted to no less than an attempt to transform the church into a Russian Armenian church as an agent of Russian integration among Russian Armenians, but also into an instrument to project Russian influence via the other Armenians into the Ottoman and Persian empires. But it was a long way from the cup to the lip, and tensions developed within the Armenian communities and between them and the Russians. The statute retained the Catholicos, elected, in theory at least, by "the entire Armenian people." He was assisted by a synod which restricted his freedom of action, and subordinated to the chief administrator in the Caucasus in Tiflis and the interior minister in Petersburg, who became, in fact, the "minister of the Armenian Church." But it proved very difficult to reconcile the role of the Catholicos as the head of the Russian Armenian church with his ambitions to become the ecclesiastical head of all Armenians, Russian, Ottoman, and Persian subjects. Mikhail Katkov, the conservative publicist, would write in 1866 that Russian interests could not allow "the presence within Russia of a Russian subject who simultaneously considers himself to be a kind of international force." We found the same problem in Russia's relations with the Catholic Church in the western theatre.[49]

North of the mountains, the settler had claimed more and more land from the nomad since the 1780s. According to the census of 1833,[50] the population of the North Caucasian steppe reached 508,700, including 405,200 Russians and Ukrainians, or 79.6 per cent of the total, leaving 88,900 "Tatars" (chiefly Nogais) and others far behind. In the so-called Lower Volga region (Saratov and Astrakhan provinces), the settled population of Russians, German colonists, and Ukrainians numbered 1,612,800 or 80.2 per cent of a total of 2,010,800. The next largest groups (in Astrakhan province) were the Kazakhs of the Inner Horde (123,800), the Kalmyks (87,800), and "Tatars" (78,800), islands of nomads gradually driven into reservation-like territories shunned by the settler, and supervised by an official (*pristav*) representing the local governor. In the Caucasus proper, the imperial territory, there were about 3,380,500 people, among whom the Russians (presumably civilians alone) were a mere 3,700. The population of the entire "Caucasian" sector of the eastern theatre was thus about 5.9 million.

The Kalmyks remained an object of major concern, despite the flight of most of them in 1771. The settler had advanced into their pastures left empty between the Ural and the Akhtuba, where they still patrolled the steppe trails to protect the shipments of salt to the Volga landings. Paul restored the *zargo* in 1800, to consist of eight members under the chairmanship of the chief of one of the seven *ulusy* making up the Kalmyk horde of about 25,000 *kibitki* in 1803. He also assumed the title of interim khan (*namestnik*) abolished after 1771, but the instruction of 1802 gave the *pristav*, subordinated to the Astrakhan military governor, considerable powers of oversight: he settled disputes between the khan and the clan leaders (*vladeltsy*) and taught them to obey him as having received his investiture and authority from the emperor, thereby imposing a hierarchical principle upon a society that had always been reluctant to accept it. Disputes over pastures were referred to the College of Foreign Affairs via the military governor. The rules of March 1825 placed the Kalmyks under the Interior Ministry, downgraded the *zargo* to the level of a *uezd* agency with a *pristav* in each of the seven *ulusy*, and created a Kalmyk Commission in Astrakhan. They also encouraged the transformation of *noions* and *zaisangs* into hereditary chieftains. This was confirmed by the statute of 1834, which also allowed them to collect taxes for administrative expenses. Finally, the statute of 1847 placed the Kalmyks under the ministry of state domains, making them *de jure* state peasants.[51] Meanwhile, they had been moving across the Akhtuba into what would be called the "Kalmyk steppe" of Astrakhan province between the Akhtuba, the Kuma, and the Ergeni Hills, where most of them are still living today. There was a way to escape this final humiliation: to convert and join the Stavropol Cossack Host, which had 920 men under their *ataman* in 1803. The Napoleonic wars made great demands on the Kalmyks. In 1811, three regular Kalmyk regiments (First and Second and Stavropolskii) were created: the first two made it to Paris in 1814, the third to northern France.[52]

In the middle sector of the eastern theatre, in the Kazan-Orenburg region, similar processes were at work. In the northern part (Viatka and Perm provinces), the Russian settler had completely swamped the native population of Udmurts and Tatars: they made up 84.8 per cent of a total population of 3 million. In the Middle Volga section (Kazan, Simbirsk, and Penza, the heart of the old Kazan khanate), the Russians had a majority of only 63 per cent due to the presence of large native groups: 473,300 Tatars, 399,000 Chuvash, and 236,600 Mordvins in a total population of 3.5 million. In Ufa/Orenburg province, the Russians remained a minority of 48.7 per cent of a total population of 1.7 million, giving a total population of 8.2 million for the entire region.[53]

Large numbers of Tatars, Mordvins, and Chuvash had migrated from the old Kazan khanate into the Orenburg Territory during the second half of the eighteenth century, fleeing the increasing integration of the native population into the categories of state and Court peasants, with the concomitant subjection to the capitation, the *obrok*, and recruiting, but the territory still remained underpopulated.[54] It remained a melting pot on the very edge of the core – there was not that much arable land across the Ural River, the Cossacks claimed it as their own, and Kazakh raids kept the edge of settlement permanently insecure. Nevertheless, the purchase of native wives and children, allowed in the 1740s, remained a significant form of inter-ethnic exchange and a contribution to ethnic integration. Both Kazakhs and Bashkirs sold them in times of famine, and although Reinsdorp forbade the practice in 1779, it continued to flourish. In 1785, the Ufa provincial board even recommended buying them with government money or bartering them for provisions from the provincial stores. However, the government was determined not to allow personal serfdom to extend, which it would do if individuals who were not allowed to purchase human beings in the core (merchants, artisans, civil officials who were not hereditary nobles) were given permission to do so in the periphery. It sought instead to foster the integration of Kazakhs especially into the category of state peasants: all these children were emancipated when they reached the age of twenty-five, even if a male had married the serf girl of his master.[55]

The most interesting feature of the policy of integration was the transformation of a large part of the Bashkir population into a Cossack "estate" (*soslovie*). The Bashkirs, a warlike people like the Kalmyks, their traditional enemies, watched the progress of social and fiscal integration with alarm. Their leaders did not want to be subordinated to the civil authorities, which they hated and despised, but wanted military ranks, and looked to the Don Cossack Host (the largest of the hosts) as a model. Nearly eight thousand Bashkirs and Meshcheriaks did patrol duty with the Orenburg Cossacks along the 2,500-kilometre-long Orenburg Line and another one thousand were detailed to the Siberian Line every other year. It was a heavy burden, which kept them away from their families and fields for long periods of time, and the Bashkir communities which had to equip them also had to keep paying the *iasak*. They knew the government had toyed with the idea of completing their social and fiscal integration into the core society. To avoid that fate, they preferred to join a Cossack world that was developing a separate identity and a sense of mission, coupled with a total disdain for the peasantry.

The reforms of 1789–98 divided the Orenburg and Ural lines into five districts (*distantsii*) from Verkhneuralsk to Gurev. Bashkirs and Meshcheriaks in 27,427 households (*dvory*) were apportioned among sixteen cantons divided into *iurts* consisting of groups of villages within a reasonable distance from the lines. The officers consisted of *starshina* and *sotniki*, all appointed by the military governor, an extremely profitable source of patronage. Each canton was assigned a specific part of the line within its district, each under a Bashkir officer responsible to the military governor. The cantons were incorporated into the Orenburg Separate Corps. These Bashkirs remained dependent on their communities, so that the new irregular force, while helping the government to tighten its grip on the border with the Kazakhs, cost it nothing. Eventually, the canton system created a huge "bureaucracy" of 5,569 officers by 1819, reduced to 3,657 by 1837. Bashkir leaders were given officer ranks, but only as long as they served, and the government refused to give them the status of hereditary nobles in 1829. Bashkirs not incorporated into the canton system remained subordinated to the civil administration. At the same time, two Teptiar Cossack regiments were created outside the canton system; they remained in existence until 1835.[56]

In the Kazakh steppe, the expanding core was approaching its natural limits. The New Ishim Line ran along the periphery of the wooded steppe with its rich black earth, beyond which began the open steppe stretching from the southern Ukraine to the Altai, still attractive to the settler with its dark chestnut brown soil despite its drier climate. Its southern boundary zigzagged along the foothills of the Kazakh Upland to Ust-Kamenogorsk on the Irtysh.[57] Beyond the open steppe began the semi-desert zone, to which the settler was as allergic as he was to the highlands and mountains of the Caucasus. It was in that intermediate zone between the wooded steppe and the semi-desert that the fate of the Kazakh nomad was sealed.

The Manchu-Zunghar conflict, the destruction of the Zunghars, and the advance of Manchu power to Lake Zaisan and Lake Balkhash had created a slow but inexorable reorientation of Kazakh politics toward the expanding core, where, in addition, a critical mass of settled population presented opportunities as well as dangers. That reorientation, which exposed the increasing vulnerability of the Kazakh frontier between the two powerful cores, the Russian and the Chinese, kept destabilizing Kazakh politics, torn between unpopular khans and clan leaders. The Russians supported the khans because encouraging the "rotting process"[58] had always been part of their policy, but they also sought support among the clans, which served the same purpose.

In the Western Horde, Nur Ali was succeeded by his brother Erali (+1794), then by his son Ishim (+1797), who was followed by his uncle Aichuvak, Nur Ali's brother. In 1805, Aichuvak's son Dzhantiura was selected in secret against the wishes of all the main actors in the steppe and was assassinated in 1809. There was no khan until 1812, when Shirgazi, Dzhantiura's brother, became khan until his death in 1823; he was so resented that he feared to show himself in the steppe. This rapid succession of khans, all mediocre figures invested by the imperial government, took place against a background of rising discontent, attacks on Russian officials and on caravans to and from Central Asia, the establishment in 1799 of a Border Commission which failed to settle disputes, and, most important, the encroachments of Cossack communities into Kazakh pastures beyond the Ural River, which only incited more anguish and despair.

In the meantime, the Western Horde had broken up. The migration of the Kazakhs continued when one of the younger sons of Nur Ali, Bukei, seeing no possibility of becoming khan, won the government's permission in 1799 to take some 5,000 *kibitki* (22,775 men and women) across the Ural into the steppe between the river and the Volga, where the Kalmyks once roamed. It was this migration which led the Kalmyks, who were on notoriously bad terms with the

Kazakhs, to move beyond the Akhtuba into the North Caucasus steppe. More Kazakhs followed later. These Kazakhs formed the Inner Horde and became "internal subjects," because they had crossed the de facto boundary of the Russian realm to enter the expanding core. The horde was placed under the jurisdiction of the Ministry of State Domains in 1838. In 1812, Bukei was given the title of khan of the new horde. He died in 1815 and was succeeded by his brother Shirgazi as khan of both the Inner and Western Horde. The next khan of the Inner Horde was Bukei's son Dzhangir (1823–45), major general in the Russian army, married to a daughter of the Orenburg *mufti*, and an active supporter of the creation of an Islamic establishment in the Inner Horde. Their oldest son was given the title of prince of the Russian empire in 1847 as "Prince Gingis," the worthy recognition of a direct descendant of the last khan of the Kipchak khanate, himself a descendant of Ezhen, brother of Batu, the conqueror of western Eurasia, both grandsons of Chingis Khan. The title of khan was abolished in the Western Horde in 1824. The horde was divided into three parts, each governed by a sultan (khan's son) assisted by a detachment of 200 Cossacks under the overall jurisdiction of the Border Commission chaired by the Orenburg commandant.[59]

The Central and Eastern Hordes were also breaking up. The disintegration of the khans' power was accelerating, and large numbers of Kazakhs under their sultans were seeking Russian "protection" – moving toward integration into the still expanding core. The statute of 1822 abolished the title of khan in both hordes, and the sultans were given unlimited administrative powers over their subjects, thereby breaking up the last vestiges of the hordes' unity. The Central Horde and the northern part of the Eastern Horde (called the Siberian Kazakhs or Kirgiz) were gradually transformed into "external districts" (*okruga*) because their population remained "external subjects," each *okrug* administered by a senior sultan in the rank of army major chosen by his clan and accountable to the commanding general in Omsk. Two such districts were created in 1824, Kokchetav and Karkaralinsk in the black earth zone, followed by more in Akmolinsk and Baian-Aul in the zone of chestnut soils in the 1830s. Kazakhs were allowed to move into the core, and Russians were allowed to settle on Kazakh lands.[60] By the later 1830s, the expanding core was finally reaching its natural periphery in the eastern theatre.

In Siberia, the census of 1833 gave the Russians an overwhelming majority of 73.8 per cent (1.7 out of 2.3 million) with a native population of 518,800, most of it in Eastern Siberia, with Buriats and Yakuts still the two largest groups.[61] Throughout the eighteenth century, the alliance with Russian authorities, based on mutual interest, had become consolidated; Buriat *noions* and Yakut *toyons* had learned to behave like the Russian ruling class, which had superimposed its dominion over their own increasingly tight control of their subjects, some converting to Orthodoxy, others remaining faithful to shamanism and Buddhism.

The abuse of authority for the purpose of self-enrichment, a typical phenomenon by which the ruling class asserted its power over the dependent population, reached its peak in Buriatia with the reign (*Dymbylovshchina*) of two *noions*, father and son, supported by the Irkutsk governor, dismissed by the governor general, supported by the minister of education and cults who kept hoping they would convert, and finally dismissed by Speransky, who removed another 255 *noions* found guilty of misrule.[62] Yakut *toyons* had asked in 1790 to be granted the rights of nobles, to become formally incorporated into the ruling class, but this was refused, even though they had already become the de facto nobility of Yakutia.[63]

Another statute of 1822 classified the non-Russian peoples of Siberia into three categories.[64] The first consisted of the "settled" population in towns and villages, including Bukharan and Tashkent merchants, as well as many groups of Tatars in the foothills of the Saian mountains, who had already become Russified. Those who had converted were simply called "Russians." They were identified with state peasants. The second category was that of "nomads," including Buriats, Yakuts, and Tungus, and other small groups. They were considered peasants by another name (*kochevye inorodtsy*), but with a different type of administration. Among them were the so-called "nomadic landtillers" (*kochevye zemledeltsy*), nomads who also engaged in some form of agriculture, chiefly among the Buriats. In 1824, for example, Buriats on both sides of Lake Baikal numbered 14,543 "settled" and 129,447 "nomadic landtillers."[65] The third category was that of hunters and fishermen of the far north and Kamchatka, who kept travelling along rivers banks and in the taiga – hence their name "vagrants" (*brodiagi*).

Buriats and Yakuts had finally become integrated into the social order of the core, of a one and indivisible Russia. Among the Buriats, "a bright and industrious people,"[66] clans were combined to form *vedomstva*, administered by steppe assemblies (*stepnye dumy*), an extravagant name for several elected members meeting under the chairmanship of a *taishi* or senior clan leader. The smaller *vedomstva* had a headman (*golova*) and two deputies (*vybornye*). These agencies were subordinated to the *uezd* land court (*zemskii sud*), the *uezd* police and land captain, and were in no way different from similar agencies among the Russian peasantry. In Yakutia, there was a steppe council (*stepnaia rada*) composed of clan chiefs. The *toyons* so abused the system that it was abolished in 1838, leaving "clan directorates" in full control of similar agencies (one headman and two deputies) in each *ulus*, forming an *inorodnaia uprava*.[67] The *toyons* were doing so well that Ivan Goncharov, travelling from Yakutsk to Irkutsk in 1854, discovered to his great surprise that the Russians in Yakutia were speaking Yakut, not only with the Yakuts but among themselves as well.[68] Integration had been so successful that it was difficult to say who had integrated whom.

The Russians had to deal with the religious issue also among the Buriats. Shamanism had been strong in Siberia, and the Buddhist lamas fought to reduce its influence. Buddhism was the third international religion after Catholicism and Islam in the territories incorporated into the expanding core. At first, the Russians supported Buddhism, but later sought to circumscribe its activities and create a Russian Buddhist Church cut off from its natural sources in Tibet and eastern Mongolia: both were under strong Manchu-Chinese influence. In 1741, the Empress Elizabeth allowed 150 Tibetan and Mongol lamas who had fled civil war in Mongolia to remain in Siberia and to proselytize among the native population. A century later, Buriat (and Buddhist Kalmyk) communities were represented in the Department of Foreign Confessions created in the Interior Ministry in February 1832. But as the number of tax-exempt lamas kept growing and the Buddhist doctrine of celibacy put a brake on population growth, Russian attitudes began to change. As the administrative-territorial integration of East Siberia proceeded apace and Russia's policy toward China became more active, the Russians sought to cut off the Buddhists' relations with their co-religionists in Mongolia and Tibet. The decree of May 1853 forbade the construction of new monasteries and the admission of new lamas.[69] Thus, from an organizational point of view, Russian policy toward the Buddhists, especially beyond Lake Baikal, resembled that followed toward the Armenians (and Catholics) to create a new ecclesiastical hierarchy parallel with that of the Orthodox Church, but managed by the minister of the interior as the "minister of non-Orthodox confessions," the civil counterpart of the senior procurator of the Holy Synod.

Judicial Integration

Russian and Muslim Courts

Religious policy aimed at converting the native peoples to Orthodoxy, thereby transforming them into Russians. Fiscal policy sought to create a uniform tax system applicable to all. Social policy was determined to integrate non-Russians, including nomads, into the social structure of the advancing community of Russian settlers, with its ruling class lording it over a vast and dependent population. Military integration gave some nomads a chance to escape this final transformation by drafting them into the irregular forces which were themselves being increasingly integrated into the overall military establishment of the expanding core.

There was yet another form of integration, to which we must now turn. Contacts with non-Russians grew with the increase of the settler population. Conversion and fiscal unification did not change customs by which people had grown used to assume what was right and what was wrong, how husbands and fathers must treat their wives and children, how individuals must regard one another outside the family and clan, and how they must look at the land. Imposing Russian law would be counterproductive, because a jurisprudence that did not recognize the litigants' assumptions and expectations cannot gain legitimacy and would only defeat its purpose. The pursuit of integration, which had to take place as the core expanded into eastern Eurasia, had to take the form of seeking an ongoing compromise between legal systems offering slightly or sharply different answers to the same questions, or supplementing one another, when one system raised and answered questions which another did not. The search for a compromise was all the more acute because the Russian legal system faced two other relatively well developed core systems, the Muslim and the Mongol. The former was in effect among the "Tatars" of various denominations in the Caspian basin and central Eurasia and among the Kazakhs; the latter, among the Kalmyks, the Buriats, and even the Yakuts.

There was no comprehensive network of courts until after the great reforms of the 1770s. In the seventeenth century, the *voevoda* at any level was a judge as well as a tax collector and garrison commander. Most disputes were settled within the peasant world, if only because the *voevoda*'s office was associated with corruption and endless delays, if not outright violence. In criminal cases, the *voevoda* took the initiative and had great powers, including the imposition of the death penalty. Whatever he could not, or did not want to, decide, he referred to the Kazan and Siberian Chanceries, where a final decision was made, unless the case had implications requiring the tsar's intervention.[70] The reform of 1708 divided the expanding core into provinces and appointed governors in each of them; that of 1719, which divided provinces into *provintsii*, required the *provintsiia voevoda* to refer their death sentences to the governor. It also made a valiant attempt to create separate (*nadvornye*) courts, of which three were established in Kazan, Tobolsk, and Yeniseisk, but the experiment was short-lived. In Siberia, their writ did not extend beyond two hundred kilometres. Beyond that perimeter, there were judicial commissioners, who tried suits valued at under fifty roubles. Suits above that sum were tried in town courts chaired by the *voevoda*; appeals went to the *nadvorny* court and then to the College of Justice in Moscow. In provincial capitals, there were *magistraty* which, among other things, settled disputes among the registered townsmen. Their decisions were appealed to the Central *Magistrat* in Moscow.[71]

The reform of 1727 cancelled this first attempt to create a judicial hierarchy separate from the administrative hierarchy by abolishing the *nadvornye* courts and *magistraty* and reintegrating the judicial function into the universal jurisdiction of governor and *voevoda*. This lasted until 1743, when the Central *Magistrat* and its provincial agencies were reopened and made "independent" of the administrative hierarchy. In 1744, the application of the death penalty was suspended, and governors had to refer their death sentences to the Senate.

In fact, the death penalty was replaced by banishment to hard labour with the governor's confirmation.[72]

The reforms of 1775–85, taken in their totality, represented a massive commitment to full integration in an expanding core that was about to reach its natural limit. Administrative unification in both western and eastern Eurasia aimed at creating an infrastructure to facilitate integration in the fiscal, judicial, and even religious realms. In every province, even if the ideal of provinces of equal size could not be attained, notably in Siberia, the reforms established a civil and a criminal chamber, each consisting of a chairman appointed by the ruler on the Senate's recommendation, and four members chosen by the Senate. In each *uezd*, it created a court with a judge and two assessors, all three elected for three years by the nobility of the district. There was also a lower court (*rasprava*) with a judge appointed by the provincial board and four assessors elected to represent the state peasantry for three years, but who did not have to be state peasants themselves. We may also include the lower land court with a land captain, who controlled the police, the investigation, and the application of corporal punishment. He also settled small disputes, and, elected as he was by the nobility, was often the most dreaded member of the repressive apparatus of the ruling class in the countryside. In the towns, there were *magistraty* which remained organs of self-government for the registered townsmen, but with a now preponderant judicial responsibility.

At the provincial level, we find a *magistrat*, which operated as an organ of self-government in the capital and as a court of appeal for the *magistraty* and separate courts set up to manage the affairs of orphans. There was also a court of equity (*sovestny*) consisting of a judge and two assessors, nobles, townsmen, or state peasants depending on the social origin of the petitioners. It received cases involving minors and the insane; it was instructed to avoid the strict application of the letter of the law (recognized to be harsh by all), and find guidance in restraint and mercy.[73] Civil cases valued at more than six hundred roubles were appealed to the Senate, which was divided in 1763 into six functional departments. The reorganization of 1805 divided it into eight departments with a territorial jurisdiction and an additional department for litigation involving challenges to the decisions of land survey agencies in the provinces. Five of the eight departments were in Petersburg, the other three in Moscow. Civil appeals from Kazan, Viatka, Perm, and Siberia went to the Fourth Department in Petersburg; those from Astrakhan and the Caucasus to the Seventh Department, those from Simbirsk, Penza, and Saratov to the Eighth Department, both in Moscow. Criminal sentences were not appealed by defendants, but the governor sent up sentences, including death, if a nobleman was stripped of his membership in the ruling class. Governors in Perm and Siberia forwarded the sentences to the Fifth Department in Petersburg; all the others in the eastern theatre went to the Sixth Department in Moscow.[74]

Such was the network of courts which the reforms introduced everywhere in the core, from the Polish to the Mongolian border. Nevertheless, the application of the reform had to deal with stubborn realities. There were hardly any nobles in Astrakhan and the northern Caucasus, let alone in Siberia, and the personnel of the courts would have to be appointed. One of the fundamental principles of the reform – the separation of the judiciary from the administration, at least at the district level – had to be abandoned. There were not enough cases, and the civil and criminal chambers were merged to form a single provincial court.[75] But a single hierarchy of courts was established everywhere, required to follow the same trial and appellate procedures and impose the same penalties. If exceptions had to be made for the time being, they could be inserted into a single uniform institutional hierarchy until circumstances ceased to justify their existence.

There was, for example, a "border court" in Orenburg, created in 1784, consisting of the commandant and two Russian officers, two merchants, and two state peasants, together with Kazakh representatives: one sultan and six elders (*starshiny*), to be replaced every three years. In 1787, three lower *raspravy* were opened in the Western Horde, one for each of the main clans, to consist of elders of the clan. The use of the term "lower *rasprava*" was very significant: in the new court hierarchy, Kazakhs were equated with state peasants until the time came when they too might be placed under the jurisdiction of the Ministry of State Domains. A similar border court was not opened in the Central Horde until 1799, under the chairmanship of the Petropavlovsk commandant; it consisted of three assessors, one sultan, and three elders, together with secretaries and clerks. A section of it sat periodically in Semipalatinsk. These border courts handled trade disputes between Russians and Kazakhs and other issues related to security in the steppe, like the ransoming of prisoners. A third border court was inaugurated in Mozdok in 1793 as a court of appeal for courts set up for the nobility in each of the Kabardian clans, with lower *raspravy* for their dependent population (*uzdeni*).[76] The place of these border courts in the hierarchy is unclear. It is likely that their decisions were never appealed, but if the court could not settle an issue, the commandant referred it to the commander of the Siberian Corps or the military governor in Orenburg and Astrakhan. It may have been too early for disputes to involve issues of substantive law; should they arise, however, the stage was set for equating the courts with *uezd* courts, whose decisions were appealed to the provincial chamber.

Another separate court deserves mention. Peter I had invited Armenians to settle in Astrakhan, and the Senate agreed in 1746 that disputes among them must be settled in their own court in accordance with their laws and customs. Such a court was created in 1747, and it produced its own law code (*sudebnik*) based on customary and canonic Armenian law, supplemented by provisions from the Russian Code of 1649 and subsequent enactments. Both parties to a case had to be Armenian. Appeals went to the Astrakhan Provincial Chancery and, after the reform, the Provincial Board, both chaired by the governor. This exception was justified by the need to spare the Armenians, who were chiefly traders, the time-consuming appellate procedures (and the heavy fines for their violation), when time was of the essence. However, the court had no jurisdiction in criminal cases, which were referred to the regular courts and tried in accordance with Russian legislation.[77] This had long been a major feature of the Russian government's attitude toward judicial integration: criminal cases were tried under Russian laws, hence the full unification of the criminal and penal law; civil cases were tried by native notables in accordance with their own laws and customs. What remained unsettled was the question of what happened when litigants appealed to Russian courts to settle disputes which they could not resolve by resorting to their own laws.

The Siberian reforms of 1822 did not depart fundamentally from the principles established or implied in the reforms of 1775–85, but took into consideration the underdeveloped condition of Siberia in relation to the more densely settled part of the core in western Eurasia. Each province had a court which combined the functions of a civil and a criminal chamber elsewhere, and each *uezd* (called *okrug*) and town had its own court; but these courts were subordinated to the *okrug* and provincial administration, which retained the old universal jurisdiction of the pre-reform *voevody*. Moreover, except for the town courts, also called *magistraty*, their personnel was entirely appointed. Appeals went to the Senate, but criminal sentences, if the governor disagreed with them, required the confirmation of the governor general in council. In Yakutia, there was no separate court, but the *oblast* administration functioned as one. In Omsk, where the *oblast* chief was a general with the authority of a divisional commander, and that of a governor in civil affairs, there was a military court and a civil one with the status of a provincial court.[78]

The reform also had to take into account relations with the Kazakhs, Buriats, and Yakuts. In the "external districts" set up in the Kazakh steppe, the *prikaz* was equated with a *uezd* court. Criminal cases, defined as treason, murder, battery (*grabezh*), *baranta* (driving away of cattle in revenge), and "clear resistance to the authorities," were decided in accordance with Russian legislation and by majority vote. All other cases were considered civil (*iskovye*) and were tried by *biis* in accordance with Kazakh laws and customs. Appellate decision by the Omsk *oblast* chief also had to follow these laws and customs.[79] Thus, the court system was fully integrated into the administrative-judicial hierarchy of Russian courts, but civil suits remained within the purview of local judges in Kazakh communities. In Buriatia and Yakutia, criminal offences were defined as rebellion (*vozmushchenie*), premeditated murder, battery, assault (*nasilie*), counterfeiting, and theft of public property. Such cases were tried in the *okrug* court under Russian law, and sentences were confirmed by the Irkutsk governor or Yakutsk chief, unless they were referred to the governor general of eastern Siberia in council. Civil disputes were settled by arbitration within the clans.[80]

In Transcaucasia, in the empire beyond the core, the Russians faced a new challenge following the Treaty of Turkmanchai (1828), which seems to have convinced them that the outer limits of the empire had been reached in the Caspian basin. At the time of the annexation in 1801, it had been intended to integrate eastern Georgia into the administrative system of the core, even though its provincial government was both simpler and bore an extravagant name. But the territorial, ethnic, and religious fragmentation of the region, together with the continuing general insecurity and growing warfare in the mountains, forced the high command in Tiflis to give priority to ad hoc experiments which ended by creating an administrative maze challenging the very assumptions behind the government's policy in 1801. Thirty years later, General Paskevich reported to Nicholas I that the administration of justice had fallen into a chaotic state.

In Georgia, where criminal offences were tried in accordance with imperial legislation, civil litigation came under the Code (*Sudebnik*) of Tsar Wakhtang VI (1675–1737), a compilation of ancient Byzantine, Armenian, and Georgian laws and customs, which had become so irrelevant that it no longer met, except in such matters as irrigation law, the needs of a more complex society. It often needed to be supplemented with provisions of Russian law, allowing judges in the *uezd* and provincial courts to pick whatever provisions they preferred in each separate case. Whatever they decided would always be lawful. Elsewhere, military rule prevailed. Criminal cases were tried by court martial. Muslims were encouraged to litigate before their elders, but if resort had to be had to the local commandant, he was likely to be guided by a mismatch of Russian and Muslim law which only encouraged his arbitrary behaviour.[81] The reform of 1840 sought to remedy this sorry state of affairs. With the introduction of the territorial division into provinces and *uezds* in effect in the core, *uezd* courts were given jurisdiction over suits exceeding fifteen silver roubles; appeals went to either of the two chambers, from which litigants could further appeal to the Senate if their suit was valued at over six hundred silver roubles. Muslims were encouraged to seek satisfaction in family disputes and inheritance cases before their own judges under Muslim law, but resort to Russian courts was not excluded. Civil procedure followed imperial legislation.[82] The framers of the reform were influenced by the views of Paskevich, who strongly believed in the "rapprochement of peoples" (*sblizhenie narodov*),[83] later so dear to Soviet publicists, overlooking the fact that by crossing the core's periphery, Russia was building an empire and no longer a one and indivisible Russia.

A major innovation had been the creation of separate territorial commands, four of them in the eastern theatre: Tiflis, Orenburg, Omsk, and Irkutsk, this last one in 1834.[84] A separate corps commander, called chief administrator in the Caucasus, military governor in Orenburg, and governor general in Siberia, was empowered to hand over to military courts all but general officers, and confirm and order the execution of sentences on all but colonels, except those to death and degradation. Others were sent to the War Ministry[85] for submission to the emperor. But a separate corps commander also wore a civilian hat. As the highest authority in the region and outranking the provincial governors, he had the final say in the confirmation of criminal sentences on civilians, unless members of the ruling class were sentenced to the loss or restriction of their rights and privileges, or if ten or more defendants were subjected to corporal punishment. In these and other cases, when the governor disagreed with the criminal chamber, the decision was sent to the relevant Senate department.[86] It is obvious that the participation of a high-ranking general gave the administration of criminal justice a strong repressive bent, especially in areas where the maintenance of security was a serious problem. There was a disturbing implication in the combination of a military command with criminal justice jurisdiction over both military personnel and civilians: the temptation to place more and more civilians under court martial jurisdiction.

The temptation was greater in the Caucasus, where the corps commander was given in 1832 the authority of a commander in chief in peacetime to confirm in the last instance sentences to death and degradation on all officers including colonels.[87] Even before the reorganization of 1840, all civilians in Georgia, Armenia, and the Muslim provinces who committed crimes had been tried by court martial. In 1844, the corps commander asked permission to try the increasing number of cases of highway robbery and battery at the place of crime and without a preliminary investigation, which in effect meant the application of wartime criminal procedures and the death penalty. This was refused; however, the repression of crimes remained the responsibility of military courts, and their sentences would now be confirmed in Tiflis.[88] In the Orenburg Territory the military governor obtained permission in 1832 to try by court martial Bashkirs who stole cattle and horses from landowners, and two years later, was empowered to try likewise all Bashkirs, Kalmyks, Teptiars, Meshcheriaks, and retired Cossacks for any type of crime, including vagrancy and the hiding of exiles.[89] In Siberia, the major problem was the theft of precious metals from the Ural mines, and perpetrators were also placed under the jurisdiction of military justice.

It may be claimed that such deviation from the norm in effect in the rest of the core implied at least a partial rejection of the policy of judicial integration, but that was not the case. Resorting to military courts to try civilians became widespread during the reign of Nicholas I,[90] and it had already been in effect before 1825, when the personnel of state-owned mines in the Urals were militarized in 1809. To steal gold, silver, and platinum, to buy and transport these stolen metals, exposed the culprits to trial by mixed civil-military commissions in Ekaterinburg and Zlatoust. Sentences on civilians were confirmed by the director of Ural mines, those on military personnel by the Orenburg military governor.[91] If anything, the use of court martials to try both Russians and non-Russians reflected the universal application of the same repressive regime throughout the core and in the emerging empire.

Russian and Islamic Law

The policy of judicial integration encountered resistance in the confessional frontier between Russia and Bukhara, Russia and Dagestan, between Orthodoxy and "Tatar" Islam, but frontiers are also zones of compromise, where an on-going process of accommodation submerges conflicts threatening the common interest of rival influences. After the Bashkir rebellion of 1754–5 and the edict of toleration of 1773, the Dagestan form of Islam, later to find its most extreme form in Muridism, lost influence in the former Kazan khanate, to be replaced by the Bukharan variant.[92] Bukhara's position as the hub of Central Asian trade was seriously threatened by the decline of the transcontinental trade routes in favour of sea-borne trade between the Indies and Europe via the Cape of Good Hope. One consequence was to reorient the trade toward Petropavlovsk, Orenburg, and Kazan, at a time when the Russians were showing a growing interest in the region; the other was to encourage the development of a conservative Islam distrustful of philosophical and scientific inquiry but relying on scholastic training and close ties with the civil authorities. The developing trade with Russia also created a prosperous Tatar bourgeoisie in Kazan and the Tatar settlement outside Orenburg (Kargal), where a large mosque would eventually become the most important centre of Islamic learning in the region, weak in the study of the Arabic language and literature, but strong in the knowledge of the Koran, which, like all sacred books, could be interpreted to suit the interests of those in power.[93] The stage was ready for the creation of a "Russian Islam."

Such was the background of the creation in 1789 of the Orenburg Ecclesiastical Assembly (*Dukhovnoe Sobranie*), another extravagant title for an agency strikingly similar to the new Russian courts. It consisted of a *mufti*, a judicial official certainly, but also a religious leader, since Muslim law was fundamentally religious law. He was assisted by two mullas, chosen from among the Kazan and Ufa Tatars; the secretary and clerks were Russian-speaking Tatars. The mullas were elected for three years, but had to pass an examination testing not only their knowledge of the law but, no doubt, their political reliability as well, and were confirmed in office by the governors of Kazan and Ufa. Since the Russian passion for uniformity required that the "assembly" be integrated into the new hierarchy of courts, it was equated with the intermediate courts, which received appeals from the *uezd* courts, and whose appeals went to the civil chamber.

In *uezds* with a substantial Muslim population there was a "court" consisting of two *akhuns*, to whom the mosques and the imams were subordinated. The assembly was later placed in the jurisdiction of the Interior Ministry, and the mullas were given the not too flattering title of "official [*ukaznye*] mullas," but one appropriate in a system patterned after the Bukharan model and the Russian ideal of an Erastian church.[94]

The position of the *mufti* elicited some controversy. In 1804, for example, Mufti Muhamad Hussein, whose grandfather had returned to Russia from Bukhara, proposed the creation in Petersburg of a College of Muslim Affairs with branches in the provinces having a Muslim population, a hierarchy resembling that of the old Central *Magistrat* with its provincial *magistraty* removed from the jurisdiction of the governors. He also wanted the assembly to have a say in the examination of criminal cases to which Muslim clerics were a party, but the government accepted the objections of the Orenburg civil governor that this would mean the importation of the millet system of the Ottoman empire.[95] Nevertheless, the government wanted to confer upon the *mufti* a status higher than that of a provincial official. When in 1811 the Orenburg criminal chamber tried a case to which Hussein was a party after the governor sent him for trial for the commission of "unlawful acts," the *mufti* refused to answer the questions put to him. This was brought to the attention of the emperor, who ordered the proceedings to stop and declared that a *mufti* could be tried only in the Senate; its sentence must be sent for the emperor's approval via the Main Administration of Foreign Confessions to which Muslim authorities were subordinated.[96]

The authorities also had to elucidate the question of the *mufti*'s social position vis-à-vis the Orthodox clergy. Hussein would eventually become one of the largest landowners in Bashkiria, and the Tatar mullas followed his example. In 1790, Nikolai Timashev, the Orenburg provincial procurator, told the civil chamber that while the Orthodox clergy was forbidden to own real property, he could not find any laws forbidding a *mufti* to buy lands from Bashkirs. He added that the government had created an unprecedented situation by appointing a "top leader [*glavny nachalnik*] over the Muslim population," who could not be compared with Orthodox bishops, as the chamber contended. The Senate ruled in Timashev's favour, claiming that since princes and *murzy*, *akhuns*, and mullas had already been allowed to buy land, the *mufti* must perforce be included among them.[97] With one stroke of the pen, the government integrated into the ruling class not only the top social layer of the native Tatar population but also its religious and judicial establishment. It was indeed a master stroke of "tolerant" behaviour. Three years later, however, the government decreed that the *mufti* was allowed to buy only empty lands from the Bashkirs; settlers would have to be non-Christians and come from abroad. They would be his personal property and his heirs would have the right to sell them.[98]

The Assembly was a civil court – misdemeanours and crimes were punished by the police and crimes by sentences of the criminal chamber in accordance with Russian law. It dealt with family law (marriage and divorce, relations between parents and children), inheritance, and burial customs. Muslim law was grounded in the Koran, other sayings of the Prophet and those of his followers, and the decisions and interpretations of four imams who founded separate schools of jurisprudence. Russian Tatars followed that of Abu Khanef (710–72), and those in the Caucasus that of Idris-al-Shchefi (772–826). Muslim law also included the work of other jurists who compiled records of judicial decisions (*fetvas*), collections of laws and commentaries, the most authoritative of which was the Khidai, going back to the twelfth century: it remained so for Russian Muslims well into the nineteenth century, especially in matters of family law. Despite the variety of its sources and the absence of a single tribunal to interpret the law for the entire Muslim community, Muslim law managed to maintain a remarkable unity and was known as the *sharia*, infusing the life of Muslim communities everywhere. Its only major (but regional) rival was the *adaty* or customs of the Caucasian highlanders, with which Muridism fought a bitter struggle for twenty years.[99]

The reverse side of this remarkable unity was an arch-conservatism, the stagnancy of Muslim law. Since it was perceived as sacred it could not be brought up to date with the development of society, especially when Muslims became part of a larger community such as the expanding Russian core. The Koran of the seventh century, schools founded in the eighth century, and commentaries dating back to the thirteenth century were not adequate to deal with issues arising in a more developed society: Muslim law, for example, hardly knew even the notion of oral contract.[100] The growth of population and increasing contacts between Russians and Muslims in daily life raised issues requiring an accommodation between the two systems of jurisprudence.

In the 1730s, for example, when the policy of Christianization was in full swing in the former Kazan khanate, the Orthodox Church encouraged marriages between Russians and newly converted Tatars in the hope that bringing a daughter-in-law or a son-in-law into a Russian or a Tatar home would strengthen his or her faith and have a multiplying effect among those who remained beyond the fold. Unfortunately, it was discovered that while the Russian father gave away his daughter with a dowry, it was a custom among the Tatars that the bride receive a dowry from her husband-to-be. It is not clear whether such a different approach to the dowry was ever tested in court before a Russian *voevoda*, but the Synod instructed its delegate to proceed cautiously and try to convince the newly converted bridegroom to accept a dowry from his future wife; barring this, to induce both sides to accept a simple exchange of dowries.[101]

In 1805, the Senate took up an appeal concerning the rights of Muslim widows to inherit property. It must have been unusual for Muslim women to seek redress in the high court against what they considered the unfairness of Muslim law. The Senate noted that the law of 1731 gave a widow one-seventh of the real property and one-fourth of the movables, but that applied only to Orthodox widows, and there was no law covering the rights of the two to four wives allowed by Muslim law. The Senate first asked the opinion of the governors of several provinces with a Muslim population, and resolved that all the widows must be treated as a single claimant. If there were children, one-eighth of both the movables and immovable must be divided equally among all the widows; if there were no children, they would inherit one-fourth of the estate, and the remaining three-fourths would go to the husband's family (*rod*).[102] It is unclear why widows without children would receive less than those with children.

In the Muslim khanates of Transcaucasia, the Russians faced different concepts of landownership. Some landowners had full hereditary title to their properties (*miulk*), others were granted land by the khans for life or for a certain time with the right to collect taxes from certain villages (*tiiul*). After the incorporation of the khanates into the emerging empire and the removal of the khans, all landowners sought to gain full title to their properties; this would give them the same social status as the landowners in the core. But the authorities were reluctant to encourage this process because of their desire to create a pool of state lands, on which the population would simply be turned into state peasants. There had long been similar issues in Bashkiria, and as late as 1803, it seems that the law was unclear. The Chancery of Land Survey considered the Bashkirs, as a non-converted native people (*inovercheskii narod*), to be the equal of state peasants, while the Ufa treasury chambers (which administered the state peasantry) considered them "owners" (*vladeltsy*).[103]

In 1830, the Senate took up the question of dual liability. A Turkmen woman filed suit in the Astrakhan court of equity against her two daughters, who had married other Turkmens without her permission. The issue was whether a case of disobedience by "Tatar" children was justiciable in Russian courts or before a Muslim judge. The Senate, noting that the daughters did not speak Russian, concluded that they had to face a Muslim judge. However, it also resolved that if litigants later filed suit for the theft of property or personal insults attending on the original suit, they had to go before the civil courts.[104] In other words, the act of disobedience by (presumably) minors belonged to family law, which came under the jurisdiction of Muslim judicial-religious authorities, but the material consequences of the violation and tort actions, for which Muslim law had few remedies, were justiciable in Russian courts.

In 1832, the Senate took up a case with broad implications and referred it to the State Council responsible for discussing new legislation. A Crimean Tatar had abducted another Tatar's wife. He was arrested and brought before the *mufti* of the Crimea, who sentenced him to receive ninety-nine blows with a stick (*palka*) in the police station and an accomplice to thirty-nine blows. He then sent both men to the governor, whose duty it was to order the police to carry out the sentence. However, the governor refused, claiming that corporal punishment under Russian law deprived a defendant of his "good name," a sentence which only a civil (Russian) court was empowered to impose, and that the *mufti* could not become a party to the administration of criminal justice: his judicial authority was restricted to the imposition of religious penalties.

The State Council found the case raised three questions. One was the relevance of Muslim law to that particular case. Muslim law did not distinguish between violations of the Seventh Commandment (thou shalt not covet thy neighbour's wife), known in Russian as *preliubodeianie*, and fornication (*liubodeianie*). Russian law (*obshchie zakony*) left the punishment of the former to religious authorities. By failing to distinguish between the two, Muslim law was found to be exceptionally harsh and in violation of Russian law. The Council cited a sentence of the Kazan criminal chamber, which in a similar case had sentenced a defendant to spend two weeks in the workhouse, while Muslim law would have dictated the strongest punishment (it did not say which). It also cited an opinion of the former Orenburg *mufti* that it was impossible to apply the severe penalties of Muslim law in Russia but also unjust to send Muslims for such a serious offence to the workhouse for only a short time. The State Council added that in Russia the police were required to watch over the morality of subjects, even without the cooperation of the church, and punished those guilty of fornication and seduction (*obolshchenie*) outside marriage.

The Council then gave the following rules for the Senate's guidance. The Muslim clergy watches over the morality of Muslim men and women and resorts to exhortation (*uveshchanie*) and other means that do not contravene "state laws." If the Muslim authorities are informed that a Muslim lead a dissolute life, they inform the police, who may already know it. The police investigate and send the case to the *magistrat* or *uezd* court, which asks the Ecclesiastical Assembly in Orenburg or the Ecclesiastical Board (*Pravlenie*) in the Crimea for an opinion (*zakliuchenie*); this opinion must discuss only the nature (*svoistvo*) and gravity (*stepen viny*) of the offence, and cite Muslim law, but may not prescribe a punishment. The duty of the court is to impose a corrective (*ispravitelnoe*) punishment, meaning detention at the police station, at the workhouse, or in prison for up to four months. Muslim authorities and the *mufti* may not take up cases of fornication and seduction between Muslims.

The case raised a second question: whether the Muslim clergy was empowered to impose sentences that included corporal punishment. The State Council referred to the ukazy of 1767 and 1802, according to which matters related to marriage were regulated by Muslim authorities, but their consequences (like theft of property and personal offences) were justiciable before the civil courts, and to that of 1827, which gave civil courts jurisdiction over matters involving Muslims, but not related to the performance of their religious obligations.

It concluded that those laws were clear enough in demarcating the respective spheres of Muslim and Russian law, and that Muslim religious authorities could not assume jurisdiction over matters of civil law.

The third question was whether a *mufti*'s personal decision had the same validity as a judicial sentence. The Council noted that the former Orenburg *mufti* had tried marriage disputes and other cases under Muslim law without the participation of the Assembly and that complaints had been received against his partiality. He had been told that his personal decisions could not be carried out. The Council confirmed this, saying that only those decisions arrived at by joint deliberation of the *mufti* and the other members had the same standing as a court decision.[105]

A similar case came up in 1837, which the Senate also forwarded to the State Council. It raised the issue of how Muslim ecclesiastical authorities should decide cases of adultery. The Council agreed with the Senate that they could impose only sentences of repentance (*pokaianie*) and correction (*ispravlenie*). If they felt that such punishment was inadequate, they had to send the case to the civil courts, which would sentence the defendant to detention not exceeding fourteen days.[106]

Yet another case raised jurisdictional issues of another kind. The Kizliar land court – the *uezd* police agency – turned to both the Orenburg Assembly and the Crimean Board to send an opinion on the legality of marriages between "followers of the sect of Ali" (Shi'ites) and those of the "sect of Omar" (Sunnis), which often took place in the Transcaucasian provinces. It wanted to know whether the children were legitimate and what were their rights to inherit property. The matter was also brought up before the Interior Ministry, which rebuked the land court, saying that it had no right to seek answers from the ecclesiastical authorities: the status of children and inheritance rights were matters of government policy and had to be brought before the civil courts, whose decisions were appealable to the Senate, responsible for the elaboration of a uniform jurisprudence throughout the empire.[107]

One can detect a certain consistency in the Russian approach to Muslim law from the middle of the eighteenth century to the 1840s. There was an assumption that conversion would bring the Muslim into the Russian community of Orthodox believers, governed by religious law in largely family matters and by Russian secular law in all others. When facing claims by those who chose to remain Muslim, the authorities endeavoured to split the unsplittable: to extract from the unitary Muslim law, which did not distinguish between religious and secular law, a religious jurisprudence – which would remain the responsibility of the religious courts – and a body of civil law to become gradually integrated into Russian civil law, while placing the punishment of crimes squarely in the Russian criminal courts. A process of integration was clearly at work here, in which Muslims would join the great mass of other subjects, but retain their religious courts with their jurisdiction over matters considered essentially religious (like marriage), much in the same way as native Russians sought redress before Orthodox courts in similar matters.

The process of integration was not driven only by the steady determination to create a one and indivisible Russia in the core and, unfortunately, in the empire as well, but also by a humanitarian concern over the harshness of Muslim law, especially its deplorable treatment of women. This harshness was the product of an age-long static social order born in the days of a pastoral economy, and frozen in time by the economic stagnation of southern Eurasia. There was no reference to a supposedly superior European model, but to a quiet and justified conviction that the settler was bringing with him a multi-faceted, more complex and more humane jurisprudence (despite all its shortcomings) to the world of the nomad or former nomad being integrated into the social and fiscal fabric of the expanding Russian core.

Russian and Mongol Law

While the existence of Islam as a core religion created a confessional frontier with Orthodoxy, in which a struggle was fought for the religious allegiance of various animist peoples in the basin of the middle Volga and the Kama, the establishment of Tibetan Buddhism (Lamaism) in Mongolia created a similar intermediate frontier occupied by Kalmyks, Buriats, and, in part, Yakuts. Such a confessional frontier was certainly a territorial one as well. The Orthodox succeeded in converting the northern Buriats from shamanism, and the Buddhists retained their hold over the southern Buriats in Transbaikalia. But it also turned into a jurisprudential frontier between the Russian and the Mongol legal systems. The rivalry was fought, as in central Eurasia between Orthodoxy and Islam, over demarcating misdemeanours from criminal offences and, in the civil law, at the appellate level, when dissatisfied parties challenged the provisions of the customary law. The Russians recognized the existence and the validity of that law but nevertheless sought to supersede and amend some of its provisions: the process was facilitated by changes in the way of life of the Buriats brought about by the arrival and the settlement of the Russians. Those amendments were thus part of a process of social, political, and economic accommodation between the settlers and the nomads in the expanding core being subjected to growing integration as it reached its natural limits.

Mongol law went back, in its official form, to the Great Yassa promulgated by Chingis Khan in 1218, known to us in only thirty fragments. It was intended to serve as the law of the Mongol Empire, but applied only to the nomadic peoples; the Russian principalities of western Eurasia, the Persian lands of southern Eurasia, and the Chinese core beyond Eurasia retained their local systems. What is known about the Yassa tells us that it emphasized the absolute power of the khan and was generous with the death penalty and other severe punishments aiming at ensuring the execution of the khan's orders; the family was patriarchal, the concept of private property unknown. Of great interest was Tamerlane's attempt in the fourteenth century to combine the provisions of the Yassa with the sharia: crimes and offences relating to religion were judged by *kadis*, while civil cases came under the Yassa. The Yassa influenced the customary law of the Kalmyks and Buriats. At the very same time that those two peoples were coming into sustained contact with the Russians, they were developing a jurisprudence that would remain the foundation of their customary law well into the nineteenth century.[108]

In 1640, a congress of Mongol princes and *taishis* of Eastern Mongols (Khalkas) and Zunghars of the Kokonor basin and the Siberian and Volga steppes met to discuss and approve the so-called Mongol-Oirat Regulations (MOR), which differed markedly from the four-hundred-year old Great Yassa, but also retained some of its provisions. They were supplemented by edicts of the Zunghar chief Galdan in 1677–8 and by administrative edicts (*yarliks*). Substantial extensions were made during the rule of Khan Donduk Dashi (1752–61), and the so-called Zinzili resolutions of 1822–7 attempted, under strong Russian influence, to bring this Kalmyk customary law up to date.

Among the Buriats, one is struck by the frequency of judicial statutes and decisions which modified or extended what may have been the same MOR of 1640. The northern Buriats produced resolutions passed by clan chieftains dealing with marriages, taxation, and tribal administration. The southern Buriats passed resolutions in 1759, 1763, and 1781, and six more between 1800 and 1823 ranging from 9 to 144 articles, dealing with issues as varied as matchmaking, divorce, intoxication, and the requisitioning of carts, but all these resolutions were only collections of customs and acts of positive law lacking a vision of the law which would create a true jurisprudence. On the other hand, they offered an overview of the tribes' thinking at a particular time on contentious issues. An attempt to create a comprehensive digest of the customary law for the nomads of Eastern Siberia (Buriats, Yakuts, Tungus, etc.) was the monster Code of Steppe Laws in 802 articles, published in 1841. It never received legislative sanction, but it would guide native courts and even Russian judges. All these resolutions and "codes" were not so much codes as digests, not unlike the Digest of Laws (*Svod Zakonov*) of the Russian empire, published in 1832 and based on the empire's Collection of Laws.

It is possible to identify the major features of Mongol law and isolate cases where Russian and Mongol law would either converge or clash. Mongol law was not significantly influenced by Lamaism, even though the Regulations of 1640 considered Buddhism the one true faith and persecuted shamanism. Insulting the clergy was severely punished; so were attacks on monastic property. The law protected the clergy's exalted position. This was a major difference between Mongol and

Islamic law. Russian jurisprudence in the eighteenth century was deeply infused with religious attitudes on crime and punishment, and sought to inculcate Orthodox values and behaviour. It stood closer to Islamic than to Mongol law.

Marriage was the most important topic of private law. Despite changing perceptions over the centuries and some differences among the various tribes, the continuing existence of a pastoral economy upheld the patriarchal nature of the family. Marriage fell into three stages, having different juristic consequences and separated by considerable periods of time: the betrothal, which took place when the bride and groom were still infants; the agreement when they were grown and the *kalim* (bride money) was paid; and the marriage ceremony. Marriage was mandatory and was the responsibility of the entire clan, who saw to it that the children would eventually have marriage partners. Polygamy continued to exist. Despite the choice made by the parents, it remained a custom to assume that the marriage took place by seizure or abduction of the bride. Hence the payment of the *kalim* (*veno* in Russian) by the bridegroom, who purchased his bride from his future in-laws. If he could not afford to pay the *kalim*, he would hire himself out to his in-laws or someone else in the extended family who would pay it for him. Marriage was the affair of the entire clan. The bride was also given a dowry. The *kalim* and dowry represented an exchange of presents, the value of which depended on the social standing of the parties. One consequence was that the wife (or at least the first wife in a polygamous marriage) was given great consideration, and mistreating her was a criminal offence. Among some of the Buriat clans, a son-in-law had to bear everything in silence and could not reply to reprimands administered by his wife's relatives.

Side by side with this relative "equality" between the sexes, which may have been a relic of an earlier time when a matriarchal society was in existence, we also find "hospitable haetarism," a practice by which a childless woman might not refuse a night's lodging and sexual favours to a traveller on pain of a fine, a reflection on the Mongols' relatively loose sexual mores. One wonders if similar practices did not exist in Siberia (and elsewhere), where armed detachments on their way to their assignments were billeted in Russian peasants' homes: the defenceless wives and daughters were certainly not going to sue the soldiers in court for rape. We also find the institution of the levirate, a custom by which a widow married the younger brother of her deceased husband, a survival from a community of wives among close relatives, justified by economic considerations such as the need to retain the widow and her dowry in the family, and the conception of the wife as the property of the family for whom a purchase price had been paid.

Divorce was simple: a husband could desert his wife, and her relatives could buy her back, but she was entitled to take the dowry with her. Gradually, the wife too obtained the right to divorce, but it was attended by material consequences (retention or return of the *kalim*), depending on the nature of the causes of the divorce.

Among the Kalmyks it was permitted to take a child from another family for the purpose of bringing it up, but after age fifteen, a girl could not be returned to her original parents. This custom probably went a long way to explain how the Russians were able to obtain boys and girls who would then become fully integrated into the Russian social order and marry Russians.

Another feature of Mongol law was its lack of recognition of the right to private ownership in immovables. The land, chiefly pastures, was the common property of the clan or groups of clans such as *hotons* and *aimaks*, and each clan and family had to camp on the land allotted to it. Valentin Riasanovsky pointed out that this was a feature common to Mongol and Muslim law – he might have added Russian law as well. Certainly, one of the most characteristic features of Russian land tenure was that land was held in common, that it was the property of the commune, and that individual plots were periodically redistributed. It was the same with the pastures of the Mongols, Kalmyks, and Buriats. That is why Russian authorities insisted that disputes attending the redistribution of pastures had to be brought before the civil courts and the governor.

With the passage of time, as the Buriats began to engage in agriculture, partly under Russian influence, or began to cultivate hay for the winter months to protect their cattle from starving, the right to own these plots entered the customary law, although the plots remained subject to redistribution if the clan insisted that they must remain the common property of all.

This phenomenon had important consequences. When nomads settled and began to grow crops, they had to recognize the right to property in immovables, which was bound to favour the clan leaders, and social differentiation set in with the blessing of the Russians because it fostered the integration of the notables into the social order of the core. Thus, paradoxically, it was in Siberia that private landholding developed, where the entire territory was considered to be the ruler's *votchina*, and where the peasantry paid an *obrok* for the right to use the land, which was, in fact, the collective property of the ruling class. The emergence of this right to private ownership of immovables seems to have made a greater impact upon the Buriat communities than among the Russians.

In Mongol law, only sons were entitled to inherit property; daughters only inherited their dowry. But the inheritance was not equally divided among the sons: the oldest received the largest share, the youngest inherited his father's household (with his widows, including his own mother, whom, however, he was forbidden to marry). The reason may have been that Mongol law recognized the separation of the sons during the lifetime of their parents. Each son received only a part of his future inheritance. By the time all the sons had separated and received their share nominally, there may have remained nothing but the household. Old Russian law also knew this concept of anticipated inheritance. Mongol law had another point in common with Russian law, as it had with other underdeveloped law: the predominance of inheritance by law (custom) over inheritance by testament. Among the Buriats, the testament was found only as a supplement to inheritance by custom. The predominance of the will, which implied the freedom of the individual to dispose of his property, would have assumed his freedom from clan and family ties – an impossible situation in a still patriarchal society structured along clan lines.

The criminal law, like Mongol law in general, lacked general principles and bore a purely concrete, casual character – not unlike Russian law. There was no equality before the law, and penalties varied not only with the object but also with the subject of the crime, very much as in Russian law, with its sharp distinction between the privileges of the ruling class and the lack of rights among the dependent population. It distinguished, again very much like Russian laws, between crimes against the clergy and religion, against the authorities, against the community, and against the person and property, as well as crimes committed by officials.

The penal law of the Yassa had been extraordinarily harsh, but the Regulations of 1640, perhaps under the mitigating influence of Lamaism, substituted corporal punishment and fines for the death penalty, over a century before Russian law did. Among the Kalmyks, penalties included, besides a few provisions for the death penalty, mutilation, flogging with the *knut*, and the full confiscation of property. Such a classification had much in common with the Russian penal system. But imprisonment was not part of Kalmyk or Buriat law because it would have been totally out of harmony with the conditions of nomadic life. A striking similarity between Russian law and native custom was subjection to ignominy, which was added to a heavy fine, for fleeing from the field of battle: the coward was dressed in a woman's sleeveless jacket. The Zinzili Congress replaced the fine in most cases with corporal punishment with the whip or rods – Russian influence was very clear here.

But even if the death penalty was no longer widely imposed after 1640, its "suspension" in Russian legislation after 1753 contributed to its de facto abolition among the Kalmyks and Buriats. In 1745, for example, the Senate accepted Nepliuev's recommendation that its continued application would be a violation of Russian law and therefore unacceptable. It appeared that when a Kalmyk committed a serious offence (*proderzost*) or aroused the hatred or fury (*zloba*) of his fellow clansmen, he was secretly strangled or butchered (*zadavit ili zarezat*) and his cattle and property (*pozhitki*) were confiscated. The Senate warned the *ulus* chiefs that if they continued to impose that penalty or "dishonoured" a Kalmyk or his family in the eyes of his own *ulus*, they would be whipped. If it was found that his offence was so great that he deserved the maximum penalty, the culprit had to be tried in court, whipped with the *knut* before his fellow clansmen, and handed back to his *ulus* chief. All sentences to natural and political death had to be sent to the Orenburg governor for confirmation, but he was now required by Russian law to forward such sentences to the Senate, which had suspended the application of the death penalty.[109]

The Senate's decision was unclear, as was often the case in the middle of the eighteenth century. The same text created a court in Stavropol for the trial of converted Kalmyks; it was given jurisdiction over Kalmyks in their *uluses*, unless the case was one of murder and highway robbery or involved disputes over pastures and other land. In these cases, and if the sentence was death or banishment, the court had to send them to the Orenburg governor. But the text seemed to imply that cases of *prozerzosti* would still be tried in court. In 1803, the government repeated that sentences to death or exile and land disputes between *uluses* had to be sent to the governor.[110]

In Eastern Siberia, the Yakut princelings were given in 1728 the right to try their own people in cases of misdemeanours (*malovazhnye prestuplenia*) such as cases involving the *kalim*, thefts of cattle, or beatings. But criminal (*kriminalnye*) cases, including murder, came under the jurisdiction of the regular courts. Complaints against the *toyons* were addressed to the *voevoda*. This was confirmed in 1752, and the government even accepted a petition of *toyons* that cancelled the right to appeal the decision of the *toyon* courts to the *voevoda*. Princes and other chieftains of *uluses* were allowed to inflict punishments of beating with sticks (*batogi*) and whipping. The natives were also encouraged to resort to mediation in order to avoid the cumbersome written procedures of the regular courts.[111] The instruction to the governor general of Siberia of 1803 also confirmed the distinction between misdemeanours and criminal cases, which must be tried in accordance with Russian law.[112] And the statute of 1822 on native peoples (*inorodtsy*) stated that crimes were tried in the regular courts in accordance with Russian laws and that civil cases not settled in the native courts had to be sent to the *uezd* court, from which they could be appealed to the civil chamber.[113]

Much archival work remains to be done before it becomes truly possible to assess the degree of interpenetration between Russian and Mongol law, the extent of Russian influence in the assimilation of Mongol law, and whether the Russians sought compromises as they did with Muslim law in Astrakhan and elsewhere. From what is already known, it appears that Russian and Mongol law were not separate species of law, that Mongol law became assimilated into the law of the conqueror. After all, law embodies the values of a society; was not the Russian a nomad like the people that had once conquered him and that he had conquered in turn? Petr Chaadaev, of Tatar ancestry, may not have been wrong.

Economic Integration

Agriculture and Industry

The success of a policy of systematic integration of the expanding core depended to a considerable extent on the creation of an agricultural base and an industrial infrastructure uniting western and eastern Eurasia. That union would also encourage the development of trade with southern Eurasia. The search for an optimum territory within which the ruling elite could create a one and indivisible Russia was a fundamental feature of Moscow's, and later Petersburg's, policy. By the end of the eighteenth century, the administrative reform had created the necessary infrastructure and the rudiments of an integrated market, whose progress, however, was severely restricted by enormous distances and poor communications. But the identification of economic space with the core territory was by then completed. Russia, consciously or not, had become the best practitioner of cameralist theory as it developed in the Germanies beginning in the 1740s.

The settlers – whether peasants, townsmen, or military personnel – suffered great hardships as they moved into steppe land favourable to agriculture, but never tilled before and rendered at times inhospitable by climatic conditions to which the Russian was not accustomed and which destroyed the settler's harvest as irremediably as they destroyed the nomad's herds. Distances made the situation worse, and it was not unusual for Cossack units in the remote Siberian northeast, the ultimate extremity of the core, to starve to death because they could not be provisioned in time. By the beginning of the nineteenth century, the state peasant managed to produce enough grain for himself and for a surplus to be disposed of, not so much in the small market towns as in the forts along the fortified lines which grew as so many market towns, more urban in fact than those towns of the interior, because Cossacks often did not have enough time to till their plots. Those forts also became trading outposts with the Kazakhs and Kalmyks coming to barter their goods for grain and metal. As a result, the military infrastructure built along the core's periphery became the determining factor in the development of regional economies in the Caspian basin and Western Siberia, linked by the grain market of Transural Bashkiria.

Agriculture provided an excellent example to help trace the fundamental demarcation between an expanding core, which had reached its natural limits, and its imperial extension, into which settlers would not cross in any significant numbers. When Nicholas I – who overlooked the distinction – stated his intention in 1830 to resettle eighty thousand Little Russian Cossacks in Transcaucasia, Paskevich answered that he could not find enough land to settle such a large number of military colonists, but might find room for less than one-tenth that number.[114] In eastern Georgia, especially in the valley of the Alezan, good land was reserved for vineyards and the cultivation of industrial crops. Karabagh was very fertile, and the Mugan steppe was suitable for the cultivation of cotton and rice. But the heat was also excessive, sharp temperature changes had a deleterious influence on agriculture, and irrigation was essential. Regular visits by locusts between the Suram range and the Caspian Sea could destroy crops in a few hours.[115] Such an environment was not favourable to the cultivation of rye, barley, and oats, the settler's preferred crops. Transcaucasia did continue to be an imperial possession, where the pre-annexation fiscal system remained in effect, while the capitation and the *obrok* formed its foundation everywhere in the core. By contrast, the growing colonization of the Stavropol upland – away from the salt-encrusted soil to the east, abandoned to the Kalmyks and Nogais – created an agricultural market for the growing population of the forts on the Caucasian Line and for the regular troops operating in the mountains and even in Transcaucasia.

It was estimated at the beginning of the nineteenth century that the minimum annual consumption of grain was two *chetverti* (16 *puds* or 262 kilograms/577.6 pounds) per person. In 1795, total cereal production in the Orenburg Territory was one million *chetverti* for a total population of 332,300 Russians and Ukrainians, or three *chetverti* per person. By 1844–5, the harvest yielded between 7 3/4 and 9 1/2 *chetverti* per male ("soul"), more than enough to create a substantial surplus. Conditions were favourable for extensive agriculture: at the beginning of the century the average allotment was 82.4 *desiatin* (222 acres) per male, but colonization reduced it to 46 *desiatins* by the 1830s – still a much higher figure than the 15 *desiatin* allotted to state peasants elsewhere, and still no incentive to practise intensive agriculture.[116]

Agriculture in the Orenburg Territory had greatly suffered during the rebellions, including that of Pugachev, and the punitive expeditions, but by the end of the century, agriculture was making progress in the valley of the Belaia, while further north and across the Urals between the Miass and Iset Rivers, where the wooded steppe turned into grassland steppe, agriculture among the Bashkirs began to occupy the same importance as animal husbandry.[117] The growth of production meant that no grain needed to be imported any longer from Kazan in the west and Siberia in the east. The surplus went to supply the distilleries and feed the working population of the ironworks and copper smelters of the Urals, or was exported from landings on the Kama and Belaia. The Territory had become the second grain market in the eastern theatre after that of the northern Caucasus; indeed the first, if we include Perm and Viatka provinces, where a grain surplus was always available for export to market towns in the region and even upstream on the Volga toward Moscow. This grain market was a replica of other such markets, all integrated – as much as communications permitted – into the grain market of the expanding core. Agriculture helped create a uniform economic landscape on the fringes of the forest and in the steppe. No wonder then that the fiscal system of the Orenburg Territory had become integrated as well by the 1830s, with the capitation and the *obrok* collected everywhere. The only, but important, exception (save for small groups of nomads) was the Stavropol (converted) Kalmyks and the Bashkirs. They had been "cossackized" at the beginning of the nineteenth century and, as such, exempted from the personal taxes, that badge of identity for the dependent population everywhere across the expanding core.

Western Siberia had the greatest potential to become the largest grain market in the eastern theatre. Statisticians assumed that the Siberian needed 2.5 *chetverti* (20 *puds* or 327.6 kilograms/722 pounds) of grain annually.[118] In the seventeenth and during much of the eighteenth century, the authorities had imposed quotas on the peasant population to secure the provisioning of troops and the civil administration. By the nineteenth century, the quotas had disappeared, to be replaced by a reliance on the state peasant to produce both for himself and for the needs of the market. But this market was not free, because occasionally poor harvests created catastrophic situations. The difficulties attending the transportation of grain over enormous distances compelled the authorities to requisition peasant grain. Peasants retaliated by hiding their grain, making the situation worse. A partial solution, of which Catherine's government was very fond, was to build grain stores with a one- or even two-year reserve.[119] One wonders, when reading contemporary texts, why local authorities had to be ordered to build them, when doing so was such a necessary precaution.

The weakness of the Siberian grain market was that "Siberia" meant at the time only a narrow band between the Old and the New Ishim Lines, between a line from Turinsk to Omsk via Yalutorovsk and Ishim on the one hand, and one from Omsk via Petropavlovsk to the confluence of the Ui and the Tobol on the other – the so-called Ishim steppe. The land was good, the climate favourable, and the population the densest in Siberia. By the mid-nineteenth century, the expanding core had found its natural limits along the Tobol and the upper course of the Ishim. Beyond the Irtysh, the Baraba and Kulunda steppes beckoned the settler to create another grain market. In 1795, the production of cereals in Tobolsk and Kolyvan provinces reached 1.4 million *chetverti* for a population of about 780,000, or 1.80 *chetverti* per person. By 1811, the harvest yielded 2.6 million *chetverti* for a population of 525,400 in Tobolsk province alone, or 4.9 *chetverti* per person, and left a surplus of 852,028 *chetverti* after consumption and storage of seed grain.[120] But the demand was great for the mining enterprises of the Altai and the military and Cossack units along the Irtysh, and occasional poor harvests could reduce consumption to subsistence levels. Some of the grain had to be transported to the settlements deep in the forest zone, which were totally destitute of that essential commodity.

In Eastern Siberia, where poor soil and terrible climate combined to impose severe limitations on the expansion of the core, shortages were an endemic threat. Irkutsk province produced only 530,000 *chetverti* of grain in 1795 for the entire territory. There were two consecutive poor harvests in 1811–12 and a third was threatening when the government banned the use of grain in distilling in 1813, and whatever was available was reserved for the population of the Nerchinsk district with its convicts and silver mines.[121] The Irkutsk district was the leading producer, followed by the Selenga valley around Verkhneudinsk (Ulan Ude). The surplus grain was shipped to Kiakhta, to provision the

Petrovskii ironworks on Lake Baikal, and via the Khilok and the Ingoda, to Nerchinsk. A third but smaller producing district was the valley of the Ilim, from which grain was shipped down the Lena to Yakutsk and beyond, to Okhotsk and Kamchatka, which the expanding core barely reached. Farther to the west, however, the Yenisei valley between Krasnoiarsk and Minusinsk was becoming the granary of Eastern Siberia. Its surplus was shipped down the Yenisei as far north as Turukhansk, but the river and road network was not favourable to eastward shipments.[122] The agricultural integration of the core suffered not so much from inadequate production as from the difficulty of shipping grain from surplus areas to areas totally dependent on imports, whenever shortages reached dangerous levels. Regional markets could not easily be converted into a global market for the entire eastern theatre.

There were hopes in the eighteenth century that Siberia might become an industrial base from which to project military power into Mongolia and even beyond the Eurasian periphery into northern China.[123] That industrial base had to be either the Urals or Eastern Siberia. The Ural industry, largely created by Peter I, had reached the peak of its development in the 1750s, and had already entered a period of relative decline by the time the Pugachev rebellion dealt it a severe blow in the 1770s. The Bashkirs had greatly suffered from the ruthless encroachments of the industrialists, who had robbed them of their forests and their lands for a song; they now took their revenge in joining peasants and workers to destroy mines, plants, and dams. An industrial revival, which would have welcomed technological improvements, was checked by a combination of parallel factors. One was the destruction of forests, from which charcoal was produced; a second was a reduction in foreign demand, notably from England; a third was the insignificant demand for iron in Siberia and Central Asia, while the Moscow region became the major producer of metal goods in the first half of the nineteenth century.[124] The result was to bind the Urals metal industry more closely than ever with the very heart of the core, and also with the northern Caucasus, to which iron articles could easily be shipped via the Volga and the Don. Transcaucasia held a promise of copper and silver mines, but substantial results would have to wait a long time.[125] Thus the Urals industry became a factor of economic integration in the Caspian basin and much of western Eurasia, while central and eastern Eurasia, nowadays the foundation of the Russian fuel industry, remained outsiders in the economy of the eastern theatre.

Siberia was not without mineral resources, the most famous ones being the copper, silver, and gold deposits in the Altai. The Demidov family had begun the exploitation of the copper mines, but also kept some of the gold for themselves at a time when Russia was almost wholly deficient in precious metals (which could be acquired only by an excess of exports over imports), save for the distant silver deposits of Nerchinsk. After the incorporation of the

Demidovs' silver and gold mines in 1747 into the properties of the ruling house managed by the Cabinet, production expanded, and the Zmeinogorsk mine, on a tributary of the Alei which flows into the Ob above Barnaul, gave most of the silver coming from Siberia in the eighteenth century. It had 3,230 workers in 1794, and in the ninety-year period from 1744 to 1834 the mine yielded 36,942 *puds* of silver and 1,000 *puds* (16,380 kilograms/36,118 pounds) of gold, or over half the total gold and silver extracted in Russia during that time. Barnaul, originally a copper plant, became the largest silver-smelting plant in the whole of Siberia. In 1781, a rich polymetal mine was discovered in the Salair range, 160 kilometres northeast of Barnaul, and in 1786 a rich silver mine (Ridderskoe), 160 kilometres south of Zmeinogorsk. The result was the creation of an enormous mining region between the Irtysh and the Tom Rivers, administered by a central mining office located in Barnaul. Copper was mined and smelted at Loktevsk on the Alei River. The oldest copper smelter was at Kolyvan, just north of Zmeinogorsk; it was closed in 1759 following the destruction of the forests around it, restored in 1790, and finally closed in 1800. The most important silver smelter in the 1830s and 1840s was at Zmeev: it smelted 20 per cent of the Altai silver.[126]

Even if the smelter was closed, the Kolyvan mines remained the major producer of copper, as well as "a training ground for young hopefuls before they entered the promotional ladder of the Mining Corps."[127] But the Altai boom ended in 1779, at the very moment when the mining district became part of the new Kolyvan *oblast*, closed in 1796. It later became part of the new Tomsk province, whose governor was also the chief of the mining administration, subordinated to the Cabinet. In 1830, the district – renamed after the Altai in 1834 – was placed under the Mining Department of the Finance Ministry. The state-owned mines of the Urals had also been under the jurisdiction of the ministry since its creation in 1802. In both regions, the labour force consisted of state peasants (who also depended on the Finance Ministry), compelled to work in the mines and smelters and bound to them for life. The Siberian mining industry thus depended on forced labour. This raises the question of Siberia's "colonial status." One may perhaps claim that the near-destruction of the fur-bearing animals in the seventeenth century was a form of colonial exploitation, even though a similar claim must also be made for the same operation and the systematic destruction of the bison in the Great Plains of North America. One must ask, however, whether the exploitation of natural resources in an expanding core, where the Russian population was becoming a substantial majority, and the near-absence of native peoples among the labour force, can be considered a similar form of colonial behaviour. One credible answer is that it cannot. This was even more the case with the Nerchinsk silver and lead mines, operated with convict labour under the jurisdiction of the College of Mining until 1787, when they were transferred to the Cabinet. By the 1820s, the main activity of the mines was to smelt gold-bearing silver and send the lead at considerable cost to the Altai plants for smelting. The decline of production was catastrophic: in the 1820s, it was already half of what it had been in the last quarter of the eighteenth century: in the 1830s, only about 190 *puds* (3,112 kilograms/6,861 pounds) were produced, and in 1859, only 10.[128]

But the production of gold and silver – all these minerals were sent to Moscow and Petersburg – did not create an industrial base for Siberia. What the region needed in order to create the rudiments of economic integration was an iron and textile industry using local raw materials, and, above all, a market. Western Siberia had no iron deposits but could meet its needs from the Urals. Most of the iron was found east of the Ob River. The tribes of the Yenisei valley had long been familiar with iron smelting on a small scale, based on local ore found close to the surface, sufficient to meet the local demand for tools, dishes, and weapons, but the local market was limited. When Siberian industrialists – who usually had made their money in the China trade and in selling vodka on behalf of the government – built ironworks in the vicinity of Krasnoiarsk and elsewhere, they discovered they could not find a sufficient labour force and could not compete with artisan forges (*ruchnye gorni*). East of Lake Baikal, the Petrovskii ironworks were built on a tributary of the Khilok in 1788 to supply iron articles to the whole of Transbaikalia, but the harsh and capricious weather took its toll. Since the plant, as elsewhere, relied on water power, it could not operate in winter, when the river froze, and in the summer, when it dried up. Its owner gave it up in 1791, when the government took it over, hoping to keep reducing the dependence of Eastern Siberia on imports from the distant Urals. It eventually became the most successful ironworks of the region.[129]

Another relative success was the Irkutsk cloth factory, built sixty kilometres downriver from Irkutsk at the confluence of the Telma and Angara Rivers. In 1731, a Velikii Ustiug merchant had decided to build a cloth factory near the Chinese border, but the operation was not profitable and was finally abandoned, showing there was no market for the cloth. It was taken over by the Commissary in 1789, and its production was intended for the troops. It was at the time the only cloth factory in the whole of Siberia, and it managed even to find a small market in Mongolia. The Buriats brought their wool; the labour force consisted largely of exiles sent to hard labour or "settlement." The quality of the cloth was poor and the factory seemed unable to produce white cloth. In 1823, it had 1,159 workers and 3,400 males attached to it to supply food and fuel. By the 1830s, there was another cloth factory in Omsk, administered by the Cossack Host, also with a labour force of convicts.[130]

It appears from this short survey that the economic integration of the eastern theatre remained an impossible dream during the first decades of the nineteenth century. What we find instead is the emergence of three regional markets in the expanding core, with a fourth in Transcaucasia beyond the core.

Agriculture and industry created a first one in the Trans-Volga part of the Caspian basin, what with the industry of the Urals and Bashkiria, the agricultural production of the lower Kama basin and the open steppe beyond, and the rising population of settlers creating a substantial demand. The West Siberian market was concentrated in a narrow zone, in the Ishim and trans-Irtysh steppes, a chiefly agrarian market without industrial resources and dependent on the Urals and Altai industry for its metal goods, but capable of expansion nevertheless, not only as a result of its growing population but also because of its organic relationship with the rest of the Kazakh steppe and its large population. The future pointed to the eventual integration of the West Siberian and Caspian markets into a huge continental market forming a semicircle embracing southern Eurasia from the west and the east, and capable of supporting enough military power to enable the government to return to Peter's policy of conquest in the region. But Eastern Siberia remained the least integrated market, both internally and within eastern Eurasia. Endowed, but inadequately, with mineral resources, cursed with a brutal climate and permafrost, it was doomed to remain underpopulated by settlers and natives alike, thus without a market for locally produced as well as imported goods. Distances, climate, and a sparse population made it impossible to maintain easy communications between its internal parts and with the rest of Eurasia; in no way could it create a sufficiently strong economic base from which to project Russian power into the Asian coastland.

Roads and Waterways

The enormous distances, the harsh climate, and the unfavourable orientation of the major rivers of the eastern theatre combined to neutralize the advantages of what appeared on the map to be a splendid hydrographic network. The Volga flowed south into an inhospitable salt-water lake with deserted northern and eastern shores. The Ob drained the whole of central Eurasia, the Yenisei and the Lena the whole of eastern Eurasia, only to end up in the wastes of the Arctic Ocean, most of their course flowing across the densely forested zone with few inhabitants and incapable of supporting more. And yet, that hydrographic network offered exceptional opportunities to the explorer, the merchant, and the serviceman, and helped bind the eastern theatre with western Eurasia while restricting, however, the possibilities of internal integration within the expanding core.

Kazan – 821 kilometres from Moscow and perched on a hill near where the Volga made a sharp southward turn toward Tsaritsyn, where it swerved again, but southeastwards, to discharge into the Caspian at Astrakhan – had always been the great hub of the mid- and lower-Volga traffic, which created an organic link between western Eurasia, the Caspian, and southern Eurasia.

The water route from Kazan to Saratov was 859 kilometres long, to Tsaritsyn another 392, and to Astrakhan a further 458, a total of 1,709 kilometres. From Moscow to Astrakhan the distance was 3,312 kilometres, and it took from thirty to forty days to reach the Caspian port nonstop.[131] The river was deep enough to accommodate large barges, but the upstream trip was difficult, as barges had to be pulled along a towpath by *burlaki*, immortalized in Ilya Repin's painting. Moreover, the river froze solid for about half the year. At the confluence of the Kama the navigation season lasted 197 days, at Tsaritsyn 210, in Astrakhan 260 days. While travellers and couriers could use the land route along the river, drive or ride on the direct overland and much shorter 1,412-kilometre-long route from Moscow via Riazan, Tambov, Borisoglebsk, and Tsaritsyn,[132] cross the Volga and follow the Akhtuba to Astrakhan, the merchandise traffic as a factor of economic integration was severely compromised from the early fall to the spring.

Difficulties increased south of Astrakhan. The barren landscape of the low-lying Caspian coast offered no shelter or even landing to water-borne traffic. To reach Kizliar on the Terek required a long journey of some 360 kilometres across a totally deserted steppe. The few postal stations were kept by Nogais and Astrakhan Tatars, who also transported heavy goods and equipment for a payment, but had to hire additional horses to carry their own provisions, water, and firewood, and oats and hay for the animals, because none could be had on the way.[133] From Kizliar one could go two ways, both beginning at the confluence of the Sunzha and the Terek and both leading to Transcaucasia. One followed the coastal road via Derbent, the "gates of gates" and the "historic highway of armies," to Baku and Shemakha, 1,000 kilometres from Astrakhan, a distance which a caravan could cover in twenty-seven days. Shemakha led via Lenkoran to Ghilan in northern Persia.[134] But the road was so unreliable, so much at the mercy of the highlanders – at Derbent the passage between the mountains and the coast was only 10 kilometres wide – that troops stationed in the area were supplied by ships sailing from Astrakhan, which deposited their provisions at Nizovaia and Derbent. The other followed the course of the Sunzha, continued to the upper Terek, crossed the Caucasus in full view of the Kazbek, rising to 5,044 metres via the Darial Gorge, and ran along the valley of the Aragvi to its confluence with the Kura near Tiflis, 1,905 kilometres from Moscow. The Terek-Aragvi route was called the Georgian Military Highway, 207 kilometres long.[135] But this road, although the best way to cross the Caucasus, was narrow, dangerous, and obstructed by heavy snows in winter, when eastern Transcaucasia was effectively cut off from the expanding core north of the mountains. Difficult communications between the northern and southern Caucasus, in sharp contrast with the ease of travel across the core, truly showed that Transcaucasia was a world apart, the constituent part of an empire and not the intrinsic building block of an expanding core.[136]

Kazan also functioned as a hub for the integration of Bashkiria across the Volga until its replacement by Ufa at the beginning of the nineteenth century. The Volga at Simbirsk, 220 kilometres downstream, received the Samara, 520 kilometres long, along which a line of forts built in the 1730s provided a highway to the Ural River and Orenburg. The Kama, from its confluence with the Volga at Laishev, led to the Belaia, on which Ufa was located, and which led along its 1,000 kilometres to the southern Urals, a short portage away from the source of the Ui River flowing east into the Tobol. The Volga, the Samara, the Kama, and their tributaries, all flowing in the direction of Kazan, created, it seemed, a convenient network of water routes for the transportation of goods toward the great markets of Moscow and Petersburg. Beyond the Samara and the Belaia, the Ural River, with its two sharp bends at Orsk and Uralsk, flowed into the Caspian east of Astrakhan and formed one of the inner boundaries of the expanding core, beyond which the Turgai River announced its natural limit. But the rich hydrographic network suffered from the climate and the low gradient so characteristic of the steppe. The Samara was a lazy river used mostly to power water mills and raft timber. The 2,380-kilometre-long Ural River was obstructed by masses of sandbars, used by the Kazakhs' and Kalmyks' cattle to ford the river in the summer. It was not navigable, froze in November, and did not open up until the spring, in April, for example, at Orenburg. The network helped integrate the region into the core, but only the steppe roads linking the provincial capitals with the district centres, the Kama, and the Volga could generate enough activity to accelerate integration beyond a bare minimum suitable for the old nomadic society. The Belaia alone was truly navigable, but its sinuous course and rapid current made it dangerous for long barges with their cargoes of metal, grain, and timber. Within the region, overland distances were still great, although shorter than the river routes. Ufa was 524 kilometres from Kazan, Orenburg 382 from Ufa, but the Orenburg Line formed a long periphery of 1,300 kilometres from Uralsk to Zverinogolovsk on the Siberian border.

Finally, Kazan led to Siberia, but crossing the middle Urals created difficulties for a long time. In the sixteenth and seventeenth centuries, Solikamsk, the capital of the Stroganov empire in the western Urals, had been the great hub toward which three roads converged from Moscow: the northern route via Vologda and Velikii Ustiug; the central route via Nizhnii Novgorod, Sanchursk, and Viatka, which linked up with the northern route; and the southern route from Nizhnii Novgorod to Kazan and up along the Kama to Solikamsk. It was from Solikamsk that the Stroganovs had sent the Cossack Ermak on that fateful expedition across the Urals which resulted in the annexation of the Siberian khanate of central Eurasia. For a long time, *voevody*, servicemen, and trappers crossed the mountains by following the Vishera, trudged over to the Lozva, which took them to the Tavda, and the Tavda discharged into the Tobol a short distance before its confluence with the Irtysh. This route was much disliked, however, because it was too long and arduous, and the Siberian side was an enormous swamp populated only by Voguls and unsuitable for settlement by Russians. In the 1590s a better route was found near the one followed by Ermak (which must have been forgotten), linking Solikamsk with the Tura, which flowed across more hospitable country and also discharged into the Tobol. In 1598, Verkhoture was founded on the upper reaches of that river and would become for 150 years the exclusive point of legal entry into Siberia. This so-called Babinov road, 270 kilometres long across the Urals, reduced the distance from Moscow to Siberia by 1,000 kilometres.[137] The founding of Ekaterinburg in 1721 necessitated the opening of a new route further south, at least for the mail and couriers. The Chusovaia, which crossed the middle Urals past Ekaterinburg to flow into the Kama near the future town of Perm, became the most convenient waterway to ship iron and copper to the Kama on their way to Kazan and Nizhnii Novgorod, but an even shorter route was found by following the Silva, which flowed past Kungur into the Chusovaia near its confluence with the Kama. However, the sparse population found it too heavy a burden to supply carriers with carts and horses, and it was not until 1763 that Kungur became a major way station on the road from the Volga to the Tobol, and Kazan the hub for official and commercial traffic between western and central Eurasia. From Kazan to Tobolsk the distance was now 1,317 kilometres.

Once in Siberia, the rich hydrographic network favoured the rapid advance of the serviceman, Cossack, and trapper out to hunt fur-bearing animals, collect the *iasak*, and find precious metals, thereby contributing to the integration of the whole of Eurasia into a huge continental fiscal and economic zone. Sailing from Tobolsk down the Irtysh and upstream on the Ob to the confluence of the Ket took between thirty-one and thirty-eight days. The 785-kilometre-long trip on the Ket took the traveller to Fort Makovskii, built by the Russians at the head of a 90-kilometre portage separating the river from the Yenisei, and took from seven to nine weeks, and another two days were necessary to cross the portage, which became until the construction of the Trans-Siberian railroad the vital link between western and eastern Eurasia, indeed between Moscow and the Sea of Okhotsk and the Amur River across nearly the whole of Eurasia.

From the town of Yeniseisk the travellers paddled their way up the Angara to the confluence of the Ilim at Ust-Ilim in six weeks, and from there could go two ways. They could continue up the Angara to Bratsk, Balagansk, Irkutsk, and Lake Baikal. The upstream trip from the Yenisei River to the lake took seventeen and a half weeks. Another three days were necessary to cross Lake Selenga, and another thirteen to reach the confluence of the Khilok. The 500-kilometre-long Khilok led to a second portage linking it with the middle course of the Ingoda near present-day Chita in fifteen days; the trip down the 560-kilometre-long Ingoda to the confluence of the Shilka and down the Shilka past Nerchinsk to its confluence with the Argun, where the Amur began, took six days.[138]

Thus the water route from Tobolsk around Lake Baikal to the Chinese border required about thirty-eight weeks, and it was interrupted in only two places.

From Ust-Ilim, travellers could also paddle up the Ilim River to a third portage in the region of good earth inviting settlement. The portage connected it with the Lena and took two days to cross. From there, a large boat needed only two weeks down the Lena to reach Yakutsk. Access to the Sea of Okhotsk was blocked by a broad upland, extremely difficult to cross on account of the deep snows. Nevertheless, the river network facilitated that access. The travellers sailed downriver to the confluence of the Aldan, 200 kilometres below Yakutsk, and moved up the 2,000-kilometre-long Aldan River, navigable over 950 kilometres. At Ust-Maia, they followed the Maia and the Yudoma to a fourth and last portage to the Urak River, which drained into the Sea of Okhotsk near where the Russians built the foundations of a port in 1732, icebound, however, beginning in October. The trip from Tobolsk to Yakutsk took about twenty-four weeks.

But there was more than met the eye. The river network was closed for over half a year by freezing weather, and conditions were especially difficult in the permafrost zone east of the Yenisei River. Meanders and rapids – there were seventy on the Angara! – sandbars and tree trunks made navigation both difficult and dangerous. Shippers needed enough provisions and had to reach suitable places for wintering or risk being caught up in the ice. Most of the rivers were too shallow – the Ket was only two feet deep – and became useless in summer so that they were not reliable for the transportation of goods. Yet the dream persisted that a continuous water route, with the potential of a strategic link between western Eurasia and China, could be built with a number of canals, and even that Yeniseisk could be linked by steamers with western Europe. The Department of Roads and Waterways instructed the director of the Tenth Region (which included Siberia) in 1809 to canalize the Ket and eliminate the portage, find a way to connect the Angara with the Lena where it became navigable at Kachug – it was eventually done by means of a road – and to link the Yudoma with the Urak.[139] This would indeed have created an uninterrupted waterway between the Volga and the Sea of Okhotsk (and the Pacific), but one totally incapable of functioning as a viable commercial highway between western Eurasia and the great ocean in the east. Only a railroad could do this.

In the meantime, a road network had to be built to accommodate traders. Alexander Radishchev wrote at the end of the eighteenth century that nature created such insurmountable obstacles that waterways would never become the ordinary method of transporting goods across Siberia. The distances were such that boats could not complete the trip in a single summer and remained idle for seven months.[140] But any road network would also face natural obstacles and have to cross one of the great rivers of the world after another, which stopped traffic for weeks on end. To take two examples: the Volga at Tsaritsyn and the Ob below the Irtysh were thirty-five kilometres wide in the spring! The technology of the day could not build hard-surface roads – even in western Eurasia roads were in miserable condition – and roads would be no more than beaten-down tracks, invisible under the deep snow, especially in central Eurasia, muddy and rutted in the spring and fall, unbearably dusty in the summer.

The first "roads" were in fact the line of forts from Zverinogolovsk across the Ishim steppe, to Omsk on the Irtysh, a distance of over 580 kilometres. Tobolsk, the "capital of Siberia," was a riverine city in the forest zone, but Omsk became, like Kazan and Irkutsk, a great hub for overland traffic. Beyond Omsk, a difficult 580-kilometre-long stretch was the Baraba steppe, sparsely populated by poor Tatars, until Russian peasants were resettled in the 1770s along a straight line to Fort Chausskii (present-day Novosibirsk) on the Ob.[141] Upriver from the fort, at Barnaul, a foreign traveller felt he had reached the centre of Eurasia. Ledyard wrote in 1787 that he was 4,539 kilometres from Petersburg and still had 4,950 to go before reaching Okhotsk, and would need to sail another 1,065 kilometres to Fort Petropavlovsk on Kamchatka before boarding ship for America.[142] From Fort Chausskii, merchants and Cossacks gradually beat down a road to Krasnoiarsk on the Yenisei along the foothills of the Saian Mountains, which continued along an almost straight line to Nizhneudinsk and Irkutsk. This road was used by Captain Vitus Bering and his Kamchatka expedition in the 1730s and became the major highway of the China trade. Beyond Irkutsk there was no overland route: merchants sailed across Lake Baikal and followed the course of the Selenga and the Kiakhta to the Mongolian border, where the Chinese had confined commercial relations with the Russians.[143]

The statute of 1822 sought to create a reliable system under the overall direction of the governors general of Western and Eastern Siberia – the former also commanded the troops in the territory – and established priorities by classifying roads into a main Siberian trail (*trakt*), major roads (*bolshie trakty*), and "country" roads (*uezdnye*), managed by a regional representative of the Main Administration of Communications in Petersburg. The main Siberian trail ran from Perm across the whole of Siberia via Ekaterinburg, Tobolsk (still the governors' residence), and Irkutsk – the Trans-Siberian railroad would follow much the same course seventy-five years later. It continued to Yakutsk and Okhotsk by following the Lena, the Aldan, and the Urak, a total length of 7,864 kilometres, 4,477 of them east of Irkutsk. Among the major roads was the Irkutsk-Kiakhta link, either around Lake Baikal – "as difficult as it is dangerous" – over 580 kilometres, or around Lake Baikal to Verkhneudinsk (Ulan Ude) and 250 kilometres overland.[144]

Despite the extraordinary difficulties attending not so much travel as the movement of goods across Siberia – travellers on sleighs could move very fast on the surface of frozen rivers – the river and road network maintained a link between western and eastern Eurasia that was more reliable and steady than the maritime link between Okhotsk and Alaska, for example. It formed many capillaries connecting forts and settlements with the larger towns, and helped create, more than anything else, the sense of a common Siberian identity among settlers, natives, and "unfortunates" (exiles). But another remarkable feature of the network was that it also linked northern and southern latitudes, central with southern Eurasia, and eastern Eurasia with Mongolia, Manchuria, and China. Nerchinsk led via the Shilka to the Nonni River of Manchuria and to Beijing beyond the Great Wall; the Selenga and its tributaries, together with the overland route, led to Urga (Ulan Bator), 304 kilometres beyond the Mongolian border, and another 500 kilometres of desolate country took the caravans to Kalgan on the Great Wall. It was also a much shorter route (by eighty days).

But the two great arteries of north-south communications were the Irtysh and its main tributary, the Ishim. The latter, 2,200 kilometres long, descended from the upland of the central Kazakh steppe, and after turning sharply northwards, flowed across the Ishim steppe, where it was navigable over 150 kilometres. It too froze over from late October to late April, and was free of ice for only 188 days; at Petropavlovsk it could be 15 kilometres wide during spring floods. It was the main artery of the Kazakh steppe, and bound the Russian settler and the Kazakh nomad for better and for worse, drawing the Central Horde irresistibly toward Russian settlements and Russians into the steppe.

The 4,260-kilometre-long Irtysh took its source in the Mongolian Altai, flowed through Lake Zaisan on to Semipalatinsk and Omsk, picked up the Tobol at Tobolsk, and drained into the Ob. From Lake Zaisan to Semipalatinsk the distance was about 585 kilometres, from Semipalatinsk to Omsk another 960, and from Omsk to the Ob a final 1,700 kilometres. But it was freely navigable only over 500 kilometres upriver from Omsk. Elsewhere, it was not deep enough in summer, there were rapids between Semipalatinsk and Ust-Kamenogorsk, and the current was often too fast. It was free of ice between 190 and 215 days, depending on the location. What took the Russians up the Irtysh from Tobolsk as early as the seventeenth century was the need for salt, found in abundance at Lake Yamyshev, to which the Zunghars also drove their herds. From Tobolsk, large boats needed four weeks to reach the lake but only half that time on the way back.[145] Later, the Irtysh waterway was also used to transport troops, provisions, and construction materials to the forts on the Irtysh Line, from which the Russians faced the Zunghars, the Kazakh Eastern Horde, and even the Chinese at Lake Zaisan.

The Ob, which led eastward via the Ket, also pointed south via the Tom. From Narym at the confluence of the Ket, the journey to Tomsk took ten days, from Tomsk to Kuznetsk another ten. One could also reach the confluence of the Biia and Katun (where the Ob began) in ten weeks from Tomsk, and another two months were needed to reach "the Chinese kingdom."[146] No wonder that the commander of the Siberian Line recommended in 1796 that a new trade route be opened from the Bukhtarma via Kobdo and Uliassutai across Mongolia. He was certain one could reach Beijing within thirty days, 1,500 kilometres away. The new road would be preferable to the 3,500-kilometre-long Kiakhta-Tobolsk route with its dangerous crossing of Lake Baikal, but the Chinese were not interested.[147] From Semipalatinsk one could also go west, to Tashkent and Bukhara, and from there to Persia and Afghanistan, into the heart of southern Eurasia.

Trade

Expansion into Transcaucasia and the expulsion of Persia from Caucasian Azerbaidjan north of the Araks River, together with increasing colonization in the core and the formation of a fringe of settlement beyond the Orenburg and Siberian Lines, stimulated the formation of market towns and the integration of isolated communities into new regional markets serving the needs of administrative and military regions. Moreover, the growth of Russian power in central and southern Eurasia created centripetal pressures with the potential to disrupt at last the east-west patterns of trade and reorient them toward the rising power in the north, raising attractive possibilities that commercial exchanges might eventually help integrate southern Eurasia into the emerging Russian empire.

The creation of a Trade Ministry in 1802 under the leadership of Nikolai Rumiantsev, a son of the field marshal and a man with an extraordinary spatial, if unrealistic, vision of Russian capabilities in the creation of a Eurasian market, set the stage for a commercial offensive that lasted until his departure in 1810.[148] The ministry was then incorporated into the powerful Finance Ministry as a Department of Foreign Trade. The ministry, also responsible for the management of state-owned industry and most of the peasant population in the eastern theatre, tended to be less carried away by expansionist visions of Russia's commercial future (which nevertheless continued to inform Russian foreign policy) and more concerned with financial returns. Under Georg von Cancrin, the finance minister from 1823 to 1844, who had been in charge of the logistics of the Russian field army between 1813 and 1820, the ministry followed a cameralist policy, equating political with economic space and aiming at the creation of an autarkic global economy within the empire. By the 1830s, four customs regions had been created: a Caucasian one for the whole of Transcaucasia, based in Tiflis, with customs houses in that city, and in Baku, Erivan, and Nakhichevan; an Astrakhan region, including the northern Caucasus and Astrakhan province to the mouth of the Ural river at Gurev; an Orenburg region stretching to Zverinogolovsk, with two customs houses in Orenburg and Troitsk; and a Siberian region from Zverinogolovsk to Fort Bukhtarma, with customs houses in Petropavlovsk, Semipalatinsk, and Bukhtarma. There was no separate region for Eastern Siberia, where the China trade was conducted at Kiakhta, which enjoyed separate status.

The construction of the Georgian Military Highway did little to facilitate trade across the mountains. It served above all a military and not a commercial purpose, to send men, provisions, and artillery to Transcaucasia, which remained an isolated backwater that could never become integrated into the spatial economy of the market towns in the northern Caucasus. The Kura was not truly navigable until the confluence of the Alazan or even of the Araks at Dzhavat; it was often too shallow and the current too swift. The Terek in the north was not navigable either, and these two rivers flowing into the Caspian could not serve as water routes from and into the interior of the isthmus between the Caspian and the Black Sea. Moreover, the Caspian coast was so devoid of safe and attractive harbours, even at Derbend, that a sea route, which in different circumstances would have encouraged trade between eastern Transcaucasia and Astrakhan, was not available. To make matters worse, the sea at Astrakhan froze from November to March, and the port shut down. As a result, the favoured trade route was the coastal road to Kizliar and further north to Astrakhan, along which Armenian and Georgian merchants took their textiles and other articles all year round and especially in wintertime.[149] Kizliar, with its large Armenian and Tatar communities, became a major trade junction, linked overland with the Cossack settlements along the Kura and the Sunzha.

In large part because of its isolation, the difficult terrain, political fragmentation, and the resulting insecurity and vexatious customs barriers, the internal trade of eastern Transcaucasia was stagnant at the beginning of the nineteenth century. Thirty years later, there still existed 17 internal trade duties (*raskhodnye stat'i*) and 120 more on industrial production in Georgia alone, a debilitating system which the Russians retained, after an early attempt to abolish it, because the duties represented a major item in the regional budget, at a time when the taxable resources remained difficult to assess.[150] On the other hand, the military unification of the isthmus after the Russian conquest revived the transit trade between the Black Sea and the Caspian and made Tiflis its major emporium and Baku its major port; it promised to give a new priority to the Persian trade, which had suffered a steep decline between the death of Nadir Shah in 1747 and the accession of Aga Muhammed Khan in 1795.

Encouraging the Persian trade was part of an expansionist commercial policy aiming to integrate the whole of southern Eurasia into the Russian sphere of influence. Catherine II told Valerian Zubov in February 1796 on the eve of his expedition, which so clearly intended to repeat Peter I's successes in 1723–4, that "peace with Persia will open to us the rich trade of the Caspian shores and within Persia; it will open a route to India shorter than that which the European powers follow around the Cape of Good Hope, and then we can turn all the profits [*vygody*] they have made to our advantage."[151]

It was too early for the empress to know that sea-borne commerce was much more reliable and much less costly than overland commerce, and that in the forthcoming race with Britain, the Russians were bound to lose. At the same time, her governor general in Irkutsk, Ivan Jacobi, was contemplating a war on China to establish a base in central and eastern Eurasia from which to create a huge market including northern China, Manchuria, and Korea dominated by Russian industrial production. He was among the first to draw the Russians' attention to Astarabad on the Caspian coast, from which a branch of the Silk Road crossed the Elburs Mountains and led to Nishapur, Meshed, and on to Herat in Afghanistan and the Indus valley of northwestern India.[152] But the report of a Russian consul written in 1797 dampened the enthusiasm for Caspian ports and overland routes. Enzeli, the major port, which led to Resht, Baghdad, and Basra on the Persian Gulf, was unprotected against the northeastern winds which made navigation on the Caspian so dangerous, and the bay was so shallow that cargoes had to be unloaded onto smaller craft before they could reach the coast. Astarabad "had no trade" because its channel was obstructed by sandbars and underwater stones, and Persian merchants coming from Kandahar and Herat found the overland route too dangerous and went to Astrakhan instead, while caravans from India preferred to cross the desert to Bukhara and continue to Khiva and the Mangyshlak Peninsula or go directly to Orenburg.[153]

But the Russians persisted in seeking advantageous conditions in Persia and a road to India. The treaties of Gulistan (1813) and Turkmanchai (1828) both reduced tariffs on Russian imports into the country to 5 per cent, without any additional charges on the transit trade to India. Exchanges grew steadily, although the market remained small: Persia's population was between five and six million during the first half of the nineteenth century.[154] By 1824–6 annual exports reached 938,287 silver roubles, a 177 per cent increase over the 1770s. Textiles and dyes remained the most profitable articles, but there was no longer any mention of foreign cloth, which by then reached Persia via the Persian Gulf. The second largest article consisted of metals (iron and copper) and metal goods. However, Russian imports reached 1.9 million roubles (a 520 per cent increase) and consisted largely of raw cotton and cotton goods, raw silk, and the highly prized scarves and shawls coming in part from Kashmir.[155] The unfavourable trade balance reflected Russia's inability to establish a dominant position for its goods in the Persian market in the face of British competition. It may very well be that Russia's difficulties in fully integrating the Persian and Transcaucasian markets into a global Russian economy was due not only to a defective infrastructure of ports and roads but also to the inability of Russian industry to produce enough goods of competitive quality and price. While colonization and a growing agricultural market facilitated integration in the core, competition from the maritime powers beyond the physical boundary of the Eurasian land mass made it difficult to integrate its outlying regions, its imperial fringe, into an imperial economy.

The threat came not only from the sea routes. Transcaucasian exchanges had always been latitudinal ones, with Turkey in the west and Persia in the east, a reminder that the transcontinental exchanges since Mongol days had followed the overland route from India and Sinkiang to the Mediterranean. The growing importance of sea-borne commerce had the effect of pulling those exchanges southward toward the Indian Ocean, the Persian Gulf, and the eastern Mediterranean, but it also gave a new importance to the land bridge between the Mediterranean and the Gulf that offered an overland shortcut to reduce the long trip around the Cape of Good Hope. Ermolov in Tiflis and others, notably Polish landowners in Right Bank Ukraine, thought the creation of a transit route from the Austrian border across the Black Sea and overland across Transcaucasia, from Redut Kale via Tiflis to Baku and on to Enzeli and Astarabad (despite all their shortcomings), would link the great hub of central European commerce in Leipzig with the Persian market and compete with the maritime route. The Transcaucasian tariff of 1821 gave chiefly Armenian traders the hope of great profits. The trade reached its peak in 1824, when Tiflis merchants sold 4.4 million roubles worth of cotton, wool, and silk fabrics in Leipzig.

But it then declined for two reasons. To contain overland costs, the goods were sent to Trieste and then by sea to Trapsund, where the British used a different overland route outside Russian territory that led via Erzerum and Bayazid to Tabriz and Tehran. From there, it led to the Persian Gulf and northward to Meshed, Herat, and even Bukhara. The other was the opposition of the Moscow merchants, supported by Cancrin. Unable to stand the competition of British and European goods, they insisted on repealing the legislation and applying instead the highly restrictive tariff of 1822, which governed the European trade. Their vision was an autarkic one, opposed to the integration of the core's imperial fringes into a larger world economy. Cancrin spoke of Transcaucasia as a Russian colony – confirming the perception of a one and indivisible Russian core and an imperial periphery – which must be integrated into the continental economy, even if that meant retarding its economic development. Latitudinal exchanges had to be transformed into longitudinal ones between north and south, so that all commercial exchanges would take place within the boundaries of a single political space dominated by Moscow and Petersburg. The 1821 tariff was indeed repealed in 1831 – it may have been no coincidence that the Polish uprising was crushed that same year.[156]

Trade with the Kazakhs and across the Kazakh steppe with Khiva, Bukhara, and Kokand was conducted in Orenburg and Petropavlovsk. Semipalatinsk ranked third, Omsk and Ust-Kamenogorsk far behind. Trade with a Central Asian population of about 5.3 million at the beginning of the nineteenth century[157] grew exponentially between the 1770s and the 1820s, reaching a total of

2.6 million silver roubles against 2.9 for the trade with Persia and Asiatic Turkey. Russia maintained a favourable trade balance, which allowed the import of gold and silver. Russian exports were chiefly textiles – an equal amount of raw cotton and cotton fabrics – with some silk and wool, but with a substantial amount of scarves and shawls of the same provenance as in the Persian trade. These and textiles in general made up 62.4 per cent of total imports, followed by cattle and horses (26.9 per cent). Exports to Central Asia were very varied, but nevertheless dominated by textiles (31.8 per cent), soft leather (*iuft*), and unprocessed hides (24.9 per cent), followed by metal goods (13 per cent), dyes, grain, cattle, horses and camels, and sugar. As in the Persian trade, textiles dominated both exports and imports, but exchanges were not simply between raw materials and finished products – Central Asia supplied both and so did Russia.[158] If it had not been for the continuing insecurity of the steppe, it is likely that the Russians would have succeeded in reorienting the Central Asian trade – in which the British could not successfully compete because it was an exclusively overland trade – toward the Volga and Siberia, toward western and central Eurasia, paving the way for an economic integration preceding the extension of the political space to eastern Persia and Afghanistan. The process would not be completed until the 1880s.

The Kazakhs were nomads, did not use money, and had little to offer save their cattle, horses, and sheep, but their eagerness to trade was matched by an instinct for plunder which created great risk for the caravans crossing the steppe. Indeed, the Kazakhs were not the only culprits. The Turkmens raided Persian caravans, and even the settled oasis societies of Khiva, Bukhara, and Kokand found a profit in hosting public sales of prisoners captured by the nomads. Trade and plunder were two sides of an economic activity driven by the attractions of immediate profit regardless of the consequences. In 1787, a customs official wrote from Orenburg that Kazakh society was in such disarray following the disintegration of the khans' power that Russia needed to create a responsible political authority to safeguard the passage of caravans. Russian merchants were not coming and the trade was in Tatar hands. Nevertheless, it was growing, but, significantly enough, the official complained that Russian industry was incapable of producing and delivering enough manufactured goods, and cited a case of the previous year, when Kazakhs brought forty thousand sheep for which they could not find buyers, and which had to be driven back into the steppe to the great indignation of their owners.[159] Ten years later, General Igelstrom expressed reservations about the future of trade with India via Bukhara: there were highway robbers, and it was so difficult to cross the Hindu Kush that goods had to be carried on human shoulders for long stretches. But his contention that the Khivan trade (linked with Bukhara via the Amu Daria) would always seek an outlet in Astrakhan rather than Orenburg was well taken, and indeed recalled the motives behind launching the Cherkassky expedition against the city in 1715. But to reach Astrakhan it was necessary to establish a commercial outpost at the tip of the Mangyshlak Peninsula facing the city across the sea. Bukharans, Khivans, and Turkmens took there their cotton and silk fabrics, lambskins, blankets, and hides, but also diamonds and pearls, and encouraged the Russians throughout the eighteenth century to build a fort. It was not done until the construction of Alexandrovsk in 1834.[160] But by then, one begins to detect a certain obsession with the capture of Khiva. An anonymous author recommended it in order to create "a Russian Gibraltar in Great Tartary" and open a safe commercial route via Kokand to Kashgar and the old Silk Road into western China and northern India via Yarkend – as Peter I had intended to do from the Irtysh also in 1715.[161] Memories were still fresh of the plundering of caravans, including one accompanied by a Cossack convoy, in 1825, when merchants lost half a million roubles.[162] But it was still premature. The attempt to conquer Khiva in 1839 ended in failure.

The powerful influence exercised by maritime commerce to the detriment of transcontinental exchanges was nowhere so visible as in the China trade. Of course, there were other factors hindering the normal operation of exchanges between Russia and China, the most important being Chinese reluctance to allow Russian trade elsewhere but in Kiakhta, and the use of trade as a political weapon to gain Russian concessions in other matters. Exchanges with China remained a form of transcontinental commerce with little effect on the internal trade of central and eastern Eurasia. Radishchev, in the already cited letter, was struck by the fact that the Siberians had barely noticed the closing of the trade in the 1780s. Cotton fabrics were replaced by linens; a local grass provided a substitute for tea; the price of furs had not come down. Only the Buriats had felt the difference, if only because they were so close to the Mongolian border.[163] Radishchev implicitly understood the difference between trade and commerce, when he noted that the major beneficiaries of the exchanges were the carriers, who transported the goods overland across the whole of Siberia to the Irbit fair near Ekaterinburg and to the Makarev fair beyond the Urals. Other beneficiaries were the supporting craftsmen: cartwrights, blacksmiths, tanners, and the catering industry. The route largely ignored the hydrographic network, even though the trip from east to west was all downstream, because the rivers flowed across such inhospitable regions.

The impact of maritime commerce on cost differentials was not strongly felt until the beginning of the nineteenth century. Radishchev estimated that the Petersburg consumers were willing to pay from three to four times more for the tea imported by the Dutch and English, and the fur trade was already suffering. An Irkutsk merchant on a visit to China in 1799 noted the decline of the trade, and Rumiantsev was alarmed by the fact that North American traders were selling their furs in Canton at much lower prices.[164] The goal of the Golovkin mission to China in 1805 was to gain permission to bring Russian furs from the

Aleutian Islands and Alaska to Canton, but the Chinese had already made their position clear. They would not even allow the inland trade on the Bukhtarma. By the 1840s, however, a *pud* (13.4 kilograms/36.1 pounds) of tea from China sold in London for thirty to forty silver kopecks, but for six silver roubles in Moscow – fifteen to twenty times more – if it came from Kiakhta; in the 1850s, tea imported by sea cost less in Petersburg than in Irkutsk, only 745 kilometres away from Kiakhta.[165]

The evolution of the customs revenue illustrates the decline of the transcontinental commerce. By 1824–6, imports from China had barely grown from the 1777–81 average, from 1.6 to 1.7 million roubles, and they consisted almost entirely of tea (89.5 per cent). Among the exports to China, which amounted to less than half the amount of exports for 1777–81, furs had almost disappeared, and they largely consisted of cloth, followed by soft leather and hides. Among the cloth exports, however, the striking revelation was the enormous share of foreign cloth (81.2 per cent), chiefly from Prussian Silesia and Russian Poland.[166] Nothing could be more revealing of the utter bankruptcy of Russia's transcontinental commerce, which had appeared so promising in the eighteenth century. But the trade of the eastern theatre was only a fraction of Russia's total foreign trade. In 1824–6, combined exports to the three regions – Persia, Central Asia, and China – averaged 2.8 million roubles or only 5.1 per cent of Russia's revenue from its European export trade (54.5 million roubles); imports averaged 5.2 million roubles or 11.3 per cent of 45.8 million of imports from Europe.[167] Yet, within this enormous area, at a slower pace lagging behind the development of the maritime economies, Russia was carving out an integrated autarkic economic empire to support the core's economic development.

Conclusion to Part III: The Eastern Theatre

To recapitulate. The eastern theatre stretched from the northern Urals, the Kama, the Volga, the Kazbek, and the Suram range, to include Persia, the basins of the Caspian and Aral Seas, Western Siberia and the Kazakh steppe, and Eastern Siberia to Kamchatka. It was so large that it easily contained three of the four territorial divisions of the Eurasian land mass – southern Eurasia with western Transcaucasia, Persia, and Central Asia; central Eurasia with Western Siberia and the Kazakh steppe; and eastern Eurasia beyond the Yenisei River to the Mongol and Manchurian border. Despite its size and diversity, it possessed one striking physical feature – that of a great amphitheatre rising toward a continuous mountain barrier of latitudinal ranges blocking easy access to the great oceans. The ground declined toward the Caspian Sea, but rose again toward the Zagros Mountains. It declined again toward the Arctic Ocean, in the great wasteland of the Siberian taiga, hardly hospitable to anyone but native hunters and fishermen, but it rose steadily toward the Tien Shan, Altai, Saian, Iablonoi, and Stanovoi mountains.

Nature divided the eastern theatre into broad latitudinal vegetation and climatic zones – from the forest zone in the north, deeply marked by the permafrost east of the Yenisei, succeeded by the wooded steppe, the steppe, the semi-desert, and the desert zones, extending beyond Central Asia to the salt-encrusted deserts of Persia, the sandy desert of the Tarim basin, and the gravelly desert of the Gobi, which to the traveller must have appeared as so many ends of the world. It was between these two extremes – the snow-covered forested north and the southern deserts and the Zagros Mountains – that the great events of Eurasian history unfolded, where the wooded steppe and the steppe became the battlefield between the settler and the nomad. That space was first unified by the Mongols, but the consolidation of political power westward to include much of western Eurasia as well was beyond the numerical strength of the nomads and the transport infrastructure of the day. Eastern Eurasia merged with China under a Mongol dynasty; southern Eurasia became a separate political organization; central Eurasia with the Mongol-dominated lands of western Eurasia, a Kipchak khanate based on the Volga on the dividing line between the two.

The gradual disintegration of the khanate was matched by the rise of three core areas – in Russia, in Persia, and in China, this last one the great Asian power. In western Eurasia, an accommodation had taken place between the Mongol overlords, which suited both sides. The Mongols needed the Russian princes to collect the tribute for them in return for recognizing some political autonomy, which only brute force could have otherwise denied. The princes needed the Mongols to develop their political autonomy and extract resources from their subjects for their own treasury. This on-going accommodation resulted in the creation of grand principalities – political regions of a kind – over which that of Moscow finally gained the upper hand. When its rise coincided with the disintegration of Mongol power, the issue was joined for Moscow to overthrow the Mongol overlordship in western Eurasia and establish its own overlordship over the three fragments of the old Mongol realm – the khanates of Kazan, Astrakhan, and Siberia. The existence of an excellent hydrographic network enabled the Russians to claim, by means of forts built at strategic points, ownership for the White Tsar of the three khanates in central Eurasia and round out their conquests by incorporating eastern Eurasia. There remained only the Kazakh steppe with its Chingissid khans, a separate horde that had also been part of the Kipchak khanate. By 1700 the expanding Muscovite core had become the true successor of the Mongol-occupied space, save for southern Eurasia, now dominated by the Persian core and its superior civilization.

The Russians in Moscow and in Tobolsk already had a definite spatial vision of what their future realm must be. The Volga led to the Caspian and the Caspian to the northern Caucasus. The great rivers of Siberia descended from the crest of the mountainous periphery and watered the central and eastern Eurasian amphitheatre, which they assumed to be the patrimony of the Russian tsar. As such, it constituted a single domain to be administered by the same rules as the western Eurasian patrimony, by means of *prikazy* at the centre and *voevody* in every fort and settlement. The vision was all the more realistic in that the core, except in the lower Volga valley, was still confined to the forest zone. To expand into the wooded steppe and the steppe, the domain needed peasants to till the land and a military infrastructure to defend the settler against the nomads still roaming between the Volga and the Altai. That was the purpose of the fortified lines built steadily beginning in the 1730s, which not only demarcated the core's outer periphery but kept moving southward until it nearly coincided by the end of the eighteenth century with that of the agricultural zone. Beyond that zone the settler would not go, because there was no land on which to grow his rye, barley, and oats, or because agriculture required irrigation with which he was not familiar in a climate to which he was allergic. The perimeter kept creeping forth, not only as a result of a strategic vision among the ruling elite, which looked upon itself as the managers of the core, but also of the interaction between Russian and native, in which the native, be it in Mozdok, the Mangyshlak Peninsula, or Orenburg/Orsk, invited the Russian to build forts for self-protection against tribal warfare or to protect traders against the plundering nomads.

Governors and *voevody* had managed the core since Peter's reign, but its territorial division was still the crazy quilt it had always been since the core began to expand. It was no coincidence that the great reforms of the 1780s created for the first time a uniform territorial pattern as a prerequisite for the systematization of management across the entire eastern theatre. It was then that the core reached the limits of its expansion, because it finally incorporated the entire zone of agricultural land, save for a fringe beyond the Terek and along the lines across the Kazakh steppe. General administration, the court system, fiscal organization and procedures, and police control were systematized with very few exceptions of no structural importance. Native rebellions had been crushed, and an accommodation had been reached with the native elites by integrating them into the hierarchy of the ruling class and securing them a share in the extraction of natural resources in return for their loyalty. The expanding core had been fully integrated, at least at the management level, and its population was overwhelmingly Russian.[1]

Across much of the eastern theatre, in the Kazan Tatar lands, in Bashkiria, Buriatia, and Yakutia, the Russians encountered already stratified societies, in which the dominant ethnic group had already imposed a system of obligations upon scattered small minorities, be it in the form of tribute or military service, as well as a set of cultural norms. That is why the encounter between Russian and native was violent at times, as the native overlords resisted the imposition upon them, in a process of superstratification, of the obligations and norms of the conqueror. The "Tatarization," "Bashkirization," of the Volga minorities, the "Buriatization" of some Turkic groups, and the "Yakutization" of scattered minorities in the far north had to give way to the steady march of Russification, not without, however, a reverse assimilation of the conquerors, as in Yakutia. A melting pot, encouraged by intermarriage or simply cohabitation with the native, worked both ways with the passage of time. The acceptance of mixed families with Bashkir, Kazakh, and especially Kalmyk women, and even highlanders on the Caucasian Line, had a powerful effect of integrating the native into the Russian peasantry and ruling class, the continuing extension of a process of assimilation which had already been taking place for a long time in western Eurasia.

It also meant the extension of public serfdom across the entire eastern theatre. The government refused to tolerate the introduction of privately held serfs in much of it, and certainly in Siberia, because few landlords would want to move that far away in the first place and absentee landownership would only result in creating a mass of roving people beyond the reach of the authorities. There also remained a persistent assumption that Siberia was the property of the ruling house. The population of "the tsar's domain" had to consist of peasants of the crown and for the most part of "state peasants," who, despite their legal status as free men, were in fact a pool of serf labour at the disposal of the ruling class as a whole. The social integration of the nomad remained a goal of government policy, which overlooked ethnic differences or subsumed them under the overarching concept of a dependent population subjugated to serve the needs of a ruling class, well known for its multi-ethnic constitution. But the realization of that goal had to remain a distant one, because nomads could not easily become agricultural settlers on grazing lands, which in some parts had shaped a nomadic way of life for centuries. Even where they could become settlers, they resisted, as a free people used to roam empty spaces would do, among whom the condition of peasant was despised. But integration proceeded nevertheless – the Bashkirs into the Cossack troops, who ranked higher in public esteem, while others were legally equated with state peasants under the jurisdiction of the Ministry of State Domains, which succeeded the Finance Ministry as the agency responsible for the state peasantry everywhere.

Charles Steinwedel writes eloquently about the successes of Russian policies of superstratification, even if he does not use that word. The eighteenth century was a time of constant intertribal warfare in the eastern theatre, and the imposition of Russian hegemony created stability and peace. Many of his conclusions apply to other sectors of that theatre. From Georgia to Yakutia, the native population grew at a rapid pace and could afford to maintain the fortified perimeters which guaranteed stability. "The Orenburg fortified line cut the Bashkirs off from the Kazakh steppe but also prevented the kinds of raids and clashes that cost lives and cattle. Compared to the horrors of the eighteenth century, it was better to be a Bashkir in the nineteenth century." Russian policies "proved crucial in creating a Russian Orthodox and Muslim elite that, while not large, had sufficient culture power, linguistic ability, and resources to compel their co-religionists to accept imperial authority." "Through co-optation of elites and control of Bashkir communities, imperial authority greatly increased its power and stability. As imperial officials relied increasingly on native elites to administer Bashkirs, the status of those elites grew."

There was a downside, however. Steinwedel bemoans the fact that ordinary Bashkirs became a pool of exploited labour at the bidding of the military governor. But was not that the ultimate form of social integration? The peasant population in the unitary state was approximately equally divided between the serfs belonging to the landed nobility and the so-called peasants of the Treasury, who were collective property of the ruling class that governed the country in offices and rural estates. The Bashkirs were aware of this and chose to become

"Cossackized" to avoid that degraded state. But was not the military establishment an institution run by the same principles as a large estate? Without mentioning the military settlements, which represented the most gruesome form of serfdom, was it not a fact that the peasant, once he was taken into the army, became a free man for a short time before becoming the tool of his regimental commander? These officers stole the solider's pay and food, used him for their personal needs, and beat him legally by invoking regimental powers. If the Bashkirs became the "serfs" of the military governor, it only meant that Bashkir society had become integrated into Russian society, its leaders strengthening their elite status, while the rank and file was downgraded into the dependent population.[2]

It was intended that the conversion of the native would erase ethnic differences and facilitate social integration. The Russian realm, which grew into an expanding core, was as much a confessional state as a political edifice, and the identity of a Russian was religious rather than ethnic. Those who converted automatically became Russian, and to refuse to convert was to insist on remaining a member of an alien political and religious family, which, in the exclusive and xenophobic world of Orthodoxy, was tantamount to treason against the ruling house and its ruling elite. Resistance had to be overcome, by brutal means if need be, but preferably by incentives in the form of tax exemptions or ranks in the political hierarchy. It also suited native leaders to convert, because Orthodoxy demanded the faithful's unconditional obedience to the secular power, including themselves, and native landowners would be allowed to keep their serfs, as would any other member of the ruling class. The persecution of Islam was in part a long-mooted revenge for a church that had once boasted of its purity, unsullied by foreign influences, while having to pray for the health of a Kipchak khan, who was a Muslim. But it also served political ends, and as such was not free of other contradictions, as when the destruction of mosques in the Kazan region took place while the governor of Orenburg invited Kazan Tatars to settle there and build mosques.

Catherine II's policy of toleration seemed to represent at first glance another such contradiction, but that was not the case. By then the Russians had become aware of the existence of three core religions – Orthodoxy, Islam, and Tibetan Buddhism – and three confessional frontiers, in which Orthodoxy had to fight for domination against Islam and Buddhism, both with centres beyond the expanding core. In eastern Eurasia, the northern Buriats and Yakuts had been converted, while the southern Buriats remained Buddhist. In the Volga region, the Mari, Udmurts, and Chuvash had also been Christianized, but the Islamic Tatar world had not succumbed to the onslaught of Orthodoxy. The government then initiated a policy designed to create a Muslim "church" under Russian auspices in Orenburg, demanding in return the loyalty of Tatar merchants and mullas in the service of Russian goals in southern Eurasia. The *mufti* and his assistants were integrated into the administrative hierarchy, and the government sought to create a jurisprudence in the application of Muslim law restricted to the settlement of purely religious issues, while the civil (and criminal) law would become integrated into the larger body of Russian law. It was integration in a roundabout way – by recognizing irreducible differences and no longer looking on the practice of Islam as a treasonable act, providing that such a concession would secure political loyalty and serve Russian ambitions beyond the expanding core.

Economic policy also served to integrate the core. As in German lands, the Russians emphasized the importance of the territory over the market, and sought to demarcate political boundaries, within which the government could pursue a policy of uniformity and equilibrium, while market-oriented policies emphasized the primacy of the market, which cut across political boundaries and created spatial disparities. One detects a distinct policy seeking to equate political, religious, and economic boundaries to form an integrated and self-sufficient whole – a "world system" on a huge continental scale – sustained by its natural resources, its faith, and its civilization, under the authoritarian leadership of a multi-ethnic elite bent on maximizing military power.

The peasant, who became a majority in the eastern theatre by the middle of the eighteenth century, brought his own occupations with him and was taxed at the same rate as the peasant in western Eurasia. The native paid the *iasak*, for which it was difficult to establish a uniform rate, but which corresponded to the *obrok* as a rent paid for the use of land belonging to someone else. Market towns arose as soon as population density reached a point beyond which it was no longer necessary to demand a grain contribution to secure the provisioning of the troops. The nomad, who was keen on plunder, was also eager to barter his animals for grain, fabrics, tools, and utensils. A three-cornered market thus naturally developed, integrating the supply of the peasant with the demand of the soldier and Cossack in the fort, and both with the economy of the nomad. The stronger the Russian presence became on the core's periphery, the greater became the centripetal pull drawing the nomad into close relationships with the settler.

Peter I's ambition to merge the regional markets of towns, forts, and customs houses by canals linking the river networks of western Eurasia with those of central, southern, and eastern Eurasia, and to create an uninterrupted waterway between Europe and Asia, was a striking vision of spatial unification and integration, but one unrealistic from the start, because of unfavourable geographic circumstances and primitive technology incapable of overcoming several major obstacles. It was indeed a characteristic feature of many of these impressive visions of Russia's future that they reflected strategic rather than commercial ambitions – the former might be realized with sufficient effort and willpower and the brutal exploitation of the dependent population; the latter were much more likely to be restricted by transportation costs, supply, and demand. The conflict was once again one between a philosophy of power seeking to create, organize, and manage a definite territory, and commercial capabilities much more dependent on the constraints of the environment. Trade was an effective factor of integration within the spatial limitations of regional markets, but was unable to accelerate the integration of the expanding core. This was also partly explained by the relative industrial decline of the late eighteenth century, which would continue unabated for two generations, owing to the exhaustion of easily accessible sources of raw materials, the destruction of forests as source of fuel, and high overland transport costs over enormous distances.

When the expanding core reached its natural limits by the end of the eighteenth century, it was well on its way to become a one and indivisible Russia. Subsequent legislation, together with the progress of colonization, could only deepen the integration. But expansion motivated by strategic ambitions to establish Russia's hegemony in the Eurasian land mass, in competition with Britain, which emerged at the same time as the leading maritime power along the periphery of that land mass, could not simply stop along the limit of the agricultural zone, but needed to reach a perimeter along which Russian and British ambitions would balance each other.

Peter I's expeditions against Khiva and Yarkend aimed at no less than creating protectorates in southern Eurasia, but were premature. The decision to annex eastern Georgia and eastern Transcaucasia was a momentous event, as Russia gained a foothold in a region which would gradually grow larger with the annexation of Central Asia and the partition of Persia itself; this came close to bringing about the reunification of the whole of Eurasia, as the Mongols had done five hundred years earlier. But the conquest of Transcaucasia did not mean the further expansion of the core, but the creation of an empire. Russian peasants would never settle there in large numbers – yet, a substantial Russian majority was a prerequisite, if the core was to remain a one and indivisible Russia. Georgians and Armenians were Christians, but their churches retained strong autocephalitic claims, and the Azeri Turks were Muslims, strongly influenced by both Persians and Turks. The core's tax system was not introduced there; the regional administration and military command acquired a deep sense of separateness. Central Asia was an alien land, even if the core in the eastern theatre had long been in touch with it via merchants and envoys. Southern Eurasia, marked for centuries by the superior civilization of the Persian core, would remain a separate world, much as it had been in the days of Hulagu, Chingis Khan's grandson.

Paradoxically, however, there were powerful forces encouraging the integration of southern Eurasia into the emerging Russian empire. The past wealth of Transcaucasia, Central Asia, and Persia had depended on the transcontinental trade routes from India to the Mediterranean. The growth of sea-borne commerce inevitably damaged the overland trade, because it was more secure and less costly, as when tea shipped from Canton via the Cape of Good Hope became fifteen times cheaper in Petersburg than the tea carted across Siberia from Kiakhta. The economic and political decline of the three fragments of southern Eurasia had the effect of making them more dependent on the growing market of their northern neighbour, so that their eventual annexation and partition was the culmination of the reorientation of their trade. The copper of Transcaucasia, the silk of Persia, and the cotton of Central Asia bound the imperial periphery to what had been the expanding core. That the core's industry remained unable to encourage and satisfy a potential demand for its manufactured products pointed to the self-inflicted damage caused by protectionist policies that neglected the importance of creating an imperial continental market, while favouring the continued integration of a one and indivisible Russian core. In the end, the core's inability to expand while remaining a core exposed fault lines that would destroy the viability of both core and frontier.

By the end of Nicholas I's reign, it seems that a certain vision of how Russia would manage the Eurasian space was crystallizing in government circles. The annexation of Transcaucasia brought the Russians to Iran's natural borders, and the advance across the Kazakh steppe to the Syr Daria and the Tien Shan Mountains was paving the way for the annexation of Central Asia: the Russians would reach the Iranian border on the other side of the Caspian. In East Siberia, they were about to incorporate the valleys of the Amur and Ussuri Rivers and build a port at Vladivostok. Fifty years later, they were implanting their influence in Mongolia and even contemplating the annexation of Manchuria, until they were stopped by the countervailing force of Japan. Russia's vision in the eastern theatre thus included the expansion of the core, the creation of an imperial fringe in Transcaucasia, Central Asia, Mongolia, and Manchuria, and the constitution of an outer periphery consisting of Iran, and northern China to the Yellow River – that was indeed Sergei Witte's vision at the beginning of the twentieth century, but a vision which Russia's spatial overstretch and the government's increasing weakness were bound to blur. The internal consistency of the three zones was bound to differ: densest in the core, softer in the imperial fringe, while in the outer periphery the Russians would encourage the "rotting process,"[3] the ultimate defence against external threats, but also a dangerous incitement to further expansion and a disastrous overstretch.

Conclusion

After a long journey across the so-called Russian Empire from the Sea of Okhotsk to the Baltic Sea via the Caspian and Black Seas, the time has come to draw a balance. A Muscovite core emerged on the margin of the Mongol-Tatar steppe empire and grew to incorporate the entire basin of the Volga River and the Caspian Sea. It was there that the Russian population settled and grew, and it was there that the Muscovite core turned into an expanding Russian core. The core spread eastwards to the borders of China on the periphery of eastern Eurasia, to the borders of Iran and Turkey on the periphery of southern Eurasia, and to the periphery of western Eurasia along the Oder and the Norwegian Alps in Poland and Sweden. As it grew, it was forced to develop policies reflecting the visions of its ruling elite, the opportunities and the restraints offered or imposed by an immensely diverse geographical and ethnic environment. The core grew as a political formation infused with a martial spirit, dominated by a ruling house insisting on its autocratic power, and a ruling class of families for which upholding the ruler's autocracy was the best way to guarantee their own. The core was also infused with a spirit of religious exceptionalism, in which the xenophobia of the Orthodox Church reinforced the political absolutism of the ruling house, and elevated the ruler to a quasi-divine status far removed from the degraded condition of its humble subjects. Such a political system, Eurasian in nature and oriental in origin, assumed control over all the sources of power, which it used for its own self-aggrandizement. In short, the expanding Russian core was a political-military-fiscal-religious conglomerate which kept renewing itself at every stage of its expansion, a Leviathan in motion toward the Eurasian periphery, always insisting on retaining its original constitution.[1]

Policies evolved slowly. The expanding Russian core of the mid-seventeenth century was a hodgepodge of ad hoc institutions created to answer the needs of the moment. During Peter's reign, when the military ethos became more preeminent than it had ever been before, a systematization of government became quite apparent. The territorial reform of 1708 divided the territory under Moscow's jurisdiction into provinces and counties everywhere, including the Baltic provinces. Governors were superimposed upon the old network of *voevody* except in those provinces. By the end of the eighteenth century, the same administrative-territorial division applied everywhere, and would be extended in the future to newly incorporated territories. As the expanding core became larger and larger, more troops were stationed in the peripheries, and more commanders assumed a dominant role in regional and local administration. The draft (*rekrutstvo*) was introduced everywhere, although special rules applied in the Baltic provinces. Regional civil and military integration went hand in hand, and in some borderlands corps commanders were also governors general. Even in Siberia, which at first glance appeared to constitute an exception, slight differences in the hierarchy and procedures did not imply differences in principle – only that circumstances required an adjustment in order to make those principles more effective. Administrative and military integration implied that the turbulence along the Eurasian periphery, so characteristic of the seventeenth and eighteenth centuries, had abated, and that Russian hegemony in the expanding core had become secure. The outer boundaries of the border provinces became the international border of the expanding core with China, Persia, Turkey, Austria, Prussia, and Sweden.

Superstratification was a form of integration. The process was found in all three theatres, but did not succeed everywhere. It worked relatively well in the eastern theatre, in part because the Russian presence remained slight – population densities were exceptionally low, especially beyond the Yenisei River. There, Buriats recognized a community of interests with the Russians, if only because the proximity of the Chinese core beyond the Eurasian periphery left them no choice. The Russian intruder recognized their customs but claimed the right to take part in the allocation of pastures – a highly sensitive matter – thereby gaining the possibility of arbitrating political disputes and shaping the upper stratum of Buriat society to recognize Russian supremacy and Russia's legitimate claim to collect the *iasak*. But further north, the reverse process took place – the Russians were Yakutized and merged with native society. Elsewhere in the same theatre, the Russians encountered similar processes – strong and cohesive societies of Tatars were already engaged in integrating and assimilating smaller native communities when the Russians arrived. The acceptance of the Russian intruder facilitated the process of superstratification and reinforced the upper stratum's hold over local societies and over its own people. In Bashkiria, rivalry over land ownership, embittered by religious hostility, resulted in bloody uprisings.

Superstratification – that is, the integration of the upper stratum of a native society into the command structure of the expanding core – worked best where Russians and natives professed the same values. One senses in the documents a certain admiration by the Russians for Kalmyks and for Georgians: a military ethos and courage in battle created a strong bond, and the Georgians were certainly among those who benefited most from their association with the Russians, while the nomadic Kalmyks fell victim to the transformation of the frontier from a war zone into a land of peaceful agricultural settlers. The same transformation affected the Cossacks. The Poles destroyed those in Right Bank Ukraine, the Russians retained those in the Left Bank, but also transformed most of them into state peasants when they did not deport them to the Caucasus. The Don, Ural, Orenburg, and Siberian Cossacks developed an *esprit de corps* inseparable from their development into frontier and elite troops in the creation of an "empire." In a different way, superstratification worked very well in the former Hetmanate. The Khmelnytsky uprising heralded a massive social transformation of Ukrainian society from below: increased stratification and the introduction of serfdom brought local society in line with Russian society, and the emerging native nobility began to gravitate more and more toward the expanding Russian core and, within it, toward its two capitals in Petersburg and Moscow.

Superstratification also worked very well in the western theatre, in Finland and the Baltic provinces, where an intruding stratum of Swedes and Germans had already made great headway in Swedifying and Germanizing local societies, as the Tatars and Bashkirs, Buriats and Yakuts, had already done in the eastern theatre. Germans especially had an interest in giving their loyalty to the Russian emperor, who promised to respect their privileges, and actually did for the most part, whereas the Swedes, in pursuit of their own ambition to create a unitary state, had been encroaching upon them and even gave serious thought to the abolition of serfdom. But superstratification failed miserably in the western provinces, where Poles had already gone very far in Polonizing Lithuania and Belarus. It was not so much this competition between Russians and Poles over who would prevail in imposing their civilization on the native population that prevented an accommodation, as the fact that both Russians and Poles belonged to core civilizations and not frontiers, and a core civilization cannot be successfully subjugated to another because both possess a universalist *Weltanschauung* demanding hegemony. The mutual antagonism between the two peoples had a long history, and the proud Polish *szlachta* could not accept being subordinated to and integrated into the Russian structure of domination. The uprising of 1831 only made matters worse.

Fiscal policy encouraged the process of superstratification. The combination of a poll tax and a quitrent was the centrepiece of the Russian fiscal system. The poll tax was collected from male peasants who lived on collectively owned government property, and its proceeds were earmarked to support the army and navy. The quitrent served to support the civil administration – that is, the institutionalized ruling class which managed the expanding Russian core. The quitrent on properties owned, no longer collectively, but by individual members of the ruling class, and paid by the peasants of a lord, went to support his way of life. The implication was that the "people" did not own the land but merely rented it and paid for the right to use it as a form of tribute. It has even been suggested that a Russian "subject" (*poddany*) was defined as someone under tributary obligations (*pod-dan-stvo*) toward a lord or the ruler. The poll tax and the quitrent were extended everywhere in the expanding core, even in Siberia, where the *iasak* was the equivalent of the quitrent: it was paid by the native population for the right to continue fishing, herding, and hunting. The fiscal system was thus one of the most powerful tools of integration at the disposal of the ruler and the ruling elite, and finance ministers were among the most forceful supporters of the creation of a unitary state.

The fiscal system was not only a tool of integration; it also contributed to the process of superstratification. The collection of the capitation and the quitrent required the conduct of periodic censuses and the systematic classification, if only for the sake of convenience, of the population into simple categories of taxpayers and non-taxpayers and of taxpayers of various rates. The peasant population was gradually forced into two categories, state peasants and privately owned serfs. As the expanding core kept growing, social categories of native people were forced into the mould: Bashkirs were made into Cossacks, Little Russian Cossacks and Kalmyks into state peasants by placing them under the jurisdiction of the Ministry of State Domains responsible for the management of state forests and state peasants. The upper stratum of the native population was incorporated into a multi-ethnic nobility of the expanding core, as in Left Bank Ukraine, the Baltic provinces, and Georgia, and attempts were even made to create a nobility where there had not been any, as in the Muslim provinces of Transcaucasia. As a result, superstratification became transformed into a simple form of integration into a ruling elite and ruling class staffing governmental institutions, the true managers of the expanding core of dependent population of townsmen and peasants.

Russian policy toward legal systems required pragmatic adjustments to local situations, yet a determination was palpable to create a unitary state, the same uniformity whenever the government felt it was no longer counterproductive. In other words, the continued existence of separate legal systems remained a residual factor contingent upon the good will of the government and the multi-ethnic elite. One must distinguish here between two types of legal system: that of nomadic societies, mainly in the eastern theatre, and that of settled societies in the west, but in both cases the government had to proceed with great caution because the adjudication of legal disputes went to the heart of family and social relations. These societies had different concepts of the role and position of the individual, parents and extended relations, and women, and of the acquisition and disposal of property, of inheritance.

One can say that, as a general rule, the Russian criminal and penal law applied from the beginning in all newly conquered territories in the east, giving the "intruder" the opportunity to exercise his powers of coercion in the process of superstratification. Coercion was used for a purpose and in the name of certain principles, chiefly religious: to instil in the native certain values inviting him to accept a higher civilization, or instil fear of retribution for his refusal to accept integration. In the civil law, where the customary law of the native could not be replaced by the statute law of the intruder for very objective reasons, the policy was to distinguish between cases coming under the jurisdiction of religious authorities in the Russian legal system and those adjudicated in the lay courts; to apply the distinction to the native law, and leave the former under the jurisdiction of the local religious authorities – in part because they were more sensitive cases on account of their religious content – and integrate the others into the civil jurisprudence of the expanding core. Doing so created two parallel legal systems – the native one being a mirror image of the Russian one – until some future time when both could be merged to become the single legal system of a unitary state, as, for example, when the nomadic society had become integrated into a society of settlers.

The consequences of introducing Russian law varied from one territory to another. Inquisitorial procedure introduced an element of regularity in proceedings at the first instance and appellate levels, resented by some, appreciated by others, both in nomadic societies and in the Polish-administered lands, as newcomers discovered, much to their surprise. Russian law was also, at least in some cases, less harsh than that of native societies. Mongol law was not merciful, and at the other end of the expanding core, Swedish law was harsher than Russian. Indeed, the widespread use of corporal punishment may have been the result to Mongol influence, and the most brutal punishment in the Russian army – running the gauntlet – was of Swedish origin. We are not used to seeing the Russians as agents of modernization, but we need to change our approach to the subject. In much the same way, Catherine II's reforms of local government democratized the ruling class of native territories, especially in the Baltic provinces, where membership in a caste of indigenous nobles was opened to other social groups, until then kept out of the political process.

The attempts to codify native law played an important role in the shaping of a policy of integration. They are often seen as reflecting a determination by the local ruling elites to assert their identity against a relentless policy, but this determination must not be taken seriously. The codification of privileges going back to the later Middle Ages (notably in the Baltic provinces) was the equivalent of casting in stone legal norms which had become obsolete beyond serving to consolidate the power position of the ruling class. Yet, despite appearances, such codification was bound to remain a very unstable achievement. It would identify, clearly and finally, the privileges, the civil, criminal, and procedural norms, but would also be immediately exposed to the scrutiny of the Russian government. These laws would be seen as a relic of a distant past, a justification of the status quo in an age of change. In the absence of local legislatures in a unitary state, they could not be amended without the legal sanction of the ruler of the expanding core. The Russian code of 1649 had become largely irrelevant by the end of the eighteenth century, and had been much amended; the new Digest of 1832 would be subjected to periodic revisions. The attempt to codify local law was an exercise in futility, a sop to those who felt some local laws deserved to be retained because they were grounded in old customs. Only in the Baltic provinces was the law codified, but the work was never completed, and what was created was demolished less than two generations after its publication to make way for an ever deeper integration into the expanding Russian core.

But there were also serious obstacles to integration, to the realization of a policy of creating a unitary state. One was trade, which can encourage integration but can also retard it. The hydrographic network of Eurasia is a magnificent one, but most of the rivers flow in the wrong direction, drain into the frozen seas, or are doomed by the low gradient of the great plain to freeze early, open up late, and not carry enough water to support heavy ships. Rapids endanger navigation on the Western Dvina and the Dnieper. Only the Volga with its two tributaries, the Oka and the Kama, constitutes an impressive network in western Eurasia, the land of the Russian people, but the Volga drains into the Caspian, a closed sea far from the great oceans, the mirror image of Russian autarky. The Volga basin constituted an integrated market of huge dimensions: the Ural region shipped its metal goods, the north its timber, the south its grain. It linked both with Siberia, but internal communications beyond the great rivers were so poor that unless production could be shipped downriver, it remained bound to its local market; its further growth was limited until the building of railroads. Therefore, there was not so much trade as commerce: goods produced in the deep interior sought an outlet on the coasts of western Eurasia, or in the steppe, where, however, the nomads' market was insufficient to stimulate production inland. The trade routes were directed west- and southwards; they did not integrate but projected the peripheries outward.

There were ways to neutralize these centrifugal forces in order to strengthen the unitary state, but they were riven with contradictions. One was to station an increasing number of troops in the frontier territories to raise the demand for agricultural products and even manufactured goods. Although the deployment of troops was governed by strategic considerations and the fear of local uprisings, it was also of great economic importance. This was true along the southern fringe of Siberia, in the northern Caucasus, in the southern Ukraine and the Grand Duchy of Lithuania, and even more so in the Baltic provinces, which happened to be near the capital where the demand was so great for food products. Troop deployment bound the peripheries more closely to the centre of the expanding core in Moscow, strengthened the economies of the peripheries, and reoriented them toward the centre. Both phenomena contributed to the development of a policy of autarky, which found its clearest manifestation in a protectionist, even a prohibitive, tariff and the creation of a Fortress Empire. The lack of an extensive frontage on the great oceans encouraged centripetal gravitation. But such a policy, even if dictated by the geographical environment, contained two major contradictions. The encouragement of the peripheral economies would stimulate the growth of education and separatist movements with identities different from those of the Russians and sap the strength of the unitary state.

The other consequence was that the restriction of trade in an age of rapidly growing international exchanges, chiefly sea-borne trade, would undermine the relative strength of the expanding core. Thus, the administrative growth of the unitary state threatened to retard its economic development and the growth of a civil society, while promoting the opposite in the peripheries. The legacy of Russian policies during the first half of the nineteenth century was pregnant with dangerous consequences.

Another serious obstacle to integration was the existence of confessional frontiers in which Orthodoxy fought existential encounters with hostile religions, Latin Christianity, Islam, and even Buddhism, all connected with power centres located beyond the realm of Russian hegemony. Orthodoxy was so much a part of the Russian consciousness and so intimately associated with the interests of the ruling elite and ruling class that the annexation of new territories inexorably entailed a determination to convert the native population. Once the natives had been converted, they became Russian, as Speransky blandly admitted in 1822. In the southern and much of the western theatres, where the population had been practising Orthodoxy for a long time, the annexation meant the incorporation of so many more "Russians" into the expanding unitary state. In the eastern theatre, converting at least the upper stratum of local societies was meant to strengthen the policy of superstratification – working out a compromise integrating the upper stratum into the command hierarchy of the expanding core – but it also widened the gap between that stratum and the dependent population, much as was already the case in the original Russian lands.

It is also quite obvious that Russian Orthodoxy was at a severe disadvantage against the great religions of the periphery. Because official Orthodoxy was so much a manifestation of state power, it emphasized the observance of rites, shied away from theological disputes, and remained very close to the paganism of the simple people – a paradoxical combination which could not make it a source of enlightenment and transcendental faith. The Jesuits in Beijing impressed their hosts with their education, their curiosity, and their faith; the clerics of the Orthodox mission – with some exceptions – made their mark with their drunkenness, a deplorable condition which led the Manchu court to ask for their recall. By contrast, Islam relied on a clergy better educated in the dialectical interpretations of the Koran than the Russian priest who tilled his land like a peasant and often enjoyed no respect at all was educated in the Bible. The Buddhists had the intellectual support of a vast community spread across China and India. In the Baltic provinces, the Protestant clergy was at the forefront of the enlightenment of their flock, and, when they were not, the Moravian Brethren were there to preach a religion of the heart. Orthodoxy was, there too, the mirror image of the closed world of the Caspian basin. In such conditions, Orthodoxy could not hope to spread far beyond the world of the Eastern Slavs, and its four rivals would offer the most insuperable resistance to religious integration.

The movement to educate the upper layers of the dependent population began in the nineteenth century, when universities were created with their network of secondary schools financed by the Central Treasury. Interestingly enough, four of the six universities were located in the peripheries, where Latin Christianity and Islam had already laid solid foundations. Like the Orthodox Church, the educational system was an instrument of state power – it taught loyalty and submission and the religion of the Orthodox God, who had also taught loyalty and submission. But more modern subjects would also arouse a historical consciousness among the youth of the peripheries. This consciousness would in turn imbue a sense of separateness resistant to integration. One could not teach the "Russian spirit" without also awakening the "spirit" of another people (*Volksgeist* in Herder's vocabulary), especially in an age of rising nationalism, that pernicious movement with a natural instinct to destroy stable structures founded in history. The joint work of these two factors – religious and educational – resisting integration was certain to wreck the policy of integration in the latter half of the nineteenth century together with the attempt to create a unitary state. By 1850, however, when our story ends, the dark clouds were still low on the horizon, and the Nikolaevan policy of creating not an empire but a unitary state appeared to be successful.

Is this to say that there was no Russian Empire? If we return to the definition given in the Introduction that an empire is a large political conglomerate in which a minority ethnic group imposes its political control and its civilization upon other peoples, we are immediately presented with a major problem. It is obvious that in Siberia, for example, where the Russians had swamped the native population by 1850, there could be no question of an empire. But what of the territories west of a line running from the Gulf of Finland to Ekaterinoslav on the Dnieper, where the Russian population was insignificant, and where this book has shown that the government of the expanding Russian core was pursuing a policy of systematic integration? Can there be a unitary state where the population of the intruder is insignificant or must this be an empire? The Russians would answer that it can be, because their reasoning was based on a fiction: that much of the population of the former Grand Duchy of Lithuania on both sides of the Pripiat marshes and in the lower Dnieper and Don valleys was Orthodox and therefore Russian. One is reminded of the objection of the Greek Patriarch of Constantinople to the creation of an Orthodox exarchate in Bulgaria in 1878, that there were no Bulgarians, only Greeks speaking Bulgarian. In Moscow, the other great Orthodox metropolis, they saw Belarusians and Ukrainians as Russians who happened to be speaking Belarusian or Ukrainian. Such an attitude was peculiar to Orthodoxy – and was of Hellenistic origin – which subsumed national differences under the general mantle of a common religion. Preposterous as it may sound today, such a view was by no means unrealistic in the eighteenth and nineteenth centuries. Therefore one can conclude that the Russians were indeed creating a unitary state of "Russians" west of that line and down to the foothills of the Caucasus.

But what of Transcaucasia – the mountains were a world apart – Poland, and Finland? Their legal status was by no means clear. All three territories were occupied by force of arms. Finland and Poland were sometimes referred to as states, but how could there be a state within a state? Finland was largely left alone because this western periphery of Eurasia and eastern periphery of Europe became a zone of peace after 1815. Russian interest was mainly naval – to secure the approaches to the capital. Poland also retained its own government, even after 1832, under a viceroy, an unusual arrangement in Russian administrative history. Transcaucasia was too fragmented to have its own government, but it was given a strong regional authority unlike any other in the expanding core, and a viceroy was also appointed in Tiflis in 1844. The fiscal system, the law, and religion remained specific to each territory and different from the Russian. We can claim with certainty that the imperial phase began with the annexation of Georgia in 1801 and would end in the 1880s with the completion of the conquest of Central Asia. The expansion of the Russian core had found a natural obstacle, and an empire was born.

And yet, the situation was not so simple. The battle between ministries and territorial administrators never stopped and would only become fiercer after the death of Nicholas I. There is enough evidence to show that the ministries – the carriers of the unitary state idea – kept undermining the powers of the territorial managers, even under powerful individuals like Paskevich. The viceregal experiment was scrapped in Poland and Transcaucasia in 1875 and 1882 respectively, and the appointment of governors general depending for the most part on the War Ministry inaugurated a new age of administrative integration. The move was followed by the introduction of Russian legislation at all levels, even in Finland, on the way to transforming the empire into a unitary state, as had already been done, on a much smaller scale, in France and the United

Kingdom. Thus the conclusion must be that Russia did create an empire in the first half of the nineteenth century only gradually but in order to transform it eventually into an extension of the unitary state.[2] Unfortunately, the policy developed in a hostile environment, in which nationalism kept raising its ugly head, and turned the whole of western and southern Eurasia into a cauldron of mutually hostile nationalisms, which finally combined to destroy the empire and cause the unitary state to implode, paving the way for the horrors of the twentieth century.

As a parting statement, I will quote from the work of a great scholar: "in history an epilogue is nothing but a prologue, and every conclusion is but an introduction … every type of research is at best a landmark in a succession of attempts to reconstruct the past … and the contribution of these efforts resides in the fact that it raises problems, destined to be taken up again and deepened by other scholars. Such is the course of historical research."[3] As an unknown scholar put it in the epigraph to this book, "may this work make it easier for others to move on."

Abbreviations

AE	Arkheograficheskii Ezhegodnik
AGS	*Arkhiv Gosudarstvennogo Sovieta*
AJ	*Asiatic Journal*
AKAK	*Akty sobrannykg Kavkazskoiu Arkheografic heskoiu Kommissieiu*
AKV	Arkhiv kniazia Vorontsova
APH	*Acta Poloniae Historica*
BH	*Baltische Hefte*
BK Slovar'	*Bantysh-Kamenskii. Slovar' dostopomiatnykh liudei russkoi zemli*
BM	*Baltische Monatschrift*
CAS	*Central Asian Survey*
CASS	*Canadian-American Slavic Studies*
Chteniia	*Chteniia v Imperatorskom Obshchestve istorii i drevnosti Rossiiskikh pri Moskovskom Universitete*
CMR(S)	*Cahiers du monde russe (et sovietique)*
DBL	*Deutschbaltisches Biographisches Lexikon* 1710–1960
DNR	*Drevniaia i Novaia Rossiia*
ES	*Entsiklopedicheskii Slovar'* (Brockhaus & Efron)
EUkr	*Encyklopedia of Ukraine*
GJ	*Geographic Journal*
HNM	*Hüpel. Nordische Miscellaneen*
HUS	*Harvard Ukrainian Studies*
IHR	*International History Review*
IZ	*Istoricheskie zapiski*
IV	*Istoricheskii Vestnik*
JE	*Jewish Encyclopedia*
JGO	*Jahrbücher fur Geschichte Osteuropas*
MERSH	*Modern Encyclopedia of Russian and Soviet History*
MS	*Morskoi sbornik*
OI	*Otechestvennaia istoriia*

OPIS	Vysochaishim ukazam i poveleniiam., Khroniashchimsia v S.-Peterburgstom Senatskom Arkhive za XVIII vek
OZ	Otechestvennye Zapiski
PSB	*Polski Slownik Biograficzny*
*PSZ**	*Polnoe Sobranie Zakonov*
RA	Russkii Arkhiv
RBS	*Russkii Biograficheskii Slovar'*
RGADA	Rossiiskii gosudarstvennyi arkhiv drevnykh aktov
RGOV	Russkoe Geograficheskoe obshchestvo. Vestnik
RGVIA	Rossiiskii gosudarstvennyi voenno-istoricheskii arkhiv
RHD	Revue d'histoire diplomatique
RS	*Russkaia Starina*
RV	Russkii Vestnik
SA	Senatskii Arkhiv
SEER	*Slavonic and East European Review*
SIM	*Sbornik istoricheskikh materialov*
SIRIO	*Sbornik Imperatorskogo russkogo is toricheskogo obshchestva*
SJH	*Scandinavian Journal of History*
SR	*Slavic Review*
SS	*Skandinavskii sbornik*
SVP	*Svod voennykh postanovlenii*, 1838 edition
SZ	*Svod Zakonov*, 1832 edition
VE	*Vestnik Evropy*
VS	*Voennyi Sbornik*
YuV	*Yuridicheskii Vestnik*
ZOOID	*Zapiksi Odesskogo obshchestva liubitelei istorii i drevnostei*
ZhGUP	*Zhurnal Grazhdanskogo i ugolovnogo Prava*
ZhMNP	*Zhurnal Ministerstva Narodnogo Prosveshcheniia*
ZhMVD	*Zhurnal Ministerstva Vnutrennykh Del*
ZhMYu	*Zhurnal Ministerstva Yustitsii*

* This *Collection of Laws of the Russian* Empire was published in two series (for the purpose of this book): the first begins with document 1 (1649) and ends with document 30,600 (November 1825); the second begins again with Document 1 (December 1825). The reader should follow the date to determine the series.

Notes

Introduction

1 To those objecting to my placing Sweden, Finland, and Poland in Eurasia, I answer that Hungarian conservatives view their country as "an extension of Eurasia into Europe," and their society as "the westernmost extension of Eurasian peoples." See Korkut, "Resentment," 71–2.
2 Goehrke, *Russland*, 319. The words "overlapping space" are also from him (317).
3 Danilevskii, *Rossiia i Evropa*, passim.
4 For studies of the Hellenistic world see Chamoux, *Hellenistic Civilization*, Baynes, *Hellenistic Tradition*, and Roussel, *La Grèce.*
5 Yemelianova, *Russia and Islam*, 38; Vasary, *Turks, Tatars*, preface.
6 Yemelianova, *Russia and Islam*, 9, 38. Maureen Perrie notes that the idea of Moscow as the centre of a new universal Orthodox empire was born after 1453, but that it was not until Tsar Alexei Mikhailovich (1645–76) that the tsar saw himself as a new Byzantine emperor pushing for the "Byzantinization of Muscovite church relations … including the assimilation of the tsar to the church hierarchy" ("Uspenskii and Zhivov," 143). Richard Wortman writes that "the emperor was bound by laws until he himself changed them," and refers to "superiority to Law." The emperor was, he adds, a "superordinate ruler from another realm, a pagan god-descendant, a Christ transfigured," and that even Peter failed to distinguish the state from his personal authority (*Russian Monarchy*, xv, xviii). Similarly, Donald Ostrowski notes that "there was no written secular articulation of limitations on the ruler's power," only self-limitation; but, quoting Marc Szeftel, "where was the guarantee that the Monarch would consistently observe this ideal of self-limitation?" (Ostrowski, *Muscovy*, 215, 217).
7 O'Brien, *Muscovy*, 22.
8 Kollmann, *Crime and Punishment*, 211, 259.
9 Burbank, "Empire and Transformation," 13–14, and Burbank and Cooper, *Empires*, passim, the most comprehensive work on the subject.

10 Wortman, “Integrity,” 8.
11 Burbank, “Imperial Rights,” 402.
12 I thank a reader for University of Toronto Press for this suggestion.
13 Wortman, “Integrity,” 25.
14 As Ekaterina Pravilova puts it in the best characterization of Russian policy: “the management of the Russian Empire in the eighteenth and nineteenth centuries rested on *toleration* of diversity and the *pursuit* of standardization” (emphasis added) (“From the Złoty,” 295).
15 LeDonne, *Ruling Russia*, 205–25.
16 LeDonne, “Administrative Regionalization,” 16–20.
17 Two excellent studies of the operation of patronage networks are Beik, *Absolutism*, for France, and Maczak, “Confessions,” for Poland. Ledonne, “Ruling Families,” for Russia. Nancy Kollman has done pioneering work for an earlier period in *Kinship and Politics*.
18 Eberhard, *Conquerors*, 27–8, 137.
19 Zalkind, *Prisoedinenie*, 114–17.

1 Laying the Foundations, 1650–1775

1 For the portages see Kerner, *Urge*, 114–19, 133–5; for the canals see “Voennoe znachenie,” 134–48.
2 Woods, *Baltic Region*, 203, and *Finland and Its Geography*, 326–73 and 376–410.
3 Woods, *Baltic Region*, 128, 173, 389. Well into the nineteenth century, only “Swedish optimists” included Finland in Scandinavia. Finland was a world apart, well to the east (Holmberg, “On the Practicability,” 171).
4 “Zapadnaia Dvina,” in *ES*, 12:242–3.
5 Nalkowski, *Poland*, 49–52.
6 Baginski, *Poland*, 35–6, 49; Nalkowski, *Poland*, 53–4.
7 Braun, *Diary*, 175.
8 Christiansen, *Northern Crusades*, 6–13.
9 Woods, *Baltic Region*, 15.
10 France, *Crusades*, 165–9, 226–7.
11 For excellent maps see Christiansen, *Northern Crusades*, passim.
12 France, *Crusades*, 168. A good history of the Order is Boockmann, *Deutsche Orden*, passim.
13 Halecki, “Evolution,” 283. Samogitia was also known for the deeply rooted Catholicism of its hard-working population (Dolgorukov, “Kniaz’ Nikolai Andreevich Dolgorukov,” 182, 188–9). Memel, which controlled the exits from the Niemen, was called “a bastion of the Teutonic Order” (Fortstreuter, *Memelland*, 7).
14 Beauvois, *Histoire*, 29–31, 65–6, 72–3. A very useful guide to help trace territorial changes is *The Historical Atlas of Poland*.
15 Beauvois, *Histoire*, 30.

16 Ibid., 16–23, 46–8.
17 Vernadsky, *Mongols*, 239–40; Vernadsky, *Russia at the Dawn*, 3–4.
18 Beauvois, *Histoire*, 93–4; Vernadsky, *Russia at the Dawn*, 246–9. For the importance of the Union see Dembkowski, *Union*, 213–21: some have claimed that it created the "Eastern Mission" of Poland at the expense of its Western interests (ibid., 217).
19 Ordin, *Pokorenie*, 1:18–33; Christiansen, *Northern Crusades*, 177–82.
20 Florinsky, *Russia*, 204–5.
21 Andersson, *History of Sweden*.
22 Vernadsky, *Tsardom*, 1:198–201.
23 Ibid., 248–57.
24 Ibid., 285; Ordin, *Pokorenie*, 1:44–6, 47–50.
25 As Vernadsky claims (*Tsardom*, 1:285–9); for a contrary view see Kirby, *Northern Europe*, 1:125.
26 Quoted in Kerner, *Urge*, 49–52; see also Roberts, *Swedish Imperial Experience*, 68.
27 Vernadsky, *Tsardom*, 1:289–91, 349–54; Beauvois, *Histoire*, 116.
28 Kirby, *Northern Europe*, 1:186; Roberts, *Swedish Imperial Experience*, 39, 99–100.
29 Florinsky, *Russia*, 1:336.
30 Kotilaine, "Opening a Window," 527, 529.
31 Andersson, *History*, 232
32 See the volume of contributions edited by Serhii Plokhy, *Poltava 1709*.
33 Ordin, *Pokorenie*, 1:52–3.
34 *PSZ*, vol. 5, 1719, no. 3380, 1713, no. 2703, 1714, no. 2831.
35 *PSZ*, vol. 12, 1744, no. 8856.
36 Upton, *Charles XI*, 162–3, 188–90; Kirby, *Concise History*, 38.
37 Amburger, *Geschichte*, 386; *DBL*, 468.
38 Lehtonen, *Polnischen Provinzen*, 202.
39 Amburger, *Geschichte*, 387; *DBL*, 173–4, 438–9.
40 *PSZ*, vol. 4, 1710, no. 2297, 2298; Lehtonen, *Polnischen Provinzen*, 199–200.
41 Amburger, *Geschichte*, 174–5.
42 *PSZ*, vol. 4, 1712, no. 2658.
43 Kirilov, *Tvetushchee sostoianie*, 71, 76, 68.
44 *PSZ*, vol. 11, 1843, no. 8798.
45 *Stoletie*, vol. 4, annex, 24–5.
46 Newbury, *Patrons, Clients*, 3–4.
47 Nordmann, *Grandeur*, 31.
48 Fahlbeck, *Der Adel*, 15.
49 Roberts, *Swedish Imperial Experience*, 92–4.
50 Cited in Kirby, *Northern Europe*, 222.
51 Kirby, ibid., 154–5; Troshchinskii, "Zapiska," 115–16, 120.
52 Roberts, *Swedish Imperial Experience*, 117–19; Nordmann, *Grandeur*, 40–63; Heckscher, *Economic History*, 117–24; Upton, *Charles XI*, 199–222. Fahlbeck bluntly

writes that the reversion was, "after the French Revolution, the most radical state-induced social transformation in any country in modern times" (*Der Adel*, 15). The standard work on the reversion remains Vasar's (for Livland).

53 *PSZ*, vol. 4, 1710, no. 2301.

54 *DBL*, 470; *RBS*, 10:127; "Zur livländischen," 248–9, 252–6; Bushkovitch, *Peter the Great*, 294–5.

55 Upton, *Charles* XI, 199.

56 *PSZ*, vol. 4, 1710, no. 2279, 2298, 2299.

57 Ibid., no. 2287.

58 Ibid., no. 2298.

59 Ibid., no. 2277, 2286, 2495.

60 Eckardt, "Livländische Landtag," 118; Roberts, *Swedish Imperial Experience*, 121.

61 Troshchinskii, "Zapiska," 122; "Extrakt," 210; *PSZ*, vol. 4, 1712, no. 2496.

62 *DBL*, 139–40, 173–4, 468.

63 *PSZ*, vol. 8, 1728, no. 5330.

64 Eckardt, "Livländische Landtag," 140–3; see also Whelan, *Adapting to Modernity*, 19–25.

65 "Zur livländischen," 283–96. For general histories of the Baltic German nobilities see Wrangell, *Die Estlandische Ritterschaft*, with abundant photographs and a long section on the emancipation of the Estland peasantry (62–95); *Kurland und seine Ritterschaft*, esp. 16–49, 60–84. There is a list of matriculated nobles on 429–63. For a list of families in the Livland *Matrikel* from 1745 until 1875 see Eckardt, *Livland*, 525–39.

66 "Zur livländischen," 284–5. For more on social divisions among the Germans see Whelan, *Adapting to Modernity*, 29, 32–4.

67 *DBL*, 404–5; Rauch, "Zur baltischen Frage," 465–6.

68 Heckscher, *Economic History*, 50, 109–12.

69 Nordmann, *Grandeur*, 290.

70 Lilja, "Swedish Urbanization," 285.

71 "Zur livländischen," 437.

72 Raun, *Estonia*, 23.

73 Plakans, *Latvians*, 52–3, 73–4.

74 Raun, *Estonia*, 230–1.

75 *PSZ*, vol. 5, 1712, no. 2501; vol. 7, 1725, no. 4743.

76 "Sostav gorodov," 399–403; Nordmann, *Grandeur*, 58–9.

77 Kabuzan, *Narody Rossii v XVIII veke*, 84.

78 Plakans, *Latvians*, 25–6.

79 Kirby, *Northern Europe*, 18–19. The Abbé de Pradt, Napoleon's envoy to the Duchy of Warsaw, felt the following in 1812: "it seemed that Europe ended when I crossed the Oder ... Poland is no longer Asia, but it is not yet Europe" (Pradt, *Histoire*, 72). The historian Hugh Seton-Watson is quoted as thinking that "the social structure of Eastern Europe more closely resembled that of Russia, or even of Asiatic

countries, than that of France, Britain, or Germany" on the eve of the Communist takeover in the late 1940s (cited in Dawisha, *Eastern Europe*, 43). Thirty years after Pradt's trip to Warsaw, the poet Fedor Tiutchev wrote the following on his way back from Europe and upon his arrival in Warsaw: "No matter how you look at it, the city on the outside is in some way akin to Moscow, and this is especially striking to someone coming from the West" (quoted in Gorizontov, *Paradoksy*, 5).

80 Plakans, *Latvians*, 25–6, 33–4.

81 Raun, *Estonia*, 20.

82 Kirby, *Northern Europe*, 158.

83 Nordmann, *Grandeur*, 59–60.

84 Kirby, *Northern Europe*, 158.

85 Raun, *Estonia*, 30.

86 Kirby, *Northern Europe*, 150–1.

87 Roberts, *Swedish Imperial Experience*, 86, 88–9.

88 Heckscher, *Economic History*, 128.

89 Kabuzan, *Izmeneniia*, 87; Plakans, *Latvians*, 63–5.

90 Raun, *Estonia*, 43.

91 Cited in Plakans, *Latvians*, 63; see also Donnert, *Agrarfrage*, 27–8; Eckardt (*Livland*, 215–31) discusses the persecution of the movement.

92 Nordmann, *Grandeur*, 45.

93 *PSZ*, vol. 1, 1661, no. 301.

94 Semenov, *Izuchenie*, chast' 1, 20.

95 Roberts, *Swedish Imperial Experience*, 105–7.

96 Kotilaine, "Opening a Window," 499–502.

97 Dale, *Indian Merchants*, 77.

98 Kotilaine, "Opening a Window," 529–30.

99 Oliva, *Misalliance*, 129.

100 *PSZ*, vol. 7, 1724, no. 4452.

101 LeDonne, *Grand Strategy*, 47.

102 Lodyzhenskii, *Istoriia*, 50, 57.

103 Mardefeld to the Prussian King, 9 June 1724, in *SIRIO*, 15:245.

104 Lodyzhenskii, *Istoriia*, 61–3.

105 Semenov, *Izuchenie*, chast' 1, 73; *PSZ*, vol. 7, 1725, no. 4712.

106 "Zur livländischen," 465; *PSZ*, vol. 10, 1737, no. 7184; 1739, no. 7980; vol. 11, 1741, no. 8430; vol. 12, 1746, no. 9258; vol. 15, 1758, no. 10879.

107 Kirby, *Northern Europe*, 358–60.

108 Lodyzhenskii, *Istoriia*, 92.

109 *History of Finland's Literature*, 11.

110 Plakans, *Concise History*, 32.

111 Orfield, *Growth*, 272.

112 For the northern crusades see France, *Crusades*, passim.

113 Paul, "Secular Power," 238, 242.

114 Plakans, *Latvians*, 31–3. On the organization of the Church in Swedish times and the reforms see *Baltische Kirchengeschichte*, 77–102.
115 Kirby, *Concise History*, 40–1.
116 Kent, *Concise History*, 53, 56.
117 Andersson, *History*, 133, 196.
118 Roberts, *Swedish Imperial Experience*, 69–70.
119 Nordmann, *Grandeur*, 33–5.
120 "Ursprungliche Einrichtung," 328–32.
121 Nordmann, *Grandeur*, 113.
122 Ordin, *Pokorenie*, 1:52.
123 Kirby, *Concise History*, 41.
124 Nordmann, *Grandeur*, 113–19.
125 Raun, *Estonia*, 32–3; Piirimiae, "Rol' Tartuskogo universiteta," passim.
126 Upton, *Charles XI*, 198–9.
127 Kent, *Concise History*, 59. The oldest university may in fact be that of Lund, founded in 1425.
128 Scott, *Sweden*, 196–8.
129 Rauch, "Reflexe," 11–12.
130 Roberts, *Swedish Imperial Experience*, 119–20.
131 Piirimiae, "Rol' Tartuskogo universiteta," 71–3; Cheshikhin, "Kak poniali"; Upton, *Charles XI*, 198; Kirby, *Northern Europe*, 280; Plakans, *Latvians*, 39–40, 56, 67; Raun, *Estonia*, 32–3.
132 Florinsky, *Russia*, 491, 592.
133 *PSZ*, vol. 8, 1728, no. 5220.
134 *PSZ*, vol. 7, 1725, no. 4781; "Zur livländischen," 431.
135 *PSZ*, vol. 10, 1739, no. 7957; vol. 13, 1751, no. 9905.
136 Jenkins, *Social Order*, 93.
137 Orfield, *Growth*, 252.
138 Upton, *Charles XI*, 237.
139 Chydenius, "Swedish Lawbook," 378.
140 Orfield, *Growth*, 284–5; Fahlcrantz, "Naemd," 838–9.
141 Orfield, *Growth*, 306–7, 256, 284–5; Upton, *Charles XI*, 166–7; Scott, *Sweden*, 186; Chydenius, "Swedish Lawbook," 306–7.
142 Chydenius, ibid., 377–9, 383.
143 Orfield, *Growth*, 280–1.
144 *History of Finland's Literature*, 42.
145 RGADA, f. 16, d. 664, 1. 2–10: from the report of the Vyborg governor of 1775.
146 A general survey of the Baltic court system beginning in the sixteenth century is in Remdul, "Nemetskie sudy."
147 "Sostav gorodov," 394–8.
148 "Pribaltiiskoe grazhdanskoe pravo," in *ES*, 118–19.
149 Roberts, *Swedish Imperial Experience*, 116; Upton, *Charles XI*, 198.

150 *PSZ*, vol. 9, 1734, no. 6548 and 1736, no. 7382. The college was firmly in the hands of Baltic Germans: Hermann von Brevern (1717–21), Sigismund von Wolff (1721–30), Hermann von Keyserling (for a brief period), Karl von Mengden (1735–40), and Friedrich von Emme (1741–64) (Amburger, *Geschichte*, 176).
151 *PSZ*, vol. 13, 1751, no. 9905.
152 Ordin, *Pokorenie*, 1:103.
153 *PSZ*, vol. 22, 1787, no. 16507; see also vol. 20, 1779, no. 14842.
154 Ordin, *Pokorenie*, 1:106–7.
155 *PSZ*, vol. 5, 1718, no. 3201 and 3202.
156 *PSZ*, vol. 12, 1744, no. 8964.
157 See the table of organization in *PSZ*, vol. 8, 1728, no. 5220 and vol. 25, 1798, no. 18675.
158 *PSZ*, vol. 7, 1726, no. 4894 and vol. 11, 1743, no. 8756.
159 Lehtonen, *Polnischen Provinzen*, 202; "Zur livländischen," 287; *PSZ*, vol. 16, 1764, no. 12250. For the mood prevailing in Petersburg in the 1830s, during the work on codification, see Ch-v, "Speranskii," 41–57.

2 Full Integration, 1775–1815

1 LeDonne, *Russian Empire*, 39.
2 *SIRIO*, 5:9–11.
3 Martens, *Recueil*, 6:71–81.
4 *Historical Atlas of Poland*, 18.
5 *PSZ*, vol. 23, 1793, no. 17141.
6 Magocsi, *Ukraine: A Historical Atlas*, 59–60.
7 *PSZ*, vol. 19, 1772, no. 13850.
8 *PSZ*, vol. 20, 1777, no. 14603, 1778, no. 14762 and 14774.
9 Zhukovich, "Upravlenie is sud," 7–8; *PSZ*, vol. 23, 1795, no. 17325, 17327, 17403.
10 Kabuzan, *Narody Rossii v XVIII veke*, 172–4.
11 LeDonne, "Russian Governors General," passim. See also, for an example, "Pis'ma Mikhailu Nikitichu Krechetnikovu," passim.
12 Zhukovich, "Upravlenie i sud," 293–9.
13 *PSZ*, vol. 19, 1773, no. 14014; Zhukovich, "Upravlenie i sud," 289–90.
14 *PSZ*, vol. 19, 1772, no. 13808.
15 Zhukovich, "Upravlenie i sud," 88–106.
16 "Chernyshev, Zakhar," in *RBS*, 22:313–18; Dobrynin, "Istinnoe povestvovanie," 98, 107–8. He quotes the Mogilev governor saying in 1778 that the Russian personnel in his province consisted of ten different kinds of crooks.
17 "Passek, Petr," in *RBS*, 13:359–61; Dobrynin, "Istinnoe povestvovanie," 108–9, 116, 137–40, 208–29; Zhukovich, "Upravlenie i sud," 350–2.
18 "Tutolmin, Timofei," in *BK Slovar'*, 1836, 5:171–4; Zhukovich, "Upravlenie i sud," 30–2. Nesvizh was a fine Radziwill estate; Minsk did not have suitable buildings

to house a governor general and the provincial agencies. See also "Pis'ma imp. Ekateriny II Tutolminu," passim.

19 Lukowski, *Partitions*, 162–75. For a general survey of this so-called northwestern region see "Severo-zapadnyi krai."

20 *PSZ*, vol. 23, 1794, no. 17264, 1795, no. 17417 and 17418.

21 Woods, *Baltic Region*, 400–1.

22 Zhukovich, "Upravlenie i sud," 31–7.

23 Kabuzan, *Narody Rossii v XVIII veke*, 173–4, 213–15, 228.

24 *PSZ*, vol. 23, 1794, no. 17264.

25 *PSZ*, vol. 23, 1795, no. 17359.

26 Zhukovich, "Upravlenie i sud," 55–6.

27 *RBS*, 113–15.

28 Lord, "Third Partition," passim.

29 Lehtonen, *Polnische Provinzen*, 105–6.

30 RGVIA, f. VUA, d. 234.

31 *PSZ*, vol. 24, 1796, no. 17606.

32 *Cambridge History of Poland*, 2:72.

33 Lukowski, *Liberty's Folly*, 9; Kutrzeba, *Grundriss*, 157–61; Lehtonen, *Polnische Provinzen*, 32–8, 56, 66–9.

34 Lord, "Third Partition," passim. Governor General Prince Nikolai Dolgorukov (of the Northwest from 1831 to 1840) gave a damning assessment of Polish society in the mid-1830s: a *szlachta* known for its haughtiness and the baseness of a slave depending on the circumstances; a clergy boasting of its exorbitant intolerance, sacrilegious behaviour, and cupidity; a middle class (*soslovie*) inclined to constant trouble-making, and a hardly existing trading community ("Kniaz' Nikolai Andreevich Dolgorukov," 174, 176–7).

35 *Cambridge History of Poland*, 2:75–6, 78.

36 Lukowski, *Liberty's Folly*, 84.

37 Roos, "Ständewesen," 310–13; Kowecki, "Transformations," 6; LeDonne, *Absolutism*, 22.

38 Kabuzan, "Izmeneniia," 107–18; Kabuzan, *Narody Rossii v XVIII veke*, 166, 171–4; Kabuzan and Troitskii, "Izmeneniia," 163.

39 Lukowski, *Partitions*, 7–8.

40 Lord, "Third Partition," passim. For the structure of the Polish nobility see Gierowski, *Polish-Lithuanian Commonwealth*, 17–19, 113–23.

41 Lord, "Third Partition," passim.

42 Zhukovich, "Upravlenie i sud," 322.

43 Leslie, *Polish Politics*, 13–14.

44 Ibid., 14–16; Lord, "Third Partition," passim.

45 Lukowski, *Liberty's Folly*, 76–7.

46 Cippola, *Before the Industrial Revolution*, 226–7.

47 Kersten, "Magnats," 131.

48 *Cambridge History of Poland*, 2:74.
49 Lehtonen, *Polnischen Provinzen*, 85; Lukowski, *Liberty's Folly*, 14–16.
50 Lukowski, *Liberty's Folly*, 126–7; for the seventeenth century see Wojcik, "Separatist Tendencies."
51 Hatton, *Charles XII*, 158–60.
52 Lukowski, *Liberty's Folly*, 37; Kula, *Economic Theory*, 147.
53 Opalinski, "Great Poland's Power Elite," 51; Pospiech and Tygielski, "Social Role," 75–8; Kersten," "Magnats," 126–7; Kula, *Economic Theory*, 148.
54 Pospiech and Tygielski, "Social Role," 85–90.
55 Plakans, *Concise History*, 93.
56 Kersten, "Magnats," 119, 125.
57 Zhukovich, "Upravlenie i sud," 322; Lehtonen, *Polnischen Provinzen*, 631.
58 *PSZ*, vol. 22, 1784, no. 15961; vol. 23, 1795, no. 17327.
59 Magocsi, *Historical Atlas of East Central Europe*, 49–50.
60 Gostautas, "Early History," 3.
61 Magocsi, *Historical Atlas*, 51–3; Zhukovich, "Shkol'noe delo," 297.
62 Zoltowski, *Border of Europe*, 22–4.
63 Gastautas, "Early History," 4–6.
64 Milosz, *History*, 90–2; Zoltowski, *Border of Europe*, 18. Barbara Skinner skirts the issue of the role of Jesuits in the creating of the Uniate Church as an instrument of Polish policy (*Western Front*, 22–5).
65 Zoltowski, *Border of Europe*, 22–4.
66 Cynarski, "Shape," 9–17; Milosz, *History*, 154.
67 Beauvois, *Histoire*, 140.
68 Lukowski, *Liberty's Folly*, 181–4; Zoltowski, *Border of Europe*, 51; Milosz, *History*, 156–7; Gierowski, *Polish-Lithuanian Commonwealth*, 159–61.
69 *PSZ*, vol. 2, 1686, no. 1213; Lukowski, *Partitions*, 21–2.
70 *PSZ*, vol. 19, 1772, no. 13921–2.
71 Zoltowski, *Border of Europe*, 68; Lehtonen, *Polnischen Provinzen*, 138.
72 *PSZ*, vol. 20, 1780, no. 15028.
73 "Church, History of," *EUkr*, 1:477; *PSZ*, vol 22, 1785, no. 16122.
74 LeDonne, *Grand Strategy*, 145.
75 Lehtonen, *Polnischen Provinzen*, 146.
76 *PSZ*, vol. 19, 1772, no. 13808.
77 *PSZ*, vol. 19, 1774, no. 14102, 1772, no. 13922. For Catherine II's policy toward the Jesuits see Moroshkin, *Iezuity v Rossii*, vol. 1, passim.
78 Zhukovich, "Shkol'noe delo," 300–2.
79 Zoltowski, *Border of Europe*, 88–9; Zhukovich, "Shkol'noe delo," 342–4.
80 Zhukovich, "Shkol'noe delo," 313.
81 Ibid., 328–9.
82 *PSZ*, vol. 17, 1766, no. 12776; vol. 18, 1769, no. 13251–2.
83 *PSZ*, vol. 19, 1772, no. 13922, 1773, no. 14073; Lehtonen, *Polnische Provinzen*, 559.

84 *PSZ*, vol. 19, 1774, no. 14122; vol. 21, 1782, no. 15356. For Sestrenshevich see *PSB*, 37:375–80.
85 Lehtonen, *Polnische Provinzen*, 546–7, 573–4; Leslie, *Polish Politics*, 6–7.
86 *PSZ*, vol. 21, 1782, no. 15326.
87 Leslie, *Polish Politics*, 6–7; Butterwick, *Polish Revolution*, 307–11.
88 *PSZ*, vol. 23, 1795, nn. 17379–80.
89 This intention to create a separate Roman Catholic Church would have a long life. Antonii Zubko, bishop of Minsk and Bobruisk, would submit such a project in 1840. Dolbilov and Staliunas do indeed use this term (*Obratnaia Uniia*, 21).
90 *PSZ*, vol. 23, 1794, no. 17199 and 17204.
91 *PSZ*, vol. 19, 1773, no. 14087. For a general study of the importance of Memel and the difficulty attending the linking of the Lithuanian and Polish trade see Forstreuter, *Die Memel*, esp. 87–9 and the two maps.
92 *PSZ*, vol. 8, 1730, no. 5573.
93 Lukowski, *Liberty's Folly*, 32.
94 Topolski, "La régréssion," 45.
95 Lesnodorski, "Pologne," 53–4.
96 Coxe, *Travels*, 2:236–8.
97 *PSZ*, vol. 19, 1772, no. 13894; Lehtonen, *Polnischen Provinzen*, 412–13.
98 *PSZ*, vol. 19, 1773, no. 13948; vol. 20, 1775, no. 14271; vol. 21, 1782, no. 15407.
99 *PSZ*, vol. 21, 1783, no. 15664; vol. 23, 1795, no. 17419.
100 Coxe, *Travels*, 2:92.
101 Lukowski, *Liberty's Folly*, 110–11; Lehtonen, *Polnische Provinzen*, 103–4.
102 Lukowski, *Liberty's Folly*, 113.
103 See Coxe, *Travels*, 2:90 for the rates.
104 Lehtonen, *Polnische Provinzen*, 49.
105 *PSZ*, vol. 19, 1772, no. 13865.
106 *PSZ*, vol. 19, 1772, no. 13923, 13973, 1774, no. 14113, 1775, no. 14312; vol. 20, 1778, no. 14689.
107 *PSZ*, vol. 21, 1783, no. 15724.
108 *PSZ*, vol. 23, 1794, no. 17222, 1795, no. 17495; vol. 24, 1797, no. 18277. On the limited development of a money economy in Belorussia see Pokhilevich, "Perevod."
109 Dollinger, *La Hanse*, 270–3, 317. Before 1772, the southern part of eastern Belorussia received its salt from the Crimea (*PSZ*, vol. 23, 1794, no. 16736).
110 LeDonne, "Indirect Taxes," 163–4.
111 *PSZ*, vol. 19, 1772, no. 13865; Lehtonen, *Polnische Provinzen*, 413.
112 *PSZ*, vol. 19, 1773, no. 13980, 1774, no. 14127; Lehtonen, *Polnische Provinzen*, 483–5, 538–9.
113 *PSZ*, vol. 23, 1794, no. 16736, 1795, no. 17366.
114 LeDonne, "Indirect Taxes," 174–5.

115 "Propinatsionnoe pravo," in *ES*, 25:453–5, 921 (for *czopowe*); see also Murphy, "Burghers."
116 *PSZ*, vol. 19, 1772, no. 13865; *Svedeniia*, 1:14–15.
117 *AGS*, I, part 2, 287; *PSZ*, vol. 20, 1779, no. 14892.
118 *PSZ*, vol. 23, 1795, no. 17327; *Svedeniia*, 1:16–17.
119 *SIRIO*, 6:284–92, 293–304.
120 Coxe, *Travels*, 2:237.
121 Roos, "Ständewesen," 350.
122 Topolski, "Problem," 213. There is an error in the original; the percentages are 15, 35, and 60; I make it 50 per cent. See also Weinryb, *Jews*, 308–20.
123 Klier, *Russia*, 55–6; Levine, *Economic Origins*, 166. On the Jews of Belorussia see Derzhavin, "Mnenie," passim.
124 Klier, *Russia*, 19; Baron, *Russian Jew*, 16, claims the first partition brought in only 27,000 Jews.
125 Kabuzan, *Narody Rossii v pervoi polovine XIX v.*, 122–3. The growing number of Jews made them more visible. State Comptroller Balthasar von Campenhausen reported in 1816: "the growing Jewish population in our Polish provinces terrifies me; this will only cause more corruption [*razvrat*] among local officials and an increase in smuggling" (Kampengausen, "Perepiska," 272).
126 Topolski, "Problem," 213.
127 Klier, *Russia*, 68.
128 Lukowski, *Liberty's Folly*, 77–8.
129 Kutrzeba, *Grundriss*, 162–3.
130 Levine, *Economic Origins*, 61–2, 72.
131 Ibid., 9, 61–2, 72, 99, 145.
132 RGADA, f. 16, d. 168, ch. 15, list 221; see also Lehtonen, *Polnische Provinzen*, 41–2.
133 Klier, *Russia*, 53.
134 *PSZ*, vol. 19, 1772, no. 13865.
135 Klier, *Russia*, 62; Kakhovskii's report is in *Sochinenia Derzhavina*, 7:308–14.
136 *PSZ*, vol. 20, 1776, no. 14522.
137 *PSZ*, vol. 20, 1779, no. 14892.
138 Klier, *Russia*, 69.
139 Zhukovich, "Upravlenie i sud," 334–45.
140 Ibid., 345–7; Stone, "Jews and Urban Question," 534.
141 *PSZ*, vol. 22, 1786, no. 16391.
142 *PSZ*, vol. 23, 1789, no. 16781, 1790, no. 16877.
143 Klier, *Russia*, 75.
144 *PSZ*, vol. 23, 1794, no. 17224.
145 Baron, *Russian Jew*, 21.
146 *PSZ*, vol. 11, 1742. no. 8673 and 8867.

147 *PSZ*, vol. 23, 1791, no. 17006. Klier, *Russia*, 75, does not emphasize enough that the edict of 1791 did not indicate at all a new policy, but was a reaffirmation of earlier views that the Jews must not be allowed into Russia.

148 As can be seen in *PSZ*, vol. 23, 1795, no. 17327. See also *Zapadnye okrainy*, 310–12.

149 Raeff, *Well-Ordered Police State*, passim; Garner, *Etat, économie, territoire*, 32, 51, 94, 167.

150 LeDonne, *Ruling Russia*, 273–4. On the role of Pietism see Donnert, *Agrarfrage*, 52–67.

151 *PSZ*, vol. 21, 1783, no. 15775, 15881; vol. 17, 1765, no. 12333; a new county centre was created for the Piltau district in Gazenpot (Hausau). After the secularization of the Livonian Order, the district had become the personal property of the Polish king (Gessen, "Evrei," 381–2).

152 *PSZ*, vol. 21, 1783, no. 15795.

153 *RBS*, 3:365–6; *DBL*, 108–9.

154 *RBS*, 2:671–3; Czartoryski, *Mémoires*, 1:225.

155 *RBS*, 13:138–9, *DBL*, 524; Czartoryski, *Mémoires*, 1:235–6.

156 *RBS*, 3:414–16.

157 RGVIA, f. VUA, d. 234.

158 *PSZ*, vol. 22, 1784, no. 15979.

159 *PSZ*, vol. 21, 1782, no. 15719; Zutis, *Ostzeiskii vopros*, 495–506.

160 *PSZ*, vol. 22, 1784, no. 16099; "Zur livländischen," 434.

161 *PSZ*, vol. 22, 1784, no. 16019. It seems that very few criminal cases had to be appealed outside the province. Catherine II told Dahl in 1777 that in Estland there had not been a single criminal case in fourteen years, and that in the Baltic provinces in general such cases were settled by mutual agreement (*poliubovno*). If they had to be taken to court, they were settled "so well" that very few decisions were appealed to Petersburg ("Besedy imp. Ekateriny II," 17).

162 *PSZ*, vol. 20, 1779, no. 14842; vol. 22, 1787, no. 16507.

163 *PSZ*, vol. 22, 1785, no. 16154 and 1786, no. 16308.

164 LeDonne, *Grand Strategy*, 146.

165 "Zur livländischen," 287–9.

166 Dukes, *Catherine the Great*, 67.

167 *PSZ*, vol. 16, 1763, no. 11743.

168 Igelstrom, "Erinnerungen," 12–14. On home education in Kurland see Bolotov, *Zhizn'*, 79–80; see, especially, Eckardt, *Livland*, 375–81, 402–7, 410–15.

169 LeDonne, *Absolutism*, 22.

170 *SIRIO*, 147:65–77, 78–82, 85–94.

171 Zutis, *Ostzeiskii vopros*, 517.

172 Troshchinskii, "Zapiska," 135–7.

173 Zutis, *Ostzeiskii vopros*, 567–72; *PSZ*, vol. 22, 1787, no. 16554.

174 "Petitsiia," 449–54.

175 *PSZ*, vol. 22, 1786, no. 16424.
176 Bil'basov, "Prisoedinenie," 238–9.
177 *PSZ*, vol. 22, 1787, no. 16584.
178 Zutis, *Ostzeiskii vopros*, 307–9; Raun, *Estonia*, 40–2.
179 Kabuzan, *Izmeneniia*, 101, 113.
180 On Eisen see Bartlett, "Russia's First Abolitionist," 165–71; Donnert, *Agrarfrage*, 70, 75; Zutis, *Ostzeiskii vopros*, 334–8.
181 Donnert, *Agrarfrage*, 188–9; Bartlett, "Russia's First Abolitionist," 171–6. But serfdom was so ingrained in the mores of the time that Eisen could not resist buying a serf boy for 12 roubles (ibid., 173).
182 Donnert, *Agrarfrage*, 141–63.
183 Ibid., 75–86; Zutis, *Ostzeiskii vopros*, 338–45.
184 "Zur livländischen," 454–67; Ibneyeva, "Journey," 139–40.
185 "Zur livländischen," 429–30, 459–65; Donnert, *Agrarfrage*, 178.
186 Heckscher, *Mercantilism*, 2:61.
187 Nordmann, *Grandeur*, 353; Kirby, *Northern Europe*, 365–6.
188 *PSZ*, vol. 17, 1766, no. 12636.
189 Lodyzhenskii, *Istoriia*, 142.
190 *PSZ*, vol. 16, 1763, no. 11785.
191 *PSZ*, vol. 16, 1764, no. 12221.
192 *PSZ*, vol. 17, 1766, no. 12735; Semenov, *Izuchenie*, chast' 2, 22–4; Eckardt, *Livland*, 464–83.
193 *PSZ*, vol. 17, 1765, no. 12518. Tables showing the number of ships entering Riga from 1669 to 1820 and the dates when the Dvina opened are in "Izvestie," 42–4.
194 *PSZ*, vol. 21, 1782, no. 15520.
195 Lodyzhenskii, *Istoriia*, 137.
196 "Neue Einrichtungen," 199–201.
197 Zutis, *Ostzeiskii vopros*, 463.
198 Ibneyeva, "Journey," 136.
199 "Zur livländischen," 440, 453; PSZ, vol. 17, 1766, no. 12612. See also Zutis, *Politika*, 43–57, and Eckardt, *Livland*, 395–402.
200 *PSZ*, vol. 21, 1783, no. 15724; Zutis, *Ostzeiskii vopros*, 538.
201 The reform was also a major factor in the peasant uprising of 1784: see Diubiuk, "Krestianskoe dvizhenie."
202 "Neue Einrichtungen," 201–2.
203 *SIRIO*, 6:291, 302.

3 Unitary State or Empire? 1815–1855

1 Nicholas Mikhailovitch, *Relations Diplomatiques*, 2:42, 54–5. For the two major operations of the Swedish war see V-n, "Zimniaia ekspeditsiia" and Anushkin, "Alandskaia ekspeditsiia."

2 Hube, “Rossiia i Shvetsiia,” 24; Kabuzan, *Narody Rossii v pervoi polovine XIX v.*, 122–3, 200–1, 203.
3 *PSZ*, vol. 6, 1831, no. 4448.
4 Ordin, *Pokorenie*, 2, annex, 3–6, 153–61.
5 Kirby, *Baltic World*, 80.
6 *RBS*, 265–8; Nordmann, *Grandeur*, 359–60; Ordin, *Pokorenie*, 1:119–22; Skalon, “Upravlenie,” 934.
7 Thaden, *Russia's Western Borderlands*, 92; Nicolas Mikhailovitch, 5:307; *RBS*, 412–14. On Steinheil and Zakrevsky see Neseman, “A Special Baltic-German Understanding.”
8 *RBS*, 195–9; Thaden, *Russia's Western Borderlands*, 92–3. On Zakrevsky's unpleasant character see Obolenskii, “Nabroski,” 352–4 and Ginsburg, “From a Family Archive.” Like Ermolov he was strongly anti-German, and with his chief of staff, Prince Petr Volkonskii, fell victim to the “coup” of 1823 engineered by the “Germans” and the Saltykov patronage network. He was greatly offended by his demotion to governor general of Finland, and felt that Finland should be fully merged with Russia (P., “Istoricheskie siluety,” 397, 668).
9 Thaden, *Russia's Western Borderlands*, 201, 203.
10 *PSZ*, vol. 10, 1835, no. 8281. For the military reforms and the location of troops see Luntinen, *Imperial Russian Army*, 49–75.
11 Thaden, *Russia's Western Borderlands*, 212; Jutikkala, *Geschichte*, 268.
12 *PSZ*, vol. 27, 1802, no. 20272 and 20274; vol. 31, 1811, no. 24831; vol. 1, 1826, no. 292; vol. 9, 1834, no. 7618; Amburger, *Geschichte*, 437–8; Divov, “Dnevnik,” 479; Kirby, *Baltic World*, 80. On the dismal condition of Vyborg province at the end of the eighteenth century see Bobovich, “Sostoianie,” 41–2. The creation of a state secretariat also convinced some Finns that they would now be able to submit their grievances directly to the emperor without going through an intermediate instance (Scheibert, “Anfänge,” 416).
13 “Imperator Aleksandr I i Graf Armfelt,” 132.
14 *RBS*, 1: 293–5; Thaden, *Russia's Western Borderlands*, 87–91.
15 *RBS*, 1:292; Thaden, *Russia's Western Borderlands*, 203.
16 *RBS*, 15:529–30; Thaden, *Russia's Western Borderlands*, 86–7, 93.
17 See for instance *PSZ*, vol. 18, 1843, no. 16717; vol. 23, 1848, no. 21927.
18 Abov, “Finliandiia,” 61–2; for the title see *SZ*, vol. 1, art 37.
19 Abov, “Finliandiia,” 58–72; Skalon, “Upravlenie,” 935. A publication of the Committee of Ministers (undated) called Russia a unitary state (*edinoe gosudarstvo*) (Abov, “Finliandiia,” 72). Jutikkala, *Geschichte*, 265, uses the term *Landtag*, not *seim/Sejm*. See also Scheibert, *Volk und Staat*, 38–47.
20 Abov, “Finliandiia,” 58–9.
21 Thaden, *Russia's Western Borderlands*, 201. The controversy over whether Finland had already become a state by the time it was incorporated into the Russian Empire or had been conquered by force of arms and annexed from Sweden is examined in Elenev, “Uchenie.”

22 Leslie, *Polish Politics*, 34–5. This must have been a bitter disappointment for at least some Polish nationalists who as late as 1813 circulated maps showing the borders of a Greater Poland deep into Russia and the annexation of East Prussia, Pomerania, and Silesia ("Bumagi," 225). Catherine II herself was quite aware of the difference: when it was suggested to her that she ought to proclaim herself queen of Poland, she answered in 1795 that she had not taken "an inch" (*piad*) of Polish territory, only what the Poles themselves did not consider as Polish territory (Shil'der, "Imperator," 292).

23 Maikop, "Tsarstvo Pol'skoe," 427.

24 Kabuzan, *Narody Rossii v pervoi polovine XIX v.*, 124, 129, 141, 152–3.

25 *PSZ*, vol. 12, 1837, no. 10203; vol. 19, 1844, no. 18136a; Thaden, *Russia's Western Borderlands*, 147.

26 The text of the Charter is in Vernadsky, *Charte*. In 1813, Czartoryski had called for the reconstitution of the old Polish Empire within the Russian: the kingdom and the duchy to become "an integral part of the empire, but may not be otherwise incorporated," an ambiguous expression at best (Czartoryski, "Mémoire (1813)," 621). Nevertheless there was a certain similarity between Czartoryski's views and the provision of the Treaty of Kiel (1814), according to which "the provinces of Norway would belong to the King of Sweden and constitute a kingdom united with (and not incorporated into) Sweden" (Weibull, "Treaty of Kiel," 297).

Charles Morley claims that "re-establishment of the Kingdom of Poland was an idée fixe of Alexander … he opposed an *independent* [emphasis in original] Poland. He was interested in a Polish state only as part of the Russian Empire and in the happiness of the Poles as Russian subjects" (Morley, "Alexander I," 411, 415). Alexander II would say much the same thing in 1856: "Poland will not be happy until she joins the great family which is the Russian Empire … the Polish tribe [*plemia*] constitute one branch of the great Slavic people [*Slavianskii narod*], but its cultural language must be Russian" (Shipov, "Rossiia i Pol'sha," 56, 59).

27 *PSZ*, vol. 37, 1820, no. 28119. Count Ignacy Sobolewski (1815–22) was followed by Stefan Grabowski (1822–33) and Ignacy Turkull (1839–56). Sobolewski resided in Warsaw, his successors in Petersburg. None had the same authority as Rehbinder, let alone Gustav Armfelt. In the Finnish case, the power centre was in Petersburg; in the Polish case, it was in Warsaw and was anti-Polish.

28 Manifesto of May 1815 in Dubrovin, "Russkaia zhizn'."

29 Boris Uspenskii comes close to a similar explanation (*Tsar i imperator*). Gorizontov, unfortunately, skirts the issue (*Paradoksy*, 6).

30 Wandycz, *Lands*, 77. Pienkos exposes Constantine's cowardice during the crisis of 1830–1. Nicholas I intended to clip his wings in Poland (*Imperfect Autocrat*, 110–12).

31 Maikop, "Tsarstvo Pol'skoe," 192–3.

32 Czartotyski, *Mémoires*, 363–5.

33 Przhetslavskii, "Kaleidoskop," 1708–42; Szyndler, *Mikolai Nowosilcow*, passim.

34 Wandycz, *Lands*, 105–17; Leslie, *Polish Politics*; *PSZ*, vol. 12, 1832, no. 5165–6. An analysis of the statute is in Mezhdu dvukh vosstanii, *Korolevstvo*, 105–16.
35 On Prince Francisek Drucki-Lubecki (1778–1846), who believed that close cooperation with Russia served Poland's best interests, see Przhetslavskii, "Kniaz' Ksaverii."
36 *PSZ*, vol. 17, 1842, no. 15518.
37 *PSZ*, vol. 16, 1841, no. 14852.
38 I have discussed this issue in LeDonne, "Russian Governors General," and "Administrative Regionalization."
39 *RBS*, 333–46. For his activities in Poland see Shcherbatov, *General-Fel'dmarshal*, vol. 5–7.
40 Shcherbatov, ibid., 5, Part 2, 600–5.
41 *PSZ*, vol. 5, 1830, no. 3768; vol. 10, 1835, no. 8355; *SVP*, chast' 1, kn. 1, annexes, 3–20; Kagan, *Military Reforms*, 224–5.
42 PSZ, vol. 8, 1833, no. 6635.
43 *PSZ*, vol. 7, 1832, no. 5192; vol. 18, 1843, no. 17038.
44 *PSZ*, vol. 14, 1839, no. 12908.
45 *PSZ*, vol. 21, 1846, no. 20669; for the Polish road network, see "Iskustvennye dorogi."
46 *PSZ*, vol. 23, 1848, no. 21907.
47 *PSZ*, vol. 26, 1851, no. 24853.
48 *PSZ*, vol. 25, 1850, no. 24533, 25000. A general survey of legislation in the *tsarstvo* is in Reinke, "Ocherk." Pravilova concludes that, by the end of the reign of Nicholas I, "Poland's finances were gradually incorporated into the financial orbit of the empire," and by the 1860s, an independent Polish budget had for all intents and purposes ceased to exist (Pravilova, "From the Złoty," 315–16).
49 Shcherbatov, *General-Fel'dmarshal*, vol. 5, Part 2, 603.
50 *PSZ*, vol. 24, 1796, no. 17634.
51 *PSZ*, vol. 27, 1802, no. 20162; vol. 26, 1801, no. 20004; vol. 30, 1808, no. 23166.
52 *PSZ*, vol. 17, 1842, no. 16347; for the creation of Kovno province see Staliunas, "Problema."
53 *PSZ*, vol. 26, 1819, no. 28041.
54 Of the 296,400 "others," 281,900 were Ukrainians in Belorussia and Lithuania. For a very detailed survey of the society of the western provinces and of the policy of sequestration see Zhukovich, "Soslovnyi sostav."
55 Amburger, *Geschichte*, 388, 392, 394, 436.
56 Gradovskii, "Istoricheskii ocherk," 335.
57 *PSZ*, vol. 24, 1796, no. 17584, 17681, and 17761; vol. 25, 1799, no. 19230; Zhukovich, "Zapadnaia Rossiia," 199–200. The procurator would also continue to operate in accordance with the 1775 Statute. The *Hofgericht* would simply be the equivalent of a chamber for both civil and criminal affairs. The system, as it existed in the 1830s, is described in detail in "Kratkoe obozrenie upravleniia."

58 Czartoryski, *Mémoires*, 313.

59 On Paulucci see *RBS*, 13:402–3; Cheshikhin, "Kak poniali," 272; *Istoricheskii obzor*, 1:404–5.

60 Amburger, *Geschichte*, 392, 394; on Rimsky-Korsakov, see *RBS*, 16:209–14; Dobrynin, "Istinnoe," 343; Przhetslavskii, "Kaleidoskop," 1719.

61 *PSZ*, vol. 38, 1822, no. 29087 and 29088.

62 Troshchinskii, "Zapiska," 155.

63 Thaden, *Russia's Western Borderlands*, 178, 187; on Pahlen see *DBL*, 572–3. "Sostav i ustroistvo zemskoi politsii" and "Sostav gorodov" are very useful and comprehensive descriptions of the local and municipal organization.

64 *PSZ*, vol. 6, 1831, no. 4244.

65 *PSZ*, vol. 6, 1831, no. 4233 and 4894; Thaden, *Russia's Western Borderlands*, 122.

66 *PSZ*, vol. 23, 1848, no. 21908.

67 Murav'ev, "Dve zapiski," 585–90 and "Chetyre zapiski," 172. For Muravev see Kropotov, *Zhizn'*. Most of the book is devoted to Muravev's activities as governor of Mogilev.

68 Dolgorukov, "Kniaz'." On Mirkovich see Mirkovich, "Iz zapisok"; he was the son of a Serb who had emigrated to Russia in 1760. For the years if his tenure as governor general see 413–34.

69 *PSZ*, vol. 6, 1831, no. 4677, art. 12.

70 *SVP*, chast' 1, kn. 2, annexes, 22–3; PSZ, vol. 8, 1833, no. 6573.

71 Amburger, *Geschichte*, 195–6; *PSZ*, vol. 4, 1829, no. 2599; vol. 6, 1831, no. 4251; vol. 7, 1832, no. 5317; vol 25, 1850, no. 24131.

72 *PSZ*, vol. 30, 1809, no. 23996; vol. 5, 1830, no. 4019 and 4020; vol. 18, 1843, no. 16998a (in vol. 19, 1844, annex, 39–109); vol. 28, 1853, no. 26953.

73 *PSZ*, vol. 8, 1831, no. 4989; for the Baltic provinces see art. 116, pt, 2

74 Florinsky, *Russia*, 775–6.

75 *PSZ*, vol. 20, 1845, no. 19086.

76 Mikhail Dolbilov writes: to appeal to the peasantry "threatened to undermine the traditional, legistimistic foundations and mechanics of the Romanov empire" and "the fear of indigenous nation-building as an unintended result of Russification proved to be stronger than the eagerness to integrate and assimilate" ("Russian Nationalism," 146, 152).

77 *History of Finland's Literature*, xxv–vi.

78 Konttinen, "Central Bureaucracy," 202.

79 Quoted in Ordin, *Pokorenie*, 2, annex, 133.

80 Konttimen, "Central Bureaucracy," 208–9.

81 *PSZ*, vol. 17, 1842, no. 15194.

82 Kirby, *Concise History*, 85–6. The clergy had supported the annexation because the Russians placed great importance on its role to win over the people (thereby enhancing its power), and the Finnish nobility no longer felt a keen attachment to Sweden (Scheibert, "Anfänge," 378, 380).

83 Kirby, *Baltic World*, 61; Raun, *Estonia*, 40.
84 Kirby, *Baltic World*.
85 Ch-v, "Speranskii," 54–6.
86 *PSZ*, vol. 33, 1816, no. 26277–8, 26280 (Estland); vol. 34, 1817, no. 27024 (Kurland); vol. 36, 1819, no. 27734–6 (Livland); Thaden, *Russia's Western Borderlands*, 104–9; Plakans, *Latvians*, 78–9; Raun, *Estonia*, 41–3, 47–9.
87 Kabuzan and Troitskii, "Izmeneniia," 163–4. Kovno province was at that time still part of Vilno province.
88 Czartoryski, *Mémoires*, 2:303.
89 Dubrovin, "Russkaia zhizn'," 1902, 1:231.
90 *PSZ*, vol. 6, 1831, no. 4869; Zoltowski, *Border of Europe*, 110–11.
91 Kabuzan and Troitskii, "Izmeneniia," 163; they do not show any decline in the number of nobles.
92 *PSZ*, vol. 10, 1835, no. 8463.
93 Rozen, *Zapiski*, 86.
94 Thaden, *Russia's Western Borderlands*, 124. Governor General Mirkovich made the crucial point: Poles had established their grip on the old Grand Duchy by moving there in significant numbers and polonizing the population. Russia had first tried to follow a similar policy by granting land to members of the elite, hoping they would settle there and bring in Russians, but they had sold their properties and did not bring any of their serfs (Mirkovich, "Iz zapisok," 428). As I stated in the Introduction, the Russians were moving eastward, not westward.
95 Dokhturov, "Pis'ma," 1115–16. Cf. Nesselrode's statement in 1813: "There is no room in a Polish heart for a Russian Poland" (Martens, *Recueil*, 3:214–16).
96 Shcherbatov, *General-Fel'dmarshal*, 5, annex, 283–5. For Repnin's statement see LeDonne, *Grand Strategy*, 144.
97 Wandycz, *Lands*, 118.
98 Leslie, *Polish Politics*, 46–7, 50, 263–5.
99 Leon Wasilewski makes an interesting case for the old Polish Commonwealth as a unitary state. He calls it an empire in his title and on p. 16 (*das polnische Reich*), and claims that despite its federal structure it also had a "unitary state organization," led by the nobility, "the nation," unitary by nationality and language. This is what would make this nobility refractory to Russian attempts to use it for purposes of integration into the expanding Russian core: see Wasilewski, *Die Ostprovinzen*, 16–17.
100 Perovsky, "O neobkhodimosti," 184. It is unclear whether Perovsky is truly the author.
101 *SZ*, 1832, vol. 1, kn.3, art 287–7. The First Department was not a judicial department.
102 *PSZ*, vol. 16, 1841, no. 14852; Amburger, *Geschichte*, 433.
103 Amburger, *Geschichte*, 80–2, and his references.
104 *PSZ*, vol. 1. 1825–6, no. 114; Amburger, *Geschichte*, 82, mentions a second director, Mikhail Balugianskii (1826–47).

105 Orfield, *Growth*, 256.
106 Thaden, *Russia's Western Borderlands*, 210: I draw this section from this work, 209–13.
107 Skalon, "Upravlenie," 939–40.
108 "Pribaltiiskoe grazhdanskoe pravo," in *ES*, 25:121.
109 Veselov, "Pribaltiiskie nemtsy," 204.
110 Thaden, *Russia's Western Borderlands*, 170–2; *DBL*, 667; Ch-v, "Speranskii," 41–57.
111 *PSZ*, vol. 20, 1845, no. 19146. For a comprehensive survey of the work of codification see Stael von Holstein, "Die Kodifizierung."
112 Veselov, "Pribaltiiskie nemtsy," 202–5.
113 "Litovskii Statut," in *ES*, 17:814–15. The 1821 decree is not in the *PSZ*, but is cited in *PSZ*, vol. 7, 1832, no. 5459.
114 *PSZ*, vol. 6, 1831, no. 4233.
115 Murav'ev, "Chetyre politicheskie zapiski," 170–2. To follow the development of the Lithuanian Statute in Belorussia see Savicki, "Historical Conspectus."
116 Lepesh, *Komitet*; for its discussion of the nobility see 55–71.
117 "Danilowicz, I.," in *PSB*, 4:412–14; Lepesh, *Komitet*, 84–93.
118 Nolde, *Ocherki*, 141.
119 *PSZ*, vol. 15, 1840, no. 13591; Thaden, *Russia's Western Borderlands*, 123–36.
120 "Pol'skoe pravo," in *ES*, 24:425. For the Code Napoleon in the Duchy of Warsaw see Grinwasser, "Le Code Napoléon."
121 Przhetslavskii, "Kaleidoskop," 1723.
122 "Pol'skoe pravo," in *ES*, 24:425.
123 Maikop, "Tsarstvo Pol'skoe," 168.
124 Thaden, *Russia's Western Borderlands*, 151–3; *PSZ*, vol. 16, 1841, no. 14852; vol. 17, 1842, no. 15428.
125 For attempts at codification in the eighteenth century see Gierowski, *Polish-Lithuanian Commonwealth*, 231–4.
126 Gilpin, *Political Economy*, 93, 95.
127 This section is based on Florinsky, *Russia*, 709–12, 789–91.
128 *PSZ*, vol. 31, 1810, no. 24464; vol. 33, 1816, no. 26218.
129 *PSZ*, vol. 36, 1819, no. 27987-27988.
130 Kindleberger, *World in Depression*, 53.
131 *PSZ*, vol. 33, 1822, no. 28965; Semenov, *Izuchenie*, chast' 2, 135–40.
132 *PSZ*, vol. 25, 1850, no. 24533.
133 *PSZ*, vol. 31, 1811, no. 24480.
134 Przhetslavskii, "Kaleidoskop," 2270–2.
135 Leslie, *Polish Politics*, 78–9.
136 On Drucki-Lubecki see Przhetslavskii, "Kniaz' Ksaverii," 625–48, 67–92.
137 Wandycz, *Lands*, 79–82, 90, 203.
138 *PSZ*, vol. 35, 1818, no. 27453.
139 *PSZ*, vol. 38, 1822, no. 29149; see also *Zapadnye okrainy*, 86–9 and *Pol'sha i Rossiia*, 219–28.

140 *PSZ*, vol. 6, 1831, no. 4941; vol. 9, 1834, no. 7542; Mezhdu dvukh vosstanii, *Korolevstvo*, 216–17, 234–7.

141 Leslie, *Polish Politics*, 47.

142 "Svedeniia o gorode Libave," 135; *PSZ*, vol. 40, 1825, no. 30467. Libava was the best hope for those wishing to develop the trade of the Baltic provinces; the sea never froze more than a couple of weeks, while it froze for three months at Riga. Others claimed it could never rival Memel, which channelled the trade of Lithuania and part of Kurland ("Na Kovnu ili na Rigu?" 25, and Kampengausen, "Perepiska," 268).

143 *PSZ*, vol. 5, 1830, no. 3708. By contrast, Revel was growing rapidly. In the 1830s, it had a population of 14,000 (men and women), and many families had from fifteen to twenty children ("Manuel-guide de Réval," 394).

144 *PSZ*, vol. 34, 1817, no. 27034.

145 Kirby, *Baltic World*, 52. For inland navigation as a factor of integration see Ukhtomskii, "Saimanskii kanal." A survey of Russia's trade with Norway is Alimova, "Russkaia."

146 *PSZ*, vol. 10, 1835, no. 8241.

147 Kirby, *Baltic World*, 99.

148 *PSZ*, vol. 25, 1850, no. 24333.

149 Uvarov's biographer rightly claims that the minister's program was a "policy of cultural imperialism" and that "the goal remained assimilation – the creation of a Great Russian identity among the various subjects of the tsar" (Whittaker, *Origins*, 189, 190).

150 *PSZ*, vol. 27, 1803, no. 20597–8.

151 Ibid., no. 20701.

152 "Vilenskii universitet," in *ES*, 328.

153 Dubrovin, "Russkaia zhizn'," 1902, 1:26–7, 15–18, 22; Bogdanovich, *Istoriia*, 6:181; Flynn, *University Reform*, 112–23.

154 Bogdanovich, *Istoriia*, 6:180–1. See Barkhatsev, "Iz istorii," for a survey of the Vilno Educational Region in the 1820s.

155 *PSZ*, vol. 34, 1817, no. 27106; Florinsky, *Russia*, 727–8.

156 Maikop, "Tsarstvo Pol'skoe," 165, 427; Bogdanovich, *Istoriia*, 6:164–7.

157 *PSZ*, vol. 14, 1839, no. 12908; vol. 25, 1850, no. 26158; Thaden, *Russia's Western Borderlands*, 148–50; Flynn, *University Reform*, 215–45.

158 *PSZ*, vol. 7, 1832, no. 5317; vol. 4, 1829, no. 2599; vol. 6, 1831, N.4251; vol. 25, 1850, no. 24131.

159 *PSZ*, vol. 3, 1828, no. 2502; vol. 8, 1833, no. 6569; vol. 9, 1834, no. 6699 and 7250; Murav'ev, "Chetyre zapiski," 166–70. For Muravev's role in the educational reforms and the closing of Vilno University see Kropotov, *Zhizn'*, 259–75.

160 *PSZ*, vol. 25, 1798, no. 18474; Cheshikhin, "Kak poniali," 269–70.

161 "Yurevskii universitet," in *ES*, 435–7.

162 *PSZ*, vol. 27, 1802, no. 20551.

163 *PSZ*, vol. 27, 1820, no. 28302.
164 *PSZ*, vol. 27, 1803, no. 20598.
165 Thaden, *Russia's Western Borderlands*, 109–12.
166 *PSZ*, vol. 10, 1835, no. 8337; vol. 12, 1837, no. 9883; vol. 25, 1850, no. 23977.
167 Thaden, *Russia's*, 172–5.
168 *History of Finland's Literature*, 50; the statement may be apocryphal.
169 Ibid., 20, 50.
170 "Gel'singforsskii universitet," in *ES*, 291.
171 Konttinen, "Central Bureaucracy," 216–17; Scheibert, *Volk und Staat*, 250.
172 *PSZ*, vol. 9, 1834, no. 7321.
173 Thaden, *Russia's Western Borderlands*, 217–18; Scheibert, *Volk und Staat*, 112–14.
174 *PSZ*, vol. 9, 1734, no. 6548; vol. 19, no. 1774, no. 14122.
175 *PSZ*, vol. 24, 1797, no. 17836; vol. 25, 1798, no. 18345; vol. 26, 1801, no. 20053; vol. 31, 1810, no. 24307; Amburger, *Geschichte*, 182; Werth, *Tsar's Foreign Faiths*, 46–64.
176 *PSZ*, vol. 34, 1817, no. 27106; vol. 39, no. 1824, no. 29914; vol. 7, 1832, no. 5126.
177 Zaveleiskiii, "Statistika," table 4 (no pagination). See also "Narodonaselenie Tsarstva Pol'skogo." The city of Warsaw had a population of 130,000 inhabitants in 1833.
178 Amburger, *Geschichte*, 182.
179 Dubrovin, "Russkaia zhizn'," 1902, 1:234. For this reason, it may not be quite true in Russia that "with a supreme head located beyond the borders of the various empires, the Catholic Church proved comparatively (though by no means entirely) impervious to imperial intervention" (Werth, "Imperiology and Religion," 54).
180 *PSZ*, vol. 26, 1801, no. 20053.
181 *PSZ*, vol. 25, 1798, no. 18504; Zhukovich, "Zapadnaia Rossiia," 257–8.
182 *PSZ*, vol. 24, 1797, no. 19156; vol. 8, 1833, no. 6161. For the Minsk diocese see Sipovich, "Diocese," 182–3.
183 *PSZ*, vol. 7, 1832, no. 5506; Murav'ev, "Chetyre zapiski," 165.
184 Wandycz, *Lands*, 118; Milosz, *History*, 226. Andrzej Walicki introduced an important correction in his 1994 lectures to the assumption that Poland had always belonged to Europe ("the West"). The Poles did not see it that way until the middle of the twentieth century. The core of Poland's historical ideology was the Sarmatian ideology, claiming for the country a cultural uniqueness in need of defending itself against pernicious influences from Europe, and claiming that its political system was infinitely superior to European monarchies. Even as late as the 1840s, "it is justified to say that anti-Westernism was more widespread among Polish emigres than Westernism" (Walicki, *Poland between East and West*, 9, 11–12).
185 The modern Polish historian Andrzej Nowak claims that "the struggle for the borderlands is a struggle for survival" ("Bor'ba za okrainy," 429).

186 *PSZ*, vol. 16, 1841, no. 15152–3.

187 Zoltowski, *Border of Europe*, 113–15. In this connection, Cynthia Whittaker quotes Daniel Beauvois as saying that the closing of Vilno University was "one of the worst examples of cultural genocide in history" (Whittaker, *Origins*, 192). For the extent of the repression see "Uprazdnenie greko-uniatskikh monastyrei," especially 520.

188 It was not published in the *PSZ*. The text is in Lescoeur, *Eglise catholique*, 434–9. See also *PSZ*, vol. 23, 1848, no. 22766 (for the dioceses); for Samogitia, see *PSZ*, vol. 15, 1840, no. 13854.

189 Amburger, *Geschichte*, 184–5; *PSZ*, vol. 25, 1798, no. 18503; Zoltowski, *Border of Europe*, 92; *PSZ*, vol. 3, 1828, no. 1977; Thaden, *Russia's Western Borderlands*, 67–8; also *PSZ*, vol. 30, 1809, no. 23482 and vol. 31, 1810, no. 24118.

190 Zhukovich, "Zapadnaia Rossiia," 239–41; *PSZ*, vol. 14, 1839, no. 12467; Zoltowski, *Border of Europe*, 111–13; Thaden, *Russia's Western Borderlands*, 129–33. On Siemashko see *PSB*, 36:606–11. See also Batiushkov, *Belorussia i Litva*, 351–76, with portraits of the major participants in the controversy. On Siemashko's role in particular see Lencyk, *Eastern Catholic Church*, 74–88 and 103–18. See also *Zapadnye okrainy*, 108–11; Werth, *Tsar's Foreign Faiths*, 74–85.

191 *PSZ*, vol. 9, 1834, no. 7021; vol. 15, 1840, N, 13841; Murav'ev, "Chetyre zapiski," 174–5, 186–97. Likewise, the Poles used the Basilian monks to polonize the Belorussians and convert them to Catholicism (Chebod'ko, "Iz vospominanii," 539–41).

192 Upton, *Charles XI*, 172.

193 Igelstrom, "Erinerrungen," 56.

194 Kirby, *Baltic World*, 73. See also *Baltische Kirchengeschichte*, 149–77.

195 Amburger, *Geschichte*, 178–80; Troshchinskii, "Zapiska," 103, 105.

196 *PSZ*, vol. 27, 1803, no. 20589.

197 *PSZ*, vol. 7, 1832, no. 5870. For the historical background of the statute see Stael von Holstein, "Zur Geschichte."

198 "Liuteranstvo v Rossii," *ES*, 18:257–58; *PSZ*, vol. 10, 1835, no. 8387.

199 Thaden, *Russia's Western Borderlands*, 177–80; Samarin, "Pravoslavnye latyshi," "Dvizhenie latyshei," and "Spravka po delu." Also *Baltische Kirchengeschichte*, 177–93, and Kovalchuk, "Der baltische Generalgouverneur." The most recent analysis is Bruggemann, "Imperiale und lokalle Loyalitäten."

200 Quoted in Veselov, "Pribaltiiskie nemtsy," 208.

Conclusion to Part I: The Western Theatre

1 Levine, *Economic Origins*, 29.

2 Jorg Ganzenmüller has exposed the contradiction between an imperial policy and the creation of a unitary state. He writes that the government of Nicholas I pursued a policy of normative integration, which sought to achieve not coordination of interests with the Polish nobility, but the enforcement of Russian (*staatliche*) norms.

On the other hand, state power did not come as an all-powerful (*ubermächtiger*) actor in the Polish provinces: it did not have the personnel, and its agents occasionally became integrated into the social networks of the Polish world (Ganzenmüller, *Russische Staatsgewalt*, 367, 369).

3 Lescoeur, *Eglise catholique,* 3.
4 Alexis De Toqueville, *Democracy in America* (New York, 2004), 476.

4 Laying the Foundations, 1650–1725

1 This section is based on a reading of entries in *ES* for each province and district of the theatre. See also Berg, *Natural Regions*, 68, 90.
2 In this work, the controversial term "Little Russia," widely used in the eighteenth century, officially and not, means the provinces of Chernihiv and Poltava (and not Kharkiv) in their nineteenth-century borders. For the larger meaning of the term see Plokhy, *Ukraine and Russia*, 49–65.
3 Lydolph, *Geography*, 114.
4 Ibid., 97.
5 Vernadsky, *Russia at the Dawn*, 253, 258–9; Lydolph, *Geography*, 95–6; Mirov, *Geography*, 215–19.
6 Potocki, *Voyages*, 2:34.
7 Mirov, *Geography*, 181, 188–9.
8 Vernadsky, *Mongols*, 52–3, 142–7, 157–9, 179–89, 202, 233–4, 279–80, 305–6.
9 Ibid., 255–63, 301–2.
10 Hrushevsky, *History*, 149–51; Fisher, *Crimean Tatars*, 3–12.
11 Vernadsky, *Russia at the Dawn*, 78–81.
12 Beauvois, *Histoire*, 68–9.
13 Vernadsky, *Russia at the Dawn*, 152.
14 Allen and Muratoff, *Caucasian Battlefields*, 8.
15 Vernadsky, *Russia at the Dawn*, 153.
16 Beauvois, *Histoire*, 96–8, 107; Vernadsky, *Russia at the Dawn*, 245–6.
17 *ES*, 12:275–7; Khoroshkin, "Voenno-istoricheskii ocherk," 97–8; Hrushevsky, *History*, 151–6.
18 Krasnov, "Proshedshee," 305–6; Korolenko, "Khopertsy," 205–7.
19 Vernadsky, *Tsardom*, 10, 16, 89–93, 118–21, 130–2.
20 Krasnov, "Proshedshee," 299, 309–11.
21 Vernadsky, *Tsardom*, 323–4.
22 Hrushevsky, *History*, 151–6.
23 Vernadsky, *Russia at the Dawn*, 284–92.
24 Subtelny, *Ukraine*, 125–6.
25 Ibid., 127–37; Beauvois, *Histoire*, 131–3; Hrushevsky, *History*, 277–301.
26 Hrushevsky, *History*, 295; *Zapadnye okrainy*, 33–49. Buturlin may have reasoned that since the Hetmanate consisted of "Russian" subjects, the tsar had no obligation to pledge anything. In this connection, it is interesting to note the position of

the Empress Elizabeth's chancellor (foreign minister), Alexei Bestuzhev-Riumin (1693–1768): "It is known and proven that the Little Russian people has from time immemorial [*izdrevle*] been a subject of Russia [*poddannoi Rossiiskoi*], then passed under Poland, and under Tsar Alexei Mikhailovich returned once again" (Bestuzhev-Riumin, "Mnenie," 340). Interestingly enough, this was the official view at a time when the empress restored the Hetmanate. See also Basarab, *Pereiaslav 1654*, 6–10.

Andreas Kappeler makes the crucial comment that the Pereiaslav agreement "stood in the tradition of the numerous agreements which Muscovy concluded with nomadic political entities in the context of the gathering of the lands of the Golden Horde," and that this has been largely overlooked by Eurocentric research. It may indeed be valuable to trace the evolution of Russian attitudes toward the Ukrainian Cossacks and the Kalmyks (LeDonne, *Russian Empire*, 64).

Finally, Mikhail Dolbilov notes that "the liquidation of the autonomy of the Hetmanate proceeded without interruption from the time of the Pereiaslav agreement." As early as April 1707 (two years before Poltava), the tsar placed "Kiev and the Little Russian towns" under the *Razriad*, the war ministry of the time. Thus, the urban sector of the territory was integrated into the Russian infrastructure (Dolbilov and Miller, *Zapadnye okrainy*, 52, 53).

27 Subtelny, *Ukraine*, 143–5; Hrushevsky, History, *History*, 306–15. Davies's *Warfare* is now the standard work for the geopolitics of the period: for the background of the 1654 agreement see 103–14, followed by what he calls the "Ukrainian quagmire" (197–311).

28 Subtelny, *Ukraine*, 145–6, 149–50; Hrushevsky, *History*, 321–8.

29 Vernadsky, *Tsardom*, 626–9; Hrushevsky, *History*, 331.

30 Zagorovskii, *Belgorodskaia cherta*, passim. For the standard account of Russian southward migration along the Belgorod Line, and the northward migration of the Ukrainians toward it, see Bagalei, *Ocherki*, 197–311.

31 Hrushevsky, *History*, 409–10.

32 Kabuzan, *Narody Rossii v XVIII veke*, 84–6.

33 Magocsi, *History*, 231.

34 Kirilov, *Tsvetushchee sostoianie*, 164–70.

35 Magocsi, *History*, 233–4; Okinshevich, *Ukrainian Society*, 74–105.

36 Subtelny, *Ukraine*, 149.

37 Magocsi, *History*, 233–5.

38 Magocsi, *History*, 234–5, Subtelny, *Mazepists*, 37–9.

39 Magocsi, *History*, 265–6; Hrushevsky, *History*, 405, 409–10.

40 Subtelny, *Ukraine*, 152–3; Samoilov, "Zhizn'," 1024–6; Magocsi, *History*, 230. A handy history of the Zaporozhian Host is March, *Cossacks*; for its demise, see 201–14. A colourful survey of Zaporozhian life and customs is in Cresson, *Cossacks*, 27–43. See also Golobutskii, *Zaporozhskoe kazachestvo*, 341–80, and Okinshevich, *Ukrainian Society*, 113–25.

41 Subtelny, *Ukraine*, 150–2.
42 Ibid., 160–5; Magocsi, *History*, 240–7. Plokhy decries his “authoritarian rule” (*Origins*, 345). A recent biography is Tairova-Yakovleva, *Ivan Mazepa*, passim.
43 *PSZ*, vol. 4, 1708, no. 2218; Paul Bushkovitch is one of the few who clearly sees the connection between the creation of the provinces and the impending Swedish offensive (*Peter the Great*, 284–6).
44 Kabuzan, *Narody Rossii v XVIII veke*, 67–9, 75–6.
45 *PSZ*, vol. 5, 1719, no. 3380.
46 Hrushevsky, *History*, 378.
47 Subtelny, *Ukraine*, 181.
48 Ibid.; Magocsi, *History*, 272.
49 *PSZ*, vol. 6, 1722, no. 3988–90, 4010.
50 Subtelny, *Ukraine*, 167.
51 LeDonne, *Grand Strategy*, 41–2.
52 *PSZ*, vol. 6, 1720, no. 3686, 1722, no. 4131.
53 *PSZ*, vol. 6, 1720, no. 4200.
54 *PSZ*, vol. 6, 1720, no. 4191.
55 Kirilov, *Tsvetushchee sostoianie*, 161.
56 Ibid., 175.
57 *PSZ*, vol. 7, 1723, no. 4200.
58 Kalachna is on the Don where the river is closest to the Volga.
59 Krasnov, “Proshedshee,” 294, 311–13.
60 Tolstoi, “I.A. Tolstoi,” 141–3; Krasnov, “Proshedshee,” 107.
61 Krasnov, “Proshedshee,” 109–10; Korolenko, “Khopertsy,” 208–9.
62 Boeck, *Imperial Boundaries*, 172–86.
63 Krasnov, “Proshedshee,” 113–15. For a fine introduction to the history of the Don Cossacks see Boeck, *Imperial Boundaries*, 27–39, 172–86, and his eloquent *Afterword* on 245–51.
64 Got'e, *Istoriia*, annexed maps.
65 Kabuzan, *Narody Rossii v XVIII veke*, 67–8, 76.
66 Krasnov, “Proshedshee,” 112–13.
67 Khoroshkin, “Voenno-istoricheskii ocherk,” 112–13. An excellent survey of the Ukrainian, Don, and Caucasus Cossacks, with maps and photographs, is Seaton, *Horsemen*, 26–62, 73, 126–58.
68 Khoroshkin, “Voenno-istoricheskii ocherk,” 106–7; Kirilov, *Tsvetushchee sostoianie*, 375.
69 Hrushevsky, *History*, 172–6.
70 “Pospolitye,” in *ES*, 24:691–3.
71 Hrushevsky, *History*, 350–1.
72 Khoroshkhin, “Voenno-istoricheskii ocherk,” 95.
73 Subtelny, *Mazepists*, 10–11.
74 “Don voisko,” in *ES*, 11:27–32.

75 Khoroshkhin, "Voenno-istoricheskii ocherk," 94.
76 Subtelny, *Mazepists*, 10–11.
77 "Starshyna malorossiiskaia," in *ES*, 31:457–8.
78 Subtelny, *Mazepists*, 133–4.
79 Hrushevsky, *History*, 347–9, 351–2.
80 *PSZ*, vol. 7, 1723, no. 4196.
81 Thaden, *Russia's Western Borderlands*, 8.
82 As Zenon Kohut put it, "the Ukrainian gentry carried out its own transformation" and "enthusiastically accepted the 1785 charter" (*Russian Centralism*, 239, 242).
83 Magocsi, *History*, 151–2.
84 Plokhy, *Origins*, and *Cossacks*, 77–86.
85 Magocsi, *History*, 213.
86 Chynczewska-Hennel, "Political, Social and National Thought," 124–8.
87 Plokhy, *Origins*, 260.
88 Chynczewska-Hennel, "Political, Social and National Thought," 132. On this whole issue see Kharlamovich, *Malorossiiskoe vlianie*, 220–31.
89 Plokhy, *Origins*, 243. What Khmelnytsky overlooked was that such an empire would eventually become a unitary state: "the policy of ethnic unification and the establishment of Russian institutions in Ukraine developed in tandem with the policy of religious unification" (Zhivov, "Question," 6).
90 Vernadsky, *Tsardom*, 560–2, 568–70.
91 Subtelny, *Mazepists*, 44; Hrushevsky, *History*, 353–4.
92 A general commemorative work is "Kiev Mohyla Academy," passim.
93 Florinsky, *Russia*, 410.
94 Cracraft, *Church Reform*, 184–98.
95 Krasnov, "Proshedshee," 116.
96 Florinsky, *Russia*, 413; Cracraft, *Church Reform*, 49–62.
97 Magocsi, *History*, 147–50; see also Magocsi, *Historical Atlas*, 34–6.
98 S. Velychenko, "Cossack Ukraine and Baltic Trade 1600–1648: Some Observations on an Unresolved Issue," in Koropeckyj, *Ukrainian Economic History*, 151–71, here 151.
99 Magocsi, *History*, 254.
100 LeDonne, *Grand Strategy*, 47, 59.
101 B. Krawchenko, "Petrine Mercantilist Economic Policies toward the Ukraine," in Koropeckyj, *Ukrainian Economic History*, 186–209, here 193.
102 *PSZ*, vol. 4, 1701, no. 1826.
103 Krawchenko, "Petrine Mercantilist Economic Policies," 197.
104 Heckscher, *Mercantilism*, 2:61. For the Greek colonies in Nezhin and the Crimea see Terent'eva, *Greki v Ukraine*, 63–86, 125–51.
105 *PSZ*, vol. 4, 1701, no. 1866.
106 Magocsi, *History*, 282; Krawchenko, "Petrine Mercantilist Economic Policies," 197.

107 *PSZ*, vol. 5, 1713, no. 2705.
108 *PSZ*, vol. 5, 1714, no. 2767–8.
109 Krawchenko, "Petrine Mercantilist Economic Policies," 198.
110 *PSZ*, vol. 5, 1716, no. 3359.
111 *PSZ*, vol. 7, 1724, no. 4532, 1727, no. 5201.
112 *PSZ*, vol. 6, 1721, no. 3860.
113 Krawchenko, "Petrine Mercantilist Economic Policies," 203.
114 Ibid., 208. Subtelny writes that as early as the sixteenth century "the towns became – and remained for centuries – foreign territories for most Ukrainians" (*Ukraine*, 87).

5 Toward Full Integration, 1725–1796

1 Subtelny, *Mazepists*, 159–60.
2 Amburger, *Geschichte*, 395–6; *PSZ*, vol. 7, 1726, no. 4901; Petrukhintsev, *Vnutrenniaia politika*, 289, 317. I thank Paul Bushkovitch for the reference.
3 *PSZ*, vol. 9, 1734, no. 6539; Subtelny, *Ukraine*, 167–8; Lazarevskii, "Ocherk," 93–4; Hrushevsky, *History*, 384–9.
4 *PSZ*, vol. 8, 1728, no. 5324; Magocsi, *History*, 273.
5 *PSZ*, vol. 9, 1734, no. 6614.
6 Got'e, *Istoriia*, 1:109.
7 The fifth, Ostrohozhskii, was included into Voronezh province.
8 *PSZ*, vol. 8, 1731, no. 5824.
9 Weissbach in *RBS* (1998), 427–30.
10 On the *haidamak* uprising see Kohut, "Myths Old and New."
11 *ES*, 12:278; Zagorovskii, "Vzaimootnosheniia," 55–6; see the very useful map in Magocsi, *Ukraine*, 11.
12 Hrushevsky, *History*, 389–90. By 1762, there were about 33,700 Cossacks and over 150,000 peasants in Zaporozh'e (Magocsi, *History*, 269).
13 Semen Sukin was Kiev governor in 1736–8. His instruction is in *PSZ*, vol. 10, 1737, no. 7161.
14 Zagorovskii, "Vzaimootnosheniia," 54–8.
15 *PSZ*, vol. 8, 1731, no. 5778, 1732, no. 6055.
16 Kabuzan, *Narody Rossii v XVIII veke*, 101–2.
17 *PSZ*, vol. 9, 1734, no. 6539, 6608. The board was given the fancy title of Governing Council of the Hetman's Office. The Russians were very fond of giving inflated titles, as in Georgia and Lithuania.
18 *PSZ*, vol. 9, 1734, no. 6619.
19 *ES*, 17:324–5; *PSZ*, vol. 8, no. 5673, 6055, 6279; vol. 9, 1736, no. 6925; vol. 11, 1743, no. 8787. For a detailed analysis of the construction of the line, see Petrukhintsev, *Vnutreniaia politika*, 224–48. I thank Paul Bushkovitch for this major reference.

20 "Razumovsky, K.," in *RBS*, 15:454–9.
21 *PSZ*, vol. 11, 1753, no. 8829.
22 *PSZ*, vol. 11, 1743, no. 8823.
23 Magocsi, *History*, 274; Subtelny, *Ukraine*, 170–2.
24 Shtrandman, "Zapiski," 294–7.
25 Krasnov, "Proshedshee," 114–16.
26 "Novorossiiskii krai," in *ES*, 290–1; Auerbach, *Die Besiedelung*, passim; *PSZ*, vol. 13, 1751, no. 9919, 9921; 1752, no. 9924, 9993; vol. 14, 1755, no. 10488, 10491; Obreskov, "Reliatsiia," 183–99. For the background see *PSZ*, vol. 9. 1736, no. 6973. In general, the Serbs made a bad impression: "in folk songs and folk tales, the image of the Serb is synonymous with that of a robber, a knave, a rake, a good-for-nothing, unwilling to work, expecting only pleasures from life, bent upon leading a prosperous, carousing and drunken existence" (Polons'ka-Vasylenko, *Settlement*, 174). See also Kirpichenok, *Serbskie poseleniia*, 46–88, 92–110.
27 LeDonne, *Grand Strategy*, 93.
28 *Nakazy* of the Chernigov, Akhtyrka, and Kharkiv nobility in *SIRIO*, 68:242–3, 254–5, 264–5.
29 *PSZ*, vol. 19, 1770, no. 13532.
30 *PSZ*, vol. 17, 1765, no. 12397, 12430, and 12440.
31 *PSZ*, vol. 16, 1764, no. 12099, 12180, 12211; vol. 17, 1765, no. 12367. Auerbach's maps are indispensable; Pylons'ka-Vasylenko, "Iz istorii," 173.
32 *PSZ*, vol. 16, 1764, no. 12180.
33 Zagorovskii, "Vzaimootnosheniia," 71.
34 Polons'ka-Vasylenko, "Iz istorii," 132–4.
35 Druzhinina, *Severnoe Prichernomor'e*, 50–3; Coxe, *Travels*, 3:421–2. In a larger sense, traditional Cossack formations were becoming obsolete: "European standards of military discipline and deployment made the old style of unregulated Cossack charge ineffective on the battlefield." What was happening was the "inescapable price of taming the steppe to agriculture" (McNeill, *Europe's Steppe Frontier*, 177, 202).
36 Subtelny, *Ukraine*, 170–1.
37 Hrushevsky, *History*, 455–6. A historian of the host notes that "the main reason for the destruction of Zaporozh'e was that the entire system [*stroi*] of the Host with its broadly democratic principles did not fit into the basic organization of Great Russia [*ne podkhodil k korennomu stroiu*]. Catherine II, like her predecessors, pursued with special perseverance the idea of centralization by seeking to put down any regional particularism [*oblastnaia obosoblennost'*]" (Evarnitskii, "Glavneishie momenty," 114). See also Golobutskii, *Zaporozhskoe kazachestvo*, 42–3. For the treaty see Druzhinina, *Kiuchuk Kainardzhiiskii mir*, 260–73, 349–60.
38 *PSZ*, vol. 20, 1775, no. 14252 and 14380; see also vol. 18, 1769, no. 13351.
39 *PSZ*, vol. 19, 1770, no. 13504.
40 *PSZ*, vol. 20, 1775, no. 14252.

41 LeDonne, *Grand Strategy*, 94, 96.
42 *PSZ*, vol. 20, 1775, no. 14251, 14330; Samoilov, "Zhizn'," 1230–1; Svatikov, *Rossiia i Don*, 225–39.
43 *PSZ*, vol. 20, 1777, no. 14607; Debu, "O nachal'nom ustanovlenii," 57–9.
44 RGVIA, f. VUA, d. 234; Druzhinina, *Severnoe Prichernomor'e*, 62.
45 Krasnov, "Proshedshee," 121.
46 *PSZ*, vol. 20, 1779, no. 14844, 1780, no. 14984, 15097.
47 *PSZ*, vol. 21, 1782, no. 15335 and 15378.
48 *PSZ*, vol. 22, 1784, no. 16028.
49 *PSZ*, vol. 22, 1784, no. 15920 and 15924.
50 Bobrovskii, "Suvorov," 13; Petrushevskii, "Suvorov," 11–12; Korolenko, "Khopertsy," 218–19; Fisher, *Russian Annexation*, 139–50.
51 LeDonne, *Russian Empire*, 110.
52 *PSZ*, vol. 23, 1795, no. 17300, 17343.
53 In 1593–1630, 1652–1709, 1734–75 (Magocsi, *Ukraine*, map 11).
54 Kabuzan, *Narody Rossii v XVIII veke*, 209–12, 217–23, 229, 240–1. A census has been described as a means of domination (*Herrschaftsmittel*), but the same could be said of just about every activity of government. Likewise, a universal military draft – even the more rudimentary "recruiting" (*rekrutstvo*) – does not necessarily lead to the creation of a nation under arms: see Leonhard and von Hirschhausen, *Empires und Nationalstaaten*, 53, 79. For the population and administrative division of the Ukrainian lands from the sixteenth century until the reform of 1775–81 see Vermenych, *Administratyvn-terytorial'nii ustrii Ukrainy* 1:228–90, unfortunately without maps and statistical tables. On the early settlement of the Crimea by Russians and Ukrainians after 1783 see Druzhinina, *Severnoe Prichernomor'e*, 104–21.
55 *PSZ*, vol. 21, 1783, no. 15769; Kohut, *Russian Centralism*, 218–33.
56 *PSZ*, vol. 22, 1784, no. 15929; Druzhinina, *Severnoe Prichernomor'e*, 147–8.
57 *PSZ*, vol. 23, 1793, no. 17122, 1794, no. 17200 and 1795, no. 17320.
58 *PSZ*, vol. 23, 1792, no. 17025; Krasnov, "Proshedshee," 121; Khoroshkin, "Voenno-istoricheskii ocherk," 112–13; Grankin and Zemlianskii, *Severnyi Kavkaz*, 117–23.
59 *PSZ*, vol. 23, 1792, no. 17055–6.
60 *PSZ*, vol. 24, 1796, no. 17606.
61 Hrushevsky, *History*, 413, 469.
62 Karasaev, "Otaman," 874–6.
63 I borrow here from various articles in *EUkr*; see also Kohut, *Russian Centralism*, 237–48.
64 Freeze, *Russian Levites*, passim; *PSZ*, vol. 9, 1734, no. 6614.
65 Lazarevskii, "Ocherk," 1884–94.
66 Vinskii, *Moe vremia*, 13–14.
67 *SIRIO*, 68:130, 137, 150–1, 193, 276–7.
68 Florinsky, *Russia*, 594–5.
69 *PSZ*, vol. 22, 1786, no. 16375.

70 *PSZ*, vol. 14, 1756, no. 10618; vol. 15, 1760, no. 11106; vol. 25, 1799, no. 19156.
71 Fisher, "Enlightened Despotism," 546–7, and *Crimean Tatars*, 21, 77, 96; *PSZ*, vol. 23, 1794, no. 17174.
72 Litwin, "Catholicization," 81–2.
73 "Basilian Monastic Order," in *EUkr*, 1:183.
74 Hrushevsky, *History*, 441–3.
75 "Pis'ma imp. Ekateriny II Tutolminu," 2291–4, 2298–2302.
76 *PSZ*, vol. 23, 1793, no. 17113, 1795, no. 17384.
77 *PSZ*, vol. 23, 1795, no. 17318; vol. 25, 1799, no. 19156. For short biographies of the Uniate and Orthodox metropolitans during Catherine's reign see Fedoriw, *History*, 187–91 and 198–200.
78 "Tribunal koronnyi," in *ES*, 33:804–5; "zemskii sud" in *ES*, 12:533; "grodskii sud" in *ES*, 9:754; "Podkomorskii sud" in *ES*. 24:86–7.
79 Bagalei, "Magdeburgskoe pravo," 5–8, 11–16, 32–4; Hrushevsky, *History*, 171–2.
80 It is not certain that Novgorod-Seversk was given a charter (Bagalei, "Magdeburgskoe pravo," 31).
81 See, for example, Mnohohrishny's articles in *PSZ*, vol. 1, 1669, no. 447.
82 "Sudy v Malorossii," in *ES*, 32:15–16.
83 *PSZ*, vol. 8, 1728, no. 5324.
84 *PSZ*, vol. 9, 1834, no. 6608 and vol. 11, no. 8823.
85 LeDonne, *Absolutism*, 190.
86 *PSZ*, vol. 15, 1760, no. 11133, 1762, no. 11541.
87 "Sudy v Malorossii," in *ES*, 32:16; *PSZ*, vol. 16, 1763, no. 11812.
88 Kabuzan, *Izmeneniia*, 107–18.
89 For the sake of convenience I follow the establishments printed in *PSZ*, vol. 23, 1796, no. 17494 (*kniga shtatov*).
90 *PSZ*, vol. 17, 1768, no. 13148; vol. 19, 1772, no. 13854.
91 LeDonne, *Absolutism*, 215; Zagorovskii, "Vzaimootnosheniia," 60–1, 67–8.
92 "Khanstvo krymskoe," in *ES*, 37:50–1.
93 Zhukovich, "Upravlenie i sud," 25–8.
94 Translated by Karl von Loewe, *The Lithuanian Statute of 1529* (Leiden, 1976).
95 See the Russian edition edited by I. Lappo, *Litovskii Statut* v *Moskovskom perevode-redaktsii* (Yur'ev, 1916). I thank Nancy Colemann for this edition.
96 Kvachevskii, "Litovskii," 222–3, 254–5.
97 Jenkins, *Social Order*, 93.
98 *SIRIO*, 68:134–6.
99 Ibid., 136.
100 *PSZ*, vol. 8, 1728, no. 5324; vol. 9, 1734, no. 6540 and 6614; "Code of Laws of 1743," in *EUkr*, 1:533–4; published by Kistiakowski in *Kievskii Universitet. Izvestia* (1875–8) and separately in 1879. See also Tkach, *Istoriia kodifikatsii dorevoliutsiinogo prava Ukrainia*, 78–122; and Petrukhiktsev, *Vnutrenniaia politika*, 341–50.

101 *PSZ*, vol. 15, 1761, no. 11317.

102 "Magdeburg Law" in *EUkr*, 3:267; Bagalei, "Magdeburgskoe pravo," 1–5, 19–29; "Gernanic Law" in *EUkr*, 2:42.

103 "Pravo Magdeburgskoe," in *ES*, 24:894–96; *PSZ*, vol. 6, 1831, no. 4319 and vol. 9, 1834, no. 7694a; Delimar'skyi, *Magdeburhz'ke pravo*, 77–101.

104 Translated by Richard Hellie, *The Muscovite Law Code* (*Ulozhenie*) *of 1649*, Part 1 (Irvine, CA, 1988).

105 "Ulozhenie" in *ES*, 682–6.

106 RGVIA, f. 44, d. 50, Part 11:201–4.

107 *PSZ*, vol. 15, 1759, no. 10997.

108 Zhukovich, "Upravlenie i sud," 30–1.

109 *PSZ*, vol. 15, 1840, no. 13591. It was quite true that "the recognition of the empire's multi-ethnic character was accompanied by a desire to eradicate local particularities in government, law, and custom," and this not only under Catherine II (Plokhy, *Ukraine and Russia*, 23).

110 "Poles in Ukraine," *EUkr*, 4:86–8. Those magnates looked upon their estates as "islands of culture in a sea of barbarism" (Beauvois, *Le Noble*, 221).

111 LeDonne, "Geopolitics," passim.

112 Kabuzan, *Narody Rossii v XVIII veke*, 229; *Narody v pervoi polovine XIX v.*, 123.

113 Dubrovin, "Russkaia zhizn'," 1902, 3:23–5.

114 LeDonne, *The Russian Empire and the World*, 78–80.

115 *PSZ*, vol. 30, 1809, no. 23806, 23893, 24035; Dubrovin, "Russkaia zhizn'," 1902, 4:23–8, 30–3.

116 Kabuzan, *Izmeneniia*, 143–54.

117 Kabuzan and Troitskii, "Izmeneniia," 164.

118 Bagalei, "Magdeburgskoe pravo," 13–14.

119 Rosman, *Lord's Jews*, 36–51, 73–4.

120 "Russia" in *JE* (1825), 10:521.

121 *PSZ*, vol. 7, 1727, no. 5063.

122 *PSZ*, vol. 9, 1734, no. 6610 and 6614.

123 *PSZ*, vol. 10, 1739, no. 7869 and vol. 11, 1740, no. 8169.

124 *PSZ*, vol. 11, 1742, no. 8673, 1743, no. 8840.

125 *PSZ*, vol. 23, 1794, no. 17224.

126 Kabuzan, *Narody Rossii v pervoi polovine XIX v.*, 123–5, 165–6.

127 "Pale of Settlement" in *JE*, 9:468–70.

128 According to the statute of 1835, the Pale included in the southern theatre the following provinces: Chernihiv and Poltava; Podolia, Volhynia, and Kiev (less Kiev city); Ekaterynoslav, Bessarabia, Kherson (less Nikolaev); and Crimea (less Sevastopol); *PSZ*, vol. 10, 1835, no. 8054, pt. 3–4.

129 "Jews" in *EUkr*, 3:385–87. For the Council of the Four Lands see *The Jews of Old Poland*, 93–109, 141–5; for the *kahals*, 132–41.

130 "Kahal" in *JE*, 7:409–11. For a project to reform the *kahal* submitted by the Jewish communities themselves see Minkina, *Syny Rakhili*, 29–43. Derzhavin called the *kahal* "a state within the state" (Klier, *Russia*, 105).

131 *PSZ*, vol. 23, 1794, no. 17224, 1795, no. 17327; Zhukovich, "Upravlenie i sud," 12–13, 23–4.

132 Aksakov, *Pis'ma*, 1:418–19.

133 *PSZ*, vol. 28, 1804, no. 21547. For the context of the reform see Minkina, *Syny Rakhili*, 80–100. For an extensive analysis see Klier, *Russia*, 116–42. Klier calls the statute "a phantom in the air" because it failed to abolish the *kahal*, for which the committee that drafted it had been created.

134 *PSZ*, vol. 36, 1819, no. 27700.

135 *PSZ*, vol. 39, 1824, no. 30004.

136 Aksakov, "Ukrainskie iarmarki," 143–5.

137 "Jews," in *EUkr*, 2:387.

138 *PSZ*, vol. 10, 1835, no. 8054.

139 *PSZ*, vol. 19, 1844, no. 18546. In 1856, Alexander II would order a review of the entire legislation concerning the Jews in order to bring in line (*soglashat'*) its provisions with the general policy (*vidy*) of "merging [*slianie*] this people with "the native [*korennoe*] population" of the region (*Zapadnye okrainy*, 318).

140 Aksakov, "Ukrainskie iarmarki," 143.

141 "Karaimy," in *ES*, 14:430–2; "Karaites and Karamism," in *JE*, 7:438–47; "Evrei-Karaimy."

142 *PSZ*, vol. 23, 1795, no. 17340.

143 On Nazism and the Karaites see *Soviet Jewish Affairs* 8:36–45.

144 *PSZ*, vol. 12, 1837, no. 9991.

145 Matuz, "Relations étrangères," 239–40. For the Crimean Tatars see O'Neill's *Between Subversion*, chapters 1 and 2, and 211–315. What is missing in her analysis is the Russians' persistent distrust of the Tatars, inherited from a history of their raids in the southern steppe and their seizure of countless captives. I think it ran very deep in the Russian consciousness and would be an obstacle to a policy of superstratification. One can make a similar case in other borderlands as well, against the Poles and Kazan Tatars, for example.

146 Shotwell and Deak, *Turkey*, 93.

147 Fisher, *Crimean Tatars*, 95. For another survey of the history, social organization in Islam and the Crimea, and an extensive bibliography, see Roslavtseva, *Krymskie Tatary*.

148 LeDonne, *Grand Strategy*, 93.

149 Kabuzan, *Narody Rossii v XVIII v.*, 229, 240–1; *Narody Rossii v pervoi polovine XIX v.*, 126, 188–91; Vodarskii et al., *Naselenie*, 85–100, 120–5.

150 "Turko-Tatary" in *ES*, 43:349; Panin, "Iz bumag," 453.

151 "Istoricheskaia spravka," 41–3; Fisher, *Crimean Tatars*, 13, 15–16, 22; a fourth clan, the Kipchak, was in full decline at the time of the annexation.

152 Fisher, *Crimean Tatars*, 22–3.
153 Ibid., 77.
154 Samoilov, "Zhizn," 1211.
155 For his ancestors see Murzakevich, "Yakub-aga."
156 Fisher, *Crimean Tatars*, 72–5.
157 Kabuzan and Troitskii, "Izmeneniia," 164.
158 *PSZ*, vol. 23, 1794, no. 17265.
159 *PSZ*, vol. 2, 1827, no. 1417.
160 *PSZ*, vol. 6, 1831, no. 5033.
161 "Nogai Tatars" in *EUkr*, 3:608.
162 "Nogai" in *ES*, 20:421–2; Panin, "Iz bumag," 453; Fisher, *Crimean Tatars*, 24–5.
163 Compare these with the fanciful figures in "Predely kochev'ia," 589–90.
164 Bobrovskii, "Suvorov," 7, 15–19; Petrushevskii, "Suvorov," 12–21.
165 *PSZ*, vol. 28, 1805, no. 21752.
166 Baddeley, *Russian Conquest*, 42.

6 Unitary State or Empire? 1796–1855

1 LeDonne, "Russian Governors General," passim.
2 LeDonne, "Administrative Regionalization," passim.
3 Amburger, *Geschichte*, 397–8.
4 *RBS*, 16:123–7. The major work is Shandra, *Malorosiis'ke general-gubernatorstvo*: she sees a process of relentless and systematic integration, especially after the dismissal of Repnin. The book also contains portraits of seven of the eight governors general: she does not include Alexander Gur'ev, who spent little time in Poltava (from December 1834 to June 1835).
5 For Bibikov see *RBS*, 3:23–6; Kudriavtsev, *Institut*, 58–62, a valuable book containing the biography of all the Kiev governors general from 1700 to the Revolution, with a portrait of each. Shandra's *Administratyvni ustanovy* contains a survey of the legislation concerning the governors general and governors of Right Bank Ukraine from 1801 to 1855.
6 Obolenskii, "Nabroski," 355–65. Bibikov wrote in 1839 that he was receiving reports from Volhynia that many local officials "of Russian origin" spoke Polish not only with Poles, but also among themselves (one is reminded of the Russians in Yakutia!). Therefore, Russification should be understood as de-Polonization (Nadolska, "Volyn within the Russian Empire," 95). For the inventories see "Sostav i znachenie," Moon, "Inventory Reform," and Beauvois, *Le Noble*, 58–66. One must also place in this context the brutal purge of the Polish *szlachta* conducted by Bibikov at the same time (Beauvois, *Le Noble*, 110–53).
7 Amburger, *Geschichte*, 400.
8 *RBS*, 16:253–62.
9 *RBS*, 10:60–5.

10 “Formuliarny spisok” in AKV, 35:v–xvi; LeDonne, “Frontier Governors General.” For a list of his accomplishments see “O trudakh.”
11 *RBS*, 21:31–2.
12 *PSZ*, vol. 27, 1803, no. 20598; vol. 39, 1824, no. 30102. The governor general of Little Russia was also the curator of Kharkiv University from 1846 to 1855 (Amburger, *Geschichte*, 196–7).
13 *PSZ*, vol. 30, 1809, no. 23996; vol. 11, 1836, no. 9030; vol. 18, 1843, no. 16998a.
14 *PSZ*, vol. 5, 1830, no. 4019.
15 *PSZ*, vol. 32, 1814, no. 25723.
16 *Composition de l’armée russe*, passim.
17 *PSZ*, vol. 5, 1830, no. 3768.
18 Puzyrevskii, *Pol’sko-russkaia voina*, passim.
19 *PSZ*, vol. 10, 1835, no. 8355.
20 *PSZ*, vol. 10, 1835, no. 8276; *SVP*, chast’ 1, book 2, annex, 11–26.
21 *PSZ*, vol. 38, 1822, no. 29087–8.
22 LeDonne, *Russian Empire*, 79.
23 *PSZ*, vol. 6, 1831, no. 5019; vol. 12, 1837, no. 10740; Amburger, *Geschichte*, 365.
24 Gamba, *Voyage*, 1:30–1.
25 Tavrov, “Vostochny bereg,” 23–5.
26 *PSZ*, vol. 31, 1811, no. 24615.
27 *PSZ*, vol. 4, 1829, no. 3199.
28 Squire, *Third Department*, passim.
29 *PSZ*, vol. 2, 1827, no. 1062; vol 11, 1836, no. 9355.
30 “Military Colonies” in *MERSH*, 22:80–4.
31 Bogdanovich, *Istoriia*, 5:350–3; *PSZ*, vol. 34, 1817, no. 26772–3, 27190 and 27192.
32 *PSZ*, vol. 39, 1824, no. 29830.
33 Bogdanovich, *Istoriia*, 5:467–72.
34 *PSZ*, vol. 33, 1816, no. 26481.
35 *PSZ*, vol. 34, 1817, no. 28508–9, 28592, 28832, 28834–5.
36 *PSZ*, vol. 1, 1826, no. 644.
37 *PSZ*, vol. 7, 1832, no. 5458.
38 *PSZ*, vol. 32, 1812, no. 25129.
39 *PSZ*, vol. 29, 1807, M. 22465; Hrushevsky, *History*, 458–9.
40 *PSZ*, vol. 4, 1829, no. 2797; vol. 7, 1832, no. 5395.
41 *PSZ*, vol. 26, 1801, no. 20445.
42 *PSZ*, vol. 27, 1803, no. 20754.
43 “Don Cossack Host” in *MERSH*, 9:218–21.
44 *PSZ*, vol. 25, no. 1798, no. 18673.
45 *PSZ*, vol. 27, 1802, no. 20156.
46 Krasnov, “Proshedshee,” 124–5; Khoroshikhin, “Voenno-istoricheskii obzor,” 311–12.
47 *PSZ*, vol. 10, 1835, no. 8163; Svatikov, *Rossiia i Don*, 274–97, 307–27.

48 *PSZ*, vol. 10, 1835, no. 8233.
49 "Black Sea Cossack Host" in *MERSH*, 4:205–7; *PSZ*, vol. 30, 1808, no. 22902; Golobutskii, *Chernomorskoe kazachestvo*, 136–42.
50 Maikop, "Gertsog Rishel'e," 46; Waresquiel, *Duc de Richelieu*, 156–9; Gamba, *Voyage*, 1:50.
51 *PSZ*, vol. 37, 1820, no. 28241; Golobutskii, *Chernomorskoe kazachestvo*, 162–73, 315–27.
52 Khoroshkin, "Voenno-istoricheskii ocherk," 312.
53 Serhii Plokhy sums up very well the plight of the Cossacks: "Ukrainian Cossackdom … was one of the social phenomena produced by the existence of an open steppe frontier between the settled agricultural population of Eastern Europe and the nomads of the Eurasian plains" (*The Cossacks and Religion*, 1). With the disappearance of the frontier in the old territories, the Cossacks were becoming irrelevant.
54 *PSZ*, vol. 21, 1783, no. 15724.
55 *SIRIO*, 1:300.
56 *Istoricheskii obzor*, 1:100.
57 *PSZ*, vol. 6, 1831, no. 4536.
58 *PSZ*, vol. 23, 1795, no. 17356.
59 *PSZ*, vol. 39, 1824, no. 29775.
60 *PSZ*, vol. 6, 1831, no. 4869.
61 *PSZ*, vol. 37, 1820, no. 28171.
62 *PSZ*, vol. 29, 1806, no. 22316; vol. 37, 1820, no. 28307.
63 *PSZ*, vol. 39, 1824, no. 29732.
64 *PSZ*, vol. 7, 1832, no. 5073.
65 *PSZ*, vol. 32, 1812, no. 25144; vol. 5, 1830, no. 3463. For the Taganrog Greeks see *PSZ*, vol. 40, 1825, no. 30268.
66 *PSZ*, vol. 25, 1709, no. 19167.
67 *PSZ*, vol. 38, 1823, no. 29324.
68 *PSZ*, vol. 38, 1823, no. 29680
69 *PSZ*, vol. 33, 1815, no. 25935.
70 *PSZ*, vol. 4, 1829, no. 2612.
71 *PSZ*, vol. 5, 1830, no. 4143.
72 *PSZ*, vol. 27, 1802, no. 20428.
73 *PSZ*, vol. 35, 1818, no. 27448.
74 *PSZ*, vol. 37, 1821, no. 28574.
75 *PSZ*, vol. 37, 1821, no. 28574.
76 *PSZ*, vol. 23, 1791, no. 16981.
77 *PSZ*, vol. 1, 1826, no. 385.
78 *PSZ*, vol. 31, 1810, no. 24361; "Polozhenie Chernigovskoi gubernii."
79 Statistics in the following section come from *SIRIO*, 6:284–91.
80 Jones, "Ukrainian Grain," 210, 215–16.

81 Ibid., 212–13; Reychman, "Commerce polonais," 236–7.
82 Jones, "Ukrainian Grain," 220–4.
83 Coxe, *Travels*, 3:413–15
84 LeDonne, "Geopolitics, Logistics," 13–16. Smolii recognizes the importance of Polish grain for the Russian army in the region but does not see its connection with the partition of the Polish Empire in the south (Smolii, *Vozz'edynannia*, 102–9). On the worsening condition of the magnate economy and the pauperization of the towns, and the increasing resort to the production of vodka (for the Russian army), see Baranovich, *Magnatskoe khoziaistvo*, 176, and Markina, *Magnatnoe pomest'e*, 226–9.
85 *PSZ*, vol. 20, 1775, no. 14355.
86 Reychman, "Commerce polonais," 235–6.
87 "Vzgliad na istoriiu," 338–9; Samoilov, "Zhizn'," 1213–14.
88 *PSZ*, vol. 21, 1782, no. 15220.
89 *PSZ*, vol. 22, 1784, no. 16093.
90 Druzhinina, *Severnoe Prichernomor'e*, 282–3.
91 LeDonne, *Grand Strategy*, 138.
92 *PSZ*, vol. 28, 1804, no. 21530; vol. 35, 1818, no. 27479.
93 "The Ports of Taganrog," 365.
94 "Vzgliad na istoriiu," 351. Patricia Herlihy discusses the opening of the free port in *Odessa*, 21–48, 96–8.
95 Gamba, *Voyage*, 1:17. For the background of the creation of the *porto franco* see Honcharuk, *Odes'ke*, 69–84. For the different approaches of Governor General Vorontsov and Finance Minister Cancrin, see ibid., 150–64.
96 "Novorossiiskie stepi," 69; "Vzgliad na istoriiu," 347–8.
97 Melnyk, "Industrial Development," 246; Magocsi, *History*, 280–1; Subtelny, *Ukraine*, 261; Aksakov, "Ukrainiskie iarmarki."
98 *PSZ*, vol. 36, 1819, no. 27987–8.
99 *PSZ*, vol. 38, 1822, no. 28964–5.
100 *PSZ*, vol. 33, 1816, no. 26218.
101 *PSZ*, vol. 16, 1841, no. 15064; Florinsky, *Russia*, 709–12, 789–91.
102 Gamba, *Voyage*, 1:37–8.
103 *PSZ*, vol. 40, 1825, 30486.
104 "Pis'ma grafa Kochubeia," 318–19.
105 "Mysli o torgovle," 301–2. On the rapid rise of Odessa but also the weakness of the port see "Pis'mo puteshestvennika."
106 "Visit to Odessa," 279–80. Despite this pessimistic appraisal, the Black Sea trade kept expanding: Druzhinina, *Yuzhnaia Ukraina*, 183–98.
107 Jones, "Ukrainian Grain," 227; Tavrov, "Vostochny bereg," 13–16.
108 Aksakov, "Ukrainskie iarmarki," 152–4; "Novorossiiskie stepi," 68–9.
109 Rozen, *Zapiski*, 392–4.
110 Rozhkova, "K voprosu," 312; Skal'kovskii, "Yarmanki," 122–8.

111 Dukes, *Catherine the Great*, 197–8.
112 *SIRIO*, 68:130.
113 *SIRIO*, 68:150–1.
114 "Zapiska gospodam deputatam," pt. 6.
115 Vinskii, *Moe vremia*, passim.
116 For the various schools mentioned here see *EUkr*, 2:450, 545,47, 457–8; 3:602–3, 836; *PSZ*, 1765, no. 12430 and 12937.
117 Zhukovich, "Shkol'noe delo," 334–41; Gierowski, *Polish-Lithuanian Commonwealth*, 198–200.
118 Dubrovin, "Russkaia zhizn'," 1902, 1:20–2.
119 Zhukovich, "Zapadnaia Rossiia," 196–201; Dubrovin, "Russkaia zhizn'," 1902, 1:27.
120 *EUkr*, 2:669; Zoltowski, *Border*, 80–2.
121 *EUkr*, 2:537–8.
122 For a handy introduction to Herder's writings see Johann Gottfried Herder, *Another Philosophy of History* and *Selected Political Writings*, trans. I. Evrigenis and D. Pellerin (Indianapolis, 2004).
123 Dubrovin, "Russkaia zhizn'," 1902. 17–18, 23–6; see also *RBS*, 22:64–70; 4:144–6.
124 Ibid. For Krylov's fable see Ivan Krylov, *Sochineniia v dvukh tomakh* (Moscow, 1984), 2:132. There are several versions of the fable.
125 Hrushevsky, *History*, 420.
126 Ibid., 469.
127 Ibid., 421.
128 *EUkr*, 370. Serhii Plokhy in his recent book claims quite credibly to have found the author of the *History* in a group of collaborators around Stepan Shirai (1761–1841) in the Starodub region. It is quite paradoxical (but no less credible), because it was there that the percentage of Cossacks in the total population was the lowest. It was also a region which had largely escaped the devastation caused by the Cossack wars of the seventeenth century (Plokhy, *Cossack Myth*, 344–50).
129 Luckyj, *Between Gogol*, 99.
130 Ibid., 99. *Khokhol* was a derogatory name for a Ukrainian.
131 Ibid., 98.
132 "Romanticism," in *EUkr*, 4:403.
133 Chyzhevs'kyi, *History*, 455–78.
134 "Cyril and Methodius Brotherhood" in *EUkr*, 1:635; Luckyj, *Between Gogol*, 162–8.
135 Milosz, *History*, 226–7.
136 *Kyrylo-Mefodiivs'ke Tovarystvo*, 3 vols. (Kiev, 1990), here 1:169–70.
137 She was the granddaughter of Kiril Razumovsky, the last hetman.
138 Luckyj, *Between Gogol*, 128–32, 154–7.
139 Ibid., 137–43. As Serhii Plokhy puts it, "it was the gentry of the Hetmanate that created the Cossack myth as a reflection of its own political needs" (*Ukraine and Russia*, 171).
140 From *The Dream*, quoted in Luckyj, *Between Gogol*, 150.

Conclusion to Part II: The Southern Theatre

1 Readers objecting to this statement may do well to remember the following. When Russia's successful operations against Turkey in 1829 raised the possibility of the dissolution of the Ottoman Empire, Minister of Foreign Affairs Karl Nesselrode made the following statement to a special committee appointed to discuss the issue on 4/16 September 1829. Russia does not seek territorial conquests and aggrandizement, let alone the destruction of the Ottoman Empire. "We always considered the preservation of the empire to be more useful than harmful to Russia's true interests. It is an advantage to have as neighbour a weak state always threatened by the spirit of revolt undermining its vassals, doomed to submit to the law of the victor and to vegetate henceforth in accordance with the goodwill of the emperor." See *Vneshniaia politika Rossii*, 8/16 (1994), 282–4. If this is not a protectorate, what is? Nearly a century later, Russia's ambitions had become much greater. A Turkish military historian writes that former Russian war minister Alexei Kuropatkin drew a plan in 1915 to annex eastern Anatolia and divide it into six Russian-type provinces. A second plan proposed the annexation of most of the remainder of Anatolia. The agriculture minister proposed to settle Russian peasants on the Black Sea coast "for the purpose of the ultimate incorporation of conquered territories" in Anatolia. I thank Huseyin Oylupinar for this reference.

Introduction to Part III: The Eastern Theatre

1 Arnold Toynbee, *A Study of History*, 2nd ed., 10 vols (Oxford, 1935–54), here 2:112.
2 Andreas Kappeler, "Formirovanie Rossiiskoi imperii v XV–nachale XVIII veke: nasledstvo Rusi, Vizantii i Ordy," in *Rossiiskaia imperiia v sravnitelnoi perspective. Sbornik statei* (Moscow, 2004), 94–112, here 99.
3 A convenient introduction to the study of empires is Howe, *Empire: A Very Short Introduction*. An all-encompassing work is that of Jane Burbank and Frederick Cooper, *Empires in World History*.
4 Edmund Demolins, *Les grandes routes des peuples. Comment la route crée le type social*, 2 vols. (Paris, 1901–3), here 1:210.
5 LeDonne, *The Grand Strategy*, 43.
6 Semple, *Influences*, 134.
7 Osterhammel, *Colonialism*, 22.
8 Ibid., 4.
9 A table in *Sibir' v sostave*, 345 shows that the Russian and other "immigrant [*prishlie*], chiefly Ukrainian[s] and Belarussian[s], populations rose from 229,227 in 1709 (both sexes) to about 2.9 million in 1858, a 1,160 per cent increase, while the native population [*inorodtsy*] rose from about 200,000 to about 648,000, a 224

per cent increase." But note that the native population kept increasing under Russian rule, while the population of Native Americans declined from about 600,000 in 1800 to 250,000 in 1890 in the United States.

10 Hrytsak, "The Post-Colonial Is Not Enough," 732. I draw the reader's attention to the review of three books on Central Asian "colonialism" by Moritz Florin in *Kritika* 8 (2017): 827–38. He quotes Adeeb Khalid: "unlike modern overseas colonial empires," Russia (here the Soviet state) "did not attempt to perpetuate differences but instead sought to 'homogenize' populations in order to attain universal goals." I claim here that to homogenize populations helped create a social foundation for the pursuit of a policy of integration.

11 Osterhammel, *Colonialism*, 68.

12 Ibid., 59.

13 Eccles, "Frontiers," 31.

14 Howe, *Empire: A Very Short Introduction*, 19. The authors of *Sibir' v sostave*, 227, claim that one difference between the Russian and European cases was that the Urals, unlike the Atlantic, did not create a zone of separateness from the mother country, that the Russians and native societies did not run parallel lives, but interpenetrated.

15 Lattimore, *Studies*, 166–7.

16 Osterhammel, *Colonialism*, 15.

17 Ibid., 64–5.

18 Monahan, *Merchants*, 165–74, and Witzenrath, *Cossacks*, 122–38. See also Remnev, *Samoderzhavie i Sibir'* and his numerous articles; Burke, *History*, 76.

19 Duverger, *Concept*, 9; Doyle, *Empires*, 12–13; Burbank and Cooper, *Empires*, 8; Howe, *Empire: A Very Short Introduction*, 30.

20 Vasilenko, "Prikazy," in *ES* 25: 186–9; Pokrovskii, *Ministerskaia vlast' v Rossii* (Yaroslav, 1906), xx–xxxi; "Viedomosti iz Sinoda, iz Senata i iz dvukh Voinskikh kollegii i ikh Kontorakh i kakis v nikh dela opravliatsia," *Chtenia* 4 (1905):1–24.

21 Wortman, "Intentions," 373.

22 Sultangalieva, "Kazakhskie chinovniki Rossiiskoi imperii XIX v.," 651.

23 Badian, *Foreign Clientelae*, 156.

24 LeDonne, "Building an Infrastructure," 585; *Vlast' v Sibiri*, 375–508 gives a short biography of each.

25 LeDonne, "Administrative Regionalization," 19.

26 The title of Robert Kerner's well-known work *The Urge to the Sea: The Course of Russian History* (Berkeley, 1942).

27 LeDonne, *Russian Empire*, 179.

28 LeDonne, *Grand Strategy*, 47.

29 Duverger, *Concept*, 17.

30 To help assess the importance and contribution of Russian rule see the concept of "hegemonic stability" in James, *The Roman Predicament*, 30.

7 Laying the Foundations, 1650–1730

1 This introduction to the geography of the eastern theatre is based on Berg, *Natural Regions*; Lydolph, *Geography*; and articles on various provinces in *ES*. There is a splendid description of the physical geography of the entire theatre in Kropotkin, "Orography of Asia."
2 Allen and Muratoff, *Caucasian Battlefields*, 5–6.
3 F. Stark, *Rome on the Euphrates: The Story of a Frontier* (New York, 1966), 97.
4 For the location of trade routes see the maps attached to Burton, *Bukharans*.
5 Vernadsky, *Kievan Russia*, 236–9 and *Mongols*, 27–45.
6 Vernadsky, *Mongols*, 45, 49–52, 57.
7 Ibid., 218, 350.
8 Ibid., 137; Starr, *Legacy*, 202.
9 Vernadsky, *Russia at the Dawn*, 3.
10 Florinsky, *Russia*, 62.
11 Ibid., 85, 88, 140–1, 166.
12 Ibid., 102–3.
13 Ivan I was the first to use this title, but only intermittently in inter-prince treaties; Ivan III was the first to use it in negotiations with a foreign country in 1493 (Vernadsky, *Russia*, 2, 86).
14 Florinsky, *Russia*, 59.
15 Vernadsky, *Russia*, 71–5, 77. Khodarkovsky calls the encounter the "Ugra standoff" (*Russia's Steppe Frontier*, 77–82).
16 Vernadsky, *Mongols*, 331–2; *Russia at the Dawn*, 81–2.
17 Sykes, *History*, 2:118–64.
18 Vernadsky, *Tsardom*, 52–9, 80–3. Romaniello emphasizes that the conquest of Kazan was an Orthodox victory over Islam. No less interesting is his description of the construction of the Arzamas Line, which heralded the construction of similar lines between the Dnieper and the Volga, in the northern Caucasus, and facing the Kazakh steppe (*Elusive Empire*, 27–36).
19 Ibid., 63, 121. Khodarkovsky, *Russia's Steppe Frontier*, 100–17.
20 Vernadsky, *Tsardom*, 175–82.
21 Kerner, *Urge to the Sea*, passim.
22 The Sea of Okhotsk, the Black Sea, and the Baltic Sea.
23 Holdich, *Political Frontiers*, 250. Willard Sunderland put it no less convincingly: "because of the apparent seamlessness of geographic contiguity, the Muscovite conquest produced no clear colonies … the steppe was not, for all that, defined as a region wholly distinct from Russia … for Russian elites, the [North Caucasus] steppe seemed as much an extension of Russia as a territory distinguishable from it" (*Taming the Wild Field*, 17, 89, 109). See also Kappeler, *Russian Empire*, 161: "the 'colonial empire' label does not aptly describe the character of the pre-modern Russian Empire."

24 Vernadsky, *Mongols*, 159, 385; *Russia at the Dawn*, 82.

25 "Muscovy's own princes had been raised and trained in the Qipchak system. The possibility that Moscow could succeed in unifying the steppe, where the Mongols had recently failed, inspired visions of imperial opportunities. As much as the Orthodox tradition justified a southward push through Ukrainian territory to reclaim 'all Rus' from the open steppe, the Mongol legacy was more than enough to plan the annexation of the Khanates of Kazan, Astrakhan, and Sibir', reunifying the western Mongol Empire (Romaniello, *Elusive Empire*, 22). Andreas Kappeler had already put it in no less compelling fashion: after the conquest of Astrakhan, not far from Sarai, the capital of the Golden Horde, "its possessor was able to consider himself to be the heir of the great Mongol Empire," and "by the end of the eighteenth century Russia had become the un-challenged heir of the great Eurasian empire of the Golden Horde." Finally, "Russian expansion to the west went hand in hand in the seventeenth and eighteenth centuries with the 'gathering of the lands of the Golden Horde'" (*Russian Empire*, 26, 52, 56).

26 Vernadsky, *Tsardom*, 301–2; Ermolaev, *Srednee Povolzh'e*, 52–60; Wood, *History*, 19–25. For the Siberian Prikaz and the *voevody* see Lantzeff, *Siberia*, 4–18, 47–61.

27 Lantzeff, *Siberia*, 67; *Vlast' v Sibiti*, 14–41.

28 Vernadsky, *Tsardom*, 184.

29 Debu, "O nachal'nom ustanovlenii," 281–4; Kostenko, "Ural'skoe," 150–72; and Vitevskii, "Yaitskoe voisko," 292–9, 436–7. For the Siberian Cossacks see Katanaev, "Istoricheskii ocherk," 42–60.

30 I mean here the Ostiaks, Samoeds, Tungus, Yukagirs, and Koriaks, among others.

31 On the Kazan Tatars see Rorlich, *Volga Tatars*, 5–6; *Istoriia Bashkortostana*, 131–2; Georgi, *Opisanie*, 125–34; for the Mordva and Cheremis and Chuvash see ibid., 71–90; see also Kappeler, *Russlands Erste Nationalitäten*, 39–66.

32 Georgi, *Opisanie*, 147–52.

33 On Armenians and Georgians see ibid., 179–86, 434–5.

34 *Istoriia Bashkortostana*, 129–41; Georgi, *Opisanie*, 205–18.

35 "Kirgiz-Kaisaki" in *ES*, 15:95–6; Georgi, *Opisanie*, 228–48.

36 Barfield, *Perilous Frontier*, 278–9; Georgi, *Opisanie*, 395–411; *Ocherki istorii Kalmytskoi ASSR*, 53–72.

37 Forsyth, *History*, 84; *Istoriia Buriatskoi ASSR*, 120; "Buriaty" in *ES*, 5:59–61; Zalkind, *Prisoedinenie*, 152–7; Georgi, *Opisanie*, 415–26.

38 Ledyard, *Journey*, 156.

39 Forsyth, *History*, 55–6; Georgi, *Opisanie*, 274–82.

40 *PSZ*, vol. 4, 1708, no. 2208; vol. 5, 1719, N.3378.

41 LeDonne, "Building an Infrastructure," 584–85; *Vlast' v Sibiri*, 41–71.

42 LeDonne, "Evolution," 86–9. For the local administration of Siberia in the eighteenth century see Anan'ev, *Voevodskoe upravlenie*, 94–114.

43 Slovtsov, *Istoricheskoe obozrenie*, 250–2; *Mezhdunarodnye otnosheniia*, 1:231–2; Courant, *Asie centrale*, 66–7; Kasymbaev, *Gosudarstvennye deiateli*, 8–11.

44 *Mezhdunarodnye otnosheniia*, 234–5.
45 Ibid., 239–40.
46 Ibid., 232–3.
47 On Gantimur see Perdue, “Boundaries,” 267–8.
48 Rossabi, *China and Inner Asia*, 107–8; Bantysh-Kamenskii, *Diplomaticheskoe sobranie*, 36–43; Chen, *Sino-Russian Relations*, 80–1; Bowden, *Modern History*, 8–9.
49 Cahen, *Histoire*, 47–9; Bantysh-Kamenskii, *Diplomaticheskoe sobranie*, 50–5; Chen, *Sino-Russian Relations*, 90–3; Prescott, *Map of Mainland Asia*, 8–10: the text of the treaty is on 13–16.
50 *Mezhdunarodnye otnosheniia*, 258–61; Prescott, *Map of Mainland Asia*, 18–25. For the text of the border treaty (Bur Treaty), which was incorporated into the Kiakhta Treaty, see Sychevskii, “Istoricheskaia zapiska,” 1725. Also Shumakher, “Nashi snosheniia,” 175–8; Bantysh-Kamenskii, *Diplomaticheskoe sobranie*, 132–49, 344–6.
51 Kirilov, *Tsvetushchee sostoianie*, 378, 403. A regiment of garrison dragoons had 1,077 men, one of garrison infantry 1,309 men: *PSZ*, 43, 1720, no. 3511, p. 37; see also *PSZ*, vol. 8, 1731, no. 5803; Slovtsov, *Istoricheskoe obozrenie*, 243.
52 Lebedev, “Bashkirskoe vosstanie,” 81–102; *Istoriia Bashkortostana*, 207–19; Kappeler, *Russlands Erste Nationalitäten*, 137–87.
53 Tkhorzhevskii, *Stenka Razin*, passim.
54 *PSZ*, vol. 4, 1708, no. 2218, vol. 5, 1717, no. 3119 and 1719, no. 3374 and 3380; vol. 7, 1727, no. 5065.
55 Baskakov, *Russkie familii*, 85–7, 94–5, 101–3.
56 On the change of course of the Amu-Darya see Jaubert, “Mémoire.”
57 Goloskov, “Pokhod v Khivu,” 308–10; *PSZ*, vol. 5, 1714, no. 2809.
58 Solov’ev, *Istoriia Rossii*, 9:366–70; Korsakov, “Artemii Petrovich Volynskii,” 52–60, 293–4; Kukanova, “Russko-iranskie torgovye otnosheniia,” 232–3, 241–9.
59 McCabe, *Shah’s Silk*, 169–70, 257–8, 275–9, 284–5.
60 Bushev, *Posol’stvo*, 257–60.
61 Lystsov, *Persidskii pokhod*, passim, and Beskrovnyi, *Russkaia armiia i flot*, 239–44.
62 *PSZ*, vol. 9, 1733, 6707.
63 LeDonne, *Grand Strategy*, 44–52; Kirilov, *Tsvetushchee sostoianie*, 377–9, 403–4.
64 Eberhard, *Conquerors*, 58. See also Lattimore, *Studies*, 530. Eberhard had in mind the superimposition of a pastoral group over an agrarian society; I use the term in the opposite sense. Superstratification was not only a political but also a socio-economic concept. The Russians, as men of the plain and tillers of the land out to create a unitary state, sought to settle the nomad, but “sedentarization was a process of downward mobility.” The nature of nomadism, “with its centrifugal forces, prevented the establishment of a tightly controlled centralized authority able to reach the periphery of society. Such a structure became possible only when a certain degree of sedentarization had occurred.” Closer relations with the Russian state brought about a split among the top stratum and a more rigid stratification within the native society, resulting in the degradation of the lower levels to the status of

peasants. "The government realized that co-optation and fostering sedentarization were the best ways to pacify the nomads" (Khodarkovsky, *Where Two Worlds Met*, 2, 17, 237, 240). Not only to pacify them, indeed, but also to integrate them into the social structure of the core power.

65 Kabuzan, *Narody Rossii v XVIII veke*, 72–4, 77, 84–6.

66 *Istoriia Tatarskoi ASSR*, 1:118–24. An excellent introduction to the great variety of Muslim peoples in the Caucasus, Siberia, and Central Asia is "Etudes géographiques" followed by a survey of Russia's policies beginning in the 1550s. See in this connection Werth, *At the Margins*, 27–47.

67 *PSZ*, vol. 3, 1697, no. 1585 (instruction to the Terek *voevoda*); vol. 4, 1700, no. 1792 (instruction to the Astrakhan *voevoda*).

68 *Istoriia Bashkortostana*, 133–41.

69 Ibid., 129, 183–4; Asfandiiarov, *Bashkirskie tarkhany*, 17–19, 27–33.

70 *Ocherki istorii Kalmytskoi ASSR*, 129–39.

71 *PSZ*, vol. 4, 1708, no. 2207 and vol. 5, 1713, no. 2702; Korsakov, "Artemii Petrovich Volynskii," 298–9; *Ocherki istorii Kalmytskoi ASSR*, 154–62, 185–8. Slave raids could be quite extensive: in 1842 alone, some 800 Karakalpaks captured 1,000 Russian women and children in Siberia: Khodarkovsky, *Russia's Steppe Frontier*, 25.

72 Zalkind, *Prisoedinenie*, 145–7, 152–7, 294–5. *Istoriia Buriatskoi ASSR*, 68–72, 151–52. On *kyshtymstvo* see Zalkind, *Prisoedinenie*, 260–1.

73 Forsyth, *History*, 86; Zalkind, *Prisoedinenie*, 38–40, 282, 295–7. For the uprisings of the seventeenth century see Kudriavtsev, *Istoriia*, 61–79. He also observes, on the other hand, that "the arrival of the Russians resulted in reducing the influence of the *noions*, but they quickly adjusted to the new political situation and became the conduit [*provodnik*] of Russian policy toward the peasantry" (118).

74 Forsyth, *History*, 55–6, 61–2.

75 Ibid., 62.

76 Vernadsky, *Mongols*, 370. Florinsky says 17 per cent of the "upper class" (*Russia*, 63). Valerie Kivelson claims that the Russians showed indifference to the religious convictions of their subjects. This is highly debatable. Why then did they persecute Muslims in the former Kazan khanate, and why did they offer incentives to convert? She also challenges the statement that converted natives became Russian automatically, yet Yemelianova, quoting a document of the Ministry of Education of 1870, writes that the final goal of education of the *inorodtsy* is "their complete and religious Russification." See also Vasary, who writes that embracing Christianity was tantamount to becoming Russian ("Clans," 101). See Kivelson, *Cartographies*, 149–50; Yemelianova, *Russian and Islam*, 72.

77 Vernadsky, *Mongols*, 379; Forsyth, *History*, 5.

78 Forsyth, *History*, 6, 52; *Istoriia Yakutskoi ASSR*, 121–2.

79 Vernadsky, *Tsardom*, 80–3.

80 Abramov, "Materialy," 20–41; Leskov, "Sibirskie kartinki," 196–7.

81 Florinsky, *Russia*, 287–95.

82 Cracraft, *Church Reform*, passim.
83 *PSZ*, vol. 2, 1684, no. 1102; Slovtsov, *Istoricheskoe obozrenie*, 238–9.
84 Khabutdinov, *Millet*, 3, 36–9.
85 Freeze, *Russian Levites*, 12, 168, 170.
86 Frank, *Muslim Religious Institutions*, 101, 111–13, 133.
87 *PSZ*, vol. 2, 1685, no. 1117, 1686, no. 1163.
88 Rorlich, *Volga Tatars*, 40. See also *PSZ*, vol. 2, 1686, no. 1179; 1682, no. 923 and 944; 1683, no. 1009.
89 Forsyth, *History*, 93; Bawden, *Modern History*, 52–8, 70; Waley-Cohen, "Religion, War," 339–41.
90 Yadrintsev, "Altaiiego," 640–1; also Forsyth, *History*, 99–100, 170. Metropolitan Filofei sent a mission to Urga to find out about Buddhism and encourage young people to learn about Mongols (Slovtsov, *Istoricheskoe obozrenie*, 233–4).
91 Andrei Kurapov observes that Russia in the eighteenth century did not look upon Buddhism as a doctrine equal to Orthodoxy, and that a debate tolerated with the bearers of Catholicism and Protestantism was simply impossible with Buddhism. There could be no dialogue between the two faiths (Kurapov, *Buddizm*, 165).
92 Florinsky, *Russia*, 274–5.
93 Ibid., 282, 362–5; LeDonne, *Absolutism*, 258–60, 27–33, and Steinwedel, *Threads of Empire*, 67–8.
94 Slovtsov, *Istoricheskoe obozrenie*, 373.
95 *Istoriia Sibiri*, 2:72–5.
96 Rossabi, *China*, 100; *Istoriia Sibiri*, 2:62–3.
97 Slovtsov, *Istoricheskoe obozrenie*, 373–4; *Istoriia Sibiri*, 2:216–17; *Istoriia Yakutskoi ASSR*, 50–1, and especially Shunkov, *Ocherki*, 174–96.
98 *Istoriia Sibiri*, 2:217.
99 Ibid., 2:76.
100 Pavlov, "Vyvoz pushniny," 134–8; Forsyth, *History*, 63–4.
101 *Istoriia Bashkortostana*, 133–41; Fisher, *Fur Trade*, 50–1; Dameshek, *Iasachnaia politika* focuses on the first half of the nineteenth century.
102 Fairbank, *World Order*, 63–5, 70–1, 79; Rossabi, *China*, 19–22, 71–3, 92.
103 Slovtsov, *Istoricheskoe obozrenie*, 100–1; *Istoriia Bashkortostana*, 199.
104 Fisher, *Fur Trade*, 59–60.
105 *Istoriia Yakutskoi ASSR*, 63–4.
106 Fisher, *Fur Trade*, 60.
107 Ibid., 41–2.
108 Ibid., 57–8.
109 Ibid., 56–7. Kabuzan estimates that the first census registered 71,744 *iasak*-payers in the whole of Siberia (*Sibir' XVII–XVIII vv.*, 153).
110 *Istoriia Buriatskoi ASSR*, 103–5; *Istoriia Sibiri*, 2:129–31.
111 Pavlov, "Vyvoz," 121; Fisher, *Fur Trade*, 52–3, 56–8.
112 *Istoriia Sibiri*, 2:130–1.

113 *Istoriia Bashkortostana*, 199.

114 Lemercier-Quelquejay, "Routes commerciales," 10; Gamrekeli, *Torgovye sviazi*, 1:25, 36, 60.

115 *PSZ*, vol. 3, 1697, no. 1585, pt. 12–13, 16; vol. 6, 1720, N.3622, pt. 55, 62–3; Kokiev, "Kabardino," 188–90.

116 Vitevskii, "Yaitskoe voisko," 203.

117 Burton's *Bukharans* is the classic work on the subject. A more recent work is Monahan, *Merchants*, which includes an excellent chapter on the Irtysh River and Lake Yamyshev. Her conclusions may not be valid for the post-Petrine period. She claims that merchants acting in a private capacity, rather than the Muscovite government, were the leading force in opening up Siberia: but the pursuit of security and wealth are not mutually exclusive. See also Khodarkovsky, *Russia's Steppe Frontier*, 27.

118 Potanin, "O karavannoi torgovle," 44–50.

119 Dale, *Indian Merchants*, 89, 96–8.

120 Ibid., 126.

121 Kukanova, "Russko-iranskie torgovye otnosheniia," 232–3, 237, 239.

122 Dale writes that Jenkonson found little trade in Astrakhan in the 1580s (*Indian Merchants*, 78).

123 Lobanov-Rostovsky, *Russia*, 64.

124 Rerikh, *Tibet*, 174–5.

125 Reading, *Anglo-Russian Commercial Treaty*, 225–6.

126 Bundas, "Morskie sily," 37–8; Kukanova, "Russko-iranskie torgovye otnosheniia," 236–9.

127 *PSZ*, vol. 5, 1717, no. 3097; Kukanova, "Russko-iranskie torgovye otnosheniia," 241–2.

128 Blanchard, *Russia's Age of Silver*, 65–8; Bassin, "Expansion."

129 Cahen, *Histoire*, 29, 72; Rossabi, *China*, 133; Vatin, *Minusinskii*,164.

130 Pavlovsky, *Chinese-Russian Relations*, 18; Cahen, *Histoire*, 100, 110–13.

131 Bantysh-Kamenskii, *Diplomaticheskoe sobranie*, 81–2, 432–3; Cahen, *Histoire*, 155–8.

132 Bantysh-Kamenskii, *Diplomaticheskoe sobranie*, 66–9; Cahen, *Histoire*, 60–1; *PSZ*, vol. 3, 1697, no. 1606.

133 This distinction between market towns and commercial cities was inspired by Fox, *History*, 25, 33–4, 47, 171–2.

8 The Progress of Integration, 1731–1782

1 LeDonne, "Evolution," 107.

2 *Gubernii Rossiiskoi imperii*, 45–6, 119.

3 Kabuzan, *Izmeneniia*, 71–3.

4 Popov, *Tatishchev*, 425–6, 645–6.

5 *PSZ*, vol. 9, 1733, no. 6496.
6 Zasedateleva, *Terskie kazaki*, l/8–226
7 *PSZ*, vol. 13, 1750, no. 9727.
8 *Istoriia Bashkortostana*, 222–5; Smirnov, *Orenburgskaia ekspeditsiia*, 16–47.
9 I was much impressed by Sven Beckert's article "American Danger: United States, Euroafrica, and the Territorialization of Industrial Capitalism 1870–1950," *American Historical Review* 122 (2017): 1137–70, here 1162, which offers interesting parallels with Russian ambitions in the Petrine and post-Petrine periods.
10 Petrukhintsev, *Vnutrenniaia politika*, 390–424, 955–63; Kirilov, *Tsvetushchee sostoianie*, 7–16; and Fisher, *Bering's Voyages*, passim.
11 *PSZ*, vol. 8, 1728, no. 5316 and 5318; vol. 10, 1743, no. 7347; *Istoriia Bashkortostana*, 183.
12 Iudin, "Baron' Igel'strom," 513–14; *PSZ*, vol. 11, 1743, no. 8783; vol. 12, 1744, no. 8902.
13 *Istoriia Bashkortostana*, 223–5.
14 Ibid., 252; Vitevskii, "Yaitskoe voisko," 388–9.
15 Ibid., 291.
16 *PSZ* vol. 8, 1730, no. 5659.
17 For a general discussion of this issue see LeDonne, "Russian Governors General," 5–30.
18 Rafienko, "Instruktsiia," 58–60. Rafienko claims the instruction remained in force until 1782, but in fact it may never have taken effect (*Istoriia Sibiri*, 2:300). Strangely enough, *Vlast' v Sibiri*, 85–7 ignores the issue of why the instruction was not included in the *PSZ*.
19 Chupin, "Burtsov," 986–7, 991–2.
20 Sychevskii, "Istoricheskaia zapiska," 82–3, 115.
21 *PSZ*, vol. 9, 1736, no. 6876.
22 *Istoriia Sibiri*, 2:181.
23 Kabuzan, *Izmeneniia*, 75–7.
24 P.-., "Kratkaia khronologiia," 217.
25 *Istoriia Sibiri*, 2:187.
26 *PSZ*, vol. 9, 1734, no. 6571.
27 *SA*, 6: 102–9, 174–85; "Materialy dlia istorii Sibiri, " 63–4, 77.
28 *PSZ*, vol. 16, 1764, no. 12269; Amburger, *Geschichte*, 405–6.
29 *PSZ*, vol. 16, 1764, no. 12137.
30 On Miatlev, see Baranov, *Opis'*, 3, no. 9108, 10241, 10785, 10833, 10842. See also Bezprozvannykh, *Priamur'e*, 156–61; Solov'ev, *Istoriia Rossii*, 13:351–2.
31 On Soimonov, see *RBS*, 19:44–8; Baranov, *Opis'*, 3, no. 10804; Pavlenko, *Anna Ioanovna*, 294–5; On Chicherin, *RBS*, 20:427–9; Gazenvinkel', "Sibirskii gubernator," 783–4; Leskov, "Sibirskie kartinki," 547–52. For short biographies of the other governors, see *Vlast' v Sibiri*, 71–89, 511–45.

32 Slovtsov, *Istoricheskoe obozrenie*, 548–50; *PSZ*, vol. 15, 1761, no. 11185, pt. 10; Potanin, "O karavannoi torgovle," 99–100; *Istoriia Sibiri*, 2:182, 185.
33 LeDonne, *Russian Empire*, 211.
34 The Siberian Line (or Lines) now meant the Ishim, Irtysh, and Kolyvan-Kuznetsk Lines: see *PSZ*, vol. 16, 1763, no. 11931.
35 *PSZ*, vol. 19, 1771, no. 13649; vol. 20, 1775, no. 14257; Krestovskii, "Chetyre," 13–25, 208–10.
36 Chuloshnikov, *Bashkirskoe vosstanie*, passim, and Islaev, *Vosstanie Batyrshi*, passim.
37 *Ocherki istorii Kalmytskoi ASSR*, 199–202, 212–20; Courant, *Asie centrale*, 129–39.
38 Vitevskii, "Yaitskoe voisko," 377–93, 435–58; Kostenko, "Ural'skoe," 155–9.
39 *PSZ*, vol. 17, 1765, no. 12432; Debu, "O nachalnom ustanovlenii," 51–2. The College of Foreign Affairs reduced the original number by half, to 112 men. For the advance of the Cossacks from Tsaritsyn to the Terek see Iudin, "S Volgi na Terek."
40 Volkov, "Zapiska," 59.
41 Debu, "O nachal'nom ustanovlenii," 49–52, 54; *PSZ*, vol. 19, 1770, N, 13404, 14476; vol. 20, 1776, no. 14464.
42 For a comprehensive study of the reforms see LeDonne, *Ruling Russia*, 57–82, and LeDonne, "The Territorial Reform," 147–85, 411–57.
43 Population data from Kabuzan, *Izmeneniia*, 95–106 and Kabuzan, *Narody Rossii v XVIII v.*, 166–71, 181–3, 227, 230.
44 I found Kabuzan a little confusing here. He gives for the northern Caucasus a total population of 37,776 people, but later adds the 115,000 Tatars. It is unclear where they actually belong.
45 A similar problem here. Figures for the native population come from Kabuzan in Kabuzan and Troitskii, "Dvizhenie naseleniia Sibiri," 139–57. I follow him here and multiply his totals by two (he gives only the male population) to obtain an approximate total. On p. 146 he gives a total Russian population of 778,000 (70.4 per cent) and a total native population of 326,000. Compare this figure with the 227,235 natives mentioned by Forsyth for the seventeenth century. How reliable these figures are remains moot (Forsyth, *History*, 71).
46 *Istoriia Bashkortostana*, 231–47; Nolde, *Formation*, 1:218–31.
47 Kappeler, *Russlands Erste Nationalitäten*, 244–320.
48 Khabutdinov, *Millet*, 29–30.
49 *Istoriia Bashkortostana*, 228.
50 Petrukhintsev, *Vnutrenniaia politika*, 382–3, 455–6, 461.
51 *PSZ*, vol. 9, 1736, no. 6890 and Steinwedel, *Threads of Empire*, 50–1.
52 Frank, *Muslim Religious Institutions*, 169; *Istoriia Bashkortostana*, 228, 230.
53 Bogoslovskii, *Kratkii istoricheskii obzor*, 14.
54 Ibid., 19–24, 72–3. A survey of the Board's activities is in Islaev, *Islam i pravoslavie*, 59–135.
55 *PSZ*, vol. 12, 1744, no. 8978.

56 *PSZ*, vol. 13, 1749, no. 9631.
57 *PSZ*, vol. 11, 1740, no. 8236 and 1743, no. 8793; vol. 12, 1744, no. 8978.
58 *PSZ*, vol. 11, 1743, no. 8793.
59 Bogoslovskii, *Kratkii istoricheskii obzor*, 23.
60 Frank, *Muslim Religious Institutions*, 172; Sultangalieva, "Russian Empire," passim.
61 Iudin, "Baron' O.A. Igel'strom," 520–1.
62 Chuloshnikov, *Bashkirskoe vosstanie*, passim, and Khabutdinov, *Millet*, 39–45.
63 Khabutdinov, *Millet*, 29–30.
64 *PSZ*, vol. 19, 1773, no. 13996; Fisher, "Enlightened Despotism," 543–9.
65 *PSZ*, vol. 20, 1775, no. 14313.
66 *PSZ*, vol. 21, 1782, no. 15324, pt. 2.
67 Khodarkovsky, "Of Russian Governors," 1–26 and *Where Two Worlds Met*, 170–235; *Ocherki istorii Kalmytskoi ASSR*, 185–96. The literature on the Kalmyks is extensive: one may begin with Khodarkovsky's works and continue with Remilev, *Oirat-Mongoly*, for a comprehensive history.
68 Sychevskii, "Istoricheskaia zapiska," 119–22; *Mezhdunarodnye otnosheniia*, 278–81. Russia's interference in the succession is well described in Khodarkovsky, "Of Russian Governors," 3–19. For the role of the khan and the administrative organization of the Kalmyks see Komandzhaev, *Administrativnaia sistema*, 23–32, 39–48, 49–52.
69 *Ocherki istorii Kalmytskoi ASSR*, 190.
70 Courant, *L'Asie*, 131–2.
71 *Ocherki istorii Kalmytskoi ASSR*, 181–2.
72 Khodarkovsky, *Where Two World Met*, 232–4; *Ocherki istorii Kalmytskoi ASSR*, 212–22. Khodarkovsky neatly describes the situation of a people occupying an ethnic frontier between two core powers: "the Kalmyks had escaped Russian tentacles only to be ensnared in Chinese ones" (*Where Two Worlds Met*, 235).
73 Kabuzan, *Narody Rossii v XVIII veke*, 84–5, 226–7. Another source claims that Ubashi left with 30,000 *kibitki* and left behind 11,200 (*Ocherki istorii Kalmytskoi ASSR*, 216).
74 *PSZ*, vol. 7, 1725, no. 4784.
75 *PSZ*, vol. 8, 1729, no. 5400; vol 10, 1739, no. 5443; vol. 27, 1803, N.21025. On Colonel Zmeev and his policies see Orlova, *Istoriia khristianizatsii*, 65–9, and Khodarkovsky, *Where Two Worlds Met*, 172, 180–2, 208.
76 *PSZ*, vol. 11. 1741, no. 8393.
77 *PSZ*, vol. 12, 1745, no. 9110.
78 *PSZ*, vol. 16, 1764, no. 12174.
79 Kabuzan, *Narody Rossii v pervoi polovine XIX v.*, 204.
80 On their way of life at the beginning of the nineteenth century see Zu., "Dr. Savva Bol'shoi's Account." For a history of the three hordes from 1750 to 1832 see Levshine, *Description*, 155–298.
81 Slovtsov, "Istoricheskii obzor," 554–5. Alexis Levshine notes that the local archives in Omsk and Orenburg are full of complaints by khans and sultans about the insubordination of their subjects and the weakness of their own power (Levshine, *Description*, 396).

82 Kasymbaev, *Gosudarstvennye deiateli*, 16–20; *PSZ*, vol. 8, 1731, no. 5703 and 5704.
83 *PSZ*, vol. 9, 1734, no. 6567. On the controversial nature of the agreement between the Russians and Abulkhair see Bodger, "Abulkhair," 55, 57.
84 Kasymbaev, *Gosudarstvennye deiateli*, 25–6, 29–31, 36–9, 71–2, 77–8.
85 Courant, *L'Asie*, 127–8; Kasymbaev, *Gosudarstvennye deiateli*, 162–5, 194–5.
86 Kasymbaev, *Gosudarstvennye deiateli*, 102–3, 108–14, 116–26.
87 *Mezhdunarodnye otnosheniia*, 2:233–4.
88 Kasymbaev, *Gosudarstvennye deiateli*, 130–5.
89 *Istoriia Buriatskoi ASSR*, 1:102, 213.
90 Ibid., 111; see Shchukin, "Buriaty" for their customs and way of life.
91 *Istoriia Buriatskoi ASSR*, 137–9; *PSZ*, vol. 26, 1851, no. 25039.
92 Shchukin, 106, 108, 174.
93 Ibid., 136, 174–6, 187.
94 LeDonne, "Proconsular Ambitions," passim.
95 "An Account of the Buriats," 589.
96 Ibid., 590.
97 *Istoriia Buriatskoi ASSR*, 249–53.
98 Forsyth, *History*, 66.
99 *Istoriia Sibiri*, 2:294; Forsyth, *History*, 163–4.
100 *Istoriia Yakutskoi ASSR*, 1:87; Forsyth, *History*, 61.
101 *Istoriia Yakutskoi ASSR*, 88, 128; Fisher, *Bering's Voyages*, 122–32.
102 Forsyth, *History*, 164.
103 *Istoriia Yakutskoi ASSR*, 123–5, 249–51.
104 Kalashnikov, "Zapiski," 203–4.
105 Mikhailovskii, *Shamanstvo*, passim.
106 LeDonne, *Absolutism*, 260–1.
107 *PSZ*, vol. 7, 1724, no. 4533.
108 *SIRIO*, 134:148–9, 186–8.
109 *Istoriia Bashkortostana*, 228.
110 Ibid., 249–51; *PSZ*, vol. 15, 1761, no. 11186.
111 *PSZ*, vol. 18, 1769, no. 13357 and 13375.
112 *PSZ*, vol. 16, 1762, no. 11633.
113 *Istoriia Sibiri*, 2:217–20.
114 *PSZ*, vol. 8, 1731, no. 5735.
115 *PSZ*, vol. 14, 1754, no. 10198; *Istoriia Bashkortostana*, 252.
116 *PSZ*, vol. 11, 1740, no. 8017.
117 *PSZ*, vol. 16., 1763, no. 11749.
118 Dameshek, *Iasachnaia politika*, 3–5; *Istoriia Sibiri*, 2:404.
119 *Istoriia Sibiri*, 2:404.
120 Ibid., 2:294–5.
121 Ibid.
122 LeDonne, *Absolutism*, 278. There is a good description of the *iasak* system in Modorov, *Rossiia i gorny Altai*, 114–40.

123 LeDonne, *Absolutism*, 269–75.
124 Indian, Persian, Armenian, and Central Asian traders residing in Astrakhan were not required to open their homes, even after they became permanent residents (*PSZ*, vol. 18, 1769, no. 13307).
125 *PSZ*, vol. 19.1771, no. 13467.
126 See the *nakazy* to the Legislative Commission in *SIRIO*, 134: 186–8, 305, 306, 335–6. See also *PSZ*, vol. 14, 1755, no. 10449; vol. 16, 1762, no. 11633; vol 19, 1770, no. 13422.
127 Forsyth, *History*, 140.
128 LeDonne, "Indirect Taxes," 161–90.
129 Gamrekeli, *Torgovye sviazi*, 1:5, 39, 81–4; 2:45, 78–80.
130 *PSZ*, vol. 8, 1732, no. 5935.
131 *AGS*, 2:686.
132 Dale, *Indian Merchants*, 131–2.
133 *PSZ*, vol. 13, 1750, no. 9751; vol. 14, no. 1755, no. 10486.
134 Petrushevskii, "Suvorov," 6–7.
135 Dale, *Indian Merchants*, 109–10.
136 Reading, *Anglo-Russian Commercial Treaty*, 258; Sokolov, "Astrakhanskii port," 473–4; *AGS*, 2:686–9.
137 Semenov, *Izuchenie*, chast' 3, 450–7.
138 *SIRIO*, 5:275–6.
139 Vitevskii, "Yaitskoe voisko," 212–13. On the Orenburg "exchange market" (*menovoi dvor*), see Kriukov, "Orenburgskii."
140 *PSZ*, vol. 13, 1749, no. 9639; vol. 16, 1763, no. 11807.
141 *PSZ*, vol. 13, 1752, no. 9995.
142 *PSZ*, vol. 14, 1755, no. 10486. For the Caspian trade with Persia, Central Asia, and China, see Coxe, *Travels*, 3:382–406.
143 "Materialy dlia istoriii Sibiri," 138–9.
144 Potanin, "O karavannoi torgovle," 42–4, 106–7.
145 Ibid., 107–8; *PSZ*, vol. 16, 1763, no. 11931.
146 Semenov, *Izuchenie*, chast' 3, 458–65.
147 Sladkovskii, *Istoriia*, 9, 149–50; *PSZ*, vol. 16, 1762, no. 11630.
148 Semenov, *Izuchenie*, chast' 3, 466–71.
149 Potanin, "O karavannoi torgovle," 85–7.
150 Bezprozvannykh, *Priamur'e*, 177–8.

9 Unitary State or Empire? 1782–1830

1 *AKAK*, 2:826. On Tsitsianov, see Rayfield, *Edge of Empires*, 261–7.
2 The Gulistan Treaty is in *PSZ*, vol. 32, 1813, no. 25466; that of Turkmanchai in vol. 3, 1828, no. 1794.
3 Fawcett, *Frontiers*, 80–1.

4 Gamba, *Voyage*, 2:413, etc.
5 *PSZ*, vol. 26, 1801, no. 20007; vol. 27, 1802, no. 20511.
6 Dubrovin, "A.P. Ermolov," 230–1; Dubrovin, "1802 god," 230–2.
7 *PSZ*, vol. 39, 1824, no. 30516; vol. 3, 1828, no. 1888.
8 For Paskevich's activities in the Caucasus see Shcherbatov, *General-Fel'dmarshal*, vols. 3 and 4. The first viceroy of the Caucasus was Count Mikhail Vorontsov (1844–54): see Rayfield, *Edge of Empires*, 286–91, and especially Rhinelander, *Prince Michael Vorontsov*, 140–97.
9 *AKAK*, 7:39.
10 *PSZ*, vol. 27, 1803, no. 20890; vol. 28, 1804, no. 21183.
11 *PSZ*, vol. 27, 1803, no. 20771.
12 On the condition of the Siberian administration before and during Pestel's tenure see "K Irkutskomu letopistsu," with amusing asides on how governors were appointed. Pestel's autobiography ("Bumagi I.B. Pestelia," 369–407) shows a total unawareness of his own responsibility for the abuses committed during his tenure.
13 LeDonne, "Frontier Governors General 1772–1825. III. The Eastern Frontier," 330–1; *Vlast' v Sibiri*, 138–44.
14 *PSZ*, vol. 38, 1822, no. 29125–36; *Vlast' v Sibiri*, 145–59, and Raeff, *Siberia*, passim.
15 On the transfer of the West Siberian administration from Tobolsk to Omsk see *PSZ*, vol. 13, 1838, no. 11690 and vol. 14, no. 12553. Omsk was considered a poor choice at the time, and the governor general, Lt.-Gen. Petr Gorchakov, was later blamed for recommending it (*Stepnoi krai Evrazii*, 52–4). For the administration of East Siberia during the reign of Nicholas I, and the careers of the governors general and governors, see Matkhanova, *Vysshaia administratsiia*, 36–42, 46–55, and Matkhanova, *General-Gubernatory*, 43–243.
16 *PSZ*, vol. 38, 1822, no. 29125.
17 *PSZ*, vol. 6, 1831, no. 4585. Speransky's statutes have been called "a variant of imperial regionalism" (*Vlast' v Sibiri*, 84).
18 *PSZ*, vol. 2, 1827, no. 878.
19 *PSZ*, vol. 15, 1840, no. 13368.
20 *PSZ*, vol. 21, 1846, no. 20701; vol. 24, 1849, no. 23303.
21 *PSZ*, vol. 26, 1851, no. 24811, 25394–5; vol. 29, 1854, 28255; vol. 25, no. 24639.
22 LeDonne, *Grand Strategy*, 108, 125.
23 *PSZ*, vol. 24, 1796, no. 17606; vol. 26, 1801, no. 19951; vol. 30, no. 1808, no. 22807–8; vol. 31, 1810, no. 24386; vol. 32, 1814, no. 25723; vol. 33, 1815, no. 26022.
24 *PSZ*, vol. 21, 1783, no. 15683; *SIRIO*, 27:387.
25 *PSZ*, vol. 26, 1801, no. 19951.
26 *PSZ*, vol. 30, 1808, no. 23239; Katanaev, "Istoricheskii ocherk," 46–66.
27 *SVP*, 1838, Part I, annex, 40–1; *PSZ*, vol. 26, 1851, no. 25039.
28 "Arkhiv grafa Igel'stroma," 367–8; *PSZ*, vol. 26, 1801, no. 19951; vol. 28, 1804, no. 21426 and 21533. On how marriages (and divorces) took place between Cossacks and natives along the lines see Malikov, *Tsars, Cossacks, and Nomads*, 59–60.

29 Beskrovnyi, *Russkaia armiia i flot*, 321.
30 "Orenburgskoe kazachie voisko," in *VS*, 1874, 3, 101, 114–16; *PSZ*, vol. 27, 1803, no. 20786.
31 *PSZ*, vol. 15, 1840, no. 14041.
32 Stebelsky, "The Frontier in Central Asia," 155.
33 Kostenko, "Ural'skoe," 160–1.
34 *SVP*, 1838, Part 1, annex, 39. Further east were the Siberian and, beginning in 1851, the Transbaikal Cossacks. On these Cossacks see Malikov, *Tsars, Cossacks and Nomads*, 77–81; on their nativization, 106–13.
35 *PSZ*, vol. 26, 1801, no. 19951. This road would later become the famous Georgian Military Highway; see "Former and Present State" and "Rukovodstvo."
36 Dubrovin, "A.P. Ermolov," 222–4.
37 *PSZ*, vol. 9. 1834, no. 6917.
38 Dubrovin, "A.P. Ermolov," 189; *PSZ*, vol. 34, 1817, no. 26840; Korolenko, "Khopertsy," 219–20. An excellent description of the Terek Line is Chernozubov, "Ocherki."
39 *SVP*, 1838, Part 1, annex, 33–8.
40 Potto, *Kavkazskaia voina*, 2:77–8.
41 Beskrovnyi, *Russkoe voennoe iskusstvo*, 8–21.
42 Allen and Muratoff, *Caucasian Battlefields*, 20.
43 Beskrovnyi, *Russkoe voennoe iskusstvo*, 166–72; Dubrovin, "Poslednie dni," 2:195–222, 7:5–37.
44 *PSZ*, vol. 27, 1803, no. 20598; vol. 6, 1831, no. 4251; vol. 23, 1848, no. 22838.
45 *PSZ*, vol. 11, 1836, no. 9030; vol. 5, 1830, no. 4019–20; vol. 13, 1838, no. 11690.
46 Lang, *Last Years*, 258, 268–9; Dubrovin, "1802 god," 571, 583–4; *PSZ*, vol. 35, 1818, no. 27605; vol. 36, 1819, no. 27821; vol. 37, 1820, no. 28405.
47 Lang, *Last Years*, 193, 283–4. I have left out of this book the highlanders of the Caucasus. They can be placed only with difficulty into the framework.
48 Adeney, *Greek and Eastern Churches*, 344–8; Gvosdev, "Russian Empire," 407–17; *PSZ*, vol. 34, no. 26858; vol. 35, 1818, no. 27605; R-ov, "Feofilakt Rusanov," 623–9.
49 Adeney, *Greek and Eastern Churches*, 539–52; Werth, "Glava tserkvi," 100–10; *PSZ*, vol., 11, 1836, no. 8970.
50 Kabuzan, *Narody Rossii v pervoi polovine XIX v.*, 121–2, 125.
51 *PSZ*, vol. 26, 1800, no. 19599, 19600; vol. 9, 1834, no. 7560a; vol., 22, 1847, no. 21144; *Ocherki istorii Kalmytskoi ASSR*, 208–9; Komandzhaev, *Administrativnaia sistema*, 65–76. See also Steinwedel, *Threads of Empire*, 78–9, 82–8, for the role played by Military Governor Osip Igelstrom, but I think Steinwedel underestimated the importance of the voluntary aspect of the reform. It may have been imposed from above, but it also reflected the social ambitions of the Bashkir elite. He is certainly aware of the social consequences of the reform: see 103.
52 *PSZ*, vol. 31, 1811, no. 24583; *Ocherki istorii Kalmytskoi ASSR*, 248–55.
53 Kabuzan, *Narody Rossii v pervoi polovine XIX v.*, 121–2.

54 Reinsdorf, "Zapiska," 90–2.

55 *Istoriia Bashkortostana*, 288; *PSZ*, vol. 30, 1808–9, no. 23038, 23039, 23040; vol. 40, 1825, no. 30224. On the purchases of Kazakh children see Malikov, *Tsars, Cossacks, and Nomads*, 84–8.

56 *PSZ*, vol. 25, 1798, no. 18477; *Istoriia Bashkortostana*, 342–3, 347–8; *PSZ*, 1798, no. 18701. The standard general work of the administration of the Bashkirs after 1798 is Asfandiiarov, *Kantonnoe upravlenie*; for its creation and development until its abolition in 1863, see 16–49.

57 Gorban, "In the South."

58 LeDonne, *Russian Empire*, 135–6.

59 *PSZ*, vol. 26, 1801, no. 19773; vol. 30, 1808, no. 23164.

60 *PSZ*, vol. 38, 1822, no. 29127. The 1822 statute was one of the reasons for the Kazakh uprising of 1824–47. Sultan Kenesar Kasymov was a grandson of Khan Ablai; he wanted to restore the position of khan and proclaimed himself khan, made war on Kokand, formed an alliance with Bukhara, and demanded the removal of Cossack units from the steppe. The rebellion was crushed and Kasymov died, but fighting the Kirgiz: see Steblin-Kamenskaia, "K istorii," 235–8, 249–51. See also Malikov, *Tsars, Cossacks and Nomads*, 151–81.

61 Kabuzan, *Narody Rossii v pervoi polovine XIX v.*, 124–5, 127.

62 *Istoriia Bashkortostana*, 241–2; Forsyth, *History*, 168.

63 *PSZ*, vol. 23, 1790, no. 16829; *Istoriia Sibiri*, 2:296.

64 *PSZ*, vol. 38, 1822, 29126; Raeff, *Siberia*, 112–28.

65 *Istoriia Bashkortostana*, 180–1.

66 Veniakov, "Zabaikal'e," 217–18.

67 *Istoriia Buriatskoi ASSR*, 224; *Istoriia Yakutskoi ASSR*, 154; Forsyth, *History*, 164.

68 Fregat Pallada Goncharov, in *Sobranie sochinenii*, 6 vols. (Moscow, 1972), here 3:369. See also Sunderland, "Russians into Yakuts," 824–5. One is reminded of Dmitrii Likhachev's comment about "the capacity of Russian culture to be enriched by foreign cultures and by the transformation of one's own, previous culture"; see his *Reflections*, 165. Conversely, Malikov mentions the interaction between Russian and Kazakh cultures, but adds that "the Kazakh language became the lingua franca of the frontier" (*Tsars, Cossacks and Nomads*, 285).

69 Schorkowitz, "Orthodox Church," 203–8. It might be worthwhile to examine certain affinities between Buddhism and Orthodoxy: for example, the concentration in both religions on ritual and the necessity to withdraw from political activity. One might begin with Shomakhmadov, *Uchenie*, 40–58, which deals only with Buddhism. For Shamanism, see Basilov, "Chosen by the Spirits," 3–48.

70 LeDonne, *Absolutism*, 181–3.

71 Slovtsov, *Istoricheskoe obozrenie*, 245–6.

72 *PSZ*, vol. 7, 1727, no. 5015; LeDonne, *Absolutism*, 190–1.

73 LeDonne, *Ruling Russia*, 152–65.

74 *PSZ*, vol. 16, 1763, no. 11989; vol. 28, 1805, no. 21605.

75 See for example, *PSZ*, vol. 28, 1804, no. 21183.

76 *PSZ*, vol. 22, 1784, no. 15991; vol. 22, 1786, no. 16482; "Arkhiv grafa Igel'stroma," 354; vol. 25, 1799, no. 18897. For Mozdok see *PSZ*, vol. 23, 1792, no. 17025; vol. 27, 1802, no. 20511.

77 *PSZ*, vol. 17, 1765, no. 12307; vol. 27, 1802, no. 20240; vol. 29, 1806, no. 22311; vol. 2, 1827, no. 1247; Pogosian, *Sudebnik*, passim.

78 *PSZ*, vol. 38, 1822, no. 29125.

79 *PSZ*, vol. 38, 1822, no. 29127.

80 *PSZ*, vol. 38, 1822, no. 29126.

81 *AKAK*, 7:35–9; Shcherbatov, *General Fel'dmarshal*, 3, annex, 122–7.

82 *PSZ*, vol. 15, 1840, no. 13368.

83 He wanted the population of Transcaucasia to "blizhatsia s Rossieiu" (*AKAK*, 7:38).

84 *PSZ*, vol. 9, 1834, no. 6810.

85 *PSZ*, vol. 33, 1815, no. 26022, pt. 16–17.

86 *PSZ*, vol. 12, 1837, no. 10303, par. 239.

87 *PSZ*, vol. 7, 1832, no. 5636.

88 *PSZ*, vol. 19, 1844, no. 17649.

89 *PSZ*, vol. 7, 1832, no. 5201; vol. 9, 1834, no. 6852.

90 LeDonne, "Civilians."

91 *PSZ*, vol. 9, no. 7065; see also vol. 3, 1828, no. 1960 and vol. 6, 1831, no. 4775.

92 Khabutdinov, *Millet*, 30.

93 Ibid., 39–45, and especially, Hamamoto, "Tatarskaia Kargala."

94 *PSZ*, vol. 22, 1788, no. 16710; vol. 23, no. 1789, no. 16759, 1793, no. 17146; Frank, *Muslim Religious Institutions*, 102–4, 109–10; Islaev, *Islam i pravoslavie*, 198–212. See also Crews, *For Prophet*, 41–67. Crews ignores the influence of the Bukhara model in imperial policy in the region.

95 Khabutdinov, *Millet*, 26.

96 *PSZ*, vol. 31, 1811, no. 24819.

97 *PSZ*, vol. 23, 1790, no. 16897.

98 *PSZ*, vol. 23, 1793, no. 17099.

99 "Pravo musul'man," in *ES*, 24:896–9. The Russians attempted to codify the *adat* in order to make it a jurisprudence capable of rivalling the shari'a, but the attempt led nowhere because the authorities concluded that Islamic law was more civilized than customary law: see Kemper, "*Adat* against *Shari'a*," 149–54. For the *adat* among the Kazakhs see Martin, *Law and Custom*, 17–32. "*Adat* was not a set of abstract rules but a broad range of economic values and principles embedded within the culture of which it was a part" (ibid., 8). See also Kemper, *Herrschaft, Recht und Islam*, 317–66 and 401–3.

100 "Pravo musul'man," 898.

101 *PSZ*, vol. 11, 1740, no. 8236.

102 *PSZ*, vol. 28, 1805, no. 21634.

103 Rozhkova, "Iz istorii," 186–7; *PSZ*, vol. 27, 1803, no. 20687. Among the nomads, "land was not 'owned'; it was only loosely identified with the clan for as long as its members pastured there" (Martin, *Law and Custom*, 21).

104 *PSZ*, vol. 5, 1830, no. 3559.

105 *PSZ*, vol. 7, 1832, no. 5500.

106 *PSZ*, vol. 12, 1837, no. 10313.

107 *PSZ*, vol. 8, 1833, no. 6591.

108 This section is based on Riasanovsky, *Fundamental Principles*.

109 *PSZ*, vol. 12, 1745, no. 9110. See Komandzhaev, "Kalmytskoe pravo," 193–209.

110 *PSZ*, vol. 27, 1803, no. 21025.

111 *Istoriia Yakutskoi ASSR*, 92–3; *PSZ*, vol. 21, 1783, no. 15680.

112 *PSZ*, vol. 27, 1803, no. 20771.

113 *PSZ*, vol. 38. 1822, no. 29126, art. 122, 256–61.

114 Shcherbatov, *General-Fel'dmarshal*, vol. 3, annex, 144–52.

115 Gamba, *Voyage*, 2:425–6, 217–21, 226–31; Aksakov, *Pis'ma*, 127.

116 *Istoriia Bashkortostona*, 337–8; *AGS*, 2:83–6.

117 *Istoriia Bashkortostana*, 267–75.

118 *Istoriia Sibiri*, 2:209.

119 *PSZ*, vol. 21, 1783, no. 15867; vol. 22, 1786, no. 16312; vol. 27, 1803, no. 20771; vol. 28, 1805, no. 21590; vol. 30, 1808, no. 23097a; "Iz bumag Golovkina," 23–4.

120 *AGS*, 2:83–86; *Istoriia Sibiri*, 2:368; Ledyard, *Journey*, 163.

121 *PSZ*, vol. 32, 1813, no. 25519.

122 *Istoriia Buriatskoi ASSR*, 175; *Istoriia Sibiri*, 2:369; Ledyard, *Journey*, 163.

123 LeDonne, "Proconsular Ambitions," 31–60.

124 Portal, *L'Oural*, 345–9, 358, 373–6.

125 Lang, *Last Years*, 195–6, 259, 272; Gamba, *Voyage*, 2:257–8.

126 *Istoriia Sibiri*, 2:232–3, 385, 87; Blanchard, *Russia's*, 80, 127, 147.

127 Blanchard, *Russia's*, 129.

128 *Istoriia Sibiri*, 2:387. For the amount of silver smelted at Nerchinsk in the eighteenth century see "O vyplavke."

129 *Istoriia Sibiri*, 2:250–1; Komogortsev, "Iz istorii," 116–19.

130 *PSZ*, vol. 24, 1797, no. 17814; vol. 23, 1791, no. 16998; vol. 28, 1804, no. 21563; *Istoriia Buriatskoi ASSR*, 198; *Istoriia Sibiri*, 2:404; Kalashnikov, "Zapiski," 626–7.

131 Lemercier-Ouelquejay, "Routes commerciales," 1–7.

132 *PSZ*, vol. 13, 1752, no. 9929.

133 Ozeretskovsky, "Pis'ma," 57–8; *PSZ*, vol. 19, 1773, no. 14081.

134 Allen and Muratov, *Caucasian Battlefields*, 4–6. The trip from Astrakhan to Ghilan took thirty days (McCabe, *Shah's Silk*, 284–5).

135 A very useful tourist guide in the form of a detailed map is *Voenno-gruzinskaia doroga* (Tiflis, 1960).

136 The Caucasus formed "a nearly complete barrier to climatic and cultural exchange between north and south" (Lydolph, *Geography*, 190).

137 Slovtsov, *Istoricheskoe obozrenie*, 144–5, 207, 287–9.
138 Kerner, *Urge to the Sea*, 168–75.
139 *PSZ*, vol. 30, 1809, no. 23996.
140 Radishchev, “Pis’mo,” 2:14–15, 20.
141 “Materialy dlia istorii Sibiri,” 11–12; Slovtsov, *Istoricheskoe obozrenie*, 377.
142 Ledyard, *Journey*, 127.
143 Slovtsov, *Istoricheskoe obozrenie*, 187–9.
144 *PSZ*, vol. 38. no. 29130
145 Kerner, *Urge to the Sea*, 172–75; Slovtsov, *Istoricheskoe obozrenie*, 377–8.
146 Kerner, *Urge to the Sea*, 175.
147 *Mezhdunarodnye otnosheniia*, 2:211–13, 242.
148 Bezprozvannykh, *Priamur’e*, 202.
149 Gamrekeli, *Torgovye sviazi*, 1:74, 106–9, 2:45–7.
150 Lang, *Last Years*, 272; Rozhkova, “Is istorii,” 171–5.
151 Dubrovin, “Pokhod,” 2:219. no. 2.
152 LeDonne, “Proconsular Ambitions,” 41.
153 *AGS*, 2:686–716.
154 Abrahamian, “Oriental Despotism,” 14–15.
155 Semenov, *Izuchenie*, chast’ 3, 450–7.
156 Rozhkova, “Iz istorii,” 175–9, 181–3, 188.
157 Kiniapina et al., *Kavkaz*, 211.
158 Semenov, *Izuchenie*, chast’ 3, 458–65.
159 “O rasprostranenii torga,” 57–64.
160 *AGS*, 2:643–52, 659–62, 709–11.
161 “Proekt o usilenii,” 400–3.
162 Kiniapina et al., *Kavkaz*, 228.
163 Radishchev, “Pis’mo,” 1:19.
164 *AGS*, 2:734–6.
165 Sladkovskii, *Istoriia*, 205–7.
166 Semenov, *Izuchenie*, chast’ 3, 466–71; Gal’perin, “Russko-kitaiskaia torgovlia,” 223–4.
167 Semenov, *Izuchenie*, chast’ 3, 499.

Conclusion to Part III: The Eastern Theatre

1 Vadim Trepavlov is quite right in saying that the policy of Muscovy and the Russian Empire was “the gradual integration of the annexed peoples and regions into the general state structure (“Kalmyki,” 69).
2 Steinwedel, *Threads of Empire*, 109–11.
3 LeDonne, *Russian Empire*, 135, 311, 350, 210. I do not share Mark Bassin’s pessimistic view that the annexation of the Amur region shattered the dream of a Californian El Dorado. Some well-placed Russians feared at the time (unjustifiably)

the the Amur would become a Russian Mississippi bringing liberal ideas into the expanding core, already threatened by the dangers from revolutionary Europe. It was true that the Amur valley was unbearably cold and inhospitable, that the valuable sable had become nearly extinct, that few Russians would want to move there, and that most of the valuable land was in the valley of the Sungari, across the river in Manchuria. But without the incorporation of the Amur, Russia would have remained a nearly land-locked country save for the almost inaccessible Kamchatka peninsula and its vulnerable port at Petropavlosk. Russia would be without Vladivostok, which gave her some pretence to be a Pacific power. But many years later, in our own time, Yakutia has revealed its abundant mineral wealth and northern Siberia its enormous reserves of oil and natural gas, which would otherwise be exported across Chinese or Japanese territory. Bassin is very critical of Muravev-Amurskii, but he was a man with a vision which "was not destroyed by a better acquaintance with reality," as Nicholas Risanovsky puts it in his introduction to Bassin's article, but which a much later reality would justify with a vengeance.

Conclusion

1 Matthew Romaniello writes (using the word "empire" to which we have become accustomed) that "the Russian Empire was a joint long-term project of the tsar, the Russian Orthodox Church, and the state's administration. It was an ongoing quest for hegemonic control," with "Orthodoxy the public face of an empire built upon Mongol roots" (Romaniello, *Elusive Empire*, 11, 13, 27).
2 George Bournoutian puts it very well: "Nicholas [I]'s administrators were divided into two broad groups, sometimes called regionalist and *centralist*. While both advocated Russian rule, the regionalists were more sensitive to local traditions and hoped for a gradual transformation, while the centralists wanted a speedy Russification of all borderlands" (*History*, 112).
3 Michael Confino, *Systèmes agraires et progrès agricole* (Paris, 1969), 360.

Bibliography

General Works

Allen, W.E.D. "The Caucasian Borderland." *Geographical Journal* 99–100 (1942): 225–37.

Amburger, E. *Geschichte der Behördenorganisation Russlands von Peter dem Grossen bis 1917* (Leiden, 1966).

Bater, J., and R. French, eds. *Studies in Russian and Historical Geography*. 2 vols. (London, 1983).

Baynes, N. *The Hellenistic Tradition and East Rome* (Oxford, 1946).

Beik, W. *Absolutism and Society in Seventeenth-Century France* (Cambridge, 1985).

Berg, L. *Natural Regions of the USSR* (New York, 1950).

Beskrovnyi, L. *Russkaia armiia i flot v 18 veke* (Moscow, 1958).

– *Russkoe voennoe iskusstvo 19 veka* (Moscow, 1974).

Bogdanovich, M. *Istoriia tsarstvovaniia Imperatora Aleksandra I i Rossii v ego vremia*, 6 vols. (Petersburg, 1869–71).

Burbank, J., ed. "Empire and Transformation: The Politics of Difference." In Uyama Tomohiko, *Comparing Modern Empires: Imperial Rule and Decolonization in the Changing World Order* (Hokkaido, 2018).

– "Imperial Rights Regime: Law and Citizenship in the Russian Empire." *Kritika* 7 (2006): 397–431.

Burbank, J., and F. Cooper. *Empires in World History: Power and the Politics of Difference* (Princeton, 2010).

Burbank, J., Mark von Hagen, and A. Remnev, eds. *Russian Empire: Space, People, Power, 1700–1930* (Bloomington, 2007).

Burke, P. *History and Social Theory*, 2nd ed. (Cambridge, 2005).

Bushkovitch, P. *Peter the Great: The Struggle for Power, 1671–1725* (Cambridge, MA, 2001).

Carlyle, R., and A. Carlyle. *A History of Medieval Political Theory in the West*. 6 vols. (London, 1962).

Chamoux, F. *Hellenistic Civilization* (London, 2003).

Composition de l'armée russe, 1819. Ministere des Affaires étrangèrs, Archives diplomatiques, Paris, vol. 27. Russie 1819–1827. Forces et colonies militaires, fol. 1–37.

Coxe, W. *Travels into Poland, Russia, Sweden and Denmark*. 5 vols. (London, 1792).

Cracraft, J. *The Church Reform of Peter the Great* (London, 1971)

Danilevskii, H. *Rossiia i Evropa* (Moscow, 1869).

Doyle, M. *Empires* (Ithaca, 1986).

Durkheim, E. *The Elementary Forms of Religious Life* (London, 1976).

Duverger. M., ed. *Le Concept d'Empire* (Paris, 1980).

Eberhard, W. *Conquerors and Rulers: Social Forces in Medieval China* (Leiden, 1965).

Florinsky, M. *Russia: A History and an Interpretation* (New York, 1953).

France, J. *The Crusades and the Expansion of Catholic Christendom, 1000–1714* (London, 2005).

Gilpin, R. *The Political Economy of International Relations* (Princeton, 1987).

Goehrke, C. *Russland: Eine Strukturgeschichte* (Paderborn, 2010).

Got'e, Yu. *Istoriia blastnogo upravleniia v Rossii ot Petra I do Ekateriny II*, vol. 1 (Moscow, 1913).

Gubernii Rossiiskoi Imperii. Istoriia i rukovoditeli 1708–1917 (Moscow, 2003).

Heckscher, E. *An Economic History of Sweden* (Cambridge, 1954).

- *Mercantilism*. 2 vols. (London, 1935).

The Historical Atlas of Poland (Warsaw, 1986).

Howe, S. *Empire: A Very Short Introduction* (Oxford, 2002).

Imperial Russian Foreign Policy, ed. H. Ragsdale (Cambridge, MA, 1993)

Imperiology: From Empirical Knowledge to Discussing the Russian Empire, ed. K. Matsuzato (Sapporo, 2007).

Istoricheskii obzor deiatel'nosti Komiteta ministrov, ed. S. Seredonin. 5 vols. in 8 (Petersburg, 1902–3).

Jones, A. *The Later Roman Empire 284–302*. 2 vols. (Baltimore, 1986).

Kabuzan, V. *Izmeneniia v razmeshchenii naseleniia Rossii v XVIII–pervoi polovine XIX v.* (Moscow, 1971).

- *Narody Rossii v XVIII veke. Chislennost' i etnicheskii sostav* (Moscow, 1990).

- *Narody Rossii v pervoi polovine XIX v. Chislennost' i etnicheskii sostav* (Moscow, 1992).

Kabuzan, V., and S. Troitskii. "Izmeneniia v chislennost, udel'nom vese i razmeshchenii dvorianstva v Rossii v 1782–1858 gg." *Istoriia SSSR* 4 (1971): 153–69.

Kappeler, A. "Formirovanie Rossiiskoi imperii v XV–nachale XVIII veka: nasledstvo Rusi, Vizantii i Ordy." In *Russiiskaia imperiia*, 94–112.

- *The Russian Empire: A Multi-Ethnic History* (London, 2001).

- *Russland als Vielvölkerreich-Entstehung. Geschichte-Zerfall* (Munich, 1993).

Khodarskovsky, M. "From Frontier to Empire: The Concept of Frontier in Russia, Sixteenth–Eighteenth Centuries." *Russian History* 19 (1992): 115–28.

Kindleberger, Ch. *The World in Depression 1929–1939*. Revised ed. (Berkeley, 1986).

Kirilov, I. *Tsvetushchee sostoianie vserossiiskogo gosudarstva* (Moscow, 1977).

Kirpichenok, A. *Serbskie poseleniia na Ukraine v seredine XVIII veka* (Petersburg, 2007).
Kivelson, V. *Cartographies of Tsardom: The Land and Its Meanings in Seventeenth-Century Russia* (Ithaca, 2006).
Kivelson, V., and R. Suny. *Russia's Empires* (New York, 2017).
Kollmann, N. *Crime and Punishment in Early Modern Russia* (Cambridge, 2012).
– *Kinship and Politics: The Making of the Muscovite Political System 1345–1457* (Stanford, 1987).
– *The Russian Empire 1450–1801* (Oxford, 2017).
Korkut, U. "Resentment and Reorganization: Anti-Western Discourse and the Making of Eurasianism in Hungary." *Acta Slavica Iaponica* 38 (2017): 71–90.
Laruelle, M. *L'idéologie eurasiste russe ou comment penser l'empire* (Paris, 1999).
LeDonne, J. *Absolutism and Ruling Class* (New York/Oxford, 1991).
– "Administrative Regionalization in the Russian Empire, 1802–1826." *CMR* 43 (2002): 5–34.
– "Civilians under Military Justice during the Reign of Nicholas I." *CASS* 7 (1973): 171–87.
– "The Evolution of the Governor's Office 1727–1764." *CASS* 12 (1978): 86–115.
– *The Formation of the Russian Political Order 1700–1825* (New York/Oxford, 1991).
– "Frontier Governors General 1772–1825." *JGO* 47 (1999): 56–88; 48 (2000): 161–83, 321–40.
– *The Grand Strategy of the Russian Empire 1650–1831* (Oxford, 2003).
– "Indirect Taxes in Catherine's Russia." *JGO* 23 (1975): 161–90; 24 (1976): 173–207.
– "Regionalism and Constitutional Reform, 1819–1826." *CMR* 43/4 (2003): 5–34.
– "Ruling Families in the Russian Political Order, 1689–1825." *CMR* (1987): 233–322.
– *Ruling Russia: Politics and Administration in the Age of Absolutism 1762–1796* (Princeton, 1984).
– *The Russian Empire and the World 1700–1917: The Geopolitics of Expansion and Containment* (Oxford, 1997).
– "Russian Governors General 1775–1825: Territorial or Functional Administration." *CMR* 42 (2001): 5–30.
– "The Territorial Reform of the Russian Empire, 1775–1796." *CHRS* 23 (1982):147–85; 24 (1983): 411–57.
Leonhard, J., and U. von Hirschhausen. *Empires und Nationalstaaten im 19. Jahrhundert* (Göttingen, 2009).
Likhachev, D. *Reflections on Russia* (Boulder, 1991).
Lodyzhenskii, K. *Istoriia russkogo tamozhennogo tarifa* (Petersburg, 1886).
Lydolph, P. *Geography of the USSR*. 2nd ed. (New York, 1970).
Mirov, N. *Geography of Russia* (New York, 1951).
Mackinder, H. *Democratic Ideals and Reality* (New York, 1919).
– "The Geographical Pivot of History." *Geographic Journal* 23 (1904): 421–44.
– "The Round World and the Winning of the Peace." *Foreign Affairs* 21 (1943): 595–605.

Mączak, A. "Confessions, Freedoms, and the Unity of Poland-Lithuania." In R. Evans and T. Thomas, eds., *Crown, Church and Estates* (New York, 1991).
Obolensky, D. *The Byzantine Commonwealth* (New York, 1971).
O'Brien, C.B. *Muscovy and the Ukraine: From the Pereiaslavl Agreement to the Truce of Andrusovo, 1654–1667* (Berkeley and Los Angeles, 1963).
Perrie, M. "Uspenskii and Zhivov on Tsar, God, and Pretenders." *Kritika* 15 (2014): 133–49.
Raczka, W. "A Sea or a Lake? The Caspian's Long Odyssey." *CAS* 19 (2000): 189–221.
Reconstruction and Interaction of Slavic Eurasia and Its Neighboring Worlds, ed. O. Ieda and T. Uyama (Sapporo, 2006).
Rossiiskaia imperiia v sraynitel'noi perspective. Sbornik statei (Moscow, 2004).
Roussel, P. *La Grèce et 1'Orient des guerres médiques à la conquête romaine* (Paris, 1928).
Semenov, A. *Izuchenie istoricheskikh svedenii o Rossiiskoi vneshnei torgovle i promyshlennosti s poloviny XVIIgo stoletiia po 1858 goda*. 2 vols. (Petersburg, 1859).
Solov'ev, S. *Istoriia Rossii s drevneishikh vremen*. 15 vols. (Moscow, 1959–66).
Squire, P. *The Third Department: The Establishment and Practices of the Political Police in the Russia of Nicholas I* (Cambridge, 1968).
Stoletie voennago ministerstva 1802–1902, ed. D. Skalom, 13 vols. (Petersburg, 1902).
Svedeniia o piteinykh sborakh v Rossii, chasti 1–5 (Petersburg, 1960–1).
Szamuely, T. *The Russian Tradition* (New York, 1974).
Trubetskoy, N. *The Legacy of Genghis Khan and Other Essays on Russian Identity* (Ann Arbor, 1991)
Vernadsky, G. *Kievan Russia* (New Haven, 1948).
– *The Mongols and Russia* (New Haven, 1953).
– *Russia at the Dawn of the Modern Age* (New Haven, 1959).
– *The Tsardom of Muscovy 1547–1682*. 2 vols. (New Haven, 1969).
Viollet-le-Duc, E. *L'art russe. Ses origines, ses éléments constitutifs, son apogée, son avenir* (Paris, 1877).
"Voennoe znachenie vodnykh putei Evropeiskoi Rossii." *VS* 9 (1905): 127–46; 10: 137–50; 11: 161–78; 12: 131–56.
Werth, P. "Imperiology and Religion: Some Thought on a Research Agenda." In *Imperiology*, 61–7.
Wortman, R. "The 'Integrity' (tselost') of the State in Imperial Russian Representation." *Ab Imperio* 2 (2011): 1–25.
– *Russian Monarchy: Representation and Rule* (Brighton, MA, 2013).
– *Scenarios of Power: Myth and Ceremony in Russian Monarchy*. 2 vols. (Princeton, 1995).

The Western Theatre

Abov, G. "Finliandiia v russkom gosudarstvennom prave." *Zhurnal Yuridicheskogo Obshchestva* 4 (1898): 58–72.

Alimova, T. "Russkaia krest'anskaia pomorskaia torgovlia s Severnoi Norvegiei." *SS* 22 (1977): 45–53.

Andersson, I. *A History of Sweden* (London, 1955).

Anisimov, M. "Rossiia i Shvetsiia v seredine XVIII veka: ot konfrontatsii k soiuzu." *OI* 6 (2004): 3–17.

Anushkin, V. "Alandskaia ekspeditsiia 1808 goda." *VS* 5 (1908): 19–42; 6: 27–52.

Bagger, H. "The Role of the Baltic in Russian Foreign Policy, 1721–1773." In *Imperial Russian Foreign Policy*, 36–72.

Baginski, H. *Poland and the Baltic: The Problem of Poland's Access to the Sea* (London, 1942).

Baltische Kirchengeschichte, ed. R. Wittram (Göttingen, 1956).

Barkhatsev, S. "Iz istorii Vilenskogo uchebnogo okruga." *RA* 1 (1874): 1149–1262.

Baron, S. *The Russian Jew under Tsar and Soviets* (New York, 1964).

Bartlett, R. "Russia's First Abolitionist: The Political Philosophy of J.G. Eisen." *JGO* 39 (1991): 161–76.

Batiushkov, P. *Belorussia i Litva* (Petersburg, 1890).

"Besedy imp. Ekateriny II s Dalem, 1772–1777." *RS* 3 (1876): 1–20.

Bienemann, F. *Die Statthalterschaft in Liv- und Estland, 1783–1796* (Leipzig, 1886).

Bil'basov, V. "Prisoedinenie Kurliandii." *RS* 8 (1895): 231–44.

Bobovich, I. "Sostoianie sel'skogo khoziaistva 'staroi Finliandii' v kontse XVIII–nachale XIX v." *SS* 27 (1977): 31–43.

Bogatyrev, S., ed. *Russia Takes Shape: Patterns of Integration from the Middle Ages to the Present* (Helsinki, 2005).

Bolotov. *Zhizn' i prikliucheniia Andreia Bolotova* (Moscow, 1986).

Boockmann, H. *Der Deutsche Orden. Zwölf Kapitel aus seiner Geschichte*. 4th ed. (Munich, 1994).

The Borders of Lithuania: The History of a Millennium (Baltos Lankos, 2010).

Boudou, A. *Le Saint Siège et la Russie: Leurs relations diplomatiques au XIXe siècle*. 2 vols. (Paris, 1922).

Braun, O. *The Diary of Otto Braun* (New York, 1924).

Bruggemann, K. "Imperiale und lokale Loyalitäten im Konflikt: Der Einzug Russlands in die Ostseeprovinzen in den 1840er Jahren" *JGO* 62 (2014): 321–44.

"Bumagi otnosiashchiesia k offitsial'noi i chastnoi perepiske grafa Arakcheeva." *SIM* (1876): 225–32, 389–405.

Bundas. "Morskie sily I narodnoe kholiaistvo Rossii pri Petre Velikom." *MS* 11 (1918): 3–43.

Butterwick, R. *The Polish Revolution and the Catholic Church, 1788–1792: A Political History* (Oxford, 2012).

Buxhoeveden, H. "Ein General und eine Mystekerin." *BH* 15 (1967): 144–74.

The Cambridge History of Poland. 2 vols. (Cambridge, 1950).

Camena d'Almeida, P. *Etats de la Baltique. Russie* (Paris, 1932).

Campe, P. "Otto Hermann v. Vietinghoff, gen. Scheel, Marienburg – der sogenannte 'Halbkönig v. Livland, 1772–1792." *BH* 6 (1960): 82–110.

Chebod'ko, Ya. "Iz vospominanii ob unii v Bielorussii v nachale XIX veka." *RA* 12 (1903): 537–44.

Cheshikhin, E. "Kak poniali v Baltiiskikh guberniiakh ukaz ob otmene pytok." *RA* 3 (1887): 449–52.

Christiansen, E. *The Northern Crusades: The Baltic and Catholic Frontier 1100–1525* (London, 1980).

Ch-v. "Speranskii i Bagul'ianskii. Uchastie ikh v sostavlenii svoda uzakonenii dlia pribaltiiskikh gubernii." *RS* 3 (1882): 41–58.

Chydenius, W. "The Swedish Lawbook of 1734: An Early Germanic Codification." *Law Quarterly Review* 20 (1904): 377–91.

Cippola, C. *Before the Industrial Revolution: European Society and Economy 1000–1700.* 2nd ed. (London, 1980).

Cynarski, St. "The Shape of Sarmatian Ideology in Poland." *APH* 19 (1968): 5–17.

Czartoryski, A. "Mémoire (1813)." *Arkhiv grafov Mordvinovykh* 9 (1903): 608–26.

– *Mémoires du Prince Adam Czartoryski et correspondence avec l'Empereur Alexandre Ier*. 2 vols. (Paris, 1887).

Dawisha, K. *Eastern Europe, Gorbachev, and Reform: The Great Challenge* (Cambridge, 1990).

Derzhavin, G. "Mnenie ob otvrashchenii V Bielorussii goloda i ustroistve byta Evreev. 1800." *Sobranie Derzhavina* 7 (1872): 229–305.

Diubiuk, E. "Krestianskoe dvizhenie v Lifliandii vo vtoroi polovine XVIII veka." *IZ* 13 (1942): 175–206.

Divov. "Dnevnik P.G. Divova." *RS* 2 (1897): 457–94; 4 (1898): 617–32.

Dobrynin. "Istinnoe povestvovanie ili zhizn' G.I. Dobrynina, im samim pisannaia (1752–1827)." *RS* 1 (1871): 119–60, 247–71, 395–420, 562–604, 651–72; 2: 1–38, 97–153, 177–222, 305–78.

Dokhturov. "Pis'ma D.S. Dokhturova k ego supruge 1805–1814." *RA* 1: 1090–1131.

Dolbilov, M. "Russian Nationalism in the Nineteenth Century Policy of Russification in the Russian Empire's Western Region." In *Imperiology*, 141–58.

– "The Stereotype of the Poles in Imperial Policy." *Russian Studies in History* 44 (2005): 45–90.

Dolbilov, M., and A. Miller, eds. *Zapadnye okrainy Rossiiskoi imperii* (Moscow, 2006).

Dolbilov, M., and D. Staliunas. *Obratnaia Uniia: iz istorii otnoshenii mezhdu katolitsizmom i pravoslaviem v Rossiiskoi imperii 1840–1873* (Vilnius, 2010).

Dolgorukov. "Kniaz' Nikolai Andreevich Dolgorukov." *Chteniia* 1 (1864): 167–97.

Dollinger, Ph. *La Hanse (XII–XVII siècles)* (Paris, 1964).

Donnert, E. *Agrarfrage und Aufklärung in Lettland und Estland* (Frankfurt am Main, 2008).

"Dvizhenie Latyshei i Estov v Livonii s 1841 goda." *Chteniia* 3 (1865): 109–43.

Eckardt, J. *Livland im Achtzehnten Jahrhundert* (Leipzig, 1876).

– "Der Livlandische Landtag in seiner historischen Entwicklung." *BM* 3 (1861): 38–78, 116–59.

Elenev, F. "Uchenie o Finlandskom gosudarstve." *RS* 3 (1893): 255–322, 455–89.

Evans, R., and T. Thomas, eds. *Crown, Church and Estate: Central European Politics in the Sixteenth and Seventeenth Centuries* (New York, 1991).

"Extrakt aus einer Deduction Wegen des Landstaates von Livland." *HNM* 2 (1781): 204–10.

Fahlbeck, P. *Der Adel Schwedens (und Finlands)* (Jena, 1903).

Fahlcrantz, G. "The Naemd or the Remnant of the Jury in Sweden." *American Law Review* 22 (1888): 837–52.

Feldbaek, O. "Denmark and the Treaty of Kiel 1814." *SJH* 15 (1990): 259–68.

Finland and Its Geography, ed. R. Platt (New York, 1955).

Flynn, J. *The University Reform of Tsar Alexander I 1802–1835* (Washington, 1988).

Forgotten Pages in Baltic History: Diversity and Inclusion, ed. M. Housden and D. Smith (New York, 2011).

Forstreuter, K. *Die Memel als Handelsstrasse Preussens nach Osten* (Konigsberg, 1931).

– *Memelland* (Elbing, 1939).

France, J. *The Crusades and the Expansion of Catholic Christendom 1000–1714* (Abingdon, 2005).

Frost, R. *After the Deluge: Poland-Lithuania and the Second Northern War 1655–1660* (Cambridge, 1993).

Galaktionov, I., and E.A.L Chistiakova. *Ordin-Nashchokin. Russkii diplomat XVII v.* (Moscow, 1961).

Ganzenmüller, J. *Russische Staatsgewalt und polnischer Adel. Elitenintegration and Staatsausbau im Westen des Zarenreiches 1772–1850* (Cologne, 2013).

Garner, G. *Etat, économie, territoire en Allemagne. L'espace dans le caméralisme et l'économie politique 1740–1820* (Paris, 2005).

Gerhard, D., ed. *Ständische Vertretungen in Europa im 17. und 18. Jahrhundert* (Göttingen, 1969).

Gessen, Yu. "Evrei v Kurliandii XVI–XVIII v." *Evreiskaia Starina* 6 (1914): 145–62, 365–84.

Ginsburg, M. "From a Family Archive, 1824–34: Aleksandr Mukhanov's Tour of Duty in Finland." *Scando-Slavica* 7 (1961): 5–19.

Golovachev, P. "Znachenie Andrussovskogo peremiriia dlia mezhdunarodnykh otnoshenii vostochnoi Evropy." *RS* 3 (1903): 159–66.

Gorizontov, L. *Paradoksy imperskoi politiki: Poliaki v Rossii i russkie v Pol'she XIX–nachalo XX v.'* (Moscow, 1999).

Gostautas, S. "The Early History of the University of Vilnius: A Crossroads between East and West." In *Universities*, 1–10.

Gradovskii, A. "Istoricheskii ocherk uchrezhdeniia general-gubernatorstva v Rossii." In *Sobranie sochinenii*, 9 vols. (Petersburg, 1899–1904), 1: 299–338.

– "Vysshaia administratsiia Rossii XVIII st. i general prokurory." In *Sobranie sochinenii*, 9 vols. (Petersburg, 1899–1904), 1: 37–297.

Grinwasser, H. "Le Code Napoléon dans le duché de Varsovie." *Revue des Etudes Napoléonienes* 2 (1917): 129–70.

Halecki, O. "L'évolution historique de l'Union polono-lituanienne." *Le Monde slave* 5 (1926): 279–93.

Hatton, R. *Charles XII of Sweden* (London, 1968).

Hill, Ch. *The Danish Sound Dues and the Command of the Baltic* (Durham, NC, 1926).

A History of Finland's Literature, ed. G. Schoolfield (Lincoln, NE, 1998).

Hoensch, J. "Der Streit um den polnischen Generalzoll 1764–66." *JGO* 18 (1970): 355–88.

Holmberg, A. "On the Practicability of Scandinavianism; Mid-Nineteenth Century Debate and Aspirations." *SJH* 9 (1984): 171–82.

Hube, P. "Rossiia i Shvetsiia pered voinoi 1808–1809 gg." *VS* 2 (1908): l–22.

Ibneyeva, G. "The Journey of Catherine II to the Baltic Lands in 1764." In Bogatyrev, *Russia*, 128–41.

Igelstrom. "Erinnerungen des Grafen Alexander Archibald Igelstrom." *BH* 16 (1970): 6–148.

"Imperator Aleksandr I i graf Armfel'd, 1811–1812 gg." *RS* 3 (1896): 127–52.

"Iskustvennye dorogi v Pol'she." *ZhMVD* 2 (1835): 434–7.

"Izvestie o chisle korablei pribyvshikh v gorod Rigu s 1669 po 1820–i god i o vremeni vskrytiia reki Dviny." *OZ* 11 (1822): 142–4.

Jutikkala, E. *Geschichte Finnlands* (Stuttgart, 1964).

Kagan, F. *The Military Reforms of Nicholas I: The Origins of the Modern Russian Army* (London, 1999).

Kampengausen. "Perepiska barona B.B. Kampengauzena s grafom Arakcheevym." *SIM* 7 (1895): 266–88.

Kent, N. *A Concise History of Sweden* (Cambridge, 2008).

Kersten, A. "Les magnats. Elite de la société nobiliaire." *APH* 36 (1977): 119–23.

Khanevich, V. "Nekotorye epizody iz vremeni vossoedineniia Uniatov v kontse proshlogo veka." *RS* 2 (1894): 97–135.

Kienewicz, S. *The Emancipation of the Polish Peasantry* (Chicago, 1969).

Kirby, D. *The Baltic World 1772–1993: Europe's Northern Periphery in an Age of Change* (London, 1995).

– *A Concise History of Finland* (Cambridge, 2006).

– *Northern Europe in the Early Modern Period: The Baltic World 1492–1772* (London, 1990).

Klier, J. *Russia Gathers Her Jews: The Origins of the "Jewish Question" in Russia, 1772–1825* (DeKalb, IL, 1986).

Koliupanov, N. "Administrativnoe i sudebnoe ustroistvo Tsarstva Pol'skogo ot Konstitutsii 1815 goda do reformy 1864 goda." *YuV* 10 (1890): 175–91, 11: 335–58.

Kolzakov. "Vospominaniia Kolzakova 1815–31." *RS* 1 (1873): 423–55, 587–615.

Konttinen, E. "Central Bureaucracy and the Restriction of Education in Early Nineteenth-Century Finland." *SJH* 21 (1996): 201–20.

Kotilaine, J. "Opening a Window on Europe: Foreign Trade and Military Conquest on Russia's Western Border in the 17th Century." *JGO* 46 (1998): 495–530.

Kovalchuk, S. "Der baltische Generalgouverneur Furst Aleksandr Suvorov und die Verfolgung der Altgläubigen in Riga." In *Russland an der Ostsee*, 191–214.
Kowecki, J. "Les transformations de la structure sociale en Pologne au XVIII siècle: la noblesse et la bourgeoisie." *APH* 26 (1972): 5–30.
"Kratkoe obozrenie upravleniia Lifliandieu i osobykh prav sei gubernii." *ZhMVD* 9 (1835): 41–64.
Kropotov, D. *Zhizn' grafa M.N. Murav'eva, v sviazi s sobytiiami ego vremeni* (Petersburg, 1874).
Kula, W. *An Economic Theory of the Feudal System: Towards a Model of the Polish Economy 1500–1800* (London, 1986).
Kurland und seine Ritterschaft (Pfaffenhofen/Ilm, 1971).
Kutrzeba, S. *Grundriss des polnischen Verfassungsgeschichte* (Berlin, 1912).
Kyrylo-Mefodiïvs'ke tovarystvo, ed. P.S. Sokhan' et al. 3 vols. (Kiev, 1990).
Lehtonen, U. *Die polnischen Provinzen Russlands unter Katharina II. in den Jahren 1772–1782* (Berlin, 1907).
Lencyk, W. *The Eastern Catholic Church and Czar Nicholas I* (Rome/New York, 1966).
"Lennye i emfiteutichnye imeniia." *AGS* 3 (1878): 561–73.
Lepesh, O. *Komitet zapadnykh gubernii: organizatsiia i deyatel'nost 1831–48 gg.* (Minsk, 2016).
Lescoeur, L. *L'Eglise catholique en Pologne sous le gouvernement russe* (Paris, 1860).
Leslie, R. *Polish Politics and the Revolution of November 1830* (Westport, CT, 1969).
Lesnodorski, B. "La Pologne et l'Europe au tournant des XVIIIe et XIXe siècles." *APH* 22 (1970): 52–72.
Levine, H. *Economic Origins of Antisemitism: Poland and Its Jews in the Early Modern Period* (New Haven, 1991).
Lialikov, F. "Revel, 1822–25." *RA* 2 (1878): 240–52.
Lilja, S. "Swedish Urbanization c 1570–1800: Chronology, Structure and Causes." *SJH* 19 (1994): 277–308.
Lindroth, S. *A History of Uppsala University 1477–1977* (Stockholm, 1977).
Lord, R. "The Third Partition of Poland." *Slavonic Review* 3 (1925): 481–98.
Lukowski, J. *Liberty's Folly: The Polish-Lithuanian Commonwealth in the Eighteenth Century, 1697–1795* (London, 1991).
– *The Partitions of Poland 1772, 1793, 1795* (London, 1999).
Lukowski, J., and H. Zawadzki. *A Concise History of Poland*. 2nd ed. (Cambridge, 2006).
Luntinen, P. *The Imperial Russian Army and Navy in Finland 1808–1918* (Helsinki, 1997).
Maczak, A. "Confessions, Freedoms, and the Unity of Poland-Lithuania." In Evans and Thomas, *Crown, Church, and Estates*, 269–86.
Maczak, A., and N. Samsonowicz. "La zone Baltique, un des éléments du marche européen." *APH* 11 (1965): 71–99.
Maikop, P. "Tsarstvo Pol'skoe posle Venskogo Kongressa." *RS* 4 (1902): 183–94; 1 (1903): 419–36: 3: 5–20; 4 (1904): 618–40; 1 (1905): 154–69.

"Manuel-guide de Réval et des environs 1833." *ZhMVD* 3 (1834): 388–404.

"Markiz Pauluchchi v pogon za tainymi obshchestvami v Ostzeiskikh guberniakh." *RS* 3 (1897): 5–32.

Martens. *Recueil des traités et conventions conclues par la Russie avec les puissances étrangères*. 15 vols. (Petersburg, 1874–1905).

Mattiesen, H. "Gebiet und Grenzen des Herzogtüms Kurland 1569–1795." *JGO* 5 (1957): 198–205.

Mediger, W. "Russland und die Ostsee im 18. Jahrhundert." *JGO* 16 (1968): 85–103.

Mezhdu dvukh vosstanii. *Korolevstvo Pol'skoe i Rossiia v 30-soe gody XIXv.*, ed. Fal'kovich (Moscow, 2016).

Mikhailovitch, Nicolas, ed. *Les relations diplomatiques de la Russie et de la France d'après les rapports des ambassadeurs d'Alexandre et de Napoléon 1808–1812*. 7 vols. (Petersburg, 1905).

Milosz, C. *The History of Polish Literature*. 2nd ed. (Berkeley, 1983).

Mirkovich. "Iz zapisok F. Ya. Mirkovicha." *RA* 3 (1890): 395–434.

Morley, Ch. "Alexander I and Czartoryski: The Polish Question from 1801 to 1813." *SEER* 25 (1946–7): 405–26.

Moroshkin, M. *Iezuity v Rossii s tsarstvovaniia Ekateriny II do nashego vremeni*. 2 vols. (Petersburg, 1867–70).

Murav'ev. "Chetyre politicheskie zapiski grafa M.N. Murav'eva-Vilenskogo." *RA* 2 (1885): 161–201.

– "Dve zapiski grafa M.N. Murav'eva." *RA* 2 (1902): 585–95.

Murphy, C. "Burghers versus Bureaucrats: Enlightened Centralism, the Royal Towns, and the Case of the Propinacja in Poland-Lithuania, 1776–1793." *SR* 71 (2012): 385–409.

"Na Kovnu ili na Rigu?" *VE* 12 (1866): 25–30.

Nalkowski, W. *Poland as a Geographical Entity* (London, 1917).

"Narodonaselenie Tsarstva Pol'skogo." *ZhMVD* 1 (1835): 180–2.

Neseman, F. "A Special Baltic-German Understanding about Finland's Autonomy in the Russian Empire? Count Fabian Steinheil as the Governor General of the Grand Duchy of Finland 1810–1823." In *Forgotten Pages*, 9–33.

"Neue Einrichtungen in Lif- und Ehstland vom Jahre 1783." *HNM* 8 (1784): 193–231.

Newbury, C. *Patrons, Clients, and Empire* (New York, 2003).

Nol'de, A. *Ocherki po istorii kodifikatsii mestnykh grazhdanskikh zakonov pro grafe Speranskom*. 2 vols. (Petersburg, 1906–14).

Nolte, H., ed. *Internal Peripheries in European History* (Göttingen, 1991).

Nordmann, C. *Grandeur et liberté de la Suède 1660–1792* (Paris, 1971).

Nosov, B. "Kurliandskoe gertsogstvo i Rossiisko-pol'skie otnosheniia v 60-e gody XVIII veka: k predistorii razdelov Rechi pospolitoi." *Slavianovedenie* 5 (1993): 54–66.

"Novosil'tsev o konstitutsii Tsarstva Pol'skogo." *RS* 1 (1905): 599–605.

"Novye svedeniia o chislennosti i obitalishchakh Litovskogo plemeni." *ZhMVD* chast' 34 (1851): 99–116.

Nowak, Andrzej. "Bor'ba za okrainy, bor'ba za vyzhyvanie: Rossiiskaia imperiia XIX v. I poliaki." In *Zapadnye okrainy Rossiiskoi imperii* (Moscow, 2006).
"Ob uchrezhdenii rimsko-katolicheskoi dukhovnoi Akademii v Vilne." *ZhMVD* 3 (1834): 365–74.
Obolenskii, D. "Nabroski iz proshlogo." *IV* 4 (1893): 349–74, 659–90.
"Obozrenie sostoianiia gorodov Velikogo Kniazhestva Finliandskogo v 1833 godu." *ZhMVD* 5 (1835): 220–5.
Obushenkova, L. *Korolevskoe Pol'skoe v 1815–1830 gg. Ekonomicheskoe i sotsial'noe razvitie* (Moscow, 1979).
Oliva, L. *Misalliance: A Study of French Policy in Russia during the Seven Years' War* (New York, 1964).
Opalinski, E. "Great Poland's Power Elite under Sigismund III 1587–1632: Defining the Elite." *APH* 42 (1980): 41–66.
"Opisanie gorodov Botnicheskogo zaliva v morskom otnoshenii." *MS* 9 (1857): 49–61.
Ordin, K. *Pokorenie Finliandii*. 2 vols. (Petersburg, 1889).
Orfield, L. *The Growth of Scandinavian Law* (Philadelphia, 1953).
P.-, V. "Istoricheskie siluety" *IV* 2 (1891): 389–409, 659–81.
Paul, M. "Secular Power and the Archbishop of Novgorod before the Muscovite Conquest." *Kritika* 8 (2007): 231–70.
Pavulan, V. "Politika Shvedskoi administratsii v Vidzeme XVIII v. v otnoshenii putei soobshchenii, tranzita, i dorozhnogo khoziaistva." *SS* 16 (1971): 48–59.
Perovskii, L. "O neobkhodimosti vesti vo vsekh guberniiakh i oblastiakh imperii russkie organicheskie zakony." *Chteniia* 3 (1865): 173–85.
"Petitsiia Pribaltiiskogo dvorianstva Imperatritse Ekaterine II na imia Pribaltiiskogo General-Gubernatora." *RA* 2 (1915): 449–54.
Pienkos, A. *The Imperfect Autocrat: Grand Duke Constantine Pavlovich and the Polish Congress Kingdom* (Boulder, CO, 1987).
Piirimiae, Kh. "Rol' Tartuskogo universiteta v istorii kul'tury XVII–nachala XVIII veka." *SS* 28 (1983): 69–83.
"Pis'ma imp. Ekateriny II k T.I. Tutolminu." *RA* 2 (1873): 2273–2317.
"Pis'ma k Mikhailu Nikitichu Krechetnikovu grafa Z.G. Chernysheva i drugikh 1769–85." *Chteniia* 4 (1863): 1–63.
Plakans, A. *A Concise History of the Baltic States* (Cambridge, 2011).
– *The Latvians: A Short History* (Stanford, 1995).
Pokhilevich, D. "Perevod gosudarstvennykh krest'ian Litvy i Bielorussii v seredine XVIII v. s denezhnoi renty na otrabotochnuiu." *IZ* 39 (1952): 121–58.
Pol'sha i Rossia v pervoi tertii XIX veka. Iz istoriia avtonomnogo Korolevtsva Pol'skogo 1815–1830, ed. Fal'kovich (Moscow, 2010).
Popov, A. *Posledniaia sud'ba Papskoi politiki v Rossii 1845–67* (Petersburg, 1868).
Pospiech, A., and W. Tygielski. "The Social Role of Magnates' Courts in Poland." *APH* 43 (1981): 75–100.
Pradt, M. de. *Histoire de l'ambassade dans le grand duché de Varsovie en 1812* (Paris, 1816).

Pravilova, E. "From the Złoty to the Ruble: The Kingdom of Poland in the Monetary Politics of the Russian Empire." In Burbank et al. *Russian Empire*, 295–319.
Przhetslavskii, O. "Kaleidoscop vospominanii 1811–71." *RA* 2 (1872): 1705–69, 1887–1954, 2269–2334.
– "Kniaz' Ksaverii Drutskoi-Liubetskii 1772–1846." *RS* 1 (1878): 625–48, 2: 67–92.
Radwan, M. *Carat wobec Kosciola grecokatolickiego w zaborze rosyjskim 1796–1839* (Lublin, 2004).
Raeff, M. *The Well-Ordered Police State: Social and Institutional Change through Law in the Germanies and Russia, 1600–1800* (New Haven, 1983).
Rauch, G. "Reflexe des abendländischen Geisteslebens an der schwedischen Universität Dorpat." In *Universities*, 11–18.
– "Zur baltischen Frage im 18. Jahrhundert." *JGO* 5 (1957): 441–87.
Raun, T. *Estonia and the Estonians* (Stanford, 1987).
Reinke, N. "Ocherk zakonodatel'stva Tsarstva Pol'skogo (1807–1881g.)." *ZhMYu* 8 (1901): 1–65; 9: 1–43.
Remdul, Y. "Nemetskie sudy v pribaltiiskom krae nakanune ikh uprazdneniia." *Yuridicheskii Vestnik* 10 (1887): 193–213; 11: 395–431.
Roberts, M. *The Swedish Imperial Experience 1560–1718* (Cambridge, 1979).
Roginskii, V. "Russia and the Treaty of Kiel 1814." *SJH* 15 (1990): 279–89.
Roos, H. "Ständewesen und parlamentarische Verfassung in Polen 1505–1772." In Gerhard, *Ständische Vertretungen*, 310–67.
Rossiiskaia imperiia: strategii stabilizatsii i opyty obnovleniia, ed. M. Karpacheva, M. Dolbilov, and A. Mimakov (Voronezh, 2004).
Rozen, A. *Zapiski Dekabrista* (Irkutsk, 1984).
Russland an der Ostsee, ed. K. Bruggermann and B. Woodworth (Vienna/Cologne, 2012).
Samarin, Yu. "Pravoslavnye latyshi 1841–1842 gody." *RA* (1969): 1224–1361.
Savicki, S. "An Historical Conspectus of the Sources of Byelorussian Law." *Journal of Byelorussian Studies* 1 (1966): 110–20, 221–31.
Scheibert, P. "Die Anfänge der finnischen Staatswerdung unter Alexander I." *JGO* 3/4 (1939): 351–430.
– *Volk und Staat in Finland in der ersten Hälfte des vorigen Jahrhundert* (Breslau, 1941).
Scott, F. *Sweden: The Nation's History* (Carbondale, IL, 1988).
"Severo-zapadnyi krai imperii v prezhnem i nastoiashchem vide." *ZhMVD* 1 (1843): 207–41, 382–449.
Shcherbatov, A. *General-Fel'dmarshal Kniaz' Paskevych. Ego zhizn' i deyatel'nost.* 7 vols. (Petersburg, 1888–1904).
Shil'der, N. "Imperator Nikolai I i Pol'sha 1825–31." *RS* 1 (1900): 277–306.
Shipov, S. "Rossiia i Pol'sha, sviaz ikh i vzaimnye otnosheniia." *Chteniia* 1 (1860): 51–60.
Sipovich, C. "The Diocese of Minsk, Its Origin, Extent and Hierarchy." *Journal of Byelorussian Studies* 2 (1969): 177–91.

Skalon, V. "Upravlenie i sudoustroistvo v Finliandii." *ES* 35: 933–40.
Skowronek, J. *Adam Jerzy Czartoryski 1770–1861* (Warsaw, 1994).
"Sostav gorodov v guberniiakh ostzeiskikh." *ZhMVD* 3 (1843): 383–428.
"Sostav i ustroistvo zemskoi politsii v guberniiakh ostzeiskikh." *ZhMVD* 4 (1843): 209–42.
"Spravka po delu o prisoedinenii k pravoslaviiu krest'ian pribaltiiskikh gubernii." *Chteniia* 3 (1865): 144–72.
Stael von Holstein, R. "Die Kodifizierung des baltischen Provinzialrechts." *BM* 52 (1901): 185–208, 249–80, 305–58.
– "Zur Geschichte des Kirchengesetz vom Jahr 1832." *BM* 52 (1901): 127–76.
Staliunas, D. "Problema administrativno-territorial'nykh granits v natsionalnoi politike' imperskoi vlasti. Kovenskaia guberniia v seredine XIX veka." In *Rossiiskaia imperiia*, 147–66.
Stanislawski, M. *Tsar Nicholas I and the Jews: The Transformation of Jewish Society in Russia, 1824–1855* (Philadelphia, 1983).
"Starostinskie imeniia." *AGS* 3 (1878): 574–604.
Stone, D. "Jews and the Urban Question in Late Eighteenth Century Poland." *SR* 50 (1991): 531–41.
La Suède et la Russie 1809–18 (Stockholm, 1985).
"Svedeniia o gorode Libave, Libavskom porte i torgovle onogo." *ZhMVD* 1 (1831): 129–36.
Szyndler, B. *Mikolai Nowosilcow 1762–1828* (Warsaw, 2004).
Thaden, E. *Russia's Western Borderlands 1710–1870* (Princeton, 1984).
Topolski, J. "The Problem of Internal Economic Peripheries in Poland in Early Modern Times." In Nolte, ed., *Internal Peripheries*, 205–17.
– "La régréssion économique en Pologne du XVIe au XVIIe siècle." *APH* 7 (1962): 28–49.
Troshchinskii. "Zapiska D.P. Troshchinskogo o ministerstvakh." *SIRIO* 3 (1868): 1–162.
Ukhtomskii, L. "Saimanskii kanal i ozero Saima." *MS* 7 (1862): 92–108.
The Universities in Dorpat/Tarku, Riga and Wilna/Vilnius 1579–1979, ed. G. von Pistohlkors, T. Raun, and P. Kaegbein (Cologne/Vienna, 1987).
"Uprazdnenie greko-uniatskikh monastyrei v Zapadnoi Rossii (1828)." 2nd ed. *RS* 1 (1870): 517–38.
Upton, A. *Charles XI and Swedish Absolutism* (Cambridge, 1998).
"Ursprungliche Einrichtung des Lieflandischen Ober-Konsistoriums." *HNM* 5/6 (1782): 328–32.
Uspenskij, B., and V. Zhivov. *"Tsar and God" and Other Essays in Russian Cultural Semiotics* (Boston, 2012).
Uspenskii, B. *Tsar i imperator. Pomazanie na tsarstvo i semantika monarshikh titulov* (Moscow, 2000).
Vasar, J. *Die grosse Livlandische Güter-Reduktion* (Tartu/Dorpat, 1931).
Vernadsky, G. *La charte constitutionnelle de l'Empire russe de l'an 1820* (Paris, 1933).
Veselov, A. "Pribaltiiskie nemtsy (istoriko-iuridicheskii ocherk)" *IV* 2 (1915): 200–11.

"Vospomimanie o Mitropolitakh R.K. tserkvei v Rossii: Stanislav Sestrentsevich Bogush i Gaspar Koliumne Tsetsishovskom." *ZhMVD* 1 (1835): 149–63; 2: 394–404.

V-n, F. "Zimniaia ekspeditsiia 1809 goda cherez Kvarken." *VS* 7 (1900): 1–26; 8: 271–89.

Walicki, A. *Poland between East and West: The Controversies over Self-Definition and Modernization in Partitioned Poland* (Cambridge, MA, 1994).

Wandycz, P. *The Lands of Partitioned Poland 1795–1918* (Seattle, 1974).

Wasilewski, L. *Die Ostprovinzen des alten Polenreichs* (Krakau, 1916).

Weibull, J. "The Treaty of Kiel and Its Political and Military Background." *SJH* 15 (1990): 291–301.

Weinryb, B. *The Jews of Poland: A Social and Economic History of the Jewish Community in Poland from 1100 to 1800* (Philadelphia, 1972).

Werth, P. *The Tsar's Foreign Faiths: Toleration and the Fate of Religious Freedom in Imperial Russia* (Oxford, 2014).

Whelan, H. *Adapting to Modernity: Family, Caste, and Capitalism among the Baltic German Nobility* (Cologne, 1999).

Whittaker, C. *The Origins of Modern Russian Education: An Intellectual Biography of Count Sergei Uvarov, 1786–1855* (DeKalb, IL, 1984).

Wimarski, B. *Les institutions politiques en Pologne au XIXe siècle* (Paris, 1924).

Wojcik, Z. "The Separatist Tendencies in the Grand Duchy of Lithuania in the 17th Century." *APH* 69 (1994): 55–62.

Woods, E. *The Baltic Region: A Study in Physical and Human Geography* (London, 1932).

Wrangell, W. *Die Estlandische Ritterschaft, ihre Ritterschaftshauptmänner und Landräte* (Limburg/Lahn, 1967).

Zapadnye okrainy rossiiskoi imperii, ed. M. Dolbilov and A. Miller (Moscow, 2006).

Zavileiskii, M. "Statistika Tsarstva Pol'skogo." *ZhMVD* (1842): 53–327.

Zhibitskaia, E. *Finliandiia. Ekonomiko-geograficheskaia kharakteristika* (Moscow, 1962).

Zhukovich, P. "Shkol'noe delo v Zapadnoi Rossii v tsarstvovanie Ekateriny II." *ZhMVD* (Dec. 1915): 296–344.

– "Soslovnyi sostav naseleniia Zapadnoi Rossii v tsarstvovanie Ekateriny II." *ZhMVD* (Jan. 1915): 76–109; (Feb.): 257–321.

– "Upravlenie i sud v Zapadnoi Rossii v tsarstvovanie Ekateriny II." *ZhMVD* (Jan.–Feb. 1914): 265–315; (March–April): 88–120, 314–55; (May–June): 1–60; (July): 1–43.

– "Zapadnaia Rossiia v tsarstvovanie imperatora Pavla." *ZhMVD* (May–June 1916):,183–276; (July–August): 207–63; (Sept.–Oct.): 186–275.

Zimmermann, M. *Etats scandinaves. Régions polaires et boréales* (Paris, 1933).

"Zur livländischen Landtagsgeschichte des 18. Jahrhunderts." *BM* 18 (1869): 247–89, 428–74; 19 (1870): 84–99, 146–54.

Zutis, Ya. *Ostzeiskii vopros v XVIII veke* (Riga, 1946).

– *Politika tsarizma v Pribaltike v pervoi polovine XVIII V.* (Moscow, 1937).

The Southern Theatre

Aksakov, I. "Ukrainskie iarmarki." *Russkaia Beseda* 2 (1858): 87–158.

Auerbach, N. *Die Besiedlung der Südukraine in den Jahren 1774–1787* (Wiesbaden, 1965).

Bagalei, D. "Magdeburgskoe pravo v Levoberezhnoi Malorossii." *ZhMVD* 1 (1892): 1–55.

– *Ocherki iz istorii kolonizatsii stepnoi okrainy Moskovskogo gosudarstva* (Moscow, 1887).

Baranovich, A. *Magnatskoe khoziaistvo na iuge Volyni v XVII v.* (Moscow, 1955).

Basarab, J. *Pereiaslav 1654: A Historical Study* (Edmonton, 1982).

Beauvois, D. *Histoire de la Pologne* (Paris, 1995).

– *Le noble, le serf et le revizor. La noblesse polonaise entre le tsarisme et les masses ukrainiennes (1831–1863)* (Paris, 1985).

– *Pouvoir russe et noblesse polonaise en Ukraine 1793–1830* (Paris, 2003).

Bestuzhev-Riumin. "Mnenie ego siiatel'stva grafa Alekseeya Petrovich Bestuzheva-Riumina o klassakh Malorossiiskikh chinov." *Arkhiv kn. Vorontsova* 35 (1882): 340–9.

Bobrovskii, P. "Suvorov na Kubani v 1788 godu i za Kubaniu v 1783." *VS* 4 (1900): 3–44.

Boeck, B. *Imperial Boundaries, Cossack Communities and Empire-Building in the Age of Peter the Great* (Cambridge, 2009).

Bogucka, M. *The Lost World of the "Sarmatians"* (Warsaw, 1996).

Chynczewska-Hennel, T. "The Political, Social and National Thought of the Ukrainian Higher Clergy, 1569–1700." *HUS* 26 (2002–3): 97–152.

Chyzhevs'kyj, D. *A History of Ukrainian Literature* (Littleton, CO, 1975).

Cresson, W. *The Cossacks: Their History and Country* (New York, 1919).

Culture, Nation and Identity: The Ukrainian-Russian Encounters (1600–1945), ed. A. Kappeler et al. (Edmonton/Toronto, 2003).

Davies, B. *Warfare, State and Society on the Black Sea Steppe, 1500–1700* (London, 2007).

Delimars'kyi, R. *Magdeburhz'ke pravo u Kyievi* (Kiev, 1996).

Dembkowski, H. *The Union of Lublin: Polish Federalism in the Golden Age* (Boulder, CO, 1982).

Druzhinina, E. *Kiuchuk-Kainardzhiiskii mir 1774 goda* (Moscow, 1955).

– *Severnoe Prichernomor'e v 1775–1800 gg.* (Moscow, 1989).

– *Yuzhnaia Ukraina v period krizisa feodalizma, 1825–1860gg.* (Moscow, 1981).

Dubrovin, N. "Russkaia zhizn' v nachale XIX veka." *RS* 1 (1904): 249–52.

Dukes, P. *Catherine the Great and the Russian Nobility* (Cambridge, 1967).

"Etnografiia Bessarabskoi oblasti." *ZOOID* 5 (1863): 491–536.

Evarnitskii, D. "Glavneishie momenty iz istorii Zaporozhskogo kozachestva." *Russkaia Mysl'* 1 (1897): 99–115.

"Evrei-karaimy." *ZhMVD* 1 (1843): 263–84.

Fedoriw, G. *History of the Church in Ukraine* (St Catharines, ON, 1984).
Fisher, A. *The Crimean Tatars* (Stanford, 1978).
– "Enlightened Despotism and Islam under Catherine II." *SR* 27 (1968): 542–53.
– *The Russian Annexation of the Crimea 1772–1783* (Cambridge, 1970).
Frontiers in Question: Eurasian Borderlands, 700–1700, ed. D. Power and N. Standen (London, 1999).
Gierowski, J. *The Polish-Lithuanian Commonwealth in the XVIIIth Century: From Anarchy to Well-Organized State* (Krakow, 1996).
Golobutskii, V. *Chernomorskoe kazachestvo* (Kiev, 1956).
– *Zaporozhskoe kazachestvo* (Kiev, 1957).
Gordeev, A. *Istoriia kazakov*. 4 vols. (Petersburg, 1992).
Grankin, Yu., and A. Zemlianskii. *Severnyi Kavkaz i ego kolonizatsiia Rossiei v 30–90 gody XVIII veka* (Piatigorsk, 2006).
Halecki, O. *Borderlands of Western Civilization: A History of East Central Europe* (New York, 1952).
Herlihy, P. *Odessa: A History 1794–1914* (Cambridge, MA, 1986).
Honcharuk, T. *Odes'ke porto-franko. Istoriia 1819–1859 gg.* (Odessa, 2005).
Hrushevsky, M. *A History of Ukraine* (New Haven, 1941).
"Istoricheskaia spravka ob obrazovanii v Tavricheskoi gubernii Tatarskikh dvorianskikh rodov." *ZOOID* 23 (1901): 41–3.
Jenkins, I. *Social Order and the Limits of the Law* (Princeton, 1980).
The Jews of Old Poland 1000–1795, ed. A. Polonsky, J. Basista, and A. Link-Lenczowski (London, 1993).
Jones, R. "Ukrainian Grain and the Russian Market in the Late Eighteenth and Early Nineteenth Centuries." In Koropeckyj, ed., *Ukrainian History*, 210–27.
Karasaev, A. "Otaman Stepan Danilovich Efremov 1753–1772 gg." *IV* 3 (1902): 870–83.
Kefeli, V., and E. Lebedeva. *Karaimy-drevnii narod Kryma* (Simferopol, 2003).
Kharlamovich, K. *Malorossiiskoe vlianie na Velikorusskuiu tserkovnuiu zhizn'* (Kazan, 1914).
Khoroshkin, M. "Voenno-istoricheskii ocherk kazach'ikh voisk." *VS* 5 (1881): 86–119; 6: 309–24.
"The Kiev Mohyla Academy: Commemorating the 350th Anniversary of Its Founding (1632)." *HUS* 8 (1984): 1–2.
Kirpichenok, A. *Serbskie poseleniia na Ukraine v seredine XVIII veka* (Petersburg, 2007).
Kohut, Z. "Myths Old and New: The Haidamak Movement and the Koliivshchina (1768) in Recent Historiography." *HUS* 1 (1977): 359–78.
– *Russian Centralism and Ukrainian Autonomy: Imperial Absorption of the Hetmanate 1760s–1830s* (Cambridge, MA, 1988).
Kokiev, G. "Kabardino. Osetinskie otnosheniia v XVII v." *IZ* 2 (1932): 153–208.
Korolenko, M. "Khopertsy." *VS* 1 (1896): 205–26.
Koropeckyj, I., ed. *Ukrainian Economic History: Interpretative Essays* (Cambridge, MA, 1991).

Krasnov, N. "Proshedshee i nastoiashchee Donskikh kazakov." *VS* 10 (1882): 293–316; 11: 107–27.
Kudriavtsev, L. *Institut gubernatorstva Ukrainy* (Kiev, 2008).
Kvachevskii, A. "Litovskii Statut, kak istochnik mestnogo prava dlia gubernii Cherni govskoi i Poltavskoi." *ZhGUP* 4 (1876): 222–55.
Lazarevskii, A. "Ocherk Malorossiiskikh familii. Materialy dlia istorii obshchestva v XVII–XVIII vekakh." *RA* 1 (1875): 9–97, 311–25, 439–52; 2: 248–64; 3: 297–308; 3 (1876): 437–55, 402–9.
LeDonne, J. "Geopolitics, Logistics, and Grain: Russia's Ambitions in the Black Sea Basin, 1737–1834." *IHR* 28 (2006): 1–41.
Litwin, N. "Catholicization among the Ruthenian Nobility and Assimilation Processes in the Ukraine During the Years 1569–1648." *APH* 55 (1987): 57–83.
Luckyj, G. *Between Gogol and Ševčenko* (Munich, 1971).
Magocsi, P. *Historical Atlas of East Central Europe* (Seattle, 1993).
– *A History of Ukraine* (Toronto, 1996).
– *Ukraine: A Historical Atlas* (Toronto, 1985).
Maikop, P. "Gertsog Rishel'e v Rossii." *RS* 3 (1897): 33–49.
March, G. *Cossacks of the Brotherhood: The Zaporog Kosh of the Dnieper River* (New York, 1990).
Markevich, M. *Istoriia Malorosii* (Kiev, 2003).
Markina, V. *Magnatnoe pomest'e pravoberezhnoi Ukrainy vtoroi poliviny XVIII v.* (Kiev, 1961).
Matuz, J. "Les relations étrangères du khanat de Crimée XVe–XVIIIe siècles." *RHP* 100 (1988): 233–49
McNeill, W. *Europe's Steppe Frontier 1500–1800* (Chicago, 1964).
Melnyk, L. "Industrial Development and the Expansion of Free Labor in the Ukraine during the First Half of the Nineteenth Century." In Koropeckyj, ed., *Ukrainian Economic History*, 246–60.
Miakotin, V. *Ocherki sotsial'noi istorii Ukrainy v XVII–XVIII v.* 3 vols. (Prague, 1924–6).
Minkina, O. *"Syny Rakhili": Evreiskie deputaty v Rossiiskoi imperii 1772–1825* (Moscow, 2011).
Moon, D. "The Inventory Reform and Peasant Unrest in Right-Bank Ukraine in 1847–48." *SEER* 79 (2001): 653–97.
Murzakevich, N. "Yakub-aga (Yakov) Rudzevich." *ZOOID* 13 (1883): 255–9.
"Mysli o torgovle Chernogo moria." *OZ* 10 (1822): 301–32; 11: 214–33, 355–65.
Nadolska, V. "Volyn within the Russian Empire: Migratory Processes and Cultural Interaction." In *Imperiology*, 85–110.
Nakko, A. "Ocherk grazhdanskogo upravleniia v Bessarabii, Moldavii i Valakhii vo vremia russko-turetskoi voiny 1808–1812 goda." *ZOOID* 11 (1879): 269–310.
Nelepin, R. *Istoriia kazachestva.* 2 vols. (Petersburg, 1995).
"Novorossiiskie stepi." *ZhMVD* 1 (1843): 5–73.

Obolenskii, D. "Nabroski iz proshlogo." *IV* 4 (1893): 349–74, 659–90.
Obreskov. "Reliatsiia nadvornogo sovietnika i rezidenta Obrazkova iz Pery Konstantinopol'skoi ot 26-go Yuniia 1754 g." *AKV* 25 (1882): 183–99.
Okinshevich, L. *Ukrainian Society and Government 1648–1781* (Munich, 1978).
O'Neill, K. *Claiming Crimea: A History of Catherine the Great's Southern Empire* (New Haven, 2017).
"O trudakh Diuka Rishel'e po chasti upravleniia v poludennoi Rossii." *ZOOID* 10 (1877): 391–406.
"Otryvok povestvovaniia o Novorossiiskom krae (1751–86)." *ZOOID* 3 (1853): 79–129
Panin. "Iz bumag gr. Nikity Ivanovicha Panina." *RA* 3 (1878): 426–82.
"Pis'ma grafa V.P, Kochubeia k M.N. Speranskomu 1823–1825 gg." *RS* 4 (1902): 301–22.
"Pis'ma imp. Ekateriny II k T.I. Tutolminu." *RA* 2 (1873): 2273–2317.
"Pis'mo puteshestvennika, byvshago v Odesse v 1804 godu." *ZOOID* 21 (1898): 3–7.
Plokhy, S. *The Cossack Myth: History and Nationhood in the Age of Empires* (Cambridge, 2001)
– *The Cossacks and Religion in Early Modern Ukraine* (Oxford, 2001).
– *The Origins of Slavic Nations: Premodern Identities in Russia, Ukraine, and Belarus* (Cambridge, 2006).
– *Ukraine and Russia: Representations of the Past* (Toronto, 2008).
Plokhy, S., ed. *Poltava 1709: The Battle and the Myth* (Cambridge, MA, 2012).
Polons'ka-Vasylenko, N. "Iz istorii iuzhnoi Ukrainy v XVIII V. Zaselenie Novorossiiskoi gubernii (1764–75)." *IZ* 13 (1942): 130–74.
– *The Settlement of the Southern Ukraine 1750–1775* (New York, 1955).
"Polozhenie Chernigovskoi gubernii gubernskogo i povietovykh marshalov o ustanovlenii aktsiza ili poshliny." *Chteniia* 2 (1864): 73–82.
"The Ports of Taganrog and Kertch in the Sea of Azov." *AJ* 17 (1824): 365–9.
Potocki, J. *Voyages au Caucase et en Chine*. 2 vols. (Paris, 1980).
"Prava sostoianiia raznykh klassov narodonaseleniia Bessarabskoi oblasti." *ZhMVD* 3 (1843): 48–64.
"Predely kochev'ia Kubantsev s Rossiiskimi vladeniami v 1789 godu." *ZOOID* 3 (1853): 589–90.
Puzyrevskii, A. *Pol'sko-russkaia voina 1831 goda* (Petersburg, 1886).
Reychman, J. "Le commerce polonaise en Mer Noire au XVIIIe siècle par le port de Kherson." *CMRS* 7 (1966): 234–48.
Roslavtseva, L. *Krymskie Tatary* (Moscow, 2008).
Rosman, M. *The Lord's Jews: Magnate-Jewish Relations in the Polish-Lithuanian Commonwealth during the Eighteenth Century* (Cambridge, MA, 1990).
Rozhkova, M. "K voprosu o znachenii iarmarok vo vnutrennei torgovle doreformennoi Rossii pervaia polovina XIX v." *IZ* 54 (1955): 298–314.
Samoilov, A. "Zhizn' i deianiia general-fel'dmarshala kn. G.K. Potemkina." *RA*, 1867, cols. 575–606, 993–1027, 1203–62, 1537–78.
Seaton, A. *The Horsemen of the Steppes: The Story of the Cossacks* (London, 1985).

Shandra, V. *Administratyvni ustanovy pravoberezhnoi Ukrainy kintsia XVIII–pochatku XX st. v rosiis'komu zakonodavstvi: Dzhreloznavchyi analitychnyi ohliad* (Kiev, 1998).

– *Malorossiis'ke general-gubernatorstvo 1802–1856* (Kiev, 2001).

Shotwell, J., and F. Deak. *Turkey at the Straits: A Short History* (New York, 1940).

Shtrandman. "Zapiski Gustava fon Shtrandmana, 1742–1803." *RS* 2 (1882): 289–318

Skal'kovskii, A. "Yarmarki, ili sukhoputnye rynki Novorossiiskogo kraia." *ZhMVD* 11 (1855): 77–154.

Skinner, B. *The Western Front of the Eastern Church* (DeKalb, IL, 2009).

Smolii, V. *Vozz'ednannia pravoberezhnoi Ukraini z Rosieiu* (Kiev, 1978).

"Sostav i znachenie inventarei v pomeshchiikh imeniiakh oblastei vozvrashchennykh ot Pol'shi." *ZhMVD* 1 (1843): 242–62.

Subtelny, O. *The Mazepists: Ukrainian Separatism in the Early Eighteenth Century* (Boulder, CO, 1981).

– *Ukraine: A History* (Toronto, 1988).

Svatikov, S. *Rossiia i Don 1549–1917* (Vienna, 1924).

Tairova-Yakovleva, T. *Ivan Mazepa i rossiiskaia imperiia. Istoriia "predatel'stva"* (Moscow, 2011).

Tavrov, N. "Vostochny bereg Chernogo moria i ego znachenie dlia razvitiia russkogo moreplavaniia." *MS* 9 (1862): 3–62; 10: 253–78.

Terent'eva, N. *Greki v Ukraine* (Kiev, 1999).

Tkach, A. *Istoriia kodifikatsii dorevoliutsionnogo prava Ukrainy* (Kiev, 1968).

Tolstoi. "Ivan Andreevich Tolstoi. Pis'ma k nemu Petra Valikogo." *RS* 2 (1879): 135–50, 249–52.

Vermenych, Ya. *Administratyvn-terytorial'nii ustrii Ukrainy*. 2 vols. (Kiev, 2009).

Vinskii, G. *Moe vremia. Zapiski* (Petersburg, 1914).

"Visit to Odessa." *AJ* 7 (1832): 279–80.

Vodarskii, Ya., O. Eliseeva, and V. Kabuzan. *Naselenie Kryma v kontse XVII–kontse XX vekov* (Moscow, 2002).

"Vzgliad na istoriiu torgovli Chernogo i Azovskogo morei." *ZhMVD* 11 (1835): 337–64.

Walicki, A. *Poland between East and West* (Cambridge, MA, 1994).

Waresquiel, E. *Le Duc de Richelieu 1766–1822* (Paris, 1990).

Weeks, Th. "Between Rome and Tsargrad: The Uniate Church in Imperial Russia." In *Of Religion and Empire*, 70–91.

Zagorovskii, V. *Belgorodskaia cherta* (Voronezh, 1969).

Zagorovskii, -. "Vzaimootnosheniia Zaporozh'ia i russkoi pravitel'stvennoi vlasti vo vremia Novoi Sichi." *ZOOID* 31 (1913): 54–74.

"Zapiska gospodam deputatam, izbrannym ot dvorian Malorossiskoi gubernii." *Chteniia* 1 (1865): 193–99.

Zhivov, V. "The Question of Ecclesiastical Jurisdiction in Russian-Ukrainian Relations (Seventeenth and Early Eighteenth Centuries." In *Culture, Nation, and Identity*, 1–18.

Zoltowski, A. *Border of Europe: A Study of the Polish Eastern Provinces* (London, 1950).

The Eastern Theatre

Abrahamian, E. "Oriental Despotism: The Case of Qajar Iran." *International Journal of Middle Eastern Studies* 5 (1974): 3–31.

Abramov, N. "Materialy, dlia istorii Khoistianskogo prosveshcheniia Sibiri so vremeni pokorenii v 1581 goda do nachala XIX stoletiia." *ZhMNP* 81 (1854): 15–56.

"An Account of the Buriats." *AJ* 18 (1824): 588–90.

Adeney, W. *The Greek and Eastern Churches* (Clifton, NJ, 1965).

Aksakov, I. *Pis'ma k rodnym 1844–1849* (Moscow, 1988).

Allen, W. "The Caucasian Borderland." *Geographical Journal* 99–100 (1942): 225–37.

Allen, W., and P. Muratoff. *Caucasian Battlefields: A History of the Wars on Turco-Caucasian Border 1828–1921* (Cambridge, 1953).

Anan'ev, D. *Voevodskoe upravlenie Sibirii v XVIII veke* (Novosibirsk, 2005).

"Arkhiv grafa Igel'stroma." *RA* 3 (1886): 341–71, 480–97.

Asfandiiarov, A. *Bashkirskie tarkhany* (Ufa, 2006).

– *Kantonnoe upravlenie v Bashkirii 1798–1865gg.* (Ufa, 2005).

Asiatic Russia: Imperial Power in Regional and International Context, ed. T. Uyama (London, 2012).

Baddeley, J. *The Russian Conquest of Caucasus* (London, 1908).

Badian, Ernst. *Foreign Clientelae 265–70 B.C.* (Oxford, 1958).

Balzer, M. *Shamanic Worlds: Rituals and Lore of Siberia and Central Asia* (New York, 1997).

Bantysh-Kamenskii, N. *Diplomaticheskoe sobranie del mezhdu Rossiiskim i Kitaiskim gosudarstvami s 1619 po 1792 god* (Kazan, 1882).

Baranov, P. *Opis' Vysochaishim ukazam i poveleniiam, khranashchimsia v St.- Peterburgskom Senatskom Arkhive za XVIII vek.* 3 vols.(Petersburg, 1872–8).

Barfield, T. *The Perilous Frontier: Nomadic Empires and China* (Oxford, 1989).

Basilov, V. "Chosen by the Spirits." In Balzer, *Shamanic Worlds*, 3–48.

Baskakov, N. *Russkie familii Tiurkskogo proiskhozhdeniia* (Moscow, 1979).

Bassin, M. "Expansion and Colonialism on the Eastern Frontier: Views of Siberia and the Far East in Pre-Petrine Russia." *Journal of Historical Geography* 14 (1988): 3–21.

Besprozvannykh, E. *Priamur'e v sisteme russko-kitaiskikh otnoshenii XVII–seredine XIXv.* (Khabarovsk, 1986).

Blanchard, I. *Russia's "Age of Silver": Precious Metals Production and Economic Growth in the Eighteenth Century* (London, 1989).

Bodger, A. "Abulkhair, Khan of the Kazakh Little Horde, and His Oath of Allegiance to Russia in October 1731." *SEER* 58 (1980): 40–57.

Bogoslovskii, G. *Kratkii istoricheskii obzor Kazanskoi eparkhii* (Kazan, 1892).

Bournoutian, G. *A History of the Armenian People.* 2 vols. (Costa Mesa, CA, 1994).

Bowden, C. *The Modern History of Mongolia* (London, 1968).

"Bumagi Ivana Borisovicha Pestelia." *RA* 1 (1875): 369–423.

Burbank, J., and F. Cooper. *Empires in World History: Power and the Politics of Differences* (Princeton, 2010).

Burton, A. *The Bukharans: A Dynastic, Diplomatic and Commercial History 1550–1702* (Richmond, UK, 1997).
Bushev, P. *Posol'stvo Artemiia Volynskogo v Iran v 1715–1718 gg.* (Moscow, 1978).
Cahen, V. *Histoire des relations de la Russie avec la Chine sous Pierre le Grand* (Paris, 1912).
Chen, V. *Sino-Russian Relations in the Seventeenth Century* (The Hague, 1966).
Chernozubov, F. "Ocherki Terskoi stariny. Na Staroi Terskoi Linii." *RA* 3 (1914): 316–45.
Chuloshnikov, A. *Bashkirskoe vosstanie 1755 gg.* (Moscow, 1946).
Chupin, N. "Burtsov, Tatishchev i Zholobov v dele Egora Stoletova, 1733–1736 gg." *RS* 2 (1873): 985–92.
Courant, M. *L'Asie centrale aux XVII et XVIIIe siècles. Empire kalmouk ou empire mantchou?* (Paris, 1912).
Crews, R. *For Prophet and Tsar: Islam and Empire in Russia and Central Asia* (Cambridge, MA, 2006).
Dale, S. *Indian Merchants and Eurasian Trade, 1600–1750* (Cambridge, 1994).
Dameshek, L. *Iasachnaia politika tsarizma v Sibiri v XlX–nachale XX veka* (Irkutsk, 1983).
Debu. "O nachal'nom ustanovlenii i rasprostranenii Kavkazskoi linii." *OZ* 16 (1823): 234–48; 18 (1824): 268–93; 19: 48–74.
– "Some Account of the Nations on the Russian Borders of Mount Caucasus." *AJ* 20 (1825): 273–8.
Demolins, Edmund. *Les grandes routes des peuples. Comment la route crée le type social.* 2 vols. (Paris, 1901–3).
Dubrovin, N. "A.P. Ermolov na Kavkaze." *VS* (1882–4, 1886).
– "1802 god v Gruzii." *VE* 3 (1868): 9–52; 4: 573–84; 5: 213–70.
– "Pokhod grafa V.A. Zubova v Persiiu v 1796 god." *VS* (1874): 2–6.
– "Poslednie dni prebyvaniia Ermolova na Kavkaz." *VS* (1886): 1–3, 7–8.
Eberhard, W. *Conquerors and Rulers: Social Forces in Medieval China* (Leiden, 1965).
Eccles, William. "The Frontiers of New France." In *Essays on Frontiers in World History*, ed. George Wolkskill and Stanley Palmer (Arlington, TX, 1981).
Egorov, V. *Istoricheskaia geografiia zolotoi ordy v XIII–XIV vv.* (Moscow, 1985).
Ermolaev, I. *Srednee Povolzh'e vo vtoroi polovine XVI–XVII v. Upravlenie Kazanskim kraem* (Kazan, 1982).
"Les étapes de la politique islamique russe." *Revue du Monde Musulman* 56 (1923): 93–166.
"Etude géographique des éléments islamisés." *Revue du Monde Musulman* 56 (1923): 12–91.
Fairbank, J., ed. *The Chinese World Order: Traditional China's Foreign Relations* (Cambridge, MA, 1968).
Fawcett, C. *Frontiers: A Study in Political Geography* (Oxford, 1918).
Fisher, A. "Enlightened Despotism and Islam under Catherine II." *SR* 27 (1968): 542–53.
Fisher, R. *Bering's Voyages* (Seattle, 1977).

– *The Russian Fur Trade 1550–1700* (Berkeley, 1943).
"Former and Present State of the Road over Mount Caucasus." *AJ* 20 (1825): 415–18.
Forsyth, M. *A History of the Peoples of Siberia: Russia's North Asian Colony, 1581–1990* (Cambridge, 1992).
Fox, Edward. *History in Geographic Perspective: The Other France* (New York, 1971).
Frank, A. *Muslim Religious Institutions: The Islamic World of Novouzensk District and the Kazakh Inner Horde 1780–1910* (Leiden, 2001).
Freeze, G. *The Russian Levites: Parish Clergy in the Eighteenth Century* (Cambridge, MA, 1977).
Gal'perin, A. "Russko-Kitaiskaia torgovlia v XVIII–pervoi polovine XIX veka." *Problemy vostokovedeniia* 5 (1959): 215–27.
Gamba, J. *Voyage dans la Russie méridionale, et particulièrement dans les provinces situées au-delà du Caucase, fait depuis 1820 jusqu'en janvier 1824*. 2 vols. (Paris, 1826).
Gammer, M. *Muslim Resistance to the Tsar: Shamil and the Conquest of Chechnia and Daghestan* (London, 1994).
Gamrekeli, V. *Torgovye sviazi vostochnoi Gruzii s Severnym Kavkazom v XVIIIv.* 2 vols. (Tbilisi, 1968–77).
Gazenvinkel', K. "Sibirskii gubernator D.I. Chicherin." *IV* 2 (1893): 783–90.
Georgi, I. *Opisanie vsekh obitaiushchikh v Rossiiskom gosudarstve narodov* (Petersburg, 2005, reprint of 1797 edition).
Glazig, J. *Die russisch-Orthodoxe Heidenmission sei Peter dem Grossen* (Munster, 1954).
Goloskov, D. "Pokhod v Khivu v 1717 godu." *VS* 10 (1861): 303–64.
Gorban, N. "In the South of Western Siberia: The New Ishim Fortified Line." *Soviet Geography* 25 (1984): 177–94).
Gromyko, M. "Tserkovnye votchiny zapadnoi Sibiri nakanune sekuliarizatsii." In *Sibir' XVII–XVIII vv.*., 158–85.
Gvosdev, N. "The Russian Empire and the Georgian Orthodox Church in the First Decades of Imperial Rule." *CAS* 14 (1995): 407–23.
Hamamoto, M. "Tatarskaia Kargala in Russia's Eastern Policies." In *Asiatic Russia*, 32–51.
Harley, J. *Siberia: A History of the People* (New Haven, 2014).
Holdich, T. *Political Frontiers and Boundary Making* (London, 1916).
Howe, S. *Empire: A Very Short Introduction* (Oxford, 2002).
Hrytsak, Y. "The Post-Colonial Is Not Enough." *Slavic Review* 74 (2015): 732–7.
Imperial Visions: Nationalist Imagination and Geographical Expansion in the Russian Far East, 1840–1865 (Cambridge, 1999).
Islaev, F. *Islam i pravoslavie v Povolzh'e XVIII stoletiia. Ot konfrontatsii k terpimosti* (Kazan, 2001).
– *Vosstanie Batyrshi. God 1755* (Kazan, 2004).
Istoriia Bashkortostana s drevneishikh vremen do 60–kh godov XIXv. (Ufa, 1997).
Istoriia Buriatskoi ASSR. 2 vols. (Ulan-Ude, 1954–9).

Istoriia Kazakhstana s drevneishikh vremen do nashikh dnei. 5 vols. (Almaty, 1997–2000).
Istoriia Sibiri. 5 vols. (Leningrad, 1968–9).
Istoriia Tatarskoi ASSR (Kazan, 1973).
Istoriia Yakutskoi ASSR. 3 vols. (Moscow, 1955–7).
Iudin, P. "Baron' O.A. Igel'strom v Orenburgskom krae." *RA* 1 (1897): 513–55.
– "S Volgi na Terek." *RA* 2 (1901): 531–44.
"Iz bumag grafa Iu. A. Golovkina." *SN* 7 (1904): 17–97.
James, Harold. *The Roman Predicament* (Princeton, 2006).
Jaubert, M. "Mémoire sur l'ancien cours de l'Oxus." *JA* 12 (1833): 481–500.
"K Irkutskomu letopistsu poiasnenie. Zapiski o Sibiri." *Chteniia* 3 (1859): 65–80.
Kabuzan, V., and S. Troitskii. "Dvizhenie naseleniia Sibiri v XVIII v." *Sibir' XVII–XVIII vv.*, 139–57.
Kalashnikov. "Zapiski Irkutskogo zhitelia (I.T. Kalashnikova)." *RS* 3 (1905): 187–25, 384–409, 609–46.
Kalmyki v mnogonatsional'noi Rossii: opyt chetyrekh stoletii (Elista, 2008).
Kappeler, A. *Russlands erste Nationalitäten. Das Zarenreich und die Völker der Mittleren Wolga vom 16. bis 19. Jahrhundert* (Cologne/Vienna, 1982).
Karatygin, P. "Graf Pavel Sergeevich Potemkin." *IV* 3 (1883): 345–71.
Kasymbaev, ZH. *Gosudarstvennye deiateli kazakhskikh khanstv XVIIIv*. (Almaty, 1999).
Katanaev, I. "Istoricheskii ocherk sluzhby Sibirskogo kazach'iogo voiska." *VS* 7 (1903): 42–60; 8: 46–66.
Kazach'i voiska Aziatskoi Rossii v XVIII–nachale XX veka. Sbornik dokumentov, ed. N. Bekmakhanova (Moscow, 2000).
Kemper, M. "*Adat* against *Shari'a*: Russian Approaches toward Daghestani 'Customary Law' in the 19th Century." *Ab Imperio* 3 (2005): 142–72.
– *Herrschaft, Recht und Islam in Daghestan* (Wiesbaden, 2005).
Kerner, R. *The Urge to the Sea: The Course of Russian History* (Berkeley, 1942).
Khabutdinov, A. *Millet Orenburgskogo sobraniia v kontse XVIII–XIX vekakh* (Kazan, 2000).
Khodarkovsky, M. "Of Russian Governors and Kalmyk Chiefs, or the Politics of the Steppe Frontier in the 1720s–1730s." *CAS* 11 (1992): 1–26.
– *Russia's Steppe Frontier: The Making of a Colonial Empire 1500–1800* (Bloomington, 2002).
– "Uneasy Alliance: Peter the Great and Ayuki Khan." *CAS* 7 (1988): 1–45.
– *Where Two Worlds Met: The Russian State and the Kalmyk Nomads 1600–1771* (Ithaca, 1992).
Kiniapina, N., et al. *Kavkaz i Sredniaia Aziia vo vneshnei politike Rossii* (Moscow, 1984).
Komandzhaev, E. *Administrativnaia sistema Kalmykov v XVIII–XIXv*. (Elista, 2009).
– "Kalmytskoe pravo XVII–XVIIIvv.: klassifikatsiaa prestuplenii." In *Kalmyki v mnogonatsionatsional'noi Rossii*, 193–209.
Komogortsev, I. "Iz istorii chernoi metallurgii Vostochnoi Sibiri v XVII–XVIIIv." In *Sibir' XVII–XVIII vv.* 97–120.

Korolenko, P. "Khopertsy." *VS* 1 (1896): 205–26.

Korsakov, D. "Artemii Petrovich Volynskii, Biograficheskii ocherk" *DNR* 1 (1876): 45–60; 1 (1877): 289–302.

Kostenko, I. "Ural'skoe kazach'e voisko." *VS* 9 (1878): 150–72.

Krestovskii, V. "Chetyre legkie polevye komandy i ikh posledushchaia sud'ba." *VS* 3 (1813): 13–46; 4: 185–228.

Kriukov, A. "Orenburgskii menovoi dvor." *OZ* 30 (1827): 127–40.

Kropotkin, P. "The Orography of Asia." *GJ* 23 (1904): 176–207, 331–61.

Kudriavtsev, F. *Istoriia Buriat-Mongol'skogo naroda (ot XVII do 60–kh godov XIXv)* (Moscow/Leningrad, 1940).

Kukanova, N. "Russko-iranskie torgovye otnosheniia v kontse XVII–nachale XVIII v." *IZ* 57 (1956): 232–54.

Kurapov, A. *Buddizm i vlast v Kalmytskom khanstve XVII–XVIII vv.* (Elista, 2007).

Lamaizm v Buriatii XVIII–nachala XX veka (Novosibirsk, 1983).

Lang, D. *The Last Years of the Georgian Monarchy 1658–1832* (New York, 1957).

Lantzeff, G. *Siberia in the Seventeenth Century: A Study of the Colonial Administration* (Berkeley, 1943).

Lattimore, O. *Studies in Frontier History: Collected Papers 1928–1958* (Paris, 1962).

Lebedev, V. "Bashkirskoe vosstanie 1705–1711 gg." *IZ* 1 (1937): 81–102.

LeDonne, John. "Building an Infrastructure of Empire in Russia's Eastern Theater 1650s–1840s." *CHR* 47 (2006): 581–608.

– "Frontier Governors General 1772–1825. III. The Eastern Frontier." *JGO* 48 (2000): 321–40.

– "Proconsular Ambitions on the Chinese Border: Governor General Iakobi's Proposal of War on China." *CMR* 45 (2004): 31–60.

Ledyard, J. *Journey through Russia and Siberia, 1787–1788* (Madison, 1966).

Lemercier-Quelquejay, C. "Les routes commerciales et militaires au Caucase du Nord au XVIe et XVIIe siècles." *CAS* 4 (1985): 1–19.

Leskov, N. "Sibirskie kartinki XVIII veka." *VE* 3 (1893): 177–200; 4: 534–61.

Levshine (Levshin), A. *Description des hordes et des steppes des Kirghiz-Kazaks* (Paris, 1840).

Lobanov-Rostovsky, A. *Russia and Asia* (Ann Arbor, 1951).

Lystsov, V. *Persidskii pokhod Petra I 1722–23* (Moscow, 1951).

Malikov, Yu. *Tsars, Cossacks, and Nomads* (Berlin, 2011).

Mancall, M. *Russia and China: Their Diplomatic Relations to 1728* (Cambridge, MA, 1971).

Martin, V. *Law and Custom in the Steppe: The Kazakhs of the Middle Horde and Russian Colonialism in the Nineteenth Century* (Richmond, UK, 2001).

"Materialy dlia istorii Sibiri." *Chteniia* 4 (1866): 1–128; 1 (1867): 129–230; 2: 231–325.

"Materialy dlia statisticheskogo opisania Samarskoi gubernii." *ZhMVD* 43 (1860): 1–96.

Matkhanova, N. *General-Gubernatory Vostochnoi Sibiri* (Novosibirsk, 1998).

– *Vysshaia administratsiia Vostochnoi Sibiri v seredine XIX veka* (Novosibirsk, 2002).
McCabe, I. *The Shah's Silk for European Silver: The Eurasian Trade of the Julfa Armenians in Safavid Iran and India, 1530–1750* (Atlanta, 1999).
Mezhdunarodnye otnosheniia v Tsentral'noi Azii v XVII–XVIII veke. Dokumenty i materialy. 2 vols. (Moscow, 1989).
Mikhailovskii, V. *Shamanstvo* (Moscow, 1892).
Modorov, N. *Rossiia i gorny Altai: politicheskie, sotsial'no-ekonomicheskie i kul'turnye otnosheniia (XVII–XIXvv.)* (Gorno-Altaisk, 1996).
"Mongoly-Buriaty v Nerchinskom okruge Irkutskoi gubernii." *ZhMVD* 3 (1893): 3–47.
Monahan, E. *The Merchants of Siberia: Trade in Early Modern Eurasia* (Ithaca, 2016).
Narody Srednei Azii i Kazakhstana. 2 vols. (Moscow, 1963).
Nolde, B. *La formation de l'empire russe*. 2 vols. (Paris, 1952–3).
"O rasprostranenii torga s oblastiami Khivinskoi, Bukharskoi i Indiiskimi. 1787." *Chteniia* 2 (1863): 57–64.
"O vyplavke na Nerchinskikh zavodax serebra s 1704 po 1768." *Chteniia* 3 (1864): 94–100.
Ocherki listorii Kalmytskoi ASSR (Moscow, 1967).
Of Religion and Empire: Missions, Conversions, and Tolerance in Tsarist Russia, ed. R. Geraci and M. Khodarkovsky (Ithaca, 2001).
Orlova, K. *Istoriia khristianizatsii Kalmykov, seredina XVII–nachalo XX v.* (Moscow, 2006).
Osterhammel, Jürgen. *Colonialism: A Theoretical Overview* (Princeton, 2005).
Ostrowski, D. *Muscovy and the Mongols: Cross-Cultural Influences on the Steppe Frontier, 1304–1589* (Cambridge, 1998).
Ozeretskovskii. "Pis'ma professora Ozeretskogo k I. I. Betskomu o puteshestvii Bobrinskogo po Rossii." *RA* 3 (1876): 40–58.
P-, M. "Kratkaia khronologiia voennykh deistvii v Sibiri 1696–1769gg." *VS* 9 (1910): 203–13.
Paine, S. *Imperial Rivals: China, Russia, and Their Disputed Frontier* (Armonk, NY, 1996).
Pavlenko, N. *Anna Ioannovna, Nemtsy pri dvore* (Moscow, 2002).
Pavlov, P. "Vyvoz pushniny iz Sibiri v XVII v." *Sibir' XVII–XVIII vv.*, 121–38.
Pavlovsky, M. *Chinese-Russian Relations* (New York, 1949).
Perdue, P. "Boundaries, Maps, and Movement: Chinese, Russian, and Mongolian Empires in Early Modern Central Eurasia." *IHR* 20 (1998): 263–86.
Petrukhintsev, N. *Vnutrenniaia politika Anny Ioannovny (1730–1740)* (Moscow, 2014).
Petrushevskii, A. "Suvorov v Astrakhani, na Kubani i v Kremenchuge 1780–1787." *VS* 1 (1882): 534.
"Poezdka na Eltonskoe ozero." *OZ* 31 (1827): 3–24, 241–65, 397–419.
Pogosian, F. *Sudebnik Astrakhanskikh Armian* (Yerevan, 1968).
Popov, N. *V.N. Tatishchev i ego vremia* (Moscow, 1861).
Portal, R. *L'Ural au XVIIIe siecle* (Paris, 1950).
Potanin, G. "O karavannoi torgovle s Dzhungarskoi Bukhariei v. XVIII stoletii." *Chteniia* 2 (1868): 21–113.

Potto, V. *Kavkazskaia voina*. 5 vols. (Stavropol, 1994).
Prescott, J. *Map of Mainland Asia by Treaty* (Melbourne, 1975).
"Proekt o usilenii Rossiiskoi s Verkhneiu Azieiu torgovli chrez Khivu i Bukhariiu." *RA* 1 (1878): 400–3.
Radishchev, A. "Pis'mo o kitaiskoi torgovle." In *Polnoe Sobranie sochinenii*, 3 vols. (Moscow, 1938–52), 2:5–35.
Raeff, M. *Siberia and the Reforms of 1822* (Seattle, 1956).
Rafienko, L. "Instruktsiia Sibirskomu gubernatoru 1741g." *AE* (1973): 58–67.
Rayfield, D. *Edge of Empires: A History of Georgia* (London, 2012).
Reading, D. *The Anglo-Russian Commercial Treaty of 1734* (New Haven, 1938).
Regional'noe upravlenie i problema effektivnosti vlasti v Rossii. XVIII–nachalo XXI veka (Orenburg, 2012).
Reinsdorf. "Zapiska Orenburgskogo gubernatora Reinsdorfa." *VIRGO* 27 (1859): 90–104.
Remilev, E. *Oirat-Mongoly. Obzor istorii evropeiskikh Kalmykov* (Weiler, 2010).
Remnev, A. "Russiia i Sibir' v meniaiashchemsia prostranstve imperii XIX nachalo XX veka." In *Rossiiskaia Imperiia*, 286–319.
Rerikh (Roerich) I. *Tibet i Tsentral'naia Aziia* (Samara, 1999).
Rhinelander, A. *Prince Michael Vorontsov: Viceroy of the Tsar* (Montreal, 1990).
Riasanovsky, V. *Fundamental Principles of Mongol Law* (Tientsin, 1939).
Romaniello, M. *The Elusive Empire: Kazan and the Creation of Russia 1552–1671* (Madison, 2012).
Rorlich, A. *The Volga Tatars: A Profile in National Resilience* (Stanford, 1986).
Rossabi, M. *China and Inner Asia from 1368 to the Present Day* (London, 1975).
Rossiiskaia imperiia v sraynitel'noi perspektiv. Sbornik statei (Moscow, 2004).
R-ov. "Feofilakt Rusanov, pervyi eksarkh Gruzii." *VE* 11 (1873): 229–58; 12: 601–29.
Rozhkova, M. "Iz istorii ekonomicheskoi politiki rossiiskogo tsarizma V Zakavkaz'e." *IZ* 18 (1946): 169–200.
"Rukovodstvo dlia proezzhaiushchikh Kavkazskie gory." *OZ* 12 (1822): 212–22.
Schorkowitz, D. "The Orthodox Church, Lamaism, and Shamanism among the Buriats and Kalmyks, 1825–1925." In *Of Religion and Empire*, 201–25.
Seaton, A. *The Horsemen of the Steppe: The Story of the Cossacks* (London, 1980).
Semple, Ellen. *Influences of Geographic Environment on the basis of Ratzel's System of Anthropo-Geography* (New York, 1911).
Shchukin, N. "Buriaty." *ZhMVD* 25 (1849): 423–48; 26: 69–103.
– "Poezhka na reku Ilim." *ZhMVD* 42 (1860): 15–40.
– "Yakuty." *ZhMVD* 7 (1854): 1–46.
Shomakhmadov, S. *Uchenie o tsarskoi vlasti: teoriiI imperskogo pravleniia v Buddizme* (Petersburg, 2007).
Shumakher, P. "Nashi snosheniia s Kitaem s 1567 po 1805." *RA* 2 (1879): 145–83.
Shunkov, V. *Ocherki po istorii kolonizatsii Sibiri v XVII–nachale XVIII vekov* (Moscow/Leningrad, 1946).

Sibir' v sostave Rossiiskoi imperii (Moscow, 2007).
Sibir' XVII–XVIII vv. (Novosibirsk, 1962).
Sladkovskii, M. *Istoriia torgovo-ekonomicheskikh otnoshenii narodov Rossii s Kitaem do 1917* (Moscow, 1974).
Slovtsov, P. *Istoricheskoe obozrenie Sibiri* (Novosibirsk, 1995).
Smirnov, I. *Orenburgskaia ekspeditsiia (komissiia) i prisoedinenie Zavolzh'ia k Rossii v 30–40-e gody XVIII veka* (Samara, 1997).
Sokolov, A. "Astrakhanskii port." *VS* 1 (1849): 108–13; 2: 466–75; 1 (1851): 1–18.
Starr, S., ed. *The Legacy of History in Russia and the New States of Eurasia* (New York, 1994).
Stebelsky, I. "The Frontier in Central Asia." In Bater and French, *Studies*, 143–73.
Steblin-Kamenskaia, M. "K istorii vosstaniia sultana Kenesary Kasymova." *IZ* 13 (1942): 234–55.
Steinwedel, Ch. *Threads of Empire: Loyalty and Tsarist Authority in Bashkiria, 1552–1917* (Bloomington, 2016).
Stepnoi krai Evrazii. Istoriko-kul'turnye vzaimodeistviia i sovremennost' (Omsk, 2007).
Sultangalieva, G. "Kazakhskie chinovniki Rossiiskoi imperii XIX v.: Osobennosti vospriiatiia vlasti." *CMR* 56 (2015): 651–79.
– "The Russian Empire and the Intermediary Role of Tatars in Kazakhstan." In *Asiatic Russia*, 52–79.
Sunderland, W. "'Russians into Yakuts?' Going Native and Problems of Russian National Identity in the Siberian North." *SR* 55 (1996): 806–25.
– *Taming the Wild Field: Colonization and Empire on the Russian Steppe* (Ithaca, 2004).
Sychevskii, G. "Istoricheskaia zapiska o Kitaiskoi granitse, 1846." *Chteniia* 2 (1875): 1–292.
Sykes, P. *A History of Persia*. 3rd ed., 2 vols. (London, 1969),
Tkhorzhevskii, S. *Stenka Razin. Istoricheskii ocherk* (Petersburg, 1913).
Trepavlov, V. "Kalmyki i Rossiia v XVII–XVIII W.: poddanyye, vassaly ili soiuzniki?" In *Kalmyki v mnogonatsional'noi Rossii*, 58–70.
Vasary, I. "Clans of Tatar Descent in the Muscovite Elite in the 14th–16th Centuries." In Vasary, *Turks, Tatars, and Russians*, 101–13.
– *Turks, Tatars, and Russians in the 13th–16th Centuries* (Ashgrave, UK, 2007).
Vatin, V. *Minusinskii krai v XVIIIv*. (Minusinsk, 1913).
Veniakov, M. "Zabaikal'e Khalka." *VS* 8 (1872): 193–230.
Vitevskii, V. "Yaitskoe voisko do poiavleniia Pugacheva." *RA* 1 (1879): 273–304, 401–43; 2: 377–428; 2: 203–41, 377–402, 435–58.
Vlast' v Sibiri XVI–nachalo XXV, ed. M. Akishin and A. Remnev (Novosibirsk, 2005).
Volkov, D. "Zapiska Volkova." *Vestnik Imperatorskogo Geograficheskogo Obshchestva* 27 (1859): 49–60
Waley-Cohen, J. "Religion, War, and Empire: Building in Eighteenth Century China." *IHR* 20 (1998): 336–52.
Werth, P. *At the Margins of Orthodoxy: Mission, Governance, and Confessional Politics in Russia's Volga-Kama Region (1827–1905)* (Ithaca, 2002).

– "Coercion and Conversion: Violence amd Mass Baptism of the Volga Peoples, 1740–55." *Kritika* 4 (2003): 543–69.

– "Glava tserkvi, poddanny imperatora: Armianskii katolikos na perekrestke vnutrennei i vneshnei politike imperii, 1828–1914."*Ab Imperio* 3 (2006): 99–138.

– "Imperial Russia and the Armenian Catholikos at Home and Abroad." In *Reconstruction and Interaction*, 203–35.

– *The Tsar's Foreign Faiths: Toleration and the Fate of Religious Freedom in Imperial Russia* (Oxford, 2014).

Witzenrath, C. *Cossacks and the Russian Empire, 1598–1725: Manipulation, Rebellion and Expansion into Siberia* (London, 2007).

Wood, A. ed. *The History of Siberia: From Conquest to Revolution* (Leiden, 1991).

Wortman, R. "Intentions and Realities in 18th-Century Monarchy." *Kritika* 17 (2016): 361–77.

Yadrintsev, N. "Altai i ego i narodcheskoe tsarstvo." *IV* 2 (1885): 607–44.

Yemelianova, G. *Russia and Islam: A Historical Survey* (New York, 2002).

Zalkind, E. *Prisoedinenie Buriatii k Rossii* (Ulan Ude, 1958).

Zasedateleva, L. *Terskie kazaki (seredina XVI–nachalo XX v.)* (Moscow, 1974).

Zmeev. "Predstavleniia polkovnika Zmeeva i postanovleniia Tatishcheva i Soimonova o poselenii Kalmytskoi kniagini Anny Taishinoi v Stavropol'skoi kreposti na Volge." In Popov, *Tatishchev*, 621–30.

Zu, Yu. "Dr. Savva Bol'shoi's Account of His Captivity among the Kirghees Kaissacs in the Year 1803–4." *AJ* 18 (1824): 113–20.

Index

www.ingramcontent.com/pod-product-compliance
Lightning Source LLC
LaVergne TN
LVHW020434080826
844660LV00033B/1285

* 9 7 8 1 4 8 7 5 4 2 1 1 5 *